Disco... ...nts

Eu

Throughout this book, we use these icons to highlight special recommendations:

 The Best…
Lists for everything from bars to wildlife – to make sure you don't miss out

 Don't Miss
A must-see – don't go home until you've been there

 Local experts reveal their top picks and secret highlights

 Detour
Special places a little off the beaten track

 If you like…
Lesser-known alternatives to world-famous attractions

These icons help you quickly identify reviews in the text and on the map:

 Sights

 Eating

 Drinking

 Sleeping

 Information

This edition written and researched by

Oliver Berry,
Brett Atkinson, Alexis Averbuck, Kerry Christiani,
Mark Elli... ...ony Ham,
Virgi... ...Sieg,
Ryan... ...ilson

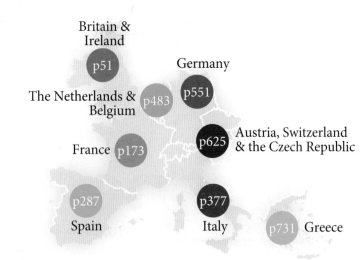

Contents

Contents

On the Road

This is Europe

Europe may be old in spirit, but in many ways it remains eternally young at heart. Whether it's sunbathing on the Côte d'Azur, cruising along the Danube, sipping wine in an Italian vineyard or simply watching the world go by from a Parisian street cafe, Europe has been setting trends and forming fashions for the rest of the world to follow for centuries, and it's still a place that really knows how to appreciate the finer things in life.

Europe is home to some of the world's most fascinating cities, as well as many of the finest museums, smartest restaurants, greatest galleries and weirdest buildings. It's plagued by more clichés than practically anywhere else on earth, and yet often seems to do everything it can to live up to them. It still leads the world in fashion, art, architecture, gastronomy and design, but often seems stubbornly resistant to change. And while it's often fascinatingly forward-thinking, it's also a place that remains perpetually in thrall to its turbulent and often troubled past.

Uncovering the contradictions is what makes travel in Europe so rewarding. The continent is complex and contrary, and while you might never quite manage to get a handle on what makes it tick, you'll have an enormous amount of fun while you try. The next surprising moment or eye-opening experience is never more than a quick train ride away: in just a few hours, you could find yourself switching the grand boulevards of Paris for the canals of Amsterdam, the coffee shops of Vienna or the ruins of ancient Rome, while watching some of the world's most magnificent landscapes unfold from the carriage window. Take your time and enjoy the trip: the journey from A to B is often all part of the essential European experience.

Au revoir, auf wiedersehn, arrivederci: however you choose to say farewell, you're in for the journey of a lifetime. Savour every moment.

> 66
> in many ways it remains eternally young at heart
> 99

Neuschwanstein Castle (p603), Germany

Europe

NORWAY

Shetland Islands

Orkney Islands

Outer Hebrides

SCOTLAND

Inverness

Aberdeen

Oban

Dundee

Glasgow **24** EDINBURGH

NORTHERN IRELAND **16**

Derry

Belfast

Newcastle-upon-Tyne

Skagerrak

DENMARK

North Sea

Galway

DUBLIN **6**

ENGLAND

York

Irish Sea

IRELAND

Liverpool

UNITED KINGDOM

Frisian Islands

Stralsund

Wismar

Hamburg

Rostock

Cork

WALES

CARDIFF

Oxford

LONDON

NETHERLANDS

Bremen

BERLIN **7**

St George's Channel

18 Bath

3

AMSTERDAM

8

Hanover

GERMANY

Plymouth

Brighton

Bruges

BRUSSELS

BELGIUM **11**

English Channel

Channel Islands

Le Havre

Caen

13 Reims

Frankfurt-am-Main

20

Plzeň

ATLANTIC OCEAN

Quimper

PARIS **2**

CHAMPAGNE

Stuttgart

Rennes

Strasbourg

Munich **17**

23

Nantes

Tours

Dijon

SWITZ.

Bavarian Alps

FRANCE

BERN **12**

Limoges

Geneva

VALAIS

ALPS

Trento

Bordeaux

Lyon

Mt Blanc (4807m)

15

Milan

5

Santiago De Compostela

Chamonix **19**

Turin

ITALY

Venice

Gijón

Po

Bologna

Vigo

Bilbao

San Sebastián

Nîmes

Genoa

Pisa

León

Toulouse

Montpellier

Nice

Perugia

Pamplona

PYRENEES

Golfe du Lion

Ligurian Sea

TUSCANY **21**

Douro

Marseille

Corsica

Elba

Salamanca

Zaragoza

ROME **1**

PORTUGAL

14 Barcelona

MADRID

SPAIN

Tagus

Badajoz

Palma De Mallorca

Sassari

Córdoba

Valencia

Sardinia

Seville

Alicante (Alicant)

Balearic Islands

Cagliari

Cádiz

10 Granada

Murcia

Mediterranean Sea

Málaga

Strait of Gibraltar

MOROCCO

ALGERIA

TUNISIA

Bay of Biscay

Loire

Seine

Rhine

Danube

Elbe

Rhône

25
Top Experiences

25 Europe's Top Experiences

Ancient Rome

Rome's famous seven hills (actually, there are nine) offer some superb vantage points. A favourite is Palatine Hill (p396), a gorgeous green expanse of evocative ruins, towering umbrella pines and unforgettable views over the Roman Forum. This is where it all began, where Romulus supposedly founded the city and where the ancient Roman emperors lived in unimaginable luxury. Nowadays, it's a truly haunting spot; as you walk the gravel paths you can almost sense the ghosts in the air. View of the Colosseum (p397) from the Roman Forum

BRUCE BI/LONELY PLANET IMAGES ©

2

The Eiffel Tower

Seven million people visit the Eiffel Tower (p186) annually, and most would agree that each visit is unique. From an evening ascent amid twinkling lights to lunch in the company of a staggering Paris panorama, there are 101 ways to 'do' it. Pedal beneath it, skip the lift and hike up, buy a crêpe from a stand or a key ring from the street, snap yourself in front of it, visit at night, or experience the odd special occasion when all 324m of it glows in different colours.

Rhythm of London

Can you hear that, music lovers? That's London (p62) calling – from the numerous theatres, concert halls, nightclubs, pubs and even tube stations where on any given night hundreds, if not thousands, of performers are taking to the stage. Search for your own iconic London experience, whether it's the Proms at the Royal Albert Hall, an East End singalong around a clunky pub piano, a performance of *Oliver!* in the West End, a superstar DJ set at Fabric nightclub or a floppy-fringed guitar band at a Hoxton boozer. Crowd outside Royal Albert Hall (p90)

The Best...
Places to Eat

PARISIAN MARKETS
Nothing feels more quintessentially French than shopping at a busy Parisian street market. (p209)

MADRID TABERNAS
The best place to try Spanish tapas is a traditional neighbourhood taberna. (p308)

ROMAN RISTORANTES
You might think you know Italian food, but your first taste of real Italian pizza will make you change your mind. (p409)

ALSATIAN WINSTUBS
For authentic Alsatian grub, head for a cosy *winstub* (wine room) in Strasbourg, France. (p235)

The Best...
Natural Wonders

ALETSCH GLACIER
The largest glacier in the Alps, covering 120 sq km. (p683)

DUNE DU PILAT
Europe's largest sand dune, on France's Atlantic coast near Arcachon. (p255)

THE GIANT'S CAUSEWAY
Spectacular volcanic rock formations off the coast of Northern Ireland. (p163)

DACHSTEIN RIESENEISHÖHLE
These ice caves extend almost 80km into the mountains near Obertraun, Austria. (p666)

SAMARIA GORGE
The walls of this 13km canyon on the Greek island of Crete reach a towering 1100m. (p765)

Imperial Vienna

The monumentally graceful Hofburg (p637) whisks you back to the age of empires as you marvel at the treasury's imperial crowns, the equine ballet of the Spanish Riding School and the chandelier-lit apartments fit for Empress Elisabeth (aka 'Sissi'). The palace, a legacy of the Habsburg era, is rivalled in grandeur only by the 1441-room Schloss Schönbrunn (p643), a Unesco World Heritage site, and the baroque Schloss Belvedere (p644), both set in exquisite gardens.

Dining room of the Hofburg

Venice in Winter

There's something magical about Venice (p424) on a sunny winter's day. With far fewer tourists around and the light sharp and clear, it's the perfect time to lap up the city's unique atmosphere. Wander Dorsoduro's shadowy backlanes, then visit two of Venice's top galleries: the Galleria dell'Accademia (p443) and the Collezione Peggy Guggenheim (p425), which houses works by many of the giants of 20th-century art.

Dublin

Ireland's capital city (p148) boasts all the attractions of a major international metropolis, but retains the friendliness and intimacy of a small town. Whether you're wandering the leafy Georgian terraces of St Stephen's Green or getting acquainted with the past at Kilmainham Gaol, you're never far from a friendly pub. And there's always the chance to sink a pint at that fountainhead of froth – the original Guinness brewery.

Remembering the Wall, Berlin

It's hard to believe that this most cosmopolitan of cities was once divided. The best way to examine the role of the Berlin Wall is to make your way – on foot or by bike – along the Berlin Wall Trail (p571). Whether you're passing the Brandenburg Gate, gazing at graffiti at the East Side Gallery or learning about the history of the Wall at the Berlin Wall Documentation Centre, the path brings it all into context. It's heartbreaking and hopeful and sombre, but integral to understanding Germany's capital. Berlin Wall mural, East Side Gallery (p571)

Amsterdam's Canals

To say Amsterdammers love the water is an understatement. Sure, the city (p494) made its first fortune in maritime trade, but that's ancient history. You can stroll next to the canals and check out some of the city's 3300 houseboats. Or, better yet, go for a ride. From boat level you'll get to see a whole new set of architectural details, like the ornamentations bedecking the bridges. And when you pass the canalside cafe terraces, you can look up and wave.

The Best...
Drinking Experiences

A PINT IN A IRISH PUB
Dublin wouldn't be Dublin without its pubs – they're still the cornerstone of the city's social life. (p154)

FRENCH VINEYARDS
If you want to learn about the fruits of the vine, head for a Bordeaux vineyard. (p254)

GERMAN BEER GARDENS
Trying the local brews at a Munich beer garden is a great way to meet the locals. (p592)

SCOTTISH WHISKY DISTILLERIES
Many of Scotland's distilleries conduct tours, but Edinburgh is a good starting point. (p141)

Prague

Emerging from behind the Iron Curtain, where it slumbered for decades, the capital of the Czech Republic is now one of Europe's most dynamic and alluring places. In some parts Prague (p694) has hardly changed since medieval times – cobbled cul-de-sacs snake through the Old Town, framed by teetering townhouses, baroque buildings and graceful bridges. And if castles are your thing, Prague has an absolute beauty (p700): a 1000-year-old fortress covering around 18 acres – the world's largest castle complex. Old Town and Prague Castle

9

The Best...
Sacred Spaces

18

RICHARD NEBESKY/LONELY PLANET IMAGES ©

10 Alhambra, Granada

The palace complex of the Alhambra (p363) is close to architectural perfection. It is perhaps the most refined example of Islamic art anywhere in the world, not to mention the most enduring symbol of 800 years of Moorish rule in what was then known as Al-Andalus. From afar, the Alhambra's red fortress towers dominate the Granada skyline, set against a backdrop of the Sierra Nevada's snow-capped peaks. Up close, the Alhambra's perfectly proportioned Generalife gardens complement the exquisite detail of the Palacio Nazaríes. Put simply, this is Spain's most beautiful monument.

Belgian Beer & Chocolate

Belgium has a brew for all seasons (p540). From tangy lambics to full-flavoured Trappists, the range of beers is exceptional. Best of all, you can sup a selection in timeless cafes, hidden away in the atmospheric cores of Belgium's great 'art' cities – Ghent, Bruges, Antwerp and Brussels – with their appealing mixtures of medieval and art nouveau architecture. And if you don't drink, there's an unparalleled range of chocolate shops (p518) selling melt-in-the-mouth pralines with ever-more-intriguing flavour combinations.

PASCALE BEROUJON/LONELY PLANET IMAGES ©

Jungfraujoch

Travelling through Switzerland often feels like one non-stop scenic adventure, and every bend in the road seems to open up a new panorama of mind-boggling views. But if it's the ultimate alpine view you're after, then Jungfraujoch (p686) is guaranteed to fit the bill. A gravity-defying train chugs up to Europe's highest railway terminus (at 3471m), opening up an unforgettable vista of icy pinnacles, knife-edge peaks and gleaming glaciers. Dress warmly, don some shades and don't forget the camera.

Champagne

Champagne houses (p229) such as Mumm, Mercier and Moët & Chandon, in the main towns of Reims and Épernay, are known the world over. Our tip? Much of Champagne's best liquid gold is made by almost 5000 small-scale *vignerons* (wine makers) in 320-odd villages. Dozens welcome visitors for a taste, a tipple and shopping at producers' prices. Travelling along the region's scenic driving routes is the best way to taste fine bubbly, amid rolling vineyards and drop-dead-gorgeous villages.

NEIL SETCHFIELD/LONELY PLANET IMAGES ©

Barcelona's La Sagrada Família

One of Spain's top sights, the Modernista brainchild of Antoni Gaudí remains a work in progress, more than 80 years after its creator's death. Fanciful and profound, inspired by nature and barely restrained by a Gothic style, Barcelona's quirky temple (p323) soars skyward with an almost playful majesty. The improbable angles and departures from architectural convention will have you shaking your head in disbelief, but the detail of the decorative flourishes on the Passion and Nativity Facades are worth studying for hours.

14

The Best...
Ancient Monuments

STONEHENGE
The world's most iconic stone circle is also one of its oldest. Some sections date back to 4500 BC. (p103)

THE ROMAN FORUM
Exploring the streets, markets and temples of ancient Rome is unforgettable. (p391)

THE ACROPOLIS
Athens' ancient temple complex remains an architectural inspiration, more than 2000 years after it was built. (p747)

THE CARNAC ALIGNMENTS
These neolithic stones stretch for miles across the Breton countryside in France. (p228)

The Best...
Weird Buildings

CENTRE POMPIDOU, PARIS
An 'inside-out' building, with pipes and girders on the outside. (p200)

KUNSTHAUSWIEN, VIENNA
An architectural mishmash of uneven floors, wonky windows and industrial materials. (p645)

LA PEDRERA, BARCELONA
Rooftop sculpture and organic lines from the imagination of Antoni Gaudí. (p330)

LEANING TOWER OF PISA
Tilting in Tuscany since 1173, it still hasn't toppled over. (p451)

OVERBLAAK, ROTTERDAM
Geometric houses like giant ice cubes tumbled together. (p512)

ATOMIUM, BRUSSELS
The 102m-tall Atomium has escalators in its connection tubes. (p522)

Gaping at the Matterhorn

It graces chocolate bar wrappers and evokes stereotypical *Heidi* scenes, but nothing prepares you for the allure of the Matterhorn (p679). In the timber-chalet-filled Swiss village of Zermatt, this mesmerising loner looms above you. Gaze at it from a tranquil sidewalk cafe, hike in its shadow along the tangle of alpine paths above town, with cowbells clinking in the distance, or pause on a ski slope and admire its majestic, chiselled peak. Left: The Matterhorn behind the village of Zermatt

LEFT: MARTIN MOOS/LONELY PLANET IMAGES ©; RIGHT: BRUCE BI/LONELY PLANET IMAGES ©

Coastal Walks in Ireland

16

Hiking the Causeway Coast (p164) between Ballycastle and Bushmills will take you through some of Northern Ireland's most inspiring and impressive coastal scenery. Its grand centrepiece is the Giant's Causeway, a strange and beautiful natural wonder that has been pulling in visitors for a couple of centuries. But there's also the nerve-testing challenge of the spectacular Carrick-a-Rede rope bridge and, waiting at journey's end, a well-deserved dram at Bushmills' whiskey distillery. Carrick-a-Rede rope bridge

Beer-Drinking in Munich

17

It's not so much that you can drink beer in Munich (p585) – everybody knows you can. It's the variety of places where you can drink that makes this city heaven for beer afficionados. There's Oktoberfest (p589), of course, and then there are the famous beer halls (p592), from the infamous Hofbräuhaus to the wonderful Augustiner Bräustuben. And why stay inside? You can drink your lager in a park in Munich's city centre, or just about anywhere.

Historical Bath

Britain boasts many great cities, but Bath (p98) is the belle of the ball. The Romans built a health resort here to take advantage of the hot water bubbling to the surface; the springs were rediscovered in the 18th century and Bath became *the* place to see and be seen by British high society. Today, the stunning Georgian architecture of grand townhouses, sweeping crescents and Palladian mansions (not to mention Roman ruins, a beautiful cathedral and a 21st-century spa) means that Bath will demand your undivided attention. Roman Baths and Bath Abbey

The Best...
Shopping Destinations

PARISIAN FLEA MARKETS
Paris' *marchés aux puces* are packed with vintage fashion and antiques. (p214)

CHRISTMAS MARKETS IN NUREMBURG
Festive markets are held all across Germany, but Nuremburg has the best. (p598)

PORTOBELLO ROAD MARKET, LONDON
Forget Oxford Street – this west London street market has the good stuff. (p91)

MILAN
Milan is awash with fancy fashion boutiques, especially around the Golden Quad. (p420)

BRUSSELS
Shop for dainty lace and handmade chocolates in the Galeries St-Hubert. (p523)

Skiing in Chamonix

19

James Bond did it and so can you: Vallée Blanche (p246) is a once-in-a-lifetime experience. You'll never forget the five hours it takes to ski the 20km off-piste descent from the spike of the Aiguille du Midi to mountaineering centre Chamonix, France – every minute will pump more adrenalin in your body than anything else you've ever done. Craving more? Hurl yourself down Europe's longest black run (16km) at Alpe d'Huez.

CHRISTIAN ASLUND/LONELY PLANET IMAGES ©

The Best...
Artistic Haunts

MONTMARTRE, PARIS
A hundred years ago, this sleepy village became one of the world's great artistic hubs. (p201)

FLORENCE
The home of the Italian Renaissance–inspired artists, including Michelangelo and Leonardo da Vinci. (p439)

MONET'S GARDEN
In rural Normandy, this was where Claude Monet created his renowned *nymphéas* (water lily) paintings. (p221)

PROVENCE
Follow in the artistic footsteps of Paul Cézanne and Vincent van Gogh. (p264)

REMBRANDTSHUIS
The Amsterdam studio where Rembrandt painted some of his most celebrated works. (p499)

20 Slow-Boating the Rhine

It sounds hokey: sitting on a boat, bobbing along, looking at the sights. Well, we dare anyone to take a cruise through Germany along the Rhine (p605) and not be utterly captivated and ready to do it again. Up on deck, you'll see the busy river framed on either side by vineyard-clad hills and, every now and then, the ruins of a castle (who doesn't like a castle?). In between are cute little towns with half-timbered buildings; don't be fooled by fakes elsewhere — these are the real thing.

IMAGE BROKER ©

Tuscany

Before dismissing a travel cliché, it pays to investigate. The gently rolling hills of Tuscany (p439), bathed in golden light and dotted with ancient vineyards, are a case in point. Battalions of books, postcards and lifestyle TV shows try to do this region justice, but nothing beats a visit. Here, picture-perfect towns vie with magnificent scenery and Italy's best food and wine – once you've had a taste of Tuscany, every cliché will ring absolutely true.

Ancient Landmarks

Greece offers some of Europe's most impressive historical sights: from the oracular Delphi (p753), perched above the sparkling Gulf of Corinth, and Olympia, home to the first Olympic Games, to the acoustically perfect theatre of Epidaurus and the mystical Sanctuary of Asclepius, an ancient healing centre. Start with the Acropolis (p747) and follow the path of history over Greece's landscape. Acropolis, Athens

Baroque Salzburg

A fortress on a hill, 17th-century cobbled streets, Mozart, the ultimate singalong – if Salzburg (p657) didn't exist, someone would have to invent it, just to keep all the acolytes who visit Austria each year happy. It's hard to say what's most popular, but you just have to see all the DVDs on sale to know that this is *The Sound of Music* country; faster than you can say 'do-re-mi' you can be whisked into gorgeous, steep hills that are alive with tour groups year-round. Picture of Mozart in a shop window, Salzburg

The Best...
Royal Residences

VERSAILLES
Louis XIV's jaw-dropping statement of architectural excess must be seen to be believed. (p216)

BUCKINGHAM PALACE
Look for the Royal Standard above the palace to see if the Queen's at home. (p67)

SCHLOSS SCHÖNNBRUNN
The Habsburg's summer retreat in Vienna is awash with rococo extravagance. (p643)

PALACIO REAL, MADRID
Wander through the 50-odd rooms on show in this 2500-room Spanish palace. (p299

PRAGUE CASTLE
The Czech monarchs are long gone, but their castle dominates Prague's old city. (p700)

Edinburgh

Edinburgh (p133) is a city of many moods, famous for its amazing festivals and especially lively in the summer. The Scottish capital is also well worth visiting out of season for the sights – like the castle silhouetted against the blue spring sky, with a yellow haze of daffodils misting the slopes below – or for the atmosphere – fog snagging the spires of the Old Town, rain on the cobblestones and a warm glow beckoning from the window of a pub on a chilly December morning. Fountain in front of Edinburgh Castle (p133)

The Best...
Wild Escapes

THE BLACK FOREST, GERMANY
This huge forest is one of the last remnants of the great woodland that once stretched over most of Europe. (p600)

THE DOLOMITES
This spiky chain of peaks is home to Italy's wildest mountain scenery. (p439)

PICOS DE EUROPA
The jagged mountains of Spain's Picos de Europa are paradise for hikers and wildlife spotters. (p316)

THE SCOTTISH HIGHLANDS
Scotland's wild, barren hills harbour some of Britain's highest peaks. (p145)

(25) The Cliffs of Santorini

The idyllic Greek island of Santorini (p760) will grab your attention and won't let go. The submerged caldera, surrounded by lava-layered cliffs topped by villages that resemble a sprinkling of icing sugar, is one of nature's great wonders. It's best experienced by a walk along the clifftops, from the main town of Fira to the northern village of Oia. The precariousness and impermanence of the place is breathtaking. Recover from your efforts with an ice-cold Mythos beer in Oia, as you wait for its famous sunset.

Europe's
Top Itineraries

London to Chartres Capital Sights

5 DAYS

This trip takes in two of Europe's mustn't-miss capitals. Start off with two days in London, then hop on the high-speed Eurostar train at St Pancras and in just over two hours – voilà! You're in la belle Paris...

LONDON

BRITAIN

BELGIUM

English Channel

FRANCE

VERSAILLES

PARIS

① London (p62)

Samuel Johnson famously quipped that when you're tired of London, you're tired of life, and this is certainly a city that's brimming with unmissable sights. Begin with the **British Museum** and its treasure trove of artefacts, then mosey around **Covent Garden** en route to **St Paul's Cathedral**. Nip across the river to **Tate Modern** before seeing a play at the **Globe Theatre**. On day two, head for **Trafalgar Square**, browse the priceless artworks of the **National Gallery**, snap yourself outside the **Houses of Parliament** and **Westminster Abbey**, then picnic in **Hyde Park**. Finish with dinner and a show in the **West End**.

LONDON ◗ PARIS

🚊 **Two hours** Via Eurostar from London St Pancras to Paris Gare du Nord. ✈ **One hour** From Heathrow or Gatwick to Roissy Charles de Gaulle.

② Paris (p186)

On day three, catch the Eurostar from London to Paris. Devote the first morning to the **Louvre**, wander around the **Jardin des Tuileries**, then travel down the Seine to Paris' Gothic masterpiece, **Notre Dame Cathedral** – don't miss the panorama from the gargoyle-topped towers. The lively **Marais** is a great area to explore after dark. On day four, spend the morning on the **Left Bank**, factoring in a trip up the **Eiffel Tower**, a walk around the **Jardin du Luxembourg** and some window-shopping along stylish **Blvd St-Germain**. Follow up with Impressionist art at the **Musée d'Orsay** or catch the metro to bohemian **Montmartre**.

PARIS ◗ VERSAILLES

🚊 **40 minutes** Via RER Line C to Versailles' Rive-Gauche, 700m from the *château*. 🚗 **40 minutes** Along the A13.

③ Versailles (p216) and Chartres (p220)

On your last day, take a day trip from the capital to Louis XIV's fabulously over-the-top palace at Versailles, then continue to **Chartres** and its Gothic cathedral, famous for the vivid blues of its stained glass.

VERSAILLES ◗ CHARTRES

🚊 **50 minutes** From Versailles' Chantiers to Chartres. 🚗 **One hour** Via N10 and A11.

Jardin du Luxembourg (p187), Paris
PHOTOGRAPHER: EURASIA/GETTY ©

5 DAYS

Biarritz to Barcelona
Into the Basque Country

A sunbaked route that starts in the stylish coastal city of Biarritz before skipping across the border into the heart of the Spanish Basque Country.

Bay of Biscay

BILBAO ③

BIARRITZ ①

SAN SEBASTIAN ②

FRANCE

SPAIN

BARCELONA ④

Mediterranean Sea

① Biarritz (p255)

Biarritz has been one of France's swishest seaside resorts since the early 19th century. The town is dominated by its imposing cathedral, but the beaches are the main attraction. Stripy tents cover **Plage Miramar** and **Grande Plage** on hot days, while surfers make a beeline for the breaks around **Anglet**. After dark, relax with a seafood meal in Biarritz' buzzy waterfront cafes.

BIARRITZ ⊙ SAN SEBASTIÁN

🚗 **One hour** 50km via A63 and A8. 🚆 **Around one hour** Depending on connections at Irun.

② San Sebastián (p339)

Regular trains and buses cross the Franco-Spanish border to San Sebastián, another lively seaside resort that boasts some of the finest city beaches in Europe, including the golden curve of **Playa de la Concha**. It's also a great place to try **pintxos**, the Basque version of tapas.

SAN SEBASTIÁN ⊙ BILBAO

🚗 **1½ hours** 98km via A8. 🚆 **Around one hour** With a change at Irun.

③ Bilbao (p341)

From San Sebastián, continue west to Bilbao, home to the **Guggenheim Museum**, one of Spain's top art galleries. Designed by the Canadian architect Frank Gehry, the building is a work of art in its own right, blending sharp angles and swooping curves into one seamless whole. Beyond the museum is Bilbao's atmospheric old quarter, **Casco Viejo**, where you'll find plenty of places to try authentic Basque cuisine.

BILBAO ⊙ BARCELONA

🚆 **Six hours** Via Zaragoza or Pamplona. 🚗 **Six hours** 605km via AP-68 and AP-2

Puppy, Jeff Koons, in front of Guggenheim Museum (p341), Bilbao
PHOTOGRAPHER: JEAN-PIERRE LESCOURRET/LONELY PLANET IMAGES ©

④ Barcelona (p319)

On day four, catch a cross-country train to Barcelona, Spain's sexiest and hippest city. Barcelona is best known for its Modernista architecture, largely thanks to the architect Antoni Gaudí whose legacy remains in the city – most obviously at **La Sagrada Família**. This dreamlike cathedral has already taken around 130 years to build and is still decades away from completion. Elsewhere around town, look out for Gaudí's touch at **Casa Batlló** and **La Pedrera**, as well as Barcelona's hilltop park, **Parc Güell**. You'll need at least a couple of days in Barcelona to see all the sights, especially once you've started delving into the achingly beautiful area around **El Raval** and the **Barri Gòtic**.

10 DAYS

Cannes to Venice
Living the High Life

Don your shades and roll the top down – this glamorous road trip travels from the exclusive beaches of the Côte d'Azur all the way to Venice's canals.

SWITZERLAND

FRANCE

VENICE ⑤

④ MILAN

ITALY

③ MONACO
① ② NICE
CANNES

MEDITERRANEAN SEA

CORSICA (FR)

➊ Cannes (p275)

Begin your trip in super-chic Cannes, which comes alive during its annual film festival, when stars, producers and directors from the film world descend on the Riviera to cut deals and show their latest opus. Outside festival season, Cannes is still a lovely place to be, whether bronzing your body on the beach or browsing around the Old Town.

CANNES ➡ NICE

🚆 **40 minutes** 🚗 **40 minutes** 34km via A8.

➋ Nice (p269)

Tourists have been flocking to Nice for more than a century, and it's still one of the Med's most popular resorts (even if the beaches are made of pebbles). The street market on **Cours Saleya** is one of France's liveliest, while **Vieux Nice** is a photogenic tangle of shady alleyways and colourful houses. There are top views from the **Parc du Château**, perched on the cliff-top at the eastern end of **Promenade des Anglais**.

NICE ➡ MONACO

🚆 **20 minutes** 🚗 **30 minutes** 20km via A8, 25km to 30km via corniche roads.

➌ Monaco (p276)

A breakneck spin along the **corniches** takes you into **Monaco**, a self-governing principality that has long been a favourite playground for the rich and famous (largely thanks to its notoriously lax tax laws). Plush apartments pack the hillside and million-dollar yachts bob in the harbour, while their owners gamble away fortunes on the roulette tables of **Monte Carlo casino**. If it's all too much, Monaco's **aquarium** and hill-top **exotic gardens** make a peaceful retreat from the hubbub.

Gondolas on a canal, Venice
PHOTOGRAPHER: RICHARD I'ANSON/LONELY PLANET IMAGES ©

MONACO ➡ MILAN

🚆 **Three hours** Via Ventimiglia. 🚗 **3½ hours** 302km via A10, A26 and A7.

➍ Milan (p420)

Monaco sits right on the Italian border, and nearby Ventimiglia has train links across northern Italy. Trendy, fashionable and effortlessly elegant, **Milan** encapsulates the essence of Italian style. The shopping is stellar, but if you'd rather just soak up the sights, don't overlook the Gothic **Duomo** and da Vinci's stunning mural of **The Last Supper**.

MILAN ➡ VENICE

🚆 **2½ hours** 🚗 **3½ hours** 284km via A4.

➎ Venice (p424)

You simply couldn't come to northern Italy and not visit **Venice**. The canal city is an ambler's paradise, but while landmarks such as **Basilica di San Marco**, the **Grand Canal** and the **Galleria dell'Accademia** are essential, you'll find another side to Venice hidden among the narrow lanes and secret canals where tourist hordes never venture.

10 DAYS

Bruges to Salzburg
Old Europe

This multi-country trip takes in the best bits of Belgium, the Netherlands, Germany and Austria. It's doable in 10 days, but more fun if you have time for side trips.

NORTH SEA

NETHERLANDS

2 AMSTERDAM

BERLIN 3

GERMANY

1 BRUGES

BELGIUM

NUREMBERG 4

FRANCE

SALZBURG 5

SWITZERLAND   AUSTRIA

❶ Bruges (p535)

Belgium might not have big mountains or superstar beaches, but it does have charming towns aplenty – chief among them being Bruges, an impossibly pretty package of cafe-lined squares, cobblestone streets, romantic canals and an iconic **bell tower**. Nearby **Ghent** is another waterfront town you'll find it hard not to fall for.

BRUGES ➲ AMSTERDAM
🚆 **Four hours** Via Brussels.

❷ Amsterdam (p494)

Regular trains run from Bruges to **Brussels** – another stately city that's worth a stop – but for this trip we're heading straight to Amsterdam, a city so laid back it's practically horizontal. Amsterdam's compact size means you can cover the centre in a day, squeezing in the **Van Gogh Museum**, **Anne Frank's House** and **Rembrandt's studio**, followed by a **canal cruise** and a visit to the **Red Light District**. Two days would allow a day trip to **Leiden** or **Delft**.

AMSTERDAM ➲ BERLIN
🚆 **6½ hours** Direct. ✈ **One hour**

❸ Berlin (p562)

Germany's capital ranks alongside London, Rome and Paris in the must-see stakes. You'll need two days: day one for the West, including the **Reichstag**, **Holocaust Memorial** and **Tiergarten**, and day two for the East, including a **Berlin Wall tour**, **Checkpoint Charlie**, the **DDR Museum** and **Potsdamer Platz**. With another day, add the landscaped gardens of **Park Sanssouci** in Potsdam.

Christmas market, Nuremberg (p596)
PHOTOGRAPHER: MARTIN RUGNER/LONELY PLANET IMAGES ©

BERLIN ➲ NUREMBERG
🚆 **Four hours** Direct. ✈ **4¼ hours** 435km via A10, A9 and A3.

❹ Nuremberg (p595)

Since the dark days of WWII, Nuremberg's **Altstadt** has been impeccably restored and now hosts one of Europe's most beautiful **Christmas markets**. The city also has a fine castle, the **Kaiserburg**, and some excellent **museums** that confront its troubled past. Best of all, the rest of **Bavaria** is right on your doorstep, with the dramatic castles of **Neuschwanstein** and **Hohenschwangau** just a short drive away.

NUREMBERG ➲ SALZBURG
🚆 **Three hours** Change at Munich. 🚗 **3½ hours** 300km via E45, E52 and E60.

❺ Salzburg (p657)

Across the Austrian border lies Salzburg, a baroque blockbuster chiefly known for its musical connections: Wolfgang Amadeus Mozart (born here) and *The Sound of Music* (filmed here). The town is at its busiest during the annual **Salzburg Festival** and **Christmas markets**, but the **Altstadt** is always animated – and the Alps are only a quick skip away. Altogether now – *the hills are alive...*

12 DAYS

London to Athens
The Grand Tour

This is the big one – end to end, top to bottom and back again. You're covering all four corners of Europe, so travelling times are long, but apart from a few flights, you can mostly let the train take the strain.

① London (p62)

Two days isn't much time in London, but you should still be able to do the highlights: the **Tower of London**, **Tate Modern**, **Big Ben** and **Buckingham Palace**, with an extra day for discovering some of the shops, restaurants and theatres of the **West End**, and perhaps a trip downriver to **Greenwich**.

LONDON ⭢ PARIS
🚆 **Two hours** On the Eurostar. ✈ **One hour** From Heathrow or Gatwick to Roissy Charles de Gaulle.

② Paris (p186)

A high-speed Eurostar train whisks you via the Channel Tunnel to Paris. It's a city you've seen a million times in the movies, but somehow nothing prepares you for your first sight of the **Eiffel Tower** appearing above the rooftops – and that's before you even get started on the **Arc de Triomphe**, the **Louvre** and **Montmartre**.

PARIS ⭢ MADRID
🚆 **10 hours** With a change at Irun. ✈ **Two hours**

③ Madrid (p298)

There's nowhere better to experience Spain than Madrid – whether that means dining out on **tapas** in one of the city's squares, heading for a meal at a top-class **taberna**, watching authentic flamenco at a traditional **tablao**, or surveying the national art collection at the **Museo Nacional del Prado**.

MADRID ⭢ ROME
✈ **Two hours**

④ Rome (p390)

The Eternal City; it is said a lifetime isn't enough to know it. During two days' sightseeing in **Rome**, choose from among the attractions of the **Colosseum**, **Vatican City**, **Pantheon**, **Spanish Steps** and the **Trevi Fountain**. For the perfect pizza, you'll want to head for the **centro storico** or **Trastevere**.

ROME ⭢ VIENNA
🚆 **13 hours** Via direct night train; other trains require change at Bologna, Venice or Florence.

Temple of Olympian Zeus (p743), Athens
PHOTOGRAPHER: SHANIA SHEGEDYN/LONELY PLANET IMAGES ©

7 **Berlin** (p562)

Another train trip transports you to the sights of Berlin, where you should spend a couple of days investigating the **Berlin Wall's** memorials and museums, plus new city sights like the **Sony Centre** and **Filmmuseum**. To experience the city's famous nightlife, **Kreuzberg** is the alternative hub, while **Prenzlauer Berg** is smarter.

BERLIN ➔ ATHENS
✈ Two hours

8 **Athens** (p742)

Finish with a cross-Europe flight to Europe's easternmost capital, **Athens**. The city is an Aladdin's Cave of ancient ruins: the **Temple of Olympian Zeus**, the **Ancient Agora** and the **Theatre of Dionysos** are all haunting in their own way, but it's the **Parthenon** that is guaranteed to stay with you long after you leave for home.

5 **Vienna** (p636)

Catch the overnight sleeper train direct to the imperial city of Vienna, where you'll spend a couple of days visiting the monomentally graceful **Hofburg**, watching the **Lipizzaner stallions** and whiling away hours over coffee and cake in one of Vienna's many grand **cafes**.

VIENNA ➔ PRAGUE
🚆 **4½ hours** Direct; longer with connections.
🚗 **Four hours** 335km via E50.

6 **Prague** (p694)

Even after decades behind the Iron Curtain, **Prague** has managed to cling to its rich cultural and architectural heritage. This isn't just the Czech Republic's loveliest city, it's also one of the loveliest in Europe, with iconic buildings such as **Charles bridge** and **Prague Castle** contributing to a truly dreamy skyline.

PRAGUE ➔ BERLIN
🚆 **4½ hours** direct 🚗 **3½ hours** 350km via A13

Europe Month by Month

February

Carnival in all its mania sweeps the Catholic regions of the Continent. Cold temperatures – even in Venice – are forgotten amid masquerades, street festivals and general bacchanalia.

 Venice Carnevale

In the period before Ash Wednesday, Venice, Italy, goes mad for masks. Costume balls enliven the social calendar in this storied old city like no other event. Even those without a coveted invite are swept up in the pageantry.

March

Let's hear it for the crocus: the tiny bulb's purple flower breaks through the ice-crusted soil to let Europe know there's a thaw in the air and spring will soon come.

 St Patrick's Day

Celebrations are held on 17 March in Irish towns big and small to honour the beloved Saint Patrick. While elsewhere the day is a commercialised romp of green beer, in his home country it's time for watching a parade with friends and family.

April

Spring arrives with a burst of colour, from the glorious bulb fields of Holland to the blooming orchards of Spain.

 Semana Santa

Parades of penitents and holy icons take to the streets of Spain, notably Seville, during Easter. Thousands of members of religious brotherhoods parade in traditional garb. Look for the pointed *capirotes* (hoods).

Top Events

🔒 **Christmas Markets, Germany & Austria,** December

🍺 **Oktoberfest, Germany,** September

✷ **Venice Carnevale, Italy,** February

★ **Edinburgh International Festival, Scotland,** August

✷ **Notting Hill Carnival, England,** August

February Masked woman, Venice Carnevale (p429), Italy

Settimana Santa

Italy celebrates Holy Week with processions and passion plays. By Holy Thursday Rome is thronged with the faithful and even non-believers are swept up in the emotion and piety of the hundreds of thousands thronging the Vatican and St Peter's Basilica.

 Feria de Abril

Hoods off! This is a week-long party held in Seville in late April to counterbalance the religious peak of Easter. The many old squares in this gorgeous city come alive during Spain's long, warm nights.

 Koninginnedag (Queen's Day)

Celebrations are held nationwide in the Netherlands on 30 April, but especially in Amsterdam, which is awash in orange costumes and fake afros, beer, balloon animals, beer, dope, Red Bull, beer, leather boys, skater dykes, temporary roller coasters, clogs, beer, fashion victims, grannies...

 # May

Expect nice weather anywhere but especially in the south where the Mediterranean summer is already full steam ahead. Yachts prowl the harbours, while beautiful people ply the sands.

 Cannes Film Festival

The famous, not-so-famous and the merely topless converge for a year's worth of movies in little more than a week in Cannes, France. Those winning awards will be sure to tell you about it in film trailers for years to come.

 Brussels Jazz Marathon

Around-the-clock jazz performances hit Brussels, Belgium, during the second-last weekend in May (www.brusselsjazz marathon.be), when the saxophone becomes the instrument of choice for this international-flavoured city's most joyous celebration.

 # June

The huge summer travel season hasn't burst out yet but the sun has burst through the clouds and the weather is gorgeous, from the hot shores in the south to the cool climes of the north.

 Glastonbury Festival

Glastonbury's youthful summer vibe peaks for this long weekend of music, theatre and New Age shenanigans (www.glaston buryfestivals.co.uk). It's one of England's favourite outdoor events and more than 100,000 turn up to writhe around in the grassy fields (or deep mud) at Pilton Farm.

 # July

Visitors have arrived from around the world and outdoor cafes, beer gardens and beach clubs are hopping. Expect beautiful – even steamy – weather anywhere you go.

 Il Palio

Siena's great annual event is the Palio on 2 July and 16 August, a pageant culminating in a bareback horse race round Il Campo. The Italian city is divided into 17 *contrade* (districts), of which 10 compete for the *palio* (silk banner) and emotions explode.

 Sanfermines ('Running of the Bulls')

Huge male bovines and people who want to be close to them invade Pamplona, Spain, from 6 to 14 July, when the town is overrun with thrill seekers, curious onlookers and, oh yeah, bulls. The *encierro* (running of the bulls) begins at 8am daily.

Bastille Day

There's fireworks, balls, processions and more for France's national day, 14 July. It's celebrated in every French town and city: go to the heart of town and get caught up in this patriotic festival.

 Notting Hill Carnival

Held over two days in August, this is Europe's largest and London's most vibrant outdoor carnival, where London's Caribbean community shows the city how to party. Food, frolicking and fun are just a part of a vast multicultural celebration.

 Edinburgh International Festival

Edinburgh, Scotland, hosts three weeks of drama, comedy, dance and music from around the globe (www.eif.co.uk). For two weeks the International Festival overlaps with the Fringe Festival (www.edfringe.com), which also draws innovative international acts. Expect cutting-edge comedy, drama and productions that defy description.

 De Gentse Feesten

Belgium's Ghent is transformed into a 10-day party of music and theatre, a highlight of which is the vast techno celebration called 10 Days Off (www.gentsefeesten.be). This gem of the low country is high on fine bars serving countless kinds of beer.

 # August

Everybody's going somewhere as half of Europe shuts down to go enjoy the traditional month of holiday with the other half. If it's near the beach, from Germany's Baltic to Spain's Balearic, it's mobbed.

 Salzburg Festival

Austria's renowned classical music festival, the Salzburg Festival (www.salzburgfestival.at) attracts international stars from late July to the end of August. That urbane person sitting by you having a glass of wine who looks like a famous cellist probably is.

 # September

It's cooling off in every sense, from the northern countries to the romance started on a dance floor in Ibiza. This may be the best time to visit: the weather's still good and the crowds have thinned.

 Venice International Film Festival

The Mostra del Cinema di Venezia is Italy's top film festival and one of the world's top indie film fests (www.labiennale.org). The judging here is seen as an early indication of what to look for at the next year's Oscars.

Oktoberfest

Germany's legendary beer-swilling party (www.oktoberfest.de) starts mid-September in Munich (don't ever tell anyone you turned up for it in October, even if you did). Millions descend for litres of beer and carousing that has no equal. If you haven't planned ahead, you'll sleep in Austria.

Festes de la Mercè

Barcelona knows how to party until dawn and it outdoes itself during the four-day Festes de la Mercè (around 24 September). Head for concerts, join the dancing and marvel at *castellers* (human castle-builders), fireworks and *correfocs* – a parade of firework-spitting dragons and devils.

 # November

Leaves have fallen and snow is about to in much of Europe. Even in the temperate zones around the Med, it can get chilly, rainy and blustery.

 ## Guy Fawkes Night

Bonfires and fireworks erupt across Britain on 5 November, recalling a failed antigovernment plot from the early 17th century. Go to high ground in London to see glowing explosions all around. It's hard to imagine what might have happened if Fawkes had succeeded.

 # Decem...

Christmas is a good excuse fo... cheer despite the weather in virt... every city and town. Decorations transform even the drabbest shopping street and every region has its own traditions.

 ## Christmas Markets

Christkindlmarkts are held across Germany and Austria. The most famous are in Nuremberg (p596) and Vienna (p647) but every town has one. Warm your hands through your mittens on a hot mug of mulled wine and find that special (or kitsch) present.

 ## Natale

Italian churches set up intricate cribs or *presepi* (nativity scenes) in the lead-up to Christmas. Some are quite famous, most are works of art and many date back hundreds of years and are venerated for their spiritual ties.

Far left: July Pageant horse at Il Palio (p454), Siena; **Left: December** Christmas market, Salzburg (p657), Austria

...over Europe, our authors have hunted down the ...hot and the happening. These are some of our fa-...ute recommendations, see lonelyplanet.com/europe.

1 THE ACROPOLIS MUSEUM, ATHENS

Despite the endless delays and overruns, Athens' flagship archaeological museum has finally opened to enormous fanfare right next to the Acropolis. The museum now houses Greece's foremost collection of ancient artefacts, sculptures and other treasures, and the stunning steel-and-glass building has won a host of architectural awards. Give yourself a whole day to explore, because this is one place that definitely deserves it (p742).

2 CENTRE POMPIDOU-METZ, PARIS

The space-age curves of Metz' gleaming white modern-art museum is as much a show-stopper as its Parisian big brother, and has brought a new sense of excitement and energy to this corner of northern France (p236).

3 DARWIN CENTRE, NATURAL HISTORY MUSEUM, LONDON

Explore the history of evolution at the striking new Darwin Centre, an eight-storey, egg-shaped structure housed inside a glass pavilion at the Natural History Museum (p73).

4 GREEN SEVILLE, SPAIN

With the opening of a new metro system and the pedestrianisation of many streets, Seville (p349) is now easier to negotiate and its monuments are finally grime-free.

5 HIGH-SPEED TRAINS FROM AMSTERDAM

Finally open (years late and well over budget), the high-speed line from Amsterdam now whisks you to Paris in under three hours, via Schiphol Airport and Rotterdam (p549).

6 LATE-NIGHT VATICAN

The Vatican Museum is now open late on most Friday evenings between early May and October – but you need to book online to be sure of a place (p401).

7 SWISS NATIONAL PARK CENTRE

Switzerland's national park may be among Europe's oldest (founded 1914), but its new visitor centre (p692) brings things right up to date. Explore conservation issues and meet the local wildlife before hitting the trails.

8 THE SHARD, LONDON

Something sleek, shiny and very tall is being built beside London Bridge... When it's completed, this huge skyscraper will be the tallest building in the EU at 310m high.

Get Inspired

 ## Books

○ **Neither Here nor There: Travels in Europe** Hilarious travelogue by best-selling author Bill Bryson, retracing his European backpacking trip of 20 years before.

○ **Europe: A History** Professor Norman Davies' sweeping overview of European history.

○ **In Europe: Travels through the Twentieth Century** Fascinating account of journalist Geert Mak's travels.

○ **Philip's Multiscale Europe** Plan your European road trip with this continent-wide travel atlas.

 ## Films

○ **The Third Man** (1949) Classic tale of wartime espionage in old Vienna, starring Orson Welles and that zither theme.

○ **The Talented Mr Ripley** (1999) This sumptuous thriller directed by Anthony Minghella makes evocative use of its Italian setting.

○ **Amélie** (2001) Endearing and tale following the quirky adventures of Parisian do-gooder Amélie Poulain.

○ **Volver** (2006) An insightful snapshot of contemporary Spain by auteur Pedro Almodóvar.

Music

○ **The Kinks: Village Green Preservation Society** Classic album exploring aspects of Englishness from Ray Davies and Co.

○ **The Original Three Tenors: 20th Anniversary Edition** Operatic classics courtesy of Pavarotti, Carreras and Domingo.

○ **The Best of Edith Piaf** The sound of France, including a selection of the Little Sparrow's greatest hits.

○ **Vinicio Capossela: Da Solo** Award-winning singer-songwriter, dubbed the Italian Tom Waits.

 ## Websites

○ **Visit Europe** (www .visiteurope.com) Extensive resource of the European Travel Commission.

○ **The Man in Seat Sixty-One** (www.seat61. com) Hands-on advice for European train travel.

○ **Eurocheapo** (www .eurocheapo.com) Budget-friendly ideas for hotels, eating, flights and sights.

○ **Auto Europe** (www.auto -europe.com) Cheap car hire from all over Europe.

Short on time?

This list will give you an instant insight into Europe.

Read *The Europe Book* is a sumptuous Lonely Planet photobook packed with images of Europe's greatest sights.

Watch *Cinema Paradiso* (1988) tells the cockle-warming tale of one boy's cinematic love affair in rural Italy.

Listen *Gipsy Kings: Greatest Hits* offers sexy Spanish rhythms married with folk, flamenco, Latin and gypsy tunes.

Log on www.raileurope. com has the info you need to plan the ultimate pan-European train trip.

Gondolas and gondoliers in Venice (p424), Italy
PHOTOGRAPHER: RUTH EASTHAM & MAX PAOLI/LONELY PLANET IMAGES ©

Need to Know

Buses

Useful for reaching smaller towns and villages, although timetables can be fiendishly complex.

Trains

High-speed trains connect many major cities, while slower trains serve regional towns. Train travel can often be faster and cheaper than flying.

Driving

Motorways in many countries incur a toll. Petrol in Europe is more expensive than in other places. Car hire is readily available.

Boat

Ferries connect the UK, Ireland and mainland Europe. Boats also link the Mediterranean coast with islands including Sicily and the Greek Islands.

Bicycles

Much of Europe is extremely bike-friendly (especially the Netherlands). Many big cities, including London, Paris and Berlin, have bike-hire schemes.

Planes

Internal flights with budget carriers are numerous, but often don't land at major airports. International hubs include London, Paris and Frankfurt.

When to Go

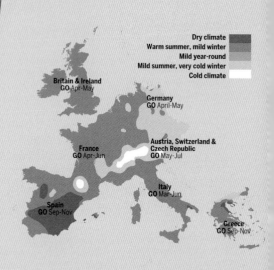

Dry climate
Warm summer, mild winter
Mild year-round
Mild summer, very cold winter
Cold climate

Britain & Ireland
GO Apr-May

Germany
GO April-May

Austria, Switzerland & Czech Republic
GO May-Jul

France
GO Apr-Jun

Italy
GO Mar-Jun

Spain
GO Sep-Nov

Greece
GO Sep-Nov

High season
(Jul & Aug)
- Hotel prices take a hefty hike in summer
- Ski-season in the Alps is between December and early March
- Accommodation can be hard to find around Easter

Shoulder
(Apr–May & Sep–Oct)
- Weather is warm and settled across much of Europe
- Crowds are lighter, but some attractions keep shorter hours

Low Season
(Nov–Mar)
- Look out for cheap deals on flights and accommodation during the winter months
- Some hotels, sights and activities close completely for the winter

Advance Planning

- **One month before** Book train tickets. Most train companies offer substantial discounts for advance bookings.
- **Two weeks before** Reserve tickets online for popular sights, such as the Alhambra in Granada, the Vatican Museums and the Colosseum in Rome.
- **When you arrive** Look into buying a travel pass if you're visiting major cities and using public transport; some travel passes also offer free or discounted admissions.

Set Your Budget

Budget less than €100
- Double room in a budget B&B: €60
- Cheap bistro lunch menu: €15
- Museum ticket: €10

Midrange €100–200
- Double room in a midrange hotel or B&B: €80–120
- Restaurant meal with a glass of wine or beer: €20–30
- Museum admission & one-day travel pass: €15

Top End more than €200
- Night in a luxury hotel: €150
- Three-course gourmet meal including wine: €35–45
- Admission costs including guided tour: €25
- Taxi fares: €10–15

Exchange Rates

Australia	A$1	€0.74	£0.67
Canada	C$1	€0.72	£0.65
Euro	€1	–	£0.90
Japan	¥100	€0.86	£0.77
Swiss	Sfr1	€0.82	£0.74
UK	£1	€1.10	–
USA	US$1	€0.69	£0.62

For current exchange rates see www.xe.com

What to bring

- **Passport or EU ID** Remember to bring your driver's licence if you're hiring a car.
- **Travel adaptors** EU countries use two-pin sockets; the UK uses three-pin sockets.
- **Sturdy shoes** You'll be doing a lot of walking, so good soles are important.
- **Raingear** In case the weather turns for the worse.
- **Travel Insurance** Check the policy wording on winter sports and flight delays.
- **Earplugs** To block out late-night revelry.
- **Flip-flops/sandals** For the beach.
- **A corkscrew** Essential for picnics.
- **Travel dictionary** Choose one with a good food section for the country you're travelling to.

Visas
- EU nationals can live and work freely throughout Europe. Citizens of most Western nations (including Australia, Canada, New Zealand, South Africa and the USA) do not require a visa to visit most EU countries for stays of up to 90 days.
- The Schengen Agreement means there are no passport controls on borders between EU nations including Austria, Belgium, France, Germany, Greece, Italy, the Netherlands, Spain, Switzerland and the Czech Republic.
- Most other nationals will need to arrange visas before they arrive.

Arriving in Europe

- **All Europe's main airports have frequent connections to city centres.**

London Express trains run from Heathrow to London Paddington, from Gatwick to London Victoria and from Stansted to Liverpool St. Piccadilly tube line runs to Heathrow terminals.

Paris Regular buses and trains run from Charles de Gaulle and Orly to central Paris.

Berlin Trains run straight to Alexanderplatz.

Madrid Line 8 of the Metro and the Aerocity minibus run to the city centre.

Amsterdam Schiphol Regular trains from Schiphol to Centraal Station.

Rome From Fiumicino, take the Leonardo Express train to Termini or the FR1 to Trastevere.

Prague The Airport Express bus runs to Prague's main train station.

Athens Metro Line 3 runs to the city centre (€6, 40 minutes).

Britain & Ireland

Few countries are as plagued by cliché as Britain and Ireland. On one side of the Irish Sea, it's all shamrocks and shillelaghs, Guinness and 40 shades of green; over in Britain, it's double-decker buses and red telephone boxes, buttoned-up emotions and stiff upper lips. And while some of the stereotypes remain true, these ancient next-door nations seem to have sloughed off most of the old clichés these days and turned their gazes firmly towards the future.

Whether it's ancient history or contemporary culture that draws you to Britain's shores, you'll really be spoiled for choice. Travelling around these pocket-sized islands is an absolute breeze, and you'll soon find you're never more than a train ride away from the next national park, tumbledown castle, world-class gallery or stately home. There are museums aplenty, galleries galore and mile upon mile of some of the most stunning coast and countryside you'll find anywhere in Europe. Buckle up, chaps – you're in for an awfully big adventure.

Castle Howard (p118), England
PHOTOGRAPHER: KARL BLACKWELL/LONELY PLANET IMAGES ©

Britain & Ireland

1 The Tower of London
2 St Paul's Cathedral, London
3 Tate Modern, London
4 Stonehenge
5 Bath
6 Castle Howard

ATLANTIC
OCEAN

NORTH
SEA

NORTH
SEA

Shetland Islands
Yell Fetlar
Foula Mainland
Lerwick

Orkney Islands

John O'Groats

Durness

Stornoway

The Minhch

Lochinver
Loch Shin
Ullapool

Uig
Dunvegan
Portree
Kyle of Lochalsh

Sea of the Hebrides

Tobermory

Lochaline

Fort William
Ben Nevis

Loch Lomond & Trossachs National Park

North Channel

Lochranza

Greenock
Glasgow

Buncrana
Coleraine
Derry
Ballymena
Strabane

Galloway Forest Park

Dumfries
Nith

Fraserburgh

Aberdeen

Moray Firth
Elgin
Inverness
Avon
Aviemore
Loch Ness

Cairngorms National Park

Avon

Dundee

Earn

Stirling
Loch Lomond

EDINBURGH

Melrose
Jedburgh

Berwick-upon-Tweed

Northumberland National Park

Hadrian's Wall

Carlisle

Newcastle-upon-Tyne

Britain & Ireland Highlights

ENTRY TO THE TRAITORS GATE

1 Tower of London & Beefeaters

One of London's world-famous landmarks, the Tower has almost 1000 years of history. Equally famous are the Yeoman Warders (or 'beefeaters') who guard the tower and the Crown Jewels. To qualify, all beefeaters must have served at least 22 years in the armed forces and earned a Long Service and Good Conduct Medal.

Need to Know

PHOTO OP On the battlements overlooking the Thames **DID YOU KNOW?** The Yeoman Guards' ceremonial outfits cost around £7000 **See our author's review on p68**.

The Tower of London Don't Miss List

BY JOHN KEOHANE, CHIEF YEOMAN WARDER

1 A TOWER TOUR

To understand the tower and its history, a guided tour with one of the Yeoman Warders is essential. Very few people appreciate that the tower is actually our home as well as our place of work; all the Warders live inside the outer walls, which once housed stables and workshops. The tower is rather like a miniature village – visitors are often rather surprised to see our washing hanging out beside the castle walls!

2 THE CROWN JEWELS

Visitors often think the Crown Jewels are the Queen's personal jewellery collection, but the Crown Jewels are actually the ceremonial regalia used during the coronation. The highlights are the Sceptre and the Imperial State Crown, which contains the diamond known as the Star of Africa.

3 THE WHITE TOWER

The White Tower is the original royal palace of the Tower of London, but hasn't been used as a royal residence since 1603. It's the most iconic building in the complex – inside you can see exhibits from the Royal Armouries, including a suit of armour belonging to Henry VIII.

4 RAVENS

A tower legend states that if its resident ravens ever left, the monarchy would topple – a royal decree states that we must keep a minimum of six ravens at any time. We currently have nine ravens, looked after by the Ravenmaster and his two assistants.

5 CEREMONY OF THE KEYS

We hold three daily ceremonies: the 9am Official Opening, the Ceremony of the Word (when the day's password is issued), and the 10pm Ceremony of the Keys, when the gates are locked after the castle has closed. Visitors are welcome to attend the latter, but must apply directly to the tower in writing.

Top: Changing of the guard;
Bottom Right: Coronation Robes, Crown Jewels

St Paul's Cathedral

The gleaming dome of St Paul's Cathedral (p72) has dominated London's skyline for over 300 years, and it remains one of the city's most recognisable landmarks. Built by the pioneering architect Sir Christopher Wren, it's not just one of Britain's most beautiful buildings, but also a masterpiece of architectural engineering – spend a few minutes in the Whispering Gallery and you'll see why.

Tate Modern

Modern art lovers absolutely mustn't miss a visit to Tate Modern (p79). This former power station on the south bank of the Thames has been transformed into Britain's top centre for contemporary art. The permanent collection takes in everything from Impressionism to pop art, but for most people the real highlight is the chance to see the latest installation inside the gigantic Turbine Hall.

Stonehenge

You've seen it a million times in photographs, magazines and TV documentaries, but nothing quite prepares you for your first sight of the real Stonehenge (p103). Built by ancient Britons in several stages between 3000 BC and 1600 BC, it's one of the world's most unforgettable structures. To see the circle at its best, book an after-hours guided tour, which will enable you to dodge the crowds and traffic noise.

Bath

Say what you like about the Romans, but one thing's for sure – they certainly knew how to build a hot tub. The natural geothermal springs of Bath (p98) have been attracting visitors for more than two thousand years, but this city has so much more to offer than a soothing soak: great restaurants, top-notch shopping and some of the finest Georgian architecture in all of England. Roman baths

Castle Howard

Stately homes don't come much statelier than Castle Howard (p118). Built during the early 18th century for the third Earl of Carlisle, it's the finest example of baroque architecture anywhere in Britain. And don't be surprised if it looks familiar – it's appeared in countless big-budget films and costume dramas, including the classic 1980s adaptation of *Brideshead Revisited*.

Britain & Ireland's Best...

Beauty Spots

o **The Lake District** (p129) Admire the landscape that inspired Wordsworth, Coleridge and Co.

o **The Yorkshire Dales** (p114) The epitome of England's green and pleasant land.

o **Snowdonia** (p131) Climb the highest mountain in Wales.

o **The Giant's Causeway** (p163) Explore Northern Ireland's great geological oddity.

o **The Ring of Kerry** (p160) Home to some of Ireland's most stunning views.

Landmarks

o **Stonehenge** (p103) The world's most famous stone circle, bar none.

o **The Eden Project** (p101) Three space-age biomes in a Cornish clay pit.

o **Buckingham Palace** (p67) Pomp and ceremony galore at the Queen's London residence.

o **The Houses of Parliament** (p66) The home of British politics.

o **The Angel of the North** (p119) Antony Gormley's winged icon has become a symbol of urban renewal.

Castles

o **Windsor Castle** (p94) Castles don't come much more regal than the Queen's weekend getaway.

o **Leeds Castle** (p95) Despite the name, this classic castle isn't anywhere near Leeds.

o **Warwick Castle** (p109) Is this England's finest fortress? You decide.

o **Edinburgh Castle** (p133) Gaze out from the battlements across Scotland's capital city.

o **Conwy Castle** (p132) A majestic medieval castle overlooking the Welsh coastline.

Need to Know

Literary Locations

○ **Brontë Parsonage Museum** (p113) Visit the house where Emily and Charlotte Brontë and their family lived from 1820 to 1861.

○ **Jane Austen's House** (p96) See the desk where Jane Austen penned *Emma*, *Mansfield Park* and *Persuasion*.

○ **Robert Burns Birthplace Museum** (p132) Pay homage to Scotland's national poet, Rabbie Burns.

○ **Charles Dickens Museum** (p69) Visit Charles Dickens' only surviving London residence.

ADVANCE PLANNING

○ **As early as possible** Arrange train tickets and car hire. Buying at least a month in advance secures the cheapest deals.

○ **One month before** Book hotels and make restaurant reservations, especially in popular cities such as London, Manchester and Bath.

○ **One week before** Book guided tours and confirm prices and opening hours.

RESOURCES

○ **Visit Britain** (www.visit britain.co.uk) The UK's main tourism site covers everything from accommodation to outdoor activities.

○ **National Rail Enquiries** (www.nationalrail.co.uk) Check out timetables and book train tickets.

○ **Traveline** (www.traveline .org.uk) Journey planning for public transport throughout the British Isles.

○ **BBC** (www.bbc.co.uk) News, programs and current affairs from Britain's iconic broadcaster.

GETTING AROUND

○ **Air** Budget flights connect most major British cities, including London, Manchester, Edinburgh and Glasgow.

○ **Car** The best option for exploring rural areas, although remember to factor in petrol and parking costs. Road distances in Britain are in miles; Ireland uses kilometres.

○ **Train** This is the best option for intercity travel. There are frequent connections between major towns.

○ **Bus** Long-distance coaches and local buses are cheap but slow. Coverage can be patchy outside major towns.

BE FOREWARNED

○ **Crowds** Top sights in popular cities get extremely crowded, especially in summer and on holiday weekends.

○ **Bank holidays** Most sights are closed and traffic on main roads can be a nightmare.

○ **Nightlife** City centres can get extremely rowdy after dark on weekends.

○ **Weather** Notoriously unpredictable, so be prepared.

Left: Skellig Michael, Ring of Kerry, Ireland;
Above: Houses of Parliament, London, England

Britain & Ireland Itineraries

It might be great by name, but Britain's surprisingly small by nature. The country's compact geography makes it easy to get around the sights; travelling by train allows you to drink in the scenery and dodge the traffic.

3 DAYS

LONDON TO BLENHEIM PALACE

The Big Smoke & Beyond

Every British adventure simply has to begin in **(1) London**. You could devote your whole holiday to exploring the capital's sights. In one day, you could just about fit in visits to Trafalgar Square, Westminster, St Paul's Cathedral and the Tower of London, before a lightning-fast detour to marvel at the Turbine Hall in Tate Modern, and finishing with an unforgettable evening performance at Shakespeare's Globe theatre.

Day two is more leisurely. Hop on a scenic boat along the River Thames to spend a morning at Britain's foremost botanical gardens, **(2) Kew Gardens**. In the afternoon, catch the boat downriver to visit Henry VIII's ostentatious abode at **(3) Hampton Court**.

On day three, take an early train out of the capital to visit **(4) Oxford**. Spend the morning wandering the quads and admiring the dreaming spires before catching a bus to **(5) Blenheim Palace**, not just one of England's finest stately homes, but also the birthplace of none other than Winston Churchill.

Top Left: Kew Gardens (p78), England;
Top Right: Oxford (p103), England

PHOTOGRAPHERS: (TOP LEFT) DOUG MCKINLAY/LONELY PLANET IMAGES ©;
(TOP RIGHT) SEAN CAFFREY/LONELY PLANET IMAGES ©

5 DAYS

OXFORD TO EDINBURGH
Northern Exposure

From **(1) Oxford**, it's an easy train trip west to the gorgeous Georgian city of **(2) Bath**, founded as a spa town by the Romans 2000 years ago and still one of England's most desirable addresses. Devote the day to exploring the Roman Baths, soaking in the Thermae Bath Spa and walking along the city's grandest streets, Royal Crescent and the Circus.

From Bath, it's on to Shakespeare's birthplace at **(3) Stratford-upon-Avon**. The town's awash with sights linked with the Bard, but don't miss the chance to catch some of his plays in action courtesy of the Royal Shakespeare Company. If there's time, history buffs might also want to squeeze in a side trip to **(4) Warwick Castle**.

Day three takes you to **(5) Manchester**, a revitalised city that has shaken off its post-industrial blues and now boasts some of Britain's top museums, galleries and restaurants. On day four, travel northwest to the Viking city of **(6) York**, with its medieval streets and landmark Minster, en route to **(7) Castle Howard**, the family seat of the aristocratic Howard family.

Finish your trip with a day in Scotland's capital, **(8) Edinburgh**, a city renowned for its arts, heritage and history, not to mention its cracking pub culture.

Discover Britain & Ireland

Royal Exchange Clock in the Square Mile (p68)

PHOTOGRAPHER: ELLIOT DANIEL/LONELY PLANET IMAGES ©

LONDON

POP 7.51 MILLION

One of the world's greatest cities, London has enough history, vitality and cultural drive to keep you occupied for weeks. This cosmopolitan capital leads international trends in music, fashion and the arts, riding a wave of 21st-century British confidence, breathing new life into established neighbourhoods like Westminster and Knightsbridge, and reinventing areas like Clerkenwell and Southwark that were formerly off the tourist track. With the Olympic Games rolling into town in 2012, and even despite the little matter of a global economic downturn, London's life and landscape never stands still.

History

London began as a Celtic village, near a ford across the River Thames. In the Roman era the settlement – now called Londinium – became properly established.

London grew prosperous and increased in global importance throughout the medieval period, surviving devastating challenges like the 1665 Plague and 1666 Great Fire.

Fuelled by mercantile wealth, the Victorian era was the city's golden age. In contrast, WWII was London's darkest hour, with the city scarred by relentless bombing – the period known as the Blitz.

The ugly postwar rebuilding phase of the 1950s gave way to the cultural renaissance of the 1960s, when London became the planet's swinging capital. Things dipped again during the 1970s, while the 1980s heralded a time of great plenty for some and hardship for others.

London in Two Days

You'll only be able to scratch the surface in two days, but here goes. Kick off on **Trafalgar Square** with a visit to the **National Portrait Gallery** and a photo-op next to **Nelson's Column**. Head south along Whitehall for a visit to **Westminster Abbey** and the **Houses of Parliament**, before heading over Westminster Bridge for an afternoon spin on the **London Eye** or a visit to **Tate Modern**. Round the day off with dinner at the **Oxo Tower Brasserie** and an evening stroll along the **South Bank**.

On day two, start with an early morning visit to either **St Paul's Cathedral** or the **Tower of London**, then head east via Covent Garden and Leicester Square to explore the lively streets around **Soho**. You could spend the afternoon with some retail therapy on **Regent St**, or expand your mind at the monumental **British Museum**. Finish up with a stylish dinner at **Wild Honey** or **Arbutus**, followed by a show in the theatre district around **Shaftesbury Avenue**.

With a couple more days to spare, you could explore some of London's other areas including the historic maritime centre of **Greenwich**, the funky neighbourhoods of **Shoreditch** and **Hoxton**, the museum district around **South Kensington** and the Botanical Gardens at **Kew**.

In 2000 the modern metropolis of London got its first elected Mayor (as opposed to the Lord Mayor of the City of London – a largely ceremonial role), and through the early years of the 21st century the city rediscovered a self-confidence that fuelled its selection as 2012 Olympic Games host.

Sights

London is teeming with magnificent buildings, world-leading museums and cutting-edge attractions. With so much to see and do, it can be hard to know where to start.

West End

Westminster may be the brains of the capital, while the parks are the lungs and the City the pockets, but if anywhere is the beating heart of London, it's the West End – a strident mix of culture and consumerism.

TRAFALGAR SQUARE   Landmark
(Map p74; ⊖Charing Cross) Trafalgar Square is a great place to start any visit to London. Dominating the square is 43m-high **Nelson's Column**, erected in 1843 to commemorate British hero Admiral Nelson's 1805 victory over Napoleon. Around the square are four plinths; three have permanent statues, the **fourth** has temporary installations.

NATIONAL GALLERY   Art Gallery
(Map p74; www.nationalgallery.org.uk; Trafalgar Sq WC2; ⊙10am-6pm Sat-Thu, to 9pm Fri; ⊖Charing Cross) Gazing grandly over Trafalgar Square, this is Britain's most important art repository. Seminal paintings from every epoch are here, including works by Giotto, Leonardo da Vinci, Michelangelo and Van Gogh.

NATIONAL PORTRAIT GALLERY Gallery
(Map p74; www.npg.org.uk; St Martin's Pl WC2; ⊙10am-6pm Sat-Wed, to 9pm Thu & Fri; ⊖Charing Cross) A visit here is like stepping into a picture book of British history.

PICCADILLY CIRCUS   Landmark
(⊖Piccadilly Circus) Neon-lit, turbo-charged Piccadilly Circus is home to a popular but unremarkable London landmark, the statue of **Eros**.

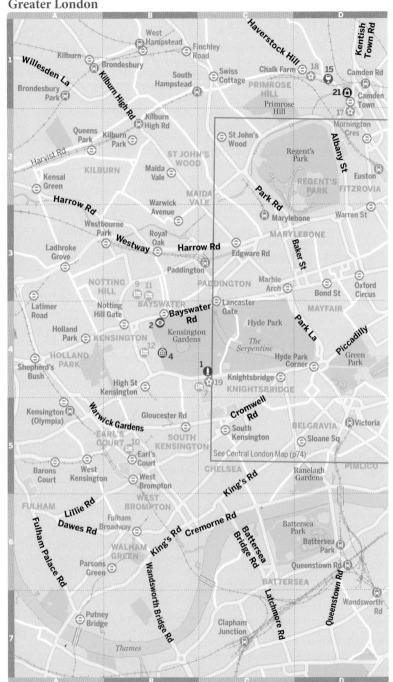

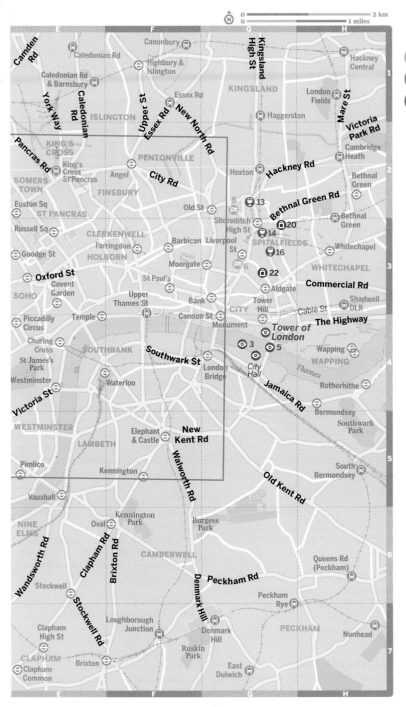

Greater London

◎ Top Sights

◎ Sights

◎ Sleeping

◎ Drinking

◎ Entertainment

◎ Shopping

COVENT GARDEN Landmark
(Map p74; ⊖Covent Garden) This is one of London's biggest tourist traps, where chain restaurants, souvenir shops, balconied bars and street entertainers vie for the punters' pound. It *was* once a garden, and then a famous market immortalised in the film *My Fair Lady*.

Westminster & Pimlico

Westminster has been the centre of political power for a millennium, and the area's many landmarks combine to form an awesome display of strength, gravitas and historical import.

WESTMINSTER ABBEY Cathedral
(Map p74; ☎020-7222 5152; www.westminster abbey.org; 20 Dean's Yard SW1; adult/child £15/6, tours £3; ⊙9.30am-4.30pm Mon, Tue, Thu & Fri, to 7pm Wed, to 2.30pm Sat; ⊖Westminster) Not merely a beautiful place of worship, Westminster Abbey serves up history cold on slabs of stone. This is where most monarchs have been crowned since 1066 (look out for the incongruously ordinary-looking **Coronation Chair**), and for centuries the great and the good have been interred here; in **Poet's Corner** you'll find the resting places of Chaucer, Dickens, Hardy, Tennyson, Dr Johnson and Kipling as well as memorials to Shakespeare, Jane Austen, Emily Brontë and more.

WESTMINSTER CATHEDRAL Cathedral
(Map p74; www.westminstercathedral.org.uk; Victoria St SW1; ⊙7am-7pm; ⊖Victoria) Not to be confused with the eponymous abbey, the neo-Byzantine Westminster Cathedral dates from 1895, and is the headquarters of Britain's Roman Catholic Church. The distinctive 83m red-brick and white-stone **tower** (adult/child £5/2.50) offers splendid views of London and, unlike St Paul's, you can take the lift.

HOUSES OF PARLIAMENT Landmark
(Map p74; www.parliament.uk; Parliament Sq SW1; ⊖Westminster) Officially called the Palace of Westminster, the oldest part of the interior is **Westminster Hall** (dating from 1097), but much of the visible building today dates from 1840. The palace's most famous feature is its clock tower, known (erroneously) as **Big Ben** – actually the name of the 13-tonne bell inside the tower. When parliament is in recess (three months over the summer, and a couple of weeks over Easter and Christmas) there are guided **tours** (☎0844 847 1672; www.ticketmaster.co.uk/housesofparliament; 75min tours adult/child £14/6) of the **House of Commons**, the **House of Lords** and other historic areas.

TATE BRITAIN Art Gallery
(Map p74; www.tate.org.uk; Millbank SW1; ⊙10am-5.40pm; ⊖Pimlico) Reaching through the time from 1500 to the present, this gallery crammed with local heavyweights such as Blake, Hogarth, Gainsborough, Whistler, Spencer and, especially, Turner, whose 'interrupted

visions' – unfinished canvasses of moody skies – wouldn't look out of place in the contemporary section, alongside works by David Hockney, Francis Bacon, Tracey Emin and Damien Hirst. There are free hour-long guided tours taking in different sections of the gallery daily at midday and 3pm, plus additional tours at 11am and 2pm on weekdays.

CHURCHILL MUSEUM & CABINET WAR ROOMS Museum
(Map p74; www.iwm.org.uk/cabinet; Clive Steps, King Charles St SW1; adult/child £15/free; ⊙9.30am-6pm; ⊖Westminster) The Cabinet War Rooms were Prime Minister Winston Churchill's underground military HQ during WWII. Now a wonderfully evocative and atmospheric museum, the restored and preserved rooms (including Churchill's bedroom) capture the drama of the time.

St James's & Mayfair
BUCKINGHAM PALACE Palace
(Map p74; ☎020-7766 7300; www.royalcollec tion.org.uk; Buckingham Palace Rd SW1; adult/ child £17/9.75; ⊙late Jul-Sep; ⊖Victoria) With so many imposing buildings in the capital, the Queen's relatively plain city

Tate-a-tate

To get between London's Tate galleries in style, the **Tate Boat** (www. thamesclippers.com) will whisk you from one to the other, stopping en route at the London Eye. Services run from 10.10am to 5.28pm daily at 40-minute intervals. A River Roamer hop-on hop-off ticket (purchased on board) costs £12, single tickets £5.

pad can be an anticlimax. When she's not visiting far-flung parts of the world, Elizabeth II splits her time between here, Windsor and Balmoral. A handy way of telling whether she's home is to check whether the 'royal standard' flag is flying on the roof. The gaudily furnished **State Rooms** are open in summer for the hordes of royal-loving tourists, but it's more fun outside watching the **changing of the guard** (⊙11.30am daily May-Jul, alternate days rest of yr).

Buckingham Palace

ST JAMES'S PARK & GREEN PARK
Parks

With its manicured flowerbeds and ornamental lake, **St James's Park** is a wonderful place to stroll and take in the views of Westminster, Buckingham Palace and St James's Palace. The expanse of **Green Park** links St James's Park to Hyde Park and Kensington Gardens, creating a green corridor from Westminster to Kensington.

The City

For centuries, the City *was* London. Today it's the central business district (also known as the '**square mile**').

TOWER OF LONDON
Castle

(Map p64; ☎0844 482 7777; www.hrp.org.uk; Tower Hill EC3; adult/child £17/9.50, audio guides £4/3; ⏰9am-5.30pm Tue-Sat, from 10am Sun & Mon, until 4.30pm Nov-Feb; ⊖Tower Hill) If you pay only one admission fee while you're here, make it the Tower of London, one of the city's three World Heritage sites. After the obligatory **Crown Jewels** visit, leave plenty of time to explore the walls, dun-

geons and museum rooms – a window on a gruesome and fascinating history, from the Roman era to the present day.

TOWER BRIDGE
Landmark

(Map p64) The south bank of the Thames was a thriving port in 1894 when elegant Tower Bridge was built. So the ships could reach the port, the bridge was designed so the roadway could be raised to allow ships to pass. It still goes up most days, although electricity has now taken over from the original steam engines. Walking across is free. For more insights, the **Tower Bridge Exhibition** (www.towerbridge.org.uk; adult/child £7/3; ⏰10am-5.30pm Apr-Sep, 9.30am-5pm Oct-Mar; ⊖Tower Hill) recounts the story with videos and animatronics.

Clerkenwell & Holborn

In these now-fashionable streets it's hard to find an echo of the notorious 'rookeries' of the 19th century, where families lived in probably the worst conditions in the city's long history, as documented so vividly in the novels of Charles Dickens.

SIR JOHN SOANE'S MUSEUM · Museum

(Map p74; www.soane.org; 13 Lincoln's Inn Fields WC2; tours £5; ☺10am-5pm Tue-Sat, 6-9pm 1st Tue of month; ⊖Holborn) Not all of this area's inhabitants were poor, aptly demonstrated by the remarkable home of a celebrated architect, now Sir John Soane's Museum.

CHARLES DICKENS MUSEUM · Museum

(Map p74; www.dickensmuseum.com; 48 Doughty St WC1; adult/child £6/3; ☺10am-5pm Mon-Sat, 11am-5pm Sun; ⊖Russell Sq) Dickens' sole surviving London residence is where his work really flourished – *The Pickwick Papers, Nicholas Nickleby* and *Oliver Twist* were all written here. The rooms are filled with fascinating memorabilia.

Southwark

SHAKESPEARE'S GLOBE · Historic Theatre

(Map p74; ☎020-7401 9919; www.shakespeares globe.org; 21 New Globe Walk SE1; adult/child £11/7; ☺10am-5pm; ⊖London Bridge) An authentic 1997 rebuild of the original London theatre where many Shakespeare plays were performed, the Globe has become a pilgrimage destination for fans of the Bard. Admission includes a guided tour of the open-roofed theatre, faithfully reconstructed from oak beams, hand-made bricks, lime plaster and thatch. Plays are still performed here (seats £15 to £35). As in Elizabethan times, 'groundlings' can watch for a modest price (£5) but there's no protection from the elements and you'll have to stand.

LONDON EYE · Views

(Map p74; ☎0871 781 3000; www.londoneye .com; adult/child £18/9.50; ☺10am-8pm; ⊖Waterloo) Originally designed as a temporary structure to celebrate the millennium, the Eye is a 135m-tall, slow-moving wheel with passengers riding in pods. The wheel takes 30 minutes to rotate completely and offers 25-mile views on a clear day. Book your ticket online to speed up your

69

Tower of London

Tackling the Tower

Although it's usually less busy in the late afternoon, don't leave your assault on the Tower until too late in the day. You could easily spend hours here and not see it all. Start by getting your bearings with the hour-long Yeoman Warder (Beefeater) tours; they're included in the cost of admission, entertaining and the only way to access the **Chapel Royal of St Peter ad Vincula ❶** which is where they finish up.

When you leave the chapel, the **Tower Green scaffold site ❷** is directly in front. The building immediately to your left is Waterloo Barracks , where the **Crown Jewels ❸** are housed. These are the absolute highlight of a Tower visit, so keep an eye on the entrance and pick a time to visit when it looks relatively quiet. Once inside, take things at your own pace. Slow-moving travelators shunt you past the dozen or so crowns that are the treasury's centrepiece, but feel free to double-back for a second or even third pass – particularly if you ended up on the rear travelator the first time around. Allow plenty of time for the **White Tower ❹**, the core of the whole complex, starting with the exhibition of royal armour. As you continue onto the 2nd floor, keep an eye out for **St John's Chapel ❺**. The famous **ravens ❻** can be seen in the courtyard around the White Tower. Head next through the towers that formed the **Medieval Palace ❼**, then take the **East Wall Walk ❽** to get a feel for the castle's mighty battlements. Spend the rest of your time poking around the many, many other fascinating nooks and crannies of the Tower complex.

BEAT THE QUEUES

Buy your fast-track ticket in advance online or at the City of London Information Centre in St Paul's Churchyard.

Palacepalooza An annual Historic Royal Palaces membership allows you to jump the queues and visit the Tower (and four other London palaces) as often as you like.

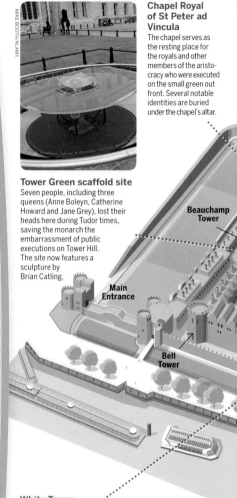

Chapel Royal of St Peter ad Vincula
The chapel serves as the resting place for the royals and other members of the aristocracy who were executed on the small green out front. Several notable identities are buried under the chapel's altar.

Tower Green scaffold site
Seven people, including three queens (Anne Boleyn, Catherine Howard and Jane Grey), lost their heads here during Tudor times, saving the monarch the embarrassment of public executions on Tower Hill. The site now features a sculpture by Brian Catling.

Beauchamp Tower

Main Entrance

Bell Tower

MIKE BOOTH/ALAMY.

White Tower
Much of the White Tower is taken up with this exhibition of 500 years of royal armour. Look for the virtually cuboid suit made to match Henry VIII's bloated body, complete with an oversized armoured pouch to protect his, ahem, crown jewels.

PAWEL LIBERA IMAGES/ALAMY

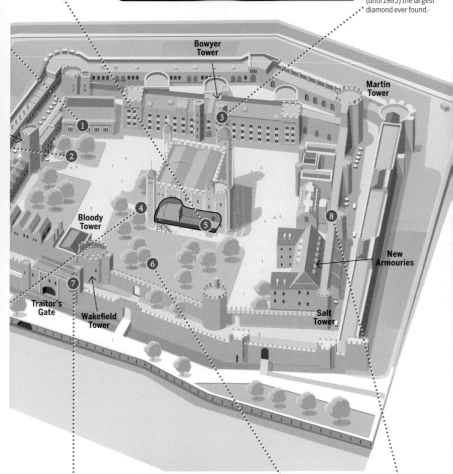

St John's Chapel
Kept as plain and unadorned as it would have been in Norman times, the White Tower's 2nd-floor chapel is the oldest surviving church in London, dating from 1080.

Crown Jewels

When they're not being worn for affairs of state, Her Majesty's bling is kept here. Among the 23,578 gems, look out for the 530-carat Cullinan diamond at the top of the Royal Sceptre, the largest part of what was (until 1985) the largest diamond ever found.

Bowyer Tower

Martin Tower

Bloody Tower

New Armouries

Traitor's Gate

Wakefield Tower

Salt Tower

Medieval Palace
This part of the Tower complex was commenced around 1220 and was home to England's medieval monarchs. Look for the recreations of the bedchamber of Edward I (1272–1307) in St Thomas's Tower and the throne room on the upper floor of the Wakefield Tower.

Ravens
This stretch of green is where the Tower's famous ravens are kept, fed on raw meat and blood-soaked bird biscuits. According to legend, if the birds were to leave the Tower, the kingdom would fall.

East Wall Walk
Follow the inner ramparts, starting from the 13th-century Salt Tower, passing through the Broad Arrow and Constable Towers, and ending at the Martin Tower, where the Crown Jewels were once stored.

ROD MCLEAN / ALAMY ©

Don't Miss St Paul's Cathedral

Dominating the City, **St Paul's Cathedral** (Map p72; www.stpauls.co.uk; adult/child £12.50/4.50; 8.30am-4pm Mon-Sat; St Paul's) was built by 'London's architect' Christopher Wren between 1675 and 1710. Inside, attractions include the **Whispering Gallery** – if you talk close to the wall it carries your words around to the opposite side – and the **Golden Gallery** at the very top, for an unforgettable view of London.

wait (you also get a 20% discount), or you can pay an additional £10 to jump the queue.

SOUTHWARK CATHEDRAL — Church
(Map p74; 020-7367 6700; Montague Close SE1; suggested donation £4-6.50; 8am-6pm Mon-Fri, 9am-6pm Sat & Sun; London Bridge) Although the central tower dates from 1520 and the choir from the 13th century, Southwark Cathedral is largely Victorian. Inside are monuments galore, including a Shakespeare Memorial.

HMAS BELFAST — Ship
(Map p64; http://hmsbelfast.iwm.org.uk; Queen's Walk SE1; adult/child £13/free; 10am-5pm; London Bridge) Launched in 1938, this battleship took part in the D-day landings and saw action in Korea. Explore the engine room, gun decks, galley, chapel and cells.

LONDON DUNGEON — Frights
(Map p74; 020-7403 7221; www.thedungeons .com; 28-34 Tooley St SE1; adult/child £20/15; 10.30am-5pm, extended hr during holidays; London Bridge) Older kids tend to love the London Dungeon, as the terrifying queues during school holidays and weekends testify. It's all spooky music, ghostly boat rides, fake blood and actors dressed as gory criminals.

SEA LIFE — Aquarium
(Map p74; 0871 663 1678; www.sealife.co.uk/ london; County Hall SE1; adult/child £18/13; 10am-6pm; Waterloo) One of the largest aquariums in Europe, with all sorts of aquatic creatures organised into different zones (coral cave, rainforest, River Thames), culminating with the shark walkway.

Chelsea, Kensington & Knightsbridge

Knightsbridge is where you'll find some of London's best-known department stores, while Kensington High St has a lively mix of chains and boutiques. Away from mammon, South Kensington boasts some of London's most beautiful and interesting museums.

VICTORIA & ALBERT MUSEUM Museum
(Map p74; V&A; www.vam.ac.uk; Cromwell Rd SW7; ⏱10am-5.45pm Sat-Thu, to 10pm Fri; ⊖South Kensington) A vast and wonderful museum of decorative art and design, the Victoria & Albert Museum is like the nation's attic, comprising four million objects collected from Britain and around the globe. In its 150 galleries you'll see ancient Chinese ceramics, Japanese swords, Asian and Islamic art, Rodin sculptures, Elizabethan gowns, an all-wooden Frank Lloyd Wright study and a pair of Doc Martens.

NATURAL HISTORY MUSEUM Museum
(Map p74; www.nhm.ac.uk; Cromwell Rd SW7; ⏱10am-5.50pm; ⊖South Kensington) A sure-fire hit with kids of all ages, the Natural History Museum on Cromwell Rd is crammed full of interesting stuff, starting with the giant dinosaur skeleton that greets you as you enter the main hall. The **Earth Galleries** are equally impressive.

SCIENCE MUSEUM
Museum
(Map p74; www.science museum.org.uk; Exhibition Rd SW7; ⏱10am-6pm; ⊖South Kensington) With seven floors of educational exhibits, the Science Museum covers everything from the Industrial Revolution to the exploration of space. There is something for all ages, from vintage cars to a flight simulator.

KENSINGTON PALACE Palace
(Map p64; www.hrp.org.uk/kensingtonpalace; Kensington Gardens W8; adult/child £13/6.25; ⏱10am-6pm; ⊖High St Kensington) Once the monarch's main residence, until George III moved across the park to Buckingham Palace, various members of the extended royal family still live here. In popular imagination it's most associated with three princesses: Victoria (born here in 1819), Margaret (sister of the current queen, who lived here until her 2002 death) and Diana (more than a million bouquets were left outside the gates following her death in 1997).

The building is undergoing major restoration work until January 2012.

HYDE PARK Park
(Map p74; ⏱5.30am- midnight; ⊖Marble Arch, Hyde Park Corner or Queensway) At 145 hectares, this is central London's largest open space. There's boating on the **Serpentine** and **Speaker's Corner** for oratorical acrobats. Nearby **Marble Arch** was designed as the entrance to Buckingham Palace, and moved here in 1851.

Hyde Park

Central London

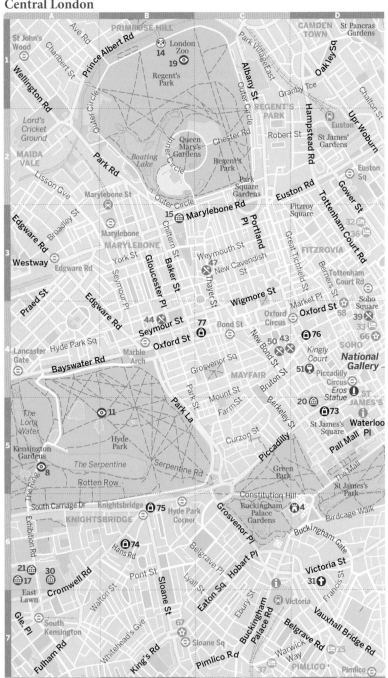

Central London

◎ Top Sights

◎ Sights

◎ Sleeping

KENSINGTON GARDENS   Park
(Map p64; ☺dawn-dusk; ⊖Queensway) Blending in with Hyde Park, these royal gardens are part of Kensington Palace. Diana devotees can visit the **Diana, Princess of Wales Memorial Playground** in its northwest corner. In contrast the **Albert Memorial** is a lavish marble, mosaic and gold affair opposite the Royal Albert Hall, built to honour Queen Victoria's husband, Albert (1819–61).

Marylebone

With one of London's best high streets and plenty of green space, increasingly hip Marylebone is a great area to wander.

REGENT'S PARK   Park
(Map p74; ⊖Regent's Park) This is London's finest open space – at once lively and serene, cosmopolitan and local – with football pitches, tennis courts and a boating lake. **Queen Mary's Gardens** are particularly pretty, with spectacular roses in summer, and the **Open Air Theatre**

(☏7935 5756; www.openairtheatre.org) hosts performances of Shakespeare, comedy and concerts on summer evenings.

LONDON ZOO   Zoo
(Map p74; www.londonzoo.co.uk; Outer Circle, Regent's Park NW1; adult/child £18/14; ☺10am-5.30pm Mar-Oct, to 4pm Nov-Feb; ⊖Camden Town) A huge amount of money has been spent to bring London Zoo, established in 1828, into the modern world. It now has a swanky £5.3 million gorilla enclosure and is involved in gorilla conservation in Gabon.

MADAME TUSSAUDS   Waxworks
(Map p74; ☏0870 400 3000; www.madame tussauds.co.uk; Marylebone Rd NW1; adult/child £26/22; ☺9.30am-5.30pm; ⊖Baker St) With so much fabulous free stuff to do in London, it's a wonder that people still join lengthy queues to visit Madame Tussauds, but in a celebrity-obsessed world the opportunity to pose beside Prince Charles and Camilla, or that other regal couple, Posh and Becks, is not short on

appeal. The wax figures are life-size and lifelike, and as close to the real thing as most of us will get.

Bloomsbury & St Pancras

In the 1930s, the pleasant streets of Bloomsbury were colonised by artists and intellectuals known as the Bloomsbury Group, which included novelists Virginia Woolf and EM Forster and the economist John Maynard Keynes.

BRITISH LIBRARY   Library

(Map p74; www.bl.uk; 96 Euston Rd NW1; ⓧ9.30am-6pm Mon & Wed-Fri, to 8pm Tue, to 5pm Sat, 11am-5pm Sun; ⓧKing's Cross St Pancras) You need to be a 'reader' (member) to use the vast collection, but the **Treasures gallery** is open to everyone. Here you'll find the 4th-century *Codex Sinaiticus* (one of the earliest Bibles), the 1215 *Magna Carta*, Shakespeare's first folio, Leonardo da Vinci's notebooks and the lyrics to 'A Hard Day's Night' scribbled on the back of Julian Lennon's birthday card.

Greenwich

An extraordinary cluster of buildings have earned 'Maritime Greenwich' its place on Unesco's World Heritage list. It's also famous for straddling the hemispheres; this is degree zero, the home of Greenwich Mean Time.

Greenwich is easily reached on the DLR. Or go by boat: **Thames River Services** (www.thamesriverservices.co.uk) depart half-hourly from Westminster Pier (single/return £9.50/12.50, one hour, every 40 minutes). Thames Clippers are cheaper.

FREE OLD ROYAL NAVAL COLLEGE
Historic Buildings

(www.oldroyalnavalcollege.org; 2 Cutty Sark Gardens SE10; ⓧ10am-5pm; ⓧDLR Cutty Sark) This magnificent example of monumental classical architecture is now partly used by the University of Greenwich and Trinity College of Music, but you can visit the **chapel** and the extraordinary **Painted Hall**, which took artist Sir James Thornhill 19 years to complete.

Tours of the complex leave at 2pm daily, taking in areas not otherwise open to the public (£5, 90 minutes).

FREE NATIONAL MARITIME MUSEUM
Museum
(020-8858 4422; www.nmm.ac.uk; Romney Rd SE10; 10am-5pm; DLR Cutty Sark) Directly behind the old college, the National Maritime Museum completes Greenwich's trump hand of historic buildings. Exhibits range from interactive displays to humdingers like Cook's journals and Nelson's uniform, complete with a hole from the bullet that killed him.

Behind Queen's House, idyllic **Greenwich Park** affords great views of London, and is capped by the **Royal Observatory** (to 7pm May-Aug), which Charles II had built in 1675 to help solve the riddle of longitude. Success was confirmed in 1884 when Greenwich was designated as the prime meridian of the world and Greenwich Mean Time (GMT) became the universal measurement of standard time.

O2
Performance Venue
(www.theo2.co.uk; Peninsula Sq SE10; North Greenwich) The world's largest dome (365m in diameter) opened on 1 January 2000 as the Millennium Dome, but closed on 31 December. Renamed the O2, it's now a 20,000-seater sports and entertainment arena surrounded by shops and restaurants.

West London

KEW GARDENS
Park
(www.kew.org.uk; Kew Rd; adult/child £14/free; 9.30am-6.30pm, earlier closing winter; Kew Gardens) In 1759 botanists began collecting specimens to plant in the 3-hectare plot known as the Royal Botanic Gardens. The gardens have bloomed to 120 hectares, and contain the most comprehensive botanical collection on earth.

HAMPTON COURT PALACE
Palace
(www.hrp.org.uk/HamptonCourtPalace; adult/child £14/7; 10am-6pm Apr-Oct, to 4.30pm Nov-Mar; Hampton Court) Built by Cardinal Thomas Wolsey in 1514 but coaxed out of him by Henry VIII, this is England's largest and grandest Tudor structure.

Take a themed tour led by costumed historians or, if you're in a rush, visit the highlights: **Henry VIII's State Apartments**, including the Great Hall with its spectacular hammer-beamed roof; the **Tudor Kitchens**; and the **Wolsey Rooms**. You could easily spend a day exploring the palace and its hectares of riverside gardens, especially if you get lost in the 300-year-old **maze**.

Hampton Court is 13 miles southwest of central London and is easily reached by train from Waterloo. Alternatively, the **riverboats** that head from Westminster to Kew continue here (return adult/child £23/12, three hours).

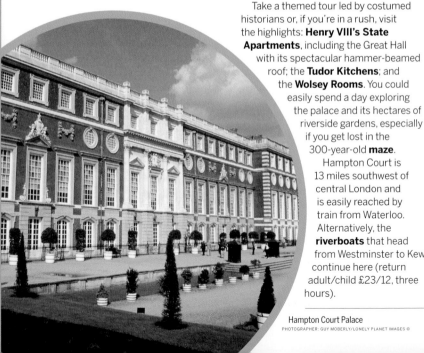

Hampton Court Palace

DAVID PEARSON / ALAMY ©

Don't Miss **Tate Modern**

This surprisingly elegant former power station is now the tremendous **Tate Modern** (www
.tate.org.uk; Queen's Walk SE1; 🕙10am-6pm Sun-Thu, to 10pm Fri & Sat; ⊖Southwark). Focusing on
modern art in all its wacky and wonderful permutations, it has been extraordinarily
successful in bringing challenging work to the masses, becoming one of London's most
popular attractions.

 Tours

One of the best ways to orient yourself
when you first arrive in London is with
a 24-hour hop-on/hop-off pass for the
double-decker bus tours. The buses loop
around interconnecting routes throughout the day, providing a commentary as
they go, and the price includes a river
cruise and three walking tours. You'll
save a couple of pounds by booking
online.

Original London Sightseeing Tour   Bus
(✆020-8877 1722; www.theoriginaltour.com;
adult/child £25/12)

Big Bus Company   Bus
(✆020-7233 9533; www.bigbustours.com;
adult/child £26/10)

London Walks   Walking
(✆020-7624 3978; www.walks.com)

London Mystery Walks   Walking
(✆07957 388280; www.tourguides.org.uk)

 Festivals & Events

University Boat Race   Boat Race
(www.theboatrace.org) Held annually in late
march since 1829.

London Marathon   Running race
(www.london-marathon.co.uk) Half a million
spectators watch whippet-thin champions and
bizarrely clad amateurs in late April.

Trooping the Colour   Royal Parade
Pomp and pageantry overload to celebrate the
Queen's official birthday in June.

The River Thames

A Floating Tour

London's history has always been determined by the Thames. The city was founded as a Roman port nearly 2000 years ago and over the centuries since then many of the capital's landmarks have lined the river's banks. A boat trip is a great way to experience the attractions.

There are piers dotted along both banks at regular intervals where you can hop-on/hop-off the regular services to visit places of interest.

The best place to board is Westminster Pier, from where boats head downstream, taking you from the City of Westminster, the seat of government, to the original City of London, now the financial district and dominated by a growing band of skyscrapers. Across the river, the once shabby and neglected South Bank now bristles with as many top attractions as its northern counterpart.

In our illustration we've concentrated on the top highlights you'll enjoy at a fish's-eye view

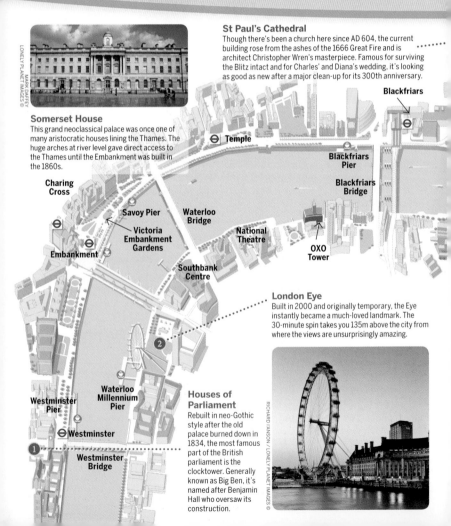

St Paul's Cathedral
Though there's been a church here since AD 604, the current building rose from the ashes of the 1666 Great Fire and is architect Christopher Wren's masterpiece. Famous for surviving the Blitz intact and for Charles' and Diana's wedding, it's looking as good as new after a major clean-up for its 300th anniversary.

MARK DAFFEY / LONELY PLANET IMAGES ©

Blackfriars

Somerset House
This grand neoclassical palace was once one of many aristocratic houses lining the Thames. The huge arches at river level gave direct access to the Thames until the Embankment was built in the 1860s.

Temple

Blackfriars Pier

Blackfriars Bridge

Charing Cross

Savoy Pier

Waterloo Bridge

National Theatre

OXO Tower

Victoria Embankment Gardens

Embankment

Southbank Centre

London Eye
Built in 2000 and originally temporary, the Eye instantly became a much-loved landmark. The 30-minute spin takes you 135m above the city from where the views are unsurprisingly amazing.

Westminster Pier

Waterloo Millennium Pier

Houses of Parliament
Rebuilt in neo-Gothic style after the old palace burned down in 1834, the most famous part of the British parliament is the clocktower. Generally known as Big Ben, it's named after Benjamin Hall who oversaw its construction.

Westminster

Westminster Bridge

RICHARD I'ANSON / LONELY PLANET IMAGES ©

as you sail along. These are, from west to east, the Houses of **Parliament** ➊, **the London Eye** ➋, **Somerset House** ➌, **St Paul's Cathedral** ➍, **Tate Modern** ➎, **Shakespeare's Globe** ➏, **the Tower of London** ➐ and **Tower Bridge** ➑.

Apart from covering this central section of the river, boats can also be taken upstream as far as Kew Gardens and Hampton Court Palace, and downstream to Greenwich and the Thames Barrier.

BOAT HOPPING

Thames Clippers hop-on/hop-off services are aimed at commuters but are equally useful for visitors, operating every 15 minutes on a loop from piers at Embankment, Waterloo, Blackfriars, Bankside, London Bridge and the Tower. Other services also go from Westminster. Oyster cardholders get a discount off the boat ticket price.

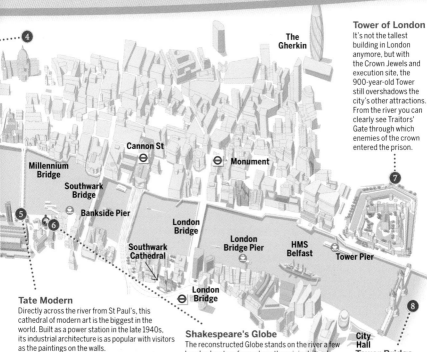

Tower of London
It's not the tallest building in London anymore, but with the Crown Jewels and execution site, the 900-year-old Tower still overshadows the city's other attractions. From the river you can clearly see Traitors' Gate through which enemies of the crown entered the prison.

The Gherkin

Cannon St

Monument

Millennium Bridge

Southwark Bridge

Bankside Pier

London Bridge

London Bridge Pier

HMS Belfast

Tower Pier

Southwark Cathedral

London Bridge

City Hall

Tate Modern
Directly across the river from St Paul's, this cathedral of modern art is the biggest in the world. Built as a power station in the late 1940s, its industrial architecture is as popular with visitors as the paintings on the walls.

DOUG MCKINLAY / LONELY PLANET IMAGES ©

Shakespeare's Globe
The reconstructed Globe stands on the river a few hundred metres from where the original stood (and burnt down in 1613 during a performance). The life's work of American actor Sam Wanamaker, the theatre runs a hugely popular season from April to October each year.

DOUG MCKINLAY / LONELY PLANET IMAGES ©

Tower Bridge
It might look as old as its namesake neighbour but one of the world's most iconic bridges was only completed in 1894. Not to be confused with London Bridge upstream, this one's famous raising bascules allowed tall ships to dock at the old wharves to the west and are still lifted up to 1000 times a year.

MARTIN MOOS/LONELY PLANET IMAGES ©

Don't Miss British Museum

This is the country's largest **museum** (Map p74; ☏ 020-7323 8000; www.britishmuseum.org; Great Russell St WC1; ⏰ 10am-5.30pm Sat-Wed, to 8.30pm Thu & Fri; ⊖ Russell Sq) and one of the oldest and finest in the world. Near the main entrance is Igor Mitoraj's **face sculpture**, *Luci di Nara*. Must-see items inside include the **Rosetta Stone**, the key to deciphering Egyptian hieroglyphics; the **Parthenon Sculptures** from Athens; the stunning **Oxus Treasure** of 7th- to 4th-century BC Persian gold; and the Anglo-Saxon **Sutton Hoo** burial relics.

The **Great Court** was restored and augmented in 2000 and now boasts a spectacular glass-and-steel roof, making it one of the capital's most impressive architectural spaces.

You'll need multiple visits to savour even the highlights here; happily there are 15 half-hour free 'eye-opener' tours between 11am and 3.45pm daily, focussing on different parts of the collection. Other tours include the 90-minute highlights tour at 10.30am, 1pm and 3pm daily (adult/child £8/5), and audio guides are available (£4.50).

Wimbledon Lawn Tennis Championships
Tennis Tournament
(www.wimbledon.org; tickets by public ballot) The world's most splendid tennis event takes place in late June.

Lovebox Music Festival
(www.lovebox.net) London's contribution to the summer music festival circuit, held in Victoria Park in mid-July.

Notting Hill Carnival Street Parades
(www.nottinghillcarnival.biz) London's Caribbean community shows the city how to party in August.

 Sleeping

Take a deep breath before reading this section because whatever your budget, London is a pricey place to sleep – in fact, one of the most expensive in the world.

West End

This is the heart of the action, so accommodation comes at a price, and a hefty one at that. A couple of hostels cater for would-be Soho hipsters of more modest means.

HAZLITT'S
Hotel £££

(☎ 020-7434 1771; www.hazlittshotel.com; 6 Frith St W1; s £206, d/ste from £259/646; @ 🛜; ⊖ Tottenham Court Rd) Staying in this charming house is a trip back into a time when four-poster beds and claw-footed baths were the norm for gentlefolk.

Westminster & Pimlico

Handy for the major sights, these areas have some good-value options.

LUNA SIMONE HOTEL
B&B £££

(Map p74; ☎ 020-7834 5897; www.lunasimone hotel.com; 47-49 Belgrave Rd SW1; s £70-75, d £95-120; @ 🛜; ⊖ Pimlico) The blue-and-yellow rooms aren't huge but they're clean and calming; the ones at the back are quieter.

WINDERMERE HOTEL
B&B £££

(Map p74; ☎ 020-7834 5163; www.winder mere-hotel.co.uk; 142-144 Warwick Way SW1; s £105-155, d £129-165; @ 🛜; ⊖ Victoria) Chintzy but comfortable early Victorian town house; the cheapest rooms share bathrooms.

Chelsea, Kensington & Knightsbridge

GORE
Hotel ££

(Map p64; ☎ 020-7584 6601; www.gorehotel .com; 190 Queen's Gate SW7; r from £135; @ 🛜; ⊖ Gloucester Rd) A short stroll from the Royal Albert Hall, the Gore serves up British grandiosity (such as antiques, carved four-posters, and a secret bathroom in the Tudor room) with a large slice of camp.

VICARAGE PRIVATE HOTEL
B&B ££

(Map p64; ☎ 020-7229 4030; www.londonvicar agehotel.com; 10 Vicarage Gate W8; s/d without bathroom £56/95, with bathroom £95/125; @ 🛜; ⊖ High St Kensington) You can see Kensington Palace from the doorstep of this grand Victorian town house. The cheaper rooms are on floors three and four, so you may get a view as well as a workout.

Bloomsbury & St Pancras

Only one step removed from the West End, the neighbourhood of Bloomsbury and adjoining Fitzrovia offer good value. You'll find a stretch of lower-priced hotels along Gower St and on pretty Cartwright Gardens. The nearby area of St Pancras is hardly salubrious but handy to absolutely everything, with some excellent budget options.

ARRAN HOUSE HOTEL
B&B ££

(Map p74; ☎ 020-7636 2186; www.arran hotel-london.com; 77-79 Gower St WC1; s/d/tr/q £70/110/128/132, without bathroom £60/80/105/111; @ 🛜; ⊖ Goodge St) Period features, pretty back garden and a comfy lounge lift this hotel from average to attractive. Squashed en suites or shared bathrooms are the trade-off for reasonable rates.

AROSFA HOTEL
B&B ££

(Map p74; ☎ 020-7636 2115; www.arosfa london.com; 83 Gower St WC1; s £60-65, d/tr/q £90/102/110; @ 🛜; ⊖ Goodge St) Immaculate if unremarkable rooms, blinged-up lounge and en suites to all 15 bedrooms – but they're tiny.

RIDGEMOUNT HOTEL
B&B £

(Map p74; ☎ 020-7636 1141; www.ridge mounthotel.co.uk; 65-67 Gower St WC1; s/d/tr/q £55/78/96/108, without bathroom £43/60/81/96; @ 🛜; ⊖ Goodge St) There's a comfortable, welcoming feel at this old-fashioned and slightly chintzy place, which has been in the same family for 40 years.

JENKINS HOTEL
B&B ££

(Map p74; ☎ 020-7387 2067; www.jenkinshotel .demon.co.uk; 45 Cartwright Gardens WC1; s/d from £52/95; ⊖ Russell Sq) This modest hotel has featured in the TV series of Agatha Christie's *Poirot*. Rooms are small but the hotel has charm.

Earl's Court & Fulham

TWENTY NEVERN SQUARE
Hotel ££

(Map p64; ☎ 020-7565 9555; www.20nevernsquare.com; 20 Nevern Sq SW5; r from £95; @ 🛜; ⊖ Earl's Court) An Ottoman theme runs through this town-house hotel, with wooden furniture and luxurious fabrics, while natural light helps maximise space.

Notting Hill, Bayswater & Paddington

NEW LINDEN HOTEL Hotel ££

(Map p64; 020-7221 4321; www.newlinden. co.uk; 58-60 Leinster Sq W2; s/d from £79/105; @ 🛜; Bayswater) Cramming in a fair amount of style for the price, with modern art in the rooms and carved wooden fixtures in the guest lounge. The quiet location, helpful staff and monsoon shower heads in the deluxe rooms make this an excellent proposition.

Hoxton, Shoreditch & Spitalfields

HOXTON Hotel £

(Map p64; 020-7550 1000; www.hoxtonhotels .com; 81 Great Eastern St EC2; d & tw £59-199; @ 🛜; Old St) All rooms are identical, but the pricing structure means the first ones each day cost £59: an absolute steal for a hotel of this calibre.

ANDAZ Hotel ££

(Map p64; 020-7961 1234; www.london. liverpoolstreet.andaz.com; 40 Liverpool St EC2; r from £145; @ 🛜; Liverpool St) The former Great Eastern Hotel is now the London flagship for Hyatt's youth-focused Andaz chain, where black-clad staff check you in on laptops. Rooms are a little generic but have free juice, snacks and wi-fi.

Booking Services

○ **At Home in London** (020-8748 1943; www.athomeinlondon.co.uk) B&Bs.

○ **London Homestead Services** (020-7286 5115; www.lhslondon.com) B&Bs.

○ **LondonTown** (020-7437 4370; www .londontown.com) Hotel and B&Bs.

○ **Uptown Reservations** (020-7937 2001; www.uptownres.co.uk) Upmarket B&Bs.

○ **Visit London** (0871 222 3118 per min 10p; www.visitlondonoffers.com) Hotels.

Eating

Dining out in London has become so fashionable that you can hardly open a menu without banging into a celebrity chef, while the range and quality of eating options has increased massively over the last few decades.

West End

Between them, Mayfair, Soho and Covent Garden are the gastronomic heart of London, with stacks of restaurants and cuisines at a wide range of budgets.

HIBISCUS French, British £££

(Map p74; 020-7629 2999; www.hibiscus restaurant.co.uk; 29 Maddox St W1; 3-course lunch/dinner £30/70; Oxford Circus) Claude and Claire Bosi have generated an avalanche of praise and two Michelin stars since moving their restaurant from Shropshire to Mayfair. Expect adventurous, intricate dishes and perfect service.

GREAT QUEEN STREET British ££

(Map p74; 020-7242 0622; 32 Great Queen St WC2; mains £9-19; ⏱lunch daily, dinner Mon-Sat; Holborn) There's no tiara on this Great Queen, but the food's still the best of British.

WILD HONEY Modern European ££

(Map p74; 020-7758 9160; www.wildhoneyres taurant.co.uk; 12 St George St W1; mains £15-24; Oxford Circus) For a good-value meal with the oak-panelled ambience of a top Mayfair restaurant, try the excellent prethea-tre set menu (£22 for three courses).

ARBUTUS Modern European ££

(Map p74; 020-7734 4545; www.arbutus restaurant.co.uk; 63-64 Frith St W1; mains £14-20; Tottenham Court Rd) Focusing on seasonal produce, inventive dishes and value for money, Anthony Demetre's Michelin-starred restaurant just keeps getting better.

Clerkenwell & Farringdon

ST JOHN British ££

(Map p74; 020-7251 0848; www.stjohnres taurant.com; 26 St John St EC1; mains £14-22;

DAVID WALL / ALAMY ©

Farringdon) Whitewashed walls and simple wooden furniture keep diners free to concentrate on world-famous 'nose-to-tail' treats.

SMITHS OF SMITHFIELD   British ££
(Map p74; 020-7251 7950; www.smithsof
smithfield.co.uk; 67-77 Charterhouse St EC1; mains 1st fl £13-15, top fl £19-30; Farringdon) This converted meat-packing warehouse is all things to all people. Hit the ground-floor bar for a beer, go upstairs to a relaxed dining space, or continue up for two more floors of feasting, each slightly smarter and pricier than the last.

Modern Pantry   Fusion ££
(Map p74; 020-7553 9210; www.themodern
pantry.co.uk; 47-48 St John's Sq EC1; mains £15-22; breakfast, lunch & dinner; Farringdon) Currently one of London's most talked-about eateries, with an innovative menu.

Southwark

You'll find plenty of touristy eateries on the riverside, making the most of the constant foot traffic and iconic London views.

OXO TOWER BRASSERIE   Fusion £££
(Map p74; 020-7803 3888; www.harvey
nichols.com; Barge House St SE1; mains £18-26;

Waterloo) The spectacular views are the big drawcard here. Choose from the restaurant, the less extravagantly priced brasserie or, if you're not hungry, the bar. Set-price menus are offered at lunchtime, before 6.15pm and after 10pm (three courses £27).

ANCHOR & HOPE   Gastropub ££
(Map p74; 36 The Cut SE1; mains £12-17; lunch Tue-Sun, dinner Mon-Sat; Southwark) The hope is that you'll get a table because you can't book at this quintessential gastropub serving unashamedly meaty British food.

Chelsea, Kensington & Knightsbridge

These highbrow neighbourhoods harbour some of London's very best (and priciest) restaurants.

MADE IN ITALY   Italian £
(020-7352 1880; www.madeinitalygroup
.co.uk; 249 King's Rd SW3; pizzas £5-11, mains £8-17; dinner Mon-Fri, lunch & dinner Sat & Sun; Sloane Sq) Pizza is served by the tasty quarter-metre at this traditional trattoria. Sit on the roof terrace and dream of Napoli.

GORDON RAMSAY
French £££

(☎020-7352 4441; www.gordonramsay.com; 68 Royal Hospital Rd SW3; 3-course lunch/dinner £45/90; ❸Sloane Sq) Like or loathe the ubiquitous celeb-chef, his eponymous restaurant is one of Britain's finest – one of only four in the country with three Michelin stars. Book ahead and dress up: jeans and T-shirts are forbidden – if you've seen the chef on the telly, you won't argue.

Marylebone

Marylebone's charming High Street has a huge range of eateries.

PROVIDORES & TAPA ROOM
Fusion £££

(Map p74; ☎020-7935 6175; www.theprovidores.co.uk; 109 Marylebone High St W1; 2/3/4/5 courses £30/43/53/60; ❸Baker St) New Zealand's greatest culinary export since kiwifruit, chef Peter Gordon works magic here, matching his creations with NZ wines.

LOCANDA LOCATELLI
Italian ££

(Map p74; ☎020-7935 9088; www.locandalocatelli.com; 8 Seymour St W1; mains £11-30; ❸Marble Arch) Known for its sublime pasta dishes, this dark but quietly glamorous

restaurant in an otherwise unremarkable hotel is one of London's hottest tables.

Islington

Allow at least an evening to explore Islington's Upper St and the lanes leading off it.

LE MERCURY
French £

(☎020-7354 4088; www.lemercury.co.uk; 140a Upper St N1; mains £7-10; ❸Highbury & Islington) A cosy Gallic haunt that appears much more expensive than it is. Sunday lunch by the open fire upstairs is a treat.

🖉 DUKE OF CAMBRIDGE
Gastropub ££

(☎020-7359 3066; www.dukeorganic.co.uk; 30 St Peter's St N1; mains £14-18; ❸Angel; 🐾) This tucked-away gastropub serves only organic food and drink, fish from sustainable sources and locally sourced vegetables and meat.

Hoxton, Shoreditch & Spitalfields

🖉 FIFTEEN
Italian ££

(Map p74; ☎0871 330 1515; www.fifteen.net; 15 Westland Pl N1; breakfast £2-8.50, trattoria £6-11, restaurant £11-25; ⊙breakfast, lunch & dinner; ❸Old St) TV-chef Jamie Oliver's culinary

Locanda Locatelli

philanthropy started here. The food is beyond excellent and even those on limited budgets can afford a visit.

ALBION British ££
(www.albioncaff.co.uk; 2-4 Boundary St E2; mains £9-13; ⊖Old St) Self-consciously retro, serving up top-quality British classics: bangers and mash, steak and kidney pies, devilled kidneys and, of course, fish and chips.

 # Drinking

As long as there's been a city, Londoners have loved to drink – and, as history shows, often immoderately.

West End

GORDON'S WINE BAR Bar
(Map p74; www.gordonswinebar.com; 47 Villiers St WC2; ⊖Embankment) What's not to love about this cavernous wine cellar lit by candles and practically unchanged over the last 120 years?

PRINCESS LOUISE Pub
(Map p74; 208 High Holborn WC1; ⊖Holborn) Arguably London's most beautiful pub, decorated with fine tiles, etched mirrors and a gorgeous central horseshoe bar, often packed with the after-work crowd.

LAMB & FLAG Pub
(Map p74; 33 Rose St WC2; ⊖Covent Garden) Everyone's favourite Covent Garden 'find', this historic pub is often jammed.

ABSOLUT ICE BAR Bar
(Map p74; ☏020-7478 8910; www.belowzerolondon.com; 31-33 Heddon St W1; admission Thu-Sat £16, Sun-Wed £13; ⊖Piccadilly Circus) At -6°C, this bar made entirely of ice is literally the coolest in London. It's a gimmick, sure, but a good one.

Clerkenwell & Farringdon

JERUSALEM TAVERN Pub
(Map p74; www.stpetersbrewery.co.uk; 55 Britton St EC1; ⊖Farringdon) Pick a wood-panelled cubbyhole at this 1720 coffee shop-turned-inn, and choose from a selection of St Peter's beers and ales.

Southwark

GEORGE INN Pub
(Map p74; www.nationaltrust.org.uk/main/w-georgeinn; 77 Borough High St SE1; ⊖London Bridge) London's last surviving galleried coaching inn, dating in its current form from 1677. Dickens and Shakespeare used to prop up the bar here (not together, obviously).

ANCHOR Pub
(Map p74; 34 Park St SE1; ⊖London Bridge) An 18th-century boozer replacing the 1615 version where Samuel Pepys witnessed the Great Fire; it still has a terrace offering superb views across the Thames.

Camden Town

LOCK TAVERN Pub, Music
(Map p64; www.lock-tavern.co.uk; 35 Chalk Farm Rd NW1; ⊖Camden Town) The archetypal Camden pub, with a rooftop terrace and a beer garden, with an interesting crowd, ready conviviality and regular live music.

Hoxton, Shoreditch & Spitalfields

TEN BELLS Pub
(cnr Commercial & Fournier Sts E1; ⊖Liverpool St) The most famous Jack the Ripper pub; admire the wonderful 18th-century tiles and ponder the past over a pint.

COMMERCIAL TAVERN Pub
(Map p64; 142 Commercial St E1; ⊖Liverpool St) The zany decor's a thing of wonder in this reformed East End boozer.

 # Entertainment

From West End luvvies to East End geezers, Londoners have always loved a spectacle. For comprehensive listings see *Time Out* or the free papers at tube stations.

Theatre

London is a world capital for theatre and there's a lot more than mammoth musicals to tempt you into the West End. On performance days, you can buy half-price tickets for West End productions (cash

only) from the official agency **tkts** (www.
tkts.co.uk; Leicester Sq WC2; ⊙10am-7pm Mon-
Sat, noon-4pm Sun; ⊖Leicester Sq). The booth
is the one with the clock tower; beware of
touts selling dodgy tickets. For more, see
www.officiallondontheatre.co.uk or www.
theatremonkey.com.

Royal Court Theatre   Theatre
(Map p74; ☎020-7565 5000; www.royalcourt
theatre.com; Sloane Sq SW1; ⊖Sloane Sq)
Patron of new British writing.

National Theatre   Theatre
(Map p74; ☎020-7452 3000; www.national
theatre.org.uk; South Bank SE1; ⊖Waterloo)
Cheaper tickets for classics and new plays from
some of the world's best companies.

Royal Shakespeare Company   Theatre
(RSC; ☎0844 800 1110; www.rsc.org.uk) The
Bard's classics and other quality stuff.

Old Vic   Theatre
(Map p74; ☎0844 871 7628; www.oldvictheatre.
com; The Cut SE1; ⊖Waterloo) Kevin Spacey
continues his run as artistic director (and
occasional performer).

Donmar Warehouse   Theatre
(Map p74; ☎0844 871 7624; www.donmar
warehouse.com; 41 Earlham St WC2; ⊖Covent
Garden) A not-for-profit company with a West
End reputation.

Almeida   Theatre
(☎020-7359 4404; www.almeida.co.uk; Almeida
St N1; ⊖Highbury & Islington)

Young Vic   Theatre
(Map p74; ☎020-7922 2922; www.youngvic.org;
66 The Cut SE1; ⊖Waterloo)

Nightclubs

London has had a lot of practice per-
fecting the art of clubbing – Samuel
Pepys used the term in 1660 – and the
variety of venues in the city today is
staggering.

The big nights are Friday and Saturday,
although you'll find some of the most
cutting-edge sessions midweek.

Admission prices vary widely; it's
often cheaper to arrive early or prebook
tickets.

Left: Shakespeare's Globe Theatre (p69); **Below:** Courtyard at Cargo

FABRIC
Superclub

(Map p74; www.fabriclondon.com; 77a Charterhouse St EC1; admission £8-18; ⊙10pm-6am Fri, 11pm-8am Sat, 11pm-6am Sun; ⊖Farringdon) Consistently rated as one of the world's greatest clubs, Friday's FabricLive offers drum'n'bass, breakbeat and hip hop; Saturdays see house, techno and electronica; while hedonistic Sundays are delivered by the Wetyourself crew.

MINISTRY OF SOUND   Superclub
(Map p74; www.ministryofsound.com; 103 Gaunt St SE1; admission £13-22; ⊙11pm-6.30am Fri & Sat; ⊖Elephant & Castle) Where the global brand started, it's London's most famous club and still packs in a diverse crew with big local and international names.

CARGO   Club
(Map p64; www.cargo-london.com; 83 Rivington St EC2; admission free-£16; ⊖Old St) A popular club with a courtyard where you can simultaneously enjoy big sounds and the great outdoors.

Rock, Pop & Jazz

Big-name gigs sell out quickly, so check www.seetickets.com before you arrive in town.

O2 ACADEMY BRIXTON   Live Music
(☎0844 477 2000; www.o2academybrixton .co.uk; 211 Stockwell Rd SW9; ⊖Brixton) Always winning awards for 'best live venue', hosting big-nae acts in a relatively intimate setting (5000 capacity).

JAZZ CAFE   Club
(Map p64; www.jazzcafe.co.uk; 5 Parkway NW1; ⊖Camden Town) Intimate club that stages a full roster of jazz, rock, pop, hip hop and dance, including famous names.

RONNIE SCOTT'S   Club
(Map p74; ☎020-7439 0747; www.ronniescotts .co.uk; 47 Frith St W1; ⊖Leicester Sq) London's legendary jazz club, pulling in the hep cats since 1959.

100 CLUB
Club

(Map p74; ☎ 020-7636 0933; www.the100club.co.uk; 100 Oxford St W1; ⊖ Oxford Circus) This legendary London venue once showcased the Stones and was at the centre of the punk revolution, now with jazz, rock and even a little swing.

ROUND HOUSE
Live Music, Theatre

(Map p64; ☎ 0844 482 8008; www.roundhouse.org.uk; Chalk Farm Rd NW1; ⊖ Chalk Farm) An iconic concert venue since the 1960s, hosting the likes of the Rolling Stones, Led Zeppelin and the Clash. It's also used for theatre and comedy.

Classical Music, Opera & Dance

ROYAL ALBERT HALL
Concert Hall

(Map p64; ☎ 020-7589 8212; www.royalalberthall.com; Kensington Gore SW7; ⊖ South Kensington) Beautiful Victorian venue that hosts classical concerts and contemporary artists.

BARBICAN CENTRE
Arts Centre

(Map p74; ☎ 0845 121 6823; www.barbican.org.uk; Silk St EC2; ⊖ Barbican) This hulking complex has a full program of film, music, theatre, art and dance, including loads of concerts from the London Symphony Orchestra (www.lso.co.uk), which is based here.

SOUTHBANK CENTRE
Concert Halls

(Map p74; ☎ 0844 875 0073; www.southbankcentre.co.uk; Belvedere Rd SE1; ⊖ Waterloo) Home to the London Philharmonic Orchestra (www.lpo.co.uk), Sinfonietta (www.londonsinfonietta.org.uk) and the Philharmonia Orchestra (www.philharmonia.co.uk), among others, this centre hosts classical, opera, jazz and choral music in three premier venues: the **Royal Festival Hall**, the smaller **Queen Elizabeth Hall** and the **Purcell Room**. Look out too for free recitals in the foyer.

ROYAL OPERA HOUSE
Opera, Ballet

(Map p74; ☎ 020-7304 4000; www.roh.org.uk; Bow St WC2; tickets £5-195; ⊖ Covent Garden) Covent Garden is synonymous with opera thanks to this world-famous venue, also the home of the Royal Ballet. Backstage tours on weekdays (£10, book ahead).

SADLER'S WELLS
Dance

(Map p74; ☎ 0844 412 4300; www.sadlerswells.com; Rosebery Ave EC1; tickets £10-49; ⊖ Angel) A glittering modern venue, Sadler's Wells has been given much credit for bringing modern dance to the mainstream.

Royal Opera House, Covent Garden

ADINA TOVY AMSEL/LONELY PLANET IMAGES ©

COLISEUM
Opera

(Map p74; ☎0871 911 0200; www.eno.org; St Martin's Lane WC2; tickets £10-87; ⊖Leicester Sq) Home of the progressive English National Opera; all performances are in English.

 ## Shopping

From world-famous department stores to quirky backstreet retail revelations, London is a veritable mecca for shoppers with an eye for style and a card to exercise.

Selfridges
Department Store

(Map p74; www.selfridges.com; 400 Oxford St W1; ⊖Bond St) The funkiest and most vital of London's one-stop shops, where fashion runs the gamut from street to formal.

Fortnum & Mason
Department Store

(Map p74; www.fortnumandmason.com; 181 Piccadilly W1; ⊖Piccadilly Circus) The byword for quality and service from a bygone era, steeped in 300 years of tradition.

Liberty
Department Store

(Map p74; www.liberty.co.uk; Great Marlborough St W1; ⊖Oxford Circus) An irresistible blend of contemporary styles and indulgent pampering in a mock-Tudor fantasyland of carved dark wood.

Harrods
Department Store

(Map p74; www.harrods.com; 87 Brompton Rd SW1; ⊖Knightsbridge) A pricy but fascinating theme park for fans of Britannia, Harrods is always crowded with slow tourists.

Harvey Nichols
Department Store

(Map p74; www.harveynichols.com; 109-125 Knightsbridge SW1; ⊖Knightsbridge) Head here for London's temple of high fashion, jewellery and perfume.

ℹ Information

Britain & London Visitor Centre

(www.visitbritain.com; 1 Regent St SW1; ⊙9am-6.30pm Mon-Fri, 10am-4pm Sat & Sun; ⊖Piccadilly Circus) Accommodation and theatre bookings, transport tickets, *bureau de change,* international telephones and internet terminals. Longer hours in summer.

Roll Out the Barrow

London has more than 350 markets selling everything from antiques and curios to flowers and fish.

Borough Market — Food
(Map p74; www.boroughmarket.org.uk; 8 Southwark St SE1; ⊙11am-5pm Thu, noon-6pm Fri, 8am-5pm Sat; ⊖London Bridge) A farmers' market sometimes called London's Larder; everything from organic falafel to boars' heads.

Camden Market — Market
(Map p64; ⊙10am-5.30pm; www.camdenmarkets.org; ⊖Camden Town) Actually a series of markets spread along Camden High St; the Lock and Stables markets are still the place for punk fashion, cheap food, hippy stuff and a whole lotta craziness.

Portobello Road Market — Clothes, Antiques
(www.portobellomarket.org; Portobello Rd W10; ⊙8am-6.30pm Mon-Sat, to 1pm Thu; ⊖Ladbroke Grove) One of London's most famous (and crowded) street markets; new and vintage clothes, antiques and food.

Brick Lane Market — Market
(Map p64; www.visitbricklane.org; Brick Lane E1; ⊙8am-2pm Sun; ⊖Liverpool St) A sprawling East End bazaar featuring everything from fruit to paintings and bric-a-brac.

Petticoat Lane Market — Market
(Map p64; Wentworth St & Middlesex St E1; ⊙9am-2pm Sun-Fri; ⊖Aldgate) A cherished East End institution overflowing with cheap consumer durables and jumble sale ware.

City of London Information Centre

(☎020-7332 1456; www.visitthecity.co.uk; ⊙9.30am-5.30pm Mon-Sat, 10am-4pm Sun; St Paul's Churchyard EC4; ⊖St Paul's) Tourist information, fast-track tickets to City attractions and guided walks (adult/child £6/4).

London's Your Oyster

Although locals love to complain, London's public transport is excellent, with tubes, trains, buses and boats all covering the capital. **Transport for London** (TFL; www.tfl.gov.uk) is the glue that binds the network together.

You can avoid queues at ticket machines by getting an Oyster card, a reusable smartcard pre-loaded with credit to give unlimited transport on tube, bus and some rail services.

London is divided into concentric transport zones, with almost all places covered in this book in Zones 1 and 2. If you're here for a week, load up your Oyster card as a weekly season ticket (£26) to travel within these zones. For four days or less, opt for the daily rate (£7.20 per day for Zones 1-2, reduced to £5.60 if you avoid peak hours). The card itself is £3, fully refundable when you leave.

ℹ Getting There & Away

Bus & Coach

The London terminus for long-distance buses (called 'coaches' in Britain) is **Victoria Coach Station** (☏020-7824 0000; 164 Buckingham Palace Rd SW1; ⊖Victoria).

Train

London's main-line rail terminals are listed below with their main destinations.

Charing Cross Canterbury

Euston Manchester, Liverpool, Carlisle, Glasgow

King's Cross Cambridge, Hull, York, Newcastle, Scotland

Liverpool Street Stansted airport, Cambridge

London Bridge Gatwick airport, Brighton

Marylebone Birmingham

Paddington Heathrow airport, Oxford, Bath, Bristol, Exeter, Plymouth, Cardiff

St Pancras Gatwick and Luton airports, Brighton, Nottingham, Sheffield, Leicester, Leeds, Paris

Victoria Gatwick airport, Brighton, Canterbury

Waterloo Windsor, Winchester, Exeter, Plymouth

ℹ Getting Around

To/From the Airports

GATWICK Trains run between Gatwick's South Terminal and Victoria (from £12, 37 minutes, every 15 minutes, hourly at night), or to/from St Pancras (from £12, 66 minutes) via London Bridge, City Thameslink, Blackfriars and Farringdon.
Gatwick Express (☏0845 850 1530; www.gatwickexpress.com) trains run to/from Victoria (one way/return £16/26, 30 minutes, every 15 minutes, first/last train 3.30am/12.32am).

HEATHROW The cheapest option to central London is the Piccadilly line on the tube, accessible from every terminal (£4.50, one hour, departing every five minutes from around 5am to 11.30pm).

Quicker is the dedicated **Heathrow Express** (☏0845 600 1515; www.heathrowexpress.co.uk), an ultramodern train to/from Paddington (one way/return £16.50/32, 15 minutes, every 15 minutes 5.12am to 11.42pm). You can purchase tickets on board (£5 extra), from self-service machines (cash and credit cards accepted) at both stations or online.

STANSTED The **Stansted Express** (☏0845 850 0150; www.stanstedexpress.com) connects with Liverpool St station (one way/return £18/27, 46 minutes, every 15 minutes 6am to 12.30am).

Bus

Single-journey bus tickets (valid for two hours) cost £2 (£1.20 on Oyster, capped at £3.90 per day); a weekly pass is £17. Children ride for free.

At stops with yellow signs, you have to buy your ticket from the automatic machine (or use an Oyster) *before* boarding. Buses stop on request, so signal the driver clearly with an outstretched arm.

Car

Don't even think about it. London was recently rated Western Europe's second most congested city (congratulations Brussels). In addition, you'll pay £8 per day simply to drive into central London from 7am to 6pm on a weekday. If you're hiring a car to continue your trip around Britain after sightseeing in London, take the tube or train to a major airport and pick it up from there.

Taxi

London's famous black cabs are available for hire when the yellow light above the windscreen is lit. Fares are metered, with flag fall of £2.20 and additional rate dependent on time of day, distance travelled and taxi speed.

Train

As well as the tube, London is served by regular urban train services (known as Overground), particularly south of the Thames. Most stations are fitted with Oyster readers and accept TFL travelcards.

Underground & DLR

London's underground train network (universally known as the tube) extends its subterranean tentacles across the city and into the surrounding counties, with services running every few minutes from roughly 5.30am to 12.30am (from 7am to 11.30pm Sunday). Tickets (or Oyster card top-ups) can be purchased from counters or machines at each station using either cash or credit card.

Waterbus

The myriad boats that ply the Thames are a great way to travel, avoiding traffic jams and giving great views. Passengers with travelcards (including an Oyster) get a third off all fares. **Thames Clippers** (www .thamesclippers.com) runs regular commuter services between Embankment, Waterloo, Blackfriars, Bankside, London Bridge, Tower, Canary Wharf, Greenwich, North Greenwich and Woolwich piers (adult/child £5.30/2.65) from 7am to midnight (from 9.30am weekends).

AROUND LONDON

'When you're tired of London, you're tired of life,' opined 18th-century Londoner Samuel Johnson.

Windsor & Eton

♫ 01753 / POP 31,000

Dominated by the massive bulk and heavy influence of Windsor Castle, these twin towns have a rather surreal atmosphere, with the morning pomp and ceremony of the changing of the guards in Windsor and the sight of schoolboys dressed in formal tailcoats wandering the streets of Eton.

Changing of the guard at Windsor Castle (p94)

WINDSOR CASTLE — Castle

(www.royalcollection.org.uk; adult/child £16/9.50; ⏲9.45am-5.15pm) The largest and oldest occupied fortress in the world, Windsor Castle is a majestic vision of battlements and towers used for state occasions and as the Queen's weekend retreat.

ETON COLLEGE — Historic School

(www.etoncollege.com; adult/child £6.20/5.20; ⏲guided tours 2pm & 3.15pm daily during school holidays, Wed, Fri, Sat & Sun during term time) A short walk through Windsor and across the River Thames brings you to this famous public school – which in Britain means a *private* school – where 18 prime ministers and endless royals were educated. As you wander around you may recognise some of the buildings; *Chariots of Fire, The Madness of King George, Mrs Brown* and *Shakespeare in Love* are just some of the classics filmed here.

ⓘ Getting There & Away

Trains from Windsor Central station on Thames St go to London Paddington (27 to 43 minutes). Trains from Windsor Riverside station go to London Waterloo (56 minutes). Services run half-hourly from both stations and tickets cost £7.90.

SOUTHEAST ENGLAND

Traditionally a day-trip playground for Londoners escaping overcrowded streets, England's southeast offers fascinating historic towns, sweeping greenbelt vistas and some vibrant seaside resorts – many just an hour or so by train from the capital.

Canterbury

POP 43,432

With its jaw-dropping cathedral surrounded by medieval cobbled streets, this World Heritage city has been a Christian pilgrimage site for several centuries, and a tourist attraction for almost as long.

◎ Sights

CANTERBURY CATHEDRAL — Cathedral

(www.canterbury-cathedral.org; adult/concession £8/7; ⏲9am-5pm Mon-Sat, 12.30pm-2.30pm Sun) The Anglican faith could not have a more imposing mother church than this extraordinary early Gothic cathedral. It's an overwhelming edifice filled with enthralling stories, striking architecture and an enduring sense of spirituality. This

Interior of Canterbury Cathedral

HOLGER LEUE/LONELY PLANET IMAGES ©

ancient structure is packed with monuments commemorating the nation's battles. The spot in the northwest transept where Archbishop Thomas Becket met his grisly end has been drawing pilgrims for more than 800 years and is marked by a flickering candle and striking modern altar. The wealth of detail in the cathedral is immense and unrelenting, so it's well worth joining a one-hour **tour** (adult/child £5/3; ◷10.30am, noon & 2.30pm Mon-Fri, 10.30am, noon & 1.30pm Sat Easter-Oct), or you can take a 40-minute self-guided **audio tour** (adult/concessions £3.50/2.50).

 ## 🛈 Getting There & Away

Train

London St Pancras high-speed service, £27.80, one hour, hourly
London Victoria £23.40, one hour 40 minutes, two to three hourly
Priory £6.50, 25 minutes, every 30 minutes

 # Brighton & Hove

POP 247,817

While some British seaside resorts are paint-peeled reminders of an earlier era, Brighton and Hove – two towns combined to form a new city in 2000 – has successfully moved on. It's now a cosmopolitan centre with a bohemian spirit, exuberant gay community, dynamic student population and a healthy number of ageing and new-age hippies, as well as traditional candy-floss fun – although the beach has never been the main attraction, mainly because it's stones, not sand.

 ## ◉ Sights

ROYAL PAVILION Historic Building
(www.royalpavilion.org.uk; adult/child £9.50/5.40; ◷9.30am-5.45pm Apr-Sep, 10am-5.15pm Oct-Mar) The city's must-see attraction is the glittering palace and party-pad of the Prince Regent (later King George IV), still an apt symbol of Brighton's reputation for hedonism. The domes and minarets outside are only a prelude to the palace's lavish oriental-themed interior.

 ## Detour:
Leeds Castle

Leeds Castle (www.leeds-castle.com; adult/child £17.50/10; ◷10am-6pm Apr-Sep) is one of the most visited attractions in Britain. This impressive structure balancing on two islands amid a large lake has been transformed from fortress to lavish palace over the centuries, and the vast estate is ideal for peaceful walks.

Leeds Castle is just east of Maidstone in Kent. Trains run from London Victoria to Bearsted (£17.10, one hour), from where you catch a special shuttle coach to the castle (£5 return).

BRIGHTON PIER Pier
(www.brightonpier.co.uk) This grand old centenarian pier is the place to come to experience the tackier side of Brighton. There are plenty of stomach-churning fairground rides and dingy amusement arcades, plus candy floss and Brighton rock to chomp.

LANES Shopping
Brighton's original fishing-village heart is the Lanes, a cobblestone web of 17th-century cottages housing a gentrified cornucopia of independent shops, pubs and one-of-a-kind eateries.

✸ Festivals & Events

There's always something fun going on in Brighton, but the main events include **Gay Pride** (www.brightonpride.org) in early August and the **Brighton Festival** (☎01273-709 709; www.brightonfestival.org) in May, the biggest in Britain after Edinburgh, drawing theatre, dance, music and comedy performers from around the globe.

Jane Austen's House

There's more than a touch of period drama at the former home of Jane Austen (1775–1817), where she wrote *Mansfield Park, Emma* and *Persuasion,* and revised *Sense and Sensibility, Pride and Prejudice* and *Northanger Abbey*. This appealing red-brick house, where the celebrated English novelist lived from 1809 to 1817, is now a **museum** (www.jane-austens-house -museum.org.uk; Chawton; adult/child £7/2; ⊙10.30am-4.30pm mid-Feb–Dec). Highlights include elegant furniture and copper pans in the kitchen, the occasional table Austen used as a desk, first editions of her novels and the delicate handkerchief she embroidered for her sister.

The museum is 18 miles east of Winchester; take bus 64 from Winchester to Chawton roundabout (50 minutes, hourly Monday to Saturday, six on Sunday) then walk the 500m to Chawton village.

 Sleeping

NEO HOTEL　　　Boutique Hotel　££
(☎01273-711104; www.neohotel.com; 19 Oriental Pl; d from £100; 🛜) With nine rooms straight out of the pages of a design magazine, other temptations include satin kimono robes and wonderful breakfasts with fruit pancakes.

 **Eating & Drinking**

TERRE À TERRE　　　Vegetarian　££
(71 East St; mains £10-15; ⊙lunch & dinner Tue-Sun; 🍴) Even staunch meat eaters will come out raving about this legendary vegetarian restaurant, famous for its modern space and inventive dishes full of robust flavours.

JB'S AMERICAN DINER　　　Diner　£
(31 King's Rd; burgers £7, mains £6.50-12; ⊙lunch & dinner) Shiny red leather booths, stars and stripes, and a '50s soundtrack provide the visual and musical background for colossal portions of burgers, fries and milkshakes.

ENGLISH'S OYSTER BAR　　　Seafood　££
(www.englishs.co.uk; 29-31 East St; mains £11-25; ⊙lunch & dinner) A 60-year institution, this Brightonian seafood paradise dishes up everything from oysters and lobster to Dover sole.

ℹ️ **Information**

Tourist office (☎0300-300 0088; www.visitbrighton.com; Royal Pavilion Shop, Royal Pavilion; ⊙10am-5.30pm)

ℹ️ **Getting There & Away**

Bus & Coach

London Victoria National Express, £11.80, two hours, hourly

Train

All London-bound services pass through Gatwick airport.

London St Pancras £16.90, 1¼ hours, half-hourly

London Victoria £13.90, 50 to 70 minutes, half-hourly

Portsmouth £13.90, 1½ hours, hourly

Winchester

POP 41,420

Calm, collegiate Winchester is a mellow must-see for all visitors. The past still echoes around the flint-flecked walls of this ancient cathedral city.

◎ **Sights**

WINCHESTER CATHEDRAL　　　Cathedral
(www.winchester-cathedral.org.uk; adult/child £6/free, combined admission & tower tour £9; ⊙9am-5pm Sat, 12.30-3pm Sun) Almost 1000 years of history are crammed into Winchester's cathedral. The exterior isn't

at first glance appealing but have a look inside – the interior is awe-inspiring, with one of the longest medieval naves (164m) in Europe and a fascinating collection of features from all eras. Jane Austen, one of England's best-loved authors, is buried near the entrance of the cathedral, in the northern aisle.

FREE GREAT HALL & ROUND TABLE
Historic Building

(Castle Ave; suggested donation adult/child £1/50p; ⏱10am-5pm) The cavernous Great Hall is the only part of 11th-century Winchester Castle that Oliver Cromwell spared from destruction. Crowning the wall is what centuries of mythology have dubbed King Arthur's Round Table. It's actually a 700-year-old copy, but is fascinating nonetheless.

HOSPITAL OF ST CROSS
Historic Building

(www.stcrosshospital.co.uk; St Cross Rd; adult/child £3/1; ⏱9.30am-5pm Mon-Sat, 1-5pm Sun Apr-Oct, 10.30am-3.30pm Mon-Sat Nov-Mar) Established in 1132 to house pilgrims and crusaders en route to the Holy Land, this hospital is the oldest charitable institution in the country.

Sleeping

WYKEHAM ARMS
Historic Inn ££

(☎01962-853834; www.fullers hotels.com; 75 Kingsgate St; s/d/ste £70/119/150; P🛜) This place is bursting with history – it used to be a brothel and also put up Nelson for a night (some say the two events coincided).

NO 21
B&B ££

(☎01962-852989; St Johns St; s/d £45/90) Gorgeous cathedral views, a flower-filled cottage garden and

rustic-chic rooms (think painted wicker and woven bedspreads) make this art-packed house a tranquil city bolthole.

Eating & Drinking

CHESIL RECTORY
Modern British ££

(☎01962-851555; www.chesilrectory.co.uk; 1 Chesil St; mains £16; ⏱lunch & dinner Mon-Sat, lunch Sun) Duck through the hobbit-sized door, settle down amid the 15th-century beams and savour perfectly prepared modern British cuisine.

BLACK BOY
Pub

(www.theblackboypub.com; 1 Wharf Hill; ⏱noon-11pm, to midnight Fri & Sat) This adorable old pub is filled with obsessive and some-times freaky collections, from pocket watches to bear traps.

Information

Tourist office (☎01962-840500; www.visit winchester.co.uk; High St; ⏱10am-5pm Mon-Sat, also 11am-4pm Sun May-Sep)

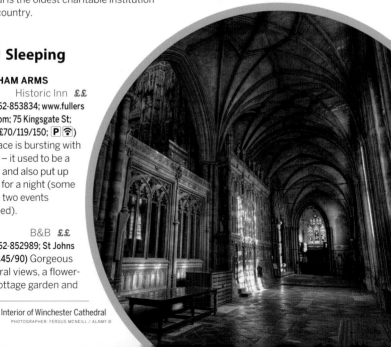

Interior of Winchester Cathedral
PHOTOGRAPHER: FERGUS McNEILL / ALAMY ©

ⓘ Getting There & Away

TRAIN Trains leave every 30 minutes for London Waterloo (£26, 1¼ hours). There are also fast links to the Midlands.

SOUTHWEST ENGLAND

Southwest England offers the pick of Britain's cities, coast and countryside – all on one verdant, sea-fringed platter.

ⓘ Getting There & Around

BUS The **Stonehenge Tour** (☏01722-336855; www.thestonehengetour.info; return adult/child £11/5) leaves Salisbury's railway and bus stations half-hourly in June and August, and hourly between September and May.

TAXI Taxis charge £35 to go to the site from Salisbury, wait for an hour and come back.

Bath

POP 90,144

A cultural trendsetter and fashionable haunt for the last 300 years, the honey-stoned city of Bath is especially renowned for its architecture. Along its stately streets you'll find a celebrated set of Roman bath-

Bath Abbey and Roman Baths

houses, a grand medieval abbey and some fine Georgian terraces. In fact, Bath has so many listed buildings the entire place has been named a World Heritage Site.

◎ Sights

ROMAN BATHS Museum
(www.romanbaths.co.uk; Abbey Churchyard; adult/child £12/7.80; ⊙9am-8pm Jul & Aug, to 6pm Mar-Jun, Sep & Oct, 9.30am-5.30pm Jan, Feb, Nov & Dec) In typically ostentatious style, the Romans constructed a glorious complex of bathhouses above the thermal waters, and 2000 years later this is one of the best-preserved ancient Roman spas in the world. The site gets very busy in summer; you can usually dodge the worst crowds by visiting early on a midweek morning.

BATH ABBEY Church
(www.bathabbey.org; requested donation £2.50; ⊙9am-6pm Mon-Sat Easter-Oct, to 4.30pm Nov-Easter, 1-2.30pm & 4.30-5.30pm Sun year-round) Constructed between 1499 and 1616, this is the last great medieval church built in England. Inside, the nave's wonderful fan vaulting was erected in the 19th century.

GLENN BEANLAND/LONELY PLANET IMAGES ©

Outside, the most striking feature is the west facade, where angels climb up and down stone ladders, commemorating a dream of the founder, Bishop Oliver King.

ROYAL CRESCENT & THE CIRCUS
Architecture

Bath's crowning glory is the **Royal Crescent**, a semicircular terrace of majestic houses, originally built for wealthy socialites, overlooking Royal Victoria Park. For a glimpse into the splendour of Georgian life, head for **No 1 Royal Crescent** (www.bath-preservation-trust.org.uk; adult/child £6/2.50; ⊙10.30am-5pm Tue-Sun mid-Feb–mid-Oct, to 4pm mid-Oct–Dec), restored using only 18th-century materials. Nearby is the **Circus**, a ring of 30 houses divided into three terraces; plaques commemorate famous residents such as Thomas Gainsborough and David Livingstone.

FREE **ASSEMBLY ROOMS**   Architecture
(Bennett St; ⊙10.30am-5pm Mar-Oct, to 4pm Nov-Feb) Opened in 1771, this was where fashionable Bath socialites gathered to waltz, play cards and listen to the latest chamber music. Today you're free to wander around the rooms.

FASHION MUSEUM
Museum

(www.fashionmuseum.co.uk; adult/child £7/5, joint ticket with Roman Baths; £ as for Assembly Rooms) In the basement of the Assembly Rooms, this museum displays costumes from the 16th to late-20th centuries, including some alarmingly small crinolines.

JANE AUSTEN CENTRE
Museum

(www.janeausten.co.uk; 40 Gay St; adult/child £6.50/3.50; ⊙9.45am-5.30pm Apr-Sep, 11am-4.30pm Oct-Mar) Bath is a location in Jane Austen's novels including *Persuasion* and *Northanger Abbey,* and the author's connections with the city are celebrated here. Other displays include period costumes.

Sleeping

HALCYON
Hotel ££

(☎01225-444100; 2/3 South Pde; www.thehalcyon.com; d £99-125; 🛜) A shabby terrace has been knocked through, polished up

---

Thermae Bath Spa

Larking about in the Roman Baths might be off the agenda, but you can sample the city's curative waters at **Thermae Bath Spa** (☎0844 888 0844; www.thermaebathspa.com; Hot Bath St; New Royal Bath spa session per 2hr/4hr/day £24/34/54, spa packages from £65; ⊙New Royal Bath 9am-10pm), where the old Cross Bath is now incorporated into an ultramodern shell of stone and plate glass. The New Royal Bath ticket includes steam rooms, waterfall shower and a choice of bathing venues – including the open-air rooftop pool, with Bath's stunning cityscape as a backdrop.

---

and totally reinvented, making this hotel far and away the best in the city centre. It's style on a budget; studio rooms even have kitchens. We like it a lot.

BROOKS
Hotel ££

(☎01225-425543; www.brooksguesthouse.com; 1 & 1a Crescent Gardens; d £69-175; 🛜) On the west side of Bath, this is a plush option, attractively blending heritage fixtures with snazzy finishes.

THREE ABBEY GREEN
B&B ££

(☎01225-428558; www.threeabbeygreen.com; 3 Abbey Green; d £85-135; 🛜) Considering the location, this place is a steal – tumble out of the front door practically onto the abbey's doorstep.

Eating & Drinking

CIRCUS
British ££

(☎01225-318918; www.thecircuscafeandrestaurant.co.uk; 34 Brock St; lunch £5.50-9.70; dinner mains £11-13.90; ⊙lunch & dinner) In a city that's often known for its snootiness, the Circus manages to be posh but not in the slightest pretentious. Quite simply, our favourite place to eat in Bath.

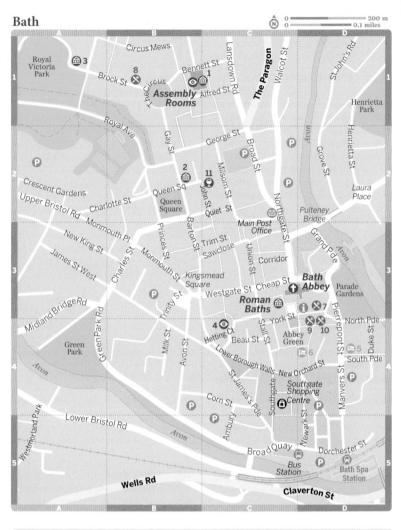

Bath

Bath

⊙ Top Sights

⊙ Sights

🛏 Sleeping

✕ Eating

✦ Drinking

Detour:
Eden Project

If any one thing is emblematic of Cornwall's regeneration, it's the **Eden Project** (☎01726-811911; www.edenproject.com; Bodelva; adult/child £15/5; ⏰10am-6pm Apr-Oct, to 4.30pm Nov-Mar). Ten years ago the site was an exhausted clay pit; a symbol of the county's industrial decline. Now it's home to the largest plant-filled greenhouses on the planet – a monumental education project about the natural world. Tropical, temperate and desert environments have been recreated inside the massive biomes, so a single visit carries you from the steaming rainforests of South America to the dry deserts of northern Africa.

MARLBOROUGH TAVERN Gastropub ££
(☎01225-423731; www.marlborough-tavern. com; 35 Marlborough Bldg; mains £10.95-15.95; ⏰lunch & dinner) Bath's best gastropub, especially if you like your flavours rich and rustic.

DEMUTH'S Vegetarian ££
(☎01225-446059; 2 North Pde Passage; mains £9.75-14.25; ⏰lunch & dinner; 🖋) For the last two decades this brilliant meat-free bistro has been turning out some of Bath's most creative and imaginative food.

CAFÉ RETRO Cafe £
(18 York St; mains £5-11; ⏰breakfast, lunch & dinner Tue-Sat, breakfast & lunch Mon) The paint job's scruffy, the crockery's ancient, but that's all part of the charm, and there's nowhere better for a stonking burger, a crumbly cake or a good mug of tea.

Sally Lunn's Tea House £
(4 North Pde Passage; lunch mains £5-6, dinner mains from £8; ⏰lunch & dinner) Classic chintzy tearoom serving the trademark Sally Lunn's bun.

SALAMANDER Pub
(3 John St) The city's bespoke brewery, Bath Ales, owns this place, and you can sample all of its produce here.

ℹ️ Information

Tourist office (☎0906-711 2000, accommodation 0844-847-5256; www.visitbath.co.uk; Abbey Churchyard; ⏰9.30am-6pm Mon-Sat, 10am-4pm Sun Jun-Sep, 9.30am-5pm Mon-Sat, 10am-4pm Sun Oct-May) Phone enquiries to the main office are charged at premium rate (50p per minute).

ℹ️ Getting There & Away

BUS Bath's new **bus and coach station** (enquiries office ⏰9am-5pm Mon-Sat) is on Dorchester St near the train station.
TRAIN Direct trains go to/from London Paddington (£22 to £39, 1½ hours, at least hourly) and Bristol (£5.80, 11 minutes, four per hour), which has connections to most major British cities.

St Ives
POP 9870

Sitting on the fringes of a glittering arc-shaped bay, St Ives was once a pilchard-fishing harbour but it's better known today as a centre of the arts. Cobbled alleyways lead through a jumble of galleries, cafes and brasseries that cater for thousands of summer visitors.

◎ Sights

TATE ST IVES Art Gallery
(☎01736-796226; www.tate.org.uk/stives; Porthmeor Beach; adult/child £5.75/3.25, joint ticket with Barbara Hepworth museum £8.75/4.50; ⏰10am-5pm Mar-Oct, to 4pm Tue-Sun Nov-Feb) This landmark gallery contains work by celebrated local artists, including Terry Frost, Patrick Heron and Barbara Hepworth, and hosts regular special exhibitions.

101

BARBARA HEPWORTH MUSEUM & SCULPTURE GARDEN Art Gallery

(☎01736-796226; www.tate.org.uk/stives; Barnoon Hill; adult/child £5.75/3.25, joint ticket with Barbara Hepworth museum £8.75/4.50; ⌚10am-5pm Mar-Oct, to 4pm Tue-Sun Nov-Feb) Barbara Hepworth (1903–75) was a leading abstract sculptor and a key figure in the St Ives art scene. Fittingly, her former studio has been transformed into a moving archive and museum.

Sleeping

PRIMROSE VALLEY Hotel £££

(☎01736-794939; www.primroseonline.co.uk; Porthminster Beach; d £105-155, ste £175-225; P 📶) A swash of sexy style on the St Ives seafront, this classy location is full of spoils – therapy room, metro-modern bar and locally sourced breakfasts.

TRELISKA B&B ££

(☎01736-797678; www.treliska.com; 3 Bedford Rd; d £60-80; 📶) The smooth decor is attractive – chrome taps, wooden furniture, cool sinks – but what really sells it is the fantastic position, literally steps from St Ives' centre.

Eating & Drinking

ALBA Seafood ££

(☎01736-797222; Old Lifeboat House; mains £11-18; ⌚lunch & dinner) Split-level sophistication next to the lifeboat house, serving excellent seafood. Tables five, six or seven have the best harbour views.

BLAS BURGERWORKS Cafe £

(The Warren; burgers £5-10; ⌚dinner Tue-Sun) This pocket-sized joint has a big reputation: sustainable sourcing, eco-friendly packaging and lots of wacky burger variations have earned it a loyal following.

Information

Tourist office (☎01736-796297; ivtic@penwith.gov.uk; Street-an-Pol; ⌚9am-5.30pm Mon-Fri, 9am-5pm Sat, 10am-4pm Sun) Inside the Guildhall.

Getting There & Away

TRAIN The gorgeous branch line from St Ives is worth taking just for the coastal views along the way. Trains terminate at St Erth (£3, 14 minutes, half-hourly), where you can then catch connections along the Penzance–Paddington main line.

St Michael's Mount

Looming up from the waters of Mount's Bay is the unmistakeable silhouette of **St Michael's Mount** (NT; ☎01736-710507; castle & gardens adult/child £8.75/4.25; ⌚house 10.30am-5.30pm Sun-Fri late Mar-Oct), a craggy island topped by an ancient monastery – one of Cornwall's most iconic landmarks.

The island is reached from the little town of **Marazion**, 3 miles from Penzance; you can walk across the causeway at low tide, or catch a ferry at high tide in the summer.

Land's End

Just 9 miles from Penzance, Land's End is the westernmost point of mainland England, where cliffs plunge dramatically into the pounding Atlantic surf. Unfortunately, the **Legendary Land's End** (☎0870 458 0099; www.landsend-landmark.co.uk; adult/child £11/7; ⌚10am-5pm summer, to 3pm winter) theme park hasn't done much to enhance the view. Take our advice: skip the tacky multimedia shows and opt for an exhilarating cliff-top stroll instead.

Bus 1/1A travels from Penzance (one hour, eight daily, five on Saturday) to Land's End.

CENTRAL ENGLAND

The geographic heartland of England is a mix of wildly differing scenes, which include historic towns like Oxford and Stratford-upon-Avon, flower-decked villages in the Cotswolds, and rejuvenated former industrial cities like Birmingham. In this section we also cover the lush dales and peaty moors of the Peak District.

DAVID WALL/LONELY PLANET IMAGES ©

Don't Miss **Stonehenge**

Stonehenge (EH; ☎ 01980-624715; www.english-heritage.org.uk; adult/child £6.90/3.50; ⊙ 9am-7pm Jun-Aug, 9.30am-6pm Mar-May & Sep-Oct, 9.30-4pm Oct-Feb) is Britain's most iconic archaeological site. This compelling ring of monolithic stones has attracted a steady stream of pilgrims, poets and philosophers for the last 5000 years. Despite the constant flow of traffic from the main road beside the monument, and the huge numbers of visitors who traipse around the perimeter on a daily basis, Stonehenge still manages to be a mystical, ethereal place – a haunting echo from Britain's forgotten past, and a reminder of the people who once walked the many ceremonial avenues across Salisbury Plain. Even more intriguingly, it's still one of Britain's great archaeological mysteries: despite countless theories about what the site was used for, ranging from a sacrificial centre to a celestial timepiece, in truth, no one really knows what drove prehistoric Britons to expend so much time and effort on its construction.

Visitors normally have to stay outside the stone circle itself. But on **Stone Circle Access Visits** (☎ 01722-343830; www.english-heritage.org.uk; adult/child £14.50/7.50) you get to wander round the core of the site, getting up-close views of the iconic bluestones and trilithons. The walks take place in the evening or early morning, so the quieter atmosphere and the slanting sunlight add to the effect. Each visit only takes 26 people; to secure a place book at least two months in advance.

Oxford

POP 134,300

Renowned as one of the world's most famous university towns, Oxford lives up to its advance billing as a colourful, history-flavoured place.

Oxford University has the eminent distinction of being the oldest university in Britain, with the first of its 39 separate colleges dating from the 13th century.

Women were first admitted to full membership of the university in 1920.

Sights

Much of the centre of Oxford is taken up by graceful university buildings, each one individual in its appearance and academic specialities. Not all are open to the public. Check www.ox.ac.uk/colleges for full details.

CHRIST CHURCH COLLEGE College
(www.chch.ox.ac.uk; St Aldate's; adult/child £6/4.50; ⏲9am-5pm Mon-Sat, 2-5pm Sun) The largest and grandest of all of Oxford's colleges, and most popular thanks to the magnificent buildings and latter-day fame as a location for the *Harry Potter* films.

MAGDALEN COLLEGE College
(www.magd.ox.ac.uk; High St; adult/child £4.50/3.50; ⏲1-6pm) Set amid 40 hectares of expansive green lawns and river walks, Magdalen (*mawd*-len) is one of the wealthiest and most beautiful of Oxford's colleges.

MERTON COLLEGE College
(www.merton.ox.ac.uk; Merton St; admission £2; ⏲2-5pm Mon-Fri, 10am-5pm Sat & Sun) From the High St, follow the wonderfully named Logic Lane to Merton College, one of Oxford's original three colleges, founded in 1264.

BODLEIAN LIBRARY Library
(www.bodley.ox.ac.uk; Broad St; ⏲9am-5pm Mon-Fri, to 4.30pm Sat, 11am-5pm Sun) This historic Bodleian is one of the oldest public libraries in the world, holding more than seven million items on 118 miles of shelving.

RADCLIFFE CAMERA Library
(Radcliffe Sq) Another library and quintessential Oxford landmark – and one of the city's most photographed buildings (no public access).

FREE ASHMOLEAN MUSEUM Museum
(www.ashmolean.org; Beaumont St; ⏲10am-6pm Tue-Sun) Britain's oldest public museum, the Ashmolean reopened in

late 2009 after a massive £61 million redevelopment that makes the once-intimidating building and stuffy collection a real joy to browse.

 # Sleeping

MALMAISON   Hotel £££
(☎ 01865-268400; www.malmaison-oxford. com; Oxford Castle; d/ste from £160/245; P @ 🛜) Lock yourself up for the night in one of Oxford's most spectacular settings, a former Victorian prison that has been converted into a sleek and slinky hotel.

ETHOS HOTEL   Hotel ££
(☎ 01865-245800; www.ethoshotels.co.uk; 59 Western Rd; d from £80; @ 🛜) This funky new hotel has spacious rooms, marble bathrooms, mini kitchen, breakfast basket and free wi-fi – all just 10 minutes' walk from the city centre. Incredible value.

 # Eating

TROUT   Modern British ££
(☎ 01865-510930; www.thetroutoxford.co.uk; 195 Godstow Rd, Wolvercote; mains £8-16) This charming old-world pub has been a favourite haunt of town and gown for many years. Book ahead.

DOOR 74   Modern British ££
(☎ 01865-203374; www.door74.co.uk; 74 Cowley Rd; mains £8-13; ⊘ closed Mon & Sun dinner) This cosy little place woos its fans with a rich mix of British and Mediterranean flavours and friendly service.

CAFÉ COCO   Mediterranean £
(www.cafe-coco.co.uk; 23 Cowley Rd; mains £6-10.50) Chilled but always buzzing, this place has classic posters on the walls and a bald clown in an ice bath. The food can be a bit hit and miss but most people come for the atmosphere.

🍷 Drinking

TURF TAVERN   Pub
(4 Bath Pl) Hidden away down narrow alleyways, this tiny medieval pub is one of the town's best loved and bills itself as 'an education in intoxication'. Home to real ales and student antics.

EAGLE & CHILD   Pub
(49 St Giles) Affectionately known as the 'Bird & Baby', this atmospheric place dates from 1650 and is a hotchpotch of nooks and crannies attracting a mellow crowd.

ℹ️ Information

Tourist office (☎01865-252200; www.visit oxford.org; 15-16 Broad St; ⏰9.30am-5pm Mon-Sat, 10am-4pm Sun)

ℹ️ Getting There & Away

BUS Services to London (£16 return) run up to every 15 minutes, day and night, and take about 90 minutes. There are also regular buses to/from Heathrow.

TRAIN There are half-hourly services to London Paddington (£19.90, one hour) and roughly hourly trains to Birmingham (£27, 1¼ hours). Hourly services to Bath (£22.50, 1¼ hours) and Bristol (£24.50, 1½ hours) require a change at Didcot Parkway.

Stratford-upon-Avon
POP 22,187

The author of some of the most quoted lines in the English language, William Shakespeare was born in Stratford in 1564 and died here in 1616. The five houses linked to his life form the centrepiece of a tourist attraction that verges on a cult of personality.

👁️ Sights & Activities

SHAKESPEARE HOUSES   Museums
(☎01789-204016; www.shakespeare.org.uk; all 5 properties adult/child £19/12, 3 in-town houses £12.50/8; ⏰9am-5pm Apr-Oct, winter hr vary) These five important buildings, associated with Shakespeare and now run by the Shakespeare Birthplace Trust, contain museums that form the core of the visitor experience.

Start your Shakespeare tour at **Shakespeare's Birthplace** (Henley St),

Shakespeare's birthplace, Henley St

Don't Miss Blenheim Palace

One of the country's greatest stately homes, **Blenheim Palace** (www.blenheimpalace.com; adult/child £18/10, park & garden only £10.30/5; ☉10.30am-5.30pm daily mid-Feb-Oct, Wed-Sun Nov-mid-Dec) is a monumental baroque fantasy designed by Sir John Vanbrugh and Nicholas Hawksmoor between 1705 and 1722. Highlights include the **Great Hall**, a vast space topped by 20m-high ceilings adorned with images of the 1st duke in battle; the opulent **Saloon**, the most important public room; the three **state rooms** with their plush decor and priceless china cabinets; and the magnificent 55m **Long Library**. You can also visit the **Churchill Exhibition**, dedicated to the life, work and writings of Sir Winston, who was born at Blenheim in 1874. Outside, you can stroll through the lavish gardens and vast parklands, parts of which were landscaped by Lancelot 'Capability' Brown.

Blenheim Palace is near the town of Woodstock, a few miles northwest of Oxford. To get there, Stagecoach bus S3 runs every half-hour (hourly on Sunday) from George St in Oxford.

the house where the world's most famous playwright supposedly spent his childhood days. When Shakespeare retired, he swapped the bright city lights of London for a comfortable town house on **New Place**. It was demolished in 1759, but the adjacent **Nash's House** (☎01789-292325; cnr Chapel St & Chapel Lane), where Shakespeare's granddaughter Elizabeth lived, describes the town's history.

Shakespeare's daughter Susanna married doctor John Hall, and **Hall's Croft** (☎01789-292107, Old Town) is their fine Elizabethan residence. Deviating from the Shakespeare theme, the exhibition here offers fascinating insights into 16th-century medicine.

Before marrying Shakespeare, Anne Hathaway lived in Shottery, a mile west of the centre, in the pretty thatched farmhouse known as **Anne Hathaway's**

Cottage (☎01789-292100, Cottage La, Shottery). As well as period furniture, there's an orchard and arboretum, with examples of all the trees mentioned in Shakespeare's plays.

Mary Arden's Farm (☎01789-293455; Station Rd, Wilmcote), the childhood home of Shakespeare's mother, is at Wilmcote, located 3 miles west of Stratford. Aimed firmly at families, the farm has exhibits that trace country life over the centuries, including nature trails, falconry displays and a collection of rare-breed farm animals.

FREE **HOLY TRINITY CHURCH** Church (☎01789-266316; www.stratford-upon-avon.org; Old Town; admission to church free, Shakespeare's grave adult/child £1.50/50p; ☺8.30am-6pm Mon-Sat, 12.30-5pm Sun Apr-Sep, shorter winter hr) The final resting place of the Bard is said to be the most visited parish church in England.

Sleeping

SHAKESPEARE HOTEL Hotel ££ (☎01789-294997; www.mercure.com; Chapel St; s/d £135/150; P @) For the full Tudor inn experience, head to this atmospheric Mercure property in a timbered medieval charmer on the main street.

WHITE SAILS Guesthouse ££ (☎01789-264326; www.white-sails.co.uk; 85 Evesham Rd; r from £95; P @ 🛜) Plush fabrics, framed prints, brass bedsteads and shabby-chic tables set the scene at this gorgeous guesthouse.

Broadlands Guest House B&B ££ (☎01789-299181; www.broadlandsguesthouse.co.uk; 23 Evesham Pl; s/d from £48/80; P) Prim and blue, with classic rooms and filling breakfasts.

Eating & Drinking

EDWARD MOON'S Modern British ££ (☎01789-267069; www.edwardmoon.com/moonsrestaurant; 9 Chapel St; mains £10-15; ☺lunch & dinner) This snug little eatery serves hearty English dishes, many of which are livened up with Asian herbs and spices.

DIRTY DUCK Pub (Waterside) Officially called the 'Black Swan', this enchanting riverside alehouse is a favourite thespian watering hole, and has a roll-call of former regulars (Olivier, Attenborough etc) that reads like an actors' *Who's Who*.

. . . .

ℹ Information

Tourist office (☎01789 264293; www.shakespeare-country.co.uk; Bridgefoot; call for opening hrs)

. . . .

ℹ Getting There & Away

Trains run to/from Birmingham (£6.30, one hour, hourly) and London Marylebone (£49.50, 2¼ hours, four daily). The Shakespeare Express steam train (☎0121-708 4960; www.shakespeareexpress.com) runs twice every Sunday in July and August between Stratford and Birmingham Snow Hill (one way adult/child £10/5).

Peak District National Park

Squeezed between the industrial Midlands to the south and the cities of Manchester and Sheffield to the west and east, the surprisingly rural Peak District

---

Royal Shakespeare Company

You just can't come to Stratford without seeing one of the Bard's plays performed by the **Royal Shakespeare Company** (RSC; ☎0844 800 1110; www.rsc.org.uk; tickets £8-38). There are often special deals for under 25-year-olds, students and seniors, and a few tickets are held back for sale on the day of performance.

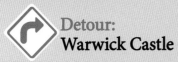

Detour:
Warwick Castle

Founded in 1068 by William the Conqueror, the stunningly preserved **Warwick Castle** (0870 442 2000; www.warwick-castle.co.uk; castle adult/child £19.95/11.95, castle & dungeon adult/child £27.45/19.45; ⊙10am-6pm Apr-Sep, to 5pm Oct-Mar; P) is the biggest show in town. With waxwork-populated private apartments, sumptuous interiors, landscaped gardens, towering ramparts, displays of arms and armour, medieval jousting and a theme-park dungeon (complete with torture chamber and ham actors in grisly make-up), there's plenty to keep the family busy for a whole day. Tickets are discounted if you buy online.

Trains run to Birmingham (£7.40, 45 minutes, every half-hour), Stratford-upon-Avon (£5.20, 30 minutes, hourly) and London (£30, 1¾ hours, every 20 minutes).

is one of the finest areas in England for walking, cycling and other outdoor activities. Don't be misled by the name; there are few peaks around here, but there are plenty of wild moors, rolling farmland and deep valleys – as well as a good scattering of hardy villages, prehistoric sites and limestone caves.

Sights

CHATSWORTH HOUSE Stately Home
(01246-582204; www.chatsworth.org; adult/child £11.25/6; ⊙11am-5.30pm Mar-Dec) Known as the 'Palace of the Peak', this vast edifice has been occupied by the Dukes of Devonshire for centuries.

Among the prime attractions in the house itself are the magnificent artworks, as well as the decorated ceilings and treasure troves of splendid furniture.

The house sits in over 42 hectares of **gardens** (adult/child £7.50/4.50), with grottoes, fountains, a maze and changing collections of modern sculptures. Beyond that is another 400 hectares of **park** (admission free), open for walking and picnicking.

Chatsworth is 3 miles northeast of Bakewell. Buses 170 and 218 run several times a day (15 minutes), plus bus 215 on Sunday.

Sleeping

The Peak District has a great selection of B&Bs, hotels and pubs. For more ideas, the local TICs can help, or see www.visit peakdistrict.com.

Buxton

Buxton is a picturesque sprawl of Georgian terraces, Victorian amusements and pretty parks, set at the very heart of the Peak District.

ROSELEIGH HOTEL B&B ££
(01298-24904; www.roseleighhotel.co.uk; 19 Broad Walk; s/d incl breakfast from £38/72; P@🛜) This gorgeous B&B has excellent rooms and a great location. The owners are seasoned travellers, with plenty of tales to tell.

Edale

Surrounded by majestic countryside, this tiny cluster of cottages is an enchanting spot.

STONECROFT B&B ££
(01433-670262; www.stonecroftguesthouse. co.uk; Grindsbrook; r from £75; P🖊) This handsome house has two comfortable bedrooms. Vegetarians and vegans are well catered for – the organic breakfast is excellent.

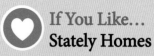

If You Like…
Stately Homes

If **Chatsworth** (p109) and **Blenheim Palace** (p107) have left you with a taste for aristocratic architecture, you won't want to miss some of England's other great estates.

1 HATFIELD HOUSE
(www.hatfield-house.co.uk; house & garden adult/child £11.50/6, gardens only £6.50/4.50; ⊗noon-5pm Wed-Sun, gardens 11am-5.30pm Wed-Sun) Twenty-one miles from central London, this magnificent Jacobean mansion is the ancestral home of the Cecils, one of England's most influential political families. Built between 1607 and 1611, the house is awash with portraits, tapestries, furnishings and armour, not to mention a ridiculously grand marble hall and carved-oak staircase.

2 SANDRINGHAM
(www.sandringhamestate.co.uk; adult/child 5-15yr £10/5, gardens & museum only £7/3.50; ⊗11am-4.30pm Apr-Oct) Six miles north of King's Lynn in Norfolk, the Queen's country estate is open to the hoi polloi when the court is not at home. Don't miss the vintage car collection, the royal pet cemetery and the house's gorgeous ground-floor rooms.

3 BURGHLEY HOUSE
(www.burghley.co.uk; adult/child incl sculpture garden £11.80/5.80; ⊗11am-5pm Sat-Thu) Ninety miles north of London, this flamboyant Elizabethan palace is a regular star of the silver screen: films including *The Da Vinci Code* and *Elizabeth: The Golden Age* have been shot here. It's famous for its lavish art collection and 17th-century Italian murals.

4 ICKWORTH HOUSE
(NT; www.nationaltrust.org/ickworth; adult/child house & park £8.30/3.30, park only £4.20/1.10; ⊗house 11am-5pm Fri-Tue Mar-Oct, gardens 10am-5pm) Thirty miles east of Cambridge, this 18th-century mansion is immediately recognisable thanks to its immense oval rotunda and wide outspread wings. The house's east wing doubles as a slick hotel.

Bakewell

The second-largest town in the Peak District, pretty Bakewell is a great base for exploring the White Peak.

MELBOURNE HOUSE　　　B&B £
(☎01629-815357; Buxton Rd; r from £55; [P])
In a picturesque building dating back more than three centuries, this is an inviting B&B on the main road leading to Buxton.

ℹ Information

Peak District National Park Authority
(☎01629-816200; www.peakdistrict.org)
There are many TICs in and around the park, including:

Bakewell (☎01629-813227; Bridge St; ⊗9.30am-5pm Apr-Oct, from 10am Nov-Mar)

Buxton (☎01298-25106; Pavilion Gardens; ⊗9.30am-5pm Oct-Mar, 10am-4pm Apr-Sep)

Castleton (☎01433-620679; Buxton Rd; ⊗9.30am-5.30pm Mar-Oct, 10am-5pm Nov-Feb)

ℹ Getting There & Around

National Express coaches run from London Victoria to Manchester and Buxton, from where you can switch to a local bus.

Trains also run between Sheffield and Manchester via Edale and several other Peak villages.

By far the handiest local bus is the hourly **Transpeak** (www.transpeak.co.uk) service that cuts across the Peak District from Nottingham and Derby to Manchester, via Matlock, Bakewell and Buxton.

EASTERN ENGLAND

The vast flatland of eastern England (or East Anglia, as it's usually called) is a contemplative and peaceful mix of lush farms, melancholy fens, big skies and the bucolic scenery that once inspired Constable and Gainsborough.

Cambridge

POP 108,863

Drowning in exquisite architecture, steeped in history and tradition, and renowned for its quirky rituals, Cambridge is a university town extraordinaire. The tightly packed core of ancient colleges, the picturesque riversides and the leafy green meadows that seem to surround the city give it a far more tranquil appeal than rival Oxford.

 Sights

Cambridge University comprises 31 colleges, though not all are open to the public. Opening hours vary from day to day, and the hours given below are only a rough guide, so contact the colleges or the tourist office for information.

CORPUS CHRISTI COLLEGE College
(www.corpus.cam.ac.uk; Trumpington St) Entry to this illustrious college is via the so-called New Court that dates back a mere 200 years.

TRINITY COLLEGE College
(www.trin.cam.ac.uk; Trinity St; adult/child £1/50p; ⊙9am-4pm) The largest of Cambridge's colleges, Trinity is entered by an impressive gateway. As you walk through, have a look at the statue of the founder, Henry VIII. His left hand holds a golden orb, while his right grips not the original sceptre but a table leg, put there by student pranksters and never replaced.

KING'S COLLEGE CHAPEL Chapel
(www.kings.cam.ac.uk/chapel; King's Pde; adult/child/under 12yr £5/3.50/free; ⊙9.30am-4.30pm Mon-Sat, 10am-5pm Sun) In a city crammed with glorious architecture, this is the show-stealer; one of the most extraordinary examples of Gothic architecture in England – most famous for its **fan-vaulted ceiling**, with intricate tracery soaring upwards before exploding into a series of stone fireworks.

BACKS Park
Behind the grandiose facades, stately courts and manicured lawns of the city's central colleges lies a series of riverside gardens and parklands collectively known as the Backs.

FREE **FITZWILLIAM MUSEUM** Museum
(www.fitzmuseum.cam.ac.uk; Trumpington St; ⊙10am-5pm Tue-Sat, noon-5pm Sun) This museum is filled with priceless treasures from ancient Egyptian sarcophagi to Greek and Roman art, Chinese ceramics to English glass, and some dazzling illuminated manuscripts. The upper galleries showcase works by Leonardo da Vinci, Titian, Rubens, Gainsborough and Constable, right through to Rembrandt and Picasso. You can join a one-hour guided tour (£3.50) of the museum on Saturdays at 2.30pm.

King's College Chapel

WOJTEK BUSS / PHOTOLIBRARY ©

 ## Sleeping

HOTEL FELIX
Hotel £££

(☎01223-277977; www.hotelfelix.co.uk; Whitehouse Lane, Huntingdon Rd; d £180-305; P @ ☎) This luxurious boutique hotel occupies a lovely villa in landscaped grounds a mile from the city centre. Its 52 rooms embody designer chic with minimalist style but lots of comfort.

TENISON TOWERS
B&B ££

(☎01223-363924; www.cambridgecitytenison towers.com; 148 Tenison Rd; s/d from £40/60) This exceptionally friendly and homely place is really handy if you're arriving by train. The rooms are bright and simple with pale colours and fresh flowers.

 ## Eating

ORIGIN8
Deli Cafe £

(www.origin8delicafes.com; 62 St Andrew's St; mains £4-6.50; ⊙breakfast & lunch Mon-Sat, lunch Sun) Bright and airy, this cafe-deli prides itself on its fresh, local organic ingredients.

OAK BISTRO
Modern British ££

(☎01223-323361; www.theoakbistro.co.uk; 6 Lensfield Rd; mains £11-17, set 2-/3-course lunch £12/15; ⊙closed Sun) This relaxed and minimalist little place serves up classic dishes with modern flair.

RAINBOW VEGETARIAN BISTRO
Vegetarian ££

(www.rainbowcafe.co.uk; 9a King's Pde; mains £8-10; ⊙lunch & dinner Tue-Sat, lunch Mon & Sun; ☑) First-rate vegetarian and organic dishes with a hint of the exotic are served in this snug subterranean gem.

 ## Drinking

EAGLE
Pub

(Bene't St) Cambridge's most famous pub has loosened the tongues and pickled the grey cells of many illustrious academics; among them Nobel Prize–winning DNA scientists Crick and Watson.

GRANTA
Pub

(☎01223-505016; Newnham Rd) If the exterior of this picturesque waterside pub looks strangely familiar, don't be surprised. It's a TV directors' favourite.

ℹ Information

Tourist office (☎0871 266 8006; www
.visitcambridge.org; Old Library, Wheeler St;
⊙10am-5.30pm Mon-Fri, to 5pm Sat, 11am-
3pm Sun)

ℹ Getting There & Away

BUS There are regular buses to/from Stansted
(£12.40, 50 minutes), Heathrow (£29.90, 2½
to three hours) and Gatwick (£31, four hours)
airports. Buses to Oxford (£10.90, 3½ hours)
are regular but they take a very convoluted
route.

TRAIN Trains to Cambridge run at least every
30 minutes to/from London's King's Cross
and Liverpool St stations (£19.10, 45 minutes
to 1¼ hours).

NORTHEAST ENGLAND

By turns wild and pretty, rural and urban, modern and historic, northeast
England contains the large and varied
counties of Yorkshire and Northumberland, and two of Britain's great
cities: historic York and resurgent
Newcastle.

Haworth

POP 6100

In the canon of English literature, it
seems that only Shakespeare himself
is held in higher esteem than the
beloved Brontë sisters. This is judging
by the eight million eager visitors a
year who make their way to this hardy
northern town, where the established
classics *Jane Eyre* and *Wuthering
Heights* were born.

Sights

BRONTË PARSONAGE MUSEUM
                                    Museum
(www.bronte.info; Church St; adult/child
£6.50/3.50; ⊙10am-5.30pm Apr-Sep, 11am-5pm
Oct-Mar) Set in a pretty garden overlooking
the church and graveyard, the house

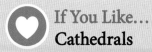

If You Like…
Cathedrals

Bowled over by the ecclesiastical
extravagance of **Canterbury** (p94) and
Winchester (p96)? Then you won't want
to miss visiting some of England's other
landmark cathedrals.

1 ELY CATHEDRAL
(www.elycathedral.org; adult/child £6/free;
⊙9am-5pm) Dubbed the 'Ship of the Fens', Ely's
magnificent cathedral is renowned for its 12th-
century Romanesque nave, 14th-century octagon
and shimmering lantern towers. Ely is 17 miles from
Cambridge; the easiest way to get there is by train
(15 minutes, every 20 minutes).

2 WELLS CATHEDRAL
(www.wellscathedral.org.uk; Chain Gate, Cathedral
Green; requested donation adult/child £5.50/2.50;
⊙7am-7pm Apr-Sep, 7am-dusk Oct-Mar) Set in a
medieval close at the heart of England's smallest city,
Wells Cathedral was built in stages between 1180
and 1508. It's best-known for its dramatic west front,
featuring a sculpture gallery decorated with more than
300 figures. The city is 18 miles from Bath; buses run
hourly.

3 SALISBURY CATHEDRAL
(www.salisburycathedral.org.uk; requested
donation adult/child £5/3; ⊙7.15am-6.15pm)
Boasting the tallest spire and longest nave of any
church in England, Salisbury Cathedral is also home
to the tomb of one of the nation's most loved authors,
Jane Austen. Trains run regularly from Bath. Trains
run half-hourly to/from London Waterloo (£32, 1½
hours), or there are hourly connections to Bath (£8,
one hour).

4 DURHAM CATHEDRAL
(www.durhamcathedral.co.uk; donation
requested; ⊙7.30am-6pm, to 5.30pm Sun)
Durham's most famous building is the definitive
example of the Romanesque style of architecture,
and one of the world's greatest places of worship.
Durham is fifteen minutes from Newcastle by train
(£5.20, five hourly).

where the Brontë family lived from 1820 till 1861 is now a museum. The rooms are meticulously furnished and decorated exactly as they were in the Brontë era, with many personal possessions of note on display.

ℹ Information

Tourist office (☎ 01535-642329; www.haworth village.org.uk; 2-4 West Lane; ⏰ 9am-5.30pm Apr-Sep, to 5pm Oct-Mar)

Yorkshire Dales National Park

From such well-known names as Wensleydale and Ribblesdale to obscure Langstrothdale and Arkengarthdale, the Yorkshire Dales is one of the most breathtakingly scenic parts of northern England. It's been protected as a national park since the 1950s, assuring its status as a walker's and cyclist's paradise.

For more details on the area, see www.yorkshire dales.org.uk.

York

POP 181,100

Nowhere in northern England says 'medieval' quite like York, a city of extraordinary historical wealth that has lost little of its preindustrial lustre. Its spider's web of narrow streets is enclosed by a magnificent circuit of 13th-century walls and the city's rich heritage is woven into virtually every brick and beam.

◎ Sights

YORK MINSTER   Church
(www.yorkminster.org; adult/child £8/free; ⏰ minster 9am-5.30pm Mon-Sat, noon-3.45pm Sun Apr-Oct, 9.30am-5.30pm Mon-Sat, noon-3.45pm Sun Nov-Mar) Not content with being Yorkshire's most important historic building, the awe-inspiring York Minster is also the largest medieval cathedral in all of northern Europe. The present minster, built mainly between 1220 and 1480, manages to encompass all the major stages of Gothic architectural development. Highlights include the **west front**, octagonal **chapter house**, the **towers** and the fabulous **stained-glass windows**.

JORVIK   Museum
(www.vikingjorvik.com; Coppergate; adult/child £8.95/6, Jorvik & Dig combined £13/9.75; ⏰ 10am-5pm Apr-Oct, to 4pm Nov-Mar) Interactive multimedia exhibits aimed at 'bringing history to life' often achieve just the opposite. But the much-hyped Jorvik, the most visited attraction in town after the minster, manages to pull it off with admirable aplomb. It's a smells-and-all reconstruction of the Viking settlement that was unearthed here during excavations in the late 1970s.

York Minster
PHOTOGRAPHER: KARL BLACKWELL/LONELY PLANET IMAGES ©

Interior of National Railway Museum, York

PHOTOLIBRARY©

FREE **CITY WALLS**   City Walls

(☼8am-dusk) If the weather's good, don't
miss the chance to walk the ramparts of
the City Walls. The full circuit is 4.5 miles
(allow 1½ to two hours); if you're pushed
for time, the short stretch from Bootham
Bar to Monk Bar is worth doing for the
views of the minster.

FREE **NATIONAL RAILWAY MUSEUM**
                                              Museum

(www.nrm.org.uk; Leeman Rd; ☼10am-6pm)
York's National Railway Museum – the
biggest in the world – is so well presented
and full of fascinating stuff that it's interesting even to folk whose eyes don't mist
over at the thought of a 4-6-2 A1 Pacific
class chuffing into a tunnel.

SHAMBLES   Medieval Street

(www.yorkshambles.com) The cobbled lane
known as the Shambles, lined with 15th-
century Tudor buildings that overhang
so much they seem to meet above your
head, is the most visited street in Europe.
It's quaint and picturesque certainly, and
hints at what a medieval street may have
looked like, but it's undeniably busy in
summer.

CLIFFORD'S TOWER   Castle

(EH; www.english-heritage.org.uk; Tower St;
adult/child £3.50/1.80; ☼10am-6pm Apr-Sep,
to 5pm Oct, to 4pm Nov-Mar) There's precious
little left of York Castle except for this
evocative stone tower. There's not much
to see inside but the views over the city
are excellent.

 Tours

For starters, check the tourist office suggestions for walking itineraries at www.
visityork.org/explore.

Ghost Hunt of York   Walking

(www.ghosthunt.co.uk; adult/child £5/3; ☼tours
7.30pm) Award-winning and highly entertaining
75-minute tour laced with authentic ghost
stories; ideal for kids. Begins at the Shambles;
no need to book.

Yorkwalk   Walking

(www.yorkwalk.co.uk; adult/child £5.50/3.50;
☼tours 10.30am & 2.15pm) A series of two-hour
themed walks on an ever-growing list of themes,
such as Roman York, women in York, and the
inevitable coffin and plague tour. Begins at
Museum Gardens Gate; no need to book.

115

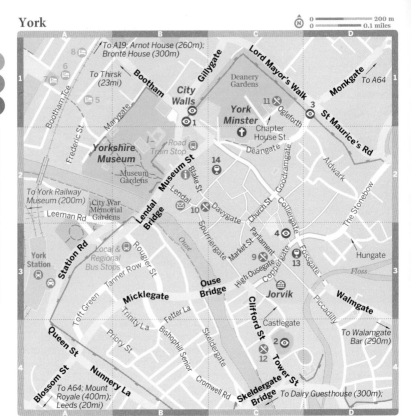

York Citysightseeing   Bus
(www.city-sightseeing.com; day tickets adult/
child £10/4; ⊙9am-5pm) Hop-on hop-off route
with 16 stops; buses leave every 10 minutes
from Exhibition Sq near York Minster.

FREE **Association of Voluntary Guides**
    Walking
(www.visityork.org; ⊙tours 10.15am, also 2.15pm
Apr-Sep & 6.45pm Jun-Aug) Free two-hour
walking tours of the city starting from Exhibition
Sq in front of York City Art Gallery.

 Sleeping

ABBEYFIELDS   B&B   ££
(☎01904-636471; www.abbeyfields.co.uk; 19
Bootham Tce; s/d from £49/78; ☎) We rate
this place very highly for its warm wel-

come, thoughtfully arranged bedrooms
and excellent breakfasts.

ELLIOTTS B&B   B&B   ££
(☎01904-623333; www.elliottshotel.co.uk;
2 Sycamore Pl; s/d from £55/80; P@☎) A
beautifully converted 'gentleman's residence' towards the boutique end of the
market with elegant rooms and hi-tech
touches. Excellent location, both quiet
and central.

23 ST MARY'S   B&B   ££
(☎01904-622738; www.23stmarys.co.uk; 23
St Mary's; s/d £55/90; P@) A smart and
stately town house with nine country
house–style rooms. Some have hand-
painted furniture, while others are
decorated with antiques and polished
mahogany.

York

 Eating

GRAY'S COURT   Cafe £££
(grayscourtyork.com; Chapter House St; mains £6-7; ⊙lunch) An unexpected find in the very heart of York, this 16th-century house has a country atmosphere, gourmet coffee and cake, a sunny garden and an oak-panelled Jacobean gallery (extra points if you grab the alcove table above the main door).

ATE O'CLOCK   Bistro £££
(☎01904-644080; www.ateoclock.co.uk; 13a High Ousegate; mains £14-17; ⊙lunch & dinner Tue-Sat) A tempting menu has made this place hugely popular with locals. Three-course dinner for £16.75 from 6pm to 7.55pm Tuesday to Thursday.

OLIVE TREE   Mediterranean £££
(☎01904-624433; www.theolivetreeyork.co.uk; 10 Tower St; mains £9-18; ⊙lunch & dinner) Local produce gets a Mediterranean makeover at this bright and breezy bistro.

BETTY'S   Tea House £££
(www.bettys.co.uk; St Helen's Sq; mains £6-11, afternoon tea £16; ⊙breakfast, lunch & dinner) Afternoon tea, old-school style, with white-aproned waitresses, linen tablecloths and a teapot collection ranged along the walls.

 Drinking

BLUE BELL   Pub
(53 Fossgate) This is what a real English pub looks like – a tiny, wood-panelled room with a smouldering fireplace, decor (and beer and smoke stains) dating from c 1798, a pile of ancient board games in the corner, friendly and efficient bar staff, and top-notch ale.

YE OLDE STARRE   Pub
(40 Stonegate) Licensed since 1644, this is York's oldest pub – a warren of small rooms and a small beer garden, with half a dozen real ales on tap.

ℹ Information

York Visitor Centre (☎01904-550099; www.visityork.org; 1 Museum St; ⊙9am-6pm Mon-Sat, 10am-5pm Sun Apr-Sep, shorter hr Oct-Mar)

ℹ Getting There & Away

York is a major railway hub with frequent direct services to/from Birmingham (£45, 2¼ hours), Newcastle (£15, one hour), Leeds (£11, 30 minutes), London's King's Cross (£80, two hours), and Manchester (£15, 1½ hours).

AROUND YORK

Newcastle-upon-Tyne
POP 189,863

Once synonymous with postindustrial decline, today's Newcastle is reborn and brimming with confidence. All of a sudden, this unfailingly friendly city, with its Geordie accent thicker than molasses, has kick-started a brand-new arts and entertainment scene – while riotous nightlife remains an established tradition.

DOUG MCKINLAY/LONELY PLANET IMAGES ©

Don't Miss **Castle Howard**

Stately homes may be two a penny in England, but you'll have to try hard to find one as breathtakingly stately as **Castle Howard** (www.castlehoward.co.uk; adult/child house & grounds £12.50/7.50, grounds only £8.50/6; ⏰ house 11am-4.30pm, grounds 10am-6.30pm Mar-Oct & 1st 3 weeks Dec), a work of theatrical grandeur and audacity, and one of the world's most beautiful buildings. It's instantly recognisable from its starring role in the 1980s TV series *Brideshead Revisited* and more recently in the 2008 film of the same name (both based on Evelyn Waugh's 1945 novel of nostalgia for the English aristocracy).

Inside, the great house is full of treasures – the breathtaking Great Hall with its soaring Corinthian pilasters, Pre-Raphaelite stained glass in the chapel, and corridors lined with classical antiquities. Outside, as you wander the grounds (populated by peacocks, naturally), views reveal Vanbrugh's playful Temple of the Four Winds and Hawksmoor's stately mausoleum, or wider vistas over the surrounding hills.

Castle Howard is 15 miles northeast of York. There are several organised tours from York – check with the tourist office.

Sights

QUAYSIDE   Neighbourhood

The Quayside, on the northern bank of the River Tyne, is ideal for a pleasant walk through the very heart of the city. You'll see the famous Tyne bridges – and the area really comes to life at night, with bars, clubs and restaurants full to bursting.

FREE BALTIC – THE CENTRE FOR CONTEMPORARY ART   Art Gallery

(www.balticmill.com; Gateshead Quays; ⏰10am-6pm Wed-Mon, from 10.30am Tue) South of the Tyne is the entirely separate city of Gateshead (the local authorities bill the pair as 'NewcastleGateshead'), home to Baltic, once a huge grain store, now a huge art gallery to rival London's Tate Modern.

Sleeping

GREYSTREETHOTEL
Hotel ££

(☎0191-230 6777; www.greystreethotel.com; 2-12 Grey St; d from £109; P) A bit of designer class along the classiest street in town has been long overdue: the rooms are gorgeous but a tad cluttered with flat-screen TVs, big beds and modern furnishings.

AVENUE
B&B ££

(☎0191-281 1396; 2 Manor House Rd; s/d £39.50/60) Buried in a sleepy residential area but just a couple of blocks from the action on Osborne Rd, this well-run B&B goes big on busy floral flounce and faux country style.

 Drinking

CROWN POSADA
Pub

(31 The Side) An unspoilt pub in the city centre and a favourite with more seasoned drinkers, be they the after-work or instead-of-work crowd.

CUMBERLAND ARMS
Pub

(off Byker Bank, Ouseburn) Sitting above the Ouseburn, this 19th-century pub has a sensational selection of ales as well as a range of Northumberland meads.

❶ **Information**

Tourist offices (www.visitnewcastlegateshead
.com) Main branch (☎0191-277 8000; Central Arcade, Market St; ⏰9.30am-5.30pm Mon-Sat); Guildhall (☎0191-277 8000; Newcastle Quayside; ⏰10am-5pm Mon-Fri, 9am-5pm Sat, 9am-4pm Sun); Sage Gateshead (☎0191-478 4222; Gateshead Quays; ⏰10am-5pm)

❶ **Getting There & Away**

Bus

Local and regional buses leave from Haymarket or Eldon Sq bus stations. National Express services:

Edinburgh £17.50, three hours, three daily

London £10 to £27, seven hours, nine daily

Manchester £19.50, five hours, five daily

Train

Destinations include:

Carlisle £14.50, 1½ hours, hourly

Edinburgh £32, 1½ hours, half-hourly

London King's Cross £103.60, three hours, half-hourly

York £23.50, one hour, every 20 minutes

Hadrian's Wall

Built in AD 122 to mark the edge of the Roman Empire, this 73-mile coast-to-coast barrier across England remains a major feature of the landscape nearly 2000 years later. Although some parts of the wall have virtually disappeared, other stretches are remarkably well preserved and utterly spectacular. The best portal site for information is www.hadrians wall.org.

 Sights

As well as the wall itself you can also marvel at the Roman forts and castles along its length.

Angel of the North

This extraordinary, gigantic, apocalyptic statue of a human frame with wings looms over the main A1 highway about 5 miles south of Newcastle. At 20m high, 200 tonnes and with a wingspan wider than a Boeing 767, it's Antony Gormley's best-known sculpture and – thanks to all those passing cars – the most viewed piece of public art in the country (though Mark Wallinger's *White Horse* in Kent may pinch the title over the next decade). You can walk right up to the base of the statue, and feel absolutely dwarfed. Buses 21 and 22 from Eldon Sq will take you there.

Hadrian's Wall

Rome's Final Frontier

Of all Britain's Roman ruins, Emperor Hadrian's 2nd-century wall, cutting across northern England from the Irish Sea to the North Sea, is by far the most spectacular; Unesco awarded it world cultural heritage status in 1987.

We've picked out the highlights, one of which is the prime remaining Roman fort on the wall, Housesteads, which we've reconstructed here.

Housesteads' granaries
Nothing like the clever underground ventilation system, which kept vital supplies of grain dry in Northumberland's damp and drizzly climate, would be seen again in these parts for 1500 years.

Milecastle

North Gate

Birdoswald Roman Fort
Explore the longest intact stretch of the wall, scramble over the remains of a large fort then head indoors to wonder at a full-scale model of the wall at its zenith. Great fun for the kids.

Housesteads Roman Fort
See Illustration Right

Interval Tower

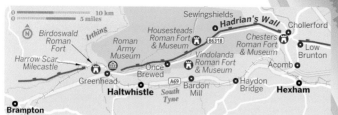

Chesters Roman Fort
Built to keep watch over a bridge spanning the River North Tyne, Britain's best-preserved Roman cavalry fort has a terrific bathhouse, essential if you have months of nippy northern winter ahead.

Hexham Abbey
This may be the finest non-Roman sight near Hadrian's Wall, but the 7th-century parts of this magnificent church were built with stone quarried by the Romans for use in their forts.

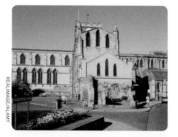

Housesteads' hospital
Operations performed at the hospital would have been surprisingly effective, even without anaesthetics; religious rituals and prayers to Aesculapius, the Roman god of healing, were possibly less helpful for a hernia or appendicitis.

Housesteads' latrines
Communal toilets were the norm in Roman times and Housesteads' are remarkably well preserved – fortunately no traces remain of the vinegar-soaked sponges that were used instead of toilet paper.

GLYN THOMAS/ALAMY

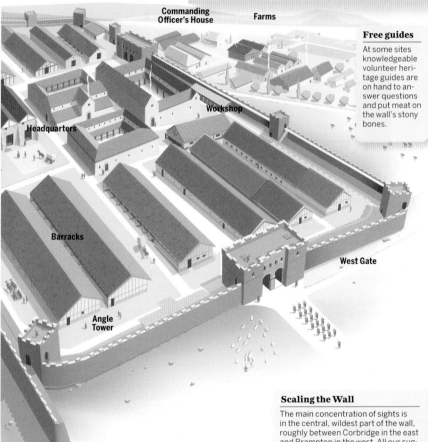

Commanding Officer's House

Farms

Free guides
At some sites knowledgeable volunteer heritage guides are on hand to answer questions and put meat on the wall's stony bones.

Workshop

Headquarters

Barracks

West Gate

Angle Tower

Scaling the Wall
The main concentration of sights is in the central, wildest part of the wall, roughly between Corbridge in the east and Brampton in the west. All our suggested stops are within this area and follow an east-west route. The easiest way to travel is by car, scooting along the B6318, but special bus AD122 will also get you there. Hiking along the designated Hadrian's Wall Path (84 miles) allows you to appreciate the achievement up close.

Housesteads' gatehouses
Unusually at Housesteads neither of the gates faces the enemy, as was the norm at a Roman fort – builders aligned them east-west. Ruts worn by cart wheels are still visible in the stone.

CHESTERS — Roman Fort

(EH; ☎ 01434-681379; Chollerford; adult/child £4.80/2.40; ⌚10am-6pm Apr-Sep) Situated near Chollerford, this well-preserved fortification includes an impressive bathhouse, while its museum displays a fascinating array of Roman sculptures and drawings unearthed in the area.

VINDOLANDA ROMAN FORT & MUSEUM — Roman Fort

(www.vindolanda.com; adult/child £5.90/3.50, with Roman Army Museum £9/5; ⌚10am-6pm Apr-Sep, to 5pm Feb, Mar & Oct) About 1.5 miles north of Bardon Mill, this extensive site offers a fascinating glimpse into the daily life of a Roman garrison town.

HOUSESTEADS ROMAN FORT & MUSEUM — Roman Fort

(EH; adult/child £4.80/2.40; ⌚10am-6pm Apr-Sep) This is the best-preserved Roman fort in the whole country, and the area's most popular ruin. It's 2.5 miles north of Bardon Mill, or a spectacular walk (3 miles) along the wall itself from Once Brewed.

ℹ Getting There & Away

The Newcastle–Carlisle train line runs parallel to the wall a mile or two to the south, with stations at Hexham, Haydon Bridge, Bardon Mill, Haltwhistle and Brampton. There are hourly buses between Carlisle and Newcastle, via most of the same towns. From June to September the hail-and-ride Hadrian's Wall Bus (number AD 122 – geddit?) shuttles between all the major sites, towns and villages along the way.

NORTHWEST ENGLAND

A place of two distinct halves, northwest England offers two very contrasting experiences: culture, music and big nights out in the world-famous cities of Manchester and Liverpool; peace, quiet, fresh air and high peaks in the mountainous Lake District.

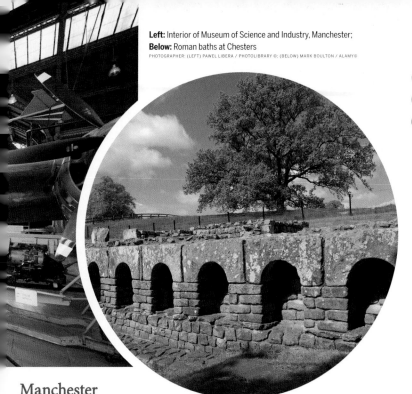

Left: Interior of Museum of Science and Industry, Manchester;
Below: Roman baths at Chesters

PHOTOGRAPHER: (LEFT) PAWEL LIBERA / PHOTOLIBRARY ©; (BELOW) MARK BOULTON / ALAMY©

Manchester

POP 394,270

This is the uncrowned capital of the north – as well as the birthplace of capitalism and the crucible of the Industrial Revolution.

 Sights

City Centre

FREE **MUSEUM OF SCIENCE & INDUSTRY** Museum

(MOSI; ☎0161-832 1830; www.msim.org.uk; Liverpool Rd; admission free, charge for special exhibitions; ⏱10am-5pm) Contains all you could want to know about the Industrial (and post-Industrial) Revolution, and Manchester's key role in it.

FREE **PEOPLE'S HISTORY MUSEUM** Museum

(☎0161-839 6061; www.phm.org.uk; Left Bank, Bridge St) One of the city's best museums, devoted to British social history and the labour movement. It's compelling stuff, and a marvellous example of a museum's relevance to our everyday lives.

NATIONAL FOOTBALL MUSEUM Museum

(☎0161-907 9099; www.nationalfootball museum.com; Urbis, Cathedral Gardens, Corporation St) It's the world's most popular game and Manchester is home to the world's most popular team, so when this museum went looking for a new home, it came to the stunning glass triangle that is Urbis. Slated to open in 2011, the museum will be a major stop on any football fan's itinerary.

FREE **MANCHESTER ART GALLERY** Art Gallery

(☎0161-235 8888; www.manchestergalleries .org; Mosley St; ⏱10am-5pm Tue-Sun) A superb collection of British art and a hefty number of European masters are on display including 37 Turner watercolours,

123

the country's best Pre-Raphaelite collection, and works by Lucian Freud, Francis Bacon, Stanley Spencer, Henry Moore and David Hockney.

Salford Quays

It's a cinch to get here from the city centre via Metrolink (£2). For the Imperial War Museum North and the Lowry, look for the Harbour City stop; get off at Old Trafford for the eponymous stadium.

FREE IMPERIAL WAR MUSEUM NORTH
Museum

(☎0161-836 4000; www.iwm.org.uk/north; Trafford Wharf Rd; ⏰10am-6pm Mar-Oct, to 5pm Nov-Feb) War museums generally appeal to those with a fascination with military hardware but this place takes a radically different approach: war is hell, it tells us, but it's a hell we revisit with tragic regularity.

FREE LOWRY
Arts Centre

(☎0161-876 2020; www.thelowry.com; Pier 8, Salford Quays; ⏰11am-8pm Tue-Fri, 10am-8pm Sat, 11am-6pm Sun & Mon) Looking more like a shiny steel ship than an arts centre,

the Lowry attracts more than a million visitors a year to its myriad functions – everything from exhibitions and performances to bars, restaurants and, inevitably, shops. The complex is home to more than 300 paintings and drawings by northern England's favourite artist, LS Lowry (1887–1976), who was born in nearby Stretford.

OLD TRAFFORD
Stadium

(☎0870 442 1994; www.manutd.com; Sir Matt Busby Way; ⏰9.30am-5pm) Home of the world's most famous club, the Old Trafford stadium is both a theatre and a temple for its millions of fans worldwide, many of whom come on a pilgrimage to pay tribute to the minor deities that others may know only as highly paid footballers. The **tour** (adult/child £12.50/8.50; ⏰every 10min 9.40am-4.30pm except match days) includes a seat in the stands, a peek at the players' lounge and a walk down the tunnel to the pitchside dugout. The **museum** (adult/child £9/7; ⏰9.30am-5pm) has a comprehensive history of the club.

Sleeping

City Centre

VELVET HOTEL Boutique Hotel ££

(☎0161-236 9003; www.velvetman chester.com; 2 Canal St; r from £99; 🛜) Beautiful bespoke rooms make this a real contender for best in the city. Despite the location and tantalising decor, it's as popular with straight visitors as it is with the same-sex crowd.

RADISSON EDWARDIAN Hotel ££

(☎0161-835 9929; www.radissonedwardian.com/ manchester; Peter St; r from £90; P @🛜) The Free Trade Hall saw it all, from Emmeline Pankhurst's

Football match at Old Trafford stadium

suffragette campaign to the Sex Pistols' legendary 1976 gig. Today, those rabble-rousing noisemakers wouldn't be allowed to set foot in the door of what is now a sumptuous five-star hotel.

PALACE HOTEL   Boutique Hotel   ££
(☎0161-288 1111; www.principal-hotels.com; Oxford St; s/d from £85/105; 🛜) An elegant refurbishment of one of Manchester's most magnificent Victorian palaces resulted in a special boutique hotel.

 Eating

YANG SING   Chinese   ££
(☎0161-236 2200; 34 Princess St; mains £9-17; ⏰lunch & dinner) A serious contender for best Chinese restaurant in England, Yang Sing attracts diners from all over with its exceptional Cantonese cuisine.

🌿**EARTH CAFE**   Vegetarian   £
(☎0161-834 1996; www.earthcafe.co.uk; 16-20 Turner St; chef's special £3.20; ⏰lunch Tue-Sat; 🔀) Below the Manchester Buddhist Centre, this gourmet vegetarian cafe's motto is 'right food, right place, right time'. The result is wonderful.

🌿**LOVE SAVES THE DAY**   Cafe   £
(☎0161-832 0777; Tib St; lunch £6-8; ⏰breakfast & lunch Mon-Wed, Sat & Sun, breakfast, lunch & dinner Thu & Fri) The Northern Quarter's most popular cafe is a New York–style deli, small supermarket and sit-down eatery in one large, airy room.

TROF   Cafe   £
(☎0161-832 1870; 5-8 Thomas St; sandwiches £4, mains around £8; ⏰lunch & dinner) Great music, top staff and a fab menu, plus a broad selection of beers and tunes (Tuesday night is acoustic night), make this hang-out a firm favourite with students.

 **Drinking**

BRITONS PROTECTION   Pub
(☎0161-236 5895; 50 Great Bridgewater St) Whisky – 200 different kinds of it – is the beverage of choice at this old-fashioned boozer with open fires in the back rooms and a cosy atmosphere.

BLUU   Bar
(☎0161-839 7740; www.bluu.co.uk; Unit 1, Smithfield Market, Thomas St; ⏰noon-midnight Sun-Mon, to 1am Tue-Thu, to 2am Fri & Sat) Our favourite of the Northern Quarter's collection of great bars; cool, comfortable and with a great terrace.

BAR CENTRO   Bar
(☎0161-835 2863; 72-74 Tib St; mains £6-9; ⏰noon-midnight Mon-Wed, to 1am Thu, to 2am Fri & Sat, 2pm-midnight Sun) A Northern Quarter stalwart, very popular with the bohemian crowd.

Old Wellington Inn   Pub
(☎0161-830 1440; 4 Cathedral Gates) One of the oldest buildings in the city and a lovely spot for a pint of genuine ale.

ℹ️ **Information**

Tourist office (☎0871 222 8223; www.visit manchester.com; Piccadilly Plaza, Portland St; ⏰10am-5.15pm Mon-Sat, to 4.30pm Sun)

ℹ️ **Getting There & Away**

Air

Manchester Airport (☎0161-489 3000; www .manchesterairport.co.uk), south of the city, is the largest airport outside London and is served by 13 locations throughout Britain as well as over 50 international destinations.

Train

Manchester Piccadilly is the main station for trains to and from the rest of the country. Trains head to Liverpool Lime St (£9, 45 minutes, half-hourly), Newcastle (£35, three hours, six daily) and London (£60, three hours, seven daily).

Chester

POP 80,130

The small city of Chester is one of English history's greatest gifts to the contemporary visitor. Its red-sandstone walls gift-wrap a tidy collection of Roman remains, and Tudor and Victorian buildings.

St George's Hall, Liverpool

TRAVELBILD.COM / ALAMY©

◉ Sights & Activities

CITY WALLS Landmark

A good way to get a sense of Chester's unique character is to walk the 2-mile circuit along the city walls that surround the historic centre. Originally built by the Romans around AD 70, the walls have been altered substantially over the following centuries but have been in their current position since around 1200.

FREE **ROMAN AMPHITHEATRE** Ruins

Just outside the city walls, this ruined arena once seated 7000 spectators (making it the country's largest). Now it's little more than steps buried in grass, but is a great place to rest your feet after walking the walls.

ROWS Architecture

A series of two-level galleried arcades line the four main streets of central Chester. The architecture is a handsome mix of Victorian and Tudor (original and mock), and houses a fantastic collection of unique, individually owned shops.

❶ Information

Tourist office (☏01244-402111; www.chester .gov.uk; Town Hall, Northgate St; ◷9am-5.30pm Mon-Sat, 10am-4pm Sun May-Oct, 10am-5pm Mon-Sat Nov-Apr)

❶ Getting There & Away

Trains travel to/from Liverpool (£4.35, 45 minutes, hourly), London Euston (£65.20, 2½ hours, hourly) and Manchester (£12.60, one hour, hourly).

Liverpool

POP 469,020

Liverpool is currently undergoing a revival: its centre is being transformed, and its magnificent cultural heritage is celebrated on the waterfront around Albert Dock.

◉ Sights

City Centre

FREE **WORLD MUSEUM** Museum

(☏0151-478 4399; www.liverpoolmuseums .org.uk/wml; William Brown St; ◷10am-5pm)

Natural history, science and technology are the themes of this sprawling museum. It also includes the country's only free planetarium.

FREE **WALKER ART GALLERY** Art Gallery
(✆0151-478 4199; www.liverpoolmuseums .org.uk/walker; William Brown St; ◷10am-5pm) Touted as the 'National Gallery of the North', the Walker houses an outstanding collection of art from the 14th to the 21st centuries.

FREE **ST GEORGE'S HALL**
Cultural Centre
(✆0151-707 2391; www.stgeorgesliverpool.co.uk; William Brown St; ◷10am-5pm Tue-Sat, 1-5pm Sun) Arguably Liverpool's most impressive building – a magnificent example of neoclassical architecture.

LIVERPOOL CATHEDRAL Church
(✆0151-709 6271; www.liverpoolcathedral.org .uk; Hope St; ◷8am-6pm) This is a building of superlatives: Britain's largest church; the world's largest Anglican cathedral; the world's third-largest bell (with the world's heaviest peal); even the world's largest organ.

Albert Dock

This former port and its surrounding buildings is now a World Heritage Site.

INTERNATIONAL SLAVERY MUSEUM Museum
(✆0151-478 4499; www .liverpool museums.org.uk/ism; Albert Dock; admission free; ◷10am-5pm) This magnificent museum reveals slavery's unimaginable horrors – including Liverpool's own role in the slave trade – and it doesn't baulk at confronting racism, through a remarkable series of multimedia and other displays.

THE BEATLES STORY Museum
(✆0151-709 1963; www.beatlesstory.com; Albert Dock; adult/student/child £12.95/8.50/6.50; ◷9am-7pm, last admission 5pm) Liverpool's most popular museum tells the story of the world's most famous foursome, with plenty of genuine memorabilia – and hardly a mention of internal discord, drugs or Yoko Ono.

FREE **MERSEYSIDE MARITIME MUSEUM**
Museum
(✆0151-478 4499; www.liverpoolmuseums .org.uk/maritime; Albert Dock; ◷10am-5pm) A graphic celebration of one of the world's great ports, including a fascinating emigration exhibit about the nine million migrants who came through on their way to North America and Australia.

FREE **TATE LIVERPOOL** Art Gallery
(✆0151-702 7400; www.tate.org.uk/liverpool; Albert Dock; special exhibitions adult/child from £5/4; ◷10am-5.50pm Jun-Aug, 10am-5.50pm Tue-Sun Sep-May) A substantial checklist of 20th-century artists.

The Beatles Story, Liverpool

North of Albert Dock

The area to the north of Albert Dock is known as **Pier Head**, still the departure point for ferries across the River Mersey. The story of the millions of migrants who sailed from Liverpool will be told in the eye-catching **Museum of Liverpool** (0151-207 0001; Mann Island), due to open in 2011. Until then, this area will continue to be dominated by a trio of buildings known as the 'Three Graces': the domed **Port of Liverpool Building**; the **Cunard Building**, in the style of an Italian palazzo; and the **Royal Liver Building** (*lie*-ver) crowned by the city's symbol, the famous copper Liver Bird.

Sleeping

RACQUET CLUB   Boutique Hotel ££
(0151-236 6676; www.racquetclub.org.uk; Hargreaves Bldg, 5 Chapel St; r £110;) Eight individually styled rooms make this one of the most elegant choices in town.

62 CASTLE ST   Boutique Hotel ££
(0151-702 7898; www.62castlest.com; 62 Castle St; r from £79; P @) This elegant

property successfully blends the traditional Victorian features of the building with a sleek, contemporary style.

HARD DAYS NIGHT HOTEL   Hotel £££
(0151-236 1964; www.harddaysnighthotel.com; Central Bldgs, North John St; r £110-160, ste £750; @) You don't have to be a Beatles fan to stay here, but it helps: the 110 ultramodern rooms are decorated with specially commissioned drawings of the band.

Eating & Drinking

EVERYMAN BISTRO   Cafe £
(0151-708 9545; www.everyman.co.uk; 13 Hope St; mains £5-8; lunch & dinner Mon-Sat, dinner Sun) Out-of-work actors and other creative types make this great cafe–restaurant (located beneath the Everyman Theatre) their second home – with good reason. Great tucker and a terrific atmosphere.

ALMA DE CUBA   Cuban ££
(0151-709 7097; www.alma-de-cuba.com; St Peter's Church, Seel St; mains £16-24; lunch

Museum of Liverpool and the Three Graces

Doing the Beatles to Death

It doesn't matter that two of them are dead or that the much-visited Cavern Club is an unfaithful reconstruction of the original, nor that, if he were alive, John Lennon would have devoted much of his cynical energy to mocking the 'Cavern Quarter' that has grown up around Mathew St. No, it doesn't matter at all, because the Beatles phenomenon lives on, and a huge chunk of the city's visitors come to visit, see and touch anything – and we mean anything – even vaguely associated with the Fab Four.

True fans will also undoubtedly want to visit the National Trust–owned **Mendips**, the home where John lived with his Aunt Mimi from 1945 to 1963, and **20 Forthlin Rd**, where Paul grew up. You can do so only by prebooked **tour** (0151-427 7231; adult/child £16.80/3.15; 10.30am & 11.20am Wed-Sun Easter-Oct), from outside the National Conservation Centre.

& dinner) This extraordinary venture has seen the transformation of a Polish church into a Miami-style Cuban extravaganza. *¡Salud!*

PHILHARMONIC Pub
(0151-707 2837; 36 Hope St; to 11.30pm) This extraordinary pub, designed by the shipwrights who built the *Lusitania,* is one of the most beautiful in all of England.

 Entertainment

Most of the city's clubs and late-night bars are concentrated in the area of Ropewalks.

Academy Music
(0151-794 6868; Liverpool University, 11-13 Hotham St) Good spot to see mid-size bands on tour.

Cavern Club Music
(0151-236 1965; 8-10 Mathew St) Reconstruction of the 'world's most famous club'; good selection of local bands.

Information

08 Place tourist office (0151-233 2008; Whitechapel; 9am-8pm Mon-Sat, 11am-4pm Sun Apr-Sep, 9am-6pm Mon-Sat, 11am-4pm Sun Oct-Mar)

Albert Dock tourist offices (0151-478 4599; 10am-6pm) At the Anchor Courtyard and Merseyside Maritime Museum.

Getting There & Away

Liverpool's main station is Lime St. It has hourly services to almost everywhere, including Chester (£5, 45 minutes), London (£65, 3¼ hours) and Manchester (£9, 45 minutes).

Lake District National Park

A dramatic landscape of high peaks, dizzying ridges and huge lakes gouged by the march of Ice Age glaciers, the Lake District is a beautiful corner of Britain. It may not be the wildest place on earth, and there are much bigger mountains in Wales and Scotland, but for England it's as extreme as it gets. Not surprisingly, the awe-inspiring geography here shaped the literary persona of one of Britain's best-known poets, William Wordsworth.

Often called simply the Lakes (but never – note, Australians – the '*Lakes* District'), the national park and surrounding area attract around 15 million visitors annually. But if you avoid summer weekends, and especially if you do a bit of hiking, it's easy enough to miss the crush.

The key valleys of the Lake District radiate from a central high point like spokes of a wheel, with most of the larger towns at the outer edge. Principal gateways include the twin towns of Windermere and Bowness in the south, Ambleside slightly nearer the centre, and Keswick in the north.

 Information

The Lake District's tourist offices are crammed with information on local hikes, activities and accommodation, and stocked with guidebooks, maps and hiking supplies.

Ambleside (☏015394-32582; tic@thehubof ambleside.com; Central Buildings, Market Cross; ⊙9am-5pm)

Bowness (☏015394-42895; bownesstic@lake district.gov.uk; Glebe Rd; ⊙9.30am-5.30pm Easter-Oct, 10am-4pm Fri-Sun Nov-Mar)

Keswick (☏017687-72645; keswicktic@lake district.gov.uk; Moot Hall, Market Pl; ⊙9.30am-5.30pm Apr-Oct, to 4.30pm Nov-Mar)

Windermere (☏015394-46499; windermeretic@ southlakeland.gov.uk; Victoria St; ⊙9am-5.30pm Mon-Sat, 9.30am-5.30pm Sun Apr-Oct)

SOUTH & WEST WALES

Lying to the west of England, the nation of Wales is a separate country within the state of Great Britain. While some areas in the south are undeniable scarred by coal mining and heavy industry, overall Wales boasts a landscape of wild mountains, rolling hills, rich farmland and some of the most beautiful beaches in all of Britain.

Cardiff

POP 324,800

The capital of Wales since only 1955, Cardiff has embraced its new role with vigour, emerging as one of Britain's leading urban centres.

Sights

Central Cardiff

CARDIFF CASTLE   Castle

(www.cardiffcastle.com; Castle St; adult/child £8.95/6.35, incl guided tour £11.95/8.50; ⊙9am-6pm Mar-Oct, to 5pm Nov-Feb) The grafting of Victorian mock-Gothic extravagance onto genuine Norman relics makes

Cardiff Castle the city's leading attraction. It's far from a traditional Welsh castle but it neatly encompasses the city's history.

MILLENNIUM STADIUM   Stadium

(☏029-2082 2228; www.millenniumstadium.com; Westgate St; tours adult/child £6.50/4; ⊙10am-5pm Mon-Sat, to 4pm Sun) This spectacular stadium squats like a stranded spaceship in the heart of the city – and in this rugby-mad nation somehow gets away with it.

Cardiff Bay

The redeveloped waterfront of Cardiff Bay is about 2 miles from the city centre and is lined with bars, restaurants and shops – and a collection of stunning buildings.

FREE WALES MILLENNIUM CENTRE   Arts Centre

(☏029-2063 6464; www.wmc.org.uk; Bute Pl) The premier arts complex of Wales, this architectural masterpiece of slate and bronze is a key feature of the bay. If you can't take in a show, wander through the public areas or take an official **guided tour** (adult/child £5.50/4.50; ⊙9am-5pm).

FREE SENEDD (NATIONAL ASSEMBLY BUILDING)   Notable Building

(☏0845 010 5500; www.assemblywales.org/sen-home; ⊙10.30am-4.30pm, extended during plenary sessions) This striking structure, surrounded by public artworks, is home to the Welsh National Assembly.

FREE PIERHEAD   Museum

(☏029-0845 010 5500; www.pierhead.org; ⊙10.30am-4.30pm) One of the area's few Victorian remnants, this red-brick building with its famous clock tower is a long-time Cardiff icon.

🛏 Sleeping

Central Cardiff

PARC HOTEL   Hotel   ££

(☏0871 376 9011; www.thistle.com/theparc hotel; Park Pl; r from £99; @ 🛜) A smart contemporary hotel located right at the heart of the main shopping area, with tasteful rooms, good facilities and helpful staff.

Cardiff Bay

ST DAVID'S HOTEL & SPA   Hotel £££
(☎029-2045 4045; www.thestdavidshotel.com;
Havannah St; r from £99; @ 🛜 ♿) A glittering,
glassy tower topped with a sail-like flour-
ish, St David's epitomises Cardiff Bay's
transformation from wasteland to stylish
place-to-be. Every room has a private
balcony with a harbour view.

 Eating & Drinking

Central Cardiff

🌿 **PLAN**   Cafe £
(28 Morgan Arcade; mains £5-8; ⏱breakfast
& lunch; ✒) Serves quite possibly Wales'
best coffee, and specialises in healthy,
organic, locally sourced food.

CLWB IFOR BACH   Club
(☎029-2023 2199; www.clwb.net; 11 Womanby
St) Truly an independent music great, *Y
Clwb* is Cardiff's most eclectic and important venue.

Cardiff Bay

WOODS BAR & BRASSERIE
   Modern European £££
(☎029-2049 2400; Stuart St; mains £11-
18; ⏱closed Sun dinner) The historic
Pilotage Building has been given
a modern makeover – zany
wallpaper, exposed stone walls
and a floor-to-ceiling glass
extension – to accommo-
date Cardiff Bay's best
restaurant.

SALT   Bar
(Mermaid Quay, Cardiff
Bay) A large, modern,
nautical-themed bar
with plenty of sofas
and armchairs for
lounging around, Salt
also has a 1st-floor
open-air terrace with
a view of yachts on the
bay.

ℹ Information

Tourist office (☎029-2087 3573; www.visit
cardiff.com; Old Library, The Hayes; ⏱9.30am-
5.30pm Mon-Sat, 10am-4pm Sun; @)

Cardiff Bay Visitor Centre (☎029-2087 7927;
Harbour Dr; ⏱10am-6pm)

ℹ Getting There & Away

Direct services from Cardiff include London
Paddington (£43, 2¾ hours) and Fishguard
Harbour (£20, 2¼ hours).

Snowdonia National Park

The jagged peaks of Snowdonia National
Park (Parc Cenedlaethol Eryri) offer the
most spectacular mountain scenery
in Wales. The most popular area is in
the north around Snowdon (at 1085m,
the highest peak in Britain south of the
Scottish Highlands), although the park
extends all the way south to Machynl-
leth. The main activities are walking and
mountain biking. For more information,
see www.visitsnowdonia.info.

Hikers in Snowdonia National Park
PHOTOGRAPHER: EOIN CLARKE/LONELY PLANET IMAGES ©

Good bases and gateways include the busy village of Betws-y-Coed on the eastern side of the park, while pretty Beddgelert is handy for the south. Most convenient for Snowdon itself is the town of Llanberis – less attractive, but with all the facilities you need.

ℹ Information

Beddgelert (☎01766-890615; Canolfan Hebog; ⊙9.30am-5.30pm Easter-Oct, 9.30am-4.30pm Fri-Sun Nov-Mar; @)

Betws-y-Coed (☎01690-710426; www.betws -y-coed.co.uk; Royal Oak Stables; ⊙9.30am-4.30pm)

LLanberis (☎01286-870765; 41 High St; ⊙9.30am-4.30pm Apr-Oct, 9.30am-3pm Fri-Mon Nov-Mar)

ℹ Getting There & Around

The handiest train line runs along the North Wales coast between Chester and Holyhead, via Llandudno Junction and Bangor (from where you can get buses into the park itself).

An excellent local bus network called the Snowdon Sherpa (☎0870 608 2608) serves the park, with connections to Llandudno, Betws-y-Coed, Bangor and Llanberis.

Conwy

On the north coast of Wales, the historic town of Conwy is utterly dominated by the Unesco-designated cultural treasure of **Conwy Castle** (Cadw; adult/child £4.60/4.10; ⊙9am-5pm, 9.30am-4pm Mon-Sat, 11am-4pm Sun low season), the most stunning of all Edward I's Welsh fortresses. Built between 1277 and 1307, it has commanding views across the estuary and Snowdonia National Park. Exploring the castle makes for a superb, living-history visit; head to the battlements for panoramic views. The 1200m-long town wall was built with the castle to guard Conwy's residents at night. Today you can walk part way round the wall for more excellent views; the best are to be had from Upper Gate.

SOUTHERN SCOTLAND

The western side of this region offers some fine scenery – high hills, moors, forests and a craggy coastline – without the attendant tour buses and crowds you might find in the Highlands.

Alloway

The pretty town of Alloway is best known as the birth-place of Robert Burns. The brand-new **Robert Burns Birthplace Museum** (NTS; www.nts.org.uk; adult/child £8; ⊙10am-5pm Oct-Mar, to 5.30pm Apr-Sep) displays a solid collection of Burnsiana, including manuscripts and possessions of the poet – like the pistols he packed in order to carry out his daily work as a taxman.

Conwy Castle

GLENN BEANLAND/LONELY PLANET IMAGES ©

To get here, aim for the town of Ayr (easily reached from Glasgow), then take bus 57 (Monday to Saturday, hourly, 10 minutes).

Melrose Abbey

Perhaps the best of the great Border **abbeys** (HS; www.historic-scotland.gov.uk; adult/child £5.20/3.10; ⏱9.30am-5.30pm Apr-Sep, to 4.30pm Oct-Mar), the red sandstone walls and remaining broken shell is pure Gothic – and famous for its decorative stonework (see if you can glimpse the pig gargoyle playing the bagpipes on the roof). You can also climb to the top for tremendous views.

EDINBURGH

☎0131 / POP 440,000

Scotland's proud and historic capital city is a visual delight, built on a grand scale around two hills – one topped by its impressive castle, the other by a big chunk of undeveloped mountain seemingly helicoptered in for effect. And with the UK's most popular and comprehensive summer festival scene, visitors who plan a brief stopover often end up staying longer.

Sights

Edinburgh's city centre is divided into two parts – Old Town and New Town – split by Princess Street Gardens.

EDINBURGH CASTLE Castle
(www.edinburghcastle.gov.uk; Castle Hill; adult/child incl audio guide £14/7.50; ⏱9.30am-6pm Apr-Sep, to 5pm Oct-Mar, last admission 45min before closing) Edinburgh Castle has played a pivotal role in Scottish history, both as a royal residence – King Malcolm Canmore (r 1058–93) and Queen Margaret first made their home here in the 11th century – and as a military stronghold. The castle last saw military action in 1745; from then until the 1920s it served as the British army's main base in Scotland.

REAL MARY KING'S CLOSE
Historic Building
(☎0845 070 6255; www.realmarykingsclose.com; 2 Warriston's Close, Writers Ct, High St; adult/child £11/6; ⏱10am-9pm Apr-Oct, to 11pm Aug, 10am-5pm Sun-Thu & 10am-9pm Fri & Sat Nov-Mar) This medieval Old Town alley survived for 250 years in the foundations

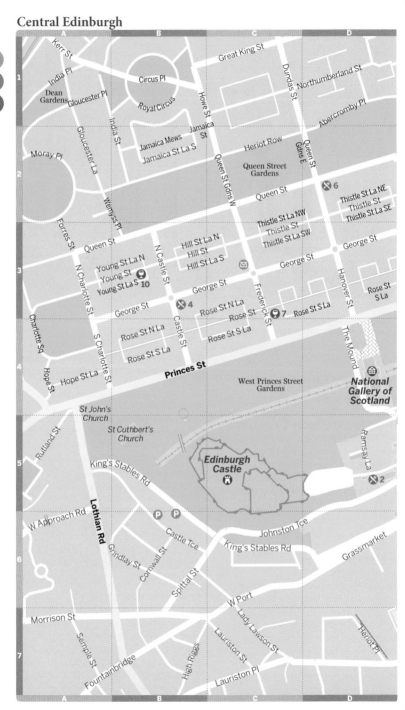

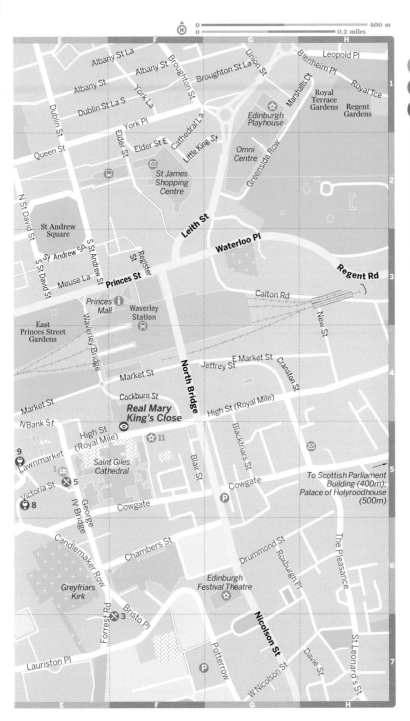

0 ———— 400 m
0 ———— 0.2 miles

E

Albany St La
Albany St
Dublin St La S
Dublin St
York La
York Pl
Queen St
N St David St
St Andrew Square
St Andrew Sq
S St Andrew St
S St David St
Meuse La
St Andrew St
Register St
Princes St
Princes Mall
East Princes Street Gardens
Waverley Bridge
Waverley Station
Market St
Cockburn St
Market St
N Bank St
Real Mary King's Close
High St (Royal Mile)
9
Lawnmarket
Saint Giles Cathedral
Victoria St
5
1
8
George IV Bridge
Cowgate
Candlemaker Row
Chambers St
Greyfriars Kirk
Forrest Rd
Bristo Pl
3
Lauriston Pl

F

Albany St
Broughton St
York La
Cathedral La
Elder St
Elder St E
Little King St
St James Shopping Centre
Leith St
Waterloo Pl
Jeffrey St
E Market St
North Bridge
High St (Royal Mile)
11
Blair St
Cowgate
Drummond St
Edinburgh Festival Theatre
Potterrow
W Nicolson St

G

Broughton St La
Union St
Blenheim Pl
Edinburgh Playhouse
Omni Centre
Greenside Row
Marshalls Ct
Royal Terrace Gardens
Calton Rd
New St
Cranston St
Blackfriars St
To Scottish Parliament Building (400m); Palace of Holyroodhouse (500m)
Roxburgh Pl
Nicolson St
Davie St

H

Leopold Pl
Royal Tce
Regent Gardens
Regent Rd
The Pleasance
St Leonard's St

135

Central Edinburgh

of the City Chambers, and now gives a fascinating insight into the daily life of 16th- and 17th-century Edinburgh.

FREE SCOTTISH PARLIAMENT BUILDING
Notable Building
(☏0131-348 5200; www.scottish.parliament.uk; ⏰9am-6.30pm Tue-Thu, 10am-5.30pm Mon & Fri in session, 10am-6pm Mon-Fri in recess Apr-Oct, 10am-4pm in recess Nov-Mar; ☏) Scotland's own parliament was officially opened in October 2005. The public areas – the Main Hall (where there is an exhibition, shop and cafe) and the **public gallery** in the Debating Chamber – are open to visitors (tickets needed for public gallery; see website for details). You can also take a free, one-hour guided tour (advance booking recommended), which includes a visit to the Debating Chamber, a committee room, the Garden Lobby and, when possible, the office of an MSP (Member of the Scottish Parliament).

PALACE OF HOLYROODHOUSE Palace
(www.royalcollection.org.uk; Canongate; adult/child £10.25/6.20; ⏰9.30am-6pm Apr-Oct, to 4.30pm Nov-Mar) This palace is the royal family's official residence in Scotland, but is most famous as the 16th-century home of the ill-fated Mary, Queen of Scots. The palace is closed to the public when the royal family is visiting and during state functions (usually in mid-May, and mid-June to early July; check the website for exact dates). The guided tour leads you through a series of impressive royal apartments, ending in the Great Gallery, where you can admire the 89 portraits of Scottish kings commissioned by Charles II, recording his unbroken lineage from Scota, the Egyptian pharaoh's daughter who discovered the infant Moses on the banks of the Nile.

HOLYROOD PARK Park
The former hunting ground of Scottish monarchs, the park covers 263 hectares of varied landscape – including crags, moorland and loch – bang in the heart of the city. The highest point is the 251m summit of **Arthur's Seat**, the deeply eroded remnant of a long-extinct volcano, and an excellent viewpoint overlooking Edinburgh.

FREE NATIONAL GALLERY OF SCOTLAND
Art Gallery
(www.nationalgalleries.org; The Mound; fee for special exhibitions; ⏰10am-5pm Fri-Wed, to 7pm Thu; ☏) This imposing classical building with its Ionic porticoes dates from the 1850s. Its octagonal rooms have been restored to their original Victorian decor of deep green carpets and dark red walls – a fitting setting for an important collection of European art from the Renaissance to postimpressionism, with works by Verrocchio (Leonardo da Vinci's teacher), Tintoretto, Titian, Holbein, Rubens, Van Dyck, Vermeer, El Greco, Poussin, Rembrandt, Gainsborough, Turner, Constable, Monet, Pissaro, Gauguin and Cézanne.

 Tours

Bus Tours
Open-topped bus tours leave from Waverley Bridge and offer hop-on, hop-off tours of the main sights.

City Sightseeing
Bus Tour

(www.edinburghtour.com; adult/child £12/5)
Bright red buses depart every 20 minutes from
Waverley Bridge.

Majestic Tour
Bus Tour

(www.edinburghtour.com; adult/child £12/5) Runs
every 30 minutes (every 20 minutes in July and
August) from Waverley Bridge to the Royal Yacht
Britannia at Ocean Terminal via the New Town,
returning via Holyrood and the Royal Mile.

Walking Tours

Black Hart Storytellers
Walking Tour

(www.blackhart.uk.com; adult/concession
£9.50/7.50) The 'City of the Dead' tour of
Greyfriars Kirkyard is probably the scariest of
Edinburgh's 'ghost' tours.

Edinburgh Literary Pub Tour
Walking Tour

(www.edinburghliterarypubtour.co.uk; adult/
student £10/8) An enlightening two-hour trawl
through Edinburgh's literary history in the
entertaining company of Messrs Clart and
McBrain.

Rebus Tours
Walking Tour

(www.rebustours.com; adult/student £10/9) Tours
of the 'hidden Edinburgh' frequented by novelist
Ian Rankin's fictional detective John Rebus.

Sleeping

HOTEL MISSONI
Boutique Hotel £££

(☎ 0131-220 6666; www.hotelmissoni.com;
1 George IV Bridge; r £180; 🛜) The Italian
fashion house Missoni has established a
style icon in the heart of the medieval Old
Town, with this bold statement of a hotel.
The place impresses with its modernistic
architecture, impeccably mannered staff
and, most importantly, very comfortable
bedrooms.

SIX MARY'S PLACE
B&B ££

(☎ 0131-332 8965; www.sixmarysplace.co.uk; 6
Mary's Pl, Raeburn Pl; s/d/f from £50/94/150;
@🛜♿) This attractive Georgian town
house mixes period features, contemporary furniture and modern colours. It also
has great (vegetarian-only) breakfasts
and a comfy lounge with free coffee.

DENE GUEST HOUSE
B&B ££

(☎ 0131-556 2700; www.deneguesthouse.com;
7 Eyre Pl; per person £25-50; ♿) This guest
house/B&B is a friendly and informal
place, with a welcoming owner and spacious bedrooms.

Festival City

Edinburgh boasts a frenzy of festivals, especially in August, with half a dozen
world-class events running at the same time. For more, see www.edinburgh
festivals.co.uk.

Edinburgh Festival Fringe (☎ 0131-226 0026; www.edfringe.com; Edinburgh Festival Fringe
Office, 180 High St) The biggest festival of the performing arts anywhere in the
world, held over 3½ weeks in August, the last two weeks overlapping with the
first two weeks of the Edinburgh International Festival.

Edinburgh International Festival (☎ 0131-473 2099; www.eif.co.uk) Festooned with
superlatives – the oldest, the biggest, the most famous, the best in the world –
with three weeks of diverse and inspirational music, opera, theatre and dance.
Tickets can be purchased at the **Hub** (www.hubtickets.co.uk).

Edinburgh Military Tattoo (☎ 0131-225 1188; www.edintattoo.co.uk; Tattoo Office, 32
Market St) A spectacular display of military marching bands, massed pipes and
drums, acrobats, cheerleaders and motorcycle display teams, all played out in
front of the magnificent backdrop of the floodlit castle during the first three
weeks of August.

Royal Mile

A Grand Day Out

Planning your own procession along the Royal Mile involves some tough decisions – it would be impossible to see everything in a single day, so it's wise to decide in advance what you don't want to miss and shape your visit around that. Remember to leave time for lunch, for exploring some of the Mile's countless side alleys and, during festival time, for enjoying the street theatre that is bound to be happening in High St.

The most pleasant way to reach the Castle Esplanade at the start of the Royal Mile is to hike up the zigzag path from the footbridge behind the Ross Bandstand in Princes Street Gardens (in springtime you'll be knee-deep in daffodils). Starting at **Edinburgh Castle** ❶ means that the rest of your walk is downhill. For a superb view up and down the length of the Mile, climb the **Camera Obscura's Outlook Tower** ❷ before visiting **Gladstone's Land** ❸ and **St Giles Cathedral** ❹. If history's your

---

Royal Visits to the Royal Mile

1561: Mary, Queen of Scots arrives from France and holds an audience with John Knox.
1745: Bonnie Prince Charlie fails to capture Edinburgh Castle, and instead sets up court in Holyroodhouse.
2004: Queen Elizabeth II officially opens the Scottish Parliament building.

JONATHAN SMITH / LONELY PLANET IMAGES ©

Edinburgh Castle
If you're pushed for time, visit the Great Hall, the Honours of Scotland and the Prisons of War exhibit. Head for the Half Moon Battery for a photo looking down the length of the Royal Mile.

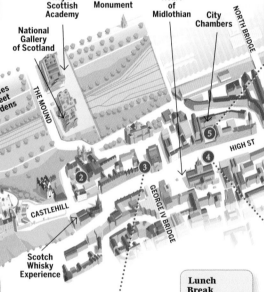

Royal Scottish Academy

Scott Monument

Heart of Midlothian

City Chambers

NORTH BRIDGE

National Gallery of Scotland

Princes Street Gardens

THE MOUND

HIGH ST

GEORGE IV BRIDGE

CASTLEHILL

Scotch Whisky Experience

KARL BLACKWELL / LONELY PLANET IMAGES ©

Gladstone's Land
The 1st floor houses a faithful recreation of how a wealthy Edinburgh merchant lived in the 17th century. Check out the beautiful Painted Bedchamber, with its ornately decorated walls and wooden ceilings.

Lunch Break

Pie and a pint at **Royal Mile Tavern**; soup and a sandwich at **Always Sunday**; bistro nosh at **Café Marlayne**.

thing, you'll want to add **Real Mary King's Close** ⑤, **John Knox House** ⑥ and the **Museum of Edinburgh** ⑦ to your must-see list.

At the foot of the mile, choose between modern and ancient seats of power – the **Scottish Parliament** ⑧ or the Palace of **Holyroodhouse** ⑨. Round off the day with an evening ascent of Arthur's Seat or, slightly less strenuously, Calton Hill. Both make great sunset viewpoints.

TAKING YOUR TIME

Minimum time needed for each attraction:

Edinburgh Castle: two hours
Gladstone's Land: 45 minutes
St Giles Cathedral: 30 minutes
Real Mary King's Close: one hour (tour)
Scottish Parliament: one hour (tour)
Palace of Holyroodhouse: one hour

Real Mary King's Close

The guided tour is heavy on ghost stories, but a highlight is standing in an original 17th-century room with tufts of horsehair poking from the crumbling plaster, and breathing in the ancient scent of stone, dust and history.

Canongate Kirk

CANONGATE

ST MARY'S ST

SOUTH BRIDGE

Tron Kirk

Our Dynamic Earth

Scottish Parliament

Don't have time for the guided tour? Pick up a *Discover the Scottish Parliament Building* leaflet from reception and take a self-guided tour of the exterior, then hike up to Salisbury Crags for a great view of the complex.

Palace of Holyroodhouse

Find the secret staircase joining Mary, Queen of Scots' bedchamber with that of her husband, Lord Darnley, who restrained the queen while his henchmen stabbed to death her secretary (and possible lover), David Rizzio.

St Giles Cathedral

Look out for the Burne-Jones stained-glass window (1873) at the west end, showing the crossing of the River Jordan, and the bronze memorial to Robert Louis Stevenson in the Moray Aisle.

Eating

ONDINE   Seafood £££
(☎0131-226 1888; www.ondinerestaurant.co.uk;
2 George IV Bridge; mains £14-24; ⊙lunch &
dinner) New on the scene in 2009, Ondine
has rapidly become one of Edinburgh's
finest seafood restaurants, with a menu
based on sustainably sourced fish. The
two-course pretheatre (5pm to 6.30pm)
dinner costs £15.

MUMS   Cafe £
(www.monstermashcafe.co.uk; 4a Forrest Rd;
mains £6-8; ⊙breakfast, lunch & dinner) The
original founder of Monster Mash has
reopened with a new name, serving up
classic British comfort food – bangers
and mash, shepherd's pie, fish and chips.

AMBER   Scottish ££
(☎0131-477 8477; www.amber-restaurant.co.uk;
354 Castlehill; mains £12-18; ⊙lunch daily, dinner
Tue-Sat) You've got to love a place where
the waiter greets you with the words, 'My

name is Craig, and I'll be your whisky
adviser for this evening.' Located in the
Scotch Whisky Experience, this restaurant manages to avoid the tourist clichés,
and creates genuinely interesting and
flavoursome dishes.

URBAN ANGEL   Cafe £
(☎0131-225 6215; www.urban-angel.co.uk; 121
Hanover St; mains £8-12; ⊙breakfast, lunch
& dinner Mon-Sat, lunch Sun) A wholesome
deli-cafe-bistro that puts the emphasis
on Fairtrade, organic and locally sourced
produce, Urban Angel serves up an all-day
brunch, tapas, and a wide range of snacky
meals.

OLOROSO   Scottish £££
(☎0131-226 7614; www.oloroso.co.uk; 33 Castle
St; mains £16-25; ⊙lunch & dinner) One of
Edinburgh's most stylish restaurants,
perched on a glass-encased rooftop with
views across to the Firth of Forth, Oloroso
serves top-notch Scottish produce with
Asian and Mediterranean touches.

Left: Palace of Holyroodhouse in Holyrood Park (p136);
Below: Beer pumps at Bow Bar
PHOTOGRAPHER: (LEFT) WILL SALTER/LONELY PLANET IMAGES ©;
(BELOW) KARL BLACKWELL/LONELY PLANET IMAGES ©

Drinking

BOW BAR Pub
(80 West Bow) One of the city's best
traditional-style pubs, serving a range of
excellent real ales and a vast selection of
malt whiskies in the evenings.

JOLLY JUDGE Pub
(www.jollyjudge.co.uk; 7a James Ct;) A snug
little pub tucked away down a close,
exuding a cosy 17th-century atmosphere.

OXFORD BAR Pub
(www.oxfordbar.com; 8 Young St) The Oxford is
that rarest of things these days: a real pub
for real people, with no 'theme', no music,
no frills and no pretensions. 'The Ox' has
been immortalised by Ian Rankin, author
of the Inspector Rebus novels, who is a
regular here, as is his fictional detective.

AMICUS APPLE Cocktail Bar
(www.amicusapple.com; 15 Frederick St) This
laid-back cocktail lounge is the hippest
hang-out in the New Town.

Information

Edinburgh & Scotland Information Centre
(ESIC; 0845 225 5121; www.edinburgh.org;
Princes Mall, 3 Princes St; 9am-9pm Mon-Sat,
10am-8pm Sun Jul & Aug, 9am-7pm Mon-Sat,
10am-7pm Sun May, Jun & Sep, 9am-5pm Mon-
Wed, to 6pm Thu-Sun Oct-Apr)

Getting There & Away

Air

Edinburgh Airport (0131-333 1000; www
.edinburghairport.com), 8 miles west of the city,
has numerous flights to other parts of Scotland
and the UK, Ireland and mainland Europe.

Bus

Scottish Citylink (0871 266 3333; www
.citylink.co.uk) coaches connect Edinburgh with
Scotland's cities and major towns.

Rosslyn Chapel

Deciphering Rosslyn

Rosslyn Chapel is a small building, but the density of decoration inside can be overwhelming. It's well worth buying the official guidebook by the Earl of Rosslyn first; find a bench in the gardens and have a skim through before going into the chapel – the background information will make your visit all the more interesting. The book also offers a useful self-guided tour of the chapel, and explains the legend of the Master Mason and the Apprentice.

Entrance is through the **north door ❶**. Take a pew and sit for a while to allow your eyes to adjust to the dim interior; then look up at the ceiling vault, decorated with engraved roses, lilies and stars (can you spot the sun and the moon?). Walk left along the north aisle to reach the Lady Chapel, separated from the rest of the church by the **Mason's Pillar ❷** and the **Apprentice Pillar ❸**. Here you'll find carvings of **Lucifer ❹**, the Fallen Angel, and the **Green Man ❺**. Nearby are **carvings ❻** that appear to resemble Indian corn (maize). Finally, go to the western end and look up at the wall – in the left corner is the head of the **Apprentice ❼**; to the right is the (rather worn) head of the **Master Mason ❽**.

ROSSLYN CHAPEL & THE DA VINCI CODE

Dan Brown was referencing Rosslyn Chapel's alleged links to the Knights Templar and the Freemasons – unusual symbols found among the carvings, and the fact that a descendant of its founder, William St Clair, was a Grand Master Mason – when he chose it as the setting for his novel's denouement. Rosslyn is indeed a coded work, written in stone, but its meaning depends on your point of view. See *The Rosslyn Hoax?* by Robert LD Cooper (www.rosslynhoax.com) for an alternative interpretation of the chapel's symbolism.

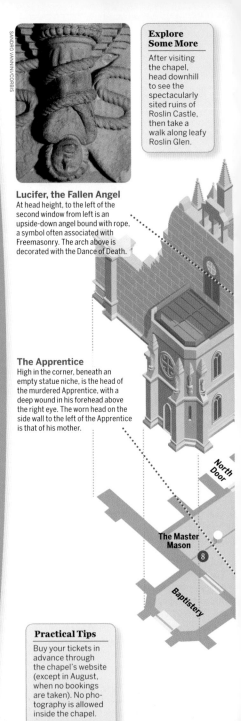

SANDRO VANNINI/CORBIS

Explore Some More

After visiting the chapel, head downhill to see the spectacularly sited ruins of Roslin Castle, then take a walk along leafy Roslin Glen.

Lucifer, the Fallen Angel
At head height, to the left of the second window from left is an upside-down angel bound with rope, a symbol often associated with Freemasonry. The arch above is decorated with the Dance of Death.

The Apprentice
High in the corner, beneath an empty statue niche, is the head of the murdered Apprentice, with a deep wound in his forehead above the right eye. The worn head on the side wall to the left of the Apprentice is that of his mother.

North Door

The Master Mason ❽

Baptistery

Practical Tips

Buy your tickets in advance through the chapel's website (except in August, when no bookings are taken). No photography is allowed inside the chapel.

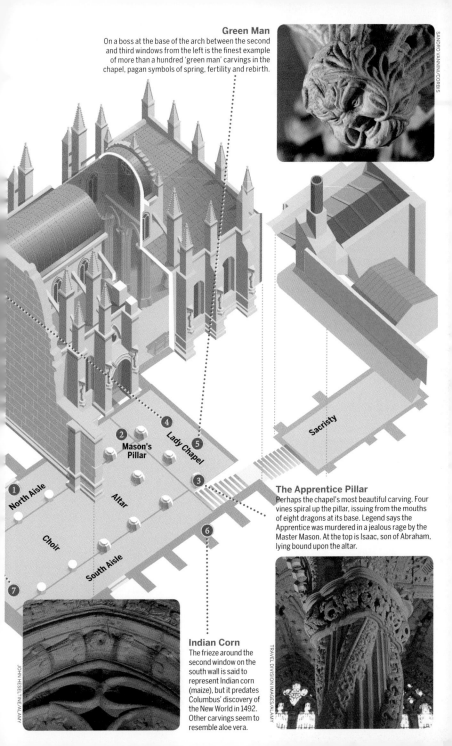

Green Man
On a boss at the base of the arch between the second and third windows from the left is the finest example of more than a hundred 'green man' carvings in the chapel, pagan symbols of spring, fertility and rebirth.

SANDRO VANNINI/CORBIS

1 North Aisle

2 Mason's Pillar

4

5 Lady Chapel

3

Altar

Choir

South Aisle

6

7

Sacristy

The Apprentice Pillar
Perhaps the chapel's most beautiful carving. Four vines spiral up the pillar, issuing from the mouths of eight dragons at its base. Legend says the Apprentice was murdered in a jealous rage by the Master Mason. At the top is Isaac, son of Abraham, lying bound upon the altar.

Indian Corn
The frieze around the second window on the south wall is said to represent Indian corn (maize), but it predates Columbus' discovery of the New World in 1492. Other carvings seem to resemble aloe vera.

JOHN HESELTINE/ALAMY

TRAVEL DIVISION IMAGES/ALAMY

Train

The main terminus in Edinburgh is Waverley train station, located in the heart of the city.

First ScotRail operates a regular shuttle service between Edinburgh and Glasgow (£11, 50 minutes, every 15 minutes), and frequent daily services to all Scottish cities including Aberdeen (£40, 2½ hours), Dundee (£20, 1¼ hours) and Inverness (£55, 3¼ hours).

CENTRAL SCOTLAND

Central Scotland is less a geographical region and more a catch-all term for everything between the Glasgow–Edinburgh conurbation and the mountains of the northwestern Highlands. Anything you ever dreamed about Scotland you can find here: lochs, hills, castles, whisky distilleries and some truly beautiful islands.

Loch Lomond

The 'bonnie banks' and 'bonnie braes' of Loch Lomond have long been Glasgow's rural retreat, and today the loch's popularity shows no sign of decreasing. The main tourist focus is on the loch's western shore, along the A82. The south-

Three Sisters, Glen Coe

ern end, around Balloch, is occasionally a nightmare of jet skis and motorboats. The eastern shore, followed by the West Highland Way long-distance footpath, is a little quieter. The region's importance was recognised when it became the heart of **Loch Lomond & the Trossachs National Park** (www.lochlomond-trossachs.org) – Scotland's first national park, created in 2002.

Getting There & Away

There are frequent trains from Glasgow to Balloch (£4.15, 45 minutes, every 30 minutes).

Stirling

POP 32,673

With an utterly impregnable position atop a mighty crag, Stirling's beautifully preserved old town is a treasure of noble buildings and cobbled streets winding up to the ramparts of its dominant castle.

◉ Sights

STIRLING CASTLE   Castle
(HS; www.historic-scotland.gov.uk; ⊘9.30am-6pm Apr-Sep, to 5pm Oct-Mar) Hold Stirling

FEARGUS COONEY/LONELY PLANET IMAGES ©

Climbing Ben Nevis

Looming over Fort William is Ben Nevis (1344m). As the highest peak in the British Isles, it attracts thousands of people who would not normally go anywhere near the summit of a Scottish mountain. Even if you're climbing 'the Ben' on a fine summer's day, an ascent should not be undertaken lightly. You will need proper walking boots (the path is rough and stony, and there may be wet snowfields on the summit), warm clothing, waterproofs, a map and compass, and plenty of food and water. And don't forget to check the weather forecast (see www.bennevisweather.co.uk).

and you control Scotland. This maxim has ensured that a fortress of some kind has existed here since prehistoric times. You cannot help drawing parallels with Edinburgh Castle, and it commands similarly superb views, but many find Stirling's fortress more atmospheric. The location, architecture and historical significance combine to make it a grand and memorable visit.

NATIONAL WALLACE MONUMENT
Monument
(www.nationalwallacemonument.com; adult/child £7.50/4.50; ⏰10am-5pm Apr-Jun, Sep & Oct, to 6pm Jul & Aug, 10.30am-4pm Nov-Mar) This nationalist memorial, commemorating the bid for Scottish independence, is so Victorian Gothic it deserves circling bats and ravens.

ℹ️ Information

Tourist office (📞01786-475019; stirling@ visitscotland.com; 41 Dumbarton Rd; ⏰10am-5pm Mon-Sat, plus Sun Jun–mid-Sep; @)

ℹ️ Getting There & Away

ScotRail services:

Aberdeen £38.60, 2¼ hours, regular services

Dundee £15.80, one hour, regular services

Edinburgh £6.90, 55 minutes, twice hourly Monday to Saturday, hourly Sunday

Glasgow £7.10, 40 minutes, twice hourly Monday to Saturday, hourly Sunday

Perth £10.40, 35 minutes, regular services

NORTHERN & WESTERN SCOTLAND

This area is a long way north, and takes effort to reach, but it is by far the best bit of Scotland, and one of the best bits of the whole of Britain too. See www .visithighlands.com for transport and accommodation advice.

Glen Coe

Scotland's most famous glen is also one of the grandest and, in bad weather, the grimmest. The southern side is dominated by three massive, brooding spurs, known as the **Three Sisters**, while the northern side is enclosed by the continuous steep wall of the knife-edged Aonach Eagach ridge. The main road threads its lonely way through the middle of all this mountain grandeur.

Glencoe was written into the history books in 1692 when the resident MacDonalds were murdered by Campbell soldiers in what became known as the Glencoe Massacre.

ℹ️ Getting There & Away

Scottish Citylink buses run to Glencoe from Fort William (£7, 30 minutes, eight daily) and Glasgow (£19, 2½ hours, eight daily).

Fort William
POP 9910

Basking on the shores of Loch Linnhe amid magnificent mountain scenery, Fort William has one of the most enviable

Stirling Castle

Planning Your Attack

Stirling's a sizeable fortress, but not so huge that you'll have to decide what to leave out – there's time to see it all. Unless you've got a working knowledge of Scottish monarchs, head to the **Castle Exhibition ❶** first: it'll help you sort one James from another. That done, take on the sights at leisure. First, stop and look around you from the **ramparts ❷**; the views high over this flat valley, a key strategic point in Scotland's history, are magnificent.

Next, head through to the back of the castle to the **Tapestry Studio ❸**, which is open for shorter hours; seeing these skilful weavers at work is a highlight. Track back towards the citadel's heart, stopping for a quick tour through the **Great Kitchens ❹**; looking at all that fake food might make you seriously hungry, though. Then enter the main courtyard. Around you are the principal castle buildings. During summer there are events (such as Renaissance dancing) in the **Great Hall ❺** – get details at the entrance. The Museum of the Argyll & Sutherland Highlanders **❻** is a treasure trove if you're interested in regimental history, but missable if you're not. Leave the best for last – crowds thin in the afternoon – and enter the sumptuous Royal **Palace ❼**.

The Way Up & Down

If you have time, take the atmospheric Back Walk, a peaceful, shady stroll around the Old Town's fortifications and up to the castle's imposing crag-top position. Afterwards, wander down through the Old Town to admire its facades.

Museum of the Argyll & Sutherland Highlanders
The history of one of Scotland's legendary regiments – now subsumed into the Royal Regiment of Scotland – is on display here, featuring memorabilia, weapons and uniforms.

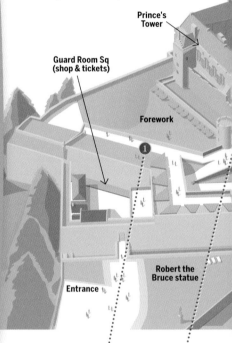

Prince's Tower

Guard Room Sq (shop & tickets)

Forework

Robert the Bruce statue

Entrance

Castle Exhibition
A great overview of the Stewart dynasty here will get your facts straight, and also offers the latest archaeological titbits from the ongoing excavations under the citadel. Analysis of skeletons has revealed surprising amounts of biographical data.

Royal Palace
The impressive new highlight of a visit to the castle is this recreation of the royal lodgings originally built by James V. The finely worked ceiling, ornate furniture and sumptuous unicorn tapestries dazzle.

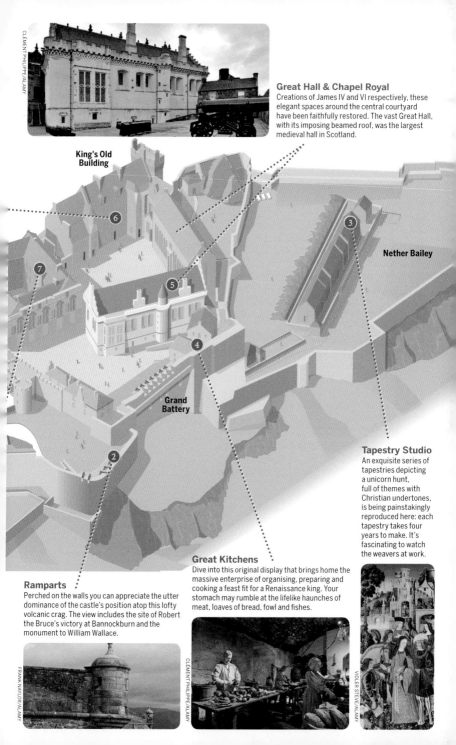

Great Hall & Chapel Royal
Creations of James IV and VI respectively, these elegant spaces around the central courtyard have been faithfully restored. The vast Great Hall, with its imposing beamed roof, was the largest medieval hall in Scotland.

King's Old Building

Nether Bailey

Grand Battery

Tapestry Studio
An exquisite series of tapestries depicting a unicorn hunt, full of themes with Christian undertones, is being painstakingly reproduced here: each tapestry takes four years to make. It's fascinating to watch the weavers at work.

Great Kitchens
Dive into this original display that brings home the massive enterprise of organising, preparing and cooking a feast fit for a Renaissance king. Your stomach may rumble at the lifelike haunches of meat, loaves of bread, fowl and fishes.

Ramparts
Perched on the walls you can appreciate the utter dominance of the castle's position atop this lofty volcanic crag. The view includes the site of Robert the Bruce's victory at Bannockburn and the monument to William Wallace.

settings in the whole of Scotland. 'Fort Bill' has carved out a reputation as 'Outdoor Capital of the UK' (www.outdoorcapital. co.uk), and its easy access by rail and bus makes it a good launch-pad for Highland exploration.

Information

Tourist office (☏01397-703781; www.visit highlands.com; 15 High St; ⏰9am-6pm Mon-Sat, 10am-5pm Sun Apr-Sep, limited hr Oct-Mar)

Getting There & Away

The spectacular West Highland line runs from Glasgow to Mallaig via Fort William. There are three trains daily (two on Sunday) from Glasgow to Fort William (£24, 3¾ hours), and four daily (three on Sunday) between Fort William and Mallaig (£10, 1½ hours). Travelling from Edinburgh (£40, five hours), you have to change at Glasgow's Queen St station.

Isle of Skye

POP 9900

The Isle of Skye is the biggest of Scotland's islands, a 50-mile-long smorgasbord of velvet moors, jagged mountains, sparkling lochs and towering sea cliffs. It takes its name from the old Norse *sky-a*, meaning 'cloud island', a Viking reference to the often mist-enshrouded Cuillin Hills. The stunning scenery is the main attraction, but there are plenty of cosy pubs to retire to when the mist closes in.

The Isle of Skye became permanently tethered to the Scottish mainland when the Skye Bridge opened in 1995. Despite the bridge, there are still a couple of ferry links between Skye and the mainland.

CalMac (www.calmac.co.uk) operates the Mallaig to Armadale ferry (driver or passenger £3.85, car £20.30, 30 minutes, eight daily Monday to Saturday, five to seven on Sunday).

Skye Ferry (www.skyeferry.co.uk) runs a tiny vessel (six cars only) on the short Glenelg to Kylerhea crossing (car and up to four passengers £12, five minutes, every 20 minutes). The ferry operates from 10am to 6pm daily from Easter to October only, till 7pm June to August.

John O'Groats

POP 500

Mainland Britain's northeasterly extreme, John O'Groats is no more than a car park surrounded by tourist shops, and offers little to the visitor beyond a means to get across to Orkney. Even the famous pub has been shut for a while now (although there are a couple of cafes). John O'Groats is best known as the endpoint of the 874-mile trek from Land's End in Cornwall, a popular if arduous challenge for cyclists and walkers, many of whom raise money for charitable causes.

IRELAND

Few countries have an image so plagued by cliché. From shamrocks and shillelaghs to leprechauns and lovable rogues, there's a plethora of platitudes to wade through before you scramble ashore on the real Ireland.

But it's well worth looking beyond the tourist tat, for the Emerald Isle is one of Europe's gems, a scenic extravaganza of lake, mountain, sea and sky.

Dublin

☏01 / POP 1.1 MILLION

Sitting in a tapas bar on Great George's St, nursing a Guinness or a hangover (or both), you think about what your favourite experience has been in Dublin so far. Was it admiring the Georgian houses along St Stephen's Green or was it wandering the grounds of Trinity College? You never come to an answer, but you do realise that, just as the waters on the banks of the Liffey River seem to rise every day, so does your affection for this city.

Sights

TRINITY COLLEGE & BOOK OF KELLS

Museum

(www.bookofkells.ie; College Green; admission to college grounds free, Old Library adult/child €9/free; ⏰9.30am-5pm Mon-Sat year-round, 9.30am-4.30pm Sun May-Sep, noon-4.30pm Sun Oct-Apr) Ireland's premier university was founded by Elizabeth I in 1592. Its full name is the University of Dublin, but **Trinity College** is the institution's sole college.

Student-guided **walking tours (per person €10)** take place twice an hour from 10.45am to 3.40pm Monday to Saturday and 10.45am to 3.15pm Sunday from mid-May to September, departing from inside the main gate on College St. The tour is a good deal since it includes admission to the **Old Library** to see the **Book of Kells**, an elaborately illuminated gospel created by monks on the Scottish isle of Iona around AD 800, and the spectacular **Long Room**, an early 18th-century library lined with marble busts of writers and philosophers.

Dublin's finest Georgian architecture, including its famed doorways, is found around **St Stephen's Green** and **Merrion Square** just south of Trinity College; both are prime picnic spots when the sun shines.

FREE **NATIONAL MUSEUM OF ARCHAEOLOGY**   Museum
(www.museum.ie; Kildare St; ◷10am-5pm Tue-Sat, 2-5pm Sun) Among the highlights of the National Museum's archaeology and history branch are its superb collection of **prehistoric gold objects**; the exquisite 12th-century **Ardagh Chalice**, the world's finest example of Celtic art; and ancient objects recovered from **Ireland's bogs**, including remarkably well-preserved human bodies.

O'CONNELL ST
            Historic Area
Dublin's grandest avenue is dominated by the needle-like **Monument of Light** (O'Connell St), better known as 'the Spire', which rises from the spot once occupied by a statue of Admiral Nelson (which disappeared in explosive fashion,

thanks to the IRA, in 1966). Soaring 120m into the sky, it is, apparently, the world's tallest sculpture.

KILMAINHAM GAOL   Museum
(www.heritageireland.com; Inchicore Rd; adult/child €6/2; ◷9.30am-6pm Apr-Sep, 9.30am-5.30pm Mon-Sat, 10am-6pm Sun Oct-Mar) The grey, threatening Kilmainham Gaol, 2km west of the city centre, played a key role in Ireland's struggle for independence and was the site of mass executions following the 1916 Easter Rising. An excellent audiovisual introduction to the building is followed by a thought-provoking one-hour tour. Buses 79, 78A and 51B from Aston Quay all pass by here.

FREE **NATIONAL GALLERY**   Art Gallery
(www.nationalgallery.ie; West Merrion Sq; ◷9.30am-5.30pm Mon-Wed, Fri & Sat, 9.30am-8.30pm Thu, noon-5.30pm Sun) A magnificent Caravaggio and a breathtaking collection of works by Jack B Yeats – William Butler's younger brother – are the main reasons to visit here. The Millennium wing has a small collection of contemporary

Long Room at Trinity College
PHOTOGRAPHER: HANNAH LEVY/LONELY PLANET IMAGES ©

Dublin

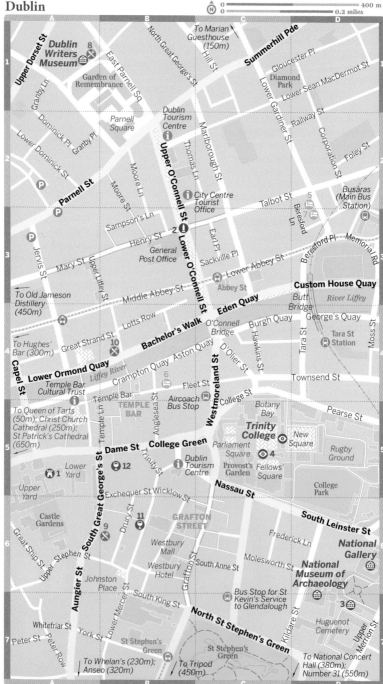

Upper Dorset St

Dublin Writers Museum · 8

Garden of Remembrance

Granby Ln

Dominick Pl · Granby Pl

Lower Dominick St

East Parnell Sq

North Great George's St

Hill St

To Marian Guesthouse (150m)

Summerhill Pde

Gloucester Pl

Diamond Park

Lower Sean MacDermot St

Lower Gardiner St

Railway St

Corporation St

Foley St

Parnell Square

Parnell St

Moore Ln

Moore St

Sampson's Ln

Henry St

Dublin Tourism Centre

Upper O'Connell St

Marlborough St

Thomas Ln

City Centre Tourist Office

Earl Pl

Sackville Pl

Talbot St · 5

Beresford

Busáras (Main Bus Station)

Beresford Pl

Memorial Rd

General Post Office · 2

Lower O'Connell St

Lower Abbey St

Mary St · Upper Liffey St · Jervis St

Middle Abbey St

Abbey St

To Old Jameson Distillery (450m)

Custom House Quay

Butt Bridge

River Liffey

Eden Quay

George's Quay

Great Strand St · 10

Lower Ormond Quay

Bachelor's Walk

Lotts Row

O'Connell Bridge

Burgh Quay

Tara St Station

Moss St

Capel St

Temple Bar Cultural Trust

Liffey River

Crampton Quay · Aston Quay

Fleet St

6

Temple Bar

Temple Ln

TEMPLE BAR

Anglesea St

Aircoach Bus Stop

Westmoreland St

D'Olier St

Hawkins St

Tara St

Townsend St

Pearse St

To Queen of Tarts (50m); Christ Church Cathedral (250m); St Patrick's Cathedral (650m)

Dame St · College Green

Trinity St

College St

Botany Bay

Trinity College · 4

New Square

Rugby Ground

South Great George's St

1 · Lower Yard

Upper Yard

Dublin Tourism Centre

Parliament Square

Provost's Garden

Fellows' Square

College Park

12

Castle Gardens

Great Ship St

Upper Stephen St

Exchequer St

Wicklow St

Nassau St

South Leinster St

Aungier St

9 · Drury St · 11

GRAFTON STREET

Westbury Mall

Westbury Hotel

South Anne St

Grafton St

Frederick Ln

Molesworth St

National Gallery

National Museum of Archaeology

Johnston Place

Lower Mercer St

South King St

Bus Stop for St Kevin's Service to Glendalough

Kildare St

3

Huguenot Cemetery

Upper Merrion St

Whitefriar St · York St · Peter Row

Peter St

North St Stephen's Green

St Stephen's Green

St Stephen's Green

To Whelan's (230m); Anseo (320m)

To Tripod (450m)

To National Concert Hall (380m); Number 31 (550m)

0 ——— 400 m
0 ——— 0.2 miles

DUBLIN SIGHTS

Dublin

Irish works. Free **guided tours** are held at 3pm on Saturday, and 2pm, 3pm and 4pm on Sunday.

CHRIST CHURCH CATHEDRAL Church
(www.cccdub.ie; Christ Church Pl; adult/concession €6/4; ⏱9am-6pm Jun-Aug, 9.45am-5pm Sep-May) Christ Church, the mother of all of Dublin's cathedrals, was a simple wood structure until 1169 when the present church was built. In the southern aisle is a monument to Strongbow, a 12th-century Norman warrior. Note the precariously leaning northern wall (it's been that way since 1562).

ST PATRICK'S CATHEDRAL Church
(www.stpatrickscathedral.ie; St Patrick's Close; adult/family €5.50/15; ⏱9am-6pm Mon-Sat, 9-11am, 12.45-3pm & 4.15-6pm Sun Mar-Oct, 9am-5pm Sat, 10-11am & 12.45-3pm Sun Nov-Feb, closed during times of worship) There was a church on the site of St Patrick's Cathedral as early as the 5th century, but the present building dates from 1191. St Patrick's choir was part of the first group to perform Handel's *Messiah* in 1742, and you can hear their successors sing the 5.45pm evensong most weeknights.

Just around the corner is the antique **Marsh's Library** (www.marshlibrary.ie; St Patrick's Close; adult/child €2.50/free; ⏱10am-1pm & 2-5pm Mon & Wed-Fri, 10.30am-1pm Sat), which is the oldest public library in the country, with an atmosphere that has hardly changed since it opened its doors in 1707.

FREE **Natural History Museum** Museum
(www.museum.ie; Merrion St; ⏱10am-5pm Tue-Sat, 2-5pm Sun) Excellent and atmospheric Victorian museum scarcely changed since 1857, when Scottish explorer Dr David Livingstone delivered the opening lecture.

Dublin Writers Museum Museum
(www.writersmuseum.com; 18-19 Parnell Sq; adult/child €7.50/4.70; ⏱10am-5pm Mon-Sat, 11am-5pm Sun year-round, to 6pm Mon-Fri Jun-Aug) The Dublin Writers Museum celebrates the city's role as a literary centre, with displays on Joyce, Swift, Yeats, Wilde, Beckett and others.

Dublin Castle Castle
(www.dublincastle.ie; adult/concession €4.50/2; ⏱10am-4.45pm Mon-Fri, 2-4.45pm Sat & Sun) The centre of British power in Ireland, dating back to the 13th century; more higgledy-piggledy palace than castle.

FREE **Irish Museum of Modern Art**
Art Gallery
(www.imma.ie; Military Rd; ⏱10am-5.30pm Tue & Thu-Sat, 10.30am-5.30pm Wed, noon-5.30pm Sun) The Irish Museum of Modern Art is renowned for its conceptual installations and temporary exhibitions. Bus 51 or 79 from Aston Quay will get you there.

Old Jameson Distillery
Whiskey Distillery
(www.jamesonwhiskey.com; Bow St; adult/child €13.50/8) Guided tours (9.30am to 6pm) covering the entire whiskey-distilling process; tastings follow.

Tours

Bus

Hop-on, hop-off city tours costing €16 (tickets valid for 24 hours) are a good way of visiting several major sights in one day.

City Sightseeing (www.city-sightseeing.com)

Dublin Bus (www.dublinbus.ie)

Walking

Each lasts two to three hours and costs around €12.

Dublin Literary Pub Crawl Literature
(670 5602; www.dublinpubcrawl.com;
⏱7.30pm daily Apr-Oct, Thu-Sun Nov-Mar) Led by actors performing pieces from Irish literature.

1916 Rebellion Walking Tour History
(086 858 3847; www.1916rising.com;
⏱11.30am Mon-Sat, 1pm Sun Mar-Oct) Visits key sites of the rebellion.

Musical Pub Crawl Music
(475 3313; www.discoverdublin.ie; ⏱7.30pm daily Apr-Oct, Thu-Sat Nov-Mar) Irish traditional music explained and demonstrated by two expert musicians in various Temple Bar pubs.

Historical Walking Tours of Dublin History
(087 688 9412; www.historicalinsights.ie;
⏱daily Apr-Oct, Fri-Sun Nov-Mar) 'Seminars on the street' conducted by history graduates of Trinity College Dublin.

Sleeping

Dublin is *always* bustling, so call ahead to book accommodation, especially at weekends. Don't forget that Dublin Tourism Centres can find and book accommodation for €5, plus a 10% deposit for the first night's stay.

North of the Liffey

TOWNHOUSE B&B €€
(878 8808; www.townhouseofdublin.com; 47-48 Lower Gardiner St; per person from €40) Elegant but unpretentious, the Georgian Townhouse has beautiful, individually designed bedrooms named after plays by the famous 19th-century writers who once lived here (Dion Boucicault and Lafcadio Hearn), and a Japanese garden out back.

Anchor Guesthouse B&B €€
(878 6913; www.anchorguesthouse. com; 49 Lower Gardiner St; s/d from €55/75; P) This lovely Georgian guest house, with its delicious wholesome breakfasts and an elegance you won't find in many of the other B&Bs along this stretch, comes highly recommended.

South of the Liffey

NUMBER 31
Boutique Hotel €€€
(676 5011; www .number31.ie; 31 Leeson Close; s/d/tr from €115/150/225; P) The

Dublin Castle (p151)
PHOTOGRAPHER: OLIVIER CIRENDINI/LONELY PLANET IMAGES ©

OLIVIER CIRENDINI/LONELY PLANET IMAGES ©

former dwelling of modernist architect Sam Stephenson (1933–2006) still feels like a 1960s designer pad with sunken sitting room, leather sofas, mirrored bar and floor-to-ceiling windows. Children under 10 are not allowed here.

MORGAN HOTEL Boutique Hotel €€€
(☎643 7000; www.themorgan.com; 10 Fleet St; r from €110; @ 🛜) Falling somewhere between *Alice in Wonderland* and a cocaine-and-hooker-fuelled rock-and-roll fantasy, the ubercool Morgan sports a sexy colour scheme of white floors and walls with dark-blue and pink lighting that extends into the bar, the rooms and even the cigar patio.

 Eating

North of the Liffey

WINDING STAIR Irish €€
(☎872 7320; www.winding-stair.com; 40 Ormond Quay; mains €22-27; ⏱noon-3.30pm & 5.30-10.30pm daily) This rustic dining room squeezed above a bookshop serves superb Irish grub, from smoked salmon and wheaten bread, to lamb chops with white bean and red onion stew, to sticky pear and ginger steam pud. Hugely popular, so book ahead.

CHAPTER ONE French €€€
(☎873 2266; www.chapteronerestaurant.com; 18-19 North Parnell Sq; mains €32-36; ⏱12.30-2.30pm Tue-Fri, 6-11pm Tue-Sat) Savour fresh Irish produce cooked in classic French style – such as rabbit loin wrapped in pancetta with carrot and black cumin purée, or turbot with fennel and citrus fruit sauce – to the tinkle of a grand piano in the vaulted basement of the Dublin Writers Museum.

South of the Liffey

L'GUEULETON French €€
(www.lgueuleton.com; 1 Fade St; mains €19-27; ⏱12.30-3pm & 6-10pm Mon-Sat, 1-3pm & 6-9pm Sun) Dubliners just can't get enough of this restaurant's take on French rustic cuisine, which ranges from regulars such as slow-roast pork belly with dauphinoise potatoes, to specials such as warm crayfish salad with paprika and flaked almonds. No reservations – queue for a table, or leave your mobile number and they'll text when a table's ready.

Queen of Tarts
Cafe €

(www.queenoftarts.ie; 3-4 Cow's Lane; mains €5-12; ⏰8am-7pm Mon-Fri, 9am-7pm Sat, 10am-7pm Sun) Pocket-sized Queen of Tarts offers a mouth-watering array of savoury tarts and filled focaccias, fruit crumbles, healthy breakfasts and weekend brunch specials. Perfect for breakfast or lunch.

 # Drinking

Temple Bar, Dublin's 'party district', is almost always packed with raucous stag and hen parties, scantily clad girls, and loud guys from Ohio wearing Guinness T-shirts. If that's not your style, there's plenty to enjoy beyond Temple Bar. In fact, most of the best old-fashioned pubs are outside the district.

STAG'S HEAD
Pub

(1 Dame Ct) Built in 1770, and remodelled in 1895, the Stag's Head is possibly the best traditional pub in Dublin (and therefore the world). You may find yourself philosophising in the ecclesiastical atmosphere, as James Joyce once did.

GROGAN'S CASTLE LOUNGE
Pub

(www.groganspub.ie; 15 South William St) A city-centre institution, Grogan's has long been a favourite haunt of Dublin's writers and painters, as well as others from the bohemian, alternative set.

HUGHES' BAR
Bar

(19 Chancery St) Directly behind Four Courts, this bar has nightly, if impromptu, traditional-music sessions that often result in a closed door – that is, they go on long past official closing time.

 # Entertainment

For events, reviews and club listings, pick up a copy of the bimonthly freebie *Event Guide* (www.eventguide.ie) or the weekly *In Dublin* (www.indublin.ie) available at cafes and hostels. Thursday's *Irish Times* has a pull-out section called 'The Ticket' that has reviews and listings of all things arty.

ℹ️ Information

Tourist Information

All Dublin tourist offices provide walk-in services only – no phone inquiries.

City Centre Tourist Office (14 O'Connell St; ⏰9am-5pm Mon-Sat)

Dublin Tourism Centre (www.visitdublin.com; St Andrew's Church, 2 Suffolk St; ⏰9am-5.30pm Mon-Sat, 10.30am-3pm Sun year-round, to 7pm Mon-Sat Jul & Aug) Tourist information for all of Ireland, accommodation bookings, car hire, maps, and tickets for tours, concerts and more. Ask about the Dublin Pass (www.dublinpass.ie), which allows entrance into more than 30 of Dublin's attractions, as well as tours and special offers.

Northern Ireland Tourist Board (NITB; ☎605 7732; www.discovernorthernireland.com) Has a desk in the Dublin Tourism Centre, with the same hours.

ℹ️ Getting There & Away

Air

Dublin airport (DUB; www.dublinairport.com) About 13km north of the city centre is Ireland's major international gateway, with direct flights from Europe, North America and Asia.

Boat

There are direct ferries that run from Holyhead in Wales to **Dublin Port**, 3km northeast of the city centre, and to **Dun Laoghaire**, 13km southeast. Boats also sail direct to Dublin Port from Liverpool.

Bus

Busáras (www.buseireann.ie; Store St), Dublin's main bus station is just north of the Liffey.

Belfast €15, 2½ hours, hourly

Cork €13, 4½ hours, six daily

Galway €14, 3¾ hours, hourly

The private company **Citylink** (www.citylink.ie) has nonstop services from Dublin airport (picking up at Bachelors Walk, near O'Connell Bridge, in the city centre) to Galway (€15, three hours, 14 daily).

Train

Iarnród Éireann Travel Centre (☎ 836 6222, bookings 703 4070; www.irishrail.ie; 35 Lower Abbey St) Can give a hand with travel information and tickets.

Regular one-way fares from Dublin:

Belfast from €18, 2¼ hours, up to eight daily

Cork €20, 2¾ hours, hourly

Galway €35, three hours, five daily

ⓘ Getting Around

To/From the Airport

Aircoach (www.aircoach.ie; one-way/return €7/12) Serves various destinations in the city; departs every 10 to 20 minutes from 5am to midnight, hourly through the night.

Airlink Express Coach (www.dublinbus.ie; one-way/return €6/10) Bus 747 runs every 10 to 20 minutes from 6am to midnight to Upper O'Connell St (35 minutes) and the central bus station (Busáras; 45 minutes). Bus 748 runs every 15 to 30 minutes from 6.50am to 10pm to Busáras (30 minutes) and Heuston train station (45 minutes).

Taxi A taxi to the city centre should cost around €20 to €25. Some Dublin airport taxi drivers can be unscrupulous, so make sure the meter is on and mention up front that you'll need a meter receipt.

Car

Traffic in Dublin is a nightmare and parking is an expensive headache. Better to leave your vehicle at the Red Cow Park & Ride just off Exit 9 on the M50 ring road, and take the Luas tram into the city centre (€4 return, 30 minutes).

Public Transport

Various public transport passes are available; one day's unlimited bus travel costs €6 (including Airlink);

bus and tram costs €7.50; and bus and DART costs €11.

BUS Dublin Bus (www.dublinbus.ie) Local buses cost from €1.15 to €2.20 for a single journey. You must pay the exact fare when boarding; drivers don't give change. The Rambler 1 Day (€6) ticket allows one day's unlimited travel on buses including Airlink.

TRAM Luas (www.luas.ie) Runs on two (unconnected) lines; the green line runs from the eastern side of St Stephen's Green southeast to Sandyford, and the red line runs from Tallaght to Connolly station, with stops along the way at Heuston station, the National Museum and Busáras. Single fares will range from €1.50 to €2.80, depending on how many zones you travel through.

TAXI For taxi service, call National Radio Cabs (☎ 677 2222).

AROUND DUBLIN

Dun Laoghaire

☎ 01

Dun Laoghaire (pronounced dun-leary), 13km south of central Dublin, is a seaside resort and busy harbour with ferry connections to Britain.

Dun Laoghaire Harbour
PHOTOGRAPHER: RICHARD CUMMINS/LONELY PLANET IMAGES ©

At Sandycove, south of the harbour, is the Martello Tower where James Joyce's epic novel *Ulysses* opens. It now houses the **James Joyce Museum** (The Fortyfoot, Sandycove; adult/child €7.25/4.55; ⏲10am-1pm & 2-5pm Mon-Sat, 2-6pm Sun Apr-Aug, by arrangement only Sep-Mar). If you fancy a cold saltwater dip, the nearby **Forty Foot Pool** (also mentioned in *Ulysses*) is the place.

Take the DART rail service (€3.80 return, 25 minutes, every 10 to 20 minutes) from Dublin to Dun Laoghaire, then bus 59 to Sandycove Rd, or walk (1km).

Malahide Castle

☎01

Despite the vicissitudes of Irish history, the Talbot family managed to keep **Malahide Castle** (www.malahidecastle.com; adult/child €7.50/4.70; ⏲10am-5pm Mon-Sat year-round, 10am-5pm Sun Apr-Sep, 11am-5pm Sun Oct-Mar) from 1185 through to 1973. The castle is packed with furniture and paintings, and Puck, the family ghost, is still in residence. The extensive **Fry Model Railway** (☎846 2184; adult/child €6/4; ⏲10am-1pm & 2-5pm Tue-Sat, 1-5pm Sun Apr-Sep, closed Oct-Mar) in the castle grounds covers 240 sq metres and re-creates Ireland's rail and public transport system (it's actually better than it sounds). Combined tickets (adult/child €11.50/7.50) give admission to the model railway and castle.

Malahide is 13km northeast of Dublin; take the DART rail service from Dublin Connolly to Malahide station (€4, return, 22 minutes, every 10 to 20 minutes).

Brú Na Bóinne

☎041

A thousand years older than Stonehenge, the extensive Neolithic necropolis known as Brú na Bóinne (Boyne Palace) is one of the most extraordinary prehistoric sites in Europe. Its tombs date from about 3200 BC, predating the great pyramids of Egypt by six centuries. The complex, including the Newgrange and Knowth passage tombs, can be visited only on a guided walk from the **Brú na Bóinne visitor cen-**

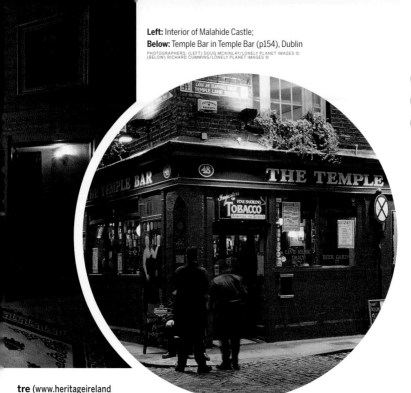

Left: Interior of Malahide Castle;
Below: Temple Bar in Temple Bar (p154), Dublin

tre (www.heritageireland .ie; Donore; adult/child visitor centre only €3/2, visitor centre & Newgrange €6/3, visitor centre & Knowth €5/3; ⊙9am-7pm Jun–mid-Sep, 9am-6.30pm May & late Sep, 9.30am-5.30pm Feb, Mar, Apr & Oct, 9.30am-5pm Nov-Jan).

The site is 50km north of Dublin, signposted off the M1. Take Bus Éireann's 100X or 101 service to Drogheda, then the 163 to Donore (total journey €15 return, 1½ to two hours, five daily), which stops at the gates of the visitor centre. Or use the **Newgrange Shuttlebus** (☎1-800 424 252; www.overthetoptours.com; return €17; ⊙daily).

Guided day tours from Dublin by **Mary Gibbons** (☎086 355 1355; www. newgrangetours.com; tour incl admission €35; ⊙daily) are excellent.

The Southwest

The southwest comes closest to the misty-eyed vision of Ireland many visitors hold in their imagination – blue lakes and green mountains, blustery beaches, bird-haunted sea cliffs, picturesque hamlets, and welcoming towns where live music sparks up every night.

Cork

☎021 / POP 120,000

There's a reason the locals call Cork (Corcaigh) 'the Real Capital' or 'the People's Republic of Cork'; something special is going on here. The city has long been dismissive of Dublin, and with a burgeoning arts, music and restaurant scene, it has a cultural reputation to rival the capital's.

⊙ Sights

CORK CITY GAOL   Museum
(www.corkcitygaol.com; Convent Ave; adult/child €7/3.50; ⊙9.30am-6pm Mar-Oct, 10am-5pm Nov-Feb) Closed down in 1923, this vast 19th-century prison is now a terrific museum about a terrifying subject. Restored cells, mannequins representing prisoners and guards, and a detailed audioguide bring home the horrors of Victorian prison life.

157

FREE CRAWFORD ART GALLERY
Art Gallery

(www.crawfordartgallery.ie; Emmet Pl; 10am-5pm Mon-Sat, to 8pm Thu) The 18th-century Cork Customs House is blended with 21st-century Dutch design in this intriguing gallery, a must-see for anyone who enjoys art and architecture. Pieces by Irish artists such as Jack Yeats and Cork's own James Barry sit among a fine permanent collection that includes artists from continental Europe.

ST FINBARRE'S CATHEDRAL
Church

(www.cathedral.cork.anglican.org; Bishop St; adult/child €4/2; 9.30am-5.30pm Mon-Sat, 12.30-5pm Sun Apr-Nov, 10am-12.45pm & 2-5pm Mon-Sat Dec-Mar) Just south of the city centre sits Cork's Protestant cathedral. Built in 1879, this beautiful Gothic Revival structure has a multitude of notable features, including a Golden Angel who sits on the eastern side of the cathedral, and whose job it is to blow her horn at the onset of the Apocalypse.

FREE CORK PUBLIC MUSEUM
Museum

(www.corkcity.ie; Fitzgerald Park; 11am-1pm & 2.15-5pm Mon-Fri, 11am-1pm & 2.15-4pm Sat year-round, 3-5pm Sun Apr-Sep) The city museum has a fine collection of artefacts that trace Cork's past from prehistory to the present, including the city's role in the fight for independence. Bus 8 goes to the University College Cork (UCC) main gates nearby.

Sleeping

GARNISH HOUSE
B&B €€

(427 5111; www.garnish.ie; Western Rd; s/d from €75/86; P) With charming rooms (think flowers and fresh fruit), gourmet breakfasts and hosts who are eager to please, Garnish House is possibly the perfect B&B.

VICTORIA HOTEL
Hotel €€

(427 8788; www.thevictoriahotel.com; St Patrick's St; r per person €49-99;) Boasting such esteemed former guests as Charles Stuart Parnell and James Joyce, the independently owned Victoria is one of Cork's oldest hotels, as well as one of its most centrally located.

Eating

FARMGATE CAFÉ
Cafe, Bistro €€

(www.farmgate.ie; English Market; mains €9-14; 8.30am-10pm Mon-Sat) An unmissable experience at the heart of the English Market, the Farmgate is perched on a balcony overlooking the market below, the source of all that fresh local produce on your plate.

IDAHO CAFÉ
Cafe €€

(19 Caroline St; dishes €7-12; 8.30am-5pm) It looks like a trad old caff from the outside, but take a gander at the menu and you'll find all sorts of creative takes on Irish standards.

NASH 19
Bistro €€

(www.nash19.com; Princes St; mains €8-20; 7.30am-5pm Mon-Fri) A sensational bistro with its own food market; local produce is honoured from breakfast to lunch and on to tea.

CAFÉ PARADISO
Vegetarian €€€

(427 7939; www.cafeparadiso.ie; 16 Lancaster Quay; mains lunch €14-15, dinner €23-25; 5.30-10pm Tue-Sat, noon-3pm Fri & Sat) Arguably the best vegetarian restaurant in Ireland, the inventive dishes on offer here will seduce even the most committed carnivore.

Drinking

Cork's pub scene is cracking, easily rivalling Dublin's. Locally brewed Murphy's is the stout of choice here, not Guinness. Check www.corkgigs.com for pubs with live music.

MUTTON LANE INN
Pub

(3 Mutton Lane) With Victorian wallpaper, rock-and-roll posters, and a covered outdoor area for drinking and smoking, Cork's oldest pub is the type of place that you'll wish you had in your home town.

SIN É
Pub

(Coburg St) There are no frills or fuss here – just a comfy, sociable pub long on atmosphere and short on pretension. There's music most nights, much of it traditional but with the odd surprise.

RICHARD CUMMINS/LONELY PLANET IMAGES ©

FRANCISCAN WELL BREWERY
Microbrewery
(www.franciscanwellbrewery.com; 14 North Mall)
The best place to enjoy the beer at this
microbrewery is in the enormous beer
garden at the back. The pub holds regular
beer festivals with other small (and often
underappreciated) Irish breweries –
check the website for details.

ℹ️ Information

Tourist office (☎ 425 5100; www.corkkerry.ie;
Grand Pde; ◷9am-6pm Mon-Sat, 10am-5pm Sun
Jul & Aug, 9.15am-5pm Mon-Fri, 9.30am-4.30pm
Sat Sep-Jun)

ℹ️ Getting There & Away

AIR Cork airport (www.corkairport.com) is
8km south of the city on the N27. Direct flights
to Belfast, Edinburgh, London, Manchester,
Amsterdam, Barcelona, Munich, Paris, Warsaw
and Rome.

BUS Aircoach (www.aircoach.ie) provides a direct
service to Dublin city and airport from St Patrick
Quay (€14, four hours, eight daily). Cork bus
station (cnr Merchants Quay & Parnell Pl) is east
of the city centre.

Dublin €13, 4½ hours, six daily

Kilkenny €19, three hours, three daily

Killarney €17, 1¾ hours, hourly

TRAIN Cork's Kent train station (Glanmire Rd
Lower) is across the river.

Dublin €20, 2¾ hours, hourly

Galway €45, five to six hours, seven daily (two
or three changes needed)

Killarney €26, 1½ to two hours, nine daily

Blarney
☎021 / POP 2150

Lying just northwest of Cork, the village
of Blarney (An Bhlarna) receives a *gazillion* visitors a year, for one sole reason:
Blarney Castle (www.blarneycastle.ie; adult/
child €10/3.50; ◷9am-6.30pm Mon-Sat, 9am-
5.30pm Sun May-Sep, to dusk daily Oct-Apr).
They come to kiss the castle's legendary
Blarney Stone and receive the 'gift of the
gab' (Queen Elizabeth I, exasperated with
Lord Blarney's ability to talk endlessly
without agreeing to her demands,
invented the term 'to talk Blarney' back
in the 16th century). The stone sits up on
the battlements, and kissing it requires a
head for heights.

Buses run regularly from Cork bus
station (€6.20 return, 30 minutes).

159

Ring of Kerry

📖 066

This 179km circuit of the Iveragh Peninsula pops up on every self-respecting tourist itinerary, and for good reason. The road winds past pristine beaches, the island-dotted Atlantic, medieval ruins, mountains and loughs (lakes). Even locals stop their cars to gawk at the rugged coastline – particularly between Waterville and Caherdaniel in the southwest of the peninsula, where the beauty dial is turned up to 11.

Tour buses travel the Ring in an anticlockwise direction. Getting stuck behind one is tedious, so driving in the opposite direction is preferred. Alternatively, you can detour from the main road – the **Ballaghbeama Pass** cuts across the peninsula's central highlands, and has spectacular views and little traffic.

The shorter **Ring of Skellig**, at the end of the peninsula, has fine views of the Skellig Rocks and is free of tourist coaches. You can forgo roads completely by walking the **Kerry Way**, which winds through the Macgillycuddy's Reeks mountains past Carrauntoohil, Ireland's highest mountain.

Daniel O'Connell was born near Cahirciveen, one of the Ring's larger towns. The excellent, wheelchair-accessible **Barracks Heritage Centre** (www.theoldbarracks.com; adult/student €4/2; ⏰10am-4.30pm Mon-Fri, 11.30am-4.30pm Sat, 1-5pm Sun Jun-Sep; shorter hours in winter) off Bridge St occupies what was once an intimidating Royal Irish Constabulary (RIC) barracks. Exhibits focus on O'Connell and on the Famine's local impact.

South of Cahirciveen the R565 branches west to Valentia Island, the 11km-long jumping-off point for an unforgettable experience: the **Skellig Rocks**, two tiny islands 12km off the coast.

The vertiginous climb up uninhabited **Skellig Michael** inspires an awe that monks could have clung to life in the meagre beehive-shaped stone huts that stand on the tiny strip of level land on top.

Calm seas permitting, boats run from spring to late summer from Portmagee, just before the bridge to Valentia, to Skellig Michael. The standard fare is around €45 return. Advance booking is essential; there are half a dozen boat operators, including **Casey's** (📞947 2437; www.skelligislands.com) and **Sea Quest** (📞947 6214; www.skelligsrock.com).

Dingle Peninsula

📖 066

Remote and beautiful, the Dingle Peninsula ends in the Irish mainland's westernmost point. This is a Gaeltacht area – if you're driving, don't bother looking for road signs that say 'Dingle Town'; they all say 'An Daingean', the Gaelic equivalent.

Cliffs of Moher

The peninsula's capital (population 1800) is a special place whose charms have long drawn runaways from across the world, making the port town a surprisingly cosmopolitan and creative place. There are loads of cafes, bookshops and art and craft galleries, and a friendly dolphin called Fungie who has lived in the bay for 25 years.

Dingle Boatmen's Association (☎915 2626; www.dingledolphin.com) operates one-hour boat trips to visit Fungie the dolphin. The cost is €16/8 per adult/child (free if Fungie doesn't show, but he usually does). There are also two-hour trips where you can swim with him (€25 per person, wetsuit hire €25 extra). Booking advisable.

West Coast

The west coast is Ireland at its wildest and most remote, a storm-battered seaboard of soaring sea cliffs and broad surf beaches. The weather is often just as wild as the landscape, but a bit of wind-torn mist and cloud just adds to the atmosphere.

Cliffs of Moher

About 8km south of Doolin are the towering 200m-high Cliffs of Moher, one of Ireland's most famous natural features.

The landscaped **Cliffs of Moher Visitor Centre** (www.cliffsofmoher.ie; adult/child €6/free; ⏰8.30am-7.30pm Jun-Aug, 9am-6pm Mar-May, Sep & Oct, 9am-5pm Nov-Feb) has exhibitions about the cliffs and the environment called the 'Atlantic Edge'. Nearby is **O'Brien's Tower**, which you can climb for €2/1 adult/child. Apparently, local landlord Cornelius O'Brien (1801–57) raised it to impress 'lady visitors'.

Galway

☎091 / POP 72,400

Arty and bohemian, Galway (Gaillimh) is legendary around the world for its entertainment scene. Cafes spill out onto cobblestone streets filled with a frenzy of fiddles, banjos, guitars and bodhráns, and jugglers, painters, puppeteers and magicians in outlandish masks enchant passers-by.

◎ Sights

FREE **GALWAY CITY MUSEUM**   Museum
(www.galwaycitymuseum.ie; Spanish Pde; ⏰10am-5pm daily Jun-Sep, to 5pm Tue-Sat Oct-May) Little remains of Galway's old city walls apart from the **Spanish Arch**, beside the river. The nearby museum has exhibits on the city's 150-year history.

EYRE SQUARE   Square
The focal point of the city centre, Eyre Square is a pleasant green space dotted with statues. In the centre of the square is **Kennedy Park**, honouring a visit by John F Kennedy in 1963.

SHOP STREET   Historic Area
Also on Shop St, parts of **Lynch Castle**, now a bank, date back to the 14th century. Lynch, so the story goes, was a mayor of Galway in the 15th century who, when his son was condemned for murder, personally acted as hangman. The stone facade that is the **Lynch Memorial Window** (Market St) marks the spot of the deed.

Across the road, in the Bowling Green area, is the **Nora Barnacle House Museum** (8 Bowling Green; admission €3; ⏰10am-5pm mid-May–mid-Sep or by appointment), the former home of the wife and lifelong muse of James Joyce, which displays the couple's letters and photographs.

✸ Festivals & Events

Galway Arts Festival   Arts
(www.galwayartsfestival.com) Held in July, this is the main event on Galway's calendar.

Galway Oyster Festival   Oysters
(www.galwayoysterfest.com) Going strong for more than 50 years now, this festival draws thousands of visitors in late September.

Sleeping

SKEFFINGTON ARMS HOTEL   Hotel €€
(☎563 173; www.skeffington.ie; Eyre Sq; r €75-190; @ 🛜) Rooms at the Skeff, overlooking Eyre Sq, are decorated in boutique style but the main reason to stay here is the renowned pub downstairs (with six bars), which also has a lunchtime carvery, an evening restaurant and a classy nightclub.

SPANISH ARCH HOTEL · Hotel €€

(☏ 569 600; www.spanisharchhotel.ie; Quay St; r €69-130; @ 🛜) In a sensational spot on the main drag, this 20-room boutique hotel is housed in a 16th-century former Carmelite convent. The hotel's solid-timber bar has a great line-up of live music, so rooms at the back, while smaller, are best for a quiet night's sleep.

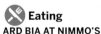 Eating

ARD BIA AT NIMMO'S · Irish €€€

(☏ 561 114; www.ardbia.com; Spanish Arch; mains €17-23; ⏱ cafe noon-3pm Wed-Fri, 10am-3.30am Sat, noon-7pm Sun, restaurant 6-10pm Tue-Sat) Tucked behind the Spanish Arch, this informal, cottage-style restaurant with whitewashed interior and mismatched furniture serves some of the finest food in the west of Ireland, from scallops and sea bass to roast Irish lamb and home-made chutneys.

ABALONE RESTAURANT · Seafood €€

(☏ 534 895; 53 Lower Dominick St; mains €20-30; ⏱ 6-10pm) There's very fine dining in this tiny yet elegant restaurant. As you'd expect from the name, seafood is the star here, but you'll also find vegetarian treats, steaks and various international dishes.

Griffins Bakery · Cafe €

(www.griffinsbakery.com; 21 Shop St; mains €5-13; ⏱ 8am-7pm Mon-Wed, 8am-8pm Thu-Sat, 9am-8pm Sun) A local institution, Griffins serves up delicious soups, sandwiches, sourdough baps and pizzas in a medieval-style tearoom.

Drinking & Entertainment

Most of Galway's pubs see musicians performing at least a couple of nights a week, whether in an informal session or as a headline act, and many swing to live music every night.

Good spots to hear trad sessions include **Monroe's Tavern** (Upper Dominick St), which has set dancing on Tuesday, **Taaffe's Bar** (19 Shop St), **Taylor's Bar** (Upper Dominick St) and **Crane Bar** (2 Sea Rd).

TIG CÓILÍ · Pub

(Mainguard St) Two live ceilidh a day draw the crowds to this authentic fire-engine-red pub, just off High St. It's where musicians go to get drunk or drunks go to become musicians...or something like that.

Róisín Dubh · Pub

(www.roisindubh.net; Upper Dominick St) A super pub complete with vast roof terrace, Róisín Dubh is *the* place to see emerging indie bands before they hit the big time.

ⓘ Information

Tourist office (☏ 537 700; www.irelandwest.ie; Forster St; ⏱ 9am-5.45pm Jun-Oct, 9am-5.45pm Mon-Sat, 9am-12.45pm Sun Jan-May, Nov & Dec)

ⓘ Getting There & Around

BUS Bus Éireann (www.buseireann.ie) buses depart from outside the train station. **Citylink** (www.citylink.ie) and **GoBus** (www.gobus.ie) stop at the **coach station** (cnr Forster St & Fairgreen Rd) a block northeast.

Clifden €12, 1½ hours, four daily

Doolin €14, 1½ hours, seven daily Monday to Saturday in summer, twice on Sunday

Dublin €14, 3¾ hours, hourly

Killarney €22, 4¾ hours, three daily

TRAIN Trains run to and from Dublin (€35, three hours, five daily).

Connemara

☏ 095

With its shimmering black lakes, pale mountains, lonely valleys and more than the occasional rainbow, Connemara in the northwestern corner of County Galway is one of the most gorgeous corners of Ireland. This is one of the most important Gaeltacht areas in the country; the lack of English signposting can be confusing at times.

The most scenic routes through Connemara are Oughterard–Recess (via the N59), Recess–Kylemore Abbey (via the R344) and the Leenane–Louisburgh route (via the R335). From Galway, **Lally Tours** (www.lallytours.com) and **O'Neachtain Tours** (www.galway.net/pages/oneachtain-tours) run day-long bus trips through Connemara for around €25 per person.

Northern Ireland

POP 1.7 MILLION

Crossing from the Republic into Northern Ireland you'll notice a couple of changes: the accent is different, the road signs are in miles and the prices are in pounds. But there's no checkpoint, no guards, not even a sign to mark the border – the two countries are in a customs union, so there's no passport control or customs declarations. All of a sudden, you're in the UK.

Dragged down for decades by the violence and uncertainty of the Troubles, Northern Ireland today is a nation rejuvenated. The 1998 Good Friday Agreement laid the groundwork for peace and raised hopes for the future, and since then the province has seen a huge influx of investment and redevelopment.

Glens of Antrim

The Antrim Coast from Larne to Ballycastle features nine beautiful valleys known as the Glens of Antrim, with lush green fields slung between black basalt crags, and picturesque harbour villages such as **Cushendall** and **Cushendun**. **Glenariff**, with its forest park and waterfalls, has been dubbed 'Queen of the Glens'.

Travelling between Cushendun and Ballycastle (with your own transport), leave the main A2 road for the narrower and more picturesque **Torr Head Scenic Road** (B92), with superb views across to the Scottish coast.

CARRICK-A-REDE ROPE BRIDGE

The 20m-long **rope bridge** (📞028-2076 9839; adult/child £5.40/2.90; ⊙10am-7pm Jun-Aug, to 6pm Mar-May, Sep & Oct, 10.30am-3.30pm Nov & Dec) that connects Carrick-a-Rede Island to the mainland, swaying some 30m above the pounding waves, is a classic test of nerve. The island is the site of a salmon fishery and is a scenic 1.25km walk from the car park. Note that the bridge is closed in high winds.

GIANT'S CAUSEWAY

This spectacular rock formation – Northern Ireland's only Unesco World Heritage site – is one of Ireland's most impressive and atmospheric landscape features. When you first see it you'll understand why the ancients thought it wasn't a natural feature – the vast expanse of regular, closely packed, hexagonal stone columns looks for all the world like the handiwork of giants.

Carrick-a-Rede Rope Bridge

CHRIS MELLOR/LONELY PLANET IMAGES ©

The more prosaic explanation is that the columns are simply contraction cracks caused by a cooling lava flow some 60 million years ago. The phenomenon is explained in an audiovisual (£1) at the **Causeway Visitors Centre** (☎028-2073 1855; www.giantscausewaycentre.com; ⏱10am-6pm Jul & Aug, 10am-5pm Mar-Jun, Sep & Oct, 10am-4.30pm Nov-Feb).

It costs nothing to visit the site, but car parking is an exorbitant £6. It's an easy 10- to 15-minute walk downhill to the Causeway itself, but a more interesting approach is to follow the clifftop path northeast for 2km to the Chimney Tops headland, then descend the Shepherd's Steps to the Causeway. For the less mobile, a minibus shuttles from the visitors centre to the Causeway (£2 return).

If you can, try to visit the Causeway out of season to avoid the crowds, and experience it at its most evocative.

BUSHMILLS

Bushmills, 4km southwest of the Giant's Causeway, makes a good base for visits to the Causeway Coast, but its real attraction is the **Bushmills Distillery**

(☎028-2073 3218; www.bushmills.com; adult/child £6/3; ⏱9.15am-5pm Mon-Sat year-round, 11am-5pm Sun Jul-Sep, noon-5.30pm Sun Mar-Jun & Oct); it's the world's oldest legal distillery, having been granted a licence by King James I in 1608. A tour of the industrial process is followed by a whiskey-tasting session; tours begin every half-hour or so.

The excellent HINI **Mill Rest Hostel** (☎028-2073 1222; 49 Main St; dm/tw £16.50/39; ⏱daily Mar-Oct, Fri-Sun only Nov-Feb; @) has small dorms and one wheelchair-friendly twin room (reserve in advance).

SURVIVAL GUIDE
Directory A-Z
Accommodation

From hip hotels to basic barns, the wide choice is all part of the attraction in Britain. There's a wide range of prices too; like-for-like, London tends to be the most expensive part of the country. In summer, popular spots (York, Canterbury, Bath etc) get very crowded, so booking ahead is often essential.

Giant's Causeway (p163)

Our reviews refer to double rooms with a private bathroom, except in hostels or where otherwise specified. Quoted rates in the Britain section are for **high season**, which is May to September.

£££	more than £130
£££	£50 to £130
£	less than £50
In Ireland:	
€€€	more than €65
€€	€30 to €65
€	less than €30

B&Bs & Guesthouses

The B&B ('bed and breakfast') is a great British institution. 'Guest house' is sometimes just another name for a B&B, or something in between B&B and hotel. Room rates are nearly always quoted per person including breakfast. Bottom-end you'll pay around £20 per person; in the midrange you're looking at around £35 or £40.

Typical costs in Ireland are around €20 to €40 per person, though more luxurious B&Bs can cost upwards of €55 per person.

Hotels

At the bargain end, you can find singles/doubles costing £30/40. Move up the scale and you'll pay £100/150 or beyond.

Business Hours

Britain

Banks Monday to Friday 9.30am to 4pm or 5pm, main branches Saturday 9.30am to 1pm.

Bars & Clubs Bars in big cities open till midnight, clubs to 2am or beyond.

Post Offices Monday to Friday, Saturday 9am to 12.30. Main branches to 5pm.

Pubs 11am to 11pm Sunday to Thursday, sometimes to midnight or 1am Friday and Saturday. Some pubs shut from 3pm to 6pm.

Restaurants Lunch around noon to 3pm, dinner 6pm to 11pm. Many close at least one day of the week.

Practicalities

○ **Electricity** British 3-pin plugs; adaptors need for European appliances. Voltage 230V @ 50Hz.

○ **Newspapers & Magazines** Broadsheets include *The Guardian, The Times, The Independent*; tabloids *The Sun, The Mirror*; right-wing *Daily Mail, Daily Express*.

○ **Radio** BBC stations nationwide: Radio 1 and 2 for music, Radio 3 for classical, Radio 4 for talk, Radio 5 Live for sport. BBC 6 Music is digital only.

○ **Smoking** Banned in enclosed public spaces.

○ **Time** GMT.

○ **Tipping** Usually not included: leave 10% in restaurants and cafes, optional in taxis.

○ **TV & Video** Publicly owned BBC operates several TV channels (BBC1, BBC2, BBC3, BBC4, BBC News). Commercial rivals ITV, Channel 4 and satellite-only Sky.

○ **Weights & Measures** Imperial: weights in pounds and ounces, distances in miles.

Shops Monday to Friday 9am to 5pm (5.30pm or 6pm in cities), Saturday 9am to 5pm, Sunday larger shops open 10am to 4pm.

Ireland

Banks 10am to 4pm Monday to Friday (to 5pm Thursday)

Post offices Northern Ireland 9am to 5.30pm Monday to Friday, 9am to 12.30pm Saturday; Republic 9am to 6pm Monday to Friday, 9am to 1pm Saturday. Smaller post offices may close at lunch and one day per week.

Pubs Northern Ireland 11.30am to 11pm Monday to Saturday, 12.30pm to 10pm Sunday. Pubs with late licences open until 1am Monday to Saturday, and midnight Sunday; Republic

Room Booking Services

Booking ahead is recommended in peak season. If you're stuck, most local **TICs** will find and book accommodation for you ahead of your arrival. This service is sometimes free but usually a fee (around £4) is charged.

In Ireland, **Fáilte Ireland** (Irish Tourist Board; www.discoverireland.ie) will book accommodation for a 10% room deposit and a fee of €5. The **Northern Ireland Tourist Board** (NITB; www.discovernorthernireland.com) books accommodation at no cost with a 10% deposit.

10.30am to 11.30pm Monday to Thursday, 10.30am to 12.30am Friday and Saturday, noon to 11pm Sunday. All pubs close Christmas Day and Good Friday.

Restaurants Noon to 10.30pm; many close one day of the week.

Shops 9am to 5.30pm or 6pm Monday to Saturday (until 8pm on Thursday and sometimes Friday), noon to 6pm Sunday (in bigger towns only). Shops in rural towns may close at lunch and one day per week.

Food

Prices for eateries in the Britain section are for a main meal unless otherwise indicated. The symbols used in each review indicate the following prices:

£££	more than £18
£££	£9 to £18
£	less than £9

Prices in Ireland are:

€€€	more than €16
€€	€8 to €16
€	less than €8

Gay & Lesbian Travellers

Most major cities – especially London, Brighton, Manchester and Glasgow – have gay and lesbian scenes, but there can still be some intolerance in smaller towns (and tabloid newspapers).

Despite the decriminalisation of homosexuality for people over 17 years of age (Northern Ireland in 1982 and the Republic in 1993), gay life is generally neither acknowledged nor understood. Only Dublin and, to a lesser extent, Belfast, Cork, Galway and Limerick have open gay and lesbian communities.

Language

The dominant language of Britain is English. Welsh is a Celtic language, entirely different to English. It almost died out in the 1960s, but today Welsh-language TV, radio and literature is increasingly popular, and all signs on roads and in public places are in both languages. In Scotland, Gaelic – another Celtic language – is spoken by about 80,000 people, mainly in the Highlands and Islands, while Lallans (or Lowland Scots) is much closer to English.

While Irish Gaelic is the official language of the Republic of Ireland, it is spoken only in a few rural areas (known as Gaeltacht) mainly in Cork, Donegal, Galway, Kerry and Mayo. English is the everyday language in the Republic and in Northern Ireland.

Money

The currency of Britain is the pound sterling (£). Paper money ('notes') comes in £5, £10, £20 and £50 denominations, although some shops don't accept £50 notes because fakes circulate. Scotland also issues its own notes, which are legal tender on both sides of the border.

The Irish Republic uses the euro (€), while Northern Ireland uses the British pound sterling (£).

In Northern Ireland several banks issue their own Northern Irish pound notes, which are equivalent to sterling but not readily accepted in mainland Britain.

ATMs

ATMs (often called 'cash machines') are easy to find in cities and even small towns.

Changing Money

Cities and larger towns have banks and bureaus for changing your money (cash or travellers cheques) into pounds. You can also change money at some post offices.

Credit & Debit Cards

Visa and MasterCard credit and debit cards are widely accepted in Britain; good for larger hotels, restaurants, shopping, flights, long-distance travel, car hire etc.

Nearly all credit and debit cards use a 'Chip and PIN' system (instead of signing). If your card isn't Chip and PIN enabled, you should be able to sign in the usual way, but some places might not accept your card.

Public Holidays

Britain & Ireland

New Year's Day 1 January

St Patrick's Day 17 March (only in Ireland)

Easter March/April (Good Friday to Easter Monday inclusive)

May Day First Monday in May

Spring Bank Holiday Last Monday in May

Summer Bank Holiday Last Monday in August

Christmas Day 25 December

Boxing Day 26 December

On public holidays (and Sundays), some small museums and places of interest close, but larger attractions have their busiest times.

Northern Ireland Only

Spring Bank Holiday Last Monday in May

Orangemen's Day 12 July (following Monday if 12th is at weekend)

August Bank Holiday Last Monday in August

Republic of Ireland Only

June Holiday First Monday in June

August Holiday First Monday in August

October Holiday Last Monday in October

Safe Travel

Britain is a remarkably safe country, but crime is not unknown in London and other cities. When travelling by tube, tram or urban train service at night, choose a carriage containing other people.

Unlicensed minicabs – a bloke with a car earning money on the side – operate in large cities, and are worth avoiding unless you know what you're doing.

Heritage Organisations

Membership of a heritage organisation gets you free admission to many historic houses and castles across Britain. We have included the relevant abbreviation (NT, NTS, EH etc) throughout this chapter.

○ **National Trust** (NT; www.nationaltrust.org.uk) annual membership costs £49 (with discounts for under-26s). A Touring Pass allows free entry to NT properties for one/two weeks (£21/26 per person). The **National Trust for Scotland** (NTS; www.nts.org.uk) is similar.

○ **English Heritage** (EH; www.english-heritage.org.uk) annual membership costs £44. An Overseas Visitors Pass allows free entry to most sites for seven/14 days for £20/25. In Wales and Scotland the equivalent organisations are: **Cadw** (www.cadw.wales.gov.uk) and **Historic Scotland** (HS; www.historic-scotland.gov.uk).

School Holidays

Roads get busy and hotel prices go up during school holidays. Exact dates vary from year to year and region to region, but are roughly:

- **Easter Holiday** Week before and week after Easter

- **Summer Holiday** Third week of July to first week of September

- **Christmas Holiday** Mid-December to first week of January.
There are also three week-long 'half-term' school holidays – usually late February (or early March), late May and late October. These vary between Scotland, England and Wales.

Telephone

Britain

Area codes in Britain do not have a standard format or length, eg 📞020 for London, 📞0161 for Manchester, 📞01225 for Bath, 📞015394 for Ambleside, followed as usual by the individual number.

To call outside the UK dial 📞00, then the country code (📞1 for USA, 📞61 for Australia etc), the area code (you usually drop the initial zero) and the number.

For directory inquiries, a host of agencies compete for your business and charge from 10p to 40p; numbers include 📞118 192, 📞118 118, 📞118 500 and 📞118 811.

Other codes include:

- 📞0500 or 📞0800 – free calls

- 📞0845 – local rate

- 📞087 – national rate

- 📞089 or 📞09 – premium rate

- 📞07 – mobile phones, more expensive than calling a landline.

- 📞100 – operator

- 📞155 – international operator; also for reverse-charge (collect) calls

Ireland

Local telephone calls from a public phone in the Republic cost a minimum of €0.50 for three minutes; in Northern Ireland a local call costs a minimum of £0.30. Prepaid phonecards by Eircom or private operators, available in newsagencies and post offices, work from all payphones and dispense with the need for coins.

To call Northern Ireland from the Republic, do not use 📞0044 as for the rest of the UK. Instead, dial 📞048 and then the local number. To dial the Republic from the North, however, use the full international code 📞00-353, then the local number.

The mobile (cell) phone network in Ireland runs on the GSM 900/1800 system compatible with the rest of Europe and Australia, but not the USA. Mobile numbers in the Republic begin with 085, 086 or 087.

Tourist Information

All British cities and towns, and some villages, have a tourist information centre (TIC) with helpful staff, books, maps and lots of free leaflets. They often also book accommodation. Britain's official tourist board is **VisitBritain** (www.visitbritain.com).

The Irish tourist board, **Fáilte Ireland** (www.discoverireland.ie), and the **Northern Ireland Tourist Board** (NITB; www.discovernorthernireland.com) operate separately.

Tourism Ireland (www.tourismireland .com) handles tourist information for both tourist boards overseas.

Visas

European Economic Area (EEA) nationals don't need a visa to visit Britain and Ireland. Citizens of Australia, Canada, New Zealand, South Africa and the USA are given leave on arrival to enter the UK for up to six months (three months for some nationalities), but are prohibited from working. For more info see www.ukvisas. gov.uk or www.ukba.homeoffice.gov.uk.

UK nationals born in Britain or Northern Ireland don't need a passport to visit the Republic, but should carry one anyway as identification.

Transport
Getting There & Away
Air

You can easily fly to Britain from just about anywhere in the world. London is a global hub, but major regional airports such as Manchester and Glasgow also handle international flights.

There are nonstop flights from Britain, continental Europe and North America to Dublin, Shannon and Belfast International, and nonstop connections from Britain and Europe to Cork.

In recent years regional airports have massively increased their choice – especially on budget ('no-frills') airlines to/from mainland Europe.

Land
BUS & COACH

You can easily get between Britain and other European countries via long-distance bus or coach. The international network **Eurolines** (www.eurolines.com) connects a huge number of destinations; buy tickets online via one of the national operators. Services to/from Britain are operated by **National Express** (www.nationalexpress.com).

TRAIN

The Channel Tunnel makes direct train travel between Britain and continental Europe a fast and enjoyable option.

High-speed **Eurostar** (www.eurostar.com) passenger services hurtle at least 10 times daily between London and Paris (2½ hours) or Brussels (two hours). The normal single fare between London and Paris/Brussels is around £150, but if you buy in advance and travel at a less busy period, deals drop to around £90 return or even less.

Drivers use **Eurotunnel** (www.eurotunnel.com). At Folkestone in England or Calais in France, you drive onto a train, get carried through the tunnel and drive off at the other end. The trains run four times an hour from 6am to 10pm, then hourly. Loading and unloading takes an hour; the journey takes 35 minutes. The one-way cost for a car and passengers is around £90 to £150 depending on the time of day (less busy times are cheaper); promotional fares bring it nearer to £50.

Sea

The main ferry routes between Britain and mainland Europe include Dover to Calais or Boulogne (France), Harwich to Hook of Holland (Netherlands), Hull to Zeebrugge (Belgium) or Rotterdam (Netherlands), Rosyth to Zeebrugge, Portsmouth to Santander or Bilbao (Spain), Newcastle to Bergen (Norway) or Gothenberg (Sweden). Routes to/from Ireland include Holyhead to Dun Laoghaire. Broker sites covering all routes and options include www.ferrybooker.com and www.directferries.co.uk.

Yacht on the Liffey River, Dublin (p148)
PHOTOGRAPHER: MARTIN MOOS/LONELY PLANET IMAGES ©

Getting Around

For getting around, your main choices are car or public transport. Having your own car makes the best use of time, and helps reach remote places, but rental and fuel costs can be expensive for budget travellers – while the hassles of parking and traffic jams in cities hit everyone – so public transport is often the way to go.

Air

Flights on longer routes (eg Exeter or Southampton to Edinburgh or Inverness) will save you time. With advance booking, fares start as low as £20 one-way, but up to £100 is more likely. On shorter or direct routes (eg London to Newcastle) train durations compare favourably with planes once airport downtime is factored in.

There are flights within Ireland between Dublin and Belfast, Cork, Derry, Donegal, Galway, Kerry, Shannon and Sligo, as well as a Belfast–Cork service. Most domestic flights take 30 to 50 minutes.

Bus

If you're on a tight budget, long-distance buses nearly always offer the cheapest way to get around, although also the slowest.

National Express (☎ 08717 818181; www .nationalexpress.com) is the main coach operator, with a wide network and frequent services between main centres. North of the border, **Scottish Citylink** (☎ 08705 505050; www.citylink.co.uk) is the leading coach company.

The Republic of Ireland's national bus line, **Bus Éireann** (☎ 01-836 6111; www.bus eireann.ie), operates across the Republic and into Northern Ireland. Intercity buses in Northern Ireland are mostly **Ulsterbus** (☎ 028-9066 6630; www.translink.co.uk).

Car & Motorcycle

Most overseas driving licences are valid in Britain for up to 12 months from the date of entry.

RENTAL

Compared to many countries (especially the USA), car rental is expensive in Britain; you'll pay around £250 per week for a small car (including insurance and unlimited mileage) but rates rise at busy times and drop at quiet times.

Car hire in Ireland is equally expensive. Extra fees may apply if you cross the North-South border.

Train on the Dingle Peninsula (p160)

ROAD RULES

Road rules in Britain and Ireland are very similar: Key points:

o drive on the left

o wear fitted seat belts in cars

o wear crash helmets on motorcycles

o give way to your right at junctions and roundabouts

o always use the left-hand lane on motorways and dual-carriageways, unless overtaking

o don't use a mobile phone while driving unless it's fully hands-free.

Speed limits are 30mph in built-up areas, 60mph on main roads and 70mph on motorways and most (but not all) dual carriageways. Drinking and driving is taken very seriously; the maximum blood-alcohol level allowed is 80mg/100mL.

Speed limits are posted in mph in Northern Ireland and km/h in the Republic: 110km/h (70mph) on motorways, 100km/h (60mph) on main roads and 50km/h (30mph) or as signposted in towns.

Car parks and other specified areas are regulated by 'pay and display' tickets or disc parking. Double yellow lines by the roadside mean no parking at any time, while single yellow lines indicate restrictions (which will be signposted).

Train

About 20 companies operate train services in Britain. **National Rail Enquiries** (☎ 08457 48 49 50; www.nationalrail.co.uk) provides timetable and fare details across the network. You can buy tickets on the spot at stations, which is fine for short journeys, but buying in advance for long journeys offers substantial discounts. The cheapest fares are nonrefundable, so if you miss your train you'll need a new ticket.

The Republic of Ireland's railway system, **Iarnród Éireann** (www.irishrail .ie), has routes radiating out from Dublin, but there is no direct north-south route along the west coast. Travelling at peak times costs substantially more. **Rail**

Users Ireland (www.railusers.ie) is more informative than the official website.

Northern Ireland Railways (www .translink.co.uk) has four lines from Belfast, one of which links up with the Republic's rail system.

CLASSES

In Britain, there are two classes of rail travel: 1st and standard. Travelling 1st class costs around 50% more than standard and, except on crowded trains, is not worth it. At weekends some train operators offer 'upgrades' for an extra £10 to £15 on top of your standard class fare.

RAIL PASSES

If you're staying in Britain for a while, passes known as 'railcards' are available:

16-25 Railcard For those aged 16 to 25, or full-time UK students.

Family & Friends Railcard Covers up to four adults and four children.

Senior Railcard For anyone over 60 years. These railcards cost around £26 (from major stations or online; valid for a year) and get you a 33% discount on most train fares, except those already discounted. With the Family card, adults get 33% and children get 60% discounts, so the fee is easily repaid in a couple of journeys. A **Disabled Person's Railcard** costs £18. For full details see www.railcard.co.uk.

For country-wide travel, **BritRail** (www. britrail.com) passes are available for visitors from overseas. They must be bought in your country of origin (not in Britain) from a specialist travel agency. They're available in three different versions (England only; all Britain; UK and Ireland) and for periods from four to 30 days. Of the other international passes, **Eurail** cards are not accepted in Britain, and **InterRail** cards are valid only if bought in another mainland European country.

In Ireland, passes include **Irish Explorer** (www.buseireann.ie; €245 for eight days' travel out of 15), which covers all rail and bus travel in the Republic. The **Irish Explorer Rail** (€145 within ROI, €180 including Northern Ireland, five days' travel out of 15) covers train-only travel.

France

Few countries provoke such passion as La Belle France.
Love it or loathe it, everyone has their own opinion about this Gallic goliath. Snooty, sexy, superior, chic, infuriating, arrogant, officious and inspired in equal measures, the French have long lived according to their own idiosyncratic rules, and if the rest of the world doesn't always see eye to eye with them, well, *tant pis* (too bad) – that's the price you pay for being a culinary trendsetter, artistic pioneer and cultural icon.

If ever there was a country of contradictions, this is it: France is a deeply traditional place: castles, chateaux and ancient churches litter the landscape while centuries-old principles of rich food, fine wine and joie de vivre underpin everyday life. Yet it is also a country that has one of Western Europe's most multicultural make-ups, not to mention a well-deserved reputation for artistic experimentation and architectural invention. Enjoy.

Fortified city of Carcassone (p256)

173

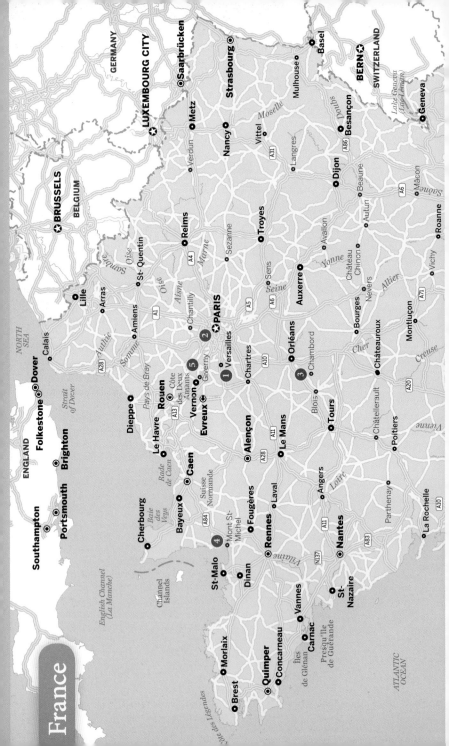

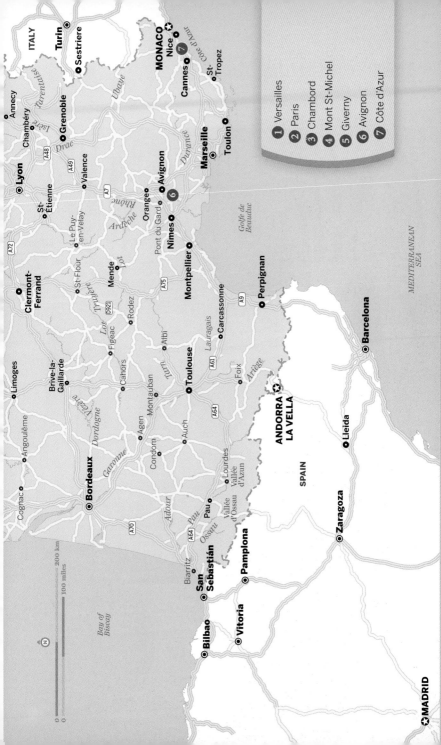

① Versailles

Versailles, as official residence of the kings of France, is magnificent – the only place where the daily life of the monarchy before the French Revolution can really be felt. My favourite time is the evening, after the crowds have gone, when I quietly walk from room to room lecturing to just a small group...extraordinary. Royal Chapel

Need to Know

AVOID QUEUES Arrive early or after 4pm **AVOID** Tuesdays, when Versailles is most crowded **MUST DO** Buy tickets early at www.chateauversailles.fr **See our author's review on p216.**

Versailles Don't Miss List

BY SYLVAIN POSTOLLE, OFFICIAL GUIDE, CHÂTEAU DE VERSAILLES

1 KING'S PRIVATE APARTMENT

This is the most fascinating part of the palace as it shows the king as a man and very much reflects his daily life in the 18th century. Of the 10 or so rooms, the most famous is his bedroom where he not only slept but also held ceremonies.

2 KING LOUIS XVI'S LIBRARY

This is a lovely room – full of books, a place where you can really imagine the king coming to read for hours and hours. Louis XVI loved geography and his copy of *The Travels of James Cook* – in English – is still here.

3 HERCULES SALON

I love one particular perspective inside the palace: from the Hercules Salon you can see all the rooms comprising the King's State Apartment, and to the right, through the gallery leading to the opera house. The salon served as a passageway, in fact, for the king to go from his state apartment to the chapel to celebrate daily Mass.

4 ROYAL CHAPEL

This is an exquisite example of the work of a very important architect of the time, Jules Hardouin-Mansart (1646–1708). The paintings are also stunning: they evoke the idea that the French king was chosen by God and was his lieutenant on earth. The chapel is where the future king Louis XVI wed Marie Antoinette in 1770.

5 ENCELADE GROVE

Versailles' gardens are extraordinary but my favourite spot has to be this grove, typical of the gardens created for Louis XIV by André Le Nôtre. A gallery of trellises surround a pool with a statue of Enceladus, chief of the Titans who was punished for his pride by the gods from Mount Olympus. When the fountains are on, it's impressive.

The Louvre

I've worked at the Louvre for 10 years and each day I still experience many emotions: we're in the heart of Paris; it is a magical place, charged with history and very intimate... The Louvre was a 12th-century fortress, then a royal palace, today one of the most famous art museums in the world, an unforgettable place with magnificent gardens.

Need to Know
FACTS 60,000 sq m of gallery, 5000 artworks, 8 million annual visitors **THE TRUTH** One visit can't cover it all **PLAN** Study www.louvre.fr beforehand **See our author's review on p195.**

Louvre Don't Miss List

BY NIKO SALVATORE MELISSANO, MUSÉE DU LOUVRE

1 WINGED VICTORY OF SAMOTHRACE
It's impossible to reduce the collections of the Louvre to a hit parade... A definite highlight is the *Winged Victory of Samothrace* atop the Daru Staircase (1st floor, Denon Wing). I adore her wings. I just cannot stop contemplating her from all angles. She is, moreover, very photogenic.

2 THE SEATED SCRIBE & MONA LISA
I could admire this statuette (Room 22, 1st floor, Sully Wing) from the ancient Egyptian empire for hours: the face of the scribe (probably that of Saqqara), like his posture (a little 'yoga') and his deep stare, say several things to me: serenity, strength of character, eternal wisdom. Then there is *La Joconde* (*Mona Lisa;* Room 6, 1st floor, Salle de la Joconde, Denon Wing) and that amazing fascination of why and how she intrigues spirits with her mysteries.

3 COUR KHORSABAD
With its enormous human-headed winged bulls, this courtyard on the ground floor of the Richelieu Wing is a jump in time into the cradle of one of the oldest cultures in the world: Mesopotamia. During the regin of King Sargon II in the 8th century, these bulls carved from alabaster guarded the Assyrian city and palace of Khorsabad (northern Iraq).

4 GRANDE GALERIE
This gallery is a real highlight (1st floor, Denon Wing), with masterpieces from the great masters of the Italian Renaissance: Leonardo de Vinci, Raphael, Arcimboldo, Andrea Mantegna... For more on all these works of art, borrow the Louvre's multimedia guide (http://monguide. louvre.fr; adult/under 18 years €6/2), available at the three main entrances (Richelieu, Sully and Denon), which makes for a fun visit at your own pace.

Bottom Right: Cour Khorsabad

Chambord

Everyone knows about Versailles, but for many people it's the incredible chateaux of the Loire Valley that best illustrate the pomp and power of the French aristocracy. If you've ever wondered what it was that annoyed the revolutionaries about the ruling elite, the opulence and extravagance of Chambord (p239) provide an eloquent answer.

2

3 Mont St-Michel

Second only to the Eiffel Tower in terms of iconic importance, the otherworldly abbey of Mont St-Michel (p224), moored off the Normandy coastline, is one of the unmissable sights of northern France. Set atop a rocky island connected to the mainland by a slender causeway, it looks like it could have dropped straight from the pages of *The Lord of the Rings*.

JOHN ELK III/LONELY PLANET IMAGES ©

Giverny

Legend has it that Claude Monet first spied Giverny (p223) from the window of a passing train. It was love at first sight: the artist moved here with his family in 1883 and never left. After he bought the house in 1890, he transformed it into his own artistic paradise, adding the lily ponds, flowerbeds and dinky Japanese bridge, which inspired some of his most famous works.

Pont du Gard

Two thousand years ago, France (then known as Gaul) was one of the most important provinces of the Roman Empire, and the country is littered with Roman remains. None, however, are as impressive as the Pont du Gard (p258) – an amazing three-tiered aqueduct near Avignon, which was designed to carry 20,000 cubic metres of water per day along the 50km of canals that stretched between Uzès and Nîmes.

Côte d'Azur

If there's one place that lives up to its name, it's the Azure Coast. Sprinkled with glittering bays, super-exclusive beaches and sun-baked Mediterranean towns, it's been one of Europe's favourite seaside retreats for as long as anyone cares to remember. Nice (p269) is essential, but for glitzy Mediterranean glamour you can't beat the pint-sized principality of Monaco (p276), where millionaires step off their yachts straight into Monte Carlo's famous casino.

France's Best...

Iconic Buildings

o **The Eiffel Tower** (p186) Brave the crowds and climb the metal asparagus.

o **Cathédrale de Notre Dame de Paris** (p194) Gothic gargoyles, gigantic bells and knockout views over Paris.

o **Chartres Cathedral** (p220) Marvel at some of France's finest stained glass.

o **Centre Pompidou** (p200) Ponder the merit of the world's first inside-out building.

o **Mont St-Michel** (p224) The island abbey graces a million postcards.

Artistic Havens

o **Musée d'Orsay** (p187) See France's national collection of Impressionist and post-Impressionist art.

o **Montmartre** (p201) Get your portrait painted on Place du Tertre.

o **Aix-en-Provence** (p264) Follow in the footsteps of Van Gogh and Cézanne.

o **Giverny** (p223) Wander among the lily ponds in Monet's beloved gardens.

o **Centre Pompidou-Metz** (p236) Visit this stunning new centre for contemporary art.

Historic Locations

o **D-Day Beaches** (p225) The liberation of Europe began on Normandy's beaches.

o **Place de la Bastille** (p202) The French Revolution began with the storming of the Bastille Prison, but it's now Paris' busiest roundabout.

o **Alignements de Carnac** (p228) Over 3000 menhirs make up the world's largest prehistoric monument.

o **Bayeux** (p222) William the Conqueror's invasion of England is recounted in the massive Bayeux Tapestry.

Need to Know

Places to Shop

○ **Parisian marchés aux puces** (p214) Paris' fascinating flea markets are a paradise for bargain hunters.

○ **Sarlat-la-Canéda** (p251) Sarlat's covered and outdoor markets groan with goodies gathered from across the Dordogne.

○ **Markets in Nice** (p269) The chaotic food and flower markets in Nice take over most of cours Saleya.

○ **Le Panier, Marseille** (p262) Shoppers have been congregating on this lively quarter of Marseille since the days of ancient Greece.

ADVANCE PLANNING

○ **Two months ahead** Book hotels for Paris, Provence, the Côte d'Azur and Corsica.

○ **Two weeks ahead** Check out SNCF train timetables online, but check our advice on p285 before you buy.

○ **When you arrive** Pick up a Paris Museum Pass or a Paris Visite Pass for discounts on sights and transport.

RESOURCES

○ **France Guide** (www .franceguide.com) Detailed advice from the government tourist office.

○ **SNCF** (www.sncf-voyages. com) Plan any train travel and buy tickets online.

○ **Météo France** (www .meteo.fr) Get the latest weather forecasts.

○ **Paris Convention & Visitors Bureau** (www .parisinfo.com) Paris' tourist site is loaded with useful tips.

GETTING AROUND

○ **Air** France's main international airports are Paris' Roissy Charles de Gaulle and Orly; regional airports serve other French cities.

○ **Bus** Handy for rural areas; otherwise you're better off with trains.

○ **Car** The country's roads are excellent, but tolls operate on most autoroutes.

○ **Sea** Cross-Channel ferries service Roscoff, St-Malo, Cherbourg and Calais. Nice and Marseille have ferry services to Corsica and Italy.

○ **Train** Fast TGVs serve most French cities, while rural areas are served by slower TERs. The Eurostar links Paris' Gare du Nord and London's St Pancras.

BE FOREWARNED

○ **Dog poo** Watch where you step, especially in Paris.

○ **Closing times** Shops, sights and museums generally shut on Sunday and Monday, and most places close for lunch between 12pm and 2pm.

○ **Manners** It's polite to say *bonjour* (hello) and *au revoir* (goodbye) when entering and leaving shops.

○ **Public transport** Remember to stamp your ticket in a *composteur* (validating machine) to avoid being fined.

France Itineraries

France is fascinating enough to fill a whole lifetime of visits, but these itineraries manage to string together the best of both north and south.

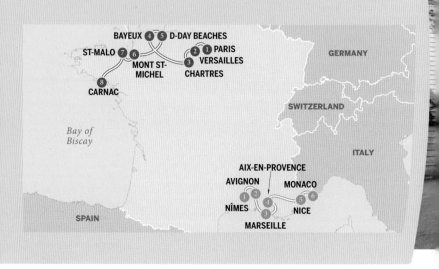

3 DAYS

PARIS TO CARNAC
Northern Sights

Everyone who visits France starts in **(1) Paris**, so this itinerary leaves the capital for a jaunt across Normandy and Brittany. On the first day, catch a train or drive west from Paris for a morning at **(2) Versailles**, Louis XIV's monumental pleasure palace. It's well worth taking one of the excellent guided tours to get the most from your visit. In the afternoon, continue to **(3) Chartres** and its cathedral, famed for the intense blues of its stained-glass windows.

On day two, travel on to **(4) Bayeux**, where you can spend the morning admiring the enormous Bayeux Tapestry before travelling to the **(5) D-Day Beaches**. Don't

miss the moving American Cemetery above Omaha Beach, which you'll instantly recognise from the opening credits of *Saving Private Ryan*. Unsurprisingly, the beach is still known to veterans as Bloody Omaha.

On day three, get up early to beat the crowds thronging around **(6) Mont St-Michel** – make sure you check the tide times if you're planning on walking in the bay itself, as the tides are treacherous. Finish up in **(7) St-Malo**, a beautiful walled city picturesquely perched on the Breton coastline. With an extra day, you could also include a visit to the stone alignments of **(8) Carnac**.

NÎMES TO MONACO

The Sultry South

5 DAYS

France's sun-drenched south is the perfect place for a road trip. This week-long itinerary begins in **(1) Nîmes**, once one of the great centres of Roman Gaul, where you can still see the remains of the amphitheatre and Roman walls. Around nearby **(2) Avignon**, you'll find two of France's most amazing structures: the mighty medieval bridge of Pont St-Bénézet and the breathtaking Roman aqueduct known as the Pont du Gard.

After a couple of days in the Provençal countryside, head for the coast. Multicultural **(3) Marseille** comes as something of a shock: it's noisy and chaotic, but if you want to taste authentic *bouillabaisse*, this is the place to do it. When the din gets too much, beat a retreat to **(4) Aix-en-Provence**, where Cézanne set up his easel over a century ago; you can visit his atmospheric studio, which has hardly changed since the artist's death in 1906.

Finish up in the quintessential city of the Côte d'Azur, **(5) Nice**, where you can while away a few days bronzing yourself on the beach, exploring the alleyways of the Old Town or tackling the hairpin curves of the corniche roads en route to the millionaires' playground of **(6) Monaco**.

Statues outside Musee d'Orsay (p187), Paris
PHOTOGRAPHER: LOU JONES/LONELY PLANET IMAGES ©

Discover France

At a Glance

- **Paris** (p186) The unmissable city of lights.

- **Brittany & Normandy** (p228 and p221) From craggy coastline to island abbeys.

- **Loire Valley** (p236) The centre of chateau country.

- **Provence** (p259) Postcard France: hilltop villages, buzzy markets, fields of lavender.

- **Cote d'Azur** (p269) France's favourite seaside getaway.

Sculptures inside Musée Rodin
PHOTOGRAPHER: BRUCE BI/LONELY PLANET IMAGES ©

PARIS

POP 2.21 MILLION

What can be said about the sexy, sophisticated City of Lights that hasn't already been said a thousand times before? Quite simply, this is one of the world's great metropolises, a trendsetter, market leader and cultural capital for over a thousand years and still going strong.

As you might expect, Paris is strewn with historic architecture, glorious galleries and cultural treasures galore. But the modern-day city is much more than just a museum piece: it's a heady hotchpotch of cultures and ideas – a place to stroll the boulevards, shop till you drop, flop riverside, or simply do as Parisians do and watch the world buzz by from a streetside cafe. Savour every moment.

Sights

Most Paris museums are closed on Mondays, but a dozen-odd, including the Louvre and Centre Pompidou, are closed on Tuesdays instead.

Left Bank

EIFFEL TOWER Landmark
(Map p188; www.tour-eiffel.fr; lifts to 2nd fl adult/child €8.10/4, to 3rd fl €13.10/9, stairs to 2nd fl €4.50/3; ⊙lifts & stairs 9am-midnight mid-Jun–Aug, lifts 9.30am-11pm, stairs 9.30am-6pm Sep–mid-Jun; M Champ de Mars–Tour Eiffel or Bir Hakeim) It's impossible now to imagine Paris (or France, for that matter) without La Tour Eiffel, the Eiffel Tower, but the 'metal asparagus', as some Parisians snidely called it, faced fierce opposition from Paris' artistic elite when it was built for the 1889 Exposition Universelle (World

Paris in Two Days

Join a **morning tour** then focus on those Parisian icons: **Notre Dame**, the **Eiffel Tower** and the **Arc de Triomphe**. Late afternoon have a coffee or pastis on **av des Champs-Élysées**, then mooch to **Montmartre** for dinner. Next day enjoy the **Musée d'Orsay**, **Ste-Chapelle** and the **Musée Rodin**. Brunch on **place des Vosges** and enjoy a night of mirth and gaiety in the nightlife-buzzy **Marais**.

With another two days, consider a **cruise** along the Seine or **Canal St-Martin** and meander further afield to **Cimetière du Père Lachaise** or **Parc de la Villette**. By night take in a concert or opera at the **Palais Garnier** or **Opéra Bastille**, or a play at the Comédie Française, and go on a bar and club crawl along Ménilmontant's **rue Oberkampf**. The **Bastille** area also translates as another great night out.

Fair). The tower was almost torn down in 1909, and was saved only by the new science of radiotelegraphy (it provided an ideal spot for transmitting antennas). Named after its designer, Gustave Eiffel, the tower is 324m high, including the TV antenna at the tip. You can either take the lifts (east, west and north pillars) or, if you're feeling fit – don't blame us if you run out of steam halfway up – the stairs in the south pillar up to the 2nd platform. Buy tickets in advance online to avoid monumental queues at the ticket office.

Spreading out around the Eiffel Tower are the **Jardins du Trocadéro** (Ⓜ Trocadéro), whose fountains and statue garden are grandly illuminated at night.

MUSÉE DU QUAI BRANLY   Art Museum
(Map p188; www.quaibranly.fr; 37 quai Branly, 7e; adult/child €8.50/free; ⏱11am-7pm Tue, Wed & Sun, to 9pm Thu-Sat; Ⓜ Pont de l'Alma or Alma-Marceau) The architecturally impressive but unimaginatively named Quai Branly Museum introduces the art and cultures of Africa, Oceania, Asia and the Americas through innovative displays, film and musical recordings.

MUSÉE D'ORSAY   Museum
(Map p188; www.musee-orsay.fr; 62 rue de Lille, 7e; adult/child €8/free; ⏱9.30am-6pm Tue, Wed & Fri-Sun, 9.30am-9.45pm Thu; Ⓜ Musée d'Orsay or Solférino) The Musée d'Orsay, housed

in a turn-of-the-century train station overlooking the Seine, displays France's national collection of paintings, sculptures and artwork produced between the 1840s and 1914.

Tickets are valid all day, so you can come and go as you please. A reduced entrance fee of €5.50 applies to everyone after 4.15pm (6pm on Thursday). A combined ticket including the Musée Rodin costs €12.

JARDIN DU LUXEMBOURG   Park
(Map p198; ⏱7.30am to 8.15am-5pm to 10pm according to the season; Ⓜ Luxembourg) When the weather is fine, Parisians of all ages come flocking to the formal terraces and chestnut groves of this 23-hectare city park to read, relax, stroll through urban **orchards** and visit the honey-producing **Rucher du Luxembourg** (Luxembourg Apiary).

Top spot for sun-soaking – always loads of chairs here – is the southern side of the palace's 19th-century, 57m-long **Orangery** (1834), where lemon and orange trees, palms, grenadiers and oleanders shelter from the cold.

MUSÉE RODIN   Garden, Museum
(Map p188; www.musee-rodin.fr; 79 rue de Varenne, 7e; adult/child incl garden €7-10/free, garden only €1; ⏱10am-5.45pm Tue-Sun; Ⓜ Varenne) One of our favourite cultural

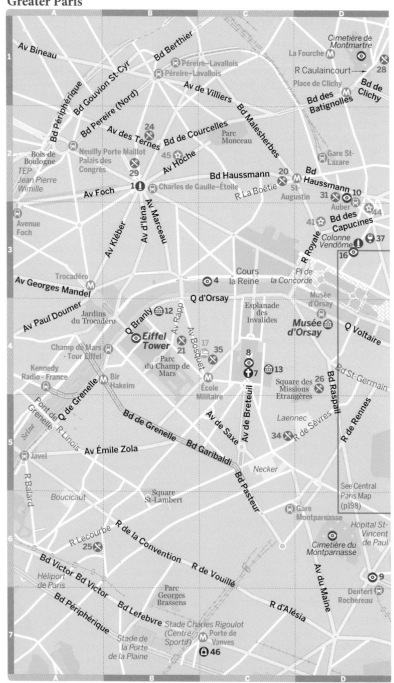

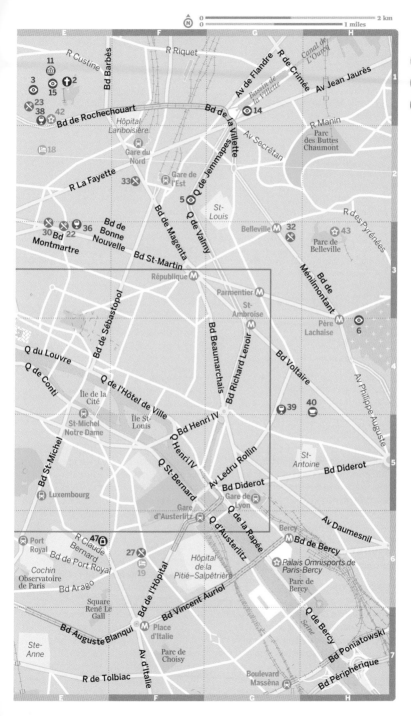

Greater Paris

attractions, the Rodin Museum is both a sublime museum and one of the most relaxing spots in the city, with a lovely sculpture garden in which to lounge. The 18th-century house displays some of Rodin's most famous works, including *The Burghers of Calais (Les Bourgeois de Calais), Cathedral, The Thinker (Le Penseur)* and *The Kiss (Le Baiser)*.

LES CATACOMBES Catacombs
(Map p188; www.catacombes.paris.fr, in French; 1 av Colonel Henri Roi-Tanguy, 14e; adult/child €8/4; ⏰10am-5pm Tue-Sun; Ⓜ Denfert-Rochereau) There are few spookier sights in Paris than the Catacombes, one of three underground cemeteries created in the late 18th century to solve the problems posed by Paris' overflowing cemeteries.

Twenty metres below street level, the catacombs consist of 1.7km of winding tunnels stacked from floor to ceiling with the bones and skulls of millions of Parisians – guaranteed to send a shiver down your spine.

PANTHÉON Monument
(Map p198; place du Panthéon, 5e; adult/child €8/ free; ⏰10am-6.30pm Apr-Sep, to 6pm Oct-Mar; Ⓜ Luxembourg) This domed landmark was commissioned around 1750 as an abbey church, but because of financial and structural problems it wasn't completed until 1789 (not a good year for opening churches in France). The crypt houses the tombs of Voltaire, Jean-Jacques Rousseau, Victor Hugo, Émile Zola, Jean Moulin and Nobel Prize winner Marie

Curie, among many others. Inside the gloomy Panthéon itself, a working model of Foucault's Pendulum demonstrates the rotation of the earth; it wowed the scientific establishment when it was presented here in 1851.

HÔTEL DES INVALIDES
Monument, Museum

(Map p188; M Varenne or La Tour Maubourg) Hôtel des Invalides was built in the 1670s as housing for 4000 *invalides* (disabled war veterans). On 14 July 1789, a mob forced its way into the building and seized 28,000 rifles before heading to the prison at Bastille, starting the French Revolution.

South are **Église St-Louis des Invalides**, once used by soldiers, and **Église du Dôme**, which contains the extraordinarily extravagant **Tombeau de Napoléon 1er** (Napoleon I's Tomb; ⊙10am-6pm Apr-Sep, 10am-5pm Oct-Mar).

JARDIN DES PLANTES
Botanical Garden

(Map p198; 57 rue Cuvier & 3 quai St-Bernard, 5e; ⊙7.30am-7pm; M Gare d'Austerlitz, Censier Daubenton or Jussieu) Paris' 24-hectare Jardin des Plantes was founded in 1626 as a medicinal herb garden for Louis XIII.

On its southern fringe is the city's main natural-history museum, the **Musée National d'Histoire Naturelle** (Map p198; www.mnhn.fr, in French; ⊙10am-5pm Wed-Mon; M Censier–Daubenton or Gare d'Austerlitz), with several galleries covering evolution, geology, palaeontology and the history of human evolution.

ÉGLISE ST-GERMAIN DES PRÉS   Church
(Map p198; 3 place St-Germain des Prés, 6e; ⊙8am-7pm Mon-Sat, 9am-8pm Sun; M St-Germain-des-Prés) Paris' oldest church, the Romanesque Église St-Germain des Prés, was built in the 11th century on the site of a 6th-century abbey and was the dominant church in Paris until the arrival of Notre Dame.

ÉGLISE ST-SULPICE
Church

(Map p198; place St-Sulpice, 6e; ⊙7.30am-7.30pm; M St-Sulpice) Lined with 21 side chapels, this beautiful Italianate church was built between 1646 and 1780.

Islands

Paris' twin set of islands could not be more different. **Île de la Cité** is bigger, full of sights and very touristed (few people live here).

Palais du Luxembourg in the Jardin du Luxembourg (p187)

Notre Dame

A Timeline

1160 Maurice de Sully becomes bishop of Paris. Mission: to grace growing Paris with a lofty new cathedral.

1182–90 The **choir with double ambulatory** ❶ is finished and work starts on the nave and side chapels.

1200–50 The **west facade** ❷, with rose window, three portals and two soaring towers, goes up. Everyone is stunned.

1345 Some 180 years after the foundation stone was laid, the Cathédrale de Notre Dame is complete. It is dedicated to *Notre Dame* (Our Lady), the Virgin Mary.

1789 Revolutionaries smash the original **Gallery of Kings** ❸, pillage the cathedral and melt all its bells except the great bell Emmanuel. The cathedral becomes a Temple of Reason, then a warehouse.

1831 Victor Hugo's novel *The Hunchback of Notre Dame* inspires new interest in the half-ruined Gothic cathedral.

1845–50 Architect Viollet-le-Duc undertakes its restoration. Twenty-eight new kings are sculpted for the west facade. The heavily decorated **portals** ❹ and **spire** ❺ are reconstructed. The neo-Gothic **treasury** ❻ is built.

1860 The area in front of Notre Dame is cleared to create the *parvis*, an alfresco classroom where Parisians can learn a catechism illustrated on sculpted stone portals.

1935 A rooster bearing part of the relics of the Crown of Thorns, St Denis and St Geneviève is put on top of the cathedral spire to protect those who pray inside.

1991 The architectural masterpiece of Notre Dame and its Seine-side riverbanks become a Unesco World Heritage Site.

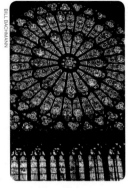

Virgin & Child
Spot all 37 artworks representing the Virgin Mary. Pilgrims have revered the pearly-cream sculpture of her in the sanctuary since the 14th century. Light a devotional candle and write some words to the *Livre de Vie* (Book of Life).

North Rose Window
See prophets, judges, kings and priests venerate Mary in vivid blue and violet glass, one of three beautiful rose blooms (1225–70), each almost 10m in diameter.

Flying Buttresses

Choir Screen
No part of the cathedral weaves biblical tales more evocatively than these ornate wooden panels, carved in the 14th century after the Black Death killed half the country's population. The faintly gaudy colours were restored in the 1960s.

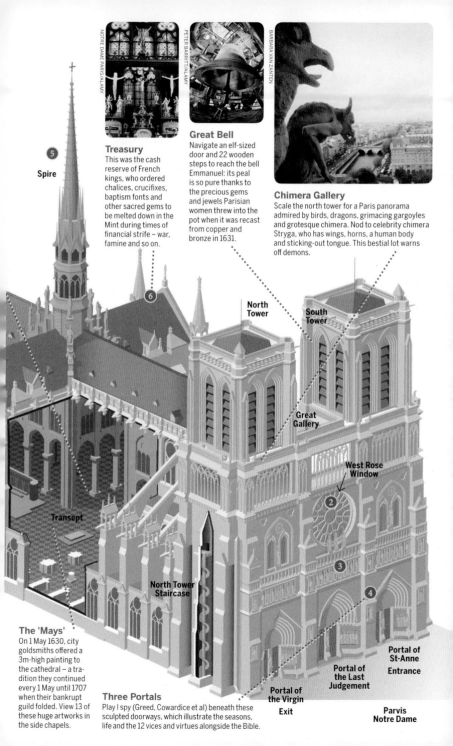

Treasury
This was the cash reserve of French kings, who ordered chalices, crucifixes, baptism fonts and other sacred gems to be melted down in the Mint during times of financial strife – war, famine and so on.

Great Bell
Navigate an elf-sized door and 22 wooden steps to reach the bell Emmanuel: its peal is so pure thanks to the precious gems and jewels Parisian women threw into the pot when it was recast from copper and bronze in 1631.

Chimera Gallery
Scale the north tower for a Paris panorama admired by birds, dragons, grimacing gargoyles and grotesque chimera. Nod to celebrity chimera Stryga, who has wings, horns, a human body and sticking-out tongue. This bestial lot warns off demons.

Spire

5

6

North Tower

South Tower

Great Gallery

West Rose Window

2

3

4

Transept

North Tower Staircase

The 'Mays'
On 1 May 1630, city goldsmiths offered a 3m-high painting to the cathedral – a tradition they continued every 1 May until 1707 when their bankrupt guild folded. View 13 of these huge artworks in the side chapels.

Three Portals
Play I spy (Greed, Cowardice et al) beneath these sculpted doorways, which illustrate the seasons, life and the 12 vices and virtues alongside the Bible.

Portal of the Virgin
Exit

Portal of the Last Judgement

Portal of St-Anne
Entrance

Parvis Notre Dame

NOTRE DAME PARIS/ALAMY

PETER BARRITT/ALAMY

BARBARA VAN ZANTEN

Smaller **Île St-Louis** is residential and quieter, with just enough boutiques and restaurants – and a legendary ice-cream maker – to attract visitors. The area around **Pont St-Louis**, the bridge across to the Île de la Cité, and **Pont Louis Philippe**, the bridge to the Marais, is one of the most romantic spots in Paris.

ÎLE DE LA CITÉ

The seven decorated arches of Paris' oldest bridge, **Pont Neuf** (Map p198; Ⓜ Pont Neuf), have linked Île de la Cité with both banks of the River Seine since 1607.

CATHÉDRALE DE NOTRE DAME DE PARIS
Church

(Map p198; www.cathedraledeparis.com; 6 place du Parvis Notre Dame, 4e; audioguide €5; ⏰ 8am-6.45pm Mon-Fri, 8am-7.15pm Sat & Sun; Ⓜ Cité) Notre Dame is the true heart of Paris: distances from Paris to all parts of metropolitan France are measured from **place du Parvis Notre Dame**, the square in front of this masterpiece of French Gothic architecture.

Constructed on a site occupied by earlier churches (and, a millennium before that, a Gallo-Roman temple), it was begun in 1163 but not completed until the mid-14th century. Free 1½-hour tours in English run at noon on Wednesday, 2pm Thursday and 2.30pm Saturday.

The entrance to its famous towers, the **Tours de Notre Dame** (Map p198; rue du Cloître Notre Dame; adult/child €7.50/free; ⏰ 10am-6.30pm daily Apr-Jun & Sep, 9am-7.30pm Mon-Fri, 9am-11pm Sat & Sun Jul & Aug, 10am-5.30pm daily Oct-Mar) is from the North Tower, to the right and around the corner as you walk out of the cathedral's main doorway. A narrow spiral staircase with 422 steps takes you to the top of the west facade for face-to-face views of countless gargoyles, the massive 13-tonne 'Emmanuel' bell in the South Tower and an unforgettable bird's-eye view of Paris. No hunchbacks, though, despite what you may have heard from Victor Hugo.

Left: Cathédrale de Notre Dame de Paris;
Below: Cruise boat on the River Seine

PHOTOGRAPHERS: (LEFT) IZZET KERIBAR/LONELY PLANET IMAGES ©;
(BELOW) RICHARD I'ANSON/LONELY PLANET IMAGES ©

STE-CHAPELLE   Church
(Map p198; 4 blvd du Palais, 1er;
adult/child €8/free; ☺9.30am-6pm Mar-
Oct, 9am-5pm Nov-Feb; Ⓜ Cité) Paris' most
exquisite Gothic monument is tucked
within the Palais de Justice (Law Courts).
Conceived by Louis IX to house his sacred relics, the chapel was consecrated
in 1248.

CONCIERGERIE   Monument
(Map p198; 2 blvd du Palais, 1er; adult/child €7/
free; ☺9.30am-5 or 6pm; Ⓜ Cité) Built as a
royal palace in the 14th century for the
concierge of the Palais de la Cité, this
atmospheric national monument was the
main prison during the Reign of Terror
(1793–94), used to incarcerate alleged
enemies of the Revolution before they
were brought before the Revolutionary
Tribunal in the Palais de Justice next door.
Among the 2700 prisoners held here
before being sent to the guillotine was
Queen Marie-Antoinette – see a repro-
duction of her cell.

A joint ticket with Ste-Chapelle is €11.

Right Bank

MUSÉE DU LOUVRE   Museum
(Map p198; www.louvre.fr; permanent col-
lections/permanent collections & temporary
exhibits €9.50/14, after 6pm Wed & Fri €6/12;
☺9am-6pm Mon, Thu, Sat & Sun, 9am-10pm
Wed & Fri; Ⓜ Palais Royal–Musée du Louvre)
The vast Palais du Louvre, overlooking the
fashionable **Jardin des Tuileries** gardens,
was constructed as a fortress by Philippe-
Auguste in the 13th century and rebuilt
in the mid-16th century for use as a royal
residence. In 1793 the Revolutionary Convention transformed it into the nation's
first national museum.

The Louvre's staggering 35,000
exhibits are spread across three wings:
Sully, Denon and Richelieu.

The collection is mind-bogglingly
diverse, ranging from Islamic artworks
and Egyptian artefacts through to a
fabulous collection of Greek and Roman
antiquities (including the *Venus de Milo*

195

The Louvre
A Half-Day Tour

Successfully visiting the Louvre is a fine art. Its complex labyrinth of galleries and staircases spiralling three wings and four floors renders discovery a snakes-and-ladders experience. Initiate yourself with this three-hour itinerary – a playful mix of *Mona Lisa* obvious and up-to-the-minute unexpected.

Arriving by the stunning main entrance, pick up colour-coded floor plans at the lower-ground-floor **information desk** ❶ beneath IM Pei's glass pyramid, ride the escalator up to the Sully Wing and swap passport for multimedia guide (there are limited descriptions in the galleries) at the wing entrance.

The Louvre is as much about spectacular architecture as masterly art. To appreciate this zip up and down Sully's Escalier Henri II to admire **Venus de Milo** ❷, then up parallel Escalier Henri IV to the palatial displays in **Cour Khorsabad** ❸. Cross room 1 to find the escalator up to the 1st floor and staircase-as-art **L'Esprit d'Escalier** ❹. Next traverse 25 consecutive galleries (thank you, floor plan!) to flip conventional contemplation on its head with Cy Twombly's **Ceiling** ❺ and the hypnotic **Winged Victory of Samothrace sculpture** ❻ – just two rooms away – which brazenly insists on being admired from all angles. End with the impossibly famous *Liberty* **Leading the People** ❼, **Mona Lisa** ❽ and **Virgin & Child** ❾.

TOP TIPS

Cent saver Visit after 3pm or in the evening when tickets are cheaper

Crowd dodgers The Denon Wing is always packed; visit on late nights Wednesday or Friday or trade Denon in for the notably quieter Richelieu Wing

2nd floor Not for first-timers: save its more specialist works for subsequent visits

Multimedia guide Worth it, if only to press the 'Where am I?' button when lost

Mission Mona Lisa

If you just want to venerate the Louvre's most famous lady, use the Porte des Lions entrance, from where it's a five-minute walk. Go up one flight of stairs and through rooms 26, 14 and 13 to the Grande Galerie and adjoining room 6.

L'Esprit d'Escalier
Escalier Lefuel, Richelieu
Discover the 'Spirit of the Staircase' through François Morellet's contemporary stained glass, which casts new light on old stone. **DETOUR»** Napoleon III's gorgeous gilt apartments.

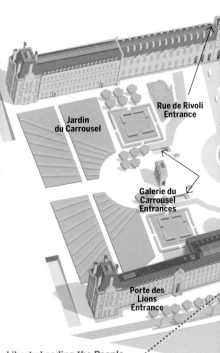

Rue de Rivoli Entrance

Jardin du Carrousel

Galerie du Carrousel Entrances

Porte des Lions Entrance

Liberty Leading the People
Room 77, 1st Floor, Denon
Decipher the politics behind French romanticism in Eugène Delacroix's rousing early 19th-century canvas and Théodore Géricault's *Raft of the Medusa*.

BILL BACHMANN/ALAMY

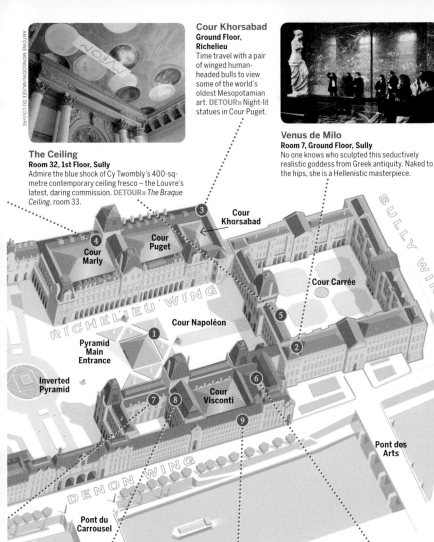

ANTOINE MONGODIN/MUSÉE DU LOUVRE

Cour Khorsabad
Ground Floor, Richelieu
Time travel with a pair of winged human-headed bulls to view some of the world's oldest Mesopotamian art. **DETOUR»** Night-lit statues in Cour Puget.

WITOLD SKRYPCZAK

Venus de Milo
Room 7, Ground Floor, Sully
No one knows who sculpted this seductively realistic goddess from Greek antiquity. Naked to the hips, she is a Hellenistic masterpiece.

The Ceiling
Room 32, 1st Floor, Sully
Admire the blue shock of Cy Twombly's 400-sq-metre contemporary ceiling fresco – the Louvre's latest, daring commission. **DETOUR»** *The Braque Ceiling*, room 33.

Cour Khorsabad ③

④ **Cour Marly**

Cour Puget

Cour Carrée

RICHELIEU WING

SULLY WING

Cour Napoléon

① **Pyramid Main Entrance**

⑤

②

Inverted Pyramid

⑥

⑦ ⑧ **Cour Visconti**

⑨

Pont des Arts

DENON WING

Pont du Carrousel

Mona Lisa
Room 6, 1st Floor, Denon
No smile is as enigmatic or bewitching as hers. Da Vinci's diminutive *La Joconde* hangs opposite the largest painting in the Louvre – sumptuous, fellow Italian Renaissance artwork *The Wedding at Cana*.

Virgin & Child
Room 5, Grande Galerie, 1st Floor, Denon
In the spirit of artistic devotion save the Louvre's most famous gallery for last: a feast of Virgin-and-child paintings by Raphael, Domenico Ghirlandaio, Giovanni Bellini and Francesco Botticini.

TERRY SMITH/ALAMY

Winged Victory of Samothrace
Escalier Daru, 1st Floor, Sully
Draw breath at the aggressive dynamism of this headless, handless Hellenistic goddess. **DETOUR»** The razzle-dazzle of the Apollo Gallery's crown jewels.

Central Paris

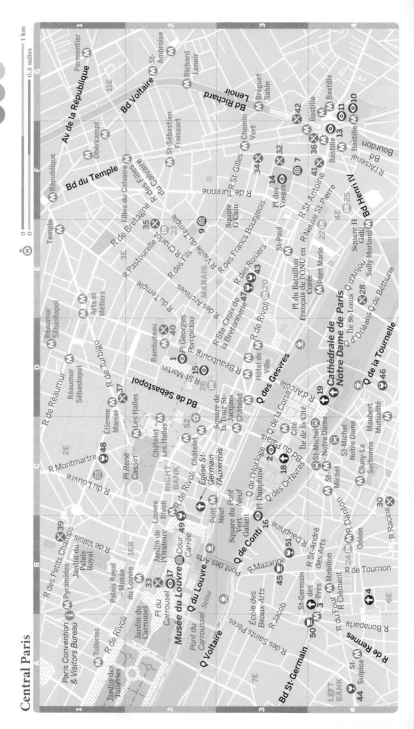

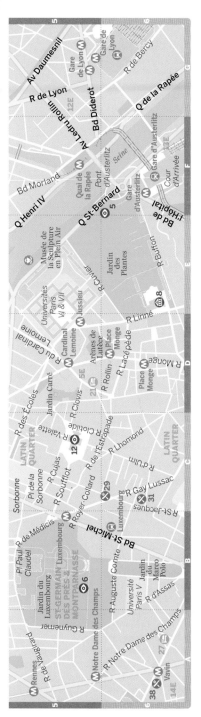

and the *Winged Victory of Samothrace*). But it's the celebrated paintings that draw most visitors; highlights include signature works by Raphael, Botticelli, Delacroix, Titian, Géricault and of course Leonardo da Vinci's slyly smiling *Mona Lisa* (Denon Wing, 1st floor, room 6). If you have time, peek at the section devoted to objets d'art, which houses a series of fabulously extravagant salons, including the apartments of Napoleon III's Minister of State, a collection of priceless Sèvres porcelain and Louis XV's dazzling crown jewels.

The gallery's main entrance and ticket windows in the Cour Napoléon are covered by the iconic 21m-high **Pyramide du Louvre** (Map p198), a glass pyramid designed by the Chinese-American architect IM Pei.

Buy tickets in advance from ticket machines in the Carrousel du Louvre shopping centre (99 rue de Rivoli) or, for an extra €1 to €1.60, from Fnac or Virgin Megastores *billetteries* (ticket offices), and walk straight in without queuing. Tickets are valid for the whole day, meaning you can come and go as you please. By 2012 you should be able to buy tickets direct on www.louvre.fr.

At the entrance to each wing rent a self-paced audioguide (€6).

English-language **guided tours** (☎ 01 40 20 52 63) depart at 11am, 2pm and (sometimes) 3.45pm Monday and Wednesday to Saturday. Tickets cost €5 in addition to the cost of admission.

ARC DE TRIOMPHE   Landmark
(Map p188; viewing platform adult/child €9/ free; ☉10am-10.30 or 11pm; Ⓜ Charles de Gaulle–Étoile) The Arc de Triomphe stands in the middle of the world's largest traffic roundabout, **place de l'Étoile**, officially known as place Charles de Gaulle. The 'triumphal arch' was commissioned in 1806 by Napoleon to commemorate his victories, but remained unfinished when he started losing battles, and wasn't completed until 1836. Since 1920, the body of an **unknown soldier** from WWI has lain beneath the arch; a memorial flame is rekindled each evening around 6.30pm.

Central Paris

The **viewing platform** (50m up via 284 steps and well worth the climb) affords wonderful views of the dozen avenues that radiate out from the arch, many of which are named after Napoleonic generals. **Av Foch** is Paris' widest boulevard, while **av des Champs Élysées** leads south to **place de la Concorde** and its famous 3300-year-old pink granite obelisk, which once stood in the Temple of Ramses at Thebes (present-day Luxor).

CENTRE POMPIDOU Museum
(Map p198; www.centrepompidou.fr; place Georges Pompidou, 4e; Ⓜ Rambuteau) Opened in 1977, the Centre Pompidou is one of central Paris' most iconic modern buildings; it was one of the first structures to have its 'insides' turned out. Its main attraction, the **Musée National d'Art Moderne** (adult/child €10-12/free; ⏱ 11am-9pm Wed-Mon), showcases France's national collection of post-1905 art, with examples from the surrealists, cubists, fauvists and pop artists all brilliantly represented.

Nearby **place Igor Stravinsky** (Map p198) delights with its colourful scuptures, including fanciful mechanical fountains of skeletons, a treble clef and a pair of ruby-red lips.

BASILIQUE DU SACRÉ COEUR Landmark
(Map p188; www.sacre-coeur-montmartre.com;
place du Parvis du Sacré Cœur, 18e; 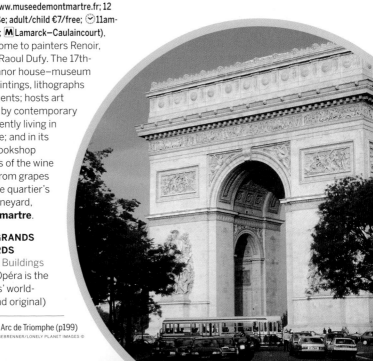6am-
10.30pm; MAnvers) The gleaming white
dome (admission €5; 9am-7pm daily Apr-Sep,
9am-6pm Oct-Mar) of this basilica has one of
Paris' most spectacular city panoramas.
It sits in the heart of Montmartre, which
lured bohemian writers and artists in
the late 19th and early 20th centuries.
Between 1908 and 1912 Picasso lived at
the studio called **Bateau Lavoir** (Map p188;
11bis place Émile Goudeau; MAbbesses).

Cafes, restaurants, endless tourists and
a concentrated cluster of caricaturists and
painters fill its main square, **place du Tertre**
(Map p188; MAbbesses) – if you're seeking your
portrait painted in Paris, this is the spot.

Just a few blocks southwest of the
tranquil residential streets of Montmartre
is lively, neon-lit Pigalle (9e and 18e),
one of Paris' two main sex districts. A
funicular connects it to the top of Butte
de Montmartre (Montmartre Hill).

No address better captures the
quartier's rebellious, bohemian and
artsy past than **Musée de Montmartre**
(Map p188; www.museedemontmartre.fr; 12
rue Cortot, 18e; adult/child €7/free; 11am-
6pm Tue-Sun; MLamarck–Caulaincourt),
one-time home to painters Renoir,
Utrillo and Raoul Dufy. The 17th-
century manor house–museum
displays paintings, lithographs
and documents; hosts art
exhibitions by contemporary
artists currently living in
Montmartre; and in its
excellent bookshop
sells bottles of the wine
produced from grapes
grown in the quartier's
very own vineyard,
Clos Montmartre.

OPÉRA & GRANDS
BOULEVARDS
Notable Buildings
Place de l'Opéra is the
site of Paris' world-
famous (and original)

opera house, **Palais Garnier** (Map p188;
guided tours 08 25 05 44 05; http://visites
.operadeparis.fr; place de l'Opéra, 9e; MOpéra).

PLACE VENDÔME Square
(Map p188; MTuileries or Opéra) The octagonal place Vendôme has long been one of
the city's smartest addresses, famous for
its 18th-century architecture, exclusive
boutiques and the superposh Hôtel Ritz-
Paris. The 43.5m-tall **Colonne Vendôme**
was fashioned from cannons captured
by Napoleon at the Battle of Austerlitz
in 1805.

MUSÉE PICASSO Museum
(Map p198; www.musee-picasso.fr, in French; 5
rue de Thorigny, 3e; 9.30am-6pm Wed-Mon;
MSt-Paul or Chemin Vert) One of Paris' best-
loved art museums, the Picasso Museum
contains more than 3500 of the *grand
maître*'s engravings, paintings, ceramics
and sculptures, as well as works from his
own art collection by Braque, Cézanne,
Matisse, Modigliani, Degas and Rousseau.
It will reopen after extensive renovations
in 2012.

PARIS SIGHTS

Arc de Triomphe (p199)

PLACE DES VOSGES   Square

(Map p198; St-Paul or Bastille) The Marais, on the Right Bank north of Île St-Louis in the 3e and 4e, was a marsh before it was transformed into one of the city's most fashionable districts by Henri IV, who constructed elegant *hôtels particuliers* (private mansions) around place Royale – today known as place des Vosges.

Novelist Victor Hugo lived here from 1832 to 1848. His home is now the **Maison de Victor Hugo** (Map p198; www .musee-hugo.paris.fr, in French; adult/child €7/ free; ☉10am-6pm Tue-Sun), with artworks and memorabilia relating to the author.

PLACE DE LA BASTILLE   Square

(Map p198; ⓜBastille) The Bastille is the most famous monument in Paris that no longer exists; the notorious prison was demolished by a Revolutionary mob on 14 July 1789, and the place de la Bastille where the prison once stood is now a busy traffic roundabout.

CIMETIÈRE DU PÈRE LACHAISE
Cemetery

(Map p188; www.pere-lachaise.com; ☉8am-6pm Mon-Fri, from 8.30am Sat, from 9am Sun; ⓜPhilippe Auguste, Gambetta or Père Lacaise)

Palais Garnier, Place de l'Opéra (p201)

The world's most-visited graveyard, Cimetière du Père Lachaise opened its one-way doors in 1804. Among the 800,000 people buried here are Chopin, Molière, Balzac, Proust, Gertrude Stein, Colette, Pissarro, Seurat, Modigliani, Sarah Bernhardt, Yves Montand, Delacroix, Édith Piaf and even the 12th-century lovers Abélard and Héloïse, whose remains were disinterred and reburied here together in 1817 beneath a neo-Gothic tombstone. The graves of **Oscar Wilde** (Division 89) and **Jim Morrison** (Division 6) are perennially popular.

CANAL ST MARTIN   Canal

(Map p188; ⓜRépublique, Jaurès or Jacques Bonsergent) The shaded towpaths of the tranquil, 4.5km-long Canal St-Martin are wonderful for a romantic stroll or bike ride past nine locks, metal bridges and Parisian neighbourhoods. Take a **canal boat tour** (see p202) to savour the real flavour.

👉 Tours

Bateaux Mouches   Boat

(Map p188; ☎01 42 25 9610; www.bateaux mouches.com; Port de la Conférence, 8e; adult/

Detour:
Bois de Boulogne & Vincennes

On Paris' western fringe, 845-hectare **Bois de Boulogne** (blvd Maillot, 16e; Ⓜ Porte Maillot) was inspired by Hyde Park in London. Attractions include formal gardens, a lake with rowing boats, **kids' amusement park** (www.jardindacclimatation.fr) and 18th-century chateau, **Château de Bagatelle** (route de Sèvres à Neuilly, 16e; adult/child €6/free; ⊙tour 3pm Sat & Sun Apr-Sep, 9am-5pm Oct-Mar), with spectacular flower gardens. Steer clear after dark, when Bois de Boulogne morphs into a playground for female and transvestite prostitutes.

Turning southeast, 995-hectare **Bois de Vincennes** (blvd Poniatowski, 12e; Ⓜ Porte de Charenton or Porte Dorée) encompasses its own fortified castle, **Château de Vincennes** (www.chateau-vincennes.fr; av de Paris, 12e; ⊙10am-5 or 6pm May-Aug, 10am-5pm Sep-Apr; Ⓜ Château de Vincennes); it's free to explore the grounds, but the keep and royal chapel can be visited only by guided **tour** (adult/child €8/free). Nearby there's a huge **floral park** (www.parcfloraldeparis.com, in French) with butterfly garden, **zoo** (www.mnhn.fr) and **aquarium** (www.acquarium-portedoree.fr).

child €10/5; ⊙Mar-Nov; Ⓜ Alma–Marceau) Cruises (70 minutes) run regularly from 10.15am to 11pm April to September and 13 times a day between 11am and 9pm the rest of the year.

Paris Canal Croisières   Boat
(Map p188; ☎ 01 42 40 96 97; www.pariscanal.com; Bassin de la Villette, 19-21 quai de la Loire, 19e; adult/child €17/10; ⊙Mar-Nov; Ⓜ Jaurès or Musée d'Orsay) This tour company runs daily 2½-hour cruises that depart from near the Musée d'Orsay (quai Anatole France, 7e) and sail to Bassin de la Villette, 19e, via the charming Canal St-Martin and Canal de l'Ourcq.

L'Open Tour   Bus
(Map p188; ☎ 01 42 66 56 56; www.pariscityrama.com; 13 rue Auber, 9e; 1 day adult/child €29/15; Ⓜ Havre–Caumartin or Opéra) This company runs open-deck buses along four circuits and you can jump on/off at more than 50 stops.

Eye Prefer Paris   Walking
(www.eyepreferparistours.com; €195 for 3 people) New Yorker turned Parisian leads offbeat tours of the city; cooking classes too.

Paris Walks   Walking
(www.paris-walks.com; adult/child €12/8) Thematic tours (fashion, chocolate, the French Revolution) in English.

Festivals & Events

Grande Parade de Paris   New Year
(www.parisparade.com) The Great Paris Parade, with marching and carnival bands, dance acts and so on, takes place on the afternoon of New Year's Day.

Paris Jazz Festival   Jazz
(www.parcfloraldeparis.com; www.paris.fr) Free jazz concerts every Saturday and Sunday afternoon in June and July in Parc Floral de Paris.

Paris Plages   Beach
(www.paris.fr) 'Paris Beaches' sees three waterfront areas transformed into sand-and-pebble 'beaches', complete with sunbeds, beach umbrellas, atomisers, lounge chairs and palm trees, for four weeks from mid-July to mid-August.

Sleeping

The **Paris Convention & Visitors Bureau** (p214) can find you a place to stay (no booking fee, but you need a credit card), though queues can be long in high season.

Louvre & Les Halles
This area is central but don't expect tranquillity or many bargains.

HÔTEL ST-MERRY   Historic Hotel   €€
(Map p198; 📞 01 42 78 14 15; www.hotelmarais
.com; 78 rue de la Verrerie, 4e; r €135-230, tr
€205-275; ❄ 🛜; **M**Châtelet) The interior
of this 12-room hostelry, with beamed
ceilings, church pews and wrought-iron
candelabra, is a neo-goth's wet dream;
you have to see the architectural elements of room 9 (flying buttress over the
bed) and the furnishings of 12 (choir-stall
bed board) to believe them. Only some of
the rooms have air-conditioning.

Marais & Bastille

Budget accommodation is a forte of
the Marais. East of Bastille, the untour-
isted 11e provides a glimpse up close of
working-class Paris.

HÔTEL DU PETIT MOULIN
                    Boutique Hotel   €€€
(Map p198; 📞 01 42 74 10 10; www.hoteldupetit
moulin.com; 29-31 rue de Poitou, 3e; r €190-290;
❄ @ 🛜; **M**Filles du Calvaire) This scrumptious boutique hotel (OK, we're impressed
that it was a bakery at the time of Henri
IV) was designed by Christian Lacroix.

Choose from medieval and rococo Marais
sporting exposed beams and dressed in
toile de Jouy wallpaper, to more-modern
surrounds with contemporary murals
and heart-shaped mirrors just this side
of kitsch.

HÔTEL CARON DE BEAUMARCHAIS
                    Boutique Hotel   €€
(Map p198; 📞 01 42 72 34 12; www.caronde
beaumarchais.com; 12 rue Vieille du Temple,
4e; r €125-162; ❄ 🛜; **M**St-Paul) Decorated
like an 18th-century private house, this
themed hotel has to be seen to be
believed. In the palatial lobby an 18th-
century pianoforte, gaming tables, gilded
mirrors, and candelabras, set the tone for
a stay that promises to be unique.

Hôtel du 7e Art   Themed Hotel   €€
(Map p198; 📞 01 44 54 85 00; www.paris-hotel
-7art.com; 20 rue St-Paul, 4e; s €75-150, d €95-
155; 🛜; **M**St-Paul) Film buffs, this fun place
with a black-and-white-movie theme running
throughout its 23 rooms is for you.

Hôtel St-Louis Marais   Historic Hotel   €€
(Map p198; 📞 01 48 87 87 04; www.saintlouis
marais.com; 1 rue Charles V, 4e; s €99, d & tw
€115-140, tr €150; 🛜; **M**Sully Morland) This
especially charming hotel in a converted 17th-
century convent sports lots of wooden beams,
terracotta tiles and heavy brocade drapes. Four
floors but no lift; wi-fi €5.

Latin Quarter

In this good-value, Left Bank
neighbourhood midrange
hotels are particularly
popular with visiting academics, making rooms
hardest to find during
conferences (March to
June and October).

HÔTEL LA DEMEURE
                    Boutique Hotel   €€
(Map p188; 📞 01 43 37 81
25; www.hotellademeure
paris.com; 51 blvd St-Marcel,
13e; s/d €165/202; ❄ @ 🛜;
MGobelins) This elegant

Hôtel Caron de Beaumarchais

KEVIN CLOGSTOUN/LONELY PLANET IMAGES ©

little number is the domain of a charming father-and-son team who speak perfect English and are always at hand to assist. Warm red and orange tones lend a 'clubby' feel to public areas; wraparound balconies add extra appeal to corner rooms; and then there's those extra nice touches – an iPod dock in every room, wineglasses for guests who like to BYO ('bring your own'), art to buy on the walls...

HÔTEL DES GRANDES ÉCOLES

Garden Hotel €€
(Map p198; 01 43 26 79 23; www.hotel -grandes-ecoles.com; 75 rue du Cardinal Lemoine, 5e; d €115-140; @ ; M Cardinal Lemoine or Place Monge) This wonderful 51-room hotel is tucked into a courtyard off a medieval street with its own garden. Choose a room in one of three buildings: our favourites are rooms 29 to 33 with direct garden access.

St-Germain, Odéon & Luxembourg

Staying in chic St-Germain des Prés (6e) is a delight. But pack your spare change – budget places just don't exist in this part of the Left Bank.

L'APOSTROPHE

Design Hotel €€
(Map p198; 01 56 54 31 31; www.apostrophe -hotel.com; 3 rue de Chevreuse, 6e; d €150-350; @ ; M Vavin) This art hotel is style. Its 16 rooms pay homage to the written word: graffiti tags one wall of room U (for 'urbain'), which has a ceiling shaped like a skateboard ramp, and room P (for 'Paris parody') sits in the clouds overlooking Paris' rooftops.

HÔTEL RELAIS ST-GERMAIN

Hotel €€€
(Map p198; 01 43 29 12 05; www.hotel-paris -relais-saint-germain.com; 9 Carrefour de l'Odéon, 7e; s/d €220/285; @ ; M Odéon) What rave reports this 17th-century town house with flower boxes and baby-pink awning gets. Ceilings are beamed, furniture is antique and fabrics are floral. Mix this with a chic contemporary air, ample art works to admire and one of Paris' most talked-about bistros, **Le Comptoir du Relais** (p208), as next-door neighbour. Delicious, darling!

Faubourg St-Germain & Invalides

The 7e is a lovely arrondissement to call home, although it's slightly removed from the action.

Top Five Pâtisseries

○ **Ladurée** (www.laduree.fr, in French; 75 av des Champs-Élysées, 8e; M George V) The most famous and decadent of Parisian pâtisseries, inventor of the *macaron* to boot.

○ **Le Nôtre** (Map p198; www.lenotre.fr, in French; 10 rue St- Antoine, 4e; M Bastille) Delectable pastries and chocolate; 10 more outlets around town.

○ **La Pâtisserie des Rêves** (www. lapatisseriedesreves.com; 93 rue du Bac, 7e; M Rue du Bac) Extraordinary cakes and tarts showcased beneath glass at the chic 'art' gallery of big-name *pâtissier* Philippe Conticini.

○ **Bruno Solques** (Map p198; 248 rue St- Jacques, 5e; M Luxembourg) Paris' most inventive *pâtissier,* Bruno Solques excels at oddly shaped flat tarts and fruit-filled brioches.

○ **Dalloyau** (Map p198; www.dalloyau. fr; 5 blvd Beaumarchais, 4e; M Bastille) Specialities include *pain aux raisins* (raisin bread), millefeuille (pastry layered with cream), *tarte au citron* (lemon tart) and *opéra* (coffee-almond cake and chocolate).

CADRAN HÔTEL   Boutique Hotel €€
(Map p188; 01 40 62 67 00; www.paris-hotel-cadran.com; 10 rue du Champ de Mars, 7e; d €144-225; M École Militaire) An address for gourmets, this concept hotel seduces guests with a clock theme and an open-plan reception spilling into a *bar à chocolat* (chocolate bar) that sells – yes – chocolate and seasonal-flavoured *macarons.*

Montmartre & Pigalle

What a charmer Montmartre is with its varied accommodation scene embracing everything from boutique to bohemian, hostel to *hôtel particulier.* The area east of Sacré Cœur can be rough – avoid Château Rouge metro station at night.

HÔTEL AMOUR   Boutique Hotel €€
(Map p188; 01 48 78 31 80; www.hotelamourparis.fr; 8 rue Navarin, 9e; s/d €100/150-280; ; M St-Georges or Pigalle) Planning a romantic escapade to Paris? Say no more. One of the 'in' hotels of the moment, the inimitable black-clad Amour is very much worthy of the hype – you won't find a more original place to lay your head in Paris at these prices. Of course, you'll have to forgo TV (none), but who needs a box when you're in love?

 Eating

As the culinary centre of the most agressively gastronomic country in the world, the city has more 'generic French', regional and ethnic restaurants than any other place in France. In pricier restaurants, ordering a *menu* (set two- or three-course meal at a fixed price) at lunchtime is invariably extraordinary good value.

Louvre & Les Halles

This area is filled with trendy restaurants, though few are outstanding – most cater to tourists.

CAFÉ MARLY   French, Cafe €€€
(Map p198; 01 46 26 06 60; cour Napoléon du Louvre, 93 rue de Rivoli, 1er; mains €20-30; 8am-2am; M Palais Royal-Musée du Louvre) This classic venue facing the Louvre's inner courtyard serves contemporary French fare throughout the day under the palace colonnades. Views of the glass pyramid (and French starlets) are priceless.

JOE ALLEN   American €€
(Map p198; 01 42 36 70 13; 30 rue Pierre Lescot, 1er; lunch menus €14, dinner menus €18.10 & €22.50; noon-1am; M Étienne Marcel) An institution since 1972, Joe Allen is a little bit of New York in Paris. The ribs are particularly recommended.

Marais & Bastille

The Marais is one of Paris' premier dining neighbourhoods; book ahead for weekend dining.

CHEZ JANOU Provençal €€
(Map p198; ☎ 01 42 72 28 41; www.chezjanou
.com; 2 rue Roger Verlomme, 3e; mains €14.50-19;
Ⓜ Chemin Vert) This lovely little spot just
east of place des Vosges attracts celebs
(last seen: John Malkovich) with its inspired cooking from the south of France,
80 types of pastis and excellent service.

LE HANGAR French, Bistro €€
(Map p198; ☎ 01 42 74 55 44; 12 impasse
Berthaud, 3e; mains €16-20; ◷ Tue-Sat; Ⓜ Les
Halles) Unusual for big mouths like us, we
almost baulk at revealing details of this
perfect little restaurant. It serves bistro
favourites in relaxing surrounds. The terrace is a delight in fine weather.

CHEZ NÉNESSE French, Bistro €
(Map p198; ☎ 01 42 78 46 49; 17 rue Saintonge,
3e; mains €18; ◷ Mon-Fri; Ⓜ Filles du Calvaire)
The atmosphere here is charmingly 'old
Parisian' and unpretentious. Dishes are
prepared with fresh, high-quality ingredients and offer good value for money.

CAFÉ HUGO French, Café €€
(Map p198; ☎ 01 42 72 64 04; 22 place des
Vosges, 4e; mains €10.70-13.30; h8am-2am;
Ⓜ Chemin Vert) Go for the plat du jour (dish

of the day) with a glass of wine (€12.50)
or brunch (€16.20) at our favourite affordable eatery on Paris' most beautiful
square – and you'll love Paris forever.

Latin Quarter & Jardin des Plantes

From cheap-eat student haunts to
chandelier-lit palaces loaded with history,
the 5e has something to suit every budget
and culinary taste.

BISTROY LES PAPILLES
French, Bistro €€
(Map p198; ☎ 01 43 25 20 79; www.lespapilles
paris.com, in French; 30 rue Gay Lussac, 5e;
menus €22-31; ◷ Tue-Sat; Ⓜ Luxembourg) This
hybrid bistro, wine cellar and *épicerie*
(specialist grocer) is one of those fabulous dining experiences that packs out
the place (reserve a few days in advance
to guarantee a table). Dining is at simply
dressed tables wedged beneath bottle-
lined walls, and fare is market-driven.

L'AGRUME French, Bistro €€
(Map p188; ☎ 01 43 31 86 48; 15 rue des
Fossés St-Marcel, 5e; mains €30, lunch menus
€14 & €16, dinner menu €35; ◷ Tue-Sat;

Café Marly

OLIVER STREWE/LONELY PLANET IMAGES ©

Censier–Daubenton) Lunching at this pocket-sized contemporary bistro is magnificent value and a real gourmet experience. Watch chefs work with seasonal products in the open kitchen while you dine; reserve several days ahead.

St-Germain, Odéon & Luxembourg

There's far more to this fabled pocket of Paris than the literary cafes of Sartre or the picnicking turf of Jardin de Luxembourg.

LE COMPTOIR DU RELAIS
French, bistro €€€
(Map p198; ☎01 44 27 07 97; 9 Carrefour de l'Odéon, 6e; dinner menus €50; MOdéon) The culinary handiwork of top chef Yves Camdeborde, this gourmet bistro serves seasonal dishes with a creative twist. Bagging a table without an advance reservation at lunchtime is doable providing you arrive sharp at 12.30pm, but forget more gastronomic evening dining without a reservation (weeks in advance for weekends).

QUATREHOMMES
Cheese Shop €
(Map p188; 62 rue de Sèvres, 6e; MVanneau) Buy the best of every French cheese at this king of *fromageries* (cheese shops).

BOUILLON RACINE Classical French €€
(Map p198; ☎01 44 32 15 60; 3 rue Racine, 6e; lunch/dinner menus €14.90/29.50; MCluny–La Sorbonne) This 'soup kitchen' built in 1906 to feed city workers is an art nouveau palace. Age-old recipes such as roast snails, *caille confite* (preserved quail) and lamb shank with liquorice inspire the menu.

Eiffel Tower Area & 16e

The museum- and monument-rich 16e arrondissement has some fine dines too.

CAFÉ CONSTANT
French, Contemporary €€
(Map p188; www.cafeconstant.com, in French; 139 rue Ste-Dominique, 7e; mains €16; ⊗Tue-Sun; MÉcole Militaire or Port de l'Alma) Take a former Michelin-starred chef, a simple corner cafe and what do you get? A Christian Constant hit with original mosaic floor, wooden tables and a queue out the door at every meal. It doesn't take reservations, so sample the bar while you wait.

LES COCOTTES
French, Concept €€
(Map p188; www.leviolondingres.com; 135 rue Ste-Dominique, 7e; starters/cocottes & mains/desserts €11/16/7; ⊗Mon-Sat; MÉcole

Militaire or Port de l'Alma) *Cocottes* are casseroles and that is what this chic space – jam-packed day and night – is all about. Get here sharp at noon or 7.15pm (or before) to get a table; no reservations.

Montparnasse

Since the 1920s, Montparnasse has been one of Paris' premier avenues for enjoying cafe life, though younger Parisians deem the quarter démodé (out of fashion) these days.

JADIS
French, Bistro €€€

(Map p188; ☎ 01 45 57 73 20; www.bistrot-jadis .com, in French; 202 rue de la Croix Nivert, 15e; lunch menus €25 & €32, dinner menus €45 & €65; ☺ Mon-Fri; M Boucicaut) This neo-bistro is one of Paris' most raved about. Traditional French dishes pack a modern punch thanks to rising-star chef Guillaume Delage, who dares to do things like braise pork cheeks in beer and use black rice instead of white.

LE DÔME
Historic Brasserie €€€

(Map p198; ☎ 01 43 35 25 81; 108 blvd du Montparnasse, 14e; starters/mains €20/40; M Vavin) A 1930s art deco extravaganza, the Dome is a monumental place for a meal of the formal white-tablecloth and bow-tied waiter variety. Stick with the basics at this historical venue and end on a high with *millefeuille* – a decadent extravaganza not to be missed.

Étoile & Champs-Élysées

The 8e arrondissement around the Champs-Élysées is known for its big-name chefs (Alain Ducasse, Pierre Gagnaire, Guy Savoy) and culinary icons (Taillevent), but there are all sorts of under-the-radar restaurants scattered in the backstreets where Parisians who live and work in the area dine.

BISTROT DU SOMMELIER
French €€€

(Map p188; ☎ 01 42 65 24 85; www.bistrotdu sommelier.com; 97 blvd Haussmann, 8e; lunch menus €33, incl wine €43, dinner menus €65-110; ☺ Mon-Fri; M St-Augustin) The whole point of this attractive eatery is to match wine with food, aided by one of the world's foremost sommeliers, Philippe Faure-Brac.

LE HIDE
French €€

(Map p188; ☎ 01 45 74 15 81; www.lehide.fr; 10 Rue du Général Lanrezac, 17e; menus €22 & €29; ☺ lunch Mon-Fri, dinner Mon-Sat; M Charles de Gaulle-Étoile) A reader favourite, Le Hide is a tiny neighbourhood bistro serving scrumptious traditional French fare: snails, baked shoulder of lamb, monkfish in lemon butter.

FROMAGERIE ALLÉOSSE
Cheese Shop €

(Map p188; 13 rue Poncelet, 17e; M Ternes) This is the best cheese shop in Paris, well worth a trip across town.

Top Five Food Markets

○ **Marché Bastille** (Map p198; blvd Richard Lenoir, 11e; ☺ 7am-2.30pm Thu & Sun; M Bastille or Richard Lenoir) Paris' best outdoor food market.

○ **Marché Belleville** (Map p188; blvd de Belleville btwn rue Jean-Pierre Timbaud & rue du Faubourg du Temple, 11e & 20e; ☺ 7am-2.30pm Tue & Fri; M Belleville or Couronnes) Fascinating entry into the large, vibrant communities of the eastern neighbourhoods, home to artists, students and immigrants from Africa, Asia and the Middle East.

○ **Marché Couvert St-Quentin** (Map p188; 85 blvd de Magenta, 10e; ☺ 8am-1pm & 3.30-7.30pm Tue-Sat, 8.30am-1pm Sun; M Gare de l'Est) Iron-and-glass covered market built in 1866, lined with gourmet food stalls.

○ **Rue Cler** (Map p188; rue Cler, 7e; ☺ 8am-7pm Tue-Sat, 8am-noon Sun; M École Militaire) Commercial street market with an almost party-like atmosphere at weekends.

○ **Rue Mouffetard** (Map p188; rue Mouffetard; ☺ 8am-7.30pm Tue-Sat, 8am-noon Sun; M Censier–Daubenton) The city's most photogenic market street.

Gourmet Glacier

Berthillon (Map p198; 31 rue St-Louis en l'Île, 4e; ice creams €2.10-5.40; ⏱10am-8pm Wed-Sun; Ⓜ Pont Marie) on Île St-Louis is the place to head to for Paris' finest ice cream. There are 70 flavours to choose from, ranging from fruity cassis to chocolate, coffee, *marrons glacés* (candied chestnuts), *Agenaise* (Armagnac and prunes), *noisette* (hazelnut) and *nougat au miel* (honey nougat).

Opéra & Grands Boulevards

The neon-lit area around blvd Montmartre forms one of the Right Bank's most animated cafe and dining districts.

LE ROI DU POT AU FEU

French, Bistro €€

(Map p188; 34 rue Vignon, 9e; menus €24-29; ⏱noon-10.30pm Mon-Sat; Ⓜ Havre–Caumartin) The typical Parisian bistro atmosphere adds to the charm of the 'King of Hotpots', but what you really come here for is its pot-au-feu (beef, root vegetable and herb stew), the stock as starter and the meat and veg as main. No bookings.

Chartier French, Bistro €
(Map p188; ☎01 47 70 86 29; www.restaurant-chartier.com; 7 rue du Faubourg Montmartre, 9e; menus with wine €19.40; Ⓜ Grands Boulevards) Chartier started life as a *bouillon* (soup kitchen) in 1896 and is a real belle époque gem. For a taste of old-fashioned Paris, it's unbeatable. No reservations.

Le J'Go Southwest French €€
(Map p188; ☎01 40 22 09 09; www.lejgo.com; 4 rue Drouot, 9e; menus €15-20; ⏱lunch Mon-Fri, dinner Mon-Sat; Ⓜ Richelieu–Drouot) This contemporary, Toulouse-style bistro magics diners away to southwestern France with every bite.

Montmartre & Pigalle

You'll still find some decent eateries in Montmartre, but beware the tourist traps.

Chez Toinette French €€
(Map p188; ☎01 42 54 44 36; 20 rue Germain Pilon, 18e; mains €17-22; ⏱dinner Mon-Sat; Ⓜ Abbesses) Chez Toinette keeps alive the tradition of old Montmartre with its simplicity and culinary expertise. Partridge, doe and duck are house specialities.

Le Café qui Parle French €€
(Map p188; ☎01 46 06 06 88; 24 rue Caulaincourt, 18e; menus €12.50 & €17; ⏱Mon-Sat, lunch Sun; 📶Ⓜ Lamarck–Caulaincourt or Blanche) We love the Talking Cafe's wall art and ancient safes below (the building was once a bank), but not as much as we love its weekend brunch (€17).

 # Drinking

The line between bars, cafes and bistros is blurred at best. And pricing is blurred most of all. Sitting at a table costs more than standing at the counter, more on a fancy square than a backstreet, more in the 8e than in the 18e. After 10pm many cafes also charge a pricier *tarif de nuit* (night rate).

Louvre & Les Halles

Le Fumoir Cocktail Bar
(Map p198; 6 rue de l'Amiral Coligny, 1er; ⏱11am-2am; Ⓜ Louvre–Rivoli) The 'Smoking Room' is a huge, stylish colonial-style bar-cafe opposite the Louvre – a fine place to sip top-notch gin while nibbling on olives.

Le Cochon à l'Oreille Bar, Cafe
(Map p198; 15 rue Montmartre, 1er; ⏱10am-11pm Tue-Sat; Ⓜ Les Halles or Étienne Marcel) A Parisian jewel, this heritage-listed hole-in-the-wall retains its belle époque tiles with market scenes of Les Halles, and just eight tiny tables.

Marais & Bastille

LE PURE CAFÉ

Cafe

(Map p188; 14 rue Jean Macé, 11e; ⏱7am-2am; Ⓜ Charonne) This old cafe moonlights as restaurant, but we like it as it was intended to be, especially over a *grand crème* (large white coffee) and the papers on Sunday morning.

Le Bistrot du Peintre
Wine Bar

(Map p188; 116 av Ledru-Rollin, 11e; ⏰8am-2am; Ⓜ Bastille) Lovely belle époque bistro and wine bar, with 1902 art nouveau bar, elegant terrace and spot-on service.

La Chaise Au Plafond
Bar

(Map p198; 10 Rue du Trésor, 4e; ⏰10am-2am; ⏰Hôtel de Ville or St-Paul) The Chair on the Ceiling is peaceful, warm and has a terrace – an oasis from the frenzy of the Marais and worth knowing about in summer.

Latin Quarter & Jardin des Plantes

CURIO PARLOR COCKTAIL CLUB
Cocktail Bar

(Map p198; 16 rue des Bernardins, 5e; ⏰7pm-2am Tue-Thu, 7pm-4am Fri & Sat; Ⓜ Maubert–Mutualité) This hybrid bar-club looks to the interwar *années folles* (crazy years) of 1920s Paris, London and New York for inspiration.

St-Germain, Odéon & Luxembourg

Au Sauvignon
Wine Bar

(Map p198; 80 rue des Sts-Pères, 7e; ⏰8am-midnight; Ⓜ Sèvres-Babylone) To savour this 1950s wine bar, order a plate of *casse-croûtes au pain Poilâne* – sandwiches made with the city's famous bread.

Prescription Cocktail Club
Cocktail Club

(Map p198; 23 rue Mazarine, 6e; ⏰7pm-2am Mon-Thu, 7pm-4am Fri & Sat; Ⓜ Odéon) With bowler and flat-top hats as lampshades and a 1930s speakeasy New York air to the place, this cocktail club is Parisian-cool.

Café La Palette
Historic Cafe

(Map p198; 43 rue de Seine, 6e; ⏰8am-2am Mon-Sat; Ⓜ Mabillon) In the heart of gallery land, this cafe where Cézanne and Braque drank attracts fashionable people and art dealers. Its summer terrace is as beautiful.

Les Deux Magots
Historic Cafe

(Map p198; www.lesdeuxmagots.fr; 170 blvd St-Germain, 6e; ⏰7am-1am; Ⓜ St-Germain des Prés) St-Germain's most famous, where Sartre, Hemingway and Picasso hung out.

Opéra & Grands Boulevards

Harry's New York Bar
American Bar

(Map p188; 5 rue Daunou, 2e; ⏰10.30am-4am; Ⓜ Opéra) Lean upon the bar where F Scott Fitzgerald and Ernest Hemingway drank and gossiped, while white-smocked waiters mix killer martinis and Bloody Marys.

Au Limonaire
Wine Bar

(Map p188; ☎01 45 23 33 33; http://limonaire .free.fr; 18 cité Bergère, 9e; ⏰7pm-midnight Mon, 6pm-midnight Tue-Sun; Ⓜ Grands Boulevards) This little wine bar is one of the best places to listen to traditional French *chansons* (songs) and local singer-song-writers. Reservations recommended.

Dining at Les Deux Magots

Montmartre & Pigalle

La Fourmi Bar
(Map p188; 74 rue des Martyrs, 18e; ⏱8am-
2am Mon-Thu, to 4am Fri & Sat, 10am-2am Sun;
Ⓜ Pigalle) A Pigalle stayer, 'the Ant' always
hits the mark: hip but not snobby, with
a laid-back crowd and a rock-oriented
playlist.

 Entertainment

To find out what's on, surf **Figaroscope**
(www.figaroscope.fr) or buy *Pariscope*
(€0.40) or *Officiel des Spectacles* (€0.35;
www.offi.fr, in French) at Parisian news
kiosks. *Billeteries* (ticket offices) in **Fnac**
(www.fnacspectacles.com, in French) and **Virgin
Megastores** (www.virginmega.fr, in French) sell
tickets.

Come on the day of a scheduled
performance to snag a half-price ticket
(plus €3 commission) for ballet, theatre,
opera etc at discount-ticket outlet
Kiosque Théâtre Madeleine (Map p188;
www.kiosquetheatre.com; opp 15 place de la
Madeleine, 8e; ⏱12.30-8pm Tue-Sat, to 4pm
Sun; Ⓜ Madeleine).

Live Music

Salle Pleyel Classical
(Map p188; 📞01 42 56 13 13; www.sallepleyel
.fr; 252 rue du Faubourg St-Honoré, 8e; concert
tickets €10-85; ⏱box office noon-7pm Mon-Sat,
to 8pm on day of performance; Ⓜ Ternes) Dating
from the 1920s, this highly regarded hall
hosts many of Paris' finest classical-
music events, including concerts by the
Orchestre de Paris (www.orchestrede
paris.com, in French).

LE VIEUX BELLEVILLE French Chansons
(Map p188; 📞01 44 62 92 66; www.le-vieux
-belleville.com; 12 rue des Envierges, 20e;
admission free; ⏱performances 8pm Thu-Sat;
Ⓜ Pyrénées) This old-fashioned bistro
at the top of Parc de Belleville is an
atmospheric venue for performances of
chansons featuring accordions and an
organ grinder three times a week. It's a
lively favourite with locals; book ahead.

Left: Galeries Lafayette at Christmas time;
Below: Berthillon ice-cream shop (p210)

PHOTOGRAPHER: (LEFT) BRUCE BI/LONELY PLANET IMAGES ©; (BELOW) JOHN SONES/LONELY PLANET IMAGES ©

LE BAISER SALÉ   Jazz
(Map p198; www.lebaisersale.com,
in French; 58 rue des Lombards, 1er;
admission free-€20; ☺5pm-6am; ☺Châtelet)
One of several clubs on this street, the
Salty Kiss hosts jazz, Afro and Latin jazz
and jazz fusion gigs, and is known for
finding new talents.

La Cigale   Rock, Jazz
(Map p188; ☎01 49 25 81 75; www.lacigale
.fr; 120 blvd de Rochechouart, 18e; admission
€25-60; Ⓜ Anvers or Pigalle) Now classed as
a historical monument, this music hall
dates from 1887 but was redecorated
100 years later by Philippe Starck.

 **Shopping**

Key areas to mooch with no particular
purchase in mind are the maze of lanes
in the Marais (3e and 4e), around St-
Germain des Prés (6e), and in Montmartre and Pigalle (9e and 18e). Or perhaps
you have something specific to buy?

Designer haute couture The world's most
famous designers stylishly jostle for window
space on Av Montaigne, av Georges V and rue
du Faubourg St-Honoré, 8e.

Chain-store fashion Find Gap, H&M, Zara and
other major, super-sized chain stores on Rue de
Rivoli in the 1er, Les Halles in the 2e, and av des
Champs-Élysées, 8e.

Department stores On and around Blvd
Haussmann, 9e, including Paris' famous
Galeries Lafayette at No 40 and
Printemps at No 64.

Hip fashion & art Young designers crowd
Rue Charlot, 3e, and beyond in the northern
Marais.

Fine art & antiques Right Bank place des
Vosges, 4e, and Left Bank Carré Rive Gauche, 6e.

Design Eames, eat your heart out! Boutique
galleries specialising in modern furniture,
art and design (1950s to present) stud rue
Mazarine and rue de Seine, 6e.

Flea Markets

○ **Marché aux Puces de Montreuil**
(av du Professeur André Lemière, 20e; ⏰8am-7.30pm Sat-Mon; Ⓜ Porte de Montreuil) This flea-market is particularly known for its secondhand clothing, designer seconds, engravings, jewellery, linen, crockery and old furniture.

○ **Marché aux Puces de St-Ouen**
(rue des Rosiers, av Michelet, rue Voltaire, rue Paul Bert & rue Jean-Henri Fabre, 18e; ⏰9am-6pm Sat, 10am-6pm Sun, 11am-5pm Mon; Ⓜ Porte de Clignancourt) Around since the late 19th century and said to be Europe's largest.

○ **Marché aux Puces de la Porte de Vanves** (Map p188; av Georges Lafenestre & av Marc Sangnier, 14e; ⏰7am-6pm or later Sat & Sun; Ⓜ Porte de Vanves) The smallest and, some say, friendliest of the trio.

ℹ Information

Dangers & Annoyances

For safety, metro stations best avoided late at night include: Châtelet–Les Halles and its seemingly endless corridors; Château Rouge in Montmartre; Gare du Nord; Strasbourg–St-Denis; Réaumur–Sébastopol; and Montparnasse Bienvenüe.

Pickpocketing and thefts from handbags and packs is a problem wherever there are crowds (especially of tourists).

Discunt Cards

Paris Museum Pass (www.parismuseumpass. fr; 2/4/6 days €32/48/64) Valid for some 38 sights including the Louvre, Centre Pompidou, Musée d'Orsay, St-Denis basilica, parts of Versailles and Fontainebleau. Buy it online, from the Paris Convention & Visitors Bureau (p214), Fnac outlets, major metro stations and all participating venues.

Tourist Information

Paris Convention & Visitors Bureau (www. parisinfo.com; 25-27 rue des Pyramides, 1er; Ⓜ Pyramides; ⏰9am-7pm Jun-Oct, 10am-7pm Mon-Sat & 11am-7pm Sun Nov-May) Main tourist office, with a clutch of smaller centres elsewhere in the city.

ℹ Getting There & Away

Air

Aéroport d'Orly (ORY; ☎39 50, 01 70 36 39 50; www.aeroportsdeparis.fr) Older and smaller of Paris' two major airports, 18km south of the city.
Aéroport Roissy Charles de Gaulle (CDG; ☎39 50, 01 70 36 39 50; www.aeroportsdeparis.fr) Three terminal complexes – Aérogare 1, 2 and 3 – 30km northeast of Paris in the suburb of Roissy.
Aéroport Beauvais (BVA; ☎08 92 68 20 66; www.aeroportbeauvais.com) Located 80km north of Paris; used by charter companies and budget airlines.

Train

Paris has six major train stations.

Gare d'Austerlitz (blvd de l'Hôpital, 13e; Ⓜ Gare d'Austerlitz) Trains to/from Spain and Portugal; Loire Valley and non-TGV trains to southwestern France (eg Bordeaux and Basque Country).

Gare de l'Est (blvd de Strasbourg, 10e; Ⓜ Gare de l'Est) Trains to/from Luxembourg, parts of Switzerland (Basel, Lucerne, Zurich), southern Germany (Frankfurt, Munich) and points further east; regular and TGV Est trains to areas of France east of Paris (Champagne, Alsace and Lorraine).

Gare de Lyon (blvd Diderot, 12e; Ⓜ Gare de Lyon) Trains to/from parts of Switzerland (eg Bern, Geneva, Lausanne), Italy and points beyond; regular and TGV Sud-Est and TGV Midi-Méditerranée trains to areas southeast of Paris, including Dijon, Lyon, Provence, the Côte d'Azur and the Alps.

Gare Montparnasse (av du Maine & blvd de Vaugirard, 15e; Ⓜ Montparnasse–Bienvenüe) Trains to/from Brittany and places en route from Paris (eg Chartres, Angers, Nantes); TGV Atlantique Ouest and TGV Atlantique Sud-Ouest trains to Tours, Nantes, Bordeaux and other destinations in southwestern France.

Gare du Nord (rue de Dunkerque, 10e; M Gare du Nord) Trains to/from the UK, Belgium, northern Germany, Scandinavia, Moscow etc (terminus of the high-speed Thalys trains to/from Amsterdam, Brussels, Cologne and Geneva and Eurostar to London); trains to the northern suburbs of Paris and northern France, including TGV Nord trains to Lille and Calais.

Gare St-Lazare (rue St-Lazare & rue d'Amsterdam, 8e; M St-Lazare) Normandy (eg Dieppe, Le Havre, Cherbourg).

Getting Around

To/From the Airports

Bus drivers sell tickets. Children aged four to nine years pay half-price on most services.

AÉROPORT D'ORLY

Air France bus 1 (0 892 350 820; http://videocdn.airfrance.com/cars-airfrance; single/return €11.50/18.50; 6.15am-11.150pm from Orly, 6am-11.30pm from Invalides) This *navette* (shuttle bus) runs every 30 minutes to/from Gare Montparnasse (rue du Commandant René Mouchotte, 15e; M Montparnasse–Bienvenüe) and Aérogare des Invalides (M Invalides) in the 7e.

Orlybus (32 46; www.ratp.fr; adult €6.60; 6am-11.20pm from Orly, 5.35am-11.05pm from Paris) RATP bus every 15 to 20 minutes to/from metro Denfert-Rochereau (20 to 30 minutes) in the 14e.

Orlyval (32 46; www.ratp.fr; adult €10.25; 6am-11pm) This RATP service links Orly with the city centre via a shuttle train and the RER. Automatic rail (€7.60) to the RER B station Antony, then RER B4 north (€2.35; 35 to 40 minutes to Châtelet, every four to 12 minutes).

RER C & shuttle (32 46; www.ratp.fr; adult €6.20; 5.30am-11.30pm) Shuttle bus every 15 to 30 minutes to RER line C station, Pont de Rungis–Aéroport d'Orly RER station, then RER C2 train to Paris' Gare d'Austerlitz (50 minutes).

AÉROPORT ROISSY CHARLES DE GAULLE

Air France bus 2 (0 892 350 820; http://videocdn.airfrance.com/cars-airfrance; single/return €15/24; 5.45am-11pm) Links airport every 30 minutes with the Arc de Triomphe outside 1 av Carnot, 17e (45 minutes), and Porte Maillot metro station, 17e (35 to 50 minutes).

Air France bus 4 (0 892 350 820; http://videocdn.airfrance.com/cars-airfrance; adult single/return €16.50/27; 7am-9pm from Roissy Charles de Gaulle, 6.30am-9.30pm from Paris) Links airport every 30 minutes with **Gare de Lyon** (20bis blvd Diderot, 12e; M Gare de Lyon) and **Gare Montparnasse** (rue du Commandant René Mouchotte, 15e; M Montparnasse–Bienvenüe).

RATP bus 350 (32 46; www.ratp.fr; adult €5.10 or 3 metro tickets 5.30am-11pm) Every 30 minutes to/from Gare de l'Est and Gare du Nord (both one hour).

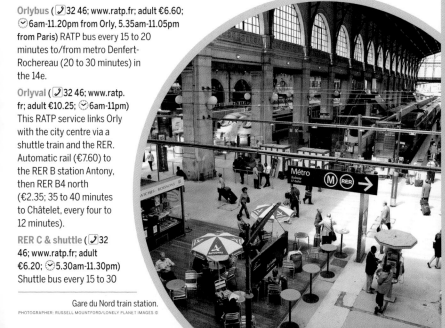

Gare du Nord train station.

BETHUNE CARMICHAEL/LONELY PLANET IMAGES ©

Don't Miss **Versailles**

The prosperous and leafy suburb of Versailles, 28km southwest of Paris, is the site of France's grandest and most famous chateau.

Dodge the worst of the crowds by visiting early morning or late afternoon, and buy your ticket in advance online (www.chateauversailles.fr) or from Fnac. Queues are longest on Tuesday (when many of Paris' museums are closed) and on Sunday.

Château de Versailles (www.chateauversailles.fr; adult/child & EU resident under 26yr €15/free; 9am-6.30pm Tue-Sun summer, 9am-5.30pm Tue-Sun winter) was built in the mid-17th century by Louis XIV to project the absolute power of the French monarchy.

The 580m-long palace is split into several wings, each with its own array of grand halls, wood-panelled corridors and sumptuous bedchambers, including the **Grand Appartement du Roi** (King's Suite) and **Galerie des Glaces** (Hall of Mirrors). Outside the main palace are vast **landscaped gardens**, filled with canals and pools, and two outbuildings, the **Grand Trianon** and the **Petit Trianon**.

Standard admission includes an English-language audioguide and entry to the state apartments, the chapel, **Appartements du Dauphin et de la Dauphine** and various galleries. A **Passeport** (adult/child & EU resident under 26yr €18-25/free) includes the same, plus the two Trianons and, in high season, the Hameau de la Reine and the Grandes Eaux Musicales fountain displays.

The current €400 million restoration project is Versailles' most ambitious yet and until 2020 at least a part of the palace is likely to be clad in scaffolding.

The palace gardens' largest fountains are the 17th-century **Bassin de Neptune** (Neptune's Fountain), a dazzling mirage of 99 spouting gushers 300m north of the palace. Watch them 'dance' in all their glory during summer's **Grandes Eaux Musicales** (adult/child €8/6; 11am-noon & 3.30-5pm Tue, Sat & Sun Apr-Sep) or after-dark **Grandes Eaux Nocturnes** (adult/child €21/17; 9-11.30pm Sat & Sun mid-Jun–Aug).

RER B (📞32 46; www.ratp.fr; adult €8.70; 🕐5.20am-midnight) Under extensive renovation at the time of research, with replacement buses on duty; RER line B3 usually links CDG1 and CDG2 with the city every 10 to 15 minutes (30 minutes).

Roissybus (📞32 46; www.ratp.fr; adult €9.40; 🕐5.30am-11pm) Direct bus every 30 minutes to/from **Opéra** (cnr rue Scribe & rue Auber, 9e).

AÉROPORT PARIS-BEAUVAIS

Navette Officielle (Official Shuttle Bus; 📞0 892 682 064, airport 0 892 682 066; adult €14) Leaves Parking Pershing, west of the Palais des Congrès de Paris, 3¼ hours before flight departures (board 15 minutes before) and leaves the airport 20 minutes after arrivals, dropping passengers south of the Palais des Congrès on place de la Porte Maillot. Journey time 1¼ hours.

Bicycle

Vélib' (www.velib.paris.fr; day/week subscription €1/5, bike hire per 1st/2nd/additional 30min free/€2/4) With this self-service bike scheme you can pick up a pearly-grey bike for peanuts from one roadside Vélib' station and drop it off at another. Its almost 1500 bike stations are accessible around the clock.

Boat

Batobus (📞08 25 05 01 01; www.batobus.com; adult 1-/2-/3-day pass €13/17/20; 🕐10am-9.30pm May-Aug, shorter hr rest of year) A fleet of glassed-in trimarans dock at eight small piers along the Seine; buy tickets at each stop or tourist offices, and jump on and off as you like.

Car & Motorcycle

If driving a car in Paris doesn't destroy your holiday sense of spontaneity, parking will.

Street parking in central Paris is limited to two hours (€1.50 to €3 per hour); to pay, buy a Paris Carte worth €10 or €30 at *tabacs* (tobacconists). Municipal car parks cost €2 to €3.50 per hour or around €25 per 24 hours.

Public Transport

Paris' public transit system is operated by the **RATP** (www.ratp.fr). The same RATP tickets are valid on the metro, RER, buses, trams and Montmartre funicular. A single ticket/*carnet* of 10 costs €1.70/12.

BUS Paris' regular bus system runs from 5.30am to 8.30pm Monday to Saturday, after which certain *service en soirée* (evening service) lines continue until midnight or 12.30am, when **Noctilien** (www.noctilien.fr) night buses, which depart every hour between 12.30am and 5.30am, kick in.

Remember to cancel (*oblitérer*) single-journey tickets in the *composteur* (cancelling machine) next to the driver.

METRO & RER Paris' underground network consists of the 14-line metro and the RER, a network of suburban train lines. The last metro train on each line begins sometime between 12.35am and 1.04am, before starting up again around 5.30am.

TOURIST PASSES The Mobilis card allows tourists unlimited travel for one day in two to six zones (€5.90 to €16.70) on the metro, the RER, buses, trams and the Montmartre funicular; while the Paris Visite pass allows you unlimited travel (including to/from airports) plus discounted entry to museums and activities. The pass will cost you €8.80/14.40/19.60/28.30 for one to three zones for one/two/three/five days.

Taxi

The flag fall is €2.10, plus €0.89 per kilometre within the city limits from 10am and 5pm Monday to Saturday (Tarif A; white light on meter), and €1.14 per kilometre from 5pm to 10am, all day Sunday, and public holidays (Tarif B; orange light on meter).

Central taxi switchboard (📞01 45 30 30 30)

Alpha Taxis (📞01 45 85 85 85; www.alpha taxis.com)

Taxis Bleus (📞01 49 36 29 48, 08 91 70 10 10; www.taxis-bleus.com)

AROUND PARIS

Bordered by five rivers – the Epte, Aisne, Eure, Yonne and Marne – the area around Paris looks rather like a giant island, and indeed is known as Île de France. Centuries ago this was where French kings retreated from hectic city life to their extravagant chateaux in Versailles and Fontainebleau.

Versailles

A Day in Court

Visiting Versailles – even just the State Apartments – may seem overwhelming at first, but think of it as a house where people ate, drank, worked, slept and conspired and you'll be on the right path.

Some two decades into his long reign, Louis XIV began turning his father's hunting lodge into a palace large enough to house his entire court (to keep closer tabs on the 6000-strong army of courtiers). Sparing no expense, the Sun King employed the greatest artists and craftspeople of the day and by 1682 he'd created the most extravagant dormitory in history.

The royal schedule was as accurate and predictable as a Swiss watch. By following this itinerary of rooms you can recreate the king's day, starting with the **King's Bedchamber** ❶ and the Queen's Bedchamber ❷, where the royal couple were roused at about the same time. The royal procession then leads through the **Hall of Mirrors** ❸ to the **Royal Chapel** ❹ for morning Mass and returns to the **Council Chamber** ❺ for late-morning meetings with ministers. After lunch the king might ride or hunt or visit the **King's Library** ❻. Later he could join courtesans for an 'apartment evening' starting from the **Hercules Drawing Room** ❼ or play billiards in the Diana **Drawing Room** ❽ before supping at 10pm.

Queen's Bedchamber
Chambre de la Reine
The queen's life was on constant public display and even the births of her children were watched by crowds of spectators in her own bedchamber. **DETOUR »** The Guardroom, with a dozen armed men at the ready.

Lunch Break

Diner-style food at Sister's Café, crêpes at Le Phare St-Louis or picnic in the park.

Guardroom

South Wing

King's Library
Bibliothèque du Roi
The last resident, bibliophile Louis XVI, loved geography and his copy of *The Travels of James Cook* (in English, which he read fluently) is still on the shelf here.

Savvy Sightseeing

Avoid Versailles on Monday (closed), Tuesday (Paris' museums close, so visitors flock here) and Sunday, the busiest day. Also, book tickets online so you don't have to queue.

VERSAILLES BY NUMBERS

Rooms 700 (11 hectares of roof)

Windows 2153

Staircases 67

Gardens and parks 800 hectares

Trees 200,000

Fountains 50 (with 620 nozzles)

Paintings 6300 (measuring 11km laid end to end)

Statues and sculptures 2100

Objets d'art and furnishings 5000

Visitors 5.3 million per year

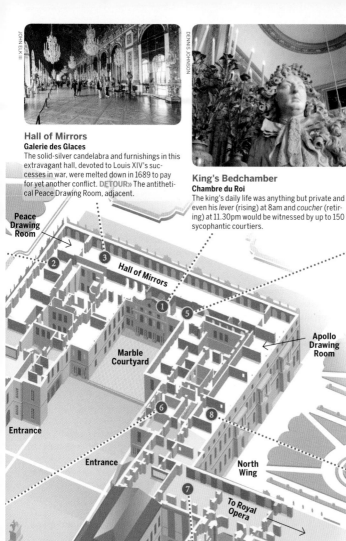

Hall of Mirrors
Galerie des Glaces
The solid-silver candelabra and furnishings in this extravagant hall, devoted to Louis XIV's successes in war, were melted down in 1689 to pay for yet another conflict. DETOUR» The antithetical Peace Drawing Room, adjacent.

King's Bedchamber
Chambre du Roi
The king's daily life was anything but private and even his *lever* (rising) at 8am and *coucher* (retiring) at 11.30pm would be witnessed by up to 150 sycophantic courtiers.

Council Chamber
Cabinet du Conseil
This chamber, with carved medallions evoking the king's work, is where the monarch met his various ministers (state, finance, religion etc) depending on the days of the week.

Peace Drawing Room

Hall of Mirrors

Marble Courtyard

Entrance

Entrance

Apollo Drawing Room

North Wing

To Royal Opera

Diana Drawing Room
Salon de Diane
With walls and ceiling covered in frescos devoted to the mythical huntress, this room contained a large billiard table reserved for Louis XIV, a keen player.

Royal Chapel
Chapelle Royale
This two-storey chapel (with gallery for the royals and important courtiers, and the ground floor for the B-list) was dedicated to St Louis, patron of French monarchs. DETOUR» The sumptuous Royal Opera.

Hercules Drawing Room
Salon d'Hercule
This salon, with its stunning ceiling fresco of the strong man, gave way to the State Apartments, which were open to courtiers three nights a week. DETOUR» Apollo Drawing Room, used for formal audiences and as a throne room.

Disneyland Paris

In 1992, Mickey Mouse, Snow White and chums set up shop on reclaimed sugar-beet fields 32km east of Paris at a cost of €4.6 billion.

The main **Disneyland Park** (⏱9am-11pm summer, 10am-8pm Mon-Fri, 9am-8pm Sat & Sun winter) comprises five *pays* (lands), including an idealised version of an American **Main St**, a recreation of the American Wild West in **Frontierland** with the legendary Big Thunder Mountain ride, futuristic **Discoveryland**, and the exotic-themed **Adventureland**, where you'll find the Pirates of the Caribbean and the spiralling 360-degrees roller coaster, Indiana Jones and the Temple of Peril. Pinocchio, Snow White and other fairy-tale characters come to life in candy-coated heart of the park, **Fantasyland**.

Adjacent **Walt Disney Studios Park** (⏱9am-6pm summer, 10am-6pm Mon-Fri, 9am-6pm Sat & Sun winter) has a sound stage, backlot and animation studios illustrating how films, TV programs and cartoons are produced.

Standard admission fees at **Disneyland Resort Paris** (www.disneylandparis.com; adult/child €52/44) cover only one park – to visit both buy a one-day pass costing €65/57 per adult/child.

Marne-la-Vallée–Chessy, Disneyland's RER station, is served by line A4; trains run every 15 minutes or so from central Paris (€6.55, 35 to 40 minutes) with the last train back to Paris just after midnight. By car follow route A4 from Porte de Bercy (direction Metz-Nancy) and take exit 14.

🛈 Getting There & Away

RER line C5 (€2.95, every 15 minutes) goes from Paris' Left Bank RER stations to Versailles-Rive Gauche, 700m southeast of the chateau.

SNCF operates up to 70 trains daily from Paris' Gare St-Lazare (€3.70) to Versailles-Rive Droite, 1.2km from the chateau.

Chartres

POP 45,600

The 130m-long **Cathédrale Notre Dame de Chartres** (www.diocese-chartres.com, in French; place de la Cathédrale; ⏱8.30am-7.30pm daily, to 10pm Tue, Fri & Sun summer) takes your breath away. The original Romanesque cathedral was devastated in a fire in 1194, but remnants of it remain in the **Portail Royal** (Royal Portal) and the 103m-high **Clocher Vieux** (Old Bell Tower, also known as the South Tower). The rest of the cathedral predominantly dates from the 13th century, including many of the 172 glorious **stained-glass windows**, which are renowned for the depth and intensity of their 'Chartres blue' tones.

A visit up the lacy Flamboyant Gothic, 112m-tall **Clocher Neuf** (New Bell Tower; adult/child €7/free, free to all 1st Sun of certain months; ⏱9.30am-12.30pm & 2-6pm Mon-Sat,

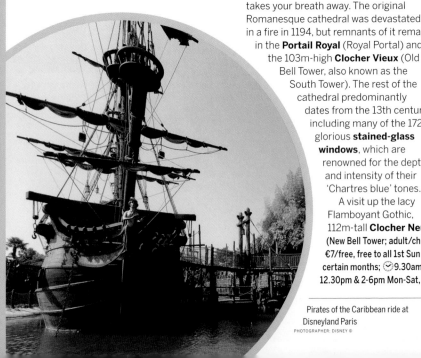

Pirates of the Caribbean ride at Disneyland Paris
PHOTOGRAPHER: DISNEY ©

Chapelle de la Vierge, Cathédrale Notre Dame, Rouen

HANNAH LEVY/LONELY PLANET IMAGES ©

2-6pm Sun summer, to 5pm winter) rewards with superb views of the three-tiered flying buttresses and the 19th-century copper roof, turned green by verdigris.

Some three dozen SNCF trains a day link Paris' Gare Montparnasse (€13.60, 55 to 70 minutes) with Chartres via Versailles-Chantiers (€11.50, 45 minutes to one hour).

NORMANDY

Famous for cows, cider and Camembert, this largely rural region (www.normandie-tourisme.fr) is one of France's most traditional – and visited thanks to such world-renowned sights as the Bayeux Tapestry, historic D-Day beaches, Monet's garden at Giverny and spectacular Mont St Michel.

Rouen

POP 120,000

With its elegant spires, beautifully restored medieval quarter and soaring Gothic cathedral, the ancient city of Rouen is a Normandy highlight. Devastated several times during the Middle Ages by fire and plague, the city was later badly damaged by WWII bombing raids, but has been meticulously rebuilt over the last six decades.

 Sights

ÉGLISE JEANNE D'ARC Church
(place du Vieux Marché) The old main thoroughfare, rue du Gros Horloge, runs from the cathedral to **place du Vieux Marché**. Dedicated in 1979, the thrillingly bizarre Église Jeanne d'Arc, with its fish-scale exterior, marks the spot 19-year-old Joan of Arc was burned at the stake in 1431.

CATHÉDRALE NOTRE DAME Cathedral
(place de la Cathédrale; 2-7pm Mon, 7.30am-7pm Tue-Sat, 8am-6pm Sun) Rouen's stunning Gothic cathedral, with its polished, brilliant-white facade, is the famous subject of a series of paintings by Monet.

MUSÉE DES BEAUX-ARTS Art Gallery
(esplanade Marcel Duchamp; adult/child €5/free; 10am-6pm Wed-Mon) In a grand structure erected in 1870, Rouen's fine-arts museum features canvases by Caravaggio, Rubens, Modigliani, Pissarro, Renoir, Sisley and several works by Monet.

221

Sleeping

Hôtel de Bourgtheroulde   Hotel   €€€
(02 35 14 50 50; www.hotelsparouen.com; 15 place de la Pucelle; r €215-380; ❄ 🤖 ♿) This stunning conversion of an old private mansion brings a dash of glamour and luxury to Rouen's hotel scene. Rooms are large and gorgeously designed and feature beautiful bathrooms.

Hôtel Dandy   Hotel   €€
(02 35 07 32 00; www.hotels-rouen.net; 93 rue Cauchoise; d €80-105; 🤖) Decorated in a grand Louis XV style, this charming place has individually designed rooms brimming with character and is passionately run by a friendly family.

Eating

LES NYMPHÉAS   Norman   €€
(02 35 89 26 69; www.lesnympheas-rouen .com, in French; 7-9 rue de la Pie; menus €30-70; Tue-Sat) Set beneath 16th-century beams, this fine restaurant gives a rich Norman twist to such dishes as farm-raised wild duck, scallops and lobster.

GILL   Gastronomic   €€
(02 35 71 16 14; www.gill.fr; 8-9 quai de la Bourse; menus €35-92; Tue-Sat) *The* place to go in Rouen for French cuisine of the highest order, served in an ultrachic, modern space. Specialities include Breton lobster, scallops with truffles, Rouen-style pigeon and, for dessert, *millefeuille à la vanille*.

LE P'TIT BEC   Bistro   €
(02 35 07 63 33; www.leptitbec.com, in French; 182 rue Eau de Robec; menus €13-15.50; lunch Mon-Sat, dinner Fri & Sat, also open dinner Tue-Thu Jun-Aug;) The down-to-earth menu here is stuffed with pasta, salads, *œufs cocottes* (eggs with grated cheese baked in cream), several vegetarian options and homemade desserts.

ℹ Information

Tourist office (02 32 08 32 40; www.rouen tourisme.com; 25 place de la Cathédrale; 9am-7pm Mon-Sat, 9.30am-12.30pm & 2-6pm Sun) Hotel reservations €3; audioguides (€5).

ℹ Getting There & Away

TRAIN From **Gare Rouen-Rive Droite** (rue Jeanne d'Arc):

Amiens €18.20, 1¼ hours, four or five daily

Caen €23.30, 1½ hours, eight to 10 daily

Dieppe €10.40, 45 minutes, up to 16 daily

Le Havre €13.60, 50 minutes, 10 to 18 daily

Paris St-Lazare €20.50, 1¼ hours, up to 25 daily

Bayeux
POP 14,350

Bayeux has become famous throughout the English-speaking world thanks to a 68m-long piece of painstakingly embroidered cloth: the 11th-century Bayeux Tapestry, whose 58 scenes vividly tell the story of the Norman invasion of England in 1066.

◎ Sights

BAYEUX TAPESTRY   Tapestry
(www.tapisserie-bayeux.fr; rue de Nesmond; admission incl audioguide €7.80; 9am-6.30pm mid-Mar–mid-Nov, to 7pm May-Aug, 9.30am-12.30pm & 2-6pm mid-Nov–mid-Mar) The world's most celebrated embroidery recounts the epic conquest of England almost a thousand years ago from an unashamedly Norman perspective. Fifty-eight scenes fill the central canvas, and smaller religious allegories and illustrations of everyday 11th-century life fill the borders. The final showdown at the Battle of Hastings is depicted in graphic fashion, complete with severed limbs and decapitated heads (along the bottom of scene 52); Halley's Comet, which blazed across the sky in 1066, appears in scene 32. Scholars believe the 68.3m-long tapestry was commissioned by Bishop Odo of Bayeux, William the Conquerer's half-brother, for the opening of Bayeux' cathedral in 1077.

MUSÉE MÉMORIAL DE LA BATAILLE DE NORMANDIE   War Museum
(Battle of Normandy Memorial Museum; blvd Fabien Ware; admission €6.50; 9.30am-6.30pm

CHRISTOPHER WOOD/LONELY PLANET IMAGES ©

Don't Miss **Maison de Claude Monet**

Monet's home for the last 43 years of his life is now the delightful **Maison et Jardins de Claude Monet** (☎ 02 32 51 28 21; www.fondation-monet.com; adult/child €6/3.50; ☉ 9.30am-6pm Apr-Oct), where you can view the Impressionist's pastel-pink house and famous gardens with lily pond, Japanese bridge draped in purple wisteria and so on. In early to late spring, daffodils, tulips, rhododendrons, wisteria and irises bloom in the flowery gardens, followed by poppies and lilies. By June, nasturtiums, roses and sweet peas are in flower, while September is the month to see dahlias, sunflowers and hollyhocks.

The gardens are in Giverny, 66km southeast of Rouen. Several trains (€10.10, 40 minutes) leave Rouen before noon; with hourly return trains between 5pm and 10pm (9pm Sat). From Paris' Gare St-Lazare two early-morning trains run to Vernon (€12.50, 50 minutes), 7km to the west of Giverny, from where **shuttle buses** (☎ 08 25 07 60 27; www.mobiregion.net; €4 return) shunt passengers to Giverny.

May-Sep, 10am-12.30pm & 2-6pm Oct-Apr)
Using well-chosen photos, as well as personal accounts from soldiers and witnesses, dioramas and a range of wartime objects, this first-rate museum offers an excellent introduction to WWII in Normandy. Don't miss the 25-minute film on the Battle of Normandy, screened in English up to five times daily. Nearby, the **Bayeux war cemetery (blvd Fabien Ware)** contains the graves of 4848 soldiers from the UK and 10 other countries (including Germany).

 **Sleeping**

CHÂTEAU DE BELLEFONTAINE

Chateau Hotel €€

(☎ 02 31 22 00 10; www.hotel-bellefontaine .com; 49 rue de Bellefontaine; d €125-150; ☎)
Swans and a bubbling brook welcome you to this majestic 18th-century chateau, surrounded by a 2-hectare private park 1.5km southeast of town. Decor mixes tradition with modernity, and the rural location couldn't be more pastoral.

DAVID TOMLINSON/LONELY PLANET IMAGES ©

Don't Miss Mont St-Michel

On a rocky island opposite the coastal town of Pontorson, the sky-scraping turrets of the abbey of **Mont St-Michel** (📞 02 33 89 80 00; www.monuments-nationaux.fr; adult/child incl guided tour €8.50/free; ⏰ 9am-7pm May-Aug, 9.30am-6pm Sep-Apr, last entry 1hr before close) provide one of France's iconic sights. The bay is notorious for fast-rising tides: at low tide the Mont is surrounded by bare sand, but six hours later, the bay and causeway may be submerged.

From the **tourist office** (📞 02 33 60 14 30; www.ot-montsaintmichel.com; ⏰ 9am-7pm Jul & Aug, 9am-12.30pm & 2-6.30pm Mon-Sat, 9am-noon & 2-6pm Sun Apr-Jun & Sep, shorter hr winter), at the base of the mount, a cobbled street winds up to the **Église Abbatiale** (Abbey Church), incorporating elements of both Norman and Gothic architecture. Other notable sights include the arched **cloître** (cloister), the barrel-roofed **réfectoire** (dining hall) and the Gothic **Salle des Hôtes** (Guest Hall), dating from 1213. A one-hour tour is included in the ticket price: English tours run hourly in summer, twice daily (11am and 3pm) in winter. In July and August, Monday to Saturday, there are illuminated *nocturnes* (night-time visits) with music from 7pm to 10pm.

Bus 6 (📞 08 00 15 00 50; www.mobi50.com, in French) links Mont St-Michel with Pontorson (€2, 13 minutes), from where there are two to three daily trains to/from Bayeux (€20.80, 1¾hr) and Cherbourg (€25.90, three hours).

 Eating

LA REINE MATHILDE Cake Shop €
(47 rue St-Martin; cakes from €2.50; ⏰ 8.30am-7.30pm Tue-Sun) A sumptuous, c 1900-style patisserie and *salon de thé* (tearoom), ideal if you're hankering for something sweet.

LA RAPIÈRE Norman €€
(📞 02 31 21 05 45; 53 rue St-Jean; menus €15-33.50; ⏰ Fri-Tue) Housed in a late 15th-century mansion held together by its original oak beams, this restaurant specialises in hearty home cooking – the *timbale de pêcheur* (fisherman's stew) is served up piping hot in a cast-iron pan.

For dessert, an excellent option is *trou normand* (apple sorbet with a dash of Calvados).

 Information

Tourist office (☏ 02 31 51 28 28; www.bayeux -bessin-tourism.com; pont St-Jean; ⏰ 9.30am- 12.30pm & 2-6pm)

 Getting There & Away

Trains link Bayeux with Caen (€5.80, 20 minutes, up to 13 daily), from where there are connections to Paris' Gare St-Lazare (€31.20, two hours) and Rouen (€22.70, 1½ hours).

D-Day Beaches

The D-Day landings, code-named 'Operation Overlord', were the largest military operation in history. Early on 6 June 1944, Allied troops stormed ashore along 80km of beaches north of Bayeux, code-named (from west to east) Utah, Omaha, Gold, Juno and Sword. The landings on D-Day – called Jour J in French – were followed by the Battle of Normandy, which ultimately led to the liberation of Europe from Nazi occupation. Memorial museums in Caen (see the boxed text, p228) and Bayeux (p222) provide a comprehensive overview, and there are many small D-Day museums dotted along the coast. For context, see www. normandiememoire.com and www.6juin1944.com.

The most brutal fighting on D-Day took place 15km northwest of Bayeux along the stretch of coastline now known as **Omaha Beach**, today a glorious stretch of fine golden sand partly lined with sand dunes and summer homes. **Circuit de la Plage d'Omaha**, trail-marked with a yellow stripe, is a self-guided tour along the beach, surveyed from

a bluff above by the huge **Normandy American Cemetery & Memorial** (www .abmc.gov; Colleville-sur-Mer; ⏰ 9am-5pm). Featured in the opening scenes of Steven Spielberg's *Saving Private Ryan*, this is the largest American cemetery in Europe.

Tours

Mémorial   Minibus
(www.memorial-caen.fr; tours €69) Excellent year-round minibus tours (four to five hours). Rates include entry to Mémorial. Book online.

Normandy Sightseeing Tours
     Walking, Bike, Minibus
(☏ 02 31 51 70 52; www.normandywebguide. com) Half-/full-day tours (€40/75) of various beaches and cemeteries.

 Getting There & Away

Bus Verts (www.busverts.fr, in French) bus 70 (two or three daily Monday to Saturday, more in summer) goes northwest from Bayeux to Colleville- sur-Mer and Omaha Beach (€2.15, 35 minutes).

WWII memorial at Omaha Beach
PHOTOGRAPHER: JOHN ELK III/LONELY PLANET IMAGES ©

Mont St-Michel

A Timeline

708 Inspired by a vision from **St Michael ①**, Bishop Aubert is compelled to 'build here and build high'.

966 Richard I, Duke of Normandy, gives the Mont to the Benedictines. The three levels of the **abbey ②** reflect their monastic hierarchy.

1017 Development of the abbey begins. Pilgrims arrive to honour the cult of St Michael. They walk barefoot across the mudflats and up the **Grande Rue ③** to be received in the almonry (now the bookshop).

1203 The monastery is burnt by the troops of Philip Augustus, who later donates money for its restoration and the Gothic 'miracle', **La Merveille ④**, is constructed.

1434 The Mont's **ramparts ⑤** and fortifications ensure it withstands the English assault during the Hundred Years War. It is the only place in northern France not to fall.

1789 After the Revolution, Monasticism is abolished and the Mont is turned into a prison. During this period the **treadmill ⑥** is built to lift up supplies.

1878 The **causeway ⑦** is created. It allows modern-day pilgrims to visit without hip-high boots, but it cuts off the flow of water and the bay silts up.

1979 The Mont is declared a Unesco World Heritage Site.

TOP TIPS

Bring a packed lunch from Pontorson to avoid the poor lunch selection on the Mont

Leave the car – it's a pleasant walk from Pontorson, with spectacular views

Pay attention to the tides – they are dangerous

Take the excellent audioguide – it tells some great stories

JOHN ELK III

Îlot de Tombelaine

Occupied by the English during the Hundred Years War, this islet is now a bird reserve. From April to July it teems with exceptional birdlife.

Treadmill
The giant treadmill was powered hamsterlike by half a dozen prisoners, who, marching two abreast, raised stone and supplies up the Mont.

The West Terrace

Chapelle St-Aubert

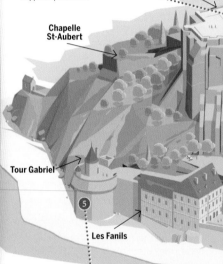

Tour Gabriel

⑤

Les Fanils

Ramparts
The Mont was also a military garrison surrounded by machicolated and turreted walls, dating from the 13th to 15th centuries. The single entrance, Porte de l'Avancée, ensured its security in the Hundred Years War. Tip: Tour du Nord (North Tower) has the best views.

ROCCO FASANO

Abbey

The abbey's three levels reflect the monastic order: monks lived isolated in church and cloister, the abbot entertained noble guests at the middle level, and lowly pilgrims were received in the basement. Tip: night visits run in July and August.

St Michael Statue & Bell Tower

A golden statue of the winged St Michael looks ready to leap heavenward from the bell tower. He is the patron of the Mont, having inspired St Aubert's original devotional chapel.

La Merveille

The highlights of La Merveille are the vast refectory hall lit through embrasured windows, the Knights Hall with its elegant ribbed vaulting, and the cloister (above), which is one of the purest examples of 13th-century architecture to survive here.

The Gardens

Église St-Pierre

Cemetery

Toilets

Tour de l'Arcade

Tourist Office

Porte de l'Avancée (Entrance)

Tour du Roi

Grande Rue

The main thoroughfare of the small village below the abbey, Grande Rue has its charm despite its rampant commercialism. Don't miss the famous Mère Poulard shop here, for souvenir cookies.

Causeway

In 2014 the causeway will be replaced by a new bridge, which will allow the water to circulate and will return the Mont to an island. Tip: join a barefoot walking tour and see the Mont as pilgrims would.

Best Views

The view from the Jardin des Plantes in nearby Avranches is unique, as are the panoramas from Pointe du Grouin du Sud near the village of St-Léonard.

Detour:
The Morbihan Megaliths

Pre-dating Stonehenge by 100 years, **Carnac** comprises the world's greatest concentration of megalithic sites. There are more than 3000 upright stones scattered between **Carnac-Ville** and **Locmariaquer** village, mostly erected between 5000 BC and 3500 BC.

Guided tours (€4) run in French year-round and in English at 3pm Wednesday, Thursday and Friday early July to late August. Sign up at the **Maison des Mégalithes** (☏ 02 97 52 89 99; rte des Alignements; ☺9am-8pm Jul & Aug, to 5.15pm Sep-Apr, to 7pm May & Jun). Opposite, the largest menhir field – with no fewer than 1099 stones – is the **Alignements du Ménec**, 1km north of Carnac-Ville. From here, the D196 heads northeast for about 1.5km to the **Alignements de Kermario**. Climb the stone observation tower midway along the site to see the alignment from above. Another 500m further on are the **Alignements de Kerlescan**, while the **Tumulus St-Michel**, 400m northeast of the Carnac-Ville tourist office, dates back to at least 5000 BC.

Caen Mémorial

Caen's hi-tech, hugely impressive **Mémorial – Un Musée pour la Paix** (Memorial – A Museum for Peace; www.memorial-caen.fr; Esplanade Général Eisenhower; adult/child €17.50/free; ☺9am-7pm Mar-Oct, 9.30am-6pm Tue-Sun Nov-Feb) uses sound, lighting, film, animation and lots of exhibits to graphically explore and evoke the events of WWII, D-Day landings and the ensuing Cold War. Tickets remain valid for 24 hours. The museum also runs D-Day beach tours (p225).

BRITTANY

Brittany is for explorers. Its wild and dramatic coastline, medieval towns, ancient thick forests and the eeriest stone circles this side of Stonehenge make a trip here well worth the detour from the beaten track.

St-Malo
POP 50,200

The mast-filled port of fortified St-Malo is inextricably tied up with the briny blue: the town became a key harbour during the 17th and 18th centuries as a base for merchant ships and government-sanctioned privateers, and these days it's a busy cross-Channel ferry port and summertime getaway.

Sights

Walking on top of the city's sturdy 17th-century ramparts (1.8km) affords fine views of the old walled city known as Intra-Muros ('within the walls') or Ville Close – access the ramparts from any of the city gates.

FORT NATIONAL   Fort
(www.fortnational.com; adult/child €5/3; ☺Easter & Jun-Sep) From the city ramparts, spot the remains of St-Malo's former prison and the rocky islet of **Île du Grand Bé**, where the great St-Malo-born 18th-century writer Chateaubriand is buried. (You can walk across at low tide, but check the tide times with the tourist office.)

AQUARIUM   Aquarium
(www.aquarium-st-malo.com; av Général Patton; adult/child €15.50/9.50; ☺10am-6pm Feb-Oct & Dec, to 8pm Jul & Aug) Allow around two hours to see St-Malo's excellent aquarium, which is located 4km south of the city centre. It's a great wet-weather alternative for kids, with a minisubmarine descent and a *bassin tactile* (touch pool), where you can get up close to rays, turbot and even a baby shark. Bus C1 from the train station passes by every half-hour.

Sleeping

HÔTEL SAN PEDRO   Hotel €

(☎ 02 99 40 88 57; www.sanpedro-hotel.com;
1 rue Ste-Anne; s €52-54, d €63-73; 🛜) Tucked
at the back of the old city, the Hôtel San Pedro
has cool, crisp, neutral-toned decor with subtle
splashes of colour, friendly service and superb
sea views.

 **Eating**

Restaurants abound between Porte
St-Vincent, the cathedral and the Grande
Porte.

RESTAURANT DELAUNAY
                    Gastronomic €€

(☎ 02 99 40 92 46; www.restaurant-delaunay
.com; 6 rue Ste-Barbe; menus €28-65; ☎ dinner
Mon-Sat, closed Mon winter) Chef Didier
Delaunay creates stand-out gastronomic
cuisine within aubergine-painted walls
at this superb address, which is sure to
please whether your personal preference
is for surf (Breton lobster's a speciality)
or turf (tender lamb).

Cliffs and mores, Brittany

LE CHALUT   Seafood €€

(☎ 02 99 56 71 58; 8 rue de la Corne-du-Cerf;
menus €25-68; ⊙ Wed-Sun) This unremarkable-
looking establishment is, in fact, St-Malo's
most celebrated restaurant.

 **Information**

Tourist office (☎ 08 25 13 52 00, 02 99 56 64
43; www.saint-malo-tourisme.com; Esplanade
St-Vincent; ⊙ 9am-7.30pm Mon-Sat, 10am-6pm
Sun Jul & Aug)

Getting There & Away

TGV train services include to/from Rennes
(€11.60, one hour) and Paris' Gare Montparnasse
(€62.40, three hours, up to 10 daily).

CHAMPAGNE

Known in Roman times as Campania,
meaning 'plain', the agricultural region
of Champagne is synonymous these
days with its world-famous bubbly. This
multimillion-dollar industry is strictly
protected under French law, ensuring
that only grapes grown in designated
Champagne vineyards can truly lay a

...

claim to the hallowed title. The town of Épernay, 30km south of the regional capital of Reims, is the best place to head for *dégustation* (tasting), and a special 'Champagne Route' wends its way through the region's most celebrated vineyards.

Reims

POP 187,650

Over the course of a millennium (816 to 1825), some 34 sovereigns – among them two dozen kings – began their reigns in Reims' famed cathedral. Meticulously reconstructed after WWI and again following WWII, the city – whose name is pronounced something like 'rance' and is often anglicised as Rheims – is endowed with handsome pedestrian zones, well-tended parks, lively nightlife and a state-of-the-art tramway.

The **Reims City Card** (€15), sold at the tourist office, gets you a tour of a Champagne house, a DIY audioguide tour of the cathedral and admission into Reims' municipal museums.

Sights

CATHÉDRALE NOTRE DAME   Church
(www.cathedrale-reims.com, in French; place du Cardinal Luçon; 7.30am-7.30pm) Begun in 1211, this cathedral served for centuries as the venue for all French royal coronations – including that of Charles VII, who was crowned here on 17 July 1429, with Joan of Arc at his side. Heavily restored since WWI, the 139m-long cathedral is a Unesco World Heritage site. Climb the 250 steps (guided tour only) of the **cathedral tower** (adult/child €7/free; at least hourly 10am-4 or 5pm Tue-Sat & Sun morning mid-Mar–Oct) for a stunning 360-degree view across France's flattest region; book tours next door at Palais du Tau.

BASILIQUE ST-RÉMI   Church
(place du Chanoine Ladame) This Benedictine abbey church, a Unesco World Heritage site, mixes Romanesque elements with early Gothic. It honours Bishop Remigius, who baptised Clovis and 3000 Frankish warriors in 498. The 12th-century-style chandelier has 96 candles, one for each year of the life of St Rémi, whose tomb lies in the choir. It's situated about 1.5km south-southeast of the tourist office.

Activities

The bottle-filled cellars (10°C to 12°C – bring a sweater!) of eight Reims-area Champagne houses can be visited by guided tour which ends, *naturellement,* with a tasting session.

MUMM   Champagne House
(www.mumm.com; 34 rue du Champ de Mars; tours €10; 9am-11am & 2-5pm Mar-Oct, Sat Nov-Feb) Mumm (pronounced 'moom'),

Basilique St-Rémi
PHOTOGRAPHER: HEMIS / ALAMY ©

founded in 1827, is the world's third-largest Champagne producer. Tours with tutored tastings of special vintages cost €15 to €20.

Taittinger Champagne House
(www.taittinger.com; 9 place St-Niçaise; tours €10; ⏰9.30-11.50am & 2pm-4.20pm, closed Sat & Sun mid-Nov–mid-Mar) Parts of these cellars, 1.5km southeast of the cathedral, occupy 4th-century Roman stone quarries; other bits were excavated by 13th-century Benedictine monks.

Sleeping

HÔTEL DE LA PAIX Hotel €€
(🖉03 26 40 04 08; www.bestwestern-lapaix-reims.com; 9 rue Buirette; d €155-205; ❄️@🛜🏊) An island of serenity just steps from hopping place Drouet d'Erlon, this modern, Best Western–affiliated hostelry has 169 classy, comfortable rooms.

HÔTEL DE LA CATHÉDRALE Hotel €
(🖉03 26 47 28 46; www.hotel-cathedrale-reims.fr; 20 rue Libergier; s/d/q from €56/59/79; 🛜) Graciousness and a resident Yorkshire terrier greet guests at this hostelry, run by a music-loving couple. Rooms, spread over four floors (no lift) are smallish but pleasingly chintzy; room 43 peeps at Basilique St-Rémi and the hills.

Eating

LE FOCH Fish €€
(🖉03 26 47 48 22; www.lefoch.com; 37 blvd Foch; menus €31-80; ⏰Tue-Fri, dinner Sat, lunch Sun) Considered by many to be one of France's best fish restaurants, elegant Le Foch – holder of one Michelin star – serves up classic cuisine that's as beautiful as it is delicious.

BRASSERIE LE BOULINGRIN
Brasserie €€
(🖉03 26 40 96 22; www.boulingrin.fr; 48 rue de Mars; menus €18-28; ⏰Mon-Sat) An old-time brasserie – the decor and zinc bar date to 1925 – whose ambience and cuisine make it an enduring favourite. September to June, the focus is *fruits de mer* (seafood).

ⓘ Information

Tourist office (www.reims-tourisme.com; 2 rue Guillaume de Machault; ⏰9am-7pm Mon-Sat, 10am-6pm Sun)

ⓘ Getting There & Away

Direct trains link Reims with Épernay (€6, 20 to 36 minutes, at least 14 daily), Laon (€9, 35 to 55 minutes, up to eight daily) and Paris' Gare de l'Est (€24, 1¾ hours, 10 to 15 daily), half of which are speedy TGVs (€32 to €41, 45 minutes).

Épernay
POP 25,225

Prosperous Épernay, 25km south of Reims, is the self-proclaimed *capitale du champagne* and home to many of the world's most celebrated Champagne houses. Beneath the town's streets, some 200 million bottles of Champagne are slowly being aged, just waiting around to be popped open for some fizz-fuelled celebration.

◎ Sights & Activities

Moët & Chandon Champagne House
(🖉03 26 51 20 20; www.moet.com; adult/child €14.50/9; 20 av de Champagne; ⏰9.30-noon & 2-4.30pm, closed Sat & Sun mid-Nov–mid-Mar, closed Jan) This prestigious *maison* offers some of the region's best cellar tours. Feeling flush? Buy a jeroboam (3L bottle) of 1998 superpremium Dom Pérignon, *millésime* (vintage Champagne) for €2100.

Mercier Champagne House
(🖉03 26 51 22 22; www.champagnemercier.com; 68-70 av de Champagne; adult/child €9/5; ⏰9.30-11.30am & 2-4.30pm, closed mid-Dec–mid-Feb) Everything here is flashy, including the 160,000L barrel that took two decades to build, the lift that transports visitors 30m underground and the laser-guided touring train.

De Castellane Champagne House
(🖉03 26 51 19 11; www.castellane.com, in French; 64 av de Champagne; adult/child €8.50/free; ⏰10-11am & 2-5pm mid-Mar-Dec, closed Jan–mid-Mar) Tours take in an informative bubbly museum, and the reward for climbing the 237 steps up the 66m-high tower (1905) is a fine panorama.

Sleeping

LE CLOS RAYMI   Historic Hotel   €€
(☎ 03 26 51 00 58; www.closraymi-hotel.com; 3 rue Joseph de Venoge; d from €100; @) Staying at this delightful three-star place is like being a personal guest of Monsieur Chandon himself, who occupied this luxurious home over a century ago. Seven romantic rooms have giant beds, 3.7m-high ceilings, ornate mouldings and parquet floors.

La Villa St-Pierre   Hotel   €
(☎ 03 26 54 40 80; www.villasaintpierre.fr; 14 av Paul Chandon; d €45-50; ☎) In an early 20th-century mansion, this homely hotel with 11 simple rooms retains much of the charm of yesteryear.

Eating

Épernay's main dining area is Rue Gambetta and adjacent place de la République.

LA CAVE À CHAMPAGNE
    French, Regional   €€
(☎ 03 26 55 50 70; www.la-cave-a-champagne .com, in French; 16 rue Gambetta; menus €17-32; ☺Thu-Mon, lunch Tue) The 'Champagne Cellar' is well regarded by locals for its *champenoise* cuisine, served in a warm, traditional, bourgeois atmosphere.

BISTROT LE 7   French   €€
(☎ 03 26 55 28 84; 13 rue des Berceaux; menus €17-23; ☺daily) One of the restaurants at Hôtel Les Berceaux has earned a Michelin star; however, the other (this one) also serves excellent French cuisine, amid semiformal, Mediterranean-chic decor.

ⓘ Information

Tourist office (☎ 03 26 53 33 00; www .ot-epernay.fr; 7 av de Champagne; ☺9.30am-12.30pm & 1.30-7pm Mon-Sat, 11am-4pm Sun, closed Sun mid-Oct–mid-Apr) Details on cellar visits, car touring and walking/cycling options. Rents GPS units (€7 per day) with DIY vineyard-driving tours in English.

Left: Church and grap wagon near vineyards, Alsace;
Below: Toasting with red wine, Lorraine

PHOTOGRAPHER: (LEFT) BARBARA VAN ZANTEN/LONELY PLANET IMAGES ©;
(BELOW) HOLGER LEUE/LONELY PLANET IMAGES ©

ⓘ Getting There & Away

Direct trains link Reims (€6.20, 20 to 36 minutes, 11 to 18 daily) and Paris' Gare de l'Est (€21, 1¼ hours, five to 10 daily).

ALSACE & LORRAINE

Alsace is a one-off cultural hybrid. With its Germanic dialect and French sense of fashion, love of foie &gras and *choucroute* (sauerkraut), fine wine *and* beer, this distinctive region often leaves you wondering quite where you are.

Strasbourg

POP 276,000

Prosperous, cosmopolitan Strasbourg (City of the Roads) is the intellectual and cultural capital of Alsace, as well as the unofficial seat of European power – the European Parliament, the Council of Europe and the European Court of Human Rights are all based here. The city's most famous landmark is its pink sandstone cathedral, towering above the restaurants, *winstubs* (traditional Alsatian eateries) and pubs of the lively old city.

Sights

GRANDE ÎLE   Old Town

With its bustling squares and upmarket shopping streets, the Grande Île – Unesco-listed since 1988 – is a paradise for the aimless ambler. Its narrow streets are especially enchanting at night, while the half-timbered buildings and flowery canals around **Petite France** on the Grande Île's southwestern corner are fairy-tale pretty. Drink in views of the River Ill and the mighty 17th-century **Barrage Vauban** (Vauban Dam), undergoing renovation at the time of reserach, from the much-photographed **Ponts Couverts** (Covered Bridges) and their trio of 13th-century towers.

233

CATHÉDRALE NOTRE-DAME   Church

(place de la Cathédrale; ⊙7am-7pm) Strasbourg's lacy, candy-coloured Gothic cathedral is one of the marvels of European architecture. Its west facade was completed in 1284, but the 142m spire wasn't finished until 1439. Inside the south entrance, the 30m-high, 16th-century **astronomical clock** (adult/child €2/free; ⊙tickets sold from 11.50am) strikes solar noon at 12.30pm, with a parade of carved wooden figures portraying the different stages of life and Jesus with his apostles.

A spiral staircase twists up to the 66m-high **platform** (adult/child €4.70/2.30; ⊙9am-7.15pm), which provides a stork's-eye view of Strasbourg.

MUSÉE D'ART MODERNE ET CONTEMPORAIN   Museum

(place Hans Jean Arp; adult/child €6/free; ⊙noon-7pm Tue, Wed & Fri, noon-9pm Thu, 10am-6pm Sat & Sun) This striking glass and steel cube showcases an outstanding collection of fine art, graphic art and photography. Kandinsky, Picasso, Magritte and Monet canvases hang out alongside curvaceous works by Strasbourg-born abstract artist Hans Jean Arp.

PALAIS ROHAN   Historic Residence

(2 place du Château; adult/child €5/free; ⊙noon-6pm Mon & Wed-Fri, 10am-6pm Sat & Sun) Hailed as a mini Versailles, this opulent 18th-century residence was built for the city's princely bishops.

Tours

Batorama   Boat

(www.batorama.fr, in French; adult/child €8.50/4.50; ⊙half-hourly 9.30am-9pm) Scenic boat trips along the storybook canals of Petite France, taking in the Vauban Dam and the glinting EU institutions. Tours depart from in front of Palais Rohan.

Cave des Hospices de Strasbourg   Wine

(www.vins-des-hospices-de-strasbourg.fr, in French; 1 place de l'Hôpital; ⊙8.30am-noon & 1.30-5.30pm Mon-Fri, 9am-12.30pm Sat) A hospice back in the days when wine was considered a cure for all ills, this brick-vaulted wine cellar produces first-rate Alsatian wines deep in the bowels of Strasbourg's hospital.

Sleeping

Hôtel du Dragon   Small Hotel €€

(☎03 88 35 79 80; www.dragon.fr; 12 rue du Dragon; s €79-112, d €89-124; @🖵) Step through a tree-shaded courtyard into the blissful calm of this bijou hotel. It offers clean, crisp interiors, attentive service and a prime location not far from Petite France.

Petite France district (p233), Strasbourg
PHOTOGRAPHER: JOHN KELLERMAN/ALAMY©

Detour:
Killing Fields

The **Battle of the Somme**, a WWI Allied offensive waged northeast of Amiens, was designed to relieve pressure on the beleaguered French troops at Verdun. On 1 July 1916, British, Commonwealth and French troops went 'over the top' in a massive assault along a 34km front.

By the time the offensive was called off in mid-November, some 1.2 million lives had been lost: the British had advanced just 12km, the French 8km. The Battle of the Somme has since become a symbol of the meaningless slaughter of war and its killing fields and cemeteries have since become a site of pilgrimage (see www.somme-battlefields.co.uk); the tourist offices in **Amiens** (03 22 71 60 50; www.amiens.com/tourisme) and **Arras** (03 21 51 26 95; www.ot-arras.fr) supply maps, guides and minibus tours.

Hôtel Gutenberg   Historic Hotel €€
(03 88 32 17 15; www.hotel-gutenberg.com; 31 rue des Serruriers; r €75-135; ❄ @ ☜) Right in the flower-filled heart of Petite France, this hotel blends 250 years of history with contemporary design – think clean lines, zesty colours and the occasional antique.

Eating

Appetising restaurants abound on Grande Île: try canalside Petite France for Alsatian fare and half-timbered romance; Grand' Rue for curbside kebabs and *tarte flambée;* and rue des Veaux or rue des Pucelles for hole-in-the-wall eateries serving the world on a plate.

LA CHOUCROUTERIE   Alsatian €€
(03 88 36 52 87; www.choucrouterie.com, in French; 20 rue St Louis; choucroute €12-16; ☺lunch Mon-Fri, dinner daily) Naked ladies straddling giant sausages (on the menu, we hasten to add) and eccentric chefs juggling plates of steaming *choucroute garnie* are just the tip of the theatrical iceberg at this inimitable bistro and playhouse double act.

MAISON KAMMERZELL   Alsatian €€
(03 88 32 42 14; www.maison-kammerzell. com; 16 place de la Cathédrale; menus €27-46) Medieval icon Maison Kammerzell serves well-executed Alsatian cuisine such as

baeckeoffe and *choucroute*. A staircase spirals up to frescoed alcoves and the 1st floor where the views – oh the views! – of the floodlit cathedral are sensational.

ℹ Information

Tourist office (03 88 52 28 28; www.otstrasbourg.fr; 17 place de la Cathédrale; ☺9am-7pm)

ℹ Getting There & Away

Air

Strasbourg's international airport (www. strasbourg.aeroport.fr) is 17km southwest of the city centre (towards Molsheim), near the village of Entzheim.

Train

DOMESTIC Destinations include Paris' Gare de l'Est (€67, 2¼ hours, 17 daily), Lille (€94, four hours, 13 daily), Lyon (€52, six hours, five daily), Marseille (€87, eight hours, five daily), Metz (€23, two hours, 20 daily) and Nancy (€22, 1½ hours, 25 daily).

INTERNATIONAL Direct services run from Basel SNCF (Bâle; €21, 1¼ hours, 25 daily), Brussels-Nord (€70, 5¼ hours, three daily), Karlsruhe (€22, 40 minutes, 16 daily) and Stuttgart (€43, 1¼ hours, four TGVs daily). On the Eurostar via Paris or Lille, London is just five hours and 15 minutes away, city centre to city centre.

Detour:
Centre Pompidou-Metz

This architecturally innovative **museum** (www.centrepompidou-metz.fr; 1 parvis des Droits de l'Homme; adult/child €7/free; ⏰11am-6pm Mon, Wed & Sun, 11am-8pm Thu, Fri & Sat), dazzling white and sinuous, is the satellite branch of Paris' Centre Pompidou. Its gallery draws on Europe's largest collection of modern art to stage ambitious temporary exhibitions. The dynamic space also hosts top-drawer cultural events.

Train it from Metz' ornate early 20th-century **train station** (pl du Général de Gaulle) to Paris' Gare de l'Est (€53, 80 minutes, 13 daily), Nancy (€9.50, 40 minutes, 48 daily) and Strasbourg (€23, 1¾ hours, 14 daily).

ROUTE DES VINS From Strasbourg, there are trains to Route des Vins destinations including Colmar (€10.50, 30 minutes, 30 daily), Dambach-la-Ville (€8, one hour, 12 daily), Obernai (€5.50, 30 minutes, 20 daily) and Sélestat (€7.50, 30 minutes, 46 daily).

LOIRE VALLEY

One step removed from the French capital, the Loire was historically the place where princes, dukes and notable nobles established their country getaways, and the countryside is littered with some of the most extravagant architecture outside Versailles.

Many of the big-name châteaux are covered by the **Pass'-Châteaux**, which offers savings of between €1.20 and €5.30 depending on which châteaux you visit; contact the tourist offices in Blois, Cheverny and Chambord.

Several companies offer a choice of itineraries, packaging Azay-le-Rideau, Villandry, Cheverny, Chambord and Chenonceau (plus wine-tasting tours) in various combinations. Half-day trips cost €18 to €33; full-day trips €43 to €50. Admission to the chateaux isn't included, but you get a discount on tickets.

○ **Acco-Dispo** (www.accodispo-tours.com)

○ **Alienor** (www.alienor.com)

○ **Quart de Tours** (www.quartdetours.com)

○ **St-Eloi Excursions** (www.saint-eloi.com)

○ **Touraine Evasion** (www.tourevasion.com)

○ **Loire Valley Tours** (www.loire-valley-tours.com)

Blois
POP 40,057

Blois' old city, heavily damaged by German attacks in 1940, retains its steep, twisting medieval streets. **Château Royal de Blois** (www.chateaudeblois.fr; place du Château; adult/child €8/4; ⏰9am-7pm Jul & Aug, 9am-6.30pm Apr-Jun & Sep, 9am-12.30pm & 1.30-5.30pm Oct-Mar) is an excellent introduction to the chateaux of the Loire Valley, with Gothic (13th century), Flamboyant Gothic (1498–1503), early Renaissance (1515–24) and classical (1630s) architecture in its four grand wings.

ⓘ Getting There & Away

Bus

TLC (✆02 54 58 55 44; www.tlcinfo.net) runs a chateau shuttle and buses from Blois' train station (tickets €2 on board). Some destinations:
BEAUGENCY Line 16, 55 minutes, four Monday to Saturday, one Sunday
CHAMBORD Line 3, 40 minutes, four Monday to Saturday, one Sunday
CHEVERNY Line 4, 45 minutes, six to eight Monday to Friday, two Saturday, one Sunday

Train

AMBOISE €11, 20 minutes, 10 daily
ORLÉANS €13 to €20, 45 minutes, hourly
PARIS' GARES D'AUSTERLITZ & MONTPARNASSE €34 to €57, two hours, 26 daily
TOURS €13 to €19, 40 minutes, 13 daily

Around Blois

Château de Cheverny

Thought by many to be the most perfectly proportioned chateau of all, **Cheverny** (☏02 54 79 96 29; www.chateau-cheverny.fr; adult/child €7.50/3.60; ⊙9.15am-6.45pm Jul & Aug, 9.15am-6.15pm Apr-Jun & Sep, 9.45am-5.30pm Oct, 9.45am-5pm Nov-Mar) represents the zenith of French classical architecture, the perfect blend of symmetry, geometry and aesthetic order. It has hardly been altered since its construction between 1625 and 1634.

Near the chateau's gateway, the kennels house pedigreed French pointer/English foxhound hunting dogs still used by the owners of Cheverny: feeding time aka the **Soupe des Chiens** (⊙5pm Apr-Sep, 3pm Oct-Mar).

Behind the chateau is the 18th-century **Orangerie**, where many priceless art works (including the *Mona Lisa*) were stashed during WWII. Hérgé used the castle as a model for Moulinsart (Marlinspike) Hall, the ancestral home of Tintin's sidekick, Captain Haddock. **Les Secrets de Moulinsart** (combined ticket with chateau adult/child €12/7) explores the Tintin connections.

Cheverny is 16km southeast of Blois and 17km southwest of Chambord. For buses to/from Blois see p236.

Amboise

POP 12,900

The childhood home of Charles VIII and final resting place of Leonardo da Vinci, elegant Amboise, 23km northeast of Tours, is pleasantly perched along the southern bank of the Loire and overlooked by its fortified château.

◉ Sights

CHÂTEAU ROYAL D'AMBOISE   Castle
(place Michel Debré; adult/child €9.70/6.30; ⊙9am-6pm, 9am-5.30pm Mar, 9am-12.30pm & 2-4.45pm Jan-Feb & mid-Nov–Dec) Sprawling across a rocky escarpment above town, this easily defendable castle presented a formidable prospect to would-be attackers – but saw little military action. It was more often used as a weekend getaway from the official royal seat at nearby Blois. Charles VIII (r 1483–98), born and bred here, was responsible for the chateau's Italianate remodelling in 1492. Today,

Château de Cheverny

If You Like…
French Chateaux

Chambord (p239) and **Cheverny** (p237) are just the start of the Loire's glorious chateaux. Here are a few more of our favourites.

1 CHENONCEAU

(www.chenonceau.com; adult/child €10.50/8; ⊙9am-8pm Jul & Aug, 9am-7.30pm Jun & Sep, 9am-7pm Apr & May, 9.30am-5pm or 6pm Oct-Mar) This 16th-century castle is one of the Loire Valley's most architecturally attractive – and one of the busiest. Framed by a glassy moat and sweeping gardens, and topped by turrets and towers, it's straight out of a fairy tale.

2 AZAY-LE-RIDEAU

(☎02 47 45 42 04; adult/child €7.50/free; ⊙9.30am-6pm, 9.30am-7pm Jul & Aug, 10am-12.30pm & 2-5.30pm Oct-Mar) Built in the 1500s on an island in the River Indre, this romantic, moat-ringed wonder flaunts geometric windows, ordered turrets and decorative stonework. Don't miss its famous loggia staircase and summertime *son et lumière*.

3 LANGEAIS

(☎02 47 96 72 60; adult/child €8.50/5; ⊙9.30am-6.30pm, 9.30am-5.30pm Feb & Mar, 9am-7pm Jul & Aug) For medieval atmosphere, head for this 15th-century fortress complete with working drawbridge, crenellated battlements and ruined 10th-century donjon. The ruined keep (France's oldest) was built by 10th-century warlord Count Foulques Nerra.

4 VILLANDRY

(www.chateauvillandry.com; adult/child €9/5, gardens only €6/3.50; ⊙chateau 9am-6pm, 9am-5.30pm Mar, 9am-5pm Feb & early Nov, gardens 9am-5pm to 7.30pm year-round) One of the last major Renaissance chateaux to be built in the Loire Valley, this one is more famous for what's outside the buildings than inside them. Its gardens are nothing short of glorious: of particular note are the Ornamental Garden and the reconstruction of a medieval *potager* (kitchen garden).

just a few of the original 15th- and 16th-century structures survive, notably the **Flamboyant Gothic wing** and **Chapelle St-Hubert**, believed to be the final resting place of da Vinci. Exit the chateau through the circular **Tour Hurtault** with its ingenious sloping spiral ramp for easy carriage access.

LE CLOS LUCÉ   Historic Manor

(www.vinci-closluce.com; 2 rue du Clos Lucé; adult/child €12.50/7.50; ⊙9am-7pm, 9am-6pm Nov-Dec, 10am-6pm Jan) Leonardo da Vinci took up residence in the grand manor house at Le Clos Lucé in 1516 on the invitation of François I, and its interior and gardens are chock-a-block with scale models of the artist's many wacky inventions.

 Sleeping

LA PAVILLON DES LYS   Boutique Hotel €€

(☎02 47 30 01 01; www.pavillondeslys.com; 9 rue d'Orange; d €98-160; 🛜) Simply take a cappuccino-coloured, 18th-century town house and fill it with designer lamps, roll-top baths, hi-fis and deep sofas, then chuck in a locally renowned restaurant and elegant patio garden, and wow, you've got one beautiful hotel!

VILLA MARY   B&B €€

(☎02 47 23 03 31; www.villa-mary.fr; 14 rue de la Concorde; d incl breakfast €90-120) Four tip-top rooms in an impeccably furnished 18th-century town house, all crammed with beeswaxed antiques, glittering chandeliers and antique rugs.

LE CLOS D'AMBOISE   Historic Hotel €€

(☎02 47 30 10 20; www.leclosamboise.com; 27 rue Rabelais; r €97-149; ♨) Another posh pad finished with oodles of style and lashings of luxurious fabrics. Features range from wood-panelling to antique beds; some rooms have separate sitting areas, others original fireplaces. Sauna and gym in the old stables.

JOHN BANAGAN/LONELY PLANET IMAGES ©

Don't Miss Château de Chambord

For full-blown chateau splendour, you can't top **Chambord** (☎02 54 50 50 20; www.chambord .org; adult/child €9.50/free; ☺9am-7.30pm mid-Jul–mid-Aug, 9am-6.15pm mid-Mar–mid-Jul & mid-Aug–Sep, 9am-5.15pm Jan–mid-Mar & Oct-Dec), constructed from 1519 by François I as a lavish base for hunting game in the Sologne forests, but eventually used for just 42 days during the king's 32-year reign (1515–47). Pick up the multilingual audioguide (adult/child €4/2), if only to avoid getting lost in Chambord's endless rooms and corridors.

The chateau's most famous feature is its **double-helix staircase**, attributed by some to Leonardo da Vinci, who lived in Amboise (34km southwest) from 1516 until his death in 1519. The Italianate **rooftop terrace** was where the royal court assembled to watch military exercises and hunting parties returning at the end of the day.

Several times daily there are 1½-hour **guided tours** (€4) in English, and during school holidays **costumed tours** entertain kids. The son et lumière show **Chambord, Rêve de Lumières** (adult/child €12/10, ☺Jul–mid-Sep), projected on the chateau's facade nightly, is a real summer highlight, as is the daily **equestrian show** (☎02 54 20 31 01; www.ecuries-chambord.com, in French; adult/child €9.50/7; ☺May-Sep).

Chambord is 16km east of Blois, 45km southwest of Orléans and 17km northeast of Cheverny.

 Eating

Chez Bruno　　　Regional Cuisine　€
(☎02 47 57 73 49; place Michel Debré; menus from €12; ☺lunch Tue-Sun, dinner Tue-Sat) Uncork a host of local vintages in a coolly contemporary setting, accompanied by honest regional cooking.

L'Épicerie　　　Traditional French　€€
(☎02 47 57 08 94; 46 place Michel Debré; menus €22-34; ☺Wed-Sun) A more time-honoured atmosphere with rich wood, neo-Renaissance decor and filling fare such as *cuisse de lapin* (rabbit leg) and *tournedos de canard* (duck fillet).

239

Bigot Tearoom €
(2 rue Nationale; ⏰9am-7.30pm Tue-Fri, 8.30am-7.30pm Sat & Sun) Since 1913 this award-winning chocolatier and pâtisserie has been whipping up some of the Loire's creamiest cakes and gooiest treats: multicoloured *macarrons*, buttery biscuits, handmade chocolates and petits fours.

ℹ️ Information

Tourist office (📞02 47 57 09 28; www.amboise -valdeloire.com; ⏰9am-7pm Mon-Sat, 10am-1pm & 2-6pm Sun)

ℹ️ Getting There & Around

Train

BLOIS €11, 20 minutes, 14 daily

TOURS €11, 20 minutes, 10 daily

PARIS' GARE D'AUSTERLITZ €38 to €56, 2¼ hours, 14 daily

PARIS' GARE MONTPARNASSE €107, 1¼ hours, 10 daily, TGV

BURGUNDY & RHÔNE VALLEY

If there's one place in France where you're really going to find out what makes the nation tick, it's Burgundy. Two of the country's enduring passions – food and wine – come together in this gorgeously rural region, and if you're a sucker for hearty food and the fruits of the vine, you'll be in seventh heaven.

Beaune

POP 22,720

Beaune (pronounced 'bone'), 44km south of Dijon, is the unofficial capital of the Côte d'Or. This thriving town's raison d'être and the source of its joie de vivre is wine: making it, tasting it, selling it but, most of all, drinking it. Consequently Beaune is one of the best places in all of France for wine tasting.

🎯 Sights & Activities

Beaune's amoeba-shaped old city is enclosed by stone **ramparts** sheltering wine cellars. Lined with overgrown gardens and ringed by a pathway, they make for a lovely stroll.

HÔTEL-DIEU DES HOSPICES DE BEAUNE Gothic Hospital
(rue de l'Hôtel-Dieu; adult/child €6.50/2.80; ⏰9am-6.30pm) Built in 1443, this magnificent Gothic hospital (until 1971) is famously topped by stunning turrets and pitched rooftops covered in multicoloured tiles. Interior highlights include the barrel-vaulted **Grande Salle** (look for the dragons and peasant heads up on the roof beams); the mural-covered **St-Hughes Room**; an 18th-century **pharmacy**

Hôtel-Dieu des Hospices de Beaune

Burgundy's Vineyards

Burgundy's most renowned vintages come from the **Côte d'Or** (Golden Hillside), a range of hills made of limestone, flint and clay that runs south from Dijon for about 60km. The northern sec¶tion, the **Côte de Nuits**, stretches from Marsannay-la-Côte south to Corgoloin and produces reds known for their robust, full-bodied character. The southern section, the **Côte de Beaune**, lies between Ladoix-Serrigny and Santenay and produces great reds and great whites.

There's also the **Route des Grands Crus** (www.road-of-the-fine-burgundy-wines.com), a signposted road route of some of the most celebrated Côte de Nuits vineyards.

Wine & Voyages (www.wineandvoyages.com; €48-58) and **Alter & Go** (www.alterandgo.fr; €60-80), with an emphasis on history and winemaking methods, run minibus tours in English; reserve online or at the Dijon tourist office.

lined with flasks once filled with elixirs and powders such as *beurre d'antimoine* (antimony butter) and *poudre de cloportes* (woodlouse powder); and the multipanelled masterpiece **Polyptych of the Last Judgement** by 15th-century Flemish painter Rogier van der Weyden, depicting Judgement Day in glorious technicolour.

CELLAR VISITS   Wine Tasting
Millions of bottles of wine age to perfection in cool dark cellars beneath Beaune's buildings, streets and ramparts. Tasting opportunities abound and dozens of cellars can be visited by guided tour. Our favourites include the candlelit cellars of the former Église des Cordeliers, **Marché aux Vins** (www.marcheauxvins.com, in French; 2 rue Nicolas Rolin; admission €10; ☺9.30-11.45am & 2-5.45pm, no midday closure mid-Jun–Aug), where 15 wines can be sampled; and **Patriarche Père et Fils** (www.patriarche.com; 5 rue du Collège; audioguide tour €10; ☺9.30-11.30am & 2-5.30pm), lined with about five million bottles of wine.

 ## Sleeping

Hôtel des Remparts   Historic Hotel €€
(☎03 80 24 94 94; www.hotel-remparts-beaune.com; 48 rue Thiers; d €75-112; ✳@🛜) Set around two delightful courtyards, rooms in

this 17th-century town house have red-tiled floors, simple antique furniture and luxurious bathrooms. Friendly staff rent bikes.

Abbaye de Maizières   Historic Hotel €€
(☎03 80 24 74 64; www.beaune-abbaye-maizieres.com; 19 rue Maizières; d €112; @) Think an idiosyncratic hotel inside a 12th-century abbey with 13 rooms featuring brickwork and wooden beams.

 ## Eating

Caves Madeleine   Burgundian €€
(☎03 80 22 93 30; 8 rue du Faubourg Madeleine; menus €14-24; ☺Mon-Wed & Sat, dinner Fri) This is a convivial Burgundian restaurant where locals tuck into regional classics like *boeuf bourguignon* and *cassolette d'escargots* at long shared tables surrounded by wine racks.

Le P'tit Paradis   Modern Burgundian €€
(☎03 80 24 91 00; 25 rue Paradis; menus €19-36; ☺Tue-Sat) Find this intimate restaurant, known for *cuisine elaborée* (creative cuisine) made with local products, on a medieval street. Summer terrace.

 ## Information

Tourist office (☎03 80 26 21 30; www.beaune-burgundy.com; 6 blvd Perpreuil; ☺9am-7pm Mon-Sat, 9am-6pm Sun)

Place des Terreaux, Lyon

CORINNE HUMPHREY/LONELY PLANET IMAGES ©

ⓘ Getting There & Away

Train

DIJON €11, 25 minutes, 40 daily

LYON-PART DIEU €31 to €46, 1¾ hours, 16 daily

MÂCON €12.90, 50 minutes, 16 daily

NUITS-ST-GEORGES €11, 10 minutes, 40 daily

PARIS GARE DE LYON €64 to €118, 2¼ hours by TGV, 20 daily, two direct TGVs daily

Lyon
POP 480,660

Gourmets, eat your heart out: Lyon is *the* gastronomic capital of France, with a lavish table of piggy-driven dishes and delicacies to savour. The city has been a commercial, industrial and banking powerhouse for the past 500 years, and is still France's second-largest conurbation, with outstanding art museums, a dynamic nightlife, green parks and a Unesco-listed Old Town.

The **Lyon City Card** (www.lyon-france.com; 1/2/3 days adult €20/30/40, child €11/15/20) covers admission to every Lyon museum and the roof of Basilique Notre Dame de Fourvière, as well as a guided city tour, a river excursion (April to October) and discounts on other selected attractions, exhibitions and shops.

The card also includes unlimited travel on city buses, trams, the funicular and metro (cheaper cards not incorporating transport are available). Pre-book online or buy from the tourist office.

◉ Sights

Vieux Lyon

Old Lyon, with its cobblestone streets and medieval and Renaissance houses below Fourvière hill, is divided into three quarters: St-Paul at the northern end, St-Jean in the middle and St-Georges in the south. Lovely old buildings languish on **rue du Bœuf, rue St-Jean** and **rue des Trois Maries**.

The partly Romanesque **Cathédrale St-Jean** (place St-Jean, 5e; ⊙8am-noon & 2-7.30pm Mon-Fri, 8am-noon & 2-7pm Sat & Sun; Ⓜ Vieux Lyon), seat of Lyon's 133rd bishop, was built from the late 11th to the early 16th centuries. Its **astronomical clock** chimes at noon, 2pm, 3pm and 4pm.

Fourvière

Over two millennia ago, the Romans built the city of Lugdunum on the slopes of Fourvière. Today, Lyon's 'hill of prayer' – topped by a basilica and the **Tour Métallique**, an Eiffel Tower–like structure built in 1893 and used as a TV transmitter – affords spectacular views of the city and its two rivers. Footpaths wind uphill, but the **funicular** (place Édouard Commette; €2.40 return) is by far the least taxing way to the top.

Crowning Fourvière hill is the **Basilique Notre Dame de Fourvière** (www.fourviere. org; ☉8am-7pm), an iconic, 27m-high basilica, a superb example of exaggerated 19th-century ecclesiastical architecture. One-hour **discovery visits** (adult/child €2/1; ☉Apr-Nov) take in the main features of the basilica and crypt; **rooftop tours** (adult/child €5/3; ☉2.30pm & 4pm Apr-Oct, 2.30pm & 3.30pm Wed & Sun Nov) climax on the stone-sculpted roof.

Presqu'île

The centrepiece of **place des Terreaux** (Ⓜ Hôtel de Ville) is the 19th-century fountain sculpted by Frédéric-Auguste Bartholdi, who was most famously the creator of the Statue of Liberty. The **Musée des Beaux-Arts** (www.mba-lyon.fr; 20 place des Terreaux, 1er; adult/child €76/ free; ☉10am-6pm Wed, Thu & Sat-Mon, 10.30am-6pm Fri; Ⓜ Hôtel de Ville) showcases France's finest collection of sculptures and paintings outside Paris.

Laid out in the 17th century, **place Bellecour** (Ⓜ Bellecour) – one of Europe's largest public squares – is pierced by an equestrian **statue of Louis XIV** .

North of place Bellecour, the charmful hilltop quarter of **Croix Rousse** (Ⓜ Croix Rousse) is famed for its bohemian inhabitants, lush outdoor food market and silk-weaving tradition, illustrated by the **Maison des Canuts** (www.maisondescanuts.com; 10-12 rue d'Ivry, 4e; adult/child €6/3; ☉10am-6pm Tue-Sat, guided tours 11am & 3.30pm; Ⓜ Croix Rousse).

Rive Gauche

MUSÉE LUMIÈRE　　　　　Film Museum
(www.institut-lumiere.org; 25 rue du Premier Film, 8e; adult/child €6/5; ☉11am-6.30pm Tue-Sun; Ⓜ Monplaisir-Lumière) Cinema's glorious beginnings are showcased at the art nouveau home of Antoine Lumière, who moved to Lyon in 1870 with his sons Auguste and Louis, two of the world's first cinematographers.

🛏 Sleeping

Hôtel de Paris　　　　　Hotel　€€
(🕿 04 78 28 00 95; www.hoteldeparis-lyon.com; 16 rue de la Platière, 1er; s €49-59, d €65-90; ✳ @ 🛜; Ⓜ Hôtel de Ville) At this fantastic-value hotel, located in a 19th-century

DISCOVER FRANCE LYON

Relief sculpture on a church wall, Lyon
PHOTOGRAPHER: GREG ELMS/LONELY PLANET IMAGES ©

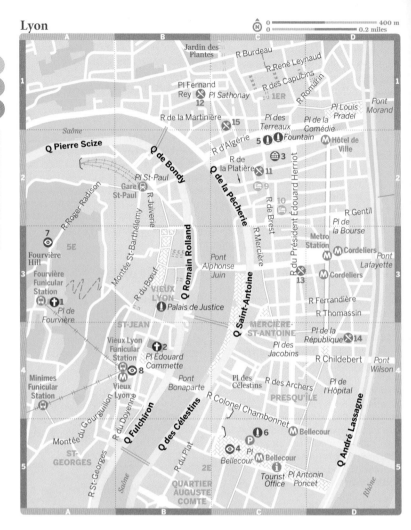

Lyon

0 ——————— 400 m
0 ——————— 0.2 miles

bourgeois building, the funkiest rooms' retro 1970s decor incorporates a palette of chocolate-and-turquoise or candy-floss-pink.

HÔTEL LE BOULEVARDIER Hotel €
(☎ 04 78 28 48 22; www.leboulevardier.fr; 5 rue de la Fromagerie, 1er; s €45-51, d €47-53; ☎; M Hôtel de Ville) Sporting quirky touches such as old skis and tennis racquets adorning the hallways, Le Boulevardier is a bargain 11-room hotel with snug, spot-less rooms. It's up a steep spiral staircase above a cool little bistro and jazz club of the same name, which doubles as reception.

HOTELO Hotel €€
(☎ 04 78 37 39 03; www.hotelo-lyon.com; 37 cours de Verdun, 2e; d from €70; M Perrache) Our hot choice around Gare de Perrache, this one stands out from the crowd for its crisp, contemporary design and touches of convenience. Studios have a kitchen-ette and one room is perfectly fitted out for travellers with disabilities.

Lyon

Eating

A flurry of big-name chefs presides over a sparkling restaurant line-up that embraces all genres: French, fusion, fast and international, as well as traditional Lyonnais *bouchons* (literally meaning 'bottle stopper' or 'traffic jam', but in Lyon a small, friendly bistro serving the city's local cuisine).

LE BEC French, Fusion €€€
(☎04 78 42 15 00; www.nicolaslebec.com, 2e; 14 rue Grolée; lunch menus €40, dinner menus €90-135; ◷Tue-Sat) With two Michelin stars, this is the flagship restaurant of Lyon's hottest chef Nicolas Le Bec, famed for his seasonal, world-influenced cuisine. Sunday brunch (€45) at his other address, innovative concept space **Rue Le Bec** (☎04 78 92 87 87; 43 quai Rambaud, 2e; mains €9-30; ◷Tue-Sun; 🚃tramline 1, Montrochet stop), on the Confluence, is equally hot.

Magali et Martin Lyonnais €€
(☎04 72 00 88 01; 11 rue Augustins, 1er; lunch/dinner menus €19.60/35; ◷Mon-Fri; Ⓜ Hôtel de Ville) Watch chefs turn out traditional but lighter,

more varied *bouchon*-influenced cuisine, at this sharp dining address.

Café des Fédérations Bouchon €€
(☎04 78 28 26 00; www.lesfedeslyon.com, in French; 8 rue Major Martin, 1er; menus €19-42; ◷Mon-Sat; Ⓜ Hôtel de Ville) Black-and-white photos of old Lyon hang on wood-panelled walls at this Lyonnais bistro, which has remained unchanged for decades.

**Comptoir-Restaurant
des Deux Places** Bouchon €€
(☎04 78 28 95 10; 5 place Fernand Rey, 1er; lunch/dinner menus €13/28; ◷Tue-Sat; Ⓜ Hôtel de Ville) Checked curtains, antique-crammed interior and ink-scribed menu contribute to the overwhelmingly traditional feel of this neighbourhood bistro with idyllic terrace beneath trees.

Grand Café des Négociants
Brasserie €€
(www.cafe-des-negociants.com, in French; 2 place Francisque Regaud, 2e; mains €17.50-34; ◷7am-3am; Ⓜ Cordeliers) This cafe-style brasserie with mirror-lined walls and tree-shaded terrace has been a favourite meeting point with Lyonnais since 1864.

LES HELLES DE LYON Market €
(http://halledelyon.free.fr, in French; 102 cours Lafayette, 3e; ◷8am-7pm Tue-Sat, 8am-noon Sun; Ⓜ Part-Dieu) Pick up a round of impossibly runny St Marcellin from legendary cheesemonger Mère Richard or a knobbly Jésus de Lyon from pork butcher Collette Sibilia at Lyon's famed indoor market.

Drinking & Entertainment

Cafe terraces on place des Terreaux buzz with all-hours drinkers, as do the multitude of British, Irish and other-styled pubs on nearby rue Ste-Catherine, 1er, and rue Lainerie and rue St-Jean, 5e, in Vieux Lyon.

Weekly what's on guides include **Lyon Poche** (www.lyonpoche.com, in French; at newsagents €1) and **Le Petit Bulletin** (www.petit-bulletin.fr, in French; free on street corners).

ℹ Information

Tourist office (☎ 04 72 77 69 69; www.lyon
-france.com; place Bellecour, 2e; ⏰ 9am-6pm;
Ⓜ Bellecour)

ℹ Getting There & Away

Air

Lyon-St-Exupéry Airport (www.lyon.aeroport.
fr), 25km east of the city, serves 120 direct
destinations across Europe and beyond, including
many budget carriers.

Train

Lyon has two main-line train stations: **Gare de la
Part-Dieu** (Ⓜ Part-Dieu) and **Gare de Perrache**
(Ⓜ Perrache). Some destinations can be reached
by direct TGV (high-speed trains):

BEAUNE €23.10, 2¼ hours, up to nine daily

DIJON €30.20, two hours, at least 12 daily

LILLE-EUROPE €92, 3¼ hours, nine daily

MARSEILLE €58.60, 1¾ hours, every 30 to 60
minutes

PARIS GARE DE LYON €64.30, two hours, every
30 to 60 minutes

STRASBOURG €55.90, 4¾ hours, five daily

ℹ Getting Around

Tramway Rhonexpress (www.rhonexpress.net,
in French) links the airport with Part-Dieu train
station in under 30 minutes. A single/return ticket
costs €13/23.

Buses, trams, a four-line metro and two
funiculars linking Vieux Lyon to Fourvière are run
by TCL (www.tcl.fr). Tickets cost €1.60/13.70 for
one/*carnet* of 10; bring coins as machines don't
accept notes (or some international credit cards).

FRENCH ALPS & JURA

Whether paragliding among the peaks,
hiking the trails or hurtling down a mountain strapped to a pair of glorified tooth-
picks, the French Alps is the undisputed
centre of adventure sports in France.

Chamonix

POP 9400 / ELEV 1037M

With the pearly white peaks of the Mont
Blanc massif as sensational backdrop,
being an icon comes naturally to Chamonix. First 'discovered' by Brits William
Windham and Richard Pococke in 1741,
this is the mecca of mountaineering. Its knife-edge peaks, plunging
slopes and massive glaciers have
enthralled generations of adventurers and thrill-seekers
ever since. Its après-ski
scene is equally pumping.

◎ Sights

AIGUILLE DU MIDI
Mountain Peak,
Cable Car
A jagged pinnacle of
rock 8km from the
domed summit of Mont
Blanc, the **Aiguille du
Midi** (3842m) is one of

View from Aiguille du Midi
PHOTOGRAPHER: JOHN ELK III/LONELY PLANET IMAGES ©

Chamonix' iconic landmarks. If you can handle the height, the 360-degree panorama from the top of the French, Swiss and Italian Alps is unforgettable.

The vertiginous **Téléphérique du l'Aiguille du Midi** (📞 04 50 53 30 80, advance reservations 24hr 04 50 53 22 75; 100 place de l'Aiguille du Midi; adult/child return Aiguille du Midi €41/33, Plan de l'Aiguille €24/19.20; ⏰8.30am-4.30pm) links Chamonix with the Aiguille du Midi. In summer you will need to obtain a boarding card (marked with the number of your departing *and* returning cable car) in addition to a ticket. Advance phone reservations incur a €2 booking fee. Bring warm clothes, as even in summer the temperature rarely rises above -10°C at the top.

Mid-May to mid-September the unrepentant can continue for a further half-hour of mind-blowing scenery – suspended glaciers, spurs, seracs and shimmering ice fields – in the smaller **Télécabine Panoramic Mont Blanc** (adult/child return from Chamonix €65/52; ⏰8.30am-3.45pm) to **Pointe Helbronner** (3466m) on the French–Italian border. From here another cable car decends to the Italian ski resort of Courmayeur.

MER DE GLACE   Glacier
The glistening **Mer de Glace** (Sea of Ice) is the second-largest glacier in the Alps, 14km long, 1800m wide and up to 400m deep. A quaint red mountain train links **Gare du Montenvers** (35 place de la Mer de Glace; adult/child €24/19; ⏰10am-4.30pm) in Chamonix with Montenvers (1913m), from where a cable car transports tourists in summer down to the glacier and the **Grotte de la Mer de Glace** (⏰Dec-May & mid-Jun–Sep), an ice cave where frozen tunnels and ice sculptures – carved anew every year since 1946 – change colour like mood rings.

A quaint red mountain train trundles up from **Gare du Montenvers** (35 place de la Mer de Glace; adult/child €24/19; ⏰10am-4.30pm) in Chamonix to Montenvers (1913m), from where a cable car takes you down to the glacier and cave. The ticket covers the 20-minute journey, entry to the caves and the cable car.

 Activities

The **Maison de la Montagne** (190 place de l'Église; ⏰8.30am-noon & 3-7pm), across the square from the tourist office, supplies details on every imaginable pastime in the Mont Blanc area.

 Sleeping

AUBERGE DU MANOIR   Chalet   €€
(📞04 50 53 10 77; http://aubergedumanoir.com, in French; 8 rte du Bouchet; s €94-108, d €104-150, q €165; 📶) This beautifully converted farmhouse, ablaze with geraniums in summer, ticks all the perfect Alpine chalet boxes: pristine mountain views, pine-panelled rooms and an inviting bar where an open fire keeps things cosy.

HOTEL SLALOM   Boutique Hotel   €€
(📞04 50 54 40 60; www.hotelslalom.net; 44 rue de Bellevue, Les Houches; r €158; 📶) Rooms are boutique chic – sleek, snowy white and draped with Egyptian cotton linens – at this gorgeous chalet-style hotel, at the foot of the slopes in Les Houches.

HOTEL L'OUSTALET   Family Hotel   €€
(📞04 50 55 54 99; www.hotel-oustalet.com; 330 rue du Lyret; d/q €140/180; 📶♨) You'll pray for snow at this Alpine chalet near Aiguille du Midi cable car, just so you can curl up by the fire with a *chocolat chaud* (hot chocolate) and hit the sauna and whirl-pool. Rooms are snug solid pine and open onto balconies with Mont Blanc views.

 **Eating**

LE BISTROT   Gastronomic   €€€
(📞04 50 53 57 64; www.lebistrotchamonix.com, in French; 151 av de l'Aiguille du Midi; menus €17-65) Sleek and monochromatic, this is a real foodie's place. Michelin-starred chef Mickey experiments with textures and seasonal flavours to create taste sensations like pan-seared Arctic char with chestnuts and divine warm chocolate macaroon with raspberry and red pepper coulis.

LE GOUTHÉ Tearoom €
(95 rue des Moulins; menus €9; ⏰9am-6.30pm Fri-Mon) Philippe's hot chocolates with pistachio and gingerbread infusions, bright macaroons and crumbly homemade tarts are the sugar fix needed for the slopes.

LE CHAUDRON Regional Cuisine €€
(📞04 50 53 57 64; 79 rue des Moulins; menus €20-23; ⏰dinner) Funky cowskin-clad benches are the backdrop for a feast of Savoyard fondues and lamb slow-cooked in red wine to melting perfection at this chic chalet.

 Drinking & Entertainment

In the centre, riverside rue des Moulins touts a line-up of drinking holes.

CHAMBRE NEUF Bar
(272 av Michel Croz; 📶) Cover bands, raucous après-ski drinking and Swedish blondes dancing on the tables make Room Nine one of Chamonix' liveliest party haunts.

MBC Microbrewery
(www.mbchx.com; 350 rte du Bouchet; ⏰4pm-2am) Be it with burgers, cheesecake, live music or amazing locally brewed beers, this trendy microbrewery delivers.

MONKEY BAR Music Bar
(81 place Edmond Desailloud; ⏰1pm-2am; 📶) Slightly grungy, very cool, this party hot spot has live gigs and DJs several times a week.

ℹ Information

Tourist office (📞04 50 53 00 24; www. chamonix.com; 85 place du Triangle de l'Amitié; ⏰8.30am-7pm)

ℹ Getting There & Away

Bus
From **Chamonix bus station** (www.sat -montblanc.com; place de la Gare), next to the train station, two to three buses run daily to/ from Geneva airport (€33, 1½ to two hours) and Courmayeur (€13, 45 minutes). Advance booking only.

Left: Ski resort, French Alps; **Below:** Hang-gliding, Annecy

PHOTOGRAPHER: (LEFT) GLENN VAN DER KNIJFF/LONELY PLANET IMAGES ©;
(BELOW) JOHN ELK III/LONELY PLANET IMAGES ©

Train

From Chamonix-Mont Blanc **train station** (place de la Gare) the Mont Blanc Express narrow-gauge train trundles to/from St-Gervais-Le Fayet (€9.50, 40 minutes, nine to 12 daily), from where there are trains to most major French cities.

Annecy

POP 53,000 / ELEV 447M

Lac d'Annecy is one of the world's purest lakes, receiving only rainwater, spring water and mountain streams. Swimming in its sapphire depths, surrounded by snowy mountains, is a real Alpine highlight. Strolling the geranium-strewn streets of the historic Vieille Ville (Old Town) is not half bad either.

 Sights & Activities

VIEILLE VILLE & LAKEFRONT
Old Town, Lake

Wandering around the Vieille Ville and the lakefront is the essence of Annecy. Behind the town hall are the **Jardins de l'Europe**, linked to the park of **Champ de Mars** by the **Pont des Amours** (Lovers' Bridge).

With labyrinthine narrow streets and colonnaded passageways, the Old Town retains much of its 17th-century appearance. On the central island, former prison **Palais de l'Isle** (3 passage de l'Île; adult/child €4.90/2.30; 🕑10.30am-6pm) now hosts local-history displays.

In the 13th- to 16th-century castle above town, the museum inside **Château d'Annecy** (adult/child €4.90/2.30; 🕑10.30am-6pm) explores traditional Savoyard art, crafts and Alpine natural history.

Parks and grassy areas line the lakefront. Public beach **Plage d'Annecy-le-Vieux** is 1km east of Champ de Mars. Closer to town, privately run **Plage Impérial** (€3.50; 🕑Jul & Aug) sits beneath the pre-WWI **Impérial Palace**. **Plage des Marquisats** (🕑Jul & Aug) is 1km south of the Vieille Ville along rue des Marquisats.

Sleeping

HÔTEL ALEXANDRA   Family Hotel €

(☎ 04 50 52 84 33; www.hotelannecy-alexandra
.fr; 19 rue Vaugelas; s/d/tr/q €48/59/70/89; 🛜)
Nice surprise: Annecy's most charming
hotel is also among its most affordable.
The welcome is five-star and rooms are
spotless – a few extra euro gets you a
balcony and canal view.

LE PRÉ CARRÉ   Boutique Hotel €€€

(☎ 04 50 52 14 14; www.hotel-annecy.net; 27 rue
Sommeiller; s/d €172/202; ❄ @ 🛜) Chic Le
Pré Carré keeps things contemporary with Zen
colours in rooms, Jacuzzi and business corner.
The staff know Annecy inside out, so you're in
very good hands.

Eating

The quays along Canal du Thiou in the
Vieille Ville are jam-packed with touristy
cafes and pizzerias.

LA CUISINE DES AMIS   Bistro €€

(☎ 04 50 10 10 80; 9 rue du Pâquier; mains
€16.50-25) Walking into this bistro is somewhat like gatecrashing a private party –
everyone is treated like one big jolly
famille. Pull up a chair, *prendre un verre*
(have a drink), scoff regional fare, pat the
dog and see if your snapshot ends up on
the wall of merry *amis*.

LA CIBOULETTE   Modern French €€

(☎ 04 50 45 74 57; www.laciboulette-annecy
.com; cour du Pré Carré, 10 rue Vaugelas; menus
€31-46; ⏰ Tue-Sat) Such class! Crisp white
linen and gold-kissed walls set the scene
at this surprisingly affordable Michelin-
starred place, and chef Georges Paccard
cooks fresh seasonal specialities, such
as slow-roasted Anjou pigeon with Midi
asparagus. Reservations are essential.

CONTRESENS   Fusion €€

(☎ 04 50 51 22 10; 10 rue de la Poste; mains
€15; ⏰ Tue-Sat) The menu reads like a
mathematic formula but it soon becomes
clear: starters are A, mains B, sides C and
desserts D. The food is as experimental
as the menu – think sun-dried tomato,
Beaufort cheese and rocket salad burger,
mussel ravioli, 'deconstructed' Snickers –
and totally divine. Kid nirvana.

ℹ Information

Tourist office (☎ 04 50 45 00
33; www.lac-annecy.com; Centre
Bonlieu, 1 rue Jean Jaurès; ⏰ 9am-
6.30pm Mon-Sat, 10am-1pm Sun)

ℹ Getting There & Away

Bus

From the bus station (rue
de l'Industrie), adjoining
the train station, Billetterie
Crolard (www.voyages
-crolard.com) sells tickets
for roughly hourly buses to
villages around the lake, local

Place de la Liberté, Sarlat-La-Canéda
PHOTOGRAPHER: ANDREW BAIN/LONELY PLANET IMAGES ©

ski resorts and Lyon St-Exupéry airport (one-way/return €33/50, 2¼ hours). **Autocars Frossard** (www.frossard.eu) sells tickets for Geneva (€10.50, 1¾ hours, 16 daily).

Train

From Annecy's **train station** (place de la Gare), there are frequent trains to many destinations, including Lyon (€23, 2¼ hours) and Paris' Gare de Lyon (€75, four hours).

DORDOGNE

If it's French heart and soul you're after, look no further. Tucked in the country's southwestern corner, the neighbouring regions of the Dordogne and Lot combine history, culture and culinary sophistication in one unforgettably scenic package.

Sarlat-La-Canéda

POP 9950

A gorgeous tangle of honey-coloured buildings, alleyways and secret squares make up this unmissable Dordogne village – a natural if touristy launch pad into the Vézère Valley.

Part of the fun of Sarlat is getting lost in its twisting alleyways and backstreets. **Rue Jean-Jacques Rousseau** or the area around **Le Présidial** are good starting points, but for the grandest buildings and *hôtels particuliers* you'll want to explore **rue des Consuls**. Whichever street you take, sooner or later you'll hit the **Cathédrale St-Sacerdos** (place du Peyrou), a real mix of architectural styles and periods: the belfry and western facade are the oldest parts.

Nearby, the former **Église Ste-Marie** (place de la Liberté) houses Sarlat's mouthwatering **Marché Couvert** (covered market) and a state-of-the-art **panoramic lift** (elevator) in its bell tower. It was designed by top French architect Jean Nouvel (whose parents live in Sarlat).

Three gold-hued, bronze-sculpted geese on **place du Marché aux Oies** ('geese market' square) attest to the enduring economic and gastronomic role of these birds in the Dordogne. Both the covered market and Sarlat's chaotic

Saturday-morning market (place de la Liberté & rue de la République) – a full-blown French market experience 'must' – sell a smorgasbord of goose-based goodies.

 Sleeping

HÔTEL LES RÉCOLLETS   Hotel €
(☎ 05 53 31 36 00; www.hotel-recollets-sarlat.com; 4 rue Jean-Jacques Rousseau; d €45-69; ❄ ☎) Lost in the Old Town medieval maze, the Récollets is a budget beauty. Nineteen topsy-turvy rooms and a charming vaulted breakfast room are rammed in around the medieval *maison*.

CLOS LA BOËTIE   Boutique Hotel €€€
(☎ 05 53 29 44 18; www.closlaboetie-sarlat.com; 95-97 av de la Selves; d €210-280; ❄ @ ☎ ☯) Each of the 11 rooms at this 19th-century mansion, a five-minute walk north of the Cité Médiévale, is a jewel.

 Eating

BISTRO DE L'OCTROI
                        Regional Cuisine €€
(☎ 05 53 30 83 40; www.lebistrodeloctroi.fr, in French; 111 av de Selves; menus €18-26) This local's tip is a little way out of town, but don't let that dissuade you. Sarladais pack into this cosy town house for the artistically presented, accomplished cooking that doesn't sacrifice substance for style.

LE GRAND BLEU   Gastronomic €€€
(☎ 05 53 29 82 14; www.legrandbleu.eu, in French; 43 av de la Gare; menus €33-90; ☺ lunch Thu-Sun, dinner Tue-Sat) Every menu at this Michelin-starred temple includes a choice of meat (such as veal sweetbreads with truffles) or seafood (such as lobster risotto with roast eggplant and truffle mousse). Cooking courses.

LE PRÉSIDIAL   Regional Cuisine €€
(☎ 05 53 28 92 47; 6 rue Landry; menus from €29; ☺ lunch Tue-Sat, dinner Mon-Sat Apr-Nov) What was a 17th-century courthouse now flaunts the city's most romantic dining

Prehistoric Paintings

Fantastic prehistoric **caves** with some of the world's finest cave art is what makes the Vézère Valley so very special. Most of the caves are closed in winter, and get very busy in summer. Visitor numbers are strictly limited, so you'll need to reserve well ahead.

Of the valley's 175 known sites, the most famous include **Grotte de Font de Gaume** (http://eyzies.monuments-nationaux.fr; adult/child €7/free; 9.30am-12.30 & 2-5.30pm Sun-Fri), 1km northeast of Les Eyzies. About 14,000 years ago, the prehistoric artists created the gallery of over 230 figures, including bison, reindeer, horses, mammoths, bears and wolves, of which 25 are on permanent display.

About 7km east of Les Eyzies, **Abri du Cap Blanc** (http://eyzies.monuments -nationaux.fr; adult/child €7/free; 9.30am-12.30 & 2-5.30pm Sun-Fri) showcases an unusual sculpture gallery of horses, bison and deer.

Then there is **Grotte de Rouffignac** (www.grottederouffignac.fr; adult/child €6.30/4; tours in French 10-11.30am & 2-5pm), sometimes known as the 'Cave of 100 Mammoths' because of its painted mammoths. Access to the caves, hidden in woodland 15km north of Les Eyzies, is aboard a trundling electric train.

Star of the show goes hands down to **Grotte de Lascaux** (Lascaux II: 05 53 51 95 03; www.semitour.com; adult/child €8.80/6; 9.30am-6pm), 2km southeast of Montignac, featuring an astonishing menagerie including oxen, deer, horses, reindeer and mammoth, as well as an amazing 5.5m bull, the largest cave drawing ever found. The original cave was closed to the public in 1963 to prevent damage to the paintings, but the most famous sections have been meticulously recreated in a second cave nearby – a massive undertaking that required some 20 artists and took 11 years.

terrace. Goose, duck and foie gras dominate the menu, and the wine list is packed with Sarlat and Cahors vintages.

ℹ Getting There & Away

The **train station** (ave de la Gare), 1.3km south of the old city, serves Périgueux (change at Le Buisson; €13.90, 1¾ hours, three daily) and Les Eyzies (change at Le Buisson; €8.60, 50 minutes to 2½ hours, three daily).

ATLANTIC COAST

Though the French Riviera is France's most popular beach spot, the many seaside resorts along the Atlantic coast are fast catching up. If you're a surf nut or a beach bum, then the sandy bays around Biarritz will be right up your alley,

while oenophiles can sample the fruits of the vine in the high temple of French winemaking, Bordeaux. Towards the Pyrenees you'll find the Basque Country, which in many ways is closer to the culture of northern Spain than to the rest of France.

Bordeaux

POP 238,900

The new millennium was a turning point for the city long nicknamed La Belle au Bois Dormant (Sleeping Beauty), when the mayor, ex-Prime Minister Alain Juppé, roused Bordeaux, pedestrianising its boulevards, restoring its neoclassical architecture, and implementing a hi-tech public-transport system. Today the city is a Unesco World Heritage site and, with its merry student population and 2.5 million-odd annual tourists, scarcely sleeps at all.

👁 Sights

CATHÉDRALE ST-ANDRÉ · Church
This Unesco-listed cathedral is almost overshadowed by the gargoyled, 50m-high Gothic belfry, **Tour Pey-Berland** (adult/child €5/free; ⊙10am-1.15pm & 2-6pm Jun-Sep, shorter hr rest of year). Scaling the tower's 232 narrow steps rewards you with a spectacular panorama of the city.

MUSEUMS · Museums
Bordeaux's museums have free entry for permanent collections. Gallo-Roman statues and relics dating back 25,000 years are among the highlights at the impressive **Musée d'Aquitaine** (20 cours Pasteur; temporary exhibitions €3; ⊙11am-6pm Tue-Sun), while more than 700 post-1960s works by 140 European and American artists are on display at the **CAPC Musée d'Art Contemporain** (Entrepôt 7, rue Ferrére; ⊙11am-6pm Tue, Thu-Sun, to 8pm Wed, closed Mon).

Jardin Public · Garden
(cours de Verdun) Home to a lovely botanical garden since 1855, the Jardin Public was laid out in 1755 and reworked in the English style a century later.

🛏 Sleeping

ECOLODGE DES CHARTRONS · B&B · €€
(☎05 56 81 49 13; www.ecolodgedeschartrons.com; 23 rue Raze; s/d incl breakfast €98/110) Hidden on a side street off the quays in Bordeaux's Chartrons wine merchants district, this *chambre d'hôte* spearheads ecofriendly sleeping in the city: think solar-heated water, hemp-based sound-proofing for the rooms and recycled antique furniture.

LA MAISON BORD'EAUX · Boutique Hotel · €€
(☎05 56 44 00 45; www.lamaisonbord-eaux.com; 113 rue du Docteur Albert Barraud; s/d from €130/150; 🛜) You'd expect to find a sumptuous 18th-century château with conifer-flanked courtyard and stable house in the countryside, but this one is smack-bang in the city. Dine after dusk on request (from €30).

LA MAISON DU LIERRE · Boutique Hotel · €€
(☎05 56 51 92 71; www.maisondulierre.com; 57 rue Huguerie; d €68-128; 🛜) A beautiful Bordelaise stone staircase (no lift) leads to

Jardin Public

BJANKA KADIC / ALAMY©

sunlit rooms with polished floorboards, rose-printed fabric furnishings and sparkling bathrooms at the delightful House of Ivy. The vine-draped garden is dreamy.

Eating

Place du Parlement, rue du Pas St-Georges, rue des Faussets and place de la Victoire are loaded with dining addresses, as is the old waterfront warehouse district around quai des Marques – great for a sunset meal or drink.

LE CHEVERUS CAFÉ
Bistro €

(📞 05 56 48 29 73; 81-83 rue du Loup; menus from €10.50; ⏰ Mon-Sat) Friendly, cosy and chaotically busy (be prepared to wait for a table at lunchtime) best describes this neighbourhood bistro. Lunch in particular is an all-out bargain.

LA TUPINA
Regional Cuisine €€

(📞 05 56 91 56 37; 6 rue Porte de la Monnaie; mains €18-40) Filled with the smell of soup simmering in an old *tupina* ('kettle' in Basque) over an open fire, this white-tableclothed place is feted far and wide for its seasonal regional specialities: minicasserole of foie gras and eggs, milk-fed lamb or goose wings with potatoes and parsley. You can get lunch here on weekdays for €16.

LA BOÎTE À HUÎTRES
Oysters €

(📞 05 56 81 64 97; 36 cours du Chapeau Rouge; mains €8) This rickety wood-panelled little place is the best spot in Bordeaux to slurp fresh Aracachon oysters, traditionally served with sausage.

L'ESTAQUADE
Gastronomic €€€

(📞 05 57 54 02 50; quai de Queyries; mains €22-26) Set on stilts jutting out from the riverbank, this restaurant is known for its seafood and magical views of Bordeaux's lovely neoclassical architecture.

Information

Tourist office (📞 05 56 00 66 00; www .bordeaux-tourisme.com; 12 cours du 30 Juillet; ⏰ 9am-7.30pm Mon-Sat, 9.30am-6.30pm Sun Jul & Aug, shorter hr rest of yr) Runs a smaller but helpful branch by the train station.

On the Wine Trail

The 1000-sq-km wine-growing area surrounding the city of Bordeaux is, along with Burgundy, France's most important producer of top-quality wines. Whet your palate with the Bordeaux tourist office's introduction wine-and-cheese courses (€24).

Bordeaux has over 5000 estates where grapes are grown, picked and turned into wine. Smaller châteaux often accept walk-in visitors, but at many places, especially better-known ones, you have to reserve in advance. One of the easiest to visit is **Château Lanessan** (📞 05 56 58 94 80; www.lanessan.com; Cussac-Fort-Medoc; adult/child €8/2; ⏰ advance reservation).

Favourite vine-framed villages in this area, brimming with charm, as well as tasting and buying opportunities, include medieval **St-Émilion** (www.saint -emilion-tourisme.com), the port town of **Pauillac** (www.pauillac-medoc.com) and **Listrac-Médoc**. In **Arsac-en-Médoc**, Philippe Raoux's vast glass-and-steel wine centre, **La Winery** (📞 05 56 39 04 90; www.lawinery.fr, in French; Rond-point des Vendangeurs, D1), stuns with regular concerts and contemporary art exhibitions. The centre also offers tastings that can help determine your *signe œnologique* ('wine sign'; booking required).

Many chateaux close during October's *vendange* (grape harvest).

Getting There & Away

Air

Bordeaux airport (www.bordeaux.aeroport.fr) is in Mérignac, 10km west of the city centre, with domestic and some international services. **Jet'Bus** (☎ 05 56 34 50 50) shuttle buses (€7, 45 minutes, every 45 minutes) link it with the train station, place Gambetta and main tourist office in town.

Train

From Bordeaux's Gare St-Jean, 3km from the centre:

NANTES €44.60, four hours

PARIS GARE MONTPARNASSE €69.80, three hours, at least 16 daily

POITIERS €35.20, 1¾ hours

TOULOUSE €33, 2¼ hours

Biarritz
POP 27,500

Edge your way south along the coast towards Spain and you arrive in stylish Biarritz, just as ritzy as its name suggests. The resort took off in the mid-19th century (Napoleon III had a rather soft spot for the place) and it still shimmers with architectural treasures from the belle époque and art deco eras. Big waves – some of Europe's best – and a beachy lifestyle are a magnet for Europe's hip surfing set.

Sights & Activities

Biarritz' fashionable beaches, particularly **Grande Plage** and **Plage Miramar**, are end-to-end bodies on hot summer days. Rent a stripey 1920s-style beach tent for €9.50 a day. North of Pointe St-Martin, the adrenaline-pumping surfing beaches of **Anglet** continue northwards for over 4km. Ride eastbound bus 9 from av Verdun (just near av Édouard VII).

Beyond long, exposed **Plage de la Côte des Basques**, some 500m south of Port Vieux, are **Plage de Marbella** and **Plage de la Milady**. Take westbound bus 9 from rue Gambetta where it crosses rue Broquedis.

Detour:
Europe's Largest Sand Dune

Between oyster beds and pine forest, the **Dune de Pilat** quite literally takes your breath away.

Sometimes called Dune de Pyla after the neighbouring resort town of **Pyla-sur-Mer**, 8km south of Arcachon, this colossal mountain of golden sand stretches south from the Bassin d'Arcachon for almost 3km. Europe's largest, it spreads 4.5m eastwards a year – swallowing trees, a road junction and a hotel in the process.

Frequent trains link Arcachon and Bordeaux (€9.80, 50 minutes).

Sleeping

HÔTEL MIRANO   Boutique Hotel   €€
(☎ 05 59 23 11 63; www.hotelmirano.fr, in French; 11 av Pasteur; d €100-110) Squiggly purple, orange and black wallpaper and oversized orange perspex light fittings are some of the rad '70s touches at this boutique retro hotel, a 10-minute stroll from the town centre.

VILLA LE GOËLAND Historic Hotel €€€
(☎ 05 59 24 25 76; www.villagoeland.com; 12 plateau de l'Atalaye; r from €170; 🛜) This stunning family home with chateau-like spires is perched high on a plateau above Pointe Atalaye. Rooms have panoramic views of town, the sea and across to Spain.

HÔTEL EDOUARD VII Historic Hotel €€
(☎ 05 59 22 39 80; www.hotel-edouardvii.com; 21 av Carnot; d from €118; 🛜) From the ornate dining room full of tick-tocking clocks to the pots of lavender designed to match the wallpaper, this beautiful and intimate hotel screams 1920s Biarritz chic.

Eating

See-and-be-seen cafes and restaurants line Biarritz' beachfront.

CASA JUAN PEDRO   Seafood   €
(📞05 59 24 00 86; Port des Pêcheurs; mains €5-15) Down by the old port – something of a hidden village of wooden fishing cottages – this cute shack restaurant cooks up tuna, sardines and squid with bags of friendly banter. There are several similar neighbouring places.

LE CRABE-TAMBOUR   Seafood   €€
(📞05 59 23 24 53; 49 rue d'Espagne; menus €13-18) Named after the famous 1977 film (the owner was the cook for the film set), this local address serves great seafood at a price that is hard to fault.

LE CLOS BASQUE   Basque   €€
(📞05 59 24 24 96; 12 rue Louis Barthou; menus €24; 🕐lunch Tue-Sun, dinner Tue-Sat) With its exposed stonework strung with abstract art, this tiny place could have strayed from Spain. Cuisine is traditional Basque with a contemporary twist. Reserve to snag a table on the terrace.

ℹ Information

Tourist office (📞05 59 22 37 00; www.biarritz .fr; Square d'Ixelles; 🕐9am-7pm Jul & Aug, 9am-6pm Mon-Sat, 10am-5pm Sun Sep-Jun)

ℹ Getting There & Away

Air

Biarritz-Anglet-Bayonne Airport (www.biarritz .aeroport.fr), 3km southeast of Biarritz, is served by easyJet, Ryanair and other low-cost carriers. STAB bus No 6 (line C on Sunday) links it once or twice hourly with Biarritz.

Train

Biarritz-La Négresse train station, 3km south of town, is linked to the centre by buses 2 and 9 (B and C on Sundays).

LANGUEDOC-ROUSSILLON

Languedoc-Roussillon comes in three distinct flavours: Bas-Languedoc (Lower Languedoc), land of bullfighting, rugby and robust red wines, where the region's major sights are; sunbaked Nîmes with its fine Roman amphitheatre; and fairy-tale Carcassonne, crowned with a ring of witch-hat turrets.

Carcassonne
POP 49,100

With its witch's hat turrets and walled city, from afar Carcassonne looks like some fairy-tale fortress – but the medieval magic's more than a little tarnished by an annual influx of over four million visitors. It can be a tourist hell in high summer, so pitch up

Château Comtal, Carcassonne
PHOTOGRAPHER: GLENN BEANLAND/LONELY PLANET IMAGES ©

GLENN BEANLAND/LONELY PLANET IMAGES ©

out of season to see the town at its best (and quietest).

The old city is dramatically illuminated at night and enclosed by two **rampart walls** punctuated by 52 stone towers, Europe's largest city fortifications. Successive generations of Gauls, Romans, Visigoths, Moors, Franks and Cathars reinforced the walls, but only the lower sections are original; the rest, including the turrets, were stuck on by the 19th-century architect Viollet-le-Duc.

A drawbridge leads to the old gate of **Porte Narbonnaise** and rue Cros Mayrevieille en route to place Château and the 12th-century **Château Comtal** (adult/child €8.50/free; ⊙10am-6.30pm Apr-Sep). Admission includes a castle meander, a short film and an optional 30- to 40-minute guided tour of the ramparts (tours in English July and August).

Carcassonne is on the main rail line to/from Toulouse (€14, 50 minutes).

Nîmes

POP 146,500

This buzzy city boasts some of France's best-preserved classical buildings, including a famous Roman amphitheatre,

although the city is most famous for its sartorial export, *serge de Nîmes* – better known to cowboys, clubbers and couturiers as denim.

Buy a **combination ticket** (adult/child €9.90/7.60), valid for three days, covering all three of Nîmes major sights. Buy one at the first sight you visit.

Sights

LES ARÈNES Roman Amphitheatre
(adult/child €7.80/4.50; ⊙9am-6.30pm)
Nîmes' magnificent Roman amphitheatre, the best preserved in the Roman Empire, was built around AD 100 to seat 24,000 spectators. It hosted animal fights to the death, stag hunts, man against lion or bear confrontations and, of course, gladiatorial combats. There's a mock-up of the gladiators' quarters and, if you time it right, you'll see a couple of actors in full combat gear slugging it out in the arena.

MAISON CARRÉE Roman Temple
(place de la Maison Carrée; adult/child €4.50/3.70; ⊙10am-6.30pm) The Square House is a remarkably well-preserved

PHILIP GAME/LONELY PLANET IMAGES ©

Don't Miss **Pont du Gard**

(www.pontdugard.fr) A Unesco World Heritage site, this three-tiered Roman aqueduct is exceptionally well preserved. It's part of a 50km-long system of canals built about 19 BC by the Romans to bring water from near Uzès to Nîmes. The scale is huge: the 35 arches of the 275m-long upper tier, running 50m above the Gard River, contain a watercourse designed to carry 20,000 cubic metres of water per day and the largest construction blocks weigh over five tonnes.

A day ticket covering the above, plus parking, is €15 for up to five passengers (€10 November to March). In July and August pay an extra €2 to teeter along the aqueduct's top tier with a guide (every half-hour from 10am to 11.30am and 2pm to 5.30pm). Admission to the site is free once the museum has closed.

The best view of the Pont du Gard is from upstream, beside the river, where you can swim on hot days.

rectangular Roman temple, constructed around AD 5 to honour Emperor Augustus' two adopted sons.

CARRÉ D'ART   MUSEUM

(www.carreeartmusee.com, in French; place de la Maison Carrée; permanent collection free, temporary exhibitions adult/child €5/3.70; ⏱10am-6pm Tue-Sun) The striking glass-and-steel building facing the Maison Carrée was designed by British architect Sir Norman Foster. Inside is the municipal library and Musée d'Art Contemporain with both permanent and temporary modern and contemporary art exhibitions from the 1960s on.

 **Sleeping**

ROYAL HÔTEL   Hotel €€

(☎04 66 58 28 27; www.royalhotel-nimes.com, in French; 3 blvd Alphonse Daudet; r €60-80; ❄ 🛜) You can't squeeze this 21-room hotel, popular with visiting artists and raffishly bohemian, into a standard mould.

HÔTEL AMPHITHÉÂTRE Hotel €

(☏ 04 66 67 28 51; http://perso.wanadoo.fr/
hotel-amphitheatre; 4 rue des Arènes; s €41-45,
d €53-70) A pair of 18th-century mansions,
the Amphitheatre Hotel just down the
road from its namesake just has 15 rooms,
each named after a writer or painter.

Eating

Nîmes' gastronomy owes as much to
Provence as to Languedoc. Look out for
cassoulet (pork, sausage and white bean
stew, sometimes served with duck), aïoli
and *rouille* (a spicy chilli mayonnaise).

Carré d'Art Classic French €€

(☏ 04 66 67 52 40; www.restaurant-lecarredart
.com, in French; 2 rue Gaston Boissier; menus
€19-29; ☺ Mon-Sat) Enjoy exceptional cuisine
in sublimely tasteful surroundings – gilded
mirrors, moulded ceilings, fresh flowers, feather-
light chandeliers and contemporary art work.

Au Plaisir des Halles French €€

(☏ 04 66 36 01 02; 4 rue Littré; mains €24-
30; ☺ Tue-Sat) Near the covered market;
ingredients here are locally sourced and the
lunchtime three-course *menu* (€20) is excellent
value. Local winegrowers feature.

ⓘ Information

Tourist office (☏ 04 66 58 38 00; www.ot
-nimes.fr; 6 rue Auguste; ☺ 8.30am-6.30pm Mon-
Fri, 9am-6.30pm Sat, 10am-5pm Sun)

ⓘ Getting There & Away

Bus

Bus station (☏ 04 66 38 59 43; rue Ste-Félicité)
PONT DU GARD €1.50, 30 minutes, two to seven
daily
UZÈS €1.50, 45 minutes, four to 10 daily

Train

ARLES €7.50, 30 minutes
AVIGNON €8.50, 30 minutes
MARSEILLE €19, 1¼ hours
PARIS GARE DE LYON €52 to €99.70, three hours

PROVENCE

Provence conjures up images of rolling
lavender fields, blue skies, gorgeous villages, wonderful food and superb wine.
It certainly delivers on all those fronts,
but it's not just worth visiting for its good
looks – dig a little deeper and you'll also
discover the multicultural metropolis of
Marseille, the artistic haven of Aix-en-
Provence and the old Roman city of Arles.

Marseille
POP 860,350

There was a time when Marseille was the
butt of French jokes. No more. The *cité
phocéenne* has made an unprecedented
comeback, undergoing a vast makeover.
Marseillais will tell you that the city's
rough-and-tumble edginess is part of
its charm and that, for all its flaws, it is
a very endearing place. They're right:
Marseille grows on you with its unique
history, souklike markets, millennia-old
port and spectacular *corniches* (coastal
roads) – all good reasons indeed why
Marseille was chosen as European Capital
of Culture in 2013.

Sights

The **Marseille City Pass** (1-/2-day pass
€22/29) gets you admission to Marseille's
museums, a guided tour of town, unlimited public transport travel, a boat trip,
entrance to Château d'If and a load of
discounts. Buy it at the tourist office.

VIEUX PORT Old Port
Guarding the harbour are **Fort St-Nicolas**
on the southern side and, across the
water, **Fort St-Jean**, founded in the 13th
century by the Knights Hospitaller of St
John of Jerusalem.

Standing guard between the old and
the 'new' port, is the striking Byzantine-
style **Cathédrale de la Major**, at the
heart of the current dynamic dockland
redevelopment around **La Joliette**. The
cathedral's distinct striped facade is built
from local white Cassis stone and green
marble from Florence in Italy.

Vieux Port

An Itinerary

Bold and busy and open-armed to the sea, Marseille is France's oldest city. Standing on the quai des Belges it's hard to get a sense of the extent of the old port, a kilometre long on either side, running down to the great bastions of St-Jean and St-Nicolas, which once had their guns trained on the rebellious population rather than out to sea. Immerse yourself in the city's history with this full-day itinerary.

Go early to experience the **fish market** ①, where you'll swap tall tales with the gregarious vendors. Hungry? Grab a balcony seat at La Caravelle, where views of the Basilique Notre Dame de la Garde accompany your morning coffee. Afterwards, take a **boat trip** ② to Château d'If, made famous by the Dumas novel, *The Count of Monte Cristo*. Alternatively, stay landside and explore the apricot-coloured alleys of **Le Panier** ③, browsing the exhibits at the **Centre de la Vieille Charité** ④.

In the afternoon, hop on the free cross-port ferry to the port's south side and wander into the **Abbaye St-Victor** ⑤ to see the bones of martyrs enshrined in gold. You can then catch the sunset from the stone benches in the **Jardin du Pharo** ⑥. As the warm southern evening sets in, join the throngs on cours **Honoré d'Estienne d'Orves**, where you can drink pastis beneath a giant statue of a lion devouring a man – the **Milo de Croton** ⑦.

CAPITAL OF CULTURE 2013

The largest urban renewal project in Europe, the Euroméditerranée project aims to rehabilitate the commercial Joliette docks along the same lines as London's Docklands. The city's green-and-white striped Cathédrale de la Major, for years abandoned in an area of urban wasteland, will form its centrepiece.

Le Panier
The site of the Greek town of Massilia, Le Panier woos walkers with its sloping streets. Grand Rue follows the ancient road and opens out into place de Lenche, the location of the Greek market. It is still the place to shop for artisan products.

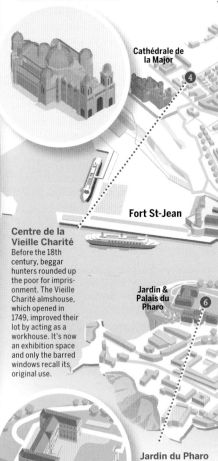

GLENN BEANLAND

Cathédrale de la Major ④

Fort St-Jean

Centre de la Vieille Charité
Before the 18th century, beggar hunters rounded up the poor for imprisonment. The Vieille Charité almshouse, which opened in 1749, improved their lot by acting as a workhouse. It's now an exhibition space and only the barred windows recall its original use.

Jardin & Palais du Pharo ⑥

Jardin du Pharo
Built by Napoléon for the Empress Eugénie, the Pharo Palace was designed with its 'feet in the water'. Today it is a private centre, but the gardens with their magnificent view are open all day.

Fish Market
Marseille's small fish market still sets up each morning to hawk the daily catch. Take a lesson in local seafood, spotting sea squirts, scorpion fish, sea urchins and conger eels. Get there before 9am if you're buying.

Milo de Croton
Subversive local artist Pierre Puget carved the savage *Milo de Croton* for Louis XIV. The statue, whose original is in the Louvre, is a meditation on man's pride and shows the Greek Olympian being devoured by a lion, his Olympic cup cast down.

Frioul If Express
Catch the Frioul If Express to Château d'If, France's equivalent to Alcatraz. Prisoners were housed according to class: the poorest at the bottom in windowless dungeons, the wealthiest in paid-for private cells, with windows and a fireplace.

Rue de la République

Quai des Belges

La Caravelle →

Quai du Port

Cross-Port Ferry →

Quai de Rive Neuve

Cours Honoré d'Estienne d'Orves

Bas Fort St-Nicolas

Lunch Break

Pick up sandwiches from Jardin des Vestiges, enjoy portside chic at Une Table au Sud, or go for earthy French-Corsican specials at La Cantine.

Abbaye St-Victor
St-Victor was built (420–30) to house the remains of tortured Christian martyrs. On Candlemas (2 February) the black Madonna is brought up from the crypt and the archbishop blesses the city and the sea.

BASILIQUE NOTRE DAME DE LA GARDE
Church

(montée de la Bonne Mère; ⏱7am-7pm, longer hr summer) Be blown away by the celestial views and knockout 19th-century architecture at the hilltop Basilique Notre Dame de la Garde, the resplendent Romano-Byzantine basilica 1km south of the Vieux Port that dominates Marseille's skyline. The domed basilica was built between 1853 and 1864 and is ornamented with coloured marble, murals and mosaics restored in 2006. Take bus 60 from the Vieux Port or walk up (30 minutes).

CHÂTEAU D'IF
Island Castle

(http://if.monuments-nationaux.fr; adult/child €5/free; ⏱9.30am-6.30pm, shorter hr & closed Mon winter) Immortalised in Alexandre Dumas' 1840s novel *Le Comte de Monte Cristo* (The Count of Monte Cristo), the 16th-century island prison of Château d'If sits 3.5km west of the Vieux Port. Political prisoners of all persuasions were incarcerated here, along with Protestants, the Revolutionary hero Mirabeau and the Communards of 1871.

Frioul If Express (www.frioul-if-express .com; 1 quai des Belges, 1er) boats (€10, 20 minutes) sail from the corner of quai de la Fraternité and quai de Rive Neuve at the Vieux Port.

LE PANIER
Historic Quarter

North of the Vieux Port, Marseille's old Le Panier quarter translates as 'the basket', and was the site of the Greek *agora* (marketplace). Today, its winding, narrow streets are a jumble of old stone houses, candy-coloured wooden shutters and artisans' shops.

LES CALANQUES
Nature Park

Marseille abuts the wild and spectacular Les Calanques, a protected 20km stretch of high, rocky promontories rising from the bright turquoise sea. They've been protected since 1975 and are slated to become a national park by 2011.

Marseille's tourist office leads guided hikes in Les Calanques and has information on walking trails (shut July and August due to forest fire risk). For great views from out at sea hop aboard a boat trip to the wine-producing port of **Cassis** (www.ot-cassis.com), 30km east along the coast, with **Croisières Marseille Calanques** (www.croisieres-marseille -calanques.com, in French; 74 quai du Port, 2e).

Lavender field, Provence

BETHUNE CARMICHAEL/LONELY PLANET IMAGES ®

Sleeping

CASA HONORÉ Boutique B&B €€€
(04 96 11 01 62; www.casahonore.com;
123 rue Sainte, 7e; d incl breakfast €150-200;
❄ 🤖 ⋈; M Vieux Port) Los Angeles
meets Marseille at this four-room
maison d'hôte, built around a central
courtyard with lap pool shaded by
banana trees.

Hôtel Saint-Ferréol Hotel €€
(04 91 33 12 21; www.hotelsaintferreol
.com; 19 rue Pisançon, 1er; d €99-120;
❄ @ 🤖; M Vieux Port) On the corner of
the city's prettiest pedestrianised street,
this plush hotel has individually decorated
rooms inspired by artists. Service is
exceptional.

Eating

The Vieux Port overflows with restaurants, but choose carefully. .
    When in Marseille eat bouillabaisse
(fish stew) and *supions* (squid pan-
fried with garlic, parsley and lemon).

Péron Contemporary €€€
(04 91 52 15 22; www.restaurant-peron
.com, in French; 56 corniche Président John
F Kennedy, 7e; mains €35; ⏱lunch Tue-Sun,
dinner Tue-Sat) Perched on the sea's edge
with magnificent views of Château d'If, Péron
is one of Marseille's top seafood tables. Arrive
before dark to watch the sunset.

La Cantinetta Italian €€
(04 91 48 10 48; 24 cours Julien; mains €9-
19; ⏱Tue-Sat; M Notre Dame du Mont-Cours
Julien) Our top choice on cours Julien serves
perfectly al dente housemade pasta and other
Italian goodies. Tables inside are cheek-by-jowl;
we prefer the sun-dappled, tiled patio garden.

Chez Madie Les Galinettes
Provençal €€
(04 91 90 40 87; 138 quai du Port, 2e; menus
€25-35; ⏱Mon-Sat, closed Sat lunch summer;
M Vieux Port) This portside terrace is always
packed, as is its arty interior when the weather
isn't cooperating. Bouillabaisse needs to be
ordered 48 hours ahead.

♥ If You Like…
French Markets

Every French region has its own mustn't
miss *marché* (market), but Provence and
the Cote d'Azur are particularly blessed.
The most famous are in **Nice** (p269) and
Marseille (p259), but you'll be able to find
one somewhere on nearly every day of the
week. Here are a few of the best…

1 VAISON-LA-ROMAINE
This delightful Provencal town has been renowned
for its thriving Tuesday market for as long as anyone
cares to remember. Hundreds of bustling stalls fill up
the cobbled medieval quarter from the crack of dawn,
selling everything from the freshest fruit to the most
fragrant lavender: the atmosphere is just about as
French as you'll get. It's 29km northeast of Orange.

2 CARPENTRAS
Market day is Friday at this lovely town 25km
northeast of Avignon. Breads, honeys, cheeses, olives,
fruit and handmade sausages are just some of the
treats in store, but the town's most famous exports are
berlingots, stripey hard-boiled sweets that come in a
rainbow of colours. From November to March, look out
for black truffles.

3 ST-TROPEZ
(www.ot-saint-tropez.com) It might be
best known for its beaches and Brigitte Bardot
connections, but St-Trop also hosts one of the Cote
d'Azur's liveliest markets. The action kicks off on
Tuesday and Saturday mornings on place des Lices:
stalls groan under plump veg, mounds of olives,
local cheeses, chestnut purée and fragrant herbs.
Afterwards you can survey the day's catch at the
fish market on place aux Herbes. St-Tropez is
84km southwest of Cannes.

Pizzaria Chez Étienne
Marseillais, Italian €€
(43 rue de Lorette, 2e; mains €12-15; ⏱Mon-Sat;
M Colbert) This family-style neighbourhood
haunt serves Marseille's best wood-fired pizza,
beef steak and *supions* (pan-fried squid). Pop in
beforehand to reserve in person (no phone). No
credit cards.

CHEZ JEANNOT Marseillais, French €€
(☎04 91 52 11 28; 129 rue du Vallon des Auffes;
mains €12-25; ⏰Tue-Sat, lunch Sun) An institution among Marseillais, the jovial rooftop terrace overlooking the port of Vallon des Auffes books out days ahead (but you can usually score an inside table). Stick to thin-crust pizzas and *supions* ('chippirons' on the menu).

MARSEILLE MARKETS   Market €
The small but enthralling **fish market** (quai des Belges; ⏰8am-1pm; Ⓜ Vieux Port) is a daily fixture at the Vieux Port. **Cours Julien** hosts a Wednesday-morning organic fruit and vegetable market.

🍷 Drinking & Entertainment

Cafes crowd cours Honoré d'Estienne d'Orves (1e), a large open square two blocks south of quai de Rive Neuve. Another cluster overlooks place de la Préfecture, at the southern end of rue St-Ferréol (1er).

ℹ️ Information

Dangers & Annoyances
Marseille isn't a hotbed of violent crime, but petty crimes and muggings are common. Avoid the Belsunce area (southwest of the train station, bounded by La Canebière, cours Belsunce and rue d'Aix, rue Bernard du Bois and blvd d'Athènes) at night. Walking La Canebiére is annoying, but generally not dangerous; expect to encounter kids peddling hash.

Tourist information
Tourist office (☎04 91 13 89 00; www
.marseille-tourisme.com; 4 La Canebière, 1er;
⏰9am-7pm Mon-Sat, 10am-5pm Sun; Ⓜ Vieux Port)

ℹ️ Getting There & Away

Air
Aéroport Marseille-Provence (www.marseille.
aeroport.fr), 25km northwest in Marignane, has numerous budget flights to various European

destinations. **Shuttle buses** (Marseille ☎04 91 50 59 34; airport ☎04 42 14 31 27; www.lepilote. com) link it with Marseille train station.

Boat
Gare Maritime (passenger ferry terminal; www
.marseille-port.fr; Ⓜ Joliette)

SNCM (www.sncm.fr; 61 blvd des Dames, 2e;
Ⓜ Joliette) Ferries to/from Corsica, Sardinia, Algeria and Tunisia.

Train
From Marseille's **Gare St-Charles**, trains including TGVs go all over France and Europe.

AVIGNON €22.80, 35 minutes, 27 daily

LYON €47.30, 1¾ hours, 16 daily

NICE €29.70, 2½ hours, 21 daily

PARIS GARE DE LYON €84.20, three hours, 21 daily

ℹ️ Getting Around
Marseille has two metro lines, two tram lines and an extensive bus network, all run by **RTM** (6 rue des Fabres, 1er; ⏰8.30am-6pm Mon-Fri, 9am-12.30pm & 2-5.30pm Sat; Ⓜ Vieux Port), where you can obtain information and transport tickets (€1.50).

Aix-en-Provence
POP 146,700

Aix-en-Provence is to Provence what the Left Bank is to Paris: a pocket of bohemian chic crawling with students. The city has been a cultural centre since the Middle Ages (two of the town's most famous sons are painter Paul Cézanne and novelist Émile Zola) but for all its polish, it's still a laid-back Provençal town at heart.

◉ Sights

CIRCUIT DE CÉZANNE   Artist Trail
Art, culture and architecture abound in Aix, especially thanks to local lad Paul Cézanne (1839–1906). To see where he ate, drank, studied and painted, you can follow the **Circuit de Cézanne**, marked by footpath-embedded bronze plaques

inscribed with the letter C. A free English-language guide to the plaques, *Cézanne's Footsteps,* is available from the tourist office.

The trail takes in Cézanne's last studio, **Atelier Paul Cézanne** (www.atelier-cezanne.com; 9 av Paul Cézanne; adult/child €5.50/2; ☺10am-noon & 2-6pm, closed Sun winter), which lies 1.5km north of the tourist office. It's painstakingly preserved as it was at the time of his death, strewn with tools and still-life models; his admirers claim that this is where Cézanne is most present.

The other two main Cézanne sights in Aix are the **Bastide du Jas de Bouffan**, the family home where Cézanne started painting, and the **Bibémus quarries**, where he did most of his Montagne Ste-Victoire paintings. Head to the tourist office for bookings (required) and information.

MUSÉE GRANET   Museum

(www.museegranet-aixenprovence.fr, in French; place St-Jean de Malte; adult/child €4/free; ☺11am-7pm Tue-Sun) Housed in a 17th-century priory, this museum's pride and joy is its nine Cézanne paintings and works by Picasso, Léger, Matisse, Tal Coat and Giacometti.

 Sleeping

L'ÉPICERIE   B&B   €€

(☏06 08 85 38 68; www.unechambreenville.eu; 12 rue du Cancel; s incl breakfast €80-120, d €100-130; ☎) This retro B&B is the fabulous creation of born-and-bred Aixois lad Luc. His breakfast room recreates a 1950s grocery store, and the flowery garden out back is a dream for evening dining (book ahead). Breakfast is a veritable feast gargantuan enough to last all day.

HÔTEL CARDINAL   Hotel   €

(☏04 42 38 32 30; www.hotel-cardinal-aix.com; 24 rue Cardinale; s/d €60/70) Hôtel Cardinal's 29 romantic rooms are beautifully furnished with antiques, tasselled curtains and newly tiled bathrooms.

HÔTEL CÉZANNE   Boutique Hotel   €€€

(☏04 42 91 11 11; http://cezanne.hotelaix.com; 40 av Victor Hugo; d €179-249; ❄ @ ☎) Aix's hippest hotel is a study in clean lines, with sharp-edged built-in desks and loveseats that feel a touch IKEA. Best is breakfast (€19), which includes smoked salmon and Champagne.

 Eating

Aix' sweetest treat is the marzipan-like local speciality, *calisson d'Aix,* a small, diamond-shaped, chewy delicacy made with ground almonds and fruit syrup. The daily **produce market** (place Richelme) sells olives, goat's cheese, garlic, lavender, honey, peaches, melons and other sun-kissed products.

Cézanne gallery

LE POIVRE D'ANE   Contemporary **€€**
(☎ 04 42 21 32 66; www.restaurantlepoivredane
.com; 40 place des Cardeurs; menus €28-45;
🕙 dinner Thu-Tue) Fancy a haddock milkshake,
duck sushi or thyme-and-cinnamon apple
tart with Baileys whipped cream? Summer
tables are smack dab on one of Aix's loveliest
pedestrian squares; reservations essential.

AMPHITRYON   Provençal **€€**
(☎ 04 42 26 54 10; www.restaurant-amphitryon
.fr; 2-4 rue Paul Doumer; menus €25-40; 🕙 Tue-
Sat) Amphitryon enjoys a solid reputation,
particularly in summer for its market-driven
cooking and alfresco dining in the cloister-
garden. Attached **Comptoir de l'Amphi**
(mains €12 to €17) is less expensive.

LE PETIT VERDOT   French **€€**
(☎ 04 42 27 30 12; www.lepetitverdot.fr; 7 rue
Entrecasteaux; mains €15-25; 🕙 dinner Mon-Sat,
lunch Sat) Wine is the primary focus at this
earthy restaurant, where tabletops are
made of cast-off wine crates. The meat-
heavy menu is designed to marry with the
wines, not the other way round.

ℹ Information

Tourist office (www.aixenprovencetourism.
com; 2 place du Général de Gaulle; 🕙 8.30am-
7pm Mon-Sat, 10am-1pm & 2-6pm Sun, longer hr
summer)

ℹ Getting There & Away

Bus

From Aix' **bus station** (av de l'Europe), which is
a 10-minute walk southwest from La Rotonde,
routes include to/from Marseille (€4.90, 35
minutes via the autoroute or one hour via the
D8), Arles (€9, 1½ hours) and Avignon (€14.70,
1¼ hours).

Half-hourly shuttle buses go to/from Aix TGV
station and Aéroport Marseille-Provence.

Train

The only useful train from Aix' **city centre train
station** (av Victor Hugo) is to/from Marseille (€7,
50 minutes). Other services use **Aix TGV station**,
15km away.

Left: Pont St-Bénezet over the Rhône River;
Below: Carved throne at Palais des Papes

PHOTOGRAPHER: (LEFT) BETHUNE CARMICHAEL/LONELY PLANET IMAGES ©;
(BELOW) BILL WASSMAN/LONELY PLANET IMAGES ©

Avignon
POP 93,560

Hooped by 4.3km of superbly preserved stone ramparts, this graceful city is the belle of Provence's ball. Famed for its annual performing arts festival and fabled bridge, Avignon is an ideal spot from which to step out into the surrounding region. Wrapping around the city, Avignon's defensive ramparts were built between 1359 and 1370, and are punctuated by a series of sturdy *portes* (gates).

Sights

PALAIS DES PAPES   Papal Palace
(www.palais-des-papes.com; place du Palais; adult/child €6/3; ⏱9am-8pm Jul & early–mid-Sep, 9am-9pm Aug, 9am-7pm mid-Mar–Jun & mid-Sep–Oct, 9am-6.30pm early–mid-Mar, 9am-5.45pm Nov-Feb) This Unesco World Heritage site, the world's largest Gothic palace, was built when Pope Clement V abandoned Rome in 1309 and settled in Avignon. The immense scale of the palace, with its cavernous stone halls and vast courtyards, testifies to the enormous wealth of the popes. The 3m-thick walls, portcullises and watchtowers, meanwhile, emphasise their need for defence.

PONT ST-BÉNEZET   Bridge
(adult/child €4.50/3.50; ⏱9am-8pm, 9.30am-5.45pm Nov-Mar) This fabled bridge, immortalised in the French nursery rhyme *Sur le Pont d'Avignon,* was completed in 1185. The 900m-long wooden bridge was repaired and rebuilt several times before all but four of its 22 spans were washed away in the mid-1600s. If you don't feel like paying, you can see it for free from the Rocher des Doms park, Pont Édouard Daladier or from across the river on the Île de la Barthelasse's chemin des Berges.

MUSÉE DU PETIT PALAIS Museum

(www.petit-palais.org; place du Palais; adult/child €6/free; ⏰10am-1pm & 2-6pm Wed-Mon) The bishops' and archbishops' palace during the 14th and 15th centuries now houses an outstanding collection of 13th- to 16th-century Italian religious paintings by artists such as Botticelli and Carpaccio.

MUSÉE ANGLADON Museum

(www.angladon.com; 5 rue Laboureur; adult/child €6/4; ⏰1-6pm Tue-Sun Apr-Nov, 1-6pm Wed-Sun Jan-Mar, closed Dec) This museum harbours the only Van Gogh painting in Provence *(Railway Wagons)*, as well as works by Cézanne, Manet, Degas and Picasso.

 ## Festivals & Events

Hundreds of artists take to the stage and streets during the world-famous **Festival d'Avignon** (www.festival-avignon.com), held every year from early July to early August. Don't miss the more experimental (cheaper) fringe **Festival Off** (www.avignonleoff.com, in French) that runs alongside the main fest.

 ## Sleeping

LE LIMAS B&B €€

(☎04 90 14 67 19; www.le-limas-avignon.com; 51 rue du Limas; d/tr incl breakfast from €120/200; ❄@) Behind its discreet lavender door, this chic address in an 18th-century town house is like something out of *Vogue Living*. It's everything interior designers strive for when mixing old and new. Breakfast by the fireplace or on a sun-drenched terrace!

HÔTEL BOQUIER Hotel €

(☎04 90 82 34 43; www.hotel-boquier.com, in French; 6 rue du Portail Boquier; d €50-70; ❄🛜) The infectious enthusiasm of owners Sylvie and Pascal Sendra sweeps through this central little place, bright, airy and spacious.

LUMANI B&B €€

(☎04 90 82 94 11; www.avignon-lumani.com; 37 rue du Rempart St-Lazare; d incl breakfast €100-170; ❄🛜) This fabulous *maison d'hôte* run by Elisabeth, whose art is hung throughout the stunning house, is a fount of inspiration for artists. Love the fountained garden.

 ## Eating

Place de l'Horloge's touristy cafes only have so-so food.

CUISINE DU DIMANCHE Provençal €€

(☎04 90 82 99 10; www.lacuisinedudimanche.com, in French; 31 rue Bonneterie; mains €15-25; ⏰closed Sun & Mon Oct-May) Spitfire chef Marie shops every morning at Les Halles to find the freshest ingredients for her earthy flavour-packed cooking. The market-driven menu changes daily, but specialities include scallops and a simple roast chicken with pan gravy.

Port de Monaco

Van Gogh's Arles

If the winding streets and colourful houses of Arles seem familiar, it's hardly surprising – Vincent van Gogh lived here for much of his life in a yellow house on place Lamartine, and the town regularly featured in his canvases. His original house was destroyed during WWII, but you can still follow in Vincent's footsteps on the **Van Gogh Trail**, marked out by footpath plaques and a brochure handed out by the **tourist office** (main office ☏ 04 90 18 41 20; www.tourisme.ville-arles.fr; esplanade Charles de Gaulle; ☺ 9am-6.45pm Apr-Sep, 9am-4.45pm Mon-Sat, 10am-12.45pm Sun Oct-Mar; train station ☏ 04 90 43 33 57; ☺ 9am-1.30pm & 2.30-4.45pm Mon-Fri Apr-Sep).

Two millennia ago, Arles was a major Roman settlement. The town's 20,000-seat amphitheatre and 12,000-seat theatre, known as the **Arénes** and the **Théâtre Antique**, are nowadays used for cultural events and bullfights.

Telleschi (☏ 04 42 28 40 22) buses go to/from Aix-en-Provence (€9, 1½ hours) and there are regular trains to/from Nîmes (€7.50, 30 minutes), Marseille (€13.55, 55 minutes) and Avignon (€6.60, 20 minutes).

AU TOUT PETIT Contemporary French €€
(☏ 04 90 82 38 86; 4 rue d'Amphoux; menus €11-24; ☺ Tue-Sat) This teensy place with just eight tables packs big flavours into every imaginative dish: it has simple, smart cooking.

L'EPICE AND LOVE French €
(☏ 04 90 82 45 96, 30 rue des Lices; mains €11-12; ☺ dinner Mon-Sat) Stews, roasts and other homestyle French dishes is what makes this tiny bohemian restaurant, decorated with antique kitchenware and mismatched chairs, so appealing. No credit cards.

ℹ️ Information

Tourist office (www.avignon-tourisme.com; 41 cours Jean Jaurès; ☺ 9am-5pm Mon-Sat, 9.45am-5pm Sun)

ℹ️ Getting There & Away

Avignon has two stations: Gare Avignon TGV, 4km southwest in Courtine; and central Gare Avignon Centre (42 blvd St-Roch) with trains to/from:

ARLES €6.70, 20 minutes

NÎMES €8.70, 30 minutes

Some TGVs to/from Paris stop at Gare Avignon Centre, but TGVs for Marseille (€22.80, 35 minutes) and Nice (€54.40, three hours) only use Gare Avignon TGV.

CÔTE D'AZUR & MONACO

With its glistening seas, idyllic beaches and lush hills, the Côte d'Azur (French Riviera) screams exclusivity, extravagance and excess. It has been a favourite getaway for European high society since Victorian times and there is nowhere more chichi or glam in France than St-Tropez, Cannes and super-rich, sovereign Monaco.

Nice
POP 352,400

Riviera queen Nice is what good living is all about – shimmering shores, the very best of Mediterranean food, a unique historical heritage, free museums, a charming Old Town, exceptional art and Alpine wilderness within an hour's drive. No wonder so many young French people aspire to live here, and the tourists just keep flooding in.

To get stuck in straight away, make a beeline upon arrival for Promenade des Anglais, Nice's curvaceous palm-lined seafront, which follows its busy pebble beach for 6km from the city centre to the airport.

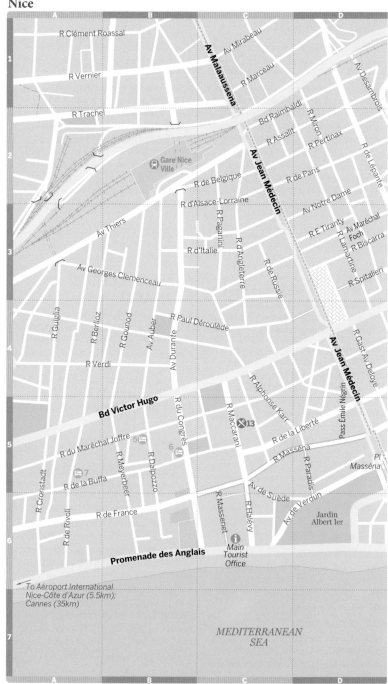

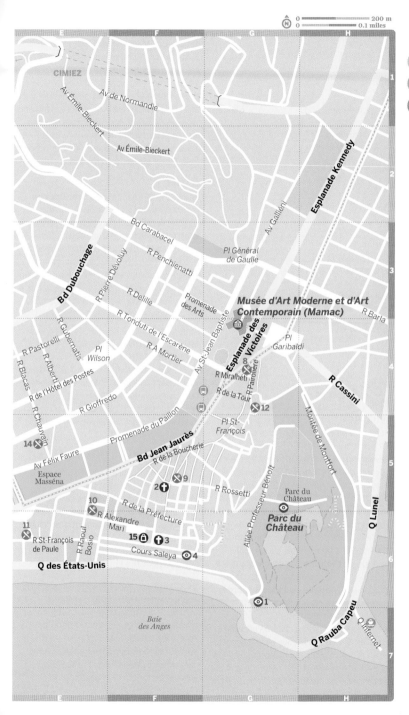

CIMIEZ

Av Émile-Bieckert

Av de Normandie

Av Émile-Bieckert

Esplanade Kennedy

Av Galléni

Bd Carabacel

R Penchienatti

Pl Général
de Gaulle

Bd Dubouchage

R Pierre Dévoluy

R Delille

Promenade
des Arts

**Musée d'Art Moderne et d'Art
Contemporain (Mamac)**

R Barla

R Tonduti de l'Escarène

R A Mortier

Av St-Jean Baptiste

**Esplanade des
Victoires**

Pl
Garibaldi

R Gubernatis

R Pastorelli

Pl
Wilson

R Blacas

R Alberti

R de l'Hôtel des Postes

R Chauvain

R Gioffredo

R Miralhéti

R Painolière

R de la Tour

R Cassini

Montée de Montfort

Promenade du Paillon

Pl St-
François

12

14

Av Félix Faure

Bd Jean Jaurès

R de la Boucherie

Espace
Masséna

2

9

R Rossetti

Parc du
Château

Allée Professeur Bénoît

*Parc du
Château*

Q Lunel

10

R Alexandre
Mari

R de la Préfecture

11

R St-François
de Paule

R Raoul
Bosio

15

3

Cours Saleya

4

Q des États-Unis

1

*Baie
des Anges*

Q Rauba Capeu

Q Internet

N 0 ———————— 200 m
     0 ———————— 0.1 miles

Nice

Sights

VIEUX NICE   Old town
Lose yourself in the Old Town's tangle of
18th-century pedestrian passages and
alleyways, historic churches and hole-in-
the-wall joints selling Niçois tapas. Cours
Saleya, running parallel to the seafront,
hosts one of France's most vibrant **food
markets** (⏰6am-1.30pm Tue-Sun), trestle
tables groaning with shiny fruit and veg,
pastries, *fruits confits* (glazed or candied
fruits such as figs, ginger, pears etc).
Baroque **Cathédrale Ste-Réparate (place
Rossetti)** with its glazed terracotta dome
(1650) and **Chapelle de la Miséricorde
(cours Saleya)** are equally exuberant.

At the eastern end of quai des États-
Unis, steep steps and a cliffside **ascenseur**
(lift; €1.10; ⏰9am-7pm Apr-Sep, shorter hr rest of
year) climb up to **Parc du Château**, a hilltop
park with great views over Old Nice and the
beachfront. The chateau itself was razed by
Louis XIV in 1706 and never rebuilt.

MUSÉE MATISSE   Museum
(www.musee-matisse-nice.org; 164 av des Arènes
de Cimiez; ⏰10am-6pm Wed-Mon) Housed in a
17th-century Genoese mansion, this small
museum reveals Matisse's evolution as an
artist rather than wowing the crowds with
masterpieces. View well-known works such
as his blue paper cutouts *Blue Nude IV* and
Woman with Amphora alongside less-well-
known sculptures and experimental pieces.
Take bus 17 from the bus station or bus 22
from Place Masséna to the Arènes stop.

MAMAC   Museum
(Musée d'Art Moderne et d'Art Contemporain;
www.mamac-nice.org; promenade des Arts;
⏰10am-6pm Tue-Sun) This one is worth a
visit for its stunning architecture alone,
but it also houses some fantastic avant-
garde art from the 1960s to the present,
including iconic pop art from Roy Lichtenstein and Andy Warhol's 1965 *Campbell's
Soup Can*. An awesome panorama of
Vieux Nice unfolds from the rooftop
garden-gallery.

**MUSÉE NATIONAL MESSAGE
BIBLIQUE MARC CHAGALL**   Museum
(www.musee-chagall.fr, in French; 4 av Dr Ménard;
adult/child €7.50/5.50; ⏰10am-5pm Wed-Mon
Oct-Jun, to 6pm Jul-Sep) This small museum
houses the largest public collection of the
Russian-born artist's seminal paintings of *Old
Testament* scenes.

CORNICHES   Scenic Drive
Some of the Riviera's most spectacular
scenery stretches east between Nice
and Monaco. A trio of corniches (coastal
roads) hugs the cliffs between the two
seaside cities, each higher up the hill than
the last. The middle corniche ends in
Monaco; the upper and lower continue to
Menton near the French-Italian border.

BEACHES   Beaches
You'll need at least a beach mat to
cushion your tush from Nice's beaches,
which are made up of round pebbles.
Free sections of beach alternate with 15
sunlounge-lined **private beaches** (www
.plagesdenice.com, in French; ⏰May-Sep),
where you pay to rent a sunlounger
(around €15 a day).

Festivals & Events

Carnaval de Nice
Carnival

(www.nicecarnaval.com) This two-week carnival, held in February, is particularly famous for its battles of the flowers, where thousands of blooms are tossed into the crowds from passing floats, as well as its fantastic fireworks display.

 # Sleeping

Nice has a suite of places to sleep, from stellar independent backpacker hostels to international art-filled icons. Prices rocket upwards in the summer season.

VILLA RIVOLI
Boutique Hotel €€

(☎04 93 88 80 25; www.villa-rivoli.com; 10 rue de Rivoli; s/d/q from 85/99/210; ❄ 🛜) Built in 1890, this stately villa feels like your own pied-à-terre in the heart of Nice. Rooms are character-rich, some with fabric walls, gilt-edged mirrors and marble fireplaces.

HÔTEL WINDSOR
Boutique Hotel €€

(☎04 93 88 59 35; www.hotelwindsornice.com; 11 rue Dalpozzo; d €120-175; ❄ @ 🛜 🏊) Graffiti casts aggressive splashes of colour on the edgy, oversize rooms of the Windsor – a real nod to contemporary art. Rooms overlooking the backyard tropical garden have a particularly lush view.

NICE GARDEN HÔTEL
Boutique Hotel €€

(☎04 93 87 35 63; www.nicegardenhotel.com; 11 rue du Congrès; s/d €75/100; ❄ 🛜) Nine beautifully appointed rooms blend old and new and overlook a delightful garden with a glorious orange tree – pure unadulterated charm and peace just two blocks from the promenade.

HÔTEL ARMENONVILLE
Hotel €€

(☎04 93 96 86 00; www.hotel-armenonville.com; 20 av des Fleurs; d €86-105; @ 🛜) Shielded by its large garden, this grand early 20th-century mansion has sober rooms, three (12, 13 and 14) with huge terrace overlooking *le jardin*.

 # Eating

Niçois nibbles include *socca* (a thin layer of chickpea flour and olive oil batter), *salade niçoise* and *farcis* (stuffed vegetables). Restaurants in Vieux Nice are a mixed bag, so choose carefully.

View from Parc du Château

GLENN VAN DER KNIJFF/LONELY PLANET IMAGES ©

LUC SALSEDO
Modern French €€€

(📞04 93 82 24 12; www.restaurant-salsedo.com, in French; 14 rue Maccarani; mains €26; 🕐lunch Fri & Sun-Tue, dinner Thu-Tue Jun-Sep, dinner only Jul-Aug) The cuisine of young chef Salsedo is local and seasonal, and is served without pomp on plates, rustic boards or cast-iron pots. The wine list is another French hit.

LUNA ROSSA
Italian €€

(📞04 93 85 55 66; www.lelunarossa.com; 3 rue Chauvain; mains €15-25; 🕐Tue-Fri, dinner Sat) The Red Moon translates as fresh pasta, perfectly cooked seafood, sun-kissed veg (artichoke hearts, sun-dried tomatoes, asparagus tips etc) and succulent meats.

LA MERENDA
Niçois €€

(4 rue Raoul Bosio; mains €12-15; 🕐Mon-Fri) This pocket-sized bistro serves some of the most unusual fare in town: stockfish (dried cod soaked in running water for a few days and then simmered with onions, tomatoes, garlic, olives and potatoes) and tripe. It also serves Bellet wines, a rare local vintage. No credit cards.

LA PETITE MAISON
French, Niçois €€€

(📞04 93 92 59 59; www.lapetitemaison-nice.com; 11 rue St-François de Paule; mains €20-40; 🕐Mon-Sat) Nice's hottest table draws celebs and politicians for its happening scene and elegantly executed Niçois specialities – tops for a splashy night out.

CHEZ RENÉ SOCCA
Niçois €

(2 rue Miralhéti; dishes from €2; 🕐9am-9pm Tue-Sun, to 10.30pm Jul & Aug, closed Nov) This address is about taste, not presentation or manners. Grab some *socca* or *petits farçis* and head across the street to the bar for a *grand pointu* (glass) of red, white or rosé.

LA TABLE ALZIARI
Niçois €

(📞04 93 80 34 03, 4 rue François Zanin; mains €9-15; 🕐Tue-Sat) Run by the grandson of the famous Alziari olive oil family, this citrus-coloured restaurant chalks up local specialities such as *morue à la niçoise* (cod served with potatoes, olives and a tomato sauce) and *daube* (stew) on its blackboard.

FENOCCHIO
Ice Cream €

(2 place Rossetti; from €2; 🕐9am-midnight Feb-Oct) Beat the summer heat with Nice's most fabulous *glacier* (ice-cream maker). Eschew predictable favourites and indulge in a new taste sensation: black olive, tomato-basil, rhubarb, avocado, rosemary, *calisson* (almond biscuit frosted with icing sugar), lavender, ginger or liquorice. There's 50 flavours in all to pick from.

ℹ Information

Main tourist office (www .nicetourisme.com; 5 promenade des Anglais; 🕐8am-8pm Mon-Sat, 9am-7pm Sun Jun-Sep, 9am-6pm Mon-Sat Oct-May) By the beach.

Train station tourist office (av Thiers; 🕐8am-8pm Mon-Sat, 9am-7pm Sun Jun-Sep, 8am-7pm Mon-Sat, 10am-5pm Sun Oct-May)

Women in festive costumes at Carnaval de Nice (p273)
PHOTOGRAPHER: JTB PHOTO/LONELY PLANET IMAGES ©

Getting There & Away

Air

Aéroport International Nice-Côte d'Azur (www .nice.aeroport.fr), 6km west of the centre, is served by numerous carriers, including several low-cost ones.

Ligne d'Azur runs two airport buses (€4). Route 99 shuttles approximately every half-hour direct between Gare Nice Ville and both airport terminals daily from around 8am to 9pm. Route 98 takes the slow route and departs from the bus station every 20 minutes (30 minutes Sunday) from around 6am to around 9pm.

Bus

From the **bus station** (5 blvd Jean Jaurès) a single €1 fare takes you anywhere in the Alpes-Maritimes *département* (with a few exceptions, such as the airport) and includes one connection, within 74 minutes. Buses run daily to Antibes (one hour), Cannes (1½ hours), Monaco (45 minutes), Vence (one hour) and St-Paul de Vence (55 minutes).

Train

From **Gare Nice Ville** (av Thiers), 1.2km north of the beach, there are frequent services to Antibes (€4, 30 minutes), Cannes (€6.10, 40 minutes), Menton (€4.60, 35 minutes) and Monaco (€3.40, 20 minutes). Direct TGV trains link Nice with Paris' Gare de Lyon (€115, 5½ hours).

Cannes

POP 71,800

Everyone's heard of Cannes and its celebrity film festival. The latter only lasts for two weeks in May, but the buzz and glitz linger all year thanks to regular visits from celebrities who come here to indulge in designer shopping, beaches and the palace hotels of the Riviera's most glamorous seafront, blvd de la Croisette.

 Sights & Activities

BEACHES　　　　　　　　　　　　　Beach

The central, sandy beaches along blvd de la Croisette are sectioned off for hotel patrons. Many accept day guests, who

pay from €20 per day for a mattress and yellow-and-white parasol on **Plage du Gray d'Albion** (⊘10am-5pm Mar-Oct) to €50-odd for a pearl-white lounge on the pier of super-stylish **Z Plage** (⊘9.30am-6pm May-Sep), the beach of Hôtel Martinez.

A microscopic strip of sand near the Palais des Festivals is free, but you'll find better free sand on **Plages du Midi** and **Plages de la Bocca**, west from the Vieux Port along blvd Jean Hibert and blvd du Midi.

PALAIS DES FESTIVALS　　　　Landmark

(Festival Palace; blvd de la Croisette) At the western end of La Croisette, this concrete bunker is the unlikely host of the world's most glamorous film festival. The tourist office runs **guided tours** (adult/child €3/free; 1½ hrs; ⊘2.30pm Jun-Apr) several times a month; book ahead.

LE SUQUET　　　　　　　　　　Old Town

Cannes' historic quarter, pre-dating the glitz and glam of the town's festival days, retains a quaint village feel with its steep, meandering alleyways. There are wonderful views of the Baie de Cannes from the top of the hill, and the fascinating **Musée de la Castre** (place de la Castre; adult/child €3.20/free; ⊘10am-7pm Jul & Aug, 10am-1pm & 2-5pm Tue-Sun Sep-Jun), an ethnographic museum.

ÎLES DE LÉRINS　　　　　　　　　Islands

Although just 20 minutes away by boat, these tranquil islands feel far from the madding crowd.

Boats leave Cannes from quai des Îles on the western side of the harbour. **Riviera Lines** (ww.riviera-lines.com) runs ferries to Île Ste-Marguerite (adult/child €11.50/6 return) and **Compagnie Planaria** (www.cannes-ilesdelerins.com) covers Île St-Honorat (adult/child €12/6).

 Sleeping

Hotel prices in Cannes fluctuate wildly according to the season, and soar during the film festival, when you'll need to book months in advance.

HÔTEL 7E ART
Boutique Hotel €

(04 93 68 66 66; www.7arthotel.com; 23 rue Maréchal Joffre; s €68, d €60-98; ❄ 🛜) Cannes' newest star puts boutique style within reach of budgeteers. The owners were schooled in Switzerland and their snappy design of putty-coloured walls, padded headboards and pop art far exceeds what you'd expect at this price.

HOTEL LE ROMANESQUE
Boutique Hotel €€

(04 93 68 04 20; www.hotelleromanesque .com; 10 rue Batéguier; r €90-150; ❄ 🛜) Every room is individually decorated at this eight-room boutique charmer in the heart of Cannes' nightlife district.

VILLA TOSCA
Hotel €€

(04 93 38 34 40; www.villa-tosca.com; 11 rue Hoche; s/d €80/100; ❄ 🛜) This elegant bourgeois town house sits on a semi-pedestrianised street in Cannes' shopping area. Rooms with balcony are perfect for people-watching.

HÔTEL SPLENDID
Boutique Hotel €€€

(04 97 06 22 22; www.splendid-hotel-cannes. com; 4-6 rue Félix Faure; s/d from €160/190; ❄) This elaborate 1871 building has everything it takes to rival Cannes' posher palaces: beautifully decorated rooms, fabulous location, stunning views – and more in the form of self-catering kitchenettes.

 Eating

MANTEL
Modern European €€

(04 93 39 13 10; www.restaurantmantel.com; 22 rue St-Antoine; menus €25-38; 🕐 Fri-Mon, dinner Tue & Thu) The Italian maître d' will make you feel like a million dollars and you'll melt for Noël Mantel's divine cuisine and great-value prices. Best of all, you get not one but two desserts with your menu (oh, the pannacotta…).

Coquillages Brun
Seafood €€

(04 93 39 21 87; www.astouxbrun.com; 27 rue Félix Faure; menus from €28; 🕐 12pm-1am) Cannes' most famous brasserie is *the* place to indulge in oysters, mussels, prawns, crayfish and other delightfully fresh shells with a glass of crisp white wine.

AUX BONS ENFANTS
Traditional French €€

(80 rue Meynadier; menus €23; 🕐 Tue-Sat) This familial little place buzzes. The lucky ones who get a table (arrive early or late) can feast on top-notch regional dishes.

ℹ Information

Tourist office (04 92 99 84 22; www.cannes .travel; blvd de la Croisette; 🕐 9am-8pm Jul & Aug, 9am-7pm Mon-Sat Sep-Jun) On the ground floor of Palais des Festivals; runs an annexe next to the train station.

ℹ Getting There & Away

Train

GRASSE €3.80, 30 minutes

MARSEILLE €22, two hours

Monaco
377 / POP 32,000

Your first glimpse of this pocket-sized principality will probably make your heart sink: after all the gorgeous medieval hilltop villages, glittering beaches and secluded peninsulas of the surrounding area, Monaco's concrete high-rises and astronomic prices come as a shock. But Monaco is beguiling. The world's second-smallest state (a smidgen bigger than the Vatican), it is as famous for its tax-haven status as for its glittering casino, sports scene (Formula One, world-famous circus festival and tennis open) and a royal family on a par with British royals for best gossip fodder.

◎ Sights & Activities

CASINO DE MONTE CARLO
Casino

(www.casinomontecarlo.com; place du Casino; 🕐 European Rooms from noon Sat & Sun, from 2pm Mon-Fri) Living out your James Bond fantasies just doesn't get any better than at Monte Carlo's monumental, richly decorated showpiece, the 1910-built casino. Admission is €10 for the European Rooms, with poker/slot machines, French roulette and *trente et quarante* (a card game), and €20 for the Private Rooms,

JEAN-PIERRE LESCOURRET/LONELY PLANET IMAGES ©

which offer baccarat, blackjack, craps and American roulette. Jacket-and-tie dress code kicks in after 10pm. Minimum entry age for both types of rooms is 18; bring photo ID.

MUSÉE OCÉANOGRAPHIQUE DE MONACO
Aquarium

(www.oceano.org; av St-Martin; adult/child €13/6.50; ⏰9.30am-7pm) Propped on a sheer cliff-face, this graceful aquarium was built in 1910 . Don't miss the spectacular views from the rooftop terrace.

PALAIS DU PRINCE
Royal Palace

(www.palais.mc; adult/child €8/3.50; ⏰10am-6pm Apr-Sep) For a glimpse into royal life, tour the state apartments with an audioguide. The palace is what you would expect of any aristocratic abode: lavish furnishings and expensive 18th- and 19th-century art. Guards are changed outside the palace at 11.55am every day.

 Sleeping

NI HÔTEL
Boutique Hotel €€

(📞97 97 51 51; www.nihotel.com; 1bis rue Grimaldi; s/d from €120/150; ❄️📶) This uber-hip design hotel makes bold use of flashy primary colours (shower walls, chairs and stairs are made of transparent coloured plastic) mixed with sobering black and white. The roof terrace is in a prime spot for evening drinks.

HÔTEL MIRAMAR
Hotel €€

(📞93 30 86 48; http://miramar.monaco-hotel .com; 1 av du Président JF Kennedy; d €145; ❄️📶) This 1950s seaside hotel with rooftop terrace bar for lazy breakfasts, lunches and evening drinks is a fabulous option right by the port. Seven of the 11 rooms have fabulous balconies overlooking the yachts.

 Eating & Drinking

LE NAUTIQUE
Cafe €

(3 av Président Kennedy; mains €9-13; ⏰Mon-Sat lunch) The clubhouse of Monaco's rowing club has million-dollar views and €10 lunches, served in a sunny linoleum-floored dining room. Look for the gym equipment at street level and the inconspicuous sign marked 'Société Nautique Fédération Monégasque Sport Avion Snack Bar'.

Monte Carlo Casino

A Timeline

1863 Charles III inaugurates the first Casino on the Plateau des Spélugues. **The atrium** ① is a small room with a wooden platform from which an orchestra 'enlivens' the gambling.

1864 Hôtel de Paris opens and the area becomes known as the 'Golden Square'.

1865 Construction of **Salon Europe** ②. Cathedral-like, it is lined with onyx columns and lit by eight Bohemian crystal chandeliers weighing 150kg each.

1868 The steam train arrives in Monaco and **Café de Paris** ③ is completed.

1878–79 Gambling moves to Hôtel de Paris while Charles Garnier is charged with building a new casino with a miniature replica of the Paris Opera House, **Salle Garnier** ④.

1890 The advent of electricity casts a glow on architect Jules Touzet's newly added **gaming rooms** ⑤ for high rollers.

1903 Inspired by female gamblers, Henri Schmit decorates **Salle Blanche** ⑥ with caryatids and the painting *Les Grâces Florentines*.

1904 Smoking is banned in the gaming rooms and **Salon Rose** ⑦, a new smoking room, is added.

1910 Salle Médecin ⑧, immense and grand, hosts the high-spending Private Circle.

1966 Celebrations mark 100 years of uninterrupted gambling despite two world wars.

TOP TIPS

Bring photo ID

Jackets are required in the private gaming rooms, and after 8pm

The cashier will exchange any currency

In the main room, the minimum bet is €10, the maximum €2000

In the Salons Privés, the minimum bet is €500, with no maximum

JOHN VLAHIDES

Salle Blanche

Look up, away from the jarring wall-to-wall slot machines, to admire Schmit's caryatids, wings spread for flight. They illustrate the emerging emancipation of women, modelled on fashionable courtesans like La Belle Otero, who placed her first bet here aged 18.

Salon Rose

Smoking was banned in the gaming rooms after a fraud involving a croupier letting his ash fall on the floor. The gaze of Gallelli's famous cigarillo-smoking nudes are said to follow you around the room.

Hôtel de Paris

Notice the horse's shiny nose (and testicles) on the lobby's statue of Louis XIV on horseback. Legend has it that rubbing them brings good luck in the casino.

Hôtel de Paris

Salle Garnier

Taking eight months to build and two years to restore (2004–06), the opera's original statuary is rehabilitated using original moulds saved by the creator's grandson. Individual air-con and heating vents are installed beneath each of the 525 seats.

JOHN VLAHIDES

Atrium

The casino's 'lobby', so to speak, is paved in marble and lined with 28 Ionic columns, which support a balustraded gallery canopied with an engraved glass ceiling.

Salon Europe

The oldest part of the casino, where they continue to play *trente-et-quarante* and European roulette, which have been played here since 1863. Tip: the bull's-eye windows around the room originally served as security observation points.

Café de Paris

With the arrival of Diaghilev as director of the Monte Carlo Opera in 1911, Café de Paris becomes the go-to address for artists and gamblers. It retains the same high-glamour ambience today. Tip: snag a seat on the terrace and people-watch.

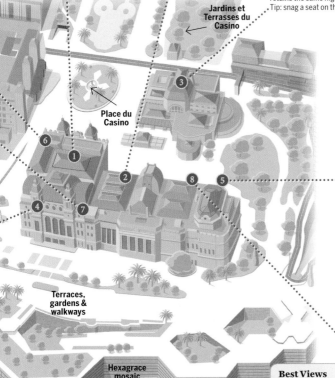

Jardins et Terrasses du Casino

Place du Casino

Terraces, gardens & walkways

Hexagrace mosaic

Fairmont Monte Carlo

Salles Touzet

This vast partitioned hall, 21m by 24m, is decorated in the most lavish style: oak, Tonkin mahogany and oriental jasper panelling are offset by vast canvases, Marseille bronzes, Italian mosaics, sculptural reliefs and stained-glass windows.

Best Views

Wander behind the casino through manicured gardens and gaze across Victor Vasarely's vibrant op-art mosaic, *Hexagrace*, to views of the harbour and the sea.

Salle Médecin

Also known as Salle Empire because of its extravagant Empire-style decor, Monégasque architect François Médecin's gaming room was originally intended for the casino's biggest gamblers. Nowadays, three adjoining Super Privés rooms keep them hidden from prying eyes.

Huit & Demi   Italian   €€

(93 50 97 02; www.huit-et-demi.com; rue Princesse Caroline; mains €13-27; ⊙noon-3pm & 7-11pm Mon-Fri, 7-11pm Sat) Chic and popular, this is the hot spot to savour Italian fare amid crimson-coloured walls lined with celebrity B&W portraits. We prefer the street terrace.

Brasserie de Monaco   Microbrewery

(www.brasseriedemonaco.com; 36 rte de la Piscine; ⊙11am-1pm Sun-Thu, 11am-3am Fri & Sat) Tourists and locals rub shoulders at Monaco's only microbrewery, which crafts rich organic ales and lager alongside tasty (pricy) antipasti plates.

🛈 Information

Telephone

Calls between Monaco and France are international calls. Dial 00 followed by Monaco's country code (377) when calling Monaco from France or elsewhere abroad. To phone France from Monaco, dial 00 and France's country code (33).

Practicalities

Electricity European two-pin plugs; voltage 230V @ 50Hz.

Newspapers & Magazines Centre-left *Le Monde*, right-leaning *Le Figaro*, left-leaning *Libération*.

Radio Radio France Info (105.5MHz), multilingual RFI (738kHz/89kHz in Paris), NRJ (www.nrj.fr), Skyrock (www.skyrock. fm), Nostalgie (www.nostalgie.fr).

Smoking Banned in most public places.

Time One hour ahead of GMT.

Tipping Small change in cafes. *Service compris* means service included; otherwise leave at least 10%.

TV & Video The channels of the national public broadcaster, France Télévisions, include France 2, 3 and 5; commercial stations include TF1 and M6.

Weights & Measures Metric.

Tourist information

Tourist office (www.visitmonaco.com; 2a blvd des Moulins; ⊙9am-7pm Mon-Sat, 11am-1pm Sun)

Getting There & Away

Monaco's **train station** (av Prince Pierre) has frequent trains to Nice (€3.40, 20 minutes), to Menton (€1.90, 10 minutes) and beyond into Italy.

SURVIVAL GUIDE
Directory A–Z

Accommodation

France has accommodation to suit every taste and pocket. In this guide we've listed reviews by author preference.

French hotels vary greatly in quality, ranging from low-budget no-star places to full-blown pleasure palaces.

€ Budget	< €70 (< €80 in Paris)
€€ Midrange	€70-175 (€80-180)
€€€ Top end	> €175 (> €180)

Business Hours

Banks 9 or 9.30am-1pm & 2-5pm Mon-Fri or Tue-Sat

Bars 7pm to 1am Mon-Sat

Cafes 7 or 8am-10 or 11pm Mon-Sat

Nightclubs 10pm-3, 4 or 5am Thu-Sat

Post offices 8.30 or 9am to 5 or 6pm Mon-Fri, 8am-noon Sat

Restaurants lunch noon-2.30 or 3pm, dinner 7-10 or 11pm

Shops 9 or 10am-noon & 2-6 or 7pm Mon-Sat

Supermarkets 9am to 7 or 8pm Mon-Sat

Food

Eating reviews throughout this chapter are ordered by preference. Price ranges for a two-course evening meal are:

€€€	more than €50
€€	€15 to €50
€	below €15

Gay & Lesbian Travellers

Most major gay and lesbian centre organisations are based in Paris. Attitudes towards homosexuality tend to be more conservative in the countryside and villages.

Legal Matters

French police have wide powers of stop-and-search and can demand proof of identity at any time. Foreigners must be able to prove their legal status in France (eg via a passport, visa or residency permit).

Money

○ Credit and debit cards, accepted almost everywhere in France, are convenient and relatively secure, and usually offer a better exchange rate than travellers cheques or cash exchanges.

○ Some places (eg 24hr petrol stations, some autoroute toll machines) only take French-style credit cards with chips and PINs.

Public Holidays

New Year's Day (Jour de l'An) 1 January

Easter Sunday & Monday (Pâques & lundi de Pâques)

May Day (Fête du Travail) 1 May – traditional parades.

Victoire 1945 8 May – commemorates the Allied victory in Europe that ended WWII.

Ascension Thursday (Ascension) May – celebrated on the 40th day after Easter.

Pentecost/Whit Sunday & Whit Monday (Pentecôte & lundi de Pentecôte) Mid-May to mid-June – celebrated on the seventh Sunday after Easter.

Bastille Day/National Day (Fête Nationale) 14 July – *the* national holiday.

Assumption Day (Assomption) 15 August

All Saints' Day (Toussaint) 1 November

Remembrance Day (L'onze novembre) 11 November – marks the WWI armistice.

Christmas (Noël) 25 December

Open or Closed?

○ The midday break is uncommon in Paris but, in general, gets longer the further south you go.

○ French law requires most businesses to close on Sunday; exceptions include grocery stores, *boulangeries*, florists and businesses catering to the tourist trade.

○ In many places shops close on Monday.

○ Restaurants generally close one or two days of the week.

○ Most (but not all) national museums are closed on Tuesday, while most local museums are closed on Monday, though in summer some open daily. Some museums close for lunch.

Telephone

MOBILE PHONES

○ French mobile phones numbers begin with ☎06 or ☎07.

○ France uses GSM 900/1800, compatible with the rest of Europe and Australia but not with the North American GSM 1900 or the totally different system in Japan (though some North Americans have tri-band phones that work here).

○ It may be cheaper to buy your own French SIM card (€20 to €30) sold at ubiquitous outlets run by France's three mobile phone companies, **Bouygues** (www.bouyguestelecom.fr), France Telecom's **Orange** (www.orange.com) and **SFR** (www.sfr.com, in French).

PHONE CODES

Calling France from abroad Dial your country's international access code, ☎33 (France's country code), and the 10-digit local number *without* the initial 0.

Calling internationally from France Dial 00 (the international access code), the country code, area code (without the initial zero if there is one) and local number.

Toilets

○ Public toilets, signposted WC or *toilettes*, are not always plentiful in France.

○ Love them (sci-fi geek) or loathe them (claustrophobe), France has its fair share of 24hr self-cleaning toilets, €0.50 in Paris and free elsewhere.

○ Some older cafes and restaurants still have the hole-in-the-floor squat toilets.

○ The French are blasé about unisex toilets, so save your blushes when tiptoeing past the urinals to reach the ladies' loo.

Visas

○ EU nationals and citizens of Iceland, Norway and Switzerland need only a passport or a national identity card in order to enter France and stay in the country, even for stays of over 90 days.

○ Citizens of Australia, the USA, Canada Israel, Hong Kong, Japan, Malaysia, New Zealand, Singapore, South, Korea and many Latin American countries do not need visas to visit France as tourists for up to 90 days.

○ Other people wishing to come to France as tourists have to apply for a **Schengen Visa** (p821).

Transport
Getting There & Away
Air

France's main international airports are **Roissy Charles de Gaulle** (CDG; 39 50, 01 70 36 39 50; www.aeroportsdeparis.fr) and **Orly** (ORY; 39 50, 01 70 36 39 50; www.aeroportsde paris.fr). Many other French towns have their own airports, which mainly handle domestic and European flights.

Car & Motorcycle

From the UK, **Eurotunnel shuttle trains** (in UK 08443-35 35 35, in France 08 10 63 03 04; www.eurotunnel.com) whisk bicycles, motorcycles, cars and coaches from Folkestone through the Channel Tunnel to Coquelles, 5km southwest of Calais, in just 35 minutes.

Train

Rail services link France with virtually every country in Europe. Tickets and information are handled by **Rail Europe** (www .raileurope.com) or in France, by **SNCF** (in France 36 35, from abroad +33 8 92 35 35 35; www.sncf.com).

Certain services between France and its continental neighbours are marketed under separate brand names:

○ **Alleo** Rail travel to Germany

○ **Artésia** (www.artesia.eu) Italian cities such as Milan

Aerial view of Paris (p186)

RICHARD I'ANSON/LONELY PLANET IMAGES ©

and, overnight, Venice, Florence and Rome.

○ **Elipsos** (www.elipsos.com) Luxurious 'train-hotel' services to Spain

○ **TGV Lyria** (www.tgv-lyria.fr) Switzerland

○ **Thalys** (www.thalys.com) Links Paris Gare du Nord with Brussels (82 minutes), Amsterdam CS (3⅓hr), Cologne Hauptbahnhof (3¼ hours) and other destinations.

○ **Eurostar** (☎ in UK 08432 186 186, in France 08 92 35 35 39; www.eurostar.com) London St-Pancras to Paris Gare du Nord in 2¼ hours with easy onward connections to destinations all over France. Ski trains connecting England with the French Alps run at weekends from mid-Dec to mid-Apr.

Sea

Regular ferries travel to France from Italy, the UK, Channel Islands and Ireland. Several ferry companies ply the waters between Corsica and Italy.

Getting Around

Air

Air France (☎ 36 54; www.airfrance.com) and its subsidiaries **Brit Air** (☎ 36 54; www.britair.fr) and **Régional** (☎ 36 54; www .regional.com) control the lion's share of France's long-protected domestic airline industry.

Budget carriers offering flights within France include **easyJet** (www.easyjet.com), **Airlinair** (www.airlinair.com), **Twin Jet** (www .twinjet.net) and **CCM** (www.aircorsica.com).

Bus

You're nearly always better off travelling by train in France if possible, as the SNCF domestic railway system is heavily subsidised by the government and is much more reliable than local bus companies. Nevertheless, buses are widely used for short-distance travel within *départements*, especially in rural areas with relatively few train lines (eg Brittany and Normandy).

Bicycle

France is a great place to cycle. Not only is much of the countryside drop-dead gorgeous but also the country has a growing number of urban and rural *pistes cyclables* (bike paths and lanes; www.voies vertes.com, in French) and an extensive network of secondary and tertiary roads with relatively light traffic. French train company SNCF does its best to make travelling with a bicycle easy and has a special website for cyclists (www.velo .sncf.com, in French).

Car & Motorcycle

A car gives you exceptional freedom and allows you to visit more-remote parts of France. But it can be expensive and, in cities, parking and traffic are frequently a major headache.

BRINGING YOUR OWN VEHICLE

All foreign motor vehicles entering France must display a sticker or licence plate identifying its country of registration. If you're bringing a right-hand-drive vehicle remember to fix deflectors on your headlights to avoid dazzling oncoming traffic.

DRIVING LICENCE & DOCUMENTS

All drivers must carry a national ID card or passport; a valid driving licence (*permis de conduire;* most foreign licences can be used in France for up to a year); car-ownership papers, known as a *carte grise* (grey card); and proof of third-party (liability) insurance.

FUEL & TOLLS

Many French motorways (autoroutes) are fitted with toll *(péage)* stations that charge a fee based on the distance you've travelled; factor in these costs when driving.

HIRE

In order to hire a car you'll usually need to be over 21 and in possession of a valid driving licence and a credit card. Auto transmissions are *very* rare in France; if you need one, you'll have to order one well in advance.

INSURANCE

Unlimited third-party liability insurance is mandatory in France. When comparing rates check the *franchise* (excess). Your credit card may cover CDW if you use it to pay for the car rental.

ROAD RULES

Cars drive on the right in France. Speed limits on French roads are as follows:

- 50km/h in built-up areas

- 90km/h (80km/h if it's raining) on N and D highways

Train on the Paris metro

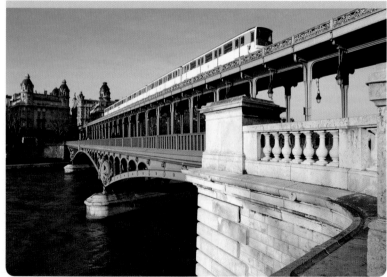

DISCOVER FRANCE TRANSPORT

Priority to the Right

Under the *priorité à droite* (priority to the right) rule, any car entering an intersection from a road on your right has the right of way, unless the intersection is marked *'vous n'avez pas la priorité'* (you do not have right of way) or *'cédez le passage'* (give way).

○ 110km/h (100km/h if it's raining) on dual carriageways

○ 130km/h (110km/h if it's raining) on autoroutes.

Other key rules of the road:

○ All passengers must wear seatbelts.

○ Children who weigh less than 18kg must travel in backward-facing child seats.

○ It is illegal to drive with a blood-alcohol concentration over 0.05% – this is the equivalent of two glasses of wine for a 75kg adult.

○ All vehicles must carry a reflective safety jacket (stored inside the car, not boot) and a reflective triangle.

○ Riders of any type of two-wheeled vehicle with a motor (except motor-assisted bicycles) must wear a helmet.

Train

France's superb rail network is operated by the state-owned **SNCF** (www.sncf.com). Many rural towns that are not on the SNCF train network are served by SNCF buses.

The flagship trains on French railways are the superfast TGVs, which reach speeds in excess of 200mph and can whisk you from Paris to the Côte d'Azur in as little as three hours.

Before boarding any train, you must validate *(composter)* your ticket by time-stamping it in a *composteur,* one of those yellow posts located on the way to the platform.

TICKETS

Buying online at the various SNCF websites can reward with you some great reductions on fares, but be warned – these are generally intended for domestic travellers, and if you're buying abroad beware of the pitfalls. Many tickets can't be posted outside France, and if you buy with a non-French credit card, you might not be able to use it in the automated ticket collection machines at many French stations.

○ Full-fare return travel costs twice as much as a one-way fare.

○ 1st-class travel, where still available, costs 20% to 30% extra.

○ Ticket prices for many trains are pricier during peak periods.

○ The further in advance you reserve, the lower the fare.

○ Children aged 4 to 11 pay half price, under 4s travel for free.

○ **Prem's** The SNCF's most heavily discounted, use-or-lose tickets, sold online, by phone and at ticket windows/machines a maximum of 90 days and minimum 14 days before you travel.

○ **Bons Plans** A grab bag of cheap options for different routes/dates, advertised online under the tab 'Dernière Minute' (Last Minute).

○ Reductions of 25% to 60% are available with several discount cards (valid for one year):

○ **Carte 12-25** (www.12-25-sncf.com in, French; €49) For travellers aged 12 to 25 years.

○ **Carte Enfant Plus** (www.enfantplus-sncf.com, in French; €70) For one to four adults travelling with a child aged four to 11 years.

○ **Carte Escapades** (www.escapades-sncf.com, in French; €85) Discounts on return journeys of at least 200km that include a Saturday night away or only involve travel on a Saturday or Sunday; for 26- to 59-year-olds.

○ **Carte Sénior** (www.senior-sncf.com, in French; €56) Over 60 years.

Spain

Passionate, sophisticated and devoted to living the good life, Spain is at once a stereotype come to life and a country more diverse than you ever imagined.

Spanish landscapes stir the soul, from the jagged Pyrenees and wildly beautiful cliffs of the Atlantic northwest to charming Mediterranean coves, while astonishing architecture spans the ages at seemingly every turn. Spain's cities march to a beguiling beat, rushing headlong into the 21st century even as timeless villages serve as beautiful signposts to Old Spain. And then there's one of Europe's most celebrated (and varied) gastronomic scenes.

But above all, Spain lives very much in the present. Perhaps you'll sense it along a crowded post-midnight street when all the world has come out to play. Or maybe that moment will come when a flamenco performer touches something deep in your soul. Whenever it happens, you'll find yourself nodding in recognition: *this* is Spain.

Palau de la Música Catalana (p322), Barcelona

Spain Highlights

1

La Sagrada Família

The Temple Expiatori de la Sagrada Família is Antoni Gaudí's masterpiece, on which he worked for 43 years. It's a slender structure devoted to geometric perfection and sacred symbolism. It's also a work in progress spanning the generations but never losing Gaudí's breathtaking originality and architectural synthesis of natural forms.

Need to Know

History Gaudí spent the last 12 years of his life preparing plans for finishing the building **Expected completion date** 2020 to 2040 **See our author's review on p324.**

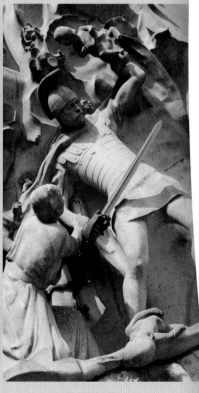

La Sagrada Família Don't Miss List

BY JORDI FAULÍ, DEPUTY ARCHITECTURAL DIRECTOR FOR LA SAGRADA FAMÍLIA

1 PASSION FACADE

Among the Fachada de la Pasión's stand-out features are the angled columns, dramatic scenes from Jesus' last hours, an extraordinary rendering of the Last Supper and a bronze door that reads like a sculpted book. But the most surprising view is from inside the door on the extreme right.

2 MAIN NAVE

The majestic Nave Principal showcases Gaudí's use of tree motifs for columns to support the domes: he described this space as a forest. But it's the skylights that give the nave its luminous quality, even more so since the scaffolding has been removed and light floods onto the apse and main altar from the skylight 75m above the floor.

3 SIDE NAVE AND NATIVITY TRANSEPT

Although beautiful in its own right with windows that project light into the interior, this is the perfect place to view the sculpted treelike columns and get an overall perspective of the main nave. Turn around and you're confronted with the inside of the Nativity Facade, an alternative view that most visitors miss; the stained-glass windows are superb.

4 NATIVITY FACADE

The Fachada del Nacimiento is Gaudí's grand hymn to Creation. Begin by viewing it front on from a distance, then draw close enough (but to one side) to make out the details of its sculpted figures. The complement to the finely wrought detail is the majesty of the four parabolic towers that reach for the sky and are topped by Venetian stained glass.

5 THE MODEL OF COLÒNIA GÜELL

Among the many original models used by Gaudí in the Museu Gaudí, the most interesting is the church at Colònia Güell. From the side you can, thanks to the model's ingenious use of rope and cloth, visualise the harmony and beauty of the interior.

Top: Passion Facade; **Bottom Right:** Nativity Facade detail

Museo del Prado

Housed in a glorious 18th-century palace (enhanced by a modern extension) in the heart of old Madrid, the Museo del Prado (p298) is Spain's foremost art museum and houses the nation's top artistic treasures. Around 7000 pieces are on show: Rubens, Rembrandt and Van Dyck are all represented, but it's the Spanish boys, Goya and el Greco, who inevitably take the prize.

3 Alhambra

This fabulous Moorish palace (p363) in Granada is one of Spain's architectural marvels. It was built for the Muslim rulers of Granada between the 13th and 15th centuries, although parts of the structure date back to the 11th century. Seeing the medieval Palacio Nazaríes (Nasrid Palace) illuminated in the evening sunlight is an image that'll stay with you long after you leave for home.

Cuenca

Spain has plenty of clifftop villages, but few of them can hold a candle to the *casas colgadas* (hanging houses) of Cuenca (p318).These balconied houses seem to have been carved straight from the cliff face, and perch precariously above the deep ravine of Río Huécar – a true marvel of medieval engineering. Unsurprisingly, the village has been named a World Heritage site by Unesco.

Flamenco

Nothing sums up the Spanish spirit better than flamenco. This ancient dance form has been a cornerstone of Spanish culture for centuries, and it's still going strong – although you'll have to choose carefully if you want to see the real thing. The best places to see authentic flamenco are Madrid (p311) and Seville (p357), where you can watch some of the country's top performers strut their fiery stuff. Flamenco dancer at Casa Patas (p312), Madrid

Teatre-Museu Dalí

Salvador Dalí is undoubtedly one of Spain's best-known artistic exports, and his museum (p330) in Figueres is a surreal sculpture in its own right. Lodged inside the converted theatre where Dalí was born, it's packed full of tricks and surprises – look out for a menagerie of monsters in the courtyard, a room upholstered in red velvet and a 'Wind Palace' decorated with Dalíesque murals.
Dalí's bedroom

Spain's Best...

Festivals

○ **Semana Santa** (p354)
This holy week is a highlight of the pre-Easter calendar.

○ **Sanfermines** (p345) See the brave (and the barmy) run with the bulls during Pamplona's hair-raising street race.

○ **Carnaval Cádiz** (p368) Spain's wildest carnival kicks off on the streets of Cádiz in February.

○ **Feria de Abril** (p354) Seville's six-day street party in April is packed with Andalucian passion.

Sacred Sites

○ **Montserrat** (p338) Make a pilgrimage to this otherworldly mountain monastery near Barcelona.

○ **Santiago de Compostela** (p355) Join the pilgrims on the last leg of the Camino de Santiago.

○ **The Mezquita** (p358) Córdoba's Moorish mosque-cum-cathedral is almost as impressive as the Alhambra.

○ **Burgos Cathedral** (p355) Pay your respects at the tomb of Spain's national hero, El Cid.

Spanish Experiences

○ **Bullfighting** (p312) Watch Spain's top *toreros* strut their stuff in Madrid's bullring.

○ **Flamenco** (p357) Experience traditional flamenco in an Andalucían *tablao*.

○ **Zarzuela** (p311) Catch this Spanish blend of dance, music and theatre.

○ **Café life** (p310) Drink till dawn with the locals.

○ **Football** (p336) Watch the soccer superstars in action at the Camp Nou.

Need to Know

Culinary Specialities

○ **Tapas** (p308) Join the locals over Spanish snacks in Madrid's lively tapas bars.

○ **Pintxos** (p341) Savour this Basque version of tapas in San Sebastián.

○ **Paella** (p349) Taste the nation's most authentic paella in Valencia.

○ **Cochinillo asado** (p308) Try this roast suckling pig in Madrid or Segovia.

○ **Basque cooking** (p343) Bilbao is a great place to experience Basque cuisine.

ADVANCE PLANNING

○ **Three months before** Book hotels and travel tickets, especially during festival season.

○ **One month before** Arrange theatre, opera and flamenco tickets, and book tables at top restaurants.

○ **One week before** Beat the queues at the Alhambra (p366) by buying your ticket online for a €1 supplement.

RESOURCES

○ **Turespaña** (www.spain .info, www.tourspain.es) The national tourism site.

○ **Renfe** (www.renfe.es) Plan your train travel.

○ **Fiestas.net** (www.fiestas .net) Handy online guide to fiestas and festivals.

○ **Tour Spain** (www.tour spain.org) Useful resource for culture and food, with links to hotels and transport.

GETTING AROUND

○ **Bus** Spain's bus network is extensive but chaotic. **ALSA** (☏902 42 22 42; www.alsa.es) is one of the largest companies.

○ **Car** Traffic and parking can be a nightmare around the big cities, so it's more convenient to get rental cars from airport kiosks. Major motorways are called *autopistas*; tolls are compulsory on many routes.

○ **Sea** Frequent ferries connect Spain with the UK, Italy, Morocco and Algeria. Major ports are in Santander, Bilbao and Barcelona.

○ **Train** Spain's railways are run by **Renfe** (☏902 24 02 02; www.renfe.es). High-speed AVE trains link Madrid, Barcelona and major towns in between, and travel across the Pyrenees into France.

BE FOREWARNED

○ **Public holidays** Most of Spain goes on holiday during August and Semana Santa (the week before Easter Sunday).

○ **Smoking** 'Officially' banned in most public places, but many Spanish people don't seem to take much notice.

○ **Scams** Watch out for pickpocketing and bag snatching, and be wary of common scams listed on p371.

Left: Ladies in flamenco dresses at Feria de Abril;
Above: Pinxtos in San Sebastián

Spain Itineraries

*Spain is famous for its laid-back approach to life –
this is, after all, the land that invented the siesta – so
take things slowly if you want to make the most of the
sights.*

3 DAYS

MADRID TO BARCELONA
City Sights

This trip gives you a taste of two of Spain's sexiest cities. Start out in **(1) Madrid**, with incredible art at the Museo Nacional del Prado, the Museo Thyssen-Bornemisza and the Caixa Forum, followed by people watching on the Plaza Mayor and an after-dark visit to the *tabernas* and tapas bars of La Latina, Chueca and Los Austrias. Book yourself a spot at a *tablao* for some late-night flamenco.

On day two, spend the morning at the Palacio Real, the monarch's Madrid residence, then visit one of the city's markets and take a picnic to the Parque del Buen Retiro. In the late afternoon, it's on to

(2) Barcelona; thanks to the high-speed AVE trains, the trip now takes under three hours, leaving you plenty of time to check in before delving into the bars and bistros of the Barrí Gòtic.

Day three's for sightseeing. Top of the list is the Sagrada Família, Gaudí's fantasy cathedral, which is still a building site almost 120 years after the first stone was laid. Spend the afternoon at the Museu Picasso, have an early evening mooch around the shops and boutiques of El Rabal and La Ribera, before finishing up with sophisticated Spanish food in the restaurants of L'Eixample.

VALENCIA TO CÁDIZ
Southern Culture

From Barcelona, catch a train along the coast to **(1) Valencia** – considered by many people to be the home of Spain's signature dish, paella – on your way towards the fiery, sunbaked region of Andalucia. The centuries-old clash of Moorish and Christian cultures has left an enduring mark on this region, and in **(2) Granada** you can glimpse one of the crowning architectural achievements of the ancient Muslim world – the mighty Alhambra, built as a palace and fortress for the region's Moorish rulers during the 14th century.

From Granada, detour northeast to **(3) Cordoba** and the stunning Mezquita, where Spain's Muslim and Christian cultures collide head on, en route to **(4) Seville**, a city that encapsulates the passion and excitement of modern Spain. This sensual city really knows how to live life to the full, with a wealth of lively *barrios,* buzzy bars and frenetic festivals, not to mention some of the most authentic flamenco in Spain.

On the last day, it's worth travelling on to **(5) Cádiz**, another enticing Andalucian city with a fascinating maritime heritage – it was from here that Christopher Columbus set out on two of his landmark voyages to discover the New World.

Vault over main stairway in Palacio Real (p299), Madrid
PHOTOGRAPHER: KRZYSZTOF DYDYNSKI/LONELY PLANET IMAGES ©

Discover Spain

Catedral de Nuestra Señora de la Almudena
PHOTOGRAPHER: DAVID TOMLINSON/LONELY PLANET IMAGES ©

MADRID
POP 3.6 MILLION

No city on earth is more alive than Madrid, a beguiling place whose sheer energy carries a simple message: this city knows how to live. Explore the old streets of the centre, relax in the plazas, soak up the culture in its excellent art museums, and take at least one night to experience the city's legendary nightlife scene.

◉ Sights & Activities

Madrid de los Austrias, the maze of mostly 15th- and 16th-century streets that surround Plaza Mayor, is the city's oldest district. Tapas-crazy La Latina, alternative Chueca, bar-riddled Huertas and Malasaña, and chic Salamanca are other districts that reward pedestrian exploration. Build in time for three of Europe's top art collections at the Prado, Reina Sofía and Thyssen-Bornemisza museums, as well as a visit to the Palacio Real.

MUSEO DEL PRADO
Art Gallery

(Map p306; www.museodelprado.es; Paseo del Prado; adult/student/child under 18yr & EU senior over 65yr €8/4/ free, free to all 6-8pm Tue-Sat & 5-8pm Sun; ⊙9am-8pm Tue-Sun; Ⓜ Banco de España) Spain's premier art museum, the Prado is an endless parade of priceless works from Spain and beyond.

The collection is roughly divided into eight major collections: Spanish paintings (1100–1850), Flemish paintings (1430–1700), Italian paintings (1300–1800), French paintings (1600–1800), German paintings (1450–1800), sculptures, decorative arts, and drawings and prints. There is generous coverage of Spanish greats including Goya, Velázquez and El Greco.

Other masters on show include Peter Paul Rubens, Pieter Bruegel, Rembrandt, Anton van Dyck, Dürer, Rafael, Titian, Tintoretto, Sorolla, Gainsborough, Fra Angelico and Tiepolo.

MUSEO THYSSEN-BORNEMISZA
Art Gallery

(Map p306; www.museothyssen.org; Paseo del Prado 8; adult/student & senior/child under 12yr €8/5.50/free; ⏰10am-7pm Tue-Sun; Ⓜ Banco de España) Opposite the Prado, the Museo Thyssen-Bornemisza is an outstanding collection of international masterpieces. Begin your visit on the 2nd floor with medieval art, and make your way down to modern works on the ground level, passing paintings by Titian, El Greco, Rubens, Rembrandt, Anton van Dyck, Canaletto, Cézanne, Monet, Sisley, Renoir, Pissarro, Degas, Constable, Van Gogh, Miró, Modigliani, Matisse, Picasso, Gris, Pollock, Dalí, Kandinsky, Toulouse-Lautrec, Lichtenstein and many others on the way.

CENTRO DE ARTE REINA SOFÍA
Art Gallery

(Map p306; www.museoreinasofia.es; Calle de Santa Isabel 52; adult/concession €6/free, free to all Sun, 7-9pm Mon & Wed-Fri, 2.30-9pm Sat; ⏰10am-9pm Mon & Wed-Sat, to 2.30pm Sun; Ⓜ Atocha) If modern art is your cup of tea, the Reina Sofía is your museum. A stunning collection of mainly Spanish modern art, the Centro de Arte Reina Sofía is home to Picasso's *Guernica* – his protest against the German bombing of the Basque town of Guernica during the Spanish Civil War in 1937 – in addition to important works by surrealist Salvador Dalí and abstract paintings by the Catalan artist Joan Miró.

FREE CAIXA FORUM
Art Gallery

(Map p306; www.fundacio.lacaixa.es, in Spanish; Paseo del Prado 36; ⏰10am-8pm; Ⓜ Atocha) The Caixa Forum, opened in 2008, seems to hover above the ground. On one wall is the *jardín colgante* (hanging garden), a lush vertical wall of greenery almost four storeys high. Inside are four floors used to hold top-quality art and multimedia exhibitions.

PALACIO REAL
Palace

(Map p306; www.patrimonionacional.es; Calle de Bailén; adult/concession €10/3.50, adult without guided tour €8, EU citizens free Wed; ⏰9am-6pm Mon-Sat, to 3pm Sun & holidays; Ⓜ Ópera) When the 16th-century Alcázar that formerly stood on this spot went up in flames on Christmas Eve 1734, King Felipe V ordered construction of a new palace on the same ground. The opulent Palacio Real was finished in 1755 and Carlos III moved in during 1764. Still used for important events of pomp and state, the palace has 2800-plus rooms, of which 50 are open to the public.

PLAZA MAYOR
Square

Ringed with cafes and restaurants, and packed with people day and night, the 17th-century arcaded Plaza Mayor (Map p306) is an elegant and bustling square Designed in 1619 by Juan Gómez de Mora, the plaza's first public ceremony was the beatification of San Isidro Labrador, Madrid's patron saint. Thereafter, bullfights watched by 50,000 spectators were a recurring spectacle until 1878, while the autos-da-fé (the ritual condemnation of heretics) of the Spanish Inquisition also took place here. Fire largely destroyed the square in 1790, but it was rebuilt and became an important market and hub of city life. Today, the uniformly ochre-tinted apartments with wrought-iron balconies are offset by the exquisite frescoes of the 17th-century **Real Casa de la Panadería** (Royal Bakery); the frescoes were added in 1992.

CHURCHES
Churches

The **Catedral de Nuestra Señora de la Almudena** (Map p306; Calle de Bailén; admission free; ⏰9am-8.30pm; Ⓜ Ópera) is just across the plaza from the Palacio Real. It's possible to climb to the cathedral's summit with fine views. En route you climb up through the cathedral's museum; follow the signs to the **Museo de la Catedral y Cúpula** (Map p306; adult/child €6/4; ⏰10am-2.30pm Mon-Sat) on the northern facade that faces the Palacio Real.

The cathedral is less captivating than the imposing 18th-century **Basílica de**

Museo del Prado

Plan of Attack

Begin on the 1st floor with **Las Meninas** ❶ by Velázquez. Although alone worth the entry price, it's a fine introduction to the 17th-century golden age of Spanish art; nearby are more of Velázquez' royal paintings and works by Zurbarán and Murillo. While on the 1st floor, seek out Goya's **La Maja Vestida and La Maja Desnuda** ❷ with more of Goya's early works in neighbouring rooms. Downstairs at the southern end of the Prado, Goya's anger is evident in the searing **El Dos de Mayo** and **El Tres de Mayo** ❸, and the torment of Goya's later years finds expression in the adjacent rooms with his **Pinturas Negras** ❹, or Black Paintings. Also on the lower floor, Hieronymus Bosch's weird and wonderful **Garden of Earthly Delights** ❺ is one of the Prado's signature masterpieces. Returning to the 1st floor, El Greco's **Adoration of the Shepherds** ❻ is an extraordinary work, as is Peter Paul Rubens' **Las Tres Gracias** ❼, which forms the centrepiece of the Prado's gathering of Flemish masters (This painting may have been moved to the 2nd floor.) A detour to the 2nd floor takes in some lesser-known Goyas, but finish in the **Edificio Jerónimos** ❽ with a visit to the cloisters and the outstanding bookshop.

Also Visit:

Nearby are Museo Thyssen-Bornemisza and Centro de Arte Reina Sofía. They form an extraordinary trio of galleries.

Las Tres Gracias (Rubens)
A late Rubens masterpiece, *The Three Graces* is a classical and masterly expression of Rubens' preoccupation with sensuality, here portraying Aglaia, Euphrosyne and Thalia, the daughters of Zeus.

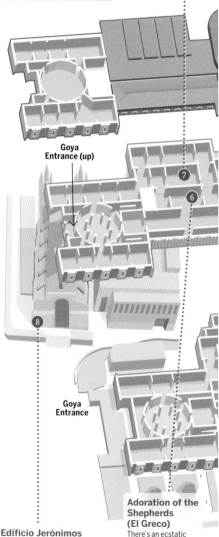

Goya Entrance (up)

Goya Entrance

Edificio Jerónimos
Opened in 2007, this state-of-the-art extension has rotating exhibitions of Prado masterpieces held in storage for decades for lack of wall space, and stunning 2nd-floor granite cloisters that date back to 1672.

Adoration of the Shepherds (El Greco)
There's an ecstatic quality to this intense painting. El Greco's distorted rendering of bodily forms came to characterise much of his later works.

Las Meninas (Velázquez)

This masterpiece depicts Velázquez and the Infanta Margarita, with the king and queen whose images appear, according to some experts, in mirrors behind Velázquez.

La Maja Vestida & La Maja Desnuda (Goya)

These enigmatic works scandalised early-19th-century Madrid society, fuelling the rumour mill as to the woman's identity and drawing the ire of the Spanish Inquisition. (La Maja Vestida pictured above.)

Edificio Villanueva

El Dos de Mayo & El Tres de Mayo (Goya)

Few paintings evoke a city's sense of self quite like Goya's portrayal of Madrid's valiant but ultimately unsuccessful uprising against French rule in 1808. (El Dos de Mayo pictured above.)

Jeronimos Entrance

Murillo Entrance

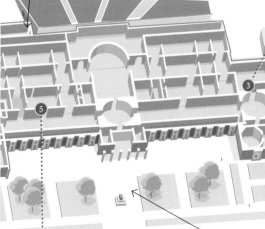

Velázquez Entrance

The Garden of Earthly Delights (Bosch)

A fantastical painting in triptych form, this overwhelming work depicts the Garden of Eden and what the Prado describes as 'the lugubrious precincts of Hell' in exquisitely bizarre detail.

Las Pinturas Negras (Goya)

Las Pinturas Negras are Goya's darkest works. *Saturno Devorando a Su Hijo* evokes a writhing mass of tortured humanity, while *La Romería de San Isidro* and *El Akelarre* are profoundly unsettling.

Greater Madrid

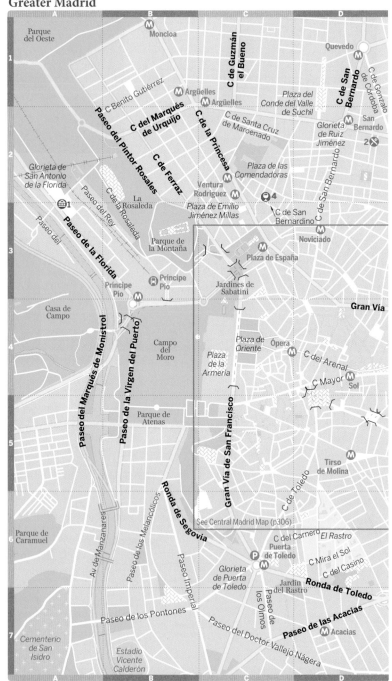

DISCOVER SPAIN MADRID

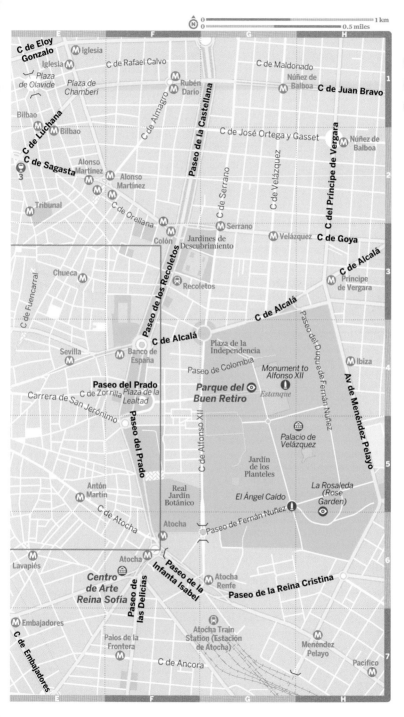

0 ———————— 1 km
0 ———————— 0.5 miles

C de Eloy Gonzalo
Ⓜ Iglesia
Iglesia Ⓜ
C de Rafael Calvo
Plaza de Olavide
Plaza de Chamberí
Rubén Darío
C de Maldonado
Núñez de Balboa Ⓜ
C de Juan Bravo
Bilbao
Ⓜ
C de Luchana
Ⓜ Bilbao
C de Almagro
Paseo de la Castellana
C de José Ortega y Gasset
Ⓜ Núñez de Balboa
C de Sagasta
Ⓜ 3
Alonso Martínez
Ⓜ Alonso Martínez
C de Orellana
C de Serrano
C de Velázquez
C del Príncipe de Vergara
Ⓜ Tribunal
Colón Ⓜ
Ⓜ Serrano
Ⓜ Velázquez
C de Goya
Jardines de Descubrimiento
C de Fuencarral
Chueca Ⓜ
Paseo de los Recoletos
🏛 Recoletos
C de Alcalá
Ⓜ Príncipe de Vergara
Sevilla Ⓜ
Ⓜ Banco de España
C de Alcalá
Plaza de la Independencia
C de Alcalá
Paseo del Duque de Fernán Núñez
Ⓜ Ibiza
Paseo del Prado
C de Zorrilla Plaza de la Lealtad
Paseo de Colombia
Monument to Alfonso XII
❶
Carrera de San Jerónimo
Paseo del Prado
Parque del Buen Retiro ⊙
Estanque
Av de Menéndez Pelayo
C de Alfonso XII
Antón Martín Ⓜ
Real Jardín Botánico
🏛 Palacio de Velázquez
Jardín de los Planteles
C de Atocha
Ⓜ Atocha
El Ángel Caído ❶
La Rosaleda (Rose Garden) ⊙
Paseo de Fernán Núñez
Ⓜ Lavapiés
Atocha Ⓜ
Centro de Arte Reina Sofía 🏛
Paseo de la Infanta Isabel
Atocha Renfe
Paseo de la Reina Cristina
Paseo de las Delicias
Ⓜ Embajadores
C de Embajadores
Palos de la Frontera Ⓜ
Atocha Train Station (Estación de Atocha) 🚆
Ⓜ Menéndez Pelayo
C de Ancora
Pacífico Ⓜ

San Francisco El Grande (Map p306; Plaza de San Francisco 1; adult/concession €3/2; ⊙mass 8am-12.30pm & 4-6pm Mon-Sat; Ⓜ La Latina or Puerta de Toledo).

PARQUE DEL BUEN RETIRO Gardens (Map p302; ⊙6am-midnight May-Sep, to 11pm Oct-Apr; Ⓜ Retiro, Príncipe de Vergara, Ibiza or Atocha) The splendid gardens of El Retiro are littered with marble monuments, landscaped lawns, the occasional elegant building and abundant greenery. It's quiet and contemplative during the week, but comes to life at weekends.

The focal point for so much of El Retiro's life is the artificial lake (*estanque*), which is watched over by the massive ornamental structure of the **Monument to Alfonso XII** on the east side of the lake, complete with marble lions.

Hidden among the trees south of the lake, the late 19th-century **Palacio de Cristal**, a magnificent metal and glass structure that is arguably El Retiro's most beautiful architectural monument, is now used for temporary exhibitions.

OTHER SIGHTS
The frescoed ceilings of the **Ermita de San Antonio de la Florida** (Map p302; Glorieta de San Antonio de la Florida 5; admission free; ⊙9.30am-8pm Tue-Fri, 10am-2pm Sat & Sun, hr vary Jul & Aug; Ⓜ Príncipe Pío) are one of Madrid's most surprising secrets. In the southern of the two small chapels you can see Goya's work in its original setting, rendered in 1798. The painter is buried in front of the altar.

 # Tours

The Centro de Turismo de Madrid offers **Descubre Madrid** (Discover Madrid; ☏91 588 29 06; www.esmadrid.com/descubremadrid; walking tours adult/concession €3.90/3.12, bus tours €6.45/5.05, bicycle tours €3.90/3.12 plus €6 bike rental), with dozens of guided walking, cycling and bus itineraries.

 # Festivals & Events

Fiesta de San Isidro City Festival
Street parties, parades, bullfights and other fun events honour Madrid's patron saint on and around 15 May.

Veranos de la Villa Summer Festival
Madrid's town hall stages a series of cultural events, shows and exhibitions known as Summers in the City, in July and August.

Suma Flamenca Flamenco
A soul-filled flamenco festival that draws some of the biggest names in the genre to the Teatros del Canal in May or June.

 # Sleeping

Madrid has high-quality accommodation across all price ranges. Los Austrias, Sol and Centro put you in the heart of the busy downtown area, while La Latina (the best *barrio* for tapas), Lavapiés and Huertas (good for nightlife) are ideal for those who love Madrid nights and don't want to stagger too far to get back to their hotel.

Los Austrias, Sol & Centro

HOTEL MENINAS Boutique Hotel €€
(Map p306; ☏91 541 28 05; www.hotelmeninas.com; Calle de Campomanes 7; s/d from €109/129; Ⓜ Ópera; ❄ 🛜) Inside a refurbished 19th-century mansion, the Meninas combines old-world comfort with modern, minimalist style. The colour scheme is blacks, whites and greys, with dark-wood floors and splashes of fuchsia and lime-green.

HOTEL PLAZA MAYOR
Hotel €€

(Map p306; ☎91 360 06 06; www.h-plazamayor.com; Calle de Atocha 2; s/d from €50/60; Ⓜ Sol or Tirso de Molina; ❋) Stylish decor, charming original elements of a 150-year-old building and helpful staff are selling points here. The rooms are attractive, some with a light colour scheme and wrought-iron furniture. The attic rooms have great views.

HOSTAL ACAPULCO
Hostal €

(Map p306; ☎91 531 19 45; www.hostalacapulco.com; Calle de la Salud 13; s/d/tr €52/62/79; Ⓜ Gran Vía; ❋ 🛜) This immaculate little *hostal* has marble floors, renovated bathrooms, double-glazed windows and comfortable beds. Street-facing rooms have balconies overlooking sunny Plaza del Carmen.

HOTEL DE LAS LETRAS
Hotel €€

(Map p306; ☎91 523 79 80; www.hoteldelasletras.com; Gran Vía 11; d from €100; Ⓜ Gran Vía) Hotel de las Letras started the rooftop hotel-bar trend in Madrid. The bar's wonderful, but the whole hotel is excellent with individually styled rooms, each with literary quotes scribbled on the walls.

Huertas & Atocha
ALICIA ROOM MATE
Boutique Hotel €€

(Map p306; ☎91 389 60 95; www.room-matehoteles.com; Calle del Prado 2; d €105-165; Ⓜ Sol, Sevilla or Antón Martín; ❋ 🛜) With beautiful, spacious rooms, Alicia overlooks Plaza de Santa Ana. It has an ultra-modern look and the downstairs bar is oh-so-cool.

HOTEL URBAN
Luxury Hotel €€€

(Map p306; ☎91 787 77 70; www.derbyhotels.com; Carrera de San Jerónimo 34; d from €190; Ⓜ Sevilla; ❋ 🛜 ☒) The towering glass edifice of Hotel Urban is the epitome of art-inspired designer cool. Dark-wood floors and dark walls are offset by plenty of light, while the bathrooms have wonderful designer fittings. The rooftop swimming pool is Madrid's best.

HOSTAL ADRIANO
Hostal €

(Map p306; ☎91 521 13 39; www.hostaladriano.com; 4th fl, Calle de la Cruz 26; s/d/tr €53/65/85; Ⓜ Sol) They don't come any better than this bright and cheerful *hostal* wedged in the streets that mark the boundary between Sol and Huertas.

Palacio de Cristal in Parque del Buen Retiro

Central Madrid

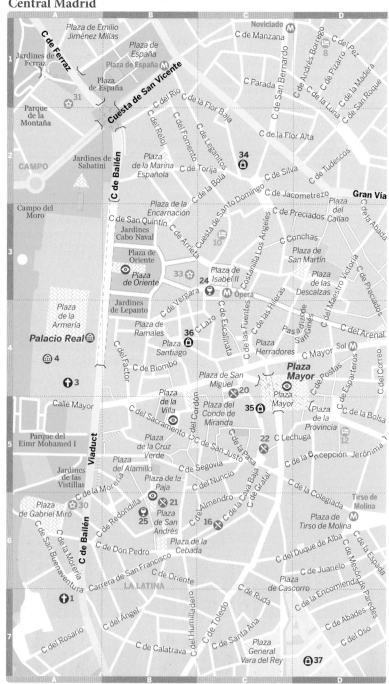

DISCOVER SPAIN MADRID

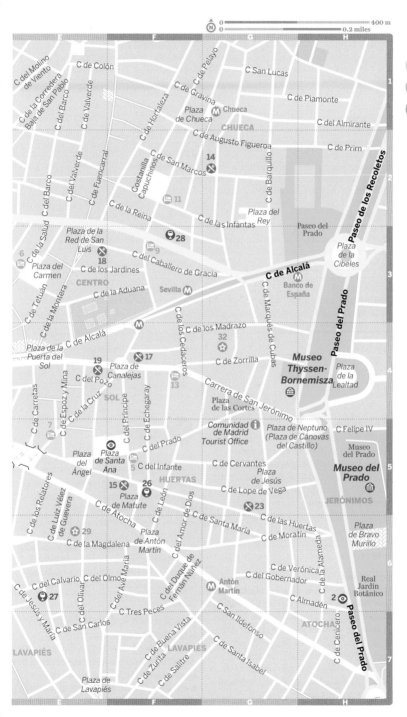

Central Madrid

Top Sights
- Museo del Prado ... H5
- Museo Thyssen-Bornemisza ... G4
- Palacio Real ... A4
- Plaza Mayor ... C4

Sights
1 Basílica de San Francisco El Grande ... A7
2 Caixa Forum ... H6
3 Catedral de Nuestra Señora de la Almudena ... A4
4 Museo de la Catedral y Cúpola ... A4

Sleeping
5 Alicia Room Mate ... F5
6 Hostal Acapulco ... E3
7 Hostal Adriano ... E5
8 Hotel Abalú ... D1
9 Hotel de Las Letras ... F3
10 Hotel Meninas ... C3
11 Hotel Óscar ... F2
12 Hotel Plaza Mayor ... D5
13 Hotel Urban ... F4

Eating
14 Bazaar ... G2
15 Casa Alberto ... F5
16 Casa Lucio ... C6
17 La Finca de Susana ... F4
18 La Gloria de Montera ... E3
19 Lhardy ... E4
20 Mercado de San Miguel ... C4
21 Naïa Restaurante ... B6
22 Restaurante Sobrino de Botín ... C5
23 Viva La Vida ... G5

Drinking
24 Café del Real ... C3
25 Delic ... B6
26 El Imperfecto ... F5
27 La Escalera de Jacob ... E6
28 Museo Chicote ... F3
Splash Óscar ... (see 11)

Entertainment
29 Casa Patas ... E6
30 Corral de la Morería ... A6
31 Las Tablas ... A1
32 Teatro de la Zarzuela ... G4
33 Teatro Real ... B3

Shopping
34 Antigua Casa Talavera ... C2
35 El Arco Artesanía ... C5
36 El Flamenco Vive ... B4
37 El Rastro ... D7

Malasaña & Chueca

HOTEL ÓSCAR Boutique Hotel **€€**
(Map p306; ☎91 701 11 73; www.room-matehoteles.com; Plaza de Vázquez de Mella 12; d €90-200; M Gran Vía; ❄ 📶 🏊) Hotel Óscar's designer rooms ooze style and sophistication. The facade – decorated with thousands of hanging Coca-Cola bottles – is a striking local landmark; there's a fine street-level tapas bar and a rooftop terrace.

HOTEL ABALÚ Boutique Hotel **€€**
(Map p306; ☎91 531 47 44; www.hotelabalu.com; Calle del Pez 19; s/d/ste from €74/90/140; M Noviciado; ❄ 📶) Hotel Abalú is an oasis of style amid Malasaña's time-worn feel. Each room has its own design drawn from the imagination of Luis Delgado, and covers the gamut from retro chintz to Zen, baroque to pure white, and most aesthetics in between.

Eating

Madrid is a focal point of cooking from around the country and is particularly attached to seafood; despite not having a sea, Madrid has the world's second-largest fish market (after Tokyo).

From the chaotic tapas bars of La Latina to countless neighbourhood favourites, you'll have no trouble tracking down specialities like *cochinillo asado* (roast suckling pig) or *cocido madrileño* (a hearty stew made of beans and various animals' innards).

Los Austrias, Sol & Centro

MERCADO DE SAN MIGUEL
Tapa & Delicatessen **€€**
(Map p306; www.casinodemadrid.es; Plaza de San Miguel; meals €15-35; ⏰10am-midnight Sun-Wed, to 2am Thu-Sat; M Sol) One of Madrid's oldest and most beautiful markets, the

Mercado de San Miguel has undergone a stunning major renovation and bills itself as a 'culinary cultural centre'. Within the early 20th-century glass walls, the market has become an inviting space strewn with tables (difficult to nab) where you can enjoy the freshest food or a drink.

RESTAURANTE SOBRINO DE BOTÍN
Traditional Spanish €€

(Map p306; 📞91 366 42 17; www.botin.es; Calle de los Cuchilleros 17; meals €40-45; Ⓜ La Latina or Sol) It's not every day that you can eat in the oldest restaurant in the world (1725), which also appears in many novels about Madrid, most notably Hemingway's *The Sun Also Rises*. The secret of its staying power is fine *cochinillo* (suckling pig; €22.90) and *cordero asado* (roast lamb; €22.90) cooked in wood-fired ovens.

LA GLORIA DE MONTERA
Spanish €€

(Map p306; Calle del Caballero de Gracia 10; meals €25-30; Ⓜ Gran Vía) Minimalist style, tasty Mediterranean dishes and great prices mean that you'll probably have to wait in line (no reservations taken) to eat here.

La Latina & Lavapiés
This area is best known for its tapas bars.

NAÏA RESTAURANTE
Fusion €€

(Map p306; 📞91 366 27 83; www.naia restaurante.com; Plaza de la Paja 3; meals €30-35; ⏱ lunch & dinner Tue-Sun; Ⓜ La Latina) On the lovely Plaza de la Paja, Naïa has a buzz about it, with a cooking laboratory overseen by Carlos López Reyes, delightful modern Spanish food and a chill-out lounge downstairs.

VIVA LA VIDA
Vegetarian €

(Map p306; www.vivalavida .vg; Costanilla de San Andrés 16; veg buffet €2.10 per 100g; ⏱ noon-midnight; Ⓜ La Latina; 🖋) This

organic food shop has an enticing vegetarian buffet that's always filled with flavour. On the cusp of Plaza de la Paja, it's a great place at any time of the day, especially outside normal Spanish eating hours.

CASA LUCIO
Traditional Spanish €€

(Map p306; 📞91 365 32 52; www.casalucio.es, in Spanish; Calle de la Cava Baja 35; meals €45-50; ⏱ lunch & dinner Sun-Fri, dinner Sat, closed Aug; Ⓜ La Latina) Lucio has been wowing *madrileños* with his light touch, quality ingredients and home-style local cooking for ages – think seafood, roasted meats and eggs (a Lucio speciality) in abundance.

Huertas & Atocha

CASA ALBERTO
Traditional Spanish €€

(Map p306; 📞91 429 93 56; www.casaalberto.es, in Spanish; .Calle de las Huertas 18; meals €25-30; ⏱ noon-1.30am Tue-Sat, to 4pm Sun; Ⓜ Antón Martín) One of the most atmospheric old *tabernas* of Madrid, Casa Alberto has been around since 1827. The secret to its staying power is vermouth on tap, excellent tapas and fine sit-down meals; *rabo de toro* (bull's tail) is a good order.

Monument to Alfonso XII in Parque del Buen Retiro (p304)

LHARDY Traditional Spanish €€€
(Map p306; 91 521 33 85; www.lhardy.com; Carrera de San Jerónimo 8; meals €60-70; lunch & dinner Mon-Sat, lunch Sun, closed Aug; MSol or Sevilla) This Madrid landmark (since 1839) is an elegant treasure trove of takeaway gourmet tapas. It's expensive, but the quality and service are unimpeachable.

LA FINCA DE SUSANA
Mediterranean €€
(Map p306; www.lafinca-restaurant.com; Calle de Arlabán 4; meals €20-25; MSevilla) It's difficult to find a better combination of price, quality cooking and classy atmosphere anywhere in Huertas. It doesn't take reservations.

Malasaña & Chueca

BAZAAR Nouvelle Spanish Cuisine €€
(Map p306; www.restaurantbazaar.com; Calle de la Libertad 21; meals €20-25; MChueca) Bazaar's popularity among the well-heeled and often-famous shows no sign of abating. Its pristine white interior design with theatre lighting may draw a crowd that looks like it stepped out of the pages of *Hola!* magazine, but the food is extremely well priced and innovative. No reservations.

NINA Nouvelle Spanish Cuisine €€
(Map p302; 91 591 00 46; Calle de Manuela Malasaña 10; meals €30-40; MBilbao) Sophisticated, intimate and wildly popular, Nina has extensive lunch, dinner and weekend brunch menus (available in English) of nouvelle Mediterranean cuisine that don't miss a trick.

Drinking

The people of Madrid like to live life on the city's streets and plazas. The bulk of Madrid's energy-filled bars are open late throughout the week: to 2am Sunday to Thursday nights, and to 3am or 3.30am Friday and Saturday nights.

Los Austrias & Centro

MUSEO CHICOTE Cocktail Bar
(Map p306; www.museo-chicote.com; Gran Vía 12; 6pm-3am Mon-Thu, to 3.30am Fri & Sat; MGran Vía) The founder of this Madrid landmark is said to have invented more than a hundred cocktails, which the likes of Ernest Hemingway, Ava Gardner, Grace Kelly, Sophia Loren and Frank Sinatra have all enjoyed at one time or another.

Café Comercial

CAFÉ DEL REAL   Bar-Cafe
(Map p306; Plaza de Isabel II 2; ⏰9am-1am Mon-Thu, to 3am Fri & Sat; Ⓜ Ópera) One of the nicest bar-cafes in central Madrid, this place serves a rich variety of creative coffees and a few cocktails to a chilled soundtrack.

La Latina & Lavapiés
DELIC   Bar-Cafe
(Map p306; Costanilla de San Andrés 14; ⏰11am-2am Sun & Tue-Thu, 7pm-2am Mon, 11am-2.30am Fri & Sat; Ⓜ La Latina) We could go on for hours about this long-standing cafe-bar, but we'll reduce it to its most basic elements: nursing an exceptionally good mojito (€8) or three on a warm summer's evening at Delic's outdoor tables on one of Madrid's prettiest plazas is one of life's great pleasures.

LA ESCALERA DE JACOB   Cocktail Bar
(Map p306; Calle de Lavapiés 11; ⏰6pm-2am; Ⓜ Antón Martín or Tirso de Molina) With magicians, storytellers, children's theatre (on Saturdays and Sundays at noon) and live music, 'Jacob's Ladder' is one of Madrid's most original bars.

Huertos & Atocha
EL IMPERFECTO   Bar
(Map p306; Plaza de Matute 2; ⏰3pm-2am Sun-Thu, to 3am Fri & Sat; Ⓜ Antón Martín) Its name notwithstanding, the 'Imperfect One' is our ideal Huertas bar, with live jazz most Tuesdays at 9pm and a drinks menu as long as a saxophone, ranging from cocktails (€6.50) and spirits to milkshakes, teas and creative coffees.

Malasaña & Chueca
CAFÉ COMERCIAL   Literary Cafe
(Map p302; Glorieta de Bilbao 7; ⏰7.30am-midnight Mon, to 1am Tue-Thu, to 2am Fri, 8.30am-2am Sat, 9am-midnight Sun; Ⓜ Bilbao) With its heavy leather seats, abundant marble and old-style waiters, this glorious old Madrid cafe proudly fights a rearguard action against progress.

SPLASH ÓSCAR   Bar
(Map p306; Plaza de Vázquez de Mella 12; ⏰4.30pm-12.30am; Ⓜ Gran Vía) Another of Madrid's stunning rooftop terraces (although this one with a small swimming pool), atop Hotel Óscar, this chilled space

with gorgeous skyline views has become a cause célèbre among A-list celebrities.

EL JARDÍN SECRETO   Bar
(Map p302; Calle del Conde Duque 2; ⏰5.30pm-12.30am Sun-Thu & Sun, 6.30pm-2.30am Fri & Sat; Ⓜ Plaza de España) The 'Secret Garden' is all about intimacy and romance in a *barrio* that's one of Madrid's best-kept secrets.

 # Entertainment

The **Guía del Ocio** (www.guiadelocio.com in Spanish; €1) is the city's classic weekly listings magazine. Also good are **Metropoli** (www.abc.es/metropolis, in Spanish) and **On Madrid** (www.elpais.com, in Spanish), respectively *ABC's* and *El País'* Friday supplements.

TEATRO DE LA ZARZUELA   Theatre
(Map p306; 📞91 524 54 00; teatrodelazarzuela.mcu.es; Calle de Jovellanos 4; Ⓜ Banco de España) This theatre, built in 1856, is the premier place to see *zarzuela,* a very Spanish mixture of dance, music and theatre.

TEATRO REAL   Opera
(Map p306; 📞902 244 848; www.teatro-real.com, in Spanish; Plaza de Oriente; Ⓜ Ópera) The Teatro Real is the city's grandest stage for elaborate operas and ballets.

Live Music
FLAMENCO
Many of flamenco's top names perform in Madrid, making it an excellent place to see interpretations of the art.

CORRAL DE LA MORERÍA   Flamenco
(Map p306; 📞91 365 84 46; www.corraldelamoreria.com; Calle de la Morería 17; admission €27-37; ⏰8.30pm-2.30am, shows 10pm & midnight Sun-Fri, 7pm, 10pm & midnight Sat; Ⓜ Ópera) One of the most prestigious flamenco stages in Madrid, with 50 years of history and top performers most nights.

LAS TABLAS   Flamenco
(Map p306; 📞91 542 05 20; www.lastablasmadrid.com; Plaza de España 9; admission €24; ⏰shows 10.30pm Sun-Thu, 8pm & 10pm Fri & Sat; Ⓜ Plaza de España) Las Tablas has quickly earned a reputation for quality

flamenco. Most nights you'll see a classic flamenco show, with plenty of throaty singing and soul-baring dancing.

CASA PATAS — Flamenco

(Map p306; 📞91 369 04 96; www.casapatas.com, in Spanish; Calle de Cañizares 10; admission €30-35; ⏰shows 10.30pm Mon-Thu, 9pm & midnight Fri & Sat; Ⓜ Antón Martín or Tirso de Molina) One of the top flamenco stages in Madrid, this *tablao* always offers unimpeachable quality.

Sport

ESTADIO SANTIAGO BERNABÉU — Football Stadium

(www.realmadrid.com; Avenida de Concha Espina 1; tour adult/under 14yr €15/10; ⏰10am-7pm Mon-Sat, 10.30am-6.30pm Sun; Ⓜ Santiago Bernabéu) The legendary Real Madrid plays at this stadium. Fans can visit the stadium and take an interesting tour through the presidential box, dressing room and field.

ESTADIO VICENTE CALDERÓN — Football Stadium

(www.clubatleticodemadrid.com; Paseo de la Virgin del Puerto; Ⓜ Pirámides) This is home to Atlético de Madrid; fans are famed as being some of the country's most devoted.

PLAZA DE TOROS LAS VENTAS — Bullfighting

(📞91 356 22 00; www.las-ventas.com, in Spanish; Calle de Alcalá 237; tours €7; ⏰tours 10am-2pm; Ⓜ Ventas) Some of Spain's top *toreros* (bullfighters) swing their capes in Plaza de Toros Las Ventas, east of Parque del Buen Retiro. Fights are held every Sunday afternoon from mid-May through to October. Purchase tickets (from €5, standing in the sun) at the plaza box office, Localidades Galicia, or from official ticket agents on Calle Victoria close to the Plaza de la Puerta del Sol. For excellent tours of the bullring in English and Spanish, contact **Tauro Tour** (📞91 556 92 37; gregorio@trazo publicidad.es; 4th fl, Paseo de la Castellana 115).

 Shopping

Shops may (and many do) open on the first Sunday of every month and throughout December.

ANTIGUA CASA TALAVERA — Traditional Ceramics

(Map p306; Calle de Isabel la Católica 2; ⏰10am-1.30pm & 5-8pm Mon-Fri, to 1.30pm Sat; Ⓜ Santo Domingo) The extraordinary tiled facade of this wonderful old shop conceals an Aladdin's Cave of ceramics from all over Spain.

EL ARCO ARTESANÍA — Souvenirs

(Map p306; www.elarcoartesania.com; Plaza Mayor 9; ⏰11am-9pm; Ⓜ Sol or La Latina) This original shop in the southwestern corner of Plaza Mayor sells an outstanding array of homemade designer souvenirs, from stone and glasswork to jewellery and home fittings.

EL FLAMENCO VIVE — Flamenco

(Map p306; www.elflamencovive.es; Calle Conde de Lemos 7; ⏰10am-2pm & 5-9pm Mon-Sat; Ⓜ Ópera) This temple to flamenco has it all, from guitars, songbooks and well-priced CDs, to polka-dotted dancing costumes, shoes, colourful plastic jewellery and literature about flamenco.

EL RASTRO — Market

(Map p306; Calle de la Ribera de Curtidores; ⏰8am-3pm Sun; Ⓜ La Latina, Puerta de Toledo or Tirso de Molina) Sunday morning at El Rastro, Europe's largest flea market, is a Madrid institution. Be aware: pickpockets love it as much as everyone else.

ℹ Information

Dangers & Annoyances

Madrid is generally safe although, as in most European cities, you should be wary of pickpockets in the centre, on the Metro and around tourist sights.

Prostitution along Calle de la Montera and in the Casa del Campo park means that you need to exercise extra caution in these areas.

Discount Cards

The Madrid Card (📞91 360 47 72; www.madrid card.com; 1/2/3 days €47/60/74) includes free entry to more than 40 museums in and around Madrid and discounts on public transport. The cheaper version (1/2/3 days for €31/35/39) covers just cultural sights.

Lampshades at El Rastro flea market

KRZYSZTOF DYDYNSKI/LONELY PLANET IMAGES ©

Emergency

Servicio de Atención al Turista Extranjero (Foreign Tourist Assistance Service; ☏ 91 548 85 37, 91 548 80 08; www.esmadrid.com/satemadrid; Calle de Leganitos 19; ☉ 9am-10pm; Ⓜ Plaza de España or Santo Domingo)

Left Luggage

At Madrid's Barajas airport, there are three consignas (left-luggage offices; ☉ 24hr). You pay €3.85 for the first 24-hour period. Similar services operate for similar prices at Atocha and Chamartín train stations (open 7am to 11pm).

Tourist Information

Centro de Turismo de Madrid (www.esmadrid .com; Plaza Mayor 27; ☉ 9.30am-8.30pm; Ⓜ Sol) Excellent city tourist office with a smaller office underneath Plaza de Colón and information points at Plaza de la Cibeles, Plaza de Callao, outside the Centro de Arte Reina Sofía and at the T4 terminal at Barajas airport.

Regional tourist office (www.turismomadrid .es; Calle del Duque de Medinaceli 2; ☉ 8am-8pm Mon-Sat, 9am-2pm Sun; Ⓜ Banco de España) Further offices at Barajas airport (T1 and T4), and Chamartín and Atocha train stations.

ⓘ Getting There & Away

Air

Madrid's international Barajas airport (MAD), 15km northeast of the city, is a busy place, with flights coming in from all over Europe and beyond.

Bus

Estación Sur de Autobuses (☏ 91 468 42 00; www.estaciondeautobuses.com, in Spanish; Calle de Méndez Álvaro 83; Ⓜ Méndez Álvaro), just south of the M-30 ring road, is the city's principal bus station.

Car & Motorcycle

The city is surrounded by two main ring roads, the outermost M-40 and the inner M-30; there are also two additional partial ring roads, the M-45 and the more-distant M-50.

Train

Madrid is served by two main train stations. The bigger of the two is **Puerta de Atocha** (Ⓜ Atocha Renfe), at the southern end of the city centre. **Chamartín train station** (Ⓜ Chamartín) lies in the north of the city. The bulk of trains for Spanish

313

destinations depart from Atocha, especially those going south. International services arrive at and leave from Chamartín.

High-speed Tren de Alta Velocidad Española (AVE) services connect Madrid with Seville (via Córdoba), Valladolid (via Segovia), Toledo, Valencia, Málaga and Barcelona (via Zaragoza and Tarragona).

🛈 Getting Around

To/From the Airport

METRO Line 8 of the metro (www.metromadrid .es, in Spanish; entrances in T2 and T4) runs to the Nuevos Ministerios transport interchange, which connects with lines 10 and 6. It operates from 6.05am to 2am. A single ticket is priced at €1 (10-ride Metrobús ticket €9); however, there's an additional €1 supplement if you're travelling to/from the airport. The journey to Nuevos Ministerios takes around 15 minutes, or around 25 minutes from T4.
BUS At time of publication, a new 24-hour bus service between Plaza de la Cibeles and the airport was due to start.

AeroCITY (📞 91 747 75 70; www.aerocity.com; €5-19 per person) is private minibus service that takes you door-to-door between central Madrid and the airport.

TAXI A taxi to the city centre will cost you around €25 in total (up to €35 from T4), depending on traffic and where you're going; in addition to what the meter says, you pay a €5.50 airport supplement.

Public Transport

Madrid's **metro** (www.metromadrid.es) is extensive and well maintained. A single ride costs €1 and a 10-ride ticket is €9. The metro is quick, clean and relatively safe, and runs from 6am until 2am.

The bus system is also good; contact **EMT** (www.emtmadrid.es) for more information. Twenty-six night-bus *búhos* (owls) routes operate from midnight to 6am, with all routes originating in Plaza de la Cibeles.

Taxi

You can pick up a taxi at ranks throughout town or simply flag one down. Flag fall is €2.05 from 6am to 10pm daily, €2.20 from 10pm to 6am Sunday to Friday and €3.10 from 10pm Saturday to 6am Sunday. Several supplementary charges, usually posted inside the taxi, apply; these include €5.50 to/from the airport and €2.95 from taxi ranks at train and bus stations.

Radio-Teléfono Taxi (📞 91 547 82 00, 91 547 82 00; www.radiotelefono-taxi.com)

Tele-Taxi (📞 91 371 21 31, 902 501 130)

CASTILLA Y LEÓN

Spain's Castilian heartland, Castilla y León is littered with hilltop towns sporting magnificent Gothic cathedrals, monumental city walls and mouth-watering restaurants.

Salamanca

POP 155,619

Whether floodlit by night or bathed in midday sun, Salamanca is a dream destination. This is a city of rare architectural splendour, awash with golden sandstone overlaid

Catedral Nueva, Salamanca

with Latin inscriptions in ochre, and with an extraordinary virtuosity of plateresque and Renaissance styles. The monumental highlights are many, with the exceptional Plaza Mayor (illuminated to stunning effect at night) an unforgettable highlight.

 ## Sights & Activities

PLAZA MAYOR
Square

The harmonious Plaza Mayor was completed in 1755 to a design by Alberto Churriguera, one of the clan behind an at times overblown variant of the baroque style that bears their name.

FREE CATEDRAL NUEVA & CATEDRAL VIEJA
Churches

Curiously, Salamanca is home to two cathedrals: the newer and larger cathedral was built beside the old Romanesque one instead of on top of it, as was the norm. The **Catedral Nueva** (New Cathedral; Plaza de Anaya; admission free; ⏰9am-8pm), completed in 1733, is a late-Gothic masterpiece that took 220 years to build. For fine views over Salamanca, head to the southwestern corner of the cathedral facade and the **Puerta de la Torre** (Ieronimus; Plaza de Juan XXIII; admission €3.25; ⏰10am-7.15pm), from where stairs lead up through the tower.

The largely Romanesque **Catedral Vieja** (Old Cathedral; admission €4.75; ⏰10am-7.30pm) is a 12th-century temple with a stunning 15th-century altarpiece whose 53 panels depict scenes from the life of Christ and Mary, topped by a representation of the Final Judgement. The entrance is inside the Catedral Nueva.

 ## Sleeping

MICROTEL PLACENTINOS
Boutique Hotel €€

(📞923 28 15 31; www.microtelplacentinos.com; Calle de Placentinos 9; s/d incl breakfast €80/95; ❄🛜) One of Salamanca's most charming boutique hotels, Microtel Placentinos is tucked away on a quiet street and has

rooms with exposed stone walls and wooden beams. The service is faultless, and the overall atmosphere one of intimacy and discretion.

HOSTAL CONCEJO
Hotel €€

(📞923 21 47 37; www.hconcejo.com, in Spanish; Plaza de la Libertad 1; s/d/tr €45/62/80; 🅿❄@🛜) A cut above the average hostal, the stylish Concejo has polished-wood floors, tasteful furnishings and a superb central location. Try to snag one of the corner rooms (like number 104) with its traditional glassed-in balcony, complete with a table, chairs and people-watching views.

 ## Eating & Drinking

MESÓN LAS CONCHAS
Grilled Meats €€

(Rúa Mayor 16; meals €25-30) Enjoy a choice of outdoor tables (in summer), an atmospheric bar or the upstairs, wood-beamed dining area. The bar caters mainly to locals who know their *embutidos* (cured meats). For sit-down meals, there's a good mix of roasts and *raciones* (large tapas portions).

EL PECADO
Modern Creative €€

(📞923 26 65 58; Plaza del Poeta Iglesias 12; meals €40, menú de degustación €45; 🍴) A trendy place that regularly attracts Spanish celebrities (eg Pedro Almodóvar and Ferran Adrià), El Pecado ('the Sin') has an intimate dining room and quirky, creative menu.

ℹ Information

Municipal tourist office (www.salamanca.es; Plaza Mayor 14; ⏰9am-2pm & 4.30-8pm Mon-Fri, 10am-8pm Sat, 10am-2pm Sun)

Regional tourist office (www.turismocastilla yleon.com; Casa de las Conchas, Rúa Mayor; ⏰9am-8pm Sun-Thu, 9am-9pm Fri & Sat)

ℹ Getting There & Away

TRAIN Up to eight trains depart daily for Madrid's Chamartín station (€19.10, 2½ hours) via Ávila (€9.65, one hour).

Detour:
Picos de Europa

These jagged mountains straddling Asturias, Cantabria and northeast Castilla y León amount to some of the finest walking country in Spain.

They comprise three limestone massifs (whose highest peak rises 2648m). The 647-sq-km **Parque Nacional de los Picos de Europa** (www.picosdeeuropa.com, in Spanish) covers all three massifs and is Spain's second-biggest national park.

There are numerous places to stay and eat all over the mountains. Getting here and around by bus can be slow going but the Picos are accessible from Santander and Oviedo (the latter is easier) by bus.

CASTILLA-LA MANCHA

Known as the stomping ground of Don Quijote and Sancho Panza, Castilla-La Mancha conjures up images of lonely windmills, medieval castles and bleak, treeless plains. The characters of Miguel de Cervantes provide the literary context, but the richly historic cities of Toledo and Cuenca are the most compelling reasons to visit.

Toledo
POP 82,291

Toledo is Spain's equivalent of a down-sized Rome. Commanding a hill rising above the Tajo River, it's crammed with monuments that attest to the waves of conquerors and communities – Roman, Visigoth, Jewish, Muslim and Christian – who have called the city home during its turbulent history.

 Sights

CATEDRAL DE TOLEDO Church
(Plaza del Ayuntamiento; adult/child €7/free; ⏱10.30am-6.30pm Mon-Sat, 2-6.30pm Sun) Toledo's cathedral dominates the skyline, reflecting the city's historical significance as the heart of Catholic Spain. Within its hefty stone walls there are stained-glass windows, tombs of kings and art in the sacristy by the likes of El Greco, Zurbarán, Crespi, Titian, Rubens and Velázquez. Look out for the **Custodia de Arfe**, by the celebrated 16th-century goldsmith Enrique de Arfe. With 18kg of pure gold and 183kg of silver, this 16th-century conceit bristles with some 260 statuettes.

SINAGOGA DEL TRÁNSITO Synagogue
(www.museosefardi.net, in Spanish; Calle Samuel Leví; adult/child €2.40/1.20, audioguide €3; ⏱10am-9pm Tue-Sat, 10am-2pm Sun) Toledo's former *judería* (Jewish quarter) was once home to 11 synagogues. Tragically, the bulk of Toledo's Jews were expelled in 1492. This magnificent synagogue was built in 1355 by special permission of Pedro I (construction of synagogues was prohibited in Christian Spain). The synagogue now houses the **Museo Sefardi** (⏱10am-9pm Tue-Sat, 10am-2pm Sun).

SAN JUAN DE LOS REYES Monastery
(Calle San Juan de los Reyes 2; admission €2.30; ⏱10am-6pm) North of the synagogues lies the early 17th-century Franciscan monastery and church of San Juan de los Reyes, notable for its delightful cloisters.

SINAGOGA DE SANTA MARÍA LA BLANCA Synagogue
(Calle de los Reyes Católicos 4; admission €2.30; ⏱10am-6pm) This more modest synagogue is characterised by the horseshoe arches that delineate the five naves – classic Almohad architecture.

FREE **MUSEO DE SANTA CRUZ** Museum
(Calle de Cervantes 3; ⏱10am-6.30pm Mon-Sat, 10am-2pm Sun) Just off the Plaza de Zocodover, the 16th-century Museo de Santa Cruz is a beguiling combination of

Gothic and Spanish Renaissance styles. The cloisters and carved wooden ceilings are superb, as are the displays of Spanish ceramics. The gallery contains a number of El Grecos, a painting attributed to Goya (*Cristo Crucificado*) and the wonderful 15th-century *Tapestry of the Astrolabes*.

IGLESIA DE SANTO TOMÉ · Church

(www.santotome.org; Plaza del Conde; admission €2.30; ⏰10am-6pm) This otherwise modest church contains El Greco's masterpiece, *El Entierro del Conde de Orgaz* (The Burial of the Count of Orgaz).

Sleeping

Accommodation is often full, especially from Easter to September.

CASA DE CISNEROS · Boutique Hotel €€

(✆925 22 88 28; www.hostal-casa-de-cisneros .com; Calle del Cardenal Cisneros; s/d €50/80; ☞✳🛜) Across from the cathedral, this seductive hotel is built on the site of an 11th-century Islamic palace, parts of which can be spied via a glass porthole in the lobby floor.

Prayer hall, Sinagoga del Tránsito

HOSTAL DEL CARDENAL · Historic Hotel €€

(✆925 22 49 00; www.hostaldelcardenal.com; Paseo de Recaredo 24; s/d €77/113; P✳🛜) A wonderful 18th-century mansion with ochre-coloured walls, arches and columns. The rooms are grand, yet welcoming, with plush fabrics and parquet floors. Several overlook the glorious terraced gardens.

Eating

AURELIO · Traditional Spanish €€€

(✆925 22 13 92; Plaza del Ayuntamiento 4; meals €35-45; ⏰lunch & dinner Tue-Sat, lunch Mon) The three restaurants under this name are among the best of Toledo's top-end eateries (the other locations are Calle de la Sinagoga 1 and 6). Game, fresh produce and traditional dishes are prepared with panache. Reservations recommended.

PALACIOS · Traditional Spanish €

(Calle Alfonso X el Sabio 3; menú €13.90, meals €14-18) An unpretentious place where stained glass, beams and efficient old-fashioned service combine with traditional no-nonsense cuisine. Hungry? Try

Gran Teatre del Liceu, La Rambla

NEIL SETCHFIELD/LONELY PLANET IMAGES ©

a gut-busting bowl of homestyle *judías con perdiz* (white beans with partridge) for starters.

ℹ Information

Main tourist office (www.toledoturismo.com; Plaza del Ayuntamiento; ⏱10.30am-2.30pm Mon, 10.30am-2.30pm & 4.30-7pm Tue-Sun)

Provincial tourist office (www.diputoledo.es; Subida de la Granja; ⏱10am-5pm Mon-Sat, 10am-3pm Sun)

ℹ Getting There & Away

For most major destinations, you'll need to backtrack to Madrid.
BUS From the **bus station** (Avenida de Castilla La Mancha), buses depart for Madrid (from €5.25,one to 1½ hours) every half-hour, 6am to 10pm daily (less often on Sundays). Services on weekdays and Sunday to Cuenca (€11.40, 2¼ hours).
TRAIN The high-speed AVE service runs every hour or so to Madrid (€9.90, 30 minutes).

Cuenca

A World Heritage site, Cuenca is one of Spain's most memorable small cities, its old centre a stage set of evocative medieval buildings and dramatic backdrops. Most emblematic are the *casas colgadas,* the hanging houses, which jut out precariously over the steep defile of Río Huécar. Dating from the 16th century, the houses with their layers of wooden balconies seem to emerge from the rock as if an extension of the cliffs. One of the finest restored examples now houses the **Museo de Arte Abstracto Español** (Museum of Abstract Art; www.march.es; adult/ child €3/free; ⏱11am-2pm & 4-6pm Tue-Fri, 11am-2pm & 4-8pm Sat, 11am-2.30pm Sun), which is an impressive contemporary art museum.

Trains run to Madrid (€11.75, 2½ hours, four to six daily) and Valencia (€12.95, 3¼ hours, four daily).

CATALONIA

Home to stylish Barcelona, ancient Tarragona, romantic Girona and countless alluring destinations along the coast, in the Pyrenees and in the rural interior, Catalonia (Catalunya in Catalan, Cataluña in Castilian) is a treasure chest waiting to be opened.

Barcelona

POP 1.59 MILLION

Barcelona is one of Europe's coolest cities. Despite two millennia of history it's a forward-thinking place, always on the cutting edge of art, design and cuisine. Whether you explore its medieval palaces and plazas, gawk at the Modernista masterpieces, shop for designer duds along its bustling boulevards, sample its exciting nightlife or just soak up the sun on the beaches, you'll find it hard not to fall in love with this vibrant city.

 Sights & Activities

LA RAMBLA   Pedestrian Boulevard
Spain's most famous boulevard, the part-pedestrianised La Rambla, explodes with life. Stretching from **Plaça de Catalunya** (Map p332) to the waterfront, it's lined with street artists, newsstands and vendors selling everything from mice to magnolias.

The colourful **Mercat de la Boqueria** (Map p332; La Rambla; ⏲8am-8pm Mon-Sat; Ⓜ Liceu), a fresh food market with a Modernista entrance, is one of La Rambla's highlights. Nearby, stop for a tour of the **Gran Teatre del Liceu** (Map p332; ☎93 485 99 14; www.liceubarcelona.com; La Rambla dels Caputxins 51-59; admission with/without guide €8.70/4; ⏲guided tour 10am, unguided visits 11.30am, noon, 12.30pm & 1pm; Ⓜ Liceu), the city's fabulous opera house.

Also stop at the **Plaça Reial** (Map p332; Ⓜ Liceu), a grand 19th-century square surrounded by arcades lined with restaurants and bars. At the waterfront end of La Rambla stands the **Mirador de Colom** (Map p332; Ⓜ Drassanes), a statue of Columbus atop a tall pedestal.

BARRI GÒTIC   Historic Area
Barcelona's Gothic **Catedral** (Map p332; Plaça de la Seu; admission free, special visit €5; ⏲8am-12.45pm & 5.15-8pm, special visit 1-5pm Mon-Sat, 2-5pm Sun & holidays; Ⓜ Jaume I) was built atop the ruins of an 11th-century Romanesque church. Highlights include the cool cloister, the crypt tomb of martyr Santa Eulàlia (one of Barcelona's two patron saints), the choir stalls (€2.20), the lift to the rooftop (€2.20) and the modest art collection in the **Sala Capitular** (chapterhouse; admission €2). You pay the individual prices only if you visit outside the special visiting hours.

Not far from the cathedral is pretty **Plaça del Rei** and the fascinating **Museu d'Història de Barcelona** (Map p332; www.museuhistoria.bcn.cat; Carrer del Veguer; adult/

Barcelona in Two Days

The first thing everyone does when they get to Barcelona is wander along **La Rambla**, one of Barcelona's most chaotic and atmospheric boulevards. Duck your head into **Mercat de la Boquería**, a lively food market, and stop for coffee on the grand square of **Plaça Reial**. Spend the afternoon getting lost among the winding streets of the **Barri Gòtic** and **El Raval**, and don't miss a visit to the excellent **Museu Picasso**. After nightfall, try some delicious tapas at **Bar Celta** or **Bar Pinotxo**.

Day two is all about architecture. Begin with a mindblowing tour around Antoni Gaudí's great unfinished masterpiece, **La Sagrada Família**, followed by visits to some of the architect's other great buildings, including **La Pedrera** and the **Casa Batlló**. Chill out in the afternoon with a picnic high above the city in **Parc Güell**, where much of the design was again dreamt up by Antoni Gaudí. Round your trip off with some authentic Catalan food at **Agut** or **Casa Leopoldo**.

Greater Barcelona

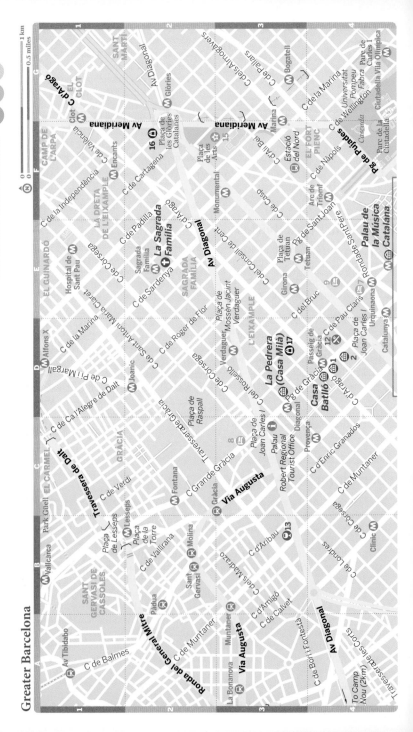

0.5 miles
1 km

SANT MARTÍ

CAMP DE L'ARPA

EL CLOT

EL GUINARDÓ

LA DRETA DE L'EIXAMPLE

SAGRADA FAMÍLIA

L'EIXAMPLE

GRÀCIA

SANT GERVASI DE CASSOLES

EL CARMEL

Park Güell

C d'Aragó

C d'Aragó

Clot

Av Diagonal

Glòries

Av Meridiana

Encants

Plaça de les Glòries Catalanes

Monumental

Av Meridiana

Marina

Estació del Nord

EL FORT PIENC

Arc de Triomf

Pg de Pujades

Parc de la Ciutadella

Parc de Carles I

Ciutadella Vila Olímpica

Pompeu Fabra

C de la Marina

C de Universitat

C de Wellington

Castella

C de la Marina

C d'Ali Bei

Plaça de les Arts

C de Sant Antoni Maria Claret

Hospital de Sant Pau

La Sagrada Família

Sagrada Família

C de Padilla

C de Cartagena

C de València

C de la Independència

C de Còrsega

C de Sardenya

C de Roger de Flor

Av Diagonal

Plaça de Mossèn Jacint Verdaguer

Verdaguer

Mossèn Verdaguer

La Pedrera (Casa Milà)

Passeig de Gràcia

Diagonal

Casa Batlló

Casa Milà

Plaça de Tetuan

Tetuan

Girona

C del Bruc

Pg de Sant Joan

Palau de la Música Catalana

Catalana

Ronda de Sant Pere

C de Nàpols

C de Casp

C del Consell de Cent

Plaça de Pau Claris

C de Pau Claris

Plaça de Joan Carles I

Urquinaona

Catalunya

Provença

C de Enric Granados

C d'Aribau

C de Muntaner

C de Còrsega

Clínic

C de Londres

Via Augusta

Plaça de Raspall

Fontana

C de Verdi

C Gran de Gràcia

Gràcia

Plaça de Joan Carles I

Palau Robert Regional Tourist Office

Travessera de Gràcia

C Grande Gràcia

Joanic

Verdaguer

C del Rosselló

C del Rosselló

Alfons X

C de la Marina

C de Pi i Margall

Lesseps

Plaça de Lesseps

Plaça de la Torre

Sant Gervasi

Muntanet

Pàdua

C de Vallirana

C dels Madrazo

C d'Armigó

C de Calvet

Av Tibidabo

La Bonanova

C de Balmes

Ronda del General Mitre

Via Augusta

Av Diagonal

C de Borrell Fontestà

To Camp Nou (2km)

Travessera

Travessera de les Corts

Vallcarca

16

15

17

13

1

12

2

7

8

9

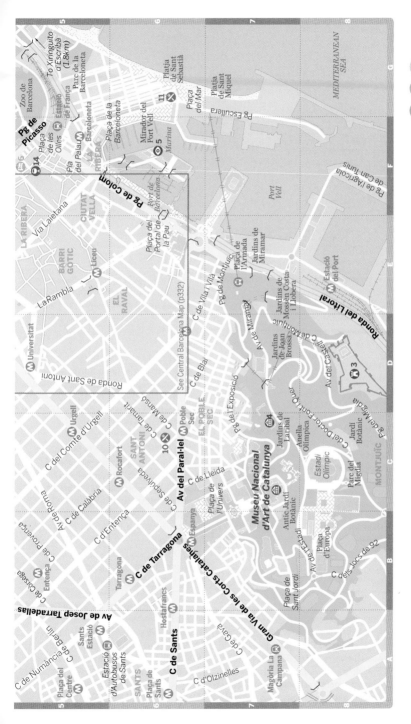

Greater Barcelona

senior & student/child under 7yr €7/5/free, free for all from 4pm 1st Sat of month & from 3pm Sun; ⊙10am-8pm Tue-Sun, to 3pm holidays; Ⓜ Jaume I), where you can visit a 4000-sq-metre excavated site of Roman Barcelona under the plaza.

EL RAVAL   Neighbourhood
To the west of La Rambla is El Raval district, a once-seedy, now-funky area overflowing with cool bars and shops. Visit the **Museu d'Art Contemporani de Barcelona** (Macba; Map p332; 🕿 93 412 08 10 www.macba.cat; Plaça dels Àngels 1; adult/concession €7.50/6; ⊙11am-8pm Mon & Wed, to midnight Thu-Fri, 10am-8pm Sat, 10am-3pm Sun & holidays; Ⓜ Universitat), which has an impressive collection of international contemporary art.

LA RIBERA   Neighbourhood
In medieval days, La Ribera was a stone's throw from the Mediterranean and the heart of Barcelona's foreign trade with homes belonging to numerous wealthy merchants. Now it's a trendy district full of boutiques, restaurants and bars.

A series of palaces where some of those wealthy merchants lived now house the **Museu Picasso** (Map p332; www.museupicasso.bcn.es; Carrer de Montcada 15-23; adult/student/senior & child under 16yr €9/6/free, temporary exhibitions adult/student €5.80/2.90, free for all 3-8pm Sun & all day 1st

Sun of month; ⊙10am-8pm Tue-Sun & holidays; Ⓜ Jaume I), home to more than 3000 Picassos, most from early in the artist's career. This is one of the most visited museums in the country, so expect queues.

The heart of the neighbourhood is the elegant **Església de Santa Maria del Mar** (Map p332; Plaça de Santa Maria del Mar; admission free; ⊙9am-1.30pm & 4.30-8pm; Ⓜ Jaume I), a stunning example of Catalan Gothic and arguably the city's most elegant church.

The opulent **Palau de la Música Catalana** (Map p320; www.palaumusica .org; Carrer de Sant Francesc de Paula 2; adult/student & EU senior/child €12/10/free; ⊙hourly 50min tours 10am-6pm Easter & Aug, 10am-3.30pm Sep-Jul; Ⓜ Urquinaona) is one of the city's most delightful Modernista works. Designed by Lluís Domènech i Montaner in 1905, it hosts concerts regularly. It is well worth joining the guided tours to get a look inside if you don't make it to a concert.

Nearby, the **Mercat de Santa Caterina** (Map p332; www.mercatsantacaterina.net, in Catalan; Avinguda de Francesc Cambó 16; ⊙7.30am-2pm Mon, to 3.30pm Tue, Wed & Sat, to 8.30pm Thu & Fri; Ⓜ Jaume I), with its loopily pastel-coloured wavy roof, is a temple to fine foods designed by the adventurous Catalan architect Enric Miralles.

WATERFRONT   Seafront

Barcelona has two major ports: **Port Vell** (Old Port), at the base of La Rambla, and **Port Olímpic** (Olympic Port), 1.5km up the coast. Shops, restaurants and nightlife options are plentiful around both marinas, particularly Port Olímpic. Between the two ports sits the onetime factory workers' and fishermen's quarter, **La Barceloneta**. It preserves a delightfully scruffy edge and abounds with crowded seafood eateries.

At the end of Moll d'Espanya in Port Vell is **L'Aquàrium** (Map p320; www.aquariumbcn.com; Moll d'Espanya; adult/senior over 60yr/child 4-12yr/under 4yr €17.50/14.50/12.50/free; ◷9.30am-11pm Jul & Aug; MDrassanes), with its 80m-long shark tunnel. Short of actually diving in among them (which can also be arranged if you like), this is as close as you could possibly get to a set of shark teeth without being bitten.

Barcelona boasts 4km of city *platjas* (beaches), beginning with the gritty **Platja de la Barceloneta** and continuing northeast, beyond Port Olímpic, with a series of cleaner, more attractive strands. All get packed in summer.

L'EIXAMPLE   Neighbourhood

Modernisme, the Catalan version of art nouveau, transformed Barcelona's cityscape in the early 20th century. Most Modernista works were built in L'Eixample, the grid-plan district that was developed from the 1870s on.

Modernisme's star architect was the eccentric Antoni Gaudí (1852–1926), a devout Catholic whose work is full of references to nature and Christianity. His masterpiece, **La Sagrada Família** (Map p320; Expiatory Temple of the Holy Family; ☎93 207 30

31; www.sagradafamilia.org; Carrer de Mallorca 401; adult/senior & student/child to 10yr €12/10/free, combined with Casa-Museu Gaudí in Park Güell €14/12/free; ◷9am-8pm Apr-Sep, to 6pm Oct-Mar; MSagrada Família), is a work in progress and Barcelona's most famous building. Construction began in 1882 and could be completed in 2020. Gaudí spent 40 years working on the church, though he saw only the crypt, the apse and the nativity facade completed. Eventually there'll be 18 towers, all more than 100m high, representing the 12 apostles, four evangelists and Mary, Mother of God, plus the tallest tower (170m) standing for Jesus Christ. Climb high inside some of the towers (or take the elevator, €2) for a new perspective.

Gaudí's **La Pedrera** (Casa Milà; Map p320; www.fundaciocaixacatalunya.es; Carrer de Provença 261-265; adult/student & EU senior/child under 13yr €10/6/free; ◷9am-8pm; MDiagonal) is his best-known secular creation, named (it translates as 'The Quarry') because of its uneven grey-stone facade, which ripples around the corner of Carrer de Provença. Inside, you can

La Pedrera

La Sagrada Família

A Timeline

1882 Francesc del Villar is commissioned to construct a neo-Gothic church.

1883 Antoni Gaudí takes over as chief architect, and plans a far more ambitious church to hold 13,000 faithful.

1926 Death of Gaudí; work continues under Domènec Sugrañes. Much of the **apse** ① and **Nativity Facade** ② is complete.

1930 Bell towers ③ of the Nativity Facade completed.

1936 Construction is interrupted by Spanish Civil War; anarchists destroy Gaudí's plans.

1939-40 Architect Francesc de Paula Quintana i Vidal restores the crypt and meticulously reassembles many of Gaudí's lost models, some of which can be seen in the **museum** ④.

1976 Completion of **Passion Facade** ⑤.

1986-2006 Sculptor Josep Subirachs adds sculptural details to the Passion Facade including the panels telling the story of Christ's last days, amid much criticism for employing a style far removed from what was thought typical of Gaudí.

2000 Central nave vault ⑥ completed.

2010 Church completely roofed over; Pope Benedict XVI consecrates the church; work begins on a high-speed rail tunnel that will pass beneath the church's **Glory Facade** ⑦.

2020-40 Projected completion date.

TOP TIPS

Light The best light through the stained-glass windows of the Passion Facade bursts through into the heart of the church in the late afternoon.

Time Visit at opening time on weekdays to avoid the worst of the crowds.

Views Head up the Nativity façade bell towers for the views, as long queues generally await at the Passion Facade towers.

KRZYSZTOF DYDYNSKI

Spiral Staircase

Nativity Facade
Gaudí used plaster casts of local people and even of the occasional corpse from the local morgue as models for the portraits in the Nativity scene.

Apse
Built just after the crypt in mostly neo-Gothic style, it is capped by pinnacles that show a hint of the genius that Gaudí would later deploy in the rest of the church.

MICHELLE CHAPLOW/ALAMY

Bell towers
The towers (eight completed) of the three facades represent the 12 Apostles. Lifts whisk visitors up one tower of the Nativity and Passion Facades (the latter gets longer queues) for fine views.

Passion Facade

See the story of Christ's last days from Last Supper to burial in an S-shaped sequence from bottom to top of the facade. Check out the cryptogram in which the numbers always add up to 33, Christ's age at his death.

STEPHEN SAKS

Completed church

Along with the Glory Facade and its four towers, six other towers remain to the completed. They will represent the four Evangelists, the Virgin Mary and, soaring above them all over the transept, a 170m colossus symbolising Christ.

Crypt

The first part of the church built, the crypt is in largely neo-Gothic style and lies under the transept. Gaudí's burial place here can be seen from the Museu Gaudí.

Escoles de Gaudi

Museu Gaudí

Jammed with old photos, drawings and restored plaster models that bring Gaudí's ambitions to life, the museum also houses an extraordinarily complex plumb-line device he used to calculate his constructions.

MANUEL COHEN/GETTY IMAGES

Glory Facade

This will be the most fanciful facade of all, with a narthex boasting 16 hyperboloid lanterns topped by cones that will look something like an organ made of melting ice cream.

visit a museum about Gaudí and his work, a Modernista apartment and the surreal rooftop with its bizarre chimneys.

Just down the street is the unique facade of the **Casa Batlló** (Map p320; www .casabatllo.es; Passeig de Gràcia 43; adult/ student, child 7-18yr & senior/child under 7yr €17.80/14.25/free; ⏱9am-8pm; Ⓜ Passeig de Gràcia), an allegory for the legend of St George (Sant Jordi in Catalan) the dragon-slayer. On the same block are two other Modernista gems, **Casa Amatller** (Map p320; Passeig de Gràcia 41) by Josep Puig i Cadafalch and the **Casa Lleó Morera** (Map p320; Passeig de Gràcia 35) by Lluís Domènech i Montaner.

High up in the Gràcia district sits Gaudí's enchanting **Park Güell** (Carrer d'Olot 7; admission free; ⏱10am-9pm; Ⓜ Lesseps or Vallcarca, 🚌24), originally designed to be a self-contained community with houses, schools and shops. The project flopped, but we're left with a Dr Seuss–style playground filled with colourful mosaics and Gaudí-designed paths and plazas.

MONTJUÏC   Neighbourhood

Southwest of the city centre and with views out to sea and over the city, Montjuïc serves as a Central Park of sorts and is a great place to go for a jog or stroll. The are is dominated by the **Castell de Montjuïc** (Map p320), a one-time fortress with quite superb views. Buses 50, 55 and 61 all head up here. Cable cars and a funicular line also access the area.

Museu Nacional d'Art de Catalunya (Map p320; www.mnac.cat; Mirador del Palau Nacional; adult/student/senior & child under 15yr €8.50/6/free, 1st Sun of month free; ⏱10am-7pm Tue-Sat, to 2.30pm Sun & holidays; Ⓜ Espanya) contains within it's walls a broad panoply of Catalan and European art.

Fundació Joan Miró (Map p320; www .bcn.fjmiro.es; Plaça de Neptu; adult/senior & child €8.50/6, temporary exhibitions €4/3; ⏱10am-8pm Tue-Wed, Fri & Sat, to 9.30pm Thu, to 2.30pm Sun & holidays) is the definitive museum that showcases Joan Miró's works.

Left: Casa Batlló; **Below:** Decorations for the Festes de la Mercè

PHOTOGRAPHER: (LEFT) KRZYSZTOF DYDYNSKI/LONELY PLANET IMAGES ©; (BELOW) DAMIEN SIMONIS/LONELY PLANET IMAGES ©

 Tours

The three routes of the **Bus Turístic** (www .tmb.net; 1 day adult/4-12yr €22/14, 2 consecutive days €29/18; ⏱9am-7.30pm) link all the major tourist sights. Buy tickets on the bus or at the tourist office.

The main tourist office also offers various **walking tours** (tours €12.50-19) in English, Spanish or Catalan.

Festivals & Events

The **Festes de la Mercè** (www.bcn.cat/ merce), held around 24 September, is the city's biggest party, with concerts, dancing, *castellers* (human castle-builders), fireworks and *correfocs* – a parade of firework-spitting dragons and devils.

The evening before the **Dia de Sant Joan** (24 June) is a colourful midsummer celebration with bonfires and fireworks. The beaches are crowded with revellers to the wee hours.

 Sleeping

La Rambla & Barri Gòtic
HOTEL NERI   Hotel €€
(Map p332; ☎93 304 06 55; www.hotelneri.com; Carrer de Sant Sever 5; d from €235; MLiceu; ❄@🛜) Occupying a beautifully adapted, centuries-old building, this stunningly renovated medieval mansion combines historic stone walls with sexy plasma TVs. Downstairs is a fine restaurant, and you can take a drink and catch some rays on the roof deck.

El Raval
HOTEL SAN AGUSTÍN   Hotel €€
(Map p332; ☎93 318 16 58; www.hotelsa.com; Plaça de Sant Agustí 3; s €123-144, d €171; MLiceu; ❄@🛜) Once an 18th-century monastery, this hotel opened in 1840, making it the city's oldest. The location is perfect: a quick stroll off La Rambla

327

Montjuïc

A Day Itinerary

Possibly the site of ancient pre-Roman settlements, Montjuïc today is a hilltop green lung looking over city and sea. Interspersed across varied gardens are major art collections, a fortress, Olympic Stadium and more. A solid one-day itinerary can take in the key spots.

Alight at Espanya metro stop and make for **CaixaForum ❶**, always host to three or four free top-class exhibitions. The **Pavelló Mies van der Rohe ❷** across the road is an intriguing look at 1920s futurist housing by one of the 20th century's greatest architects. Uphill, the Romanesque art collection in the **Museu Nacional d'Art de Catalunya ❸** should not be missed. The restaurant here makes a pleasant lunch stop. Escalators lead further up the hill towards the **Estadi Olímpic ❹**, scene of the 1992 Olympic Games. The road leads east to the **Fundació Joan Miró ❺**, a shrine to the surrealist artist's creativity. Relax in the **Jardins de Mossèn Cinto Verdaguer ❻**, the prettiest on the hill, before taking the cable car to the **Castell de Montjuïc ❼**. If you pick the right day, you can round off by contemplating the gorgeously kitsch **La Font Màgica ❽** sound and light show.

TOP TIPS

Moving views Take the Transbordador Aeri from La Barceloneta for a bird's eye approach to Montjuïc. Or use the Teleféric de Montjuïc cable car to the Castell for more aerial views.

Summer fun The Castell de Montjuïc is the scene for outdoor summer cinema and concerts (see http://salamontjuic.org).

Beautiful bloomers Bursting with colour and serenity, the Jardins de Mossèn Cinto Verdaguer are exquisitely laid out with bulbs, especially tulips, and aquatic flowers.

JEAN-PIERRE LESCOURRET

CaixaForum

This former factory and barracks designed by Josep Puig i Cadafalch is an outstanding work of Modernista architecture; like a Lego fantasy in brick.

Piscines Bernat Picornell

Olympic Needle

Poble Espanyol

Amid the rich variety of traditional Spanish architecture created in replica for the 1929 Barcelona World Exhibition, seek out the art on show in the Fundació Fran Daurel.

NEIL SETCHFIELD

Pavelló Mies van der Rohe

Admire the inventiveness of the great German architect Ludwig Mies van der Rohe in this recreation of his avant garde German pavillion for the 1929 World Exhibition.

La Font Màgica

Take a summer evening to behold the Magic Fountain come to life in a unique 15-minute sound and light performance, when the water looks like a mystical cauldron of colour.

⑧

Museu Nacional d'Art de Catalunya

Make a beeline for the Romanesque art selection and the 12th-century polychrome image of Christ in majesty recovered from the apse of a country chapel in northwest Catalonia.

③

Museu Etnològic

Teatre Grec

⑤

⑥

Museu Olímpic i de l'Esport

④

Estadi Olímpic

Jardí Botànic

⑦

Jardins de Mossèn Cinto Verdaguer

Castell de Montjuïc

Enjoy the sweeping views of the sea and city from atop this 17th-century fortress, once a political prison and long a symbol of oppression.

Fundació Joan Miró

Take in some of Joan Miró's giant bright canvases, and discover little-known works of his early years in the Sala Joan Prats and Sala Pilar Juncosa.

Museu d'Arqueologia de Catalunya

Seek out the Roman mosaic depicting the Three Graces, one of the most beautiful items in this museum, dedicated to the ancient past of Catalonia and neighbouring parts of Spain.

Detour:
Dalí's Catalonia

A short train ride north of Girona, Figueres is home to the zany **Teatre-Museu Dalí** (www.salvador-dali.org; Plaça de Gala i Salvador Dalí 5; adult/under 9yr €11/free; ☉9am-8pm Jul-Sep, 9.30am-6pm Mar-Jun & Oct, 10.30am-6pm Nov-Feb, closed Mon Oct-Jun), housed in a 19th-century theatre converted by Salvador Dalí (who was born here). 'Theatre-museum' is an apt label for this multidimensional trip through one of the most fertile (or disturbed) imaginations of the 20th century. It's full of surprises, tricks and illusions, and contains a substantial portion of Dalí's life's work.

Dalí fans will want to travel south to visit the equally kooky **Castell de Púbol** (☏972 48 86 55; www.salvador-dali.org; La Pera; adult/under 9yr €7/free; ☉10am-8pm, closed Jan–mid-Mar & Mon outside high season) at La Pera, 22km northwest of Palafrugell, and the **Casa Museu Dalí** (☏972 25 10 15; www.salvador-dali.org; Port Lligat; adult/child €10/free) at his summer getaway in Port Lligat (1.25km from Cadaqués), where entry is by advance reservation only.

BARCELONA SLEEPING

on a curious square. Rooms sparkle, are mostly spacious and light, and have parquet floors.

CASA CAMPER   Hotel €€€
(Map p332; ☏93 342 62 80; www.casacamper.com; Carrer d'Elisabets 11; s/d €228/255; MLiceu; ⊜❄@) Run by the Mallorcan shoe people in the better end of El Raval, these designer digs offer rooms with a few surprises, like the Vinçon furniture. Across the corridor from each room is a separate, private sitting room, with balcony, TV and hammock.

La Ribera & La Barceloneta
HOTEL BANYS ORIENTALS
Boutique Hotel €€
(Map p332; ☏93 268 84 60; www.hotelbanysorientals.com; Carrer de l'Argenteria 37; s/d €93/107; MJaume I; ❄@) Cool blues and aquamarines combined with dark-hued parquet floors lend this boutique beauty an understated charm. All rooms – admittedly on the small side but impeccably presented – look onto the street or back lanes.

CHIC & BASIC   Hotel €€
(Map p320; ☏93 295 46 52; www.chicandbasic.com; Carrer de la Princesa 50; s €96, d €132-171; MJaume I; ❄@) In a completely reno-

vated building are 31 spotlessly white rooms. They have high ceilings, enormous beds (room types are classed as M, L and XL!) and lots of detailed touches (LED lighting, TFT TV screens and the retention of many beautiful old features of the original building, such as the marble staircase).

L'Eixample
HOTEL CONSTANZA
Boutique Hotel €€
(Map p320; ☏93 270 19 10; www.hotelconstanza.com; Carrer del Bruc 33; s/d €110/130; MGirona or Urquinaona; ❄@) Constanza is a boutique belle that has stolen the heart of many a visitor to Barcelona.

HOSTAL GOYA   Hostal €€
(Map p320; ☏93 302 25 65; www.hostalgoya.com; Carrer de Pau Claris 74; s €70, d €96-113; MPasseig de Gràcia; ❄) The Goya is a gem of a spot on the chichi side of l'Eixample and a short stroll from Plaça de Catalunya. In the bathrooms, the original mosaic floors have largely been retained, combined with contemporary design features.

HOTEL CASA FUSTER   Hotel €€€
(Map p320; ☏93 255 30 00, 902 202345; www.hotelcasafuster.com; Passeig de Gràcia 132; s/d from €294/321; MDiagonal; P⊜❄@🌐🖙) It is hard to believe the wrecking ball once

threatened this Modernista mansion turned luxury hotel. Standard rooms are plush if smallish.

Eating

Barcelona is foodie heaven. Some of the most creative chefs are one-time students of world-renowned chef Ferran Adrià, whose influence on the city's cuisine is strong.

Although Barcelona has a reputation as a hot spot of 'new Spanish cuisine', you'll still find local eateries serving up time-honoured local grub, from squid-ink *fideuà* (a satisfying paella-like noodle dish) through pigs' trotters, rabbit with snails, and *butifarra* (a tasty local sausage).

La Rambla & Barri Gòtic

Skip the overpriced traps along La Rambla and get into the winding lanes of the Barri Gòtic.

BAR CELTA   Tapa €€
(Map p332; 93 315 00 06; Carrer de la Mercè 16; meals €20-25; noon-midnight Tue-Sun; Drassanes) Specialists in *pulpo* (octopus)

and other seaside delights from Galicia in the country's northwest; the waiters waste no time in serving up bottles of crisp white Ribeiro wine to wash down the *raciones*.

AGUT   Catalan €€
(Map p332; 93 315 17 09; Carrer d'En Gignàs 16; meals €35; lunch & dinner Tue-Sat, lunch Sun;) Contemporary paintings contrast with the fine traditional Catalan dishes offered in this timeless restaurant. You might start with something like the *bouillabaisse con cigalitas de playa* (little seawater crayfish) for €11 and follow with an oak-grilled meat dish.

PLA   Modern €€
(Map p332; 93 412 65 52; www.pla-repla.com; Carrer de Bellafila 5; meals €45-50; dinner;) In this modern den of inventive cooking with music worthy of a club, the chefs present deliciously strange combinations such as *bacallà amb salsa de pomes verdes* (cod in a green apple sauce). Exotic meats like kangaroo turn up on the menu too.

CAN CONESA   Snacks €
(Map p332; 93 310 57 95; Carrer de la Llibreteria 1; rolls & toasted sandwiches €3-5; Mon-Sat; Jaume I) This place has been

Seafood platter, Barcelona

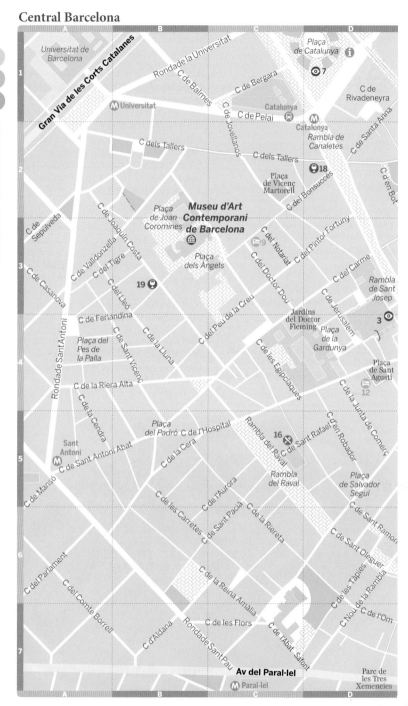

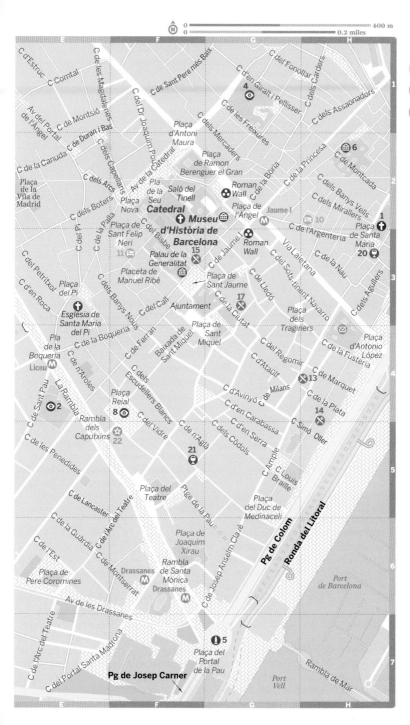

0 — 400 m
0 — 0.2 miles

C d'Estruc

C Comtal

C de les Magdalenes

C de Sant Pere més Baix

C d'en Giralt i Pellisser

C del Fonollar

C dels Carders

Av del Portal
de l'Angel

C de Montsió

C de la Canuda

C de Duran i Bas

C del Dr Joaquim Pou

C de les Freixures

4

C dels Assaonadors

C de les Mercaders

Plaça
d'Antoni
Maura

C dels Capellans

Av de la Catedral

Plaça de Ramon
Berenguer el Gran

C de la Bòria

C de la Princesa

C de Montcada

6

Plaça
de la
Vila de
Madrid

C dels Arcs

C dels Boters

Pla
de
la
Seu

Saló del
Tinell

Roman
Wall

C dels Banys Vells

C dels Miralles

Plaça
Nova

Catedral

Plaça de
l'Angel

Jaume I

C de l'Argenteria

C de la Nau

1

Plaça
de Santa
Maria

C del Pi

C del Bisbe

Museu
d'Història de
Barcelona

Roman
Wall

C de Jaume I

Via Laietana

20

C de la Palla

Plaça de
Sant Felip
Neri

11

15

Palau de la
Generalitat

C del Sots-tinent Navarro

C del Petritxol

Plaça
del Pi

C dels Banys Nous

Placeta de
Manuel Ribé

C del Call

Plaça de
Sant Jaume

C de Lledó

C d'en Roca

Ajuntament

Plaça de
Sant
Miquel

C de la Ciutat

17

Plaça
dels
Traginers

C dels Aguilers

Església de
Santa Maria
del Pi

Baixada de
Sant Miquel

C de Ferran

C del Regomir

C de la Fusteria

Plaça
d'Antonio
López

Pla
de la
Boqueria

C de la Boqueria

C d'Ataúlf

Liceu

C de n'Arolas

C dels
Escudellers Blancs

C de Milans

13

C de Marquet

La Rambla

2

C de Sant Pau

Plaça
Reial

8

C del Vidre

C d'Avinyó

C de la Plata

14

C Simó Oller

Rambla
dels
Caputxins

22

C de n'Aigla

C d'en Carabassa

C d'en Serra

C dels Còdols

C Ample

C Louis
Braille

C de les Penedies

21

Plaça del
Teatre

Ptge de la Pau

Plaça
del Duc de
Medinaceli

Pg de Colom

Ronda del Litoral

C de Lancaster

C de l'Arc del Teatre

C de la Guàrdia

C de l'Est

C de Montserrat

Plaça de
Joaquim
Xirau

Plaça de
Pere Coromines

Drassanes

Rambla
de Santa
Mònica

C de Josep Anselm Clavé

Port
de Barcelona

Drassanes

Av de les Drassanes

C de l'Arc del Teatre

C del Portal Santa Madrona

5

Plaça del
Portal
de la Pau

Pg de Josep Carner

Port
Vell

Rambla de Mar

333

Central Barcelona

doling out delicious *entrepans* (bread rolls with filling), frankfurters and toasted sandwiches here for more than 50 years – *barcelonins* swear by it and queue for them.

El Raval

BAR PINOTXO   Tapa €€
(Map p332; Mercat de la Boqueria; meals €20; ◷6am-5pm Mon-Sat Sep-Jul; Ⓜ Liceu) Of the half-dozen or so tapas bars and informal eateries within the market, this one near the Rambla entrance is about the most popular.

CASA LEOPOLDO   Catalan €€
(Map p332; ☏ 93 441 30 14; www.casaleopoldo .com; Carrer de Sant Rafael 24; meals €50; ◷lunch & dinner Tue-Sat, lunch Sun Sep-Jul; ☏) Several rambling dining areas with magnificent tiled walls and exposed timber-beam ceilings make this a fine option. The seafood menu is extensive and the local wine list strong. This is an old-town classic beloved of writers and artists down the decades.

La Ribera & Waterfront

La Barceloneta is the place to go for seafood; Passeig Joan de Borbó is lined with eateries but locals head for the back lanes.

XIRINGUITO D'ESCRIBÀ   Seafood €€
(☏ 93 221 07 29; www.escriba.es; Ronda Litoral 42, Platja de Bogatell; meals €40-50; ◷lunch; Ⓜ Llacuna) The Barcelona pastry family serves up top-quality seafood at this popular waterfront eatery. This is one of the few places where one person can order from their selection of paella and *fideuá* (normally a minimum of two people).

SUQUET DE L'ALMIRALL   Seafood €€
(Map p320; ☏ 93 221 62 33; Passeig de Joan de Borbó 65; meals €45-50; ◷lunch & dinner Tue-Sat, lunch Sun; Ⓜ Barceloneta, ☒ 17, 39, 57 or 64; ☏) At this family business, run by one of the acolytes of Ferran Adrià's El Bulli restaurant, the order of the day is top-class seafood.

L'Eixample & Gràcia

TAPAÇ 24   Tapa €€
(Map p320; www.carlesabellan.com; Carrer de la Diputació 269; meals €30-35; ◷9am-midnight Mon-Sat; Ⓜ Passeig de Gràcia) Specials in this basement tapas temple include the *bikini* (toasted ham and cheese sandwich; here the ham is cured and the truffle makes all the difference!), a thick black *arròs negre de sípia* (squid ink black rice) and, for dessert, *xocolata amb pa, sal i oli* (delicious balls of chocolate in olive oil with a touch of salt and wafer).

INOPIA
Tapa €€

(Map p320; ☎ 93 424 52 31; www.barinopia.com; Carrer de Tamarit 104; meals €25-30; ☺ dinner Tue-Sat, lunch Sat; M Rocafort) Albert Adrià, brother of star chef Ferran, has his hands full with this constantly busy gourmet tapas temple. Select a *pintxo de cuixa de pollastre a l'ast* (chunk of rotisserie chicken thigh) or the lightly fried, tempura-style vegetables.

 Drinking

Barcelona abounds with day-time cafes, laid-back lounges and lively night-time bars. Closing time is generally 2am Sunday to Thursday and 3am on Friday and Saturday.

Barri Gòtic

SOUL CLUB
Music Bar

(Map p332; Carrer Nou de Sant Francesc 7; ☺ 10pm-2.30am Mon-Thu, to 3am Fri & Sat, 8pm-2.30am Sun; M Drassanes) Each night the DJs change the musical theme, which ranges from deep funk to Latin grooves. The tiny front bar is for drinking and chatting (get in early for a stool or the sole lounge).

El Raval

BOADAS
Cocktail Bar

(Map p332; Carrer dels Tallers 1; ☺ noon-2am Mon-Thu, to 3am Fri & Sat; M Catalunya) Inside the unprepossessing entrance is one of the city's oldest cocktail bars (famed for its daiquiris). The bow-tied waiters have been serving up their poison since 1933; Joan Miró and Hemingway tippled here.

CASA ALMIRALL
Bar

(Map p332; Carrer de Joaquín Costa 33; ☺ 5.30pm-2.30am Sun-Thu, 7pm-3am Fri & Sat;

M Universitat) In business since the 1860s, this unchanged corner bar is dark and intriguing, with Modernista decor and a mixed clientele. There are some great original pieces in here, like the marble counter.

La Ribera

GIMLET
Cocktail Bar

(Map p320; Carrer del Rec 24; ☺ 10pm-3am; M Jaume I) White-jacketed bar staff with all the appropriate aplomb will whip you up a gimlet or any other classic cocktail (around €10) your heart desires. Barcelona cocktail guru Javier Muelas is behind this and several other cocktail bars around the city, so you can be sure of excellent drinks, some with a creative twist.

LA VINYA DEL SENYOR
Wine Bar

(Map p332; Plaça de Santa Maria del Mar 5; ☺ noon-1am Tue-Sun; M Jaume I) The wine list is as long as *War and Peace,* and the terrace lies in the shadow of Santa Maria del Mar. You can crowd inside the tiny wine bar itself or take a bottle upstairs.

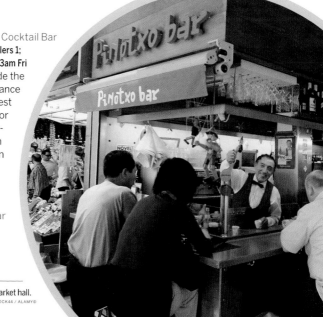

Bar Pinotxo in La Rambla market hall.
PHOTOGRAPHER: TRAVELSTOCK44 / ALAMY©

L'Eixample & Gràcia

BERLIN   Bar

(Map p320; Carrer de Muntaner 240; ⊙10am-2am Mon-Wed, to 2.30am Thu, to 3am Fri & Sat; **M**Diagonal or Hospital Clínic) This elegant corner bar attracts waves of night animals starting up for a long night.

 Entertainment

To keep up with what's on, pick up a copy of the weekly listings magazine, *Guía del Ocio* (€1) from newsstands.

Most theatre in the city is in Catalan.

There are quite a few venues that stage vanguard drama and dance, including **Teatre Nacional de Catalunya** (Map p320; ☎93 306 57 00; www.tnc.cat; Plaça de les Arts 1; admission €12-32; ⊙box office 3-7pm Wed-Fri, to 8.30pm Sat, to 5pm Sun & 1hr before show; **M**Glòries or Monumental).

Live Music

SALA TARANTOS   Music Bar

(Map p332; ☎93 319 17 89; www.masimas.net; Plaça Reial 17; admission from €7; ⊙performances 8.30pm, 9.30pm & 10.30pm; **M**Liceu)

This basement locale is the stage for some of the best flamenco to pass through Barcelona.

Sport

FC Barcelona (Barça for aficionados) has one of the best stadiums in Europe – the 99,000-capacity **Camp Nou** (☎902 189 900; Carrer d'Aristides Maillol; ⊙box office 9am-1.30pm & 3.30-6pm Mon-Fri; **M**Palau Reial or Collblanc) situated in the west of the city. Tickets for national-league games are available at the stadium, by phone or online. If going for the latter two options, be sure to plan ahead – nonmembers must book tickets 15 days before the match.

 Shopping

Most mainstream fashion stores are along a shopping 'axis' that runs from Plaça de Catalunya along Passeig de Gràcia, then left (west) along Avinguda Diagonal.

The El Born area in La Ribera is awash with tiny boutiques, especially those purveying young, fun fashion. There are

Teatre Nacional de Catalunya

No More Bulls?

On 28 July 2010 Catalonia became the first region in mainland Spain to ban bullfighting; the Canary Islands voted to make bullfighting illegal in 1991. The vote, which came as a result of a 180,000-strong petition, follows moves by 23 municipalities (including Barcelona) that have declared themselves to be antibullfighting cities in recent years. With Catalonia never the strongest bastion of bullfighting tradition and with Spain's major national political parties opposing Catalonia's ban, the chances of other Spanish regions following suit seem remote. However, other factors do pose a significant (albeit longer-term) threat to bullfighting. Recent surveys have found that around 50% of Spaniards oppose bullfighting, with the figures much higher among younger Spaniards. The recent global economic crisis has also taken its toll – there was a 50% drop in the number of bullfights in 2009, with many small towns forced to cancel their annual fiestas.

plenty of shops scattered throughout the Barri Gòtic (stroll Carrer d'Avinyò and Carrer de Portaferrissa).

JOAN MURRIÀ Food & Drink
(Map p320; www.murria.cat; Carrer de Roger de Llúria 85; Passeig de Gràcia) Ramon Casas designed the Modernista shop-front ads for this delicious delicatessen, where the shelves groan under the weight of speciality food from around Catalonia and beyond.

ELS ENCANTS VELLS Market
(Map p320; 'The Old Charms'; www.encantsbcn.com, in Catalan; Plaça de les Glòries Catalanes; 7am-6pm Mon, Wed, Fri & Sat; Glòries) Bargain hunters love this free-for-all flea market.

ℹ Information

Dangers & Annoyances
Purse snatching and pickpocketing are major problems, especially around Plaça de Catalunya, La Rambla and Plaça Reial.

Emergency
Tourists who want to report thefts need to go to the Catalan police, known as the Mossos d'Esquadra (☎088; Carrer Nou de la Rambla 80), or the Guàrdia Urbana (Local Police; ☎092; La Rambla 43).

Money
Banks (with ATMs) and foreign-exchange offices abound in Barcelona. Interchange (Rambla dels Caputxins 74; 9am-11pm; Liceu) represents American Express.

Tourist Information
Oficina d'Informació de Turisme de Barcelona

Main branch (www.barcelonaturisme.com; Plaça de Catalunya 17-S underground; 9am-9pm)

Aeroport del Prat (Terminals 1, 2B and 2A arrivals halls; 9am-9pm)

Estació Sants (8am-8pm late Jun-late Sep, 8am-8pm Mon-Fri, 8am-2pm Sat, Sun & holidays Oct-May; Sants Estació)

Town hall (Carrer de la Ciutat 2; 9am-8pm Mon-Fri, 10am-8pm Sat, 10am-2pm Sun & holidays; Jaume I)

Regional tourist office (www.gencat.net/probert; Passeig de Gràcia 107; 10am-7pm Mon-Sat, to 2.30pm Sun; Diagonal)

ℹ Getting There & Away

Air
Barcelona's airport, El Prat de Llobregat (902 404 704; www.aena.es), is 12km southwest of the city centre.

337

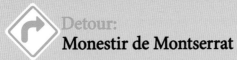

Detour:
Monestir de Montserrat

The monks who built the Monestir de Montserrat (Monastery of the Serrated Mountain), 50km northwest of Barcelona, chose a spectacular spot. The Benedictine **monastery** (www.abadiamontserrat.net; ⊙9am-6pm) sits on the side of a 1236m mountain of weird, bulbous peaks. The monastery was founded in 1025 and pilgrims still come from all over Christendom to kiss the Black Virgin (La Moreneta), the 12th-century wooden sculpture of the Virgin Mary.

If you're around the basilica at the right time, you'll catch a brief performance by the **Montserrat Boys' Choir** (Escolania; www.escolania.net; admission free; ⊙performances 1pm & 6.45pm Mon-Fri, 11am & 6.45pm Sun Sep-Jun).

You can explore the mountain above the monastery on a web of paths leading to some of the peaks and to 13 empty and rather dilapidated hermitages. Running every 20 minutes, the **Funicular de Sant Joan** (one way/return €4.50/7.20; ⊙10am-5.40pm Apr-Oct, to 7pm mid-Jul–Aug, to 4.30pm Mar & Nov, 11am-4.30pm Dec, closed Jan-Feb) will carry you up the first 250m from the monastery.

Montserrat is an easy day trip from Barcelona. The R5 line trains operated by FGC run from Plaça d'Espanya station in Barcelona to Monistrol de Montserrat up to 18 times daily starting at 5.16am. They connect with the rack-and-pinion train, or **cremallera** (www.cremalleradmontserrat.com), which takes 17 minutes to make the upwards journey and costs €5.15/8.20 one way/return.

Boat

Regular passenger and vehicular ferries to/from the Balearic Islands, operated by Acciona Trasmediterránea (☎902 454 645; www.trasmediterranea.es), dock along both sides of the Moll de Barcelona wharf in Port Vell.

Bus

The main terminal for most domestic and international buses is the Estació del Nord (☎902 303 222; www.barcelonanord.com; Carrer d'Ali Bei 80; MArc de Triomf). ALSA goes to Madrid (€28.18, eight hours, up to 16 daily), Valencia (€25.34, 4½ to 6½ hours, up to 14 daily) and many other destinations.

Car & Motorcycle

Autopistas (tollways) head out of Barcelona in most directions, including the C31/C32 to the southern Costa Brava; the C32 to Sitges; the C16 to Manresa (with a turn-off for Montserrat); and the AP7 north to Girona, Figueres and France, and south to Tarragona and Valencia (turn off along the AP2 for Lleida, Zaragoza and Madrid).

Train

Virtually all trains travelling to and from destinations within Spain stop at Estació Sants (MSants-Estació). High-speed trains to Madrid via Lleida and Zaragoza take as little as two hours 40 minutes; prices vary wildly. Other trains run to Valencia (€38.50 to €43.10, three to 4½ hours, 15 daily) and Burgos (from €49, six to seven hours, four daily).

❶ Getting Around

To/From the Airport

The **A1 Aerobús** (☎93 415 60 20; one way €5) runs from the airport (Terminal 1) to Plaça de Catalunya from 6.05am to 1.05am, taking 30 to 40 minutes. A2 Aerobús does the same run from Terminal 2, from 6am to 12.30am. Buy your tickets on the bus.

Renfe's R2 Nord train line runs between the airport and Passeig de Gràcia (via Estació Sants) in central Barcelona (about 35 minutes). Tickets cost €3, unless you have a T-10 multitrip public-transport ticket.

A taxi to/from the city centre is about a half-hour ride, depending on traffic, and should cost around €20 to €25.

Public Transport

Barcelona's metro system spreads its tentacles around the city in such a way that most places of interest are within a 10-minute walk of a station. A single metro, bus or suburban train ride costs €1.40, but a T-1 ticket, valid for 10 rides, costs €7.85.

Taxi

Barcelona's black-and-yellow taxis are plentiful and reasonably priced. The flag fall is €2. If you can't find a street taxi, call 📞93 303 30 33 to book one.

ARAGÓN, BASQUE COUNTRY & NAVARRA

This northeast area of Spain is brimming with fascinating destinations: the arid hills and proud history of Aragón; the lush coastline and gourmet delights of the Basque Country (País Vasco); and the wine country and famous festivals of Navarra.

San Sebastián

POP 183,300

Stylish San Sebastián (Donostia in Basque) has the air of an upscale resort, complete with an idyllic location on the shell-shaped Bahía de la Concha. The natural setting – crystalline waters, a flawless beach, green hills on all sides – is captivating. But this is one of Spain's true culinary capitals, with more Michelin stars per capita here than anywhere else on earth.

Sights & Activities

BEACHES & ISLA DE SANTA CLARA

Beaches

Fulfilling almost every idea of how a perfect city beach should be formed, **Playa de la Concha** and its westerly extension **Playa de Ondarreta** are easily among the best city beaches in Europe. The **Isla de Santa Clara**, about 700m from the beach, is accessible by boats that run every half-hour from June to September. Less popular, but just as showy, **Playa de Gros**, east of Río Urumea, is the city's main surf beach.

Striped sunshades at Playa de la Concha

MUSEO CHILLIDA LEKU Museum, Park
(www.museochillidaleku.com; adult/child €8.50/
free; ⏰10.30am-8pm Mon-Sat, to 3pm Sun
Jul & Aug, shorter hr rest of yr) This open-air
museum, situated south of San Sebastián, is the most engaging museum in
rural Basque Country. Amid the beech,
oak and magnolia trees, you'll find 40
sculptures of granite and iron created by
the renowned Basque sculptor Eduardo
Chillida. Many more of Chillida's works
appear inside the renovated 16th-century
farmhouse.

To get here, take the G2 bus (€1.35)
for Hernani from Calle de Okendo in San
Sebastián and get off at Zabalaga.

MONTE IGUELDO Lookout
The views from the summit of Monte
Igueldo, just west of town, will make you
feel like a circling hawk staring over the
vast panorama of the Bahía de la Concha
and the surrounding coastline and mountains. The best way to get there is via the
old-world **funicular railway** (return adult/
under 7yr €2.60/1.90; ⏰10am-10pm mid-Jul &
Aug, shorter hr rest of yr).

MONTE URGULL Castle, Museum
You can walk to the top of Monte Urgull,
topped by low castle walls and a grand
statue of Christ, by taking a path from
Plaza de Zuloaga or from behind the
aquarium. The views are breathtaking.
The castle houses the well-presented
Mirando a San Sebastián (admission free;
⏰11am-8pm May-mid-Sep, shorter hr rest of
yr), a small museum focusing on the city's
history.

🛏 Sleeping

PENSIÓN BELLAS ARTES
Boutique Hotel €€
(📞943 47 49 05; www.pension-bellasartes.com;
Calle de Urbieta 64; s/d from €75/95; 🛜) To
call this magnificent place a mere *pensión*
is to do it something of a disservice. Its
spacious rooms (some with glassed-in
balconies) with exposed stone walls and
excellent bathrooms should be the envy
of many a more expensive hotel.

PENSIÓN AMAIUR OSTATUA
Boutique Hotel €
(📞943 42 96 54; www.pensionamaiur.com;
Calle de 31 de Agosto 44; s without bathroom
€40-45, d without bathroom €50-65; @🛜)
Sprawling over three floors of an old
town house, this excellent *pensión*
continues to improve. The rooms,
all of which share bathrooms,
are generally fairly small but
have had a great deal of
thought put into them,
and every room and
every floor is different
– maybe you'll get one
with chintzy wallpaper
or maybe you'll go
for one with brazen
primary colours.

PENSIÓN ALTAIR
Boutique Pensión €
(📞943 29 31 33; www
.pension-altair.com; Calle
Padre Larroca 3; s/d €60/84;

View from Monte Urgull

❄ @ 🛜) This brand-new *pensión* might well be the future of the San Sebastián accommodation scene. It's a beautifully restored town house with unusual arched windows that look like they've come from a church, and spacious minimalist rooms a world away from the fusty decor of the old town *pensión*s. Reception is closed between 1.30pm and 5pm.

Eating

San Sebastián is paradise for food lovers. Considered the birthplace of *nueva cocina española*, this area is home to some of the country's top chefs. Head to the Parte Vieja for San Sebastián's *pintxos*, Basque-style tapas.

LA CUCHARA DE SAN TELMO Tapa €
(Calle de 31 de Agosto 28) This unfussy, hidden-away (and hard to find) bar offers miniature *nueva cocina vasca* (Basque nouvelle cuisine) from a supremely creative kitchen, where chefs Alex Montiel and Iñaki Gulin conjure up such delights as *carrílera de ternera al vino tinto* (calf cheeks in red wine).

ARZAK Basque Fine Dining €€€
(🕿943 27 84 65; www.arzak.info; Avenida Alcalde Jose Elosegui 273; meals around €150; 🕘closed last 2 weeks Jun & all Nov) With three shining Michelin stars, acclaimed chef Juan Mari Arzak takes some beating when it comes to *nueva cocina vasca* and his restaurant is, not surprisingly, considered one of the best places to eat in Spain. Reservations, well in advance, are obligatory. The restaurant is about 1.5km east of San Sebastián.

ASTELANA Tapa €
(Calle de Iñigo 1) The *pintxos* draped across the counter in this bar, tucked into the corner of Plaza de la Constitución, stand out as some of the best in the city.

LA MEJÍLLONERA Tapa €
(Calle del Puerto 15) If you thought mussels came only with garlic sauce, come here and discover mussels (from €3) by the thousand in all their glorious forms. Mus-

sels not for you? Opt for the calamari and spicy *patatas bravas*. We promise you won't regret it.

ℹ Information

Street signs are in Basque and Spanish.

Oficina de Turismo (🕿943 48 11 66; www .sansebastianturismo.com; Alameda de Blvd 8; 🕘9am-8pm Mon-Sat, 10am-7pm Sun Jun-Sep, 9am-1.30pm & 3.30-7pm Mon-Thu, 9.30am-7pm Fri & Sat, 10am-2pm Sun Oct-May)

ℹ Getting There & Away

TRAIN There are regular services to Madrid (from €52.60, five hours) and Barcelona (from €36.90, eight hours).

Bilbao
POP 354,200

The commercial hub of the Basque Country, Bilbao (Bilbo in Basque) is best known for the magnificent Guggenheim Museum. An architectural masterpiece by Frank Gehry, the museum was the catalyst of a turn-around that saw Bilbao transformed from an industrial port city into a vibrant cultural centre.

◉ Sights

MUSEO GUGGENHEIM Art Gallery
(www.guggenheim-bilbao.es; Avenida Abandoibarra 2; adult/child €13/free; 🕘10am-8pm Jul & Aug, closed Mon Sep-Jun) Opened in 1997, Bilbao's Museo Guggenheim lifted modern architecture and Bilbao into the 21st century – with sensation. Some would say that structure overwhelms function and that the Guggenheim is more famous for its architecture than its content. But Canadian architect Frank Gehry's inspired use of flowing canopies, cliffs, promontories, ship shapes, towers and flying fins is irresistible. The interior of the Guggenheim is purposefully vast – the atrium is more than 45m high; light pours through glass cliffs and exhibits filling the ground floor include such wonders as mazes of metal and phrases of light reaching for the skies.

MUSEO DE BELLAS ARTES   Art Gallery
(Fine Arts Museum; www.museobilbao.com; Plaza del Museo 2; adult/child €6/free, admission free Wed; ⊙10am-8pm Tue-Sun) A mere five minutes from Museo Guggenheim is Bilbao's Museo de Bellas Artes. There are three main subcollections: Classical Art, with works by Murillo, Zurbarán, El Greco, Goya and van Dyck; Contemporary Art, featuring works by Gauguin, Francis Bacon and Anthony Caro; and Basque Art, with the works of the great sculptors Jorge de Oteiza and Eduardo Chillida, and also strong paintings by the likes of Ignacio Zuloaga and Juan de Echevarria.

CASCO VIEJO   Old Town
The compact Casco Viejo, Bilbao's atmospheric old quarter, is full of charming streets, boisterous bars, and plenty of quirky and independent shops. At the heart of the Casco are Bilbao's original 'seven streets', Las Siete Calles, which date from the 1400s.

    The 14th-century Gothic **Catedral de Santiago** (⊙10am-1pm & 4-7pm Tue-Sat, 10.30am-1.30pm Sun) has a splendid Renaissance portico and pretty little cloister. Further north, the 19th-century arcaded **Plaza Nueva** is a rewarding *pintxo* haunt.

EUSKAL MUSEOA (MUSEO VASCO)
   Museum
(Museum of Basque Archaeology, Ethnography & History; www.euskal-museoa.org; Plaza Miguel Unamuno 4; adult/child €3/free, admission free Thu; ⊙11am-5pm Tue-Sat, to 2pm Sun) This is probably the most complete museum of Basque culture and history in all the Basque regions. The Museum of Basque Archaeology, Ethnography & History is housed in a fine old building, at whose centre is a peaceful cloister that was part of an original 17th-century Jesuit college.

 Sleeping

The Bilbao tourism authority has a useful **reservations department** (⊙902 877 298; www.bilbaoreservas.com) for accommodation.

Left: Museo Guggenheim (p341); **Below:** Plaza Nueva
PHOTOGRAPHER: (LEFT) KIMBERLEY COOLE/LONELY PLANET IMAGES ©; (BELOW) ANDREW DUKE/ALAMY ©

PENSIÓN ITURRIENEA OSTATUA
Boutique Hotel €€

(☎ 944 16 15 00; www.iturrieneaostatua.com; Calle de Santa María 14; d/tr €66/80; ☎) Easily the most eccentric hotel in Bilbao, the Pensión Iturrienea Ostatua is part farmyard, part old-fashioned toyshop, and a work of art in its own right. Try to get a double room on the 1st floor (singles don't come with quite as many frills and ribbons); they are so full of character there'll be barely enough room for your own!

GRAN HOTEL DOMINE
Designer Hotel €€€

(☎ 944 25 33 00; www.granhoteldominebilbao .com; Alameda Mazarredo 61; d from €140; P ❄ @ ☎) Designer chic all the way, from the Javier Mariscal main interiors to the Philippe Starck and Arne Jacobsen fittings – and that's just in the loos. This stellar showpiece of the Silken chain has views of the Guggenheim from some of its pricier rooms and from the roof terrace.

 ## Eating

RIO-OJA
Basque €

(☎ 944 15 08 71; Calle de Perro 4; mains €9-12) An institution that shouldn't be missed. It specialises in light Basque seafood and heavy inland fare, but to most foreigners the sheep brains and squid floating in pools of its own ink are the makings of a culinary adventure story they'll be recounting for years. Don't worry: it really does taste much better than it sounds.

RESTAURANTE GUGGENHEIM
Basque Fine Dining €€€

(☎ 944 23 93 33; www.restauranteguggenheim .com; bistro menu €19.66, restaurant menu €75, mains €30-35 ☉ closed Mon & Christmas period) El Goog's modernist, chic restaurant and cafe are under the direction of super chef Josean Martínez Alija. The *nueva cocina vasca* is breathtaking and the adventurous menu ever-changing.

Reservations are essential in the evening, but at lunch it's first-come, first-served from 1.30pm.

CAFÉ IRUÑA   Basque €
(cnr Calles de Colón de Larreátegui & Berástegui; menú del día €13.50) Moorish style and a century of gossip are the defining characteristics of this grand old dame. It's the perfect place to indulge in a bit of people-watching and while you're at it you might as well also indulge in a meal or, in the evening, some *pinchos morunos* (spicy kebabs with bread; €2.20).

ℹ️ Information

Tourist office (www.bilbao.net/bilbaoturismo; Plaza del Ensanche 11; ☺9am-2pm & 4-7.30pm Mon-Fri) Other branches at the Teatro Arriaga, Museo Guggenheim and airport.

ℹ️ Getting There & Away

AIR Bilbao's airport (BIO), with domestic and a handful of international flights, is near Sondika, 12km northeast of the city. The airport bus

Bizkaibus A3247 (€1.20, 30 minutes) runs to/from Termibus (bus station), where there is a tram stop and a metro station.
TRAIN Two Renfe trains runs daily to Madrid (from €48.60, six hours) and Barcelona (€62.30, six hours) from the Abando train station.

Navarra

Navarra, historically and culturally linked to the Basque Country, is known for its fine wines and for the Sanfermines festival in Pamplona.

Pamplona
POP 195,800

Immortalised by Ernest Hemingway in *The Sun Also Rises,* the pre-Pyrenean city of Pamplona (Iruña in Basque) is home of the wild Sanfermines (aka Encierro or Running of the Bulls) festival, but is also an extremely walkable city that's managed to mix the charm of old plazas and buildings with modern shops and a lively nightlife.

◎ Sights

CATHEDRAL   Church
(Calle Dormitalería; guided tours adult/child €4.40/2.60; ☺10am-7pm Mon-Fri, to 2pm Sat mid-Jul–mid-Sep, closed for lunch mid-Sep–mid-Jul) Pamplona's main cathedral stands on a rise just inside the city ramparts amid a dark thicket of narrow streets. It's a late-medieval Gothic gem spoiled only by its rather dull neoclassical facade.

CIUDADELA & PARKS   Park
(Avenida del Ejército) The walls and bulwarks of the grand fortified citadel, the star-shaped Ciudadela, lurk amid the verdant grass and trees in what is now a charming park, the portal to three more parks that unfold to the north and lend the city a beautiful green escape.

Crowded street in Pamplona during Sanfermines
PHOTOGRAPHER: MICAH WRIGHT/LONELY PLANET IMAGES ©

Surviving Sanfermines

The Sanfermines festival is held on 6 to 14 July, when Pamplona is overrun with thrill-seekers, curious onlookers and, oh yeah, bulls. The Encierro (Running of the Bulls) begins at 8am daily, when bulls are let loose from the Coralillos Santo Domingo. The 825m race lasts just three minutes, so don't be late. The safest place to watch the Encierro is on TV. If that's too tame for you, try to sweet-talk your way onto a balcony or book a room in a hotel with views.

MUSEO OTEIZA — Museum
(www.museooteiza.org; Calle de la Cuesta 7; adult/student/child €4/2/free, all admission free Fri; ⏰11am-7pm Tue-Sat, to 3pm Sun Jun-Sep) Around 9km northeast of Pamplona in the town of Alzuza, this impressive museum contains almost 3000 pieces by the renowned Navarran sculptor Jorge Oteiza. You can reach it via the three buses a day that run to Alzuza from Pamplona's bus station.

Sleeping

Accommodation is hard to come by during Sanfermines – book months in advance. Prices below don't reflect the huge (up to fivefold) mark-up you'll find in mid-July.

PALACIO GUENDULAIN
Historic Hotel €€€
(☎948 22 55 22; www.palacioguendulain.com; Calle Zapatería 53; d from €128; P✳🛜) To call this stunning new hotel sumptuous is an understatement. Inside the converted former home of the Viceroy of New Granada, the rooms contain 'Princess and the Pea' soft beds, enormous showers and regal armchairs.

HOTEL PUERTA DEL CAMINO
Boutique Hotel €€
(☎948 22 66 88; www.hotelpuertadelcamino.com; Calle dos de Mayo 4; s/d €69.55/81.32; P✳@) A very stylish new hotel inside a converted convent (clearly the nuns appreciated the finer things in life!) beside the northern gates to the old city. The functional rooms have clean, modern lines and it's positioned in one of the prettier, and quieter, parts of town.

Eating & Drinking

Central streets such as Calle de San Nicolás and Calle de la Estafeta are lined with tapas bars, many of which morph into nightspots at weekends.

BASERRI — Basque €
(Calle de San Nicolás 32; menú del día €14) This place has won so many awards that we could fill this book just listing them. As you'd expect, the pintxos are superb but sadly the full meals play something of a second fiddle in comparison.

CASA OTAÑO — Basque €
(☎948 22 50 95; Calle de San Nicolás 5; mains €15-18) A little pricier than many on this street but worth the extra. Its formal atmosphere is eased by the dazzling array of pink and red flowers spilling off the balcony. Great dishes range from the locally caught trout to heavenly duck dishes.

CAFÉ IRUÑA — Cafe
(Plaza del Castillo 44) Opened on the eve of Sanfermines in 1888, Café Iruña's dominant position, sense of history and belle époque decor make it the most famous and popular watering hole in the city.

ℹ Information

Tourist office (www.turismo.navarra.es; Calle de Esclava 1; ⏰9am-8pm Mon-Sat, to 2pm Sun)

ℹ Getting There & Away

TRAIN Pamplona's train station is linked to the city centre by bus 9 from Paseo de Sarasate every 15 minutes. Trains run to/from Madrid (€56, three hours, four daily) and San Sebastián (from €20.40, two hours, two daily).

KRZYSZTOF DYDYNSKI/LONELY PLANET IMAGES ©

VALENCIA & MURCIA

A warm climate, an abundance of seaside resorts, and interesting cities make this area of Spain a popular destination. The beaches of the Costa Blanca (White Coast) draw most of the visitors, but you should venture beyond the shore to get a real feel for the region.

Valencia

POP 814,200

Valencia, where paella first simmered over a wood fire, is a vibrant, friendly, slightly chaotic place. It has two outstanding fine-arts museums, an accessible old quarter, Europe's newest cultural and scientific complex, and one of Spain's most exciting nightlife scenes.

 Sights & Activities

CIUDAD DE LAS ARTES Y LAS CIENCIAS
Science Centre

(City of Arts & Sciences; ☏reservations 902 10 00 31; www.cac.es; combined ticket adult/child €31.50/24) The aesthetically stunning City of Arts & Sciences occupies a massive 350,000-sq-metre swath of the old Turia riverbed. It's mostly the work of stellar local architect, the world-renowned Santiago Calatrava. The complex includes the **Oceanogràfic** (adult/child €24/18; ☉10am-6pm), a stunning aquarium; **Hemisfèric** (adult/child €7.50/5.80), a planetarium and IMAX cinema; **Museo de las Ciencias Príncipe Felipe** (adult/child €7.50/6; ☉10am-7pm), an interactive science museum designed by architect Santiago Calatrava; and the extraordinary **Palau de les Arts Reina Sofía** (www.lesarts.com; Autovía a El Saler) concert hall. It's 3km southeast of the Plaza de la Virgen; take bus 35 from Plaza del Ayuntamiento or bus 95 from Torres de Serranos or Plaza de América.

BARRIO DEL CARMEN   Historic Area
You'll see Valencia's best face by simply wandering around the Barrio del Carmen. Valencia's Romanesque-Gothic-baroque-Renaissance **catedral** (adult/child incl audioguide €4/2.70; ☉10am-5.30pm Mon-Sat, 2-5.30pm Sun) is a compendium of centuries of architectural history and home to the **Capilla del Santo Cáliz**, a chapel said to contain the Holy Grail. Climb the 207 stairs of the **Micalet bell tower** (Miguelete bell tower; adult/child €2/1; ☉10am-7pm) for sweeping city views.

PLAZA DEL MERCADO
Plaza

Over on historic Plaza del Mercado, two emblematic buildings, each an architectural masterpiece of its era, face each other. Valencia's Modernista covered market, the **Mercado Central** (⊙7.30am-2.30pm Mon-Sat), recently scrubbed and now looking as good as new, was constructed in 1928. **La Lonja** (⊙10am-2pm & 4.30-8.30pm Mon-Sat, 10am-3pm Sun), which stands on the opposite side of the plaza, is a splendid late-15th-century building. It's listed as a Unesco World Heritage site, and was originally the location of Valencia's silk and commodity exchange.

INSTITUTO VALENCIANO DE ARTE MODERNO (IVAM)
Art Gallery

(www.ivam.es; Calle de Guillem de Castro 118; adult/child €2/1; ⊙10am-8pm Tue-Sun) IVAM (ee-bam) hosts excellent temporary exhibitions and houses an impressive permanent collection of 20th-century Spanish art.

FREE MUSEO DE BELLAS ARTES
Art Museum

(Calle San Pío V 9; ⊙10am-8pm Tue-Sun) Bright and spacious, the Museo de Bellas Artes ranks among Spain's best art museums. Highlights include the grandiose Roman *Mosaic of the Nine Muses,* a collection of magnificent late-medieval altarpieces and works by El Greco, Goya, Velázquez, Murillo, Ribalta and artists such as Sorolla and Pinazo of the Valencian Impressionist school.

BEACHES
Beaches

Playa de la Malvarrosa runs into **Playa de las Arenas**. Each is bordered by the **Paseo Marítimo** promenade and a string of restaurants. **Playa El Salér**, 10km south, is backed by shady pine woods.

 ## Sleeping

AD HOC
Hotel €€

(☏96 391 91 40; www.adhochoteles.com; Calle Boix 4; s €65-101, d €76-125; ❄ 🛜) Friendly, welcoming Ad Hoc offers comfort and charm deep within the old quarter. The late 19th-century building has been restored to its former splendour with great sensitivity.

PETIT PALACE BRISTOL
Boutique Hotel €€

(☏96 394 51 00; www.hthoteles.com; Calle Abadía San Martín 3; r €60-130; ❄ @ 🛜) Hip and minimalist, this lovely boutique hotel, a comprehensively made-over 19th-century mansion, retains the best of its past and does a particularly scrumptious buffet breakfast. Free bikes for guests.

CHILL ART JARDÍN BOTÁNICO
Boutique Hotel €€

(☏96 315 40 12; www.hoteljardinbotanico.com; Calle Doctor Peset Cervera 6; s €94-133, d €94-149; ❄ 🛜) Welcoming and megacool, this intimate, 16-room hotel is furnished with great flair. Candles flicker in the lounge and each bedroom has original artwork. The Instituto Valenciano de Arte Moderno (IVAM) is nearby.

Burn Baby Burn

In mid-March, Valencia hosts one of Europe's wildest street parties: **Las Fallas de San José** (www.fallas.es, in Spanish). For one week (12 to 19 March), the city is engulfed by an anarchic swirl of fireworks, music, festive bonfires and all-night partying. On the final night, giant *ninots* (effigies), many of political and social personages, are torched in the main plaza.

If you're not in Valencia then, see the *ninots* saved from the flames by popular vote at the **Museo Fallero** (Plaza Monteolivete 4; adult/child €2/1; ⊙10am-2pm & 4.30-8pm Tue-Sat, 10am-3pm Sun).

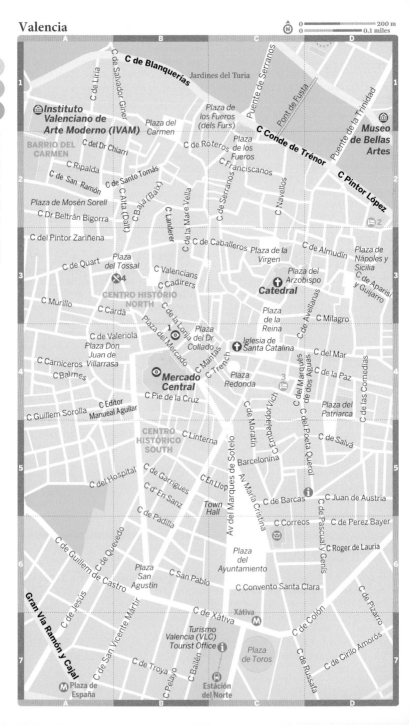

Valencia

0   200 m
0   0.1 miles

C de Liria
C de Salvador Giner
C de Blanquerías
Jardines del Turia
Puente de Serranos
Pont de Fusta
Puente de la Trinidad

🏛 **Instituto Valenciano de Arte Moderno (IVAM)**

Plaza del Carmen

Plaza de los Fueros (dels Furs)

C Conde de Trénor

🏛 **Museo de Bellas Artes**

BARRIO DEL CARMEN

C del Dr Chiarri

Plaza de los Fueros

Plaza de los Franciscanos

C Pintor López

C Ripalda
C de San Ramón
C de Santo Tomás
C Alta (Dalt)
C Baix (Baix)

C de Serranos

C Navellos

Plaza de Mosén Sorell
C Dr Beltrán Bigorra

C de la Mare Vella

C del Pintor Zariñena

C de Caballeros
Plaza de la Virgen

C de Almudín

Plaza de Nápoles y Sicilia

C de Quart
Plaza del Tossal
C Valencians
C Cadirers

Plaza del Arzobispo

Catedral ✚

C de Aparisi y Guijarro

❌ 4

CENTRO HISTÓRICO NORTH

C de la Lonja

Plaza de la Reina

C de Avellanas
C Milagro

C Murillo
C Cardà
C Landerer

Plaza del Mercado

Plaza del Dr Collado

Iglesia de Santa Catalina ✚

C del Mar

C de Valeriola
Plaza Don Juan de Villarrasa

1 ⊙

C Mantas

C de la Paz

C Carniceros
C Balmes

C Trench

Plaza Redonda

3

C del Marqués de dos Aguas

C de las Comedias

⊙ **Mercado Central**

C Pie de la Cruz

C de Moratín

C del Poeta Querol

Plaza del Patriarca

C Guillem Sorolla
C Editor Manuel Aguilar

CENTRO HISTÓRICO SOUTH

C Linterna

C de Salvá

C del Hospital
C de Garrigues
C d'En Sanz

C En Llop

Barcelonina

C de Barcas ℹ

C Juan de Austria

C de Padilla

Av del Marqués de Sotelo
Av María Cristina

Town Hall

C Correos ✉

C de Perez Bayer

C de Guillem de Castro
C de Quevedo

Plaza San Agustín

C San Pablo

Plaza del Ayuntamiento

C de Pascual y Genís
C Roger de Lauria

C Convento Santa Clara

Gran Vía Ramón y Cajal

C de Jesús
C de San Vicente Mártir
C de Troya
C Pelayo
C Bailén

C de Xàtiva
Xàtiva Ⓜ

Turismo Valencia (VLC) Tourist Office ℹ

Plaza de Toros

C de Colón
C de Russafa
C de Pizarro
C de Cirilo Amorós

Ⓜ Plaza de España

Estación del Norte 🚉

Valencia

⊚ Top Sights
Catedral...C3
Instituto Valenciano de Arte
    Moderno (IVAM) A1
Mercado Central....................................B4
Museo de Bellas Artes D1

⊚ Sights
1 La Lonja...B4

⊚ Sleeping
2 Ad Hoc...D2
3 Petit Palace Bristol C4

⊗ Eating
4 Bar Pilar..B3

 # Eating

At weekends, locals in their hundreds
head for Las Arenas, just north of the port,
where a long line of restaurants overlooking the beach all serve up authentic paella
in a three-course meal costing around €15.

LA PEPICA   Seafood €€
(☎96 371 03 66; Paseo Neptuno 6; meals around
€25; ☺lunch & dinner Mon-Sat, lunch Sun)
More expensive than its competitors, La
Pepica is renowned for its rice dishes and
seafood. Here, Ernest Hemingway, among
many other luminaries, once strutted.

TRIDENTE   Fusion €€€
(☎96 371 03 66; Paseo Neptuno; menú €45-65,
mains €22-30; ☺Tue-Sat & lunch Sun) Begin
with an aperitif on the broad beachfront
terrace, then move inside, where there's
an ample à la carte selection but you
won't find details of the day's *menús* in
front of you – they're delivered orally by
the maître d', who speaks good English.

BAR PILAR   Tapa €
(C del Moro Zeit 13; ☺noon-midnight) Cramped,
earthy Bar Pilar is great for hearty tapas
and *clóchinas,* small, juicy local mussels,
available between May and August. For
the rest of the year, *mejillones* are served,
altogether fatter if less tasty. Ask for an
entero, a platterful in a spicy broth that
you scoop up with a spare shell.

 ## ⓘ Information

Regional tourist office (www.comunitat
valenciana.com; Calle Paz 48; ☺9am-8pm Mon-
Sat, 10am-2pm Sun)

Turismo Valencia (VLC) (www.turisvalencia.es;
Plaza de la Reina 19; ☺9am-7pm Mon-Sat, 10am-
2pm Sun)

ⓘ Getting There & Away

AIR Valencia's **Aeropuerto de Manises** (☎96
159 85 00) is 10km west of the city centre. It's
served by metro lines 3 and 5.

TRAIN From Valencia's Estación del Norte, major
destinations include Alicante (€29, 1¾ hours,
eight daily) and Barcelona (€39 to €43, three to
3½ hours, at least 12 daily). The AVE, the high-
speed train, now links Madrid and Valencia, with
up to 15 high-speed services daily and a journey
time of around 1¾ hours.

ⓘ Getting Around

Metro line 5 connects the airport, downtown and
port. The high-speed tram leaves from the FGV
tram station, 500m north of the cathedral, at the
Pont de Fusta. This is a pleasant way to get to the
beach, the paella restaurants of Las Arenas and
the port.

ANDALUCÍA

Images of Andalucía are so potent,
so quintessentially Spanish that it's
sometimes difficult not to feel a sense of
déjà vu when you come here. It's almost
as if you've already been there in your
dreams: a solemn Easter parade, an ebul-
lient spring festival, exotic nights in the
Alhambra.

Seville
POP 703,000

A sexy, gutsy and gorgeous city, Seville
is home to two of Spain's most colourful
festivals, fascinating and distinctive *barrios* and a local population that lives life
to the fullest. A fiery place (as you'll soon
see in its packed and noisy tapas bars),
it is also hot climatewise – avoid July and
August!

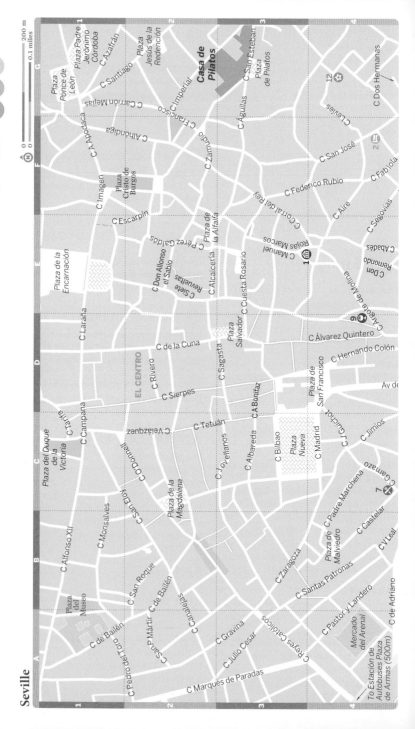

Seville

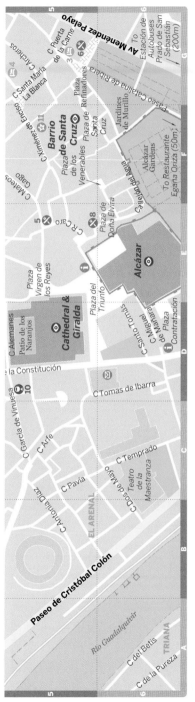

Seville

◎ Top Sights

◎ Sights

🛏 Sleeping

✗ Eating

◎ Drinking

◎ Entertainment

◎ Sights & Activities

CATHEDRAL & GIRALDA Church

(adult/concession/under 16yr €8/2/free;
🕑11am-5.30pm Mon-Sat, 2.30-6.30pm Sun Sep-
Jun, 9.30am-4.30pm Mon-Sat, 2.30-6.30pm Sun
Jul & Aug) After Seville fell to the Christians
in 1248, its main mosque was used as a
church until 1401, when it was knocked
down to make way for what would become one of the world's largest cathedrals
and an icon of Gothic architecture. The
building wasn't completed until 1507. Over
90m high, the perfectly proportioned and
exquisitely decorated **La Giralda** was the
minaret of the mosque that stood on the
site before the cathedral. The views from
the summit are exceptional.

ALCÁZAR Castle

(adult/child & concession €7.50/free; 🕑9.30am-
7pm Apr-Sep, to 6pm Oct-Mar) Seville's Alcázar, a royal residence for many centuries,
was founded in 913 as a Muslim fortress.
The Alcázar has been expanded and

Seville Cathedral

What To Look For

'We're going to construct a church so large future generations will think we were mad,' declared the inspired architects of Seville in 1402 at the beginning of one of the most grandiose building projects in medieval history. Just over a century later their madness was triumphantly confirmed.

To avoid getting lost, orient yourself by the main highlights. Directly inside the southern (main) entrance is the grand **mausoleum of Christopher Columbus** ❶. Turn right here and head into the south-eastern corner to uncover some major art treasures: a Goya in the Sacristía de los Cálices, a Zurbarán in the **Sacristía Mayor** ❷, and Murillo's shining Immaculada in the Sala Capitular. Skirt the cathedral's eastern wall taking a look inside the **Capilla Real** ❸ with its important royal tombs. By now it's impossible to avoid the lure of **Capilla Mayor** ❹ with its fantastical altarpiece. Hidden over in the northwest corner is the **Capilla de San Antonio** ❺ with a legendary Murillo. That huge doorway almost in front of you is rarely opened **Puerta de la Asunción** ❻. Make for the **Giralda** ❼ next, stealing admiring looks at the high, vaulted ceiling on the way. After looking down on the cathedral's immense footprint, descend and depart via the **Patio de los Naranjos** ❽.

TOP TIPS

Queue-dodge Reserve tickets online at www.servicaixa.com for an extra €1 up to six weeks in advance.

Pace yourself Don't visit the Alcazar and Cathedral on the same day. There is far too much to take in.

Viewpoints Take time to admire the cathedral from the outside. It's particularly stunning at night from the Plaza Virgen de los Reyes, and from across the river in Triana.

Capilla Mayor
Behold! The cathedral's main focal point contains its greatest treasure, a magnificent gold-plated altarpiece depicting various scenes in the life of Christ. It constitutes the life's work of one man, Flemish artist Pieter Dancart.

Patio de los Naranjos
Inhale the perfume of 60 Sevillan orange trees in a cool patio bordered by fortress-like walls – a surviving remnant of the original 12th-century mosque. Exit is gained via the horseshoe-shaped Puerta del Perdón.

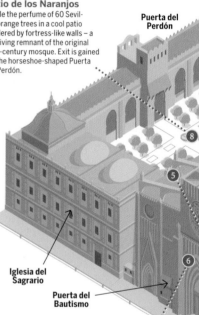

Puerta del Perdón

Iglesia del Sagrario

Puerta del Bautismo

Puerta de la Asunción
Located on the western side of the cathedral and also known as the Puerta Mayor, these huge, rarely opened doors are pushed back during Semana Santa to allow solemn processions of Catholic *hermanadades* (brotherhoods) to pass through.

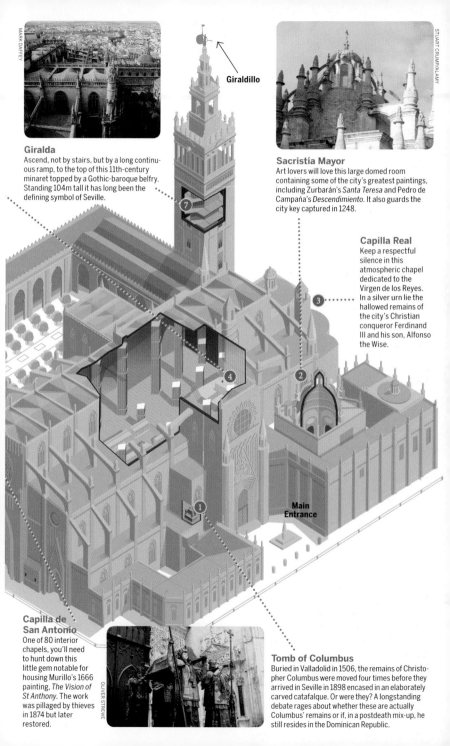

Giraldillo

Giralda
Ascend, not by stairs, but by a long continuous ramp, to the top of this 11th-century minaret topped by a Gothic-baroque belfry. Standing 104m tall it has long been the defining symbol of Seville.

Sacristía Mayor
Art lovers will love this large domed room containing some of the city's greatest paintings, including Zurbarán's *Santa Teresa* and Pedro de Campaña's *Descendimiento*. It also guards the city key captured in 1248.

Capilla Real
Keep a respectful silence in this atmospheric chapel dedicated to the Virgen de los Reyes. In a silver urn lie the hallowed remains of the city's Christian conqueror Ferdinand III and his son, Alfonso the Wise.

Main Entrance

Capilla de San Antonio
One of 80 interior chapels, you'll need to hunt down this little gem notable for housing Murillo's 1666 painting, *The Vision of St Anthony*. The work was pillaged by thieves in 1874 but later restored.

Tomb of Columbus
Buried in Valladolid in 1506, the remains of Christopher Columbus were moved four times before they arrived in Seville in 1898 encased in an elaborately carved catafalque. Or were they? A longstanding debate rages about whether these are actually Columbus' remains or if, in a postdeath mix-up, he still resides in the Dominican Republic.

MARK DAFFEY

STUART CRUMP/ALAMY

OLIVER STREWE

rebuilt many times in its 11 centuries of existence. The Catholic Monarchs, Fernando and Isabel, set up court here in the 1480s as they prepared for the conquest of Granada. Later rulers created the Alcázar's lovely gardens.

BARRIO DE SANTA CRUZ Jewish Quarter

Seville's medieval *judería*, east of the cathedral and Alcázar, is today a tangle of atmospheric, winding streets and lovely plant-decked plazas perfumed with orange blossom. Among its most characteristic plazas is **Plaza de Santa Cruz**, which gives the *barrio* its name. **Plaza de Doña Elvira** is another romantic perch, especially in the evening.

MUSEO DEL BAILE FLAMENCO Museum

(www.museoflamenco.com; Calle Manuel Rojas Marcos 3; adult/child €10/6; ⏱9.30am-7pm) The brainchild of Sevillana flamenco dancer Cristina Hoyos, Seville's newest museum is spread over three floors of an 18th-century palace, although at €10 a pop it's more than a little overpriced. Exhibits include sketches, paintings, photos of erstwhile (and contemporary) flamenco greats, plus a collection of dresses and shawls.

PARQUE DE MARÍA LUISA & PLAZA DE ESPAÑA Park

(⏱8am-10pm) A large area south of the tobacco factory was transformed for Seville's 1929 international fair, the Exposición Iberoamericana, when architects adorned it with fantastical buildings, many of them harking back to Seville's past glory or imitating the native styles of Spain's former colonies. In its midst is the large Parque de María Luisa, a living expression of Seville's Moorish and Christian past.

 Festivals & Events

The first of Seville's two great festivals is **Semana Santa**, the week leading up to Easter Sunday. Throughout the week, thousands of members of religious brotherhoods parade in penitents' garb with tall, pointed *capirotes* (hoods) accompanying sacred images through the city, while huge crowds look on.

The **Feria de Abril**, a week in late April, is a welcome release after this solemnity: the festivities involve six days of music, dancing, horse riding and traditional dress, plus daily bullfights.

Men in ceremonidal dress during Semana Santa

The city also stages Spain's largest flamenco festival, the month-long **Bienal de Flamenco**. It's held in September in even-numbered years.

🛏 Sleeping

Prices over the Semana Santa and Feria de Abril festival periods can be up to double the high-season prices that are cited here. The city's accommodation is often full at weekends and is always booked solid during festivals, so be sure to make reservations well ahead.

HOTEL AMADEUS
Hotel €€

(📞 954 50 14 43; www.hotelamadeussevilla.com; Calle Farnesio 6; s/d €85/95; 🅿 ❄ 🛜) This musician family converted their 18th-century mansion into a stylish hotel with 14 elegant rooms of which Mozart would have been proud. A couple of the newer rooms have been soundproofed for piano or violin practice.

LAS CASAS DE LA JUDERÍA
Hotel €€€

(📞 954 41 51 50; www.casasypalacios.com; Callejón Dos Hermanas 7; s/d from €140/175; 🅿 ❄ 🛜) At last – a five-star hotel that might actually be worth the extra cash. Countless patios and corridors link this veritable palace that was once 18 different houses situated on the cusp of the Santa Cruz quarter. The decor is exquisite, from the trickling fountains to the antique furniture and paintings.

HOTEL PUERTA DE SEVILLA
Hotel €€

(📞 954 98 72 70; www.hotelpuertadesevilla.com; Calle Puerta de la Carne 2; s/d €66/86; 🅿 ❄ @ 🛜) A small shiny hotel in a great location, the Hotel Puerta de Sevilla has tin-glazed painted *azulejos* tiles, flower-pattern textiles and wrought-iron beds, all for the cost of just one star. An extra bonus is the first-class and friendly service.

If You Like...
Spanish Churches

Spain is awash with fabulous churches and cathedrals. After you've visited the stunning examples in **Seville** (p351) and **Salamanca** (p315), don't miss:

1 LÉON
(www.catedraldeleon.org; ⏱ 8.30am-1.30pm & 4-8pm Mon-Sat, 8.30am-2.30pm & 5-8pm Sun) With its soaring towers, flying buttresses and truly breathtaking interior, León's 13th-century cathedral is the city's spiritual heart. It's particularly renowned for its stunning stained-glass windows – all 128 of them.

2 SANTIAGO DE COMPOSTELA
(www.catedraldesantiago.es; Praza do Obradoiro; ⏱ 7am-9pm) For centuries, this monumental cathedral has marked the end of one of Europe's great pilgrimage routes, the Camino de Santiago. Don't miss the rooftop tour (per person €10; ⏱ 10am-2pm & 4-8pm).

3 BURGOS
(Plaza del Rey Fernando; adult/child €5/2.50; ⏱ 9.30am-6.30pm) The incredible Gothic cathedral in Burgos largely dates from the 13th century. One of Spain's great heros, El Cid, lies buried beneath the star-vaulted central dome.

4 GIRONA
(www.catedraldegirona.org; cathedral museum adult/under 7yr €5/free, admission free Sun; ⏱ 10am-8pm Apr-Oct, 10am-7pm Nov-Mar, 10am-2pm Sun & holidays) Girona's cathedral boasts the widest nave of any Gothic cathedral in Europe, measuring an impressive 23m. The Romanesque cloister and baroque facade are also noteworthy.

5 BASÍLICA DE NUESTRA SEÑORA DEL PILAR
(Plaza del Pilar s/n; admission free; ⏱ 7am-8.30pm) Zaragoza's multidomed basilica supposedly marks the site where Santiago (St James the Apostle) was visited by the Virgin Mary on 2 January AD 40. A **lift** (admission €2; ⏱ 10am-1.30pm & 4-6.30pm Tue-Sun) whisks you most of the way up the north tower (Torre Pilar) for fine views.

Eating

CATALINA Tapa €
(Paseo Catalina de Ribera 4; raciones €10) If your view of tapas is glorified bar snacks; then your ideas could be blown out of the water here with a creative mix of just about every ingredient known to Iberian cooking.

BODEGA SANTA CRUZ Tapa €
(Calle Mateos Gago; tapas €1.50-2) Forever crowded, and with a mountain of paper piled on the floor, Bodega Santa Cruz is usually a standing-room-only place. Enjoy your tapas and drinks alfresco as you dodge the marching army of tourists squeezing through Santa Cruz's narrow streets.

RESTAURANT LA CUEVA
Traditional Spanish €€
(☎ 954 21 31 43; Calle Rodrigo Caro 18 & Plaza de Doña Elvira 1; menú €16, mains €11-24) Slightly frosty service is made up for by excellent paella and a storming fish *zarzuela* (cas-serole; €30 for two). The interior is roomy while alfresco tables overlook dreamy Plaza de Doña Elvira.

MESÓN CINCO JOTAS Tapa €
(Calle Castelar 1; tapas/media raciones €3.80/9.45) Try some of the best *jamón* in town here, then move on to the *solomillo ibérico* (Iberian pork sirloin) in sweet Pedro Ximénez wine for the peak of porcine flavour.

Drinking

Bars in Seville usually open 6pm to 2am weekdays, 8pm till 3am at weekends. Drinking and partying really get going around midnight on Friday and Saturday (daily when it's hot). In summer, dozens of open-air late-night bars *(terrazas de verano)* spring up along both banks of the river.

ANTIGÜEDADES Bar
(Calle Argote de Molina 40) Antigüedades blends mellow beats with kooky, offbeat decor. The tiled window seats – with a view of the bustling street outside – are the best places to sit and nurse your drink.

CASA MORALES Bar
(Garcia de Vinuesa 11) Not much has changed in this defiantly old-world bar, founded way back in 1850. There are charming anachronisms here wherever you look.

CAFÉ CENTRAL Bar
(Alameda de Hércules 64) One of the oldest and most popular on the street, Café Central has yellow bar lights and wooden flea-market chairs. Be warned – the Central attracts a massive crowd at weekends.

Bar in Casa Morales

Patio of Restaurant La Cueva

WITOLD SKRYPCZAK/LONELY PLANET IMAGES ©

Entertainment

Seville is arguably Spain's flamenco capital and you're most likely to catch a spontaneous atmosphere (of unpredictable quality) in one of the bars staging regular nights of flamenco with no admission fee.

LA CARBONERÍA Flamenco Bar
(Calle Levíes 18; admission free; ⊙8pm-4am)
During the day there is no indication that this happening place is anything but a large garage. But come after 8pm and this converted coal yard in the Barrio de Santa Cruz reveals two large bars, and nightly live flamenco (11pm and midnight) for no extra charge.

CASA DE LA MEMORIA DE AL-ANDALUS
Flamenco Tablao
(☎954 56 06 70; Calle Ximénez de Enciso 28; tickets €15; ⊙9pm) This is probably the most intimate and authentic nightly *tablao* (flamenco show), offering a wide variety of flamenco styles in a room of shifting shadows. Space is limited to 100, so reserve tickets in advance.

CASA ANSELMA Flamenco Bar
(Pagés de Corro 49, Triana; ⊙midnight to late Mon-Sat) Casa Anslema (there's no sign, just a doorway embellished with *azulejos* tiles) is the antithesis of a tourist flamenco *tablao*, with cheek-to-jowl crowds, thick cigarette smoke, zero amplification and spontaneous outbreaks of incredible, dexterous dancing. Pure magic.

❶ Information

Regional tourist office Avenida de la Constitución (**Avenida de la Constitución 21;** ⊙9am-7pm Mon-Fri, 10am-2pm & 3-7pm Sat, 10am-2pm Sun, closed holidays); Estación de Santa Justa (⊙9am-8pm Mon-Fri, 10am-2pm Sat & Sun, closed holidays)

Turismo Sevilla (www.turismosevilla.org; Plaza del Triunfo 1; ⊙10.30am-7pm Mon-Fri)

❶ Getting There & Away

Air

A range of domestic and international flights land in Seville's **Aeropuerto San Pablo**, 7km from the city centre.

Train

The modern, efficient Estación de Santa Justa (Avenida Kansas City) is 1.5km northeast of the city centre.

Twenty or more superfast AVE trains, which can reach speeds of 280km/h, whiz daily to/from Madrid (€80.70, 2½ hours) and to Barcelona (€130, 6½ hours, one daily). Other services include trains to Barcelona (€61 to €88, 10½ to 13 hours, three daily), Cádiz (€12.75, 1¾ hours, 13 daily), Córdoba (€16 to €32, 40 minutes to 1½ hours, 21 or more daily), Granada (€24, three hours, four daily), Málaga (€19.10 to €36.40, 2½ hours, five daily) and Mérida (€14, five hours, one daily).

Getting Around

Los Amarillos (www.losamarillos.es) runs buses between the airport and the Avenida del Cid near the San Sebastión bus station (€2.20 to €2.50, at 15 and 45 minutes past the hour). A taxi costs about €20.

Buses run by Seville's urban transport authority Tussam (www.tussam.es), C1, C2, C3 and C4, do useful circular routes linking the main transport terminals and the city centre.

Tussam's Tranvia (www.tussam.es, in Spanish), the city's sleek tram service, was launched in 2007. Individual rides cost €1.20,

or you can buy a *Bono* (travel pass offering five rides for €5) from many newspaper stands and tobacconists.

Córdoba

POP 302,000

Córdoba was once one of the most enlightened Islamic cities on earth, and enough remains to place it in the contemporary top three Andalucian draws. The centrepiece is the gigantic and exquisitely rendered Mezquita. Surrounding it is an intricate web of winding streets, geranium-sprouting flower boxes and cool intimate patios that are at their most beguiling in late spring.

Sights & Activities

MEZQUITA Mosque
(adult/child €8/4, free 8.30-10am Mon-Sat; ⏱10am-7pm Mon-Sat Apr-Oct, 9-10.45am & 1.30-6.30pm Sun) Founded in 785, Córdoba's gigantic mosque is a wonderful architectural hybrid with delicate horseshoe arches making this unlike anywhere else in Spain. The main entrance is the **Puerta del Perdón**, a 14th-century Mudéjar gateway,

Pool and gardens of Alcázar de los Reyes Cristianos

with the ticket office immediately inside. Inside the gateway is the aptly named **Patio de los Naranjos** (Courtyard of the Orange Trees). Once inside, you can see straight ahead to the **mihrab**, the prayer niche in the mosque's *qibla* (the wall indicating the direction of Mecca) that was the focus of prayer. The first 12 transverse aisles inside the entrance, a forest of pillars and arches, comprise the original **8th-century mosque**.

JUDERÍA   Neighbourhood

The medieval *judería*, extending northwest from the Mezquita almost to Avenida del Gran Capitán, is today a maze of narrow streets and white-washed buildings with flowery window boxes. The beautiful little 14th-century **Sinagoga** (Calle de los Judíos 20; adult/ EU citizen €0.30/free; ⊙9.30am-2pm & 3.30-5.30pm Tue-Sat, 9.30am-1.30pm Sun & holidays) is one of only three surviving medieval synagogues in Spain and the only one in Andalucía.

ALCÁZAR DE LOS REYES CRISTIANOS   Castle

(Castle of the Christian Monarchs; Campo Santo de Los Mártires s/n; adult/concession €4/2, free Fri; ⊙10am-2pm & 5.30-7.30pm Tue-Sat, 9.30am-2.30pm Sun & holidays) Just southwest of the Mezquita, the Alcázar began as a palace and fort for Alfonso X in the 13th century. From 1490 to 1821 the Inquisition operated from here. Today its gardens are among the most beautiful in Andalucía.

 Sleeping

HOTEL HACIENDA POSADA DE VALLINA   Hotel **€€**

(✆957 49 87 50; ww.hhposadadevallina cordoba.com; Calle del Corregidor Luís de la Cerda 83; s/d €50/70; P ✳ @ ⊛) In an enviable nook on the quiet side of the Mezquita (the building actually predates it), this cleverly renovated hotel uses portraits and period furniture to enhance a plush and modern interior. Columbus allegedly once stayed here.

If You Like…
Spanish Architecture

Judging by the amazing hanging houses of **Cuenca** (p318), the Spanish certainly have a taste for eye-catching architecture. Here are a few more landmark structures to look out for:

1 SEGOVIA
(www.segoviaturismo.es; Plaza Mayor 10) This quintessentially Spanish town is idyllically set amid the rolling hills of Castilla. Its most prominent landmark is the **Alcázar**, a fairy-tale castle said to have inspired Walt Disney. Elsewhere around town are some of Spain's finest Roman ruins and a monumental 894m-long Roman aqueduct. Trains run daily from Madrid to Segovia (one way €6.50, two hours, around nine daily).

2 ÁVILA
(www.avilaturismo.com; Avenida de Madrid 39) Ávila's old city is one of the best-preserved medieval bastions in all of Spain. It's famous for its 12th-century **murallas**, a dramatic complex of city walls comprising eight monumental gates, 88 watchtowers and more than 2500 turrets. Trains run to Madrid (from €8.25, one to two hours, up to 30 daily) and Salamanca (€9.65, one to 1½ hours, nine daily).

3 RONDA
(www.turismoderonda.es; Paseo de Blas Infante) Perched on an inland plateau above El Tajo gorge, Ronda is the most dramatically sited of Andalucía's **pueblos blancos** (white villages). Look out for the amazing 18th-century Puente Nuevo (New Bridge), an incredible engineering feat crossing the gorge to the Muslim Old Town (La Ciudad). Frequent trains travel to Granada (€13.50, two hours, three daily) and Córdoba (€31.50, two hours, two daily).

HOTEL MEZQUITA   Hotel **€€**

(✆957 47 55 85; hotelmezquita.com; Plaza Santa Catalina 1; s/d €42/74; ✳) One of the best-value places in town, Hotel Mezquita is right opposite the Mezquita itself. This 16th-century mansion has sparkling bath-rooms and elegant rooms, some with views of the great mosque across the street.

Mezquita

A Timeline

AD 600 Foundation of the Christian Visigothic church of St Vincent on the site of the present Mezquita.

AD 785 Salvaging Visigoth and Roman ruins, Emir Abd ar-Rahman I converts the Mezquita into a mosque.

AD 822-5 Mosque enlarged in reign of Abd-ar-Rahman II.

AD 912-961 A new minaret is ordered by Abd ar-Rahman III.

AD 961-6 Mosque enlarged by Al-Hakam II who also enriches the **mihrab** ❶.

AD 987 Mosque enlarged for the last time by Al-Mansur Ibn Abi Aamir. With the addition of the Patio de los **Naranjos** ❷, the building reaches its current dimensions.

1236 Mosque reconverted into a Christian church after Córdoba is recaptured by Ferdinand III of Castile.

1271 Instead of destroying the mosque, the overawed Christians elect to modify it. Alfonso X orders the construction of the **Capilla de Villaviciosa** ❸ and **Capilla Real** ❹.

1300s Original minaret is replaced by the baroque **Torre del Alminar** ❺.

1520s A Renaissance-style cathedral nave ❻ is added by Charles V. 'I have destroyed something unique to the world,' he laments on seeing the finished work.

2004 Spanish Muslims petition to be able to worship in the Mezquita again. The Vatican doesn't consent.

TOP TIPS

Among the oranges The Patio de los Naranjos can be enjoyed free of charge at any time.

Early birds Entry to the rest of the Mezquita is offered free every morning except Sunday between 8.30am and 10am.

Quiet time Group visits are prohibited before 10am, meaning the building is quieter and more atmospheric in the early morning.

Capilla de Villaviciosa

Sift through the building's numerous chapels till you find this gem, an early Christian modification added in 1277 which fused existing Moorish features with Gothic arches and pillars. It served as the Capilla Mayor until the 1520s.

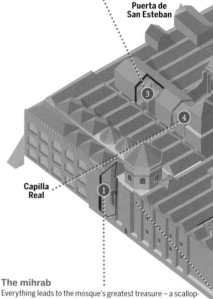

Puerta de San Esteban

Capilla Real

The mihrab

Everything leads to the mosque's greatest treasure – a scallop-shell-shaped prayer niche facing Mecca that was added in the 10th century. Cast your eyes over the gold mosaic cubes crafted by imported Byzantium sculptors.

The cathedral choir
Few ignore the impressive *coro* (choir): a late-Christian addition dating from the 1750s. Once you've admired the skilfully carved mahogany choir stalls depicting scenes from the Bible, look up at the impressive baroque ceiling.

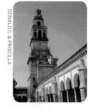

Torre del Alminar
This is the Mezquita's cheapest sight because you don't have to pay to see it. Rising 93m and viewable from much of the city, the baroque-style bell tower was built over the mosque's original minaret.

The Mezquita arches
No, you're not hallucinating. The Mezquita's most defining characteristic is its unique terracotta-and-white striped arches that support 856 pillars salvaged from Roman and Visigoth ruins. Glimpsed through the dull light they're at once spooky and striking.

Puerta del Perdón

Patio de los Naranjos
Abandon architectural preconceptions all ye who enter here. The ablutions area of the former mosque is a shady courtyard embellished with orange trees that acts as the Mezquita's main entry point.

Capilla Mayor
A Christian monument inside an Islamic mosque sounds beautifully ironic, yet here it is: a Gothic church commissioned by Charles V in the 16th century and planted in the middle of the world's third largest mosque.

The maksura
Guiding you towards the mihrab, the maksura is a former royal enclosure where the caliphs and their retinues prayed. Its lavish, elaborate arches were designed to draw the eye of worshippers towards the mihrab and Mecca.

 Eating & Drinking

Most bars in the medieval centre close around midnight.

TABERNA SAN MIGUEL
EL PISTO
Tapa €€

(Plaza San Miguel 1; tapas €3, media raciones €5-10; ⏱closed Sun & Aug) Fine wine, great atmosphere, professional waiters, zero pretension and a clamorous yet handsome decor make El Pisto (the barrel) a Córdoban and Andalucian tapa classic.

TABERNA SALINAS
Tapa €

(Calle Tundidores 3; tapas/raciones €2.50/8; ⏱closed Sun & Aug) Dating back to 1879, this large patio restaurant fills up fast. The tavern side is quieter in the early evening, and the friendly bar staff will fill your glass with local Montilla whenever you look thirsty.

CASA PEPE DE LA JUDERÍA
Andalucian €€€

(☎957 20 07 44; Calle Romero 1; tapas/media raciones €2.50-9.50, mains €11-18, menú €27)

Casa Pepe de la Judería has a great roof terrace with views of the Mezquita and a labyrinth of busy dining rooms. Down a complimentary glass of Montilla before launching into the house specials, including Cordoban oxtails or venison fillets.

ℹ Information

Municipal tourist office (Plaza de Judá Levi; ⏱8.30am-2.30pm Mon-Fri)

Regional tourist office (Calle de Torrijos 10; ⏱9am-7.30pm Mon-Fri, 9.30am-3pm Sat, Sun & holidays)

ℹ Getting There & Away

TRAIN From Córdoba's **train station** (Avenida de América), destinations include Seville (€10.60 to €32.10, 40 to 90 minutes, 23 or more daily), Madrid (€52 to €66.30, 1¾ to 6¼ hours, 23 or more daily), Málaga (€21 to €39.60, one to 2½ hours, nine daily) and Barcelona (€59.40 to €133, 10½ hours, four daily).

Left: Interior of Mezquita (p358); **Below:** Food and wine at Taberna Salinas

Granada

POP 300,000 / ELEV 685M

Granada's eight centuries as a Muslim capital are symbolised in its keynote emblem, the remarkable Alhambra, one of the most graceful architectural achievements in the Muslim world. Islam was never completely expunged here, and today it seems more present than ever in the shops, restaurants, tearooms and mosque of a growing North African community in and around the maze of the Albayzín.

 Sights & Activities

ALHAMBRA   Palace
(☎ 902 441221; www.alhambra-tickets.es, www.servicaixa.com; adult/EU senior/EU student/under 8yr €12/9/9/free, Generalife only €6; ☉ 8.30am-8pm 16 Mar-31 Oct, to 6pm 1 Nov-14 Mar) The mighty Alhambra is breathtaking. Much has been written about its fortress, palace, patios and gardens, but nothing can prepare you for the real thing.

The **Alcazaba**, the Alhambra's fortress, dates from the 11th to the 13th centuries. There are spectacular views from the tops of its towers. The **Palacio Nazaríes** (Nasrid Palace), built for Granada's Muslim rulers in their 13th- to 15th-century heyday, is the centrepiece of the Alhambra. The beauty of its patios and intricacy of its stuccoes and woodwork, epitomised by the **Patio de los Leones** (Patio of the Lions) and **Sala de las Dos Hermanas** (Hall of the Two Sisters), are stunning. The **Generalife** (Palace Gardens) is a great spot to relax and contemplate the complex from a little distance.

The Palacio Nazaríes is also open for **night visits** (☉ 10pm-11.30pm Tue-Sat Mar-Oct, 8pm-9.30pm Fri & Sat Nov-Feb).

ALBAYZÍN   Historic Area
Exploring the narrow, hilly streets of the Albayzín, the old Moorish quarter across the river from the Alhambra, is the perfect complement to the Alhambra. The cob-

363

Alhambra

A timeline

900 The first reference to *al-qala'at al-hamra* (red castle) atop Granada's Sabika Hill.

1237 Founder of the Nasrid dynasty, Muhammad I, moves his court to Granada. Threatened by belligerent Christian armies he builds a new defensive fort, the **Alcazaba ①**.

1302-09 Designed as a summer palace-cum-country estate for Granada's foppish rulers, the bucolic **Generalife ②** is begun by Muhammad III.

1333-54 Yusuf I initiates the construction of the **Palacio Nazaríes ③**, still considered the highpoint of Islamic culture in Europe.

1350-60 Up goes the **Palacio de Comares ④** taking Nasrid lavishness to a whole new level.

1362-91 The second coming of Muhammad V ushers in even greater architectural brilliance exemplified by the construction of the **Patio de los Leones ⑤**.

1527 The Christians add the **Palacio de Carlos V ⑥**. Inspired Renaissance palace or incongruous crime against the Moorish art? You decide.

1829 The languishing, half-forgotten Alhambra is 'rediscovered' by American writer Washington Irving during a protracted sleep-over.

1954 The Generalife gardens are extended southwards to accommodate an outdoor theatre.

Sala de la Barca
Throw your head back in the anteroom to the Comares Palace where the gilded ceiling is shaped like an upturned boat. Destroyed by fire in the 1890s, it has been painstakingly restored.

MICHAEL TAYLOR

Mexuar

Patio de Machuca

Palacio de Carlos V
It's easy to miss the stylistic merits of this Renaissance palace added in 1527. Check out the ground floor Museo de la Alhambra with artefacts directly related to the palace's history.

Palacio Nazaríes

Detail

Puerta de Justica

Alcazaba
Find time to explore the towers of the original citadel, the most important of which – the Torre de la Vela – takes you, via a winding staircase, to the Alhambra's best viewpoint.

DAVID TOMLINSON

Patio de Arrayanes

If only you could linger longer beside the rows of myrtle bushes *(arrayanes)* that border this calming rectangular pool. Shaded porticos with seven harmonious arches invite further contemplation.

Palacio de Comares

The neck-ache continues in the largest room in the Comares Palace renowned for its rich geometric ceiling. A negotiating room for the emirs, the Salón de los Embajadores is a masterpiece of Moorish design.

Sala de Dos Hermanas

Focus on the *dos hermanas:* two marble slabs either side of the fountain, before enjoying the intricate cupola embellished with 5000 tiny moulded stalactites. Poetic calligraphy decorates the walls.

Torre de Comares

Baños Reales

Washington Irving Apartments

Patio de Arrayanes

❹

❺

Jardín de Lindaraja

Palacio del Partal

Sala de los Abencerrajes

Jardines del Partal

Patio de los Leones

Count the 12 lions sculpted from marble holding up a gurgling fountain. Then pan back and take in the delicate columns and arches built to signify an Islamic vision of paradise.

Generalife

A coda to most people's visits, the 'architect's garden' is no afterthought. While Nasrid in origin, the horticulture is relatively new: the pools and arcades were added in the early 20th century.

Alhambra Tickets

Up to 6600 tickets to the Alhambra are available for each day. About a third of these are sold at the ticket office on the day, but they sell out early and you need to start queuing by 7am to be reasonably sure of getting one. It's highly advisable to book in advance (you pay €1 extra per ticket).

○ **Alhambra Advance Booking**
(☎national calls 902 88 80 01, international calls 0034 934 92 37 50; www.alhambra-tickets.es; ☻8am-9pm)

○ **Servicaixa** (www.servicaixa.com) Online booking in Spanish and English. You can also buy tickets in advance from Servicaixa cash machines (8am to 7pm March to October, 8am to 5pm November to February), but only in the Alhambra grounds.

For internet or phone bookings you need a Visa card, MasterCard or Eurocard. You receive a reference number, which you must show, along with your passport, national identity card or credit card, at the Alhambra ticket office when you pick up the ticket on the day of your visit.

blestone streets are lined with gorgeous *cármenes* (large mansions with walled gardens, from the Arabic *karm* for garden).

Head uphill to reach the **Mirador de San Nicolás** – a viewpoint with breathtaking vistas and a relaxed scene.

Sleeping

CASA MORISCA HOTEL
Historic Hotel €€€
(☎958 22 11 00; www.hotelcasamorisca.com; Cuesta de la Victoria 9; d interior/exterior €118/148; ❄@🛜) The Morisca could

easily compete with the finest of Marrakech's *riads* with its 14 rooms occupying a gorgeous late 15th-century Albayzín mansion. Everything is arranged around an atmospheric patio with an ornamental pool and overlooking wooden galleries. The pinnacle: an exquisite Mirador suite, affording views of the great palace itself.

CARMEN DE LA ALCUBILLA
Historic Hotel €€
(☎958 21 55 51; www.alcubilladelcaracol.com; Aire Alta 12; s/d €100/120; ❄@🛜) Tranquil Granadian beauty, this time perched on the Realejo hill in a restored Carmen (house with an internal garden) with a terraced garden overflowing with jasmine and lemon trees. The house is (almost refreshingly) light on antiques, but the views of the Sierra Nevada are stunning and the service flawless.

PARADOR DE GRANADA
Historic Hotel €€
(☎958 22 14 40; www.parador.es; Calle Real de la Alhambra; r €315; P❄@🛜) The most expensive *parador* in Spain can't be beaten for its location within the walls of the Alhambra and its historical connections (it was a former convent). Live like a Nasrid king, for one night at least. Book ahead.

HOTEL CASA DEL CAPITEL NAZARÍ
Historic Hotel €€
(☎958 21 52 60; www.hotelcasacapitel.com; Cuesta Aceituneros 6; s/d €88/110; ❄@🛜) More Albayzín magic in a 1503 Renaissance palace that is as much architectural history lesson as plush hotel. Rooms have Moroccan inflections and the courtyard hosts art exhibits.

Eating

Granada is one of the last bastions of that fantastic practice of free tapas with every drink, and some have an international flavour.

RESTAURANTE ARRAYANES
Moroccan €€
(☎958 22 84 01; Cuesta Marañas 4; mains €8.50-19; ☻from 8pm) Could this be the

best Moroccan food in a city that is well known for its Moorish throwbacks? Recline on the lavish patterned seating here, try the rich fruity tagine casseroles and make your decision. No alcohol.

PARADOR DE GRANADA
International €€€

(📞958 22 14 40; Calle Real de la Alhambra; mains €19-22; ⏰8am-11pm) Even a jaded, jilted, world-weary cynic would come over all romantic in this dreamy setting. The Spanish food has Moroccan and French influences, and it tastes all the better for being taken inside the Alhambra.

RECA
Tapa €€

(Plaza de la Trinidad; raciones €8; ⏰closed Tue) A tapas classic rightly famous for its *salmorejo* (thicker version of gazpacho) and its all-through-the-afternoon food service.

 Entertainment

The excellent monthly *Guía de Granada* (€1), available from kiosks, lists entertainment venues and tapas bars.

Situated above and to the northwest of the city centre, and offering panoramic views over the Alhambra, the Sacromonte is Granada's centuries-old *gitano* quarter.

The Sacromonte caves harbour touristy flamenco haunts, which you can prebook through hotels and travel agencies; some offer free transport.

Try the Friday or Saturday midnight shows at **Los Tarantos** (📞day 958 22 45 25, night 958 22 24 92; Camino del Sacromonte 9; admission €24) for a lively experience.

PEÑA DE LA PLATERÍA
Flamenco

(Placeta de Toqueros 7) Buried deep in the Albayzín warren, this is a genuine aficionados' club. Dramatic 9.30pm performances take place on Thursday or Saturday in an adjacent room and cost €12.

ℹ️ Information

Regional tourist office (www.turismode granada.org; Plaza de Mariana Pineda 10; ⏰9am-8pm Mon-Fri, 10am-2pm & 4-7pm Sat, 10am-3pm Sun May-Sep)

Municipal tourist office (www.granadatur.com; Calle Almona del Campillo, 2; ⏰9am-7pm Mon-Fri, to 6pm Sat, 10am-2pm Sun)

ℹ️ Getting There & Away

TRAIN The **train station** (Avenida de Andaluces) is 1.5km west of the centre. Trains run to/from Seville (€23.85, three hours, four daily), Almería (€15.90, 2¼ hours, four daily), Ronda (€13.50, three hours, three daily), Algeciras (€20.10, 4½ hours, three daily), Madrid (€66.80, four to five hours, one or two daily), Valencia (€50.60, 7½ to eight hours, one daily) and Barcelona (€62.10, 12 hours, one daily).

Street in Albayzín district (p363)
PHOTOGRAPHER: MARK AVELLINO/LONELY PLANET IMAGES ©

Cádiz

POP 128,600

Cádiz is widely considered the oldest continuously inhabited settlement in Europe. It's crammed onto the head of a promontory like an overcrowded ocean liner. Columbus sailed from here on his second and fourth voyages, and after his success in the Americas, Cádiz grew into Spain's richest and most cosmopolitan city during the 18th century. The best time to visit is during the February *carnaval* (carnival), which manages to rival Rio in terms of outrageous exuberance.

Sights & Activities

CATEDRAL   Church
(Plaza de la Catedral; adult/student €5/3, free 7-8pm Tue-Fri, 11am-1pm Sun; ⊙10am-6.30pm Mon-Sat, 1.30-6.30pm Sun) The yellow-domed 18th-century cathedral is the city's most striking landmark. From a separate entrance on Plaza de la Catedral, climb to the top of the **Torre de Poniente** (Western Tower; adult/child/senior €4/3/3; ⊙10am-6pm, to 8pm 15 Jun-15 Sep) for marvellous vistas of the streets and sea below.

You can also get your bearings by climbing up the baroque **Torre Tavira** (Calle Marqués del Real Tesoro 10; adult/student €4/3.30; ⊙10am-6pm, to 8pm 15 Jun-15 Sep), the highest of Cádiz' old watchtowers, which features sweeping views of the city.

MUSEO DE CÁDIZ   Museum
(Plaza de Mina; adult/EU citizen €1.50/free; ⊙2.30-8.30pm Tue, 9am-8.30pm Wed-Sat, 9.30am-2.30pm Sun) The Museo de Cádiz has a magnificent collection of archaeological remains, as well as an excellent fine-art collection.

For more history, the city's lively **central market** (Plaza de las Flores) is on the site of a former Phoenician temple.

Sleeping & Eating

HOTEL ARGANTONIO   Hotel   €€
(☏956 21 16 40; www.hotelargantonio.com; Calle Argantonio 3; s/d incl breakfast €90/107; ❄@☎) Hotel Argantonio is a very attrac-

Cádiz Catedral

HOLGER LEUE/LONELY PLANET IMAGES ©

tive small new hotel in the old city with an appealing Mudéjar accent to its decor. Staff are welcoming, and the rooms are comfortable with wi-fi access and flat-screen TVs.

HOSPEDERÍA LAS CORTES DE CÁDIZ
Hotel €€€

(956 21 26 68; www.hotellascortes.com; Calle San Francisco 9; s/d incl breakfast €107/148; P ✴ @ 🤶) The excellent Hospedería Las Cortes de Cádiz occupies a remodelled 1850s mansion. The 36 rooms, each themed around a figure, place or event associated with the Cortes de Cádiz, sport classical furnishings and modern comforts.

ARROCERÍA LA PEPA
Rice Dishes €€

(956 26 38 21; Paseo Maritimo 14; paella per person €12-17) To get a decent paella you have to leave the old town behind and head for a few kilometres southeast along Playa de la Victoria – an appetite-rousing predinner walk or a quick ride on the number 1 bus.

EL ALJIBE
Tapa €€

(www.pablogrosso.com; Calle Plocia 25; tapas €2-3.50, mains €10-15) *Gaditano* chef Pablo Grosso concocts delicious and intriguing-combinations of both the traditional and adventurous varieties. Try the pheasant breast stuffed with dates and the *solomillo ibérico* (Iberian pork sirloin) with Emmental cheese, ham and piquant peppers.

ℹ️ Information

Municipal tourist office (Paseo de Canalejas s/n; ⏰8.30am-6pm Mon-Fri, 9am-5pm Sat & Sun)

Regional tourist office (Avenida Ramón de Carranza s/n; ⏰9am-7.30pm Mon-Fri, 10am-2pm Sat, Sun & holidays)

ℹ️ Getting There & Away

TRAIN From the train station (902 24 02 02) trains run daily to Seville (€12.75, two hours), three per day to Córdoba (€23.85 to €38.20, three hours) and two to Madrid (€70, five hours). High-speed AVE services to Madrid are slated for commencement by 2012.

SURVIVAL GUIDE
Directory A–Z

Accommodation

In this chapter, budget options include dorm-style youth hostels, family-style *pensiones* and slightly better-heeled *hostales*. At the upper end of this category you'll find rooms with air-conditioning and private bathrooms. Midrange *hostales* and hotels are more comfortable, most with standard hotel services.

Throughout this chapter, each place to stay is accompanied by one of the following symbols (the price relates to a double room with private bathroom):

€€€	more than €120 (more than €200 for Madrid/Barcelona)
€€	€60 to €120 (€70 to €200 for Madrid/Barcelona)
€	less than €60 (less than €70 for Madrid/Barcelona)

Among the more tempting hotels for those with a little fiscal room to manoeuvre are the 90 or so **paradores** (in Spain 902 547 979; www.parador. es), a state-funded chain of hotels in often stunning locations, among them towering castles and former medieval convents.

Business Hours

Reviews in this guidebook won't list business hours unless they differ from the following standards:

Banks 8.30am to 2pm Monday to Friday; some also open 4pm to 7pm Thursday and 9am and 1pm Saturday

Central post offices 8.30am to 9.30pm Monday to Friday, 8.30am to 2pm Saturday

Nightclubs midnight or 1am to 5am or 6am

Restaurants lunch 1pm to 4pm, dinner 8.30pm to midnight or later

Shops 10am to 2pm and 4.30pm to 7.30pm or 5pm to 8pm; big supermarkets and department stores generally open from 10am to 10pm Monday to Saturday

Practicalities

Electricity European two-pin plugs; voltage 230V @ 50Hz.

Newspapers & Magazines Left-wing El País, conservative ABC, populist El Mundo, Catalonia-focused La Vanguardia.

Radio Broad mix of talk radio and music stations. The national pop-rock station is RNE 3.

Smoking 'Officially' banned in most public places.

Time One hour ahead of GMT.

Tipping Optional. In cafes and restaurants, most people leave some small change; 5% is plenty, 10% is generous.

TV & Video Most TVs receive at least eight channels: two state-run (TVE1 and La2), five private (Antena 3, Tele 5, Cuatro, La Sexta and Canal Plus) and one regional.

Weights & Measures Metric system: distances in kilometres, weights in kilograms.

Food

Throughout this chapter, each place to eat is accompanied by one of the following symbols (the price relates to a three-course meal with house wine per person):

€€€   more than €50

€€   €20 to €50

€   less than €20

Gay & Lesbian Travellers

Homosexuality is legal in Spain. In 2005 the Socialist president, José Luis Rodríguez Zapatero, gave the country's conservative Catholic foundations a shake with the legalisation of same-sex marriages in Spain.

Lesbians and gay men generally keep a fairly low profile, but are quite open in the cities. Madrid, Barcelona, Sitges, Torremolinos and Ibiza have particularly lively scenes.

Legal Matters

Drugs Cannabis is legal but only for personal use and in very small quantities. Public consumption of any drug is illegal.

Driving age 18

Drinking age 18

Smoking Not permitted in any enclosed public space, including bars, restaurants and nightclubs.

Money

ATMs Many credit and debit cards can be used for withdrawing money from *cajeros automáticos* (automatic teller machines) that display the relevant symbols such as Visa, MasterCard, Cirrus etc.

Cash Most banks will exchange major foreign currencies and offer the best rates. Ask about commissions and take your passport.

Credit & Debit Cards Can be used to pay for most purchases. You'll often be asked to show your passport or some other form of identification.

Moneychangers Exchange offices, indicated by the word *cambio* (exchange), offer longer opening hours than banks, but worse exchange rates and higher commissions.

Taxes & Refunds In Spain, value-added tax (VAT) is known as IVA (*ee-ba; impuesto sobre el valor añadido*). Visitors are entitled to a refund of the 16% IVA on purchases costing more than €90.16 from any shop if they are taking them out of the EU within three months.

Tipping Menu prices include a service charge. Most people leave some small change. Taxi drivers don't have to be tipped but a little rounding up won't go amiss.

Travellers Cheques Can be changed (for a commission) at most banks and exchange offices.

Post

The Spanish postal system, **Correos** (☎902 197 197; www.correos.es), is generally reliable, if a little slow at times. Ordinary mail to other Western European countries can take up to a week (although it often takes as little as three days). Post to North America can take up to 10 days, and to Australia or New Zealand (NZ) it can take between 10 days and three weeks.

Sellos (stamps) are sold at most *estancos* (tobacconists' shops that have 'Tabacos' in yellow letters on a maroon background), and post offices.

Public Holidays

The two main periods when Spaniards go on holiday are Semana Santa (the week leading up to Easter Sunday) and July or August.

National holidays:

Año Nuevo (New Year's Day) 1 January

Viernes Santo (Good Friday) March/April

Fiesta del Trabajo (Labour Day) 1 May

La Asunción (Feast of the Assumption) 15 August

Fiesta Nacional de España (National Day) 12 October

La Inmaculada Concepción (Feast of the Immaculate Conception) 8 December

Navidad (Christmas) 25 December

Regional governments set five holidays and local councils two more. Common dates:

Epifanía (Epiphany) or **Día de los Reyes Magos** (Three Kings' Day) 6 January

Día de San José (St Joseph's Day) 19 March

Jueves Santo (Good Thursday) March/April. Not observed in Catalonia and Valencia.

Corpus Christi June. The Thursday after the eighth Sunday after Easter Sunday.

Día de San Juan Bautista (Feast of St John the Baptist) 24 June

Día de Santiago Apóstol (Feast of St James the Apostle) 25 July

Día de Todos los Santos (All Saints Day) 1 November

Día de la Constitución (Constitution Day) 6 December

Safe Travel

Most visitors to Spain never feel remotely threatened, but a sufficient number have unpleasant experiences to warrant an alert. The main thing to be wary of is petty theft (which may of course not seem so petty if your passport, cash, travellers cheques, credit card and camera go missing).

Algeciras, Barcelona, Madrid and Seville are the worst offenders, as are popular beaches in summer (never leave belongings unattended). Common scams include the following:

○ Kids crowding around you asking for directions or help.

Girona Cathedral (p355)

○ A person pointing out bird droppings on your shoulder (some substance their friend has sprinkled on you) – as they help clean it off they are probably emptying your pockets.

○ The guys who tell you that you have a flat tyre. While you and your new friend check the tyre, his pal is emptying the car.

○ The classic snatch-and-run. Never leave your purse, bag, wallet, mobile phone etc unattended or alone on a table.

○ An old classic: the ladies offering flowers for good luck. We don't know how they do it, but afterwards your pockets always wind up empty.

Telephone

Blue public payphones are common in Spain and fairly easy to use. They accept coins, phonecards and, in some cases, credit cards. Phonecards come in €6 and €12 denominations and, like postage stamps, are sold at post offices and tobacconists.

International reverse-charge (collect) calls are simple to make: dial ☎900 99 followed by the appropriate code. For example: ☎900 99 00 61 for Australia, ☎900 99 00 44 for the UK, ☎900 99 00 11 (AT&T) for the USA etc.

To speak to an English-speaking Spanish international operator, dial ☎1008 (for calls within Europe) or ☎1005 (rest of the world).

MOBILE PHONES

All Spanish mobile phone companies (Telefónica's MoviStar, Orange and Vodafone) offer *prepagado* (prepaid) accounts for mobiles. The SIM card costs from €50, which includes some prepaid phone time. Mobile phone numbers in Spain start with the number 6.

PHONE CODES

Telephone codes in Spain are an integral part of the phone number. All numbers are nine digits and you just dial that nine-digit number.

Numbers starting with 900 are national toll-free numbers, while those starting 901 to 905 come with varying costs; most can only be dialled from within Spain. In a similar category are numbers starting with 800, 803, 806 and 807.

Tourist Information

All cities and many smaller towns have an *oficina de turismo*. National and natural parks also often have visitor centres offering useful information.

Turespaña (www.spain.info) is the country's national tourism body.

Visas

Spain is one of 25 member countries of the Schengen Convention and Schengen visa rules apply.

Transport
Getting There & Away

Entering the Country

Immigration and customs checks usually involve a minimum of fuss, although there are exceptions. Your vehicle could be searched on arrival from Morocco; they're looking for controlled substances.

Air

Flights from all over Europe, including numerous budget airlines, serve main Spanish airports. All of Spain's airports share the user-friendly website and flight information telephone number of **Aena** (☎902 404 704; www.aena.es), the national airports authority.

Madrid's Aeropuerto de Barajas is Spain's busiest (Europe's fourth-busiest) airport. Other major airports include Barcelona's Aeroport del Prat (BCN) and the airports of Palma de Mallorca (PMI), Málaga (AGP), Alicante (ALC), Girona (GRO), Valencia (VLC), Ibiza (IBZ), Seville (SVQ), Bilbao (BIO) and Zaragoza (ZAZ).

Land

Spain shares land borders with France, Portugal and Andorra.

FRANCE

The main road crossing into Spain from France is the highway that links up with Spain's AP7 tollway, which runs down to

DAVID TOMLINSON/LONELY PLANET IMAGES ©

Barcelona and follows the Spanish coast south (with a branch, the AP2, going to Madrid via Zaragoza).

In addition to the options listed below, TGV (high-speed) trains connect Paris Montparnasse with Irún, where you change to a normal train for the Basque Country and on towards Madrid. Up to three TGVs also put you on track to Barcelona (leaving from Paris Gare de Lyon), with a change at Montpellier or Narbonne.

Paris Austerlitz to Madrid Chamartín (chair/sleeper class €166.50/194.20, 13½ hours, one daily) *Trenhotel Francisco de Goya* runs via Orléans, Blois, Poitiers, Vitoria, Burgos and Valladolid.

Paris Austerlitz to Barcelona Estacio de Franca (sleeper class €188, 12 hours, one daily) *Trenhotel Joan Miró* runs via Orléans, Limoges, Figueres and Girona.

Montpellier to Lorca (twice daily) Talgo service along the Mediterranean coast via Girona, Barcelona, Tarragona, Valencia, Alicante, Murcia and Cartagena.

PORTUGAL

The A5 freeway linking Madrid with Badajoz crosses the Portuguese frontier and continues to Lisbon, and there are many other road connections up and down the length of the Hispano–Portuguese frontier.

From Portugal, the main train line runs from Lisbon across Extremadura to Madrid.

Lisbon–Madrid chair/sleeper class €58.60/83.20, 10½ hours, one daily

Lisbon–Irún chair/sleeper class €68.80/96.60, 14½ hours, one daily

Sea

Ferries run to mainland Spain regularly from the Canary Islands, Italy, North Africa (Algeria, Morocco and the Spanish enclaves of Ceuta and Melilla) and the UK. Most services are run by the Spanish national ferry company, **Acciona Trasmediterránea** (☎ 902 45 46 45; www.trasmediterranea.es).

Getting Around

Air

Domestic Spanish routes are operated by the following airlines:

Air Berlin (www.airberlin.com) German budget airline with flights from Madrid to Valencia,

Courtyard in the Alcázar, Seville (p351)

OLIVER STREWE/LONELY PLANET IMAGES ©

Palma de Mallorca, Seville, Jerez de la Frontera and Asturias.

Air Europa (www.aireuropa.com) Dozens of domestic Spanish routes.

easyJet (www.easyjet.com) To Ibiza from Madrid and Bilbao.

Iberia (www.iberia.es) Spain's national airline and its subsidiary, Iberia Regional-Air Nostrum, covering most of Spain.

Ryanair (www.ryanair.com) More than a dozen domestic Spanish routes.

Spanair (www.spanair.com) Numerous domestic Spanish services.

Vueling (www.vueling.com) Spanish low-cost company with loads of domestic flights.

Bus

Spain's bus network is operated by many independent companies, and reaches into the most remote towns and villages in the country. Many towns and cities have one main bus station, and these usually have an information desk that gives details on all services. Tourist offices can also help with information on buses.

Among the hundreds of bus companies operating in Spain, the following have the largest networks:

ALSA (902 422 242; www.alsa.es)

Avanza (902 020 999; www.avanzabus.com)

Car & Motorcycle

Spain's roads vary enormously but are generally good. Fastest are the *autopistas;* on some, you have to pay hefty tolls. Minor routes can be slow going but are usually more scenic. Trying to find a parking spot in larger towns and cities can be a nightmare.

Spanish cities do not have parking meters at every spot. Instead, if you park in a blue or green zone (frequently from 8am to 2pm or from 4pm to 8pm), you need to obtain a ticket from a streetside meter, which may be a block away. Make sure you display the ticket on the dashboard.

DRIVING LICENCES

All EU member states' driving licences are recognised. Other foreign licences should be accompanied by an International Driving Permit.

HIRE

To rent a car in Spain you have to have a licence, be aged 21 or over and have a credit or debit card. Expect a compact car to cost around €30 or more per day.

INSURANCE

Third-party motor insurance is a minimum requirement and it is compulsory to have an internationally recognised proof of insurance, which can be obtained from your insurer.

ROAD RULES

Blood-alcohol limit 0.05%.

Legal driving age for cars 18.

Legal driving age for motorcycles & scooters 16 (80cc and over) or 14 (50cc and under). A licence is required.

Motorcyclists Must use headlights at all times and wear a helmet if riding a bike of 125cc or more.

Side of the road Drive on the right.

Speed limits In built-up areas 50km/h (and in some cases, such as inner-city Barcelona, 30km/h), which increases to 100km/h on major roads and up to 120km/h on *autovías* and *autopistas* (toll-free and tolled dual-lane highways, respectively).

Train

Renfe (☎ 902 240 202; www.renfe.es) is the national railway company.

You can buy tickets and make reservations online, at stations, at travel agencies displaying the Renfe logo and in Renfe offices in many city centres.

Alaris, Altaria, Alvia, Arco and Avant Long-distance intermediate-speed services.

Cercanías For short hops and services to outlying suburbs and satellite towns in Madrid, Barcelona and 11 other cities.

Regionales Trains operating within one region, usually stopping at all stations.

Talgo and Intercity Slower long-distance trains.

Tren de Alta Velocidad Española (AVE) High-speed trains that link Madrid with Barcelona, Burgos, Córdoba, Cuenca, Huesca, Lerida, Málaga, Seville, Valencia, Valladolid and Zaragoza. There is also a Barcelona–Seville service. In coming years Madrid–Cádiz and Madrid–Bilbao should come on line.

CLASSES & COSTS

All long-distance trains have 2nd and 1st classes, known as *turista* and *preferente,* respectively.

Tickets for AVE trains are by far the most expensive.

Children aged between four and 12 years are entitled to a 40% discount; those aged under four travel for free (except on high-speed trains, for which they pay the same as those aged four to 12).

Italy

The land that has turned its lifestyle into a designer accessory, Italy is one of Europe's great seducers. Ever since the days of the 18th-century Grand Tour, travellers have been falling under its spell and still today it stirs strong emotions. The rush of seeing the Colosseum for the first time or cruising down Venice's surreal canals are experiences you'll remember for life.

Of course, Italy is not all about Michelangelo masterpieces and frescoed churches. There's also the food, imitated the world over, and a landscape that boasts beautiful Alpine peaks, stunning coastlines and remote, silent valleys. So if the cities don't do it for you, if their noise, heat and chaos start getting to you – as they get to many locals – change gear and head out to the country for a taste of the sun-kissed slow life.

Trevi Fountain (p403), Rome
PHOTOGRAPHER: MARTIN MOOS/LONELY PLANET IMAGES ©

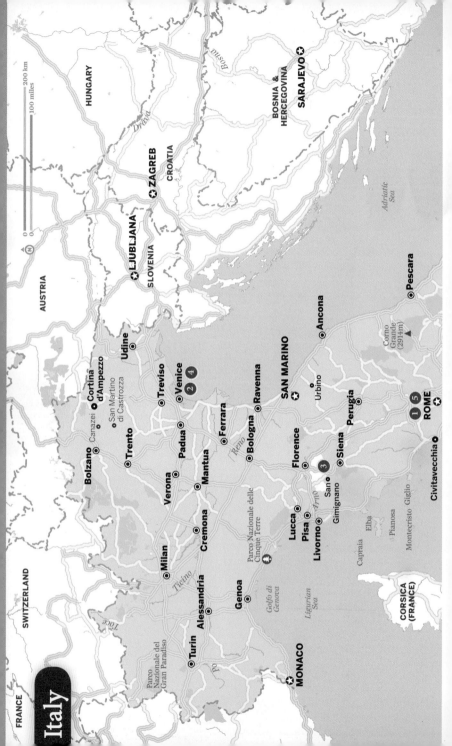

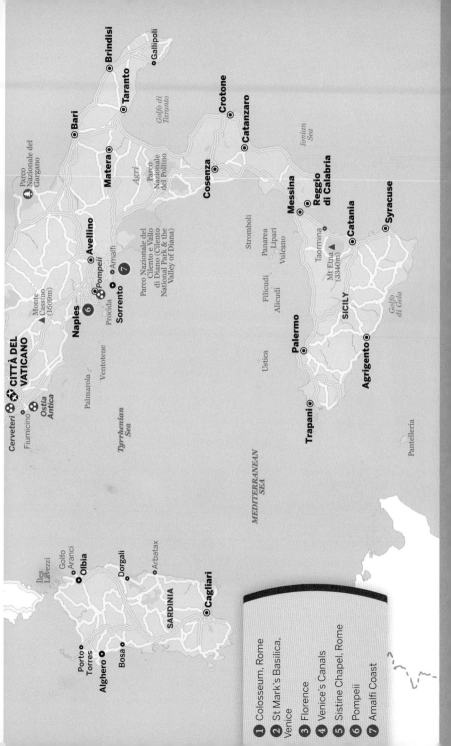

Italy Highlights

1 Colosseum

Even before setting foot in the ancient stadium, most visitors are gobsmacked to find the Colosseum looming before them in all its glory when they leave the metro station. Not only is this Roman arena impressive for its size and endurance, but its well-preserved condition makes for an evocative insight into ancient life.

Need to Know

Best route Head for the 2nd floor for the temporary exhibitions and view of the Roman Forum **Tickets** Buy online (www.pierreci.it) to avoid queuing **See our author's review on p397.**

The Colosseum Don't Miss List

BY VINCENZO MACCARRONE,
COLOSSEUM STAFF MEMBER

1 THE ARENA

The arena had a wooden floor covered in sand to prevent combatants from slipping and to soak up blood. Gladiators arrived directly from their training ground via underground passageways, and were hoisted onto the arena by a complicated system of pulleys.

2 THE CAVEA AND THE PODIUM

The cavea, for spectator seating, was divided into three tiers: knights sat in the lowest, wealthy citizens in the middle and plebs at the top. The podium – close to the action but protected from the animals on stage by nets made of hemp – was reserved for emperors, senators and VIPs.

3 THE FACADE

The exterior mimics the **Teatro di Marcello**; the walls were once clad in travertine, with marble statues filling the niches on the 2nd and 3rd floors. On the top level you'll see square holes that held wooden masts supporting the Velarium (a canvas awning over the arena).

4 TEMPORARY EXHIBITIONS

The 2nd floor hosts some fantastic exhibitions, either about the Colosseum or on the wider history of Rome. Walk past the bookshop to the end of the corridor and look towards the eastern side of the **Roman Forum** (p391) – there's a wonderful view of the Tempio di Venere e Roma (Temple of Venus and Rome), hard to see from the ground.

5 THE PERFECT PHOTO

Towards closing time, the Colosseum is bathed in a beautiful light. For great views of the building, head up Colle Oppio (Oppio Hill) right above the Colosseo metro station, or up Colle Celio (Celio Hill) opposite the Palatino and Colosseum exit.

Basilica di San Marco

An incredible layering of different eras and architectural styles inspired me to write my book on the Basilica; a building whose evolution can be divided into three phases, from its foundation in 829 and reconstruction in 976, to the construction of the 11th-century Byzantine wonder that forms the basis of what we see today.

Need to Know

Best photo Photography is forbidden inside; outside, check out the area between the Basilica and the Palazzo Ducale (the church was once the palazzo's chapel) **See our author's review on p424.**

Basilica di San Marco Don't Miss List

BY ETTORE VIO, CHIEF ARCHITECT & AUTHOR

1 MOSAICS

Look up at the arch mosaics above the facade's doorways. The one on the left depicts the arrival of St Mark's body in Venice, smuggled here in the 9th century. Inside, the sparkling mosaics begin in the narthex (atrium) and culminate in the sumptuous panels of the central Ascension dome and the Pentecost dome in the nave.

2 THE PALO D'ORO & THE TESORO

Behind the high altar is the gold-, enamel- and jewel-encrusted Palo D'Oro altarpiece. Made in Constantinople in AD 976, it was reworked in 1105, enlarged by Venetian goldsmiths in 1209 and reset in the 14th century. Accessible from the right transept, the Tesoro (Treasury) houses priceless items seized from the 1204 raid of Constantinople.

3 LOGGIA DEI CAVALLI

Accessible via the museum, the Loggia dei Cavalli has an unforgettable view of Piazza San Marco. You can also see the island of San Giorgio and the sinuous Lido, which separates the Venetian lagoon from the sea.

4 EAST MEETING WEST

The distance traversed from the entrance to the altar encapsulates the European philosophical concept of a distant God with whom communion is achieved through a long, personal journey. The Oriental domes, representing the divine, span the entire building, symbolising God's omnipresence and intimacy with humankind.

5 THE CRYPT

Considered Venice's most sacred site, the crypt harbours the 9th-century walls of the first basilica and the tomb in which St Mark's remains rested for 10 centuries. (They are now housed beneath the basilica's high altar.) Book at least a week ahead (☎041 270 8330; tecnico. proc@patriarcatovenezia.it).

Top and Left: Mosaics in Basilica di San Marco

Florence

If it's art you're after, look no further than Florence (p439). During the Middle Ages the Medicis transformed this merchant town into the centre of the Italian Renaissance, and it's brimful of artistic treasures. Marvel at the priceless canvases of the Uffizi, admire the architecture of the Duomo or join the queues to glimpse Michelangelo's masterpiece, *David* – just don't expect to have the city to yourself. Galleria Palatina (p443), Florence

Venice's Canals

What else is there to say about Venice (p424)? Quite simply, this is one of the world's unmissable cities, renowned for its glorious architecture, romantic canals, historic churches and stunning museums. Whether it's riding the gondolas, wandering the alleyways or joining the throngs in Piazza San Marco, you'll find it impossible not to fall head over heels for this Italian beauty.

Sistine Chapel

It's a tough call, but if we had to pick out Italy's most important artistic landmark, we'd go for the Sistine Chapel (p405). Michelangelo's celebrated four-year fresco on the chapel's ceiling is the highlight, but his seven-year labour of love, *The Last Judgment,* runs it a close second. Trust us – this is one artwork that really does live up to the hype.

Pompeii

You know the story: 2000 years ago, the bustling Roman town of Pompeii (p468) was devastated by a catastrophic eruption from nearby Mt Vesuvius. But nothing can prepare you for the eerie experience of standing in Pompeii itself; the deserted streets, abandoned squares and spooky body casts bring a whole new meaning to the term 'ghost town'.

Amalfi Coast

For a classic Italian road trip, nowhere can hold a candle to the Amalfi Coast (p472). Stretching for 50km along the southern Sorrento Peninsula, this glittering coastline is one of the most beautiful spots in the Mediterranean – studded with sparkling beaches, secluded bays and clifftop towns. It's tailor-made for cruising with the top down – just watch out for those hairpin bends.

Italy's Best...

Artistic Treasures

○ **David** (p443)
Michelangelo's sculptural masterpiece, in the Galleria dell'Accademia in Florence, is a celebration of the human form.

○ **Sistine Chapel** (p405)
This incredible ceiling fresco needs no introduction.

○ **St Peter's Basilica** (p399)
Rome's most impressive architectural landmark.

○ **Ravenna Mosaics** (p437)
These wonderful mosaics are mentioned in Danté's Divine Comedy.

○ **Spring** and **Venus** (p442)
Botticelli's finest works are both at the Uffizi.

Roman Remains

○ **Colosseum** (p397) See where the gladiators slugged it out.

○ **Roman Forum** (p391)
Stand in the heart of the Roman Republic.

○ **Via Appia Antica** (p407)
Walk on one of the world's oldest roads.

○ **Villa Adriana** (p391)
Take a day trip from Rome to Hadrian's incredible weekend retreat.

○ **Ostia Antica** (p391)
Explore the quays of ancient Rome's port.

Festivals

○ **Carnevale** (p429) Don your costume for Venice's crazy carnival.

○ **Scoppio del Carro** (p446)
Fireworks explode above Florence on Easter Sunday.

○ **Il Palio** (p454) Siena's annual horse races are a real spectacle.

○ **Venice International Film Festival** (p429) Italy's most prestigious film festival brings big-name stars to the city.

○ **Natale di Roma** (p407)
Rome celebrates its birthday in style.

Need to Know

City Views

- **Leaning Tower of Pisa** (p451) Where else?

- **Duomo, Florence** (p453) Climb the campanile for the quintessential Florence photo op.

- **Basilica di San Marco** (p424) See the Piazza San Marco from the basilica's bell tower.

- **Pincio Hill** (p404) Fantastic outlook over Rome.

- **Torre del Mangia** (p453) Gaze over Siena's rooftops to the Tuscan countryside beyond.

ADVANCE PLANNING

- **As early as possible** Book accommodation in major cities, especially Rome, Venice, Milan, Florence and Bologna.

- **Two weeks before** Beat the queues by booking online for major sights such as the Leaning Tower of Pisa, the Colosseum and the Vatican Museums.

- **When you arrive** Pick up discount tickets covering Rome, Venice, Florence's museums and Cinque Terre.

RESOURCES

- **Italia** (www.italia.it) Inspiration, ideas and planning tips.

- **Trenitalia** (www.ferrovie dellostato.it) Plan your train trips.

- **Agriturismo** (www. agriturismo.com) Find the perfect Italian farmstay.

- **Turismo Roma** (www. turismoroma.it) Rome Tourist Board's website.

- **Pierreci** (www.pierreci. it) Online booking for many museums and monuments.

GETTING AROUND

- **Air** Italy's largest airport is Leonardo da Vinci (aka Fiumicino) in Rome.

International flights also serve Milan, Pisa, Venice and other main cities.

- **Train** Italy's main rail hubs are Rome, Milan and Venice. High-speed services operate on the main line from Milan to Rome/Naples via Bologna and Florence. Other routes operate local *regionale* or faster InterCity (IC) services.

- **Sea** Dozens of options to France, Spain and various other Mediterranean destinations; main ports are in Rome, Ancona and Genoa.

- **Bus** Extensive and often the only option to many rural areas.

- **Car** Autostradas (motorways) are quick but often charge a toll; regional roads are better for sightseeing.

BE FOREWARNED

- **Scams** Watch out for pickpockets and moped thieves in Rome, Florence and Venice, and count your change carefully.

- **Driving** Expect the unexpected – Italians have a notoriously relaxed attitude to road rules.

- **Prices** Prices for everything skyrocket during peak season and major holidays.

Left: Michaelangelo's *David*;
Above: Cathedral and Leaning Tower of Pisa, Pisa.

Italy Itineraries

Maybe it's the art, maybe it's the architecture or maybe it's just the atmosphere – but there's something about Italy that seems to get under your skin. Don't be surprised if you're smitten.

3 DAYS

ROME TO THE AMALFI COAST
A Tale of Two Cities

Its empire may have long since sailed into the sunset, but there's still nowhere better to experience Italy at its passionate, pompous, pizza-spinning best than **(1) Rome**. There are too many sights to squeeze into a couple of days, so you'll need to plan carefully. On day one, you could do the Colosseum and the Roman Forum, followed by an early evening visit to the Pantheon, the city's best pizza at Bafetto and a late-night wander around vibrant Trastevere. Devote day two to the Vatican, allowing time for St Peter's Basilica, the Vatican Museums and the jaw-dropping Sistine Chapel.

On day three, catch the train south to **(2) Naples**, a raucous, unruly city that provides a fascinating contrast to Rome's stately sights. It's loud, it's filthy and the traffic is a nightmare, but there's still something utterly intoxicating about this chaotic city – and if you're into pizza, Naples is most definitely the place to be. Best of all, the swish island of **(3) Capri**, the ghost city of **(4) Pompeii** and the stunning scenery of the **(5) Amalfi Coast** are all within a short drive of Naples – so it also makes a great base for side trips if you have a bit more time at your disposal.

LUCCA TO FLORENCE

A Taste of Tuscany

5 DAYS

If anywhere encapsulates the Italian character, it's Tuscany. This sunbaked corner of Italy is one of the country's most rewarding regions for culture vultures. **(1) Lucca** makes a fine place to start thanks to its hilltop architecture, but it can't hold a candle to the scenic splendour of the **(2) Cinque Terre National Park**. Spend a day exploring before braving the crowds at **(3) Pisa**'s punch-drunk tower – book online and get there early or late to dodge the queues.

On day four, swing south via another of Tuscany's heart-meltingly beautiful hilltop towns, **(4) San Gimignano**. From here it's a short drive to **(5) Siena**, renowned for its medieval buildings and fabulous restaurants. The annual horse race of Il Palio takes over the town for two hectic days in July and August, but you'll need to book way ahead if you're planning on joining the party.

Complete your Tuscan trip in **(6) Florence**, a city that's literally brimming with artistic and architectural treasures. From landmark buildings such as the Gothic Duomo to the priceless artworks housed at the Uffizi and the Galleria dell'Accademia, Florence is a place where it's literally impossible not to feel inspired.

Florence Duomo (cathedral) and city
PHOTOGRAPHER: RICHARD I'ANSON/LONELY PLANET IMAGES ©

Discover Italy

ROME

POP 2.72 MILLION

An epic, monumental metropolis, Rome has been in the spotlight for close to 3000 years. As the showcase seat of the Roman Empire, it was the all-powerful *Caput Mundi* (Capital of the World). Later, as the Renaissance capital of the Catholic world, its name sent shivers of holy terror through believers and infidels alike. Some 500 years on, its name still exerts a powerful hold. Fortunately, its reality is every bit as enticing as its reputation. With its architectural and artistic treasures, its romantic corners and noisy, colourful markets, Rome is a city that knows how to impress.

History

According to legend Rome was founded by Romulus and Remus in 753 BC. Whether this is true, it's accepted that Romulus *was* the first king of Rome and that the city was an amalgamation of Etruscan, Latin and Sabine settlements on the Palatino, Esquilino and Quirinale Hills.

In 509 BC the Roman Republic was founded. Civil war put an end to the republic following the murder of Julius Caesar in 44 BC and a bitter civil war between Octavian and Mark Antony. Octavian emerged victorious and was made the first Roman emperor and given the title Augustus.

By AD 100 Rome had a population of 1.5 million and was the *Caput Mundi* (Capital of the World). But by the 5th century decline had set in and in 476 Romulus Augustulus, the last emperor of the Western Roman Empire, was deposed.

By this time Rome's Christian roots had taken firm hold. Christianity had

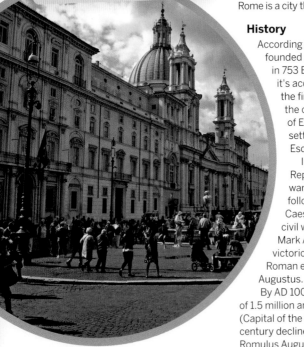

Piazza Navona (p403)
PHOTOGRAPHER: GEOFF STRINGER/LONELY PLANET IMAGES ©

been spreading since the 1st century AD, and under Constantine it received official recognition. Pope Gregory I (590–604) did much to strengthen the Church's grip over the city, laying the foundations for its later role as capital of the Catholic Church.

Sights

With more world-class sights than many small nations, Rome can be a daunting prospect. The trick is to relax and not worry about seeing everything – half the fun of the city is just hanging out, enjoying the atmosphere. Most sights are concentrated in the area between Stazione Termini and the Vatican. Halfway between the two, the Pantheon and Piazza Navona lie at the heart of the *centro storico* (historic centre). To the southeast, the Colosseum is an obvious landmark.

Ancient Rome

ROMAN FORUM   Ruins
(Map p400; Largo della Salara Vecchia; adult/ EU child incl Colosseum & Palatino €12/free, audioguide €4; ☺8.30am-1hr before sunset; Ⓜ Colosseo) Now a collection of fascinating, if rather confusing, ruins, the Roman Forum (Foro Romano) was once the showpiece centre of the Roman Republic. Originally an Etruscan burial ground, it was first developed in the 7th century BC, expanding to become the social, political and commercial core of the Roman world.

As you enter from Largo della Salaria Vecchia, ahead to your left is the **Tempio di Antonino e Faustina**, built by the senate in AD 141 and transformed into a church in the 8th century. To your right, the **Basilica Aemilia**, built in 179 BC, was 100m long with a two-storey porticoed facade lined with shops. At the end of the short path, **Via Sacra** traverses the Forum from northwest to southeast. Opposite the Basilica Aemilia stands the **Tempio di Giulio Cesare**, erected by Augustus in 29 BC on the site where Caesar's body had been burned.

Head right up Via Sacra and you reach the **Curia**, once the meeting place of the

Roman senate and later converted into a church. In front is the **Lapis Niger**, a large piece of black marble that purportedly covered Romulus' grave.

At the end of Via Sacra, the **Arco di Settimio Severo** was erected in 203 to honour Emperor Septimus Severus and his two sons and celebrate victory over the Parthians. Nearby, the **Millarium Aureum** marked the centre of ancient Rome, from which distances to the city were measured.

Southwest of the arch, eight granite columns are all that remain of the **Tempio di Saturno**, one of ancient Rome's most important temples.

To the southeast, you'll see the **Piazza del Foro**, the Forum's main market and meeting place, marked by the 7th-century **Colonna di Foca** (Column of Phocus).

Back towards Via Sacra, the **Casa delle Vestali** was home of the virgins whose job it was to keep the sacred flame alight in the adjoining **Tempio di Vesta**. The vestal virgins were selected at the age of 10 for their beauty and virtue and were required to stay chaste and committed to keeping the flame for 30 years.

Continuing up Via Sacra, you come to the vast **Basilica di Costantino**, also known as the Basilica di Massenzio, whose impressive design inspired Renaissance architects. The **Arco di Tito**, at the Colosseum end of the Forum, was built in AD 81 in honour of the victories of the emperors Titus and Vespasian against Jerusalem.

Roman Forum

In ancient times, a forum was a market place, civic centre and religious complex all rolled into one, and the greatest of all was the Roman Forum (Foro Romano). Situated between the Palatino (Palatine Hill), ancient Rome's most exclusive neighbourhood, and the Campidoglio (Capitoline Hill), it was the city's busy, bustling centre. On any given day it teemed with activity. Senators debated affairs of state in the **Curia** ❶, shoppers thronged the squares and traffic-free streets, crowds gathered under the **Colonna di Foca** ❷ to listen to politicians holding forth from the **Rostrum** ❷. Elsewhere, lawyers worked the courts in basilicas including the **Basilica di Massenzio** ❸, while the Vestal Virgins quietly went about their business in the **Casa delle Vestali** ❹.

Special occasions were also celebrated in the Forum: religious holidays were marked with ceremonies at temples such as the **Tempio di Saturno** ❺ and the **Tempio di Castore e Polluce** ❻, and military victories were honoured with dramatic processions up Via Sacra and the building of monumental arches like the **Arco di Settimio Severo** ❼ and the **Arco di Tito** ❽.

The ruins you see today are impressive but they can be confusing without a clear picture of what the Forum once looked like. This spread shows the Forum in its heyday, complete with temples, civic buildings and towering monuments to heroes of the Roman Empire.

TOP TIPS

Get grandstand views of the Forum from the Palatino and Campidoglio.

Visit first thing in the morning or late afternoon; crowds are worst between 11am and 2pm.

In summer it gets hot in the Forum and there's little shade, so take a hat and plenty of water.

Admission

Although valid for two days, admission tickets only allow for one entry into the Forum, Colosseum and Palatino.

Campidoglio (Capitoline Hill)

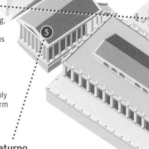

Colonna di Foca & Rostrum

The free-standing, 13.5m-high Column of Phocus is the Forum's youngest monument, dating to AD 608. Behind it, the Rostrum provided a suitably grandiose platform for pontificating public speakers.

Tempio di Saturno

Ancient Rome's Fort Knox, the Temple of Saturn was the city treasury. In Caesar's day it housed 13 tonnes of gold, 114 tonnes of silver and 30 million *sestertii* worth of silver coins.

JONATHAN SMITH / LONELY PLANET IMAGES ©

GEOFF STRINGER / LONELY PLANET IMAGES ©

Tempio di Castore e Polluce

Only three columns of the Temple of Castor and Pollux remain. The temple was dedicated to the Heavenly Twins after they supposedly led the Romans to victory over the Etruscans.

Arco di Settimio Severo

One of the Forum's signature monuments, this imposing triumphal arch commemorates the military victories of Septimius Severus. Relief panels depict his campaigns against the Parthians.

Curia

This big barnlike building was the official seat of the Roman Senate. Most of what you see is a reconstruction, but the interior marble floor dates to the 3rd-century reign of Diocletian.

Via Sacra

Julius Caesar RIP

Julius Caesar was cremated on the site where the Tempio di Giulio Cesare now stands.

Basilica di Massenzio

Marvel at the scale of this vast 4th-century basilica. In its original form the central hall was divided into enormous naves; now only part of the northern nave survives.

Tempio di Giulio Cesare

Casa delle Vestali

White statues line the grassy atrium of what was once the luxurious 50-room home of the Vestal Virgins. The virgins played an important role in Roman religion, serving the goddess Vesta.

Arco di Tito

Said to be the inspiration for the Arc de Triomphe in Paris, the well-preserved Arch of Titus was built by the emperor Domitian to honour his elder brother Titus.

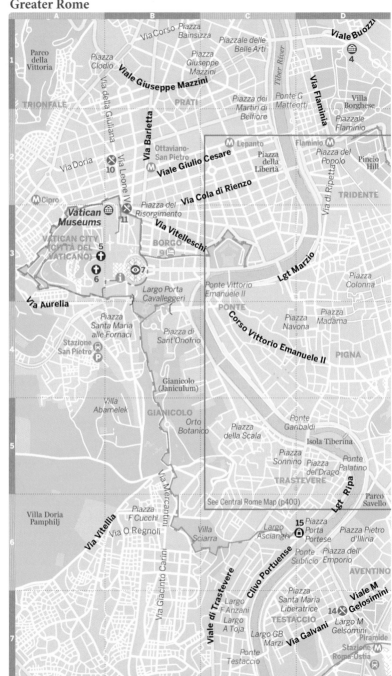

See Central Rome Map (p400)

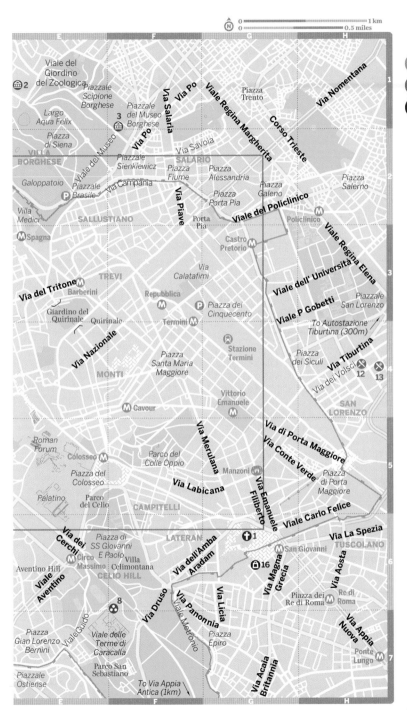

Viale del Giordino del Zoologica

Piazzale Scipione Borghese

Largo Aqua Felix

Piazza di Siena

Piazzale del Museo Borghese

VILLA BORGHESE

Galoppatoio

Villa Medici

Piazzale Brasile

Piazzale Sienkiewicz

Via Salaria

Via Po

Via Po

Via del Museo

Viale del Museo

Via Savoia

SALARIO

Via Campania

Via Piave

Via Regina Margherita

Corso Trieste

Piazza Trento

Via Nomentana

Piazza Fiume

Piazza Alessandria

Piazza Porta Pia

Piazza Galeno

Piazza Salerno

Viale del Policlinico

SALLUSTIANO

Spagna

Porta Pia

Policlinico

Castro Pretorio

Via Calatafimi

Viale dell' Università

Viale Regina Elena

Piazza Salerno

Via del Tritone

Barberini

Giardino del Quirinale

Quirinale

TREVI

Repubblica

Via Nazionale

Termini

Piazza dei Cinquecento

Viale P Gobetti

Piazzale San Lorenzo

To Autostazione Tiburtina (300m)

Piazza Santa Maria Maggiore

MONTI

Cavour

Stazione Termini

Vittorio Emanuele

Piazza dei Siculi

Via Tiburtina

Via dei Volsci

12

13

SAN LORENZO

Roman Forum

Colosseo

Piazza del Colosseo

Palatino

Parco del Celio

Parco del Colle Oppio

CAMPITELLI

Via Merulana

Manzoni

Via Labicana

Via di Porta Maggiore

Via Conte Verde

Piazza di Porta Maggiore

Via dei Cerchi

Circo Massimo

Aventino Hill

Viale Aventino

Piazza di SS Giovanni E Paolo

Villa Celimontana

CELIO HILL

LATERAN

Via dell'Amba Aradam

Via Emanuele Filiberto

1

16

San Giovanni

Via Magna Grecia

Viale Carlo Felice

Via La Spezia

TUSCOLANO

Via Aosta

Piazza Gian Lorenzo Bernini

Viale Guido

8

Viale delle Terme di Caracalla

Via Druso

Via Panonnia

Viale Metronio

Via Licia

Piazza Epiro

Piazza dei Re di Roma

Re di Roma

Via Appia Nuova

Piazzale Ostiense

Parco San Sebastiano

To Via Appia Antica (1km)

Via Acaia

Via Britannia

Ponte Lungo

2

3

0 ——————————————— 1 km
0 ——————————————— 0.5 miles

Greater Rome

PALATINO (PALATINE HILL)   Ruins
(Map p400; Via di San Gregorio 30; adult/EU child incl Colosseum & Roman Forum €12/free, audioguide €4; ⊙8.30am-1hr before sunset; MColosseo) Rising above the Roman Forum, this beautiful area is where Romulus is said to have founded the city in 753 BC. Archaeological evidence shows that the earliest settlements in the area were in fact on the Palatino and date back to the 8th century BC. This was ancient Rome's poshest neighbourhood and the emperor Augustus lived here all his life. After Rome's fall, it fell into disrepair and in the Middle Ages churches and castles were built over the ruins. Most of the Palatino is covered by the ruins of Emperor Domitian's vast complex, which served as the main imperial palace for 300 years.

Among the best-preserved buildings on the Palatino is the **Casa di Livia**, home of Augustus' wife Livia, and, in front, Augustus' separate residence, the **Casa di Augusto** (⊙11am-3.30pm Mon, Wed, Sat & Sun), which boasts exceptional frescos.

MUSEO DEI FORI IMPERIALI   Museum
(Map p400; www.mercatiditraiano.it; Via IV Novembre 94; adult/child €9/free; ⊙9am-7pm Tue-Sun; ⊟Via IV Novembre) This striking museum brings to life the **Mercati di Traiano**, Emperor Trajan's great 2nd-century market complex. From the main hallway, a lift whisks you up to the **Torre delle Milizie** (Militia Tower), a 13th-century red-brick tower, and the upper levels of the vast three-storey semicircular construction that once housed hundreds of traders. From the top there are sweeping views over the Imperial Forums.

PIAZZA DEL CAMPIDOGLIO   Square
(Map p400; ⊟Piazza Venezia) This striking piazza sits atop the Capitoline Hill (Campidoglio), the lowest of Rome's seven hills. In ancient times, it was home to the city's two most important temples: one dedicated to Juno Moneta and another to Jupiter Capitolinus, where Brutus is said to have hidden after assassinating Caesar. The Michelangelo-designed piazza, accessible by the graceful **Cordonata** staircase, is bordered by **Palazzo Nuovo** on the left, **Palazzo dei Conservatori** on the right, and **Palazzo Senatorio**, the seat of city government since 1143. In the centre, the bronze **statue of Marcus Aurelius** is a copy; the original is in Palazzo Nuovo.

MUSEI CAPITOLINI   Museum
(Capitoline Museums; Map p400; www.musei capitolini.org; Piazza del Campidoglio; adult/child €7.50/free, audioguide €5; ⊙9am-8pm Tue-Sun, last entry 7pm; ⊟Piazza Venezia) Housed in Palazzo Nuovo and Palazzo dei Conservatori, the Capitoline Museums are the oldest public museums in the world, dating to 1471. Their collection of classical art is one of Italy's finest, including masterpieces such as the *Lupa capitolina* (She

KRZYSZTOF DYDYNSKI/LONELY PLANET IMAGES ©

Don't Miss **Colosseum**

Rome's iconic monument is a thrilling sight. The 50,000-seat Colosseum (Map p400; ☏ 06 3996 7700; Piazza del Colosseo; adult/EU child incl Roman Forum & Palatino €12/free, audioguide €4; ⊙8.30am-1hr before sunset; Ⓜ Colosseo) was ancient Rome's most feared arena and attracts between 16,000 and 19,000 people on an average day.

Originally known as the Flavian Amphitheatre, the Colosseum was started by Emperor Vespasian in AD 72 and finished by his son Titus in AD 80. It was clad in travertine and covered by a huge canvas awning that was held aloft by 240 masts. Inside, tiered seating encircled the sand-covered arena, itself built over underground chambers where animals were caged. Games involved gladiators fighting wild animals or each other. The top tier and underground corridors, known as the hypogeum, have recently been opened to the public. Visits (€8 on top of the norma ticket) and are by guided tour only, require advance booking.

To the west of the Colosseum, the **Arco di Costantino** was built to celebrate Constantine's victory over rival Maxentius at the battle of Milvian Bridge (AD 312).

Follow these tips to beat the Colosseum queues:

○ Buy your ticket from the Palatino entrance (about 250m away at Via di San Gregorio 30) or the Roman Forum entrance (Largo della Salara Vecchia).

○ Get the Roma Pass, which is valid for three days and a whole host of sites.

○ Book your ticket online at www.pierreci.it (plus booking fee of €1.50).

○ Join an official English-language tour (€4 extra).

Outside the Colosseum, you'll almost certainly be hailed by centurions offering to pose for a photo. They will expect payment. There's no set rate but €5 is an acceptable sum – and that's €5 in total, not €5 per person.

Wolf), a sculpture of Romulus and Remus under a wolf, and the *Galata morente* (Dying Gaul), a moving depiction of a dying Gaul.

CHIESA DI SANTA MARIA D'ARACOELI
Church

(Piazza del Campidoglio 4; ◷9am-12.30pm & 3-6.30pm; 🚇Piazza Venezia) Marking the high point of the Campidoglio, this 6th-century church sits on the site of the Roman temple to Juno Moneta. According to legend it was here that the Tiburtine Sybil told Augustus of the coming birth of Christ, and today the church still has a strong association with the nativity.

PIAZZA VENEZIA
Square

Piazza Venezia is dominated by the mountain of white marble that is **Il Vittoriano** (Map p400; 🚇Piazza Venezia), aka the Altare della Patria. Begun in 1885 to commemorate Italian unification and honour Victor Emmanuel II, it incorporates the **tomb of the Unknown Soldier**, as well as the **Museo Centrale del Risorgimento**

(Map p400; admission free; ◷9.30am-6.30pm), documenting Italian unification. For Rome's best 360-degree views, take the **panoramic lift** (Map p400; adult/concession €7/3.50; ◷9.30am-6.30pm Mon-Thu, to 7.30pm Fri-Sun) to the top.

Over the square, the 15th-century **Palazzo Venezia** (Via del Plebiscito 118; adult/concession €4/2; ◷8.30am-7.30pm Tue-Sun) was the first of Rome's great Renaissance *palazzi*. Mussolini had his office here and there's now a museum of medieval and Renaissance art.

BOCCA DELLA VERITÀ
Artefact

(Map p400; Piazza Bocca della Verità 18; ◷10am-5pm; 🚇Via dei Cerchi) A round piece of marble once used as an ancient manhole cover, the Bocca della Verità (Mouth of Truth) is one of Rome's great curiosities. According to legend, if you put your hand in the carved mouth and tell a lie, it will bite your hand off. The mouth lives in the portico of the **Chiesa di Santa Maria in Cosmedin**, one of Rome's most beautiful medieval churches.

The Vatican

Covering just 0.44 sq km, this tiny nation is the modern vestige of the Papal States, the papal empire that ruled Rome and much of central Italy for more than a thousand years until it was forcibly incorporated into the Italian state during unification in 1861. Relations between Italy and the landless papacy remained strained until 1929 when Mussolini and Pope Pius XI signed the Lateran Treaty and formally established the Vatican State.

ST PETER'S BASILICA   Church

(Map p394; St Peter's Sq; admission free, audio guide €5; ☺7am-7pm Apr-Sep, to 6.30pm Oct-Mar; Ⓜ Ottaviano-San Pietro) In a city of churches, none can hold a candle to St Peter's Basilica (Basilica di San Pietro), Italy's biggest, richest and most spectacular church.

Built over the spot where St Peter was buried, the first basilica was consecrated by Constantine in the 4th century. Later, in 1503, Bramante designed a new basilica, which took more than 150 years to complete.

Michelangelo took over the project in 1547, designing the grand dome, which soars 120m above the altar. The cavernous 187m-long interior contains numerous treasures, including two of Italy's most celebrated masterpieces: Michelangelo's *Pietà,* the only known work to carry his signature; and Bernini's 29m-high baldachin over the high altar.

The entrance to the **dome (**☺**8am-6pm Apr-Sep, 8am-5pm Oct-Mar)** is to the right as you climb the stairs to the basilica's atrium. Make the climb on foot (€5) or by lift (€7).

Note that the basilica is one of Rome's busiest attractions, so expect long queues during peak periods. Dress rules and security are stringently enforced, so no shorts, miniskirts or sleeveless tops, and be prepared to have your bags searched.

Central Rome

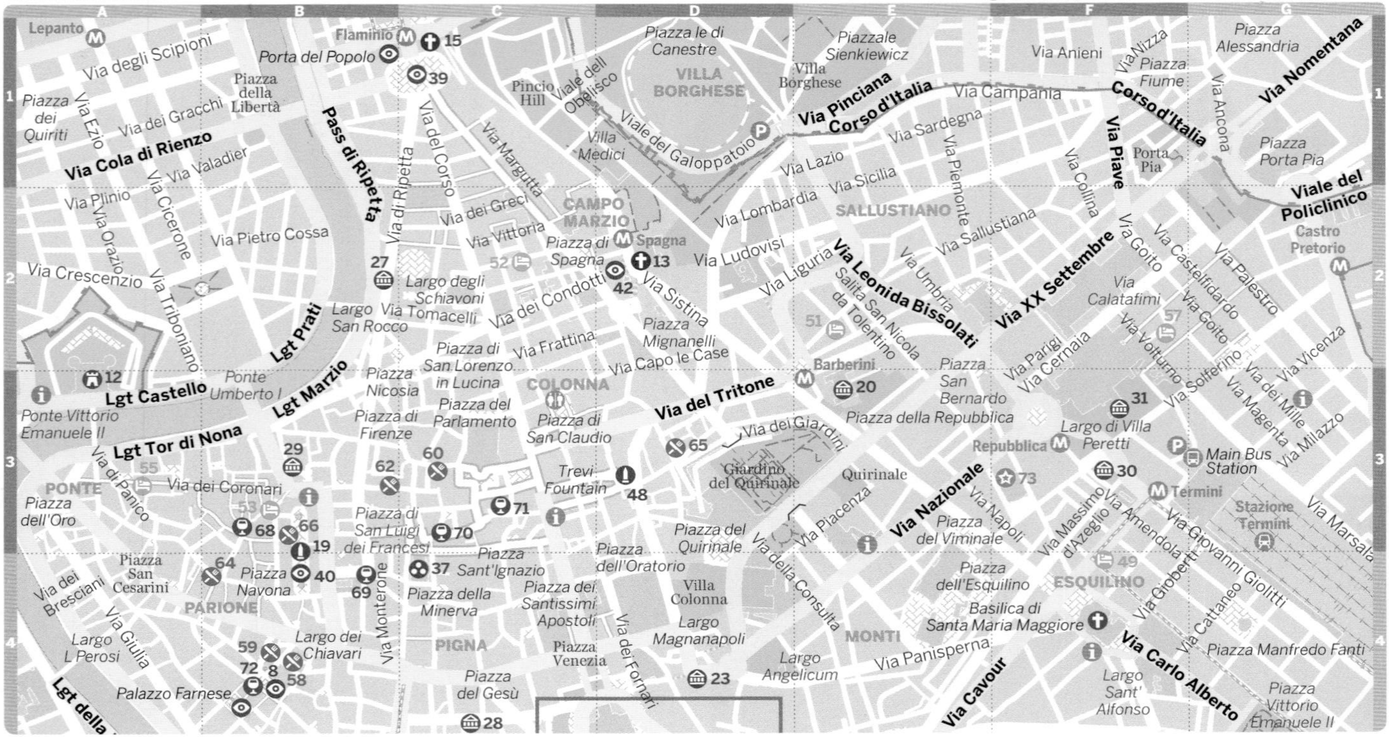

0.4 miles

500 m

Via Nomentana

Viale del Policlinico

Corso d'Italia

Via Piave

Via XX Settembre

Via Leonida Bissolati

Via Pinciana

Corso d'Italia

SALLUSTIANO

Piazza
Alessandria

Piazza
Fiume

Via Nizza

Via Vicenza

Via Marsala

Castro
Pretorio

Piazza
Porta Pia

Via Ancona

Via Palestro

Via Castelfidardo

Via dei Mille

Via San
Martino della Battaglia

Main Bus
Station

Stazione
Termini

Piazza dei
Cinquecento

Via Cavour

Piazza Manfredo Fanti

Piazza
Vittorio
Emanuele II

Via Carlo Alberto

Via Giolitti

Via Cattaneo

ESQUILINO

Basilica di
Santa Maria Maggiore

Sant'
Alfonso

MONTI

VILLA
BORGHESE

CAMPO
MARZIO

COLONNA

PIGNA

PARIONE

PONTE

Trevi
Fountain

Spagna

Flaminio

Lepanto

Via Cola di Rienzo

Lgt Prati

Pass di Ripetta

Via del Corso

Via Nazionale

Barberini

Repubblica

Quirinale

ST PETER'S SQUARE — Square

(Map p394; **M** Ottaviano-San Pietro) The Vatican's central piazza, St Peter's Sq (Piazza San Pietro) was designed by baroque artist Gian Lorenzo Bernini and laid out between 1656 and 1667. Seen from above it resembles a giant keyhole: two semicircular colonnades, each consisting of four rows of Doric columns, bound by a giant ellipse that straightens out to funnel believers into the basilica. The effect was deliberate – Bernini described the colonnade as representing 'the motherly arms of the church'.

In the centre, the 25m obelisk was brought to Rome by Caligula from Heliopolis in Egypt and later used by Nero as a turning post for the chariot races in his circus.

VATICAN MUSEUMS — Museum

(Map p394; ☎ 06 6988 4676; Viale Vaticano; adult/child €15/free, admission free last Sun of month, audioguide €7; ⊙ 9am-6pm, last entry 4pm Mon-Sat, 9am-2pm, last entry 12.30pm last Sun of month; **M** Ottaviano-San Pietro) Boasting one of the world's great art collections, the Vatican Museums are housed in the Palazzo Apostolico Vaticano, a vast 5.5-hectare complex, which consists of two large palaces and three internal courtyards.

Home to some spectacular classical statuary, the **Museo Pio-Clementino** is one of the museums' must-sees. Highlights include the *Apollo belvedere* and the 1st-century *Laocoön*, both in the Cortile Ottagono. Further on, the 175m-long **Galleria delle Carte Geografiche** (Map Gallery) is hung with 40 huge topographical maps. Beyond that are the magnificent **Stanze di Raffaello** (Raphael Rooms), which were once Pope Julius II's private apartments and are decorated with frescos by Raphael.

CASTEL SANT'ANGELO — Castle

(Map p400; Lungotevere Castello 50; adult/ EU child €8.50/free; ⊙ 9am-8pm Tue-Sun; ☐ Piazza Pia) An instantly recognisable landmark, the chunky, round-keeped Castel Sant'Angelo was commissioned

Central Rome

by Emperor Hadrian in 123 BC as a mausoleum for himself and his family. In the 6th century, it was converted into a papal fortress, and it's now a museum with an assorted collection of sculptures, paintings, weapons and furniture. The terrace offers fine views.

Rome in Two Days

Get to grips with ancient Rome at the **Colosseum**, the **Roman Forum** and **Palatino (Palatine Hill)**. Spend the afternoon exploring the **Musei Capitolini** before an evening in **Trastevere**. On day two, hit the Vatican. Marvel at **St Peter's Basilica** and the **Sistine Chapel** in the vast **Vatican Museums**. Afterwards, ditch your guidebook and get happily lost in the animated streets around **Piazza Navona** and the **Pantheon**.

With a couple of extra days, you could add in visits to the **Museo e Galleria Borghese** and venture out to **Via Appia Antica** and the catacombs. Alternatively, you could take a day trip to the ancient port of **Ostia Antica**, or visit Emperor Hadrian's summer country retreat, **Villa Adriana**.

Historic Centre

FREE **PANTHEON**　Monument
(Map p400; Piazza della Rotonda; audioguide €5; ⏱8.30am-7.30pm Mon-Sat, 9am-6pm Sun, 9am-1pm holidays; 🚌Largo di Torre Argentina) A striking 2000-year-old temple, now church, the Pantheon is the best preserved of ancient Rome's great monuments. In its current form it dates to around AD 120 when the Emperor Hadrian built over Marcus Agrippa's original 27 BC temple (Agrippa's name remains inscribed on the pediment). The dome, considered the Romans' most important architectural achievement, was the largest in the world until the 15th century and is still the largest unreinforced concrete dome ever built. Inside, you'll find the tomb of Raphael, alongside those of kings Vittorio Emanuele II and Umberto I.

PIAZZA NAVONA　Square
(Map p400; 🚌Corso del Rinascimento) With its ornate fountains, baroque *palazzi,* pavement cafes and colourful cast of street artists, hawkers and pigeons, Piazza Navona is central Rome's most celebrated square. Built over the ruins of the 1st-century Stadio di Domiziano, it was paved over in the 15th century and for almost 300 years served as the city's main market. Of the piazza's three fountains, the grand centrepiece is Bernini's 1651 **Fontana dei Quattro Fiumi (Fountain of the Four Rivers)**, a monumental affair depicting the rivers Nile, Ganges, Danube and Plate.

TREVI FOUNTAIN　Fountain
(Map p400; 🅼Barberini) Immortalised by Anita Ekberg's sensual dip in Fellini's *La dolce vita,* the Fontana di Trevi is Rome's largest and most famous fountain. The flamboyant baroque ensemble was designed by Nicola Salvi in 1732 and depicts Neptune's chariot being led by Tritons, with sea horses representing the moods of the sea. The water comes from the *aqua virgo,* a 1st-century-BC underground aqueduct, and the name 'Trevi' refers to the *tre vie* (three roads) that converge at the fountain. The custom is to throw a coin into the fountain, thus ensuring your return to Rome. On average about €3000 is chucked away every day.

GALLERIA NAZIONALE D'ARTE ANTICA
　Art Gallery
(Map p400; www.galleriaborghese.it; Via Quattro Fontane 13; adult/EU child €5/free; ⏱9am-7.30pm Tue-Sun; 🅼Barberini) A must for anyone into Renaissance and baroque art, this sumptuous gallery is housed in Palazzo Barberini, one of Rome's most spectacular *palazzi*. Inside, you'll find works by Raphael, Caravaggio, Guido Reni, Bernini, Filippo Lippi and Holbein, as well as Pietro da Cortona's breathtaking *Trionfo della Divina Provvidenza* (Triumph of Divine Providence) in the main salon.

SPANISH STEPS　Monument
(Map p400; Piazza di Spagna; 🅼Spagna) Rising above **Piazza di Spagna**, the Spanish Steps, aka the Scalinata della Trinità dei

Monti, have been a magnet for foreigners since the 18th century. The piazza was named after the Spanish embassy to the Holy See, although the staircase, which was built with French money in 1725, leads to the French church, **Chiesa della Trinità dei Monti**.

PIAZZA DEL POPOLO   Square

(Map p400; M Flaminio) This elegant landmark square was laid out in 1538 at the point of convergence of three roads – Via di Ripetta, Via del Corso and Via del Babuino – at what was then Rome's northern entrance. In the centre, the 36m-high **obelisk** was brought by Augustus from Heliopolis in ancient Egypt. Rising above the piazza, **Pincio Hill** affords great views.

On the piazza's northern flank, the **Chiesa di Santa Maria del Popolo** (⊙7am-noon & 4-7pm Mon-Sat, 8am-1.30pm & 4.30-7.30pm Sun) is one of Rome's earliest and richest Renaissance churches. Inside, the star attractions on display, and not to be missed, are the two magnificent Caravaggio paintings: the *Conversione di San Paolo* (Conversion of St Paul) and the *Crocifissione di San Pietro* (Crucifixion of St Peter).

Papal Audiences

At 11am on Wednesday, the Pope addresses his flock at the Vatican (in July and August in Castel Gandolfo near Rome). For free tickets, download the request form from the Vatican website (www.vatican.va) and fax it to the **Prefettura della Casa Pontificia** (fax 06 698 85 863). Pick them up at the office through the bronze doors under the colonnade to the right of St Peter's.

When he is in Rome, the Pope blesses the crowd in St Peter's Sq on Sunday at noon. No tickets are required.

MUSEO DELL'ARA PACIS AUGUSTAE
Museum

(Map p400; www.arapacis.it; Lungotevere in Augusta; adult/child €6.50/free; ⊙9am-7pm Tue-Sun; M Flaminio) The first modern construction in Rome's historic centre, Richard Meier's controversial white pavilion houses the Ara Pacis Augustae (Altar of Peace), one of the most important works of ancient Roman sculpture. The vast marble altar (it measures 11.6m by 10.6m by 3.6m) was completed in 13 BC as a monument to the peace that Augustus established both at home and abroad.

Villa Borghese

Just north of the historic centre, Villa Borghese is Rome's best-known park, a good spot for a picnic and a breath of fresh air.

MUSEO E GALLERIA BORGHESE
Museum, Art Gallery

(Map p394; ☎06 3 28 10; www.galleriaborghese. it; Piazzale del Museo Borghese; adult/EU child €8.50/2; ⊙8.30am-7.30pm Tue-Sun; ☐ Via Pinciana) If you have time, or inclination, for only one art gallery in Rome, make it this one. Housing the 'queen of all private art collections', it boasts paintings by Caravaggio, Botticelli and Raphael, as well as some spectacular sculptures by Gian Lorenzo Bernini.

MUSEO NAZIONALE ETRUSCO DI VILLA GIULIA
Museum

(Map p394; Piazzale di Villa Giulia; adult/EU child €4/free; ⊙8.30am-7.30pm Tue-Sun; ☐ Viale delle Belle Arti) Italy's finest collection of Etruscan treasures is beautifully housed in the 16th-century Villa Giulia. Many of the exhibits come from Etruscan burial tombs in northern Lazio, with standouts including a polychrome terracotta statue of *Apollo* and the 6th-century-BC *Sarcofago degli Sposi* (Sarcophagus of the Betrothed).

Galleria Nazionale d'Arte Moderna
Museum

(Map p394; www.gnam.beniculturali.it; Viale delle Belle Arti 131; adult/EU child €8/free; ⊙8.30am-7.30pm Tue-Sun; ☐ Viale delle Belle Arti) In this vast belle époque palace, you'll find works by some of the most important expo-

Don't Miss **Sistine Chapel**

This is the one place in the Vatican Museums that not one of the 4.5 million annual visitors wants to miss. Home to two of the world's most famous works of art, the 15th-century **Sistine Chapel** (Cappella Sistina; Map p394) is where the papal conclave is locked to elect the Pope. It was originally built in 1484 for Pope Sixtus IV, after whom it is named, but it was Pope Julius II who commissioned Michelangelo to decorate it in 1508. Over the next four years, the artist painted the remarkable *Genesis* (Creation; 1508–12) on the barrel-vaulted ceiling. Twenty-two years later he returned at the behest of Pope Clement VII to paint the *Giudizio universale* (Last Judgement; 1534–41) on the end wall.

The other walls of the chapel were painted by artists including Botticelli, Ghirlandaio, Pinturicchio and Signorelli.

nents of modern art, including Canova, Modigliani, De Chirico, Klimt, Pollock and Henry Moore.

Trastevere

Trastevere is one of central Rome's most vivacious neighbourhoods, a tightly packed warren of ochre *palazzi,* ivy-clad facades and photogenic lanes, ideal for aimless wandering. Taking its name from the Latin *trans Tiberium,* meaning over the Tiber, it was originally a working-class district but has since been gentrified and is today a trendy hang-out full of bars, trattorias and restaurants.

BASILICA DI SANTA MARIA IN TRASTEVERE   Church
(Piazza Santa Maria in Trastevere; Map p400; ⊙7.30am-8pm; 🚊 Viale di Trastevere) Nestled in a quiet corner of Piazza Santa Maria in Trastevere, Trastevere's picturesque focal square, this exquisite basilica is believed to be the oldest Roman church dedicated to the Virgin Mary. The original church dates to the 4th century, but a 12th-century makeover saw the addition of a Romanesque bell tower and frescoed facade. Inside it's the glittering 12th-century mosaics that are the main drawcard.

WILL SALTER/LONELY PLANET IMAGES ©

Don't Miss Museo Nazionale Romano

Spread over four sites, the **Museo Nazionale Romano** (National Roman Museum; Map p400) houses one of the world's most important collection of classical art and statuary. A combined ticket including each of the sites costs adult/EU child €7/free and is valid for three days.

Palazzo Massimo alle Terme   Museum
(Largo di Villa Peretti 1; ⏱9am-7.45pm Tue-Sun; M Termini) A fabulous museum with amazing frescos and wall paintings.

Terme di Diocleziano   Museum
(Via Enrico de Nicola 79; ⏱9am-7.45pm Tue-Sun; M Termini) Housed in the Terme di Diocleziano (Diocletian's Baths), ancient Rome's largest baths complex.

Palazzo Altemps   Museum
(Piazza Sant'Apollinare 44; ⏱9am-7.45pm Tue-Sun; 🚌Corso del Rinascimento) Boasts the best of the museum's classical sculpture, including the famous Ludovisi collection.

Crypta Balbi   Museum
(Via delle Botteghe Oscure 31; ⏱9am-7.45pm Tue-Sun; Largo di Torre Argentina) Set atop an ancient Roman theatre, the Teatro di Balbus (13 BC).

San Giovanni & Celio

BASILICA DI SAN GIOVANNI IN LATERANO   Church
(Map p394; Piazza di San Giovanni in Laterano 4; ⏱7am-6.30pm; M San Giovanni) For a thousand years, this huge white basilica was the most important church in Christen-dom. Consecrated in 324, it was the first Christian basilica to be built in Rome and, until the late 14th century, functioned as the pope's principal residence.

Nowadays it's Rome's official cathedral, as well as the pope's seat as Bishop of Rome.

Queue Jumping at the Vatican Museums

Here's how to jump the ticket queue – although we can't help with lines for the security checks.

◉ Book tickets at http://biglietteriamusei.vatican.va/musei/tickets (plus booking fee of €4). You can also book authorised guided tours (adult/concession €31/25).

◉ Time your visit: Wednesday mornings are a good bet, as everyone is at the Pope's weekly audience at St Peter's; lunchtime is better than the morning; avoid Mondays, when many other museums are shut.

TERME DI CARACALLA   Ruins
(Map p394; Via delle Terme di Caracalla 52; adult/EU child €6/free; ☾9am-1hr before sunset Tue-Sun, to 2pm Mon; Ⓜ Circo Massimo) The vast ruins of the Terme di Caracalla are an awe-inspiring sight. Begun by Caracalla and inaugurated in 217, the 10-hectare leisure complex could hold up to 1600 people and included richly decorated pools, gymnasiums, libraries, shops and gardens. The ruins are now used to stage summer opera.

Via Appia Antica

The *regina viarum* (queen of roads), Via Appia Antica (Appian Way) is one of the world's oldest roads. Named after Appius Claudius Caecus, who laid the first 90km section in 312 BC, it was extended in 190 BC to reach Brindisi some 540km away on the Adriatic coast. The road, which is flanked by exclusive residential villas, is rich in ruins and history – this is where Spartacus and 6000 of his slave rebels were crucified in 71 BC, and it's here that you'll find Rome's most celebrated catacombs.

To get to Via Appia Antica, take Metro Line A to Colli Albani, then bus 660, or alternatively bus 118, from the Piramide metro station. It's traffic-free on Sunday if you want to walk or cycle it. For information, bike hire or to join a guided tour, head to the **Appia Antica Regional Park Information Point** (☎06 513 53 16; www.parcoappiaantica.org; Via Appia Antica 58-60; ☾9.30am-1.30pm & 2-5.30pm; ☐ Via Appia Antica).

CATACOMBS OF SAN CALLISTO   Catacombs
(www.catacombe.roma.it; Via Appia Antica 110; adult/child €8/free; ☾9am-noon & 2-5pm Thu-Tue, closed Feb; ☐ Via Appia Antica) These are Rome's largest, most famous and busiest catacombs. Dating to the end of the 2nd century, they once formed part of a tunnel complex extending for some 20km. Excavations have so far unearthed the tombs of 16 popes and thousands of early Christians.

CATACOMBS OF SAN SEBASTIANO   Catacombs
(www.catacombe.org; Via Appia Antica 136; adult/concession €8/5; ☾9am-noon & 2-5pm Mon-Sat, closed mid-Nov–mid-Dec; ☐ Via Appia Antica) Extending beneath the Basilica di San Sebastiano, these catacombs provided a safe haven for the remains of St Peter and St Paul during the reign of Vespasian. Frescos, stucco work and mausoleums can be seen on the second level.

 Festivals & Events

Settimana della Cultura   Culture Week
(March/May) Public museums and galleries open free of charge during culture week.

Natale di Roma   Historic Festivities
(21 April) Rome celebrates its birthday with music, historical recreations, fireworks and free entry to many museums.

Estate Romana   Cultural Festival
(June to September) Rome's big cultural festival hosts events ranging from book fairs to raves

and gay parties – see www.estateromana. comune.roma.it for details.

Festa dei Santi Pietro e Paolo Religious Celebration
(29 June) Romans celebrate their patron saints Peter and Paul around St Peter's Basilica and Via Ostiense.

Festa di Noantri Neighbourhood Party
(last two weeks in July) Trastevere's annual party involves plenty of food, wine, prayer and dancing.

Festival Internazionale del Film di Roma Film Festival
(late October) Held at the Auditorium Parco della Musica, Rome's film festival rolls out the red carpet for big-screen big shots – see www. romacinemafest.it.

Sleeping

While there's plenty of choice, accommodation in Rome tends to be expensive. If you can afford it, the best place to stay is in the *centro storico*, but if you're on a tight budget you'll probably end up in the Termini area, where most of the hostels and cheap *pensioni* (guest houses) are located.

Always try to book ahead, even if it's just for the first night.

Ancient Rome

NICOLAS INN B&B €€
(Map p400; ☎06 976 18 483; www.nicolasinn. com; Via Cavour 295; d €100-180; ❄ 🖾) Visitors love this bright B&B at the bottom of Via Cavour, a stone's throw from the Imperial Forums. Run by a welcoming couple, it has four big guestrooms, each with homely furnishings, colourful pictures and en suite bathrooms.

The Vatican

HOTEL BRAMANTE Hotel €€€
(Map p394; ☎06 688 06 426; www.hotel bramante.com; Via delle Palline 24; s €100-160, d €140-230; ❄ 🖾) Housed in a Renaissance *palazzo* in the shadow of the Vatican walls, the charming Hotel Bramante is a model of classical elegance and style.

Antique furniture, wood-beamed ceilings, marble bathrooms and fresh flowers all combine to create an lovely, inviting small-inn feel.

Historic Centre

DAPHNE INN Boutique Hotel €€
(Map p400; ☎06 874 50 086; www. daphne-rome.com; Via di San Basilio 55 & Via degli Avignonesi 20; s €110-160, d €90-200, ste €320-550; ❄ @ 🖾) Daphne is a gem. Spread over two sites near Piazza Barberini, it offers value for money, exceptional service and chic rooms. These come in various shapes and sizes but the overall look is minimalist modern with cooling earth tones and linear, unfussy furniture.

HOTEL PANDA Hotel €
(Map p400; ☎06 678 01 79; www.hotelpanda. it; Via della Croce 35; s €65-80, d €85-110, tr €120-140, ❄ 🖾) A superb position near the Spanish Steps, attractive high-ceilinged rooms, and honest rates ensure a year-round stream of travellers to this budget classic. Air-con costs €6 and you can get breakfast at a nearby bar for €5. Cheaper rooms with shared bathrooms are available.

RELAIS PALAZZO TAVERNA Boutique Hotel €€
(Map p400; ☎06 203 98 064; www.relaispalazzo taverna.com; Via dei Gabrielli 92; s €70-140, d €100-180; ❄ 🖾) This cracking boutique hotel is superbly located in the heart of the historic centre. Its 11 individually decorated rooms sport a contemporary look with grey parquet floors, hand-printed wallpaper and funky, floral motifs.

HOTEL RAPHAËL Luxury Hotel €€€
(Map p400; ☎06 68 28 31; www.raphaelhotel. com; Largo Febo 2; s €160-300, d €220-350; ❄ @) An ivy-clad landmark just off Piazza Navona, the Raphaël is a Roman institution. With its gallery lobby (look out for the Picasso ceramics and Miro lithographs) sleek Richard Meier–designed rooms and panoramic rooftop restaurant, it knows how to lay out the red carpet. Breakfast costs extra.

Trastevere

ARCO DEL LAURO
B&B €€

(Map p400; ☎06 978 40 350; www.arcodel
lauro.it; Via Arco de' Tolomei 27-29; d €85-145,
q €130-180; ❄@ ⎙) This friendly B&B
is in a medieval *palazzo* in Trastevere's
quieter eastern half. The five decent-
sized double rooms, all on the ground
floor, sport an understated modern look
with white walls, parquet and modern
furnishings, while the one quad retains a
high, wood-beamed ceiling. Reception is
open until 3pm, after which you'll need
to phone.

VILLA DELLA FONTE
Hotel €€

(Map p400; ☎06 580 37 97; www.villafonte.com;
Via della Fonte dell'Olio 8; s €90-130, d €130-190;
❄⎙) Near Piazza Santa Maria in Trastevere, this charming little hotel is housed in
an ivy-clad 17th-century *palazzo*. Its five
rooms are small but tastefully decorated
with white walls, earth-coloured floors
and modern en suite bathrooms.

Termini & Esquilino

58 LE REAL B&B
B&B €€

(Map p400; ☎06 482 35 66; www.lerealdeluxe.
com; Via Cavour 58; r €70-155; ❄⎙) This
swish nine-room B&B is on the 4th floor
of a town house on busy Via Cavour.
Rooms are small but stylish with leather
armchairs, plasma TVs, Murano chandeliers, polished-wood bedsteads and
parquet floors.

WELROME
Pension €

(Map p400; ☎06 478 24 343; www.welrome.it;
Via Calatafimi 15-19; s €50-100, d €60-110; ⎙)
This is a lovely, low-key hotel not far from
Termini. Owner Mary takes great pride in
looking after her guests, and her seven
rooms provide welcome respite from
Rome's relentless streets. Breakfast costs
extra, but there are kettles and fridges for
guest use.

Eating

Eating out is one of the great joys of visiting Rome and everywhere you go you'll
find trattorias, pizzerias and restaurants.
The focus is very much on traditional
Italian cooking, and the vast majority of
places, particularly the smaller family-
run trattorias, keep to tried-and-tested
Roman dishes.

Inside the Pantheon (p403)

ROME **EATING**

Roman specialities include *trippa alla romana* (tripe with potatoes, tomato and pecorino cheese), *fiori di zucca* (fried courgette flowers) and *carciofi alla romana* (artichokes with garlic, mint and parsley). Of the pastas, *cacio e pepe* (with pecorino cheese, black pepper and olive oil) and *all'amatriciana* (with tomato, pancetta and chilli) are Roman favourites.

The Vatican

DINO E TONY
Trattoria €€

(Map p394; 📞06 3973 3284; Via Leone IV 60; mains €12; 🕐Mon-Sat) Something of a rarity, Dino e Tony is an authentic trattoria in the Vatican area. Kick off with the monumental antipasto, a minor meal in its own right, before plunging into its signature dish, *rigatoni all'amatriciana*.

Historic Centre

PIZZERIA DA BAFFETTO
Pizza €

(Map p400; Via del Governo Vecchio 114; pizzas €6-9; 🕐6.30pm-midnight) For the full-on Roman pizza experience get down to this local institution. Meals here are raucous, chaotic and fast, but the thin-crust pizzas are good and the vibe is fun. To partake,

join the queue and wait to be squeezed in wherever there's room. There's also a **Baffetto 2** (Map p400; Piazza del Teatro di Pompeo 18; 🕐6.30pm-12.30am Mon-Fri, 12.30-3.30pm & 6.30pm-12.30am Sat & Sun) near Campo de' Fiori.

MACCHERONI
Trattoria €€

(Map p400; 📞06 6830 7895; Piazza delle Coppelle 44; mains €13; 🕐Mon-Sat) With its classic vintage interior, attractive setting near the Pantheon and traditional menu, this is the archetypal *centro storico* trattoria. Locals and tourists flock here to dine on Roman stalwarts such as *tonnarelli al cacio e pepe* (pasta with cheese and pepper) and *carciofo alla romana* (Roman style artichoke).

DITIRAMBO
Trattoria €€

(Map p400; 📞06 687 16 26; Piazza della Cancelleria 72; mains €16; 🕐closed Mon lunch; 🖋) This hugely popular new-wave trattoria near Campo de' Fiori offers a laid-back, unpretentious atmosphere and innovative, organic cooking. Vegetarians are well catered for, as are seafood fans, with dishes such as turbot roulade with aubergine and mint. Book ahead.

VINERIA ROSCIOLI

Delicatessen, Restaurant €€€

(Map p400; ☎ 06 687 52 87; Via dei Giubbonari 21; mains €20; ⏱ Mon-Sat) This deli-cum-restaurant is a foodie paradise. Under the brick arches, you'll find a mouth-watering array of olive oils, conserves, cheeses and hams, while out back the chic restaurant serves sophisticated Italian dishes.

Trastevere

OSTERIA DA LUCIA

Trattoria €€

(Map p401; ☎ 06 580 36 01; Vicolo del Mattinato 2; mains €12.50; ⏱ Tue-Sun) Hidden away on an atmospheric cobbled backstreet, da Lucia is a terrific neighbourhood trattoria. It's a wonderful place to get your teeth into some authentic Roman soul food, such as *spaghetti alla gricia* (with pancetta and cheese) and tiramisu.

LE MANI IN PASTA

Restaurant €€€

(Map p400; ☎ 06 581 60 17; Via dei Genovesi 37; mains €18; ⏱ Tue-Sun) This rustic Trastevere restaurant has an open kitchen that serves up delicious fresh pasta dishes, grilled meats and fresh seafood. It's a well-known spot, so try to book ahead for dinner.

Testaccio

VOLPETTI PIÙ

Tavola Calda €

(Map p394; Via Volta 8; mains €6; ⏱ Mon-Sat) Next to the ravishing deli of the same name, this upmarket canteen is one of the few places in town where you can sit down and eat well for less than €15. Grab a tray and choose from the sumptuous spread of pizza, pasta, soup, meat, vegetables and fried nibbles.

Termini & Esquilino

POMMIDORO

Trattoria €€

(Map p394; ☎ 06 445 26 92; Piazza dei Sanniti 44; mains €12; ⏱ Mon-Sat) A long-standing favourite in the San Lorenzo area east of Termini, Pommidoro continues to win diners over with its no-fuss traditional food. Celebs sometimes drop by – Nicole Kidman and Fabio Capello have both dined here – but it remains an unpretentious spot with a laid-back vibe and excellent food.

TRAM TRAM

Trattoria €€

(Map p394; ☎ 06 49 04 16; Via dei Reti 44; mains €16; ⏱ Tue-Sun) Dressed up to look like an old-fashioned trattoria, and named after the trams that rattle past outside, this is a trendy San Lorenzo eatery. It offers traditional dishes with a focus on seafood and rustic southern Italian cuisine. There's also an excellent local wine list.

Drinking

Drinking in Rome is all about looking the part and enjoying the atmosphere. There are hundreds of bars and cafes across the city, ranging from neighbourhood hangouts to elegant streetside cafes, dressy lounge bars and Irish-theme pubs.

Castel Sant'Angelo (p401)

PHOTOGRAPHER: DAVID TOMLINSON/LONELY PLANET IMAGES ©

Much of the action is in the *centro storico*. Campo de' Fiori is popular with young drinkers and can get very rowdy. For a more upmarket scene check out the bars in the lanes around Piazza Navona.

SALOTTO 42   Bar

(Map p400; www.salotto42.it; Piazza di Pietra; ◷10am-2am Tue-Sat, to midnight Sun) Run by a Swedish model and her Italian partner, this hip, glamorous lounge bar sports soft sofas, coffee-table books and an excellent *aperitivo* spread. Brunch is also served at weekends.

CAFFÈ SANT'EUSTACHIO   Cafe

(Map p400; Piazza Sant'Eustachio 82; ◷8.30am-1am) This small unassuming place, generally three-deep at the bar, boasts Rome's best coffee.

LA TAZZA D'ORO   Cafe

(Map p400; Via degli Orfani 84-86; ◷Mon-Sat) A busy, stand-up bar that serves a superb espresso and a range of delicious coffee concoctions, such as *granita di caffè*, a crushed-ice coffee with a big dollop of cream, and *parfait di caffè*, a €3 coffee mousse.

Outside Caffè della Pace

VINERIA REGGIO   Wine Bar

(Map p400; Campo de' Fiori 15; ◷8.30am-2am Mon-Sat) The coolest of the Campo de' Fiori bars, this is a good spot to watch the nightly *campo* circus. It has a small, bottle-lined interior and several outside tables.

CAFFÈ DELLA PACE   Cafe

(Map p400; Via della Pace 3-7; ◷8.30am-3am Tue-Sun, 5pm-3am Mon) The archetypal dolce vita bar. With its art nouveau interior, ivy-clad facade and well-dressed customers, it's the very epitome of Italian style.

Entertainment

Rome has a thriving cultural scene, with a year-round calendar of concerts, performances and festivals.

Listings guides include *Roma C'è* (www.romace.it, in Italian; €1) and *Trova Roma,* a free insert that comes with a copy of *La Repubblica* newspaper every Thursday. Both publications are available at newsstands. Up-coming events are also listed on www.turismoroma.it and www.inromenow.com.

MARTIN MOOS/LONELY PLANET IMAGES ©

Two good ticket agencies are **Orbis** (📞06 482 74 03; Piazza dell'Esquilino 37; ⏰9.30am-1pm & 4-7.30pm Mon-Fri, 9.30am-1pm Sat), which accepts cash payment only, and the online agency **Hello** (📞800 90 70 80; www.helloticket.it, in Italian).

Classical Music & Opera

Rome's cultural hub and premier concert complex is the **Auditorium Parco della Musica** (📞06 8024 1281; www.auditorium.com; Viale Pietro de Coubertin 34). With its three concert halls and 3000-seat open-air arena, it stages everything from classical-music concerts to tango exhibitions, book readings and film screenings. The auditorium is also home to Rome's top orchestra, the world-class **Orchestra dell'Accademia Nazionale di Santa Cecilia** (📞box office 06 808 20 58; www.santacecilia.it).

The **Accademia Filarmonica Romana** (📞06 320 17 52; www.filarmonicaromana.org) organises classical- and chamber-music concerts, as well as opera, ballet and multimedia events at the **Teatro Olimpico** (📞06 326 59 91; www.teatroolimpico.it; Piazza Gentile da Fabriano 17).

Rome's opera season runs from December to June. The main venue is the **Teatro dell'Opera** (Map p400; 📞box office 06 481 60 255; www.operaroma.it; Piazza Beniamino Gigli 7), which also houses the city's ballet company. Ticket prices tend to be steep. In summer, opera is performed outdoors at the spectacular Terme di Caracalla.

Shopping

With everything from designer flag-ship stores to antique emporiums, flea markets and bohemian boutiques, shopping is fun in Rome. For the big-gun designer names head to Via dei Condotti and the area between Piazza di Spagna and Via del Corso. Moving down a euro or two, Via Nazionale, Via del Corso, Via dei Giubbonari and Via Cola di Rienzo are good for midrange clothing stores. For something more left field, try the small fashion boutiques and vintage clothes shops on Via del Governo Vecchio and around Campo de' Fiori. If you're looking

---

Gelato Galore

To get the best out of Rome's *gelaterie* (ice-cream shops) look for the words *'produzione proprio'*, meaning 'own production'. Here is a choice of the city's finest:

San Crispino (Map p400; Via della Panetteria 42) Near the Trevi Fountain, it serves natural, seasonal flavours – think crema with honey – in tubs only.

Old Bridge (Map p394; Via Bastioni di Michelangelo 5) Just right for a pick-me-up after the Vatican Museums.

Tre Scalini (Map p400; Piazza Navona 30) A Piazza Navona spot famous for *tartufo nero*, a €10 ball of chocolate ice cream filled with chunks of choc and served with cream.

Gelateria Giolitti (Map p400; Via degli Uffici del Vicario 40) Rome's most famous gelateria, near the Pantheon.

---

for high-quality (read expensive) antiques or gifts, head to Via dei Coronari and Via Margutta. Rome's markets are a great place for bargain hunting. The most famous, **Porta Portese** (Map p394; Piazza Porta Portese; ⏰6am-2pm Sun) is held every Sunday morning near Trastevere, and sells everything from antiques to clothes, bikes, bags and furniture. Near Porta San Giovanni, the **Via Sannio market** (Map p394; Via Sannio; ⏰9am-1.30pm Mon-Sat) sells new and secondhand clothes.

ℹ️ Information

Emergency

Police station (Questura; 📞06 4 68 61; Via San Vitale 15)

Money

ATMs are liberally scattered around the city.

American Express (📞06 6 76 41; Piazza di Spagna 38; ⏰9am-5.30pm Mon-Fri, 9am-12.30pm Sat) Has an ATM and offers exchange facilities and travel services.

Tourist Information

Centro Servizi Pellegrini e Turisti (☏06 698 81 662; St Peter's Sq; ⏱8.30am-6.15pm Mon-Sat) The Vatican's official tourist office.

Enjoy Rome (☏06 445 18 43; www.enjoyrome. com; Via Marghera 8a; ⏱8.30am-7pm Mon-Fri, to 2pm Sat) A private tourist office that arranges tours, airport transfers and hotel reservations.

I Fori di Roma Centro Espositivo Informativo (Via dei Fori Imperiali; ⏱9.30am-6.30pm) An information centre dedicated to the Forums.

🛈 Getting There & Away

Air

Rome's main international airport **Leonardo da Vinci** (FCO; ☏06 6 59 51; www.adr.it), better known as Fiumicino, is on the coast 30km west of the city. The much smaller **Ciampino airport** (CIA; ☏06 6 59 51; www.adr.it), 15km southeast of the city centre, is the hub for low-cost carriers including **Ryanair** (www.ryanair.com) and **easyJet** (www.easyjet.com).

Left-luggage (International Arrivals, Terminal 3; per 24hr €6; ⏱6.30am-11.30pm) is available at Fiumicino.

Boat

Rome's port is at Civitavecchia, about 80km north of Rome. Regular ferries run to Sardinia, Sicily and other points around the Mediterranean.

Half-hourly trains depart from Roma Termini to Civitavecchia (€4.50 to €12.50, one hour). On arrival, it's about 700 to the port (to your right) as you exit the station.

Bus

Long-distance national and international buses use the **Autostazione Tiburtina** (Piazzale Tiburtina) in front of Stazione Tiburtina.

Car & Motorcycle

Driving into central Rome is a challenge, involving traffic restrictions, one-way systems, a shortage of street parking, and aggressive drivers.

Rome is circled by the Grande Raccordo Anulare (GRA), to which all autostradas

Left: Stage at Teatro Olimpico (p413);
Below: St Peter's Square (p401), The Vatican

PHOTOGRAPHER: (LEFT) RUSSELL MOUNTFORD/LONELY PLANET IMAGES ©;
(BELOW) JOHN HAY/LONELY PLANET IMAGES ©

(motorways) connect, including the main A1 north–south artery (the Autostrada del Sole), and the A12, which connects Rome to Civitavecchia and Fiumicino airport.

CAR HIRE Rental cars are available at the airport and Stazione Termini:

Avis (☏ 06 481 43 73; www.avis.com)

Europcar (☏ 06 488 28 54; www.europ car.com)

Hertz (☏ 06 474 03 89; www.hertz.com)

Maggiore National (☏ 06 488 00 49; www. maggiore.com).

Train

Almost all trains arrive at and depart from Stazione Termini. Train information is available from the **Sala Viaggiatori** (⊙6am-midnight) next to platform 1, online at www. ferroviedellostato.it or, if you speak Italian, by calling ☏ 89 20 21. **Left luggage (1st 5hr €4, 6-12hr per hr €0.60, 13hr & over per hr €0.20;** ⊙**6am-11.50pm)** is on the lower-ground floor under platform 24.

ⓘ Getting Around

To/From the Airport

FIUMICINO The easiest way to get to/from the airport is by train but there are also bus services.

FR1 train (one-way €8) Connects the airport to Trastevere, Ostiense and Tiburtina stations. Departures from the airport every 15 minutes (hourly on Sunday and public holidays) between 5.57am and 11.27pm, from Tiburtina between 5.05am and 10.33pm.

Leonardo Express train (adult/child €14/free) Runs to/from platforms 27 and 28 at Stazione Termini. Departures from Termini every 30 minutes between 5.52am and 10.52pm, from the airport between 6.36am and 11.36pm. Journey time is 30 minutes.

Taxi The set fare to/from the city centre is €40, which is valid for up to four passengers with luggage.

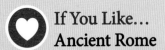

If You Like…
Ancient Rome

If the magnificent ruins of **Rome** (p390) and **Pompeii** (p468) have fired your passion for the ancient world, here are a few more sites to discover:

1 OSTIA ANTICA

(adult/concession €6.50/3.25; ⏱8.30am-7pm Tue-Sun Apr-Oct, 8.30am-6pm Mar, 8.30am-5pm Nov, Dec, Jan & Feb) Rome's **ancient port** is well worth a day trip. The ruins of restaurants, laundries, shops, houses and meeting places give a good impression of what life must once have been like in the 100,000-strong town. The Ostia Lido train (25 minutes, half-hourly) runs to Ostia Antica from Stazione Porta San Paolo.

2 VILLA ADRIANA

(adult/EU child €6.50/free, plus possible €3.50 for exhibition; ⏱9am-1hr before sunset) Emperor Hadrian's sprawling **summer residence** was one of the most sumptuous villas in the Roman Empire, and even in its ruined state, it's still mightily impressive. It's around 35km east of Rome, near the handsome Renaissance town of Tivoli.

3 ETRUSCAN TOMBS, TARQUINIA

(Via Ripagretta; admission €6, incl Museo Nazionale Tarquiniense €8; ⏱8.30am-30min before sunset Tue-Sun) Ninety kilometres northwest of Rome, Tarquinia was a centre for the Etruscan empire, and its 7th-century **necropolis** boasts Italy's most important painted tombs. Around 6000 have been discovered, although only 19 are currently open to the public. Regular trains run to Tarquinia from Rome.

CIAMPINO The best option is to take one of the regular bus services into the city centre.

Cotral bus (www.cotralspa.it; one-way/return €3.90/6.90) Runs frequent services to/from Ciampino train station (€1.20), where you can connect with trains to Stazione Termini (€1.30) or Anagnina metro station (€1.20).

SIT bus (www.sitbusshuttle.com; one-way/return €6/8) Regular departures from Via Marsala outside Stazione Termini between 4.30am and 9.30pm, from the airport between 7.45am and 11.15pm. Tickets available on the bus. Journey time is 45 minutes.

Taxi The set rate to/from the airport is €30.

Terravision bus (www.terravision.eu; one-way/return €4/8) Twice-hourly departures to/from Via Marsala outside Stazione Termini. From the airport, services are between 8.15am and 12.15pm, from Via Marsala between 4.30am and 9.20pm. Buy tickets at Terracafè in front of the Via Marsala bus stop. Journey time is 40 minutes.

Public Transport

Rome's public transport system includes buses, trams, metro and a suburban train network.

TICKETS Valid for all forms of transport and come in various forms:

Single (BIT; €1) Valid for 75 minutes, during which time you can use as many buses or trams as you like but only go once on the metro.

Daily (BIG; €4) Unlimited travel until midnight of the day of purchase.

Three-day (BTI; €11) Unlimited travel for three days.

Weekly (CIS; €16) Unlimited travel for seven days.

Buy tickets at *tabacchi,* newsstands and from vending machines at main bus stops and metro stations. They must be purchased before you start your journey and validated in the yellow machines on buses, at the entrance gates to the metro or at train stations.

BUSES Buses and trams are run by ATAC (☎06 57 003; www.atac.roma.it). Buses generally run from about 5.30am until midnight, with limited services throughout the night.

METRO There are two metro lines, A and B, which both pass through Termini. Take line A for the Trevi Fountain (Barberini), Spanish Steps (Spagna) and Vatican (Ottaviano-San Pietro); and line B for the Colosseum (Colosseo) and Circus Maximus (Circo Massimo). Trains run between 5.30am and 11.30pm (to 1.30am on Friday and Saturday).

Taxi

Official licensed taxis are white with the symbol of Rome on the doors. Always go with the metered fare, never an arranged price (the set fares to and from the airports are exceptions).

You can hail a taxi, but it's often easier to wait at a rank or phone for one.

La Capitale ( 06 49 94)

Pronto Taxi (06 66 45)

Radio Taxi (06 35 70)

Samarcanda (06 55 51)

Tevere (06 41 57)

NORTHERN ITALY

Italy's well-heeled north is a fascinating area of historical wealth and broad natural diversity. Bordered by the northern Alps and boasting some of the country's most spectacular coastline, it also encompasses Italy's largest lowland area, the decidedly nonpicturesque Po Valley plain.

Of the cities it's Venice that hogs the limelight, but in their own way Turin, Genoa and Bologna offer plenty to the open-minded traveller.

Cinque Terre

Liguria's eastern Riviera boasts some of Italy's most dramatic coastline, the highlight of which is the Unesco-listed **Parco Nazionale delle Cinque Terre** (Cinque Terre National Park) just north of La Spezia. Stretching for 18km, this awesome stretch of plunging cliffs and vine-covered hills is named after its five tiny villages – Riomaggiore, Manarola, Corniglia, Vernazza and Monterosso.

It gets very crowded in summer, so try to visit in spring or autumn. You can either visit on a day trip from Genoa or La Spezia, or stay overnight in one of the five villages.

Sights & Activities

The Cinque Terre villages are linked by the 9km **Blue Trail** (Sentiero Azzurro; admission with Cinque Terre Card), a magnificent, mildly challenging five-hour trail. The walk is in four stages. The first two stages – from Riomaggiore to Manarola (Via d'Amore, 20 minutes) and from Manarola to Corniglia (one hour) – are the easiest. For the final two stages – from Corniglia to Venazza (1½ hours) and Vernazza to Monterosso (two hours) – you'll need to be fit and wearing proper walking shoes. Make sure you bring a hat, sunscreen and plenty of water if walking in hot weather.

The Blue Trail is just one of a network of footpaths and cycle trails that crisscross the park; details are available from the park offices. If water sports are more your thing, you can hire snorkelling gear (€10 per day) and kayaks (single/double €5/10 per hour) at the **Diving Center 5 Terre** (www.5terrediving.com; Via San Giacomo) in Riomaggiore. It also offers a snorkelling boat tour for €18.

Riomaggiore village, Cinque Terre
PHOTOGRAPHER: WITOLD SKRYPCZAK/LONELY PLANET IMAGES ©

Sleeping & Eating

L'EREMO SUL MARE
B&B €

(☎ 346 019 58 80; www.eremosulmare.com; Sentiero Azzurro, Vernazza; r €80-110; ❄) This romantic cliffside B&B (its name means Hermitage by the Sea) is beautifully situated on the Blue Trail about 500m uphill from Vernazza train station. It has three rooms, a panoramic sun terrace and a kitchen for guests' use. Cash only.

HOTEL CA' D'ANDREAN
Hotel €

(☎ 0187 92 00 40; www.cadandrean.it; Via Doscovolo 101, Manarola; s €55-72, d €70-100; ❄) An excellent family-run hotel in the upper part of Manarola. Rooms are big and cool with tiled floors and unobtrusive furniture, and some also have private terraces. Breakfast, which is served in the garden, costs €6. No credit cards.

MARINA PICCOLA
Seafood €€

(☎ 0187 92 01 03; www.hotelmarinapiccola. com; Via Birolli 120, Manarola; mains €12) Dine on fresh-off-the-boat seafood overlooking the small bay at Manarola. The harbourside setting is ideal for *zuppa di pesce* (fish soup) or seafood risotto. The adjoining hotel has small but comfortable air-conditioned rooms (single/double €87/115).

TRATTORIA LA LANTERNA
Seafood €€

(☎ 0187 92 05 89; Via San Giacomo 46, Riomaggiore; mains €16) This busy restaurant is perched above the snug harbour in Riomaggiore. Tables are on a small terrace or in a bright, breezy dining room and the menu features seafood pastas and simple fish dishes.

ⓘ Information

The park's main information office (☎ 0187 92 06 33; ⏱ 8am-9.30pm) is to the right as you exit the train station at Riomaggiore. There are other offices in the train stations at Manarola, Corniglia, Vernazza, Monterosso and La Spezia (most open from 8am to 8pm).

Online information is available at www. parconazionale5terre.it and www.cinqueterre.com.

ⓘ Getting There & Away

Boat

Between July and September, Golfo Paradiso (☎ 0185 77 20 91; www.golfoparadiso.it) operates

Piazza Castello and the Palazzo Reale, Turin

DENNIS JOHNSON/LONELY PLANET IMAGES ©

boat excursions from Genoa's Porto Antico to Vernazza, Monterosso and Riomaggiore. These cost €18 one-way, €33 return.

From late March to October, **Consorzio Marittimo Turistico 5 Terre** (☎0187 73 29 87; www.navigazionegolfodeipoeti.it) runs daily ferries between La Spezia and four of the villages (not Corniglia), costing €16 one-way including all the stops.

Train

Regional trains run from Genoa Brignole to Riomaggiore (€4.80, 1½ to two hours, 20 daily), stopping at each of the Cinque Terre villages.

Between 4.30am and 11.10pm, one to three trains an hour crawl up the coast from La Spezia to Levanto (€3.30, 30 minutes), stopping at all of the villages en route. If you're doing this journey and you want to walk the Blue Trail, you'll save money buying the Cinque Terre Treno Card.

Turin

POP 908,825

First-time visitors are often surprised by Turin (Torino). Expecting a bleak, industrial sprawl dominated by Fiat factories, they are instead confronted with a dynamic and attractive city full of royal *palazzi*, historic cafes, baroque piazzas and world-class museums.

 Sights

Serious sightseers should consider the **Torino & Piedmont Card** (48hr card adult/child €20/10), available at tourist offices, which gives free public transport (not the metro) and discounts or entry to 170 museums, monuments and castles.

PIAZZA CASTELLO　　　　　Square

Turin's grandest square is bordered by porticoed promenades and regal palaces. Dominating the piazza, **Palazzo Madama** (www.palazzomadamatorino.it) was the original seat of the Italian parliament. It is now home to the **Museo Civico d'Arte Antica** (Piazza Castello; adult/child €7.50/free; ☺10am-6pm Tue-Sat, to 8pm Sun), whose impressive collection includes Gothic and early Renaissance paintings and some interesting majolica work. To the north, statues

---

Cinque Terre Card

To walk the Blue Trail (Sentiero Azzurro) coastal path you'll need a Cinque Terre Card. This comes in three forms:

● **Cinque Terre Card** (adult/child 1 day €5/2.50, 2 days €8/4) Available at all park offices.

● **Cinque Terre Treno Card** (adult/child 1 day €8.50/4.30, 2 days €14.70/7.40) Covers the Blue Trail plus unlimited train travel between Levanto and La Spezia, including all five villages.

● **Cinque Terre Card Batello** (adult/child 1 day €19.50/9.80) The Blue Trail and unlimited boat travel within the Area Marina Protetta 5 Terre.

---

of Castor and Pollux guard the entrance to the enormous and lavishly decorated **Palazzo Reale** (Royal Palace; Piazza Castello; adult/child €6.50/free; ☺8.30am-7.30pm Tue-Sun), built for Carlo Emanuele II in the mid-17th century. The palace's **Giardino Reale** (Royal Garden; admission free; ☺9am-1hr before sunset) was designed in 1697 by Louis le Nôtre, noted for his work at Versailles.

A short walk away, **Piazza San Carlo**, known as Turin's drawing room, is famous for its cafes and twin baroque churches **San Carlo** and **Santa Cristina**.

CATTEDRALE DI SAN GIOVANNI BATTISTA　　　　　Church

(Piazza San Giovanni; ☺8am-noon & 3-7pm Mon-Sat, from 7am Sun) Turin's 15th-century cathedral houses the famous Shroud of Turin (*Sindone*), supposedly the cloth used to wrap the crucified Christ. A copy is on permanent display in front of the altar, while the real thing is kept in a vacuum-sealed box and rarely revealed.

MOLE ANTONELLIANA　　　　　Museum

(Via Montebello 20) Turin's famous landmark towers 167m over the city skyline. Originally intended as a synagogue, the Mole now houses the enormously enjoyable

Museo Nazionale del Cinema (www.museo cinema.it; adult/child €7/2; ⏱ 9am-8pm Tue-Fri & Sun, to 11pm Sat) and its comprehensive collection of cinematic memorabilia. Don't miss the glass **panoramic lift** (adult/child €5/3.50; ⏱ 10am-8pm Tue-Fri & Sun, to 11pm Sat), which whisks you up 85m in 59 seconds. Joint tickets for the museum and lift cost €9/4.50.

Museo Egizio Museum
(www.museoegizio.it; Via Accademia delle Scienze 6; adult/child €7.50/free; ⏱ 8.30am-7.30pm Tue-Sun) This fabulous museum houses an engrossing collection of ancient Egyptian art that is considered the world's most important outside Cairo and London.

 Sleeping

ART HOTEL BOSTON
Boutique Hotel €€€
(☎ 011 50 03 59; www.hotelbostontorino.it; Via Massena 70; s €80-150, d €110-190, ste €250-500; ❄ @ 🛜) The Boston's austere facade gives no clues as to its chic modern interior. The public spaces are littered with impressive works of contemporary art, while many of the 86 individually decorated rooms are themed on such subjects as Lavazza coffee, Ayrton Senna and Pablo Picasso.

Alpi Resort Hotel Business Hotel €
(☎ 011 812 96 77; www.hotelalpiresort.it; Via A Bonafous 5; s €54-65, d €69-85; P ❄) A business-like three-star place in an excellent location just off Piazza Vittorio Veneto. Its impeccably clean carpeted rooms are quiet and comfortable, if rather characterless.

 Eating & Drinking

DA CIRO Pizza €
(☎ 011 53 19 25; Corso Vinzaglio 17; pizzas from €5.50; ⏱ closed Sat lunch & Sun) A favourite of Juventus footballers – ex-Juve legend Ciro Ferrara is a part-owner – this is a little bit of Naples in the north. Diners pile into the cheery, unpretentious interior to tear into delicious wood-fired pizzas. Booking recommended.

OTTO ETRE QUARTI
Pizza, Restaurant €€
(☎ 011 517 63 67; Piazza Solferino 8c; pizzas from €5, mains €12) Claim a table in one of 8¾'s high-ceilinged dining rooms or on the square-side terrace and feast on fab pizzas or tasty pastas such as *paccheri con tonno* (big pasta tubes with tuna).

ℹ **Information**

The city's efficient **tourist office** (☎ 010 53 51 81; www.turismotorino.org; ⏱ 9am-7pm daily) has branches at Porta Nuova station, Piazza Castello and Via Giuseppe Verdi near the Mole Antonelliana.

ℹ **Getting There & Around**

In Caselle, which lies 16km northwest of the city centre, **Turin airport** (TRN; ☎ 011 567 63 61; www.turin-airport.com) serves flights to/from European and national destinations. **Sadem** (☎ 800 801 600; www.sadem.it, in Italian) runs an airport shuttle (€5.50 or €6 on board, 40 minutes, half-hourly) between the airport and Porta Nuova train station. A taxi costs approximately €35 to €40.

Direct trains connect Turin with Milan (€14.50, two hours, up to 30 daily), Florence (€67, three hours, five daily), Genoa (€15, two hours, up to 20 daily) and Rome (€93, 4¼hr, seven daily).

Milan

POP 1.29 MILLION

Few Italian cities polarise opinion like Milan, Italy's financial and fashion capital. Some people love the cosmopolitan, can-do atmosphere, the vibrant cultural scene and sophisticated shopping; others grumble that it's dirty, ugly and expensive. Certainly, it lacks the picture-postcard beauty of many Italian towns, but in among the urban hustle are some truly great sights: Leonardo da Vinci's *Last Supper,* the immense Duomo, the world-famous La Scala opera house.

 Sights

Milan's main attractions are concentrated in the area between Piazza del Duomo and Castello Sforzesco.

Central Milan

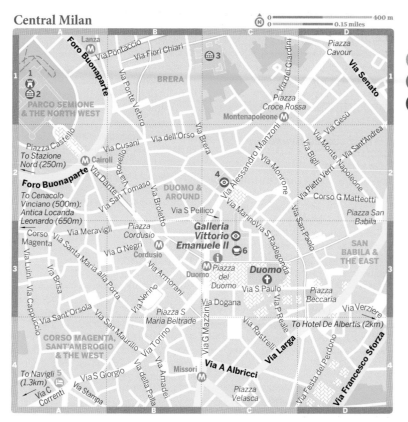

DUOMO
Church

(Piazza del Duomo; admission free; ⏰7am-7pm)
With a capacity of 40,000 people, this is the world's largest Gothic cathedral. It's also the third-largest church in Europe. Commissioned in 1386 to a florid French-Gothic design and finished nearly 600 years later, it's a fairy-tale ensemble of 3400 statues, 135 spires and 155 gargoyles.

Climb up to the **roof** (stairs/elevator €5/8; ⏰stairs 9am-5.20pm, lift 9am-9.15pm) for memorable city views.

GALLERIA VITTORIO EMANUELE II
Shopping Arcade

(Piazza del Duomo) This elegant iron-and-glass shopping arcade opens off the northern flank of Piazza del Duomo. Local tradition claims you can ward off bad luck

by grinding your heel into the balls of the mosaic bull on the floor near the central cross.

TEATRO ALLA SCALA   Opera House

(www.teatroallascala.org; Piazza della Scala; admission €5; ⏰9am-12.30pm & 1.30-5.30pm) Milan's legendary opera house hides its sumptuous six-tiered interior behind a surprisingly severe facade. You can peek inside as part of a visit to the theatre's museum providing there are no performances or rehearsals in progress.

THE LAST SUPPER (CENACOLO VINCIANO)   Painting

(☎02 9280 0360; www.vivaticket.it; Piazza Santa Maria delle Grazie 2; adult/EU child €6.50/ free plus booking fee of €1.50; ⏰8.15am-6.45pm Tue-Sun) Milan's most famous tourist attraction – Leonardo da Vinci's mural of *The Last Supper* – is in the Cenacolo Vinciano, the refectory of the Chiesa di Santa Maria delle Grazie, west of the city centre. To see it you need to book ahead or take a city tour.

FREE CASTELLO SFORZESCO   Castle

(www.milanocastello.it; Piazza Castello 3; ⏰7am-7pm) This dramatic 15th-century castle was the Renaissance residence of the Sforza dynasty. It now houses the **Musei del Castello** (adult/child €3/free; ⏰9am-5.30pm Tue-Sun), a group of museums dedicated to art, sculpture, furniture, archaeology and music. Entry is free on Friday between 2pm and 5.30pm and from Tuesday to Sunday between 4.30pm and 5.30pm.

Pinacoteca di Brera   Art Gallery

(www.brera.beniculturali.it; Via Brera 28; adult/ EU child €11/free; ⏰8.30am-7.15pm Tue-Sun) Art amassed by Napoleon forms the basis for the Pinacoteca's heavyweight collection, which includes Andrea Mantegna's masterpiece, the *Dead Christ,* and Raphael's *Betrothal of the Virgin*.

 ## Tours

Autostradale (www.autostradale.it) runs three-hour multilingual bus tours that take in the major sights and include entry to *The Last Supper*. Departures are at 9.30am from Piazza del Duomo every day except Monday. There are also two daily walking tours (€20) between Monday and Saturday, departing from the tourist office on Piazza del Duomo at 10am and 11.30am. Tickets for both tours are available from the tourist office at Piazza del Duomo.

Sleeping

Milan is a business city, which means hotels are expensive and it can be hard to find a room, particularly when trade fairs are on (which is often). Booking is essential at all times.

ANTICA LOCANDA LEONARDO   Hotel €€

(☎02 4801 4197; antica locandaleonardo.com; Corso Magenta 78; s €69-105,

Galleria Vittorio Emanuele II arcade (p421)

d €99-230; ❄ 📶) A charming little hotel with characterful rooms and a gregarious, hospitable owner. Housed in a 19th-century *palazzo* near the Cenacolo Vinciano, it's decorated in classic style with polished wood furniture, parquet floors, rugs and pot plants.

ARISTON HOTEL Hotel €€€
(☎ 02 7200 0556; www.aristonhotel.com; Largo Carrobbio 2; s €65-380, d €80-380; P ❄ @ 📶) Claiming to be Milan's first 'ecological hotel', the centrally located Ariston offers smart modern rooms and environmentally friendly touches such as organic breakfasts, all-natural soaps and free bike hire. Check the website for excellent low-season deals.

 Eating & Drinking

Local specialities include *risotto alla milanese* (saffron-infused risotto cooked in bone-marrow stock) and *cotoletta alla milanese* (breaded veal cutlet).

PIZZERIA PICCOLA ISCHIA Pizza €
(☎ 02 204 76 13; Via Morgani 7; pizzas €6.50; ⏱ closed Wed & lunch Sat & Sun) You might be in the heart of Milan, but this bustling, boisterous pizzeria is pure Naples. Everything from the wonderful wood-fired pizza to the fried antipasti and exuberant decor screams of the sunny south. It's hugely popular, so expect queues. Also does takeaway.

EL BRELLIN Restaurant €€€
(☎ 02 5810 1351; Via Alzaia Naviglio Grande 14; mains €20, set menus €35-40; ⏱ lunch daily, Mon-Sat dinner) Atmosphere-laden El Brellin is set in an 18th-century Navigli laundry. Its candlelit garden is a great place to linger over classic Milanese food while watching the evening canalside parade. *Aperitivi* (€8) are served in the bar between 7pm and 9pm.

Zucca in Galleria Cafe €
(Galleria Vittorio Emanuele II 21) Grab a coffee (but skip the overpriced food) at the cafe where Giuseppe Verdi used to drink after performances at the Teatro all Scala.

 Entertainment

Milan offers a rich and vibrant cultural scene, ranging from opera at La Scala to world-class football and cutting-edge club nights. September is a good time for classical-music fans, as the city co-hosts the **Torino Milano Festival Internazionale della Musica** (www.mitosettembremusica.it).

 Information

Police station (Questura; ☎ 02 6 22 61; Via Fatebenefratelli 11)

Tourist offices Piazza del Duomo (☎ 02 7740 4343; www.visitamilano.it; Piazza Duomo 19a; ⏱ 8.45am-1pm & 2-6pm Mon-Sat, 9am-1pm & 2-5pm Sun); Stazione Centrale (☎ 02 7740 4318; opposite platform 13; ⏱ 9am-6pm Mon-Sat, 9am-1pm & 2-5pm Sun) Pick up the free guides *Hello Milano* and *Milanomese*.

 Getting There & Away

Air

Most international flights fly into Malpensa airport (MXP; ☎ 02 23 23 23; www.sea-aeroporti milano.it), about 50km northwest of Milan. Domestic and some European flights use Linate airport (LIN; ☎ 02 23 23 23; www.sea-aeroporti milano.it), about 7km east of the city. Low-cost airlines often use Orio al Serio airport (BGY; ☎ 035 32 63 23; www.sacbo.it), near Bergamo.

Train

Regular daily trains depart Stazione Centrale for Venice (€30.15, 2½ hours), Bologna (€41, one hour), Florence (€52, 1¾ hours), Rome (€89, 3½ hours) and other Italian and European cities. Most regional trains stop at Stazione Nord in Piazzale Cadorna. Note that these prices are for the fast Eurostar Alta Velocità services.

 Getting Around

To/From the Airport

MALPENSA Malpensa Shuttle (www.malpensa shuttle.it; adult/concession €7.50/3.75) Buses run to/from Piazza Luigi di Savoia next to Stazione Centrale every 20 minutes between

4.15am and 12.30pm. Buy tickets at Stazione Centrale or the airport. Journey time is 50 minutes.

Malpensa Express (www.malpensaexpress.it; adult/concession €11/5.50) Trains from Cadorna underground station half-hourly between 5.57am and 11pm, and then a bus at 11.27pm. Journey time is approximately 35 minutes.

LINATE Starfly (www.starfly.net; tickets €4) Buses to/from Piazza Luigi di Savoia half-hourly between 5.40am and 9.30pm. Journey time is 30 minutes.

ORIO AL SERIO Autostradale (www.autostradale. it; adult/concession €8.90/4.45) Half-hourly buses to/from Piazza Luigi di Savoia between 4am and 11.30pm. Journey time is one hour.

Bus & Metro

Milan's excellent public transport system is run by ATM (www.atm-mi.it). Tickets (€1) are valid for one underground ride or up to 75 minutes' travel on city buses and trams. You can buy them at metro stations, *tabacchi* and newsstands.

Venice

POP 270,100

Venice (Venezia) is a hauntingly beautiful city. At every turn you're assailed by un-forgettable images – tiny bridges crossing limpid canals, delivery barges jostling chintzy gondolas, excited tourists posing for photographs under flocks of pigeons. To gain an understanding of its rich and melancholic culture you really need to walk its hidden back lanes. Parts of the Cannaregio, Dorsoduro and Castello *sestieri* (districts) rarely see many tourists, and you can lose yourself for hours in the streets between the Accademia and the train station. Stroll late at night to feel an eerie atmosphere, redolent of dark passions and dangerous secrets.

Despite its romantic reputation, the reality of modern Venice is a city besieged by rising tides and up to 20 million visitors a year.

History

First ruled by the Byzantines from Ravenna, it wasn't until 726 that the Venetians elected their first *doge* (duke).

Over successive centuries, the Venetian Republic grew into a great merchant power, dominating half the Mediterranean, the Adriatic and the trade routes to the Levant – it was from Venice that Marco Polo set out for China in 1271. Decline began in the 16th century and in 1797 the city authorities opened the gates to Napoleon, who, in turn, handed the city over to the Austrians. In 1866, Venice was incorporated into the Kingdom of Italy.

Orientation

Everybody gets lost in Venice. With 117 islands, 150-odd canals and 400 bridges (only four of which – the Rialto, the Accademia and, at the train station, the Scalzi and the Calatrava – cross the Grand Canal) it's impossible not to.

It gets worse: Venetian addresses are almost meaningless to all but local posties. Instead of a street and civic number, local addresses often consist of no more than the *sestiere* (Venice is divided into six districts: Cannaregio, Castello, San Marco, Dorsoduro, San Polo and Santa Croce) followed by a long number.

 Sights

A good way to whet your sightseeing appetite is to take vaporetto (small passenger ferry) No 1 along the **Grand Canal**, which is lined with rococo, Gothic, Moorish and Renaissance palaces. Alight at Piazza San Marco, Venice's most famous sight.

PIAZZA SAN MARCO   Square
Piazza San Marco beautifully encapsulates the splendour of Venice's past. Flanked by the arcaded **Procuratie Vecchie** and **Procuratie Nuove**, it's filled for much of the day with tourists, pigeons and policemen. While you're taking it all in, you might see the bronze *mori* (Moors) strike the bell of the 15th-century **Torre dell'Orologio** (clock tower).

But it's to the remarkable **Basilica di San Marco** (www.basilicasanmarco.it; Piazza San Marco; admission free; ⏱9.45am-5pm Mon-Sat & 2-5pm Sun Easter-Oct, 9.45am-5pm Mon-Sat & 2-4pm Sun Nov-Easter) that all eyes

KRZYSZTOF DYDYNSKI/LONELY PLANET IMAGES ©

are drawn. Sporting spangled spires, Byzantine domes, luminous mosaics and lavish marble work, it was originally built to house the remains of St Mark. The original chapel was destroyed by fire in 932 and a new basilica was consecrated in its place in 1094. For the next 500 years it was a work in progress as successive *doges* added mosaics and embellishments looted from the East. Behind the main altar is the **Pala d'Oro** (admission €2.50; ⏱9.45am-5pm Mon-Sat & 2-5pm Sun Easter-Oct, 9.45am-4pm Mon-Sat & 2-4pm Sun Nov-Easter), a stunning gold altarpiece decorated with priceless jewels.

The basilica's 99m freestanding **campanile** (bell tower; adult/child €8/4; ⏱9am-7pm Easter-Jun & Oct, to 9pm Jul-Sep, 9.30am-3.45pm Nov-Easter) dates from the 10th century, although it suddenly collapsed on 14 July 1902 and had to be rebuilt.

PALAZZO DUCALE Palace

(Piazzetta di San Marco; admission with Museum Pass or San Marco Museum Plus Ticket; ⏱9am-7pm Apr-Oct, to 6pm Nov-Mar) The official residence of the *doges* from the 9th century and the seat of the republic's government, Palazzo Ducale also housed Venice's prisons. On the 2nd floor, the massive **Sala del Maggiore Consiglio** is dominated by Tintoretto's *Paradiso* (Paradise), one of the world's largest oil paintings, which measures 22m by 7m.

The **Ponte dei Sospiri** (Bridge of Sighs) connects the palace to an additional wing of the city dungeons. It's named after the sighs that prisoners – including Giacomo Casanova – emitted en route from court to cell.

GALLERIE DELL'ACCADEMIA Art Gallery

(www.gallerieaccademia.org; Dorsoduro 1050; adult/EU child €6.50/free; ⏱8.15am-2pm Mon, to 7.15pm Tue-Sun) One of Venice's top galleries, the Galleria dell'Accademia traces the development of Venetian art from the 14th to the 18th century. You'll find works by Bellini, Titian, Carpaccio, Tintoretto, Giorgione and Veronese.

COLLEZIONE PEGGY GUGGENHEIM
Art Gallery

(www.guggenheim-venice.it; Palazzo Venier dei Leoni, Dorsoduro 701; adult/child €12/free; ⏱10am-6pm Wed-Mon) For something more contemporary, visit the Peggy Guggenheim Collection. Housed in the American heiress's former home, the spellbinding collection runs the gamut of modern art

Venice

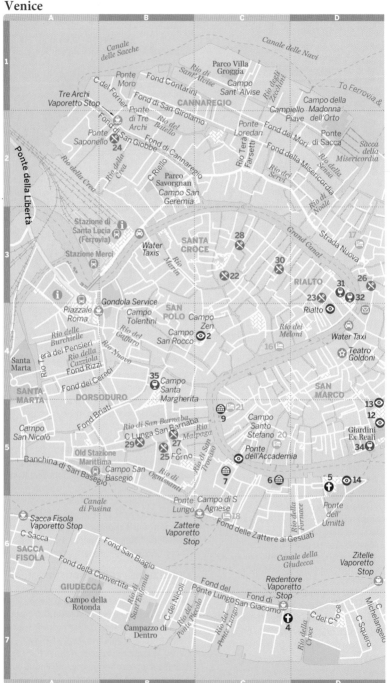

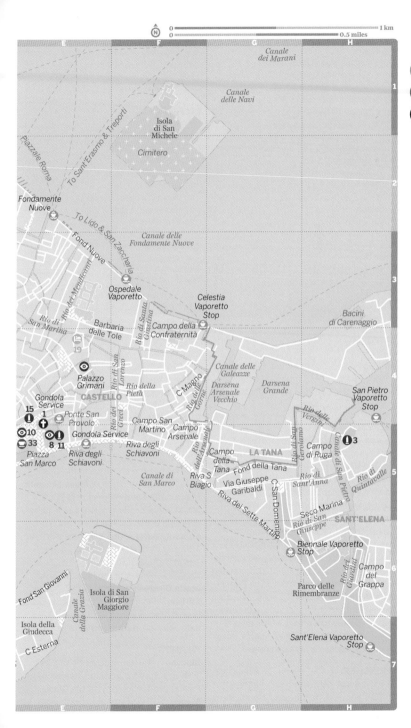

Canale
dei Marani

Canale
delle Navi

Isola
di San
Michele

Cimitero

Piazzale Roma

To Sant'Erasmo & Treporti

Fondamente
Nuove

Fond Nuove

To Lido & San Zaccharia

Canale delle
Fondamente Nuove

Rio dei Mendicanti

Ospedale
Vaporetto

Celestia
Vaporetto
Stop

Bacini
di Carenaggio

Rio di
San Marina

Barbaria
delle Tole

Rio di Santa Ginestra

Campo della
Confraternita

19

Rio di San Lorenzo

Canale delle
Galeazze

Palazzo
Grimani

CASTELLO

Rio della
Pietà

C Magno

Rio delle Gorne

Darsena
Arsenale
Vecchio

Darsena
Grande

San Pietro
Vaporetto
Stop

Gondola
Service

15
1

Ponte San
Provolo

Campo San
Martino

Campo
Arsenale

Rio dell'Arsenale

Rio delle
Vergini

Rio di Gerolamo

Campo
di Ruga

Canale di San Pietro

3

10
33

8 11

Gondola Service

Riva degli
Schiavoni

Riva degli
Schiavoni

Campo
della
Tana

LA TANA

Fond della Tana

Rio di San Pietro

Rio di
Quintavalle

Piazza
San Marco

Riva degli
Schiavoni

Riva S
Biagio

Via Giuseppe
Garibaldi

C San Domenico

Rio di
Sant'Anna

SANT'ELENA

Canale di
San Marco

Riva dei Sette Martiri

Rio di San
Giuseppe

Seco Marina

Fond San Giovanni

Canale della Grazia

Isola di San
Giorgio
Maggiore

Biennale Vaporetto
Stop

Rio del Giardino

Campo
del
Grappa

Parco delle
Rimembranze

Isola della
Giudecca

C Esterna

Sant'Elena Vaporetto
Stop

427

Venice

with works by, among others, Picasso, Pollock, Braque, Duchamp and Brancusi. In the sculpture garden you'll find the graves of Peggy and her dogs.

PALAZZO GRASSI   Art Gallery
(www.palazzograssi.it; Campo San Samuele 3231; admission price varies with exhibitions; ⊙10am-7pm Wed-Mon) In 2005, French businessman and art collector François Pinault purchased one of the Grand Canal's most impressive buildings, the 18th-century Palazzo Grassi, and commissioned Japanese architect Tadeo Ando to renovate the building. Since opening, it has hosted a series of impressive temporary exhibitions. In 2009 the museum opened a companion exhibition space in Dorsoduro, the **Punta della Dogana** (www.palazzograssi.it; Campo San Samuele 3231; admission price varies with exhibitions; ⊙10am-7pm Wed-Mon), where pieces from Pinault's extensive and eclectic collection of modern art are on show.

CHURCHES   Churches
As in much of Italy, Venice's churches harbour innumerable treasures; unusu-ally, though, you have to pay to get into many of them.

The **Chiesa del Santissimo Redentore** (Church of the Redeemer; Campo del SS Redentore 194; admission €3, included in Chorus Pass; ⊙10am-5pm Mon-Sat) was built by Palladio to commemorate the end of the Great Plague in 1577.

Guarding the entrance to the Grand Canal, the 17th-century **Chiesa di Santa Maria della Salute** (Campo della Salute 1/b; sacristy €2; ⊙9am-noon & 3.30-5.30pm) contains works by Tintoretto and Titian, arguably the greatest of Venice's artists. Titian's celebrated masterpiece, the *Assunta* (Assumption; 1518), hangs above the high altar in the **Basilica di Santa Maria Gloriosa dei Frari** (Campo dei Frari, San Polo 3004; admission €3, included in Chorus Pass; ⊙10am-6pm Mon-Sat, 1-6pm Sun), the same church in which he's buried.

ISLANDS   Islands
Murano is the home of Venetian glass. Tour a factory for a behind-the-scenes look at production or visit the **Glass Museum** (Fondamenta Giustinian 8; adult/

EU concession €6.50/3; ⊙10am-5pm Thu-Tue Nov-Mar, 10am-6pm Apr-Oct); you'll find it near the Museo vaporetto stop. **Burano**, with its cheery pastel-coloured houses, is renowned for its lace. **Torcello**, the republic's original island settlement, was largely abandoned due to malaria and now counts no more than 80 residents. Its not-to-be-missed Byzantine cathedral, **Santa Maria Assunta** (Piazza Torcello; adult/child €5/free; ⊙10.30am-6pm Mar-Oct, 10am-5pm Nov-Feb), is Venice's oldest.

Vaporetti 41 and 42 service Murano from the San Zaccaria vaporetto stop. Vaporetto LN services Murano and Burano from the vaporetto stop at Fondamente Nove in the northeast of the city. Vaporetto T connects Burano and Torcello.

Activities

Be prepared to pay through the nose for that most quintessential of Venetian experiences, a **gondola ride**. Official rates per gondola (maximum six people) start at €80 (€100 at night) for a short trip including the Rialto but not the Grand Canal, and €120 (€150 at night) for a 50-minute trip including the Grand Canal. Haggling is unlikely to get you a reduction.

If you're a solo traveller in Venice, the cheapest way for you to enjoy a gondola ride is to book in for the two-hour 'Ice-cream & Gondola' tour (€40) offered by **Turismo Ricettivo Veneziano** (www.turive. it). This includes a guided walking tour (conducted in English), a gelato and a 40-minute gondola ride. It leaves from the San Marco tourist office every day at 3pm. The same company offers a 2½hr 'Walking Venice' tour (€35), leaving from the tourist office every day at 9.10am. Both tours run between 1 April and 31 October only.

 Festivals & Events

Carnevale Religious Celebration
The major event of the year, when some Venetians and loads of tourists don Venetian-made masks and costumes for a week-long party in the lead-up to Ash Wednesday. It's been going since 1268.

Admission Discounts

The **Rolling Venice Card** (www.hellovenezia.com; €4) is for visitors aged 14 to 29 years; it offers discounts on food, accommodation, shopping, transport and museums. You can get it at tourist offices, and at HelloVenezia booths throughout the city. You'll need ID.

The **Venice Card Orange** (www.hellovenezia.com; under 30yr 3/7 days €66/87, 30yr & over €73/96) entitles holders to free entry to 12 city museums (including Palazzo Ducale), free entry to the 16 Chorus churches, unlimited use of ACTV public transport, limited use of public toilets, and reduced admissions to various museums and events. It doesn't always represent a saving, so check before buying. It's sold at tourist and HelloVenezia offices.

To visit the museums on Piazza San Marco you'll need to buy either a **Museum Pass** (www.museicivicivenezia ni.it; adult/EU senior & EU student under 25yr/child under 6yr €18/12/free), which gives entry to the museums on Piazza San Marco and eight other civic museums; or a **San Marco Museum Plus Ticket** (adult/EU senior & EU student under 25yr/child under 6yr €13/7.50/free), which gives entry to the San Marco museums and your choice of one other civic museum. Both are available at participating museums.

Regata Storica
Gondola Races

Costumed parades precede gondola races on the Grand Canal; held on the first Sunday in September.

Venice International Film Festival
Film Festival

(Mostra del Cinema di Venezia) Italy's top film fest is held in late August and September at the Lido's Palazzo del Cinema.

 ## Sleeping

Venice is Italy's most expensive city. It's always advisable to book ahead, especially at weekends, in May and September, and during Carnevale and other holidays.

San Marco

PALAZZINA GRASSI
Boutique Hotel €€€

(✆ 041 528 46 44; www.palazzinagrassi.com; San Marco 3247; rooms from €260; ❄ 🐾) Phillipe Stark has endowed this formidably fashionable hotel with his signature style, and we're pleased to report that his design lives up to the magnificent Grand Canal location. The hotel's Krug champagne bar is the ultimate in exclusiveness.

NOVECENTO
Boutique Hotel €€€

(✆ 041 241 37 65; www.novecento.biz; Celle del Dose, Campo San Maurizio 2683; r €150-300; ❄ @ 🐾) The decor here is redolent of the exotic East, and the garden is a gorgeous spot for a leisurely breakfast. The hotel sometimes hosts art exhibitions, meaning that you may well bump into artists and local connoisseurs in the enticing communal lounge.

Dorsoduro

LA CALCINA
Hotel €€

(✆ 041 520 64 66; www.lacalcina.com; Fondamenta Zattere ai Gesuati 780; s €90-140, d €110-310; ❄) A charming place with 29 rooms and a small garden, La Calcina offers immaculate and elegant rooms with parquet floors and timber furnishings. In summer, breakfast is served on a terrace overlooking the Guidecca Canal.

Left: Masked costume wearers at the Venice Carnevale (p429);
Below: Interior of Chiesa di Santa Maria della Salute (p429)

PHOTOGRAPHER: (LEFT) RUTH EASTHAM & MAX PAOLI/LONELY PLANET IMAGES ©;
(BELOW) RUSSELL MOUNTFORD/LONELY PLANET IMAGES ©

San Polo & Santa Croce

CA' ANGELI Boutique Hotel €€
(☎041 523 24 80; www.caangeli.it; Calle del Tragheto della Madoneta, San Polo 1434; s €85-150, d €105-215, ste €195-315; ✱) Overlooking the Grand Canal, Ca' Angeli is notable for its extremely comfortable rooms, helpful staff and truly magnificent breakfast spread. If you can afford it, opt for a suite overlooking the Grand Canal.

Cannaregio

HOTEL BERNARDI Hotel €
(☎041 522 72 57; www.hotelbernardi.com; SS Apostoli Calle dell'Oca 4366; s without bathroom €25-32, d without bathroom €45-62, s €48-72, d €52-85; ✱@) Comfortable rooms (opt for No 25 or 26), hospitable owners and keen prices mean that this top choice is always heavily booked. A recently opened annexe just around the corner (doubles €57 to €90, family rooms €75 to €130) offers large rooms with modern bathrooms, free wi-fi and disabled access.

Castello

LOCANDA CA' DEL CONSOLE B&B €€
(☎041 523 31 64; www.locandacadelconsole.com; Castello 6217; s €90-110, d €120-180; ✱@🛜) This former residence of a 19th-century Austrian consul is now an elegant, family-run hotel offering rooms decorated with rugs, richly coloured fabrics and period furniture.

 Eating

Venetian specialities include *risi e bisi* (pea soup thickened with rice) and *sarde di saor* (fried sardines marinated in vinegar and onions).

Dorsoduro

RISTORANTE LA BITTA Restaurant €€
(☎041 523 05 31; Calle Lunga San Barnaba 2753a; mains €18-24; ☽closed Sun) The bottle-lined dining room and attractive

431

internal courtyard are a lovely setting in which to enjoy your choice from a small, meat-dominated menu that changes with the season. No credit cards.

GROM
Gelateria €

(Campo San Barnaba 2761; ice creams from €2.20) Ah, Grom. How do we love thee? Let us count the ways: Colombian extra-dark chocolate, Bronte pistachio, marrons glacé, ricotta & fig... There's another outlet on the Strada Nuova in Cannaregio that opens only between April and September.

Enoteca Ai Artisti
Wine Bar €€

(☎ 041 523 89 44; www.enotecaartisti.com; Fondamenta della Toletta 1169a; mains €15; ⊙closed Sun) This tiny place takes its wine seriously (there's a great choice by the glass) and serves delicious cheeses, bruschetta (toast with toppings) and bowls of pasta.

San Polo & Santa Croce
VECIO FRITOLIN
Restaurant €€€

(☎ 041 522 28 81; www.veciofritolin.it; Calle della Regina, Santa Croce 2262; mains €25; ⊙dinner Tue, lunch & dinner Wed-Mon) Traditionally, a *fritolin* was an eatery where diners sat at a common table and tucked into fried seafood and polenta. This is the modern equivalent, only the food is sophisticated, the menu is varied and the decor is stylish rather than rustic. The owners also run a cafe in the Palazzo Grassi.

OSTERIA LA ZUCCA
Wine Bar, Restaurant €€

(www.lazucca.it; Calle del Tentor, Santa Croce 1762; mains €10; ⊙closed Sun; ⚡) An unpretentious little restaurant in an out-of-the-way spot, 'the Pumpkin' serves a range of innovative Mediterranean dishes prepared with fresh, seasonal ingredients. Most are small and perfect to share; many are vegetarian.

All'Arco
Wine Bar €

(Calle dell'Arco, San Polo 436; chiceti €1.50-4; ⊙7.30am-8pm Mon-Sat) Popular with locals, this tiny *osteria* serves delicious bruschetta and a range of good-quality wine by the glass.

Ae Oche
Pizza €

(www.aeoche.com; Calle del Tentor, Santa Croce 1552a/b; pizzas €4-9.50) Students adore the Tex-Mex decor and huge pizza list at this bustling place. It's on the main path between the *ferrovia* and San Marco.

Cannaregio
DA MARISA
Trattoria €€

(☎ 041 72 02 11; Fondamenta di San Giobbe 652b; lunch incl wine & coffee €15, dinner incl wine & coffee €35-40; ⊙lunch daily, dinner Tue & Thu-Sat) You can watch the sun setting over the lagoon from the canalside tables here. Local devotees overlook the fact that service can be brusque, meal times are set (noon and 8pm), credit cards aren't accepted and there's no opportunity to vary the excellent daily menu, which is mostly meat but sometimes seafood.

Entrance to Caffè Florian

FIASCHETTERIA TOSCANA
Restaurant €€€

(041 528 52 81; www.fiaschetteriatoscana.it; Salizada S Giovanni Grisostomo 5719; mains €14-32; closed all day Tue & lunch Wed) Don't worry about the name, this old-fashioned favourite near the Rialto specialises in Venetian dishes but varies the formula with a few Tuscan triumphs such as chianina beef fillet in red-wine sauce. Seafood dominates the menu – the house speciality is fried fish 'Serenissima' style – and the desserts are delectable.

 Drinking

AL MERCÁ
Bar

(Campo Cesare Battisti, San Polo 212-213; closed Sun) One of the city's best bars, this tiny place serves excellent and keenly priced wines by the glass accompanied by a lavish array of chiceti – arrive around 6.30pm for the best choice. No seating, just loads of atmosphere.

CAFFÈ FLORIAN
Cafe

(www.caffeflorian.com; Piazza San Marco 56/59) If you think it's worth paying up to four times the usual price for a coffee, emulate Byron, Goethe and Rousseau and pull up a seat at Piazza San Marco's most famous cafe.

IL CAFFÈ
Bar

(Campo Santa Margherita, Dorsoduro 2963; closed Sun) Popular with foreign and Italian students, this is one of Venice's historic drinking spots. Known to locals as Caffè Rosso because of its red frontage, it's got outdoor seating and serves a great spritz (Venetian cocktail made with prosecco – Venetian sparkling white, soda water and aperol or campari).

HARRY'S BAR
Bar

(www.harrysbarvenezia.com; Calle Vallaresso, San Marco 1323) To drink a Bellini (white-peach pulp and prosecco) at the bar that invented them is an expensive experience to tick off the list rather than a holiday highlight. Nevertheless, this bar to the stars is always full.

Ancorà
Bar

(Fabbriche Vecchie, San Polo; closed Sun) Enjoy your aperitivo with a Grand Canal view while sitting at one of the three outdoor tables on the waterside terrace here.

 Entertainment

Tickets for the majority of events in Venice are available from **HelloVenezia ticket outlets** (www.hellovenezia.it; 7am-10.45pm), run by the ACTV transport network. You'll find them in front of the train station and at Piazzale Roma.

GRAN TEATRO LA FENICE
Opera House

(for guided tours 041 24 24; www.teatrolafenice.it; Campo San Fantin, San Marco 1977; opera tickets from €20) One of Italy's most important opera houses, the fully restored Fenice is back to its sumptuous self after being destroyed by fire in 1996. The opera season runs from May to November.

Information

Emergency

Police station (Questura; 041 271 55 11; Fondamenta di San Lorenzo, Castello 5053) There's also a small branch at Piazza San Marco 67.

Tourist Information

Azienda di Promozione Turistica (Venice Tourist Board; central information line 041 529 87 11; www.turismovenezia.it) Lido (Gran Viale Santa Maria Elisabetta 6a; 9am-noon & 3-6pm Jun-Sep); Marco Polo airport (Arrivals Hall; 9am-9pm); Piazza San Marco (Piazza San Marco 71f; 9am-3.30pm); Piazzale Roma (9.30am-4.30pm Jun-Sep); train station (8am-6.30pm).

Getting There & Away

Air

Most European and domestic flights land at Marco Polo airport (VCE; 041 260 92 60; www.veniceairport.it), 12km outside Venice. Ryanair flies to Treviso airport (TSF; 0422 31 51 11; www.trevisoairport.it), about 30km from Venice.

Bus

ACTV (041 24 24; www.actv.it) buses service surrounding areas, including Mestre, Padua and Treviso. Tickets and information are available at the bus station in Piazzale Roma.

Train

Venice's Stazione di Santa Lucia is directly linked by regional trains to Padua (€2.90, 45 minutes, every 20 minutes), Verona (€18.50, 1¼ hours, half-hourly) and Ferrara (€6.15, 1½ hours, every two hours).

Getting Around

To/From the Airport

To travel between Venice and Marco Polo airport there are various options. Alilaguna (www.alilaguna.com) operates four fast-ferry lines between the airport ferry dock and different parts of the city (€13, 70 minutes, approximately every hour); the Rossa (Red) line goes to Piazza San Marco and the Oro (Gold) line goes to both Rialto and San Marco. ATVO (041 520 55 30; www.atvo.it, in Italian) runs 'Venezia Express' buses (€3/5.50 one-way/return, 20 minutes, every half-hour) between the airport and Piazzale Roma, and ACTV operates bus 5d (€2.50, 25 minutes, every half-hour). Water taxis from the airport cost €100 for up to five passengers; it's an extra €50 to travel via the Grand Canal.

For Treviso airport, take the ATVO Ryanair bus (€5, 70 minutes, 16 daily) from Piazzale Roma two hours and 10 minutes before your flight departure. The last service is at 7.40pm.

Boat

The city's main mode of public transport is the vaporetto. The most useful routes:

1 From Piazzale Roma to the train station and down the Grand Canal to San Marco and the Lido.

2 From S Zaccaria (near San Marco) to the Lido via Giudecca, Piazzale Roma, the train station and the Rialto.

DM From Piazzale Roma to Murano.

LN From Fondamenta Nuove to S Zaccaria via Murano and Burano.

T Runs between Burano and Torcello.

Tickets, available from ACTV booths at the major vaporetti stops, are expensive: €6.50 for a single trip; €16 for 12 hours; €18 for 24 hours; €23 for 36 hours; €28 for two days; €33 for three days; and €50 for seven days. There are significant discounts for holders of the Rolling Venice Card (eg €18 instead of €33 for the three-day ticket) and all tickets are 15% cheaper if you purchase them online (www.veniceconnected.com) in advance of your trip.

The poor man's gondola, *traghetti* (€0.50 per crossing) are used by Venetians to cross the Grand Canal where there's no nearby bridge.

Bologna

POP 375,000

Boasting a boisterous bonhomie rare in Italy's reserved north, Bologna is worth a few days of anyone's itinerary, not so much for its specific attractions, as for the sheer fun of strolling its animated, arcaded streets. A university town since 1088 (Europe's oldest), it is also one of Italy's foremost foodie destinations. Besides the eponymous bolognese sauce (*ragù*), classic pasta dishes such as tortellini and lasagne were invented here, as was mortadella (aka baloney or Bologna sausage).

 Sights

PIAZZA MAGGIORE　　　　Square

Pedestrianised Piazza Maggiore is Bologna's focal showpiece square. On the southern flank, the Gothic **Basilica di San Petronio** (Piazza Maggiore; ⏰7.45am-12.30pm & 3-6pm), currently covered in scaffolding, is dedicated to the city's patron saint, Petronius. Its partially complete facade doesn't diminish its status as the world's fifth-largest basilica. Inside, don't miss Giovanni da Modena's bizarre *l'Inferno* fresco in the fourth chapel on the left.

To the west is the **Palazzo Comunale** (Town Hall), home to the city's art collection, the **Collezioni Comunali d'Arte** (admission free; ⏰9am-3pm Tue-Fri, 10am-6.30pm Sat & Sun) and the **Museo Morandi** (admission free; ⏰9am-3pm Tue-Fri, 10am-6.30pm Sat & Sun) dedicated to the work of Giorgio Morandi.

Cafe tables and Palazzo Comunale in Piazza Maggiore, Bologna

RUTH EASTHAM & MAX PAOLI/LONELY PLANET IMAGES ©

LE DUE TORRI Medieval Towers

Rising above **Piazza di Porta Ravegnana** are Bologna's two leaning towers, Le Due Torri. The taller of the two, the 97m-high **Torre degli Asinelli** (admission €3; ⊙9am-6pm, to 5pm Nov-Mar), was built between 1109 and 1119 and is now open to the public. Climb the 498 steps for some superb city views from the top. The neighbouring tower, **Torre Garisenda**, stands nearby at 48m.

BASILICA DI SAN DOMENICO Church

(Piazza San Domenico 13; ⊙9.30am-12.30pm & 3.30-6.30pm Mon-Sat, 3.30-5.30pm Sun) This 13th-century church is noteworthy for the elaborate sarcophagus of San Domenico, founder of the Dominican order. The tomb stands in the **Capella di San Domenico**, which was designed by Nicolò Pisano and later added to by, among others, Michelangelo.

Also recommended:

FREE **Museo Civico Archeologico**
Museum

(Via dell'Archiginnasio 2; ⊙9am-3pm Tue-Fri, 10am-6.30pm Sat & Sun) Exhibits Egyptian and Roman artefacts and one of Italy's best Etruscan collections.

FREE **Museo d'Arte Moderna do Bologna** Museum

(MAMBO, Museum of Modern Art; www.mambo-bologna-org; Via Don Minzoni 14; ⊙10am-6pm Tue, Wed & Fri-Sun, to 10pm Thu) An excellent modern-art museum in a converted bakery.

 Sleeping

Accommodation is largely geared to the business market. It's expensive (particularly during trade fairs) and can be difficult to find unless you book ahead.

IL CONVENTO DEI FIORI DI SETA
Boutique Hotel €€€

(☎051 27 20 39; www.silkflowersnunnery.com; Via Orfeo 34; d €130-300; ❄@☎) This hotel is a model of sophisticated design. Housed in a 15th-century convent, it features contemporary furniture juxtaposed against exposed-brick walls and religious frescos, a wine bar in a former sacristy, and Mapplethorpe-inspired flower motifs.

HOTEL NOVECENTO Hotel €€€

(☎051 745 73 11; www.bolognarthotels.it; Piazza Galileo 4; s €113-340, d €149-370; P❄@☎)

435

RUSSELL MOUNTFORD/LONELY PLANET IMAGES ©

Decorated in the Viennese Succession style, this refined boutique offering is one of four hotels run by Bologna Arts Hotels. All have comfortable and well-equipped rooms, excellent locations and lashings of style.

Eating

The university district northeast of Via Rizzoli harbours hundreds of restaurants, trattorias, takeaways and cafes catering to hard-up students and gourmet diners alike.

OSTERIA DE' POETI   Restaurant €€
(☎051 23 61 66; Via de' Poeti 1b; mains €10; ☺Tue-Sun) In the cellar of a 14th-century *palazzo*, this atmospheric place is a bastion of old-style service and top-notch regional cuisine. Pasta dishes are driven by what's fresh in the markets, and mains include delicious meat dishes such as succulent roast beef served with rocket and Grana Padano cheese.

IL SARACENO   Restaurant, Pizza €€
(☎051 23 66 28; Via Calcavinazzi 2; pizzas from €5, mains €13) Popular with lunching locals,

this is a good all-purpose eatery just off central Via Ugo Basso. Tables are on a small outdoor terrace or in the yellow air-conditioned interior, and the menu covers all bases, from pizza to pasta, seafood and meats.

Pizzeria Belle Arti   Pizza €
(☎051 22 55 81; Via delle Belle Arti 14; pizzas €5-9, mains €8) This sprawling place near the university serves delicious wood-fired thin-crust pizzas and a full menu of pastas and main courses. You'll find it near the Odeon cinema.

Bologna also boasts two superb gelaterie:

Gelateria Stefino   Gelateria
(Via Galleria 49b; ☺noon-midnight daily)

La Sorbetteria Castiglione   Gelateria
(Via Castiglione 44; ☺8am-midnight Tue-Sat, to 11.30pm Mon, to 10.30pm Sun).

 Drinking & Entertainment

Bologna's drinking and nightlife scene is one of the most vibrant in the country, with a huge number of bars, cafe's and clubs. Thirsty students congregate on and around Piazza Verdi, while the fashionable Quadrilatero district hosts a dressier, more upmarket scene. Popular spots:

Café de Paris Bar
(Piazza del Francia 1c; ☉8am-1am Mon-Thu, 8am-late Fri & Sat) Modish bar with daily aperitif between 6pm and 10pm.

Caffè degli Orefici Cafe
(Via Orefici 6; ☉Mon-Sat) A modern cafe next to a historic coffee shop.

Cantina Bentivoglio Jazz Club
(☏051 26 54 16; www.cantinabentivoglio.it; Via Mascarella 4b; ☉8pm-2am) Bologna's top jazz club. Also a wine bar and restaurant.

Cassero Club
(www.cassero.it; Via Don Minzoni 18) Legendary gay and lesbian (but not exclusively) club. Home of Italy's Arcigay movement.

🛈 Information

Ospedale Maggiore (Hospital; ☏051 647 81 11; Largo Nigrisoli 2)

Police station (Questura; ☏051 640 11 11; Piazza Galileo 7)

Tourist information (☏051 23 96 60; www.bolognaturismo.info) Airport (☉9am-7pm); Piazza Maggiore 1 (☉9am-7pm)

🛈 Getting There & Around

Air

European and domestic flights arrive at **Guglielmo Marconi airport** (BLQ; ☏051 647 96 15; www.bologna-airport.it), 6km northwest of the city. An Aerobus shuttle (€5, 30 minutes, every 10 minutes) departs from the main train station; buy your ticket at the ATC office behind the taxi rank or on board.

Bus

National and international coaches depart from the **bus station** (Piazza XX Settembre), southeast of the train station.

To get to the centre from the train station take bus A, 25 or 30 (€1).

Train

Bologna is a major rail hub. From the **central train station** (Piazza delle Medaglie d'Oro), fast Eurostar Alta Velocità (ES AV) trains run to the following destinations: Venice (€28, 1½ hours, hourly), Florence (€24, 40 minutes, half-hourly), Rome (€58, 2¾ hours, half-hourly) and Milan (€41, one hour, hourly).

Ravenna
POP 156,000

Most people visit Ravenna to see its remarkable Unesco-protected mosaics. Relics of the city's golden age as capital of the Western Roman and Byzantine empires, they are described by Dante in his *Divine Comedy*, much of which was written here.

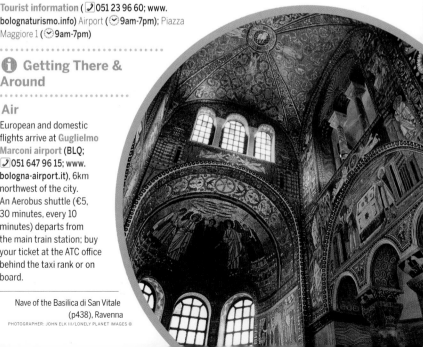

Nave of the Basilica di San Vitale (p438), Ravenna
PHOTOGRAPHER: JOHN ELK III/LONELY PLANET IMAGES ©

◉ Sights

EARLY CHRISTIAN MOSAICS   Mosaics
Ravenna's mosaics are spread over five
sites in the centre: the Basilica di San
Vitale, the Mausoleo di Galla Placida, the
Basilica di Sant'Apollinare Nuovo, the
Museo Arcivescovile and the Battistero
Neoniano. These are covered by a single
ticket (adult/child €8.50/free), which is
available at any of the five sites. Note that
the hours reported here are for April to
September; outside these months they
are slightly shorter, typically 9.30am or
10am until 5pm or 5.30pm.

On the northern edge of the *centro
storico,* the sombre exterior of 6th-
century **Basilica di San Vitale** (Via Fiandrini;
⊙9am-7pm) hides a dazzling interior with
mosaics depicting Old Testament scenes.

In the same complex, the small
Mausoleo di Galla Placidia (Via Fiandrini;
⊙9am-7pm) contains the city's oldest
mosaics. Between March and mid-
September there's an extra €2 booking
fee for the Mausoleo.

Adjoining Ravenna's unremarkable
cathedral, **Museo Arcivescovile** (Piazza
Arcivescovado; ⊙9am-7pm) boasts an
exquisite 6th-century ivory throne, while
next door in the **Battistero Neoniano**
(Via Battistero; ⊙9am-7pm), the baptism of
Christ and the apostles is represented in
the domed roof mosaics.

To the east, the **Basilica di
Sant'Apollinare Nuovo** (Via di Roma;
⊙9am-7pm) boasts, among other things,
a superb mosaic depicting a procession
of martyrs headed towards Christ and his
apostles.

Five kilometres southeast of the
city, the apse mosaic of **Basilica di
Sant'Apollinare in Classe** (Via Romea Sud,
Classe; adult/EU child €3/free; ⊙8.30am-
7.30pm Mon-Sat, 1-7.30pm Sun) is a must-see.
Take bus 4 (€1) from Piazza Caduti per la
Libertà.

🛏 Sleeping & Eating

CÁ DE VÉN   Wine Bar, Restaurant   €€
(www.cadeven.it; Via Corrado Ricci 24; mains €15;
⊙Tue-Sun) OK, we'll admit it's touristy, but
Ravenna's most famous eatery is still an
atmospheric spot for a meal and glass
of wine.

Mosaic in the Basilica di Sant'Apollinare Nuovo, Ravenna

Hotel Sant'Andrea
Hotel €€

(0544 21 55 64; www.santandreahotel.com;
Via Cattaneo 33; s €80-100, d €110-140; ❄ @)
A real find, this charming three-star hotel
offers elegant accommodation in a converted
convent. A grand wooden staircase leads up to
smart, carpeted rooms overlooking a lawned
garden.

ℹ️ Information

Tourist offices Main office (0544 354 04;
www.turismo.ravenna.it; Via Salara 8/12;
🕐8.30am-7pm Mon-Sat, 10am-6pm Sun);
Teodorico (0544 45 15 39; Via delle Industrie
14; 🕐9.30am-12.30pm & 3.30-6.30pm); Classe
(0544 47 36 61; Via Romea Sud 266, Classe;
🕐9.30am-12.30pm & 3.30-6.30pm)

Between October and May hours are slightly
shorter; typically closing time is an hour or so
earlier.

ℹ️ Getting There & Around

Regional trains connect the city with Bologna
(€6.20, 1½ hours, 14 daily) and Ferrara (€5.70, 1¼
hours, 14 daily).

In town, cycling is popular. The tourist office
runs a free bike-hire service to visitors aged 18
years or over (take ID).

TUSCANY

Tuscany is one of those places that well
and truly lives up to its press. Some
people never venture beyond Florence,
but with some of Italy's most charming towns an easy trip away, to do so
would be a grievous waste, particularly
as there are so many chances to sample
the region's famous food and wine along
the way.

Florence
POP 365,700

Poets of the 18th and 19th centuries
swooned at the beauty of Florence
(Firenze), and once here you'll appreciate why. An essential stop on everyone's
Italian itinerary, this Renaissance treasure
trove is busy year-round. Fortunately, the
huge crowds fail to diminish the city's
lustre.

Detour: Dolomites

A Unesco natural heritage site since
2009, the Dolomites stretch across
the northern regions of Trentino-
Alto Adige and the Veneto. Their
stabbing sawtooth peaks provide
some of Italy's most thrilling
scenery, as well as superb skiing and
hiking.

Area-wide information can be
obtained from tourist offices in
Trento (0461 21 60 00; www.apt.
trento.it; Via Manci 2; 🕐9am-7pm) and
Bolzano (0471 30 70 00; www.
bolzano-bozen.it; Piazza Walther 8; 🕐9am-
1pm & 2-7pm Mon-Fri, 9am-2pm Sat).
The best online resource is www.
dolomiti.org.

History

A rich merchant city by the 12th century,
Florence's golden age arrived in the 15th
century. Under the Medici prince Lorenzo
il Magnifico (1469–92), the city's cultural,
artistic and political fecundity culminated
in the Renaissance.

The Medici were succeeded in the 18th
century by the French House of Lorraine,
which ruled until 1860, when the city was
incorporated into the kingdom of Italy.

Sights

There are seven major neighbourhoods
in the historic centre: Duomo and Piazza
della Signoria, Santa Maria Novella, San
Lorenzo, San Marco, Santa Croce, Ol-
trarno and Boboli/San Miniato al Monte.

PIAZZA DEL DUOMO & AROUND
Churches

Pictures don't do justice to the exterior
of Florence's Gothic **Duomo** (cathedral;

Florence

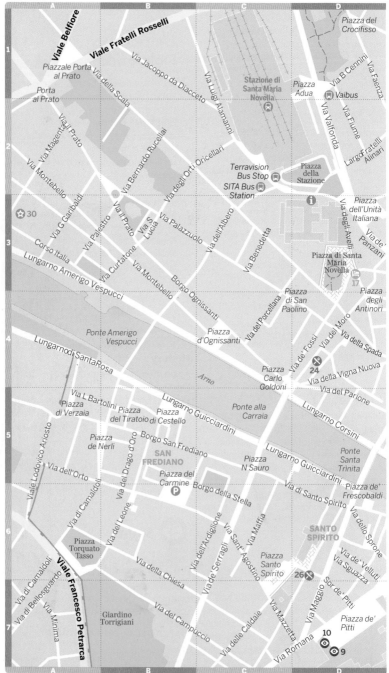

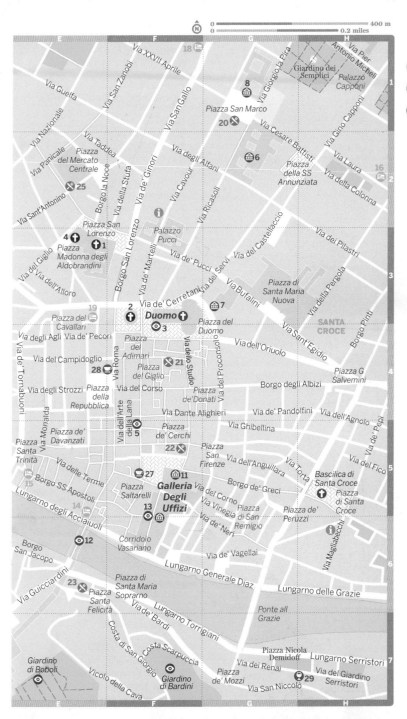

Florence

www.duomofirenze.it; ◷10am-5pm Mon-Wed & Fri, 10am-3.30pm Thu, 10am-4.45pm Sat, 10am-3.30pm 1st Sat of every month, 1.30-4.45pm Sun). While they reproduce the startling colours of the tiered red, green and white marble facade and the beautiful symmetry of the dome, they fail to give any sense of its monumental size. Officially known as the Cattedrale di Santa Maria del Fiore, its construction begun in 1294 by Sienese architect Arnolfo di Cambio, but it wasn't consecrated until 1436. Its most famous feature, the enormous octagonal **Cupola** (dome; admission €8; ◷8.30am-6.20pm Mon-Fri, to 5pm Sat) was built by Brunelleschi after his design won a public competition in 1420. The interior is decorated with frescoes by Vasari and Zuccari, and the stained-glass windows are by Donatello, Paolo Uccello and Lorenzo Ghiberti. The facade is a 19th-century replacement of the unfinished original, pulled down in the 16th century.

Beside the cathedral, the 82m **Campanile** (admission €6; ◷8.30am-6.50pm) was begun by Giotto in 1334 and completed after his death by Andrea

Pisano and Francesco Talenti. The views from the top make the 414-step climb worthwhile.

To the west, the Romanesque **Battistero** (Baptistry; Piazza di San Giovanni; admission €4; ◷12.15-6.30pm Mon-Sat, 8.30am-1.30pm 1st Sat of every month, 8.30am-1.30pm Sun) is one of the oldest buildings in Florence. Built on the site of a Roman temple between the 5th and 11th centuries, it's famous for its gilded-bronze doors, particularly Lorenzo Ghiberti's *Gate of Paradise*.

Surprisingly overlooked by the crowds, the **Museo dell'Opera del Duomo** (Cathedral Museum; www.operaduomo.firenze.it; admission €6; ◷9am-6.50pm Mon-Sat & 9am-1pm Sun) on the northern (street) side of the cathedral safeguards treasures that once adorned the Duomo, baptistry and campanile and is one of the city's most impressive museums.

GALLERIA DEGLI UFFIZI　　Art Gallery
(Uffizi Gallery; www.uffizi.firenze.it; Piazza degli Uffizi 6; adult/EU concession €10/5; ◷8.15am-6.05pm Tue-Sun) Home to the world's greatest collection of Italian Renaissance art,

the Galleria degli Uffizi attracts some 1.5 million visitors annually.

The gallery houses the Medici family collection, bequeathed to the city in 1743 on the condition that it never leave the city. Highlights include *La nascita di Venere* (Birth of Venus) and *Allegoria della primavera* (Allegory of Spring) in the Botticelli Rooms (10 to 14); Leonardo da Vinci's *Annunciazione* (Annunciation; room 15); Michelangelo's *Tondo doni* (Holy Family; Room 25); and Titian's *Venere d'Urbino* (Venus of Urbino; Room 28). Elsewhere you'll find works by Giotto, Cimabue, Filippo Lippi, Fra' Angelico, Uccello, Raphael, Andrea del Sarto, Tintoretto and Caravaggio. Tickets are cheaper if there are no temporary exhibitions.

PIAZZA DELLA SIGNORIA Square
Traditional hub of Florence's political life, Piazza della Signoria is dominated by the **Palazzo Vecchio (Old Palace; www. palazzovecchio-museoragazzi.it; adult/child €6/2;** 9am-7pm Fri-Wed, to 2pm Thu**)**, the historical seat of the Florentine government. Characterised by the 94m **Torre d'Arnolfo**, it was designed by Arnolfo di Cambio and built between 1298 and 1340. The **guided tours (** 055 276 82 24; info .museoragazzi@comune.fi.it**)** here are great – particularly those for children. Make sure you book in advance.

The statue of *David* outside the *palazzo* is a copy of Michelangelo's original, which stood here until 1873 but is now in the Galleria dell'Accademia.

PONTE VECCHIO Bridge
The 14th-century Ponte Vecchio was originally flanked by butchers' shops, but when the Medici built a corridor through the bridge to link Palazzo Pitti with Palazzo Vecchio, they ordered that the smelly butchers be replaced with goldsmiths and jewellery shops, which are still found along its length.

PALAZZO PITTI Palace
(Piazza de' Pitti) Built for the Pitti family, great rivals of the Medici, the vast 15th-century Palazzo Pitti was bought by the Medici in 1549 and became their family residence. Today it houses four museums, of which the **Galleria Palatina (** 8.15am-6.50pm Tue-Sun) is the most important. Works by Raphael, Filippo Lippi, Titian and Rubens adorn lavishly decorated rooms.

GALLERIA DELL'ACCADEMIA Art Gallery
(Via Ricasoli 60; adult/concession €10/5; 8.15am-6.20pm Tue-Sun) The people queuing outside Galleria dell'Accademia are waiting to see *David,* arguably the Western world's most famous sculpture. Michelangelo carved the giant figure from a single block of marble, finishing it in 1504 when he was just 29.

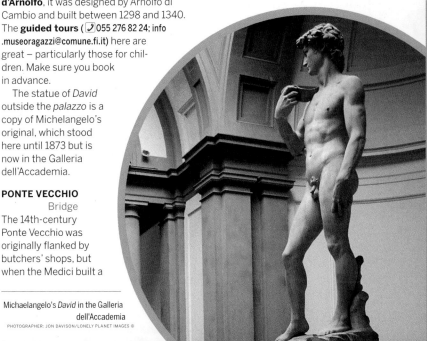

Michaelangelo's *David* in the Galleria dell'Accademia
PHOTOGRAPHER: JON DAVISON/LONELY PLANET IMAGES ©

The Uffizi

Journey into the Renaissance

Navigating the Uffizi's main art collection, chronologically arranged in 45 rooms on one floor, is straightforward; knowing which of the 1500-odd masterpieces to view before gallery fatigue strikes is not. Swap coat and bag (travel light) for floor plan and audioguide on the ground floor, then meet 16th-century Tuscany head-on with a walk up the *palazzo's* magnificent bust-lined staircase (skip the lift – the Uffizi is as much about masterly architecture as art).

Allow four hours for this journey into the High Renaissance. At the top of the staircase, 2nd floor, show your ticket, turn left and pause to admire the full length of the first corridor sweeping south towards the river Arno. Then duck left into room 2 to witness first steps in Tuscan art – shimmering altarpieces by **Giotto** ❶ et al. Journey through medieval art to room 8 and **Piero della Francesca's** ❷ impossibly famous portrait, then break in the corridor with playful **ceiling art** ❸. After Renaissance heavyweights **Botticelli** ❹ and **da Vinci** ❺, meander past the Tribuna (potential detour) and enjoy the daylight streaming in through the vast windows and panorama of the **riverside second corridor** ❻. Lap up soul-stirring views of the Arno, crossed by Ponte Vecchio and its echo of four bridges drifting towards the Apuane Alps on the horizon. Then saunter into the third corridor, pausing between rooms 25 and 34 to ponder the entrance to the enigmatic Vasari Corridor. End on a high with High Renaissance maestros **Michelangelo** ❼ and **Raphael** ❽.

Diptych of Duke & Duchess of Urbino
Room 8
Revel in realism's voyage with these uncompromising, warts-and-all portraits (1465–72) by Piero della Francesca. No larger than A3 size, they originally slotted into a portable, hinged frame that folded like a book.

The Ognissanti Madonna
Room 2
Draw breath at the shy blush and curvaceous breast of Giotto's humanised Virgin (*Maestà*; 1310) – so feminine compared to those of Duccio and Cimabue painted just 25 years before.

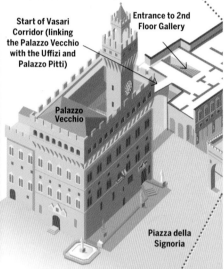

Start of Vasari Corridor (linking the Palazzo Vecchio with the Uffizi and Palazzo Pitti)

Entrance to 2nd Floor Gallery

Palazzo Vecchio

Piazza della Signoria

Grotesque Ceiling Frescoes
First Corridor
Take time to study the make-believe monsters and most unexpected of burlesques (spot the arrow-shooting satyr outside room 15) waltzing across this eastern corridor's fabulous frescoed ceiling (1581).

IMAGE REPRODUCED WITH THE PERMISSION OF MINISTERO PER I BENI E LE ATTIVITÀ CULTURALI

ALINARI ARCHIVES, FLORENCE

The Genius of Botticelli
Room 10–14
The miniature form of *The Discovery of the Body of Holofernes* (c 1470) makes Botticelli's early Renaissance masterpiece all the more impressive. Don't miss the artist watching you in *Adoration of the Magi* (1475), left of the exit.

View of the Arno
Indulge in intoxicating city views from this short glassed-in corridor – an architectural masterpiece. Near the top of the hill, spot one of 73 outer towers built to defend Florence and its 15 city gates below.

Arno River

Second Corridor

Tribuna

First Corridor

① ② ③ ④ ⑤ ⑥ ⑦ ⑧

Portrait of Pope Leo X
Room 26
Stare into the eyes of the trio in this Raphael masterpiece (1518) and work out what the devil they're thinking – a perfect portrayal of High Renaissance intrigue.

Third Corridor

Entrance to Vasari Corridor

Matter of Fact
The Uffizi collection spans the 13th to 18th centuries, but its 15th- and 16th-century Renaissance works are second to none.

Doni Tondo
Room 25
David's creator, Michelangelo, was essentially a sculptor and no painting expresses this better than *Doni Tondo* (1506–08). Mary's muscular arms against a backdrop of curvaceous nudes are practically 3D in their shapeliness.

Value Lunchbox
Try the Uffizi rooftop cafe or – better value – gourmet *panini* at 'Ino (www.ino-firenze.com; Via dei Georgofili 3-7r).

Annunciation
Room 15
Admire the exquisite portrayal of the Tuscan landscape in this painting (c 1475–80), one of few by Leonardo da Vinci to remain in Florence.

BASILICA DI SAN LORENZO Church

(www.basilicasanlorenzofirenze.com, in Italian; Piazza San Lorenzo; admission €3.50; ⏰10am-5pm Mon-Sat year-round, 1.30-5pm Sun Mar-Oct) One of the city's finest examples of Renaissance architecture, this basilica was built by Brunelleschi in the 15th century and includes his **Sagrestia Vecchia**, with sculptural decoration by Donatello.

Around the corner, at the rear of the basilica, is the sumptuous **Cappelle Medicee** (Medici Chapels; Piazza Madonna degli Aldobrandini; adult/concession €6/3; ⏰8.15am-4pm Tue-Sat, 2nd & 4th Mon & 1st, 3rd & 5th Sun of month), the principal burial place of the Medici grand dukes. Its jewel is the incomplete **Sagrestia Nuova**, Michelangelo's first architectural effort, which contains some exquisite sculptures.

MUSEO DI SAN MARCO Museum

(Piazza San Marco 1; adult/concession €4/2; ⏰8.15am-1.50pm Tue-Fri, to 4.50pm Sat & 2nd & 4th Sun & 1st, 3rd & 5th Mon of month) Housed in a Dominican monastery, this museum is a showcase of the work of Fra' Angelico, who decorated the cells between 1440 and 1441 with devotional frescos to guide the meditation of his fellow friars.

Tours

Freya's Florence Walking
(☎349 074 89 07; freyasflorence@yahoo.com; €60 per hr for private tours) English-language walking tours with an enthusiastic and expert guide.

Walking Tours of Florence Walking
(☎055 264 50 33; www.italy.artviva.com; Via de' Sassetti 1; tours per person from €25) The Artviva outfit offers a range of city tours, all led by English-speaking guides.

Festivals & Events

Scoppio del Carro
Religious Celebration
(Explosion of the Cart) A cart full of fireworks is exploded in front of the Duomo on Easter Sunday.

Maggio Musicale Fiorentino
Music Festival
(www.maggiofiorentino.com, in Italian) Italy's longest-running music festival, held from April to June.

Inside the Galleria degli Uffizi (p444)

JEAN-PIERRE LESCOURRET/LONELY PLANET IMAGES ©

Cutting the Queues

Sightseeing in Florence inevitably means queues. You'll never avoid them altogether, but by pre-booking museum tickets you'll save time. For €4 extra per museum you can book tickets for the Uffizi and Galleria dell'Accademia (the two most popular museums) through **Firenze Musei** (☎ 055 29 48 83; www.firenzemusei. it; ⏱ booking line 8.30am-6.30pm Mon-Fri, to 12.30pm Sat, ticket offices 8.15am-6pm daily). Book ahead of your visit by telephone or online, or purchase in person from the Firenze Musei desks at the Uffizi, Accademia, Palazzo Pitti or Museo di San Marco. There's also a ticket window at the rear of the Chiesa di Orsanmichele.

 # Sleeping

Although there are hundreds of hotels in Florence, it's still prudent to book ahead.

Duomo & Piazza della Signoria

RELAIS DEL DUOMO   B&B   €€
(⏱ 055 21 01 47; www.relaisdelduomo.it, in Italian; Piazza dell'Olio 2; s €48-85, d €70-130; ❄ @ 🛜) Florentine B&Bs don't come much better than this one. Located in the shadow of the Duomo, it has four light and airy rooms with attractive furnishings and lovely little bathrooms.

HOTEL CESTELLI   B&B   €
(☎ 055 21 42 13; www.hotelcestelli.com; Borgo SS Apostoli 25; s without bathroom €40-60, d without bathroom €50-80, d €70-100; ⏱ closed 2 weeks Jan, 3 weeks Aug) Run by Florentine photographer Alessio and his Japanese partner Asumi, this eight-room hotel on the first floor of a 12th-century *palazzo* is wonderfully located. Though dark, the rooms are attractively furnished, quiet and cool.

Santa Maria Novella

HOTEL SANTA MARIA NOVELLA
Hotel   €€
(☎ 055 27 18 40; www.hotelsantamarianovella. it; Piazza di Santa Maria Novella 1; d €135-195, ste €178-235; ❄ @ 🛜) The bland exterior of this excellent four-star choice gives no hint of the spacious and elegant rooms within. All are beautifully appointed, featuring marble bathrooms and comfortable beds. The breakfast spread is lavish.

CONTINENTALE   Boutique Hotel   €€€
(☎ 055 2 72 62; www.lungarnohotels.com; Viccolo dell'Oro 6r; s €240-300, d €290-530; ❄ @) Owned by the fashion house Ferragamo and designed by fashionable Florentine architect Michele Bönan, this glamorous hotel references 1950s Italy in its vibrant decor, and is about as hip as Florence gets.

San Lorenzo

Johlea & Johanna   B&B   €€
(☎ 055 463 32 92; www.johanna.it; Via San Gallo 80; s €70-120, d €80-170; ❄) This highly regarded B&B has more than a dozen tasteful, individually decorated rooms housed in five historic residences. There are also two charming suite apartments (€92 to €280).

San Marco

Hotel Morandi alla Crocetta
Boutique Hotel   €€
(☎ 055 234 47 47; www.hotelmorandi.it; Via Laura 50; s €70-109, d €100-169; P ❄ @ 🛜) This medieval convent-turned-boutique-hotel is truly stunning. Rooms are charmingly decorated (try for the frescoed No 29) and extremely well equipped. The location is wonderfully quiet.

 # Eating

Classic Tuscan dishes include *ribollita,* a heavy vegetable soup, and *bistecca alla fiorentina* (Florentine steak served rare). Chianti is the local tipple.

Duomo & Piazza della Signoria

LA CANOVA DI GUSTAVINO

Wine Bar €€

(Via della Condotta 29r; mains €8-12) The rear dining room of this atmospheric *enoteca* is lined with shelves full of Tuscan wine – the perfect accompaniment to a simple bowl of soup, a bruschetta, a pasta dish or a hearty main.

Santa Maria Novella

L'OSTERIA DI GIOVANNI Trattoria €€€

(☎055 28 48 97; www.osteriadigiovanni.com, in Italian; Via del Moro 22; mains €18-26; ☺lunch & dinner Fri-Mon, dinner only Tue-Thu) The house antipasto is a great way to sample Tuscan specialities such as *crostini* and *lardo,* and the *bistecca alla fiorentina* is sensational. Everything a perfect neighbourhood eatery should be, and then some.

COQUINARIUS Wine Bar €€

(☎055 230 21 53; Via delle Oche 15r; mains €15; ☎) Close to Piazza Signoria, this modern *enoteca* is a perfect spot for lunch or a light dinner. The pasta dishes are uniformly good, and there's almost always a few unusual and delicious salads on the menu.

San Lorenzo

NERBONE Tavola Calda €

(☎055 21 99 49; inside Mercato Centrale, Piazza del Mercato Centrale; panini €3-4, mains €5-6.50; ☺7am-2pm Mon-Sat) This unpretentious market stall has been serving its rustic dishes to queues of shoppers and stall-holders since 1872. It's a great place to try local staples such as *trippa alla fiorentina* (€6.50) and *panini con bollito* (a boiled beef bun, €3).

San Marco

ACCADEMIA RISTORANTE

Trattoria €€

(www.ristoranteaccademia.it, in italian; Piazza San Marco 7r; mains €12-18) There aren't too many decent eateries in this area, which is one of the reasons why this family-run restaurant is perennially packed. Such factors as friendly staff, cheerful decor and consistently good food help, too.

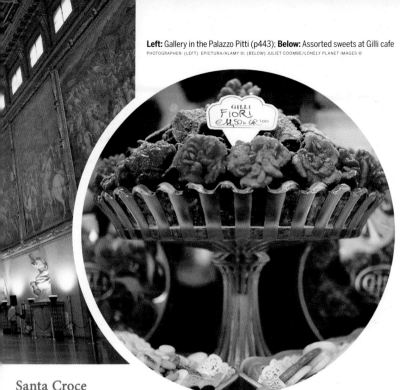

Left: Gallery in the Palazzo Pitti (p443); **Below:** Assorted sweets at Gilli cafe

PHOTOGRAPHER: (LEFT) EPICTURA/ALAMY ©; (BELOW) JULIET COOMBE/LONELY PLANET IMAGES ©

FLORENCE DRINKING

Santa Croce

TRATTORIA CIBRÈO (CIBRÉINO)   Trattoria €€

(www.edizioniteatrodelsalecibreofirenze.it, in Italian; Viadei Macci 122r; mains €13-16; ⏰Tue-Sat, closed Aug) The small dining room here is run with charm and efficiency by a maître d' who will happily explain the menu and suggest a matching wine. *Secondi* comprise a small main dish matched with a side of seasonal vegetables; everything is delicious and exceptionally well priced considering its quality. No reservations and no credit cards.

Oltrano

LE VOLPI E L'UVA   Wine Bar €

(www.levolpieluva.com; Piazza dei Rossi 1; ⏰11am-9pm Mon-Sat) Near the Ponte Vecchio, this intimate *enoteca* has an impressive list of wines by the glass and serves a delectable array of accompanying antipasti, including juicy *prosciutto di Parma*, *lardo*-topped *crostini* and boutique Tuscan cheeses. There's a tiny outdoor terrace and a small number of bar stools.

TRATTORIA LA CASALINGA   Trattoria €

(Via de' Michelozzi 9r; mains €6-9; ⏰closed Sun) Family run and much loved by locals, this unpretentious and always busy place is one of the city's cheapest trattorias. You'll be relegated behind locals in the queue – it's a fact of life and not worth protesting about – with the eventual reward being hearty and dirt-cheap peasant dishes.

🍷 Drinking

GILLI   Cafe, Bar

(www.gilli.it; Piazza della Repubblica 39r; ⏰Wed-Mon) The city's grandest cafe, Gilli has been serving excellent coffee and delicious cakes since 1733. Claiming a table on the piazza is *molto* expensive – we prefer standing at the spacious Liberty-style bar.

449

Caffè Rivoire Cafe, Bar

(www.rivoire.it, in Italian; Piazza della Signoria; ⏱closed Mon & 2nd half Jan) Rivoire's terrace has the best view in the city. Settle in for a long *aperitivo* or coffee break – it's worth the high prices.

Negroni Bar

(www.negronibar.com, in Italian; Via dei Renai 17r; ⏱8am-2am Mon-Sat, from 7pm Sun) The famous Florentine cocktail gives its name to this popular bar in the San Nicolò district. Come here after admiring the sun set over the city from Piazzale Michelangelo.

 # Entertainment

Florence's definitive monthly listings guide, *Firenze Spettacolo* (€1.80), is sold at newsstands.

Concerts, opera and dance are performed year-round at the **Teatro Comunale** (☎800 11 22 11; Corso Italia 16), which is also the venue for events organised by the Maggio Musicale Fiorentino (see Festivals & Events, p446).

 ## ℹ Information

Emergency

Police station (Questura; ☎055 497 71; Via Zara 2)

Tourist Information

Tourist offices (www.firenzeturismo.it) main office (☎055 29 08 32; Via Cavour 1r; ⏱8.30am-6.30pm Mon-Sat, to 1.30pm Sun); airport (☎055 31 58 74; ⏱8.30am-8.30pm); Santa Croce (☎055 234 04 44; Borgo Santa Croce 29r; ⏱9am-7pm Mon-Sat, to 2pm Sun Mar-Oct, 9am-5pm Mon-Sat, to 2pm Sun Nov-Feb); Piazza della Stazione (☎055 21 22 45; www.commune.fi.it; Piazza della Stazione 4; ⏱8.30am-7pm Mon-Sat, to 2pm Sun)

ℹ Getting There & Away

Air

The main airports serving Florence are Pisa international airport (Aeroporto Galileo Galilei; PSA; ☎050 84 93 00; www.pisa-airport.com) and Bologna airport (Aeroporto G. Marconi; BLQ; ☎051 647 96 15; www.bologna-airport.it).

Bus

The SITA bus station (☎800 37 37 60; www.sitabus.it, in Italian; Via Santa Caterina da Siena 17) is just south of the train station. Buses leave for Siena (€7.10, 1½ hours, every 30 to 60 minutes) and San Gimignano via Poggibonsi (€6.25, 1¼ hours, 14 daily).

Car & Motorcycle

Florence is connected by the A1 *autostrada* to Bologna and Milan in the north and Rome and Naples to the south. The A11 links Florence with Pisa and the coast, and a *superstrada* (expressway) joins the city to Siena.

Leaning Tower of Pisa

Train

There are regular services to/from Pisa (Regional €5.80, 1¼ hours, every 30 minutes), Rome (Eurostar AV, €44, 90 minutes, hourly), Venice (Eurostar AV €52, 1¾ hours, 12 daily) and Milan (Eurostar AV, €16.20, one hour, hourly).

 Getting Around

To/From the Airport

Terravision (☏ 06 321 20 011; www.terravision.it) runs a bus service between the paved bus park in front of the train station and Pisa (Galileo Galilei) airport (adult/child aged five to 12 years €10/4, 70 minutes, 12 daily). Buy your tickets at the Terravision desk inside Deanna Café, opposite. Otherwise there are regular trains (€5.10, 1½ hours, hourly between 6.37am and 8.37pm).

ATAF (☏ 800 42 45 00; www.ataf.net) runs a shuttle bus (€5, 25 minutes, half-hourly from 5.30am to 11pm) connecting Florence airport with the SITA bus station.

Eurostar's Frecciarossa service travels between Florence and Bologna Centrale train station (€24, 40 minutes, every 30 minutes).

Car & Motorcycle

Access to much of the city centre is restricted, so the best advice is to leave your car in a car park and use public transport.

Pisa
POP 87,400

Most people know Pisa as the home of an architectural project gone terribly wrong, but the Leaning Tower is just one of a number of noteworthy sights in this compact and compelling university city.

From Piazza Sant' Antonio, just west of the train station, the Leaning Tower is a straightforward 1.5km walk – follow Viale F Crispi north, cross the Ponte Solferino over the Arno and continue straight up Via Roma to Campo dei Miracoli.

 Sights & Activities

CAMPO DEI MIRACOLI   Cathedrals
(Field of Miracles) Pisans claim that Campo dei Miracoli is among the most beautiful urban spaces in the world. Certainly, the immaculate walled lawns provide a gorgeous setting for the Cathedral, Baptistry and Tower; on the other hand, few places boast so many tat-waving hawkers.

Forming the centrepiece of the Campo's Romanesque trio, the candy-striped **Cathedral** (Duomo; ⏱10am-12.45pm & 2-5pm Nov-Feb, 10am-6pm Mar, 10am-8pm Apr-Sep, 10am-7pm Oct), begun in 1063, has a graceful tiered facade and cavernous interior. The transept's bronze doors are by Bonanno Pisano, and the 16th-century entrance doors are by Giambologna.

To the west, the cupcake-like **Baptistry** (Battistero; ⏱10am-5pm Nov-Feb, 9am-6pm Mar, 8am-8pm Apr-Sep, 9am-7pm Oct) was started in 1153 and completed by Nicola and Giovanni Pisano in 1260. Inside, note Nicola Pisano's beautiful pulpit.

But it's to the campanile, better known as the **Leaning Tower** (Torre Pendente; ⏱10am-4.30pm Dec & Jan, 9.30am-5.30pm Feb, 9am-5.30pm Mar, 8.30am-8pm Apr-Sep, 9am-7pm Oct, 9.30am-5.30pm Nov), that all eyes are drawn. Bonanno Pisano began building in 1173, but almost immediately his plans came a cropper in a layer of shifting soil. Only three of the tower's seven tiers were completed before it started tilting – continuing at a rate of about 1mm per year. By 1990 the lean had reached 5.5 degrees – a tenth of a degree beyond the critical point established by computer models. Stability was finally ensured in 1998 when a combination of biased weighting and soil drilling forced the tower into a safer position. Today it's almost 4.1m off the perpendicular.

Visits are limited to groups of 40 and children under eight years are not allowed entrance; entry times are staggered and queuing is predictably inevitable.

Pisatour (⏱328 144 68 55; www.pisatour.it; adult/child under 15yr €12/free; ⏱tours Mon & Thu 3pm, Sat 10.30am) offers excellent two-to-three-hour English-language guided walking tours around the historic centre and can also organise guides for the Campo dei Miracoli.

Campo dei Miracoli Ticketing

Tickets to the **Tower** (€15 at ticket office, €17 when booked online) and **Cathedral** (€2 Mar-Oct, free Nov-Feb) are sold individually, but for the remaining sights combined tickets are available. These cost €5/6/10 for one/two/five sights and cover the Cathedral, Baptistry, Camposanto, Museo dell'Opera del Duomo and Museo delle Sinópie. Entry for children aged under 10 years is free for all sights except the tower.

Tickets are sold at two **ticket offices** (www.opapisa.it) on the piazza: the central ticket office is located behind the tower and a second office is located in the entrance foyer of the Museo delle Sinópie. To ensure your visit to the tower, book tickets via the website at least 15 days in advance.

Sleeping

HOTEL FRANCESCO   Hotel   €€
(📞050 55 54 53; www.hotelfrancesco.com; Via Santa Maria 129; r €60-150; ❄ @) The best of the hotels lining busy Via Santa Maria (just off Campo dei Miracoli), the small family-run Francesco offers a warm welcome and bright rooms with mod cons. Breakfast isn't included in the price of the room.

Eating & Drinking

BAR PASTICCERIA SALZA   Cafe   €
(📞050 58 02 44; Borgo Stretto 44; ⏰8am-8.30pm Apr-Oct, hr vary Tue-Sun Nov-Mar) Salza has been tempting patrons into sugar-induced wickedness ever since the 1920s. Claim one of the tables in the arcade, or save some money by standing at the bar – the excellent coffee and dangerously delicious cakes and chocolates will satisfy regardless of where they are sampled.

RISTORO AL VECCHIO TEATRO   Trattoria   €€
(📞050 20 21 0; Piazza Dante; set menus €25 & €35, mains €8-12; ⏰lunch Mon-Sat, dinner Tue-Sat) The Vecchio Teatro's genial host is proud of his set menu, and with good reason. The four courses are dominated by local seafood specialities and the dessert finale includes a *castagnaccio* (sweet chestnut cake) that has been known to prompt diners to spontaneous applause.

Information

For city information, check out www.pisaturismo. it or ask at one of the three **tourist offices** at the following locations: airport (📞050 50 25 18; ⏰9.30am-11.30pm); city centre (📞050 4 22 91; Piazza Vittorio Emanuele II 16; ⏰9am-7pm Mon-Sat, to 4pm Sun); Piazza dei Miracoli (📞334 641 94 08; ⏰9.30am-7.30pm).

Getting There & Away

The city's **Pisa international airport** (Galileo Galilei airport; PSA; 📞050 84 93 00; www.pisa-airport.com) is linked to the centre by train (€1.10, five minutes, 15 daily), or by the CPT Linea Rossa bus (www.cpt.pisa.it, in Italian; €1, 10 minutes, every 10 minutes). Buy bus tickets at the newsstand at the train station.

Regular trains run to the following destinations: Lucca (Regional €2.40, 30 minutes, every 30 to 60 minutes), Florence (Regional €5.80, 1¼ hours, every 30 minutes), Rome (Eurostar €39.50, three hours, nine daily) and Genoa (InterCity €16, 2½ hours, eight daily).

Siena
POP 54,200

Siena is one of Italy's most enchanting medieval towns. Its walled centre, a beautifully preserved warren of dark lanes punctuated with Gothic *palazzi*, pretty piazzas and eye-catching churches, has at its centre Piazza del Campo (known as Il Campo), the sloping square that is the venue for the city's famous annual horse race, Il Palio.

Sights

A joint ticket for the Duomo, Battistero, Museo dell'Opera, Diocesan Museum, Crypt and Santa Maria della Scala – all clustered around the Duomo – costs adult/child under 6 years/student/over 65 years €12/free/5/8. See www.opera duomo.siena.it for details.

PIAZZA DEL CAMPO Square

Ever since the 14th century, the slanting, shell-shaped Piazza del Campo has been the city's civic centre. Forming the base of the piazza, the **Palazzo Pubblico (Palazzo Comunale)** is a good example of Sienese Gothic architecture. Inside, the **Museo Civico** (adult/concession €8/4.50; ☉10am-6.15pm mid-Mar–Oct, to 4.45pm Nov–mid-Mar) houses some extraordinary frescos, including Simone Martini's famous *Maestà* (Virgin Mary in Majesty) and Ambroglio Lorenzetti's *Allegories of Good and Bad Government*. Soaring above the *palazzo* is the 102m (400-step) **Torre del Mangia** (admission €8; ☉10am-6.15pm mid-Mar–end Oct, to 3.15pm Nov–mid-Mar), which dates from 1297. A combined ticket to the two

costs adult/child under 6 years €13/free and is available only at the Torre del Mangia ticket office.

DUOMO Church

(Cathedral; Piazza del Duomo; admission €3; ☉10.30am-7.30pm Mon-Sat & 1.30-5.30pm Sun Mar-May & Sep-Oct, 10.30am-8pm Mon-Sat & 1.30-6pm Sun Jun-Aug, 10.30am-6.30pm Mon-Sat & 1.30-5.30pm Sun Nov-Feb) The spectacular Duomo is one of Italy's Gothic masterpieces. Begun in 1196, it was completed in 1215, although work continued well into the 13th century. The striking facade of green, red and white marble was designed by Giovanni Pisano, who also helped his dad, Nicola, craft the cathedral's intricate pulpit.

Behind the cathedral and down a flight of stairs, the **Battistero** (Baptistry; admission €3; Piazza San Giovanni; ☉9.30am-7pm Mar-May & Sep-Oct, to 8pm Jun-Aug, 10am-5pm Nov-Feb) has a Gothic facade and a rich interior of 15th-century frescos.

MUSEO DELL'OPERA Museum

(Piazza del Duomo; admission €6; ☉9.30am-7pm Mar-May & Sep-Oct, to 8pm Jun-Aug, to 5pm Nov-Feb) This museum is home to a large collection of Sienese painting and sculpture,

Duomo, Siena

RICHARD I'ANSON/LONELY PLANET IMAGES ©

City walls, Lucca

DAVID LYONS / ALAMY©

including an entire room dedicated to the work of Duccio di Buoninsegna, the most significant painter of the Sienese School.

 ## Festivals & Events

Siena's great annual event is the **Palio** (2 Jul & 16 Aug), a pageant culminating in a bareback horse race round Il Campo. The city is divided into 17 *contrade* (districts), of which 10 are chosen annually to compete for the *palio* (silk banner). The only rule in the three-lap race is that jockeys can't tug the reins of other horses.

Sleeping

It's always advisable to book in advance, but for August and the Palio, it's essential.

PENSIONE PALAZZO RAVIZZA
Boutique Hotel €€
(☎0577 28 04 62; www.palazzoravizza.com; Pian dei Mantellini 34; s €95-150, d €115-200; P ❄ 🛜) *Pensione* is a far too modest title for this intimate, sumptuous place, which occupies a delightful Renaissance *palazzo*. Frescoed

ceilings and antique furniture co-exist with flat-screen TVs and comprehensive wi-fi coverage. Service is courteous and efficient, and there's a small, leafy garden.

ANTICA RESIDENZA CICOGNA   B&B   €
(☎347 007 28 88; www.anticaresidenzacicogna.it; Via dei Termini 67; s €75-90, d €85-100; P ❄ 🛜) Springless beds, soundproof windows, ornate frescos, antique furniture and a lavish buffet breakfast make this central option justifiably popular. Reception has limited core hours (8am to 1pm), so arrange your arrival in advance.

 ## Eating & Drinking

Among many traditional Sienese dishes are *panzanella* (summer salad of soaked bread, basil, onion and tomatoes), *pappardelle con la lepre* (ribbon pasta with hare) and panforte (a rich cake of almonds, honey and candied fruit).

Caffè Fiorella   Cafe   €
(Via di Città 13; ⏰Mon-Sat 7am-8pm) Squeeze into this tiny space behind Il Campo to enjoy Siena's best coffee. In summer, the coffee granita with a dollop of cream is a wonderful indulgence.

OSTERIA LE LOGGE Restaurant €€€

(☎ 0577 4 80 13; www.osterialelogge.it; Via dei Porrione 33; mains €19-24; ☺ Mon-Sat) This place changes its menu of creative and delicious Tuscan cuisine almost daily. The downstairs dining room, once a pharmacy, is an atmospheric space in which to dine and there are also streetside tables.

HOSTERIA IL CARROCCIO Trattoria €€

(☎ 0577 4 11 65; Via del Casato di Sotto 32; mains €13-25; ☺ Thu-Tue) Recommended by the prestigious Slow Food movement, Il Carroccio specialises in traditional Sienese cooking. Staples include *pici* (thick spaghetti) and succulent *bistecca di chianina alla brace* (grilled steak).

Pasticceria Nannini Cafe €

(24 Via Banchi di Sopra; ☺ 7.30am-11pm) Come here for the finest *cenci* (fried sweet pastry), panforte and *ricciarelli* (almond biscuits) in town, enjoyed with a cup of excellent coffee.

ⓘ Information

Tourist office (☎ 0577 28 05 51; www.terresiena.it; Piazza del Campo 56; ☺ 9am-7pm).

ⓘ Getting There & Away

Siena is not on a main train line, so it's easier to arrive by bus. From the bus station on Piazza Gramsci, Train SPA (www.trainspa.it) and SITA buses run to/from Florence (€7.10, 1½ hours, every 30 to 60 minutes), Pisa airport (€14, two daily) and San Gimignano (€5.50, 1¼ hours, hourly), either direct or via Poggibonsi.

Sena (☎ 0577 28 32 03; www.sena.it) operates services to/from Rome (€21, three hours, 10 daily).

Lucca

POP 84,200

Lucca is a love-at-first-sight type of place. Hidden behind monumental Renaissance walls, its historic centre is chock-full of handsome churches, excellent restaurants and tempting *pasticcerie*. Founded by the Etruscans, it became a city state in the 12th century and stayed that way for 600 years. Most of its streets and monuments date from this period.

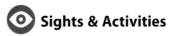

◉ Sights & Activities

CITY WALLS City Walls

Lucca's 12m-high city walls were built around the old city in the 16th and 17th centuries and were once defended by 126 cannons. In the 19th century they were crowned with a wide, tree-lined footpath that is now the centre of local Lucchese life. To join the locals in walking, jogging, rollerblading or cycling the 4km-long footpath, access it via Piazzale Verdi or Piazza Santa Maria; bike hire is available at the tourist office at Piazzale Verdi (per hour €2.50) or at one of two bike-rental shops (bikes per hour €2.50, tandems €5.50) at Piazza Santa Maria.

CATTEDRALE DI SAN MARTINO Church

(www.museocattedralelucca.it, in Italian; Piazza San Martino; ☺ 9.30am-5.45pm Mon-Fri, to 6.45pm Sat, 9am-10.45am & noon-6pm Sun Mar-Oct, 9.30am-4.45pm Mon-Fri, to 6.45pm Sat, 11.20am-11.50am & 1-4.45pm Sun Nov-Feb) The predominantly Romanesque cathedral dates to the 11th century. Its exquisite facade was designed to accommodate the pre-existing campanile, and the reliefs over the left doorway of the portico are believed to be by Nicola Pisano. Inside, there's a magnificent *Last Supper* by Tintoretto.

CHIESA E BATTISTERO DEI SS GIOVANNI E REPARATA Church

The 12th-century interior of this deconsecrated church is a hauntingly atmospheric setting for early-evening opera recitals staged by **Puccini e la sua Lucca** (☎ 340 810 60 42; www.puccinielasualucca.com; adult/concession €17/12), which are held at 7pm every evening from mid-March to October, and on every evening except Thursday from November to mid-March. Professional singers present a one-hour program of arias and duets dominated by the music of Puccini. Tickets are available from the church between 10am and 6pm.

Opera buffs should visit in July and August, when the **Puccini Festival** (☎ 0584 35 93 22; www.puccinifestival.it; Lucca ticket office Piazza Anfiteatro, tickets €33-160) is held in a purpose-built outdoor theatre in the nearby settlement of Torre del Lago.

Sleeping

AFFITTACAMERE STELLA   Pension   €
(☏0583 31 10 22; www.affittacamerestella. com; Via Pisana Traversa 2; s €45-55, d €60-70; P❋🛜) Just outside the Porta Sant'Anna, this well-regarded guest house in an early 20th-century apartment building offers comfortable and attractive rooms with wooden ceilings, a kitchen for guests' use and private parking. No breakfast.

Eating

LA PECORA NERA   Trattoria   €€
(☏0583 46 97 38; Piazza San Francesco 4; mains €9-12; ⊘closed Mon, Tue dinner, Sun lunch) The only Lucchese restaurant recommended by the Slow Food movement, La Pecora Nera also scores Brownie points for social responsibility, as its profits go to fund workshops for young people with Down syndrome.

TADDEUCCI   Cafe   €
(www.taddeucci.com; Piazza San Michele 34; ⊘8.30am-7.45pm, closed Thu Nov-Mar) This *pasticceria* is where the traditional Lucchesi treat of *buccellato* was created in 1881. A ring-shaped loaf made with flour, sultanas, aniseed seeds and sugar, it's the perfect espresso accompaniment.

Forno Giusti   Bakery   €
(Via Santa Lucia 20; pizzas & filled focaccias per kg €7-16; ⊘7am-1pm & 4-7.30pm, closed Wed afternoon & all day Sun) The best way to enjoy a Lucchese lunch is to picnic on the walls, particularly if you buy delectable provisions from this excellent bakery.

ℹ️ Information

For tourist information, go to one of Lucca's three **tourist offices** (☏0583 355 51 00; www. luccatourist.it; Piazza Napoleone (⊘10am-1pm & 2-6pm Mon-Sat); Piazza Santa Maria (⊘9am-7.30pm Apr-Oct, 9am-12.30pm & 3-6.30pm Nov-Mar); Piazza Verdi (⊘9am-7pm).

ℹ️ Getting There & Away

Lucca is on the Florence–Pisa–Viareggio train line. Regional trains run to/from Florence (Regional €5.20, 1½ hours, every 30 to 90 minutes) and Pisa (€2.40, 30 minutes, every 30 to 60 minutes).

Assisi

POP 27,600

Seen from afar, the only clue to Assisi's importance is the imposing form of the Basilica di San Francesco jutting over the hillside. Thanks to St Francis, born here in 1182, this quaint medieval town is a major destination for millions of pilgrims.

Sights

Dress rules are applied rigidly at the main religious sights, so no shorts,

Basilica di San Francesco, Assisi
PHOTOGRAPHER: RUSSELL MOUNTFORD/LONELY PLANET IMAGES ©

OLIVIER CIRENDINI/LONELY PLANET IMAGES ©

Don't Miss San Gimignano

Dubbed the medieval Manhattan, San Gimignano is a tiny hilltop town deep in the Tuscan countryside. A mecca for day trippers from Florence and Siena, it owes its nickname to the 11th-century towers that soar above its pristine *centro storico* (historic centre). Originally 72 were built as monuments to the town's wealth but only 14 remain. To avoid the worst of the crowds try to visit midweek, preferably in deep winter.

On the southern edge of Piazza del Duomo, the **Palazzo Comunale** (Piazza del Duomo; adult/concession €5/4; ⊙9.30am-7pm Mar-Oct, 10am-5.30pm Nov-Feb) houses San Gimignano's art gallery (the **Pinacoteca**) and tallest tower, the **Torre Grossa**. Climb to the top for some unforgettable views.

Nearby, the Romanesque **basilica** (Piazza del Duomo; adult/child €3.50/1.50; ⊙10am-7pm Mon-Fri, 10am-5.30pm Sat & 12.30-5.30pm Sun Apr-Oct, 10am-5pm Mon-Sat & 12.30-5pm Sun Nov-Mar), known also as the Collegiata, boasts frescos by Ghirlandaio.

While here, be sure to sample the local wine, vernaccia, while marvelling at the spectacular view from the terrace of the **Museo del Vino** (glasses €3-5; ⊙11.30am-6.30pm), which is located next to the Rocca (fortress).

Regular buses link San Gimignano with Florence (€6.50, 1¼ hours, 14 daily), travelling via Poggibonsi, and Siena (€5.50, 1¼ hours, hourly).

miniskirts, low-cut dresses or tops. To book guided tours (in English) of the Basilica di San Francesco, telephone its **information office** (📞075 819 00 84; www.sanfrancescoassisi.org; Piazza San Francesco; ⊙9am-noon & 2-5pm Mon-Sat) or use the booking form on its website.

The **Basilica di San Francesco** (Piazza di San Francesco) comprises two churches. The **upper church** (⊙8.30am-6.45pm Easter-Nov, to 5.45pm daily Nov-Easter) was damaged during a severe earthquake in 1997, but has since been restored to its former state. Built between 1230 and 1253 in the

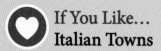

If You Like...
Italian Towns

Italy is awash with photogenic towns, although it's tough to top **San Gimignano** (p458) and **Lecce** (p475) for sheer architectural splendour.

1 VERONA
(Town centre tourist office ☎ 045 806 86 80; www.tourism.verona.it; Piazza Brà) The setting for Shakespeare's *Romeo and Juliet* is unsurprisingly one of Italy's most romantic cities. The **Casa Giulietta** where Romeo wooed Juliet is actually a modern reconstruction; legend has it that rubbing the right breast of Juliet's statue will bring you a new lover. Frequent trains to Milan, Bologna and Rome.

2 MANTUA
(Tourist office ☎ 0376 43 24 32; www.turismo.mantova.it; Piazza Andrea Mantegna 6) An easy day trip from Verona, the beautiful Unesco-listed town of Mantua was the medieval stronghold of the Gonzaga family, one of Italy's most powerful Renaissance dynasties. Their enormous palace, the **Palazzo Ducale**, houses extraordinary 15th-century frescoes by Andrea Mantegna. Frequent trains from Verona.

3 ASSISI
(Tourist office ☎ 075 81 25 34; www.assisi.regioneumbria.eu; Piazza del Comune 22) Famous for its associations with St Francis, the quaint medieval town is a major pilgrimage destination. Its main churches, the Basilica di San Francesco and the Basilica di Santa Chiara, are both hauntingly beautiful, but you'll need to dress modestly. Sulga buses connect Assisi with Rome and Florence.

Italian Gothic style, it features superb frescos by Giotto and works by Cimabue and Pietro Cavallini.

Downstairs in the dimly lit **lower church** (⏰6am-6.45pm Easter-Nov, to 5.45pm Nov-Easter), constructed between 1228 and 1230, you'll find a series of colourful frescos by Simone Martini, Cimabue and Pietro Lorenzetti. The crypt where St Francis is buried is below the church.

The 13th-century **Basilica di Santa Chiara** (075 81 22 82; Piazza Santa Chiara; ⏰6.30am-noon & 2-7pm Apr-Oct, to 6pm Nov-Mar) contains the remains of St Clare, friend of St Francis and founder of the Order of Poor Clares.

🛏 Sleeping & Eating

You'll need to book ahead during peak times: Easter, August and September, and the Feast of St Francis (3 and 4 October).

HOTEL ALEXANDER   Hotel €€
(075 81 61 90; www.hotelalexanderassisi.it; Piazza Chiesa Nuova 6; s €60-80, d €90-120; ❄🛜) Smack-bang in the centre of town, this recently renovated place is a safe choice. There are only nine rooms, but all are clean and well equipped. The roof terrace has great views.

TRATTORIA DA ERMINIO
                                    Trattoria €
(075 81 25 06; www.trattoriadaerminio.it; Via Montecavallo 19; mains €7-11, set menus €16; ⏰closed Thu, Feb & first half of Jul) Da Ermino is known for its grilled meats, which are prepared on a huge fireplace in the main dining area. In summer, tables on the pretty cobbled street are hot property, and no wonder – this is old-fashioned Umbrian dining at its rustic best. You'll find it in the upper town near Piazza Matteotti.

ℹ Information

Tourist office (☎075 81 25 34; www.assisi.regioneumbria.eu; Piazza del Comune 22; ⏰8am-2pm & 3-6pm Mon-Sat, 10am-1pm Sun) Supplies maps, brochures and practical information.

ℹ Getting There & Away

It is better to travel to Assisi by bus rather than train, as the train station is 4km from Assisi proper, in Santa Maria degli Angeli.

Sulga buses connect Assisi with Perugia (€3.20, 50 minutes, eight daily), Rome (€18, three hours, one daily) and Florence (€12.50, 2½ hours, twice weekly).

Urbino

POP 15,600

If you visit only one town in Le Marche, make it Urbino. It's difficult to get to, but as you wander its steep, Unesco-protected streets you'll appreciate the effort. Birthplace of Raphael and Bramante and a university town since 1564, it continues to be a bustling centre of culture and learning. In July, it hosts the internationally famous ancient music festival, **Urbino Musica Antica** (www.fima-online.org).

Sights

Interest is centred on Urbino's immaculate hilltop *centro storico*. To get there from the bus terminal on Borgo Mercatale, head up Via Mazzini or take the *ascensore* (lift) up to Via Garibaldi (€0.50).

PALAZZO DUCALE   Palace
(Piazza Duca Federico; adult/child €4/free;
⏰8.30am-7.15pm Tue-Sun, to 2pm Mon)
Completed in 1482. Inside, the **Galleria Nazionale delle Marche** features works by Raphael, Paolo Uccello, della Francesca and Verrocchio.

A short walk away is the **Casa Natale di Raffaello** (Via Raffaello 57; admission €3; ⏰9am-1pm & 3-7pm Mon-Sat, 10am-1pm Sun), the house where Raphael spent his first 16 years.

Information

Tourist offices
(☎0722 26 13; www.urbinoculturaturismo.it) Centre (**Via Puccinoti 35;** ⏰9am-7pm); Bus Terminus (⏰9am-6pm Mon-Sat) Also useful is www.turismo.pesarourbino.it.

Getting There & Around

The only way to get to Urbino by public transport is by bus. **Adriabus** (☎800 66 43 32; www.adriabus.eu) runs up to 20 daily buses to Pesaro (€2.75 to €3), from where you can catch a train to Bologna, and two daily services to Rome (€27, 4¼ hours).

Autolinee Ruocco (☎800 90 15 91; www.viaggiruocco.eu) runs a daily bus to Perugia (€15, 1¾ hours), for which it is essential to book in advance.

SOUTHERN ITALY

A sun-bleached land of spectacular coastlines, windswept hills and proud towns, southern Italy is a robust contrast to the genteel north. Its stunning scenery, graphic ruins and fabulous beaches often go hand in hand with urban sprawl and scruffy coastal development, sometimes in the space of a few kilometres.

Yet for all its troubles, *il mezzogiorno* (the midday sun, as southern Italy is known) has much to offer, specifically

Piazza Duca Federico, Urbino
PHOTOGRAPHER: RUSSELL MOUNTFORD/LONELY PLANET IMAGES ©

Piazza del Plebiscito, Naples

KARL BLACKWELL/LONELY PLANET IMAGES ©

the fruitful fusion of architectural, artistic and culinary styles that is the legacy of centuries of foreign dominion.

Naples

POP 963,700

Naples (Napoli) is loud, anarchic, dirty and edgy. Its manic streets and energy leave you disoriented, bewildered and hungry for more. Founded by Greek colonists, it became a thriving Roman city and was later the Bourbon capital of the Kingdom of the Two Sicilies. In the 18th century it was one of Europe's great cities, something you'll readily believe as you marvel at its imperious palaces. Many of Naples' finest *palazzi* now house museums and art galleries, the best of which is the Museo Archeologico Nazionale, one of Italy's premier museums and reason enough for a city stopover.

 Sights

CENTRO STORICO & AROUND

Neighbourhood

If you visit only one museum in southern Italy, make it the **Museo Archeologico**

Nazionale (http://museoarcheologiconazionale .campaniabeniculturali.it/, in Italian; Piazza Museo Nazionale 19; adult/EU concession €10/5; ⊙9am-7.30pm Wed-Mon), home to one of the world's most important collections of Graeco-Roman antiquities. Many of the exhibits once belonged to the Farnese family, including the colossal *Toro Farnese* (Farnese Bull) and gigantic *Ercole* (Hercules). On the mezzanine floor, *La battaglia di Alessandro contro Dario* (The Battle of Alexander against Darius) is one of many awe-inspiring mosaics from Pompeii.

A short walk south of the museum, Piazza del Gesù Nuovo is flanked by the 16th-century ashlar facade of the **Chiesa del Gesù Nuovo** (⊙7am-1pm & 4-7.30pm) and the **Basilica di Santa Chiara** (www. monasterodisantachiara.eu; Via Santa Chiara 49; ⊙7.30am-1pm & 4-8pm Mon-Sat). This hulking Gothic complex was restored to its original 14th-century look after being severely damaged by WWII bombing. The main attraction in the basilica complex is the tiled **Chiostro delle Clarisse** (Nuns' Cloisters; admission €5/3.50; ⊙9.30am-5.30pm Mon-Sat, 10am-2.30pm Sun), adjacent to the main basilica.

Just off Via Benedetto Croce, the **Museo Cappella Sansevero** (www.museosansevero.it; Via de Sanctis 19; adult/concession €7/5; ☻10am-5.40pm Mon & Wed-Sat, 10am-1.10pm Sun) reveals a sumptuous baroque interior and the *Cristo velato* (Veiled Christ), Giuseppe Sanmartino's incredibly lifelike depiction of Jesus covered by a veil.

Naples' spiritual heart is the **Duomo** (www.duomodinapoli.com; Via Duomo; ☻8am-12.30pm & 4.30-7pm Mon-Sat, 8.30am-1pm & 5-7.30pm Sun). Built by the Angevins at the end of the 13th century, it has a 19th-century neo-Gothic facade and a largely baroque interior. Inside, the holy of holies is the 17th-century **Cappella di San Gennaro**, containing the head of St Januarius (the city's patron saint) and two vials of his congealed blood. The saint is said to have saved the city from disasters on various occasions.

At the western end of Via dei Tribunali, **Port' Alba** was one of the city's 17th-century gates.

CHIAIA & SANTA LUCIA

Neighbourhood

At the bottom of Via Toledo, beyond the glass atrium of the **Galleria Umberto I** shopping arcade, Piazza Trieste e Trento leads onto **Piazza del Plebiscito**, Naples' most ostentatious piazza. Forming one side of the square, the rusty-red **Palazzo Reale** (www.palazzorealenapoli.it; Piazza del Plebiscito I; adult/EU concession €4/2; ☻9am-7pm Thu-Tue) was the official residence of the Bourbon and Savoy kings and now houses a rich collection of baroque and neoclassical furnishings, statues and paintings.

Overlooking the seafront, **Castel Nuovo** is one of Naples' landmark sites, a hulking 13th-century castle known to locals as the Maschio Angioino (Angevin Keep). Inside, the **Museo Civico** (adult/concession €5/4; ☻9am-7pm Mon-Sat) displays some interesting 14th- and 15th-century frescos and sculptures.

A second castle, the improbably named **Castel dell'Ovo** (Castle of the Egg; Borgo Marinaro; admission free; ☻8am-6pm Mon-Sat, to 1pm Sun), originally a Norman castle and then an Angevin fortress, marks the eastern end of the *lungomare* (seaside promenade). The strip of seafront here is known as Borgo Marinaro and is now given over to restaurants and bars.

VOMERO

Neighbourhood

The high point (quite literally) of Neapolitan baroque, the stunning c is one of Naples' must-see sights. Originally a 14th-century Carthusian monastery, it was given a 17th-century facelift by baroque maestro Cosimo Fanzago, and now houses the **Museo Nazionale di San Martino** (Largo San Martino 5; adult/EU concession €8/4; ☻8.30am-7.30pm Thu-Tue). Highlights include the main church, the Chiostro Grande (Great Cloister), the 'Images and Memories of Naples' exhibit in the Quarto del Priore (Priors' Quarters), and the Sezione Presepiale, dedicated to rare 18th- and 19th-centrury *presepi* (nativity scenes).

It's not worth paying the entrance fee to enter the next-door **Castel Sant' Elmo** – its views are the same as those from the Certosa.

The easiest way up to Vomero is to take the Funicolare Centrale (€1.10) from Stazione Cumana di Montesanto, near Via Toledo.

CAPODIMONTE

Museum

A 30-minute bus ride from the city centre, Capodimonte is worth a day of anyone's time. The colossal 18th-century Palazzo Reale di Capodimonte houses one of southern Italy's top fine-art museums, and the 130-hectare park is a top picnic spot.

The **Museo di Capodimonte** (Parco di Capodimonte; adult/child €10/5; ☻8.30am-7.30pm Thu-Tue) is spread over three floors and 160 rooms. You'll never see everything, but a morning should be enough for an abridged tour. With works by Bellini, Botticelli, Titian and Andy Warhol, there's no shortage of talking points, but the piece that many come to see is Caravaggio's striking *Flagellazione* (Flagellation).

Take bus 110, M4 or M5 from Stazione Centrale to get here.

Naples

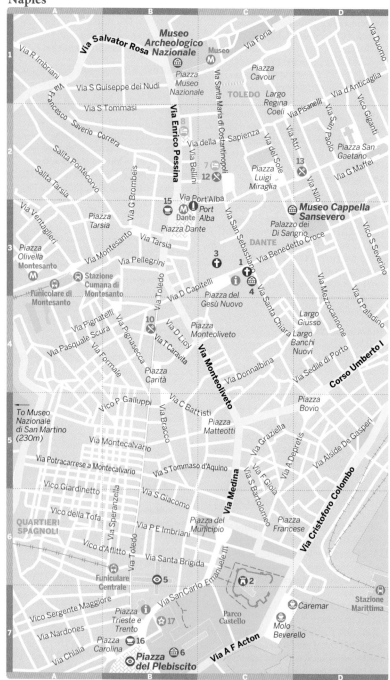

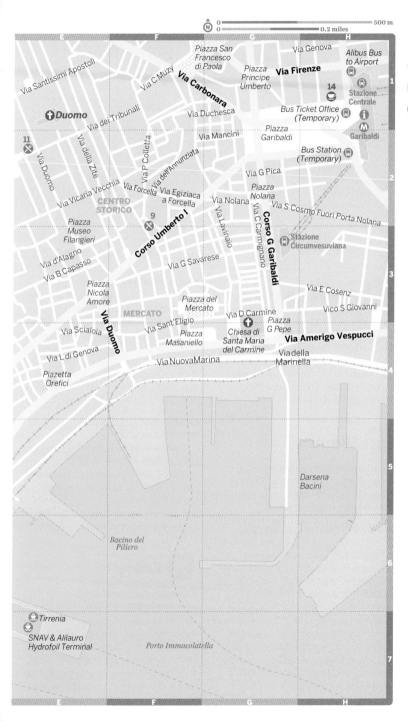

Naples

 Festivals & Events

The **Festa di San Gennaro** honours the city's patron saint and is held three times a year (first Sunday in May, 19 September and 16 December). Thousands pack into the Duomo to witness the saint's blood liquefy, a miracle said to save the city from potential disasters.

 Sleeping

You'll have no problem finding somewhere to stay, though be warned that many places suffer from street noise, and double-glazing isn't common.

ART RESORT GALLERIA UMBERTO
Boutique Hotel €€

(✆ 081 497 62 81; www.artresortgalleria umberto.it; 4th fl, Galleria Umberto I 83, Via Toledo, Quartieri Spagnoli; s €110-156, d €140-193; ✳@🛜) For a taste of Neapolitan glitz and grandeur, book into this gorgeous boutique hotel secreted on an upper floor of the magnificent Galleria Umberto I. The quiet rooms are lavishly appointed, and the price includes a delicious buffet breakfast and evening *aperitivo*. You'll need €0.10 for the lift.

COSTANTINOPOLI 104
Boutique Hotel €€€

(✆ 081 557 10 35; www.costantinopoli104.com; Via Santa Maria di Costantinopoli 104; s €170, d €220; P✳@🛜♿) Set in a neoclassical villa in the city's bohemian heartland, this quiet and elegant place is an excellent choice. The front terrace, lush garden and small swimming pool are wonderful places to relax after a long day.

LA LOCANDA DELL'ARTE & VICTORIA HOUSE B&B €

(✆ 081 564 46 40; www.bbnapoli.org; Via E Pessina 66; s €45-55, d €60-70; ✳@🛜) Spread over two floors in a grand but crumbling *palazzo* near Piazza Dante, the large rooms here have high ceilings, satellite TV and a simple but attractive decor. Excellent value, but remember €0.10 for the lift.

 Eating

Neapolitans are justifiably proud of their food. The pizza was created here – there are any number of toppings but locals favour margherita (tomato, mozzarella and basil) or marinara (tomato, garlic, oregano and olive oil), cooked in a wood-fired oven. Pizzerias serving the 'real thing' have a sign on their door – *la vera pizza napoletana* (the real Neapolitan pizza).

For something sweet try a *sfogliatella* (a flaky pastry filled with sweet orange-flavoured ricotta, and ideally served warm).

PIZZERIA SORBILLO
Pizza €

(Via dei Tribunali 32; pizzas from €4; ☾Mon-Sat) The smartest of the Via dei Tribunali pizzerias, the Sorbillo is hugely popular, so much so that eating here is much like sitting down to a meal in rush hour.

DA MICHELE
Pizza €

(www.damichele.net; Via Cesare Sersale 1/3; pizzas €4-5; ☾10am-11pm Mon-Sat) The god-father of Neapolitan pizzerias (it opened in 1870), this place near Piazza Garibaldi takes the no-frills ethos to its extremes. It's dingy and old-fashioned, and serves only two types of pizza – margherita and marinara.

IL PIZZAIOLO DEL PRESIDENTE
Pizza €

(Via dei Tribunali 120/121; pizzas from €4; ☾closed Sun) This is where British uberchef Heston Blumenthal came when he was researching pizza for his TV series *In Search of Perfection,* and for good reason. Be prepared for crowds and service with attitude.

LA STANZA DEL GUSTO
Wine Bar €€

(☎081 40 15 78; www.lastanzadel gusto.com, in Italian; Via Santa Maria di Costantinopoli 100; set menus €35-65, pastas €14, antipasto platters €22; ☾10.30am-midnight, closed Sun & Mon dinner) Gourmet set menus are served in the upstairs dining room, but the downstairs *enoteca* is more relaxed. We highly recommend the antipasto platters and a thorough investigation of the impressive wine list.

DA DORA
Seafood €€€

(☎081 68 05 19; Via Ferdinando Palasciano 30, Chiaia; mains €12-22; ☾dinner Mon-Sat, lunch Tue-Sat) This Neopolitan institution is known throughout the city for its fresh seafood. The old-fashioned interior is charming, as are the somewhat elderly waiters and the singing chef.

FANTASIA GELATI
Gelateria €

(Via Toledo 381; cones from €2; ☾7.30am-midnight) It claims to be the '*maesti gelatieri in Napoli*' ('master gelato makers in Naples'), and we thoroughly concur. Make your way to this location or the second store in **Vomero** (Piazza Vanvitelli 22; ☾7.30am-midnight).

 **Drinking**

CAFFÈ MEXICO
Cafe

(Piazza Dante 86; ☾7am-8.30pm Mon-Sat) This retro gem makes the best coffee in the city. The espresso is served *zuccherato* (sweetened), so request it *amaro* if you drink it unadorned. In summer, the

Castel Nuovo (p461)

caffè freddo con panna (iced coffee with cream) is a treat. There's another branch just near Stazione Centrale at Piazza Garibaldi 70.

GRAN CAFFÈ GAMBRINUS　　　Cafe
(www.caffegambrinus.com; Via Chiaia 1-2; ⏱7am-2am) Naples' most venerable cafe features a showy art nouveau interior and a cast of self-conscious drinkers served by smart, waistcoated waiters. It's great value when you stand at the bar.

 Entertainment

You can buy tickets for most sporting and cultural events at **Box Office** (☎081 551 91 88; www.boxofficenapoli.it; Galleria Umberto I 17).

Opera fans will enjoy an evening at **Teatro San Carlo** (☎box office 081 797 23 31; www.teatrosancarlo.it; Via San Carlo 98; box office ⏱10am-7pm Mon-Sat, 10am-3.30p Sun; tickets from €25), the oldest opera house in Italy. The opera season runs from December to

May and performances of music and ballet are held at other times of the year.

ℹ **Information**

Dangers & Annoyances

Despite Naples' notoriety as a Mafia hot spot, the city is actually pretty safe. That said, travellers should be careful about walking alone late at night near Stazione Centrale and Piazza Dante. Petty crime is also widespread – be vigilant for pickpockets and moped bandits, and make sure you never leave anything visible in a parked car.

Discount Cards

Campania ArteCard (☎800 600 601; www.campaniaartecard.it; €12-30) gives free or discounted admission to museums in Naples and the whole region. Choose the version that suits you best; some include free public transport. The Napoli e Campi Flegrei card is valid for three days, includes free public transport and will give you free entrance to three museums and 50% disount on the entrance charge for 11 others. Available at

participating museums, online or
through the call centre.

Emergency

Police station (Questura; ☎081 794 11 11; Via
Medina 75)

Medical Services

Ospedale Loreto-Mare (Hospital; ☎081 254 27
93; Via Amerigo Vespucci 26) On the waterfront,
near the train station.

Tourist Information

There are several tourist information points
(www.inaples.it) around town: Piazza del Gesù
Nuovo (☎081 551 27 01; ⊙9.30am-1.30pm &
2.30-6pm Mon-Sat, 9am-1.30pm Sun); Via Santa
Lucia (☎081 240 09 14; ⊙9am-7pm daily); Via
San Carlo (☎081 40 23 94; ⊙9.30am-1.30pm
& 2.30-6pm Mon-Sat, 9am-1.30pm Sun).

All of these stock *Qui Napoli,* a useful bilingual
monthly publication with details of sights,
transport, accommodation and major events in
Naples.

ⓘ Getting There & Away

Air

Capodichino airport (NAP; ☎848 88 87 77;
www.gesac.it), 7km northeast of the city centre,
is southern Italy's main airport. Flights operate
to most Italian cities and up to 30 European
destinations, as well as New York. Some 27 airlines
serve the airport, including Alitalia, Air One,
easyJet, Meridiana, Lufthansa, BMI and Air France.

Boat

A fleet of *traghetti* (ferries), *aliscafi* (hydrofoils)
and *navi veloci* (fast ships) connect Naples with
Sorrento, the bay islands, the Amalfi Coast,
Salerno, Sicily and Sardinia. Hydrofoils leave from
Molo Beverello and Megellina; ferries depart from
the Porta di Massa ferry terminal.

Tickets for shorter journeys can be bought at
Molo Beverello or Mergellina. For longer journeys
try ferry company offices at Porto di Massa or a
travel agent. You can also buy online.

MARTIN MOOS/LONELY PLANET IMAGES ©

Don't Miss Pompeii

An ancient town frozen in its 2000-year-old death throes, Pompeii was a thriving commercial settlement until Mt Vesuvius erupted on 24 August AD 79, burying it under a layer of *lapilli* (burning fragments of pumice stone) and killing some 2000 people. The Unesco-listed **ruins** (081 857 53 47; www.pompeiisites.org; adult/EU concession €11/5.50, audioguide €6.50; 8.30am-7.30pm Apr-Oct, 8.30am-5pm Nov-Mar, last entry 1½ hr before closing) provide a remarkable model of a working Roman city, complete with temples, a forum, an amphitheatre, apartments, a shopping district and a brothel. Dotted around the 44-hectare site are a number of creepy body casts, made in the late 19th century by pouring plaster into the hollows left by disintegrated bodies. They are so lifelike you can still see clothing folds, hair, even the expressions of terror on their faces.

There is a **tourist office** (081 536 32 93; www.pompeiturismo.it; Piazza Porta Marina Inferiore 12; 8am-6pm Mon-Sat, 8.30am-2pm Sun Aug & Sep, 8.30am-3.30pm Mon-Fri, 8.30am-2pm Sat Oct-Jul) just outside the excavations at Porta Marina.

The easiest way to get to Pompeii is by the Ferrovia Circumvesuviana from Naples (€2.40, 35 minutes, half-hourly) or Sorrento (€1.90, 30 minutes, half-hourly). Get off at Pompeii Scavi-Villa dei Misteri; the Porta Marina entrance is nearby.

Note, however, that ferry services are pared back in winter and adverse sea conditions may affect sailing schedules.

Bus

Most buses leave from Piazza Garibaldi. SITA (199 73 07 49; www.sitabus.it, in Italian) runs buses to the following destinations: Pompeii (€2.40, 40 minutes, hourly), Sorrento (€3.40, one hour 20 minutes, three daily), Positano (€3.40, two hours, three daily), Amalfi (€3.40, two hours, eight daily) and Bari (€20, three hours, one daily). Buy tickets and catch buses from the terminus near Porto di Massa or from the front of Stazione Centrale.

Miccolis (081 200 380; www.miccolis-spa. it, in Italian) serves Lecce (€29, 5½ hours) and Brindisi (€26.60, five hours).

Train

Naples is southern Italy's main rail hub. Most trains stop at Stazione Centrale, which incorporates Stazione Garibaldi. There are up to 30 trains daily to Rome (InterCity €20.50, 2¼ hours) and some 15 to Salerno (InterCity €7, 35 minutes).

The **Circumvesuviana** (800 05 39 39; www.vesuviana.it), accessible through Stazione Centrale, operates trains to Sorrento (€3.40, 65 minutes) via Pompeii (€2.40, 35 minutes) and other towns along the coast. There are about 40 trains daily running between 5am and 10.40pm, with reduced services on Sunday.

ⓘ Getting Around

To/From the Airport

By public transport you can either take the regular **ANM** (✆ 800 639 525; www.anm.it) bus 3S (€1.10, 30 minutes, half-hourly) from Piazza Garibaldi, or the Alibus airport shuttle (€3, 20 minutes, every 20 minutes) from Piazza del Municipio or Stazione Centrale.

Taxi fares are set at €19 to/from the historic centre.

Car & Motorcycle

The public car park outside Castel Nuovo charges €1.50 per hour (€2 for successive hours).

Public Transport

You can travel around Naples by bus, metro and funicular. Journeys are covered by the **Unico Napoli ticket** (www.unicocampania.it), which comes in various forms: the standard ticket, valid for 90 minutes, costs €1.10; a daily pass is €3.10; and a weekend daily ticket is €2.60. Note that these tickets are not valid on the Circumvesuviana line.

Taxi

Taxi fares are set at €10.50 between the historic centre and Piazza Garibaldi and €10 from the centre to the port. There's a €3 surcharge after 10pm (€5.50 on Sunday).

Capri

POP 7330

The most visited of Naples' Bay islands, Capri is far more interesting than a quick day trip would suggest. Get beyond the glamorous veneer of chichi piazzas and designer boutiques and you'll discover an island of rugged seascapes, desolate Roman ruins and a surprisingly unspoiled rural hinterland.

Capri's fame dates to Roman times, when Emperor Augustus made it his private playground and Tiberius retired there in AD 27. Its modern incarnation as a tourist destination dates to the early 20th century when it was invaded by an army of European artists, writers and revolutionaries, drawn by both the beauty of the locals and the thrilling landscape.

The island is easily reached from Naples and Sorrento. Hydrofoils and ferries dock at Marina Grande, from where it's a short funicular ride up to Capri, the main town. A further bus ride takes you up to Anacapri.

For the best views on the island, take the **seggiovia** (chairlift; one-way/return €7/9; ⏱9.30am-5pm Mar-Oct, 10.30am-3pm Nov-Feb) up from Piazza Vittoria to the summit of **Mt Solaro** (589m), Capri's highest point.

◎ Sights & Activities

GROTTA AZZURRA   Cave
(Blue Grotto; admission €4; ⏱9am-3pm) Capri's single most famous attraction is the Blue Grotto, a stunning sea cave illuminated by an other-worldly blue light. The best time to visit is in the morning. Boats leave from Marina Grande and the return trip costs €19.50 (€12 for the trip and €7.50 for the row boat into the grotto) plus the entrance fee to the grotto; allow a good hour. You can also take a bus from Viale Tommaso de Tommaso in Anacapri (15 minutes) or walk along Viale Tommaso de Tommaso, Via Pagliaro and Via Grotta Azzurra (50 minutes). Note that the grotto cannot be visited when seas are rough or tides are high.

GIARDINI DI AUGUSTO   Garden
(Gardens of Augustus; admission free; ⏱9am-1hr before sunset) Once you've explored Capri Town's dinky whitewashed streets, head over to the Giardini di Augusto for some breathtaking views. From here the magnificent **Via Krupp** zigzags vertiginously down to Marina Piccola.

VILLA JOVIS   Ancient Site

(admission €2; ⊙9am-1hr before sunset) East of Capri Town, an hour-long walk along Via Tiberio, are the ruins of the largest and most sumptuous of the island's 12 Roman villas, once Tiberius' main Capri residence. A short walk away, down Via Tiberio and Via Matermània, is **Arco Naturale**, a huge rock arch formed by the pounding sea.

VILLA SAN MICHELE   Garden

(☎081 837 14 01; Via Axel Munthe; admission €6; ⊙9am-6pm May-Sep, to 5pm Oct & Apr, to 3.30pm Nov-Feb, to 4.30pm Mar) Up in Anacapri, Villa San Michele boasts some Roman antiquities and beautiful, panoramic gardens.

Sleeping

Capri has plenty of top-end hotels but few genuinely budget options. Always book ahead, as hotel space is at a premium during summer and many places close in winter.

HOTEL LA TOSCA   Pension €€

(☎081 837 09 89; www.latoscahotel.com; Via Dalmazio Birago 5; s €48-95, d €75-150; ⊙Apr-Oct; ❄ 🎧) La Tosca is one of the island's top budget hotels. With 10 sparkling white rooms, a central location and a roof terrace with panoramic views, it presses all the right buttons.

CAPRI PALACE   Hotel €€€

(☎081 978 01 11; www.capripalace.com; Via Capodimonte 2b; s €270-360, d €350-1450; ⊙Apr-Nov; ❄ @ 🎧 ≋) This fashionable retreat has a stylish Mediterranean-style decor and is full of contemporary art. Guests rarely leave the hotel grounds, taking full advantage of the huge pool, on-site health spa and top-notch **L'Olivo** restaurant.

Eating & Drinking

Be warned that restaurants on Capri are overpriced and underwhelming. The major exception to this rule (second part only) is L'Olivo restaurant at the Capri Palace Hotel, which is the proud possessor of two Michelin stars.

DA TONINO   Restaurant €€€

(☎081 837 67 18; Via Dentecale 12; mains €22-26; ⊙closed Wed & Jan-Mar) A tranquil setting and traditional Campanian dishes await at this popular place near Piazzetta della Noci. The menu is dominated by seafood – try the grilled calamari or the salt-and-pepper prawns – and there are delicious lemon profiteroles on offer for dessert.

R Buonocore   Gelateria €

(35 Via Vittorio Emanuele; medium cone €3) Come here for the best gelato in town. You'll find it near the corner of Via Carlo Serena.

ℹ Information

Information is available online at www.capri.it, www.capritourism.com or from one of the three tourist offices (Anacapri ☎081 837 15 24; Via G Orlandi 59; ⊙9am-3pm Mon-Sat; Capri Town ☎081 837 06 86; Piazza Umberto I; ⊙8.30am-8.30pm Mon-Sat, 9am-3pm Sun Apr-Sep, 9am-1pm & 3.30-6.45pm Mon-Sat Nov-Mar; Marina Grande ☎081 837 06 34; ⊙9am-1pm & 3.30-6.45pm Mon-Sat). The offices open occasionally on Sundays in summer between 9am and 3pm.

ℹ Getting There & Around

There are year-round hydrofoils and ferries to Capri from Naples and Sorrento.

From Naples, ferries depart from Porto di Massa and hydrofoils from Molo Beverello and Mergellina. Tickets cost €16 (hydrofoil), €14.50 (fast ferry) and €9.60 (ferry) – see p467 for further details.

From Sorrento, there are more than 25 sailings a day (less in winter). You'll pay €14 for the 20-minute hydrofoil crossing, €9.80 for the 25-minute fast ferry trip.

In summer, hydrofoils and ferries connect Capri with Positano (€15.50 to €16.50) and Amalfi (€15 to €17).

On the island, buses run from Capri Town to/from Marina Grande, Anacapri and Marina Piccola. There are also buses from Marina Grande to Anacapri. Single tickets cost €1.40 on all routes, as does the funicular that links Marina Grande with Capri Town in a four-minute trip.

DAVID TOMLINSON/LONELY PLANET IMAGES ©

A tour around the island by motorboat (stopping for a swim and at the Grotta Azzurra on the way) costs €160 per group. A reputable operator is **Capri Relax** (www.caprirelaxboats.com), which has a small office near the chemist shop at Marina Grande.

Sorrento

POP 16,600

Overlooking the Bay of Naples and Mt Vesuvius, Sorrento is southern Italy's main package holiday resort. Despite this, and despite the lack of a decent beach, it's an appealing place whose laid-back charm defies all attempts to swamp it in souvenir tat. There are few must-see sights but the *centro storico* is lively and the town makes a good jumping-off point for the Amalfi Coast, Pompeii and Capri.

 **Sights & Activities**

You'll probably spend most of your time in the *centro storico,* a tight-knit area of narrow streets lined with loud souvenir stores, cafes, churches and restaurants. To the north, the **Villa Comunale park** (ad-mission free; ⏱8am-midnight Apr-Sep, 8am-8pm Nov-Mar) commands grand views over the sea to Mt Vesuvius.

The two main swimming spots are **Marina Piccola** and **Marina Grande**, although neither is especially appealing. Nicer by far is **Bagni Regina Giovanna**, a rocky beach set among the ruins of a Roman villa, 2km west of town. To get there take the SITA bus for Massalubrense.

 Sleeping

CASA ASTARITA B&B €
(☎081 877 49 06; www.casastarita.com; Corso Italia 67; d €70-110; ✳@) The six rooms in this handsome 18th-century building near Piazza Tasso are individually decorated and have all the mod cons you will need.

 Eating & Drinking

IL BUCO Restaurant €€€
(☎081 878 23 54; www.ilbucoristorante.it; II Rampa Marina Piccola 5; mains €35-40; ⏱Thu-Tue) Traditional regional specialities are given a modern makeover at Sorrento's

471

best restaurant. Housed in a monks' former wine cellar – hence the name, which means 'the hole' – it well deserves its Michelin star. In summer, seating is outside near one of the city's ancient gates.

L'ANTICA TRATTORIA Trattoria €€€ (☎ 081 807 10 82; www.anticatrattoria.it; Via P Reginaldo 33; set 4-course menu €40-46) Another excellent fine-dining option, this place has been pleasing local palettes since 1930. Choose between the tempting four-course set menus on offer (one from the sea and another from the land), or opt for a gluten-free or vegetarian version.

ℹ Information

Tourist information office (☎ 081 807 40 33; www.sorrentotourism.com; Via Luigi de Maio 35; ⏱ 8.45am-6.15pm Mon-Sat, to 12.45 Sun Aug only) In the Circolo dei Forestieri (Foreigners' Club) in front of Marina Piccola.

If you are travelling in Sorrento and along the Amalfi Coast on a SITA bus, you will save money and time by investing in a Unico Costiera travel card, available for durations of 45 minutes (€2.40) 90 minutes (€3.60), 24 hours (€7.20) and 72 hours (€18). The 24-hour and 72-hour tickets also cover one trip on the city sightseeing bus that travels between Amalfi and Ravello and Amalfi and Maiori. Buy the cards from bars, *tabacchi* and SITA or Circumvesuviana ticket offices.

ℹ Getting There & Away

Circumvesuviana trains run half-hourly between Sorrento and Naples (€3.40, 65 minutes) via Pompeii (€1.90). Regular SITA buses leave from the train station for the Amalfi Coast, stopping in Positano (50 minutes) and then Amalfi (1½ hours). Both trips are covered by a 90-minute or greater Unico Costiera travel card.

Sorrento is the main jumping-off point for Capri and ferries/hydrofoils run year-round from Marina Piccola.

Amalfi Coast

Stretching 50km along the southern side of the Sorrentine Peninsula, the Amalfi Coast (Costiera Amalfitana) is a postcard vision of Mediterranean beauty. Against a shimmering blue backdrop, whitewashed villages and terraced lemon groves cling to vertiginous cliffs backed by the craggy Lattari mountains. This Unesco-protected area is one of Italy's top tourist destinations, attracting hundreds of thousands of visitors each year, 70% of them between June and September.

ℹ Getting There & Away

There are two main entry points to the Amalfi Coast: Sorrento and Salerno. Regular SITA buses run from Sorrento to Positano (50 minutes) and Amalfi (1½ hours) and from Salerno to Amalfi (1¼ hours). All trips are covered by a 90-minute or greater Unico Costiera travel card.

Grotta dello Smeraldo, Amalfi
PHOTOGRAPHER: ALFIO GIANNOTTI/PHOTOLIBRARY ©

Between April and September, **Metrò del Mare** runs boats from Naples to Sorrento (€6.50, 45 minutes), Positano (€14, 55 minutes) and Amalfi (€15, 1½ hours). A trip from Amalfi to Positano costs €9; to Sorrento it's €11. **TravelMar** (📞089 81 19 86; www.travelmar.it) runs ferries from Amalfi to Salerno (€6) and Positano (€6) and from Salerno to Positano (€10).

By car, take the SS163 coastal road at Vietri sul Mare.

Positano
POP 3970

Approaching Positano by boat, you will be greeted by an unforgettable view of colourful, steeply stacked houses packed onto near-vertical green slopes. In town, the main activities are hanging out on the small beach and browsing the expensive boutiques that are scattered around town.

Sleeping & Eating

ALBERGO MIRAMARE   Hotel €€€
(📞089 87 50 02; www.starnet.it/miramare; Via Trara Genoino 29; s €135-150, d €185-250; ⊙Mar-Oct; ❄@🔊) Every room at this gorgeous hotel has a terrace with sea view, just one of the features that make it a dream holiday destination. Rooms are extremely comfortable, sporting all mod cons, and the common areas include a comfortable lounge and breakfast room with spectacular views.

IL SAN PIETRO   Restaurant €€€
(📞089 87 54 55; www.ilsanpietro.it; Via Laurito 2; mains €45-55; ⊙Apr-Oct) Positano's only claim to haute cuisine has fans throughout Europe. Located in the luxe hotel of the same name, it is a perfect spot for a romantic candlelit dinner. The Michelin-starred chef is Belgian, but has well and truly mastered the Italian culinary repertoire.

DA VINCENZO   Trattoria €€€
(📞089 87 51 28; www.davincenzo.it; Via Pasitea 172-178; mains €18-30; ⊙dinner daily, lunch Wed-Mon Apr-Nov) The best of the town's trattorias, Da Vincenzo has been serving *cucina di territorio* (cuisine of the territory) since 1958.

Amalfi
POP 5400

An attractive tangle of souvenir shops, dark alleyways and busy piazzas, Amalfi is the coast's main hub. Large-scale tourism has enriched the town, but it maintains a laid-back, small-town vibe, especially outside the busy summer months.

Looming over the central piazza is the town's landmark **Duomo** (Piazza del Duomo; admission 10am-5pm €2.50, 7.30am-10am & 5pm-7.30pm free; ⊙7.30am-7.30pm), one of the few relics of Amalfi's past as an 11th-century maritime superpower. Between 10am and 5pm, entry is through the adjacent **Chiostro del Paradiso** (Cloisters of Paradise; ⊙9am-7.45pm; adult/child €3/1).

Four kilometres west of town, the **Grotta dello Smeraldo** (Emerald Grotto; admission €5; ⊙9am-4pm) is the local version of Capri's famous sea cave. One-hour boat trips from Amalfi cost €10 return and operate between 9.20am and 3pm daily.

Sleeping & Eating

HOTEL LIDOMARE   Hotel €€
(📞089 87 13 32; www.lidomare.it; Largo Duchi Piccolomini 9; s €55-65, d €103-145; ❄🔊) Housed in a 14th-century building on a petite piazza, the Lidomare is a lovely, family-run hotel. The spacious rooms are full of character, with majolica tiles and fine old antiques. Some also have jacuzzis and sea views.

LA CARAVELLA   Restaurant €€€
(📞089 87 10 29; www.ristorantelacaravella.it; Via Matteo Camera 12; mains €45-55; ⊙Fri-Wed) The location leaves a lot to be desired, but if you're serious about food this is where you should eat when in Amalfi. Michelin starred, it specialises in seafood and has an amazing wine list.

Matera
POP 60,400

Set atop two rocky gorges, Matera is one of Italy's most remarkable towns. Dotting the ravines are the famous *sassi* (cave dwellings), where up to half the town's population lived until the late 1950s. Ironically, the *sassi* are now Matera's fortune,

Detour: Ravello

The refined, polished town of Ravello commands some of the finest views on the Amalfi Coast. A hair-raising 7km road trip from Amalfi, it has been home to an impressive array of bohemians including Wagner, DH Lawrence, Virginia Woolf and Gore Vidal. The main attractions are the beautiful gardens at **Villa Cimbrone** and **Villa Ruffolo**. The **tourist office** (☎089 85 70 96; www.ravellotime.it; Via Roma 18bis; ⏰9am-8pm) can provide details on these and Ravello's famous summer festival.

Regular SITA buses run from Amalfi to Ravello (€3.60; 70 minutes).

attracting visitors from all over the world, and inspiring Mel Gibson to film *The Passion of the Christ* here.

Sights & Activities

SASSI Cave Dwellings

Within Matera there are two *sassi* areas, **Barisano** and **Caveoso**. With a map you can explore them on your own, although you might find an audioguide (€8) from Viaggi Lionetti (Via XX Settembre 9) helpful.

Inhabited since the Paleolithic age, the *sassi* were brought to public attention with the publication of Carlo Levi's book *Cristo si é fermato a Eboli* (Christ Stopped at Eboli, 1954). His description of children begging for quinine to stave off endemic malaria shamed the authorities into action and about 15,000 people were forcibly relocated in the late 1950s. In 1993 the *sassi* were declared a Unesco World Heritage site.

Accessible from Via Ridola, **Sasso Caveoso** is the older and more evocative of the two *sassi*. Highlights include the **chiese rupestre** (rock churches) of **Santa Maria de Idris** and **Santa Lucia alle Malve** (both admission free; ⏰9.30am-1.30pm & 4-10pm) with their well-preserved 13th-century Byzantine frescoes.

To see how people lived in the *sassi*, the **Casa-Grotta di Vico Solitario** (off Via Bruno Buozzi; admission €1.50; ⏰9am-9pm Apr-Sep, 9.30am-5.30pm Nov-Mar) has been set up to show a typical cave house of 40 years ago.

The countryside outside Matera, the **Murgia Plateau**, is littered with dozens of Palaeolithic caves and monastic developments. It's best explored with a guide.

Tours

Viaggi Lionetti (☎0835 33 40 33; www.viaggilionetti.com; Via XX Settembre 9) and **Ferula Viaggi** (☎0835 33 65 72; www.ferulaviaggi.it; Via Cappelluti 34) offer guided tours of the *sassi* – about €13 per person for a three-hour tour – as well as excursions into Basilicata.

Sleeping

HOTEL IN PIETRA Boutique Hotel €€
(☎0835 34 40 40; www.hotelinpietra.it; Via San Giovanni Vecchio 22; s €70, d €110-150; ❄) Housed in a 13th-century church in the Sasso Barisano, this is a fabulously seductive boutique hotel. Everything about the place charms, from the glowing butter-yellow stone walls and soaring arches to the chic minimalist decor and rocky bathrooms. Unforgettable.

SASSI HOTEL Hotel €
(☎0835 33 10 09; www.hotelsassi.it; Via San Giovanni Vecchio 89; s/d €70/90, ste €105-125; ❄) In the Barisano, this friendly *sasso* hotel has a range of rooms in a rambling 18th-century *palazzo*. No two are identical, but the best are bright and spacious with tasteful, modern furniture, terraces and panoramic views.

Eating & Drinking

IL CANTUCCIO   Trattoria €€
(☑0835 33 20 90; Via delle Beccherie 33; mains
€13; ☺Tue-Sun) Family-run Il Cantuccio
is a Slow Food–recommended trattoria
serving creative regional fare. Speciality of the house is a lavish, seven-dish
antipasto, which includes a deliciously
creamy ricotta with fig syrup and a tasty
caponata (a sweet-and-sour aubergine
ratatouille).

IL TERRAZZINO   Trattoria €
(Vico San Giuseppe 7; tourist menus €18,
evening pizza menus €6; ☺closed Tue) Just
off Piazza Vittorio Veneto, this teeming
trattoria does a roaring trade in filling,
no-nonsense pastas and simple meat
dishes. Get into the swing of things with a
delicious rustic antipasto of olives, salami
and cheese.

ⓘ Information

Get *sassi* maps from the tourist information
kiosk (Via Ridola; ☺9am-12.30pm & 3-6pm)
near the entrance to Sasso Caveoso. Online
information is available at www.aptbasilicata.it
and www.sassiweb.it.

ⓘ Getting There & Away

The best way to reach Matera is by bus. From
Rome's Stazione Tiburtina, Marozzi (www.
marozzivt.it, in Italian) runs three daily buses
(€34.50, 4½ to 6½ hours). Matera's bus
terminus is north of Piazza Matteotti near the
train station.

   By train, the Ferrovie Appulo Lucano (☑080
572 52 29; www.fal-srl.it) runs hourly services to/
from Bari (€4, 1¼ hours).

Lecce
POP 94,800

Lecce's bombastic displays of jaw-
dropping baroque architecture are one of
southern Italy's highlights. Opulent to the
point of excess, the local *barocco leccese*
(Lecce baroque) style has earned this
urbane city a reputation as the 'Florence
of the South'.

Sights

BASILICA DI SANTA CROCE   Church
(☑0832 24 19 57; Via Umberto I; ☺8am-1pm &
4-9pm) The most celebrated example of
Lecce's baroque architecture is the eye-
popping Basilica di Santa Croce. It took a
team of 16th- and 17th-century craftsmen
more than 100 years to create the swirling facade that you see today. If you look
carefully you can actually see a profile of
Giuseppe Zimbalo, the chief architect,
carved into the facade to the left of the
rose window.

PIAZZA DEL DUOMO   Square
A short walk from the Basilica, Lecce's
showpiece square is yet another orgy of
architectural extravagance, much of it
down to Giuseppe Zimbalo. He restored
the 12th-century **cathedral** (☺8am-12.30pm
& 4-8pm), considered by many to be his
masterpiece, and fashioned the 68m-high
bell tower. Facing the cathedral is the
15th-century **Palazzo Vescovile** (Bishop's
Palace) and the 17th-century **Seminario**.

PIAZZA SANT'ORONZO   Square
Lecce's social and commercial hub,
Piazza Sant'Oronzo is built round the
remains of a 2nd-century **Roman amphitheatre**. Originally this was the largest in
Puglia, with a capacity for 15,000 people,
but only the lower half of the grandstand
survives.

Sleeping

SUITE 68   Boutique B&B €€
(☑0832 30 35 06; www.kalekora.it; Via Prato
7-9; s €60-80, d €80-120; ❄) Decorated with
works by local artists, the seven stylish
rooms at this city-centre B&B have been
designed with immaculate taste.

B&B CENTRO STORICO PRESTIGE
                   B&B €
(☑0832 24 33 53; www.bbprestige-lecce.it; Via
S Maria del Paradiso 4; s €50-60, d €70-90, apt
€65-90; @ ☏) A cheerful home away from
home, this is a cracking little B&B. The
irrepressible Renata ushers guests into

YANNICK LUTHY / ALAMY ©

her lovingly tended 2nd-floor flat, where sunlight floods into understated white guestrooms. There's also a pretty rooftop terrace and a ground-floor apartment for four people.

CENTRO STORICO   B&B €

(☎ 0832 24 27 27; www.bedandbreakfast.lecce.it; Via Vignes 2/b; d €70-80, ste €90-100; P ❄ 🖤) A characterful hideaway on the 2nd floor of a 16th-century *palazzo*. The high-ceilinged rooms are bright and colourful, decked out with parquet, wrought-iron beds and thoughtful extras such as kettles and ironing boards. Upstairs, there's a sun terrace where evening wine tastings are held.

Eating & Drinking

ALLE DUE CORTI   Restaurant €

(☎ 0832 24 22 23; www.alleduecorti.com; Corte dei Giugni 1; mains €9; ⏰ Mon-Sat) This traditional restaurant is a fine place to get to grips with Salento's gastronomic heritage. The menu, written in dialect, features classics such as *la taieddha* (rice, potatoes and mussels) and *pupette alla sucu* (meatballs in tomato sauce).

VICO PATARNELLO   Pizza, Restaurant €

(Vico Mondo Nuovo 2; pizzas €8; ⏰ 8pm-1.30am Tue-Sun) Follow signs to the Chiesa Greca to find this popular pizzeria-cum-restaurant in the backstreets of the historic centre. With outside seating and a modern interior, it's a lovely spot to munch on pizza or pasta dishes such as *linguine all'astice* (thin pasta ribbons with lobster).

TRATTORIA LE ZIE   Trattoria €€

(☎ 0832 24 51 78; Via Colonnello Costadura 19; mains €10; ⏰ closed Mon & dinner Sun) Also known as 'Cucina Casareccia', this family-run trattoria serves exactly what you hope it will – classic, *nonna*-style cooking. Booking essential.

ℹ Information

Tourist office (☎ 0832 24 80 92; Corso Vittorio Emanuele 24; ⏰ 9am-1pm & 4-8pm Mon-Sat Apr-Sep, to 7pm Nov-Mar)

Ufficio Informazioni Duomo (☎ 0832 52 18 77; www.infolecce.it; Piazza del Duomo 2; ⏰ 9.30am-8pm Mon-Fri, 10am-8pm Sat & Sun) Rents out bikes (per hour/day €3/15) and runs guided tours (per person €7).

❶ Getting There & Away

Lecce is the end of the main southeastern rail line and there are frequent direct trains to/from Brindisi (€2.30, 30 minutes, hourly), Bari (€8.60, 1½ to two hours), and Rome (€62, six hours, seven daily), as well as to points throughout Puglia.

By car, take the SS16 to Bari via Monopoli and Brindisi. For Taranto take the SS7.

SURVIVAL GUIDE
Directory A–Z

Accommodation

The bulk of Italy's accommodation is made up of *alberghi* (hotels) and *pensioni* – often housed in converted apartments. Other options are youth hostels, camping grounds, B&Bs, *agriturismi* (farm-stays), mountain *rifugi* (Alpine refuges), monasteries and villa/apartment rentals.

Prices fluctuate enormously between high and low season. High-season rates apply at Easter, in summer (mid-June to August), and over the Christmas to New Year period. Peak season in the ski resorts runs from December to March.

PRICE RANGES

In this chapter prices quoted are the minimum-maximum for rooms with a private bathroom and, unless otherwise stated, include breakfast. The following price indicators apply (for a high-season double room):

€€€	more than €200
€€	€110 to €200
€	less than €110

Business Hours

In this chapter, opening hours have only been provided in Information, Eating, Drinking, Entertainment and Shopping sections when they differ from the following standard hours:

Banks 8.30am-1.30pm & 3-4.30pm Mon-Fri

Bars & Cafes 7.30am-8pm; many open earlier and some stay open until the small hours; pubs often open noon-2am

Post offices major offices 8am-7pm Mon-Fri, to 1.15pm Sat; branch offices 8.30am-2pm Mon-Fri, to 1pm Sat

Restaurants noon-3pm & 7.30-11pm or midnight; most restaurants close one day a week

Shops 9am-1pm & 3.30-7.30pm, or 4-8pm Mon-Sat; in larger cities many chain stores and supermarkets open from 9am to 7.30pm Mon-Sat; some also open Sun morning, typically 9am -1pm; food shops are generally closed Thu afternoon; some other shops are closed Mon morning

Many museums, galleries and archaeological sites operate summer and winter opening hours. Winter hours are usually between November and late March or early April.

Food

Throughout this chapter, the following price indicators have been used (prices refer to the cost of a main course):

€€€	more than €18
€€	€10 to €18
€	less than €10

Practicalities

Electricity European two-pin plugs; voltage 230V @ 50Hz.

Newspapers & Magazines Leading daily *Corriere della Sera*, Rome-based *Il Messaggero*, centre-left *La Repubblica*.

Radio State-owned RAI-1, RAI-2 and RAI-3 broadcast nationwide. Big cities have their own commercial stations.

Smoking Banned in enclosed public spaces.

Time GMT +1.

Tipping Not expected, but leave an optional 10% in restaurants and small change in bars (€0.10 or €0.20).

TV & Video State-run RAI-1, RAI-2 and RAI-3 (www.rai.it), plus commercial stations Canale 5, Italia 1, Rete 4 and La 7.

Weights & Measures Metric system.

Gay & Lesbian Travellers

● Homosexuality is legal in Italy.

● It is well tolerated in major cities but overt displays of affection could attract a negative response, particularly in small towns and in the more conservative south.

Money

● Italy's currency is the euro.

● ATMs, known in Italy as *bancomat,* are widespread and will accept cards displaying the appropriate sign.

● Credit cards are widely accepted, although they are not as prevalent as in the USA or UK. Many small trattorias, pizzerias and *pensioni* only take cash. Don't assume museums, galleries and the like accept credit cards.

● You're not expected to tip on top of restaurant service charges but, if you think the service warrants it, feel free to round up the bill or leave a little extra – 10% is fine. In bars, Italians often leave small change (€0.10 or €0.20).

Post

● Italy's postal system, **Poste Italiane** (🔊 803 160; www.poste.it), is reasonably reliable.

● The standard service is *posta prioritaria.* Registered mail is known as *posta raccomandata,* insured mail as *posta assicurato.*

● *Francobolli* (stamps) are available at post offices and *tabacchi* (tobacconists) – look for a big white 'T' against a blue/black background. Tobacconists keep regular shop hours.

Public Holidays

Most Italians take their annual holiday in August. This means that many businesses and shops close down for at least a part of the month, usually around Ferragosto (15 August). Easter is another busy holiday.

New Year's Day (Capodanno) 1 January

Epiphany (Epifania) 6 January

Easter Monday (Pasquetta) March/April

Liberation Day (Giorno delle Liberazione) 25 April

Labour Day (Festa del Lavoro) 1 May

Republic Day (Festa della Repubblica) 2 June

Feast of the Assumption (Ferragosto) 15 August

All Saint's Day (Ognisanti) 1 November

Feast of the Immaculate Conception (Immacolata Concezione) 8 December

Christmas Day (Natale) 25 December

Boxing Day (Festa di Santo Stefano) 26 December

Individual towns also have holidays to celebrate their patron saints:

St Mark (Venice) 25 April

St John the Baptist (Florence, Genoa and Turin) 24 June

Saints Peter and Paul (Rome) 29 June

St Rosalia (Palermo) 15 July

St Janarius (Naples) First Sunday in May, 19 September and 16 December

St Ambrose (Milan) 7 December

Telephone

● Area codes are an integral part of all Italian phone numbers and must be dialled even when calling locally. The area codes have been listed in telephone numbers throughout this chapter.

● To call abroad from Italy, dial 🔊 00, then the relevant country code followed by the telephone number.

● To make a reverse-charge (collect) international call, dial 🔊 170. All operators speak English.

PHONE CODES

● Italy's country code is 🔊 39.

● Mobile phone numbers begin with a three-digit prefix starting with a 3.

● Toll-free (free-phone) numbers are known as *numeri verdi* and start with 800.

PHONECARDS

To phone from a public payphone you'll need a *scheda telefonica* (telephone card; (€2.50, €5). Buy these at post offices, *tabacchi* and newsstands.

Travellers with Disabilities

Italy is not an easy country for travellers with disabilities. Cobbled streets, blocked pavements and tiny lifts all make life difficult. Rome-based **Consorzio Cooperative Integrate** (COIN; ☎ 06 2326 9231; www. coinsociale.it) is the best point of reference for travellers with disabilities. Other useful websites:

Handyturismo (www.handyturismo.it) Information on Rome.

Milanopertutti (www.milanopertutti.it) Focuses on Milan.

Terre di Mare (www.terredimare.it) Covers Liguria, including Genoa and the Cinque Terre.

If you're travelling by train, **Trenitalia** (www.ferroviedellostato.it) runs a telephone info line (☎ 199 30 30 60) with details of assistance available at stations.

Visas

Schengen visa rules apply for entry.

Transport

Getting There & Away

Air

Italy's main international airports:

Leonardo da Vinci (www .adr.it) Rome; Italy's main airport, also known as Fiumicino.

Malpensa (www.sea -aeroportimilano.it) Milan's principal airport.

Ciampino (www.adr.it) Rome's second airport. For low-cost European carriers.

Pisa International Galileo Galilei (www. pisa-airport.com) Main gateway for Florence and Tuscany.

Venice Marco Polo (www.veniceairport.it)

Bologna Guglielmo Marconi (www.bologna -airport.it)

Cagliari Elmas (www.sogaer.it)

Naples Capodichino (www.gesac.it)
Italy's national carrier is **Alitalia** (www. alitalia.com).

Land

BORDER CROSSINGS

Italy borders France, Switzerland, Austria and Slovenia. The main points of entry:

From France The coast road from Nice; the Mont Blanc tunnel from Chamonix.

From Switzerland The Grand St Bernard tunnel; the Simplon tunnel; Lötschberg Base tunnel.

From Austria The Brenner Pass.

View across the Giudecca canal, Venice (p424)

CAR & MOTORCYCLE

If traversing the Alps, note that all the border crossings listed above are open year-round. Other mountain passes are often closed in winter and sometimes even in spring and autumn. Make sure you have snow chains in your car.

When driving into Italy always carry proof of ownership of a private vehicle. You'll also need third-party motor insurance.

TRAIN

International trains connect with various cities:

Milan To/from Barcelona, Paris, Basel, Geneva, Zürich and Vienna.

Rome To/from Paris, Munich and Vienna.

Venice To/from Paris, Basel, Geneva, Lucerne, Vienna, Ljubljana, Zagreb, Belgrade and Budapest.

There are also international trains from Genoa, Turin, Verona, Bologna, Florence and Naples. Details are available online at www.ferroviedellostato.it.

Eurail and Inter-Rail passes are both valid in Italy.

Sea

Dozens of ferry companies connect Italy with other Mediterranean countries. Timetables are seasonal, so always check ahead – you'll find details of routes, companies and online booking on **Traghettiweb** (www.traghettiweb.it).

Getting Around

Air

Domestic flights serve most major Italian cities and the main islands (Sardinia and Sicily), but are relatively expensive.

The main airports are in Rome, Pisa, Milan, Bologna, Genoa, Turin, Naples, Venice, Catania, Palermo and Cagliari.

Boat

Navi (large ferries) service Sicily and Sardinia; *traghetti* (smaller ferries) and *aliscafi* (hydrofoils) cover the smaller islands.

The main embarkation points for Sardinia are Genoa, Livorno, Civitavecchia and Naples; for Sicily, it's Naples and Villa San Giovanni in Calabria.

Train in the hills above Bolzano (p439), The Dolomites

Bus

○ Italy boasts an extensive and largely reliable bus network.

○ Buses are not necessarily cheaper than trains, but in mountainous areas such as Umbria, Sicily and Sardinia they are often the only choice.

Car & Motorcycle

○ Roads are generally good throughout the country and there's an excellent system of autostradas (motorways).

○ There's a toll to use most autostradas, payable in cash or by credit card at exit barriers.

○ Motorways are indicated by an A with a number (eg A1) on a green background; *strade statali* (main roads) are shown by an S or SS and number (eg SS7) against a blue background.

DRIVING LICENCES

All EU driving licences are recognised in Italy. Holders of non-EU licences must get an International Driving Permit (IDP) to accompany their national licence.

HIRE

To hire a car:

○ You must have a valid driving licence (plus IDP if required).

○ You must have had your licence for at least a year.

○ You must be aged 21 years or over. Under-25s will often have to pay a young-driver's supplement on top of the usual rates.

○ You must have a credit card.

You'll have no trouble hiring a scooter or motorcycle (provided you're over 18); there are rental agencies in all Italian cities. Rates start at about €30 a day for a 50cc scooter.

INSURANCE

If you're driving your own car, you'll need an international insurance certificate, known as a Carta Verde (Green Card), available from your insurance company.

ROAD RULES

○ Drive on the right, overtake on the left and give way to cars coming from the right.

○ It's obligatory to wear seatbelts, to drive with your headlights on outside built-up areas, and to carry a warning triangle and fluorescent waistcoat in case of breakdown.

○ Wearing a helmet is compulsory on all two-wheeled vehicles.

○ The blood alcohol limit is 0.05%.

○ Unless otherwise indicated, speed limits are as follows:

130km/h (in rain 110km/h) on autostradas

110km/h (in rain 90km/h) on all main, non-urban roads

90km/h on secondary, non-urban roads

50km/h in built-up areas

Train

Italy has an extensive rail network. Most services are run by **Trenitalia** (☎89 20 21; www.ferroviedellostato.it). There are several types of train:

Regionale or interregionale (R) Slow local services.

InterCity (IC) Fast trains between major cities.

Eurostar (ES) Similar to InterCity but faster.

Eurostar Alta Velocità (ES AV) High-speed trains operating on the Turin–Milan–Bologna–Florence–Rome–Naples–Salerno line.

TICKETS

○ Ticket prices depend on type of train and class (1st class is almost double 2nd class).

○ InterCity trains require a supplement, which is incorporated in the ticket price.

○ Generally, it's cheaper to buy all local train tickets in Italy – check for yourself on the Trenitalia website.

○ Tickets must be validated – in the yellow machines at the entrance to platforms – before boarding trains.

○ Children under four travel free, while kids between four and 12 years are entitled to discounts of between 30% and 50%.

The Netherlands & Belgium

They might be next-door neighbours, but Belgium and the Netherlands couldn't be more different in attitude and outlook. On the one side, there's Belgium: best known for its bubbly beer, top-quality chocolate and political position at the heart of the EU. But look beyond these well-worn clichés and you'll discover an eccentric little nation packed with centuries of history, art and architecture, not to mention a longstanding identity crisis between its Flemish and Walloon sides.

On the other side, there's the Netherlands: liberal, laid-back and flat as a pancake, famous for its brown cafes, spinning windmills and colourful tulip fields. But again, the stereotypes tell only half the story. Look beyond Amsterdam's canals and you'll discover a whole different side to Holland, from buzzy urban centres like Rotterdam, gorgeous medieval towns such as Leiden and Delft, and wide-open spaces such as the stunning national parks of Duinen van Texel and Hoge Veluwe.

Woman cycling on frozen river, the Netherlands
PHOTOGRAPHER: FRANS LEMMENS/LONELY PLANET IMAGES ©

The Netherlands & Belgium

NORTH SEA

Ems

RUHRGEBIET

Münster

Bad Bentheim

Groningen

Winschoterdiep

Assen

Emmen

Schiermonnikoog

Ameland

Terschelling

Vlieland

Leeuwarden

Waddenzee

Enschede

Dwingelderveld National Park

Zwolle

Deventer

IJssel

Veluwezoom National Park

Hoge Veluwe National Park

Arnhem

Waal

Nijmegen

Eindhoven

IJsselmeer

Texel

Den Helder

Alkmaar

Edam

AMSTERDAM

Amersfoort

Utrecht

Lek

Den Bosch

Tilburg

Haarlem

Aalsmeer

Gouda

Rotterdam

De Biesbosch National Park

Breda

Leiden

Delft

Kinderdijk

Dordrecht

Den Haag

Willemstad

Roosendaal

Schouwen-Duiveland

Domburg

Middelburg

4

4

4

1 2

3

4

N

0 — 20 miles

0 — 60 km

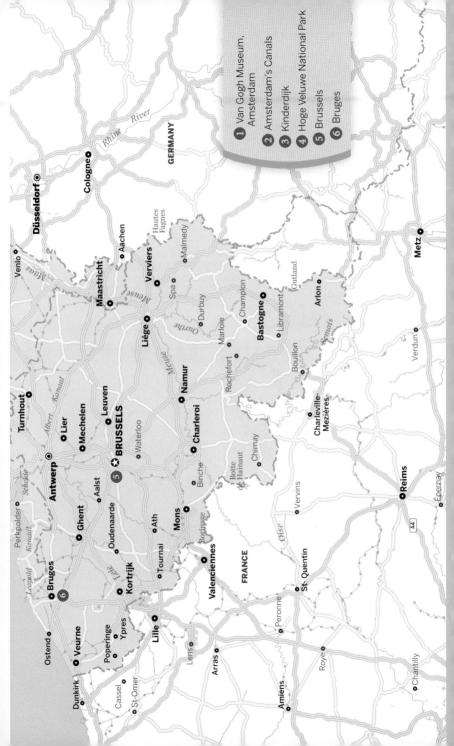

1 Van Gogh Museum, Amsterdam
2 Amsterdam's Canals
3 Kinderdijk
4 Hoge Veluwe National Park
5 Brussels
6 Bruges

The Netherlands & Belgium Highlights

JEAN-PIERRE LESCOURRET/LONELY PLANET IMAGES ©

VINCENT VAN GOGH 1853–1890

①

Van Gogh Museum

Van Gogh may have spent a lot of his life in the south of France, but he was a Dutchman by birth, and we're lucky enough to have the world's finest collection of his works right here in the heart of Amsterdam. The museum, designed by architect Kisho Kurokawa, also owns an amazing collection by his contemporaries, some of which were owned by the Van Gogh brothers themselves.

Need to Know

AUDIOGUIDES Are available in nine languages **DID YOU KNOW?** Van Gogh produced over 900 paintings between 1881 and 1890 **For full details on the Van Gogh Museum, see p498.**

Van Gogh Museum Don't Miss List

BY TEIO MEEDENDORP, RESEARCHER

1 SUNFLOWERS

If there's one painting that springs to mind when you think of Van Gogh, it's this one. It's his best-known work, and is famous for the intensity and vividness of its colours – much like the painting of his bedroom in Arles, which we also have on display at the museum. Paintings like these, with their bright colours and expressive brushwork, are Van Gogh icons, and are still inspiring people over a century later.

2 LANDSCAPE AT TWILIGHT

My favourite Van Gogh painting changes all the time, but one I keep coming back to is *Landscape at Twilight*. Van Gogh painted it in Auvers-sur-Oise in June 1890, almost a month before he took his life. The short, sharp brushstrokes, and the dramatic contrast of dark trees against an intense orange and green-yellowish sky, never seem to wear you out.

3 SPRIG OF FLOWERING ALMOND IN A GLASS

This exquisite little painting is easily missed since it's only 24cm x 19cm, the size of a sheet of paper. It's a still life with some almond blossoms just opening up. Almonds are among the first trees to bloom in spring, and this is Van Gogh's first attempt at painting them in Arles. His more famous depictions of blossoming peach, plum and pear trees followed soon afterwards, but for me this remains one of his most charming pictures.

4 THE HARVEST

Van Gogh's stunning panoramic view of yellow and green fields disappearing in the distance under a blazing hot sun was painted in Arles in the middle of the summer of 1888. Just after he finished it, the artist himself declared that it 'absolutely killed all the rest' of his work. I don't know if I'd go that far, but it's certainly stunning.

Top: Van Gogh's *Sunflowers*; **Bottom Right:** Museum exterior

Amsterdam's Canals

If any European city was tailor-made for a romantic break, it's Amsterdam (p494). The city is criss-crossed by a web of waterways left over from its days as a maritime hub, and they're still a fundamental part of the city's laid-back character. Take a river cruise, hire a houseboat, cycle along the cobbled quays or just sit back in a canalside cafe and watch the world spin by.

2

WILL SALTER/LONELY PLANET IMAGES ©

3 Kinderdijk

If you're looking for the quintessential Dutch landscape, look no further than Kinderdijk (p513). This Unesco-protected landscape southeast of Rotterdam boasts some of the Netherlands' oldest dikes and windmills, built during the 18th century to drain agricultural land. Regular boat cruises run from Rotterdam, and bikes are readily available for hire once you arrive.

JEAN-PIERRE LESCOURRET/PHOTOLIBRARY©

Hoge Veluwe National Park

4

The Netherlands might be one of the most crowded countries on the planet, but that doesn't mean you can't escape the crowds. In Hoge Veluwe, the Netherlands' largest national park, deer, wild boar and mouflon wander freely through 55 sq km of moorland, forest and dunes. The park even has its own excellent art museum, just in case the weather takes a turn for the worse. Red deer

Bruges

5

With its beautiful medieval centre and charmingly old-world atmosphere, Bruges (p535) is a true Belgian treasure. The city's most famous landmark is the huge Belfort (413m; belltower) overlooking the central marketplace – 366 winding steps lead to the top for one of the best views in Belgium. The only drawback is its popularity – try to visit the city in the low season if you possibly can.

Brussels

6

With its impressive squares, colonnaded arcades and Art Nouveau architecture, Brussels (p518) is a city that oozes grace and sophistication. Browse for antiques, taste handmade chocolates and shop till you drop, then sit back and immerse yourself in the city's famous cafe culture on Grand Place. Arcade du Cinquantenaire (p519) in Parc du Cinquantenaire

The Netherlands & Belgium's Best...

Shopping Spots

o **Albert Cuypmarkt** (p506) Haggle for some bargains in Amsterdam's biggest street market.

o **Waterlooplein** (p506) This huge flea market is great for antiques, bric-a-brac and vintage fashion.

o **Aalsmeer** (p506) Browse the technicolour blooms at this huge Dutch flower market.

o **Galeries St-Hubert** (p523) Window-shop along this elegant shopping arcade.

Views

o **The Canal Belt** (p495) Watch narrowboats putter past in Amsterdam's canal quarter.

o **Belfort, Bruges** (p536) Bruges' iconic belltower offers knockout views across the city.

o **Euromast** (p513) This striking 185m-high tower soars above Rotterdam's historic harbour.

o **Kinderdijk** (p513) The classic Dutch landscape: pancake-flat fields and spinning windmills.

o **Domtoren** (p516) 465 steps lead to the top of Utrecht's church tower.

Places for a Beer

o **Délirium Café** (p525) Brussels' largest selection of beers: 2000 and counting!

o **In de Vrede** (p540) Super-rare beers brewed by Trappist monks.

o **Heineken Experience** (p499) Visit the home of Heineken, just outside Amsterdam.

o **Musée Bruxellois de la Gueuze** (p522) Sip lambic beers at this Brussels brewery.

o **De Garre** (p539) Tiny Belgian brewpub hidden in Bruges' tangled alleyways.

Need to Know

Art Galleries

○ Rijksmuseum (p498)
Still the daddy of Dutch art galleries (despite the endless renovations).

○ Van Gogh Museum (p498) The world's largest collection of Vincent's works.

○ Museum het Rembrandthuis (p499)
Visit Rembrandt's studio in Amsterdam.

○ Museum Boijmans van Beuningen (p512)
Admire Dutch old masters, surrealists and pop artists at this Rotterdam landmark.

○ SMAK (p532) Belgium's top contemporary gallery, near Ghent.

ADVANCE PLANNING

○ Two months before
Book accommodation for popular cities, especially Amsterdam, Bruges and Ghent

○ At least a month before Book Eurostar tickets for the cheapest deals

○ When you arrive Pick up a Museumkaart (p543), which covers entry to 400 Dutch museums

RESOURCES

○ Netherlands Tourism Board (www.holland.com) Hotels, sights, restaurants and more

○ Dutch Railways (www .ns.nl) Plan your travel on the Dutch railways

○ Flanders (www.visitflanders .com) Specific information for the Flanders region

○ Brussels (www.brussels international.be and www.otp .be) The latest lowdown on Belgium's capital

○ Belgian beer tourism (www.belgianstyle.com) All you need to know about Belgian beer

GETTING AROUND

○ Air The Netherlands' main airports are at Schiphol (Amsterdam) and Rotterdam. Most Belgian flights land in Brussels, Antwerp, Charleroi or Liège. All airports have shuttle buses and/or trains serving the relevant cities.

○ Bus Regular buses serve major Dutch cities plus Brussels, Antwerp, Ghent and Liège

○ Car Rental costs and petrol can be pricey, but you can hire a car easily in most cities and from regional airports

○ Train Belgium and the Netherlands both have good rail networks, with high-speed trains (known as Thalys in Belgium and Hispeed in the Netherlands) connecting several major cities

BE FOREWARNED

○ Public transport The prepaid OV-chipkaart covers all public transport in the Netherlands (p549)

○ Drugs In the Netherlands, soft drugs are tolerated, but hard drugs are a serious crime. You can smoke pot *without* tobacco in coffee shops (but not cafes!).

○ Languages Belgium has three official languages – French, German and Dutch (also called Flemish). Many Dutch people speak excellent English.

The Netherlands & Belgium Itineraries

The Netherlands and Belgium both have a lot to offer – great museums, groundbreaking architecture and some of Europe's most interesting cities.

AMSTERDAM ❶

LEIDEN ❷

DELFT ❶

ROTTERDAM ❷   KINDERDIJK ❸

ANTWERP ❹

GHENT ❻

BRUSSELS ❺

3 DAYS

AMSTERDAM TO ROTTERDAM
The Dutch Essentials

For an introduction to the Netherlands, you simply can't beat **(1) Amsterdam**. It won't take you long to fall head over heels for this lovely, laid-back city. On day one you could do the Rijksmuseum, Van Gogh Museum and Rembrandtshuis, and spend the evening exploring the Red Light District.

On day two visit Anne Frank's house, where the teenager penned her diary during the Nazi occupation. Spend the afternoon exploring the canals along Prinsengracht and Herengracht and the lovely area around Jordaan. Finish up with the essential Amsterdam experience – a romantic canal cruise.

On your last day, hop on a train to **(2) Rotterdam**, Holland's funky second city, home to some of its wackiest architecture. Don't miss the experimental Overblaak development and the 185m tall Euromast, but make sure you leave time for the city's excellent arts museum, the Museum Boijmans van Beuningen. Spend the evening drinking and dining in the old harbour area of Delfshaven.

Top Left: Performance artist in Amsterdam (p494), the Netherlands; **Top Right:** Grand Place (p523) in Brussels, Belgium

5
DAYS

DELFT TO GHENT

The Road to Belgium

After the big Dutch cities, it's time to explore further afield. Two historic towns are within easy reach of Rotterdam – **(1) Delft**, famous for its decorative china, and **(2) Leiden**, Rembrandt's home town. Frequent train links make reaching either town a breeze, so devote a day to each. Then it's on to **(3) Kinderdijk**, a wonderfully Dutch landscape of 19 antique windmills spinning above pancake-flat polders. The best way to get there is by the Waterbus from central Rotterdam.

On day four, catch the train south into Belgium and hop off at **(4) Antwerp**, a fascinating old city that deserves at least a day of your time. Its main claim to fame is as the birthplace of Rubens; you can even visit the artist's original studio.

On day five, catch the train south to **(5) Brussels**, Belgium's elegant capital and one of the EU's most important cities. All roads lead to Grande Place, Brussels' magnificent main square, where you can browse for Belgian goodies in the historic Galeries St-Hubert before sampling some locally brewed beers in one of the city's many belle époque cafes.

Finish with a visit to one of Belgium's best-kept secrets, **(6) Ghent**: with its haphazard streets, old squares and waterfront cafes, it feels a lot like Bruges but without the crowds.

Discover
the Netherlands & Belgium

THE NETHERLANDS
Amsterdam

020 / POP 747,000

If Amsterdam were a staid place it would still be one of Europe's most beautiful and historic cities, right up there with Venice and Paris. But add the qualities that make it Amsterdam – the funky and mellow bars, brown cafes full of characters, pervasive irreverence, whiffs of pot and an open-air marketplace for sleaze and sex – and you have a literally intoxicating mix.

Wander the 17th-century streets, tour the iconic canals, stop off to enjoy a masterpiece and discover a funky shop. Walk or ride a bike around the concentric rings of the centre then explore the historic lanes of the Jordaan district or the Plantage and bask in the many worlds-within-worlds, where nothing ever seems the same twice.

Sights & Activities

Amsterdam is compact, and you can roam the city on foot. Hop on the occasional tram to rest your feet – or stop off in a cafe.

City Centre

The not-overly-impressive Royal Palace and the square that puts the Dam in Amsterdam anchor Amsterdam's oldest quarter. This is the busiest part of town for tourists, with many barely getting out of the train station before hitting coffee shops and the Red Light District.

NIEUWE KERK   Church

(New Church; www.nieuwekerk.nl; Dam; adult/child €5/free; ⊙10am-5pm) Just north of the Royal Palace, the late-Gothic basilica Nieuwe Kerk is the coronation church of

Oude Kerk

PHOTOGRAPHER: WILL SALTER/LONELY PLANET IMAGES ©

Amsterdam in Two Days

Start with a morning exploring Amsterdam's museum district, **Museumsplein**. The **Rijksmuseum** is still undergoing renovations, but you can glimpse a few old masters before your visit to the **Van Gogh Museum**. Have lunch at **Van Dobben**, followed by an afternoon exploring the **Canal Quarter**, especially photogenic Prinsengracht, Keizersgracht and Herengracht. If time allows, squeeze in a visit to **Anne Frank's House**, and spend the evening exploring the saucy sights and brown cafes of the **Red Light District**.

Day two begins with more sightseeing: visit Amsterdam's impressive main square, **Dam**, tick off the twin churches of the **Oude Kerk** and **Nieuwe Kerk**, take in some local history at the **Amsterdams Historisch Museum** and see Rembrandt's former studio at the **Museum het Rembrandthuis**. Take it easy in the afternoon with a leisurely wander around **Vondelpark** and a twilight **canal cruise**, and round the trip off with a gourmet dinner at **De Belhamel**.

Dutch royalty, with a carved oak chancel, a bronze choir screen, a massive, gilded organ and stained-glass windows. It's now used for exhibitions and organ concerts.

OUDE KERK — Church

(Old Church; www.oudekerk.nl; Oudekerksplein 23; adult/child €7/1; ⊙11am-5pm Mon-Sat, 1-5pm Sun) Amsterdam's oldest building, the 14th-century Oude Kerk was built to honour the city's patron saint, St Nicholas. Inside there's a dramatic Müller organ, gilded oak vaults and impressive stained-glass windows.

RED LIGHT DISTRICT — District

The Red Light District retains the power to make your jaw go limp, even if near-naked prostitutes propositioning passers-by from black-lit windows is the oldest Amsterdam cliché. Note that even in the dark heart of the district there are charming shops and cafes where the only thing that vibrates is your mobile phone. Despite the neon-lit sleaze, the district is tightly regulated and reasonably safe for strolling. The city government has been steadfastly reducing the number of licensed windows.

AMSTERDAM MUSEUM — Museum

(www.ahm.nl; Kalverstraat 92; adult/child €10/5; ⊙10am-5pm Mon-Fri, 11am-5pm Sat & Sun) Housed in the old civic orphanage, the Amsterdam Museum takes you through all the fascinating twists and turns of Amsterdam's convoluted history. Look for a re-creation of the original Café het Mandje, a touchstone in the gay-rights movement.

Canal Belt

Created in the 17th century as an upscale neighbourhood, the Canal Belt, especially in the west and south, remains Amsterdam's top district. Wandering here amid architectural treasures and their reflections on the narrow waters of the Prinsengracht, Keizersgracht and Herengracht can cause days to vanish quicker than some of Amsterdam's more lurid pursuits. No two buildings are alike, yet they combine in ever-changing, ever-pleasing harmony.

ANNE FRANK HUIS — Historic Building

(Anne Frank House; ☎556 71 00; www.annefrank .org; Prinsengracht 267; adult/child €8.50/free; ⊙9am-9pm mid-Mar–mid-Sep, to 7pm other times) The Anne Frank Huis, where Anne wrote her famous diary, lures almost a million visitors annually with its secret annexe, reconstruction of Anne's melancholy bedroom, and her actual diary, with its sunnily optimistic writing tempered by quiet despair. Look for the photo of Peter Schiff, her 'one true love'. Try going in the

Central Amsterdam

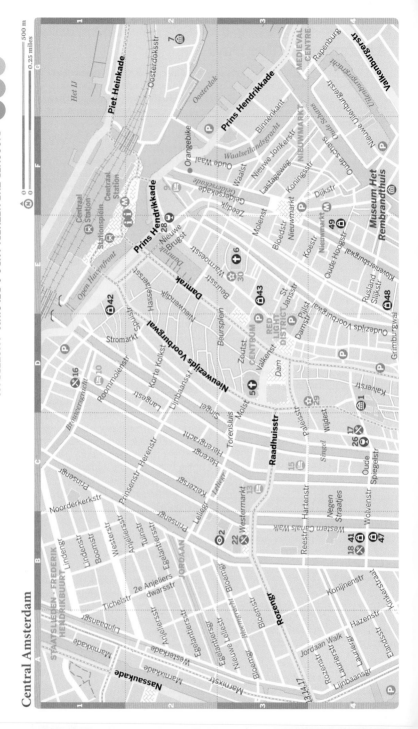

500 m
0.25 miles

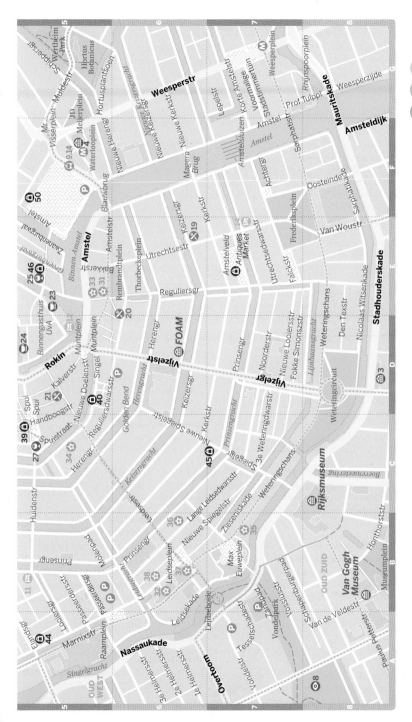

Central Amsterdam

early morning or evening when crowds are lightest; book online to avoid long queues.

FOAM   Art Gallery
(Fotografie Museum Amsterdam; www.foam.nl; Keizersgracht 609; adult/child €8/free; ⊘10am-6pm Sat-Wed, to 9pm Thu & Fri) FOAM is an airy gallery devoted to painting with light. Two storeys of changing exhibitions feature such world-renowned photographers as Sir Cecil Beaton, Annie Leibovitz and Henri Cartier-Bresson.

Museumplein

The genteel streets are a bit bland but what you'll find inside Amsterdam's big three museums will knock your wooden shoes off (if they can ever get them all open again, that is).

VAN GOGH MUSEUM   Museum
(www.vangoghmuseum.nl; Paulus Potterstraat 7; adult/child €14/free; ⊘10am-6pm Sat-Thu, to 10pm Fri) This museum houses the world's largest Van Gogh collection. Trace the artist's life from his tentative start though to the black cloud that descended over him and his work. There's also works by contemporaries Gauguin, Toulouse-Lautrec, Monet and Bernard.

RIJKSMUSEUM   Museum
(www.rijksmuseum.nl; Stadhouderskade 42; adult/child €12.50/free; ⊘9am-6pm) The nation's most revered museum boasts a collection

valued in the billions, but until renovations finish in 2013 (or later) there are only a few masterpieces displayed, including a couple of Vermeers and the crowning glory, Rembrandt's *Nightwatch* (1650). On most days crowds make the entire experience unpleasant. The rooms are tight and you'll find the Louvre's *Mona Lisa* mobs snapping pics with abandon. Save one queue by buying your ticket online.

STEDELIJK MUSEUM Museum
(www.stedelijkindestad.nl; Museumplein) When open, the Stedelijk Museum features around 100,000 pieces, including Impressionist works from Monet, Picasso and Chagall; sculptures from Rodin and Moore; De Stijl landmarks by Mondrian; and pop art from Warhol and Lichtenstein. Renovations and a new other-worldly addition mean the museum is closed until at least late 2011.

VONDELPARK Park
(www.vondelpark.nl) Vondelpark is an English-style park with free concerts, ponds, lawns, thickets, winding footpaths and three outdoor cafes. It was named after the poet and playwright Joost van den Vondel, the 'Dutch Shakespeare', and is popular with joggers, skaters, buskers and lovers.

Jordaan
Originally a stronghold of the working class, the Jordaan is now one of the most desirable areas to live in Amsterdam. It's a pastiche of modest 17th- and 18th-century merchants' houses, humble workers' homes and a few modern carbuncles, squashed into a grid of tiny lanes peppered with bite-sized cafes and shops.

De Pijp
HEINEKEN EXPERIENCE Brewery
(www.heinekenexperience.com; Stadhouderskade 78; admission €15; ☉11am-7pm) The Heineken Experience is the much-gussied-up reincarnation of the brewer's old brewery tour, featuring multimedia displays, rides and plenty of gift shops. At Amsterdam's most popular attraction, acolytes enjoy samples of the beer, which (like Stella Artois et al) is dismissed as an 'old man's beer' domestically and sold at a premium abroad.

Nieuwmarkt & Plantage
The streets around the Rembrandt House are prime wandering territory, offering a vibrant mix of old Amsterdam, canals and quirky shops and cafes.

MUSEUM HET REMBRANDTHUIS
Historic Building
(Rembrandt House Museum;www.rembrandthuis.nl; Jodenbreestraat 4; adult/child €8/1.50; ☉10am-5pm) You almost expect to find the master himself at the Museum het Rembrandthuis, the house where Rembrandt van Rijn ran his painting studio, only to lose the lot when profligacy set in, enemies swooped and bankruptcy came knocking.

JOODS HISTORISCH MUSEUM Museum
(Jewish Historical Museum; www.jhm.nl; JD Meijerplein 2-4; adult/child €7.50/3; ☉11am-5pm) A beautifully restored complex of four Ashkenazic synagogues from the 17th and 18th centuries shows the history of Jews in the Netherlands. It vividly captures the vibrant Jewish community snuffed out by WWII.

HOLLANDSCHE SCHOUWBURG
Memorial
(Holland Theatre; www.hollandscheschouwburg.nl; Plantage Middenlaan 24; admission free; ☉11am-4pm) After 1942 this theatre became a detention centre for Jews awaiting deportation. Up to 80,000 people passed through here on their way to the death camps. Among the stories told through the displays, that of Bram and Eva Beem is particularly heartbreaking (the Nazis paid a 750-guilder reward – about €15,000 today – for people who betrayed Jews in hiding).

 ## Tours

ST NICOLAAS BOAT CLUB Boat
(www.amsterdamboatclub.com; suggested donation €10) The alternative to the big staid boats bumping around the canals, these small boats are piloted by characters as interesting as the passing sights. Have a beer and a smoke and

learn about alternative Amsterdam. Departure times vary; sign up at Boom Chicago.

Sleeping

Book ahead for weekends and in summer. Many cheaper places cater specifically to party animals with booze flowing, pot smoking and general mayhem around the clock. Others exude refined old-world charm. Wi-fi is near universal but elevators are not.

MIAUW SUITES   Hotel €€€
(☎ 717 34 29; www.miauw.com; Hartenstraat 36; r from €150, 2-night minimum; 🛜) Located above the same-named fashion shop in the hip Western Canal Belt, Miauw's spacious quarters are just what the doctor ordered for a weekend's shopping blitz. Mixing stylish and vintage decor, suites here are more like one-bedroom flats.

HOTEL AMSTERDAM WIECHMANN
Hotel €€
(☎ 626 33 21; www.hotelwiechmann.nl; Prinsengracht 328; r €65-200; @ 🛜) This family-run hotel occupies three houses on the edge of the Jordaan. It has a marvellous canalside location, cosy but lovingly cared-for rooms furnished with country quilts and chintz.

HOTEL DE L'EUROPE   Grand Hotel €€€
(☎ 531 17 77; www.leurope.nl; Nieuwe Doelenstraat 2-8; r from €250; ❄ @ 🏊) Oozing Victorian elegance, L'Europe welcomes you with a marble lobby, 100 gloriously large rooms (some with terraces, most with canal views) and a sense of serene calm that makes it a blissful oasis amid the hurly-burly. Service is gracious. You can designate your stay carbon-neutral.

CHIC & BASIC AMSTERDAM   Hotel €€
(☎ 522 23 45; www.chicandbasic.com; Herengracht 13-19; s/d from €120/140; @ 🛜) Spread across three canal houses, the modern rooms here merge minimalism with cosiness and flair. The ad-sized photos

of skinny models might make you wish you hadn't wolfed down those *frites,* but if you score a Herengracht-facing room all diet thoughts will disappear out the window and into the canal.

HOTEL NADIA
Hotel €€

(620 15 50; www.nadia.nl; Raadhuisstraat 51; r €60-150; @) This handsome building has a precipitous set of stairs but the energetic staff will tote your luggage up them. Rooms are immaculate and breakfast is included. Rooms to the front have great views of the Westerkerk and the Jordaan.

HOTEL PRINSENHOF
Hotel €

(623 17 72; www.hotelprinsenhof.com; Prinsengracht 810; s/d without bathroom €49/69, s/d with bathroom €84/89;) Honest value, this 18th-century house features canal views, rooms with mismatched furniture and 'Captain Hook', the electric luggage hoist. The attic quarters provide top views and are most sought-after.

 Eating

Amsterdam abounds in food choices. Happy streets for hunting include Utrechtsestraat, Spuistraat and any of the little streets lining and connecting the west canals, such as Berenstraat.

Restaurants

DE BELHAMEL French-Italian €€€
(Brouwersgracht 60; mains €20-25) In warm weather the canalside tables at the head of the Herengracht are an aphrodisiac, and the sumptuous art nouveau interior of the De Belhamel provides the perfect backdrop for excellent French- and Italian-inspired dishes such as silky roast beef.

PANCAKES! Dutch €
(Berenstraat 38; mains from €4) A great place to sample Dutch pancakes amid cool shops along the Western Canals, in an at-

mosphere free of clogs and other kitsch – and there are just as many locals here as tourists. Kids love it.

LUCIUS — Seafood €€€
(Spuistraat 247; mains €20-30; ⏲dinner) Simple, delicious and consistently full, this seafood place is known for fresh ingredients and for not overdoing the sauce and spice. The interior is all fish tanks and tiles, and service is thorough and efficient.

TUJUH MARET — Indonesian €€
(Utrechtsestraat 73; mains €14-20) Grab a wicker chair and tuck into spicy Sulawesi-style dishes like dried, fried beef or chicken in red-pepper sauce. *Rijsttafel* is laid out according to spice intensity; *makanan kecil* is a mini-*rijsttafel*.

Cafes

Cafes run the spectrum between classic places to update your blog over coffee to full-on pubs.

CAFÉ DE JAREN — Grand Cafe €€
(Nieuwe Doelenstraat 20) Watch the Amstel float by from the balcony and waterside terraces of this soaring, bright grand cafe. The great reading table has loads of foreign publications for whiling away hours over beers.

CREA — Cafe €
(Turfdraagsterpad 17; mains €4-10) Walking along Grimburgwal, you can't help but notice the prime cafe chairs across the canal. They're part of the University of Amsterdam's cultural centre, a laid-back spot that's a superb urban escape.

Quick Eats

VAN DOBBEN — Dutch €
(Korte Reguliersdwarsstraat 5; mains from €4) The venerable Van Dobben has white tile walls and white-coated counter men who specialise in snappy banter. Trad Dutch fare is the speciality: try the *pekelvlees* (like corned beef). The best *kroketten* (croquettes) and pea soup in town.

VLEMINCKX — Frites €
(Voetboogstraat 31; frites from €2; ⏲11am-6pm) This hole-in-the-wall takeaway has drawn hordes for its monumental *frites* since 1887. The standard is smothered in mayonnaise, though you can ask for tomato sauce, peanut sauce or a variety of spicy toppings.

WIL GRAANSTRA FRITESHUIS — Frites €
(Westermarkt 11; frites from €2; ⏲11am-6pm) This little stall near the Anne Frank Huis has been serving up light and crispy fries with mayo since 1956. Nearby stalls offer local staples such as herring on a stick.

Drinking

A particular Amsterdam joy is discovering your own brown cafe. They are found everywhere, often tucked into the most atmospheric of locations. Many serve food.

Concertgebouw
PHOTOGRAPHER: IMAGEBROKER©

HOPPE Brown Cafe
(Spuistraat 18) This gritty *bruin cafe* has been luring drinkers for more than 300 years. Journalists, bums, socialites and raconteurs toss back brews amid the ancient wood panelling.

DOELEN Brown Cafe
(Kloveniersburgwal 125) On a busy cross-roads between the Amstel and De Wallen (the Red Light District), this cafe dates back to 1895 and looks it: carved wooden goat's head, stained-glass lamps, sand on the floor. During fine weather the tables spill across the street for picture-perfect canal views.

IN 'T AEPJEN Brown Cafe
(Zeedijk 1) Candles burn even during the day at this bar based in a 15th-century house, which is one of the city's two remaining wooden buildings. The name allegedly comes from the bar's role in the 16th and 17th centuries as a crash pad for sailors from the Far East, who often toted *aapjes* (monkeys) with them.

GOLLEM Bar
(Raamsteeg 4) All the brew-related para-phernalia in this minuscule space barely leaves room for the 150 beers and the connoisseurs who come to try them. The bartenders are happy to advise.

 Entertainment

Find out what's on in Thursday's papers or the monthly *Time Out Amsterdam*.

Coffee Shops

Cafes have coffee, 'coffee shops' are where one buys pot. Smoking regulations mean you can puff pot but not tobacco.

ABRAXAS Coffee Shop
(Jonge Roelensteeg 12) The Abraxas manage-ment knows what stoners want: mellow music, comfy sofas, rooms with different energy levels, and thick milkshakes. The considerate staff and mellow clientele make this a great place for coffee-shop newbies. Get stoned and send strange emails from the computers.

ROKERIJ Coffee Shop
(Lange Leidsedwarsstraat 41) Behind the black hole of an entrance you'll find Asian decor and candlelight for those tired of the Rastafarian vibe. One of many friendly locations.

Nightclubs
SUGAR FACTORY Club
(www.sugarfactory.nl; Lijnbaansgracht 238) One night it's Balkan beats; another, it's 'wicked jazz sounds' – the Sugar Factory has all kinds of live entertainment.

ESCAPE Club
(www.escape.nl; Rembrandtplein 11) Amster-dam's biggest, glitziest club has man-aged to keep the bass pumping since the '80s.

ODEON Club
(www.odeontheater.nl; Singel 460) Set in a skinny canal house, the Odeon has been a creative party spot for decades.

Live Music
PARADISO Live Music
(www.paradiso.nl; Weteringschans 6) This con-verted church has been a premier rock venue since the '60s.

CONCERTGEBOUW Live music
(🎫 for tickets 10am-5pm 671 83 45; www .concertgebouw.nl; Concertgebouwplein 2-6) Each year, this neo-Renaissance centre presents around 650 concerts attracting 840,000 visitors, making it the world's busiest concert hall (with reputedly the best acoustics).

MELKWEG Live Music
(www.melkweg.nl; Lijnbaansgracht 234A) Melkweg ('Milky Way'), which is housed in a former dairy, must be the coolest club-gallery-cinema-cafe-concert hall in Amsterdam.

Theatre
STADSSCHOUWBURG Theatre
(www.stadsschouwburgamsterdam.nl; Leidse-plein 26) Amsterdam's most beautiful theatre was built in 1894. It features large-scale productions, operettas, dance and summer English-language productions and performances.

Gay & Lesbian Amsterdam

INFORMATION

- **Gay News Amsterdam** (www.gayamsterdam.nl) Website and free paper.
- **Pink Point** (www.pinkpoint.org; ⏰noon-6pm Mar-Aug, limited hrs Sep-Feb) On the Keizersgracht, behind the Westerkerk.

ACCOMMODATION

Most hotels in town are lesbian and gay friendly, but some cater specifically to queer clientele:

BLACK TULIP HOTEL
Hotel €€

(☎427 09 33; www.blacktulip.nl; Geldersekade 16; s €125, d €145-195; @ 📶) This small hotel has more bondage gear than you can crack a whip at. Everything is fashionable and most rooms contain sling and bondage hooks; a few contain bondage chairs and steel cages. There's a three-night minimum stay at weekends.

ENTERTAINMENT

Argos
Bar

(www.argosbar.com; Warmoesstraat 95) Amsterdam's oldest leather bar. Dress code for the regular 'SOS' (Sex On Sunday) party: nude or seminude.

Montmartre
Bar

(www.cafemontmartre.nl; Halvemaansteeg 17) Beneath outrageous ceiling decorations, patrons sing loudly to Dutch ballads and top-40 songs. It's like a gay Eurovision. Regarded by many as the Benelux's best gay bar.

 Shopping

The big department stores cluster around the Dam; chains line the pedestrian (in more ways than one) Kalverstraat.

Centraal Station Area

Chills & Thrills
Headshop

(Nieuwendijk 17) Herbal trips, truffles, psychoactive cacti, novelty bongs and life-sized alien sculptures.

Red Light District

Condomerie
Condoms

(Warmoesstraat 141) Puts the 'pro' back in prophylactic: rarely can you shop for a condom in such a tasteful setting and grapple with so many choices.

Western Canals

Mendo
Designer Goods

(Berenstraat 11) A striking combination of visually stunning books, art, candy and even umbrellas.

Boekie Woekie
Books

(Berenstraat 16) Sells books by artists, whether that means a self-published monograph or an illustrated story handcrafted down to the paper.

Southern Canal Belt

Eduard Kramer
Antiques

(Nieuwe Spiegelstraat 64) One of many cute little oddball shops on this street. This one specialises in antique Dutch tiles and lots of other interesting old knick-knacks.

American Book Center
Books

(Spui 12) Amsterdam's biggest selection of English-language books, travel guides, newspapers and magazines.

Nieumarkt

Juggle   Juggling Equipment
(Staalstraat 3) Keeps many balls in the air selling juggling goods.

't Klompenhuisje   Clogs
(Nieuwe Hoogstraat 9a) A couple of canals north of Juggle, with surprisingly comfortable, traditional Dutch *klompen* (clogs).

Information

I Amsterdam Card (www.iamsterdam.com; per 24/48/72hr €38/48/58) Available at VVV offices and some hotels. Gives admission to most museums, canal boat trips, and discounts at shops, attractions and restaurants; includes a transit pass.

Tourist office (VVV; www.vvvamsterdam.nl; Stationsplein 10; ⏰9am-7pm) Maps, guides and transit passes.

Getting There & Away

Air

Most major airlines serve Schiphol (AMS; www .schiphol.nl), which lies 18km southwest of the city centre.

Bus

For details of regional transport in the Netherlands, call the transport information service (0900-9292; www.9292ov.nl); it costs €0.70 per minute.
     Amsterdam has good long-distance bus links with the rest of Europe.

Train

Amsterdam's main train station is fabled Centraal Station (CS), with service to the rest of the country and major European cities.

Getting Around

To/From the Airport

A taxi into Amsterdam from Schiphol airport takes 25 to 45 minutes and costs about €45. Trains to Centraal Station leave every few minutes, take 15 to 20 minutes, and cost €4/7 per single/return.

Bicycle

Amsterdam is cycling nirvana: flat, beautiful, with dedicated paths. About 150,000 bicycles are stolen yearly, so always lock up. Rental agencies include:
Bike City (www.bikecity.nl; Bloemgracht 68-70; per day/week €14/57) In the Jordaan; has no advertising on the bikes.

Facade of the Stadsschouwburg theatre (p503)

Markets

Markets of just about every description are scattered across the city.

Amsterdam's largest and busiest market, **Albert Cuypmarkt** (www.decuyp.nl; Albert Cuypstraat; ⊙10am-5pm Mon-Sat) has a 100-year history. Here you can find food of every description, flowers, souvenirs, clothing, hardware and household goods.

Bloemenmarkt (Singel; ⊙9am-5pm, closed Sun Dec-Feb) is a touristy 'floating' flower market that's actually on pilings. Still, at the stalls that actually stock flowers (as opposed to plastic clogs), the vibrant colours burst forth.

You can pick up jewellery, furniture, art and collectables at **De Looier Antiques Market** (www.looier.nl; Elandsgracht 109; ⊙11am-5pm Sat-Thu).

A favourite with academics, **Oudemanhuis Book Market** (Oudemanhuispoort; ⊙11am-4pm Mon-Fri) is a moody, old, covered alleyway connecting two streets and it's lined with secondhand booksellers.

Waterlooplein Flea Market (Waterlooplein; ⊙9am-5pm Mon-Fri, 8.30am-5.30pm Sat) is Amsterdam's most famous flea market: unique curios, secondhand clothing, music, used footwear, ageing electronic gear, New Age gifts and cheap bicycle parts.

Orangebike (www.orangebike.nl; Geldersekade 37; per day/week €10/43) Also offers a range of city tours (from €20).

Boat

Amsterdam's canal boats are a popular way to tour the town but most are actually a bit claustrophobic, with steamed-up glass windows surrounding passengers. Look for a boat with an open seating area.

Rederij Lovers (www.lovers.nl; Prins Hendrikkade 25-27; adult/child €10/5) Runs several routes that stop at major sights, allowing you to hop on and off; circuits last about an hour.

There are also free ferries from behind Centraal Station to destinations around the IJ, notably Amsterdam Noord.

Car & Motorcycle

Amsterdam is horrendous for parking, with charges averaging €5 per hour. Your best bet is to ditch the car at an outlying train station and ride in.

Public Transport

Services – including the iconic trams – are run by the local transit authority, the GVB; national railway (NS) tickets are not valid on local transport. The GVB has a highly useful information office (www.gvb.nl; Stationsplein 10; ⊙7am-9pm Mon-Fri, 8am-9pm Sat & Sun) across the tram tracks from the Centraal Station main entrance.

Public transport in Amsterdam uses the *OV-chipkaart* (p549). Cards for one/two hours cost €2.50/3.50 on trams and buses. Better deals are the unlimited ride tickets sold by the GVB (from machines and the office), which are good for 24/48/72/96 hours and cost €7/11.50/15.50/19.50.

Taxi

Amsterdam taxis are expensive, even if only taken over short journeys. Try Taxicentrale Amsterdam (☎677 77 77).

Around Amsterdam

Aalsmeer

☎0297 / POP 20,000

Here, at the world's biggest **flower auction** (www.floraholland.com; Legmeerdijk 313; adult/child €5/3; ⊙7-10am Mon-Fri), 21 million flowers and plants worth around €6 million change hands daily; the rose is the biggest seller, outselling the tulip three to one. Bidding usually takes place between 7am and 9.30am; Monday, Tuesday and Friday are the best days.

Take Connexxion bus 172 from Amsterdam Centraal Station to the Aalsmeer VBA stop (50 minutes, four times hourly).

Alkmaar

☎ 072 / POP 93,500

This picturesque town stages its famous **cheese market** (Waagplein; ⌚10am-noon Fri, Apr-early Sep) in the historic main square. The market dates from the 17th century. Dealers in officious white smocks insert a hollow rod to extract cheese samples, sniffing and crumbling for fat and moisture content. Then the porters, wearing colourful hats to signify their cheese guild, heft the cheeses on wooden sledges to a large scale. An average 30,000kg of cheese is on display at the Alkmaar market at any one time.

Arrive early for more than fleeting glimpses. There are four trains per hour from Amsterdam Centraal (€6.70, 40 minutes).

Randstad

When people think of Holland outside Amsterdam, they are often really thinking about the Randstad. One of the most densely populated places on the planet, it stretches from Amsterdam to Rotterdam and features the classically Dutch towns and cities of Den Haag, Utrecht, Haarlem, Leiden, Delft and Gouda. Most people focus their visit to Holland here, enjoying the peerless cycling network that links the towns amid tulip fields.

Haarlem

☎ 023 / POP 149,000

Haarlem is the Netherlands in microcosm, with canals, gabled buildings and cobblestone streets. Its historic buildings, grand churches, museums, cosy bars, good restaurants and antique shops draw scores of day trippers – it's only 15 minutes by train from Amsterdam.

 Sights

A couple of hours' stroll – with stops for refreshments – will cover Haarlem's tidy centre, which radiates out from the **Grote Markt**, where there are markets on many days.

GROTE KERK VAN ST BAVO Church
(www.grotekerk.nl; Oude Groenmarkt 23; adult/ child €2.50/free; ⌚10am-5pm Mon-Sat) This 15th-century Gothic cathedral has a

Grote Kerk Van St Bavo. Haarlem

50m-high steeple that can be seen from almost anywhere in Haarlem. It has a striking Müller organ, 30m high with around 5000 pipes.

FRANS HALS MUSEUM   Museum

(www.franshalsmuseum.nl; Groot Heiligland 62; adult/child €7.50/free; ⏱11am-5pm Tue-Sat, noon-5pm Sun) Kept in an almshouse where Frans Hals spent his final, impoverished years, the superb collection in this museum features Hals' two paintings known collectively as the *Regents & the Regentesses of the Old Men's Alms House* (1664).

CORRIE TEN BOOM HOUSE   Historic Building

(www.corrietenboom.com; Barteljorisstraat; admission free; ⏱10am-4pm Tue-Sat Apr-Oct, 11am-3pm Nov-Mar) Also known as 'the hiding place', the Corrie Ten Boom House is named for the matriarch of a family that lived in the house during WWII. Using a secret compartment in her bedroom, she hid hundreds of Jews and Dutch resistors until they could be spirited to safety. In 1944 the family was betrayed and sent to concentration camps, where three died. Later, Corrie Ten Boom toured the world preaching peace. Tours in English are offered each day.

Sleeping

HOTEL CARILLON   Hotel   €€

(☎531 05 91; www.hotelcarillon.com; Grote Markt 27; s/d from €60/80; 🛜) Small but tidy white rooms in the shadow of the Grote Kerk are the hallmark here. A few share bathrooms and cost from €40.

STEMPELS   Hotel   €€

(☎512 39 10; www.stempelsinhaarlem.nl; Klokhuisplein 9; r €90-155; @ 🛜) Haarlem's most interesting lodging has 17 spacious rooms, set in a gorgeous old printing house, on the eastern side of the Grote Kerk.

Eating & Drinking

Lange Veerstraat has a bounty of cafes, while Schagchelstraat is lined with restaurants. The Saturday morning market on Grote Markt is one of Holland's best; try the fresh *Stroopwafels* (small caramel-filled waffles).

DE HAERLEMSCHE VLAAMSE   Fast Food   €

(Spekstraat 3; frites €2) Practically on the doorstep of the Grote Kerk, this *frites* joint not much bigger than a telephone box is a local institution.

LAMBERMON'S GRAND CAFÉ   Bistro   €€

(Korte Veerstraat 1; dishes €8-25) The 'grand' in the name is almost an understatement at this oh-so-chic corner hot spot in a beautiful former fashion store. Bottles of champagne are on ice for sips by the glass; the waitstaff even manages a bit of attitude coupled with elan.

Keukenhof Gardens

PHOTOGRAPHER: MANFRED GOTTSCHALK/LONELY PLANET IMAGES

Information

The **tourist office** (www.vvvhaarlem.nl; Verwulft 11; ⏱9.30am-5.30pm Mon-Fri, 10am-5pm Sat, 11am-3pm Sun Apr-Sep, 9.30am-5.30pm Mon-Fri, 10am-5pm Sat Oct-Mar) is located in a free-standing glass house in the middle of the main shopping district.

 Getting There & Away

Trains serve Haarlem's stunning art deco station, a 10-minute walk from the centre.

Leiden

📞071 / POP 116,800

Leiden is a busy, vibrant town that is another popular day trip from Amsterdam. Claims to fame: it's Rembrandt's birthplace, it's home to the Netherlands' oldest university (and 20,000 students) and it's where America's pilgrims raised money to lease the leaky *Mayflower* that took them to the New World in 1620. Large, dignified 17th-century buildings with tall, almost regal windows line the canals.

Sights & Activities

The best way to experience Leiden is by strolling the historic centre, especially along the Rapenburg canal.

Follow the huge steeple to **Pieterskerk** (Pieterskerkhof; ⏱1-4pm), which shines after a grand restoration (a good thing as it's been prone to collapse since it was built in the 14th century). The precinct here is as old Leiden as you'll get and includes the gabled old **Latin School** (Schoolstraat), which – before it became a commercial building – was graced by a pupil named Rembrandt from 1616 to 1620.

Trains from Haarlem

DESTINATION	PRICE (€)	DURATION (MIN)	FREQUENCY (PER HR)
Amsterdam	3.80	15	5-8
Den Haag	7.30	35-40	4-6
Rotterdam	10.50	50	4

Detour:
Keukenhof Gardens

One of the Netherlands' top attractions is near Lisse, between Haarlem and Leiden: **Keukenhof** (www.keukenhof.nl; adult/child €14.50/7; ⏱8am-7.30pm mid-Mar–mid-May, last entry 6pm) is the world's largest bulb-flower garden, attracting nearly 800,000 visitors during a season almost as short-lived as the blooms on the millions of multicoloured tulips, daffodils and hyacinths.

Connexxion bus 54 travels from Leiden Centraal Station to Keukenhof (30 minutes, four times per hour).

Head east to the 15th-century **St Pancraskerk** (Nieuwstraat), which is surrounded by tiny buildings unchanged since the pilgrims were here in 1620.

LAKENHAL   Museum
(Cloth Hall; www.lakenhal.nl; Oude Singel 28-32; adult/under 18yr €7.50/free; ⏱10am-5pm Tue-Fri, noon-5pm Sat & Sun) This 17th-century museum has an assortment of works by old masters (including a few Rembrandts) as well as period rooms and temporary exhibits.

DE VALK   Historic Building
(Falcon; www.molenmuseumdevalk.nl; 2e Binnenvestgracht 1; adult/child €3/2; ⏱10am-5pm Tue-Sat, 1-5pm Sun) Leiden's carefully restored windmill sadly notes that local boy Rembrandt, though a miller's son, didn't paint many windmills.

RIJKSMUSEUM VAN OUDHEDEN
                                                Museum
(National Museum of Antiquities; www.rmo.nl; Rapenburg 28; adult/child €9/free; ⏱10am-5pm Tue-Sun) Hieroglyphs and almost 100 human and animal mummies are the supporting cast to the Temple of Taffeh, a

gift from Egypt for Dutch help in rescuing ancient monuments when the Aswan High Dam was built in the 1960s.

Sleeping

HOTEL NIEUW MINERVA   Hotel €€
(☏ 512 63 58; www.nieuwminerva.nl; Boommarkt 23; r €80-150; @ 🛜) The Minerva has a traditional look and a quiet canalside location. Some of the 40 rooms have themed decor. The Rembrandt Room features an old-style walled bed with thick privacy curtains.

REMBRANDT HOTEL   Hotel €€
(☏ 514 42 33; www.rembrandthotel.nl; Nieuwe Beestenmarkt 10; r €85-125; @) Light pouring in the windows makes the white decor of the 20 rooms that much brighter at this historic but well-cared-for inn.

 Eating & Drinking

MANGERIE DE JONGE KOEKOP
                    Bistro €€€
(Lange Mare 60; meals from €30; ⏱ dinner Mon-Sat) Always popular, this bistro has fresh and inventive fare. Dine under the stars at tables outside in summer.

BRASSERIE HET KOETSHUIS   Bistro €
(Burgsteg 13; mains from €8) Right in the shadow of De Burcht (an 11th-century citadel), you can sit on the large terrace and ponder the ramparts or huddle inside at a long table in what was once stables. Cafe classics dominate the long and varied menu.

CAFÉ L'ESPERANCE   Brown Cafe €
(Kaiserstraat 1) Long, dark and handsome, all decked out in nostalgic wood panelling *and* overlooking an evocative bend in the canal.

・・・・・・・・・・・・・・・・・・・・・・・・・・・・・・

ℹ Information

The **tourist office** (www.vvvleiden.nl; Stationsweg 41; ⏱ 8am-6pm Mon-Fri, 10am-4pm Sat, 11am-3pm Sun), across from the train station, has good maps and historic info.

・・・・・・・・・・・・・・・・・・・・・・・・・・・・・・

ℹ Getting There & Away

Buses leave from directly in front of Centraal Station.

Trains from Leiden

DESTINATION	PRICE (€)	DURATION (MIN)	FREQUENCY (PER HR)
Amsterdam	8	34	6
Den Haag	3.20	10	6
Schiphol Airport	5.30	15	6

Delft

☏ 015 / POP 96,600

Compact, charming and relaxed, Delft may be the perfect Dutch day trip. Founded around 1100, it maintains tangible links to its romantic past despite the pressures of modernisation and tourist hordes. Many of the canalside vistas could be scenes from *Girl with a Pearl Earring,* the novel about Golden Age painter Johannes Vermeer, which was made into a movie (and partially shot here) in 2003. His *View of Delft* is an enigmatic vision of the town (it hangs in the Mauritshuis in Den Haag). Delft is also famous for its 'delftware', the distinctive blue-and-white pottery originally duplicated from Chinese porcelain by 17th-century artisans.

Sights

The 14th-century **Nieuwe Kerk** (www.nieuwekerk-delft.nl; Markt; adult/child €3.50/1.50; ⏱ 9am-6pm Apr-Oct, 11am-4pm Nov-Mar, closed Sun) houses the crypt of the Dutch royal family and the mausoleum of Willem the Silent. The fee includes entrance to the **Oude Kerk** (www.oudekerk-delft.nl; Heilige Geestkerkhof; ⏱ 9am-6pm Apr-Oct, 11am-4pm Nov-Mar, closed Sun). The latter, 800 years old, is a surreal sight: its tower leans 2m from the vertical. Among the tombs inside is Vermeer's. The **town hall** and the **Waag** on the Markt are right out of the 17th century.

VERMEER CENTRE DELFT
                    Tourist Attraction
(Voldersgracht 21; adult/child €7/3; ⏱ 10am-5pm) The nonprolific painter (only 35

works are firmly attributed to him) stars at this touristy attraction, which looks at his artistry and life in detail but actually has none of his paintings.

MUNICIPAL MUSEUM HET PRINSENHOF
Museum

(www.prinsenhof-delft.nl; St Agathaplein 1; adult/child €7.50/free; ⏰10am-5pm Tue-Sat, 1-5pm Sun) This museum, in a former convent where Willem the Silent was assassinated in 1584, displays various objects telling the story of the 80-year war with Spain, as well as 17th-century paintings.

DE CANDELAER
Studio

(www.candelaer.nl; Kerkstraat 13; ⏰9am-5.30pm Mon-Fri, 9am-5pm Sat year-round, 9am-5pm Sun Mar-May) Just five artists produce iconic Delftware here. When it's quiet they'll give you a detailed tour of the manufacturing process.

ROYAL DELFT
Factory

(www.royaldelft.com; Rotterdamseweg 196; ⏰9am-5pm daily Apr-Oct, closed Sun Nov-Mar) The only original Delftware factory, operating since the 1650s. Bus 129 from the train station stops nearby at Jaffalaan, or it's a 15-minute walk.

Statue of Willem the Silent in Nieuwe Kerk, Delft

Sleeping & Eating

HOTEL DE ARK
Hotel €€

(☎215 79 99; www.deark.nl; Koornmarkt 65; r €115-160; @ 📶) Four 17th-century canalside houses have been turned into this gracious and luxurious small hotel. Rooms have vintage beauty that isn't stuffy. Out back there's a small garden; nearby are apartments for longer stays.

EETCAFÉ DE RUIFTHE
Bistro €€

(Kerkstraat 22; mains €12-18; ⏰lunch & dinner) Wonderfully rustic, with a low ceiling and canal views from a rear terrace. Try the much-loved local Stellendam shrimps.

BARRIQUE
Cafe €

(Beestenmarkt 33; meals from €8) Just east of the Markt, cafes sprawl across the shady Beestenmarkt. This slick cafe specialises in wine for the beer-weary, tapas and smooth jazz.

Information

The **tourist office** (☎0900-515 15 55; www.delft .nl; Hippolytusbuurt 4; ⏰10am-4pm Mon, 9am-6pm Tue-Fri, to 5pm Sat, to 4pm Sun) has free internet; the thematic walking guides are excellent.

Trains from Delft

DESTINATION	PRICE (€)	DURATION (MIN)	FREQUENCY (PER HR)
Amsterdam	11.60	60	2
Den Haag	2.50	12	4
Rotterdam	3.20	12	4

ⓘ Getting There & Away

The area around the train station will be a vast construction site for years to come as the lines are moved underground.

Rotterdam

☎010 / POP 606,000

Rotterdam bursts with energy. Vibrant nightlife, a diverse, multi-ethnic community, an intensely interesting maritime tradition and a wealth of top-class museums all make it a must-see part of any visit to Holland, especially if you are passing by on the new high-speed trains.

The Netherlands' 'second city', Rotterdam was bombed flat during WWII and spent the following decades rebuilding.

◉ Sights & Activities

Rotterdam is split by the vast Nieuwe Maas shipping channel, which is crossed by a series of tunnels and bridges, notably the fabulously postmodern Erasmusbrug. The centre is on the north side of the water and is easily strolled. The historic neighbourhood of Delfshaven is 3km west.

MUSEUM BOIJMANS VAN BEUNINGEN

Museum

(www.boijmans.nl; Museumpark 18-20; adult/child €9/free, Wed free; ⊙11am-5pm Tue-Sun) Museum Boijmans van Beuningen is among Europe's very finest museums and has a permanent collection taking in Dutch and European art (Bosch, Van Eyck, Rembrandt, Tintoretto, Titian and Bruegel's *Tower of Babel*). The surrealist wing features ephemera, paraphernalia and famous works from Dalí, Duchamp, Magritte, Man Ray and more.

ARCHITECTURE

Notable Buildings

Like those mod visions of the future that never seem to come to pass, Rotterdam's architecture is both fanciful and arresting.

The **Overblaak development** (1978–84), designed by Piet Blom, is marked by its pencil-shaped tower and arresting up-ended, cube-shaped apartments. One unit, the **Kijk-Kubus Museum-House** (www.kubuswoning.nl; adult/child €2.50/1.50; ⊙11am-5pm), lets you see what it's like to live at odd angles.

Designed by Ben van Berkel, the 1996 800m-long **Erasmusbrug** bridge is a city icon. Nearby, on the south bank, look for

Erasmusbrug bridge, Rotterdam
PHOTOGRAPHER: GLENN VAN DER KNIJFF/LONELY PLANET IMAGES ©

KPN Telecom headquarters, built in 2000 and designed by Renzo Piano, who also designed Paris' Pompidou Centre. The building leans at a sharp angle, seemingly resting on a long pole. There's also the very tall new **MaasToren** and **De Rotterdam**, which broke ground in 2009 and will be the largest building in the country.

MARITIEM MUSEUM ROTTERDAM
Museum

(www.maritiemmuseum.nl; Leuvehaven 1; adult/child €7.50/4; ⊙10am-5pm Tue-Sat, 11am-5pm Sun year-round, plus 10am-5pm Mon Jul & Aug) This engaging museum looks at the Netherlands' rich maritime traditions. There's an array of models that any youngster would love to take into the tub, plus more interesting and explanatory displays.

SPIDO
Harbour Cruise

(www.spido.nl; Willemsplein 85; adult/child €9.50/6; ⊙9.30am-5pm Jun-Sep, shorter hr Oct-May) Offers daily harbour tours.

EUROMAST
Observation Deck

(www.euromast.com; Parkhaven 20; adult/child €9/6; ⊙10am-11pm) At 185m, a shimmy up the Euromast is a must. It offers unparalleled 360-degree views of Rotterdam, with its rotating, glass-walled 'Euroscope' contraption ascending to near the summit, from where you'll fully appreciate just how mighty the harbour is.

DELFSHAVEN
Historic Area

Delfshaven was once the main seaport for the city of Delft and today it's a twee-free piece of Rotterdam's past. A reconstructed 18th-century **windmill** (Voorhaven 210) still grinds flour, while the **Oude Kerk** on Voorhaven is where the Pilgrim Fathers prayed for the last time before leaving the city on 22 July 1620. Get here on tram 4, which cruises lively Nieuwe Binnenweg.

Sleeping

HOTEL NEW YORK
Hotel €€

(☎439 05 00; www.hotelnewyork.nl; Koninginnenhoofd 1; r €110-220; @ 🛜) The city's most appealing hotel is housed in the former headquarters of the Holland-America passenger-ship line. The 72 art nouveau rooms – with many original and painstakingly restored decor items and fittings – are worthy of any luxury ocean liner.

HOTEL BAZAR
Hotel €€

(☎206 51 51; www.hotelbazar.nl; Witte de Withstraat 16; r €70-130) Bazar is deservedly popular for its 27 rooms styled on Middle Eastern, African and South American themes: lush, brocaded curtains, exotically tiled bathrooms and more. Top-floor rooms have balconies and views.

🍴 Eating

CENTRAL ROTTERDAM

DE BALLENTENT
Dutch €

(www.deballentent.nl; Parkkade 1; meals from €5; ⊙9am-11pm) Rotterdam's best waterfront pub-cafe is also a great spot for a meal. Mussels, schnitzels and more line the menu but the real speciality here are *bals*, huge home-made meatloafy meatballs.

Blowing in the Wind

In 1740 a series of windmills were built to drain a polder about 12km southeast of Rotterdam. Today 19 of the Dutch icons survive at **Kinderdijk** (www.kinderdijk.nl), which is a Unesco monument. You can wander the dikes for over 3km amid the spinning sails and visit inside one of the **windmills** (adult/child €3.50/2; ⊙9.30am-5.30pm). It's a good bicycle ride; you can rent bikes once there or travel from Rotterdam (16km); get a map from the tourist office.

A fantastic day trip is by the **Waterbus** (www.waterbus.nl; Willemskade; day pass adult/child €11.50/7). The fast ferries leave from Rotterdam every 30 minutes and a connection puts you at Kinderdijk, 1km from the first mill. After the visit, continue by ferry to utterly charming **Dordrecht** and then return to Rotterdam by train.

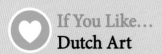

If You Like...
Dutch Art

If wandering through the **Rijksmuseum** (p498) and **Museum Boijmans van Beuningen** (p512) have piqued your interest in Dutch art, you might want to pay a visit to some of the Netherlands' more out-of-the-way museums:

1 MAURITSHUIS
(www.mauritshuis.nl; Korte Vijverberg 8; adult/child €11/free; ⏰10am-5pm Tue-Sat, 11am-5pm Sun) This small museum nestled in Den Haag (the Hague), provides a painless introduction to Dutch art. It's housed in an old city palace, and some of the highlights on display include a wistful Rembrandt self-portrait and Verneer's *Girl with a Pearl Earring*.

2 BONNEFANTENMUSEUM
(www.bonnefantenmuseum.nl; Ave Céramique 250; adult/child €8/free; ⏰11am-5pm Tue-Sun) This postmodern fantasy in Maastricht features a striking 28m tower that houses various provocative exhibits. The collection mixes Flemish masterpieces with controversial modern works.

3 GRONINGER MUSEUM
(www.groningermuseum.nl; Museumeiland 1; adult/child €10/3; ⏰10am-5pm Tue-Sun, 10am-10pm Fri) The striking, polymorphous and recently rehabbed local museum occupies three islands in the middle of the canal in front of the station and hosts contemporary design and photography exhibitions alongside classic Golden Age Dutch paintings.

4 GEMEENTEMUSEUM
(Municipal Museum; www.gemeentemuseum.nl; Stadhouderslaan 41; adult/child €10/free; ⏰11am-5pm Tue-Sun). Admirers of modernist artists such as De Stijl and Piet Mondrian mustn't miss this Berlage-designed museum in Den Haag. Mondrian's unfinished *Victory Boogie Woogie* takes pride of place (as it should: the museum paid €30 million for it), alongside other 20th-century names.

BAZAR Middle Eastern €€
(Witte de Withstraat 16; mains €7-15) On the ground floor of the inventive Hotel Bazar, this eatery comes up with creative Middle Eastern fusion fare that complements the stylised decor. Dolmades haven't tasted this good any place west of Istanbul.

DUDOK Grand Cafe €€
(Meent 88; dishes €6-20) There are always crowds at this sprawling brasserie near the centre. Inside it's all high ceilings and walls of glass; outside you have your pick of an array of tables lining the street. Meals range from breakfast to snacks to cafe fare such as soups and pasta.

DELFSHAVEN

HET EETHUISJE Dutch €
(Mathenesserdijk 436; mains €8-10) Trad Dutch food is served from this little storefront near the canal. Utterly tourist-free. Tuck into meaty fare served with rib-sticking starchy sides.

STADSBROUWERIJ DE PELGRIM Dutch €€
(Aelbrechtkolk 12; mains €7-20) This place is named for the religious folk who passed through on their way to America. Now you can come here to make your own voyage – through the various beers brewed in the vintage surrounds.

Drinking

DE OUDE SLUIS Brown Cafe
(Havenstraat 7, Delfshaven) The view up the canal from the tables outside goes right out to Delftshaven's windmill at this ideal brown cafe. Inside you'll find good beers on tap, including the hoppy Brigand IPA.

WEIMAR Cafe
(Haringvliet 637) Named for the Hotel Weimer, which used to stand here before it was blasted to rubble in 1940, this is one of scores of waterside cafes in Oude Haven.

ℹ️ Information

The Rotterdam Welcome Card (from €9) offers discounts for sights, hotels and restaurants and free public transport. Buy it from the tourist office.

Tourist office (www.rotterdam.info) City (Coolsingel 197; ⏱9am-6pm Mon-Sat, 10am-5pm Sun); Groothandelsgebouw (Weena; ⏱9am-5.30pm Mon-Sat, 10am-5pm Sun) You can get free internet here, as well as pick up the essential *R Zine*. The main (city) branch is located in the City Information Centre, with a good display on architecture since the war and a huge town model. A second location is near the train station in the landmark Groothandelsgebouw.

Use-It (www.use-it.nl; Schaatsbaan 41-45; ⏱9am-6pm Tue-Sun mid-May–mid-Sep, to 5pm Tue-Sat mid-Sep–mid-May) Offbeat independent tourist organisation all but lost amid the station construction.

ℹ️ Getting There & Away

The area around Rotterdam Centraal Station will be one big construction site until the stunning new station – set above and below ground – is completed in 2013.

Trains from Rotterdam

DESTINATION	PRICE (€)	DURATION (MIN)	FREQUENCY (PER HR)
Amsterdam via Lieden	13.30	65	5
Amsterdam (high speed)	21	40	2
Brussels	27-43	75-107	1
Schiphol	10.70	47	3
Utrecht	9.10	40	4

ℹ️ Getting Around

Rotterdam's trams, buses and metro are provided by RET (www.ret.nl). Most converge in front of CS, where there is an information booth (⏱6am-11pm Mon-Fri, 8am-11pm Sat & Sun) that also sells tickets. There are other information windows in the major metro stations. Day passes are €6.

Rent bikes from Use-it (p509) for €6 per day.

Delfshaven harbour (p513)

FRANS LEMMENS/LONELY PLANET IMAGES ©

Utrecht

📞030 / POP 302,000

Utrecht is one of the Netherlands' oldest cities and boasts a beautiful, vibrant, old-world city centre, ringed by striking 13th-century canal wharves. The wharves, well below street level, are unique to Utrecht. Canalside streets alongside brim with shops, restaurants and cafes.

Initial impressions may be less auspicious. When you step off the train you'll find yourself lost in the maze that is the Hoog Catharijne shopping centre. The Hoog is huge, attached to the station, and it seemingly goes on forever. It's really a nightmare but a vast construction project is transforming the entire area.

👁 Sights

Focus your wanderings on the **Domplein** and south along the tree-lined **Oudegracht**.

DOMTOREN
Historic Building

(www.domtoren.nl; Domplein; adult/child €8/4.50; ⏰11am-4pm) The Domtoren is 112m high, with 465 steps. It's a tough haul to the top but well worth the exertion: the tower gives unbeatable city views. The guided tour in Dutch and English is detailed and gives privileged insight into this beautiful structure. Buy tickets nearby at the tourist office.

CENTRAAL MUSEUM
Museum

(www.centraalmuseum.nl; Nicolaaskerkhof 10; adult/child €9/4; ⏰11am-5pm Tue-Sun) This museum has a wide-ranging collection: applied arts dating back to the 17th century as well as paintings by some of the Utrecht School artists. There's even a 12th-century boat that was dug out of the local mud, and a 400-year-old dollhouse. Admission also includes the following:

DICK BRUNA HUIS

(www.dickbrunahuis.nl; Nicolaaskerkhof 10) One of Utrecht's favourite sons, Dick Bruna is the creator of beloved cartoon rabbit Miffy and she naturally takes pride of place at his studio across from the museum. Kids get a huge kick out of it, but so do adults who appreciate superlative graphic design.

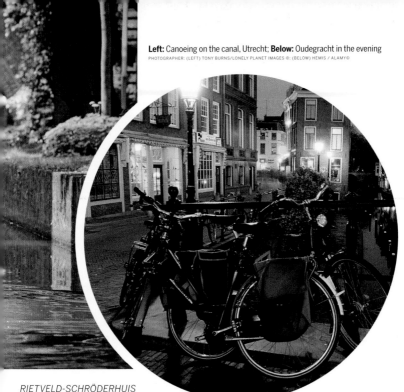

Left: Canoeing on the canal, Utrecht; **Below:** Oudegracht in the evening

RIETVELD-SCHRÖDERHUIS
This Unesco-recognised
house is just outside the centre.
Built in 1924 by Utrecht architect Gerrit
Rietveld, it is a stark example of 'form
follows function'. There's a €3 surcharge
for the mandatory tour; the museum will
give you a map for the 25-minute stroll
to the house or loan you a free bike.

 Sleeping

GRAND HOTEL KAREL V   Hotel €€€
(☎ 233 75 55; www.karelv.nl; Geertebolwerk
1, off Walsteeg; r €140-300; ❄ @ ⓦ) The
lushest accommodation in Utrecht can
be found in this former knights' gathering
hall from the 14th century. The service
and decor are understated. The 117
rooms are split between the old manor
and a new wing. Taking tea in the walled
garden is sublime.

STROWIS BUDGET HOSTEL   Hostel €
(☎ 238 02 80; www.strowis.nl; Boothstraat 8;
dm from €16, r €63; @ ⓦ) This 17th-century
building is near the town centre and has
been lovingly restored and converted

into a hostel (four- to 14-bed rooms). It
has a cosy bar and rents bikes.

 Eating

When Utrecht groans with visiting mobs,
you can escape down to the waterside
canal piers with a picnic.

BLAUW   Indonesian €€€
(www.restaurantblauw.nl; Springweg 64; set
menu from €20; ⊙dinner) Blauw is *the*
place to go for stylish Indonesian food
in Utrecht. Young and old alike enjoy
spicy, fresh fare amid the stunning red
decor, which mixes vintage art with hip
minimalism.

DEEG   Mediterranean €€€
(www.restaurantdeeg.nl; Lange Nieuwstraat
71; menus from €34; ⊙dinner) A charming
corner location in the museum quarter
is but the first draw at this casual bistro,
which has nightly set menus that
change regularly. Fresh local produce

517

Trains from Utrecht

DESTINATION	PRICE (€)	DURATION (MIN)	FREQUENCY (PER HR)
Amsterdam	6.70	30	4
Maastricht	23.50	120	2
Rotterdam	9.10	40	4

gets a Mediterranean accent and many items – such as the cheeses – are organic.

 Information

The tourist office (www.utrechtyourway.nl; Domplein 9; ⏰10am-6pm Mon-Fri, 10am-5pm Sat, noon-5pm Sun) sells maps and tours of the nearby Domtoren.

 Getting There & Away

Utrecht is easily walked (once you escape the shopping mall). The train station is a major connection point and is Holland's busiest. It is on the line linking Amsterdam to Cologne.

BELGIUM

Stereotypes of comic books, remarkable beers and sublime chocolates are just the start in this eccentric little country, whose self-deprecating people have quietly spent centuries producing some of Europe's finest art and architecture. Bilingual Brussels is the dynamic yet personable EU capital, but also sports what's arguably the world's most beautiful city square. And anyone with a love of the good life will quickly come to appreciate a country where *café*-culture is king and fine food is almost a birthright.

Brussels

POP 1.03 MILLION

Like the country it represents, Brussels (Bruxelles, Brussel) is a surreal, multi-layered place pulling several disparate identities into one enigmatic core. It subtly seduces with great art, tempting chocolate shops and classic cafes. Note that Brussels is officially bilingual, so all names – from streets to train stations – have both Dutch and French versions, but for simplicity we use only the French versions in this chapter.

 Sights

Central Brussels

Although Brussels is very spread out, most key sights and numerous unmissable *cafés* are within leisurely walking distance of the fabulous Grand Place.

MANNEKEN PIS Monument

Making a suitably surreal national symbol, the **Manneken Pis** is a diminutive fountain in the form of a little boy cheerfully taking a leak into a fountain pool. Sexual equality is ensured by his lesser-known squatting sister, the **Jeanneke Pis** (www.jeannekepis official.be; Impasse de la Fidélité).

MUSÉES ROYAUX DES BEAUX-ARTS Gallery

(Royal Museum of Fine Arts; www.fine-arts -museum.be; Rue de la Régence 3; adult/ senior/student/BrusselsCard €8/5/2/free; ⏰10am-5pm Tue-Sun) Belgium's premier collection of both ancient and modern art is remarkably well endowed with works by Flemish Primitives, the Breugel (Breughel) family and Rubens. However, many rooms are closed for long-term renovation. Headphones (for English explanations) cost an extra €2.50; special exhibitions also cost extra. A €13 combination ticket includes the Magritte Museum next door.

MAGRITTE MUSEUM Art Gallery

(www.musee-magritte-museum.be; Place Royale; adult/under 26yr/BrusselsCard €8/2/free; ⏰10am-5pm Tue-Sun) This state-of-the-art 2009 museum celebrates the life and work of Belgian surrealist artist René Magritte, taking visitors well beyond his stereotypically witty canvases of pipes and bowler hats. Consider pre-purchasing tickets online to save queuing.

MIM   Museum, Architecture

(Musical Instrument Museum; www.mim.be; Rue Montagne de la Cour 2; adult/BrusselsCard €5/free; ☺10am-5pm Tue-Sun) MIM makes one of the world's biggest collections of musical instruments much more accessible by providing a wordless audioguide that lets you hear how most of them sound.

PLACE ROYALE   Neighbourhood

Dominating this neoclassical square is a bold equestrian **statue of Godefroid de Bouillon**, the Belgian crusader knight who very briefly became the first European 'king' of Jerusalem in 1099. Around the corner, the 19th-century **Palais Royal** (www.monarchy.be/palace-and-heritage/palace-brussels; Place des Palais; admission free; ☺10.30am-4.00pm Tue-Sun late Jul-early Sep) is Belgium's slightly less-inspired cousin to Buckingham Palace. It's the Belgian king's office, but the royals no longer live here.

SABLON   Neighbourhood

Dominated by the flamboyantly Gothic church, **Église Notre-Dame du Sablon** (Rue de la Régence; ☺9am-7pm), the cobbled **Grand Place du Sablon** is lined with upmarket cafes, restaurants and chocolatier boutiques. Nearby streets are dotted with fascinating antique shops and the **Place du Petit Sablon** features a garden of 48 bronze statuettes representing the medieval guilds. A pavement outside offers rooftop panoramas towards the distant Atomium and **Koekelberg Basilica**. A glass **elevator** (☺7.30am-11.45pm) leads down into the quirky, downmarket (but slowly gentrifying) Marolles quarter.

Ixelles

MUSÉE HORTA   Museum

(www.hortamuseum.be; Rue Américaine 25; adult/child €7/3; ☺2-5.30pm Tue-Sun; M Horta, 🚊91 or 92) Architect Victor Horta's 1898 house-museum makes a fine introduction to Brussels' art nouveau heritage. Decorated with numerous century-old ornaments, the building's sinuous wrought iron and shaped wood are augmented by a partially stained-glass roof. The ticket stub includes a small map, helping you to seek out other

---

If You Like…
National Parks

If you've enjoyed the wide-open skies and wildlife of **Hoge Veluwe**, you might like to spend a few days exploring one of the Netherlands' other national parks.

1 DUINEN VAN TEXEL NATIONAL PARK
The island of Texel (*tes*-sel) is 3km off the coast of Noord Holland and makes a superb getaway from the mainland. Some 25km long and 9km wide, it's known for its sandy beaches, nature reserves, forests and picture-book villages. The entire western coast of the island is designated as a national park, where salt fens and heath alternate with grass-covered dunes. Much of the area is bird sanctuary and accessible only on foot.

2 NATIONAL PARK OOSTERSCHELDE
(www.npoosterschelde.nl; visitor centre admission free; ☺10am-5pm) The province of Zeeland (Sea Land) sits at the centre of a vast, flat delta and is one of the Netherlands' most flood-prone regions. A disastrous flood in 1953 was the impetus for the enormous Delta Project, which established a network of dams, dikes and a 3.2km storm-surge barrier to protect the area from future flooding. You can see the flood defences while exploring this lovely national park, which stretches along much of the Zeeland coastline.

---

art nouveau monuments scattered around the surrounding area. For more, see www.brusselsartnouveau.be or buy the €3 Brussels art nouveau guide from tourist offices.

Cinquantenaire

Hop off metro line 1 or 5 at Mérode to see Leopold II's triumphal arch and associated grand museums.

ARCADE DU CINQUANTENAIRE   Triumphal Arch

Reminiscent of Paris' *Arc de Triomphe,* the Cinquantenaire was designed to celebrate Belgium's 50th anniversary, but building over-ran by 25 years! To climb it, find the stairs within the free **Military Museum** (www.klm-mra.be; Parc du Cinquantenaire 3; admission/audioguide free/€3; ☺9am-11.45 &

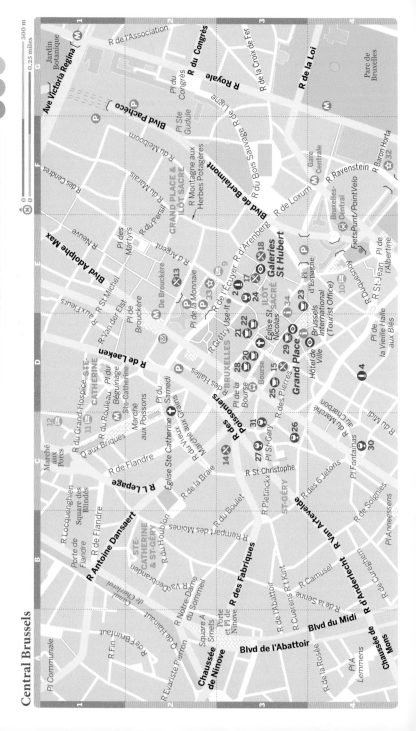

Central Brussels

0.25 miles

500 m

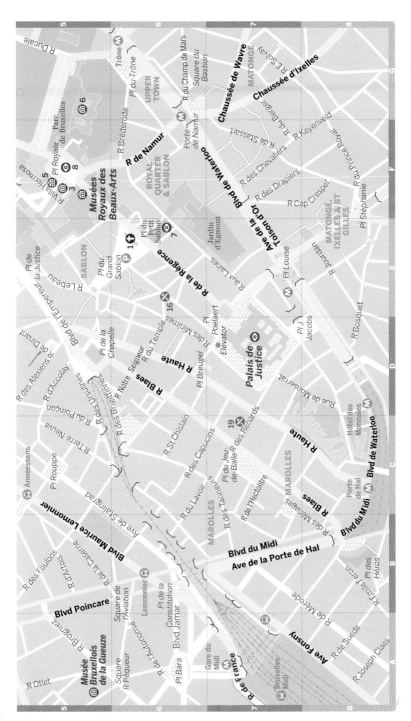

R Ducale

Trône Ⓜ

Pl du Trône

UPPER
TOWN

Ⓜ

R Bréderode

Parc
de Bruxelles

🏛 6

Pl Royale

R Villa Hermosa

5 🏛
3 🏛
8

Musées
Royaux des
Beaux-Arts

R de Namur

Porte
de Namur

ROYAL
QUARTER
& SABLON

R du Champ de Mars
Square du
Bastion

Chaussée de Wavre

MATONGE

R E Solvay

Chaussée d'Ixelles

R du Berger

R des Chevaliers

R de Stassart

R Keyenveld

R du Prince Royal

SABLON

Pl du
Grand
Sablon

1 ℹ

P

Pl du
Petit
Sablon

7 ⊙

R de la Régence

Jardin
d'Egmont

Bld de Waterloo

Ave de la Toison d'Or

R des Drapiers

R Cap Crespel

MATONGE,
IXELLES & ST
GILLES

Pl Stéphanie

Pl de
la Justice

R Lebeau

R aux Laines

Pl Louise

R Jourdan

R Bosquet

Blvd de l'Empereur

Pl de la
Chapelle

R du Temple

R des Minimes

16 ✗

R Breughel

Poelaert

Elevator

Palais de
Justice ⊙

Pl J
Jacobs

Ⓜ

R Bosquet

R de Dinant

R d'Accolay

R des Alexiens

Pl Breughel

R Haute

R Blaes

R Notre Seigneur

R des Brigittines

R des Usines

R Terre-Neuve

R du Poinçon

St Chislain

R des Capucins

19 ✗

Pl du Jeu-
de-Balle

R des Renards

R de l'Hectolitre

R Haute

Hotel des
Monnaies

Ⓜ

Blvd de Waterloo

R de Monserat

Anneessens Ⓗ

Pl Rouppe

Blvd Maurice Lemonnier

Ave de Stalingrad

R du Lavoir

MAROLLES

R des Tanneurs

R des Ménages

MAROLLES

R Blaes

Porte
de Hal Ⓜ

Blvd du Midi

Pl des
Héros

R Emile Feron

R de la Caserne

R d'Artois

R des Foulons

Square de
l'Aviation

Pl de
l'Aéroport

Lemonnier Ⓗ

Pl de la
Constitution

Blvd Jamar

Blvd Poincare

Blvd du Midi

Ave de la Porte de Hal

Blvd du Midi

R de Suède

R de Mérode

R Otlet

Musée
Bruxellois
de la Gueuze 🏛

R Broigniez

R des Foulons

R Péqueur

Square
R Péqueur

Pl Bara

Gare du
Midi

Ⓜ

Bruxelles-
Midi 🚈

R de France

Ave Fonsny

R Joseph Claes

🚈

Central Brussels

1-4.30pm Tue-Sun), which boasts a vast collection of all things military.

MUSÉE DU CINQUANTENAIRE Museum
(www.kmkg-mrah.be; Parc du Cinquantenaire 10; adult/concession/BrusselsCard €5/4/free; ⊙10am-5pm Tue-Sun) Belgium's most underestimated museum has an astonishingly rich, global collection ranging from ancient Egyptian sarcophagi to Meso-American masks, to icons to wooden bicycles. You'd need days to appreciate it all. The English-language audioguide (€3 extra) is worth considering.

Tervuren
AFRICA MUSEUM Museum
(www.africamuseum.be; Leuvensesteenweg 13, Tervuren; adult/concession/BrusselsCard €5/4/free, audioguide €2; ⊙10am-5pm Tue-Sun) In a vast formal park of lakes and manicured lawns, this veritable palace of a building was purpose-built by King Léopold II to show off Europe's most impressive array of African artefacts. Take tram 44 to its eastern terminus from metro Montgomery.

Anderlecht
MUSÉE BRUXELLOIS DE LA GUEUZE
Brewery
(www.cantillon.be; Rue Gheude 56; admission €5; ⊙9am-5pm Mon-Fri, 10am-5pm Sat; MClemenceau) In this fascinating working brewery, cobwebs and 19th-century equipment contribute to a curious spontaneous fermentation process that produces ultra-tart lambic beers, a Brussels speciality. Two tasters are included in the price of a self-guided tour. From Brussels-Midi station walk 800m north via Place Bara and Rue Limnander.

Heysel
ATOMIUM Monument, Museum
(www.atomium.be; Sq de l'Atomium; adult/concession/with BrusselsCard €11/8/9; ⊙10am-7pm May-Sep, 10am-6pm Oct-Apr; MHeyzel, ☐51) This Brussels icon is a space-age leftover

JONATHAN SMITH/LONELY PLANET IMAGES ©

Don't Miss **Grand Place**

Brussels' incomparable central square tops any itinerary. Its splendidly spired Gothic **Hôtel de Ville** was the only building to escape bombardment by the French in 1695, quite ironic considering that it was their main target. Today the pedestrianised square's splendour is due largely to its intact collection of **guildhalls**, rebuilt by merchant guilds after 1695 and fancifully adorned with gilded statues. A block northeast of Grand Place, the 1847 **Galeries St-Hubert** (www.galeries-saint-hubert.com) was Europe's first shopping arcade and remains a must-visit. Enchantingly colourful lanes of close-packed fish restaurants lead south from here down the **Rue des Bouchers**, but beware that (with some exceptions) many are notorious tourist traps.

from the 1958 World Fair consisting of nine gigantic gleaming balls impressively representing an iron crystal lattice enlarged 165 billion times. However, the interior exhibitions are less compelling and you might be happy just glimpsing the Atomium distantly from outside the vast **Palais de Justice** in central Brussels.

 Sleeping

Brussels' business hotels drop prices dramatically at weekends, during the July and August summer holidays and whenever the 'Eurocrats' are away. At such times, internet deals can get you a top-end room for little more than a midrange option and €69 walk-in deals become possible at several places around the southern entrance of the Galeries St-Hubert.

HÔTEL LE DIXSEPTIÈME

Boutique Hotel €€€

(02 502 57 44; www.ledixseptieme.be; Rue de la Madeleine 25; s/d/ste €180/200/270, weekend d/ste from €100/170;) This alluring boutique hotel occupies part of a 17th-century ambassadorial mansion. Its understated opulence reigns in all but the very cheapest rooms.

BrusselsCard

The **BrusselsCard** (www.bitc.be; 24/48/72hr €24/34/40) allows free visits to 32 Brussels-area museums (including those indicated in reviews) and gives a few bar and restaurant discounts, plus unlimited free use of city public transport. Only seriously hyperactive museum fans will save much money but, if you do buy a BrusselsCard, the following (not reviewed) are central and worth adding to your busy schedule:

National Bank Money Museum

Lace Museum

Porte de Hal (ancient city gate-fort)

Maison du Roi Includes the Manneken Pis' costumes.

Porte de Hal Ancient city gate-fort.

Brewing Museum on the Grand Place (if only for the free beer)

DOMINICAN   Business Hotel **€€€**
(02 203 08 08; www.thedominican.be; Rue Léopold 9; r weekday/weekend from €180/115; ❄ 🛜 @) Combines classic elegance with understated modern chic on the site of a former abbey. The location is brilliantly central, albeit on a side street favoured by beggars next door. Breakfast is delivered at 8am; make your own Nespresso.

MAISON NOBLE   Luxury B&B **€€**
(02 219 23 39; www.maison-noble.eu; Rue du Marcq 10; r €139-159; ❄ @ 🛜) Splendidly refined four-room guest house, in a quiet street near Place St-Catherine, features a steam room and a piano lounge.

HÔTEL NOGA   Family Hotel **€€**
(02 218 67 63; www.nogahotel.com; Rue du Béguinage 38; r weekday/weekend from €95/70; ❄ @ 🛜) Model yachts, sepia photos of Belgian royalty and assorted random kitsch lead up to rooms that are neat and clean without any particular luxuries. Prices include breakfast and one hour's wi-fi.

 Eating

Central Brussels

L'OGENBLIK   Seafood, Steak **€€€**
(02 511 61 51; www.ogenblik.be; Galerie des Princes 1; lunch €11, mains €23-28; ⏱ noon-2.30pm & 7pm-midnight) This archetypal historic bistro-restaurant has sawdust floors, close-packed tables and feels more convivially casual than most upmarket Brussels fish restaurants. Nearby, similarly priced recommendations include **Scheltema**, **Vincent**, **Chez Leon** and **Aux Armes de Bruxelles**. However, beware of many other outwardly cheaper options that give a brilliant buzz to the Rue des Bouchers and Petite Rue des Bouchers – several have been known to operate sneaky tourist-catching scams.

FIN DE SIÈCLE   Belgian **€€**
(Rue des Chartreux 9; mains €10.93-18.97; ⏱ bar 4.30pm-1am, kitchen 6pm-12.30am) A low-lit cult place with rough tables, youthful *café* ambience and great-value Belgian favourites, along with meze and tandoori chicken. There's no sign and, with no reservations accepted, you might need to queue.

BELGA QUEEN BRUSSELS   Belgian **€€**
(02 217 21 87; www.belgaqueen.be; Rue Fossé aux Loups 32; mains €16-25, weekday lunch €16; ⏱ noon-2.30pm & 7pm-midnight) Belgian cuisine is given a chic, modern twist within a magnificent, if reverberant, 19th-century bank building with classical stained-glass ceilings. There's a good wine and beer list.

Mokafé   Waffles **€**
(Galerie du Roi; ⏱ 7.30am-11.30pm) This timeless cafe in the awesome Galeries St-Hubert is ideal for coffee and cakes or €2.60 Brussels waffles.

Fritland   Chips
(Rue Henri Maus 49; ⏱ 11am-1am Sun-Thu, 10am-3am Fri & Sat) Sit-down or takeaway *frites* (chips).

Marroles & Sablon

The Sablon has many interesting, relatively upmarket eateries. Dotted along Rue Haute are several more idiosyncratic choices.

Restobières
Belgian €€

(☎02 502 72 51; www.restobieres.eu; Rue des Renards 32; mains €12-22, menus €18-38; ⏰noon-3pm Tue-Sat, 6.30pm-11pm Thu-Sat, 4pm-11pm Sun) Beer-based Belgian meals served in a Marolles backstreet amid bottles, grinders and countless antique souvenir biscuit tins featuring Belgian royalty.

Le Perroquet
Cafe €

(Rue Watteeu 31; light meals €6.50-11; ⏰noon-1am) This glorious yet relaxed art nouveau cafe serves drinks, good-value salads and an imaginative range of stuffed pitas, some vegetarian.

Drinking

Café culture is one of Brussels' greatest attractions. On the Grand Place itself, 300-year-old gems, like **Roy d'Espagne** (Grand Place 1) and **Chaloupe d'Or** (Grand Place 24), are magnificent but pricey. Cheaper classics lie around the Bourse, several down easily missed shoulder-wide alleys. Livelier pubs are ranged around Place St-Géry. The fashion-conscious head further south to Flagey.

AROUND THE BOURSE
Area

Many of Brussels's most iconic cafes are within stumbling distance of the Bourse. Don't miss century-old masterpieces **Falstaff** (Rue Henri Maus 17; ⏰10am-1am; 🍴), with its festival of stained glass ceilings, nor **Le Cirio** (Rue de la Bourse 18; ⏰10am-midnight; 🍴), a sumptuous yet affordable 1866 marvel full of polished brasswork and serving great-value pub meals. Three more classics are hidden up shoulder-wide alleys: the medieval yet unpretentious **A l'Image de Nostre-Dame** (off Rue du Marché aux Herbes 5; ⏰noon-midnight Mon-Fri, 3pm-1am Sat, 4pm-10.30pm Sun), the 1695 Rubenseque **Au Bon Vieux Temps** (Impasse Saint Michel; ⏰11am-midnight), which sometimes stocks ultra-rare Westvletteren beers (albeit charging €10!), and the 1877 lambic specialist **À la Bécasse** (Rue de Tabora 11; ⏰11am-midnight; 🍴), with its vaguely Puritan rows of wooden tables.

DÉLIRIUM CAFÉ
Beer Bar

(www.deliriumcafe.be; Impasse de la Fidélité 4A; ⏰10am-4am Mon-Sat, 10am-2am Sun) The smoky main cellar pub has barrel tables, beer-tray ceilings and over 2000 beers.

Falstaff restaurant

Upstairs, the smoke-free **tap house** (www
.deliriumtaphouse.be) features copper stills,
metal panelling and 25 beers on draft.

PLACE ST-GÉRY   Area
Sip a quiet coffee by day or be buffeted
by music at night in youthful yet characterful bars, like **Zebra**, **Gecko** and **Floreo**,
that surround **Café des Halles** (www
.cafedeshalles.be), an 1881 market hall
that's now part cafe, part exhibition hall.
It also hosts a free weekend nightclub in
its cellars.

Moeder Lambic Fontainas   Beer Bar
(Place Fontainas 8; ⊙10am-4am Mon-Sat,
10am-2am Sun; 😐) A pub with designer decor,
dangling trumpet lamps, backlit wall panels
and an incredible 40 brews on draft including
Cantillon lambics and gueuze.

⭐ Entertainment

La Monnaie/De Munt   Opera
(www.demunt.be; Place de la Monnaie) Opera,
theatre and dance.

BoZar   Arts Centre
(www.bozar.be; Palais des Beaux-Arts, Rue
Ravenstein 23) Music, dance, exhibitions, theatre
and more.

🛍 Shopping

Tourist-oriented shops stretch between
the Grand Place and Manneken Pis. For
better **chocolate shops** in grander settings, peruse the resplendent **Galeries
St-Hubert** or the upmarket Sablon area.

ℹ Information

Tourist Information
There are info counters at Brussels Airport and
Bruxelles-Midi station.

Brussels International (📞02 513 89 40; www.
brusselsinternational.be; Grand Place; ⊙9am-6pm
Mon-Sat, plus Sundays in summer) Cramped and
often packed city info office within the town hall.

Flanders Info (📞02 504 03 90; www.visit
flanders.com; Rue du Marché aux Herbes 61;
⊙9am-6pm Mon-Sat, 10am-5pm Sun; 📶)

ℹ Getting There & Away

TRAIN Eurostar, TGV and Thalys high-speed
trains stop only at Bruxelles-Midi (Brussel-
Zuid). Jump on any local service for the
four-minute hop to conveniently central
Bruxelles-Central.

ℹ Getting Around

To/From the Airport
TRAIN Four trains depart
each hour from 5.30am
to 11.50pm. It costs €5.10
and takes 16 minutes
from Bruxelles-Central,
20 minutes from Bruxelles-
Midi.
TAXI Fares cost around €35.
Bad idea in rush hour traffic.

Onze Lieve Vrouwekathedraal, Antwerp

Bicycle

SHORT-TERM HIRE With **Villo!** (www.villo.
be; ⏱24hr), you can ride a bike from A to B,
drop it off, then take a new one for the next hop.
The first 30 minutes is free, but costs, charged
automatically to your credit card, rise rapidly
if you keep it longer (one/two/three hours
€0.50/3.50/7.50). Keep the bike 24hr and you've
automatically 'bought' it (€150). Some of the
180 automated rental pick-up/drop-off stations
are credit-card equipped for paying the initial
membership subscription (per day/week/year
€1.50/7/30). High-toll helpline ☎078 05 11 10
works only during office hours.

LONGER HIRE FietsPunt/PointVelo (www.
recyclo.org; per 1/3 days €7.50/15; ⏱7am-7pm
Mon-Fri) is located outside Bruxelles-Central's
Madeleine exit. You'll need ID, plus a credit card or
a €150 cash deposit.

TOURS Brussels Bike Tours (www.brussels
biketours.com; tour incl bicycle rental adult/
student €30/25; ⏱10am & 3pm Apr-Sep, 11am
Oct), with a maximum group size of 12, start from
the Grand Place tourist office and take around 3½
hours, including stops for beer and *frites*.

Public Transport

INFORMATION Fare/route information at www
.stib.be.

COSTS Tickets, once validated, can be used
on any combination of the metro, trams and
city buses, with the exception of reaching the
airport. A one-hour 'jump' ticket costs €1.70/2
when pre-purchased/bought aboard. Booklets of
five/10 tickets cost €7.30/11.20. A one-/three-day
unlimited pass costs €4.50/9.50.

Taxi

Taxis cost €2.40 flag fall plus €1.35 per kilometre
in Brussels, €2.70 per beyond city limits (eg
airport, Tervuren).

Flanders

Antwerp

POP 457,000

Cosmopolitan, confident and full of
contrasts, Antwerp (Antwerpen in Dutch,
Anvers in French) was one of northern Europe's foremost cities in the 17th century
when it also was home to Pieter Paul Rubens, diplomat, philosopher and northern
Europe's greatest baroque artist. Today it
once again revels in fame and fortune attracting art lovers and mode moguls, club
queens and diamond dealers.

◎ Sights

Sold at tourist offices, the two-day **Museumkaart** (€20) provides free city transport
and entrance to 15 museums and five significant churches, including all sights reviewed below. Most city-run museums are
free anyway if you're under 19 or over 65.
Many, including Museum Plantin-Moretus
and Rubenshuis, are free for everyone on
the last Wednesday of each month.

GROTE MARKT   Square
Antwerp's photogenic epicentre, this
pedestrianised square is graced by a
Renaissance-style **Stadhuis** and the
baroque **Brabo Fountain**, featuring a
bronze hero throwing the severed hand
of a dastardly giant. This illustrates the
legend that romantics still use to explain
Antwerp's disputed etymology, 'Hand
Werpen' (hand throwing) becoming
Antwerpen.

ONZE-LIEVE-VROUWEKATHEDRAAL
                                                    Cathedral
(www.dekathedraal.be; Handschoenmarkt; adult/
concession €5/3; ⏱10am-5pm Mon-Fri, 10am-
3pm Sat, 10am-4pm Sun) Belgium's largest
Gothic cathedral, built between 1352
and 1521, still dominates the city skyline
thanks to a steeple that is arguably the
most magnificent in Europe. Priceless
artworks inside include two world-famous
Rubens tableaux.

MUSEUM PLANTIN-MORETUS
                                        Historic Building
(www.museumplantinmoretus.be; Vrijdag Markt
22; adult/under 26yr €6/4; ⏱10am-5pm Tue-Sun)
Antwerp has saved numerous historic
homes as art-filled museums, but none
can compare with this enchanting medieval building that once housed the world's
first industrial printing works. Highlights
include the formal courtyard garden, 1640
library and historic print shop.

RUBENSHUIS   Historic Building
(www.museum.antwerpen.be; Wapper 9-11;
adult/concession €6/4; ⏱10am-5pm Tue-Sun)
Rubens' Antwerp home and studio has

been meticulously restored and rebuilt along original lines and filled with 17th-century artworks, albeit relatively few by the master himself. The full 90-minute audioguide visit may prove overly detailed for many visitors.

SCHELDT RIVERBANK Neighbourhood
The Scheldt River (Schelde in Dutch) is Antwerp's economic lifeline. For a riverside stroll, follow **Zuiderterras**, a raised promenade that runs south from **Het Steen**, Antwerp's partly medieval castle. At the pretty tree-lined square **St-Jansvliet**, a lift descends to the 1930s **St-Annatunnel** (free), allowing pedestrians and cyclists to cross 570m beneath the river to the **Linkeroever** (Left Bank) for a city panorama.

MEIR Neighbourhood
If walking from Antwerpen-Centraal station to Groenplaats, revel in the grand, statue-draped architecture of pedestrianised Meir and Leystraat. Look inside gilt-overloaded **Stadsfeestzaal** (Meir 76), one of the world's most indulgently decorated shopping malls. Watch top-quality chocolates being made at **Chocolate Line** (www.thechocolateline.be; ⏰10.30am-6.30pm) in the mural-overloaded 1745 **Paleis op de Meir** (www.paleisopdemeir.be; Meir 50).

STATION AREA
Antwerpen-Centraal train station is an attraction in itself and the famous **Antwerp zoo** is just outside.

DIAMOND QUARTER Neighbourhood
(www.awdc.be) An astounding 80% of all the world's uncut diamonds are traded in Antwerp's architecturally miserable diamond district, immediately southwest of Antwerpen-Centraal station. For the cost of a smile you can see gem polishers at work at **Diamondland** (www.diamondland.be; Appelmansstraat 33a; admission free; ⏰9.30am-5pm Mon-Sat), which is essentially a zero-pressure lure to get visitors into a diamond salesroom. The well-explained **Diamond Museum** (Koningin Astridplein 19-23; adult/concession €8/4; ⏰10am-5.30pm Tue-Thu) has changing jewellery 'treasure shows'

Trains from Antwerpen-Centraal

DESTINATION	FARE (€)	DURATION (MIN)	FREQUENCY (PER HR)
Amsterdam	26.90	190	1
Bruges	14.20	70	1
Brussels	6.30	35-50	5
Ghent	9.90	50	2
Lier	2.50	15	2
Leuven	6.60	45	2
Liège	14.80	125	1
Mechelen	2.90	15	2

and similar live gem-polishing demonstrations.

'T ZUID
Around 1km south of the fashion quarter, 't Zuid is a conspicuously prosperous area dotted with century-old architecture, hip bars, fine restaurants and interesting museums.

KMSKA Art Gallery
(www.kmska.be; Leopold De Waelplaats; 🚊1 or 23) Opened in 1890, the palatial Koninklijk Museum voor Schone Kunsten is one of northern Europe's finest art galleries, but wholesale renovations mean it will be largely closed until at least 2012. Highlights of its exceptional collection (yes, plenty of Rubens) will be on show at the brand new city museum, **MAS** (www.mas.be; Hanzestedenplaats), which opened in May 2011.

Sleeping
HOTEL JULIEN Boutique Hotel €€€
(☎03 229 06 00; www.hotel-julien.com; Korte Nieuwstraat 24; r €170-290; ❄@🛜) This very discreet boutique mansion-hotel exudes a tastefully understated elegance and subtle modernist style. Many of the characterful rooms have exposed beams or old brick-tile floors. Reception feels like a designer's office and there's a library and indulgent dining room with a faceted ceiling.

HOTEL LES NUITS
Hotel €€€

(☏03 225 02 04; www.hotellesnuits.be; Lange Gasthuisstraat; d/ste from €135/215; 🛜) Black on black corridors that are fashionable fantasies more than Halloween howlers lead to 24 designer-modernist rooms, each with its own special touches, super-comfy bed and rain-forest shower. Sauna and *hamam* are free. Breakfast (€12.50) is taken in the casually suave restaurant where you check in; there's no reception.

Matelote Hotel
Boutique Hotel €€

(☏03 201 88 00; www.hotel-matelote.be; Haarstraat 11; r €90-190; @🛜) Discreet new design hotel on a pedestrianised backstreet in the heart of the city, with 10 contemporary rooms, tastefully arranged in a 16th-century building. Breakfast costs €12.

Eating

For cheap, central snacks, stroll Hoogstraat. For cosy, pricier options look in parallel Pelgrimstraat (with its 'secret' medieval alley, Vlaaikeusgang) or the picturesque lanes leading to Rubens' wonderful but fire-damaged St-Carolus-Borromeuskerk. For confectioners and chocolate shops, try the lanes around Lombardia.

DE GROOTE WITTE AREND
Belgian €€

(☏03 233 50 33; www.degrootewittearend.be; Braderijstraat 24; snacks €4-9, mains €12-20; ⏱10.30am-midnight) Well-cooked Belgian classics, including *stoemp*, eel, shrimp croquettes and rabbit in Westmalle, are served around the open cloister of a partly 16th-century former convent with its own preserved chapel. Non-diners can sip one of over 80 Belgian beers.

HET VERMOEIDE MODEL
Belgian €€

(☏03 233 52 61; http://hetvermoeidemodel.com; Lijnwaadmarkt 2; mains €16.50-25, set menu €26; ⏱4-10pm Tue-Sun) This atmospheric medieval house-restaurant is full of exposed brickwork and chandeliers, with a creaky stairway leading up to a secret little roof terrace (bookings advised in summer). The menu includes steaks, ribs, *waterzooi* (€17.50) and seasonal mussels in Calvados.

De Kleine Zavel
Mediterranean €€€

(☏03 231 96 91; www.kleinezavel.be; Stoofstraat 2; mains €23-30; ⏱noon-2.30pm & 6-11pm Wed-Sun) The informal bistro-style decor belies this restaurant's high gastronomic standing for fusion cuisine with an accent on fish and Mediterranean flavours.

Museum Plantin-Moretus (p527)

DISCOVER THE NETHERLANDS & BELGIUM FLANDERS

529

Zuiderterras
European €€

(☎ 03 234 12 75; www.zuiderterras.be; Ernest van Dijckkaai 37; mains €16-25; ⏱9am-midnight) This bustling contemporary cafe-restaurant is an Antwerp landmark, with summer terrace and year-round river views, if somewhat patchy service. Reservations advised.

🍷 Drinking

To sound like a local, stride into a pub and ask for a *bolleke*. Don't worry, that means a 'little bowl' (ie glass) of De Koninck, the city's favourite ale. Cheap places to try it include classic, smoky 'brown cafes' **Oud Arsenaal** (Pijpelincxstraat 4; ⏱9am-7.30pm Fri-Wed), **De Kat** (Wolstraat 22), **De Ware Jacob** (Vlasmarkt 19) and the livelier **Pelikaan** (Melkmarkt 14).

Den Engel
Bar

(Grote Markt 5; ⏱9am-2am) Historic watering hole whose terrace provides perfect views across the main square.

De Vagant
Gin Cafe

(www.devagant.be; Reyndersstraat 25; ⏱11am-2am) More than 200 types of *jenever* (Dutch gin; €2.20 to €7.50) served in a bare-boards local cafe or sold by bottle from their bottle shop, which resembles an old-style pharmacy.

't Elfde Gebod
Bar

(www.kathedraalcafe.be; Torfbrug 10; ⏱noon-11pm Mon-Sat, noon-10pm Sun; 🍴) This ivy-clad medieval masterpiece has an utterly astounding interior decked with angels, saints, pulpits and several deliciously sacrilegious visual jokes.

Bierhuis Kulminator
Beer Pub

(Vleminckveld 32; ⏱8pm-midnight Mon, 11am-midnight Tue-Fri, 5pm-late Sat) Classic pub boasting 700 mostly Belgian brews, including rare vintage bottles.

ℹ Information

Tourism Antwerp (☎ 03 232 01 03; www.visitantwerpen.be; Grote Markt 13; ⏱9am-5.45pm Mon-Sat, 9am-4.45pm Sun) Central tourist office with a branch on level zero of Antwerpen-Centraal train station.

ℹ Getting There & Away

BUS Regional **De Lijn** (www.delijn.be) and international **Eurolines** (☎ 03 233 86 62; Van Stralenstraat 8; ⏱9am-5.45pm Mon-Fri, 9am-3.15pm Sat) buses both depart from points near Franklin Rooseveltplaats. **Ecolines** (www.ecolines.net) buses for Eastern Europe depart from near Antwerpen-Berchem train station.

TRAIN Antwerpen-Centraal Station (🚉Diamant), 1.5km east of the historic centre, is a cathedral of a building, considered among the world's most handsome stations. Seven daily high-speed trains run to Paris (from €48, 125 minutes).

ℹ Getting Around

Rooseveltplaats and Koningin Astridplein are hubs for the integrated network of **De Lijn** (www.delijn.be) buses and trams.

Diamond and tools in the Diamond Museum (p528), Antwerp
PHOTOGRAPHER: DEA/P LIACI/PHOTOLIBRARY ©

Ghent

POP 235,000

Known as Gent in Dutch and Gand in French, Ghent is Flanders' unsung historic city. Like a grittier Bruges without the crush of tourists, it sports photogenic canals, medieval towers, great cafes and some of Belgium's most inspired museums. Always a lively student city, things go crazy in mid-July during the 10-day **Gentse Feesten** (www.gentsefeesten.be), a citywide party of music and theatre incorporating **10 Days Off** (www.10daysoff.be), one of Europe's biggest techno parties.

Sights

CITY CENTRE

The main sights are strolling distance from Korenmarkt, the westernmost of three interlinked squares that form the heart of Ghent's historic core.

GRASLEI & PATERSHOL Neighbourhood
For one of Belgium's most picturesque views, cross **Grasbrug** bridge and look towards **Graslei**, the city's favoured waterfront promenade, lined with archetypal step-gabled warehouses and town houses. Touristy **canal tours** (adult/child €6/3.50; ⊙10am-6pm Mar–mid-Oct, weekends only mid-Oct–Feb) depart regularly from near here or you can stroll aimlessly around the picturesque alleys of the medieval **Patershol district**. If you have a Museumpass, don't miss the delightful **Huis van Alijn** (www.huisvanalijn.be; Kraanlei 65; adult/under 26yr €5/1; ⊙11am-5pm Tue-Sat, 10am-5pm Sun) in a restored 1363 children's hospice. The museum's theme is life in the 20th century and, although little is in English, the engrossing exhibits are self-explanatory.

ST-BAAFSKATHEDRAAL Cathedral
(St-Baafsplein; ⊙8.30am-6pm) This vast cathedral is an essential stop for fans of Flemish Primitive art who flock in to see Jan van Eyck's world-famous 1432 masterpiece the **Adoration of the Mystic Lamb** (adult/child €3/1.50; ⊙9.30am-4.30pm Mon-Sat, 1-4.30pm Sun). To see what the fuss is about without queuing or paying, see the photo replica in side-chapel 30.

Digging it up

At the time of writing, a vast project to revitalise Ghent's city centre means that Botermarkt has become one giant archaeological site. Tram tracks are being relaid, causing temporary rerouting of transport. But by mid-2012 the effect should make Ghent lovelier than ever. A model of what's planned is displayed in the city hall's **lobby** (admission free; ⊙7am-7.30pm Mon-Thu).

BELFORT Medieval Tower
(Botermarkt; adult/concession €3/2.50; ⊙10am-5.30pm mid-Mar–mid-Nov) Ghent's 14th-century belfry affords spectacular views of the city, while an audioguide provides historical commentary. A lift takes you most of the way up, but there are still some narrow stairs to negotiate.

GRAVENSTEEN Castle
(St-Veerleplein; adult/concession €8/6; ⊙9am-5pm) Lovingly restored, the Gravensteen once more looks like a quintessential 12th-century castle, even though it spent the 19th century recycled as a factory. An imaginative video story-tour compensates for a relative lack of period furnishings.

MIAT Museum
(www.miat.gent.be; Minnemeers 9; adult/under 26yr €5/1; ⊙10am-6pm Tue-Sun) In a five-floor 19th-century mill-factory building, this innovative museum celebrates Ghent's history of textile production with thought-provoking exhibits about industrialisation's effects on society (mostly in Dutch). Prepare for sensory overload on Tuesday or Thursday mornings when the working machinery is unleashed.

Design Museum Museum
(www.designmuseumgent.be; J Breydelstraat 5; adult/child €5/free; ⊙10am-6pm Tue-Sun) One of Ghent's lesser-known gems, the Design Museum displays furnishings from the Renaissance through to contemporary styles.

Werregarensteeg Offbeat Sights
Graffiti-filled alley.

OUT OF THE CENTRE
SMAK Art Gallery
(www.smak.be; Citadelpark; adult/under 26yr
€6/1, 10am-1pm Sun free; ⏱10am-6pm Tue-Sun;
🚌5) Regularly changing exhibitions of cutting-
edge installation art.

Museum voor Schone Kunsten
Art Gallery
(www.mskgent.be; Citadelpark; adult/under 26yr
€5/1; ⏱10am-6pm Tue-Sun; 🚌5) This stately
maze of light, airy rooms houses a good selection
of Belgian art from the 14th to 20th centuries.

Sleeping
Bed & Breakfast Ghent (www.bedandbreak
fast-gent.be).

CHAMBRES D'HÔTES VERHAEGEN
B&B €€€
(☎09 265 07 60; www.hotelverhaegen.be;
Oude Houtlei 110; d €195-265; ⏱reception
2-6pm) This 1770s rococo mansion is a
sumptuous blend of historical restoration
and certain well-placed modernist and
retro touches. There's a dazzling salon,
18th-century dining room and neatly
manicured parterre garden. Superb
'Paola's Room' has hosted Belgian royalty.
Breakfast costs €15 extra.

Accipio B&B
(☎0486 559498; www.accipio.be; St-
Elisabethplein 26; s/d/q €80/95/160; @) Two
super-stylish family-sized suites in a historic
house with 19th-century beams and lots of
personality. Each includes a kitchenette with
Senseo coffee-maker.

HOTEL HARMONY Boutique Hotel €€€
(☎09 324 26 80; www.hotel-harmony.be;
Kraanlei 37; s/d/ste from €135/150/225; @🏊)
This old-meets-new boutique hotel offers
luxuriously heaped pillows, fine white
linens, Miró-inspired art and chocolate-
and-raspberry colour schemes beneath
antique beams. River views from 'exceptional' rooms (s/d €160/185) are possibly
the best in all of Ghent. The rear deck has
an 8m-by-4m outdoor pool. Breakfast is
included.

Left: Gravensteen Castle (p531), Ghent;
Below: Handmade chocolates, Belgium

PHOTOGRAPHER: (LEFT) CHRIS CHRISTO/LONELY PLANET IMAGES ©;
(BELOW) GEORGIA GLYNN SMITH/LONELY PLANET IMAGES ©

Eating

As well as our recommendations, there's an endlessly tempting selection of eateries in the alleys of Patershol, along Graslei's photogenic canal and up Oudburg. Prices fall the further north you go.

HOUSE OF ELIOTT   Lobster   €€
(09 225 21 28; www.thehouseofeliott.be; J Brey-delstraat 36; mains €15-24; noon-2pm & 6-11pm Thu-Mon, closed Sep) Flapper mannequins and sepia photos exude pseudo-1920s charm in this canal-side gem with an exceptional waterside terrace. The speciality is lobster in multifarious preparations.

BRASSERIE PAKHUIS
                European, Oysters   €€
(09 223 55 55; www.pakhuis.be; Schuurkenstraat 4; mains €13.50-29, set lunch €12.90, set dinners €25-42; lunch & dinner Mon-Sat, bar from lunch to 1am) This hip, if mildly ostentatious, brasserie and bar is set in an elegantly restored former textile warehouse, whose century-old wrought ironwork is well worth admiring, even if you only stop for a drink.

AMADEUS   Ribs   €€
(www.amadeusspareribrestaurant.be; mains €12.50-17; 6.30pm-11pm) Patershol (09 225 13 85; Plotersgracht 8/10); Botermarkt (09 223 37 75; Goudenleeuwplein 7) Great value all-you-can-eat spare ribs (€13.95) served at two equally enticing addresses, both dressed up like Parisian brasseries, full of mirrors, stained glass, and the bustle of cheerful conversation.

EETHUIS AVALON   Vegetarian   €
(09 224 37 24; www.restaurantavalon.be; Geldmunt 32; meals €9-13; lunch Mon-Sat;) Reliably delicious, organic vegetarian food served in a warren of little rooms or outside on a small, tree-shaded terrace.

Drinking
For character, variety and eccentricity, Ghent's cafes are world-beaters.

533

'T VELOOTJE
Bar

(Kalversteeg 2; beer €4; ☺usually from 9pm) Crammed from floor to ceiling with all manner of junk and riches, including gorgeous antique bicycles, this somewhat bewildering cafe has dodgy toilets, a temperamental owner and only two types of unreliably chilled beer. But you won't forget it.

HOTSY TOTSY
Cafe

(www.hotsytotsy.be; Hoogstraat 1; ☺6pm-1am Mon-Fri, 8pm-2am Sat & Sun; 🚇1) This 'artists cafe' sports a classic zinc bar, silver-floral wallpaper and black-and-white film photos. There are chess sets, poetry nights and free live jazz most Thursday evenings, October to April.

HET WATERHUIS AAN DE BIERKANT
Beer Pub

(www.waterhuisaandebierkant.be; Groentenmarkt 12; ☺11am-1am) Draped in dried hop fronds and serving exclusive house beers, the building is a photogenic sight in its own right. It shares an enticing waterfront terrace with **'t Dreupelkot** (☺4pm-late), a *jenever* (Dutch gin) specialist.

Rococo
Cafe

(Corduwaniersstraat 5; coffee/beer/wine €2.50/4/4; ☺from 10pm) Brilliantly lavish late-night cafe-bar with carved wooden ceilings and lighting provided entirely by candles.

Pink Flamingo's
Pub, Cafe

(www.pinkflamingos.be; Onderstraat 55; ☺noon-midnight Sun-Thu, 2pm-3am Fri & Sat) Kitsch-overloaded cafe with Barbie lamps, 1970s wallpaper and oodles of plastic fruit.

Ghent Moneysavers

The good value **Museumpass** (www.visitgent.be; €20) provides three days' free entrance to all the sights reviewed below (except for boat tours), six more attractions and all city transport. It's sold at museums, De Lijn booths and the tourist office.

Herberg de Dulle Griet
Beer Pub

(Vrijdagmarkt 50; ☺4.30pm-1am Tue-Sat, noon-7.30pm Mon) Heavy beams, heraldic ceilings, barrel tables and the odd boar's head all add character to one of Ghent's best-known pubs.

't Caffetse
Cafe

(beer/Cava €1.30/3.50; ☺11am-5pm Tue-Sat) Remarkably inexpensive cafe set within the cloister of the 14th-century Huis van Alijn. Lawn seating in summer.

Callisto Tearoom
Cafe

(Hooiaard; ☺varies seasonally) Tourist-oriented, with unbeatable waterway views, balloon lanterns and traditional glass chandeliers.

⭐ Entertainment

For listings of what's on, see *Week-Up* (www.weekup.be/gent/week), *Zone 09* magazine (free from distribution boxes round town) or www.democrazy.be.

Vooruit
Theatre

(www.vooruit.be; St-Pietersnieuwstraat 23; 🚇5) This prominent venue for dance, rock concerts, film and visiting theatre companies occupies a striking 1912 building, whose architecture was a visionary premonition of art deco.

De Bijloke
Convert Hall

(www.debijloke.be; Jozef Kluyskensstraat 2) Medieval abbey-hospital recycled into a classical music venue.

De Vlaamse Opera
Opera

(www.vlaamseopera.be; Schouwburgstraat 3) An 1840 beauty with horseshoe-shaped tiered balconies and elegant salons.

Handelsbeurs
Concert Hall

(www.handelsbeurs.be; Kouter 29) Anything from classics to Latin to blues.

ℹ Information

Tourist office (☎09 266 52 32; www.visitgent.be; Botermarkt 17; ☺9.30am-6.30pm) should move to the old fish-market building on St-Veerleplein during late 2011.

ℹ Getting There & Away

Bus

REGIONAL Many De Lijn (www.delijn.be) services currently start from Gent-Zuid bus station

JEAN-BERNARD CARILLET/LONELY PLANET IMAGES ©

(Woodrow Wilsonplein), but a new bus station is under construction beside Gent-St-Pieters.

Train

Gent-Dampoort, 1km west of the old city, is the handiest station, with useful trains to Antwerp (€8.60, fast/slow 42/64 minutes, three per hour), Bruges (€5.90, 35 minutes, hourly) and Lille, France (€15.20, 68 minutes, hourly), via Kortrijk.

Ghent's main station, **Gent-St-Pieters** (2.5km south of centre) has more choice, including Brussels (€8.10, 36 minutes, twice hourly) and Bruges (fast/slow 24/42 minutes, five per hour).

ⓘ Getting Around

Bicycle

HIRE Hire bicycles from Gent-St-Pieters **station luggage room** (bagagekantoor; per day €9.50, deposit €12.50) or **Biker** (Steendam 16; per half/full day €6.50/9; ⊙9am-12.30pm & 1.30-6pm Tue-Sat). Id required.

WARNING Police confiscate illegally parked bikes.

Bus & Tram

TICKETS One-hour/all-day tickets cost €1.20/5 if purchased ahead of time from ticket machines or **De Lijn offices**

Gent-St-Pieters Kiosk (⊙7am-7pm Mon-Fri); Botermarkt (⊙7am-7pm Mon-Fri, 10.30am-5.30pm Sat).

TRAM 1 Picks up within the tunnel to the left as you exit Gent-St-Pieters station then runs to Korenmarkt, Gravensteen and beyond.

BUS 5 From Vlasmarkt passing Vooruit and Heuvelpoort (handy for the Citadelpark galleries).

Bruges

POP 117,000

Cobblestone lanes, dreamy canals, soaring spires and whitewashed old almshouses combine to make central Bruges (Brugge in Dutch) one of Europe's most picture-perfect historic cities. The only problem is that everyone knows.

◉ Sights

Beyond the sights listed, the real joy of Bruges is simply wandering alongside the canals, soaking up the atmosphere. To avoid the worst crowds, explore east of pretty Jan van Eyckplein. Or maybe seek out the windmills beside the city's eastern 'moat', heading north of the fortified Kruispoort gate-tower at Langestraat's eastern end.

Bruges

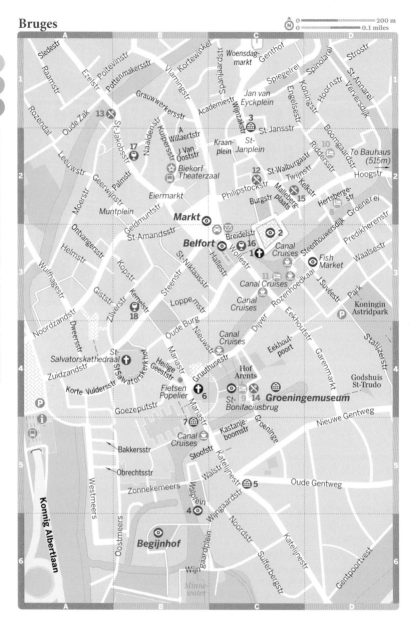

MARKT   Square

The heart of ancient Bruges, the old market square is lined with pavement cafes beneath step-gabled facades. The buildings aren't always quite as medieval as they look, but together they create a fabulous scene and even the neo-Gothic **post office** is architecturally magnificent. The scene is dominated by the **Belfort**, Belgium's most famous belfry whose iconic octagonal tower is arguably better appreciated from afar than by climbing

Bruges

366 claustrophobic **steps to the top** (adult/concession €8/6; ☺9.30am-5pm, last tickets 4.15pm).

BURG   Square

Bruges' 1420 **Stadhuis** (City Hall; Burg 12) is smothered in statuettes and contains a breathtaking **Gotishe Zaal** (Gothic Hall; adult/concession €2/1; ☺9.30am-4.30pm),featuring dazzling polychromatic ceilings, hanging vaults and historicist murals. Tickets include entry to part of the early baroque **Brugse Vrije** (Burg 11a; ☺9.30am-noon & 1.30-4.30), which is next door.

The easily missed **Basilica of the Holy Blood** (Burg 5; ☺9.30-11.50am & 2-5.50pm) is named for its highly revered relic, a few coagulated drops of Christ's blood, venerated daily (usually 2pm). Pay €1.50 to see the one-room treasury housing a reliquary used to display the phial

of blood during the elaborate Heilig-Bloedprocessie (Holy Blood Procession) every Ascension Day (17 May 2012, 9 May 2013).

GROENINGEMUSEUM   Art Gallery

(Dijver 12; adult/concession €8/6; ☺9.30am-5pm Tue-Sun) This small but extraordinarily valuable collection covers Flemish art from the 14th to 20th centuries, including some priceless Renaissance and Flemish Primitive works.

ONZE LIEVE VROUWEKERK   Church

(Mariastraat; ☺9.30am-4.50pm Mon-Sat, 1.30-4.50pm Sun) This large, sober 13th-century church is best known for Michelangelo's serenely contemplative 1504 *Madonna and Child* statue. The church's **treasury section** (adult/concession €2/1) houses royal graves plus 15th- and 16th-century artworks.

ST-JANSHOSPITAAL   Museum

(Mariastraat 38; adult/concession €8/6; ☺9.30am-5pm Tue-Sun) The chapel of a 12th-century hospital displays historical medical implements, medically themed paintings and six masterpieces by 15th-century artist Hans Memling. Tickets allows visits to a restored 17th-century pharmacy, poorly signposted off a small courtyard beside.

BEGIJNHOF   Garden

(admission free; ☺6.30am-6.30pm) One of Bruges' quaintest spots, the walled Begijnhof is an area of hushed calm just 10 minutes' walk south of the Markt, close to the romantic **Minnewater** (Lake of Love).

CHOCO-STORY   Museum

(www.choco-story.be; Wijnzakstraat 2; adult/child €6/4; ☺10am-5pm) Trace the cocoa bean's crooked path from Aztec currency to a dieter's dilemma in this absorbing museum, which culminates in tasting a praline that's made as you watch. The last demonstration is at 4.45pm.

DE HALVE MAAN   Brewery

(www.halvemaan.be; Walplein 26) Find where the 'Bruges Fool' *(Brugse Zot)* originated on crowded 45-minute **guided tours** (tour incl 1 drink €5.50; ☺hourly 11am-4pm) of this 1856 brewery. Or just sip a 'Strong Henry' *(Straffe Hendrik;* 9%) in the appealing cafe.

MUSEUM VOOR VOLKSKUNDE

Museum

(Balstraat 43; adult/concession €2/1; ⊙9.30am-5pm Tue-Sun) In an attractive former almshouse, 18 themed tableaux illustrate Flemish life in times gone by.

Sleeping

GUESTHOUSE NUIT BLANCHE

B&B €€€

(☎0494 400447; www.bruges-bb.com; Groeninge 2; d €175-195) Step into a Van Eyck painting where original gothic fireplaces and period furniture cunningly hide many of the modern fittings. The historic house once hosted Churchill, as well as Belgian royalty, and room rates cover the bottle of bubbly in your minibar.

RELAIS BOURGONDISCH CRUYCE

Boutique Hotel €€€

(☎050 33 79 26; www.relaisbourgondischcruyce .be; Wollestraat 41-47; d €185-375; ⊙Mar-Dec) Luxury and history intertwine in this part-timbered medieval house full of designer fittings, genuine antiques, trunks, Persian rugs and even an original Matisse. Watch the tourists drool enviously as they pass in their cruise barges. Room sizes vary significantly.

HOTEL PATRITIUS

Family Hotel €€

(☎050 33 84 54; www.hotelpatritius.be; Riddersstraat 11; d €80-122, tr €129-147; P ❄ 🛜) This proud 1830s town house has high ceilings, a snug bar-lounge and a pleasant garden. The 16 guest rooms vary radically in size and style: some new, some with exposed beams, some mildly chintzy. A decent breakfast is included.

B&B Huyze Hertsberge

B&B €€

(☎050 33 35 42; www.huyzehertsberge.be; Hertsbergestraat 8; r €125-165) Oozing with good taste, this late 17th-century house has a tranquil little canal-side garden and gorgeous period salon decked with antiques and sepia photos. Rooms are comfortably grand.

Eating

Touristy terraces crowd the Markt and line pedestrianised St-Amandsstraat where there are many cheaper eateries. Along eclectic Langestraat, you'll find everything from kebabs to Michelin stars. About town, numerous taverns and bakeries serve snacks and several hostels offer great meal deals.

DEN GOUDEN HARYNCK

Fine Dining €€€

(☎050 33 76 37; www.dengouden harynck.be; Groeninge 25; mains €38-45, set lunch menu €35, 3-/4-course menus €74/89; ⊙lunch & dinner Tue-Sat) Jackets or pearls are appropriate garb in this Michelin-starred restaurant, where even the set lunch is a faultless exercise in artistic nouveau cuisine.

DE BOTTELIER

Mediterranean €€

(☎050 33 18 60; www. debottelier.com; St-Jakob-

Old bottling machine at De Halve Mann brewery (p537)

sstraat 63; pasta/veg dishes from €8.80/13.50, other mains from €16; ⏰lunch & dinner Tue-Fri, dinner Sat) Decorated with hats and old clocks, this adorable little restaurant overlooks a handkerchief of canal-side garden. It's consistently popular with local diners, so book ahead.

CAMBRINUS   Brasserie   **€€**
(www.cambrinus.eu; Philipstockstraat 19; snacks €7, mains €17-23; ⏰noon-11pm) Cambrinus keeps its kitchen open all day for mussels and other Belgian favourites, including many beer-based meals, and offers hundreds of brews to wash them down with. It's family friendly, but the decor and service are in stereotypical British pub style.

't Gulden Vlies   Belgian   **€€**
(☎050 33 47 09; www.tguldenvlies.be; Mallebergplaats 17; mains €14-22, 2-/3-course menu €16/27; ⏰7pm-3am Wed-Sun) Intimate latenight restaurant with old-fashioned decor and good-value Belgian cuisine.

Drinking & Entertainment

De Garre   Pub
(Garre 1; ⏰noon-midnight) Hidden down a minuscule alley between candy shops, this antique pub serves dozens of Belgian ales. Served nowhere else, Garre Tripel (€3) is a magnificent 11% mind-blower.

De Republiek   Pub
(www.derepubliek.be; St-Jakobsstraat 36; ⏰from 11am) Spacious local favourite with candlelit tables, backlit bottles and a youthful buzz, it has a garden terrace and cheap food till late.

't Brugs Beertje   Pub
(Kemelstraat 5; ⏰4pm-1am Thu-Tue) Classic brew pub decorated with time-yellowed beer mats and enamel brewery signs.

ⓘ Information

Tourist Office (☎050 44 46 46; www.brugge .be) Concertgebouw ('t Zand 34; ⏰10am-6pm); Train Station (⏰10am-5pm Mon-Fri, 10am-2pm Sat & Sun) Standard city maps cost €0.50, but the arguably better *Use-It* maps (www.use-it.be) are free if you ask for one.

Bruggecentraal (www.bruggecentraal.be) Events listings.

Bruges Moneysavers

A three-day **Musea Brugge Pass** (adult/child €15/5) allows free entry to 16 city-owned attractions. Even if you visit only the Belfort and Groeningemuseum, you'll already save money.

Private attractions like Choco-Story and De Halve Maan (plus an interesting **diamond museum** and a less-successful **chip museum**) aren't included, but you can save a little on each with a **Bruges Card** (www .brugescard.be) or **Welkom@Brugge Card** (www.welkom-brugge.be), free to guests from most hostels and hotels.

ⓘ Getting There & Away

Bruges' train station is about 1.5km south of the Markt, a lovely walk via the Begijnhof. Every hour, trains run twice to Brussels (€12.90, one hour), five times to Ghent (€5.60, fast/slow 23/39 minutes), and once to Antwerp (€12.90, 70 minutes). For Ypres (Ieper in Dutch), take a train to Roeselare (€4.50, fast/slow 22/33 minutes), then bus 94 or 95: both buses pass key WWI sites en route.

ⓘ Getting Around

BUS From the train station to Markt, take any bus marked 'Centrum'. In reverse, they pick up at Biekorf.

BICYCLE Bauhaus hostel (per half/full day €6/9), Fietsen Popelier (Mariastraat 26; per hr/half day/full day €3.50/7/10; ⏰10am-7pm), and Rent-a-Bike (Bruges Station; per day/week €12/72; ⏰7.30am-7pm Mon-Fri, 9am-9pm Sat & Sun) all offer bicycle hire.

Quasimundo (☎050 33 07 75; www.quasi mundo.eu; adult/student €24/22; ⏰mid-Mar–mid-Oct) offers half-day bicycle tours around Bruges and its surroundings, with rental included. Book ahead.

BOAT Canal Tours (adult/child €6.90/3.20; ⏰10am-6pm Easter-early Nov) depart every 20 minutes from several jetties, notably on Dijver. Tours last 30 minutes.

HORSE-DRAWN CARRIAGE Up to five people per carriage (€36) on a well-trodden 35-minute route from the Markt. Includes a five-minute nosebag stop near the Begijnhof.

Ypres
POP 35,500

Especially when viewed from the southeast, Ypres' Grote Markt is one of the most breathtaking market squares in Flanders. It's all the more astonishing once you discover that virtually all of its convincingly 'medieval' buildings are in fact 20th-century copies. The originals had been brutally bombarded into oblivion between 1914 and 1918 when the historic city failed to capitulate to German advances. WWI battles in the surrounding poppy fields, known as the Ypres Salient, killed hundreds of thousands of soldiers. A century later, countless lovingly tended cemeteries remain, along with numerous widely spread WWI-based museums and trench remnants.

 Sights

CENTRAL YPRES

GROTE MARKT   Square

The brilliantly rebuilt **Lakenhallen**, a vast Gothic edifice originally serving as the 13th-century cloth market, dominates this very photogenic central square. It sports a 70m-high belfry, reminiscent of London's Big Ben, and hosts the gripping museum **In Flanders Fields** (www.inflanders fields.be; Grote Markt 34; adult/child €8/4; ⊙10am-6pm), a multimedia WWI experience honouring ordinary people's experiences of wartime horrors. It's very highly recommended, but will be closed from mid-September 2011 till April 2012 for refitting. The ticket allows free entry to three other minor city museums.

MENIN GATE & CITY RAMPARTS
                   Neighbourhood

A block east of Grote Markt, the famous **Menin Gate** is a large stone gateway straddling the main road at the city moat. It's inscribed with the names of 54,896 'lost' British and other Commonwealth WWI troops whose bodies were never found. Every evening at 8pm, traffic is halted while buglers sound the **Last Post** (www.lastpost.be) in moving remembrance.

A pleasant 20-minute parkland stroll takes you south atop the hefty city **rampart remnants**, emerging at **Rijselpoort** where there's a pretty moat-side **war cemetery**. Beneath is the intriguing little **Ramparts War Museum**

Beer Country

Dotted with windmills, the almost pan-flat hop fields north and west of Ypres produce many of Belgium's most sought-after beers. **De Dolle** (www. dedollebrouwers.be; ⊙brewery visits 2pm Sun) creates **Oerbier** at Esen near attractive Diksmuide which, like Ypres, had its historic core totally rebuilt after WWI. Watou is known for the full-flavoured **St-Bernardus** (www.sintbernardus.be). Like liquid alcoholic chocolate, extraordinary **Pannepot** (http://struise.noordhoek.com/eng) is brewed at the dreary-looking **Deca Brewery** in Woesten on the windmill-dotted road between Ypres and the gorgeous medieval town of Veurne. But the 'holy grail' of pubs is **In de Vrede** (www.indevrede.be; Donkerstraat 13, Westvleteren; ⊙10am-8pm Sat-Wed), opposite **Abdij St-Sixtus** (St Sixtus Abbey; www.sintsixtus.be; ⊙closed to visitors). While the pub's decor is far from memorable, it's the only place anywhere on earth where there's a reasonably assured chance of drinking (not taking away) the rarest of Trappist beers, **Westvletteren 12°** (€4.50). It's often cited as the world's best brew. Once you've tasted its fruity complexity, you might well agree.

DENNIS JOHNSON/LONELY PLANET IMAGES ©

(Rijselsestraat 208; admission €3; ⌚11am-8pm), which displays WWI mementos through a series of subterranean mannequin scenes. Enter through the inexpensive **'t Klein Rijsel** pub, which serves its own caramel-rich beer (€2) in specially made tankards.

YPRES SALIENT

Many Salient sites are awkward to reach without a car or tour bus. However, the following are accessible by the Ypres–Roeselare bus routes 94 and 95, so could be visited en route to or from Bruges.

MEMORIAL MUSEUM
PASSCHENDAELE 1917   Museum

(www.passchendaele.be; Ieperstraat 5, Zonnebeke; admission €5; ⌚10am-6pm Feb-Nov) The highlight of this slick, very informative WWI museum is walking through recreated dugouts and trench emplacements in the basement. It's in the 1922 'castle' of Zonnebeke village, 6km east of Ypres. Bus 94 stops 200m away.

TYNE COT   Cemetery

(admission free; ⌚24hr) The world's largest Commonwealth war cemetery, 11,956 soldiers are buried here in maudlin straight rows. A further 35,000 names of the missing are engraved on the rear wall. Enter via a sparse but well-designed **visitor centre** (⌚9am-6pm Feb-Nov). It's 3km beyond Zonnebeke, 500m from the nearest 94 bus stop.

DEUTSCHER SOLDATENFRIEDHOF
  Cemetery

The Salient's small, intensely moving German cemetery has up to 10 bodies per grave and is eerily watched over by four shadowy statues. Enter through a black concrete 'tunnel' that clanks and hisses spookily with distant war sounds while four short video montages commemorate the tragedy of war. Bus 95 stops outside at 'Duits Kerkhof'. That's 1km north of Langemark, 17 minutes from Ypres.

 Tours

There are dozens more WWI sites to seek out. If you have wheels, the tourist office has useful pamphlets. The following two bookshops between Grote Markt and Menin Gate sell a range of specialist books and offer twice-daily, half-day guided mini-bus tours of selected war sites. Advance booking is wise.

Over the Top (057 42 43 20; www.overthe toptours.be; Meensestraat 41; ⏰9am–12.30pm, 1.30pm–5.30pm & 7.30pm–8.30pm)

British Grenadier (☎057 21 46 57; www .salienttours.com; Meensestraat 5; ⏰9.30am-1pm, 2-6pm & 7.30-8.30pm)

🛏 Sleeping & Eating

Ariane Hotel   Hotel €€
(☎057 21 82 18; www.ariane.be; Slachthuis-straat 58; s/d from €94/120; P 🌐) This is a peaceful, professionally managed larger hotel with contemporary designer rooms, wartime memorabilia in common rooms and a swish restaurant that's a popular Ypres institution.

Hotel Regina   Hotel €€
(☎057 21 88 88; www.hotelregina.be; Grote Markt 45; s/d from €70/85) Right on the Markt, the location is ideal. Attempts at 'artistic' decor generally backfire but the Ensor room is a worthy exception, with an old-world timber interior and unbeatable views.

In 't Klein Stadhuis
                    Cafe, Restaurant €€
(www.kleinstadhuis.be; Grote Markt 32; mains €12-21; ⏰closed Sun Oct-May) Tucked away in an eccentrically decorated historic guildhall

beside the Stadhuis, this split-level cafe serves gigantic, good-value meals. Even when the main kitchen is closed, it still offers a few limited options.

ℹ Information

Temple.com (Tempelstraat 18; per hr €2; ⏰11am-7pm Fri-Wed) Internet in a grocery shop.
Toerisme Ieper (☎057 23 92 20; www.ieper. be; Grote Markt 34; ⏰9am-6pm) Inside the Lakenhallen.

ℹ Getting There & Around

BUS Services pick up passengers in Grote Markt's northeast corner (check the direction of the bus carefully!), including Roeselare-bound routes 94 (roughly twice hourly on weekdays, five daily on weekends) and 95 (hourly on weekdays, five daily at weekends).
TRAIN Services run hourly to Ghent (€9.90, one hour) and Brussels (€15.20, 1½ hours) via Kortrijk (€4.50, 30 minutes), where you could change for Bruges or Antwerp.
BICYCLE Hire bicycles from **Hotel Ambrosia** (☎057 36 63 66; www.ambrosiahotel.be; D'Hondtstraat 54; per day €10; ⏰9am-7pm); you'll need to provide a credit card as a guarantee.

Galeries St-Hubert (p523), Brussels

SURVIVAL GUIDE
Directory A-Z

Accommodation
THE NETHERLANDS
In this chapter, prices are for double rooms and include private bathroom unless otherwise stated and are quoted at high-season rates. Breakfast is not included in rates unless specified. Most rooms are nonsmoking. The following price indicators apply:

€€€	more than €150
€€	€80 to €150
€	below €80

BELGIUM
Our reviews refer to double rooms with private bathroom except in hostels or where otherwise specified. Quoted rates are for high season, which means May to September in Bruges, Ypres and the Ardennes, September to June in business cities.

€€€	€150
€€	€60 to €150
€	below €60

Business Hours
THE NETHERLANDS

Banks & government offices 9.30am-4pm Mon-Fri

Bars & cafes 11am-1am

Clubs Mostly 10pm-4am

Museums Most closed Monday

Post offices 9am-6pm Mon-Fri

Restaurants 10am or 11am-10pm, with a 3-6pm break

Shops noon-6pm Mon, 9am-6pm Tue-Sat (also Sun in large cities), also to 9pm Thu; supermarkets to 8pm

BELGIUM

Banks 9am-3.30pm Mon-Fri

Brasseries 11am-1am

Clubs 11pm-6am Fri-Sun

Pubs and cafes till 1am or later

Restaurants 11.30am-2.30pm & 6.30-10.30pm

Practicalities

○ **Electricity** Two-pin European plugs. Voltage 230V @ 50hz.

○ **Smoking** Smoking is banned in public places, including bars – but note that in the Netherlands you can still smoke pot in coffee shops as long as there's no tobacco mixed in.

○ **Time** European, one hour ahead of GMT.

○ **Tipping** Not compulsory since most restaurant bills include a service charge.

○ **Weights & Measures** Metric system.

Shops 10am-6pm Mon-Sat, limited opening Sun, some close for lunch

Supermarkets 9am-8pm Mon-Sat, some open Sun

Discount Cards
Available from museums, a Museumkaart gives access to 400 museums across the Netherlands for €40 (€20 for under 25s).

Food
THE NETHERLANDS
The following price categories for the cost of a main course are used in the listings.

€€€	more than €20
€€	€10 to €20
€	less than €10

BELGIUM
Price ranges for average main courses are as follows:

€€€	more than €25
€€	€14 to €25
€	less than €14

Legal Matters
Drugs are illegal in the Netherlands. Possession of soft drugs up to 5g is tolerated but larger amounts can get you jailed. Hard drugs are treated as a serious crime.

Money
THE NETHERLANDS

Credit Cards All major international cards are recognised in the Netherlands, and you will find that most hotels, restaurants and major stores accept them (although not the Dutch railway).

ATMs Automatic teller machines can be found outside banks and at train stations.

Tipping Not essential as restaurants, hotels, bars etc include a service charge.

BELGIUM

Exchange Banks usually offer better rates than exchange bureaux (*wisselkantoren* in Dutch, *bureaux de change* in French), though sometimes this is only for their banking clients.

ATMs Widespread, often hidden within bank buildings.

Tipping Not expected in restaurants (service and VAT is always included).

Public Holidays
THE NETHERLANDS

Public holidays in the Netherlands:

Nieuwjaarsdag New Year's Day

Goede Vrijdag Good Friday

Eerste Paasdag Easter Sunday

Tweede Paasdag Easter Monday

Koninginnedag (Queen's Day) 30 April

Bevrijdingsdag (Liberation Day) 5 May

Hemelvaartsdag Ascension Day

Eerste Pinksterdag Whit Sunday (Pentecost)

Tweede Pinksterdag Whit Monday

Eerste Kerstdag (Christmas Day) 25 December

Tweede Kerstdag (Boxing Day) 26 December

BELGIUM

School holidays are July and August; one week in November; two weeks at Christmas; one week around Carnival; two weeks at Easter; and one week in May.
Public holidays:

New Year's Day 1 January

Easter Monday March/April

Labour Day 1 May

Ascension Day Fortieth day after Easter

Whit Monday Seventh Monday after Easter

Flemish Community Festival 11 July (Flanders only)

National Day 21 July

Assumption 15 August

Francophone Community Festival 27 September (Wallonia only)

All Saints' Day 1 November

Armistice Day 11 November

Germanophone Community Festival 15 November (Eastern Cantons only)

Christmas Day 25 December

Traditional Dutch clogs , the Netherlands
PHOTOGRAPHER: TONY BURNS/LONELY PLANET IMAGES ©

Canal at night, Amsterdam

JEAN-PIERRE LESCOURRET/LONELY PLANET IMAGES ©

Telephone
THE NETHERLANDS

Most public phones will accept credit cards as well as various phonecards.

Country code ☎31

International access code ☎00

Collect call *(gesprek)*; domestic ☎0800 01 01; international ☎0800 04 10

International directory inquiries ☎0900 84 18

National directory inquiries ☎1888

Operator assistance ☎0800 04 10

BELGIUM

Dial full numbers: there's no droppable area code.

International operator ☎1324

Directory assistance ☎1405; costs a hefty €3

Reverse charge ☎1224

☎**0800** numbers toll free, others are metered

☎**0900** or ☎**070** numbers are high toll

☎**0472** to **0479**, **0482** to **0489** and **0492** to **0499** are mobile numbers

Visas

Schengen visa rules apply.

Transport
Getting There & Away

Air
THE NETHERLANDS

Schiphol airport (AMS; www.schiphol.nl) is the Netherlands' main international airport. **Rotterdam airport** (RTM; www.rotterdam-airport.nl) and **Eindhoven airport** (EIN; www.eindhovenairport.nl) are small.

BELGIUM

Belgium's main international airports:

Antwerp (ANR; www.antwerpairport.be) Tiny with just a few flights to the UK on **CityJet** (www.cityjet.com).

Brussels (BRU; www.brusselsairport.be) Belgium's main long-haul gateway.

Charleroi (CRL; www.charleroi-airport.com) Budget airlines **Ryanair** (www.ryanair.com), **JetAirFly** (www.jetairfly.com) and **WizzAir** (www.wizzair.com) use the misleadingly named Brussels-South Charleroi Airport, which is actually 55km south of Brussels, and 6km north of the ragged, post-industrial city of Charleroi.

Liège (LGG; www.liegeairport.com) Mostly charter flights.

JEAN-BERNARD CARILLET/LONELY PLANET IMAGES ©

Land
THE NETHERLANDS

The most extensive European bus network is maintained by **Eurolines** (www.eurolines.com).

Busabout (www.busabout.com) is a UK-based budget alternative. It runs coaches on circuits in continental Europe, including one through Amsterdam; passes are available in a variety of flavours.

If driving, you'll need the vehicle's registration papers, third-party insurance and an International Driving Permit in addition to your domestic driving licence. The national auto club, **ANWB** (www.anwb.nl), has offices across the country and will provide info if you can show an auto-club card from your home country (eg AAA in the US and AA in the UK).

The Netherlands has good train links to Germany, Belgium and France. All Eurail, Inter-Rail, Europass and Flexipass tickets are valid on the Dutch national train service, **Nederlandse Spoorwegen** (Netherlands Railway, NS; www.ns.nl). Many international services, including those on the high-speed line to Belgium, are operated under the **Hispeed** (www.nshispeed.nl) and **Fyra** (www.fyra.com) brands. In addition, **Thalys** (www.thalys.com) fast trains serve Brussels (where you can connect to Eurostar) and Paris.

Finally open (years late and far over budget), the high-speed line from Amsterdam (via Schipol and Rotterdam) speeds travel times to Antwerp (70 minutes), Brussels (1¾ hours) and Paris (three hours).

German ICE high-speed trains run six times a day between Amsterdam and Cologne (2½ hours) via Utrecht.

BELGIUM

Ecolines (☎ 02 279 2057; www.ecolines.net) and **Eurobus** (☎ 02 527 5012; www.eurobus.pl) operate buses from Brussels and Antwerp to various destinations in Eastern Europe.

Eurolines (☎ 02 274 1350; www.eurolines.be; ☉ 9am-7.30pm Mon-Fri, 9am-5pm Sat) Prebookings are compulsory with Eurolines, but although nine Belgian cities are served, only Brussels, Antwerp, Ghent and Liège have ticket offices.

Border Crossings Not usually controlled.

Petrol Cheaper in Luxembourg, so fill up there if passing by.

Driving licence Home driving licences will usually suffice for foreign drivers.

Priorité à droite As in France; see p285.

For comprehensive train timetables and international bookings see www.b-rail.be.

International high-speed trains have compulsory prebooking requirements and charge radically different prices according to availability so advance booking can save a packet. Operating companies:

Thalys (www.thalys.com) Paris–Brussels–Antwerp–Rotterdam–Schipol–Amsterdam (eight daily). Brussels–Amsterdam takes 113 minutes. Brussels–Paris takes 80 minutes with summer-only connections to Avignon and Marseille (5¾ hours). Brussels–Liège–Aachen–Cologne (108 minutes) runs four times daily.

Eurostar (www.eurostar.com) Brussels–Lille–London St-Pancras (two hours) up to nine times daily.

ICE (www.db.de) Brussels–Liège–Aachen–Cologne–Frankfurt (3¼ hours) six times daily via Frankfurt airport (three hours).

TGV (www.sncf.com) Numerous Belgium–France routes, including Brussels–CDG airport (100 minutes, seven daily). No service to central Paris.

FYRA (www.fyra.com) Brussels–Amsterdam high-speed service (1¾ hours) due to start 2013.

Sea
THE NETHERLANDS

Several companies operate car/passenger ferries between the Netherlands and the UK:

DFDS Seaways (www.dfds.co.uk) Sails between Newcastle and IJmuiden (near Amsterdam).

P&O Ferries (www.poferries.com) Operates an overnight ferry every evening between Hull and Europoort (near Rotterdam).

Stena Line (www.stenaline.co.uk) Sails between Harwich and Hoek van Holland.

BELGIUM

Most UK-bound motorists drive a couple of hours west to Dunkirk (Dunkerque) or Calais in France. However, there are two direct options from Belgium:

Zeebrugge–Hull From €159, overnight 14 hours, with **P&O** (www.poferries.com). Pedestrians can reach Zeebrugge port on a bus leaving Bruges train station at 7.30pm (€3.50).

Ostend–Ramsgate €55 to €62, four hours, four daily, with **TransEuropa Ferries** (www.transeuropaferries.com). No pedestrians carried.

Getting Around

Bicycle
THE NETHERLANDS

The Netherlands has more than 20,000km of dedicated bike paths *(fietspaden)*, which makes it the most bike-friendly place on the planet.

Many day-trippers avail themselves of the train-station bicycle shops, called **Rijwiel shops** (www.ov-fiets.nl), found in more than 100 train stations. Operating

Bloemenmarkt (p506), Amsterdam
PHOTOGRAPHER: WILL SALTER/LONELY PLANET IMAGES ©

long hours (6am to midnight is common), the shops hire out bikes from €6 to €8 per day with discounts by the week. You'll have to show an ID and leave a deposit.

You may bring your bicycle onto any train as long as there is room; a day pass for bikes (*dagkaart fiets;* €6) is valid.

BELGIUM

Cycling is a great way to get around in flat Flanders, less so in chaotic Brussels or undulating Wallonia. The Belgian countryside is riddled with cycling routes (see www.veloroutes.be) and most tourist offices sell helpful regional cycle maps.

To take your bike onto a train costs €5 one way (or €8 all day) on top of the rail fare. A few other busy city-centre train stations don't allow bicycle transportation.

Bicycle hire is available from private operators and many major train stations from around €6.50/9.50 per half-/full day. Deposit and/or ID usually required.

Car & Motorcycle
THE NETHERLANDS

Speed limits 50km/h in built-up areas, 80km/h in the country, 100km/h on major through roads and 120km/h on freeways (sometimes 100km/h, clearly indicated).

Bicycle with flower basket, Belgium

Blood alcohol limit 0.05%.

Car hire You must be at least 23 years of age to hire a car in the Netherlands. Some car-hire firms levy a small surcharge for drivers under 25 years.

Road rules Traffic travels on the right and the minimum driving age is 18 for vehicles and 16 for motorcycles. Seat belts are required and children under 12 years must ride in the back if there's room. Trams always have right of way and, if turning right, bikes have priority.

BELGIUM

Motorways Toll-free.

Speed limits 50km/h in most towns (30km/h near schools), 70 to 90km/h on intertown roads and 120km/h on motorways.

Blood alcohol limit 0.05%.

Car hire Available at airports and major train stations, but usually cheaper from city-centre offices.

Road rules Traffic travels on the right. Minimum driving age is 18. Seat belts are compulsory. At roundabouts and junctions, approaching vehicles have priority unless otherwise indicated.

Train

THE NETHERLANDS

The train network is run by **NS (Nederlandse Spoorwegen; www.ns.nl)**. First-class sections are barely different from the 2nd-class areas, but they are less crowded.

The new universal form of transport payment in the Netherlands, the **OV-chipkaart** (www.ov-chipkaart.nl) is a smartcard that you use in place of cash. When you enter and exit a bus, tram or train, you hold the card against a reader at the doors or station gates. The system then calculates your fare and deducts it from the card. Fares for the chip cards are much lower than a ticket bought from the driver or conductor on buses and trams.

Other tickets:

Enkele reis One way; you can break your journey along the direct route.

Dagretour Day return; 10% to 15% cheaper than two one-way tickets.

Weekendretour Weekend return; costs the same as a normal return and is valid from 7pm Friday to 4am Monday.

Dagkaart Day pass; allows unlimited train travel throughout the country. Good value only if you're planning to spend the day on the train.

BELGIUM

NMBS/SNCB (Belgian Railways; ☎02 528 2828; www.b-rail.be) trains are completely nonsmoking.

Children After 9am, kids under 12 years travel for free if accompanied by an adult.

Seniors People over 65 years pay only €5 for a return 2nd-class trip anywhere in Belgium (some exclusions apply).

B-Excursions Good value one-day excursion fares including return rail ticket plus selected entry fees.

Go Pass/Rail Pass Ten one-way 2nd-class trips to anywhere in Belgium (except frontier points) cost €46/74 for people under/over 26 years.

Weekend Return Tickets Valid from 7pm Friday to Sunday night, for just 20% more than a single.

Trains & Tribulations

Buying a train ticket is the hardest part of riding Dutch trains. Among the challenges:

○ Only some ticket machines accept cash, and those are coins-only, meaning that buying a ticket to go any distance will require a pocketful of change.

○ Ticket machines that accept plastic will not work with most non-Dutch credit and ATM cards.

○ Ticket windows (excepting one each at Schiphol and Amsterdam) do not accept credit or ATM cards, although they will accept paper euros. Lines are often long and there is a surcharge for the often-unavoidable need to use a ticket window.

○ Deeply discounted tickets for Hispeed and Fyra trains sold on the web require a Dutch credit card, a policy unheard of in other countries. And the cheap fares can't be bought at ticket windows.

○ The once-popular Voordeeluren-abonnement, good for a 40% discount on train travel, is now sold only to people with Dutch bank accounts.

Germany

Beer or wine? That sums up the German conundrum. One is at the heart of a pilsner-swilling culture, is the very reason for one of the world's great parties (Oktoberfest) and is consumed with pleasure across the land. The other is responsible for gorgeous vine-covered valleys, comes in myriad forms and is enjoyed everywhere, often from cute little green-stemmed glasses.

And the questions about Germany continue. Berlin or Munich? Castle or club? Ski or hike? East or west? BMW or Mercedes? In fact, the answers are simple: both. The beauty of Germany is that rather than choosing, you can revel in the contrasts. Berlin, edgy and vibrant, is a grand capital in a constant state of reinvention. Munich rules Bavaria, the centre of national traditions. Half-timbered villages bring smiles as you wander their cobblestoned and castle-shadowed lanes. Exploring this country and all its facets keeps visitors happy for weeks.

Three Girls and a Boy sculpture by Wilfried Fitzenreiter on the bank of Spree River, Berlin

Germany

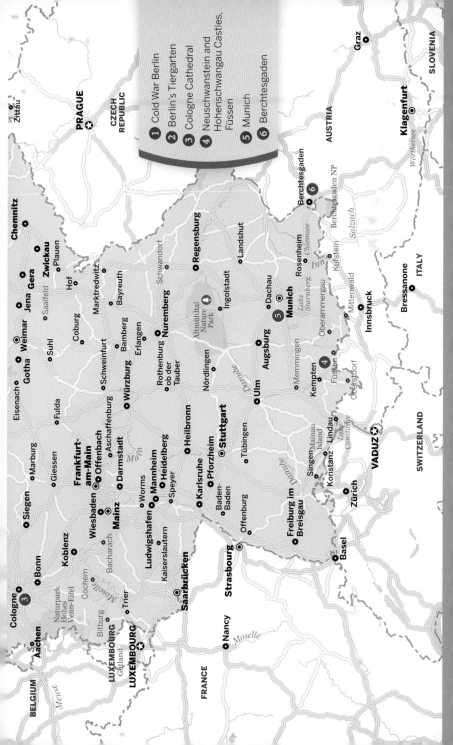

1 Cold War Berlin
2 Berlin's Tiergarten
3 Cologne Cathedral
4 Neuschwanstein and Hohenschwangau Castles, Füssen
5 Munich
6 Berchtesgaden

Germany Highlights

① Cold War Berlin

It's hard to believe, but two decades ago Berlin was still one of the most infamous symbols of the Cold War. For 28 years between 1961 and 1989, the Berlin Wall divided the city in two, separating the democratic West from the communist-controlled East. Berlin has moved on since reunification, but the shadow of the Cold War still lingers in some places. Stasi headquarters, Stasi Museum (p569)

Need to Know

TOP TIP Bikes are a great way to explore the wall **DID YOU KNOW?** There were two Berlin walls, separated by a gap of between 27 and 91m **For full details on Cold War Berlin, see p571.**

Cold War Berlin Don't Miss List

BY MIKE STACK, BERLIN TOUR GUIDE

1 BERLINER MAUER DOKUMENTATIONSZENTRUM

For an introduction to Berlin's divided history, don't miss this open-air **memorial** (p571) on Bernauer Strasse, one of the city's most infamous Cold War streets. It's the only place in Berlin where the so-called death strip between the two walls still exists, and you can see two exhibitions documenting the wall's 28-year history. The memorial is opposite the Nordbahnhof S-Bahn station, where there's another exhibition on the 'ghost stations' that were closed after the wall was built in 1961.

2 STASI EXHIBITION

This free exhibition on Zimmer Strasse opened in 2011 next to **Checkpoint Charlie** and documents the practices of East Germany's secret police, the Stasi – the biggest spy organisation of the Cold War. The exhibition explores the techniques the Stasi used to keep people under surveillance, and the web of spies they used to hunt down the 'enemies' of the East German state.

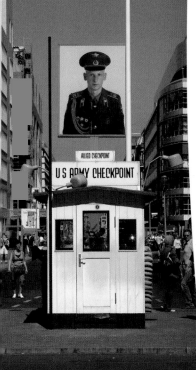

3 DDR MUSEUM

This brilliant museum (p567) on Alexanderplatz allows you to experience daily life in East Berlin. It's really hands-on and explores what it was like to live behind the Iron Curtain: you can sit in an old Trabi car, see a communist concrete-slab apartment and even experience East Berlin's nudist beaches! There's a great restaurant next door, which sells classic East German dishes, too.

4 BORNHOLMER STRASSE CHECKPOINT

Don't miss the chance to stand on one of the most important locations of the 20th century – the first checkpoint forced open by protesters on 9 November 1989, an event that marked the beginning of the end for the entire Berlin Wall. The exhibition gives an hour-by-hour explanation of the last days of the wall's existence, and the amazing events behind its fall.

Top: Berliner Mauer Dokumentationszentrum
Bottom Right: Checkpoint Charlie

Berlin Tiergarten

Most cities have green spaces, but not many have a park as breathtakingly beautiful as Berlin's Tiergarten (p568). This oasis of calm in the heart of the city is traversed by a tangle of paths, cycleways and wooded trails, and on sunny days it seems like half of Berlin heads for the park and lets it all hang out. Literally.

Cologne Cathedral

Travelling around Europe can bring on a bad case of cathedral fatigue, but even if you've seen a hundred churches, you still can't fail to be wowed by Cologne's gargantuan cathedral (Kölner Dom, p609). Blackened with age and festooned with gargoyles, flying buttresses and luminous stained glass, it's quite simply one of the world's most dramatic structures. Absolutely not to be missed.

Neuschwanstein and Hohenschwangau Castles

These towering castles (p603) could have fallen from the pages of an old European fairy tale, but they both date from the 18th century. Their history is inextricably bound with King Ludwig II, whose twin obsessions – Wagnerian operas and swans – have left an indelible mark on the castles' decor. If you have time to visit only a couple of German castles, make sure it's these. Hohenschwangau Castle

Munich's Beer Gardens

Germany is one of Europe's great beer-guzzling nations, but the sheer variety of brews on offer can be bewildering for visitors. Regardless of whether you're a first-time tippler or a hardened hophead, there's nowhere better to get to grips with Germany's favourite drink than Munich's many beer gardens (p592) – and if you can time your visit to coincide with the annual outdoor booze-up known as Oktoberfest, all the better. Drinking at the Hofbräuhaus (p592), Munich

Eagle's Nest

Hemmed in by mountains, Berchtesgaden would be worth visiting simply for its location, but this peaceful valley conceals a murky past. High above the valley on Mt Kehlstein, Hitler constructed a lofty retreat known as the Eagle's Nest (p604), from where he could gaze across the snow-capped peaks while planning world domination. Looking out at the very same view is a profoundly eerie experience.

Germany's Best...

Relaxing Retreats

○ **Park Sanssouci** (p578) Explore the stately palaces and gardens of this landscaped Potsdam park.

○ **Tiergarten, Berlin** (p568) Kick back with the locals in Berlin's idyllic city park.

○ **Baden-Baden** (p600) Lose your inhibitions and bathe like a German – in the nude.

○ **Lake Constance** (p607) Catch a boat across Germany's loveliest lake.

Historic Sites

○ **Checkpoint Charlie** (p571) This infamous checkpoint between East and West Berlin was once a symbol of divided Germany.

○ **Dokumentation Obersalzburg** (p599) This fascinating museum near Berchtesgarden explores the area's links with the Nazi regime.

○ **Buchenwald** (p587) Pay your respects at this chilling concentration camp.

○ **Nuremberg** (p595) Look beyond the Nazi connections to discover one of Germany's most historic old quarters.

Historic Buildings

○ **Reichstag** (p563) This landmark Berlin building was built to house the German parliament.

○ **Cologne Cathedral** (p609) Germany's most celebrated church: a masterpiece of Gothic grandeur.

○ **Residenz, Munich** (p586) Bavarian rulers occupied this vast palace for over six centuries.

○ **Wieiskirche** (p602) The rococo splendour of this 18th-century church has earned it a place on Unesco's World Heritage list.

Need to Know

Places for a Drink

○ **Beer gardens, Munich**
(p592) There's nowhere better to sink a few German brews than Munich's Englischer Garten.

○ **Bars of East Berlin** (p574)
Drink and dance till dawn in Berlin's hippest quarters.

○ **Beach bars, Hamburg**
(p614) Sunbathe on the sand just a stone's throw from central Hamburg.

○ **Moselle Valley** (p601)
Take a tipple in Germany's wine-making heartland.

ADVANCE PLANNING

○ **As early as possible**
In summer book accommodation as early as you can, especially in popular spots such as the Black Forest, the Moselle and Rhine Valleys and the Bavarian Alps

○ **One month before** Arrange hotel accommodation and car hire

○ **Two weeks before** Book city tours in Berlin, Munich and other cities, and plan train journeys using the Deutsche Bahn website (www.bahn.de)

RESOURCES

○ **German National Tourist Office** (www.germany-tourism.de) The official site for the German National Tourist Board

○ **Facts about Germany** (www.tatsachen-ueber-deutschland.de) Full of fascinating facts about the German nation

○ **Online German Course** (www.deutsch-lernen.com) Brush up your Deutsch before you go

GETTING AROUND

○ **Air** Germany is well served by major airlines, but be aware that budget carriers often use small regional airports. Frankfurt and Munich are the main hubs.

○ **Car** Germany's road system is fast and efficient; autobahns (motorways) are fastest, but regional roads are much more pleasant to drive on. Traffic can be a problem on summer weekends and around holidays.

○ **Train** Germany's rail system, operated by **Deutsche Bahn** (www.bahn.de), is one of the best in Europe. Trains are frequent, fast and very comfortable.

○ **Bus** Buses are much less comfortable and efficient than trains, but can often be the only option for rural towns and villages

BE FOREWARNED

○ **Autobahns** Unless otherwise indicated, there is no official speed limit on German motorways

○ **Accommodation** Can be hard to come by in peak seasons such as Oktoberfest and the Christmas markets

Left: Statues in Park Sanssouci, Potsdam;
Above: Lake Constance, Bavaria

Germany Itineraries

From chocolate box mountain views to edgy urban art galleries, Germany is a place that constantly confounds your expectations. Look beyond the tired old clichés and you'll discover a very different Deutschland.

BERLIN TO DRESDEN

Berlin & Beyond

Those in the know rate **(1) Berlin** as Europe's most exciting city. Since reunification the city has rediscovered its sense of self, and is home to a host of fascinating museums, art galleries and historic sites – and that's before you even get started on the nightlife. In a couple of days you can tick off the major sights: day one covers the Brandenburg Gate, the Reichstag, the Holocaust Memorial and the Tiergarten, with day two set aside for East Berlin, Alexanderplatz, Checkpoint Charlie and the DDR and Stasi Museums. After dark is when you'll really start to see what makes Berlin tick – Kreuzberg and Prenzlauerberg are both excellent areas to experience the Berlin underground.

On day three, travel south on one of Germany's efficient high-speed trains to **(2) Dresden**, a city effectively wiped off the map during WWII. Thankfully, the city's baroque centre has been rebuilt in elegant style along with its landmark cathedral, the Frauenkirche. For something more up to date, cross the River Elbe to explore the Neustadt's latest new bars and restaurants.

Top Left: Frauenkirche (p580), Dresden;
Top Right: Kaiserburg Castle (p596), Nuremberg

5 DAYS

MUNICH TO BAMBERG

A Bavarian Adventure

From Dresden, it's a two-hour train trip to the Bavarian capital, **(1) Munich**, an excellent base from which to launch forays around the wider Bavarian region. You'll need at least a day to do the city justice: key sights include the Residenz and the royal retreat of Schloss Nymphenburg, but for many people Munich's main highlights are its beer halls and beer gardens, which really come alive during the city's annual booze-up, Oktoberfest.

On day two, it's a couple of hours by train or car to the **(2) Bavarian Alps**, which brood along the border with Austria and provide some of Germany's finest hiking and climbing. The mountains were a favourite haunt of the Nazi elite in the years before WWII, and you should set aside time to visit the Führer's infamous mountain-top retreat, the Eagle's Nest, as well as the former Nazi HQ at Obersalzburg, which now houses a superb history museum.

On day three, head east to **(3) Füssen**, where you can tour two of Germany's most picturesque castles, Neuschwanstein and Hohenshwangau. Fussen also marks the start of one of Germany's most scenic drives, the Romantic Road, which links together a string of picturesque German towns including **(4) Nuremberg** and **(5) Bamberg**.

Discover Germany

BERLIN

🎵 030 / POP 3.41 MILLION

Renowned for its diversity and its tolerance, its alternative culture and its night-owl stamina, the best thing about the German capital is the way it reinvents itself and isn't shackled by its mind-numbing history. And the world is knows this – expatriates and steady increase of out-of-towners flock to see what all the fuss is about.

Some arrive seeking (and finding) Hemingway's Paris or Warhol's New York, but everyone unearths something extraordinary that often makes home seem, well, banal and conservative.

In short, all human life is here, and don't expect to get much sleep.

History

United, divided, united again, Berlin has a roller-coaster past. The merger of two medieval trading posts, it enjoyed its first stint as a capital in 1701, when it became the leading city of the state of Brandenburg-Prussia. Under Prussian King Friedrich I and his son, Friedrich II, it flourished culturally and politically.

As workers flooded to Berlin's factories, its population doubled between 1850 and 1870. 'Deutschland' was a latecomer to the table of nationhood, but in 1871 Berlin was again proclaimed a capital, this time of the newly unified Germany. By 1900 the city was home to almost two million people, but after WWI it fell into decline and, like the rest of Germany, it suffered an economic crisis and hyperinflation.

In the mid-1930s Berlin became a centrepiece of Nazi power and suffered

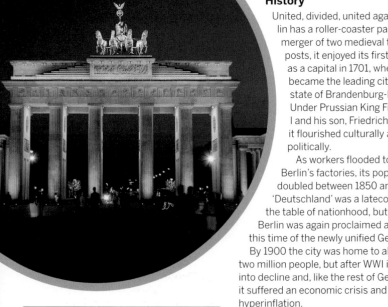

Brandenburg Gate
PHOTOGRAPHER: MARK DAFFEY/LONELY PLANET IMAGES ©

Glass cupola on top of the Reichstag

PAOLO CORDELLI/LONELY PLANET IMAGES ©

heavily during WWII. During the Battle of Berlin from August 1943 to March 1944, British bombers targeted the city nightly. The Soviets also shelled Berlin and invaded from the east.

The Potsdam Conference took place in August 1945 and split the capital into zones occupied by the four victorious powers – the USA, Britain, France and the Soviet Union.

The Berlin Wall, built in August 1961, was originally intended to prevent the drain of skilled labour from the East, but soon became a Cold War symbol. For decades East Berlin and West Berlin developed separately, until Hungarians breached the Iron Curtain in May 1989; the Berlin Wall followed on 9 November.

 Sights

BRANDENBURG GATE Landmark
(Map p572; Brandenburger Tor; Pariser Platz; M S-Bahn Unter den Linden) Finished in 1791 as one of 18 city gates, the neoclassical Brandenburg Gate became an east-west crossing point after the Berlin Wall was built in 1961. A symbol of Berlin's division, it was a

place US presidents loved to grandstand. John F Kennedy passed by in 1963. Ronald Reagan appeared in 1987 to appeal to the Russian leader, 'Mr Gorbachev, tear down this wall!' In 1989 more than 100,000 Germans poured through it as the wall fell. Five years later, Bill Clinton somewhat belatedly noted: 'Berlin is free.' The crowning Quadriga statue, a winged goddess in a horse-drawn chariot (once kidnapped by Napoleon and briefly taken to Paris), was cleaned in 2000 along with the rest of the structure.

REICHSTAG Historic Building
(Parliament; Map p572; 2273 2152; www .bundes/tag.de; Platz der Republik 1; admission free; ⊙8am-midnight, last admission 10pm) Just west of the Brandenburg Gate stands the glass-domed landmark with four national flags fluttering. A fire here in 1933 allowed Hitler to blame the communists and grab power, while the Soviets raised their flag here in 1945 to signal Nazi Germany's defeat. Today the building is once again the German seat of power, but it's the glass cupola added during the 1999 refurbishment that roughly 10,000 people a day flock to see. Walking along the internal spiral walkway by British star architect

Berlin

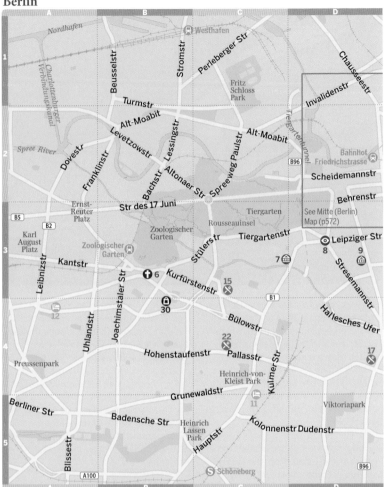

Norman Foster feels like being in a postmodern beehive. To beat the queues, book a table at the upmarket rooftop restaurant **Käfer** (☎ 2262 9935; www.feinkost -kaefer.de), which uses a separate entrance. With young children in tow, you're allowed to bypass the queue, too.

HOLOCAUST MEMORIAL   Memorial
(Map p572; Denkmal für die ermordeten Juden Europas; ☎ 2639 4336; www.stiftung-denkmal .de; Cora-Berliner-Strasse 1; admission free; ⊙field 24hr, information centre 10am-8pm Tue-Sun, last

entry 7.15pm Apr-Sep, 10am-7pm Tue-Sun, last entry 6.15pm Oct-Mar; Ⓜ S-Bahn Unter den Linden) Just south of the Reichstag, this grid of 2711 'stelae', or differently shaped concrete columns, is set over 19,000 sq metres of gently undulating ground. For historical background, designer Peter Eisenman has created an underground information centre in the southeast corner of the site.

UNTER DEN LINDEN   Historic Avenue
(Map p564) Celebrated in literature and lined with lime (or linden) trees, the street

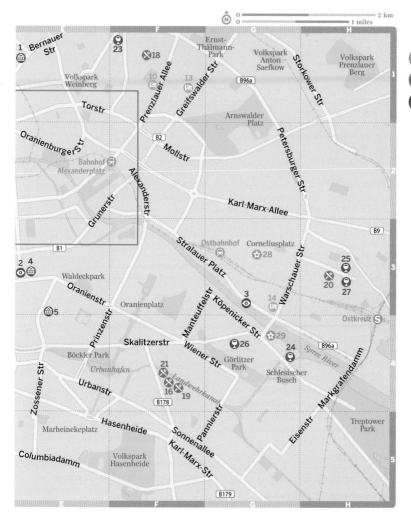

Unter den Linden was the fashionable avenue of old Berlin. Today, after decades of communist neglect, it's been rebuilt and regained that status.

MUSEUMSINSEL   Museum
(Map p572; Museums Island; ☎ all museums 2090 5577; www.smb.museum; adult/concession per museum €10/5, combined ticket for all museums €14/7; ☺10am-6pm Tue-Sun, to 10pm Thu; Ⓜ S-Bahn Hackescher Markt) Lying along the Spree River, the Museumsinsel contains the **Pergamonmuseum** (Am Kupfergraben

5), which is to Berlin what the British Museum is to London: a feast of Mesopotamian, Greek and Roman antiquities looted by archaeologists.

The **Alte Nationalgalerie** (Old National Gallery; Bodestrasse 1-3) houses 19th-century European sculpture and painting; the **Altes Museum** (Am Lustgarten) features classical antiquities but is scheduled for restoration and may be closed in the coming years; and the **Bodemuseum** (Monbijoubrücke) houses sculpture, Byzantine art and painting from the

565

Berlin

Middle Ages to the 19th century. Watch for special exhibitions at each. The entire Museumsinsel is currently being renovated and redeveloped – a new main visitor reception area is in the works and construction is expected to last until 2015. One of the newest additions was the reopening of the **Neues Museum** (New Museum; adult/concession €10/5; ⊙10am-6pm Sun-Wed, to 8pm Thu-Sat), which was reduced to rubble during WWII. It has been fully rebuilt and opened in late 2009. It houses Queen Nefertiti and Egyptian artefacts and the pre- and early history. See www .museumsinsel-berlin.de for details.

BERLINER DOM   Church
(Berlin Cathedral; Map p572; ☎2026 9136 www .berliner-dom.de; adult/under 14/concession €5/ free/3; ⊙9am-8pm Mon-Sat, from noon Sun Apr-Sep, to 7pm Oct-Mar) Overlooking the 'island' is this stately former royal court church – come here mainly for the exceptional view of the city from its top gallery, to see glass mosaics of the dome and to glimpse the Sauer organ (over 7000 pipes).

DEUTSCHES HISTORISCHES MUSEUM
                                        Museum
(German History Museum; Map p572; ☎203 040; www.dhm.de; Unter den Linden 2; admission €6,

⊙10am-6pm) Some come for the permanent exhibition on German history, but the museum is still arguably most notable for the glass-walled spiral staircase by modernist architect IM Pei (creator of the Louvre's glass pyramid).

HACKESCHER MARKT   Historic Area
(Ⓜ S-Bahn Hackescher Markt) A complex of shops and apartments around eight courtyards, the **Hackesche Höfe** (Map p572) is commercial and touristy, but it's definitely good fun to wander around the big-name brand shops and smaller boutiques or simply people watch in the cafes and restaurants – the atmosphere is always lively.

HAMBURGER BAHNHOF   Museum
(Map p572; ☎3978 3439; www.hamburgerbahn hof.de; Invalidenstrasse 50, Mitte; adult/concession €12/6; ⊙10am-6pm Tue-Fri, 11am-8pm Sat, 11am-6pm Sun; Ⓜ Hauptbahnhof/Lehrter Stadtbahnhof) This contemporary-art museum is housed in a former neoclassical train station and showcases works by Warhol, Lichtenstein, Cy Twombly and Keith Haring.

FERNSEHTURM TV TOWER   Landmark
(Map p572; ☎242 3333; www.berlinerfernseh turm.de; adult/concession €10/6.50; ⊙9am-mid-

night Mar-Oct, from 10am Nov-Feb; **M**Alexanderplatz) Call it Freudian or call it *Ostalgie* (nostalgia for the communist East or *Ost*), but Berlin's once-mocked socialist Fernsehturm TV tower is fast becoming its most-loved symbol. Originally erected in 1969 and the city's tallest structure, its central bauble was decorated as a giant football for the 2006 FIFA World Cup, while its 368m outline still pops up in numerous souvenirs.

The Turm dominates **Alexanderplatz**, a former livestock and wool market that became the low-life district chronicled by Alfred Döblin's 1929 novel *Berlin Alexanderplatz* and then developed as a 1960s communist showpiece.

NEUE NATIONALGALERIE　　Museum
(Map p564; ☏266 2951; www.neue-nationalgalerie.de; Potsdamer Strasse 50; adult/concession €10/5; ☉10am-6pm Tue, Wed & Fri, to 10pm Thu, 11am-6pm Sat & Sun; **M**S-Bahn Potzdamer Platz) Berlin's best collection of 20th-century works by Picasso, Klee, Munch, Dalí, Kandinsky and many German expressionists are housed in an exquisite 'temple of light and glass' built by Bauhaus director Ludwig Mies van der Rohe.

POTSDAMER PLATZ　　Historic Area
(Map p564; **M**S-Bahn Potsdamer Platz) The lid was symbolically sealed on capitalism's victory over socialism in Berlin when this postmodern temple to Mammon was erected in 2000 over the former death strip. Under the big-top, glass-tent roof of the **Sony Center** and along the malls of the Legolike **Daimler City**, people swarm in and around shops, restaurants, offices, loft apartments, clubs, a cinema, a luxury hotel and a casino – all revitalising what was the busiest square in prewar Europe.

During the International Film Festival Berlin (see p589), Potsdamer Platz welcomes Hollywood A-listers. In between you can rub shoulders with German cinematic heroes at the **Filmmuseum** (☏300 9030; www.filmmuseum-berlin.de; Potsdamer Strasse 2; adult/concession €6/4.50; ☉10am-6pm Tue, Wed & Fri-Sun, to 8pm Thu). There's also 'Europe's fastest lift' to the 100m-high **Panorama Observation Deck** (www.panoramapunkt.de; adult/concession €4.50/3; ☉11am-8pm, last entry 7.30pm).

But, as ever in Berlin, the past refuses to go quietly. Just north of Potsdamer Platz lies the **former site of Hitler's Bunker** (Map p572).

TOPOGRAPHIE DES TERRORS Memorial
(Map p564; ☏2548 6703; www.topographie.de; Niederkirchner Strasse 8; admission free; ☉10am-8pm May-Sep, to dusk Oct-Apr; **M**S-Bahn Potsdamer Platz) This is an eye-opening and graphic collection of text and images

Berlin in Two Days

Investigate the **Brandenburg Gate** area, including the **Reichstag** and the **Holocaust Memorial**. Walk east along Unter den Linden, stopping at the **Bebelplatz book-burning memorial**. Veer through the Museumsinsel for window shopping and cafe-hopping through **Hackescher Markt**. In the evening, explore the bars of **Prenzlauer Berg**, along Kastanieanallee and Pappelallee.

Start the next day at the East Side Gallery remnant of the **Berlin Wall**, before heading to **Checkpoint Charlie** and the nearby **Jewish Museum**. You could spend the afternoon exploring the sights around **Alexanderplatz** – don't miss the **DDR Museum** and a photo op beside the **Fernsehturm TV Tower**. Alternatively, take a leisurely wander around the **Tiergarten**, Berlin's largest green space. After dark, explore the nightlife around Kreuzberg and stop off for a beer at Madame Claude or Hops & Barley.

JOHN FREEMAN/LONELY PLANET IMAGES ©

Don't Miss **Berlin's Tiergarten**

Lolling about in the grass on a sunny afternoon is the quintessential Berlin pastime. Germans adore the outdoors and flock to urban green spaces. They also dislike tan lines so don't be surprised if you stumble upon locals sunbathing in the nude.

The Tiergarten is criss-crossed by a series of major roads and anchored by the Brandenburg Gate and the Riechstag on its northwestern edge. It's a tangle of curved walking and cycling paths, tiny ponds, open fields and thick woods. You'll probably get lost, but there are dozens of maps scattered about to help you find your way.

From the Reichstag, the Tiergarten's **carillon** (John-Foster-Dulles-Allee; 🚌 100 or 200) and the **Haus der Kulturen der Welt** (House of World Cultures; John-Foster-Dulles-Allee) are clearly visible. The latter was the US contribution to the 1957 International Building Exposition and it's easy to see why locals call it the 'pregnant oyster'.

Further west, the wings of the **Siegessäule** (Victory Column; 🚌 100 or 200) were the *Wings of Desire* in that famous Wim Wenders film. This golden angel was built to commemorate Prussian military victories in the 19th century. Today, as the end point of the annual Christopher Street Parade, she's also a gay icon. However, there are better views than those at the column's peak. Soviet War Memorial, Tiergarten

surrounding WWII, mounted on the ruins of the Gestapo and SS headquarters. Note: may not be suitable for children.

JEWISH MUSEUM Museum
(Juedisches Museum; Map p564; 📞 2599 3300; www.juedisches-museum-berlin.de; Lindenstrasse 9-14; adult/concession €5/2.50; ⊙ 10am-10pm Mon, to 8pm Tue-Sun, last entry 1hr before closing; Ⓜ Hallesches Tor) The Daniel Libeskind building that is the Jüdisches Museum is as much the attraction as the collection within. Designed to disorient and unbalance with its 'voids', cul-de-sacs, barbed metal fittings, slit windows and uneven floors, this still-somehow-beautiful structure swiftly conveys the uncertainty and sometime-terror of past Jewish life in Germany.

KAISER-WILHELM-GEDÄCHTNISKIRCHE
& KURFÜRSTENDAMM Church
(Map p564; ☎ 218 5023; www.gedaechtniskirche
-berlin.de; Breitscheidplatz; ☉ memorial hall
10am-4pm Mon-Sat, hall of worship 9am-7pm;
ⓜ Halleschen Tor) West Berlin's legendary
shopping thoroughfare and avenue, the
Ku'damm (the nickname for its full name
Kurfürstendamm), has lost some of its ca-
chet since the wall fell, but is worth visiting
for its landmark church, which remains in
ruins – just as British bombers left it on 22
November 1943 – as an antiwar memorial.
Only the broken west tower still stands.

STASI MUSEUM Museum
(☎ 553 6854; www.stasimuseum.de; House
22, Ruschestrasse 103; adult/concession
€5/4; ☉ 11am-6pm Tue-Fri, 2-6pm Sat & Sun;
ⓜ Magdalenenstrasse) This imposing
compound, formerly the secret police
headquarters, now contains the Stasi
Museum. It's largely in German, but well
worth it to get a sense of the impact the
Stasi had on the daily lives of GDR citizens
through the museum's extensive photos
and displays of the astounding range of
surveillance devices, as well as exhibits of
the tightly sealed jars used to retain cloths
containing body-odour samples.

Tours

Guided tours are phenomenally
popular; you can choose Third
Reich, Wall, bunker, communist, boat or bicycle tours, as
well as guided pub crawls.
Expect to pay around €15
or more.

NEW BERLIN Walking
(☎ 017-9973 0397; www
.newberlintours.com) Free
(yup, free) 3½-hour in-
troductory walking tours.
These leave at 10.30am
and 12.30pm from Dunkin'
Donuts opposite the Zoologisher Garten train station,

and 11am and 1pm outside Starbucks at
Pariser Platz near the Brandenburg Gate.
Guides are enthusiastic, knowledgeable...
and accept tips.

Trabi Safari Car
(☎ 275 2273; www.trabi-safari.de; €30-80)
Operates from the Berlin Hi-Flyer near
Checkpoint Charlie.

Fat Tire Bike Tours Bicycle
(http://fattirebiketours.com/berlin) Offers a huge
range of tours, from standard city tours to themed
tours along the former course of the Berlin Wall
and/or a Cold War tour, historical tours and more.

Sleeping

Mitte & Prenzlauer Berg
HOTEL GREIFSWALD Hotel €
(Map p564; ☎ 4442 7888; www.hotel-greifswald
.de; Greifswalderstrasse 211; s/d/tr/apt from
€57.50/69/90/75; @ 🛜; ⓜ Senefelder Platz)
You'd never guess this informal, quiet hotel
set back from the street around a sweet
courtyard is regularly home to bands and

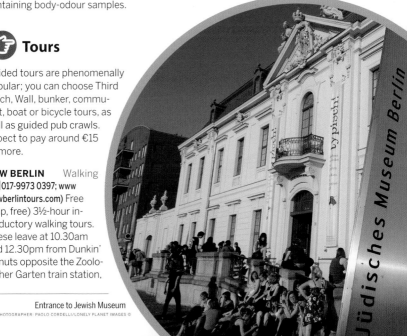

Entrance to Jewish Museum
PHOTOGRAPHER: PAOLO CORDELLI/LONELY PLANET IMAGES ©

even rock stars – until you see their photos in the lobby. We love the sumptuous breakfast buffet (€7.50) served until noon.

CIRCUS HOTEL
Hotel €€

(Map p572; ☎ 2000 3939; www.circus-berlin.de; Rosenthalerstrasse 1; s €70, d from €80, ste €100, apt €115-170; ⊖ @ 🛜; Ⓜ U-Bahn Rosenthaler Platz) The fancier younger sister to the Circus Hostel across the intersection, this hotel has given careful attention to every detail – the result is a retro twist on minimalism, airy rooms, bold-coloured walls and super-shiny wood flooring.

ACKSELHAUS & BLUEHOME
Hotel €€

(Map p564; ☎ 4433 7633; www.ackselhaus.de; Belforter Strasse 21; ste from €105, apt from €150; @ 🛜; Ⓜ Senefelder Platz) This Zen oasis, spread across two buildings, offers exquisitely designed suites or apartments (most with kitchenettes). Each has a different theme, from Italian to Hollywood; all exude an element of exquisite class, calm and humour – the African suite, for example, has stuffed animal heads mounted on the wall.

LUX 11
Hotel €€€

(Map p572; ☎ 936 2800; www.lux-eleven.com; Rosa-Luxemburg-Strasse 9-13; r/ste from €165/205; ⊖ @ 🛜; Ⓜ Weinmeisterstrasse/Alexanderplatz) A liberal use of white makes this slick, streamlined hotel a haven of unpretentious minimalism. All rooms feature a tiny kitchenette (kettle, coffee makers, two-pot stove and a handful of cookware).

Kreuzberg & Friedrichshain

MICHELBERGER HOTEL
Hostel €

(Map p564; ☎ 2977 8590; www.michelbergerhotel.com; Warschauer Strasse 39; s/d/tr from €60/70/150; 🛜; Ⓜ Prinzenstrasse, Hallesches Tor) This trendy design hotel is funky and fun and offers downmarket rates in stylish digs – think loft beds and sleek furniture. Minimalism dominates but the clean lines mean small spaces still feel roomy.

Charlottenburg & Schöneberg

BERLINER BED & BREAKFAST
Hotel €

(Map p564; ☎ 2437 3962; www.berliner-bed-and-breakfast.de; Langenscheidtstrasse 5; s/d/tr/q without bathroom €35/55/68/78; Ⓜ Kleistpark) Lofty ceilings and gorgeous wood floors dominate in this small, unique space with themed rooms (Asia, retro, fashionable). Excellent breakfast provisions are left for guests each day, which you prepare yourself in the communal kitchen.

HOTEL BOGOTA
Hotel €€

(Map p564; ☎ 881 5001; www.bogota.de; Schülterstrasse 45; d without bathroom from €65, with bathroom €90-150; ⊖ 🛜; Ⓜ Uhlandstrasse) With oodles of charm and character at affordable prices, this is a must for vintage-furniture lovers.

Eating

Berliners love to eat out – it's relaxed and affordable and patrons often linger long after finishing their meals. Many of the

Berliner Mauer Dokumentationszentrum

If Walls Could Talk

Remnants of the 155km Berlin Wall are scattered across the city, but you can follow all or sections of its former path along the 160km-long **Berliner Mauerweg** (Berlin Wall Trail; www.berlin.de/mauer), a signposted walking and cycling path that follows the former border fortifications, either along customs-patrol roads in West Berlin or border-control roads used by GDR guards.

The longest surviving stretch of the wall is the **East Side Gallery** (Map p564; www.eastsidegallery.com; Mühlenstrasse; **M** S-Bahn Warschauer Strasse) in Friedrichshain.

The sombre **Berliner Mauer Dokumentationszentrum** (Berlin Wall Documentation Centre; Map p564; ☎ 464 1030; www.berliner-mauer-dokumentationszentrum.de; Bernauer Strasse 111; admission free; ◷ 10am-6pm Tue-Sun Apr-Oct, to 5pm Nov-Mar; **M** U-Bahn Bernauersrasse) is a memorial containing a section of the original wall, photos of the surrounding area (before and during the lifespan of the wall), newspaper clippings and listening stations featuring old West and East Berlin radio programs as well as eyewitness testimonies.

In Kreuzberg, the famous sign at **Checkpoint Charlie** (Map p564) still boasts: 'You are now leaving the American sector.' But it and the reconstructed US guardhouse are just tourist attractions now. For a less light-hearted view of the past, visit **Haus am Checkpoint Charlie** (Map p564; ☎ 253 7250; www.mauer-museum .com; Friedrichstrasse 43-45; adult/concession €12.50/9.50; ◷ 9am-10pm; **M** Kochstrasse/Stadtmitte). Tales of spectacular escape attempts include through tunnels, in hot-air balloons and even using a one-man submarine.

best finds are in the budget category. Restaurants usually open from 11am to midnight, with varying *Ruhetage* or rest days. Cafes often close around 8pm, though just as many stay open until 2am or later.

There's the excellent organic **Kollwitzplatz market** (Map p564; ◷ 9am-4pm Sat & Sun; **M** Senefelderplatz), the relaxed **Winterfeldtplatz farmers market** (Map p564; ◷ Wed & Sat) and the bustling, ultracheap **Türkenmarkt** (Map p564; Turkish market; ◷ noon-6:30pm Tue & Fri).

Mitte & Prenzlauer Berg

SANKT OBERHOLZ International €
(Map p572; Rosenthaler Strasse 72a; dishes €5-8; 🛜; **M** Rosenthaler Platz) Berlin's *'Urbanen Pennern'* (officeless, self-employed creative types) have been flocking here for years with their laptops for the free wi-fi access, but we like it for the people-watching – especially from the lofty life-guard chairs out front. Soups, sandwiches and salads are always satisfying.

ASSEL German €€
(Map p572; ☎ 281 2056; Oranienburger Strasse 21; mains €5-16; **M** Oranienburger Strasse or Hackescher Markt) One of the few exceptional picks on a particularly touristy and busy stretch of Mitte. Come for coffee, a bite or a full meal and stretch out in the wooden booths made from old S-Bahn seats. Plus, the toilets are entertaining (you'll see).

ODERQUELLE German €€
(☎ 4400 8080; Oderberger Strasse 27; mains €8-16; ◷ dinner; **M** Eberswalder Strasse) Modern German food in such mellow, convivial digs is rare, almost as rare as snagging a table here after 7pm, so be sure to reserve. This is one of the best places in Berlin for consistently excellent service, exceptional wine and typical German dishes – think elegant, modern comfort food.

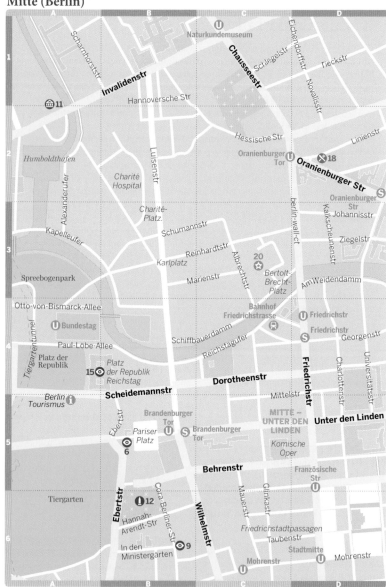

Kreuzberg & Friedrichshain

SCHNEEWEISS German €
(Map p564; ☎ 2904 9704; Simplonstrasse 16; day menu €7-10, Ⓜ S-Bahn Warschauer Strasse) Subtly embossed vanilla wallpaper, a long, central table and parquet flooring keep the neutral 'Snow White' feeling more après-ski than icy. The vaguely German ' Alpine' food here is really excellent.

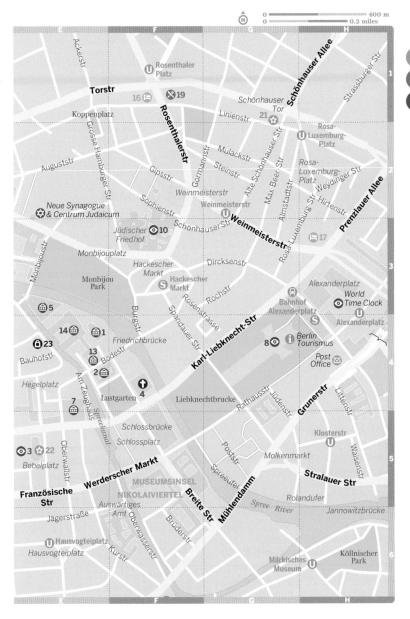

NANSEN International €€
(Map p564; ☎301 1438; Maybachufer 39; mains
€10-19; ⏱dinner; Ⓜ Schönlein Strasse) You can
dine on seasonal modern German cuisine
in a romantic, candlelit space – most
menu items are sourced locally.

CAFE JACQUES International €€
(Map p564; ☎694 1048; Maybachufer 8;
mains €12-20; Ⓜ Schönleinstrasse) Dishes
hover around French and North African
mainstays but Italian fare features
too – frankly, it's all so lovingly and

Mitte (Berlin)

exceptionally prepared, you can't go wrong with anything you order. Reserve or be disappointed – one peek inside and you'll want to hop in and get a piece of this unfussy space and inviting atmosphere.

Curry 36　　　　　　Sausages €

(Map p564; Mehringdamm 36; snacks €2-6; ☉9am-4pm Mon-Sat, to 3pm Sun; Ⓜ Mehringdamm) This is Kreuzberg's most popular sausage stand, as evidenced by the daily queues (yes, it really is worth the wait).

Charlottenburg & Schöneberg

CAFÉ EINSTEIN STAMMHAUS

Austrian €€

(Map p564; ☎261 5096; www.cafeeinstein.com, in German; Kurfürstenstrasse 58; mains €15-23; ☉9am-1am; Ⓜ Nollendorfplatz) You'll think you've hopped to another capital at this

Viennese coffee house. Choose from schnitzel, strudel and other Austrian fare in the polished, palatial digs.

ENGELBECKEN　　　　Bavarian €€

(☎615 2810; Witzleben Strasse 31; mains €8-20; ☉dinner daily, lunch Sun; Ⓜ Sophie Charlotte Platz) Come here for what many rate as Berlin's best Bavarian food, with *Schweinbraten* (pork sausages), schnitzels, dumplings and sauerkraut. All meats are organic.

 # Drinking

Gemütlichkeit, which roughly translates as 'cosy, warm and friendly, with a decided lack of anything hectic', dominates the upscale bars of the west as well as the hipper, more underground venues in the east.

Bars without food open between 5pm and 8pm and may close as late as 5am (if at all).

MADAME CLAUDE　　　　　　Bar

(Map p564; Lübbener Strasse 19; Ⓜ Schlesiches Tor) Kick back with a beer and pretend you've stepped into the pages of Alice in Wonderland. True to Berlin it's shabby and slightly gritty, with secondhand furniture and a DJ doling out tracks from a hip Mac.

HOPS & BARLEY　　　　　　Pub

(Map p564; ☎2936 7534; Wühlisch Strasse 40; Ⓜ S-Bahn Warschauer Strasse) Excellent ciders and beers – brewed on site at this convivial microbrewery – pack them in every night. It's set inside a former butcher shop littered with aged-but-refurbished wood tables and school desks.

FLEISCHMÖBEL　　　　　　Bar

(Map p564; Oderberger Strasse 2; ☉from noon; Ⓜ Eberswalder Strasse) Despite its odd name, the furniture is merely secondhand at this loungey cafe. It morphs into a convivial drinking den after dark, with serious locals engaging in intense conversations.

SÜSS WAR GESTERN　　　　　Bar

(Map p564; Wülischstrasse 43; Ⓜ S-Bahn Ostkreuz). Street-art-covered walls, 1970s decorations and comfortable sofas make this outpost worth the trek. Most nights feature a DJ spinning anything from funk to soul to electric music.

Prater
Beer Garden

(Kastanienallee 7-9; Ⓜ Eberswalder Strasse) A summer institution, Berlin's oldest beer garden (since 1837) invites you in for a tall chilled draft under the canopy of chestnut trees.

Wohnzimmer
Bar

(☎ 445 5458; Lettestrasse 6; ⏰10am-4am; Ⓜ Eberswalder Strasse) The vintage furnishings often match up well with the style of its patrons in this laid-back Prenlauer Berg stalwart.

Freischwimmer
Bar

(Map p564; Vor dem Schlesischen Tor 2a; ⏰from 2pm Mon-Fri, from 11am Sat & Sun, reduced hr in winter; Ⓜ Schlesisches Tor). It was a boathouse, now it's a bar that entices with its chill vibe and a view of the tranquil canal.

 # Entertainment

Berlin's legendary nightlife needs little introduction. Whether alternative, underground, cutting edge, saucy, flamboyant or even highbrow, it all crops up here.

Nightclubs

Few clubs open before 11pm (and if you arrive before midnight you may be dancing solo) but they stay open well into the early hours – usually sunrise at least. Admission charges, when they apply, range from €5 to €20.

BERGHAIN/PANORAMABAR
Club

(Map p564; www.berghain.de; Wrienzer Bahnhof; ⏰from midnight Thu-Sat; Ⓜ Ostbahnhof) If you make it to only one club in Berlin, this is where you need to go. Expect cutting-edge sounds in industrial surrounds.

KAFFEE BURGER
Club

(Map p572; ☎ 2804 6495; www.kaffeeburger .de; Torstrasse 60; Ⓜ Rosa-Luxemburg-Platz) The original GDR '60s wallpaper is part of the decor at this arty bar, club and music venue in Mitte.

WATERGATE
Club

(Map p564; ☎ 6128 0394; www.water-gate.de; Falckensteinstrasse 49a; ⏰from 11pm Fri & Sat; Ⓜ Schlesisches Tor) Watch the sun rise over the Spree River through the floor-to-ceiling windows of this fantastic lounge. The music is mainly electro, drum'n'bass and hip hop.

Riechstag (p563)

Berlin also has a healthy and thriving scene of no-holds-barred sex clubs. The notorious **Kit Kat Club** (☏7889 9704; Bessemerstrasse 14; MAlt-Tempelhof) is the original and the best.

Music & Theatre

STAATSOPER UNTER DEN LINDEN
Opera House

(Map p572; ☏information 203 540, tickets 2035 4555; www.staatsoper-berlin.de; Unter den Linden 5-7; MS-Bahn Unter den Linden) The Staatsoper Unter den Linden is the handiest and most prestigious of Berlin's three opera houses, where unsold seats go on sale cheap an hour before curtains-up.

BERLINER ENSEMBLE
Theatre

(Map p572; ☏information 284 080, tickets 2840 8155; www.berliner-ensemble.de; Bertolt-Brecht-Platz 1; MFriedrichstrasse) The famous song 'Mack the Knife' had its first public airing here, during the *Threepenny Opera's* premiere in 1928. Bertolt Brecht's former theatrical home continues to present his plays.

Shopping

KADEWE Department Store
(Map p564; www.kadewe.de; Tauentzienstrasse 21-24; ⊙10am-8pm Mon Thu, to 9pm Fri, 9.30am-8pm Sat; MU-Bahn Wittenbergplatz) Germany's most renowned retail emporium, equivalent to Harrods. The 6th-floor gourmet food halls are extraordinary, and the store is near the principal western shopping thoroughfare of Kurfürstendamm.

Flea market–hopping is a popular local pastime at the weekend, particularly Sundays. The **Berlin Art & Nostalgia Market** (Map p572; Georgenstrasse, Mitte; ⊙8am-5pm Sat & Sun; MS-Bahn Friedrichstrasse) is heavy on collectables, books, crafts and GDR memorabilia; the **Flohmarkt am Mauerpark** (Bernauer Strasse 63, Mauerpark; ⊙10am-5pm Sun; MEberwalder Strasse) is known for its vintage wear and young-designer retro fashions; and the **Flohmarkt am Arkonaplatz** (Arkonaplatz; ⊙10am-5pm Sun; MBernauerstrasse) is best for 1960s and 1970s furniture and accessories.

Information

Berlin Tourismus (☏250 025; http://visit berlin.de/de) Alexanderplatz **(Alexa Shopping Centre;** ⊙10am-6pm); Brandenburg Gate (⊙10am-6pm); Hauptbahnhof **(Ground floor, Europa Platz entrance;** ⊙8am-10pm); Reichstag (⊙10am-6pm); Zoologisher Garten station (Kurfürstendamm 21; ⊙10am-8pm Mon-Sat, to 6pm Sun)

Berlin Welcome Card (www.berlin-welcomecard .de; 48/72hr €16.90/22.90, incl Potsdam & up to 3 children €18.90/25.90) Free use of public transport, plus museum and entertainment discounts.

Corinthian colonnade, Park Sanssouci (p578), Potsdam
PHOTOGRAPHER: MARK AVELLINO/LONELY PLANET IMAGES ©

ℹ Getting There & Away

Air

Berlin has two international airports, reflecting the legacy of the divided city. The larger one is in the northwestern suburb of **Tegel** (TXL), about 8km from the city centre; the other is in **Schönefeld** (SXF), about 22km southeast. For information about either, go to www.berlin-airport.de or call ☎0180-500 0186. Schönefeld is being expanded into **Berlin Brandenburg International** (BBI). It has an estimated completion date of mid-2012.

Car

Lifts can be organised by ride-share agency **ADM Mitfahrzentrale** (ride-share agencies; www .mitfahrzentralen.org, in German) Hardenbergplatz (☎194 420; Hardenbergplatz 14; ⏲9am-8pm Mon-Fri, 10am-2pm Sat, 10am-4pm Sun); Zoo station (☎194 240; ⏲9am-8pm Mon-Fri, 10am-6pm Sat & Sun).

Train

Regular long-distance services arrive at the architecturally spectacular **Hauptbahnhof** (www .berlin-hauptbahnhof.de), with many continuing east to Ostbahnhof. Sample fares include to Leipzig (€36, 1¼ hours), Hamburg (€68, 1½ to two hours), Stralsund (€38 to €46, 2¾ to 3¼ hours) and Prague (€62, 4½ to five hours). The few lockers available are hidden in the parking garage.

ℹ Getting Around

To/From the Airport

SCHÖNEFELD The S9 train travels through all the major downtown stations, taking 40 minutes to Alexanderplatz.

The faster 'Airport Express' trains travel the same route half-hourly to Bahnhof Zoo (30 minutes), Friedrichstrasse (23 minutes), Alexanderplatz (20 minutes) and Ostbahnhof (15 minutes). Note that these are regular regional RE or RB trains designated as Airport Express in the timetable. Trains stop about 400m from the terminals, which are served by a free shuttle bus every 10 minutes. Walking takes five to 10 minutes.

Buses 171 and X7 link the terminals directly with the U-Bahn station Rudow (U7), with onward connections to central Berlin.

The fare for any of these trips is €2.80. A taxi to central Berlin costs about €35.

TEGEL Tegel (TXL) is connected to Mitte by the JetExpressBus TXL (30 minutes) and to Bahnhof Zoo (Zoo Station) in Charlottenburg by express bus X9 (20 minutes). Bus 109 serves the western city – it's slower but useful if you're headed somewhere along Kurfürstendamm (30 minutes). Tegel is not directly served by the U-Bahn, but both bus 109 and X9 stop at Jakob-Kaiser-Platz (U7), the station closest to the airport.

Any of these trips costs €2.10. Taxi rides cost about €20 to Bahnhof Zoo and €23 to Alexanderplatz.

Car & Motorcycle

Garage parking is expensive (about €2 per hour) and vehicles entering the environmental zone (within the S-Bahn rail ring) must display a special sticker (*Umweltplakette*; €5 to €15). Order it online at www.berlin.delabo/kfz/dienstleistungen/ feinstaubplakette.php. Non-German-speakers can also order it at www.umweltplakette.de, operated by a private company that charges around €37. The fine for getting caught without the sticker is €40. One type of ticket is valid on all transport – including the U-Bahn, buses, trams and ferries run by **Berliner Verkehrsbetriebe** (☎194 49; www.bvg.de), the S-Bahn and RE, SE and RB trains operated by **Deutsche Bahn** (www.bahn.de).

Most tickets are available from vending machines located in the stations, but must be validated before use. If you're caught without a validated ticket, there's a €40 on-the-spot fine.

Services operate from 4am until just after midnight on weekdays, with many *Nachtbus* (night bus) services in between. At weekends, they run all night long (except the U4).

Taxi

Taxi stands are located at main train stations and throughout the city. Order on ☎0800-222 2255.

Potsdam

☎0331 / POP 150,000

The Prussian royal seat of Potsdam is the most popular day trip from Berlin. Friedrich II (Frederick the Great) commissioned most of the palaces in the mid-18th century.

In August 1945 the victorious WWII Allies chose nearby Schloss Cecilienhof for the Potsdam Conference, which set the stage for the division of Berlin and Germany into occupation zones.

Public Transport Tickets

Three tariff zones exist – A, B and C. Unless venturing to Potsdam, the outer suburbs or Schönefeld Airport, you'll only need an AB ticket.

TICKET	AB (€)	BC (€)	ABC (€)
Single	2.10	2.50	2.80
Day pass	6.10	6.30	6.50
Group day pass (up to 5 people)	15.40	15.90	16.10
7-day pass	26.20	27.00	32.30

Potsdam Hauptbahnhof is just southeast of the city centre, across the Havel River. As this is still quite a way – 2km – from Park Sansoucci, you might like to change here for a train going one or two stops to Charlottenhof (for Schloss Sanssouci) or Sanssouci (for Neues Palais).

 Sights

PARK SANSSOUCI   Historic Site
(admission free; ☉dawn to dusk) At the heart of Park Sanssouci lies a celebrated rococo palace, **Schloss Sanssouci** (☏969 4190; adult/concession Apr-Oct €12/8, Nov-Mar €8/5; ☉10am-6pm Tue-Sun Apr-Oct, to 5pm Nov-Mar). Built in 1747, it has some glorious interiors. Only 2000 visitors are allowed entry each day (a Unesco rule), so tickets are usually sold by 2.30pm, even in quiet seasons. Tours run by the tourist office guarantee entry.

The late-baroque **Neues Palais** (New Palace; ☏969 4255; adult/concession €6/5; ☉10am-6pm Wed-Mon Apr-Oct, to 5pm Nov-Mar) was built in 1769 as the royal family's summer residence. It's one of the most imposing buildings in the park and the one to see if your time is limited.

The **Bildergalerie** (Picture Gallery; ☏969 4181; adult/concession €2/1.50; ☉10am-6pm Tue-Sun mid-May–Oct) contains a rich collection of 17th-century paintings by Rubens, Caravaggio and other big names.

Many consider the **Chinesisches Haus** (Chinese House; ☏969 4222; admission €2; ☉10am-6pm Tue-Sun mid-May–Oct) to be the pearl of the park. It's a circular pavilion of gilded columns, palm trees and figures of Chinese musicians and animals, built in 1757.

SCHLOSS CECILIENHOF   Palace
(☏969 4244; tours adult/concession €6/5; ☉9am-6pm Tue-Sun Apr-Oct, to 5pm Nov-Mar) When outgoing British Prime Minister Winston Churchill and his accompanying successor Clement Attlee arrived at this palace in 1945 they must have immediately felt at home. Located in the separate New Garden, northeast of the centre on the bank of the Heiliger See, this is an incongruously English-style country manor in rococo-heavy Potsdam.

FILMPARK BABELSBERG   Museum
(☏721 2755; www.filmpark.de; Grossbeeren-strasse; adult/child/concession €19/13/16; ☉10am-6pm Apr-Oct) Germany's **UFA Film Studios** was where Fritz Lang's *Metropolis* was shot and FW Murnau filmed the first Dracula movie, *Nosferatu*. Since a relaunch in 1999, it's helped Berlin regain its film-making crown, with Roman Polanski's *The Pianist* and Quentin Tarantino's *Inglorious Basterds* both made here. The visitor experience includes theme-park rides and a studio tour – the daily stunt show (2pm) is worth catching. The studios are east of the city centre.

ℹ Information

Potsdam tourist office (275 580; www
.potsdamtourismus.de; Brandenburger Strasse 3;
⊙9.30am-6pm Mon-Fri, 9.30am-4pm Sat & Sun
Apr-Oct, 10am-6pm Mon-Fri, 9.30am-2pm Sat &
Sun Nov-Mar) Near the Hauptbahnhof.

Park Sanssouci Besucherzentrum (Park
Sanssouci Visitor Centre; ✆969 4202; www.
spsg.de; An der Orangerie 1; ⊙8.30am-5pm Mar-
Oct, 9am-4pm Nov-Feb) Near the windmill and
Schloss Sanssouci.

ℹ Getting There & Away

S-Bahn line S7 links central Berlin with Potsdam
Hauptbahnhof about every 10 minutes. Some
regional (RB/RE) trains from Berlin stop at all
three stations in Potsdam. Your ticket must cover
Berlin Zones A, B and C (€2.80) to travel here.

SAXONY

With its restored 'old German' roots,
Saxony has emerged as one of the biggest
draws for visitors to Germany. Restored
and revitalised Dresden combines classicism with creativity. Just up the fabled

Elbe River, Meissen is a gem of a medieval
town with a palace and cathedral high on
a hill.

Dresden

✆0351 / POP 484,000

Proof that there is life after death, Dresden
has become one of Germany's most
popular attractions, and for good reason.
Restorations have returned the city to the
glory days when it was famous throughout
Europe as 'Florence on the Elbe', owing
to the efforts of Italian artists, musicians,
actors and master craftsmen who flocked
to the court of Augustus the Strong, be-
stowing countless masterpieces upon the
city. Death came suddenly when, shortly
before the end of WWII, Allied bombers
blasted and incinerated much of the
baroque centre, a beautiful jewel-like area
dating from the 18th century. More than
25,000 died, and in bookstores throughout town you can peruse texts showing
the destruction (or read about it in Kurt
Vonnegut's classic *Slaughterhouse Five*).

The city celebrated its 800th
anniversary in 2006 and, while much
focus is on the restored centre, you
should cross the River Elbe to the

Elbe River, Dresden

IMAGE BROKER©

Neustadt, where edgy new clubs and cafes open every week, joining the scores already there.

 ## Sights

FRAUENKIRCHE   Cathedral
(Church of Our Lady; www.frauenkirche-dresden. org; Neumarkt; ⏰10am-6pm) One of Dresden's most beloved icons, the Frauenkirche was rebuilt in time for the city's 800th anniversary celebrations in 2006. Initially constructed between 1726 and 1743 under the direction of baroque architect George Bähr, it was Germany's greatest Protestant church until February 1945, when bombing raids flattened it. The communists decided to leave the rubble as a war memorial; after reunification, calls for reconstruction prevailed, although the paucity of charcoal-tinged original stones shows just how much is new. You can also climb to the top for good views.

SEMPEROPER   Historic Building
(www.semperoper-erleben.de; Theaterplatz; tour adult/child €8/4; ⏰varies) Designed by Gustav Semper, this neo-Renaissance opera house *is* Dresden. The original building opened in 1841 but burned down less than three decades later. Rebuilt in 1878, it was pummelled in WWII and reopened in 1985 after the communists invested a fortune restoring it.

RESIDENZSCHLOSS   Palace
(www.skd.museum; Schlossplatz) The Residenzschloss, a massive neo-Renaissance palace, has ongoing restoration projects. Its many features include the **Hausmannsturm** (Servants' Tower; adult/child €3/2; ⏰10am-6pm Wed-Mon), which has sobering pictures of the complete WWII destruction.

ZWINGER   Museums
(www.skd.museum; Theaterplatz 1; ⏰10am-6pm Tue-Sun) Dresden's elaborate 1728 fortress, an attraction in its own right with a popular ornamental courtyard, also houses six major museums. The most important is the **Galerie Alte Meister** (adult/child €10/7.50), which features masterpieces including Raphael's *Sistine Madonna*. The **Rüstkammer** (Armoury; adult/child €3/2) has a superb collection of ceremonial weapons. The dazzling

DISCOVER GERMANY DRESDEN

Porzelansammlung (Porcelain Collection; adult/child €6/3.50) is filled with flamboyant breakables.

ALBERTINUM
Art Gallery

(www.skd.museum; Brühlsche Terrasse; adult/child €8/6; ⏱10am-6pm) Massive renovations ended in 2010 and the results are stunning. A light-filled enclosed courtyard welcomes you into this treasure trove of art. Highlights include the **Münzkabinett** collection of antique coins and medals, and the **Skulpturensammlung**, which includes classical and Egyptian works. The **Galerie Neue Meister** has renowned 19th- and 20th-century paintings from leading French and German Impressionists.

 Tours

SÄCHSISCHE DAMPFSCHIFFAHRT
River Tour

(www.saechsische-dampfschiffahrt.de; adult/child from €16/8) Ninety-minute Elbe tours leave from the Terrassenufer dock several times daily in summer aboard the world's oldest fleet of paddle-wheel steamers. There's also service to villages along the river such as Meissen.

 Sleeping

KEMPINSKI HOTEL TASCHENBERGPALAIS
Hotel €€€

(☎491 20; www.kempinski-dresden.de; Taschenberg 3; r €200-400; ❄@🛜🏊) This restored 18th-century mansion is Dresden's heavyweight, with views over the Zwinger, incredibly quiet corridors, and doors that seem impervious to anything outside, protecting the 214 rooms and suites.

HOTEL MARTHA HOSPIZ
Hotel €€

(☎817 60; www.hotel-martha-hospiz.de; Nieritzstrasse 11; r €80-140; 🛜) Fifty rooms decked out in Biedermeier style, an attractive winter garden and a sound on-site restaurant with Saxon cooking and local wine make this a very pleasant place to lay your hat.

HOTEL KIPPING
Hotel €€

(☎478 500; www.hotel-kipping.de; Winckelmannstrasse 6; s/d from €70/80; @🛜) Just south of the Hauptbahnhof, this is a family-run, family-friendly hotel that comes with 20 comfortable rooms in a house right out of the *Addams Family*.

 Eating

WENZEL PRAGER BIERSTUBEN
Czech €€

(Königstrasse 1; mains €7-20; ⏱11am-midnight) This busy beer hall serves up oceans of Czech lager under arched brick ceilings. Always crowded, the menu leans towards traditional meaty mains.

RASKOLNIKOFF
Cafe €

(www.raskolnikoff.de; Böhmische Strasse 34; mains €5-14) This bohemian cafe in a former artists' squat was one of the Neustadt's first post-Wende pubs.

GÄNSEDIEB
German €€

(Weisse Gasse 1; mains €8-18) One of nearly a dozen choices on Weisse Gasse, the 'Goose Thief' serves hearty schnitzels, goulash and steaks alongside a full range of Bavarian Paulaner beers.

Café Europa
Cafe €€

(Königsbrücker Strasse 68; mains €6-15; ⏱24hr; 🛜) Smart open-all-hours cafe with newspapers and free internet. Come here to regroup during the early hours.

Grand Café
Cafe €€

(An der Frauenkirche 12; mains €10-20; ⏱10am-1am) Yummy cakes and more ambitious mains in the gold-trimmed Coselpalais, plus tables on a large patio and good views of Frauenkirche.

 Information

Dresden City-Card (per 48hr €21) Provides admission to museums, discounted city tours and boat tours and free public transport. Buy it at the tourist office.

Dresden Regio-Card (per 72hr €32) Everything offered by the City-Card plus free transport on the entire regional transport network. Valid as far as the Czech border and Meissen.

Tourist office (www.dresden-tourist.de; Kulturpalast, Schlossstrasse; ☺10am-7pm Mon-Fri, 10am-6pm Sat, 10am-3pm Sun)

❶ Getting There & Around

Dresden's **airport** (DRS; www.dresden-airport.de), served by Lufthansa and Air Berlin among others, is 9km north of the city centre, on S-Bahn line 2 (€1.90, 20 minutes).

Dresden is well linked with regular train services through the day to Leipzig (€29, 70 minutes), Berlin-Hauptbahnhof by IC/EC train (€36, 2¼ hours) and Frankfurt-am-Main by ICE (€89, 4½ hours).

Dresden's **public transport network** (www.dvbag.de) charges €1.90 for a single-trip ticket; day tickets cost €5 and can be bought on trams. Trams 3, 7, 8 and 9 provide good links between the Hauptbahnhof, Altstadt and Neustadt.

THURINGIA

Thuringia likes to trade on its reputation as the 'Green Heart' of Germany, an honour helped by the former GDR's dodgy economy, which limited development.

These days its main towns of Erfurt and Weimar are popular for their historic centres and long histories. In fact the latter is a microcosm of German history – high and low – over the last 500 years.

Weimar

☏03643 / POP 65,000

Neither a monumental town nor a medieval one, Weimar appeals to those whose tastes run to cultural and intellectual pleasures. After all, this is the epicentre of the German Enlightenment, a symbol for all that is good and great in German culture. An entire pantheon of intellectual and creative giants lived and worked here: Goethe, Schiller, Bach, Cranach, Liszt, Nietzsche, Gropius, Herder, Feininger, Kandinsky, Klee...the list goes on.

Internationally, of course, Weimar is better known as the place where the constitution of the Weimar Republic was drafted after WWI, though there are few reminders of this historical moment. The ghostly ruins of the Buchenwald concentration camp, on the other hand, provide haunting evidence of the terrors of the Nazi regime. The Bauhaus and classical Weimar locations are protected as Unesco World Heritage sites.

 Sights

A good place to begin a tour is in front of the neo-Gothic 1841 **Rathaus** on the Markt. Directly east is the **Cranachhaus**, where painter Lucas Cranach the Elder lived for two years before his death in 1553.

GOETHE SITES

Historic Sites

The **Goethe National-museum** (Frauenplan 1; adult/child €8.50/2.50; ☺9am-6pm Tue-Sun) focuses not so much on the

Schloss Schwerin, Mecklenburg-Western Pomerania
PHOTOGRAPHER: WITOLD SKRYPCZAK/LONELY PLANET IMAGES ©

man as on his movement, offering a broad overview of German classicism, from its proponents to its patrons. The adjoining **Goethe Haus**, where such works as *Faust* were written, focuses much more on the man himself. He lived here from 1775 until his death in 1832.

Goethes Gartenhaus (adult/child €4.50/2; ☺10am-6pm Apr-Oct, to 4pm Nov-Mar) was his beloved retreat and stands in the alluring **Park an der Ilm**.

BAUHAUS MUSEUM   Museum
(Theaterplatz; adult/child €5/1; ☺10am-6pm) The Bauhaus School and movement were founded here in 1919 by Walter Gropius, who managed to draw such artists as Kandinsky, Klee, Feininger and Schlemmer as teachers. The exhibition at the museum chronicles the evolution of the group and explains its design innovations, which continue to shape our lives.

SCHLOSSMUSEUM   Museum
(Burgplatz 4; adult/child €6/2.50; ☺10am-6pm Tue-Sun Apr-Oct, 10am-4pm Nov-Mar) Housed in the **Stadtschloss**, the former residence of the ducal family of Saxe-Weimar, the museum boasts the Cranach Gallery, several portraits by Albrecht Dürer and collections of Dutch masters and German romanticists. A €90-million project for a full restoration is now in the works.

OTHER HISTORIC SITES
    Historic Sites
Goethe's fellow dramatist Friedrich von Schiller lived in Weimar from 1799 until his early death in 1805; his house is now the **Schiller Museum** (Schillerstrasse 12; adult/child €5/2; ☺9am-6pm Wed-Mon). The study at the end of the 2nd floor contains the desk where he penned *Wilhelm Tell* and other works.

Liszt Haus (Marienstrasse 17; adult/child €4/1; ☺10am-6pm Tue-Sun Apr-Oct) is on the western edge of Park an der Ilm. Composer and pianist Franz Liszt lived here in 1848 and again from 1869 to 1886, when he wrote *Hungarian Rhapsody* and *Faust Symphony*. It reopened in 2011 (the official year of Liszt!) after a major rehab.

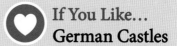

If You Like…
German Castles

The dramatic castles at **Neuschwanstein** and **Hohenschwangau** (p603) are the most famous fortresses in Germany, but they're certainly not the only ones.

1 SCHLOSS HEIDELBERG
(www.schloss-heidelberg.de; adult/child €5/3, tours €4; ☺8am-5.30pm) Heidelberg's castle is one of Germany's finest examples of grand Gothic-Renaissance architecture. The building's half-ruined state only enhances its romantic appeal. There are regular trains to Heidelberg from Frankfurt and Stuttgart; change at Mannheim for other German cities.

2 WARTBURG
(www.wartburg-eisenach.de; tour adult/child €8/5; ☺tours 8.30am-5pm Mar-Oct, 9am-3.30pm Nov-Feb) The Wartburg in Eisenach is the only German castle to be named a Unesco World Heritage site. Although parts of the castle date back to the 11th century, its fame is largely due to the Protestant reformer Martin Luther, who went into hiding here from 1521 to 1522 after being excommunicated. You can still visit his study, along with an extravagant Great Hall, which inspired Wagner's opera *Tannhäuser*. Frequent trains run to Erfurt and Weimar.

3 SCHLOSS SCHWERIN
(☎525 2920; www.schloss-schwerin.de; adult/child €4/2.50; ☺10am-6pm mid-Apr–mid-Oct, 10am-5pm Tue-Sun mid-Oct–mid-Apr) This striking neo-Gothic castle was built in the mid-1800s and dominates the charming lakeside town of Schwerin, the oldest city in Mecklenburg-Western Pomerania. Regular trains run to Schwerin from Hamburg and Berlin-Hauptbahnhof.

Sleeping

HOTEL ELEPHANT   Hotel **€€€**
(☎8020; www.starwood.de; Markt 19; r from €120-250; @☎) A true classic, the 1937 marble Bauhaus-Deco splendour of the 99-room, five-star Elephant has seen most of Weimar's great and good come and go. Just to make the point, a golden Thomas Mann looks out over the Markt from a balcony in front.

HOTEL AMALIENHOF   Hotel €€

(☎5490; www.amalienhof-weimar.de; Amalien-strasse 2; r €90-110) The charms of this 35-room church-affiliated hotel are manifold: classy antique furnishings, richly styled rooms that point to history without burying you in it, and a late breakfast buffet for those who take their holidays seriously.

 Eating

JO HANNS   Bistro €€

(Scherfgasse 1; mains €10-20) The food is satisfying but it's the 130 wines from the Saale-Unstrut region – many served by the glass – that draw people inside the cosy maroon walls or outside on the terrace. Food is inventive, with many specials.

GASTHAUS ZUM WEISSEN SCHWAN
German €€

(Frauentorstrasse 23; mains €11-20; ⏰noon-midnight Wed-Sun) At this venerable inn, you can fill your tummy with Goethe's favourite dish (boiled beef with herb sauce, red beet salad and potatoes), which actually hails from his home town of Frankfurt.

RESIDENZ-CAFÉ   Cafe €€

(Grüner Markt 4; mains €6-16) The 'Resi', one of Weimar's enduring favourites, is a Jack of all trades: everyone should find something to their taste here. The Lovers' Breakfast is €20 for two, but the inspired meat and vegetarian dishes may well have you swooning, too.

ℹ Information

Tourist information (www.weimar.de; Markt 10; ⏰9.30am-7pm Mon-Fri, to 4pm Sat & Sun) Discount cards start at €10.

ℹ Getting There & Away

Weimar's Hauptbahnhof is a 20-minute walk from the centre. It's on a line with frequent services linking Leipzig (€24, one hour) and Erfurt (€8, 15 minutes). Two-hourly ICE/IC services go to Berlin-Hauptbahnhof (€53, 2¼ hours).

Left: Statue in front of the Residenzmuseum (p586), Munich;
Below: Feeding birds at Schloss Nymphenburg (p586), Munich
PHOTOGRAPHER: (LEFT) PAUL BERNHARDT/LONELY PLANET IMAGES ©;
(BELOW) LEE FOSTER/LONELY PLANET IMAGES ©

Most buses serve Goetheplatz, on the northwestern edge of the Altstadt. No time for the 20-minute walk before the next train departs? A cab costs €6.

BAVARIA

Bavaria (Bayern) can seem like every German stereotype rolled into one. Lederhosen, beer halls, oompah bands and romantic castles are just some of the clichés. But as any Bavarian will tell you, the state thinks of itself as Bavarian first and German second.

Bavaria draws visitors year-round. If you have time for only one part of Germany after Berlin, this is it. Munich, the capital, is the heart and soul. The Bavarian Alps, Nuremberg and the medieval towns on the Romantic Road are other important attractions.

Munich

📞 089 / POP 1.35 MILLION

Pulsing with prosperity and *Gemütlich keit* (cosiness), Munich (München) revels in contradictions. Age-old traditions exist side by side with sleek BMWs and designer boutiques. Its museums include world-class collections, and its music and cultural scenes rival Berlin.

Despite all its sophistication, Munich retains a touch of provincialism that visitors find charming. The people's attitude is one of live and let live – and Müncheners will be the first to admit that their 'metropolis' is little more than a *Weltdorf,* a world village. During Oktoberfest visitors descend on the Bavarian capital in their zillions to raise a glass to this fascinating city.

🎯 Sights

Munich is a sprawling metropolis. Wandering the centre is rewarding but you'll need public transport to reach some of the key sights like the palaces.

585

Meissen

Straddling the Elbe around 25km upstream from Dresden, Meissen is a compact, perfectly preserved Saxon town, popular with day trippers.

Meissen has long been renowned for its chinaware, with its trademark insignia of blue crossed swords. Meissen's porcelain factory is now 1km southwest of the Altstadt in an appropriately beautiful building, the **Porzellan-Museum** (www.meissen.com; Talstrasse 9; adult/child €9/4.50; ⊙9am-6pm May-Oct, to 5pm Nov-Apr), which dates to 1916. There are often long queues for the workshop demonstrations, but you can view the porcelain collection upstairs at your leisure.

RESIDENZ　　　　　　　Palace
(Max-Joseph-Platz 3) Bavarian rulers lived in this vast pile from 1385 to 1918. Apart from the palace itself, the **Residenzmuseum** (www.residenz-muenchen.de; adult/child €6/free; ⊙9am-6pm Apr–mid-Oct, 10am-5pm mid-Oct–Mar) has an extraordinary array of 100 rooms containing no end of treasures and artworks. In the same building, the **Schatzkammer** (Treasure Chamber; adult/child €6/free) exhibits jewels, crowns and ornate gold.

SCHLOSS NYMPHENBURG　　Palace
(www.schloesser.bayern.de; adult/child €5/4; ⊙9am-6pm Apr–mid-Oct, 10am-4pm mid-Oct–Mar) This was the royal family's equally impressive summer home. Parts of it date from the 17th century. The surrounding park deserves a long, regal stroll. All this splendour is northwest of the city centre, via tram 17 from the Hauptbahnhof.

ALTE PINAKOTHEK　　Art Gallery
(www.pinakothek.de; Barer Strasse 27; adult/child €7/5, Sun €1; ⊙10am-8pm Tue, to 6pm Wed-Sun) A short stroll northeast of the centre, the Alte Pinakothek is a treasure house full of paintings by European masters from the 14th to 18th centuries. Highlights on display include Dürer's Christ-like *Self Portrait* and his *Four Apostles,* Rogier van der Weyden's *Adoration of the Magi* and Botticelli's *Pietà.*

NEUE PINAKOTHEK　　Art Gallery
(www.pinakothek.de; Barer Strasse 29; adult/child €7/5, Sun €1; ⊙10am-5pm Thu-Mon, to 8pm Wed) Immediately north of the Alte Pinakothek, this is home to mainly 19th-century works, including Van Gogh's *Sunflowers,* and sculpture. Enter from Theresienstrasse.

DEUTSCHES MUSEUM Science Museum
(www.deutsches-museum.de; Museumsinsel 1; adult/child €8.50/3; ⊙9am-5pm) This enormous science and technology museum celebrates the many achievements of humanity – Germans in particular. Kids become gleeful as they interact with the exhibits. Take the S-Bahn to Isartor.

BAYERISCHES NATIONALMUSEUM
　　　　　　　　　　　　　Museum
(www.bayerisches-nationalmuseum.de; Prinzregentenstrasse 3; adult/child €5/free, Sun €1; ⊙10am-5pm Tue, Wed & Fri-Sun, to 8pm Thu) East of the Hofgarten, break bread with old, dead Bavarians, from peasants to knights.

JÜDISCHES MUSEUM　　Museum
(www.juedisches-museum-muenchen.de; St-Jakobs-Platz 16; adult/child €6/3; ⊙10am-6pm Tue-Sun) Offers insight into Jewish history, life and culture in Munich.

STADTMUSEUM　　　　　Museum
(www.stadtmuseum-online.de; St-Jakobs-Platz 1; adult/child €4/2, Sun free; ⊙10am-6pm Tue-Sun) You went in for an hour and spent two; this superbly redone city museum

puts the foam on the stein of Munich history – good and bad.

BMW MUSEUM
Car Museum
(www.bmw-welt.de; adult/child €12/6; ⏰10am-6pm Tue-Sun) North of the city, auto fetishists get stroked at this bowl-shaped temple adjacent to BMW's headquarters and factory. Take the U3 to Olympiazentrum.

ENGLISCHER GARTEN
Park
One of the largest city parks in Europe, this grand park is a great place for strolling, especially along the Schwabinger Bach. In summer nude sunbathing is the rule rather than the exception. If they're not doing this, they're probably drinking merrily at one of the park's three beer gardens (see the boxed text, p592).

BOTANICAL GARDENS
Garden
(www.botmuc.de; Menzinger Strasse 65; adult/child €4/free; ⏰varies with season, generally 9am-6pm) The gorgeous municipal gardens are two stops past Schloss Nymphenburg on tram 17.

OLYMPIA PARK COMPLEX
Park
The glorious grounds of the 1972 Olympics continue to thrill today. If you like heights, take a ride up the lift of the 290m **Olympiaturm** (Olympic Tower; adult/child €4.50/3; ⏰9am-midnight). And if you fancy a swim, the **Olympic Pool Complex** (Olympic Park; admission €4; ⏰7am-11pm) will have you feeling like Mark Spitz while you imagine seven gold medals around your neck – or just work on your breaststroke. Take the U3 to Olympia Zentrum.

 Tours

Mike's Bike Tours
Bicycle
(www.mikesbiketours.com; tours from €24) Enjoyable (and leisurely) city cycling tours in English. Tours depart from the archway at the Altes Rathaus on Marienplatz.

Munich Walk Tours
Walking
(www.munichwalktours.de; tours from €12) Walking tours of the city on topics from Nazis to beer. Meet under the Glockenspiel on Marienplatz.

City Bus 100
Bus
Ordinary city bus that runs from the Hauptbahn-hof to the Ostbahnhof via 21 of the city's museums and galleries. This includes all three Pinakothek, the Residenz and the Bayerisches National-museum.

Buchenwald

This **concentration-camp museum** (www.buchenwald.de; ⏰9am-6pm Apr-Oct, 9am-4pm Nov-Mar) and memorial are located just 10km north of Weimar.

Between 1937 and 1945, more than a fifth of the 250,000 people incarcerated here died. The location on the side of a hill only added to the torture of the inmates, as there are sweeping views of the region – an area where people were free while those here died. Various parts of the camp have been restored and there is an essential **museum** with excellent exhibits. There's also a heartbreaking display of art created by the prisoners.

After the war, the Soviets turned the tables but continued the brutality by establishing Special Camp No 2, in which 7000 so-called anticommunists and ex-Nazis were literally worked to death. Their bodies were found after the reunification in mass graves north of the camp, near the Hauptbahnhof.

In Weimar, **Buchenwald Information** (Markt 10; ⏰9.30am-6pm Mon-Fri, to 3pm Sat & Sun) is an excellent resource.

To reach the camp, take bus 6 (€1.80, 15 minutes, hourly) from Weimar.

Central Munich

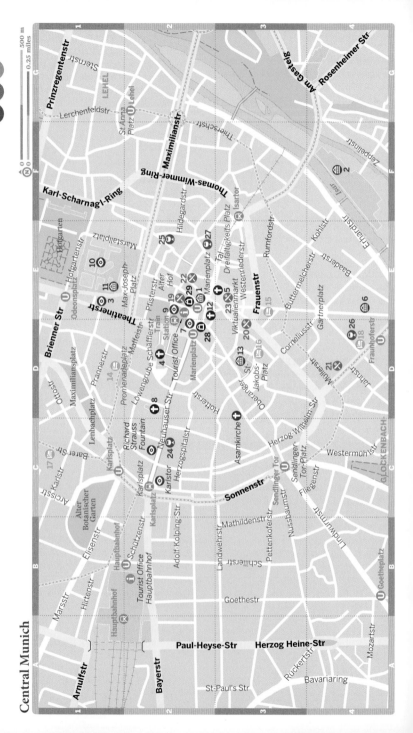

Central Munich

Festivals & Events

Oktoberfest   Beer
(www.oktoberfest.de; ⊙10am-11.30pm, from 9am Sat & Sun) Hordes come to Munich in the 15 days before the first Sunday in October. While there is no entrance fee, those steins of beer (called *mass*) add up fast. Although its origins are in the marriage celebrations of Crown Prince Ludwig in 1810, there's nothing regal about this beery bacchanalia now: expect mobs and expect to make some new drunken friends!

Sleeping

Munich has no shortage of places to stay – except during Oktoberfest or some busy summer periods, when the wise (meaning those with a room) will have booked.

HOTEL BLAUER BOCK   Hotel €€
(☎231 780; www.hotelblauerbock.de; Sebastiansplatz 9; r €60-150; 🛜) A whiff of roasted almonds away from the Viktualienmarkt, this tidy hotel once provided shelter for Benedictine monks and has an ideal location that's the envy of more prestigious abodes. It's comfy, familiar and spacious. Cheaper rooms share bathrooms.

BAYERISCHER HOF   Hotel €€€
(☎212 00; www.bayerischerhof.de; Promenadeplatz 2-6; r €180-400; ✳@🛜⛲) Room doors fold away into the stucco mouldings at the Hof, one of the grande dames of the Munich hotel trade. It boasts a super-central location, a pool and a jazz club. Rates include a champagne breakfast.

PENSION GÄRTNERPLATZ   Hotel €€
(☎202 5170; www.pension-gaertnerplatztheater .de; Klenzestrasse 45; r €80-130; 🛜) Escape the tourist rabble, or reality altogether, in this eccentric establishment where rooms are a stylish interpretation of Alpine pomp. The room named 'Sisi' will have you sleeping in a canopy bed guarded by a giant porcelain mastiff.

HOTEL AM VIKTUALIENMARKT
    Hotel €€
(☎231 1090; www.hotel-am-viktualienmarkt.de; Utzschneiderstrasse 14; r €50-120; 🛜) Owners Elke and her daughter Stephanie run this perfectly located property with panache and a sunny attitude. A steep staircase (no lift) leads to rooms, the nicest of which have wooden floors and framed poster art. Book far ahead.

LEONARDO BOUTIQUE HOTEL SAVOY
    Hotel €€
(☎287 870; www.leonardo-hotels.com; Amalienstrasse 25; r €80-180; 🛜) In a Maxvorstadt area thick with modest hotels and cafes,

A Munich Stroll

The pivotal **Marienplatz** is a good starting point for a tour of Munich's heart. Dominating the square is the towering neo-Gothic **Neues Rathaus** (new town hall), with its ever-dancing **Glockenspiel** (carillon), which performs at 11am and noon (also at 5pm from March to October), bringing the square to an expectant standstill (note the fate of the Austrian knight...). Two important churches are on this square: the baroque star **St Peterskirche** (Rindermarkt 1; church free, tower adult/child €1.50/1; ⏰ 9am-7pm Apr-Oct, to 6pm Nov-Mar) and, behind the **Altes Rathaus**, the often-forgotten **Heiliggeistkirche** (Tal 77; ⏰ 7am-6pm).

Walk north along the genteel Theatinerstrasse, a staid street today with a notorious past. On 9 November 1923, Hitler and his followers marched up the street during their 'beer hall putsch' to seize control of Bavaria. A hail of gunfire at the **Feldherrnhall** in front of Odeonsplatz ended the revolution – but not for long.

Return south on Theatinerstrasse, and cut west to the landmark of Munich, the late-Gothic **Frauenkirche** (Church of Our Lady; Frauenplatz 1; ⏰ 7am-7pm Sat-Wed, 7am-8.30pm Thu, 7am-6pm Fri) with its then-trendy 16th-century twin onion domes. Go inside and join the hordes gazing at the grandeur of the place, or scale the 98m **tower** (adult/child €3/1.50; ⏰ 10am-5pm Mon-Sat Apr-Oct) for some Alps spotting. Continue west to the large, grey 16th-century **Michaelskirche** (Neuhauserstrasse 52; ⏰ 8am-7pm), Germany's earliest and grandest Renaissance church.

the Savoy stands out after a stylish refit that has given it trappings of luxury. Big windows look across to other inns so you can compare rooms.

HOTEL MARIENBAD
Hotel €€

(☎ 595 585; www.hotelmarienbad.de; Barer Strasse 11, Maxvorstadt; r €50-150; 🛜) Back in the 19th century, Wagner, Puccini and Rilke shacked up in what once ranked among Munich's finest hotels. Still friendly and well maintained, it now flaunts an endearing alchemy of styles, from playful art nouveau to campy 1960s utilitarian.

 ## Eating

DER PSCHORR
German €€

(Viktualienmarkt 15; mains €10-18) Shining like a jewel box across a square, this modern high-ceilinged restaurant, operated by a local brewer, is the 21st-century version of a beer hall. Creative dishes, including new takes on old German classics, stream out from the open kitchen.

WEISSES BRAUHAUS
Bavarian €€

(Tal 7; mains €9-20) The place for classic Bavarian fare in an ancient beer-hall setting. Everything from *Weissewurst* (beloved local white sausage) to hearty traditional fare such as boiled ox cheeks is on offer. The menu has changed little in decades.

HAXNBAUER
German €€

(Sparkassenstrasse; mains €10-22) Meats of all kinds roast in the windows of this modern take on a trad restaurant. The roast goose is much favoured. Always popular; excellent quality.

FRAUNHOFER
German €€

(Fraunhoferstrasse 9; mains €6-16; ⏰ 4.30pm-1am) This classic brewpub contrasts olde-worlde atmosphere (mounted animal heads and a portrait of Ludwig II) with a menu that offers progressive takes on classical fare.

GÖTTERSPEISE
Cafe €

(Jahnstrasse 30; snacks from €3) If the Aztecs thought of chocolate as the elixir of the gods, then this shop-cum-cafe must be heaven. Cocoa addicts can satisfy their cravings here with rave-worthy French chocolate cake, thick, hot drinking chocolate and chocolate-flavoured 'body paint' for those wishing to double their sins.

VIKTUALIENMARKT — Outdoor Market
(⏰ Mon-Fri & Sat morning) Just south of Marienplatz is a large open-air market, where you can put together a picnic feast to take to the Englischer Garten.

ALOIS DALLMAYR — Food Hall
(Dienerstrasse 14) You'll find one of the world's great delicatessens behind the mustard-yellow awnings, its sparkling cases filled with fine foods.

Drinking

Apart from the beer halls and gardens, Munich has no shortage of lively pubs. Schwabing and Glockenback-Viertel are good places to follow your ears. Many places serve food; most are open until 1am or later at weekends.

ALTER SIMPL — Pub
(Türkenstrasse 57, Maxvorstadt; meals from €8) Thomas Mann and Hermann Hesse used to knock 'em back at this legendary thirst parlour. Alter Simpl is also a good place to satisfy midnight munchies as bar bites are available until one hour before closing time.

MORIZZ — Bar
(Klenzestrasse 43) This mod art deco–style lounge with red leather armchairs and mirrors for posing and preening goes for a more moneyed clientele and even gets the occasional local celebrity drop-in. Packed at weekends.

TRACHTENVOGL — Lounge
(Reichenbachstrasse 47, Gärtnerplatzviertel; ⏰ 10am-1am) At night you'll have to shoe-horn your way into this buzzy lair favoured by a chatty, boozy crowd of scenesters, artists and students. Daytimes are mellower at this former folkloric garment shop.

Shopping

All shoppers converge on the **Marienplatz** to buy designer shoes or kitschy souvenirs. The stylish department store **Ludwig Beck**

Beer tent at Oktoberfest (p589)

KRZYSZTOF DYDYNSKI/LONELY PLANET IMAGES ©

JON ARNOLD IMAGES LTD / ALAMY©

Don't Miss Beer Halls & Beer Gardens

Beer drinking is not just an integral part of Munich's entertainment scene, it's a reason to visit. Germans drink an average of 130L of the amber liquid each per year, while Munich residents manage much more.

On a warm day there's nothing better than sitting and sipping among the greenery at one of the Englischer Garten's classic beer gardens. **Chinesischer Turm** (above) is justifiably popular while the nearby **Hirschau** on the banks of Kleinhesseloher See is less crowded.

Augustiner Bräustuben (Landsberger Strasse 19) Depending on the wind, an aroma of hops envelops you as you approach this ultra-authentic beer hall inside the actual Augustiner brewery.

Hofbräuhaus (Am Platzl 9) The ultimate cliché of Munich beer halls. Tourists arrive by the busload but no one seems to mind that this could be Disneyland (although the theme park wasn't once home to Hitler's early speeches, like this place was).

Zum Dürnbrau (Tal 21) Tucked into a corner off Tal, this is a great and authentic little alternative to the Hofbräuhaus. There's a small beer garden, and drinkers of dark draughts enjoy pewter-topped mugs.

Augustiner Bierhalle (Neuhauser Strasse 27) What you probably imagine an old-style Munich beer hall looks like, filled with laughter, smoke and clinking glasses.

(☏ 236 910; Marienplatz 11) has something for everyone. Bypass Calvin et al for more unusual European choices. Nearby **Maximilianstrasse** is a fashionable street that is ideal for simply strolling and window shopping. Close by, **Hugendubel** (Salvatorplatz 2) is crammed with English-language titles.

To truly 'unchain' yourself, though, you should hit the **Gärtnerplatzviertel** and **Glockenbach-Viertel**, bastions of well-edited indie stores and local-designer boutiques.

Munich has eight **Christmas markets** from late November, including a big one on Marienplatz. For more on these popular events, see p598.

 Information

Discount Cards

City Tour Card (www.citytourcard.com; 1/3 days €9.80/18.80) Includes transport and discounts of between 10% and 50% for about 30 attractions. Available at some hotels, MVV (Munich public transport authority) offices and U-Bahn and S-Bahn vending machines.

Tourist Information

EurAide (593 889; www.euraide.de; Hauptbahnhof; 9am–noon & 1-5pm, longer hr in summer) Dispenses savvy travel advice in English, sells and validates rail passes, explains train-ticket savings and discounts many tours; staff work in the DB Travel Centre at counter 1.

Tourist office (www.muenchen.de) Hauptbahnhof (Bahnhofplatz 2; 9.30am-6.30pm Mon-Sat, 10am-6pm Sun, longer hr in summer & during holidays); Marienplatz (Neues Rathaus, Marienplatz 8; 10am-8pm Mon-Fri, to 4pm Sat) Be sure to ask for the excellent and free guides *Young and About in Munich, National Socialism in Munich* and various neighbourhood guides.

 Getting There & Away

Air

Munich's sparkling white **airport** (MUC; www.munich-airport.de) is second in importance only to Frankfurt for international and national connections.

Bus

Munich has a new **bus station** (ZOB; www.zob-muenchen.de; Arnulfstrasse). It's 500m west of the Hauptbahnhof, at the S-Bahn stop Hackerbrücke.

Munich is a stop for the **Romantic Road bus** (www.romanticroadcoach.de); see p616.

Car & Motorcycle

The main hire companies have counters together on the second level of the Hauptbahnhof. For arranged rides, the **Mitfahrzentrale** (194 40;

www.itfahrzentrale.de; Lämmerstrasse 6; 8am-8pm) is near the Hauptbahnhof. The cost is split with the driver and you can reach most parts of Germany for well under €40.

Train

Train services to/from Munich are excellent. There are rapid connections at least every two hours to all major cities in Germany, as well as daily trains to other European cities.

 Getting Around

To/From the Airport

Munich's international airport is connected by the S8 and the S1 to Marienplatz and the Hauptbahnhof (€9.60). The service takes about 40 minutes and there is a train every 10 minutes from 4am until around 12.30am. The S8 route is slightly faster. For €10.40 you can get a ticket that's good all day.

Taxis make the long haul for at least €60.

Car & Motorcycle

It's not worth driving in the city centre – many streets are pedestrian-only.

Public Transport

Munich's excellent **public transport network** (MVV; www.mvv-muenchen.de) is zone-based, and most places of interest to tourists (except Dachau and the airport) are within the 'blue' inner zone (*Innenraum;* €2.40). MVV tickets are valid for the S-Bahn, U-Bahn, trams and buses, but they must be validated before use.

Kurzstrecke (short rides) cost €1.20 and are good for no more than four stops on buses and

ICE Trains to Munich (hourly)

DESTINATION	PRICE	DURATION (HR)
Berlin	€113	5¾
Frankfurt	€89	3
Hamburg	€115	5½

Trains to Munich

DESTINATION	PRICE	DURATION (HR)
Paris	€140	6
Vienna	€75	4
Zürich	€65	4¼

trams, and two stops on the U- and S-Bahns. *Tageskarte* (day passes) for the inner zone cost €5.20, while three-day tickets cost €12.80.

Dachau

The first Nazi concentration camp was **Dachau** (www.kz-gedenkstaette-dachau. de; Alte-Roemerstrasse 75; admission free; ⊙9am-5pm Tue-Sun), built in March 1933. Jews, political prisoners, homosexuals and others deemed 'undesirable' by the Third Reich were imprisoned in the camp. More than 200,000 people were sent here; more than 30,000 died at Dachau, and countless others died after being transferred to other death camps. An English-language documentary is shown at 11.30am and 3.30pm. A visit includes camp relics, memorials and a very sobering museum.

Take the S2 (direction: Petershausen) to Dachau and then bus 726 to the camp. A Munich XXL day ticket (€7) will cover the trip.

Romantic Road

The popular and schmaltzily named Romantic Road (Romantische Strasse) links a series of picturesque Bavarian towns and cities. It's not actually one road per se, but rather a 353km route chosen to highlight as many quaint towns and cities as possible in western Bavaria. A good first stop is the info-packed website www .romanticroad.de.

A popular way to tour the Romantic Road is the **Romantic Road bus** (☎069 719126-268; www.romanticroadcoach.de; ⊙phone line 9am-6pm Mon-Fri). The total fare (tickets are bought on board) is a pricey €105.

Bamberg

♫0951 / POP 71,000

Off the major tourist routes, Bamberg is revered by those in the know. It boasts a beautifully preserved collection of 17th- and 18th-century merchants' houses, palaces and churches. No wonder it has been recognised by Unesco as a World Heritage site. Could it be the best small town in Germany?

◉ Sights

Bamberg's main appeal is its fine buildings – the sheer number, their jumble of styles and the ambience this creates. Most attractions are spread on either side of the Regnitz River, but the **Altes Rathaus** (Obere Brücke) is actually solidly perched on its own islet. Its lavish murals are among many around town.

The princely and ecclesiastical district is centred on **Domplatz**, where the Romanesque and Gothic **cathedral** (Domplatz; ⊙8am-6pm Apr-Sep, to 5pm Oct-Mar), housing the statue of the chivalric king-knight, the *Bamberger Reiter*, is the biggest attraction. Look for the enigmatic statue, the *Lächelnde Engel* (Smiling Angel).

Across the square, the imposing 17th-century **Neue Residenz** (www.schloesser .bayern.de; Domplatz 8; adult/child €4/3; ⊙9am-6pm Apr-Sep, 10am-4pm Oct-Mar) has 40 rooms filled with treasures and opulent decor.

Above Domplatz is the former Benedictine monastery of **St Michael**, at the top of Michaelsberg. The **Kirche St Michael** (Franziskanergasse 2; ⊙9am-6pm) is a must-see for its baroque art and the herbal compendium painted on its ceiling.

🛏 Sleeping

HOTEL SANKT NEPOMUK　　Hotel　€€
(☎984 20; www.hotel-nepomuk.de; Obere Mühlbrücke 9; r €95-145; 🛜) This is a classy establishment in a half-timbered former mill right on the Regnitz. It has a superb restaurant (mains €15 to €30) with a terrace, 24 comfy rustic rooms and bikes for rent.

HOTEL EUROPA
Hotel €€

(☎ 309 3020; www.hotel-europa-bamberg.de; Untere Königstrasse 6-8; r €75-120) Smell the spaghetti from one of the 46 rooms above Bamberg's best Italian restaurant. Ask for a room at the front with views of the Dom and the red-tiled roofs of the Altstadt. Breakfast is in the restaurant or out in the sunny courtyard.

 Eating & Drinking

Bamberg's unique style of beer is called *Rauchbier,* which literally means smoked beer.

SCHLENKERLA
German €€

(Dominikanerstrasse 6; mains €8-15; ☺ Wed-Mon) Featuring a warren of rooms decked out with lamps fashioned from antlers, this 16th-century restaurant is famous for tasty Franconian specialities and *Rauchbier,* served directly from oak barrels.

KLOSTERBRÄU
German €

(Obere Mühlbrücke 1-3; mains €6-12) This beautiful half-timbered brewery is Bamberg's oldest. It draws *Stammgäste* (regular local drinkers) and tourists alike, who wash down filling slabs of meat and dumplings with its excellent range of ales.

 Information

The tourist office (www.bamberg.info; Geyerswörthstrasse 3; ☺ 9.30am-6pm Mon-Fri, 9.30am-2.30pm Sat & Sun) is in the old town.

 Getting There & Away

Two trains per hour go to/from both Würzburg (€17, one hour) and Nuremberg (€20, one hour). Bamberg is also served by ICE trains running between Munich (€58, two hours) and Berlin (€74, 3¾ hours) every two hours.

Nuremberg
☎ 0911 / POP 498,000

Nuremberg (Nürnberg) woos visitors with its wonderfully restored medieval Altstadt, its grand castle and its magical *Christkindlesmarkt* (Christmas market). Thriving traditions also include sizzling *Nürnberger Bratwürste* (finger-sized sausages) and *Lebkuchen* – large, soft gingerbread cookies, traditionally eaten at Christmastime but available here year-round. Both within and beyond the

Altes Rathaus, Bamberg

DAVID PEEVERS/LONELY PLANET IMAGES ©

high stone wall encircling the Altstadt is a wealth of major museums that shed light on Nuremberg's significant history.

Nuremberg played a major role during the Nazi years, as documented in Leni Riefenstahl's film *Triumph of the Will* and during the war-crimes trials afterwards. It has done an admirable job of confronting this ugly past with museums and exhibits.

Sights

The scenic **Altstadt** is easily covered on foot. On Lorenzer Platz there's the **St Lorenzkirche**, noted for the 15th-century tabernacle that climbs like a vine up a pillar to the vaulted ceiling.

To the north is the bustling **Hauptmarkt**, where the most famous **Christkindlmarkt** in Germany is held from the Friday before Advent to Christmas Eve. The church here is the ornate **Pfarrkirche Unsere Liebe Frau**; the clock's figures go strolling at noon. Near the Rathaus is **St Sebalduskirche** (9.30am-6pm), Nuremberg's oldest church (dating from the 13th century), with the shrine of St Sebaldus.

KAISERBURG   Castle
(www.schloesser.bayern.de; adult/child incl museum €6/5; 9am-6pm Apr-Sep, 10am-4pm Oct-Mar) Climb up Burgstrasse to this enormous 15th-century fortress for good views of the city. The walls spread west to the tunnel-gate of **Tiergärtnertor**, where you can stroll behind the castle to the gardens.

GERMANISCHES NATIONALMUSEUM
Museum
(www.gnm.de; Kartäusergasse 1; adult/child €8/5; 10am-6pm Tue & Thu-Sun, to 9pm Wed) The most important general museum of German culture in the country, this stunner displays works by German painters and sculptors, an archaeological collection, arms and armour, musical and scientific instruments and, of course, toys.

NUREMBERG TRIALS MEMORIAL
Historical Site
(www.memorium-nuremberg.de; Bärenschanzstrasse 72; adult/child €5/3; 10am-6pm Wed-Mon) From 1945 to 1949 suspected Nazis were tried for war crimes in Nuremberg, which was chosen because it had been the spiritual home of the Third Reich. The courthouse where the trials were held is still in use and is now home to a compel-

Christkindlmarkt at Hauptmarkt, Nuremberg

RICHARD NEBESKY/LONELY PLANET IMAGES ©

ling and comprehensive **exhibit** about the world's first efforts to prosecute genocide. **Courtroom 600**, where the trials were held, can be toured when it is not in use.

LUITPOLDHAIN Historical Site

Nuremberg's role during the Third Reich is well known. The Nazis chose this city as their propaganda centre and for mass rallies, which were held at Luitpoldhain, a (never completed) sports complex of megalomaniac proportions.

Don't miss the **Dokumentationzentrum** (www.museen.nuernberg.de; Bayernstrasse 110; adult/child €5/3; ◷9am-6pm Mon-Fri, 10am-6pm Sat & Sun) in the north wing of the huge unfinished Congress Hall, which would have held 50,000 people. The museum's absorbing exhibits trace the rise of Hitler and the Nazis, and the important role Nuremberg played in the mythology. Take tram 9 or 6 to Doku-Zentrum.

 Sleeping

HOTEL ELCH Hotel €€

(☑249 2980; www.hotel-elch.com; Irrerstrasse 9; r €65-110; ⑳) This historic hotel, with a logo of the namesake elk, occupies a 14th-century half-timbered house that wears its years on its skew facade. The spotless and petite rooms are up a narrow medieval staircase.

HOTEL DREI RABEN Hotel €€

(☑274 380; www.hotel3raben.de; Königstrasse 63; r €100-185; ⑳) This designer theme hotel builds upon the legend of three ravens perched on the building's chimney stack, who tell each other stories from Nuremberg lore. Each of the 21 rooms uses its style and humour to tell a particular tale – from the life of Dürer to the history of the locomotive.

 Eating

BRATWURSTHÄUSLE German €€

(http://die-nuernberger-bratwurst.de; Rathausplatz 2; meals €6-14; ◷closed Sun) A local

If You Like…
Picturesque German Towns

If you've fallen for the charms of **Bamberg** (p594), here are a few more gorgeous German towns to discover.

1 LÜBECK

(www.lubeck-tourism.de) With its crooked gates, medieval merchants' homes and spired churches, Lübeck has unsurprisingly made it onto Unesco's World Heritage list. Don't miss a boat tour on the Trave River, which forms a moat around the Old Town. Regular trains travel from Lübeck's Hauptbahnhof to Hamburg.

2 ROTHENBURG OB DER TAUBER

(www.rothenburg.de) This is the classic German walled town, ringed on every side by sturdy medieval battlements. It gets extremely busy – visit late in the day to avoid the worst crowds. There are hourly trains to/from Würzburg via Steinach (total journey €13, 70 minutes). Romantic Road buses (p594) stop here for 35 minutes.

3 QUEDLINBURG

(www.quedlinburg.de) Another Unesco-listed gem, Quedlinburg is famous for its spectacular castle district, perched on a 25m-high plateau above town. Established during the reign of Heinrich I (919–36), the present-day Renaissance Schloss dates from the 16th century. From nearby Magdeburg, there are frequent trains to Berlin and Leipzig.

4 HAMELIN

(www.hamelin.de/touristinfo) Famous for its fairy-tale connections with the Pied Piper, the quaint town of Hamelin is one of the prettiest in Lower Saxony. Needless to say, the best way to explore is by following the Pied Piper trail – marked, of course, by white rats on the pavement. Frequent S-Bahn trains (S5) head from Hanover to Hamelin.

legend and *the* place for flame-grilled and scrumptious local sausages. Get them with *Kartoffelsalat* (potato salad). There are also nice tree-shaded tables outside.

Christmas Markets

Beginning in late November every year, central squares across Germany – especially those in Bavaria – are transformed into Christmas markets or *Christkindlmarkts* (also known as *Weihnachtsmärkte*). Folks stamp about between the wooden stalls, perusing seasonal trinkets (from treasures to schlock) while warming themselves with tasty *glühwein* (mulled, spiced red wine) and such treats as sausages and potato pancakes. The markets are popular with tourists but locals love 'em too, and bundle themselves up and carouse for hours. Nuremberg's **market** (www.chriskindlesmarkt.de) fills much of the centre and attracts two million people.

HÜTT'N
German €€

(Burgstrasse 19; mains €8-15; ⊙dinner Wed-Mon) Be prepared to queue for a table at this local haunt. The special here is the *ofenfrische Krustenbraten:* roast pork with crackling, dumplings and sauerkraut salad. There's also a near-endless variety of schnapps and beers.

CAFÉ AM TRÖDELMARKT
Cafe €

(Trödelmarkt 42; dishes €3-5; ⊙9am-6pm) A gorgeous place on a sunny day, this multilevel waterfront cafe overlooks the covered Henkersteg bridge.

KETTENSTEG
Beer Garden €

(Maxplatz 35; mains €6-14) Right by the river and with its own suspension bridge to the other side, this beer garden and restaurant is fine on a summer day and cosy in winter.

ⓘ Information

Nürnberg + Fürth Card (€21) Good for two days of unlimited public transport and admissions.

Tourist office (www.tourismus.nuernberg.de) Künstlerhaus (**Königstrasse 93;** ⊙9am-7pm Mon-Sat, 10am-4pm Sun); Hauptmarkt (**Hauptmarkt 18;** ⊙9am-6pm Mon-Sat, 10am-4pm Sun)

ⓘ Getting There & Around

Nuremberg's **airport** (NUE; www.airport-nuernberg.de) is a hub for budget carrier Air Berlin, which has services throughout Germany, as well as flights to London. There's frequent service to the airport on the S-2 line (€2, 12 minutes).

BAVARIAN ALPS

While not quite as high as their sister summits further south in Austria and Switzerland, the Bavarian Alps (Bayerische Alpen) still are standouts, owing to their abrupt rise from the rolling Bavarian foothills. Stretching westward from Germany's southeastern corner to the Allgäu region near Lake Constance, the Alps take in most of the mountainous country fringing the southern border with Austria.

Berchtesgaden

☑08652 / POP 7900

Steeped in myth and legend, the Berchtesgadener Land enjoys a natural beauty so abundant that it's almost preternatural. Framed by six formidable mountain ranges and home to Germany's second-highest mountain, the Watzmann (2713m), the dreamy, fir-lined valleys are filled with gurgling streams and peaceful Alpine villages.

Much of the terrain is protected by law as the Nationalpark Berchtesgaden, which embraces the pristine Königssee, one of Germany's most photogenic lakes. Yet, Berchtesgaden's history is also indelibly entwined with the Nazi period, as chronicled at the disturbing Dokumentation Obersalzberg. The Eagle's Nest, a mountaintop lodge built for Hitler, is now a major tourist attraction.

⊙ Sights & Activities

DOKUMENTATION OBERSALZBERG
Museum

(www.obersalzberg.de; Salzbergstrasse 41, Obersalzberg; adult/child & student €3/free; ⊙9am-5pm daily Apr-Oct, 10am-3pm Tue-Sun Nov-Mar) In 1933 quiet Obersalzberg (some 3km from Berchtesgaden) became the southern headquarters of Hitler's government, a dark period that's given the full historical treatment at this compelling museum. You can visit tunnels that were dug for a fortunately unfulfilled Nazi last stand but the exhibits – including the erudite English audio guide (€2) – are the real draw. It shows how Hitler gained the support of the masses through his demonization of 'elites' while cigarette companies increased sales by including a picture of the dictator in every pack.

To get there take bus 838 from the 1938-vintage Hauptbahnhof in Berchtesgaden. It's hourly weekdays but infrequent at weekends. A cab costs about €20.

KÖNIGSSEE
Lake

Crossing the beautiful, emerald-green Königssee, an alpine lake situated 5km south of Berchtesgaden (and linked by hourly buses in summer) is sublime. There are frequent boat tours (€13) across the lake to the pixel-perfect chapel at **St Bartholomä**.

ⓘ Getting There & Away

There is hourly train service to Berchtesgaden from Munich (€30, 2½ hours), which usually requires a change in Frilassing. There are hourly connections to nearby Salzburg in Austria (€10, one hour); bus 840 from the station takes 45 minutes.

Oberammergau
📞08822 / POP 5500

A blend of genuine piety, religious kitsch and monumental commercial greed, Oberammergau sometimes seems to sink under the weight of day trippers. Sadly, the crush of humanity may distract from the town's triple charms: its gorgeous valley setting below the jagged Kofel peak, a 500-year-old woodcarving tradition and a wealth of houses painted with *Lüftlmalerei* (idealised murals on outside walls).

About 20km north of Garmisch-Partenkirchen, Oberammergau is known worldwide for hosting the famous **Passion Play** (www.passionplay-oberammergau.com), acted out by much of the towns' folk roughly every 10 years since 1634 to give thanks for being spared from the plague. The next one is in 2020.

Hourly trains connect Munich with Oberammergau (€18, 1¾ hours) with a change at Murnau. **RVO bus 9606** (www.rvo-bus.de) links Oberammergau with Füssen and the Wieskirche as well as Garmisch-Partenkirchen five to six times daily.

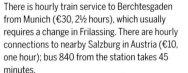

Trains to Nuremberg

DESTINATION	PRICE	DURATION (HR)
Berlin-Hauptbahnhof	€89	4½
Frankfurt	€48	2
Munich	€49	1
Stuttgart	€38	2¼

Tickets on the bus, tram and U-Bahn system cost €2 each. Day passes are €4.

Baden-Baden

07221 / POP 55,000

Who wouldn't want to bathe naked with a bunch of strangers? That's the question at the heart of the matter in Baden-Baden, the storied and ritzy spa town.

The natural hot springs have attracted visitors since Roman times, but this small city really became fashionable only in the 19th century, when it became a destination of royalty. It is stately, closely cropped and salubrious. Take the 69°C plunge. The 19th-century **Friedrichsbad** (www.roemisch-irisches-bad.de; Römerplatz 1; bathing program €21-31; 9am-10pm) is the reason for your journey. It's decadently Roman in style and provides a muscle-melting 16-step bathing program. No clothing is allowed inside, and several bathing sections are mixed on most days. The more modern **Caracalla-Therme** (www.caracalla.de; Römerplatz 1; entrance from €14; 8am-10pm) is a vast, modern complex of outdoor and indoor pools, and hot- and cold-water grottoes.

Baden-Baden is on the busy Mannheim–Basel train line. Frequent local trains serve Karlsruhe (€8, 15 minutes) and Offenburg (€9, 20 minutes), from where you can make connections to much of Germany.

BLACK FOREST

The Black Forest (Schwarzwald) gets its name from the dark canopy of evergreens, which evoke mystery and allure in many. Although some parts heave with visitors, a 20-minute walk from even the most crowded spots will put you in quiet countryside interspersed with enormous traditional farmhouses and patrolled by amiable dairy cows. It's not nature wild and remote, but bucolic and picturesque.

The Black Forest is east of the Rhine between Karlsruhe and Basel. It's shaped like a bean, about 160km long and 50km wide. From north to south there are four good bases for your visit: Freudenstadt, Schiltach, Triberg and Titisee. Each has good train links.

Those with a car will find their visit especially rewarding, as you can wander the rolling hills and deep valleys at will. One of the main tourist roads is the Schwarzwald-Hochstrasse (B500), which runs from Baden-Baden to Freudenstadt and from Triberg to Waldshut. Other thematic roads with maps provided by tourist offices include Schwarzwald Bäderstrasse (spa town route), Schwarzwald Panoramastrasse (panoramic view route) and Badische Weinstrasse (wine route). Whatever you do, make certain you have an excellent commercial regional road map with you.

RHINELAND-PALATINATE

Rhineland-Palatinate (Rheinland-Pfalz) is deeply riven by rivers, and the names of two – Rhine and Moselle – are synonymous with the wines made from the grapes growing on its hillsides.

Moselle Valley

Exploring the vineyards and wineries of the Moselle (Mosel) Valley is an ideal way to get a taste of German culture and people – and, of course, the crisp, light wines.

Castles and half-timbered towns are built along the sinuous river below steep, rocky cliffs planted with vineyards (they say locals are born with one leg shorter than the other so that they can easily work the vines).

❶ Getting There & Around

The most scenic part of the Moselle Valley runs 195km northeast from Trier to Koblenz; it's most practical to begin your Moselle Valley trip from either of these two.

Local and fast trains run every hour between Trier and Koblenz, but the only riverside stretch of this line is between Cochem and Koblenz (however, it's a scenic dandy).

Detour: Wieskirche

This Unesco World Heritage–listed **church** (www.wieskirche.de; ⊙8am-7pm May-Oct, to 5pm Nov-Apr) is a jaw-dropping spectacle of 18th-century rococo excess. Its white pillars tower over a tiny village 25km northeast of Füssen. The church can be reached by the **Romantic Road bus** (www.romanticroadcoach.de) or **RVO bus 9606** (www.rvo-bus.de), which runs between Füssen and Garmisch-Partenkirchen via Wieskirche and Oberammergau (five to six daily).

From May to early October, Köln-Düsseldorfer (KD) Line (www.k-d.com) ferries sail daily between Koblenz and Cochem (€25 one way, 5¼ hours upstream, 4¼ hours downstream).

Koblenz

☏0261 / POP 110,000

South of Koblenz, at the head of the beautiful Eltz Valley, **Burg Eltz** (www.burg-eltz.de; adult/child €8/5.50; ⊙9.30am-5.30pm Apr-Oct) is not to be missed. Towering over the surrounding hills, this superb medieval castle has frescoes, paintings, furniture and ornately decorated rooms. Burg Eltz is best reached by train to Moselkern on the Trier line, from where it's a 50-minute walk up through the forest. Alternatively, a shuttle bus runs in peak season.

Cochem

☏02671 / POP 5400

This often-crowded German town has narrow alleyways and one of the most beautiful castles in the region.

For a great view, head up to the **Pinnerkreuz** with the chairlift on Endertstrasse (€5). The perfect crown on the 100m-high hill, **Reichsburg Castle** (www.reichsburg-cochem.de; adult/6-17yr €5/3; ⊙9am-5pm) is a 15-minute walk from

town. Its idealised form can be credited to its 1877 construction (it was never needed to actually *function* as a castle).

Many local vineyards offer tours that include a chance to wander the vines, enjoy the views, have a picnic, sample some cheese, visit the gift shop and, oh, try the wine.

This is the terminus for KD Line boats from Koblenz. Trains on the Trier–Koblenz line run twice hourly to Bullay (€5, 10 minutes), where you can pick up the Moselbahn bus.

Trier

☏0651 / POP 101,000

Trier is touted as Germany's oldest town and you'll find more Roman ruins here than anywhere else north of the Alps.

Sights

A **Combi-Ticket** (adult/child €6/5) is good for most of the historical sites.

ROMAN RUINS   Ruins

The town's chief landmark is the **Porta Nigra** (adult/child €3/1.50; ⊙9am-6pm Apr-Sep, to 5pm Mar & Oct, to 4pm Nov-Feb), the imposing city gate on the northern edge of the town centre, which dates back to the 2nd century AD.

Additional Roman sites include the **Amphitheatre** (Olewigerstrasse; adult/child €3/1.50; ⊙9am-6pm Apr-Sep, to 5pm Mar & Oct, to 4pm Nov-Feb) and the gloomy underground caverns of the **Kaiserthermen** (Im Palastgarten).

MIDDLE AGES BUILDINGS
       Historical Buildings

Trier's massive Romanesque **Dom** (www.dominformation.de; Liebfrauenstrasse 12; ⊙6.30am-6pm Apr-Oct, to 5.30pm Nov-Mar) shares a 1600-year history with the nearby and equally impressive **Konstantin Basilika** (☏724 68; Konstantinplatz; ⊙10am-6pm Mon-Fri, noon-6pm Sun Apr-Oct).

The early Gothic **Dreikönigenhaus** (Simeonstrasse 19) was built around 1230 as a protective tower; the original entrance was on the second level, accessible only by way of a retractable rope ladder.

DENNIS JOHNSON/LONELY PLANET IMAGES ©

Don't Miss **Neuschwanstein & Hohenschwangau Castles**

Close to the Austrian border and the foothills of the Alps, the small town of Füssen is completely shadowed by two monumental castles associated with King Ludwig II in nearby Schwangau, which fulfil everyone's fantasy image of a castle.

Hohenschwangau is where Ludwig lived as a child. Both castles are 19th-century constructions but this one draws less crowds. The adjacent Neuschwanstein is Ludwig's own creation (with the help of a theatrical designer). Although it was unfinished when he died in 1886, there is plenty of evidence of Ludwig's twin obsessions: swans and Wagnerian operas. The pastiche of architectural styles, alternatively overwhelmingly beautiful and a little too much, reputedly inspired Disney's Fantasyland castle.

Tickets may be bought only from the **ticket centre** (www.ticket-center-hohenschwangau .de; Alpenseestrasse 12, Hohenschwangau; adult/child €9/free, incl Schloss Hohenschwangau €17/ free; ☉tickets 8am-5.30pm Apr-Sep, 9am-3.30pm Oct-Mar). In summer it's worth the €1.80 surcharge each to reserve ahead. To walk to Hohenschwangau from there takes about 20 minutes, while Neuschwanstein is a 45-minute steep hike. Horse-drawn carriages (€6) and shuttle buses (€2) shorten but don't eliminate the hike.

Take the bus from Füssen train station (€2, 15 minutes, hourly) or share a **taxi** (☏7700; up to 4 people €10). Go early to avoid the worst of the rush.

Train connections to Munich and Augsburg (€23, two hours) run every hour. Füssen is the start of the Romantic Road and the **Romantic Road bus** (www .romanticroadcoach.de; ☉8am daily mid-Apr–mid-Oct) service. Neuschwanstein Castle

MUSEUMS

Museums

The **Karl Marx Haus** (www.fes.de/marx; Brückenstrasse 10; adult/child €3/2; ☉10am-6pm daily Apr-Oct, 2-5pm Tue-Sun Nov-Mar) is the suitably modest birthplace of the man.

SCOTT KEMPER / ALAMY ©

Don't Miss Eagle's Nest

Berchtesgaden's creepiest – yet impressive – draw is the Eagle's Nest atop Mt Kehlstein, a sheer-sided peak at Obersalzberg. Perched at 1834m, the innocent-looking lodge (called Kehlsteinhaus in German) has sweeping views across the mountains and down into the valley where the Königssee shimmers. Ironically, though it was built for him, Hitler is said to have suffered from vertigo and rarely visited.

Drive or take bus 849 from Dokumentation Obersalzberg to Kehlstein, where you board a special **bus** (www.kehlsteinhaus.de; adult/child €16/9) that drives you up the mountain. It runs between 9am and 4pm, and takes 35 minutes.

Eagle's Nest Tours (649 71; www.eagles-nest-tours.com; Königsseer Strasse 2; adult/6-12yr €48/30; ⏱1.30pm mid-May–Oct) has four-hour tours in English that cover the war years; they leave from near the train station.

Near Porta Nigra, **Städtisches Museum** (www.museum-trier.de; Simeonstrasse 60; adult/child €5/free; ⏱9.30am-6pm Tue-Sun) fills a renovated 11th-century Trier monastery with two millennia of Trier history.

 Sleeping

HOTEL RÖMISCHER KAISER

Hotel €€

(977 00; www.friedrich-hotels.de; Am Porta-Nigra-Platz 6; r €75-150; ✉) The Kaiser is in an elegant old corner building. The 43 rooms inside are comfortable, decorated in soft colours and have parquet floors; some also have balconies. Ceilings are regally high.

HOTEL PAULIN

Hotel €€

(147 4010; www.hotel-paulin-trier.de; Paulinstrasse 13; r €60-120; ✉) In a low-key modern building right across from the old centre, this tidy 24-room hotel offers something even a weary Roman can appreciate: a comfy night's sleep at a good price.

Eating

WALDERDORFF'S   Cafe €€
(www.walderdorffs.de; Domfreihof 1a; mains
€8-16) A high-concept wine bar and cafe
across from the Dom. Score one of the
dozens of tables out front or inside in the
stylish surrounds.

ZUM DOMSTEIN   Bistro €€
(www.domstein.de; Am Hauptmarkt 5; mains
€10-20, Roman dinner €15-33) A touristy but
fun German-style bistro where you can
either feast like the ancient Romans
(fried zucchini? not bad) or dine on more
conventional German and international
fare.

KARTOFFEL KISTE   Spud Cafe €€
(www.kiste-trier.de; Fahrstrasse 13-14; mains €8-
16) A local favourite, this place specialises
in baked, breaded, soupified and sauce-
engulfed potatoes, as well as steaks.

Information

Tourist office (www.trier.de; An der Porta Nigra;
⏱9am-6pm Mon-Sat, 10am-5pm Sun May-Oct,
reduced hr in winter)

Getting There & Away

Trier has a train service to Koblenz (€20, 1½
hours, hourly) via Bullay and Cochem, as well as to
Luxembourg (€16, 50 minutes, hourly).

Rhine Valley

A trip along the mighty Rhine is a highlight for most travellers, as it should be.
The section between Koblenz and Mainz
provides vistas of steep vineyard-covered
mountains punctuated by brooding
castles. Spring and autumn are the best
times to visit the Rhine Valley; in summer
it's overrun and in winter most towns go
into hibernation.

The **Köln-Düsseldorfer (KD) Line**
(www.k-d.com) runs slow and fast boats daily
between Koblenz and Mainz (as well as the
less-interesting stretch between Cologne
and Koblenz). The journey takes about four
hours downstream and about 5½ hours
upstream (€47, free with rail pass). Boats
stop at riverside towns along the way.

Frequent train services operate on both
sides of the Rhine River, but are more
convenient on the left bank. The ride is
amazing; sit on the right heading north
and on the left heading south.

Lake Constance (p607)

GLENN VAN DER KNIJFF/LONELY PLANET IMAGES ©

St Goar & St Goarshausen

☎ 06741 / POP 3100

These two towns are on opposite sides of the Rhine; St Goar is on the left bank and St Goarshausen on the right. One of the most impressive castles on the river is **Burg Rheinfels** (www.st-goar.de; adult/child €5/2.50; ☺ 9am-6pm Apr-Oct, 11am-5pm Sat & Sun in good weather Nov-Mar) in St Goar. An absolute must-see, the labyrinthine ruins reflect the greed and ambition of Count Dieter V of Katzenelnbogen, who built the castle in 1245 to help levy tolls on passing ships ('African or European?'). Across the river, just south of St Goarshausen, is the Rhine's most famous sight, the **Loreley Cliff**. Legend has it that a maiden sang and lured sailors to their deaths against its base.

Mainz

☎ 06131 / POP 185,000

A short train ride from Frankfurt, Mainz has an attractive old town that makes for a good day trip. Though it can't compare to the compact beauty of the nearby towns along the Rhine, Mainz impresses with its massive **Dom (Domstrasse 3; ☺ 9am-6pm Tue-Fri, to 4pm Sat, 1-3pm Sun)**,

which has a smorgasbord of architecture: Romanesque, Gothic and baroque. **St Stephanskirche (Weisspetrolse 12; ☺ 10am-noon & 2-5pm)** has stained-glass windows by Marc Chagall.

NORTH RHINE-WESTPHALIA

From vibrant Cologne to elegant Düsseldorf to stately Bonn, the heavily populated Rhine-Ruhr region goes far beyond its coal and steel industries and offers historic towns and cities, each with a distinct life and atmosphere.

Cologne

☎ 0221 / POP 1 MILLION

Cologne (Köln) seems almost ridiculously proud to be home to Germany's largest cathedral. The twin-tower shape of its weather-beaten Gothic hulk adorns the strangest souvenirs – from egg cosies and slippers to glassware and expensive jewellery. Today it's one of Germany's most multicultural spots, with a vibrant nightlife only partly fuelled by the local *Kölsch* beer.

Frau Nr 13, Thomas Schütte, outside the Museum Ludwig, Cologne

Detour:
Lake Constance

Lake Constance (Bodensee) is an oasis in landlocked southern Germany. Historic towns line its vineyard-dappled periphery, which can be explored by boat or bicycle or on foot. While sun is nice, the lake is best on one of the many misty days, when it is shrouded in mystery.

Constance's southern side belongs to Switzerland and Austria, where the snow-capped Alps provide backdrops across the lake so ideal that you may decide unwisely to chuck it all and start a postcard business. The German side of Lake Constance features three often-crowded tourist centres in Constance, Meersburg and the island of Lindau. It's essentially a summer area, when it abounds with aquatic joy.

Trains link Lindau and Constance, and buses fill in the gaps to places like Meersburg. By car, the B31 hugs the northern shore of Lake Constance, but it can get rather busy. The Constance–Meersburg car ferry run by BSB ferries provides a vital link for those who don't want to circumnavigate the entire lake and a chance for some watery vistas.

The most enjoyable, albeit slowest, way to get around is on the **Bodensee-Schiffsbetriebe** (BSB; www.bsb-online.com) boats, which, from Easter to late October, call several times a day at the larger towns along the lake; there are discounts for rail-pass holders.

⊙ Sights & Activities

Two prominent museums sit next to the cathedral. The **Römisch-Germanisches Museum** (Roman Germanic Museum; ☏ 2212 2304; www.museenkoeln.de; Roncalliplatz 4; adult/concession €8/4; ⏱ 10am-5pm Tue-Sun) displays artefacts from the Roman settlement in the Rhine Valley. The **Museum Ludwig** (☏ 2212 6165; www.museenkoeln.de; Bischofsgartenstrasse 1; adult/concession €9/6, 50% off after 5pm first Thu of each month; ⏱ 10am-6pm Tue-Sun, to 10pm first Thu of each month) has an astoundingly good collection of 1960s pop art, German expressionism Russian avant-garde painting, as well as photography.

KOLUMBA   Museum
(☏ 933 1930; Kolumbastrasse 4; adult/under 18yr/concession €5/free/3; ⏱ noon-5pm Wed-Mon) Encased in the ruins of the late-Gothic church St Kolumba, with layers of foundations going back to Roman times, this is a magnificent design by Swiss architect Peter Zumthor, 2009 winner of the Pritzker Prize, the 'architectural Oscar'. Exhibits span the arc of religious artistry from the early days of Christianity to the present. Coptic textiles, Gothic reliquary and medieval painting are juxtaposed with works by Bauhaus legend Andor Weiniger and edgy room installations.

NS DOKUMENTATIONSZENTRUM
     Museum
(☏ 2212 6332; Appellhofplatz 23-25; adult/concession €3.60/1.50; ⏱ 10am-4pm Tue, Wed & Fri, 10am-6pm Thu, 11am-4pm Sat & Sun) Cologne's Third Reich history is poignantly documented here. The basement of the building was the local Gestapo prison, where scores of people were interrogated, tortured and killed.

CHOCOLATE MUSEUM   Museum
(☏ 931 8880; www.schokoladenmuseum.de; Am Schokoladenmuseum 1a; adult/concession €7.50/7; ⏱ 10am-6pm Tue-Fri, 11am-7pm Sat & Sun, last entry 1hr before closing) South along the riverbank is this glass-walled museum where you nibble on samples while learning about chocolate-making.

Tours

Day cruises and Rhine journeys can be organised through **KD River Cruises** (📞 208 8318; www.k-d.com; Frankenwerft 35). Day trips (10.30am, noon, 2pm and 6pm) cost €7.20. Sample one-way fare to Bonn is €12.50.

Sleeping

KLEINE STAPELHÄUSCHEN   Hotel €
(📞 272 7777; www.koeln-altstadt.de/stapel haeuschen; Fischmarkt 1-3; s/d from €45/68; @ 📶) A small, friendly hotel housed in a 12th-century building in the centre of the old town, just off the riverbank. Exposed beams, antique furnishings and simple but cosy touches give rooms a homey feel.

HOTEL HOPPER ET CETERA   Hotel €€
(📞 924 400; www.hopper.de; Brüsseler Strasse 26; s €80-270, d €120-295; @) Parquet flooring, white linen and red chairs lend an elegant simplicity to this former monastery's rooms. The package is rounded off with a bar and sauna in separate parts of the vaulted cellar.

HOTEL CRISTALL   Hotel €€
(📞 163 00; www.hotelcristall.de; Ursulaplatz 9-11; s €72-184, d €90-235; @ 📶) Angular sofas greet you in the lobby of this recently expanded boutique hotel. Rooms in the newest wing feature minimalist spaces with slate showers and black carpeting; the main building has simpler rooms with a stylish but less-modern look.

Eating

FEYNSINN   International €€
(📞 240 9210; Rathenauplatz 7; mains €7-18) Inside, under murals, students, creative types and tourists tuck into seasonal cuisine (menu changes weekly) as well as traditional Cologne fare such as *Himmel and Aad* (literally Heaven and Earth, which is mashed potatoes and apple sauce).

WEINSTUBE BACCHUS   International €€
(📞 217 986; Rathenauplatz 17; mains €9-20; 🕐 dinner) Dark-wood tables, yellow walls that are lined with paintings by local artists (all pieces are for sale), a seasonal international menu and an almost exclusively German wine list make this casual wine bar–restaurant popular among the locals.

Drinking

As in Munich, beer in Cologne reigns supreme. More than 20 local breweries turn out a variety called *Kölsch,* which is relatively light and slightly bitter. The breweries run their own

Chocolate Museum (p607)
PHOTOGRAPHER: GUIDO SCHIEFER / ALAMY ©

ALFREDO MAIQUEZ/LONELY PLANET IMAGES ©

Don't Miss Kölner Dom

As easy as it is to get church fatigue in Germany, the huge **Kölner Dom** (www.koelner-dom.de; admission free; ⏰6am-7.30pm, no visitors during services) is one you shouldn't miss. Blackened with age, this gargoyle-festooned Gothic cathedral has a footprint of 12,470 sq metres, with twin spires soaring to 157m. Although its ground stone was laid in 1248, stop-start construction meant it wasn't finished until 1880, as a symbol of Prussia's drive for unification. Just over 60 years later it escaped WWII's heavy night bombing largely intact.

Behind the altar lies the cathedral's most precious reliquary, the **Shrine of the Three Magi** (c 1150–1210), which reputedly contains the bones of the Three Wise Men.

To see the shrine properly, you need to take a **guided tour** (adult/concession €6/4; ⏰in English 10.30am & 2.30pm Mon-Sat, 2.30pm Sun). Alternatively, you can embark on the strenuous endeavour of climbing the 509 steps of the Dom's **south tower** (adult/concession €2.50/1.50; ⏰9am-6pm May-Sep, to 5pm Mar, Apr & Oct, to 4pm Nov-Feb). You pass the 24-tonne **Peter Bell**, the world's largest working clanger, before emerging at 98.25m to magnificent views.

beer halls and serve their wares in skinny 200mL glasses.

FRÜH AM DOM
Beer Hall

(☎258 0394; Am Hof 12-14) This three-storey beer hall and restaurant (including cellar bar), the most central in the city, has black-and-white flooring, copper pans and tiled ovens keeping it real, despite the souvenir shop. It's also open for breakfast.

PÄFFGENÄ
Beer Hall

(☎135 461; Friesenstrasse 64-66) Another favourite, this thrumming wood-lined room has its own beer garden. It's not far from the bars of the Belgisches Viertel.

ⓘ Information

Köln Welcome Card (24/48/72hr €9/14/19) Discount card that includes free public transport (including Bonn) and discounted museum admission. Available from the tourist office.

Tourist office (2213 0400; www.koeln tourismus.de; Unter Fettenhennen 19; ⊙9am-8pm Mon-Sat, 10am-5pm Sun)

ⓘ Getting There & Away

Air

Cologne-Bonn airport (CGN; www.airport-cgn .de) is growing in importance. There are now direct flights to New York, while budget airlines German Wings and easyJet, among others, fly here.

Car

The city is on a main north-south autobahn route and is easily accessible for drivers and hitchhikers. The popular German ride-share agency **ADM-Mitfahrzentrale** (194 40; www.citynetz -mitfahrzentrale.de; Maximinen Strasse 2) is near the train station.

Train

There are frequent RE services operating to Düsseldorf (€11 to €16, 25 to 30 minutes) and Aachen (€13.90, 50 minutes to one hour). Frequent EC, IC or ICE trains go to Hanover (from €55, 2¾ to three hours), Frankfurt-am-Main (from €39, one to 2¼ hours, three hourly) and Berlin (€104, 4¼ hours, hourly). Frequent Thalys high-speed services connect Cologne to Paris (from €95, four hours) via Brussels, and ICE trains go to Amsterdam (from €59, 2½ hours).

Düsseldorf

0211 / POP 585,000

'D-Town' or 'the City D', as local magazine editors like to call Düsseldorf, is Germany's fashion capital.

This elegant and wealthy town could feel stiflingly bourgeois if it weren't for its lively old-town pubs, its position on the Rhine, its excellent art galleries and the postmodern architecture of its Mediahafen.

◉ Sights & Activities

Düsseldorf has a lively **Altstadt** (Old Town), which is filled with enough restaurants, beer halls and pubs to have earned it the slightly exaggerated title of the 'longest bar in the world'.

What really sets the city apart, however, is the contemporary architecture of its **Mediahafen**. Here, in the city's south, docks have been transformed into an interesting commercial park, most notably including the **Neuer Zollhof**, three typically curved and twisting buildings by Bilbao Guggenheim architect Frank Gehry.

For a bird's-eye view of the Mediahafen, and indeed all of Düsseldorf, catch the express elevator to the 168m viewing platform of the neighbouring **Rheinturm** (adult/child €3.50/1.90; ⊙10am-11.30pm). There's also a revolving restaurant and cocktail bar a level above, at 172.5m.

The **K20** (838 10; www.kunstsammlung .de; Grabbeplatz 5; adult/concession €10/5, combination ticket K20 & K21 €17/8.50; ⊙10am-6pm Tue-Fri, 11am-6pm Sat & Sun) museum features a brand-new wing and early 20th-century masters, including an extensive Paul Klee collection.

K21 (838 1600; www.kunstsammlung .de; Ständehausstrasse 1; same prices as K20) concentrates on art from 1990 onwards. Highlights include Nam June Paik's *TV Garden*, local artist Katarina Fritsch's giant black mouse sitting on a sleeping man, the psychedelically decorated bar and the glassed-in roof.

KIT – Kunst Im Tunnel (892 0769; www.kunst-im-tunnel.de; Mannesmannufer 1b; adult/concession €4/3) literally translates as 'Art in the Tunnel', which is exactly what you get in the former road tunnel. Revolving exhibits – often by local students from the Düsseldorfer Art Academy – line the concrete curved walls of this surreal, subterranean space.

Sleeping

HOTEL BERIAL Hotel €
(490 0490; www.hotelberial.de; Gartenstrasse 30; s/d from €40/60; @ 🛜) An inviting ambience reigns here, thanks to the friendly staff and the contemporary furnishings. The breakfast buffet is truly gargantuan.

STAGE 47 Boutique Hotel €€€
(388 030; www.stage47.de; Graf-Adolf-Strasse 47; s/d from €160/180; P @ 🛜) Behind

the drab exterior, movie glamour meets design chic at this urban boutique hotel. Rooms are named for famous people, some of whom have actually stayed in the environs dominated by black, white and grey tones. Nice touches: an iHome and a Nespresso coffee maker.

 Eating & Drinking

OHME JUPP Bistro €
(☏326 406; Ratinger Strasse 19; ⏰8am-1am) Casual, artsy cafe serving breakfast and seasonal blackboard specials; also a popular after-work drinking den.

ZUM UERIGE Brewpub
(☏866 990; Berger Strasse 1) In this noisy, cavernous place, the trademark Uerige Alt beer (a dark and semisweet brew typical of Düsseldorf) flows so quickly that the waiters just carry around trays and give you a glass whenever they spy one empty. It also serves hearty German fare, so it doubles as an excellent place for a bite.

LIDO Bar
(☏1576 8730; www.lido1960.de; Am Handels hafen 15) A glass-and-steel cube extends out over the water in the Mediahafen and its smooth outdoor lounge-deck is *the* place to see and be seen on a hot summer night.

ⓘ Information

Düsseldorf Welcome Card (24/48/72hr €9/14/19) Discount card offering free public transport and discounted museum admission. Available from the tourist office.

Tourist office (www.duesseldorf-tourismus. de) main office (☏172 0222; Immermannstrasse 65b; ⏰9.30am-6.30pm Mon-Sat); old town (☏1720 2840; Marktstrasse/Ecke Rheinstrasse; ⏰10am-6pm)

ⓘ Getting There & Away

From **Düsseldorf International Airport** (DUS; www.duesseldorf-international.de), trains go directly to other German cities, while frequent S-Bahn services (1 and 7) head to Düsseldorf train station.

The many train services from Düsseldorf include to Cologne (€10.50 to €16, 25 to 30 minutes), Frankfurt-am-Main (€70, 1½ to 1¾ hours), Hanover (€53, 2½ hours) and Berlin (€97, 4¼ hours).

Mediahafen, Düsseldorf

JORG GREUEL/LONELY PLANET IMAGES ©

ⓘ Getting Around

The metro, trams and buses are useful to cover Düsseldorf's distances. Most trips within the city cost €2.30; longer trips to the suburbs are €4.50. Day passes are €5.30.

HAMBURG

☎ 040 / POP 1.77 MILLION

It comes as no surprise that Hamburg is stylishly expanding itself by 40% without batting an eyelid – this is a city where ambition flows through the waterways and designer-clad residents cycle to their jobs with a self-assurance unmatched by any other German city. The site of Europe's largest urban-renewal project is a never-ending forest of cranes that are efficiently transforming old city docks into an extension of the city – it all makes you wonder: what *can't* this city achieve?

Germany's leading port city has always been forward-thinking and liberal. Nowadays it's also a media capital and the wealthiest city in Germany.

◎ Sights & Activities

OLD TOWN　　　　　　　Historic Area

Hamburg's medieval **Rathaus** (☎ 4283 120 10; tours adult/child €3/0.50, ⊙ English-language tours hourly 10.15am-3.15pm Mon-Thu, to 1.15pm Fri, to 5.15pm Sat, to 4.15pm Sun; Ⓜ Rathausmarkt or Jungfernstieg) is one of Europe's most opulent. North of here, you can wander through the **Alsterarkaden**, the Renaissance-style arcades sheltering shops and cafes alongside a canal or 'fleet'.

For many visitors, however, the city's most memorable building is south in the Merchants' District. The 1920s, brown-brick **Chile Haus** (cnr Burchardstrasse & Johanniswall; Ⓜ Mönckebergstrasse/Messberg) is shaped like an ocean liner, with remarkable curved walls meeting in the shape of a ship's bow and staggered balconies that look like decks.

ALSTER LAKES　　　　　　　Lakes

A cruise on the Binnenalster and Aussenalster is one of the best ways to appreciate the elegant side of the city. **ATG Alster-Touristik** (☎ 3574 2419; www.alstertouristik .de; 2hr trip adult/child €9.50/4.25; ⊙ Apr-Oct; Ⓜ Jungfernstieg) is a good bet. The company also offers 'fleet' tours and winter tours through the icy waters.

Better yet, hire your own rowboat or canoe. Opposite the Atlantic Hotel you'll find **Segelschule Pieper** (☎ 247 578; www.segels chule-pieper.de; An der Alster; per hr from €15; ⊙ Apr-Oct; Ⓜ Hauptbahnhof).

SPEICHERSTADT & HARBOUR

Historic Area

The beautiful red-brick, neo-Gothic warehouses lining the Elbe archipelago south of the Altstadt once stored exotic goods from around the world. Now the so-called **Speicherstadt** (Ⓜ Messberg/

Waterfront buildings, Old Hamburg

Feeding swans at Alsterarkaden, Hamburg

THOMAS WINZ/LONELY PLANET IMAGES ©

Baumwall) is a popular sightseeing attraction. It's best appreciated by simply wandering through its streets or taking a Barkassen boat up its canals. **Kapitän Prüsse** (☎ 313 130; www.kapitaen-pruesse. de; Landungsbrücke No 3; adult/child from €12.50/5.50) offers regular Speicherstadt tours, leaving from the port. Other Barkassen operators simply tout for business opposite the archipelago.

The Speicherstadt merges into the **HafenCity**, an area where the old docks are being transformed into a 155-hectare extension of the city – what looks like a never-ending construction zone is actually Europe's largest inner-city development project. When finished, the area will house a university, approximately 6000 apartments and more. It's estimated that in the next 20 years, it will extend the centre city of Hamburg by about 40%.

REEPERBAHN   Red Light District

(M Reeperbahn) No discussion of Hamburg is complete without mentioning St Pauli, home of the Reeperbahn, Europe's biggest red-light district. Sex shops, peep shows, dim bars and strip clubs line the streets, which generally start getting crowded with

the masses after 8pm or 9pm. This is also where the notorious **Herbertstrasse** (a block-long street lined with brothels that's off-limits to men under 18 and to female visitors of all ages) is located as well as the **Erotic Art Museum** (☎ 317 4757; www.erotic artmuseum.de; Bernhard-Nocht-Strasse 69; adult €5; ☉ noon-10pm, to midnight Fri & Sat) and the **Condomerie** (☎ 319 3100; www.condomerie .de; Spielbudenplatz 18; ☉ noon-midnight), with its extensive collection of prophylactics and sex toys.

INTERNATIONAL MARITIME MUSEUM
                                   Museum

(☎ 300 93 300; www.internationales-maritimes -museum.de; Koreastrasse 1; adult/concession €10/7; ☉ 10am-6pm Tue, Wed & Fri-Sun, 10am-8pm Thu; M Messberg) Esconced within HafenCity, this nine-floor, enormous space examines 3000 years of maritime history through displays of model ships, naval paintings, navigation tools and educational exhibits explaining the seas and its tides and currents.

MUSEUM FÜR VÖLKERKUNDE Museum
(☎ 01805-308 888; www.voelkerkundemuseum .com; Rothenbaumchaussee 64; admission €5, after 4pm Fri free; ☉ 10am-6pm Tue, Wed &

Life's a Beach Bar

Beach bars in Hamburg are *the* place to be in the summer. The city beach season kicks off around April and lasts until at least September, as patrons come to drink, listen to music, dance and generally hang out on the waterfront. Leading venues, open daily, include **Lago Bay** (www.lago.cc, in German; Grosse Elbstrasse 150; Ⓜ Königstrasse), a stylish retreat where you can actually swim, and where free exercise classes will help you keep fit, er, between cocktails. **StrandPauli** (www.strandpauli.de, in German; St-Pauli-Hafenstrasse 84; 🚌 112) is a more laid-back stretch of sand with a youthful feel, and **Strandperle** (www.strandperle -hamburg.de, in German; Övelgönne 1; 🚌 112), the original Hamburg beach bar. It's little more than a kiosk but the people-watching is excellent, as many patrons linger over the newspaper with a drink or a coffee – think of it as a sandy, al fresco cafe-lounge.

Fri-Sun, to 9pm Thu; Ⓜ Hallerstrasse or Dammtor) The Museum of Ethnology demonstrates sea-going Hamburg's acute awareness of multiculturalism and aims to promote respect for the world and its cultures. You'll be awestruck by the giant statues from Papua New Guinea at the top of the stairs.

HAMBURGER KUNSTHALLE
Art Gallery

(☎ 428 131 200; www.hamburger-kunsthalle. de; Glockengiesserwall; adult/concession €8.50/5; ◷ 10am-6pm Tue, Wed & Fri-Sun, to 9pm Thu); Ⓜ Hauptbahnhof) The Hamburger Kunsthalle consists of two buildings, the old one housing old masters and 19th-century art, and a white concrete cube – the Galerie der Gegenwart – showcasing contemporary German artists, including Rebecca Horn, Georg Baselitz and Gerhard Richter, alongside international stars such as David Hockney, Jeff Koons and Barbara Kruger.

ST MICHAELISKIRCHE
Church

(tower adult/concession €3/2; ◷ 10am-6pm Apr-Oct, to 5pm Nov-Mar; Ⓜ Stadthausbrücke) This is one of Hamburg's most recognisable landmarks. It's also northern Germany's largest Protestant baroque church. From the tower of 'Der Michel', as it's commonly called, you have panoramic views.

 ## Sleeping

FRITZ HOTEL
Boutique Hotel €€

(☎ 8222 2830; www.fritzhotel.com; Schanzenstrasse 101-103; s/d €60/90; 🛜; Ⓜ Sternshanze) Run by fun, friendly staff, this stylish town-house hotel is as cool as a cucumber in shades of white and grey and splashes of red.

HOTEL VILLAGE
Hotel €€

(☎ 480 6490; www.hotel-village.de; Steindamm 4; s without/with bathroom incl breakfast from €52/72, d without/with bathroom incl breakfast from €68/95; @ 🛜; Ⓜ Hauptbahnhof) A former bordello going straight, it has boudoirs that feature various mixes of red velvet, gold flock wallpaper, leopard prints and sometimes even blue-neon-lit bathrooms or mirrors above the bed – don't be surprised if you stumble upon a photo shoot during your stay.

HOTEL FRESENA
Hotel €€

(☎ 410 4892; www.hotelfresena.de; Moorweidenstrasse 34; s €75-99, d €88-130; P 🚭 @; Ⓜ Dammtor) Palatial, with clean modern rooms, high ceilings, African statues and cool theatre photographs, Hotel Fresna is all character and no clutter. If it's full, the building houses four other pensions and the friendly staff will help you find a room somewhere else. Breakfast is €9 extra.

HOTEL WEDINA
Hotel €€

(📞280 8900; www.wedina.de; Gurlittstrasse 23; s/d main bldg incl breakfast from €98/118, other bldg incl breakfast from €108/138; 🅿🛜; Ⓜ Hauptbahnhof) You might find a novel instead of a chocolate on your pillow at Wedina, a hotel that's a must for bookworms and literary groupies. Jonathan Franzen, Vladimir Nabokov and JK Rowling are just some of the authors who've stayed and left behind signed books.

GALERIE-HOTEL SARAH PETERSEN
Hotel €€

(📞249 826, 0173 200 0746; www.galerie-hotel-sarah-petersen.de; Lange Reihe 50; s €88-155, d €98-165; ❄@; Ⓜ Hauptbahnhof) This delightful guest house inside a historic 1790 town house is an extension of its welcoming artist-owner's personality, whose paintings decorate the walls. Furnishings include a mix of contemporary, antique and art deco styles.

Eating

FRANK UND FREI
Pub fare €

(Schanzenstrasse 93; mains €5-16; Ⓜ Sternschanze) Big, bustling and laid-back restaurant and pub offering simple German fare, salads and pastas with brick walls, wooden booths, shiny pillars and a stylish curved wooden bar.

FLEETSCHLÖSSCHEN
International €€

(Brooktorkai 17; snacks €7-10; ⏰8am-8pm Mon-Fri, 11am-6pm Sat & Sun; Ⓜ Messberg) This former customs post overlooks a Speicherstadt canal and the HafenCity development and has a narrow, steel spiral staircase to the toilets. There's barely room for 20 inside, but its several outdoor seating areas are brilliant in sunny weather.

GEEL HAUS
German €€

(Koppel 76; dishes €5-10; ⏰from 6pm; 🍴; Ⓜ Hauptbahnhof) Geel Haus is a neighbourhood favourite, tucked away on a quiet street in St Georg, with an emphasis on Austrian and German fare. Plenty of veggie options.

CAFÉ PARIS
French €€

(Rathausstrasse 4; mains €10-19; ⏰from 9am Mon-Fri, from 10am Sat & Sun; Ⓜ Rathaus) At this stalwart in the city centre, be sure to admire the spectacular ceiling murals and tiles on maritime and industrial themes. On weekends breakfast is served until 4pm in this bustling French brasserie.

 Drinking & Entertainment

SÜDHANG
Wine Bar

(📞4309 9099; www.suedhang-hamburg.de; Susannenstrasse 29; ⏰from noon Mon-Sat, from 4pm Sun; Ⓜ Sternschanze) Walk through the shoe store, head up the stairs and enter this friendly wine bar with polished mahogany tables and low lighting perched right above the hustle of the neighbourhood.

Soupy Eel

Tired of wurst and dumplings? Well, you're in a port city now so specialities generally involve seafood, veering away from stereotypical German fare. *Labskaus* is a dish of boiled, marinated beef put through the grinder with mashed potatoes and herring and served with a fried egg, red beets and pickles. Or perhaps you'd prefer *Aalsuppe* (eel soup) spiced with dried fruit, ham, vegetables and herbs? **Deichgraf** (📞364 208; www.deichgraf-hamburg.de; Deichstrasse 23; mains €18-29; ⏰lunch Mon-Sat, dinner Sat; Ⓜ Rödingsmarkt) is one leading local restaurant that can acquaint you with these and other local dishes.

TOWER BAR Cocktail Bar
(www.hotel-hafen-hamburg.de; Seewartenstrasse 9; ⊗6pm-1am Mon-Thu, 6pm-2.30am Fri-Sun; Ⓜ Landungsbrücken) For a more elegant, mature evening, repair to this 14th-floor eyrie at the Hotel Hafen for unbeatable harbour views.

ⓘ Information

Dangers & Annoyances

Although safe, Hamburg contains several red-light districts around the train station and Reeperbahn. The Hansaplatz in St Georg can feel a bit dicey after dark.

Emergency

Police station Hauptbahnhof (Kirchenallee exit); St Pauli (Davidwache, Spielbudenplatz 31; Ⓜ Reeperbahn)

Tourist Information

Hamburg Tourismus (✆ information 3005 1200, hotel bookings 3005 1300; www.hamburg -tourismus.de) Hauptbahnhof (Kirchenallee exit; ⊗8am-9pm Mon-Sat, 10am-6pm Sun); Landungsbrücken (btwn piers 4 & 5; ⊗8am-6pm Apr-Oct, 10am-6pm Nov-Mar; Ⓜ Landungsbrücken); airport (✆ 5075 1010; ⊗6am-11pm) Sells the **Hamburg Card** (one/three/five days €8.50/19.90/34.90), which offers free public transport and museum discounts.

ⓘ Getting There & Away

Air

Hamburg's **airport** (HAM: www.flughafen-hamburg .de) has frequent flights to domestic and European cities, including on low-cost carrier Air Berlin.

Bus

The **Zentral Omnibus Busbahnhof** (ZOB, central bus station; ✆ 247 5765; www.zob-hamburg.de; Adenauer Allee 78) is most popular for services to Central and Eastern Europe.

Car & Motorcycle

The A1 (Bremen–Lübeck) and A7 (Hanover–Kiel) cross south of the Elbe River.

Left: Rathaus (p612), Hamburg; **Below:** View over Hamburg

PHOTOGRAPHER: (LEFT) JOHN FREEMAN/LONELY PLANET IMAGES ©;
(BELOW) THOMAS WINZ/LONELY PLANET IMAGES ©

Train

When reading train timetables, remember that there are two main train stations: Hamburg Hauptbahnhof and Hamburg-Altona. There are frequent RE/RB trains to Lübeck (€11.50, 45 minutes), as well as various services to Hanover (from €35, 1¼ to 1½ hours) and Bremen (from €20.90, one to 1¼ hours). In addition there are EC/ICE trains to Berlin (from €65, 1½ to two hours), Cologne (from €78, four hours) and Munich (from €125, 5½ to six hours) as well as EC trains to Copenhagen (from €81, 4¾ hours).

Getting Around

To/From the Airport

The S1 S-Bahn connects the airport directly with the city centre, including the Hauptbahnhof. The journey takes 24 minutes and costs €2.70.

Public Transport

There is an integrated system of buses and U-Bahn and S-Bahn trains. A single journey costs €2.70; day tickets, bought from machines before boarding, cost €6.30, or €5.30 after 9am.

SURVIVAL GUIDE
Directory A–Z

Accommodation

Germany has all types of places to unpack your suitcase. Reservations are a good idea, especially if you're travelling in the busy summer season (June to September). Local tourist offices will often go out of their way to find something in your price range.

PRICE RANGES

In this chapter, prices include private bathroom unless otherwise stated and are quoted at high-season rates. Breakfast is not included in rates unless specified. Most rooms are non-smoking.

€€€	more than €150
€€	€80 to €150
€	less than €80

617

Hamburger Kunsthalle (p614), Hamburg

DAVID PEEVERS/LONELY PLANET IMAGES ©

Business Hours

Banks & government offices 9.30am-4pm Mon-Fri

Bars & cafes 11am-1am

Clubs Mostly 10pm-4am

Post offices 9am-6pm Mon-Fri

Restaurants 10am or 11am to 10pm, with a 3-6pm break

Shops 9am-6pm Mon-Sat (also Sun in large cities); many more are staying open to 8pm or later on days other than Thursday

Discount Cards

Many cities offer discount cards, usually combining up to three days' public transport use with free or reduced admission to major local museums and attractions.

Food

The following price categories for the cost of a main course are used in the listings in this chapter.

€€€	more than €20
€€	€10 to €20
€	less than €10

Gay & Lesbian Travellers

Overall, Germans are fairly tolerant of gays *(Schwule)* and lesbians *(Lesben)*, although, as elsewhere in the world, cities such as Berlin are more liberal than rural areas, and younger people tend to be more open-minded than older generations.

Legal Matters

By law you must carry some form of photographic identification, such as your passport, national identity card or driving licence.

If driving in Germany, you should carry your driving licence and obey road rules carefully (see p621). The permissible blood-alcohol limit is 0.05%; drivers caught exceeding this amount are subject to stiff fines, a confiscated licence and even jail time. Drinking in public is not illegal, but make sure you are discreet about it.

Money

ATMS

Automatic teller machines can be found outside banks and at train stations.

CREDIT CARDS

All major international cards are recognised, and you will find that most hotels, restaurants and major stores accept them (although *not* all railway ticket offices). Always check first to avoid disappointment. Shops may levy a 5% surcharge (or more) on credit cards to offset the commissions charged by card providers.

EXCHANGE

The easiest places to change cash are at banks or foreign-exchange counters at airports and train stations, particularly those of the Reisebank. Main banks in larger cities generally have money-changing machines for after-hours use, although they don't often offer reasonable rates.

Public Holidays

Germany observes eight religious and three secular holidays nationwide. Shops, banks, government offices and post offices are closed on these days. States with predominantly Catholic populations, such as Bavaria and Baden-Württemberg, also celebrate Epiphany (6 January), Corpus Christi (10 days after Pentecost), Assumption Day (15 August) and All Saints' Day (1 November). Reformation Day (31 October) is observed only in eastern Germany.

The following are *gesetzliche Feiertage* (public holidays):

Neujahrstag (New Year's Day) 1 January

Ostern (Easter) Good Friday, Easter Sunday and Easter Monday

Christi Himmelfahrt (Ascension Day) Forty days after Easter.

Maifeiertag/Tag der Arbeit (Labour Day) 1 May

Pfingsten (Whit/Pentecost Sunday & Monday) Fifty days after Easter.

Tag der Deutschen Einheit (Day of German Unity) 3 October

Weihnachtstag (Christmas Day) 25 December

Zweite Weihnachtstag (Boxing Day) 26 December

Safe Travel

Although the usual cautions should be taken, theft and other crimes against travellers are rare in Germany. Africans, Asians and southern Europeans may encounter racial prejudice, especially in eastern Germany, where they can be singled out as scapegoats for economic hardship.

Telephone

Country code 📞 49

International access code 📞 00

International directory inquiries 📞 118 34 for an English-speaking operator

National directory inquiries 📞 118 37 for an English-speaking operator, or www.telefonbuch.de

Operator assistance 📞 0180-200 1033

Travellers with Disabilities

Germany is fair at best (but better than much of Europe) for the needs of physically disabled travellers, with access ramps for wheelchairs and/or lifts in some public buildings.

Practicalities

Electricity European two-pin plugs; voltage 230V @ 50hz.

Newspapers & Magazines Widely read newspapers include *Die Welt*, *Frankfurter Allgemeine*, left-leaning *Die Tageszeitung* and tabloid *Bild*.

Smoking Generally banned in schools, hospitals, airports and train stations, but each state has its own rules for bars and clubs.

Time One hour ahead of GMT.

Tipping Restaurant bills include a service charge (Bedienung); add another 10% unless service was really awful. Tip bartenders around 5%, taxi drivers around 10%.

TV & Video Two national public channels ARD and ZDF, plus cable channels such as Pro7, SAT1 and RTL.

Weights & Measures Metric: distances in kilometres, weights in kilograms.

Deutsche Bahn Mobility Service Centre
(☏ 01805-996 633, ext 9 for English operator; www.bahn.de; ⊙8am-8pm Mon-Fri, 8am-4pm Sat) Train access information and help with route planning. The website has useful information in English.

German National Tourism Office (www .deutschland-tourismus.de) Has an entire section (under Travel Tips) about barrier-free travel in Germany.

Transport
Getting There & Away
Air
Budget carriers, Lufthansa and international airlines serve numerous German airports. Frankfurt and Munich remain the main hubs.

Berlin Schönefeld (SXF; www.berlin-airport.de)

Berlin Tegel (TXL; www.berlin-airport.de)

Cologne/Bonn (CGN; www.airport-cgn.de)

Düsseldorf (DUS; www.duesseldorf -international.de)

Frankfurt (FRA; www.frankfurt-airport.de)

Frankfurt-Hahn (HHN; www.hahn-airport.de)

Hamburg (HAM; www.flughafen-hamburg.de)

Munich (MUC; www.munich-airport.de)

Stuttgart (STR; www.stuttgartairport.com)

Land
CAR & MOTORCYCLE
Germany is served by an excellent highway system. If you're coming from the UK, the quickest option is the Channel Tunnel. Ferries take longer but are cheaper. You can be in Germany three hours after the ferry docks.

Within Europe, autobahns and highways become jammed at weekends in summer and before and after holidays.

TRAIN
A favourite way to get to Germany from elsewhere in Europe is by train. The main German hubs with the best connections for major European cities include:

Cologne High-speed Thalys trains to France and Belgium (with Eurostar connections from Brussels to London), ICE trains to the Netherlands.

Frankfurt ICE trains to Paris.

Hamburg Scandinavia.

Munich High-speed trains to Paris and Vienna; regular trains to southern and southeastern Europe.

Stuttgart High-speed trains to Italy and Switzerland.

Sea
Germany's main ferry ports are Kiel, Lübeck and Travemünde in Schleswig-Holstein, and Rostock and Sassnitz (on Rügen Island) in Mecklenburg-Western Pomerania.

Getting Around
Air
There are lots of flights within the country, many by budget carriers such as **Air Berlin** (www.airberlin.com) and **Germanwings** (www.germanwings.com) as well as **Lufthansa** (www.lufthansa.de). Be aware, however, that with check-in and transit times, flying is seldom as efficient as a fast train.

Bus
The bus network in Germany functions primarily as support for the train network. Bus stations or stops are usually located near the train station in any town.

Berlin Linien Bus (www.berlinlinienbus.de) Connects major cities (primarily Berlin, but also Munich, Düsseldorf and Frankfurt) with each other as well as holiday regions such as the Harz Mountains and the Bavarian Alps. The express service between Berlin and Hamburg is one of the more popular (€9 to €22, 3¼ hours, 12 daily).

Touring (www.touring.com) The German affiliate of **Eurolines** (www.eurolines.com) has services that include the popular Romantic Road bus in Bavaria and overnight buses that run routes between major cities.

Car & Motorcycle

AUTOMOBILE ASSOCIATIONS

Germany's main motoring organisation, **ADAC (Allgemeiner Deutscher Automobil-Club;**  **roadside assistance 0180-222 2222, if calling from mobile phone 222 222; www.adac.de)** offers roadside assistance to members of its affiliates, including British AA, American AAA and Canadian CAA.

DRIVING LICENCES

Visitors do not need an international driving licence to drive in Germany; bring your licence from home.

HIRE

You usually must be at least 21 years of age to hire a car in Germany. You'll need to show your licence and passport, and make sure you keep the insurance certificate for the vehicle with you at all times.

Agencies include:

Avis (☎ 0180-555 77; www.avis.de)

Europcar (☎ 0180-580 00; www.europcar.de)

Hertz (☎ 0180-533 3535; www.hertz.de)

Sixt (☎ 0180-526 0250; www.sixt.de)

INSURANCE

You must have third-party insurance to enter Germany with a vehicle.

ROAD CONDITIONS

The autobahn system of motorways runs throughout Germany. Road signs (and most motoring maps) indicate national autobahn routes in blue with an 'A' number, while international routes have green signs with an 'E'. Though efficient, the autobahns are often busy, and visitors frequently have trouble coping with the high speeds. Secondary roads (usually designated with a 'B' number) are easier on the nerves and much more scenic, but can be slow going.

Cars are impractical in urban areas. Vending machines on many streets sell parking vouchers that must be displayed clearly behind the windscreen. Leaving your car in a central *Parkhaus* (car park) can cost a fortune, as much as €20 per day or more.

ROAD RULES

Road rules are easy to understand, and standard international signs are in use. You drive on the right, and cars are

Warehouses and canal in the Speicherstadt (p612), Hamburg

GUY VANDERELST/LONELY PLANET IMAGES ©

right-hand drive. Right of way is usually signed, with major roads given priority, but at unmarked intersections traffic coming from the right always has right of way.

The blood-alcohol limit for drivers is 0.05%. Obey the road rules carefully: the German police are very efficient and issue heavy on-the-spot fines. Germany also has one of the highest concentrations of speed cameras in Europe.

Speed limits:

Towns & cities 50km/h

Open road/country 100km/h

Autobahn Unlimited but many exceptions as posted

Public Transport

Public transport is excellent within big cities and small towns, and is generally based on buses, *Strassenbahn* (trams), S-Bahn and/or U-Bahn (underground trains). Tickets cover all forms of transit, and fares are determined by zones or time travelled, sometimes both.

Make certain that you have a ticket when boarding – only buses and some trams let you buy tickets from the driver.

In some cases you will have to validate the ticket on the platform or once aboard. Ticket inspections are frequent (especially at night and on holidays) and the fine is a non-negotiable €50 or more.

Train

Operated almost entirely by **Deutsche Bahn** (DB; www.bahn.de), the German train system is the finest in Europe and is generally the best way to get around the country.

CLASSES

It's rarely worth buying a 1st-class ticket on German trains; 2nd class is usually quite comfortable.

Train types include the following:

CNL, EN, D These are night trains, although an occasional D may be an extra daytime train.

ICE Sleek InterCityExpress services run at speeds up to 300km/h. The trains are very comfortable and feature cafe cars.

IC/EC Called InterCity or EuroCity, these are the premier conventional trains of DB. When trains are crowded, the open-seating coaches are much more comfortable than the older carriages with compartments.

Sony Centre at Potsdamer Platz (p567), Berlin

RE RegionalExpress trains are local trains that make limited stops. They are fairly fast and run at one- or two-hourly intervals.

RB RegionalBahn are the slowest DB trains, not missing a single town or cow.

S-Bahn These suburban trains run frequent services in larger urban areas and rail passes are usually valid. Not to be confused with U-Bahns, which are run by local authorities that don't honour rail passes.

COSTS

Standard DB ticket prices are distance-based. You will usually be sold a ticket for the shortest distance to your destination.

Sample fares for one-way, 2nd-class ICE travel include Frankfurt–Berlin (€113), Frankfurt–Hamburg (€109) and Frankfurt–Munich (€91).

Regular full-fare tickets are good for four days from the day you tell the agent your journey will begin, and you can make unlimited stopovers along your route during that time.

DISCOUNTS

The following are among the most popular discounts offered by DB (2nd class):

BahnCard 25/50/100 Only worthwhile for extended visits to Germany, these discount cards entitle holders to 25/50/100% off regular fares and cost €57/2225/3650.

Dauer-Spezial 'Saver fare' tickets sold at a huge discount on the web.

Savings Fare 25 Round-trip tickets bought three or more days in advance and restricted to specific trains save 25%.

Savings Fare 50 Same conditions as the fare above but also including a Saturday-night stay.

Schönes Wochenende 'Happy Weekend' tickets allow unlimited use of RE, RB and S-Bahn trains on a Saturday or Sunday between midnight and 3am the next day, for up to five people travelling together, or one or both parents and all their children/grandchildren for €37.

RESERVATIONS

During peak periods, a seat reservation (€3.50) on a long-distance train can mean the difference between squatting near the toilet or relaxing in your own seat. Reservations can be made using vending machines or the web.

SCHEDULE INFORMATION

The **DB website** (www.bahn.de) is excellent. There is extensive info in English and you can use it to sort out all the discount offers and schemes.

Telephone information is also available: reservations ☎118 61; toll-free automated timetable ☎0800-150 7090.

TICKETS

Many train stations have a *Reisezentrum* (travel centre), where staff sell tickets and can help you plan an itinerary (ask for an English-speaking agent). Smaller stations may have only a few ticket windows and the smallest ones aren't staffed at all. In this case, you must buy tickets from multilingual vending machines. Buying your ticket on the train carries a surcharge (€3 to €8). Not having a ticket carries a stiff penalty.

TRAIN PASSES

Agencies outside Germany sell German Rail Passes for unlimited travel on all DB trains for a number of days in a 30-day period. Sample 2nd-class prices for adults/under 26 are €188/150 for four days. Given the discounts available, especially on the web, passes may not be good value. Try building an itinerary at the DB website and compare.

Most Eurail and Inter-Rail passes are valid in Germany.

Austria, Switzerland & the Czech Republic

If it's mountain scenery that inspires you, then Austria and Switzerland will seem like seventh heaven. This is a corner of Europe where Mother Nature has done her work on a grand scale: icy peaks, sheer cliffs and silver glaciers stand out against the open sky, providing the perfect mountain playground for skiers and snow-boarders. While winter sports are the main attraction, there are plenty more reasons to visit: from the grand cities of Vienna and Salzburg to the sparkling waters of Lake Geneva.

Out to the east, the Czech Republic has emerged from behind the Iron Curtain to become one of Europe's most captivating places to travel. The charming city of Prague is packed with incredible architecture and historic sights, and further afield you could spend your time exploring the splendid castles of Konopiště and Karlštejn, hiking the trails of the Bohemian Switzerland National Park or sampling the world-class beer for which the Czech Republic is rightly renowned.

North face of the Eiger mountain, Grindelwald (p685)

Fountain outside the Church of St Nicholas, Prague (p695)

Austria, Switzerland & the Czech Republic

1. Prague
2. Salzburg
3. Jungfraujoch
4. Zermatt
5. Český Krumlov Castle
6. Vienna

200 km
100 miles

POLAND

SLOVAKIA

★ BRATISLAVA ⑥

HUNGARY

Lake Balaton

CROATIA

Dráva

SLOVENIA

LJUBLJANA ★

Klagenfurt ●

Drava

Trutnov
Rychnov
Pardubice
Chrudim
35
Liberec

Olomouc

Blansko

Brno ●

Jihlava
D1
38

Horn
Hollabrunn
Stockerau
Schwechat
VIENNA ★ ⑥
Neusiedler See
Wiener Neustadt
B17
Schneeberg
S33
B25
Amstetten
Mürzzuschlag
Bruck an der Mur
Leoben
Oberwart
Feldbach
Graz ●
A2

PRAGUE ★ ①

CZECH REPUBLIC

Strakonice
Klatovy
Český Krumlov
20
D5

Karlovy Vary
Cheb ●

Liberec

The Wachau
Freistadt ⑤
Linz ●
Steyr
Nationalpark Kalkalpen ④
Stainach
Radstadt
Tamsweg
Spittal an der Drau
Lienz
Villach ●

AUSTRIA

Passau
Braunau am Inn
Inn
Traun
Enns

Salzburg ● ②
Berchtesgaden NP
Bad Reichenhall
Berchtesgaden NP
Zell am See
Krimml Falls
Hohe Tauern National Park
Grossglockner

Regensburg

GERMANY

Danube

Ulm

Lake Starnberg

Munich ●

Chiemsee

Kufstein
Hall
A12
Zugspitze ▲
Ötz
Wildspitze ▲
A13
S16
27

ITALY

Adige

Ötro

Vienna

VADUZ ★

Schaffhausen
Mainau Island
Lake Constance
Winterthur
Aarau
Lake Zürich
Zürich
LIECHTENSTEIN
Chur
St Moritz
Flims- Laax

Basel
Solothurn
Biel
Delémont
Neuchâtel
Lac de Neuchâtel
Fribourg
BERN ★
10
Lucerne
Lake Lucerne
SWITZERLAND
Bellinzona ●
Lugano ●
Lago di Como
Isola di San Giulio
Lago Maggiore

FRANCE

Forêt des la Joux
Gruyères
Lausanne
Montreux
9
Jungfraujoch ③
Zermatt ④
Isole di Brissago
Parc National de la Vanoise

Drava

Austria, Switzerland & the Czech Republic Highlights

① Prague's Architecture

Prague has a unique collection of historical monuments, built over the course of a thousand years by many generations of princes, kings and powerful aristocrats. Its historical centre stretches out along the banks of the Vltava River, creating one of Europe's most enchanting and romantic cityscapes. Vladislav Hall (p701), Prague Castle

Need to Know

TOP TIP Tickets to Prague Castle remain valid for two days **PHOTO OP** Standing in the centre of Charles Bridge **For full details on Prague's historic sights, see p694.**

Prague's Architecture Don't Miss List

BY MARTINA ŠVAJCROVÁ, PRAGUE INFORMATION SERVICE

1 PRAGUE CASTLE

For a millennia, Prague Castle has been a symbol of the Czech state. It was built in the 9th century for the princes and kings of Bohemia, but since 1918 it has served as the official seat of the Czech president. It represents an incredible mix of architectural styles – ecclesiastical, residential, military, regal – and comprises one of the largest ancient castles in the world.

2 CHARLES BRIDGE AND BRIDGE TOWERS

Prague's oldest and most iconic structure is Charles Bridge, begun by King Charles IV in 1357 and completed in 1402. The bridge's ends are fortified by towers – the smallest one is a relic of the 12th-century Judita's Bridge, the first stone bridge ever built in Prague. On the other side overlooking the Old Town, the bridge's tallest tower is considered to be one of Prague's most beautiful Gothic structures. The bridge is also decorated by 30 saints, added between 1683 and 1928.

3 OLD TOWN HALL AND THE ASTRONOMICAL CLOCK

Prague's town hall was established in 1338 to house the Old Town authorities. The oldest part of the complex includes a beautiful tower, an oriel chapel and a fabulous astronomical clock, where the 12 apostles appear every hour between 9am and 9pm. The eastern wing was destroyed during the Prague uprising on 8 May 1945, and has never been rebuilt.

4 VYŠEHRAD

For astonishing views, this clifftop castle is one of the best-kept secrets in Prague. It began as a fort built around the 10th century, and briefly served as a residence for the Czech royalty. Its notable buildings include the precious Romanesque rotunda of St Martin and the Gothic church of St Peter and Paul, but don't miss a walk around Vyšehrad cemetery, where many significant Czech personalities have been buried since 1869.

Top: Astronomical clock, Old Town Hall;
Bottom Right: St Vitus Cathedral (p701), Prague Castle

Salzburg

Salzburg (p657) has a lot more to offer than just Mozart and *The Sound of Music*. There's one of Austria's most atmospheric Altstadts to explore, for a start. Then there are boat trips down the Danube, a wealth of Baroque architecture to admire and a fantastic funicular ride up to the clifftop castle of Festung Hohensalzburg, offering unforgettable views across Salzburg's higgledy-piggledy rooftops.

Jungfraujoch

You'll be king of the mountain at Europe's highest train station, Jungfraujoch (p686). At a dizzying 3741m, this icy wonderland of glaciers inspires scores of people to make the journey, so start early. Whatever you do, save the trip for a clear day – the ride's not worth the price of the ticket if all you see up there are clouds.

AFLO CO. LTD. / ALAMY©

Zermatt

4

For Alpine atmosphere, it's hard to top Zermatt (p679). This car-free Swiss town is hemmed in by some of the Alps' most impressive peaks, including the spiky profile of the Matterhorn, an irresistible draw for aspiring mountaineers. Nowadays it's the skiing and snowboarding that attracts the crowds – not to mention the once-in-a-lifetime vista from the top of Gornergrat. Hikers at Gornergrat

5

Český Krumlov Castle

Prague Castle might be the most famous in the Czech Republic, but the castle at Český Krumlov (p717) comes a close second. You can take three different guided tours, each revealing a slightly different side to the castle – one even allows you to peek inside the castle's original theatre, which still has its stage machinery in situ.

6

Vienna's Coffee Houses

There's one pastime that the Viennese know how to do better than almost anyone else, and that's drink coffee (preferably accompanied by a thick slice of cake). The city's coffee houses have been the favourite haunt of intellectuals, impoverished artists and cultural types for centuries, and they're still by far the best place to take the city's pulse. We've listed some of the city's best on p649. Café Sperl (p649), Vienna

Austria, Switzerland & the Czech Republic's Best...

Palaces & Chateaux

○ **Hofburg** (p637) The might of the Austrian monarchy is summed up by this monumental Viennese palace.

○ **Prague Castle** (p700) The world's largest castle complex sprawls over old Prague.

○ **Konopiště Chateau** (p712) Archduke Franz Ferdinand d'Este's country estate.

○ **Schloss Schönbrunn** (p643) The Habsburg dynasty's summer palace is a Unesco-listed treasure.

○ **Schloss Hellbrunn** (p664) A palace renowned for its watery wonders.

Old Towns

○ **Malá Strana** (p703) This rabbit warren of medieval streets is the place to lose yourself in Prague.

○ **Salzburg** (p657) Winding alleyways, cobbled streets and photo ops aplenty.

○ **Vienna** (p637) Re-enact some of those famous scenes from *The Third Man*.

○ **Bern** (p681) Switzerland's dynamic capital conceals a much older heart.

○ **Olomouc** (p704) This ancient Czech town is well off the tourist radar.

Places to Relax

○ **Hallstatt** (p667) Watch the boats chug out across the lake in one of Austria's most picturesque corners.

○ **Wolfgangsee** (p668) Join the locals for a spot of sunbathing and swimming by a glittering lake.

○ **Lednice-Valtice Cultural Landscape** (p719) Enjoy this vast landscaped garden developed by the dukes of Liechtenstein.

○ **Lucerne** (p683) Feel the stress seep away in this über-stylish Swiss city.

Need to Know

Lofty Views

○ **Gornergrat** (p679) Catch the cable car in Zermatt and behold the mighty Matterhorn.

○ **Schilthorn** (p686) Enjoy one of the most dramatic mountain panoramas in the Swiss Alps.

○ **Bergisel** (p669) Hold your nerve at the top of this gravity-defying ski jump in Innsbruck.

○ **Grindelwald** (p685) Gaze over Grindelwald's sparkling glacier.

ADVANCE PLANNING

○ **Two Months Before** Reserve as early as possible in the Alps during the ski season.

○ **One Month Before** Book hotels for summer travel in Prague, Vienna, Salzburg and other big-ticket cities.

○ **Two Weeks Before** Reserve tickets for the State Opera House and the Spanish Riding School in Vienna.

RESOURCES

○ **Österreich Werbung** (www.austria.info) Austria's national tourism authority.

○ **Prague Information Service** (www.praguewelcome.cz) Official Prague info.

○ **Czech Tourism** (www.czechtourism.com) Czech-wide travel planning from the state tourism body.

○ **Switzerland Tourism** (www.myswitzerland.com) The full Swiss lowdown: accommodation, activities and more.

GETTING AROUND

○ **Boat** Ferry services and cruiseboats ply many Austrian and Swiss lakes.

○ **Bus** Postbuses supplement regional train lines in Austria and Switzerland, and serve many smaller Czech towns and villages.

○ **Car** As always, driving is best for rural areas, but pricey parking and incomprehensible one-way systems make Prague, Vienna, Salzburg and Zürich a no-no. *Vignettes* (motorway taxes) are charged on Austrian autobahns, and many tunnels incur a toll.

○ **Train** Train services in all three countries are fast, frequent and efficient, although Switzerland really shines.

BE FOREWARNED

○ **Czech Manners** It's customary to say *dobrý den* (good day) when entering a shop, cafe or quiet bar, and *na shledanou* (goodbye) when leaving.

○ **Mountain Passes** Many road-passes in Austria and Switzerland are closed in winter due to snowfall.

○ **Scams** Prague pickpockets work the crowds at the astronomical clock, Prague Castle and Charles Bridge. Book through a reputable taxi firm to avoid unscrupulous drivers.

Left: Detail of a house in Lucerne, Switzerland; **Above:** Hallstatt, Austria.

Austria, Switzerland & the Czech Republic Itineraries

Take in the stirring scenery of the Alps, as well as the culture and architecture of the Czech Republic.

FRANCE

CZECH REPUBLIC

GERMANY

VIENNA ①

SALZBURG ②

SALZKAMMERGUT ① ② BAD ISCHL

ZÜRICH ④

INNSBRUCK ③

AUSTRIA

SWITZERLAND

INTERLAKEN ⑤

⑥ JUNGFRAU

ITALY

SLOVENIA

---

3 DAYS

VIENNA TO SALZBURG
Baroque Beauty

Three days will give you just enough time to explore Austria's two must-see cities. Start off with two days in the capital, **(1) Vienna**, a city that's been synonymous with culture and refinement since the days of the Habsburg dynasty. You'll need a full day to explore its incredible palaces, the Hofburg and Schloss Schönnbrunn, which illustrate the immense wealth and political power this ancient dynasty wielded until it was forcibly deposed in 1918 following the end of WWII.

On day two, take in more baroque splendour at the Schloss Belvedere and Liechstenstein Palace, then venture into the world of contemporary art at the wonderfully weird KunstHausWien. Leave a few hours aside for discovering the city's wonderful cafes – nowhere does coffee and cake quite like Vienna.

On day three, catch the train to **(2) Salzburg**, another Austrian city that's awash with impressive baroque architecture, especially around the Altstadt. Salzburg is most famous as the birthplace of Mozart, but for many people it's the chance to tour the locations from *The Sound of Music* that are the real draw. Don't miss the creaky cable car up to the Festung Hohensalzburg, a clifftop castle offering unparalleled vistas over the whole of Salzburg.

SALZKAMMERGUT TO JUNGFRAU
Into the Alps

5 DAYS

From Salzburg, you're within reach of some of the most breathtaking mountain scenery in Europe. Spend at least a day exploring the attractions of **(1) Salzkammergut**, including the old salt mines and the ice caves, before detouring via **(2) Bad Ischl** to visit Franz Ferdinand's opulent summer residence, decorated with the Archduke's hunting trophies. On day three, catch a train west to **(3) Innsbruck**, the capital of the Tirol region and a thriving centre for outdoor sports. The Nordketten Bahnen whisks you via a funicular and two cable cars from the centre of town to the tip of Hafelekar peak (2256m) in just 25 minutes.

From here, the mighty Alps unfold all the way into Switzerland and France. Fast and frequent trains run west from Innsbruck to **(4) Zürich**, a squeaky-clean Swiss city with a surprisingly lively heart, but the real scenery starts further south at **(5) Interlaken**, where you can paraglide, ice-climb or zorb the days away beneath the shadow of the Eiger, Mönch and Jungfrau peaks. Further south lies the **(6) Jungfrau** region, where some of Europe's largest glaciers snake their way among the snow-dusted peaks, including the mighty Grindelwald and Aletsch Glaciers.

Jungfrau peak, Bernese Oberland (p683)

Discover Austria, Switzerland & the Czech Republic

AUSTRIA

For such a small country, Austria has made it big. This is, after all, the land where Mozart was born, where Strauss taught the world to waltz and where Julie Andrews grabbed the spotlight with her twirling entrance in *The Sound of Music*. This is also the place where the Habsburgs built their 600-year empire, and where past glories still shine in the resplendent baroque palaces and chandelier-lit coffee houses of Vienna, Innsbruck and Salzburg. This is a perfectionist of a country and whatever it does – mountains, classical music, new media, castles, cake, you name it – it does exceedingly well.

Vienna

♩ 01 / POP 1.68 MILLION

Few cities in the world glide so effortlessly between the past and the present like Vienna. Its splendid historical face is easily recognised: grand imperial palaces, bombastic baroque interiors, and superb museums flanking magnificent squares.

But Vienna is also one of Europe's most dynamic urban spaces. A stone's throw from the Hofburg, the Museums Quartier houses some of the world's most provocative contemporary artworks behind a striking basalt facade.

Throw in the mass of green space within the confines of the city limits (almost half the city expanse is given over to parkland) and the 'blue' Danube cutting a path east of the historical centre, and you have a capital that is distinctly Austrian.

Pulpit at Stephansdom
PHOTOGRAPHER: GREG ELMS/LONELY PLANET IMAGES ©

Fiakers (horse-drawn carriages) outside the Hofburg

PICTUREPROJECT / ALAMY©

 Sights

Vienna's stately buildings and beautifully tended parks are made for the aimless ambler.

Some former homes of the great composers – including those of Mozart and Beethoven – are open to the public; ask at the tourist office.

If you're planning on doing a lot of sightseeing, consider purchasing the **Wien-Karte** (Vienna Card; €18.50) for 72 hours of unlimited travel plus discounts at selected museums, attractions, cafes and shops. It's available from hotels and ticket offices.

The City of Vienna runs some 20 **municipal museums** (www.museum.vienna. at), which are included in a free booklet available at the **Rathaus**. Permanent exhibitions in all are free on Sunday.

STEPHANSDOM Cathedral
(www.stephanskirche.at; 01, Stephansplatz; admission free; ⏲6am-10pm Mon-Sat, 7am-10pm Sun) Rising high and mighty above Vienna with its dazzling mosaic tiled roof is Stephansdom, or Steffl (little Stephen) as the Viennese call it. The cathedral

was built on the site of a 12th-century church but its most distinctive features are Gothic.

Taking centre stage inside is the magnificent Gothic **stone pulpit**, fashioned in 1515 by Anton Pilgram. The baroque **high altar** in the main chancel depicts the stoning of St Stephen; the left chancel contains a winged altarpiece from Wiener Neustadt, dating from 1447; the right chancel houses the Renaissance–style red marble tomb of Friedrich III.

Dominating the cathedral is the skeletal, 136.7m-high **Südturm** (adult/child €3.50/1; ⏲9am-5.30pm). Negotiating 343 steps brings you to a cramped viewing platform for a stunning panorama of Vienna. You can also explore the cathedral's **Katakomben** (catacombs; tours adult/child €4/1.50; ⏲10-11.30am & 1.30-4.30pm Mon-Sat, 1.30-4.30pm Sun), housing the remains of plague victims in a bone house and urns containing some of the organs of Habsburg rulers – gripping stuff.

HOFBURG Palace
(Imperial Palace; www.hofburg-wien.at) Nothing symbolises the culture and heritage of Austria more than its Hofburg, home base of the Habsburgs for six centuries, from the

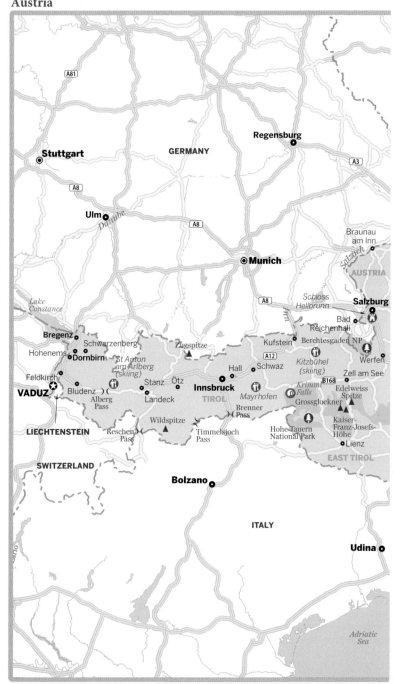

0 ———— 100 km
0 ———— 50 miles

CZECH REPUBLIC

20

R43

Brno

Drosendorf

Retz

Horn

Hollabrunn

SLOVAKIA

Passau

Freistadt

Krems an der Donau

Dürnstein

Stockerau

Tulln

VIENNA

Schwechat

BRATISLAVA

D2

UPPER AUSTRIA

Linz

Traun

Ansfelden

Melk

A1

Perchtoldsdorf

Mödling

Neusiedl am See

A8

Wels

Amstetten

Baden bei Wien

Bad Vöslau

A3

Eisenstadt

M1

THE SALZKAMMERGUT

Steyr

Wiener Neustadt

A1

Gmunden

Nationalpark Kalkalpen

Mariazell

Schneeberg

Neunkirchen

Attersee

Ebensee

St Gilgen

Bad Ischl

Hoher Nock

AUSTRIA

Admont

Gloggnitz

Mürzzuschlag

S6

Oberpullendorf

Neusiedler See

Bad Aussee

B320

Stainach

Eisenerz

Kapfenberg

STYRIA

BURGENLAND

Haus

A9

Leoben

Bruck an der Mur

Radstadt

Unzmarkt-Frauenburg

Oberwart

HUNGARY

Tamsweg

Judenburg

Hundertwasser Spa

Bad Blumau

Murau

Köflach

Graz

Güssing

Rennweg

Voitsberg

CARINTHIA

Feldbach

St Veit an der Glan

Wolfsberg

A9

Spittal an der Drau

Feldkirchen

St Andrä

Ehrenhausen

Bad Radkersburg

Wörthersee

Völkermarkt

Villach

Klagenfurt

Drava

A2

E57

LJUBLJANA

Sava

E59

Drava

SLOVENIA

ZAGREB

CROATIA

Kupa

Sava

Central Vienna

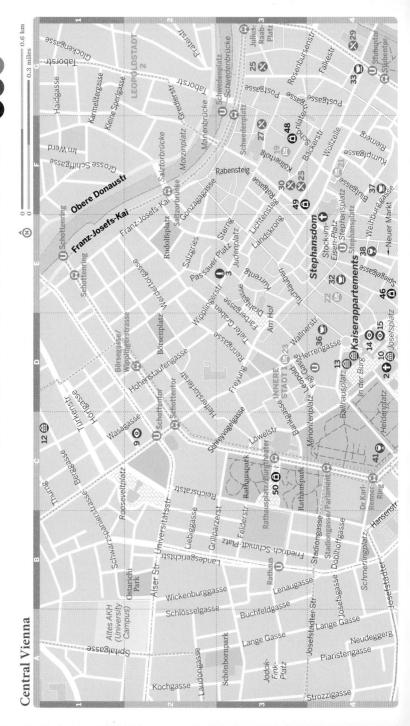

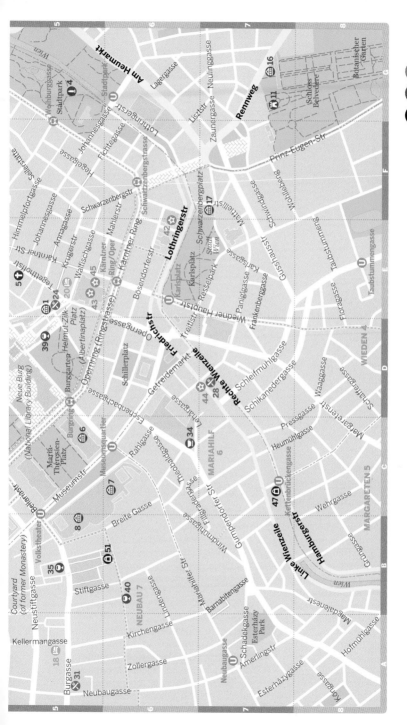

Central Vienna

first emperor (Rudolf I in 1273) to the last (Karl I in 1918). The Hofburg owes its size and architectural diversity to plain old one-upmanship; the oldest section is the 13th-century **Schweizerhof** (Swiss Courtyard).

The **Kaiserappartements (Imperial Apartments; Hofburg; adult/child €9.90/5.90; ◷9.30am-5.30pm)**, once occupied by Franz Josef I and Empress Elisabeth, are extraordinary for their chandelier-lit opulence. Included in the entry price, the **Sisi Museum** is devoted to the life of Austria's beauty-obsessed Empress Elisabeth, nicknamed 'Sisi'. Highlights

include a reconstruction of her luxurious coach and the dress she wore on the eve of her wedding. A ticket to the Kaiserappartements also includes entry to the **Silberkammer** (silver chamber), showcasing fine silverware and porcelain.

Among several other points of interest within the Hofburg you'll find the **Burgkapelle** (Royal Chapel), where the Vienna Boys Choir performs, the **Spanische Hofreitschule** (Spanish Riding School) and the **Schatzkammer (Imperial Treasury; 01, Schweizerhof; adult/child €12/ free; ◷10am-6pm Wed-Mon)**, which holds all manner of wonders including the 10th-century Imperial Crown, a 2860-carat Columbian emerald and even a thorn from Christ's crown.

ALBERTINA — Art Gallery

(www.albertina.at; 01, Albertinaplatz 3; adult/child €9.50/free; ⏱10am-6pm, to 9pm Wed) Simply reading the highlights should have any art fan lining up for entry into this gallery. Among its enormous collection (1.5 million prints and 50,000 drawings) are 70 Rembrandts, 145 Dürers (including the famous *Hare*), 43 Raphaels, as well as works by Da Vinci, Michelangelo, Rubens, Cézanne, Picasso, Klimt and Kokoschka.

In addition to the mostly temporary exhibitions, a series of Habsburg staterooms are always open.

SCHLOSS SCHÖNBRUNN — Palace, Museum

(www.schoenbrunn.at; 13, Schönbrunner Schlossstrasse 47; Imperial Tour with audio adult/child €9.50/6.50; ⏱8.30am-5pm) The Habsburgs' overwhelmingly opulent summer palace is now a Unesco World Heritage site. Of the palace's 1441 rooms, 40 are open to the public. The Imperial Tour takes you into 26 of these. Because of the popularity of the palace, tickets are stamped with a departure time, and there may be a time lag, so buy your ticket straight away and then explore the gardens.

Fountains dance in the French-style formal **gardens** (admission free; ⏱6am-dusk). The gardens harbour the world's oldest zoo – the **Tiergarten** (www.zoovienna.at; adult/child €14/6; ⏱9am-6.30pm), founded in 1752 – a 630m-long hedge **maze** (adult/child €2.90/1.70; ⏱9am-6pm) and the **Gloriette** (adult/child €2/1.40; ⏱9am-6pm), whose roof offers a wonderful view over the palace grounds and beyond.

KAISERGRUFT — Church

(Imperial Burial Vault; www.kapuziner.at/wien, in German; 01 Neuer Markt; adult/child €4/1.50; ⏱10am-6pm) Beneath the Kapuzinerkirche (Church of the Capuchin Friars), the high-peaked Kaisergruft is the final resting place of most of the Habsburg elite. The tombs range from simple to elaborate, such as the 18th-century baroque double casket of Maria Theresia and Franz Stephan. Empress Elisabeth's ('Sissi's') coffin receives the most attentionr: lying alongside that of her husband, Franz Josef, it is often strewn with fresh flowers.

Schloss Schönbrunn

KUNSTHISTORISCHES MUSEUM
Museum, Art Gallery

(Museum of Fine Arts; www.khm.at; 01, Burgring 5; adult/child €12/free; ⏱10am-6pm Tue-Sun, to 9pm Thu) For classical works of art, nothing comes close to the Kunsthistorisches Museum. The building houses a huge range of treasured pieces amassed over the years by the Habsburgs and includes works by Rubens, Van Dyck, Holbein and Caravaggio. Some paintings by Peter Brueghel the Elder, including *Hunters in the Snow,* also feature. There is an entire wing of ornaments, clocks and glassware, and Greek, Roman and Egyptian antiquities.

MUSEUMS QUARTIER
Museums

(Museum Quarter; www.mqw.at; 07, Museumsplatz 1, ⏱information & ticket centre 10am-7pm) This remarkable ensemble of museums, cafes, restaurants and bars occupies the former imperial stables designed by Fischer von Erlach. Spanning 60,000 sq metres, it is one of the world's most ambitious cultural spaces.

The highpoint is undoubtedly the **Leopold Museum** (www.leopoldmuseum. org; adult/child €10/free; ⏱10am-6pm, to 9pm Thu), which showcases the world's largest collection of Egon Schiele paintings, alongside some fine works by Austrian artists like Klimt, Kokoschka and Albin Egger-Lienz.

The dark basalt **MUMOK** (www.mumok. at; 07, Museumsplatz 1; adult/child €9/free; ⏱10am-6pm, to 9pm Thu) is alive with Vienna's premier collection of 20th-century art, centred on fluxus, nouveau realism, pop art and photo-realism.

SCHLOSS BELVEDERE
Palace, Art Gallery

(www.belvedere.at; combined ticket adult/child €13.50/free) The Belvedere is a masterpiece of total art and one of the world's finest baroque palaces, designed by Johann Lukas von Hildebrandt (1668–1745).

The first of the palace's two main buildings is the **Oberes Belvedere** (Upper Belvedere; 03, Prinz-Eugen-Strasse 27; adult/child €9.50/free; ⏱10am-6pm). Pride and

joy of the gallery is Gustav Klimt's rich gold *The Kiss* (1908), which perfectly embodies Viennese Art Nouveau, accompanied by other late-19th- to early-20th-century Austrian works. The second is the grandiose **Unteres Belvedere** (Lower Belvedere; 03, Rennweg 6; adult/child €9.50/free; ◷10am-6pm Thu-Tue, to 9pm Wed), which contains a baroque museum. The buildings sit at opposite ends of a manicured garden.

KUNSTHAUSWIEN   Art Gallery
(www.kunsthauswien.com; 03, Untere Weiss-gerberstrasse 13; adult/child €9/4.50) Like something out of a toy shop, this gallery was designed by eccentric Viennese artist and architect Friedensreich Hundert-wasser (1928–2000), whose love of uneven floors, colourful mosaic ceramics, irregular corners and rooftop greenery shines through. The permanent collection is a tribute to Hundertwasser, showcasing his paintings, graphics and philosophy on ecology and architecture.

Down the road from the Kunsthauswien there's a block of residential flats by Hundertwasser, the **Hundertwassershaus** (cnr Löwengasse &Kegelgasse). It's not possible to see inside, but you can visit the **Kalke Village** (www.kalke-village.at; ◷9am-7pm), also the handiwork of Hundertwasser, created from an old Michelin factory.

PRATER   Amusement Park
(www.wien-prater.at; 02; admission free) This large park encompasses grassy meadows, woodlands, an amusement park known as the **Würstelprater** and one of the city's icons, the **Riesenrad** (www.wienerriesenrad.com; 02, Prater 90; adult/child €8.50/3.50; ◷9am-11.45pm). Built in 1897, the 65m-high wheel takes about 20 minutes to rotate its 430-tonne weight, offering far-reaching views of Vienna. It achieved celluloid fame in the film *The Third Man*.

Schloss Belvedere (p644)

KRZYSZTOF DYDYNSKI/LONELY PLANET IMAGES ©

PALAIS LIECHTENSTEIN Museum
(www.liechtensteinmuseum.at; 09, Fürstengasse
1; adult/child €10/free; ⏰10am-5pm Fri-Tue)
The collection of Duke Hans-Adam II of
Liechtenstein is on show at Vienna's gorgeous baroque Liechtenstein Palace. It's
one of the largest private collections in
the world, and presents a feast of classical paintings including Raphael's *Portrait
of a Man* (1503) and Rubens' *Decius Mus*
cycle (1618).

Holocaust Memorial Memorial
(01, Judenplatz) On Judenplatz is Austria's first
Holocaust memorial, the 'Nameless Library'.
This squat, boxlike structure pays homage to
the 65,000 Austrian Jews who were killed during
the Holocaust.

Sigmund Freud Museum Museum
(www.freud-museum.at; 09, Berggasse 19; adult/
child €7/2.50; ⏰9am-5pm) Former house
of the famous psychologist, now housing a
small museum featuring some of his personal
belongings.

Wien Museum Museum
(www.museum.vienna.at, in German; 04,
Karlsplatz 5; adult/child €6/free; ⏰10am-6pm
Tue-Sun) Provides a snapshot of the city's

history, and contains a handsome art collection
with paintings by Klimt and Schiele.

 Tours

The tourist office publishes a monthly list
of guided walks, *Wiener Spaziergänge*,
and can advise on bus tours and river
cruises.

VIENNA TOUR GUIDES Walking
(www.wienguide.at; adult/child €14/7) Con-
ducts 60 different guided walking tours,
some of which are in English, from art
nouveau architecture to Jewish traditions
and the ever-popular *Third Man* Tour.

 Festivals & Events

Pick up a copy of the monthly booklet of
events from the tourist office. Tickets for
many events are available at Wien-Ticket
Pavillon in the hut by the Staatsoper.

Wiener Festwochen (www.festwochen.or.at)
Wide-ranging program of arts from around the
world, from May to mid-June.

VIENNA TOURS

Viennale (www.viennale.at) The country's biggest and best film festival, featuring fringe and independent films from around the world, in October.

Christkindlmärkte Vienna's much-loved Christmas market season runs from mid-November to Christmas Day.

Opernball (01, Staatsoper) Of the 300 or so balls held in January and February, the Opernball (Opera Ball) is the ultimate. It's a supremely lavish affair, with the men in tails and women in shining white gowns.

Sleeping

Central Vienna is first to fill up, especially in summer, so be sure to book well ahead if you're keen to be close to the major sights.

HOTEL KAERTNERHOF Hotel €€
(☎512 19 23; www.karntnerhof.com; 01, Grashof-gasse 4; s/d from €95/140; @ 🎧) Tucked away from the bustle, this treasure oozes old Vienna charm, from the period paintings and the wood- and frosted-glass-panelled lift to the roof terrace. With Stephansplatz less than five minutes away, this place is a steal.

PENSION HARGITA Pension €
(☎526 19 28; www.hargita.at; 07, Andreasgasse 1; s/d from €57/68; 🎧) Ignore the bland exterior – stepping into the wood-panelled lobby is like entering a mountain chalet. This Hungarian–Austrian family-operated place is tastefully simple. Fresh colours and flowers decorate the homey rooms, and the breakfast room has a country feel.

BOUTIQUEHOTEL STADTHALLE
Hotel €€
(☎982 42 72; www.hotelstadthalle.at; 15, Hackengasse 20; s/d from €68/98) Welcome to Vienna's most sustainable hotel, which makes the most of solar power, rainwater collection and LED lighting. Rooms are a blend of modern with polished antiques. You'll get a 10% discount if you arrive by bike or train.

HOTEL SACHER Hotel €€€
(☎514 56-0; www.sacher.com; 01, Philharmonik-erstrasse 4; d from €375; @ 🎧) Walking into the Sacher is like turning the clocks back 100 years. The reception, with its dark-wood panelling, deep red shades and heavy gold chandelier, recalls an expensive *fin-de-siècle* bordello. All rooms boast baroque furnishings and 19th-century oil paintings, and the top-floor spa pampers with chocolate treatments.

ALTSTADT Pension €€
(☎522 66 66; www.altstadt.at; 07, Kirchengasse 41; s/d from €149/249; @ 🎧) One of Vienna's finest pensions, Altstadt has charming, individually decorated rooms, with high ceilings, plenty of space and a cosy lounge with free afternoon tea and cakes. Staff are genuinely affable and artworks are from the owner's personal collection.

PENSION PERTSCHY Pension €€
(☎534 49-0; www.pertschy.com; 01, Habsburgergasse 5; s/d from €79/119; 🎧) This quiet pension, just off the Graben, is hard to beat. The spacious rooms sport bright colours and period pieces, the staff are extremely friendly, and children are welcomed with gusto (toys and highchairs are available).

KÖNIG VON UNGARN Hotel €€
(☎515 84-0; www.kvu.at; 01, Schulerstrasse 10; s/d from €150/219; 🎧) Vienna's oldest hotel (1746) balances class and informality. Rooms are individually furnished with antiques (the best face Domgasse) and the inner courtyard is wonderful.

STYLE HOTEL Boutique Hotel €€€
(☎22 780 0; www.stylehotel.at; 01, Herrengasse 12; r from €250) Top contender for the title of Vienna's most fashionable hotel, with art nouveau and art deco overtones.

Eating

Vienna has thousands of restaurants covering all budgets and styles of cuisine, but dining doesn't stop there. *Kaffeehäuser* (coffee houses), *Beisln* (beer houses) and *Heurigen* (wine taverns) are just as fine

Naschmarkt Nibbles

The sprawling **Naschmarkt** (06, Linke & Rechte Wienzeile; ⊗6am-6.30pm Mon-Fri, to 5pm Sat) is *the* place to *nasch* (snack) in Vienna. Big and bold, the market is a foodie's dream. The food stalls selling meats, fruits, vegetables, cheeses and spices are perfect for assembling your own picnic. There are also plenty of people-watching cafes, restaurants dishing up good-value lunches, delis and takeaway stands where you can grab a falafel or baguette.

for a good meal. *Würstel Stande* (sausage stands) are conveniently located on street corners and squares.

FIGLMÜLLER
Beer Hall €€

(☑512 61 77; 01, Wollzeile 5; mains €7-15; ⊗lunch & dinner, closed Aug) This famous *Beisl* serves some of the biggest (and best) schnitzels in town. Sure, the rural decor is contrived and beer isn't served (only wine from the owner's vineyard), but it doesn't get more Viennese than this.

STOMACH
Austrian €€

(☑310 20 99; 09, Seegasse 26; mains €10-18; ⊗dinner Wed-Sat, lunch & dinner Sun) Once a butcher's shop, Stomach serves seriously good Austrian food, from Styrian roast beef to buttery, rich pumpkin soup. The interior is rural Austrian, and the overgrown garden creates a picturesque backdrop. Reservations are recommended.

GRIECHENBEISL
Beer Hall €€

(☑533 19 77; 01, Fleischmarkt 11; mains €11-24; ⊗11am-1am) This is Vienna's oldest *Beisl* (dating from 1447), once frequented by the likes of Beethoven, Schubert and Brahms. The vaulted, wood-panelled rooms are a cosy setting for classic Viennese dishes. Bag a spot in the front garden in summer.

ZU DEN ZWEI LIESLN
Beer Hall €

(☑523 32 82; 07, Burggasse 63; lunch menu €4.90-5.30, mains €6-11.90) Six varieties of schnitzel crowd the menu at this classic budget *Beisl* of legendary status.

EXPEDIT
Italian €€

(☑512 33 13 23; 01, Wiesingerstrasse 6; mains €8-25; ⊗10am-1am Mon-Sat, to 10pm Sun) Expedit has moulded itself on a Ligurian *Osteria*. Its warehouse decor creates a busy yet informal atmosphere and a clean, smart look. Every day brings new, seasonal dishes to the menu. Reservations are recommended.

ÖSTERREICHER IM MAK
Austrian €€

(☑7140 121; 01, Stubenring 5; lunch €6.40, mains €14.50-20.80; ⊗8.30am-1am) This is the brainchild of Helmut Österreicher, one of Austria's leading chefs. He jazzes up back-to-the-roots Austrian dishes such as *Tafelspitz* with exotic or nonregional ingredients.

Bitzinger Würstelstand am Albertinaplatz
Sausage Stand €

(01, Albertinaplatz; sausages €2.80-3.50; ⊗24hr) Located behind the Staatsoper, this is one of Vienna's best sausage stands.

Zanoni & Zanoni
Ice Cream €

(Lugeck 7; ice cream from €2; ⊗7am-midnight) An Italian gelataria and *pasticceria* open 365 days a year. Great for creamy gelati and late-night desserts.

 **Drinking**

Vienna is riddled with late-night drinking dens, with concentrations of pulsating bars north and south of the Naschmarkt, around Spittelberg (many double as restaurants) and along the Gürtel (mainly around the U6 stops of Josefstädter Strasse and Nussdorfer Strasse).

Vienna's age-old *Heurigen* (wine taverns) are identified by a *Busch'n* (a green wreath or branch) hanging over the door; many have outside tables in large gardens or courtyards, while inside the atmosphere is rustic. Opening times are approximately from 4pm to 11pm, and wine costs around €2.50 per *Viertel* (250mL).

PALMENHAUS Bar, Cafe

(01, Burggarten; ⏱10am-2am, closed Mon & Tue Jan-Feb) Housed in a beautifully restored Victorian palm house, the Palmenhaus has a relaxed vibe. In summer, tables spill out onto the pavement overlooking the green of the Burggarten, and there are occasional club nights.

DAS MÖBEL Bar, Cafe

(07, Burggasse 10; ⏱10am-1am; 📶) The interior is never dull at this bar near the Museums Quartier. It's remarkable for its funky decor and furniture – cube stools, assorted moulded lamps – and everything is up for sale.

LOOS AMERICAN BAR Cocktail Bar

(01, Kärntner Durchgang 10; ⏱noon-4am Sun-Wed, to 5am Thu-Sat) Designed by Adolf Loos in 1908, this tiny box decked head-to-toe in onyx is *the* spot for a classic cocktail in the Innere Stadt, expertly whipped up by talented mixologists.

10ER MARIE Wine Bar

(16, Ottakringerstrasse 222-224; ⏱3pm-midnight Mon-Sat) Vienna's oldest *Heuriger* has been going strong since 1740 – Schubert, Strauss and Crown Prince Rudolf all kicked back a glass or three here. The usual buffet is available.

WEIN & WASSER Wine Bar

(08, Laudongasse 57; ⏱6pm-1am Mon-Sat) At 'Wine & Water', the staff warmly guide you through the lengthy list, which includes over 20 Austrian wines served by the glass. The brick arches, lit by flickering candles, create a cosy space for imbibing.

♥ If You Like... Coffee House Culture

Vienna's legendary *Kaffeehäuser* (coffee houses) are wonderful places for people-watching, daydreaming and catching up on gossip or world news. Most serve light meals alongside a mouth-watering array of cakes and tortes. Expect to pay around €7 for a coffee with a slice of cake.

Café Sperl
(06, Gumpendorfer Strasse 11; ⏱7am-11pm Mon-Sat, 11am-8pm Sun, closed Sun in summer; 📶) With its gorgeous Jugendstil fittings, grand dimensions and cosy booths, Sperl is one of Vienna's finest coffee houses. The must-try is *Sperl Torte* – an almond-and-chocolate-cream dream.

Café Hawelka
(01, Dorotheergasse 6; ⏱8am-2am Mon & Wed-Sat, from 10am Sun) A traditional haunt for artists and writers, this shabby-chic coffee house attracts the gamut of Viennese society.

Café Sacher
(01, Philharmonikerstrasse 4; ⏱8am-11.30pm) This opulent coffee house is celebrated for its *Sacher Torte* (€4), a rich chocolate cake with apricot jam once favoured by Emperor Franz Josef.

Café Prückel
(01, Stubenring 24; ⏱8.30am-10pm) Intimate booths, strong coffee and diet-destroying cakes are all attractions at this 1950s gem. There's live piano music from 7pm to 10pm Monday, Wednesday and Friday.

Demel
(01, Kohlmarkt 14; ⏱10am-7pm) An elegant, regal cafe near the Hofburg. Demel's speciality is the *Anna Torte,* a chocolate and nougat calorie-bomb.

Kleines Café
(01, Franziskanerplatz 3; ⏱10am-2am) Tiny bohemian cafe with wonderful summer seating on Franziskanerplatz.

Siebensternbräu Brewery, Pub

(www.7stern.at; 07, Siebensterngasse 19; ⏱10am-midnight) Large brewery with all the main varieties, plus hemp beer, chilli beer and smoky beer.

Imperial Entertainment

Founded over five centuries ago by Maximilian I as the imperial choir, the world-famous **Vienna Boys' Choir** (Wiener Sängerknaben; www.wsk.at) is the original boy band. These cherubic angels in sailor suits still hold a fond place in Austrian hearts. **Tickets** (☏533 99 27; www.bmbwk.gv.at, in German) for their Sunday performances at 9.15am (October to June) in the Burgkapelle (Royal Chapel) in the Hofburg should be booked around six weeks in advance. The group also performs regularly in the Musikverein.

Another throwback to the Habsburg glory days is the **Spanische Hofreitschule** (Spanish Riding School; ☏533 90 31; www.srs.at; 01, Michaelerplatz 1; ⏰performances 11am Sat & Sun mid-Feb–Jun & late Aug-Dec). White Lipizzaner stallions gracefully perform equine ballet to classical music, while brilliant chandeliers shimmer from above and the audience cranes forward to see from pillared balconies. Tickets, costing between €23 and €143, are ordered through the website, but be warned that performances usually sell out months in advance. Unclaimed tickets are sold about two hours before performances. **Morning Training** (adult/child/family €12/6/24; ⏰10am-noon Tue-Sat Feb-Jun & mid-Aug–Dec) same-day tickets are available at the **visitor centre** (⏰9am-4pm Tue-Fri) on Michaelerplatz.

Volksgarten Pavillon   Bar
(01, Burgring 1; ⏰11am-2am Apr–mid-Sep)
A lovely 1950s-style pavilion with views of Heldenplatz and an ever-popular garden.

 Entertainment

Vienna is, and probably will be till the end of time, the European capital of opera and classical music. The program of music events is never-ending and even the city's buskers are often classically trained. The tourist office produces a handy monthly listing of concerts and other events.

FLEX   Club
(www.flex.at; 01, Donaukanal, Augartenbrücke; ⏰6pm-4am) Vienna's most celebrated low-life club, Flex has one of the best sound systems in Europe, puts on great shows and features the top DJs from Vienna and abroad.

STAATSOPER   Concert Venue
(☏514 44 7880; www.wiener-staatsoper. at; 01, Opernring 2; ⏰box office closed Sun) Performances at Vienna's premier opera and classical music venue are lavish, formal affairs, where people dress up. Standing-room tickets (€3 to €4) are sold 80 minutes before performances begin.

MUSIKVEREIN   Concert Venue
(☏505 81 90; www.musikverein.at; 01, Bösendorferstrasse 12; ⏰box office closed Sun) The opulent Musikverein, home to the Vienna Philharmonic Orchestra, is celebrated for its acoustics. Standing-room tickets in the main hall cost €4 to €6.

VOLKSOPER   Concert Venue
(People's Opera; ☏514 44 3670; www.volks oper.at; 09, Währinger Strasse 78; ⏰box office closed Sun) Vienna's second opera house features operettas, dance and musicals. Standing tickets can go for as little as €2 to €6.

THEATRE AN DER WIEN   Theatre
(www.musicalvienna.at; 06, Linke Wienzeile 6). Once the host of monumental premiers such as Mozart's *Die Zauberflöte,* this theatre now showcases opera, dance and concerts. Tickets start from €7 for standing room.

Shopping

The Innere Stadt does a brisk trade in designer labels, sweets and jewellery, while most Viennese head to Mariahilfer Strasse for high-street brands. Idiosyncratic local stores cluster in Neubau. Neubaugasse is good for secondhand hunters and collectors, and Josefstädter Strasse is a quaint, old-fashioned shopping experience.

DOROTHEUM Auction House
(www.dorotheum.com; 01, Dorotheergasse 17; ◷10am-6pm Mon-Fri, 9am-5pm Sat) One of Europe's largest auction houses where, surprisingly, not every item is priced out of this world. Stop by and simply browse the collection – it's as entertaining as visiting many of Vienna's museums.

MANNER Confectionary
(www.manner.com; 01, Stephansplatz 7; ◷10am-6.30pm Sun-Fri, 9.30am-8.30pm Sat) One bite and you'll be hooked on the *Manner Schnitten* (wafers filled with hazelnut cream) sold at this old-world confectionary store since 1898.

ⓘ Information

Tourist Info Wien (☎211 14-555; www.wien.info; 01, Albertinaplatz; ◷9am-7pm) Vienna's main tourist office, with a ticket agency, hotel booking service, free maps and every brochure you could ever want.

ⓘ Getting There & Away

Air

Vienna is the main centre for international flights. Although there are frequent flights to Graz, Klagenfurt, Salzburg, Linz and Innsbruck with Austrian Airlines (www.austrian.com) from Vienna, flying domestic routes offers few benefits over trains.

Boat

Heading west, a series of boats plies the Danube between Krems and Melk, with a handful of services originating in Vienna. Two respectable operators include DDSG Blue Danube and Brandner (☎07433-25 90; www.brandner.at), the latter located in Wallsee. Both run trips from April through October that start at around €11 one way. For trips into Germany, contact Donauschiffahrt Wurm + Köck (☎0732 783607; www.donauschiffahrt.de; Untere Donaulände 1, Linz).

Bus

Vienna currently has no central bus station and national Bundesbuses arrive and depart from several different locations, depending on the destination.

Car & Motorcycle

The Gürtel is an outer ring road that joins up with the A22 on the north bank of the Danube and the A23 southeast of town. All the main road routes intersect with this system, including the A1 from Linz and Salzburg, and the A2 from Graz.

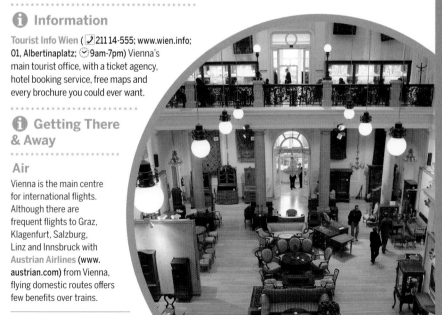

Dorotheum auction house
PHOTOGRAPHER: GREG ELMS/LONELY PLANET IMAGES ©

To Market

Vienna's atmospheric **Flohmarkt** (flea market; 05, Kettenbrückengasse; ◷dawn-4pm Sat) shouldn't be missed, with goods piled up in apparent chaos on the walkway. Books, clothes, records, ancient electrical goods, old postcards, ornaments, carpets...you name it, it's all here. Come prepared to haggle.

From mid-November, *Christkindlmärkte* (Christmas Markets) bring a festive sparkle to Vienna, their stalls laden with gifts, *Glühwein* (mulled wine) and *Maroni* (roasted chestnuts). Some of the best include the pretty but touristy **Rathausplatz market**, the traditional **Spittelberg market** in Spittelberg's cobbled streets, where you can pick up quality crafts, and the authentic, oft-forgotten **Heiligenkreuzerhof market**.

Train

Vienna is one of central Europe's man rail hubs. Österreiche Bundesbahn (ÖBB; Austrian Federal Railway; www.oebb.at) is the main operator. There are direct services and connections to many European cities. Sample train times include: Berlin (nine to 10 hours), Budapest (2¾ to four hours), Munich (four to five hours), Paris (12 to 13 hours), Prague (4½ to 5½ hours) and Venice (eight to nine hours).

Vienna has multiple train stations. At press time, a massive construction project was in progress at Vienna's former Südbahnhof: essentially, the station was shut but an eastern section had been set up as a temporary station to serve some regional trains to/from the east, including Bratislava. The complex is due to reopen as Hauptbahnhof Wien (Vienna Central Station) in late 2012 or early 2013, and as the main station in the city it will receive international trains.

ℹ Getting Around

To/From the Airport

It is 19km from the city centre to Vienna International Airport (VIE; www.viennaairport.com) in Schwechat. The City Airport Train (CAT; www.cityairporttrain.com; return adult/child €18/free; ◷5.38am-11.08pm) runs every 30 minutes and takes 16 minutes between the airport and Wien Mitte; book online for a €2 discount. The S-Bahn (S7) does the same journey (single €3.60) but in 26 minutes.

Buses run every 20 or 30 minutes, between 5am and 11pm, from the airport (one way/return €6/11). Services run to Meidling, Westbahnhof and Schwedenplatz.

Taxis cost about €35. C&K Airport Service (☎44 444) charges €33 one way for shared vans.

Bicycle

Vienna's city bike scheme is called Vienna City Bike (www.citybikewien.at, in German; 1st/2nd/3rd hr free/€1/2, per hr thereafter €4), with more than 60 bicycle stands across the city. A credit card is required to rent bikes – just swipe your card in the machine and follow the instructions (in a number of languages).

Car & Motorcycle

Due to a system of one-way streets and expensive parking, you're better off using the excellent public transport system. If you do plan to drive in the city, take special care of the trams; they always have priority and vehicles must wait behind trams when they stop to pick up or set down passengers.

Fiakers

More of a tourist novelty than anything else, a *Fiaker* is a traditional-style horse-drawn carriage. Bowler-hatted drivers generally speak English and point out places of interest en route. Expect to pay a cool €65/95 for a 40-/60-minute ride from Stephansplatz, Albertinaplatz or Heldenplatz.

Public Transport

Vienna has a unified public transport network that encompasses trains, trams, buses, and underground

(U-Bahn) and suburban (S-Bahn) trains. Free maps and information pamphlets are available from **Wiener Linien** (www.wienerlinien.at, in German).

Before use, all tickets must be validated at the entrance to U-Bahn stations and on buses and trams (except for weekly and monthly tickets). Tickets are cheaper to buy from ticket machines in U-Bahn stations and in *Tabakladen*, where singles cost €1.80. On board, they cost €2.20. Singles are valid for an hour, and you may change lines on the same trip.

A 24-hour ticket costs €5.70, a 48-hour ticket €10, a 72-hour ticket €13.60 and an eight-day ticket €28.80 (validate the ticket once per day as and when you need it). Weekly tickets (valid Monday to Sunday) cost €14; the Vienna Card (€18.50) includes travel on public transport for up to three days.

Taxi

Taxis are metered for city journeys and cost €2.60 flag fall during the day and €2.70 at night, plus a small per-kilometre fee. It's safe to hail taxis from the street, and there's generally a fair few about.

The Danube Valley

The stretch of the Danube between Krems and Melk, known locally as the Wachau, is arguably the loveliest along the entire length of the mighty river. Both banks are dotted with ruined castles and medieval towns, and lined with terraced vineyards.

Krems An Der Donau

☑02732 / POP 23,800

Sitting on the northern bank of the Danube against a backdrop of terraced vineyards, Krems marks the beginning of the Wachau. It has an attractive cobbled centre, a small university, some good restaurants and the gallery-dotted Kunstmeile (Art Mile).

◉ Sights & Activities

It's a pleasure to wander the cobblestone streets of Krems and Stein, especially at night – don't miss the baroque treasures of Schürerplatz and Rathausplatz squares in Stein.

KUNSTHALLE Art Gallery
(www.kunsthalle.at; Franz-Zeller-Platz 3; adult/child €9/3.50; ◷10am-6pm) The flagship of Krems' **Kunstmeile** (www.kunstmeile-krems.at), an eclectic collection of galleries and museums, the Kunsthalle has an ever-changing program of small but excellent exhibitions.

Castle ruins and town on the Danube River, Wachau area

MAN/IMAGEBROKER©

Sleeping & Eating

ARTE HOTEL KREMS Hotel €€
(☎711 23; www.arte-hotel.at, in German; Dr-Karl-Dorrek-Strasse 23; s €89-105, d €128-162;
🅿♿🛜) This comfortable new art hotel close to the university has large, well-styled rooms in bright colours and with open-plan bathrooms.

 MÖRWALD KLOSTER UND
Austrian €€
(☎704 930; www.moerwald.at; Undstrasse 6; mains €20-33, 5-course menu €85, 3-course lunch €25; ⏰closed Sun & Mon; ♿) Run by celebrity chef and winemaker Toni Mörwald, this is one of the Wachau's best restaurants. Delicacies from roast pigeon breast to fish dishes with French touches are married with top wines.

Getting There & Away

Frequent daily trains connect Krems with Vienna's Franz-Josefs-Bahnhof (€13.90, one hour). The quickest way to Melk is by train to Spitz, continuing by bus (€7.30,

one hour, five times daily). The boat station is near Donaustrasse, about 2km west of the train station.

Melk

☎02752 / POP 5200

With its sparkling and majestic abbey-fortress, Melk is a highlight of any visit to the Danube Valley. Many visitors cycle here for the day – wearily pushing their bikes through the cobblestone streets.

◉ Sights

STIFT MELK Abbey
(Benedictine Abbey of Melk; ☎5550; www.stiftmelk.at; Abt Berthold Dietmayr Strasse 1; adult/child/family €7.70/4.50/15.40, with guided tour €9.50/6.30/19; ⏰9am-5.30pm) Rising like a vision on a hill overlooking the town, Stift Melk is Austria's most famous abbey. It has been home to Benedictine monks since the 11th century, though it owes its current good looks to 18th-century mastermind Jakob Prandtauer.

The interior of the monastery church is baroque gone barmy, with endless prancing angels and gold twirls. Other highlights include the **Bibliothek** (library) and the **Marmorsaal** (Marble Hall); the trompe l'oeil on the ceiling (by Paul Troger) gives the illusion of greater height. Eleven of the imperial rooms, where dignitaries (including Napoleon) stayed, now house a **museum**. From around November to March, the monastery can only be visited by guided tour (11am and 2pm daily). Always phone ahead to ensure you get an English-language tour.

ⓘ Getting There & Away

Boats leave from the canal by Pionierstrasse, 400m north of the abbey. There are hourly trains to Vienna (€15.70, 1¼ hours).

Stift Melk abbey, Melk

Detour: St Florian

One of Austria's finest Augustinian abbeys is St Florian's **Augustiner Chorherrenstift** (www.stift-st-florian.at; Stiftstrasse 1; tours adult/child €8/5; ☺tours 11am, 1pm, 3pm May-Sep), 18km southeast of Linz. The abbey dates to at least 819 but is now overwhelmingly baroque in style. A guided tour leads you through the opulent library, Marble Hall and the Altdorfer Gallery, displaying 14 paintings by Albrecht Altdorfer (1480–1538) of the Danube School. A vision of pink marble and gilding, the resplendent abbey church harbours the huge 18th-century organ upon which famous Romantic composer Anton Bruckner played during his stint as organist (1850–55).

Buses run frequently between St Florian and Linz Hauptbahnhof (€2.60, 22 minutes); there is a reduced service on Sunday.

The South

Austria's two main southern states, Styria (Steiermark) and Carinthia (Kärnten), often feel worlds apart from the rest of the country, both in climate and attitude. Styria is a blissful amalgamation of genteel architecture, rolling green hills, vine-covered slopes and soaring mountains. Its capital, Graz, is one of Austria's most attractive cities.

A jet-setting, fashion-conscious crowd heads to sun-drenched Carinthia for summer holidays. The region (right on the border with Italy) exudes an atmosphere that's as close to Mediterranean as this staunch country gets.

Graz

☑0316 / POP 257,350

Austria's second-largest city is probably its most relaxed and, after Vienna, its liveliest for after-hours pursuits. It's an attractive place with bristling green parkland, red rooftops and a small, fast-flowing river gushing through its centre. Architecturally, it has Renaissance courtyards and provincial baroque palaces, complemented by innovative modern designs.

◎ Sights & Activities

Admission to all of the major museums with a 24-hour ticket costs €11/14 for adults/children.

UNIVERSALMUSEUM JOANNEUM

Museum

(www.museum-joanneum.at; Raubergasse 10) With its 19 locations, this ensemble of museums is the gardener of Graz' rich cultural landscape. Until work is completed, some museums will be closed until late 2011, including **Neue Galerie Graz** (adult/child €8/3; 10am-6pm, closed Mon), Styria's most important historical and contemporary art collection.

KUNSTHAUS GRAZ

Art Gallery

(www.kunsthausgraz.at; Lendkai 1; adult/child €7/3; ☺10am-6pm, closed Mon) Designed by British architects Peter Cook and Colin Fournier, this world-class contemporary art space looks something like a space-age sea slug from the outside. Exhibitions here change every three to four months.

SCHLOSS EGGENBERG

Palace

(Eggenberger Allee 90; adult/child €7/3; ☺10am-5pm, closed Mon & Nov-Palm Sunday) A blend of Gothic, Renaissance and baroque styles, this beautiful palace can be reached by tram 1 from Hauptplatz. Admission includes a guided tour (from 10am to 4pm, on the hour except at 1pm), taking in 24 *Prunkräume* (staterooms), with interiors based around astronomy, the zodiac and classical or religious mythology.

MURINSEL · Bridge

This artificial island-cum-bridge in the River Mur is an open seashell of glass, concrete and steel, by New York artist Vito Acconci. It houses a trendy cafe-bar in aqua blue and a small stage. In summer, further downstream, a beach bar is set up.

SCHLOSSBERG · Viewpoint

The wooded slopes of Schlossberg (473m) can be reached on foot, with the funicular **Schlossbergbahn** (Castle Hill Railway; 1hr ticket €1.90) from Kaiser-Franz-Josef-Kai, or by **Glass Lift** (1hr ticket €1.90) from Schlossbergplatz. Napoleon was hard-pressed to raze this fortress, but raze it he did. Today the medieval **Uhrturm** (Clock Tower) and a small **Garnison Museum** (Schlossberg 5a; adult/child €1/free; ⌚10am-4pm, closed Mon–Wed & Nov–mid-May) are the legacies.

Landeszeughaus · Armoury

(www.zeughaus.at; Herrengasse 16; adult/child €7/3; ⌚10am-6pm) A must-see for fans of armour and weapons, housing an astounding array of 30,000 gleaming exhibits.

FREE BURG · Castle

(Hofgasse) At the far end of Graz' 15th-century castle is an ingenious double staircase (1499). Adjoining it is the Stadtpark, the city's largest green space.

Sleeping

HOTEL DANIEL · Hotel €€

(☎711 080; www.hoteldaniel.com; Europaplatz 1; r €59-79, breakfast €9 per person; **P** ⊜ ❄ @) Perched at the top of Annenstrasse, the Daniel is an exclusive design hotel. All rooms are tastefully furnished in minimalist designs; you can rent a Vespa (€15 per day) and there's a 24-hour espresso bar.

HOTEL STRASSER · Hotel €

(☎71 39 77; www.hotel-strasser.at; Eggenberger Gürtel 11; s/d/tr/apt €45/65/93/180; **P** @ 🛜) Strasser has some fascinating pseudo-neoclassical and Mediterranean touches, with Tuscan gold blending with mirrors and cast-iron balustrades. It's handy to the train station.

 Eating

With leafy salads dressed in delicious pumpkin-seed oil, fish specialities and *Pfand'l* (pan-grilled) dishes, Styrian cuisine is Austrian cooking at its light and healthy best.

AIOLA UPSTAIRS · International €€

(http://upstairs.aiola.at, in German; Schlossberg 2; pasta €9.50-15, mains €17.50-25; ⌚9am-midnight, closed Sun) This wonderful restaurant on Schlossberg has great views, delicious international flavours, a superb wine list, spot-on cocktails and very chilled music.

DER STEIRER · Beer Hall €€

(www.dersteirer.at, in German; Belgiergasse 1; mains €9-18.50, tapas €2, lunch menu €6.90; ⌚11am-midnight) This Styrian neo-*Beisl* and wine bar has a small but excellent selection of local dishes and a large choice of wines. The goulash with fried polenta is easily one of the best in the country.

ℹ Information

Graz Tourismus (☎80 75-0; www.graztourismus.at; Herrengasse 16; ⌚10am-6pm) Graz's main tourist office, with loads of free information on the city. Inside the train station is an information stand and terminal, and free hotline to the tourist office.

ℹ Getting There & Away

Ryanair (www.ryanair.com) has regular flights from London Stansted to **Graz airport** (☎290 20; www.flughafen-graz.at), 10km south of the centre, while **Air Berlin** (www.airberlin.com) connects the city with Berlin.

Trains to Vienna depart hourly (€34, 2½ hours), and six daily go to Salzburg (€48, four hours). International train connections from Graz include Ljubljana (€34, 3½ hours) and Budapest (€46, 5½ hours).

Single tickets (€1.90) for buses, trams and the Schlossbergbahn are valid for one hour, but you're usually better off buying a 24-hour pass (€4.10).

Bicycle rental is available from **Bicycle** (☎68 86 45; Körösistrasse 5; per 24hr €10; ⌚7am-1pm & 2-6pm, closed Sat & Sun).

ROBERTO GEROMETTA/LONELY PLANET IMAGES ©

Salzburg

☏0662 / POP 147,600

The joke 'if it's baroque, don't fix it' is a perfect maxim for Salzburg; the tranquil Old Town burrowed in below steep hills looks much as it did when Mozart lived here 250 years ago. Second only to Vienna in numbers of visitors, this compact city is centred on a tight grouping of narrow, cobbled streets overshadowed by ornate 17th-century buildings, which are in turn dominated by the medieval Hohensalzburg fortress from high above. Across the fast-flowing Salzach River rests the baroque Schloss Mirabell, surrounded by gorgeous manicured gardens.

If this doesn't whet your appetite, then bypass the grandeur and head straight for kitsch-country by joining a tour of *The Sound of Music* film locations.

Sights

The money-saving **Salzburg Card** (1-/2-/3-day card €25/33/38) gains you entry to all of the major sights and attractions in the city, a free river cruise, unlimited use of public transport (including cable cars) plus numerous discounts on tours and events.

A Unesco World Heritage site, Salzburg's **Old Town** centre is equally entrancing whether viewed from ground level or the hills above.

The grand **Residenzplatz**, with its horse-drawn carriages and mythical fountain, is a good starting point for a wander. The overwhelmingly baroque **Dom** (cathedral; Domplatz; admission free; ⌚8am-7pm Mon-Sat, 1-7pm Sun), slightly to the south, is entered via bronze doors that symbolise faith, hope and charity. The adjacent **Dommuseum** (adult/child €6/2; ⌚10am-5pm Mon-Sat, 11am-6pm Sun) is worth a visit: it's a treasure trove of ecclesiastical art.

From here, head west along Franziskanergasse and turn left into a courtyard for **Stiftskirche St Peter** (St Peter Bezirk 1/2; admission free; ⌚8.30am-noon & 2.30-6.30pm), an abbey church founded around 700. Among the lovingly tended graves in the grounds you'll find the **Katakomben** (catacombs; adult/student €1/0.60; ⌚10.30am-5pm Tue-Sun).

657

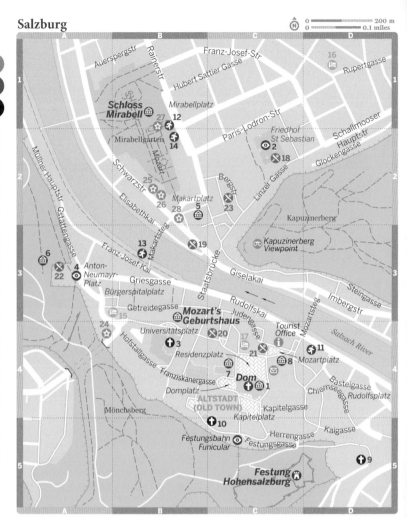

The western end of Franziskanergasse opens out into Max Reinhardt Platz, where you'll see the back of Fisher von Erlach's **Kollegienkirche (Universitätsplatz; admission free; ☺8am-6pm)**, another outstanding example of baroque architecture.

The **Stift Nonnberg (Nonnberg Convent; admission free; ☺7am-dusk)**, where Maria first appears in *The Sound of Music*, is back in the other direction, a short climb up the hill to the east of the Festung Hohensalzburg.

FESTUNG HOHENSALZBURG
Historical Building

(www.salzburg-burgen.at; Mönchsberg 34; adult with/without funicular €10.50/7.40; child €6/4.20; ☺9am-8pm) Salzburg's most visible icon is this mighty clifftop fortress, one of the best preserved in Europe. Built in 1077, the fortress was home to many prince-archbishops (who ruled Salzburg from 798). Inside are the impressively ornate staterooms, torture chambers and two museums.

Salzburg

It takes 15 minutes to walk up the hill to the fortress, or you can catch the **Festungsbahn funicular** (Festungsgasse 4; adult/child one way €3.60/1.80; return €6/3.20; ⊙9am-8pm).

SALZBURG MUSEUM Museum
(www.smca.at; Mozartplatz 1; adult/child €7/3; ⊙9am-5pm Tue-Sun, to 8pm Thu) Housed in the baroque Neue Residenz palace, Salzburg's flagship museum hosts contemporary art exhibitions and celebrates the city's famous citizens, like 16th-century physician Paracelsus, in an interactive way. Salzburg's famous 35-bell **glockenspiel**, which chimes daily at 7am, 11am and 6pm, is on the palace's western flank.

SCHLOSS MIRABELL Palace, Park
(⊙dawn-dusk) Prince-Archbishop Wolf Dietrich built this splendid palace in 1606 for his beloved mistress Salome Alt. The only way to see the sublime baroque interior is by attending an evening concert in the **Marmorsaal** (Marble Hall).

It's free to visit the manicured, fountain-dotted **gardens**, which are less overrun first thing in the morning and early evening. The *Tänzerin* (dancer) sculpture is a great spot from which to photograph the fortress. *The Sound of Music* fans will of course recognise the Pegasus statue, the gnomes and the steps where the mini Von Trapps practised 'Do-Re-Mi'.

MOZART'S GEBURTSHAUS Museum
(Mozart's Birthplace; www.mozarteum.at; Getreidegasse 9; adult/child €7/2.50; ⊙9am-5.30pm) Mozart was born in this bright-yellow town house in 1756 and spent the first 17 years of his life here. Today's museum harbours a collection of memorabilia, including the mini violin the child prodigy played, plus a lock of his hair and buttons from his jacket.

MOZART'S WOHNHAUS Museum
(Mozart's Residence; www.mozarteum.at; Makartplatz 8; adult/child €7/2.50; ⊙9am-5.30pm) The Mozart family moved to this more spacious abode in 1773, where a prolific Mozart composed works such as the *Shepherd King* (K208) and *Idomeneo* (K366). Alongside family portraits and documents, you'll find Mozart's original fortepiano.

659

The museum also houses the free **Mozart Ton-und Filmmuseum** (⊙9am-1pm Mon, Tue & Fri, 1-5pm Wed & Thu), a film and music archive for the ultra-enthusiast.

RESIDENZ — Palace

(www.residenzgalerie.at; Residenzplatz 1; adult/child €8.50/2.70; ⊙10am-5pm Tue-Sun) This resplendent baroque palace is where the prince-archbishops held court until the 19th century. You can visit their opulently frescoed staterooms, and the gallery, which spotlights Dutch and Flemish masters of the Rubens and Rembrandt ilk.

MUSEUM DER MODERNE — Art Gallery

(www.museumdermoderne.at; Mönchsberg 32; adult/child €8/6; ⊙10am-6pm, to 8pm Wed) This ultramodern gallery shows first-rate modern art exhibitions. The works of Gerhard Richter, Max Ernst and Hiroshi Sugimoto have previously featured.

The **Mönchsberg Lift** (Gstättengasse 13; with/without gallery ticket return €1.70/2.90; ⊙8am-7pm, to 9pm Wed) whizzes up to the gallery year-round.

FREE FRIEDHOF ST SEBASTIAN — Cemetery

(Nonnberggasse 2; ⊙7am-dusk) Tucked behind the baroque St Sebastian's Church, this peaceful cemetery is the final resting place of Mozart family members, as well as 16th-century physician Paracelsus. Outpomping them all, though, is Prince-Archbishop Wolf Dietrich von Raitenau's mosaic-tiled **mausoleum**, an incredibly elaborate memorial to himself.

Tours

The horse-drawn carriages (*Fiaker*) in front of Residenz do guided Altstadt tours; prices depend on your itinerary.

One-hour guided tours of the historic centre depart daily at 12.15pm and 2pm on Mozartplatz and cost €9. You can borrow a two-hour iGuide from the tourist office (€7.50) to take in the sights at your own speed.

Left: Sculptures in the gardens of Schloss Mirabell (p659);
Below: *Fiaker* (horse-drawn carriage) in the Old Town (p657), Salzburg

PHOTOGRAPHER: (LEFT) DENNIS JOHNSON/LONELY PLANET IMAGES ©; (BELOW) FVP/IMAGEBROKER ©

Fräulein Maria's Bicycle Tours
Bicycle Tours

(www.mariasbicycletours.com; adult/
child incl bike hire €24/15; ⏲9.30am May-
Sep) Wannabe Marias on bicycles. No booking
required; just turn up at the Mirabellplatz
meeting point.

Bob's Special Tours
Coach Tours

(☎849 511; www.bobstours.com; Rudolfskai
38; ⏲office 10am-3pm Mon-Fri, noon-2pm Sat
& Sun) Minibus tours to *The Sound of Music*
locations (€40), the Bavarian Alps (€40) and
Grossglockner (€80). Reservations essential.

Salzburg Sightseeing Tours
Coach Tours

(☎881 616; www.salzburg-sightseeingtours.at;
Mirabellplatz 2; adult/child €20/7; ⏲office 8am-
6pm) Sells a 24-hour ticket for a multilingual
hop-on, hop-off bus tour of the city and *The
Sound of Music* locations.

Salzburg Schiffsfahrt
River Cruises

(www.salzburgschifffahrt.at; adult/child €13/7,
to Schloss Hellbrunn €16/10; ⏲Apr-Oct) Hour-
long cruises depart from Makartsteg bridge,

with some chugging on to Schloss Hellbrunn
(the ticket price does not cover entry to the
palace).

Festivals & Events

Austria's most renowned classical music
festival, the **Salzburg Festival** (www.salz-
burgfestival.at) attracts international stars
from late July to late August. Book on its
website before January, or ask the **ticket
office** (☎804 5-500; Herbert-von- Karajan-
Platz 11; ⏲10am-6pm) about cancellations
during the festival.

Sleeping

HAUS WARTENBERG   Guesthouse €€
(☎848 400; www.hauswartenberg.com;
Riedenburgerstrasse 2; s/d €65/95; [P] [@]) Set
in vine-strewn gardens, this 17th-century

No Tourist Trapp

Did you know that there were 10 (not seven) Trapp children? Or that Rupert was the eldest (so long Liesl) and the captain a gentle-natured man? For the truth behind the Hollywood legend, stay at **Villa Trapp** (☎63 08 60; www.villa-trapp. com; Traunstrasse 34; d €109-500) in Aigen district, 3km from the Altstadt. Marianne and Christopher have transformed the von Trapp's elegant 19th-century villa into a beautiful guesthouse, brimming with family heirlooms and snapshots. The villa sits in Salzburg's biggest private park.

chalet guesthouse is a 10-minute stroll from the Altstadt. Country-style rooms done out in chunky pinewood and florals are in keeping with the character of the place.

HOTEL & VILLA AUERSPERG Hotel €€
(☎889 440; www.auersperg.at; Auerspergstrasse 61; s €109-139, d €145-188, ste €205; P@ 📶) This charismatic villa-hotel hybrid fuses late-19th-century flair with contemporary design. Relax by the lily pond in the garden or in the rooftop wellness area with mountain views. Free bike hire is a bonus.

HOTEL AM DOM Hotel €€
(☎842 765; www.hotelamdom.at; Goldgasse 17; s €90-180, d €140-260; ❄@📶) Antique meets boutique at this Altstadt hotel, where the original vaults and beams of the 800-year-old building contrast with razor-sharp design features.

HOTEL SCHLOSS MÖNCHSTEIN
Hotel €€€
(☎848 555-0; www.monchstein.at; Mönchsberg Park 26; d €335-445, ste €595-1450; P❄📶) On a fairy-tale perch atop Mönchsberg, this 16th-century castle is honeymoon (and second mortgage) material. Rooms are lavishly decorated with Persian rugs and oil paintings. A massage in the spa, a candlelit tower dinner for two, a helicopter ride – just say the word.

ARTHOTEL BLAUE GANS Hotel €€
(☎842 491-50; www.hotel-blaue-gans-salzburg. at; Getreidegasse 43; s €120-140, d €140-200;

❄📶) Contemporary design blends harmoniously with the original vaulting and beams of this 650-year-old hotel, which has sleek yet comfortable rooms.

 Eating

Old-fashioned taverns, world flavours, kitschy Mozart dinners – you'll find the lot in the Altstadt.

ALTER FUCHS Austrian €
(☎882 022; Linzer Gasse 47-49; mains €9-16; ⏰Mon-Sat) This old fox prides itself on old-fashioned Austrian fare like schnitzel fried to golden perfection. Bandana-clad foxes guard the bar in the vaulted interior and there's a courtyard for good-weather dining.

RIEDENBURG Austrian €€€
(☎830 815; www.riedenburg.at, in German; Neutorstrasse 31; lunch €18, mains €26-35; ⏰Tue-Sat) At this lovely and romantic Michelin-starred pick, Richard Brunnauer's creative Austrian signatures, such as venison and guinea fowl crêpes with wild herbs, are expertly matched with top wines.

ZUM FIDELEN AFFEN Austrian €€
(☎877 361; Priesterhausgasse 8; mains €10.50-16.50; ⏰dinner Mon-Sat) At the jovial monkey you'll dine heartily on Austrian classics like goulash and sweet curd dumplings in the vaulted interior or on the pavement terrace. Reservations are recommended.

M32 Fusion **€€**

(☏841 000; www.m32.at, in German; Mönchsberg 32; mains €14-26; ☺9am-1am Tue-Sun)
Bold colours and a forest of stag antlers
reveal architect Matteo Thun's imprint
at Museum der Moderne's glass-walled
restaurant.

⭐ Entertainment

High-brow venues include the
Schlosskonzerte (☏848 586; www.salzburger
-schlosskonzerte.at), in Schloss Mirabell's
sublime baroque Marble Hall, and the **Mo-
zarteum** (www.mozarteum.at; Schwarzstrasse
26). Marionettes bring *The Sound of Music*
and Mozart's operas magically to life at
Salzburger Marionettentheater (☏87
24 06; www.marionetten.at; Schwarzstrasse 24;
☺May-Sep, Christmas, Easter).

Most bands with a modern bent will
invariably play at either the **Rockhouse**
(www.rockhouse.at, in German; Schallmooser
Hauptstrasse 46) or **ARGEkultur** (www.
argekultur.at, in German; Josef-Preis-Allee 16);
both double as popular bars.

ℹ Information

The main tourist office in Salzburg (☏889
87-330; www.salzburg.info; Mozartplatz 5;
☺9am-7pm) has plenty of useful information
about the city and its immediate surrounds;
there's also a very handy ticket booking
agency located in the same building. For
information on the rest of the province,
visit the Salzburgerland Tourismus (www.
salzburgerland.com) website.

ℹ Getting There & Away

Air

Salzburg airport (www.salzburg-airport.com), a
20-minute bus ride from the centre, has regular
scheduled flights to destinations all over Austria
and Europe.

Bus

Buses depart from just outside the Hauptbahnhof
on Südtiroler Platz, where timetables are
displayed. Bus information and tickets are
available from the information points on the main
concourse.

Coffee Break

Get *gemütlich* (comfy) over coffee, cake and people-watching in Salzburg's
grandest cafes:

DEMEL
(www.demel.at; Mozartplatz 2; ☺9am-8pm; 📶) Demel's 1st-floor balcony has a prime
view of Mozartplatz. The must-try cake on the menu is *Anna Torte:* moist
chocolate sponge with a splash of orange liqueur, topped with a chocolate-
nougat swirl.

CAFÉ BAZAR
(www.cafe-bazar.at; Schwarzstrasse 3; ☺7.30am-11pm Mon-Sat, 9am-6pm Sat) All
chandeliers, polished wood and intelligent conversation. Enjoy breakfast or a
cream-filled torte on the terrace overlooking the Salzach River.

CAFÉ TOMASELLI
(www.tomaselli.at, in German; Alter Markt 9; ☺7am-9pm) Going strong since 1705, this
marble and wood-panelled cafe is a former Mozart haunt. It's famous for having
Salzburg's flakiest strudels, best *Einspänner* (coffee with whipped cream) and
grumpiest waiters.

Hourly buses leave for the Salzkammergut including Bad Ischl (€9.10, 1½ hours), Mondsee (€5.70, 50 minutes), St Wolfgang (€8.40, 1¾ hours) and St Gilgen (€5.70, 50 minutes). For more information on buses in Salzburgerland and the Salzkammergut and an online timetable, see www.svv.at.

Car & Motorcycle

Three motorways converge on Salzburg to form a loop around the city: the A1/E60 from Linz, Vienna and the east; the A8/E52 from Munich and the west; and the A10/E55 from Villach and the south. The quickest way to Tyrol is to take the road to Bad Reichenhall in Germany and continue to Lofer (B178) and St Johann in Tyrol.

Train

Fast trains leave for Vienna (€47.50, three hours) via Linz (€22, 1¼ hours) hourly. The express service to Klagenfurt (€35.50, three hours) goes via Villach. There are trains every hour or so to Munich (€34).

ℹ Getting Around

Salzburg airport is located 4km west of the city centre. Bus 2 goes there from the Hauptbahnhof (€2.10, 19 minutes). A taxi costs about €15.

Bus drivers sell singles for €2.10. Other tickets, including day (€5) and week (€12.80) passes, must be bought from the automatic machines at stops or *Tabak* shops.

The majority of the Old Town is pedestrianised. **Top Bike** (www.topbike.at; 2hr/4hr/day €6/10/15, 20% discount with all train tickets) rents bikes from just outside the train station.

Around Salzburg
Schloss Hellbrunn

A prince-archbishop with a wicked sense of humour, Markus Sittikus built Italianate **Schloss Hellbrunn** (www.hellbrunn.at; Fürstenweg 37; adult/child €9.50/4.50; ◷9am-5.30pm, to 9pm Jul & Aug) as a 17th-century summer palace and an escape from his Residenz functions.

The ingenious trick fountains and water-powered figures are the big draw. When the tour guides set them off, expect to get wet! Admission includes entry to the baroque palace. The rest of the sculpture-dotted gardens are free to visit. Look out for the *The Sound of Music* pavilion of 'Sixteen Going on Seventeen' fame.

Bus 25 runs to Hellbrunn, 4.5km south of Salzburg, every 20 minutes from Rudolfskai in the Altstadt.

Gardens of Schloss Hellbrunn

Salzkammergut

A picture-perfect wonderland of glassy blue lakes and tall craggy peaks, Austria's Lake District is a long-time favourite holiday destination, attracting visitors in droves from Salzburg and beyond.

You can also tour the salt mines that made the region wealthy or plunge into the depths of the fantastic Dachstein caves, where glittering towers of ice are masterfully illuminated in the depths of a mountain.

ⓘ Getting There & Around

The major rail routes bypass the heart of Salzkammergut, but regional trains cross the area north to south. This route begins at Attnang-Puchheim on the Salzburg–Linz line. The track from here connects to Bad Ischl, Hallstatt and Obertraun in one direction and Gmunden in another. At small, unstaffed stations (*unbesetzter Bahnhof*), tickets can be bought on the train; no surcharge applies.

Regular buses connect the region's towns and villages, though less frequently on weekends.

Passenger boats ply the waters of the Attersee, Traunsee, Mondsee, Hallstätter See and Wolfgangsee.

Bad Ischl

☏ 06132 / POP 14,050

During the last century of the Habsburg reign, Bad Ischl became the favourite summertime retreat for the imperial family and their entourage. Today the town and many of its digni-fied buildings still have a stately aura, while a very high proportion of the local women still go about their daily busi-ness in *Dirndl* (Austria's traditional full, pleated skirt).

◎ Sights & Activities

KAISERVILLA Palace

(Jainzen 38; www.kaiservilla.com; adult/child €12/7.50, grounds only €4.50/3.50; ⊙9.30am-4.45pm, closed Thu-Tue Jan-Mar, closed Nov) This Italianate building was Franz Josef's summer residence and shows that he loved huntin', shootin' and fishin' – it's dec-

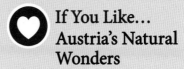

If You Like...
Austria's Natural Wonders

Austria is blessed with some truly astonishing scenery.

1 EISRIESENWELT
(www.eisriesenwelt.at; adult/child €8.50/4.50, with cable car €19/9.50; ⊙9am-3.30pm May-Oct) One thousand metres above the village of Werfen are the world's largest accessible ice caves. This glittering empire is a once-seen-never-forgotten experience. The one-hour tour takes you through twinkling passageways and chambers; unsurprisingly you'll need to dress for subzero temperatures. Werfen can be reached from Salzburg on the A10/E55 motorway or by train (€9.20, 40 minutes); regular minibuses run to the caves throughout summer.

2 DACHSTEIN RIESENEISHÖHLE
(www.dachsteinwelterbe.at; cable car return plus 1 cave adult/child €27/15, 1 cave only adult/child €10.80/6) At nearby Obertraun is another fabulous cave complex, extending into the mountain for almost 80km. The ice itself is around 500 years old, but is increasing in thickness each year – the 'ice mountain', at 8m high, is twice as high now as it was when the caves were first explored in 1910.

3 KRIMML FALLS
(www.wasserfaelle-krimml.at; adult/child €2/0.50, free Dec-Apr; ⊙ticket office 8am-6pm mid-Apr-late Oct) This thunderous, three-tier waterfall is Europe's highest, at 380m. It's also one of Austria's most unforgettable sights. Krimml is on Hwy 168 (which becomes Hwy 165). Buses run year-round from Krimml to Zell am See (€8.40, 1¼ hours, hourly).

orated with an obscene number of animal trophies. It can be visited only by guided tour, during which you'll pick up little gems – like the fact that Franz Josef was conceived in Bad Ischl after his mother, Princess Sophie, took a treatment to cure her infertility in 1828. It was also here that the Kaiser signed the letter declaring war on Serbia, which led to WWI.

Obertraun

At nearby Obertraun you'll find the intriguing **Dachstein Rieseneishöhle** (see p 669). The caves are millions of years old and extend into the mountain for almost 80km in places.

From Obertraun it's also possible to catch a cable car to **Krippenstein** (return adult/child €23/14; ⊙closed mid-Oct–Nov & Easter–mid-May), where you'll find the freaky **5Fingers viewing platform**, which protrudes over a sheer cliff face. Not for sufferers of vertigo.

Cable Car   Cable Car
(www.katrinseilbahn.com; return adult/child €17.50/11.50, ⊙closed Apr–mid-May & Nov–mid-Dec) The local mountain (1542m), with walking trails and limited skiing in winter, is served by a cable car.

Kaiser Therme   Spa
(www.eurothermen.co.at; Bahnhofstrasse 1; adult/child €13.50/9.50; ⊙9am-midnight) If you'd like to follow in Princess Sophie's footsteps, check out the indulgent treatments at this spa.

 Sleeping & Eating

HOTEL GARNI SONNHOF
                                              Hotel €€
(📞230 78; www.sonnhof.at; Bahnhofstrasse 4; s €65-95, d €90-150; P 📶) Nestled in a leafy glade of maple trees next to the station, the Hotel Garni Sonnhof has cosy, traditional decor, a beautiful garden, chickens that deliver breakfast eggs, and a sunny conservatory.

GOLDENES SCHIFF   Hotel €€
(📞242 41; www.goldenes-schiff.at; Adalbert Stifterkai 3; s €98-109, d €144-176, apt €192; mains €14-18; P @ 📶) The best rooms at this comfortable pick have large windows overlooking the river.

WEINHAUS ATTWENGER   Austrian €€
(📞233 27; www.weinhaus-attwenger.com, in German; Lehárkai 12; mains €14-22; ⊙lunch & dinner, closed Mon, closed Tue Nov-Apr; ➡) This quaint chalet with a riverside garden serves prime-quality Austrian cuisine

from a seasonal menu, with excellent wines to match.

GRAND CAFÉ & RESTAURANT ZAUNER ESPLANADE   Austrian €€
(Hasner Allee 2; mains €10-18.50; ⊙10am-10pm) This offshoot of Café Zauner, the famous pastry shop at Pfarrgasse 7, serves Austrian staples, some using local organic meats, in a pleasant location beside the river.

ⓘ **Information**

Salzkammergut Info-Center (📞240 00-0; www.salzkammergut.co.at; Götzstrasse 12; ⊙9am-8pm, closed Sun Oct-Mar)

Tourist office (📞277 57-0; www.badischl. at; Auböckplatz 5; ⊙8am-6pm Mon-Fri, 9am-6pm Sat, 10am-1pm Sun) Also has a telephone service (8am to 10pm) for rooms and information.

ⓘ **Getting There & Around**

Buses depart from outside the train station, with hourly buses to Salzburg (€9.10, 1½ hours) via St Gilgen (€4.80, 40 minutes).

Hourly trains to Hallstatt (€3.60, 25 minutes) go via Steeg/Hallstätter See, at the northern end of the lake, and continue on the eastern side via Hallstatt station to Obertraun (€4.30, 30 minutes).

A boat from Hallstatt station (€2.20) takes you to the township. There are also frequent trains to Gmunden (€7.20, 40 minutes) and Salzburg (€21, two hours) via Attnang-Puchheim.

Hallstatt

 06134 / POP 840

With pastel-hued homes, swans and towering mountains on either side of a glassy green lake, Hallstatt looks like a greeting card for tranquillity. Boats chug lazily across the water from the train station to the village itself, which clings precariously to a tiny bit of land between mountain and shore.

Sights & Activities

Hallstatt has been classified a Unesco World Heritage site for its natural beauty and for evidence of human settlement dating back 4500 years. Over 2000 graves have been discovered in and around the village, most dating from 1000 to 500 BC.

SALZBERGWERK Salt Mine
(Salt Mine; funicular return & tour adult/child €24/12, tour only €12/6; ☺9.30am-4.30pm, closed mid-Oct–Apr) The region's major cultural attraction is situated high above Hallstatt on Salzberg (Salt Mountain). In 1734 the fully preserved body of a prehistoric miner was found; today he is known as the 'Man in Salt'. The standard tour revolves around his fate, with visitors travelling down an underground railway and miner's slides to an illuminated subterranean salt lake.

The mine can be reached on foot or with the **funicular railway** (one way adult/child €7/3.50).

BEINHAUS Church
(Bone House; Kirchenweg 40; admission €1; ☺10am-6pm, closed Nov-Apr) Don't miss the macabre yet beautiful Beinhaus behind Hallstatt's parish church. It contains rows of stacked skulls painted with flowery designs and names of the deceased. The old Celtic pagan custom of mass burial has been practised here since

1600 (mainly due to the lack of graveyard space), and the last skull in the collection was added in 1995.

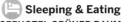 Sleeping & Eating

SEEHOTEL GRÜNER BAUM Hotel €€
(☎8263; Marktplatz 104; s €80, d without view €140, d or ste with lake view €170-210; P @ ☎) This hotel has its own pontoon and tastefully furnished rooms (most with balconies). Breakfast delivered to your bedside and sparkling lake views make this ideal for romantic sojourns.

BALTHAZAR IM RUDOLFSTURM Cafe €
(Rudolfsturm; mains €10-13.50; ☺9am-6pm, closed Nov-Apr; ☻) With the most spectacular terrace in the region, Balthazar is situated 855m above Hallstatt. Both the views over the lake and the food are excellent.

🛈 Information

Tourist office (☎8208; www.dachstein-salzkammergut.at; Seestrasse 169; ☺9am-6pm Mon-Fri, to 4pm Sat, to noon Sun, closed Sat & Sun Sep-Jun)

DISCOVER AUSTRIA, SWITZERLAND & THE CZECH REPUBLIC

Cable car, Bad Ischl (p665)
PHOTOGRAPHER: TERENCE WAELAND / ALAMY ©

ℹ Getting There & Away

BOAT The last ferry connection leaves Hallstatt train station at 6.55pm (€2.20, 10 minutes). Ferry excursions do the circuit Hallstatt Lahn via Hallstatt Markt, Obersee, Untersee and Steeg return (€9.50, 90 minutes) three times daily from mid-July to August.

TRAIN Hallstatt train station is across the lake. The boat service from there to the village coincides with train arrivals. About a dozen trains daily connect Hallstatt and Bad Ischl (€3.60, 22 minutes) and Hallstatt with Bad Aussee (€3.60, 15 minutes).

Wolfgangsee

Wolfgangsee is a hugely popular place to spend the summer swimming, boating, walking or simply lazing by its soothing waters. Its two main resorts are St Wolfgang and St Gilgen, with the former taking first prize in the beauty stakes.

Coming from Salzburg, the first town you come across is **St Gilgen**.

St Wolfgang, towards the southern end of Wolfgangsee, is squeezed between the northern shoreline of the lake and the towering peak of **Scharfberg** (1783m). Reaching the top of Schafberg is an easy exercise – from May to October, a cogwheel railway climbs to its summit in 40 minutes (one way/return €19.60/28.60).

A ferry operates May to October between Strobl and St Gilgen (one way €8.80, 75 minutes), stopping at points en route. Boats run from St Wolfgang to St Gilgen almost hourly during the day (one way €6.50, 50 minutes); the free *Eintauchen & Aufsteigen* timetable from the local tourist offices gives exact times.

Northern Salzkammergut

Mondsee is popular for two reasons – its close proximity to Salzburg (only 30km) and its warm water. The main village on the lake, also called Mondsee, is home to an attractive 15th-century church that was used in the wedding scene of *The Sound of Music* and a small and helpful **tourist office** (☎ 2270; www.mondsee.at; Dr Franz Müller Strasse 3; ⏱ 8am-6pm Mon-Fri, 9am-6pm Sat & Sun, closed Sat & Sun Oct-May).

Lying to the east of Mondsee is **Attersee**, Salzkammergut's largest lake and a favourite with sailors. East again from Attersee you'll find **Traunsee** and its three main resorts: Gmunden, Traunkirchen and Ebensee. **Gmunden** is

Church and hotel, St Wolfgang

MARTIN MOOS/LONELY PLANET IMAGES ©

famous for its twin castles, linked by a causeway on the lake, and its green-and-white ceramics.

Buses run every hour to Mondsee from Salzburg (€5.70, 55 minutes). Gmunden is connected to Salzburg by train (€15.70, 1¼ hours) via Attnang-Puchheim.

Tirol

With converging mountain ranges behind lofty pastures and tranquil meadows, Tirol (also Tyrol) captures a quintessential Alpine panoramic view. Occupying a central position is Innsbruck, the region's jewel, while in the northeast and southwest are superb ski resorts. In the southeast, separated somewhat from the main state since part of South Tirol was ceded to Italy at the end of WWI, lies the protected natural landscape of the Hohe Tauern National Park, an alpine wonderland of 3000m peaks, including the country's highest, the Grossglockner (3798m).

Innsbruck

☏ 0512 / POP 118,000

Tirol's capital is a sight to behold. The mountains are so close that within 25 minutes it's possible to travel from the heart of the city to over 2000m above sea level. Summer and winter outdoor activities abound, and it's understandable why some visitors only take a peek at Innsbruck proper before heading for the hills.

◎ Sights

GOLDENES DACHL & MUSEUM Museum
(Golden Roof; Herzog-Friedrich-Strasse 15; adult/child €4/2; ⊙10am-5pm, closed Mon Oct-Apr) Innsbruck's golden wonder is this Gothic oriel, built for Emperor Maximilian I and glittering with 2657 fire-gilt copper tiles. An audioguide whizzes you through the history in the museum; look for the grotesque tournament helmets designed to resemble the slit-eyed Turks of the rival Ottoman Empire.

HOFKIRCHE & VOLKSKUNSTMUSEUM
Church, Museum
(www.tiroler-landesmuseum.at; Universität-strasse; combined ticket adult/child €8/4; ⊙10am-6pm Mon-Sat, from 12.30pm Sun)

The 16th-century Hofkirche is one of Europe's finest royal court churches. Top billing goes to the empty **sarcophagus** of Emperor Maximilian I (1459–1519), a masterpiece of German Renaissance sculpture, guarded by 28 giant bronze figures including Dürer's legendary King Arthur. You're now forbidden to touch the statues, but numerous inquisitive hands have already polished parts of the dull bronze, including Kaiser Rudolf's codpiece!

Next door the **Volkskunstmuseum** (Folk Art Museum; www.tiroler-landesmuseum. at; Universitätstrasse; combined Hofkirche ticket adult/child €8/4; ⊙10am-6pm Mon-Sat, from 12.30pm Sun) houses Tyrolean folk art, from handcarved sleighs and Christmas cribs to carnival masks and cow bells.

The **Innsbruck Card** gives you one visit to Innsbruck's main sights and attractions, a return journey on all cable cars and unlimited use of public transport, including the Sightseer bus, which makes getting to some of the more remote sights easier. It's available at the tourist office and costs €29/34/39 for 24/48/72 hours (half price for children).

HOFBURG Palace
(Imperial Palace; www.hofburg-innsbruck. at; Rennweg 1; adult/child €8/free; ⊙9am-5pm) Empress Maria Theresia gave this Habsburg palace a total baroque makeover in the 16th century. The highlight of the state apartments is the Riesensaal (Giant's Hall), lavishly adorned with frescoes and paintings of Maria Theresia and her 16 children, including Marie Antoinette.

Tucked behind the palace is the **Hofgarten** (admission free; ⊙daylight hr), an attractive garden for a botanical stroll.

BERGISEL Ski Jump
(www.bergisel.info; adult/child €8.50/4; ⊙10am-6pm) Rising above Innsbruck like a celestial staircase, this glass-and-steel ski jump was designed by much-lauded Iraqi architect Zaha Hadid.

It's 455 steps or a two-minute funicular ride to the 50m-high **viewing platform**. Here, the panorama of the Nordkette range, Inn Valley and Innsbruck is breathtaking, though the cemetery at the bottom has undoubtedly made a few ski jumping pros quiver in their boots, not least plucky Brit Eddie 'the Eagle' Edwards.

Bus 4143 and line TS run from the Hauptbahnhof to Bergisel.

TIROLER LANDESMUSEUM FERDINANDEUM
Art Gallery, Museum

(www.tiroler-landesmuseum.at; Museumstrasse 15; adult/child €8/4; ⊙10am-6pm Tue-Sun) This treasure-trove of Tyrolean history and art contains the original reliefs used to design the Goldenes Dachl. In the gallery you'll find old master paintings, Gothic altarpieces, a handful of Kokoschka and Klimt originals, and Viennese Actionist works with shock factor.

SCHLOSS AMBRAS
Palace

(www.khm.at/ambras; Schlossstrasse 20; adult/child €10/free; ⊙10am-5pm) Archduke Ferdinand II transformed Schloss Ambras from a fortress into a Renaissance palace in 1564. A visit takes in the ever-so-grand banquet hall, shining armour (look out for the 2.6m suit created for giant Bartlmä Bon) and room upon room of Habsburg portraits, with Titian, Velázquez and Van Dyck originals. It's free to stroll or picnic in the expansive **gardens** (⊙6am-8pm).

Schloss Ambras is 4.5km southeast of the centre. Take bus 4134 from the Hauptbahnhof to the castle for discounted entry and a free return journey.

🏃 Activities

Anyone who loves the great outdoors will be itching to head up into the Alps in Innsbruck.

Zaha Hadid's space-age **Nordketten Bahnen** (www.nordkette.com; ⊙every 15min, 8.30am-5.30pm) funicular whizzes you from the Congress Centre to the slopes in just 25 minutes. Tickets cost €14.10/23.40 one way/return to Seegrube and €15.60/26 to Hafelekar. Both afford superb views of Innsbruck and the Alps, and appeal to walkers and mountain bikers.

From late May to October, Innsbruck Information arranges daily guided hikes – from sunrise walks to lantern-lit strolls – free to those with a Club Innsbruck Card. Pop into the tourist office to register and browse the program.

Innsbruck is the gateway to the massive **Olympia SkiWorld Innsbruck** (www.ski-innsbruck.at) ski arena, covering nine surrounding resorts and 282km of slopes to test all abilities. The most central place to pound powder is the **Nordpark**, accessed by **cable car** (⊙8am-7pm) running every 15 minutes. A three-/seven-day Innsbruck Glacier Ski Pass covering all areas costs €105/200; ski buses are free to anyone with an Innsbruck Card.

🛏 Sleeping

HOTEL WEISSES KREUZ
Hotel €€

(☎594 79; www.weisseskreuz.at; Herzog-Friedrich-Strasse 31; s €36-72, d €100-132; P @ 🛜) Beneath the Altstadt's arcades, this atmospheric 500-year-old hotel has played host to famous guests including a 13-year-old Mozart. It remains comfortable to this day.

ROMANTIK HOTEL SCHWARZER ADLER
Hotel €€€

(☎587 109; www.deradler.com; Kaiserjäger-strasse 2; s €110-159, d €150-211, ste €295-480; P @ ⛆) This boutique hotel's fabulously over-the-top suites glitter with Swarovski crystals; one features the solid marble bed Versace once slept in.

GOLDENER ADLER
Hotel €€

(☎571 111; www.goldeneradler.com; Herzog-Friedrich-Strasse 6; s/d €92/135; P ❄ 🛜) Since opening in 1390, the grand Goldener Adler has welcomed kings, queens and Salzburg's two biggest exports: Mozart and Mrs Von Trapp. Rooms are elegant, with gold drapes and squeaky-clean marble bathrooms.

🍴 Eating

Bistros, cafes and traditional taverns line Altstadt lanes like Herzog-Friedrich-Strasse, Hofgasse and Kiebachgasse; most have alfresco seating in summer.

CHEZ NICO
Vegetarian €€

(📞586 398; www.chez-nico.at; Maria-Theresien-Strasse 49; lunch €12.50, 7-course menu €45; ⏰lunch & dinner Tue-Fri, dinner Sat; 🍴) Take a creative Parisian chef with an artistic eye and a passion for herbs, *et voilà*, you get Chez Nico. Nicolas Curtil (Nico) cooks seasonal vegetarian delights like chanterelle-apricot goulash and porcini-sage ravioli at this intimate bistro.

GASTHAUS GOLDENES DACHL
Tyrolean €€

(📞589 370; www.gasthaus-goldenesdachl.at; Hofgasse 1; mains €10-18) Portions are generous and the menu typically Tyrolean at this tavern, a cosy spot to try *Gröstl* (potatoes and bacon topped with a fried egg).

OTTOBURG
Austrian €€

(📞584 338; www.ottoburg.at; Herzog-Friedrich-Strasse 1; lunch €6-9, mains €17-26; ⏰Tue-Sun; 🍴) This 12th-century castle hides a warren of wood-panelled *Stuben* (parlours). Dig into tournedos of venison, *Topfenknödel* (cottage cheese dumplings) and other hearty fare.

🛈 Information

Innsbruck Information (📞535 60; www.innsbruck.info; Burggraben 3; ⏰9am-6pm) Main tourist office with truckloads of info on the city and surrounds, including skiing and walking. Sells ski passes, public-transport tickets and city maps (€1); will book accommodation (€3 commission) and has an attached ticketing service.

🛈 Getting There & Away

AIR Innsbruck Airport (www.innsbruck-airport.com), 4km to the west of the city centre, caters to national and international flights, handled mostly by Austrian Airlines, BA, easyJet and Welcome Air.

TRAIN Fast trains depart every two hours for Bregenz (€31.30, 2¾ hours), Salzburg (€37.80, two hours), Kitzbühel (€17.60, 1¾ hours) and Munich (€37, two hours).

🛈 Getting Around

TO/FROM THE AIRPORT The airport is 4km west of the centre and served by bus F. Buses depart every 15 or 20 minutes from Maria-Theresien-Strasse (€1.80); taxis charge about €8 to €10 for the same trip.

PUBLIC TRANSPORT Single tickets on buses and trams cost €1.80 (from the driver; valid upon issue). A 24-hour ticket is €4.10.

Hohe Tauern National Park

If you thought Mother Nature pulled out all the stops in the Austrian Alps, Hohe Tauern National Park was her magnum opus. Straddling Tirol, Salzburg and Carinthia, this national park is the largest in the Alps; a 1786-sq-km wilderness of 3000m peaks, alpine meadows and waterfalls. At its heart lies **Grossglockner** (3798m), Austria's highest mountain, which towers over the 8km-long Pasterze Glacier, best

Walker in Tirol (p669)

PHOTOGRAPHER: GARETH MCCORMACK/LONELY PLANET IMAGES ©

seen from the outlook at **Kaiser-Franz-Josefs-Höhe** (2369m).

The 48km **Grossglockner Road** (Hwy 107; www.grossglockner.at, in German), from Bruck in Salzburgerland to Heiligenblut in Carinthia, is one of Europe's greatest alpine drives. A feat of 1930s engineering, the road swings giddily around 36 switchbacks, passing jewel-coloured lakes, forested slopes and wondrous glaciers.

If you have wheels, you'll have more flexibility, although the road is open only between May and October, and you must pay tolls (per car/motorcycle €28/18).

SWITZERLAND

What giddy romance Zermatt, St Moritz and other glitterati-encrusted names evoke: from the intoxicating chink of multimillionaires hobnobbing over cocktails served in ice-carved flutes to the comforting jangle of the cows coming home, seduction is head-over-heels.

This is Sonderfall Schweiz ('special case Switzerland'), a rare and refined breed, a privileged country set apart from others, but Europe's bijou land of plenty is as proudly idiosyncratic and unique as ever.

Geneva

POP 185,700

Supersleek, slick and cosmopolitan, Geneva (Genève in French, Genf in German) is a rare breed of city. It's one of Europe's priciest. Its people chatter in every language under the sun (184 nationalities comprise 45% of the city's population) and it's constantly thought of as the Swiss capital – which it isn't. This gem of a city superbly strung around the sparkling shores of Europe's largest alpine lake is, in fact, Switzerland's second-largest city.

👁 Sights & Activities

The city centre is so compact it's very easy to see many of the main sights on foot.

LAKE GENEVA   Lake

Begin your exploration of Europe's largest alpine lake by having a coffee on **Île Rousseau**, where a statue honours the celebrated freethinker. Cross to the southern side of the lake and walk west to the **Horloge Fleurie (Flower Clock; Quai du Général-Guisan)** in the Jardin Anglais. Geneva's most photographed clock, crafted from 6500 flowers, has ticked since 1955 and sports the world's longest second hand (2.5m).

The 140m-tall **Jet d'Eau** on the lake's southern shore is impossible to miss. At any one time there are 7 tonnes of water in the air, shooting up with incredible force –

Cathédrale de St-Pierre, Old Town
PHOTOGRAPHER: PCL/ALAMY©

Illuminated chateau, Lake Geneva

ANDY CHRISTIANI/LONELY PLANET IMAGES ©

200km/h, 1360 horsepower – to create its sky-high plume, kissed by a rainbow on sunny days.

OLD TOWN   Historic Area
The main street, Grand-Rue, shelters the **Espace Rousseau** at No 40, where the 18th-century philosopher was born.

Nearby, the part-Romanesque, part-Gothic **Cathédrale de St-Pierre** is where Protestant John Calvin preached from 1536 to 1564. Beneath the cathedral is a **site archéologique** (✆ 022 311 75 74; www.site-archeologique.ch; Cour St-Pierre 6; adult/child Sfr8/4; ⊙ 10am-5pm Tue-Sun), an interactive space safeguarding fine 4th-century mosaics and a 5th-century baptismal font.

You can trace Calvin's life in the neighbouring **Musée Internationale de la Réforme** (International Museum of the Reformation; ✆ 022 310 24 31; www.musee -reforme.ch; Rue du Clootre 4; adult/student/ child Sfr8/3/2; ⊙ 10am-5pm Tue-Sun).

PALAIS DES NATIONS   Landmark
(✆ 022 907 48 96; www.unog.ch; Ave de la Paix 14; tours Sfr10; ⊙ 10am-noon & 2-4pm Apr-Oct, to 5pm Jul & Aug, 10am-noon & 2-4pm Mon-Fri Nov-Mar) The art deco Palais des Nations is the European arm of the UN and the home of 3000 international civil servants. You can see where decisions about world affairs are made on the hour-long tour. ID or passport is obligatory for admission.

FREE CERN   Laboratory
(✆ 022 767 84 84; www.cern.ch; ⊙ tours 10.30am Mon-Sat) The World Wide Web was one of the many creations to come out of the European Organisation for Nuclear Research (CERN), a laboratory for research into particle physics funded by 20 nations, which lies 8km west near Meyrin. The free guided visits need to be booked at least one month in advance if you want to guarantee your preferred date, and you will need to present your ID or passport for entry. Equally riveting is **Microcosm** (✆ 022 767 84 84; http://microcosm.web.cern.ch; admission free; ⊙ 8.15am-5.30pm Mon-Fri, 8.30am-5pm Sat), CERN's on-site multimedia and interactive visitors centre.

From the train station, take tram 14 or 16 to Avanchet, then bus 56 to its terminus in front of CERN (Sfr3, 40 minutes).

Switzerland

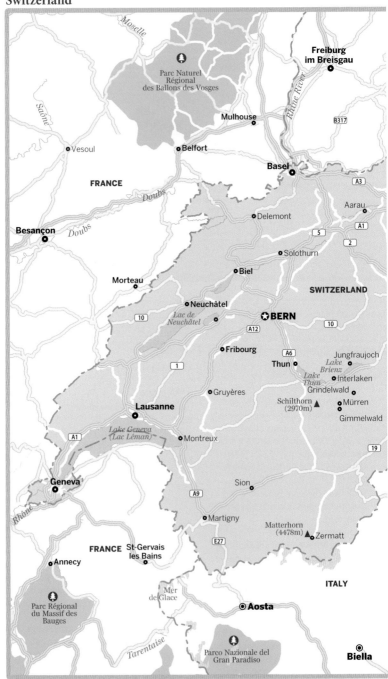

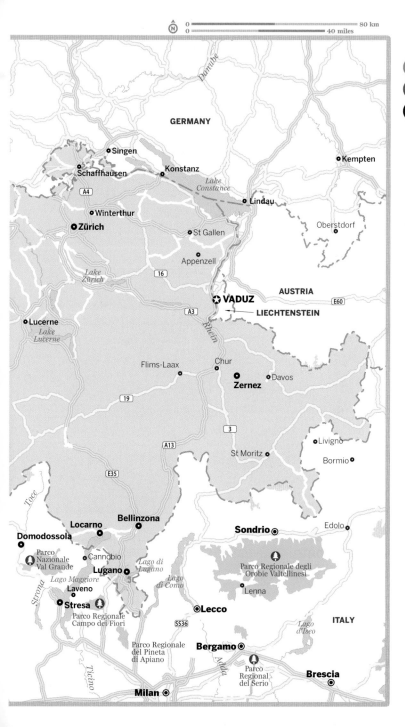

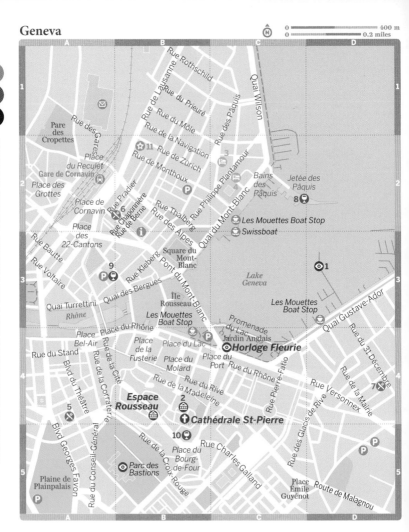

Sleeping

When checking-in, ask for your free public transport ticket covering unlimited bus travel for the duration of your hotel stay.

HÔTEL DE LA CLOCHE   Hotel €€
(☎ 022 732 94 81; www.geneva-hotel.ch/cloche; Rue de la Cloche 6; s Sfr95-128, d Sfr110-149, s without bathroom Sfr65-95, d Sfr98-120; ☝☎) Elegant fireplaces, bourgeois furnishings, wooden floors and the odd

chandelier add a touch of grandeur to this old-fashioned one-star hotel.

LA COUR DES AUGUSTINS   Hotel €€€
(☎ 022 322 21 00; www.lacourdesaugustins. com; s/d from Sfr175/250; Rue Jean-Violette 15; P @ ☎) Disguised by a 19th-century facade, the crisp white interior of this 'boutique gallery hotel' sports the latest technology and screams cutting edge.

EDELWEISS   Hotel €€€
(☎ 022 544 51 51; www.manotel.com; Place de la Navigation 2; d from Sfr290; ☎) Plunge

676

Geneva

yourself into the heart of the Swiss Alps *en ville* at this Heidi-style hideout, with its big cuddly St Bernard, fireplace and chalet-styled restaurant.

Eating

L'ADRESSE International €

(☎022 736 32 32; www.ladresse.ch; Rue du 31 Decembre 32; mains Sfr24-37; ☉lunch & dinner Tue-Sat) An urban loft with rooftop terrace and hybrid lifestyle boutique-contemporary bistro, this hip address is at home in converted artist workshops. *The* place for lunch, brunch or (in the words of the Swiss) Saturday slunch...

AU GRÜTLI International €

(☎022 328 98 68; www.cafedu grutli.ch; Rue du Général Dufour 16; mains Sfr28-36; ☉breakfast, lunch & dinner Mon-Fri, dinner Sat & Sun) Indonesian lamb, moussaka, scallops with ginger and citrus fruits or Provençal chicken are among the international flavours at this razor-sharp theatre restaurant.

CAFÉ DE PARIS French €

(rue du Mont Blanc 26; salad, steak & chips Sfr40; ☉lunch & dinner) A memorable dining experience that's been feeding the hungry since 1930. Everyone goes for the same thing here: green salad, beef steak with a killer-calorie herb-and-butter sauce, and as many fries as you can handle.

Drinking & Entertainment

Pâquis, the district in between the train station and lake; is particularly well endowed with bars. In summer the **paillote** (Quai du Mont-Blanc 30; ☉to midnight), with wooden tables inches from the water, gets crammed.

SCANDALE Bar

(☎022 731 83 73; www.scandale.ch; Rue de Lausanne 24; ☉11am-2am Tue-Fri, 5pm-2am Sat) Retro 1950s furnishings in a cavernous interior with comfy sofas ensure that this lounge bar is never empty. Regular happenings at Scandale include art exhibitions, Saturday-night DJs and bands.

BUVETTE DES BAINS Bar

(☎022 738 16 16; www.bains-des-paquis.ch; Quai du Mont-Blanc 30; ☉8am-10pm) Meet Genevans at this earthy beach bar at Bains des Pâquis. Dining is on trays and, in summer, alfresco.

LA BRETELLE Bar

(☎022 732 75 96; Rue des Étuves 17; ☉6pm-2am) Little has changed since the 1970s, when this legendary bar opened. Live accordion-accompanied French *chansons* most nights.

LA CLÉMENCE Bar

(☎022 312 24 98; www.laclemence.ch; Place du Bourg-de-Four 20; ☉7am-1am Mon-Thu & Sun, to 2am Fri & Sat) Indulge in a glass of local wine or an artisanal beer at La Clémence: a venerable old cafe-bar excellently located on Geneva's loveliest square.

DISCOVER AUSTRIA, SWITZERLAND & THE CZECH REPUBLIC GENEVA

ℹ Information

Tourist office (☎022 909 70 00; www.geneve -tourisme.ch; Rue du Mont-Blanc 18; ⏰10am-6pm Mon, from 9am Tue-Sat)

ℹ Getting There & Away

AIR Aéroport International de Genève (GVA; ☎0900 57 15 00; www.gva.ch), 4km from town, has connections to major European cities and many others worldwide. It is also an easyJet hub.

BOAT CGN (Compagnie Générale de Navigation; ☎0848 811 848; www.cgn.ch) operates a steamer service from its Jardin Anglais jetty to other villages on Lake Geneva. Many only sail May to September, including those to/from Lausanne (Sfr37.60, 3½ hours). Eurail and Swiss Pass holders are valid on CGN boats or there is a one-day CGN boat pass (Sfr49).

TRAIN Trains run to most Swiss towns including at least hourly to/from Lausanne (Sfr20.60, 40 minutes), Bern (Sfr46, 1¾ hours) and Zürich (Sfr80, 2¾ hours).

International daily rail connections from Geneva include Paris (TGV from Sfr130, 3½ hours), Hamburg (from Sfr278, 9½ hours), Milan (from Sfr97, 4½ hours) and Barcelona (from Sfr125, 10 hours).

ℹ Getting Around

TO/FROM THE AIRPORT Getting from the airport is easy with regular trains into Gare de Cornavin (Sfr3, eight minutes). A metered taxi costs Sfr30 to Sfr50.

PUBLIC TRANSPORT Buses, trams, trains and boats service the city, and ticket dispensers are found at all stops. Tickets cost Sfr2 (within one zone, 30 minutes) or Sfr3 (two zones, one hour), and a city/canton day pass is Sfr7/12. The same tickets are also valid on the yellow shuttle boats known as Les Mouettes (the seagulls) that criss-cross the lake every 10 minutes between 7.30am and 6pm.

Valais

Matterhorn country: an intoxicating land that seduces the toughest of critics with its endless breathtaking panoramic vistas.

This is an area of extraordinary natural beauty: Switzerland's 10 highest

mountains – all climbing to over 4000m – rise to the sky here.

Snow fiends can ski and board in one of Europe's top resorts, Zermatt.

Zermatt

POP 5830

Since the mid-19th century, Zermatt has starred among Switzerland's glitziest resorts. Today it attracts intrepid mountaineers and hikers, skiers who cruise at snail's pace, spellbound by the scenery, and style-conscious darlings flashing designer togs in the lounge bars. But all are smitten with the Matterhorn (4478m), the Alps' most famous peak and an unfathomable monolith, synonymous with Switzerland, that you simply can't stop looking at.

◉ Sights & Activities

GORNERGRAT   Mountain
Alpine views of Gornergrat (3090m) from the cable cars and gondolas are uniformly breathtaking, especially from the **cogwheel train** (one way Sfr38), which takes 35 to 45 minutes with two to three departures per hour. Sit on the right-hand side to gawk at the Matterhorn.

CEMETERY   Cemetery
A walk in Zermatt's cemetery is a sobering experience for any would-be mountaineer, as numerous monuments tell of untimely deaths on Monte Rosa and the Matterhorn.

MATTERHORN MUSEUM   Museum
(☏ 027 967 41 00; www.matterhornmuseum.ch; Kirchplatz; adult/student/10-16yr/under 10yr Sfr10/8/5/free; ⏱11am-6pm mid-Dec–Sep, 2-6pm Oct, closed Nov–mid-Dec) On 13 July 1865 Edward Whymper led the first successful ascent of the mountain. The climb took 32 hours but the descent was marred by tragedy when four team members crashed to their deaths in a 1200m fall down the North Wall. Visit the museum to see the infamous rope that broke.

ALPIN CENTER
Ski School

(027 966 24 60; www.alpincenter-zermatt.ch; Bahnhofstrasse 58; ⏰8.30am-noon & 3-7pm mid-Nov–Apr & Jul-Sep) Climbs led by mountain guides can be arranged to major 4000ers, including Breithorn (Sfr165), Riffelhorn (Sfr257) and, for experts willing to acclimatise for a week, Matterhorn (Sfr998). The program also covers multiday hikes, glacier hikes to Gorner (Sfr120), snowshoeing (Sfr140) and ice-climbing (Sfr175).

SKIING
Skiing

For skiers and snowboarders, Zermatt is cruising heaven, with mostly long, scenic red runs, plus a scattering of blues for beginners and knuckle-whitening black runs for experts. The three main skiing areas are **Rothorn**, **Stockhorn** (good for mogul fans) and **Klein Matterhorn** (snowboarding freestyle park and half-pipe) – holding 300km of ski runs in all, with free buses shuttling skiers between areas. February to April is peak time. Snow can be sketchy in early summer but lifts are significantly quieter.

A day pass that coves all ski lifts in Zermatt (excluding Cervinia) costs Sfr67/57/34 per adult/student/child. Including Cervinia, the costs are Sfr75/64/38.

Sleeping & Eating

Most places close May to mid-June and from October to mid-November.

HOTEL BAHNHOF
Hotel €€

(📞027 967 24 06; www.hotelbahnhof.com; Bahnhofstrasse; dm/s/d Sfr40/70/110; 🛜) Opposite the station, these spruce budget digs have a lounge, a snazzy open-plan kitchen, and proper beds that are a godsend after scaling or schussing down mountains all day. Free wi-fi.

WHYMPER STUBE
Swiss €€

(📞027 967 22 96; Bahnhofstrasse 80; mains Sfr23-42) The mantra at this alpine classic serving the tastiest fondue in Zermatt (including variations with pears and gorgonzola). Gorge today, climb tomorrow.

BAYARD METZGEREI
Swiss €

(📞027 967 22 66; Bahnhofstrasse 9; sausages from Sfr6; ⏰noon-6.30pm Jul-Sep, from 4pm Dec-Mar) Follow your nose to this butcher's grill for to-go bratwurst, chicken and other carnivorous bites.

Handmade Swiss chocolates, Bern

BRUCE BI/LONELY PLANET IMAGES ©

❶ Information

Tourist office (☎ 027 966 81 00; www.zermatt.
ch; Bahnhofplatz 5; ⊗8.30am-6pm Mon-Sat, to
noon & 1.30-6pm Sun mid-Jun–Sep, 8.30am-noon
& 1.30-6pm Mon-Sat, 9.30am-noon & 4-6pm Sun
Oct–mid-Jun)

❶ Getting There & Around

CAR Zermatt is car-free, and dinky electric
vehicles are used to transport goods and serve
as taxis around town. Drivers have to leave their
vehicles in one of the garages or the open-air car
park in Täsch (Sfr13.50 per day) and take the train
(Sfr7.60, 12 minutes) into Zermatt.

TRAIN Trains depart roughly every 20 minutes
from Brig (Sfr35, 1½ hours), stopping at Visp en
route. Zermatt is also the starting point of the
Glacier Express to Graubünden, one of the most
spectacular train rides in the world.

Bern

POP 123,400

One of the planet's most underrated
capitals, Bern is a fabulous find. With
the genteel old soul of a Renaissance
man and the heart of a high-flying 21st-
century gal, the riverside city is both
medieval and modern. The 15th-century
Old Town is gorgeous enough to sweep
you off your feet and make you forget the
century (it's definitely worthy of its 1983
Unesco World Heritage site protection
order). But the edgy vintage boutiques,
artsy-intellectual bars and Renzo Piano's
futuristic art museum crammed with
Paul Klee pieces slam you firmly back
into the present.

◉ Sights

OLD TOWN   Historic Area

Bern's flag-bedecked medieval centre is
an attraction in its own right, with 6km
of covered arcades, and cellar shops and
bars descending from the streets. After a
devastating fire in 1405, the wooden city
was rebuilt in today's sandstone.

Bern's **Zytglogge** (clock tower) is a
focal point; crowds congregate to watch
its revolving figures twirl at four minutes

before the hour, after which the actual
chimes begin. Tours enter the tower
to see the clock mechanism May to
October; contact the tourist office for
details.

Equally enchanting are the 11
decorative **fountains** (1545) depicting
historical and folkloric characters. Most
are along Marktgasse as it becomes
Kramgasse and Gerechtigkeitsgasse,
but the most famous of these lies in
Kornhausplatz: the **Kindlifresserbrunnen**
(Ogre Fountain), a giant snacking…on
children.

Inside the 15th-century Gothic **Münster**
(cathedral; tower adult/7-16yr Sfr4/2, audioguide
Sfr5; ⊗10am-5pm Tue-Sat, from 11.30am Sun
Easter-Nov, 10am-noon & 2-4pm Tue-Fri, to 5pm
Sat, 11.30am-2pm Sun rest of yr, tower closes
30min earlier), a dizzying hike up the lofty
spire – Switzerland's tallest – is worth the
344-step hike.

PAUL KLEE CENTRE   Art Gallery

(☎ 031 359 01 01; www.zpk.org; Monument in
Fruchtland 3; adult/6-16yr Sfr18/6, audioguides
Sfr5; ⊗10am-5pm Tue-Sun) Bern's Guggenheim, the fabulous Zentrum Paul Klee is
an eye-catching 150m-long building designed by Renzo Piano, 3km east on the
outskirts of town. Inside the three-peak
structure, the middle 'hill' showcases
4000 rotating works from Paul Klee's pro-
digious and often playful career.

Take bus 12 from Bubenbergplatz to
Zentrum Paul Klee (Sfr3.80; sit on the
right for the best views of the city on
your way out there). By car the museum
is right next to the Bern-Ostring exit of
the A6.

EINSTEIN MUSEUM   Museum

(☎ 031 312 00 91; www.einstein-bern.ch; Kramgasse 49; adult/student Sfr6/4.50; ⊗10am-7pm
Mon-Fri, to 4pm Sat Feb-Dec) The world's
most famous scientist developed his
theory of relativity in Bern in 1905. Find
out more at the Einstein Haus, in the
humble apartment where Einstein lived
between 1903 and 1905 while working as
a low-paid clerk in the Bern patent office.
Upstairs, a 20-minute biographical film
tells Einstein's life story.

FREE **HOUSES OF PARLIAMENT** Parliament

(☎031 332 85 22; www.parliament.ch; Bundesplatz; ☺hourly tours 9am-4pm Mon-Sat) The 1902 Bundeshäuser, home of the Swiss Federal Assembly, is impressively ornate, with statues of the nation's founding fathers, a stained-glass dome adorned with cantonal emblems and a huge chandelier. Tours are offered when parliament is in recess; otherwise watch from the public gallery. Bring your passport to get in.

BÄRENGRABEN Bear Park

(www.baerenpark-bern.ch, in German; ☺9.30am-5pm) Bern was founded in 1191 by Berchtold V and named for the unfortunate bear (*bärn* in local dialect) that was his first hunting victim. The bear remains the city's heraldic mascot, hence the bear pits. Since 2009 the bears live in a new, spacious, riverside park. Buy a paper cone of fresh fruit (Sfr3) for the bears but don't feed them anything else.

KUNSTMUSEUM Museum

(☎031 328 09 44; www.kunstmuseumbern.ch, in German; Hodlerstrasse 8-12; adult/student main collection Sfr8/5, temporary exhibitions Sfr8-18; ☺10am-9pm Tue, to 5pm Wed-Sun) The permanent collection at the Museum of Fine Arts includes works by Italian artists such as Fra Angelico, Swiss artists such as Ferdinand Hodler, and works by Picasso and Dalí.

🛏 Sleeping

HOTEL LANDHAUS Hotel €

(☎031 331 41 66; www.landhausbern.ch; Altenbergstrasse 4; dm from Sfr33, d from Sfr160, without bathroom from Sfr120; P☺@🛜) Backed by the grassy slope of a city park and fronted by the river and Old Town spires, this historic hotel oozes character. Its soulful ground-floor **restaurant**, a tad bohemian, draws a staunchly local crowd.

BELLEVUE PALACE Hotel €€€

(☎031 320 45 45; www.bellevue-palace. ch; Kochergasse 3-5; s/d from Sfr360/390; P☺❄@🛜) Bern's power brokers and international statesmen such as Nelson Mandela gravitate towards Bern's only five-star hotel. Near the parliament, it's *the* address to impress. Cheaper weekend rates.

HOTEL BELLE EPOQUE Hotel €€€

(☎031 311 43 36; www.belle-epoque.ch; Gerechtigkeitsgasse 18; s/d from Sfr250/350; ☺@🛜) Standards are so exacting at this romantic hotel with art deco furnishings that modern aberrations are cleverly hidden – such as the TV in the steamer-trunk-style cupboard – so as not to spoil the look.

Eating

Waterside or Old Town, Bern cooks up a delicious choice of dining, handy for all budgets.

LÖTSCHBERG AOC Swiss €€

(☎031 311 34 55; Zeughausgasse 16; mains Sfr14-28) Take an all-Swiss wine and beer list, add cheese specialities from the Valais (including fondue and raclette, of course), decorate the cheerful yellow walls with circular wood wine racks, add chequered tablecloths and you have one of the most dynamic Swiss restaurants in the country.

ALTES TRAMDEPOT Swiss €€

(☎031 368 14 15; Am Bärengraben; mains Sfr16-20; ☺lunch & dinner) Even locals recommend this cavernous microbrewery by the bear pits. Swiss specialities snuggle up to wok-cooked stir-fries, pasta and international dishes on its bistro-styled menu.

KORNHAUSKELLER Swiss €€€

(☎031 327 72 72; Kornhausplatz 18; mains Sfr32-52; ☺lunch & dinner Mon-Sat, dinner Sun) Dress well and dine fine beneath vaulted frescoed arches at Bern's former granary, where beautiful people sip cocktails alongside historic stained-glass on the mezzanine above.

ℹ Information

BernCard (per 24/48/72hr Sfr20/31/38) Discount card providing admission to permanent collections at 27 museums, free public transport and city tour discounts.

Tourist office (📞 031 328 12 12; Bärengraben; ⏱9am-6pm Jun-Sep, 10am-4pm Mar-May & Oct, from 11am Nov-Feb) By the bear pits.

🛈 Getting There & Around

AIR Bern-Belp airport (BRN; 📞 031 960 21 21; www.alpar.ch), 9km southeast of the city centre, is a small airport with direct flights to/from Munich (from where there are onward connections pretty much everywhere). **Airport shuttles** (📞 031 971 28 88, 079 651 70 70) coordinated with flight departures pick up/drop off at the train station (Sfr15, 20 minutes).

TRAIN Hourly trains connect to most Swiss towns, including Geneva (Sfr46, 1¾ hours), Basel (Sfr37, 70 minutes) and Zürich (Sfr46, one hour).

Central Switzerland & Bernese Oberland

The Bernese Oberland should come with a health warning – caution: may cause trembling in the north face of Eiger, uncontrollable bouts of euphoria at the foot of Jungfrau, 007 delusions at Schilthorn and A-list fever in Gstaad. This area is also home to Europe's highest train station, Jungfraujoch, and the serpentine Aletsch Glacier, surrounded by 4000m turrets and an eerie, frosty stillness.

Lucerne

POP 59,500

Recipe for a gorgeous Swiss city: take a cobalt lake ringed by magestic mountains, add a medieval Old Town and sprinkle with a good assortment of covered bridges, sunny plazas, candy-coloured houses and waterfront promenades. Lucerne is bright, beautiful and has been a popular destination since the likes of Goethe, Queen Victoria and Wagner savoured her views in the 19th century.

◉ Sights

OLD TOWN   Historic Area

Your first port of call should be the medieval Old Town, with its ancient rampart walls and towers, 15th-century buildings with painted facades and the much-photographed covered bridges. **Kapellbrücke** (Chapel Bridge), dating from 1333, is Lucerne's best-known landmark. It's famous for its distinctive water tower and the spectacular 1993 fire that nearly destroyed it. Though it has been rebuilt, fire damage is still obvious on the 17th-century pictorial panels under the roof.

SAMMLUNG ROSENGART   Museum

(📞 041 220 16 60; www.rosengart.ch; Pilatusstrasse 10; adult/student Sfr18/16; ⏱10am-6pm Apr-Oct, 11am-5pm Nov-Mar) Lucerne's blockbuster cultural attraction is the Rosengart Collection, occupying a graceful neoclassical pile. It showcases the outstanding stash of Angela Rosengart, a Swiss art dealer and close friend of Picasso. Alongside works by the great Spanish master are paintings and sketches by Cézanne, Klee,

Kapellbrücke (Chapel Bridge), Lucerne
PHOTOGRAPHER: IZZET KERIBAR/LONELY PLANET IMAGES ©

Traditional house in Mürren

ROBERTO GEROMETTA/LONELY PLANET IMAGES ©

Kandinsky, Miró, Matisse and Monet. Standouts include Miró's electric-blue *Dancer II* (1925) and Klee's childlike *X-chen* (1938).

🛏 Sleeping

HOTEL ALPHA   Hotel   €
(📞 041 240 42 80; www.hotelalpha.ch; Zähringerstrasse 24; s/d from Sfr75/110; @ 🛜) Easy on the eye and wallet, this hotel is in a quiet residential area, 10 minutes' walk from the centre. Rooms are simple, light and spotlessly clean.

THE HOTEL   Hotel   €€€
(📞 041 226 86 86; www.the-hotel.ch; Sempacherstrasse 14; ste from Sfr420; ❄ @ 🛜) Streamlined and jet black, 10 ultramodern suites reveal stainless-steel fittings, open-plan bathrooms peeking through to garden foliage, and stills from movie classics, which grace the ceilings at this Jean Nouvel creation. Downstairs **Bam Bou** is one of Lucerne's hippest restaurants.

🍴 Eating & Drinking

RESTAURANT SCHIFF   Swiss   €€
(📞 041 418 52 52; Unter der Egg 8; mains Sfr20-45) Under the waterfront arcades and lit by tea lights at night, this restaurant has bags of charm. For a meal with a local flavour, try fish from Lake Lucerne and some of the city's most celebrated *Chögalipaschtetli* (vol-au-vents stuffed with meat and mushrooms).

SCHÜTZENGARTEN   International   €
(📞 041 240 01 10; Bruchstrasse 20; mains Sfr19-45; 🕐 Mon-Sat; 🍴) As well as a cracking sense of humour, Schützengarten has friendly service, wood-panelled surrounds, appetising vegetarian and vegan dishes, and organic wine. Sit on the vine-strewn terrace in summer.

RATHAUS BRÄUEREI   Pub   €
(📞 041 410 52 57; Unter den Egg 2; 🕐 8am-midnight Mon-Sat, to 11pm Sun) Sip home-brewed beer under the vaulted arches of this buzzy tavern, or nab a pavement table and watch the river flow.

ℹ Getting There & Away

Frequent trains connect Lucerne to Interlaken West (Sfr33.40, two hours, via the scenic Brünig Pass), Bern (Sfr35, 1¾ hours), Lugano (Sfr55, 2¾ hours), Geneva (Sfr72, 3¾ hours, via Olten or Langnau) and Zürich (Sfr23, one hour).

Jungfrau Region

If the Bernese Oberland is Switzerland's alpine heart, the Jungfrau region is where yours will skip a beat. Presided over by glacier-encrusted monoliths Eiger, Mönch and Jungfrau (Ogre, Monk and Virgin), the scenery stirs the soul and strains the neck muscles.

Grindelwald

POP 3815

Once a simple farming village nestled in a valley under the north face of the Eiger, Grindelwald's charms were discovered in the late 19th century, making it one of Switzerland's oldest, and the Jungfrau's largest, resorts. It has lost none of its appeal over the decades, with archetypal alpine chalets and verdant pastures set against an Oscar-worthy backdrop.

Hourly trains link Grindelwald with Interlaken Ost (Sfr10.20, 40 minutes, hourly).

◉ Sights & Activities

OBERER GLETSCHER　　　　　Glacier
(Upper Glacier; adult/child Sfr6/3; ⊙9am-6pm mid-May–Oct) The shimmering, slowly melting Oberer Gletscher is a 1½-hour hike from the village, or catch a bus (marked Terrasen Weg-Oberer Gletscher) to Hotel-Restaurant Wetterhorn. Walk 10 minutes from the bus stop, then pant up 890 log stairs to reach a terrace offering dramatic vistas. A crowd-puller is the vertiginous hanging bridge spanning the gorge.

GLETSCHERSCHLUCHT　　　　Glacier
(Glacier Gorge; admission Sfr7; ⊙10am-5pm May-Oct, to 6pm Jul & Aug) Turbulent waters carve a path through the craggy Gletscherschlucht, a 30-minute walk south of the centre. A footpath weaves through tunnels hacked into cliffs – a popular spot for canyon and bungee-jumping expeditions.

GRINDELWALD-FIRST　　　　Skiing
First is the main skiing area, with runs stretching from **Oberjoch** at 2486m to the village at 1050m. In the summer it caters to **hikers**, with 90km of trails, 48km of which are open year-round.

Catch the longest **cable car** (📞033 854 80 80; www.maennli chen.ch) in Europe from Grindelwald-Grund to Männlichen (single/return Sfr31/Sfr51), where there are more extraordinary views and hikes.

Gimmelwald

POP 118

Decades ago an anonymous backpacker scribbled these words in the Mountain Hostel's guest book: 'If heaven isn't what it's cracked up to be, send me back to Gimmelwald.' Enough said. When the sun is out in Gimmelwald, this pipsqueak of a village will take your breath away. Once a secret bolthole for hikers and adventurers keen to escape the region's worst tourist excesses, Gimmelwald gets a fair whack of foot traffic these days – though even crowds can't diminish its scintillating Swiss scenery and charm.

Surrounding hiking trails include one down from Mürren (30 to 40 minutes) and one up from Stechelberg (1¼ hours). Cable cars are also an option (Mürren or Stechelberg Sfr5.60).

Mürren

POP 438

Arrive on a clear evening when the sun hangs low on the horizon, and you'll think you've died and gone to heaven. Car-free Mürren is storybook Switzerland.

In summer, the **Allmendhubel funicular** (single/return Sfr12/7.40) takes you above Mürren to a panoramic restaurant. From here, you can set out on many walks, including the famous **Northface Trail** (1½ hours) via Schiltalp to the west, with spellbinding views of the Lauterbrunnen Valley and monstrous Eiger north face – bring binoculars to spy intrepid climbers.

Sleeping options include **Eiger Guesthouse** (📞033 856 54 60; www. eigerguesthouse.com; dm Sfr40-70, d Sfr160, without bathroom Sfr120; @), by the train station, with the downstairs pub serving tasty grub; and **Hotel Jungfrau** (📞033 856 64 64; www.hoteljungfrau.ch; s Sfr88-110, d Sfr270-300; @), overlooking the nursery slopes from its perch above Mürren. It dates to 1894 and has a beamed lounge with open fire. Ten out of 10 to much-

BRUCE BI/LONELY PLANET IMAGES ©

lauded chalet **Hotel Alpenruh** (☎033 856 88 00; www.alpenruh-muerren.ch; s/d Sfr145/270; ☕@), for service, food and unbeatable views to Jungfrau massif.

Schilthorn

There's a tremendous 360-degree panorama from the 2970m **Schilthorn** (www.schilthorn.ch). On a clear day, you can see from Titlis to Mont Blanc and across to the German Black Forest.

Buy a Sfr116 excursion trip (Half-Fare Card and Eurail Pass 50% off, Swiss Pass 65% off) to Lauterbrunnen, Grütschalp, Mürren, Schilthorn and returning through Stechelberg to Interlaken. A return from Lauterbrunnen (via Grütschalp) and Mürren costs about Sfr100. Ditto the return journey via the Stechelberg cable car.

Jungfraujoch

The whole world wants to see Jungfraujoch (3471m) and yes, tickets are expensive, but don't let that stop you. It's a once-in-a-lifetime trip and there's a reason why two million people a year visit this Holy Grail, Europe's highest train station. The icy wilderness of swirling glaciers and 4000m turrets that unfolds is truly enchanting.

Clear weather is essential for the trip; check www.jungfrau.ch or call ☎033 828 79 31 and don't forget warm clothing, sunglasses and sunscreen. Up top, when you tire of the view (is this possible?), dash downhill on a snow disc (free), zip across the frozen plateau on a flying fox (Sfr20), enjoy a bit of tame skiing or boarding (Sfr33), drive a team of Greenland dogs or do your best Tiger-Woods-in-moon-boots impersonation with a round of glacier golf. At Sfr10 a shot it isn't cheap, but get a hole-in-one and you win the Sfr100,000 jackpot (which nobody has yet won).

From Interlaken Ost, journey time is 2½ hours each way (Sfr177.80 return, Swiss Pass/Eurail Sfr133).

Zürich

POP 365,400

Zürich used to be Europe's best-kept secret. Conservative bankers and perfect, medieval landmarks stood at the forefront, with no hint that a city as cool and hip as Berlin or Amsterdam lurked within this financial centre's impeccably clean streets. But somewhere between ranking as the top city in the world for quality of life seven

DISCOVER AUSTRIA, SWITZERLAND & THE CZECH REPUBLIC ZÜRICH

years running, hosting Europe's largest street party and erecting a flagship store made entirely of 16 stacked shipping containers, the secret got out and the international press started writing about the real Zürich: a cool, stylish and surprising city.

Sights

OLD TOWN
Historic Area

Explore the cobbled streets of the pedestrian Old Town lining both sides of the river.

The bank vaults beneath **Bahnhofstrasse**, the city's most elegant street, are said to be crammed with gold and silver.

On Sundays all of Zürich strolls around the lake – the locals are on to something, and one short meander tells you why. It's simply sublime and relaxing; on a clear day, you'll even glimpse the Alps in the distance.

FRAUMÜNSTER
Church

(cathedral; www.frau muenster.ch; Münsterplatz; ⏰9am-6pm May-Sep, 10am-5pm Oct-Apr) On the west bank of the Limmat River, the 13th-century Fraumünster is Zürich's most noteworthy attraction: it has some of the most distinctive and attractive stained-glass windows in the world.

GROSSMÜNSTER
Church

(Grossmünsterplatz; www.grossmuenster.ch; ⏰9am-6pm midMar–Oct, 10am-5pm Nov–midMar, tower closed Sun morning midMar–Oct & Sun Nov–midMar) Across the river, the dual-towered Grossmünster was where, in the 16th century, the Protestant preacher Huldrych Zwingli first spread his message of 'pray and work' during the Reformation – a seminal period in Zürich's history.

ST PETERSKIRCHE
Church

(St Peter's Church; St Peterhofstatt; ⏰8am-6pm Mon-Fri, to 4pm Sat, 11am-5pm Sun) From any position in the city, it's impossible to overlook the 13th-century tower of St Peterskirche. Its prominent clock face, 8.7m in diameter, is Europe's largest.

KUNSTHAUS
Art Gallery

(☏044 253 84 84; www.kunsthaus.ch; Heimplatz 1; adult/student/child Sfr18/8/free, Sun free; ⏰10am-8pm Wed-Fri, to 6pm Tue & Sat & Sun) Zürich's impressive Fine Arts Museum boasts a rich collection of Alberto Giacometti sculptures, Monets, Van Goghs, Rodin sculptures and other 19th- and 20th-century works of art. Swiss artist Ferdinand Hodler is also represented.

Activities

Zürich comes into its own in summer, when its green lakeshore parks buzz with bathers, sun-seekers, in-line skaters, footballers, lovers, picnickers, party animals, preeners and police patrolling on rollerblades!

Schilthorn cable car

Zürich

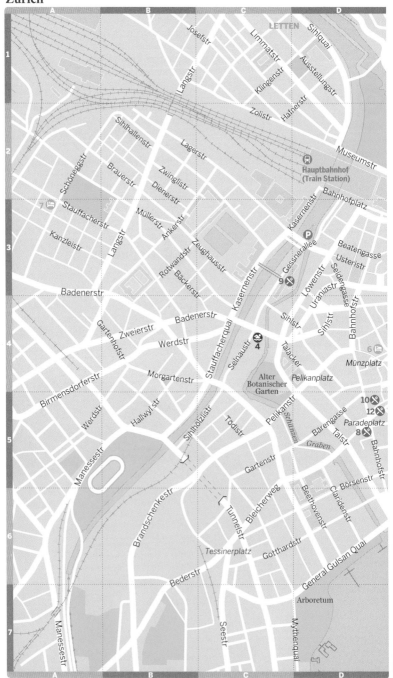

Zürich

SWIMMING AREAS   Swimming
(admission Sfr6; ⊙9am-7pm May & Sep, to 8pm
Jun-Aug) From May to mid-September,
outdoor swimming areas – think a rectangular wooden pier partly covered by
a pavilion – open around the lake and up
the Limmat River.

   Along the river, 19th-century
Frauenbad (Stadthausquai) is open
to women only during the day, and
Männerbad (Schanzengraben) is men-only.
Both open their trendy bars to both sexes
at night – leave shoes at the entrance and
drink with feet dipped in the water.

Sleeping

PENSION FÜR DICH   Pension €€
(☎044 317 91 60; www.fuerdich.ch; Stauffauch-
erstrasse 141; d without bathroom from Sfr95;
⊖ 🔊) These simple but fabulous apartments have been converted into comfy
rooms – think retro furnishings meets Ikea.
A number of rooms have balconies, and
breakfast can be had for a steal at its cafe
downstairs, plus you're smack in the centre
of the Kreis 4 nightlife action. There's no
reception – just head to the bar in the cafe.

HOTEL WIDDER Hotel €€€
(☎ 044 224 25 26; www.widderhotel.ch; Rennweg 7; s/d from Sfr530/725; P ✳ @ 🛜)
A stylish hotel in the equally grand Augustiner district, the Widder is a pleasing fusion of modernity and traditional charm. Rooms and public areas across the eight town houses that make up this place are stuffed with art and designer furniture.

HOTEL DU THÈÂTRE Hotel €€
(☎ 044-2672670; www.hotel-du-theatre.ch; Seilergraben 69; s/d from Sfr100/110; 🛜) Located in the lively Niederdorf and within walking distance of the train station, this friendly boutique hotel is decorated with designer furniture and old film stills. These are an ode to the hotel's past – in the 1950s it operated as a combined theatre and hotel.

 # Eating

Zürich has a thriving cafe culture and hundreds of restaurants – explore Niederdorfstrasse and its nearby backstreets.

ZEUGHAUSKELLER Beer Hall €€
(☎ 044 211 26 90; www.zeughauskeller.ch; Bahnhofstrasse 28a; mains Sfr18-35; ⏱ 11.30am-11pm; 🖈) The menu at this huge, atmospheric beer hall – set inside a former armoury (look for the shields and various protective antiques hanging from the walls) – offers 20 different kinds of sausages in eight languages, as well as numerous other Swiss specialities of a carnivorous and vegetarian variety.

RESTAURANT ZUM KROPF Swiss €€
(☎ 044 221 18 05; www.zum kropf.ch; In Gassen 16; mains Sfr23-48; ⏱ closed Sun) Notable for its historic interior, with marble columns, stained glass and ceiling murals, Kropf has been favoured by locals since 1888 for its hearty Swiss staples and fine beers.

REITHALLE International €€
(☎ 044 212 07 66; www.restaurant-reithalle.ch; Gessnerallee 8; mains Sfr22-35; ⏱ lunch & dinner Mon-Fri, dinner Sat & Sun) Fancy dining in the stables of a former barracks complex? The walls at this boisterous, convivial spot are still lined with the cavalry horses' feeding and drinking troughs. Cuisine is Swiss and international, and tables are cleared at 11.30pm, when the place metamorphoses into a dance club.

CAFÉ SPRÜNGLI Swiss €
(☎ 044 224 47 31; www.spruengli.ch; Bahnhofstrasse 21; mains Sfr9-15; ⏱ 7am-6.30pm Mon-Fri, 8am-6pm Sat, 9.30am-5.30pm Sun) Indulge in cakes, chocolate and coffee at this epicentre of sweet Switzerland, in business since 1836.

STERNEN GRILL Sausage Stand €
(Theatrestrasse 22; snacks from Sfr6; ⏱ 11.30am-midnight) This is the city's most famous – and busiest – sausage stand; just follow the crowds streaming into Bellevueplatz for a tasty greasefest.

Drinking & Entertainment

Buzzing drinking options congregate in the happening Kreis 4 district (the former red-light district known as the Langstrasse area – it's safe to wander though you may be offered drugs or sex – with loads of popular bars quietly humming off its side streets) and Kreis 5 districts, together known as Züri-West. Mid-May to mid-September, Wednesday to Sunday, the trendy water bars at the **lake baths** are hot places to hang barefooted.

ⓘ Information

Zürich Tourism (☎ 044 215 40 00, hotel reservations 044 215 40 40; www.zuerich.com; train station; ⏱ 8am-8.30pm Mon-Sat, 8.30am-6.30pm Sun May-Oct, 8.30am-7pm Mon-Sat, 9am-6.30pm Sun Nov-Apr)

ZürichCard (per 24/72hr Sfr17/24) Discount card available from the tourist office and airport train station; provides free public transport, free museum admission and more.

ℹ️ Getting There & Away

AIR Zürich airport (ZRH; ☎ 043 816 22 11; www.zurich-airport.com), 10km north of the centre, is a small international hub with two terminals.

CAR The A3 approaches Zürich from the south along the shore of Lake Zürich. The A1 is the fastest route from Bern and Basel.

TRAIN Direct daily trains run to Stuttgart (Sfr76, three hours), Munich (Sfr104, 4½ hours) and Innsbruck (Sfr79, four hours), plus many other international destinations. There are regular direct departures to most major Swiss towns, such as Lucerne (Sfr23, 46 to 50 minutes), Bern (Sfr46, 57 minutes) and Basel (Sfr31, 55 minutes).

ℹ️ Getting Around

TO/FROM THE AIRPORT Up to nine trains an hour yo-yo between the airport and main train station between 6am and midnight (Sfr6, nine to 14 minutes).

PUBLIC TRANSPORT There is a comprehensive unified bus, tram and S-Bahn service in the city, which includes boats plying the Limmat River. Short trips under five stops are Sfr2.40. A 24-hour pass for the centre is Sfr7.80.

Northern Switzerland

This region is left off most people's Switzerland itineraries – precisely why you should visit! Sure, it's known for industry and commerce, but it also has some great attractions. Breathe in the sweet (OK slightly stinky) odours of black-and-white cows as you roll through the bucolic countryside. Take time to explore the tiny rural towns set among green rolling hills, and on Lake Constance (Bodensee) and the Rhine River on the German border.

Graubünden

Don't be fooled by Graubünden's diminutive size on a map. This is topographic origami at its finest. Unfold the rippled landscape to find an outdoor adventurer's paradise riddled with more than 11,000km of walking trails, 600-plus lakes and 1500km of downhill ski slopes – including super swanky St Moritz and backpacker mecca Flims-Laax. Linguistically wired to flick from Italian to German to Romansch, locals keep you guessing too.

Flims-Laax

They say if the snow ain't falling anywhere else, you'll surely find some around Flims-Laax. These towns, along with tiny Falera, 20km west of Chur, form a single ski area known as the **Weisses Arena** (White Arena), with 220km of slopes catering for all levels. Laax in particular is a mecca for snowboarders, who spice up the local nightlife too. The resort is barely two hours by train and bus (less by car) from Zürich airport.

The ski slopes range as high as 3000m and are mostly intermediate or easy, although there are some 45km of more challenging runs. A one-day ski pass includes ski buses and costs Sfr62 (plus Sfr5 for the KeyCard that you use to access the lifts).

Chalets in Graubünden
PHOTOGRAPHER: BRUCE BI/LONELY PLANET IMAGES ©

St Moritz

POP 5070

Switzerland's original winter wonderland and the cradle of Alpine tourism, St Moritz (San Murezzan in Romansch) has been luring royals, the filthy rich and moneyed wannabes since 1864. With its smugly perfect lake and aloof mountains, the town looks a million dollars.

Skiers and snowboarders will revel in the 350km of runs in three key areas. For groomed slopes with big mountain vistas, head to Corviglia (2486m), accessible by funicular from Dorf. From Bad a cable car goes to Signal (shorter queues), giving access to the slopes of Piz Nair. A ski pass for both areas costs Sfr67 (child/youth Sfr23/45) for one day.

Silhouetted by glaciated 4000ers, Diavolezza (2978m) is a must-ski for free-riders and fans of jaw-dropping descents.

Sleeping & Eating

CHESA CHANTARELLA Hotel €€

(☎ 081 833 33 55; www.chesachantarella.ch; Via Salastrains; s/d from Sfr120/210; ☺ Jun-Sep & Dec-Apr; P) Sitting above the town, this is a lively choice with bright, modern rooms. Sip hot chocolate on the terrace, venture down to the wine cellar or dine on hearty local fare in the restaurant.

HATECKE Swiss €€

(☎ 081 864 11 75; www.hatecke.ch; snacks & mains Sfr16-28; ☺ 9am-6.30pm Mon-Fri, to 6pm Sat) Edible art is the only way to describe the organic, locally sourced delicacies at Hatecke. *Bündnerfleisch* and venison ham are carved into wafer-thin slices on a century-old slicing machine in the speciality shop. Sit on a sheepskin stool in the funky cafe next door to lunch on delicious Engadine beef carpaccio or *Bündnerfleisch* with truffle oil.

ENGIADINA Swiss €€

(☎ 081 833 32 65; Plazza da Scuola 2; fondue Sfr29-46; ☺ Mon-Sat) A proper locals' place, Engiadina is famous for fondue, and that's the best thing to eat here. Champagne gives the melted cheese a kick. It's open year-round.

ⓘ Information

Tourist office (☎ 081 837 33 33; www.stmoritz. ch; Via Maistra 12; ☺ 9am-6.30pm Mon-Fri, to noon & 1.30-6pm Sat, 4-6pm Sun Dec-Easter & mid-Jun–mid-Sep, 9am-noon & 2-6pm Mon-Fri, to noon Sat rest of yr)

ⓘ Getting There & Away

The **Glacier Express** (www.glacierexpress.ch) plies one of Switzerland's most famous scenic train routes, connecting St Moritz to Zermatt (Sfr138 plus Sfr15 or Sfr30 reservation fee in summer, 7½ hours, daily) via the 2033m Oberalp Pass. It covers 290km and crosses 291 bridges. Novelty drink glasses in the dining car have sloping bases to compensate for the hills – remember to keep turning them around!

Swiss National Park

The road west from Müstair stretches 34km over the Ofenpass (Pass dal Fuorn, 2149m), through the thick woods of Switzerland's only **national park** (www. nationalpark.ch; ☺ Jun-Oct) and on to **Zernez** and the hands-on **Swiss National Park Centre** (☎ 081 851 41 41; www.nationalpark. ch; adult/child Sfr7/3; ☺ 8.30am-6pm Jun-Oct, 9am-noon & 2-5pm Nov-May), where you can explore a marmot hole, eyeball adders in the vivarium and learn about conservation and environmental change.

The national park was established in 1914 – the first such park in Europe – and spans 172 sq km.

Entry to the park and its car parks is free. Walkers can enter by trails from Zernez, S-chanf and Scuol. Conservation is paramount here, so stick to footpaths and respect regulations prohibiting camping, littering, lighting fires, cycling, picking flowers and disturbing the animals.

THE CZECH REPUBLIC

More than two decades after the fall of the Berlin Wall, a host of European cities and countries have been touted as the 'new Prague' or the 'next Czech Republic'. The 'where to next?' focus may have shifted to other destinations, but the original Prague and Czech Republic remain essential stops on any European sojourn.

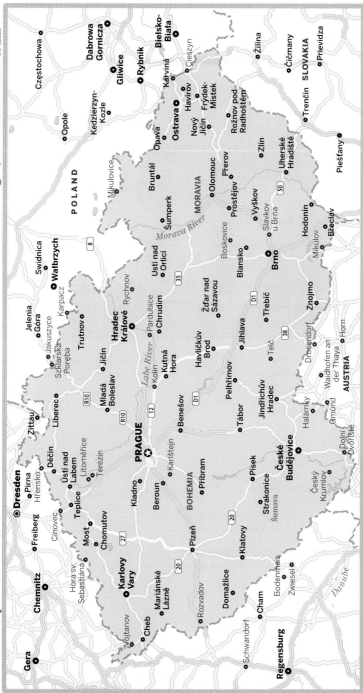

DISCOVER AUSTRIA, SWITZERLAND & THE CZECH REPUBLIC THE CZECH REPUBLIC

Prague's inevitable transition from communist capital to modern metropolis is now complete, as centuries of history and glorious architecture compete with thoroughly 21st-century energy and impetus.

Prague

POP 1.22 MILLION

It's the perfect irony of Prague: you are lured to the city by the past, but compelled to linger by the present and the future. Fill your days with its artistic and architectural heritage – from Gothic and Renaissance to art nouveau and cubist – but after dark move your focus to the lively restaurants, bars and clubs in emerging neighbourhoods like Vinohrady and Žižkov.

And if Prague's seasonal legions of tourists wear you down, that's OK. Just drink a glass of the country's legendary lager, relax and be reassured that quiet moments still exist: a private dawn on Charles Bridge, a chilled beer in Letná as you gaze upon the glorious cityscape of

Staré Město, or getting reassuringly lost in the intimate lanes of Malá Strana or Josefov.

◉ Sights

Central Prague nestles on the Vltava River, separating Hradčany (the medieval castle district) and Malá Strana (Little Quarter) on the west bank, from Staré Město (Old Town) and Nové Město (New Town) on the east.

Prague Castle overlooks Malá Strana, while the twin Gothic spires of Týn Church dominate Old Town Sq (Staroměstské nám). The broad avenue of Wenceslas Sq (Václavské nám) stretches southeast from Staré Město towards the National Museum and main train station.

Staré Město

OLD TOWN SQUARE　　　Historic Area
(Staroměstské nám; M Staroměstská)
Kick off in Prague's Old Town Square (Staroměstské nám), dominated by the

Left: Týn Church in Staroměstské nám (Old Town Square), Staré Město;
Below: Astronomical Clock on the Old Town Hall

PHOTOGRAPHERS: (LEFT) RICHARD NEBESKY/LONELY PLANET IMAGES ©;
(BELOW) JONATHAN SMITH/LONELY PLANET IMAGES ©

twin Gothic steeples of **Týn Church** (1365), the baroque **Church of St Nicholas** (Kostel sv Mikuláše) and the **Old Town Hall clock tower** (adult/child 70/50Kč; 11am-6pm Mon, 9am-6pm Tue-Sun). From the top spy on the crowds below watching the **astronomical clock** (1410), which springs to life every hour with assorted apostles and a bell-ringing skeleton. In the square's centre is the **Jan Hus Monument**, erected in 1915 on the 500th anniversary of the religious reformer's execution.

PRAGUE JEWISH MUSEUM   Museum
(221 711 511; www.jewishmuseum.cz; Ticket Reservation Centre, U Starého hřbitova 3a; adult/child 300/200Kč; 9am-6pm Sun-Fri Apr-Oct, to 4.30pm Nov-Mar; M Staroměstská) North and northwest of the Old Town Square, **Josefov** was Prague's Jewish Quarter. Six monuments form the Prague Jewish Museum. The museum's collection exists only because in 1942 the Nazis gathered objects from 153 Jewish communities in Bohemia and Moravia, planning to establish a 'museum of an extinct race' after completing their extermination program.

The **Klaus Synagogue** (U Starého hřbitova 1) exhibits Jewish customs and traditions, and the **Pinkas Synagogue** (Široká 3) is a memorial to the Holocaust. Its walls are inscribed with the names of 77,297 Czech Jews, including Franz Kafka's three sisters. A few blocks northeast is the **Spanish Synagogue** (Spanélská Synagóga; Dušní 12), built in a Moorish style in 1868.

The oldest still-functioning synagogue in Europe, the early Gothic **Old-New Synagogue** (Červená 1; adult/child 200/140Kč; 9.30am-5pm Sun-Thu, 9am-4pm Fri), dates from 1270. Opposite is the **Jewish town hall** (Židovská radnice; closed to the public) with its picturesque 16th-century clock tower. A combined ticket (adult/child 480/320Kč) is available for entry to the six sites of the Prague Jewish Museum and the Old-New Synagogue.

Central Prague

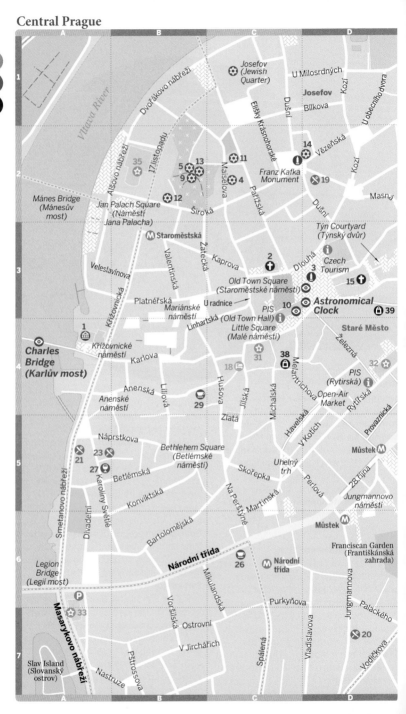

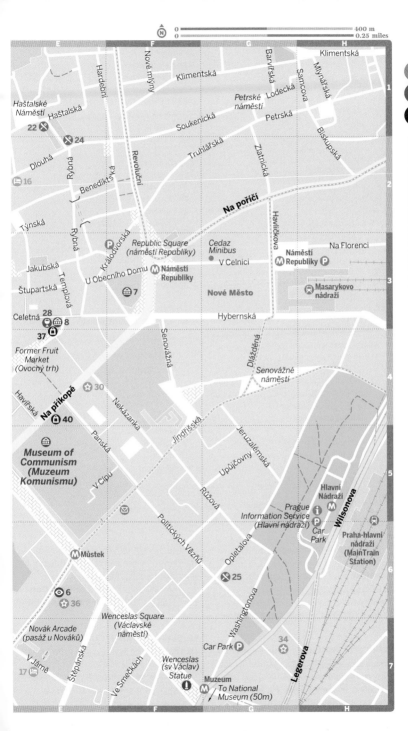

N

0 — 400 m
0 — 0.25 miles

Klimentská

Nové mlýny

Klimentská

Baňvířská

Lodecká

Samcova

Mlynářská

Haštalské
Náměstí Haštalská

Petrské
náměstí

Petrská

Biskupská

22 ✗

✗ 24

Soukenická

Dlouhá

Rybná

Benedikská

Truhlářská

Revoluční

Zlatnická

Na poříčí

Havlíčkova

16

Týnská

Rybná

Králodvorská

Republic Square
(náměstí Republiky)

Cedaz
Minibus

V Celnici

Na Florenci

Jakubská

Štupartská

Templová

U Obecního Domu M Náměstí
Republiky

Náměstí
M Republiky P

Masarykovo
nádraží

Celetná 28

7

Nové Město

8

Hybernská

37

Senovážná

Dlážděná

Former Fruit
Market
(Ovocný trh)

Senovážné
náměstí

30

Na příkopě

Nekázanka

Jindřišská

Jeruzalémská

Havířská

40

Panská

Upůjčovny

Museum of
Communism
(Muzeum
Komunismu)

V Cípu

Růžová

Hlavní
Nádraží M

Wilsonova

Prague
Information Service
(Hlavní nádraží)

Car
Park

Praha-hlavní
nádraží
(MainTrain
Station)

M Můstek

Politických Vězňů

Opletalova

Washingtonova

✗ 25

6

36

Novák Arcade
(pasáž u Nováků)

Štěpánská

Wenceslas Square
(Václavské
náměstí)

Car Park P

34

Legerova

17

V Jámě

Ve Smečkách

Wenceslas
(sv Václav)
Statue

Muzeum
M

To National
Museum (50m)

697

Central Prague

The **Old Jewish Cemetery**, entered from the Pinkas Synagogue, is Josefov's most evocative corner. The oldest of its 12,000 graves date from 1439. Use of the cemetery ceased in 1787 as it was becoming so crowded that burials were up to 12 layers deep.

MUNICIPAL HOUSE   Historic Building
(Obecní dům; www.obecni-dum.cz; nám Republiky 5; day tours adult/child 270/220Kč; night tours 310/260Kč; ◷10am-9.30pm; Ⓜ nám Republiky) The shopping street of Celetná leads

east to the art nouveau Municipal House, decorated by the early 20th century's finest Czech artists. Included in the guided tour are the impressive **Smetana Concert Hall** and other beautifully decorated rooms.

MUSEUM OF CZECH CUBISM   Museum
(Muzeum Českého Kubismu; www.ngprague.cz; Ovocný trh 19; adult/child 100/50Kč; ◷10am-6pm Tue-Sun; Ⓜ nám Republiky) Located in Josef Gočár's House of the Black Madonna, the angular collection of art

Prague in Two Days

Beat the tourist hordes with an early-morning stroll across **Charles Bridge**, and continue uphill on Nerudova to Hradčany and the glories of **Prague Castle**. Don't miss also seeing the superb 'Princely Collections' at the **Lobkowicz Palace**. Head back down to the **Franz Kafka Museum** and cross the river again to the **Charles Bridge Museum**.

On day two, explore **Josefov** – Prague's original Jewish quarter – and then pack a hilltop picnic for the view-friendly fortress at **Vyšehrad**. Make time for a few Czech brews at the excellent **Pivovarský Klub**, before sampling robust Czech food at **U Ferdinanda**, or tapas and seafood at **U malé velryby.** For a nightcap head to a cool late-night spot like **Duende**.

and furniture is yet another branch of Prague's National Gallery. On the ground floor is the excellent Grand Cafe Orient.

Nové Město & Vyšehrad

WENCESLAS SQUARE Historic Area
(Václavské nám; MMůstek) Dating from 1348, Nové Město (New Town) is only 'new' when compared with the older Staré Město. The sloping avenue of Wenceslas Sq, lined with shops, banks and restaurants, is dominated by a **statue of St Wenceslas** on horseback. Wenceslas Sq has always been a focus for demonstrations and public gatherings. Beneath the statue is a shrine to the victims of communism, including students Jan Palach and Jan Zajíc, who burned themselves alive in 1969 in protest against the Soviet invasion.

NATIONAL MUSEUM Museum
(www.nm.cz; Václavské nám 68; adult/child 150/50Kč, free admission 1st Thu of month; ⊙10am-6pm, closed 1st Tue of month; MMuzeum) The imposing National Museum has ho-hum collections covering prehistory, mineralogy and stuffed animals, but the grand interior is worth seeing for the pantheon of Czech historical luminaries. In 2010, a new annex showcasing special exhibitions opened across the street in a building that has been used – at different times – as the Prague Stock Exchange, the Czechoslovak Parliament and the studios of Radio Free Europe. Guided tours

of this building run at 10am and 1pm on Wednesdays. In 2011 the main building of the museum is scheduled to close for five years for major renovations. Ask at the Prague Information Service for the latest news.

CHARLES BRIDGE MUSEUM Museum
(www.muzeumkarlovamostu.cz; Křížovnické nám; adult/child 150/70Kč; ⊙10am-8pm, to 6pm Oct-Apr; ⊞17, 18 to Karlovy lázě) Before or after strolling across Charles Bridge, examine the history of the Vltava's most famous crossing with displays on ancient bridge-building techniques, masonry and carpentry.

FREE **VYŠEHRAD** Fort
(www.praha-vysehrad.cz; ⊙9.30am-6pm Apr-Oct, to 5pm Nov-Mar; MVyšehrad) Pack a picnic and head to the ancient clifftop fortress Vyšehrad, perched above the Vltava. Dominated by the towers of **Church of SS Peter & Paul** (Kostel sv Petra a Pavla) and founded in the 11th century, Vyšehrad was rebuilt in the neo-Gothic style between 1885 and 1903. The adjacent **Slavín Cemetery** contains the graves of many Czechs, including the composers Smetana and Dvořák. The view from the citadel's southern battlements is superb.

CITY OF PRAGUE MUSEUM Museum
(www.muzeumprahy.cz; Na Poříčí 52, Karlín; adult/child 120/50Kč; ⊙9am-6pm Tue-Sun; MFlorenc) This museum, housed in a

The Challenging Mr Černý

David Černý's work polarises people. In Prague's Lucerna pasáž, he's hung St Wenceslas and his horse upside down, and across the river outside the Kafka Museum, Černý's *Piss* sculpture invites contributions by SMS. Rising above the city, like a faded relic from *Star Wars,* is the Žižkov Tower with Černý's giant babies crawling up the exterior.

Černý's other recent project is MeetFactory (www.meetfactory.cz) a multipurpose gallery, artists' collective and performance space in a former railways workshop across the river in Smíchov.

grand, neo-Renaissance building near Florenc metro station, charts Prague's evolution from prehistory to the 19th century.

LUCERNA PASÁŽ   Historic Building
(Lucerna Passage; Ⓜ Můstek) Just off Wenceslas Sq, the Lucerna pasáž is an art nouveau shopping arcade. It's now graced with David Černý's *Horse* sculpture.

MUSEUM OF COMMUNISM   Museum
(www.muzeumkomunismu.cz; Na příkopě 10; adult/child 180/140Kč; ⊗9am-9pm; Ⓜ Můstek) The Museum of Communism is tucked (ironically) behind McDonald's. The exhibition is fascinating through its use of simple everyday objects to illuminate the restrictions of life under communism. Be sure to watch the video about protests leading up to the Velvet Revolution. You'll never think of it as a pushover again.

Hradčany

The Hradčany area west from Prague Castle is mainly residential, with shops and restaurants on Loretánská and Pohořelec. In 1598 Hradčany was almost levelled by Hussites and fire, and the 17th-century palaces were built on the ruins.

PRAGUE CASTLE   Castle
(Pražský hrad; www.hrad.cz; ⊗castle 9am-6pm Apr-Oct, to 4pm Nov-Mar, grounds 5am-midnight Apr-Oct, 9am-11pm Nov-Mar, gardens closed Nov-Mar; 🚃22, 23 to Pražský hrad). The biggest castle complex in the world, Prague Castle is the seat of Czech power, housing the president's office and the ancient Bohemian crown jewels.

The **long tour** (adult/child 350/175Kč) includes the Old Royal Palace, the Story of Prague Castle exhibit, the Basilica of St George, St Vitus Cathedral, the Convent of St George, the Prague Castle Picture Gallery, and Golden Lane with Daliborka Tower. The **short tour** (adult/child 250/125Kč) focuses only on the Old Royal Palace, St Vitus Cathedral, the Basilica of St George, Golden Lane and the Story of Prague Castle exhibit. Buy tickets at the **Castle Information Centre** in the Second Courtyard. Most areas are wheelchair accessible. Count on about three hours for the long tour and two hours for the short tour. Tickets are valid for two days, but you can only visit each attraction once. DIY audio guides can also be rented. Entry to the castle courtyards and the gardens is free.

The main entrance is at the western end. The **changing of the guard**, with stylish uniforms created by Theodor Pistek (costume designer for the film *Amadeus*), takes place every hour, on the hour.

The **Matthias Gate** (Matyášova Brána) leads to the Second Courtyard and the **Chapel of the Holy Cross** (Kaple sv Kríže). On the north side is the **Prague Castle Picture Gallery** (adult/child 150/80Kč, admission free 4-6pm Mon; ⊗9am-5pm Apr-Oct, to 4pm Nov-Mar), with a collection of European baroque art.

The Third Courtyard is dominated by **St Vitus Cathedral** (Katedrala sv Víta; included on long and short tours), a French Gothic structure begun in 1344 by Emperor Charles IV, but not completed until 1929. Stained-glass windows created by early-20th-century Czech artists illuminate the interior, including one by Alfons Mucha (third chapel on the left as you enter the cathedral) featuring SS Cyril and Methodius.

The 14th-century chapel on the cathedral's southern side with the black imperial eagle on the door contains the **tomb of St Wenceslas**, the Czechs' patron saint and the Good King Wenceslas of Christmas–carol fame.

On the southern side of the cathedral's exterior is the **Golden Gate** (Zlatá brána), a triple-arched doorway topped by a 14th-century mosaic of the Last Judgment.

Also on the southern side is the **Story of Prague Castle** (www.story-castle.cz; adult/child 140/70Kč, free with short and long tour tickets) exhibition. This multimedia take on history includes a 40-minute **documentary** (⊙in English 9.45am, 11.14am, 12.45pm, 2.15pm & 3.45pm).

Opposite is the entrance to the **Old Royal Palace** (Starý Královský Palác) with its elegantly vaulted **Vladislav Hall** (1486–1502). Horsemen used to ride into the hall up the ramp at the far end for indoor jousts.

Beyond, the crowds surge into the **Golden Lane**, a 16th-century tradesmen's quarter of tiny houses in the castle walls. Kafka lived and wrote at his sister's place at No 22 in 1916 and 1917.

On the right, before the castle's exit, is the **Lobkowicz Palace** (www.lobkowiczevents.cz/palace; Jiřská 3; adult/concession 275/175Kč; ⊙10.30am-6pm). Built in the 1570s, this palace was home to the aristocratic Lobkowicz family until WWII when it was co-opted by the Nazis. The communists confiscated it in 1948, and it was only returned to the family in 2002. Now it is a private museum focused on the **Princely Collections**, with highlights including paintings by Canaletto and original sheet music by Mozart, Beethoven and Hadyn.

From the castle's eastern end, the Old Castle Steps lead to Malostranská metro station, or turn sharp right to wind through the **Garden on the Ramparts**.

Prague Castle, Charles Bridge (p703) and Malá Strana

Prague Castle

200 m
0.1 miles

Daliborka Tower

Entrance to Castle

Black Tower

Golden Lane (Zlatá Ulička)

Palace Gardens Beneath Prague Castle (Palácové Zahrady pod Pražským Hradem)

2

White Tower (Bílaá Věž)

George St (Jiřská)

Valdštejnská

7

Stag Moat (Jelení příkop)

Wallenstein Garden (Valdštejnská zahrada)

Malá Strana

To Summer Palace (250m)

All Saints' Chapel (Kaple Všech Svatých)

St George Square (Jiřské náměstí)

Wallenstein Square (Valdštejnské náměstí)

Tomášská

Sněmovní

Brusnice

St Vitus Cathedral (Katedrala sv Víta)

Gardens on the Ramparts (Zahrada Na Valech)

Royal Garden (Královská zahrada)

Mihulka (Powder Tower)

5

4

6

Ludwik Wing

Thunovská

To Pražský Hrad Tram Stop (50m)

Powder Bridge (Prašná most) Tunnel

Plečnik Monolith

1

Third Courtyard

Castle Steps (Zámecké schody)

U Prašného mostu

Imperial Stable

i

1

Second Courtyard Passage

Hradčany

Zahrada Na Baště

i

3

First Courtyard

Prague Castle Entrance

Archbishop's Palace (Arcibiskupský Palác)

Hradčany Square (Hradčanské náměstí)

Prague Castle

There are two main routes to the castle. You can catch the metro to Malostranská or tram 12, 20, 22 or 23 to Malostranská nám and look forward to a brisk walk up Nerudova. Alternatively take tram 22 or 23 to the Pražský hrad stop, where you can enter at the Second Courtyard.

ŠTERNBERG PALACE　　Art Gallery
(www.ngprague.cz; adult/child 150/80Kč; ⊙10am-6pm Tue-Sun; ◻22, 23 to Pražský hrad) The 18th-century Šternberg Palace outside the castle entrance houses the National Gallery with the country's principal collection of 14th- to 18th-century European art.

Malá Strana

Downhill from the castle are the baroque backstreets of Malá Strana (Little Quarter), built in the 17th and 18th centuries by victorious Catholic clerics and nobles on the foundations of their Protestant predecessors' Renaissance palaces.

CHARLES BRIDGE　　Bridge
(◻17, 18 to Karlovy lázně) Malá Strana is linked to Staré Město by Charles Bridge. Built in 1357, and graced by thirty 18th-century statues, it was the city's only bridge until 1841. Climb the **Malá Strana bridge tower** (adult/child 50/30Kč; ⊙10am-6pm Apr-Nov) for excellent views. In the middle of the bridge is a bronze statue (1683) of St John of Nepomuk, a priest thrown to his death from the bridge in 1393 for refusing to reveal the queen's confessions to King Wenceslas IV. Visit the bridge at dawn before the tourist hordes arrive. Gangs of pickpockets work the bridge day and night, so watch your valuables.

ST NICHOLAS CHURCH　　Church
(www.psalterium.cz; adult/child 70/35Kč; ⊙9am-5pm Mar-Oct, to 4pm Nov-Feb; ◻12, 20, 22, 23 to Malostranské nam) Near the cafe-crowded main square of Malostranské nám is the beautiful baroque St Nicholas Church. Take the stairs to the gallery to see the 17th-century *Passion Cycle* paintings. From April to October the church is used for **classical music concerts** (adult/child 490/300Kč; ⊙6pm Wed-Mon).

FREE **WALLENSTEIN PALACE**　　Palace
(⊙10am-4pm Sat & Sun; ◻12, 20, 22, 23 to Malostranské nam) East along Tomášská is the Wallenstein Palace, built in 1630 and now home to the Czech Republic's Senate. The adjacent **Wallenstein Gardens** boast a Renaissance loggia and bronze (replica) sculptures.

FRANZ KAFKA MUSEUM　　Museum
(www.kafkamuseum.cz; Cihelná 2b; adult/child 120/60Kč; ⊙10am-6pm; Ⓜ Malostranská) North of Charles Bridge is the innovative and arty Franz Kafka Museum. Kafka's diaries, letters and first editions provide a poignant balance to the T-shirt cliché the writer has become in tourist shops. In front is the **Piss sculpture** by Czech artist David Černý with two animatronic figures piddling in a puddle shaped like the Czech Republic.

FUNICULAR RAILWAY　　Landmark
(tram ticket 26Kč; ⊙every 10-20 min 9.15am-8.45pm; ◻12, 20, 22, 23 to Újezd) Escape the tourist throngs on the cable car from Újezd to the rose gardens on **Petřín Hill**. Ascend 299 steps to the top of the view-friendly iron-framed **Petřín Lookout Tower** (adult/child 100/50Kč, lift 50Kč extra; ⊙10am-10pm May-Sep, to 7pm Apr & Oct, to 5pm Sat & Sun Nov-Mar), built in 1891 in imitation of the Eiffel Tower. Behind the tower, a staircase leads to lanes winding back to Malostranské nám.

If You Like...
Czech Architecture

Prague (p694) and **Český Krumlov** (p716) are justly famous for their architecture, but if you're allergic to crowds you might want to discover some of the Czech Republic's lesser-known gems.

1 OLOMOUC
With an Old Town to rival Prague, a wealth of religious structures and the nation's finest ecclesiastical museums, Olomouc is a wonderful place to experience the real Czech Republic. Better still, with tourist numbers at a trickle, you'll be able to soak up the sights away from the crowds. There are frequent trains from Prague.

2 SLAVONICE
Barely 1km from the Austrian border, Slavonice is a little town any country would be proud to have. It's famous for its twin squares, dotted with stunning Renaissance architecture left over from its strategic importance during the Thirty Years' War. Happily, the town's architectural treasures were spared the socialist makeover and now make up one of the Czech Republic's most unspoilt towns. Slavonice is on a little-used train line from Telč (45Kč, one hour).

3 MIKULOV
Described by Czech poet Jan Skácel as a 'piece of Italy moved to Moravia by God's hand', Mikulov is topped with an imposing chateau and studded with baroque and Renaissance facades. It's also an excellent base for exploring the Moravian wine country. Trains run to Brno and Bratislava; some also link from Břeclav to Vienna.

Tours

Prague Tours   Walking
(📞775 369 121; www.praguer.com; per person 400-1200Kč) Includes a Ghost Tour and specialist Kafka and architecture tours.

Prague Walks   Walking
(📞608 339 099; www.praguewalks.com; per person 300-800Kč) From communism to Old Town pubs.

Wittmann Tours   Cultural
(📞222 252 472; www.wittmann-tours.com; per person from 750Kč) Specialises in tours of Jewish interest, including day trips (1250Kč) to the Museum of the Ghetto at Terezín and visits to the Moravian town of Třebíč.

Festivals & Events

Prague Spring   Classical Music
(www.festival.cz) From 12 May to 4 June, classical music kicks off summer.

Prague Fringe Festival   Arts
(www.praguefringe.com) Eclectic action in late May and early June.

Czech Beer Festival   Beer
(www.ceskypivnifestival.cz) Lots of food, music and about 70 beers from around the country. Mid to late May.

Khamoro   Music, Culture
(www.khamoro.cz) Late May's annual celebration of Roma culture.

United Islands   World Music
(www.unitedislands.cz) In mid-June.

Prague International Jazz Festival   Jazz
(www.jazzfestivalpraha.cz) Late November.

Christmas Market   Seasonal Festival
1 to 24 December in the Old Town Square.

Sleeping

At New Year, Christmas or Easter, and also from May to September, book in advance. Prices quoted are for the high season: generally April to October. Rates can increase up to 15%.

Staré Město

HOTEL ANTIK   Hotel €€
(📞222 322 288; www.antikhotels.com; Dlouhá 22; s/d 2590/2990Kč; P@🛜; Mnám Republiky) The popular Antik has a modern tinge with flash bathrooms and flat screen TVs, but heritage fans can still celebrate its 15th-century building (no lift) beside an antique shop. It's a great area for bars and restaurants, so ask for a quieter back room.

SAVIC HOTEL   Luxury Hotel   €€€
(☎ 233 920 118; www.hotelsavic.cz; Jilská 7; d/ste
€169/239; P @ 🛜; M Staroměstská) Looking
for somewhere romantic and central?
Originally a Dominican convent, the
Savic's combination of 14th-century heritage and 21st-century amenities avoids the
chintzy overkill of other top-end places.

Nové Město

DAHLIA INN   Pension   €
(☎ 222 517 518; www.dahlia.inn; Lípová 1444/20
16; s/d €49/59; 😊 @ 🛜; M Karlovo nám) From
the outside the building is nondescript,
but a few floors up there is a relaxed and
friendly B&B with spacious rooms decorated in designer style, flat-screen TVs,
and cool and classy bathrooms. The well-
travelled British–Czech owner is a wealth
of information on local restaurants, bars
and clubs.

ICON HOTEL   Boutique Hotel   €€€
(☎ 221 634 100; www.iconhotel.eu; V Jámě 6; d &
ste €180-240; @ 🛜; 🚋 3, 9, 14, 24 to Vodičkova)
Here's design-savvy cool concealed down
a quiet laneway. The handmade beds are
extra-wide, and the crew at reception is
unpretentious and hip.

THE AUGUSTINE   Luxury Hotel   €€€
(☎ 266 112 233; www.theaugustine.com; Letenská
12/33; d/ste from €340/800; P ✳ @ 🛜; 🚋 12,
20, 22, 23 to Malostranské nám). Occupying a
rambling former Augustinian monastery
in Malá Strana, the Augustine has elegant
and spacious rooms, beautiful gardens
and a premium spa with relax-at-all-costs
services. The hotel's own specially brewed
beer is served in a spectacular cellar bar.

APARTHOTEL ANGEL   Apartment   €€
(☎ 242 211; www.aparthotelangel.com; Karla
Engliše 2/3221, Smíchov; d/q from €69/79;
P 🛜; M Anděl) These spacious and
modern, self-contained apartments in the
midst of Smíchov's 21st-century regeneration are excellent value for travelling
families. The Old Town and Prague Castle
are a short tram ride away, and nearby
are good local restaurants.

HOTEL SAX   Boutique Hotel   €€
(☎ 257 531 268; www.hotelsax.cz; Jánský Vršek
328/3; d from €120; P @ 🛜; 🚋 12, 20, 22, 23
to Malostranské nám) In a quiet, atmospheric
corner of Malá Strana, the eclectically
furnished Hotel Sax has huge baths, big
flat-screen TVs, primary-coloured leather

Christmas market, Staroměstské nám (Old Town Square)

couches and striking abstract photography; all tinged with a thoroughly retro 1960s design aesthetic.

Eating

Eating in Prague's tourist areas is pricey, but cheaper eats are available a block or two away. Regular lunch specials (look for 'denní menu') will stretch your budget.

Most restaurants open from 11am to 11pm. Phone numbers are included for restaurants where bookings are recommended for dinner.

Staré Město

CÉLESTE BISTRO Mediterranean €€
(☎773 222 422; www.celestebistro.cz; V Kolkovně 7; mains 275-415Kč; ⏰11.30am-2.30pm & 6pm-midnight Mon-Sat; Ⓜ Staroměstská) Tucked away on one of the Old Town's loveliest streets, Céleste presents French and Mediterranean flavours in an expansive and modern space. Lunch (two/three courses 290/390Kč) is a good-value option.

LA DEGUSTATION Czech €€€
(☎222 311 234; www.ladegustation.cz; Haštalská 18; degustation menus 1000-2250Kč; ⏰noon-2.30pm Tue-Thu, 6pm-midnight Mon-Sat; Ⓜ nám Republiky) Traditional Bohemian flavours, some inspired by 19th-century cookbooks, are delivered across a variety of multicourse tasting menus. Allow three hours for the seven-course menu (2250Kč) or, if you're pushed for time, try the shorter 'post-theatre' menu (1000Kč).

LEHKÁ HLAVA Vegetarian €€
(☎222 220 665; www.lehkahlava.cz; Boršov 2; mains 120-210Kč; ✍; ☒17, 18 to Karlovy lázně) Lehká Hlava means 'clear head' and that's the normal outcome after a meal at this hip little cafe. In the kitchen the emphasis is on healthy, freshly prepared vegetarian and vegan dishes, ranging from hummus and roast vegetables to spinach burritos and a spicy oriental stir-fry. Lehká Hlava is very popular, so it's worth booking ahead.

LOKAL Czech €
(Dlouhá 33; mains 130-240Kč; ☺; Ⓜ nám Republiky) Welcome to a slick reinvention of a traditional Czech pub for the 21st century. Lokal specialises in traditional Czech recipes – usually prepared with a lighter, less fatty touch – and is very good value given its Old Town location.

Nové Město, Smíchov & Vinohrady

KARAVANSERÁJ Middle Eastern €
(Masarykovo nábřeží 22, Nové Město; mains 130-250Kč; ✍; ☒6, 9, 17, 18, 21 to Národní divadlo) Lebanese flavours dominate at this relaxed spot that's part ethnic eatery and part travellers' cafe, but the menu also touches down in India and Morocco. There's an ever-changing array of large-format travel photography on the walls.

Grand Cafe Orient (p708)
PHOTOGRAPHER: DOUG MCKINLAY/LONELY PLANET IMAGES ©

RESTAURACE U ŠUMAVY — Czech €
(Štěpánská 3, Nové Město; mains 100-150Kč; Ⓜ IP Pavlova) Here's emphatic and tasty proof that good-value Bohemian fare still exists in central Prague. Ensconced in a country-cottage decor, canny locals crowd in for lunch specials that remind them of their grandmother's cooking. The roast duck is good, and it's always worth taking a chance on the daily soup (*polévka*) special.

U FERDINANDA — Czech €
(cnr ulice Opletalova & Politických Vězňů, Nové Město; mains 100-180Kč; Ⓜ Muzeum) Welcome to a thoroughly modern spin on a classic Czech pub with beer, courtesy of the Ferdinand brewery from nearby Benešov. Quirky gardening implements in corrugated iron decorate the raucous interior, and a younger local clientele crowds in for well-priced Czech food.

HOME KITCHEN — Cafe €
(Jungmannova 8, Nové Město; mains 65-120Kč; ⏱7.30am-7pm Mon-Fri, 8.30am-3pm Sat; 🖋; 🚊3, 9, 14, 24 to Lazarská) Organic soups, salads and home-style daily specials provide the perfect escape for lunch at this cosy brick-lined spot away from the tourist sprawl of Old Town Square.

ZLATÝ KLAS — Czech €€
(Plzeňská 9, Smíchov; mains 120-230Kč; Ⓜ Anděl) Easily the best of the traditional Czech pubs in the immediate Anděl area, Zlatý klas offers super-fresh 'tank beer' (*tankové pivo*), meaning the beer is served from large tanks and is free of the carbon dioxide used to pump beer through the taps. It also offers good Czech grub, such as roast pork, goulash and fried breast of chicken. From the Anděl metro walk west on Plzeňská for 100m.

Hradčany & Malá Strana

U MALÉ VELRYBY — Seafood €€
(☎257 214 703; www.umalevelryby.cz; Maltézské nám 15, Malá Strana; tapas 55-65Kč, mains 365-375Kč; ⏱noon-3pm & 6-11pm; 🚊12, 20, 22, 23 to Malostranské nám) With only eight tables, you'll need to book at this cosy backstreets eatery where the friendly chef-owner from Ireland creates tasty miracles with (mainly) seafood. Try the seafood tagliatelle, the Basque chicken with saffron risotto, or settle in with a few tapas and a good bottle of wine.

CUKRKÁVALIMONÁDA — Cafe €
(☎257 530 628; Lázeňská 7, Malá Strana; mains 100-180Kč; ⏱9am-11pm; 🚊12, 20, 22, 23 to Malostranské nám) By day, homemade pastas, frittatas, ciabattas, and salads are delicious diversions at this lovely courtyard cafe, combining a modern look with beautiful Renaissance painted timber beams. After dark a more sophisticated bistro menu kicks in. Mid-afternoon pick-me-up drinks include elderflower flavoured with mint and lemon. The name translates to 'sugar, coffee, lemonade' – the Czech equivalent of 'eeny-meeny-miny-moe'.

ARTISAN RESTAURANT & CAFE — International €€
(☎257 218 277; Rosickych 4, Malá Strana; mains 170-380Kč; ⏱; 🚊6, 9, 12, 20, 23 to Újezd) Good steaks, gourmet burgers and robust seafood dishes are the standouts at this well-priced and unpretentious bistro on the quieter edge of Malá Strana. Two- or three-course lunches from 95Kč are great value.

 ## Drinking

Czech beers are among the world's best. The most famous brands are Budvar, Plzeňský Prazdroj (Pilsner Urquell) and Prague's own Staropramen. Independent microbreweries and regional Czech beers are also becoming more popular in Prague.

Avoid the tourist areas, and you'll find local bars selling half-litres for 35Kč or less.

PIVOVARSKÝ KLUB — Beer Hall
(Křižíkova 17, Karlín; ⏱; Ⓜ Florenc) Submit to your inner hophead at this pub-restaurant-beer shop with interesting limited-volume draught beers, and bottled brews from around the Czech Republic. Come for lunch, as it gets full of loyal regulars later on.

PIVOVARSKÝ DŮM — Beer Hall
(cnr Ječná & Lipová, Nové Město; 🚊4, 6, 22, 23 to Štepánská) The 'Brewery House' microbrewery conjures everything from a refreshing wheat beer to coffee- and banana-flavoured styles – even a beer 'champagne'.

DUENDE — Bar
(Karoliny Světlé 30, Nové Město; ⏱1pm-midnight Mon-Fri, from 3pm Sat, from 4pm Sun; MNárodní třída) Barely five minutes' walk from the tourist hubbub of Charles Bridge, this bohemian drinking den pulls in an arty, mixed-age crowd of locals.

HOSTINEC U KOCOURA — Pub
(Nerudova 2, Malá Strana; 🚊12, 20, 22, 23 to Malostranské nám) 'The Tomcat' is a long-established traditional pub, still enjoying its reputation as a favourite of ex-president Václav Havel, and still managing to pull in a mostly Czech crowd. Old-school authenticity and citrusy *kvasnicové* ('yeast beer') from the Bernard brewery make it an essential post-Castle stop.

BOKOVKA — Wine Bar
(Pštrossova 8, Nové Město; ⏱4pm-1am Sun-Thu, to 3am Fri & Sat; MKarlovo nám) This compact wine bar is named after the movie *Sideways* (*bokovka* in Czech), and is owned by film-making wine lovers. Wines include a great selection of excellent Moravian vintages, and good-value food platters are perfect for two or more.

LETNA BEER GARDEN — Beer Garden
(Letna Gardens, Bubeneč; 🚊12, 17 to Čechův most) This garden bar has views across the river of the Old Town and southwest to the castle. In summer it's packed with a young crowd enjoying cheap beer and grilled sausages. Sometimes the simple things in life are the best.

LITERÁRNÍ KAVÁRNA ŘETĚZOVÁ — Cafe
(Řetězová, Staré Město; ⏱noon-11pm Mon-Fri, from 5 Sat & Sun; 🚊17,21 to Karlovy lažně) This is where you would have headed post-1989 to become the next great expat novelist. Two decades on, leave your laptop and notebook at home, take in the vintage black-and-white pics of famous Czech writers, and treat yourself to a coffee or a beer. When someone asks you, 'So what was the best cafe you went to in Prague?', this is the correct answer.

GRAND CAFE ORIENT — Cafe
(Ovocný trh 19, Nové Město; Mnám Republiky) In the 'House of the Black Madonna', Josef Gočár's cubist gem, the reborn Grand Cafe Orient also features Gočár-designed lampshades and furnishings.

CAFE LOUVRE — Cafe
(1st fl, Národní třída 2; ⏱; MNárodní Třída) Others are more famous, but the French-style Louvre is arguably Prague's most amenable grand cafe.

Entertainment

From clubbing to classical music, puppetry to performance art, Prague offers plenty of entertainment. It's an established centre of classical music and jazz. For current listings see www.prague.tv or www.praguewelcome.cz.

Rudolfinum — Music
(📞227 059 227; www.ceskafilharmonie.cz; nám Jana Palacha, Staré Město; ⏱box office 10am-6pm Mon-Fri, plus 1hr before performances; MStaroměstka) One of Prague's main concert venues is the Dvořák Hall in the neo-Renaissance Ruldolfinum, home to the Czech Philharmonic Orchestra.

Smetana Hall — Music
(📞222 002 101; www.obecni-dum.cz; nám Republiky 5, Staré Město; ⏱box office 10am-6pm Mon-Fri; Mnám Republiky) Another main concert venue in the city is Smetana Hall, located in the art nouveau Municipal House. A highlight is the opening of the Prague Spring Festival.

Prague State Opera — Opera
(Státní opera Praha; 📞224 227 266; www.opera.cz; Legerova 75, Nové Město; ⏱box office 10am-5.30pm Mon-Fri, to noon & 1-5pm Sat & Sun; MMuzeum) Opera, ballet and classical drama (in Czech) are performed at this neo-Renaissance theatre. The box office is at Wilsonova 4.

Balcony of the National Theatre

RICHARD NEBESKY/LONELY PLANET IMAGES ©

National Theatre
Theatre

(Národní divadlo; 224 913 437; www.narodni-divadlo.cz; Národní třída 2, Nové Město; ☺box office open 10am-6pm; Ⓜ Národní třída) Classical drama, opera and ballet feature at this venue.

Estates Theatre
Opera

(Stavovské divadlo; 224 902 322; www.narodni-divadlo.cz; Ovocný trh 1, Staré Město; ☺box office 10am-6pm; Ⓜ Staroměstska) Every night from mid-July to the end of August, **Opera Mozart** (271 741 403; www.mozart-praha.cz) performs *Don Giovanni*, which premiered here in 1787.

Divadlo Minor
Children's Theatre

(222 231 351; www.minor.cz; Vodičkova 6, Nové Město; ☺box office 9am-1.30pm & 2.30-8pm Mon-Fri, 11am-6pm Sat & Sun; 🚊3, 9, 14, 24, Vodičkova) Kid-friendly shows including puppets and pantomime.

Try the following ticket agencies:

Bohemia Ticket International (224 227 832; www.ticketsbti.cz) Nové Město (Na příkopě 16, ☺10am-7pm Mon-Fri, to 5pm Sat, to 3pm Sun; Ⓜ nám Republiky); Staré Město (Malé nám 13; ☺9am-5pm Mon-Fri, to 1pm Sat; Ⓜ Staroměstská)

Ticketpro (296 333 333; www.ticket pro.cz; Lucerna pasáž, Šétěpánská 61, Nové Město; ☺noon-8.30pmMon-Fri; Ⓜ Můstek) Also has branches of the Prague Information Service.

Ticketstream (www.ticketstream.cz) Online bookings for events in Prague.

Shopping

PIVNÍ GALERIE
Beer

(www.pivnigalerie.cz; U Průhonu 9, ☺noon-8pm Tue-Fri; 🚊1, 3, 5, 25 to U Průhonu) Just a quick tram ride from central Prague, you can purchase beers from across the Czech Republic – we counted around 170 from more than 30 breweries. Note the limited opening hours, so head to the Pivovarský Klub bar/restaurant/beer shop if you're in town from Saturday to Monday.

KUBISTA
Design

(www.kubista.cz; Ovocný trh 19, Staré Město; Ⓜ nám Republiky) Kubista specialises in limited-edition reproductions of distinctive cubist furniture and ceramics, and designs by masters of the form such as Josef Gočár and Pavel Janák. It also has a few original pieces for serious collectors.

MODERNISTA

Design

(www.modernista.cz; Celetná 12, Staré Město; ⏰11am-7pm; Ⓜnám Republiky) This classy showcase of Czech cubism, art deco and similar design features covetable but reasonably affordable ceramics, jewellery, posters and books. Downstairs a renovated vaulted Gothic space provides the ultimate showcase for larger examples of home and office furniture and lighting.

Manufaktura

Handicrafts

(www.manufaktura.biz; Melantrichova 17, Staré Město; ⓂStaroměstska) Sells traditional Czech handicrafts, wooden toys and handmade cosmetics.

Moser

Crystal

(www.moser-glass.com; Na příkopě 12, Nové Město; ⏰10am-8pm Mon-Fri, to 7pm Sat & Sun; Ⓜnám Republiky) Top-quality Bohemian crystal.

ⓘ Information

Tourist Information

The Prague Information Service (Pražská informační služba, PIS; ☎12 444, in English & German; www.praguewelcome.cz) provides free tourist information with good maps. Branches are listed below.

PIS Malá Strana Bridge Tower (Charles Bridge; ⏰10am-6pm Apr-Oct; 🚋12, 20, 22, 23 to Malostranské nám)

PIS Old Town Hall (Staroměstské nám 5, Staré Město; ⏰9am-7pm Mon-Fri, to 6pm Sat & Sun Apr-Oct, to 6pm Mon-Fri, to 5pm Sat & Sun Nov-Mar; ⓂStaroměstská) The main branch.

PIS Rytirská (Rytirská 31; ⏰9am-7pm Apr-Oct, 9am-6pm Nov-Mar; ⓂMůstek)

If you're venturing beyond Prague, Czech Tourism (www.czechtourism.com; Staroměstské nám, Staré Město; ⏰9am-5pm Mon-Fri; ⓂStaroměstská) has an office in Prague's Old Town Square.

ⓘ Getting There & Away

Bus

The main terminal for international and domestic buses is Florenc bus station (ÚAN Florenc Křižíkova 4, Karlín; ⓂFlorenc), 600m northeast of the main train station. Some regional buses depart from near metro stations Anděl, Dejvická, Černý Most, Nádraží Holešovice, Smíchovské Nádraží or Želivského, and some buses to České Budějovice or Český Krumlov depart from the Ná Knížecí or outside the Roztyly metro station.

Train

Prague's main train station is Praha-hlavní nádraží (☎221 111 122; Wilsonova, Nové Město; ⓂHlavní nádraží). At the time of writing it was undergoing major redevelopment. Buy train tickets and get timetable information from ČD Centrum (⏰6am-7.30pm) at the southern end of level 2.

Some international trains stop at Praha-Holešovice station, which is on the northern side of the city, while

Handcrafted Easter eggs in Manufaktura

PHOTOGRAPHER: RICHARD NEBESKY/LONELY PLANET IMAGES ©

some domestic services terminate at Praha-Smíchov, south of Malá Strana. Check timetables and departure points at www.idos.cz.

ℹ Getting Around

To/From the Airport

Prague's Ruzyně airport is 17km west of the city centre.

The **Airport Express** (50Kč; ☺5am-10pm) bus service goes directly to the upper level of Prague's main train station (Praha-hlavní nádraží) from where you can access the metro system. Luggage is free on this service; buy your ticket from the driver.

Cedaz Minibus (☏220 111 111; www.cedaz. cz; ☺every 30min 7.30am-7pm) leaves from outside arrivals; buy your ticket from the driver. The minibus stops at the **Czech Airlines** (V Celnici 5; Mnám Republiky) office near the Hilton around nám Republiky (120Kč) or further out at the Dejvická metro station (90Kč). You can also get a Cedaz minibus from your hotel or any other address (480Kč for one to four people, 960Kč for five to eight).

Otherwise, see the (Dopravní podnik; DPP) desk in arrivals and take bus 119 (26Kč, 20 minutes, every 15 minutes) to the end of the line (Dejvická), then continue by metro into the city centre (another 10 minutes; no extra ticket needed). You'll also need a half-fare (13Kč) ticket for your backpack or suitcase if it's larger than 25cm x 45cm x 70cm.

AAA Taxis (☏14 014; www.aaataxi.cz; around 650Kč) are reputable and the drivers speak good English.

Bicycle

City Bike (☏776 180 284; www.citybike -prague.com; Královdvorská 5, Staré Město; per day 500Kč; ☺9am-7pm May-Sep; MStaroměstská)

Car & Motorcycle

Central Prague has many pedestrian-only streets, marked with Pěší Zóná (Pedestrian Zone) signs, where only service vehicles and taxis are allowed; parking can be a nightmare. Meter time limits range from two to six hours at around 50Kč per hour. Parking in one-way streets is normally only allowed on the right-hand side.

Public Transport

All public transport is operated by **Dopravní podnik hl. m. Prahy** (DPP; ☏800 191 817; www.dpp.cz).

Tickets are sold from machines at metro stations and major tram stops, at news-stands, Trafiky snack shops, PNS and other tobacco kiosks, hotels, all metro station ticket offices and DPP information offices.

A *jízdenka* (transfer ticket) is valid on tram, metro, bus and the Petřín funicular and costs 26Kč (half-price for six- to 15-year-olds); large suitcases and backpacks (anything larger than 25cm x 45cm x 70cm) also need a 13Kč ticket. Once validated, tickets remain valid for 75 minutes from the time of stamping if validated between 5am and 10pm on weekdays, and for 90 minutes at other times. Within this period, you can make unlimited transfers between all types of public transport (you don't need to punch the ticket again).

Tickets for 24 hours (100Kč) and three/five days (330/500Kč).

The metro operates from 5am to midnight daily.

Taxi

Try to avoid getting a taxi in tourist areas such as Wenceslas Sq and outside the main train station. To avoid being ripped off, phone a reliable company such as **AAA** (☏14 014; www. aaaradiotaxi.cz) or **City Taxi** (☏257 257 257; www.citytaxi.cz). Both companies also offer online bookings.

Around Prague
Karlštejn

Erected by the Emperor Charles IV in the mid-14th century, **Karlštejn Castle** (☏274 008 154; www.hradkarlstejn.cz; Karlštejn; ☺9am-6pm Tue-Sun Jul & Aug, to 5pm May, Jun & Sep, to 4pm Apr & Oct), crowns a ridge above Karlštejn village. It's a 20-minute walk from the train station.

The highlight is the **Chapel of the Holy Rood**, where the Bohemian crown jewels were kept until 1420. The 55-minute guided tours (in English) on **Route I** costs 250/150Kč per adult/child. **Route II**, which includes the chapel (June to October only), are 300/200Kč adult/child and must be prebooked. See online for details.

Trains from Praha-hlavní nádraží station to Beroun stop at Karlštejn (49Kč, 45 minutes, hourly).

Konopiště

The assassination of the heir to the Austro-Hungarian throne, Archduke Franz Ferdinand d'Este, sparked WWI. For the last 20 years of his life he hid southeast of Prague in his country retreat at **Konopiště Chateau** (www. zamek-konopiste.cz; Benešov; ☺9am-5pm Tue-Sun May-Aug, to 4pm Tue-Fri, to 5pm Sat & Sun Sep, 9am-3pm Tue-Fri, to 4pm Sat & Sun Apr & Oct).

Three guided tours are available. **Tour III** (adult/child 300/200Kč) is the most interesting, visiting the archduke's private apartments, unchanged since the state took over the chateau in 1921. **Tour II** (adult/child 200/130Kč) takes in the **Great Armoury**, one of Europe's most impressive collections.

Having renovated the massive Gothic and Renaissance building in the 1890s, Franz Ferdinand decorated his home with some of his 300,000 hunting kills. About 100,000 of them adorn the walls, each marked with when and where it was slain. The **Trophy Corridor** and **Chamois Room** (both on Tour III) are truly bizarre.

There are direct trains from Prague's Praha-hlavní nádraží station to Benešov u Prahy (68Kč, 1¼ hours, hourly). Konopiště is 2.5km west of Benešov. Local bus 2 (11Kč, six minutes, hourly) runs from a stop on Dukelská, 400m north of the train station (turn left out of the station, then first right on Tyršova and first left) to the castle car park. Otherwise it's a 30-minute walk.

Bohemia

The ancient land of Bohemia makes up the western two-thirds of the Czech Republic. The modern term 'bohemian' comes to us via the French, who thought that Roma came from Bohemia. The word *bohémien* was later used to describe to people living an unconventional lifestyle.

Left: Karlštejn Castle (p711); **Below:** Bear at Konopiště Chateau

PHOTOGRAPHERS: (LEFT) SILOTO/ALAMY ©; (BELOW) AD PHOTO/ALAMY©

Terezín

The massive fortress at Terezín (Therie-senstadt in German) was built by the Habsburgs in the 18th century to repel the Prussian army, but the place is better known as a notorious WWII prison and concentration camp. Around 150,000 men, women and children, mostly Jews, passed through en route to the extermination camps of Auschwitz-Birkenau: 35,000 of them died here of hunger, disease or suicide, and only 4000 survived. From 1945 to 1948 the fortress served as an internment camp for the Sudeten Germans, who were expelled from Czechoslovakia after the war.

The **Terezín Memorial** (www.pamatnik -terezin.cz) consists of the Museum of the Ghetto in the Main Fortress, and the Lesser Fortress, a 10-minute walk east across the Ohře River. Admission to one of these costs 160/130Kč per adult/ child; and a combined ticket for both is 200/150Kč.

The **Museum of the Ghetto** (⏰9am-5.30pm) records daily life in the camp during WWII, through moving displays of paintings, letters and personal possessions. Entry to the Museum of the Ghetto includes entry to the Magdeburg Barracks and vice versa.

Around 32,000 prisoners, many of them Czech partisans, were incarcerated in the **Lesser Fortress** (⏰8am-6pm Apr-Oct, to 4.30pm Nov-Mar). Take the grimly fascinating self-guided tour through the prison barracks, workshops, morgues and mass graves, before arriving at the bleak execution grounds, where more than 250 prisoners were shot.

At the **Magdeburg Barracks** (cnr Tyršova & Vodárenská; ⏰9am-6pm Apr-Oct, to 5.30pm Nov-Mar), the former base of the Jewish 'government', are exhibits on the rich cultural life – music, theatre, fine arts and literature – that flourished against this backdrop of fear.

ℹ️ Getting There & Away

Buses (80Kč, one hour) leave hourly from outside Prague's Holešovice metro station. Most continue on to Litoměřice.

Bohemian Switzerland National Park

The main road and rail route between Prague and Dresden follows the fast-flowing Labe (Elbe) River, gouging a sinuous, steep-sided valley through a sandstone plateau on the border between the Czech Republic and Germany. The landscape of sandstone pinnacles, giddy gorges, dark forests and high meadows is the Bohemian Switzerland National Park (Národní park České Švýcarsko), named after two 19th-century Swiss artists who settled here.

Just south of the German border, **Hřensko** is a cute village of half-timbered houses crammed into a sandstone gorge where the Kamenice River joins the Labe.

A signposted 16km (five to six hours) circular **hike** explores the main sights. From Hřensko's eastern end a trail leads via ledges and tunnels through the mossy chasms of the **Kamenice River Gorge**.

From May to September, the **Poseidon** (www.labskaplavebni.cz) travels along the Labe River from Děčín to **Hřensko** (adult/child 100/50Kč; 🕑9.30am Mon-Fri, 9am & 1pm Sat & Sun) and back to **Děčín** (adult/child 120/60Kč; 🕑10.30am Mon-Fri, 10am & 2pm Sat & Sun).

Plzeň

POP 175,000

Plzeň (Pilsen in German) is the hometown of Pilsner Urquell (Plzeňský prazdroj), the world's original lager beer. 'Urquell' (in German; *prazdroj* in Czech) means 'original source' or 'fountainhead', and the local style is now imitated across the world.

Pilsner Urquell is now owned by international conglomerate SAB-Miller, and some beer buffs claim the brew's not as good as before. One taste of the town's tasty *nefiltrované pivo* (unfiltered beer) will have you disputing that claim, and the original brewery is still an essential stop for beer aficionados.

Plzeň is an easy day trip from Prague, but the buzzing pubs and smaller microbreweries of this university town also reward an overnight stay.

Kamenic River, Bohemian Switzerland National Park

IMAGEBROKER / ALAMY©

Sights

BREWERY MUSEUM Museum
(www.prazdroj.cz; Veleslavínova 6; guided tour
adult/child 120/90Kč, with English text 90/60Kč;
⊙10am-5pm) The Brewery Museum is in a
medieval malt house. A **combined entry**
(adult/child 250/130Kč) that includes the
Pilsner Urquell Brewery is also available.

PILSNER URQUELL BREWERY Brewery
(www.prazdroj.cz; guided tour adult/child
150/80Kč; ⊙10am-5pm) Beer fans should
make the pilgrimage east across the river
to the famous Pilsner Urquell Brewery.
Visiting the hallowed brewery involves
travelling deep into a series of tunnels,
with the ultimate reward of a superior,
just-tapped glass of Pilsner Urquell.

PLZEŇ HISTORICAL UNDERGROUND
Historic Area
(www.plzenskepodzemi.cz; adult/child 90/60Kč;
⊙10am-5pm) In previous centuries beer
was brewed, stored and served in the
tunnels beneath the Old Town. Take a
30-minute guided tour through 500m of
tunnels at the Plzeň Historical Underground. The temperature is a chilly 10°C,
so wrap up and bring a torch (flashlight).
Tours begin at the Brewery Museum.

GREAT SYNAGOGUE Synagogue
(Sady Pětatřicátníků 11; adult/child 55/35Kč;
⊙10am-6pm Sun-Fri Apr-Oct) The Great
Synagogue, west of the Old Town, is the
third-largest in the world – only those in
Jerusalem and Budapest are bigger. It
was built in the Moorish style in 1892 by
the 2000 Jews who lived in Plzeň at the
time. An English guide costs 500Kč extra.
The building is often used for concerts
and art and photography exhibitions.

CHURCH OF ST BARTHOLOMEW
Church
(adult/child 20/10Kč; ⊙10am-4pm Mon-Fri) In
summer people congregate at the outdoor
beer bar in nám Republiky, the sunny Old
Town square, beneath the Gothic Church
of St Bartholomew. Inside the 13th-century
structure there's a Gothic *Madonna* (1390)
on the high altar and fine stained-glass windows. Climb the 102m church **tower** (adult/

child 30/10Kč; ⊙10am-6pm, weather dependent),
the highest in Bohemia, for great views of
Plzeň's rugged sprawl.

Sleeping

HOTEL ROUS Boutique Hotel €€
(☎602 320 294; www.hotelrous.cz; Zbrojnicka
113/7; s/d from 1690/2290Kč; [P][@][🖝]) This
600-year-old building incorporates the
warmth of the original stone walls with
modern furnishings. Breakfast is taken in
a garden cafe concealed amid remnants
of Plzeň's defensive walls. Downstairs, the
Caffe Emily serves the hotel's very own
microbrewed beer.

PENSION CITY Pension €
(☎377 326 069; www.pensioncityplzen.cz; Sady
5 května 52; s/d 1050/1400Kč; [P][🖝]) On a quiet, central street near the river, the City
is popular with both local and overseas
guests. Welcoming English-speaking staff
are a good source of local information.
Rooms are showing a bit of wear and the
wi-fi is patchy, but the buffet breakfast
continues to be one of Bohemia's best.

Eating & Drinking

NA PARKANU Pub €
(Veleslavínova 4; mains 100-150Kč) Attached to
the Brewery Museum, Na Parkanu lures
a mix of tourists and locals with good-
value meals and a summer garden. Don't
leave without trying the *nefiltrované pivo*
(unfiltered beer). It's not our fault if you
stay for another.

MĚŠŤANSKÁ BESEDA Cafe
(Kopeckého sady 13) Cool heritage café,
sunny beer garden, expansive exhibition
space and occasional arthouse cinema –
Měšťanská Beseda is hands-down Plzeň's
most versatile venue. The beautifully
restored Viennese-style coffee house is
perfect for a leisurely coffee and cake.

Information

City Information Centre (www.plzen.eu) nám
Republiky (městské informační středisko; ☎378
035 330; nám Republiky 41; ⊙9am-6pm); train
station (☎972 524 313; ⊙9am-7pm Apr-Sep, to
6pm Oct-Mar)

Getting There & Away

BUS Express buses run to/from Prague Florence (110Kč, 1½ hours, hourly). Buses also link Plzeň to Karlovy Vary (84Kč, 1¾ hours, five daily) and Mariáns ké Lázně (80Kč, 1¼ hours, four daily).
TRAIN Fast trains link Plzeň and Prague (147Kč, 1½ hours, eight daily), České Budějovice (174Kč, two hours, five daily) and Mariáns ké Lázně (101Kč, 1½ hours, eight daily).

Český Krumlov

POP 14,600

Crowned by a stunning castle, Český Krumlov's Renaissance and baroque buildings enclose the meandering arc of the Vltava river. In 1992 Český Krumlov was granted Unesco World Heritage status.

For too many travellers, Český Krumlov is just a hurried day trip, but its combination of dazzling architecture and watery fun on the Vltava deserve more attention. After dark in the Old Town is a magical time, and you can easily fill three days by adding a day trip to the nearby Newcastle mountains area.

Sights

NÁM SVORNOSTI   Square
Across the river is nám Svornosti, the Old Town square, overlooked by the Gothic **Town Hall**. Above the square is the striking Gothic **Church of St Vitus** (1439).

EGON SCHIELE ART CENTRUM
Art Gallery
(www.schieleartcentrum.cz; Široká 70-72; adult/child 120/700Kč; ⊙10am-6pm) The Egon Schiele Art Centrum is an excellent art gallery that showcases works by the Viennese painter Egon Schiele (1890–1918).

FOTOATELIÉR SEIDEL   Museum
(www.seidel.cz; Linecká 272; admission 130K; ⊙9am-4pm) The Fotoateliér Seidel presents a retrospective of the work of local photographers Josef Seidel and his son František. Especially poignant are the images recording early-20th-century life in nearby mountain villages.

Sebastian Tours   Tours
(☎607 100 234; www.sebastianck-tours.com; 5 Května Ul, Plešivec; per person 599Kč) Offers southern Bohemia guided tours, including stops at Hluboká nad Vltavou and České Budějovice.

Oldřiška Baloušková   Walking Tours
(oldriskab@gmail.com) Offers tailored walking tours for 450Kč per hour. It's recommended you contact her by email a few days before you arrive.

Festivals & Events

Infocentrum (see p 722) sells tickets to most festivals.

Five-Petalled Rose Festival   Folk Culture
In mid-June; features two days of street performers and medieval games.

Chamber Music Festival Classical Music
Late June to early July.

Český Krumlov International Music Festival   Classical Music
(www.festivalkrumlov.cz) July to August.

Jazz at Summer's End Festival   Jazz
(www.jazz-krumlov.cz) Mid-September.

Sleeping

PENSION SEBASTIAN   Pension €
(☎608 357 581; www.sebastianck.com; 5 Května Ul, Plešivec; s/d/tr incl breakfast 1090/1250/1590Kč; ⊙Apr-Oct; P �𝄢) An excellent option just 10 minutes' walk from the Old Town. Larger four-bed rooms (1780Kč) are good for families and there's a pretty garden for end-of-day drinks and diary writing. The well-travelled owners also run tours of the surrounding region.

PENSION KAPR   Pension €
(☎602 409 360; www.penzionkapr.cz; Rybářská 28; s 1000Kč, d 1220-1600Kč; P @ �𝄢) This riverside pension with exposed bricks and 500 years of history has a quiet location and wonderful views of the Old Town. The lovely rooms with whitewashed walls and wooden floors are all named after the owners' children.

CASTLE VIEW APARTMENTS
Apartments €€
(☎731 108 677; http://accommodation-cesky-krumlov.castleview.cz; Satlavska 140; d 2000-

Don't Miss Český Krumlov Castle

The Old Town, almost encircled by the Vltava River, is watched over by **Český Krumlov Castle** (☎ 380 704 721; www.castle.ckrumlov.cz; ⊗ 9am-6pm Tue-Sun Jun-Aug, to 5pm Apr, May, Sep & Oct) and its ornately decorated **Round Tower** (50/30Kč). Three different guided tours are on offer: **Tour I** (adult/child 240/140Kč) takes in the Renaissance and baroque apartments that the aristocratic Rožmberk and Schwarzenberg families called home; **Tour II** (adult/child 180/110Kč) visits the Schwarzenberg apartments used in the 19th century; and the **Theatre Tour** (adult/child 380/220Kč; ⊗ 10am-4pm Tue-Sun May-Oct) explores the chateau's remarkable rococo theatre, complete with original stage machinery. Wandering through the courtyards and gardens is free.

3500Kč) Furnished apartments are better value than top-end hotels in Český Krumlov. Castle View has seven apartments with spacious bathrooms, and decor combining sophistication and romance in equal measure. Five of the apartments can sleep up to five people. Infocentrum (see p 722) can also recommend other furnished apartments.

Eating

LAIBON   Vegetarian **€**
(☎ 728 676 654; Parkán 105; mains 100-180Kč)
Candles and vaulted ceilings create a great boho ambience in the best little vegetarian teahouse in Bohemia. The riverside setting's pretty fine as well. Order the blueberry dumplings for dessert and don't miss the special 'yeast beer' from the Bernard brewery.

U DWAU MARYÍ   Czech **€**
(☎ 380 717 228; Parkán 104; mains 110-220Kč)
The 'Two Marys' medieval tavern recreates old recipes and is your best chance to try dishes made with buckwheat and millet: all tastier than they sound. Wash the food down with a goblet of mead (a drink made with honey) or a 21st-century pilsner. In summer it's a tad touristy, but the stunning riverside castle views easily compensate.

🍷 Drinking

NA LOUŽI   Pub
(Kájovská 66) Nothing's changed in this *pivo* parlour for almost a century. Locals and tourists come for huge meals and tasty beer from the Eggenberg brewery.

DIVADELNÍ KLUB ÁNTRÉ   Cafe
(602 336 320; Horní Braná 2; ⊜ 📶) This nonsmoking cafe-bar in the town theatre has a terrace overlooking the river. There's free wi-fi, and it's always worth dropping by to see if any live music is scheduled.

Cikánská jizba   Czech €€
(380 717 585; Dlouhá 31; mains 140-230Kč; ⊙3pm-midnight Mon-Sat) At 'The Gypsy Room' there's live Roma music at the weekends to go with the menu of meaty Czech favourites.

ℹ Information

Infocentrum (380 704 622; www.ckrumlov. cz; nám Svornosti 1; ⊙9am-6pm) Transport and accommodation info, maps, internet access (5Kč per five minutes) and audio guides (100Kč per hour). A guide for disabled visitors is available.

ℹ Getting There & Away

Direct shuttle buses to Austria are offered by several companies. For a train, you'll need to first head to České Budějovice.

Stiff competition keeps prices relatively low: Vienna (1100Kč), Salzburg (1100Kč) and Linz (450Kč). From Linz there are regular trains to Vienna, Salzburg and Munich. Public transport to Austria involves heading to north to České Budějovice and catching a train to Linz (two hours).

Adršpach-Teplice Rocks

The Czech Republic's most extraordinary scenery lies near Poland, in a protected landscape region known as the Adršpach-Teplice Rocks (Adršpašsko-Teplické skály). Thick layers of stratified sandstone have been eroded and fissured by water and frost to form giant towers and deep, narrow chasms. Discovered by mountaineers in the 19th century, the region is popular with rock climbers and hikers. Sandy trails lead through pine-scented forests and loop through the pinnacles, assisted occasionally by ladders and stairs.

Two main formations – **Adršpach Rock Town** (Adršpašské skalní město) and **Teplice Rock Town** (Teplické skalní město) – comprise a single nature reserve. At each entrance there's a **ticket booth** (adult/child 60/30Kč; ⊙8am-6pm Apr-Nov) with handy 1:25,000 trail maps on offer. There are direct buses from Prague's Černý Most metro station to Trutnov (160Kč, 2¾ hours, hourly). From Trutnov catch a train to Teplice nad Metují-Skály (46kč, 1¼ hours) via Adršpach (40Kč, one hour).

Moravia

Away from the tourist commotion of Prague and Bohemia, Moravia

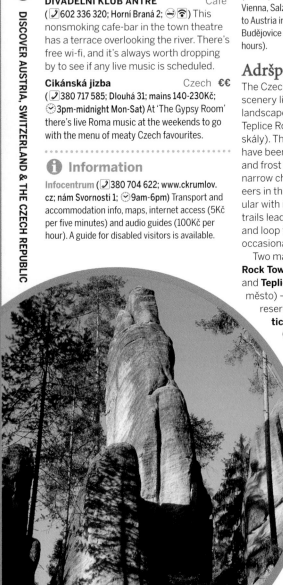

Sandstone formation at Adršpach-Teplice Rocks reserve
PHOTOGRAPHER: RICHARD NEBESKY/LONELY PLANET IMAGES ©

provides a quietly authentic experience. Mildly active travellers can explore the stunning landscapes of the Moravian Karst region, and everyone can celebrate with a good vintage from the Moravian wine country.

Moravian Karst

The limestone plateau of the Moravian Karst (Moravský kras) is riddled with caves and canyons carved by the subterranean Punkva River. There's a car park at **Skalní Mlýn** with an information desk and ticket office.

The **Punkva Caves tour** (Punkevní jeskyně; www.smk.cz; adult/child 160/80Kč; ⊗8.20am-3.50pm Apr-Sep, 8.40am-2pm Mon-Fri, to 3.40pm Sat & Sun Oct, 8.40am-2pm Tue-Sun Nov-Mar) involves a 1km walk through limestone caverns to the bottom of the **Macocha Abyss**, a 140m-deep sinkhole. Small, electric-powered boats then cruise along the underground river back to the entrance. On weekends and in July and August tickets for cave tours can sell out in advance, so book ahead online.

Beyond the Punkva Caves entrance, a **cable car** (adult/child return 80/70Kč, combined tourist train & cable-car ticket 120/100Kč) travels to the upper rim of the Macocha Abyss.

Kateřinská Cave (Kateřinská eskyně; adult/child 70/50Kč; ⊗8.20am-4pm Apr-Sep, to 2pm Oct, 10am, noon & 2pm Feb-Mar) is 300m from the Skalní Mlýn car park. Usually less crowded, the 40-minute tour explores two massive chambers.

From Brno trains run to Blansko (35Kč, 30 minutes, hourly).

Moravian Wine Country

Heading south from Brno to Vienna is the Moravian wine country. Czech wine has improved greatly since the fall of communism in 1989, with small producers concentrating on the high-quality end of the market. Czech red wines, such as the local speciality Svatovavřinecké (St Lawrence), are mediocre, but dry and fruity whites can be good, especially the riesling (*Vlašský Ryzlink*) and Müller-Thurgau varietals.

There are lots of *vinné sklepy* (wine cellars), *vinoteky* (wine shops) and *vinárny* (wine bars) to explore, as well as spectacular chateaux. See www.wineofczechrepublic.cz for touring routes and more information.

Lednice & Valtice

The **Lednice–Valtice Cultural Landscape** consists of 200 sq km of woodland, artificial lakes and tree-lined avenues dotted with baroque, neoclassical and neo-Gothic chateaux. Europe's biggest landscaped garden, it was created over several centuries by the dukes of Liechtenstein and is now a Unesco World Heritage site.

The massive neo-Gothic **Lednice Chateau** (✆519 340 128; www.zamek-lednice. com; ⊗9am-6pm Tue-Sun May-Aug, to 5pm Tue-Sun Sep, to 4pm Sat & Sun only Apr & Oct), was the Liechtensteins' summer palace. Studded with battlements, pinnacles and gargoyles, it gazes across an island-dotted artificial lake. **Tour 1** (adult/child 120/70Kč, 45 min) visits the major rooms, while **Tour 2** (adult/child 120/70Kč, 45 min) concentrates on the Liechtenstein apartments. Visit the gardens for free, or cruise on a **pleasure boat** (⊗9.30am-5pm Jul & Aug, Tue-Sun May, Jun & Sep, Sat & Sun Apr & Oct). Routes include between the chateau and an incongruous minaret (adult/child 80/40Kč) and between the minaret to nearby Janův castle (adult/child 120/60Kč).

SURVIVAL GUIDE
Directory A-Z

Accommodation
AUSTRIA

From simple mountain huts to five-star hotels fit for kings – you'll find the lot in Austria. Tourist offices invariably keep lists and details, and some arrange bookings for free or for a nominal fee. It's wise to book ahead at all times, particularly during the high seasons July and August, and December to April in ski resorts. Some places require email

Practicalities

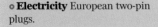

- **Electricity** European two-pin plugs.

- **Smoking** Illegal in most public places in Austria, Switzerland & the Czech Republic, although still permitted in some bars and restaurants.

- **Time** GMT +1.

- **Tipping** Optional in Austria and the Czech Republic, but generally expected in restaurants (5% to 10%). Tips in Switzerland are included in meal prices.

- **Weights & Measures** Metric.

confirmation but many places are also bookable online.

In some resorts (not often in cities) a *Gästekarte* (guest card) is issued if you stay overnight, which offers discounts on things such as cable cars and admission.

Accommodation prices in this chapter are for the high summer season (April to October). Price ranges for a double room including breakfast:

€€€	more than €200
€€	€80 to €200
€	below €80

SWITZERLAND

Even the most inexpensive places are pricey compared with other parts of Europe. The upside is that hostels, hotels and B&Bs almost always include a generous breakfast in their price and the standard of accommodation is high – divine fluffy feather duvet included.

In mountain resorts prices are seasonal: low season (mid-September to mid-December, mid-April to mid-June); mid-season (January to mid-February, mid-June to early July, September); and high season (July to August, Christmas, mid-February to Easter).

€€€	more than Sfr250
€€	Sfr150 to Sfr250
€	less than Sfr150

THE CZECH REPUBLIC

Prices quoted are for rooms with a private bathroom and a simple breakfast, unless otherwise stated. The following indicators apply for a high-season double room:

€€€	more than 3700Kč
€€	1600Kč to 3700Kč
€	less than 1600Kč

Business Hours

AUSTRIA

Banks 8am or 9am-3pm Mon-Fri, to 5.30pm Thu

Cafes 7.30am-8pm; hours vary widely

Post offices 8am-noon & 2-6pm Mon-Fri, to noon Sat

Pubs & bars Close between midnight and 4am

Restaurants Lunch noon-2.30pm or 3pm, dinner 7-10pm or 11pm

Shops 9am-6.30pm Mon-Fri, to 5pm Sat

SWITZERLAND

Banks 8.30am-4.30pm Mon-Fri, with late opening usually 1 day a week

Cafes & bars Hours vary widely

Restaurants Lunch noon-2pm or 3pm, dinner 7-10pm

Shops 8am-6.30pm Mon-Fri, with a one- to two-hour break for lunch at noon

THE CZECH REPUBLIC

Banks 8.30am-4.30pm Mon-Fri

Bars 11am-midnight

Castles Usually closed Mon year-round

Museums Usually closed Mon year-round

Post offices 8.30am-6pm Mon-Fri, to noon Sat

Restaurants 11am-11pm

Shops 8.30am-6pm Mon-Fri, to noon Sat

Food

Price ranges for main meals in restaurants listed in this chapter, are indicated by the following:

AUSTRIA

€€€	more than €200
€€	€80 to €200
€	less than €80

SWITZERLAND

€€€	more than Sfr30
€€	Sfr15 to Sfr30
€	less than Sfr15

THE CZECH REPUBLIC

€€€	more than 500Kč
€€	200Kč to 500Kč
€	less than 200Kč

Gay & Lesbian Travellers

Vienna is more tolerant towards gays and lesbians than the rest of the country. The attitude of most Austrians is close to that of Western Europeans.

Attitudes towards homosexuality are reasonably tolerant in Switzerland. Zürich and Geneva have lively gay scenes.

Homosexuality is legal in the Czech Republic, but Czechs are not yet used to seeing public displays of affection; it's best to be discreet.

Languages

Austria German

Switzerland Has three official federal languages: German (spoken by 64% of people), French (19%) and Italian (8%).

The Czech Republic Czech

Money

AUSTRIA

Currency Austria uses the euro. Major train stations have currency offices, and there are plenty of banks and *bureaux de change*.

ATMs Some *Bankomaten* (ATMs) operate 24-hourly. Most accept at the very least Maestro debit cards and Visa and MasterCard credit cards.

Credit cards Visa and MasterCard (Eurocard) are accepted a little more widely than American Express and Diners Club.

Fiaker (horse-drawn carriage) in Salzburg (p657)

CHARLOTTE HINDLE/LONELY PLANET IMAGES ©

Tipping About 10% in restaurants, bars and cafes, and in taxis; hand over the bill and the tip together. It also doesn't hurt to tip hairdressers, hotel porters, cloak-room attendants, cleaning staff and tour guides €1 or €2.

SWITZERLAND

Currency Swiss francs, divided into 100 centimes (*Rappen* in German-speaking Switzerland).

Credit cards All major travellers cheques and credit cards are accepted.

Exchanging money Nearly all train stations have currency-exchange facilities open daily and ATMs are everywhere.

Tipping Included in meal prices; there's no need to tip unless the service was superlative.

THE CZECH REPUBLIC

Currency Czech crown (Koruna česká). Keep small change handy for use in public toilets, telephones and tram-ticket machines.

Credit cards Widely accepted in petrol stations, midrange and top-end hotels, restaurants and shops.

Exchanging money Beware of *směnárna* (private exchange offices), especially when in Prague – they advertise misleading rates, and often charge exorbitant commissions or 'handling fees'.

Tipping Optional, but increasingly expected in Prague. Round the bill up the next 20Kč or 30Kč (5% to 10%). Leave small change in bars.

Public Holidays
AUSTRIA

New Year's Day (Neujahr) 1 January

Epiphany (Heilige Drei Könige) 6 January

Easter Monday (Ostermontag)

Labour Day (Tag der Arbeit) 1 May

Whit Monday (Pfingstmontag) 6th Monday after Easter

Ascension Day (Christi Himmelfahrt) 6th Thursday after Easter

Corpus Christi (Fronleichnam) 2nd Thursday after Whitsunday

Assumption (Maria Himmelfahrt) 15 August

National Day (Nationalfeiertag) 26 October

All Saints' Day (Allerheiligen) 1 November

Immaculate Conception (Mariä Empfängnis) 8 December

Christmas Day (Christfest) 25 December

St Stephen's Day (Stephanitag) 26 December

SWITZERLAND

New Year's Day 1 January

Easter March/April; Good Friday, Easter Sunday and Monday

Ascension Day Fortieth day after Easter

Whit Sunday & Monday Seventh week after Easter

National Day 1 August

Christmas Day 25 December

St Stephen's Day 26 December

THE CZECH REPUBLIC

New Year's Day 1 January; also anniversary of the founding of the Czech Republic.

Easter Monday March/April

Labour Day 1 May

Liberation Day 8 May

SS Cyril and Methodius Day 5 July

Jan Hus Day 6 July

Czech Statehood Day 28 September

Republic Day 28 October

Struggle for Freedom and Democracy Day 17 November

Christmas 24 to 26 December

Telephone
AUSTRIA

Country code ☎0043

Area codes Begin with '0' (eg '01' for Vienna). Drop this when calling from outside Austria; use it for all landline calls inside Austria except for local calls or to special toll and toll-free numbers.

Mobile phones The network works on GSM 1800 and is compatible with GSM 900 phones.

Austrian mobile *(Handy)* telephone numbers begin with 0650 or higher up to 0683. Phone shops sell prepaid SIM cards for about €10.

Payphones Take phonecards or coins; €0.20 is the minimum for a local call.

SWITZERLAND

Country code ☎ 0041

Area codes Do not exist in Switzerland or Liechtenstein. Always dial numbers in full.

Mobile phones Mobile phone numbers start with 079. Prepaid local SIM cards (Sfr30 to Sfr100) are available from the three network operators (Orange, Sunrise and Swisscom mobile).

Payphones Minimum charge is Sfr0.50 and phones take Swiss franc or euro coins, as well as phonecards. The latter can be purchased from post offices and newsagencies.

THE CZECH REPUBLIC

Country code ☎ 420

Area codes All Czech phone numbers have nine digits; dial all nine for any call.

Mobile phones Mobile phone coverage (GSM 900) is excellent. Purchase a Czech SIM card from any mobile phone shop for around 500Kč (including 300Kč of calling credit). Local mobile phone numbers start with 601 to 608 and 720 to 779.

Phonecards You can buy phonecards from post offices and news stands from 1000Kč.

Tourist Information

AUSTRIA

The **Austrian National Tourist Office** (ANTO; www.austria.info) has a number of overseas offices. There is a comprehensive listing on the ANTO website. Tourist offices within Austria are dispersed far and wide, and the hours tend to be very seasonal.

SWITZERLAND

Your first port of call for information should be **Switzerland Tourism** (www.myswitzerland.com). Local tourist offices are extremely helpful and have reams of literature to give out, including maps (nearly always free).

THE CZECH REPUBLIC

The official **Czech tourist office** (www.czechtourism.com) and the **Prague Information Service** (www.praguewelcome.cz) are excellent resources for first-time visitors to the Czech Republic. Smaller tourist offices can be found in many regional towns and cities.

Visas

AUSTRIA

Not required for stays of up to three months for EU citizens, or citizens of much of Eastern Europe, Israel, USA, Canada, the majority of Central and South American nations, Japan, Korea, Malaysia, Singapore, Australia or New Zealand. All other nationalities require a

Evening in Malá Strana (p703), Prague
PHOTOGRAPHER: RICHARD NEBESKY/LONELY PLANET IMAGES ©

RICHARD MILLS/LONELY PLANET IMAGES ©

visa; the website for the **Ministry of Foreign Affairs** (www.bmaa.gv.at) has a list of embassies where you can apply for one.

SWITZERLAND

Not required for passport holders from the UK, EU, Ireland, the USA, Canada, Australia, New Zealand, South Africa, Norway and Iceland. For up-to-date details on visa requirements, go to the **Swiss Federal Office for Migration** (www.eda.admin.ch).

THE CZECH REPUBLIC

Czech citizens of most countries can spend up to 90 days in the country in a six-month period without a visa. For travellers from some other countries, a Schengen Visa is required; you can only apply for this from your country of residence. Check www.czech.cz for the latest information.

Transport

Getting There & Away

Air

AUSTRIA

Vienna is the main transport hub for Austria, but Graz, Linz, Klagenfurt, Salzburg and Innsbruck all receive international flights. Flights to these cities are often a cheaper option than those to the capital, as are flights to Airport Letisko (Bratislava airport), 60km east of Vienna in Slovakia.

Graz airport (GRZ; ☎ 0316-29 02-0; www.flughafen-graz.at)

Innsbruck airport (INN; ☎ 0512-225 25-0; www.innsbruck-airport.com)

Klagenfurt airport (KLU; ☎ 0463-415 00-0; www.klagenfurt-airport.com)

Linz airport (LNZ; ☎ 07221-600-0; www.flughafen-linz.at)

Salzburg airport (SZG; ☎ 0662-85800; www.salzburg-airport.com)

Vienna airport (VIE; ☎ 01-7007 22233; www.viennaairport.com)

SWITZERLAND

The main international airports are in Zürich and Geneva.

Geneva airport (GVA; ☎ 0900 57 15 00; www.gva.ch)

Zürich airport (ZRH; ☎ 043 816 22 11, flight information by SMS ☎ send message ZRH plus flight number to 9292; www.zurich-airport.com)

THE CZECH REPUBLIC

Most international flights arrive in Prague, with Frankfurt, Amsterdam or Munich being the most relevant major European hubs if flying from Asia, Oceania or North America.

The Czech Republic's second city, Brno, receives regular flights from London. **Czech Airlines** (www.czechairlines. com) has a good safety record and is a member of the Skyteam airline alliance.

Brno-Tuřany airport (www.airport-brno.cz)

Prague-Ruzyně airport (www.prg.aero)

Land

AUSTRIA

Bus Buses depart from Austria for as far afield as England, the Baltic countries, the Netherlands, Germany and Switzerland, as well as many Eastern European cities.

Car & motorcycle There are numerous entry points into Austria by road from Germany, the Czech Republic, Slovakia, Hungary, Slovenia, Italy and Switzerland. All border-crossing points are open 24 hours.

Train Austria has excellent rail connections. The main services in and out of the country from the west normally pass through Bregenz, Innsbruck or Salzburg en route to Vienna. Express services to Italy go via Innsbruck or Villach; trains to Slovenia are routed through Graz.

SWITZERLAND

Car & motorcycle Roads into Switzerland are good despite the terrain, but special care is needed to negotiate mountain passes. Upon entering Switzerland you need to decide whether you wish to use the motorways: there is a one-off charge of Sfr40 payable in cash, including euros, at the border or, better still, in advance through Switzerland Tourism or a motoring organisation. The sticker (*vignette* in French and German, *contrassegno* in Italian) you receive is valid for a year and must be stuck on the windscreen. For more details see www.vignette.ch. Some Alpine tunnels incur additional tolls.

Train Located in the heart of Europe, Switzerland is a hub for train connections to the rest of the continent. Zürich is the busiest international terminus, with two direct day trains and one night train to Vienna. Regular trains travel from Paris to Geneva, Lausanne, Bern and Basel. Most connections from Germany, including Frankfurt and Berlin, pass though Zürich or Basel.

THE CZECH REPUBLIC

The Czech Republic has border crossings with Germany, Poland, Slovakia and Austria.

Bus Prague's main international bus terminal is Florenc bus station. The peak season for bus travel is mid-June to the end of September, with daily buses to major European cities. Outside this season, frequency falls to two or three a week.

Car & motorcycle Motorists need to buy a *nálepka* (motorway tax coupon) – on sale at border crossings and petrol stations – in order to use Czech motorways. See www.ceskedalnice. cz for more information.

Train International train tickets can be purchased online with **České Dráhy** (Czech Railways; www. cd.cz). International trains arrive at Prague's main train station (Praha-hlavní nádraží, or Praha hl. n.), or the outlying Holešovice (Praha Hol.) and Smíchov (Praha Smv.) stations.

Getting Around

Air

AUSTRIA

Flying within a country the size of Austria is not usually necessary. A couple of airlines serving longer routes:

Austrian Airlines (www.austrian.com) The national carrier and its subsidiaries Tyrolean Airways and Austrian Arrows offer several flights daily between Vienna and Graz, Innsbruck, Klagenfurt, Linz and Salzburg.

Welcome Air (www.welcomeair.at) Flights from Innsbruck to Graz.

SWITZERLAND

Swiss International Air Lines (www.swiss. com) serves the major hubs of EuroAirport (Basel), Geneva and Zürich airports, with return fares fluctuating wildly in price – anything from Sfr70 to Sfr300. Swiss no-frills carrier **Fly Baboo** (www.flybaboo. com) flies Geneva–Lugano.

THE CZECH REPUBLIC

The Czech Republic is compact and internal flights are limited.

Czech Airlines (📞 800 310 310; www.czechairlines.com) Links Prague with Brno, Karlovy Vary, Ostrava and Brno.

Bus
AUSTRIA

Rail routes are often complemented by Postbus services, which usually depart from outside train stations. In remote regions, services are reduced on Saturday, often nonexistent on Sunday. Generally you can only buy tickets from the drivers. For information inside Austria, visit the website www.postbus.at.

SWITZERLAND

Yellow postal buses are a supplement to the rail network, following postal routes and linking towns to the more inaccessible regions in the mountains. In all, routes cover some 8000km of terrain. Services are regular, and departures tie in with train arrivals. Postbus stations are next to train stations and offer destination and timetable information.

THE CZECH REPUBLIC

Within the Czech Republic buses are often faster, cheaper and more convenient than trains. Many bus routes have reduced frequency (or none) on weekends. Buses occasionally leave early, so get to the station at least 15 minutes before the official departure time. Check bus timetables and prices at www.idos.cz.

Car & Motorcycle
AUSTRIA

Autobahns are marked 'A', *Bundesstrassen* or 'B' roads are major roads, while *Landstrassen* (L) are places to enjoy the ride and are usually good for cyclists. Vienna is linked by a daily motorail service to Innsbruck, Salzburg and Villach.

Driving licence A driving licence should always be carried. If it's not in German, you need to carry a translation or International Driving Permit as well.

Hire Multinational car-hire firms all have offices in major cities; ask at tourist offices for details. The minimum age for hiring small cars is 19 years, or 25 years for larger, 'prestige' cars. Customers must have held a driving licence for at least a year. Many contracts forbid customers to take cars outside Austria, particularly into Eastern Europe.

Motorway & tunnel tolls A *Vignette* (motorway tax) is imposed on all autobahn; charges for cars/motorbikes are €7.90/4.50 for 10 days and €22.90/11.50 for two months. *Vignette* can be purchased at border crossings, petrol stations and *Tabak* shops. There are additional tolls (usually €2.50 to €10) for some mountain tunnels.

Road rules Minimum driving age is 18 years of age. Driving is on the right-hand side of the road. Give way to the right at all times except when a priority road sign indicates otherwise. Trams always have priority. Seatbelts are compulsory. The penalty for drink driving – over 0.05% – is a hefty on-the-spot fine and confiscation of your driving licence.

Speed limits The limit is 50km/h in built-up areas, 130km/h on motorways and 100km/h on other roads. Except for the A1 (Vienna–Salzburg) and the A2 (Vienna–Villach), the speed limit is 110km/h on the autobahn from 10pm to 5am.

SWITZERLAND

Driving licence You do not need an International Driving Permit to operate a vehicle in Switzerland. A driving licence from your home country is sufficient.

Hire For the best deals on car hire, prebook; particularly competitive rates are often found on Auto Europe (www.autoeurope.com).

Mountain roads Stay in low gear whenever possible and remember that ascending traffic has the right of way over descending traffic. Some minor Alpine passes are closed from November to May – check with the local tourist offices before setting off. Snow chains are recommended during winter.

Road rules Driving is on the right-hand side. Seatbelts are compulsory, and you must use dipped lights in *all* road tunnels. Postbuses always have right of way. If your blood alcohol level is over 0.05%, you face a large fine or imprisonment.

Speed limits The limit is 50km/h in towns, 120km/h on motorways, 100km/h on semimotorways (designated by roadside rectangular pictograms showing a white car on a green background) and 80km/h on other roads.

THE CZECH REPUBLIC

Driving licence Foreign driving licences are valid for up to 90 days. Strictly speaking, licences that do not include photo identification need an International Driving Permit as well, although this rule is rarely enforced.

Fuel Leaded petrol is available as *special* (91 octane) and *super* (96 octane), and unleaded as *natural* (95 octane) or *natural plus* (98 octane). The Czech for diesel is *nafta* or just *diesel*. *Autoplyn* (LPG gas) is available in every major town but at very few outlets.

Hire Small local companies offer better prices, but are less likely to have fluent, English-speaking staff. It's often easier to book by email than by phone. Typical rates for a Škoda Fabia are around 700Kč a day, including unlimited kilometres, collision-damage waiver and value-added tax (VAT). Bring your credit card as a deposit. A motorway tax coupon is included with most rental cars.

Road rules Driving is on the right-hand side of the road, and road rules reflect the rest of Europe. Vehicles must be equipped with a first-aid kit and a red-and-white warning triangle. Using seat belts is compulsory. Drinking and driving is forbidden; the blood alcohol level is zero.

Speed limits Cars are limited to 30km/h or 50km/h in built-up areas, 90km/h on open roads and 130km/h on motorways. Motorbikes are limited to 80km/h. Police can hit you with on-the-spot fines of up to 2000Kč for speeding and other traffic offences (be sure to insist on a receipt).

Train

AUSTRIA

Austria has a clean, efficient rail system, and if you use a discount card it's very inexpensive.

Disabled passengers Use the ☎05-1717 number from 7am to 10pm for special travel assistance. Staff at stations will help with boarding and alighting. Do this at least 24 hours

Staroměstské nám (Old Town Square, p694), Prague

ahead of travel (72 hours ahead for international services).

Fares The fares quoted in this chapter are for 2nd-class tickets.

Information The main operator is **ÖBB** (☏ 05 17 17; www.oebb.at), supplemented with a handful of private lines. Tickets and timetables are available online.

Rail passes The Vorteilscard (adult/under 26 years/senior €100/20/27) reduces fares by at least 45% and is valid for a year, but can't be used on buses. Bring a photo and your passport or ID.

Reservations In 2nd class within Austria this costs €3.50 for most express services; recommended for travel on weekends.

SWITZERLAND

The Swiss rail network consists of a combination of state-run and private lines, and covers 5000km. Trains are clean, reliable and frequent. Prices are high, and if you plan on taking more than one or two train trips it's best to purchase a travel pass.

Information Train schedules are revised yearly; be sure to double-check details before travelling either online with **Swiss Federal Railways** (www.rail.ch, www.sbb.ch/en), or call its **Rail Service** (☏ 0900 300 300, per min Sfr1.19).

Fares All fares are for 2nd class; 1st-class fares are about 65% higher.

Rail passes The **Swiss Pass** (www.swisstravelsystem.ch) allows unlimited travel on almost all public transport, plus trams and buses in 38 towns, and 50% off funiculars, cable cars and private railways, such as Jungfrau Railways. These passes are available for four days (Sfr260), eight days (Sfr376), 15 days (Sfr455), 22 days (Sfr525) and one month (Sfr578); prices are for 2nd-class tickets. The Swiss Flexi Pass allows free, unlimited trips for three to six days within a month and costs Sfr249 to Sfr397 (2nd class). With either pass, two people travelling together get 15% off. Passes also include free admission to all Swiss museums. Passes can be purchased in advance at www.swisstravelsystem.com or in the UK from the **Swiss Travel Centre** (☏ 0207 420 49 00; 30 Bedford St, London WC2E 9ED).

THE CZECH REPUBLIC

Czech Railways provides efficient train services to almost every part of the country.

Buying tickets The sales clerks at ticket counters outside of Prague may not speak English, so write down your destination with the date and time you wish to travel. If you're paying by credit card, let them know *before* they issue the ticket.

Fares Quoted prices are for 2nd class unless otherwise indicated.

Information Fares and information can be found online at www.idos.cz and www.cd.cz.

Ski lift in Tirol (p669), Austria
PHOTOGRAPHER: RICHARD NEBESKY/LONELY PLANET IMAGES ©

Train travelling through the Bernese Oberland (p683), Switzerland

GLENN VAN DER KNIJFF/LONELY PLANET IMAGES ©

Train types The cost of train travel in the Czech Republic varies according to the train class. The fastest services are EC (EuroCity) and IC (InterCity), which have a choice of 1st- and 2nd-class coaches and incur a fare supplement. The main domestic network is served by R *(rychlík)* trains, which don't incur a supplement and are usually marked in red on timetables. Slower Os *(osobní)* and Sp *(spěšný)* trains are 2nd-class only.

Greece

Don't let headline-grabbing financial woes put you off going to Greece. The elements that have made Greece one of the most popular destinations on the planet are still all there, and now is as good a time as any to turn up for some fun in the sun.

That alluring combination of history and hedonism continues to beckon. Within easy reach of magnificent archaeological sites are breathtaking beaches and relaxed tavernas serving everything from ouzo to octopus. Wanderers can island-hop to their hearts content, while party types can enjoy pulsating nightlife in Greece's vibrant modern cities and on such islands as Mykonos, Ios and Santorini. Throw in welcoming locals with an enticing culture and it's easy to see why most visitors head home vowing to come back.

Travellers to Greece inevitably end up with a favourite site they long to return to – get out there and find yours.

Ancient Delphi (p753)

Greece

1 Acropolis
2 Acropolis Museum
3 Monasteries, Meteora
4 Knossos, Crete
5 Santorini
6 Tavernas, Thessaloniki

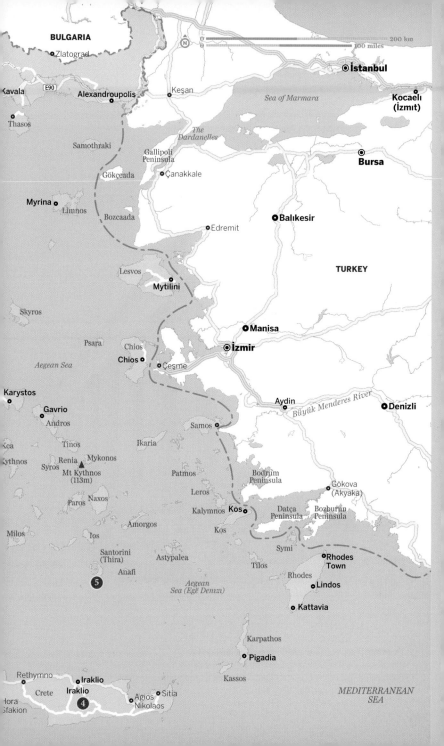

Greece Highlights

① Acropolis

The Acropolis (p747) is a masterpiece of classical architecture and an absolutely essential item on any Athens itinerary. The complex was largely developed during the rule of Pericles, and even in its part-ruined state it's impossible not to find yourself transported back into the glory of Greece from long ago. Parthenon

Need to Know

TOP TIP The best time is early morning before it gets too busy and hot **DID YOU KNOW?** It has suffered horribly from pollution over the years **For full details on the Acropolis, see p747.**

Acropolis Don't Miss List

BY CATHERINE TRIANTIS,
PROFESSIONAL LICENSED TOURIST
GUIDE

1 PARTHENON

This is the crowning achievement of Greek architecture. Walk around the temple to get a feel for its geometry. Stop at the northeastern corner to see the curves of the building. By looking at the eastern steps, you can see them gradually ascend and then descend, forming a curve.

2 ERECHTHEION

Have a look at each side of this ornate and architecturally unique temple, characterised by elegance, grace and elaborate decoration. The most interesting side is the porch of the caryatids with six female Korae statues. Although the statues are copies, the artists' craftmanship is evident in the transparency of the clothing and unique hairstyles.

3 VIEWS OF ATHENS

The Acropolis offers an aerial view of the city. To the north you'll see Plaka and Ancient Agora; to the east, the Temple of Olympian Zeus, Hadrian's Arch and the National Gardens; to the south, the new Acropolis Museum and Filopappou Hill; and to the west, the Athenian Observatory.

4 COLOURFUL PAST

Built to protect the Acropolis after the Persian Wars in 479 BC, the massive northern fortification walls were made from columns taken from the sites of earlier temples. Look closely to spot hints of colour on these columns – almost everything was rendered with colour in the past.

5 TEMPLE OF ATHENA NIKE

An absolute jewel, this temple was dedicated to the victory goddess, Athena Nike, and contained a wingless statue of her to keep her from flying away from Athens and therefore keeping the city victorious.

Top: Caryatids of Erechtheion;
Bottom Right: Temple of Athena Nike

735

Acropolis Museum

It may have taken over three decades to bring to fruition, but Athens has finally got the archaeological museum (p742) it's always deserved. Prominently positioned in the shadow of the Acropolis, the museum has been specially designed to house the nation's greatest ancient treasures and provide fascinating historical context to the real-life ruins themselves.

2

Meteora

3

The dramatic rock pinnacles at Meteora (p757) grace many a Grecian postcard, but nothing compares to seeing them for yourself. Inhabited by monks since the 11th century, these rocky spires are still home to a string of peaceful monasteries, best seen in the light of the setting sun. You can travel between them by road, but hiking the ancient paths provides a much more authentic pilgrimage.

Agias Triados monastery (p757), Meteora

Knossos

4

The capital of Minoan Crete, Knossos (p769) is another essential attraction for aficionados of ancient history. According to legend, the city was once the site of the infamous Labyrinth inhabited by the beastly half-man, half-bull known as the Minotaur. Whatever the truth of the story, it's still a stunning sight – but you'll need to get there early to avoid the crowds. Palace of Knossos

5

Santorini

With its ancient ruins, seaside ports and rugged hillsides, Greece is irresistibly photogenic – but nowhere quite compares to Santorini (p760) in the scenery stakes. This idyllic island overlooks a glittering lagoon formed by a prehistoric volcanic explosion, and its clifftop churches, stark white buildings and azure waters are a photographer's dream come true. Oia (p760), Santorini

6

Greek Tavernas

Dining al fresco at a neighbourhood taverna (p755) in Thessaloniki or Athens is a wonderful way to immerse yourself in Grecian culture. Peer into the pots to see what's cooking, order a plate of *mezedhes* (mixed appetisers) and settle in to meet the locals – you're in for a culinary experience you'll never forget. Just try to leave room for dessert! Cooking at a taverna in Athens

Greece's Best...

Ancient Sites

○ **Parthenon, Athens** (p747) The mother of all Doric structures, completed in 438BC.

○ **Temple of Zeus, Ancient Olympia** (p754) The spiritual home of the Olympic Games.

○ **Sanctuary of Athena, Delphi** (p753) Where Ancient Greeks once consulted the Oracle.

○ **Knossos, Crete** (p769) The legendary lair of the Minotaur was rediscovered in 1900.

○ **Delos** (p760) The island birthplace of Apollo.

Old-World Towns

○ **Nafplio, Peloponnese** (p752) With its elegant houses and seaside mansions overlooking a turquoise sea, Nafplio is made for wandering.

○ **Rhodes Town** (p766) Protected by massive 12m thick walls, this is one of the most authentic medieval towns anywhere in Greece.

○ **Corfu Town** (p772) A tangle of winding alleyways and hidden plazas, over-looked by two medieval fortresses.

Island Getaways

○ **Paros** (p763) Sparkling beaches and marbled hills make for one of the loveliest islands of the Cyclades.

○ **Samos** (p763) The jewel of the Aegean archipelago was once an important centre of Hellenic culture.

○ **Kefallonia** (p773) Explore the island immortalised in Louis de Bernières' classic novel *Captain Corelli's Mandolin*.

○ **Ithaki** (p773) Escape to the legendary home of the Greek hero Odysseus.

Need to Know

Greek Food

○ **Oikeio** (p750) For home-style Greek cooking, you won't do better than this taverna in Athens' Kolonaki neighbourhood.

○ **Tzitzikas & Mermingas** (p749) This cheery Athens restaurant is famous for its creative *mezedhes*.

○ **Gastrodromio El Olympio** (p756) One of Greece's best country restaurants, with gorgeous Olympus views to boot.

○ **To Meltemi** (Map p767) Rhodes' finest seafood in a superb beachside setting.

Left: Temple of Zeus, Ancient Olympia;
Above: Old town square of Rhodes
PHOTOGRAPHERS: (LEFT) DIANA MAYFIELD/LONELY PLANET IMAGES ©;
(ABOVE) CHRISTOPHER GROENHOUT/LONELY PLANET IMAGES ©

ADVANCE PLANNING

○ **As far as possible ahead** Book for popular ferry routes, especially in high summer.

○ **At least a month ahead** Top hotels are generally booked out in the high season, so it pays to reserve as early as you can.

○ **When you arrive** If you're visiting the Acropolis, the €12 ticket covers entry to several other of Athens' ancient sites.

RESOURCES

○ **Greek National Tourist Organisation** (www.gnto.gr) Known as EOT within Greece.

○ **Ministry of Culture** (www.culture.gr) Crammed with cultural information.

○ **Ancient Greece** (www.ancientgreece.com) Handy online guide to the ancient world.

○ **Greek Ferries** (www.greekferries.gr) Essential resource for island-hoppers.

GETTING AROUND

○ **Boat** Nearly every island has a boat service, but timetables are notoriously erratic – sailings can be cancelled at short notice due to bad weather.

○ **Bus** Often the only option for reaching smaller towns and villages. Scooters are a good option on many islands.

○ **Car** Allows for maximum freedom, but Greece's roads require nerves of steel.

○ **Train** Greece's train network is limited to two main lines (connecting Athens with the Peloponnese and northern Greece), plus a few small branch lines.

BE FOREWARED

○ **Theft** Watch out for pickpockets in crowded spots, especially in big cities such as Athens, at markets and in popular tourist areas. Never leave your belongings unattended on the beach.

○ **Toilets** Public toilets in Greece are rare, and many can't handle toilet paper!

○ **Driving** Take extra care – Greece has the highest road-fatality rate in Europe.

○ **Ferries** Sailings are extremely weather dependent, so it pays to be flexible with your travel plans.

Greece Itineraries

With its mystic temples and magnificent ruins, travelling through Greece often feels like a journey through time. It's a wonderful place to let your imagination wander.

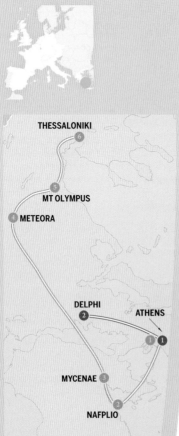

THESSALONIKI

MT OLYMPUS

METEORA

DELPHI

ATHENS

MYCENAE

NAFPLIO

3
DAYS

ATHENS TO DELPHI

Ancient Wonders

For an introduction to the world of ancient Greece, nowhere compares with **(1) Athens**. Magnificent monuments are scattered across the city, but for the historical background it's sensible to start at the Acropolis Museum, which brings together the surviving art treasures unearthed at the actual Acropolis nearby. In the afternoon, hike up to the Parthenon and the Ancient Agora, and spend the evening exploring some of Athens' atmospheric tavernas. Spend the following day seeing the rest of Athens, including the National Archaeological Museum and the Benaki Museum, finishing up with a tour of the Temple of Olympian Zeus and the nearby Panathenaic Stadium, the spiritual home of the modern Olympics.

On day three, take a trip north to **(2) Delphi** and feel the potent spirit on the slopes of Mt Parnassos. The ancient Greeks considered this the centre of the world. You can follow in the pilgrims' footsteps along the Sacred Way, which leads uphill to the Temple of Apollo. Nearby is another impressive ruin, the 20-column Sanctuary of Athena.

Top Left: Statues at Ancient Agora (p743), Athens;
Top Right: Climbing stairs to a monastery at Meteora (p757)

5 DAYS

ATHENS TO THESSALONIKI

Mansions & Monasteries

With five days at your disposal, you can venture out from **(1) Athens** on some fantastic day trips. A couple of hours west is **(2) Nafplio** and its smart hillside mansions tumbling down towards the sparkling Mediterranean. The best views are from the Venetian Palamidi Fortress, which dates back to the early 18th century.

An hour from Nafplio is another unmissable relic of the ancient world, the ruined city of **(3) Mycenae**, once one of the most powerful in ancient Greece. Try and imagine the sights and sounds that would have greeted you as you walk through the monumental Lion's Gate, the city's main entrance, and one of the largest surviving ancient sculptures in Greece.

On day three, head back towards Athens for a pilgrimage to the bewitchingly beautiful rock-top monasteries of **(4) Meteora**. Take a bus up to the top and work your way back down or walk the ancient paths; you can usually visit at least four of the religious communities in a day.

Spend the last couple of days exploring the sacred home of the gods, **(5) Mt Olympus**, and indulging in the fine food and sinful sweets of **(6) Thessaloniki**. The city's ancient walls and Byzantine churches form a perfect backdrop for the cafe-lined waterfront.

Discover Greece

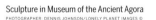

Sculpture in Museum of the Ancient Agora
PHOTOGRAPHER: DENNIS JOHNSON/LONELY PLANET IMAGES ©

ATHENS

POP 3.2 MILLION

Stroll around Athens and you'll quickly stumble across breathtaking archaeological treasures, reminders of the city's enormous historical influence on Western civilisation. Though the city still suffers from traffic congestion, pollution and urban sprawl, take the time to look beneath her skin and you will discover a complex metropolis full of vibrant subcultures.

Athens' golden age, the pinnacle of the classical era, came after the Persian empire was repulsed at the battles of Salamis and Plataea (480–479 BC). The city has passed through many hands and cast off myriad invaders from Sparta to Philip II of Macedon, the Roman and Byzantine Empires and, most recently, the Ottoman Empire. In 1834 Athens superseded Nafplio as the capital of independent Greece.

 Sights

ACROPOLIS MUSEUM

Museum

(☎210 900 0901; www.theacropolis museum.gr; Dionysiou Areopagitou 15; admission €5; ☺8am-8pm Tue-Sun; ☎; Ⓜ Akropoli) Don't miss this superb new museum on the southern base of the hill, and magnificently reflecting the Parthenon on its glass facade; it houses the surviving treasures of the Acropolis.

The museum's crowning glory is the top-floor **Parthenon Gallery**, a glass hall built in alignment with the Parthenon, visible through the windows. It showcases the temple's metopes and 160m frieze shown in sequence for the first time in over 200 years. Interspersed between

Athens in Two Days

There's only one way to spend your first day in Athens, and that's exploring the wonders of ancient Greece. In the morning, get the historical context at the impressive new **Acropolis Museum**, and then devote the whole afternoon to investigating the **Acropolis** itself. If you still have an hour or two, it's worth taking the time to visit Athens' two thousand-year-old marketplace, the **Ancient Agora**, as well as the **Temple of Olympian Zeus**. Discuss your day over quality *mezedhes* at a traditional taverna such as **Tzitzikas & Mermingas** or **Taverna tou Psarra**.

On day two, you can soak up the city's other sights. Catch the ceremonial **Changing of the Guard** outside parliament, then ponder the artefacts at the **Benaki Museum** or the **National Archaeological Museum**. In the afternoon, stroll up **Lykavittos Hill** for stunning vistas across Athens, then reward yourself with fantastic food and a knockout view of the Acropolis at **Varoulko**.

the golden-hued originals, white plaster replicates the controversial Parthenon Marbles removed by Lord Elgin in 1801 and later sold to the British Museum.

Other highlights include five **caryatids**, the maiden columns that held up the Erechtheion (the sixth is in the British Museum), a giant floral akrotirion and a **movie** illustrating the history of the Acropolis.

ANCIENT AGORA   Ancient Monument
(☏ 210 321 0185; Adrianou 24; adult/child €4/free; ⊗ 8.30am-8pm Apr-Oct, 8am-5.30pm Nov-Mar; Ⓜ Monastiraki) The Ancient Agora was the marketplace of early Athens and the focal point of civic and social life.

ROMAN AGORA   Ancient Monument
(☏ 210 324 5220; cnr Pelopida & Eolou; adult/child €2/free; ⊗ 8.30am-8pm Apr-Oct, 8am-5.30pm Nov-Mar; Ⓜ Monastiraki) The Romans built their agora just east of the ancient Athenian Agora. The wonderful **Tower of the Winds** was built in the 1st century BC by Syrian astronomer Andronicus.

TEMPLE OF OLYMPIAN ZEUS & PANATHENAIC STADIUM
Ancient Monuments
(☏ 210 922 6330; adult/child €2/free; ⊗ 8.30am-8pm Apr-Oct, 8am-5.30pm Nov-Mar; Ⓜ Akropoli) Begun in the 6th century BC, Greece's largest temple is impressive for the sheer size of its Corinthian columns:

17m high with a base diameter of 1.7m. East of the temple, the Panathenaic Stadium, built in the 4th century BC as a venue for the Panathenaic athletic contests, hosted the first modern Olympic Games in 1896.

NATIONAL ARCHAEOLOGICAL MUSEUM
Museum
(☏ 210 821 7717; www.namuseum.gr; 28 Oktovriou-Patision 44; adult/child €7/free; ⊗ 1.30-8pm Mon, 8am-8pm Tue-Sun Apr-Oct, 8.30am-3pm Nov-Mar; Ⓜ Viktoria) One of the world's great museums, it contains significant finds from major archaeological sites throughout Greece.

BENAKI MUSEUM   Museum
(☏ 210 367 1000; www.benaki.gr; cnr Leoforos Vasilissis Sofias & Koumbari 1, Kolonaki; adult/child €6/free, free Thu; ⊗ 9am-5pm Mon, Wed, Fri & Sat, 9am-midnight Thu, 9am-3pm Sun; Ⓜ Syntagma) This superb museum houses the extravagant collection of Antoine Benaki, the son of an Alexandrian cotton magnate. Splendid displays include ancient sculpture, Persian, Byzantine and Coptic objects, Chinese ceramics, icons, El Greco paintings and fabulous traditional costumes.

LYKAVITTOS HILL   Park
(Ⓜ Evangelismos) Pine-covered Lykavittos is the highest of the eight hills dotting Athens. Climb to the summit for stunning views of

Central Athens

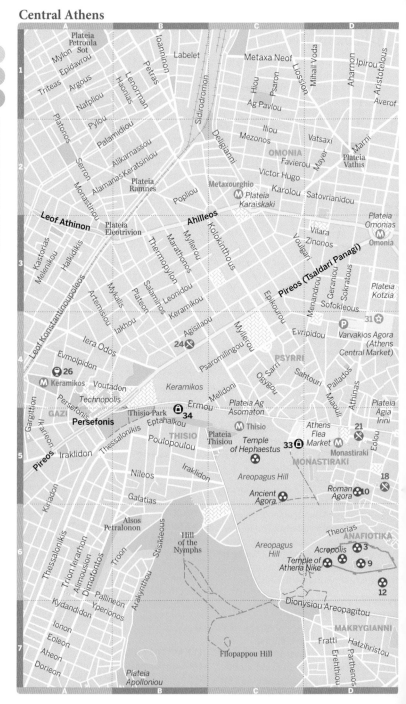

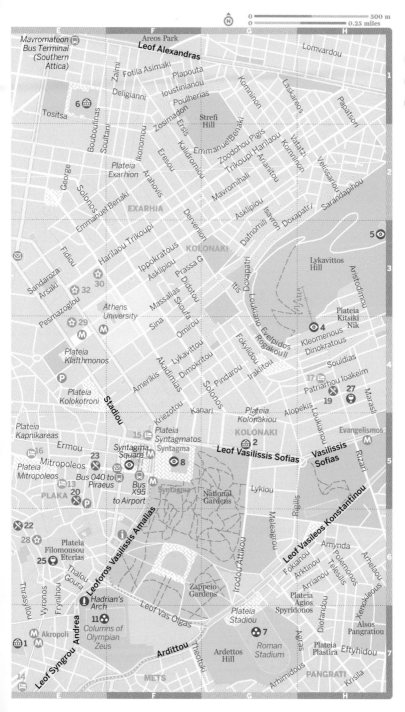

0 ———————— 500 m
0 ———————— 0.25 miles

Mavromateon Bus Terminal (Southern Attica)

Areos Park

Leof Alexandras

Lomvardou

Tositsa

6

Zaimi
Fotila Asimaki
Plapouta
Deligianni
Ioustinianou
Poulherias

Komninon
Laskareos
Papatsori

Bouboulinas
Soultani
Zosimadon
Ersis
Ikonomou

Strefi Hill

Emmanuel Benaki
Zoodohou Pigis
Trikoupi Hariaou
Komninon
Vatatzi
Velissariou
Sarandapihou

George
Solonos
Emmanuel Benaki
Arahovis
Dervenion

Plateia Exarhion

Kalidromiou
Eresou

Mavromihali

EXARHIA

Asklipiou
Isavron
Doxapatri

Fidiou
Harilaou Trikoupi
KOLONAKI

Dafnomili

5

Sandaroza Arsaki
Ippokratous
Asklipiou
Prassa G
Didotou
Skoura

Ittis
Doxapatri
Loukianou

Lykavittos Hill

Aristodimou

32
30

Pesmazoglou

Athens University

Massalias
Sina
Omirou

Fokylidou
Rogakou II

Plateia Kitsiki Nik

29

Akadimias
Lykavittou
Dimokritou

Pindarou
Iraklitou

Kleomenous
Dinokratous

4

Plateia Klafthmonos

Amerikis

Solonos

Souidias

17

Plateia Kolokotroni

Stadiou
Kriezotou
Kanari

Plateia Kolonakiou

Patriarhou Ioakeim

19
27

Marasli

Plateia Kapnikareas

Ermou

15
Plateia Syntagmatos
Syntagma

Alopekis

KOLONAKI

Evangelismos

16
Mitropoleos
Plateia Mitropoleos

23
Syntagma Square
Syntagma

2

Leof Vasilissis Sofias

Loukianou

Vasilissis Sofias

13
PLAKA
20

Bus 040 to Piraeus
Bus X95 to Airport

8

Lykiou

Rizari

22
28

National Gardens

Leof Vasileos Konstantinou

25

Plateia Filomousou Eterias

Thalou
Goura

Vyronos
Frynihou

Akropoli

Hadrian's Arch

11
Columns of Olympian Zeus

Leoforos Vasilissis Amalias

Meleagrou

Irodou Attikou

Rigilis

Amynda
Fokianou
Arktinou
Arrianou
Telesilis
Polemonos

Xenokleous
Arhelaou

1

Leof Syngrou Andrea

14

METS

Zappeio Gardens

Leof Vas Olgas

Ardittou

Ardettos Hill

Plateia Agios Spyridonos

Plateia Stadiou

7

Roman Stadium

Agras
Diofandou

Alsos Pangratiou

Plateia Plastira
Eftyhidou

PANGRATI

Arhimidous
Krisila

Theotoki

745

Central Athens

the city, the Attic basin and the islands of Salamis and Aegina (pollution permitting).

The main path to the summit starts at the top of Loukianou, or take the **funicular railway** (return €6; ⊘9am-3am) from the top of Ploutarhou.

PARLIAMENT & CHANGING OF THE GUARD   Cultural Ritual
In front of the parliament building on Plateia Syntagmatos (Syntagma Sq), the traditionally costumed *evzones* (guards) of the **Tomb of the Unknown Soldier** change every hour on the hour. On Sunday at 11am, a whole platoon marches down Vasilissis Sofias to the tomb, accompanied by a band.

 Tours

Athens Sightseeing Public Bus Line   Bus
(Bus Route 400; tickets €5) Stops at 20 key sites. Buy tickets (valid for 24 hours on all public transport, excluding airport services) on board.

CitySightseeing Athens   Bus
(📞210 922 0604; www.city-sightseeing.com; adult/concession €18/8; ⊘every 30min 9am-6pm) Open-top double-decker buses on a 90-minute circuit.

 Festivals & Events

Hellenic Festival   Performing Arts
(📞210 327 2000; www.greekfestival.gr; box office Panepistimiou 39, Syntagma; ⊘8.30am-4pm Mon-Fri, 9am-2pm Sat; Ⓜ Panepistimio) The city's most important cultural event runs from mid-June to August.

 Sleeping

Book well ahead for July and August.

Syntagma & Monastiraki
HOTEL GRANDE BRETAGNE
                Luxury Hotel €€€
(📞210 333 0000; www.grandebretagne.gr; Vasileos Georgiou 1, Syntagma; r/ste from

DENNIS JOHNSON/LONELY PLANET IMAGES ®

Don't Miss **The Acropolis**

Arguably the most important ancient monument in the Western world, the **Acropolis** (☏210 321 0219; adult/child €12/free; ⊙8.30am-8pm Apr-Oct, 8am-5pm Nov-Mar; Ⓜ Akropoli) attracts multitudes of tourists, so visit in the early morning or late afternoon.

People lived on the Acropolis until the late 6th century BC, but in 510 BC the Delphic oracle declared that the Acropolis should be the province of the gods. When all of the buildings were reduced to ashes by the Persians on the eve of the Battle of Salamis (480 BC), Pericles set about rebuilding a city purely of temples.

It's the **Parthenon** (above), however, that epitomises the glory of ancient Greece. Completed in 438 BC, it's unsurpassed in grace and harmony. To achieve the appearance of perfect form, columns become narrower towards the top and the bases curve upward slightly towards the ends – effects that make them look straight.

To the north, lies the **Erechtheion** and its much-photographed Caryatids, the six maidens who support its southern portico. These are plaster casts – the originals are in the Acropolis Museum.

On the southern slope of the Acropolis, the importance of theatre in the everyday lives of ancient Athenians is made manifest in the enormous **Theatre of Dionysos**. Built between 340 and 330 BC on the site of an earlier theatre dating to the 6th century BC, it held 17,000 people.

The €12 ticket at the Acropolis (valid for four days) includes entry to the other significant ancient sites: Ancient Agora, Roman Agora, Keramikos, Temple of Olympian Zeus and the Theatre of Dionysos.

€275/420; Ⓟ ❄ @ 🛜 ⊠; Ⓜ Syntagma) Dripping with elegance and old-world charm, *the* place to stay in Athens has always has been these deluxe digs. The guest rooms, divine spa and rooftop restaurant are built for pampering.

Magna Grecia Boutique Hotel **€€**
(☎210 324 0314; www.magnagreciahotel.com; Mitropoleos 54, Monastiraki; s/d incl breakfast from €110/130; ❄ @ 📶; M Syntagma) Enjoy Acropolis views from the front rooms and rooftop terrace in a historic building opposite the cathedral. Rooms with murals sport comfortable mattresses, DVD players and minibars.

Plaka, Makrygianni & Koukaki

CENTRAL HOTEL Boutique Hotel **€€**
(☎210 323 4357; www.centralhotel.gr; Apollonos 21, Plaka; r incl breakfast €93-155; 🚭 ❄ @; M Syntagma) Pass through the sleek lobby and by the attentive staff to spacious white rooms hung with original art and decked out with all the mod cons. Some balconies have Acropolis views, as does the rooftop, where you can sunbake and relax in the Jacuzzi.

HERA HOTEL Boutique Hotel **€€**
(☎210 923 6682; www.herahotel.gr; Falirou 9, Makrygianni; r from €115; ❄ @; M Akropoli) The interior of this exquisite boutique hotel matches its lovely neoclassical facade. The rooftop garden, restaurant and bar boast spectacular views and it is a short walk to the Acropolis and Plaka.

Kolonaki

PERISCOPE Boutique Hotel **€€€**
(☎210 729 7200; www.periscope.gr; Haritos 22, Kolonaki; r from €135; 🚭 ❄ @ 📶; M Evangelismos) A hip hotel with a cool, edgy look (Mini Cooper seats for chairs in the cafe-bar), this place has comfortable minimalist rooms with all the mod cons and a quiet location.

Eating

Wear your most stylish togs at night: Athenians dress up to eat out. Eat streets include Mitropoleos, Adrianou and Navarchou Apostoli in Monastiraki, the area around Plateia Psyrri, and Gazi near Keramikos metro.

Listings without opening hours specified are open for lunch and dinner daily during high season.

Left: Chapel on Lykavittos Hill (p743);
Below: View of Athens from Lykavittos Hill
PHOTOGRAPHERS: (LEFT) GEORGE TSAFOS/LONELY PLANET IMAGES ©;
(BELOW) GEORGE TSAFOS/LONELY PLANET IMAGES ©

Syntagma & Monastiraki

TZITZIKAS & MERMINGAS
Mezedhes €€
(Mitropoleos 12-14, Syntagma; mezedhes €6-8; M Syntagma) Greek merchandise lines the walls of this cheery, modern *mezedhopoleio*. The great range of delicious *mezedhes* draws a bustling local crowd.

SAVAS
Souvlaki €
(Mitropoleos 86-88, Monastiraki; gyros €2; M Monastiraki) This joint serves enormous grilled-meat plates (€8.50) and the tastiest gyros (pork, beef or chicken) in Athens. Take away or sit down in what becomes one of the city's busiest eat streets late at night.

Plaka & Makrygianni

Paradosiako
Taverna €
(☎ 210 321 4121; Voulis 44a, Plaka; mains €7-14; M Syntagma) For great traditional fare you can't beat this inconspicuous, no-frills taverna on the periphery of Plaka. Choose from daily specials such as delicious shrimp *saganaki*.

TAVERNA TOU PSARRA
Taverna €€
(☎ 210 321 8734; Eretheos 16, Plaka; mains €8-23; M Monastiraki) On a path leading up towards the Acropolis, this gem of a taverna is one of Plaka's best, serving scrumptious *mezedhes* and excellent fish and meat classics on a tree-lined terrace.

O Platanos
Taverna €
(☎ 210 322 0666; Diogenous 4, Monastiraki, Plaka; mains €7-9; M Monastiraki) Laid-back O Platanos 'Plane Tree' serves tasty, home-cooked-style Greek cuisine. The lamb dishes are delicious and we love the leafy courtyard.

Psyrri, Thissio & Gazi

VAROULKO
Gourmet Seafood €€€
(☎ 210 522 8400; www.varoulko.gr; Pireos 80, Gazi; mains €22-30; ☾ closed Sun; M Keramikos) For a magical Greek dining experience, you can't beat the winning combination of

Acropolis views and delicious seafood by celebrated chef Lefteris Lazarou.

Kolonaki & Pangrati

OIKEIO Bistro €
(210 725 9216; Ploutarhou 15, Kolonaki; mains €8-11; M Evangelismos) With excellent home-style cooking, this modern taverna lives up to its name ('Homey'). The intimate bistro atmosphere spills out to tables on the pavement for glitterati-watching. Reservations recommended.

SPONDI Gourmet Greek €€€
(210 756 4021; www.spondi.gr; Pyrronos 5, Pangrati; mains €36-50; 8pm-midnight) Chef Arnaud Bignon has won two Michelin stars using local ingredients and adhering to French technique but embodying vibrant Greek flavours.

 # Drinking

Athenians know how to party. Everyone has their favourite *steki* (hang-out), but expect people to show up after midnight.

Hoxton Bar
(210 341 3395; Voutadon 42, Gazi; M Keramikos) Kick back on overstuffed leather couches under modern art in this industrial space that fills up late with bohemians, ruggers and the occasional pop star.

Brettos Bar
(210 323 2110; Kydathineon 41, Plaka; M Syntagma) This distillery and bar is back-lit by an eye-catching collection of coloured bottles.

Mai-Tai Bar
(Ploutarhou 18, Kolonaki; M Evangelismos) Jam-packed with well-heeled young Athenians, this is just one in a group of happening spots in Kolonaki.

 # Entertainment

The *Kathimerini* supplement inside the *International Herald Tribune* contains event listings and a cinema guide, or check www.breathtakingathens.gr, www .ticketservices.gr and www.tickethour. com. **Ticket House** (Map p744; 210 360 8366; Panepistimiou 42) sells concert tickets.

Classical Music, Theatre & Dance

Megaron Mousikis Concert Hall
(210 728 2333; www.megaron.gr; cnr Leoforos Vasilissis Sofias & Kokkali) Superb concert venue hosting winter performances by local and international artists.

Olympia Theatre Opera, Ballet
(210 361 2461; www.national opera.gr; Akadimias 59, Exarhia) November to June: ballet, symphony and the Greek National Opera (www .nationalopera.gr).

Dora Stratou Dance Company Dance
(210 921 4650; www .grdance.org; Filopappou Hill, ticket office Scholiou 8; tickets €15; 9.30pm)

Evzone (guard) at the Tomb of the Unknown Soldier (p746)
PHOTOGRAPHER: ANDREW BAIN/LONELY PLANET IMAGES ©

Tue-Sat, 8.15pm Sun May-Sep) Traditional folk-dancing shows feature more than 75 musicians and dancers in an open-air amphitheatre.

Most authentic *rembetika* venues close during summer, but you can see a popularised version at some tavernas in Psyrri.

Rembetika Stoa Athanaton   Traditional Music

(☏ 210 321 4362; Sofokleous 19; ⏰ 3.30-6pm & midnight-late Mon-Sat Oct-May) Located above the meat market, this is still *the* place to listen to *rembetika*.

Shopping

Athens is the place to shop for cool jewellery, clothes and shoes, and souvenirs such as backgammon sets, hand-woven textiles, olive oil beauty products, worry beads and ceramics.

Monastiraki Flea Market   Flea Market
Enthralling; spreads daily from Plateia Monastirakiou (Monastiraki Sq).

Sunday Market   Flea Market
(⏰ 7am-2pm Sun) At the end of Ermou, towards Gazi.

 Information

Emergency

Tourist Police (☏ 24hr 171, 210 920 0724; Veïkou 43-45, Koukaki; ⏰ 8am-10pm)

Athens Police Station Central (☏ 210 770 5711/17; Leoforos Alexandras 173, Ambelokipi; Ⓜ Ambelokipi); Plateia Syntagmatos (☏ 210 725 7000)

Money

Most banks have branches around Plateia Syntagmatos.

Eurochange Syntagma (☏ 210 331 2462; Karageorgi Servias 2; ⏰ 8am-9pm; Ⓜ Syntagma); Monastiraki (☏ 210 322 2657; Areos 1)

Tourist Information

EOT (Greek National Tourist Organisation; ☏ 210 870 7000; www.gnto.gr) Syntagma (☏ 210 331

0392; Leoforos Vasilissis Amalias 26; ⏰ 9am-7pm Mon-Fri, 10am-4pm Sat & Sun; Ⓜ Syntagma); airport (☏ 210 353 0445; Arrivals Hall; ⏰ 9am-7pm Mon-Fri, 10am-4pm Sat & Sun); head office (Tsoha 24; ⏰ 9am-2pm Mon-Fri; Ⓜ Ambelokipi)

 Getting There & Away

Air

Modern **Eleftherios Venizelos International Airport** (ATH; ☏ 210 353 0000; www.aia.gr), 27km east of Athens, has a 24-hour information desk.

Boat

Most ferries, hydrofoils and high-speed catamarans leave from the massive port at Piraeus. Some services depart from smaller ports at Rafina and Lavrio.

Bus

Athens has two main intercity **KTEL** (www.ktel .org) bus stations, one 5km, and one 7km to the north of Omonia.

Train

Intercity trains to central and northern Greece depart from the central **Larisis train station**, about 1km northwest of Plateia Omonias.

OSE Offices (☏ 1110; www.ose.gr) Syntagma (☏ 210 362 4402; Sina 6; ⏰ 8am-3pm Mon-Sat); Omonia (☏ 210 524 0647; Karolou 1; ⏰ 8am-3pm Mon-Fri)

Getting Around

To/From the Airport

METRO Line 3 links the airport to the city centre in around 40 minutes; it operates from Monastiraki from 5.50am to midnight, and from the airport from 5.30am to 11.30pm. Tickets (€6) are valid for all public transport for 90 minutes.
TAXI Fares vary according to the time of day and level of traffic; expect at least €30 from the airport to the centre, and €40 to Piraeus.

Public Transport

The metro, tram and bus system makes getting around central Athens and to Piraeus easy. Tickets (€1), good for 90 minutes, and a 24-hour travel pass (€3) work on all forms of public transport except for airport services.

BUS & TROLLEYBUS Buses and electric trolleybuses operate every 15 minutes from 5am to midnight. Purchase tickets before boarding (from the metro, a bus-ticket booth or a kiosk). Validate as you board.

Piraeus Buses operate 24 hours: every 20 minutes from 6am to midnight, and then hourly.

METRO Trains operate from 5am to midnight: every three minutes during peak periods and every 10 minutes off-peak. Get timetables at www.ametro.gr. Validate tickets as you enter the platforms.

METRO Fast suburban rail (☎1110; www .trainose.com) links Athens with the airport, Piraeus, the outer regions and the northern Peloponnese. It connects to the metro at Larisis, Doukissis Plakentias and Nerantziotissa stations, and goes from the airport to Kiato.

PELOPONNESE ΠΕΛΟΠΟΝΝΗΣΟΣ

The Peloponnese encompasses a breathtaking array of landscapes, villages and ruins.

Nafplio ΝΑΥΠΛΙΟ
POP 14,500

Elegant Venetian houses and neoclassical mansions dripping with crimson bougainvillea cascade down Nafplio's hillside to the azure sea. Vibrant cafes, shops and restaurants fill winding pedestrian streets. Crenulated Palamidi Fortress perches above it all. What's not to love?

 Sights

Palamidi Fortress Fortress
(☎27520 28036; admission €4; ⏰8am-6.45pm Jun-Aug, to 2.45pm Sep-May) Enjoy spectacular views of the town and surrounding coast from the magnificent hilltop fortress built by the Venetians between 1711 and 1714.

Archaeological Museum Museum
(Plateia Syntagmatos; ⏰8.30am-3pm Tue-Sun; adult/concession €2/1) Fine exhibits include fire middens from 32,000 BC and bronze armour from near Mycenae (12th to 13th centuries BC).

Peloponnese Folklore Foundation Museum Museum
(☎27520 28379; 1 Vas Alexandrou St; admission €4; ⏰9am-2.30pm & 5.30-10.30pm) One of

Greece's best small museums, with displays of vibrant regional costumes and rotating exhibitions.

 **Sleeping**

The Old Town is *the* place to stay, but has limited budget options.

AMFITRITI PENSION Pension €€
(☎27520 96250; www.amfitriti-pension.gr; Kapodistriou 24; d incl breakfast €85-110) Quaint antiques fill these intimate rooms in an Old Town house. Enjoy stellar views at its nearby sister hotel, Amfitriti Belvedere, which is chock full of brightly coloured tapestries and emits a feeling of cheery serenity.

Hotel Grande Bretagne
Luxury Hotel €€€
(☎27520 96200; www.grandebretagne.com.gr; Filellinon Sq; s/d incl breakfast €130/180) In the heart of Nafplio's cafe action and overlooking the sea, this splendidly restored hotel with high ceilings, antiques and chandeliers radiates plush opulence.

 Eating

Taverna Aeolos Traditional Greek €
(☎27520 26828; V Olgas 30; mains €5-13) This boisterous taverna lined with copper pans gets packed with locals sharing generous mixed-grill plates (€8.50). Live music during summer.

Omorfi Poli Greek, Italian €
(☎27520 29452; Bouboulinas 75; mains €6-16; ⏰dinner) Greek favourites and *mezedhes* (€5) with a slight Italian twist (there's mushroom risotto), plus friendly service and good wine list.

Antica Gelateria di Roma
Ice Creamery €
(☎27520 23520; cnr Farmakopoulou 6 & Komninou) The best (yes, best) traditional gelati outside Italy.

ⓘ Information

TOURIST INFORMATION Kasteli Travel & Tourist Agency (☎27520 29395; 38 Vas Konstantinou; ⏰9am-2pm year-round & 6-8pm Jun-Sep) At Syngrou; friendly English-speaking.

Municipal Tourist Office (☎27520 24444; 25 Martiou; ⏰9am-1pm & 4-8pm)

ⓘ Getting There & Away

Services from **KTEL Argolis Bus Station** (☎27520 27323; Syngrou 8):

Argos (for Peloponnese connections) €1.40, 30 minutes, half-hourly

Athens €12, 2½ hours, hourly (via Corinth)

Epidavros €2.60, 45 minutes, four daily

Mycenae €2.60, one hour, two daily

Mycenae ΜΥΚΗΝΕΣ

Although settled as early as the 6th millennium BC, **Ancient Mycenae** (☎27510 76585; admission €8; ⏰8am-8pm Jun-Sep, to 6pm Oct, to 3pm Nov-May) was at its most powerful from 1600 to 1200 BC. Mycenae's entrance, the **Lion Gate**, is Europe's oldest monumental sculpture. Homer accurately described Mycenae as being 'rich in gold': excavations of **Grave Circle A** by Heinrich Schliemann in the 1870s uncovered magnificent gold treasures, such as the Mask of Agamemnon, now on display at Athens' National Archaeological Museum.

Two buses go daily to Mycenae from Argos (€1.60, 30 minutes) and Nafplio (€2.60, one hour).

CENTRAL GREECE ΚΕΝΤΡΙΚΗ ΕΛΛΑΔΑ

This dramatic landscape of deep gorges, rugged mountains and fertile valleys is home to the magical stone pinnacle-topping monasteries of Meteora and the iconic ruins of ancient Delphi, where Alexander the Great sought advice from the Delphic oracle.

Delphi ΔΕΛΦΟΙ

POP 2800

The ancient Greeks regarded Delphi as the centre of the world. According to mythology, Zeus released two eagles at opposite ends of the world and they met here. By the 6th century BC, **Ancient Delphi** (☎22650 82312; site or museum €6, combined adult/child €9/5, free Sun Nov-Mar; ⏰1.30-7.45pm Mon, 8am-7.45pm Tue-Sun Apr-Oct, 8.30am-2.45pm Nov-Mar) had become the Sanctuary of Apollo. Thousands of pilgrims flocked here to consult the middle-aged female oracle who sat at the

Tomb of Agamemnon at Mycenae

753

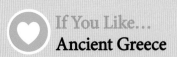

If You Like…
Ancient Greece

If your imagination has been fired by the ruins of the **Acropolis** (p747) and **Mt Olympus** (p756), you'll want to seek out some of the other treasures of ancient Greece.

1 EPIDAVROS
(☎27530 22006; admission €6; ⏰8am-7pm Apr-Sep, 8am-5pm Oct-Mar) This spectacular Unesco World Heritage site was the sanctuary of Asclepius, god of medicine. It has a splendid ancient spa and healing centre, and the magnificent **theatre** is still used during the Hellenic Festival. The site is 36km east of Nafplio.

2 MYSTRAS
(☎27310 83377; adult/child €6/3; ⏰8am-7.30pm Apr-Oct, 8.30am-3pm Nov-Mar) Mystras was once the effective capital of the Byzantine Empire. Ruins of palaces, monasteries and churches, most of them dating from between 1271 and 1460, nestle at the base of the Taÿgetos Mountains, and are surrounded by verdant olive and orange groves. The site is about 7km from Sparta.

3 ANCIENT OLYMPIA
(☎26240 22517; adult/child €6/3, site & museum €9/5; ⏰8am-8pm Apr-Oct, 8.30am-3pm Nov-Mar) The first ever Olympic Games were staged here in 776 BC, and every four years thereafter until AD 394 when Emperor Theodosius I banned them. Today the site is dominated by the immense ruined **Temple of Zeus**, to whom the games were dedicated. It's 20km east of Pyrgos.

mouth of a fume-emitting chasm. From the entrance, take the **Sacred Way** up to the **Temple of Apollo**, where the oracle sat. From here the path continues to the **theatre** and **stadium**.

Opposite the main site and down the hill some 100m, don't miss the **Sanctuary of Athena** and the much-photographed **Tholos**, a 4th-century-BC columned rotunda of Pentelic marble.

Six buses a day go to Athens (€13.60, three hours). Take a bus to Lamia (€8.20,

two hours, two daily) or Trikala (€13.80, 4½ hours, two daily) to transfer for Meteora.

NORTHERN GREECE

Northern Greece is stunning, graced as it is with magnificent mountains, thick forests, tranquil lakes and archaeological sites. Most of all, it's easy to get off the beaten track and experience aspects of Greece noticeably different from other mainland areas and the islands.

Thessaloniki
ΘΕΣΣΑΛΟΝΙΚΗ
POP 800,800

Dodge cherry sellers in the street, smell spices in the air and enjoy waterfront breezes in Thessaloniki (thess-ah-lo-nee-kih), also known as Salonica. The second city of Byzantium and of modern Greece boasts countless Byzantine churches, a smattering of Roman ruins, engaging museums, shopping to rival Athens, fine restaurants and a lively cafe scene and nightlife.

Check out the seafront **White Tower** (Lefkos Pyrgos; www.lpth.org; admission free; ⏰8am-3pm Tue-Sun) and wander *hamams* (Turkish baths) and churches such as the enormous, 5th-century **Church of Agios Dimitrios** (Agiou Dimitriou 97; admission free; ⏰8am-10pm). The award-winning **Museum of Byzantine Culture** (☎2310 868 570; www.mbp.gr; Leoforos Stratou 2; admission €4; ⏰8am-8pm Tue-Sun, 1.30-8pm Mon) beautifully displays splendid sculptures, mosaics, icons and other intriguing artefacts. The **Archaeological Museum** (☎2310 830 538; Manoli Andronikou 6; admission €6; ⏰8.30am-8pm) showcases prehistoric, ancient Macedonian and Hellenistic finds.

🛏 Sleeping

Electra Palace Hotel Luxury Hotel €€
(☎2310 294 000; www.electrahotels.gr; Plateia Aristotelous 9; d €130-210; ❄ @ 🛜 🏊) Dive

into five-star seafront pampering: impeccable service, plush rooms, a rooftop bar, indoor and outdoor swimming pools, and a *hamam*.

City Hotel Business Hotel €€
(2310 269 421; www.cityhotel.gr; Komninon 11; s/d incl breakfast €120/135; ✳ @ 🛜) Ask for a light-filled front room in this excellently located, sleek and stylish hotel.

 Eating & Drinking

Tavernas dot Plateia Athonos and cafes pack Leoforos Nikis. Head to **Modiano Market** for fresh fruit and vegetables.

ZYTHOS Traditional Greek €
(Katouni 5; mains €6-12) Popular with locals, this excellent taverna with friendly staff serves delicious standards, interesting regional specialities, good wines by the glass and beers on tap. Its second outlet is **Dore Zythos** (🖉 2310 279 010; Tsirogianni 7), near the White Tower.

Kitchen Bar Eclectic International €
(🖉 2310 528 108; Warehouse B, Thessaloniki Port; mains €7-13) This perennial favourite offers both drinks and artfully prepared food, in a

sumptuously decorated, renovated warehouse with waterfront tables.

Paparouna Creative Greek €
(🖉 2310 510 852; www.paparouna.com; Syngrou 7; mains €8-16; 🕐1pm-1am; 🛜) Built a century ago as a bank, this lively restaurant whips up inventive cuisine like chicken with peppermint and honey.

White Tower, Thessaloniki

GEORGE TSAFOS/LONELY PLANET IMAGES ©

Bus

The **main bus station** (23105 95408; Monastiriou 319) services Athens (€35, 6¼ hours, 10 daily), Ioannina (€28.50, 4¾ hours, six daily) and other destinations.

Train

The **train station** (2310 599 421; Monastiriou) serves Athens (regular/IC €28/36, 6¾/5½ hours, seven/10 daily), Alexandroupolis (€13.60, six hours, three daily) and beyond.

Mt Olympus
ΟΛΥΜΠΟΣ ΟΡΟΣ

Just as it did for the ancients, Greece's highest mountain, the cloud-covered lair of the Greek pantheon, fires the visitor's imagination today. The highest of Olympus' eight peaks is **Mytikas** (2917m), popular with trekkers, who use **Litohoro** (elevation 305m), 5km inland from the Athens–Thessaloniki highway, as their base. The main route up takes two days, with a stay overnight at one of the **refuges** (May-Oct). Good protective

clothing is essential, even in summer. **EOS** (Greek Alpine Club; 23520 84544; Plateia Kentriki; 9.30am-12.30pm & 6-8pm Mon-Sat Jun-Sep) has information on treks.

The romantic guest house **Xenonas Papanikolaou** (23520 81236; xenpap@ otenet.gr; Nikolaou Episkopou Kitrous 1; s/d €45/50;) sits in a flowery garden up in the backstreets, a world away from the tourist crowds.

Gastrodromio El Olympio (23520 21300; Plateia Eleftherias; mains €7-13), one of Greece's best country restaurants, serves such specialities as *soutzoukakia* (minced meat with cumin and mint) and delicious wild mushrooms with an impressive regional wine list and gorgeous Olympus views.

From the **bus station** (23520 81271) 13 buses daily go to Thessaloniki (€8, 1¼ hours) and three to Athens (€28, 5½ hours).

CYCLADES ΚΥΚΛΑΔΕΣ

The Cyclades (kih-*klah*-dez) are Greek islands to dream about. Named after the rough *kyklos* (circle) they form around the island of Delos, they are rugged outcrops of rock in the azure Aegean, speckled with white cubist buildings and blue-domed Byzantine churches.

Some of the islands, such as Mykonos, Ios and Santorini, have seized tourism with great enthusiasm. Prepare to battle the crowds if you turn up at the height of summer.

Mykonos
ΜΥΚΟΝΟΣ
POP 9700

Sophisticated Mykonos glitters happily under the Aegean sun, shamelessly surviving on tourism. The island has something for everyone, with marvellous beaches,

Sanctuary of Athena (p754), Delphi
PHOTOGRAPHER: NOBORU KOMINE/LONELY PLANET IMAGES ©

MARK DAFFEY/LONELY PLANET IMAGES ©

Don't Miss Meteora ΜΕΤΕΩΡΑ

Meteora (meh-*teh*-o-rah) should be a certified Wonder of the World with its magnificent late-14th-century monasteries perched dramatically atop enormous rocky pinnacles. Try not to miss it. The tranquil village of **Kastraki** (above), 2km from Kalambaka, is the best base for visiting.

While there were once monasteries on all 24 pinnacles, only six are still occupied: **Megalou Meteorou** (Grand Meteoron; 9am-5pm Wed-Mon Apr-Oct, 9am-4pm Thu-Mon Nov-Mar), **Varlaam** (9am-4pm Wed-Mon Apr-Oct, Thu-Mon Nov-Mar), **Agiou Stefanou** (9am-1.30pm & 3.30-5.30pm Tue-Sun Apr-Oct, 9.30am-1pm & 3-5pm Nov-Mar), **Agias Triados** (Holy Trinity; 9am-5pm Fri-Wed Apr-Oct, 10am-3pm Nov-Mar), **Agiou Nikolaou Anapafsa** (9am-3.30pm Sat-Thu) and **Agias Varvaras Rousanou** (9am-6pm Thu-Tue Apr-Oct, 9am-4pm Nov-Mar). Admission is €2 for each monastery and strict dress codes apply (no bare shoulders or knees and women must wear skirts; borrow a long skirt at the door if you don't have one).

Local buses shuttle between Kalambaka and Kastraki (€1.90); a bus goes up to the monasteries in the morning. From Kalambaka, express trains run to Athens (regular/IC €14.60/24.30, 5½hr/4½, two/two daily) and Thessaloniki (€12.10, four hours, three daily).

romantic sunsets, chic boutiques, excellent restaurants and bars, and its long-held reputation as a mecca for gay travellers.

Sights & Activities

A stroll around Mykonos Town, shuffling through snaking streets with blinding white walls and balconies of flowers, is a must for any visitor. **Little Venice**, where the sea laps up to the edge of the restaurants and bars, and Mykonos' famous hilltop row of **windmills** should be included in the spots-to-see list. You're bound to run into one of Mykonos' famous resident pelicans on your walk.

The island's most popular beaches are on the southern coast. **Platys Gialos** has wall-to-wall sun lounges, while nudity is not uncommon at **Paradise Beach**, **Super Paradise**, **Agrari** and gay-friendly **Elia**.

Mykonos

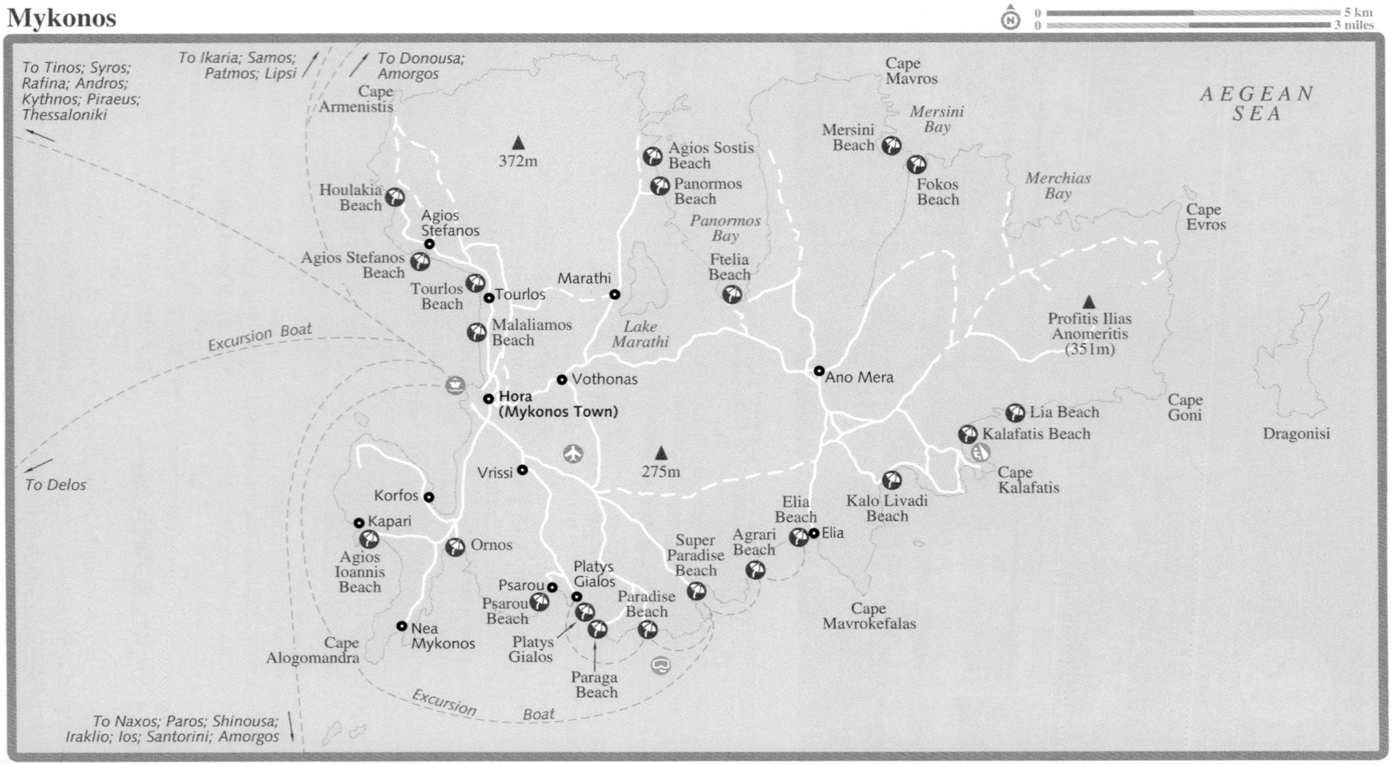

5 km
3 miles

AEGEAN SEA

Dragonisi

Cape Evros

Cape Goni

Lia Beach

Kalafatis Beach

Cape Kalafatis

Merchias Bay

Profitis Ilias Anomeritis (351m)

Cape Mavros

Mersini Bay

Fokos Beach

Mersini Beach

Kalo Livadi Beach

Cape Mavrokefalas

Ano Mera

Elia Beach

Elia

Agrari Beach

Panormos Bay

Agios Sostis Beach

Panormos Beach

Ftelia Beach

Lake Marathi

Super Paradise Beach

Paradise Beach

Marathi

Vothonas

275m

Platys Gialos

Paraga Beach

Tourlos

Malaliamos Beach

Hora (Mykonos Town)

Vrissi

Psarou Beach

Platys Gialos

372m

Agios Stefanos

Tourlos Beach

Ornos

Cape Armenistis

Houlakia Beach

Agios Stefanos Beach

Nea Mykonos

Korfos

Kapari

Agios Ioannis Beach

Cape Alogomandra

Excursion Boat

To Ikaria; Samos;
Patmos; Lipsi /
/ To Donousa;
Amorgos

To Tinos; Syros;
Rafina; Andros;
Kythnos; Piraeus;
Thessaloniki

To Naxos; Paros; Shinousa;
Iraklio; Ios; Santorini; Amorgos

To Delos

Excursion Boat

Sleeping

Hotel Lefteris Hotel €€
(☎22890 27117; www.lefterishotel.gr; 9 Apollonas, Mykonos Town; s/d €95/120, studios €220-260; ❄) Tucked away just up from Taxi Sq, Lefteris has bright and comfy rooms, and a relaxing sun terrace with superb views over town. A good international meeting place.

HOTEL PHILIPPI Hotel €€
(☎22890 22294; chriko@otenet.gr; 25 Kalogera, Mykonos Town; s €60-90, d €75-120; ❄⌨) In the heart of the *hora,* Philippi has spacious, bright, clean rooms that open onto a railed veranda overlooking a lush garden.

 # Eating

There is no shortage of places to eat and drink in Mykonos Town.

Fato a Mano Mediterranean €
(☎22890 26256; Meletopoulou Sq; mains €8-15) In the middle of the maze, this place is worth taking the effort to find. It serves up tasty Mediterranean and traditional Greek dishes with pride.

 # Drinking & Entertainment

The waterfront is perfect for sitting with a drink and watching an interesting array of passers-by, while Little Venice has bars with dreamy views and water lapping below your feet.

Information

Tourist information office (☎22890 25250; www.mykonos.gr; ⊙9am-9pm Jul & Aug, 10am-5pm Easter-Jun, Sep & Oct) At the western end of the waterfront, just up from the Delos boat ticket office.

Getting There & Around

AIR There are daily flights connecting **Mykonos airport** (JMK) to Athens. The airport is 3km southeast of the town centre; €1.50 by bus from the southern bus station.

BOAT Daily ferries (€30, five hours) and catamarans (€45, three hours) arrive from Piraeus. From Mykonos, there are daily ferries and hydrofoils to most major Cycladic islands, daily services to Crete, and less-frequent

Waterside bar in Little Venice (p757), Mykonos

Detour:
Delos ΔΗΛΟΣ

Southwest of Mykonos, the island of **Delos** (sites & museum €5; ⊘9am-3pm Tue-Sun) is the Cyclades' archaeological jewel.

According to mythology, Delos was the birthplace of Apollo – the god of light, poetry, music, healing and prophecy. The island flourished as an important religious and commercial centre from the 3rd millennium BC, reaching its apex of power in the 5th century BC.

Ruins include the **Sanctuary of Apollo**, containing temples dedicated to him, and the **Terrace of the Lions**. These proud beasts were carved in the early 6th century BC using marble from Naxos to guard the sacred area. The original lions are in the island's **museum**, with replicas on the original site. The **Sacred Lake** (dry since 1926) is where Leto supposedly gave birth to Apollo, while the **Theatre Quarter** is where private houses were built around the **Theatre of Delos**.

Numerous boat companies offer trips from Mykonos to Delos (€15 return, 30 minutes) between 9am and 1pm.

services to the northeastern Aegean Islands and the Dodecanese.

Santorini (Thira) ΣΑΝΤΟΡΙΝΗ (ΘΗΡΑ)

POP 13,500

Stunning Santorini is unique and should not be missed. The startling sight of the submerged caldera almost encircled by sheer lava-layered cliffs – topped off by clifftop towns that look like a dusting of icing sugar – will grab your attention and not let it go. If you turn up in high season, though, be prepared for relentless crowds and commercialism – Santorini survives on tourism.

 **Sights & Activities**

Fira

The stunning caldera views from Fira are unparalleled.

The exceptional **Museum of Prehistoric Thira** (admission €3; ⊘8.30am-8pm Tue-Sun), which has wonderful displays of artefacts predominantly from ancient Akrotiri, is two blocks south of the main square. **Megaron Gyzi Museum** (admission €3.50; ⊘10.30am-1pm & 5-8pm Mon-Sat, 10.30am-4.30pm Sun), behind the Catholic cathedral, houses local memorabilia, including photographs of Fira before and after the 1956 earthquake.

Around the Island

Excavations in 1967 uncovered the remarkably well-preserved Minoan settlement of **Akrotiri** at the south of the island, with its remains of two- and three-storey buildings. A section of the roof collapsed in 2005, killing one visitor, and at the time of research, the site's future as a visitor attraction was up in the air.

At the north of the island, the intriguing village of **Oia** (ee-ah), famed for its postcard sunsets, is less hectic than Fira and is a must-visit. Its caldera-facing tavernas are superb spots for brunch. There's a path from Fira to Oia along the top of the caldera that takes three to four hours to walk.

Santorini's black-sand **beaches** of **Perissa** and **Kamari** sizzle – beach mats are essential.

Of the surrounding islets, only **Thirasia** is inhabited. Visitors can clamber around on volcanic lava on **Nea Kameni** then swim into warm springs in the sea at **Palia Kameni**; there are various excursions available to get you there.

 Sleeping

HOTEL KETI Traditional Hotel €€
(☎ 22860 22324; www.hotelketi.gr; Agiou Mina, Fira; d/tr €95/120; ✳ @) Overlooking the caldera, with views to die for, Hotel Keti has traditional rooms carved into the cliffs. Some rooms have Jacuzzis.

HOTEL ATLANTIS Hotel €€€
(☎ 22860 22232; www.atlantishotel.gr; Fira; s/d incl breakfast €200/300; P ✳ @ ☲) Perfectly positioned and epitomising San-torini style, Atlantis is the oldest and most impressive place in Fira. With bright, airy rooms, swimming pool, relaxing terraces and lounges, it is a superb place to stay.

ⓘ Getting There & Around

AIR Santorini airport (JTR) has daily flight connections with Athens, plus seasonal scheduled flights with Iraklio and Rhodes. The airport is 5km southeast of Fira; frequent buses (€1.50) and taxis (€12).

BOAT There are daily ferries (€33.50, nine hours) and fast boats (€47, 5¼ hours) to

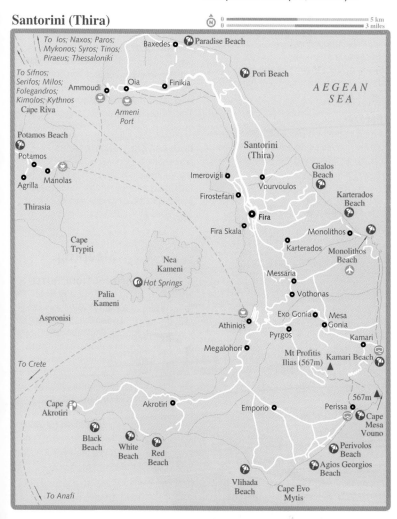

Santorini (Thira)

Piraeus; daily connections in summer to Mykonos, Ios, Naxos, Paros and Iraklio; and ferries to the smaller islands in the Cyclades.

CAR & MOTORCYCLE A rental car or scooter is a great option on Santorini.

CRETE KPHTH
POP 540,000

Crete is Greece's largest and southern-most island and its size and distance from the rest of Greece gives it the feel of a different country. With its dramatic landscape and unique cultural identity, Crete is a delight to explore.

While Crete's proud, friendly and hospitable people have enthusiastically embraced tourism, they continue to fiercely protect their traditions and culture – they remain a major part of the island's appeal.

History

Crete was the birthplace of Minoan culture, Europe's first advanced civilisation, which flourished between 2800 and 1450 BC. Very little is known of Minoan civilisation, which came to an abrupt end, possibly destroyed by Santorini's volcanic eruption in around 1650 BC.

Iraklio HPAKΛEIO
POP 131,000

Iraklio (ee-*rah*-klee-oh; often spelt Herak-lion), Crete's capital, is a bustling modern city and the fifth largest in Greece. It has a lively city centre and an excellent archaeological museum, and is close to Knossos, Crete's major visitor attraction.

 Sights

ARCHAEOLOGICAL MUSEUM Museum (Xanthoudidou 2; adult/student €6/3; ☯8am-1pm Mon, 8am-8pm Tue-Sun) The outstanding Minoan collection here is second only to that of the national museum in Athens. The museum was under long-term recon-struction at the time of research.

KOULES VENETIAN FORTRESS Fortress (admission €2; ☯9am-6pm Tue-Sun) Pro-tecting the old harbour, this impressive fortress is also known as Rocca al Mare, which, like the city walls, was built by the Venetians in the 16th century.

 Sleeping

LATO BOUTIQUE HOTEL Boutique Hotel €€ (☎28102 28103; www.lato.gr; Epimenidou 15; s/d €100/127; ❄@) This stylish hotel is a top place to stay. Ask for a room with harbour views. The con-temporary interior de-sign extends to the bar, breakfast restaurant and **Brilliant** (☎28103 34959), the superb fine-dining restaurant on the ground floor.

Island of Naxos in the Cyclades

Eating & Drinking

The places around the park are packed at night. A bustling, colourful market runs all the way along 1866, with a number of reasonably priced tavernas.

Giakoumis Taverna   Taverna **€**
(📞28102 80277) One of the best, offering up Cretan specialities hot off the grill.

ℹ Information

Tourist office (📞28102 46299; Xanthoudidou 1; ⏱8.30am-8.30pm Apr-Oct, to 3pm Nov-Mar) Opposite the Archaeological Museum.

KTEL (www.ktel.org) Runs the buses on Crete; has useful tourist information inside Bus Station A.

ℹ Getting There & Around

AIR Daily flights from Iraklio's Nikos Kazantzakis airport (HER) to Athens; regular flights in summer to Thessaloniki and Rhodes. Bus 1 travels to/from the airport (5km east of town) and city centre (€1.20) every 15 minutes from 6am to 1am.

BOAT Daily ferries service Piraeus (€37, seven hours), and catamarans head daily to Santorini and continue to other Cycladic islands. Twice weekly, ferries sail east to Rhodes (€28, 12 hours) via Agios Nikolaos, Sitia, Kassos, Karpathos and Halki.

Phaestos & Other Minoan Sites ΦΑΙΣΤΟΣ

Phaestos (📞29820 42315; admission €6; ⏱8am-7pm May-Oct, to 5pm Nov-Apr), 63km southwest of Iraklio, is Crete's second-most important Minoan site. While not as impressive as Knossos, this is still worth a visit for stunning views of the surrounding Mesara plain and Mt Psiloritis (or Mt Ida). Eight buses a day head to Phaestos from Iraklio's Bus Station B (€5.90, 1½ hours).

Other important Minoan sites can be found at **Malia**, 34km east of Iraklio, where there's a palace complex and

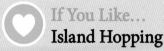 ## If You Like…
Island Hopping

If you've fallen for the laid-back pace of life on the Ionian Islands (p771), then you're in luck – there are plenty more Greek archipelagos to explore.

1 CYCLADES
Beyond Mykonos and Santorini, there are several more islands to explore in the Cyclades. The island of **Naxos** is the largest and lushest; **Paros** is known for its lovely beaches and terraced hills; and **Ios** is for party animals. All can be reached by boat from Piraeus on the mainland and Iraklio on Crete.

2 AEGEAN ISLANDS
These far-flung islands are strewn across the northeastern corner of the Aegean, closer to Turkey than mainland Greece. **Samos** was an important centre of Hellenic culture, while **Lesvos** is the third largest of the Greek islands. There are regular flights from Athens and frequent ferries from Piraeus. Seasonal boats also connect Samos from the Cyclades, the Dodecanese and other Greek ports.

3 DODECANESE
Beyond the main islands of the Dodecanese, traditional Greek culture still holds sway. To the north of Rhodes, the island of **Symi** is home to the ancient **Monastery of Panormitis** (admission free; ⏱dawn-sunset), while the mountainous island of **Karpathos** (*kar*-pah-thos), midway between Crete and Rhodes, is a scenic, hype-free place with a cosy port, numerous beaches and unspoilt villages. Both can be easily reached by boat from Rhodes.

adjoining town, and **Zakros**, 40km southeast of Sitia, the last Minoan palace to have been discovered, in 1962.

Hania XANIA
POP 53,500

Crete's most romantic, evocative and alluring town, Hania (hahn-*yah*; often spelt Chania) is the former capital and the island's second-largest city. There is a rich mosaic of Venetian and Ottoman architecture, particularly in the area of the old harbour, which lures tourists in droves.

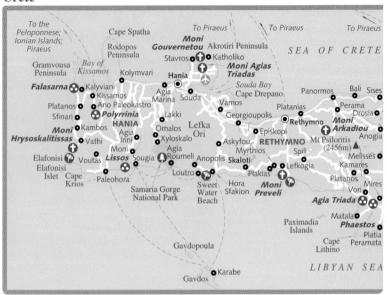

To the
Peloponnese;
Ionian Islands;
Piraeus

Cape Spatha

To Piraeus   To Piraeus   To Piraeus

Moni Gouvernetou Akrotiri Peninsula

Gramvousa   *Bay of*   Rodopos   Stavros Katholiko   SEA OF CRETE
Peninsula   *Kissamos*   Peninsula
         Kolymvari   **Hania**   *Moni Agias Triadas*
Falasarna   Kalyviani   Souda Bay
      Kissamos   Agia   Souda   Cape Drepano   Panormos   Bali   Sises
Platanos   Ano Paleokastro   Marina   Vamos   Perama   Drosia
Sfinari   **HANIA**   Platanias   **Rethymno**   *Moni Arkadiou*   Anogia
Moni   Kambos   Agia   Omalos   Lefka   Georgioupolis   Episkopi   Mt Psiloritis   Melisses
Hrysoskalitissas   Vathi   Irini   Xyloskalo   Ori   Askyfou   **RETHYMNO**   (2456m)   Kamares
Elafonisi   Voutas   Moni   Agia   Myrthios   Spili   Lefkogia   Platanos
Elafonisi   *Lissos*   Sougia   Roumeli   Anopolis   Skaloti   Plakias   Mires
Islet   Cape   Paleohora   Loutro   Hora   *Moni*   Vori
Krios   Samaria Gorge   Sweet   Sfakion   *Preveli*   *Agia Triada*
      National Park   Water   Matala
         Beach   Paximadia   *Phaestos*
      Gavdopoula   Islands   Cape   Platia
            Lithino   Perama

Gavdos   Karabe   *LIBYAN SEA*

👁 Sights & Activities

OLD HARBOUR   Sea Wall, Lighthouse
From Plateia 1866, the **old harbour** is a short walk down Halidon. A stroll around here is a must for any visitor to Hania. It is worth the 1.5km walk around the sea wall to get to the Venetian **lighthouse** at the entrance to the harbour.

ARCHAEOLOGICAL MUSEUM   Museum
(Halidon 30; admission €2; ⏰8.30am-3pm Tue-Sun) The museum is housed in a 16th-century Venetian church that the Turks made into a mosque. The building became a movie theatre in 1913 and then was a munitions depot for the Germans during WWII.

🛏 Sleeping

PENSION LENA   Pension €
(☎28210 86860; www.lenachania.gr; Ritsou 5; s/d €35/55; ❄) For some real character in where you stay, Lena's pension in an old Turkish building near the mouth of the old harbour is the place to go. Help yourself

to one of the appealing rooms if Lena isn't there – pick from the available ones on the list on the blackboard.

AMPHORA HOTEL   Hotel €€
(☎28210 93224; www.amphora.gr; Parodos Theotokopoulou 20; s/d €95/110; ❄) Most easily found from the waterfront, this is Hania's most historically evocative hotel. Amphora is in an impressively restored Venetian mansion with elegantly decorated rooms around a courtyard. The hotel also runs the **waterfront restaurant**, which ranks as the best along that golden mile.

🍴 Eating & Drinking

The entire waterfront of the old harbour is lined with restaurants and tavernas, many of which qualify as tourist traps. Watch out for touts trying to reel you in. There are a number of good options one street back.

Taverna Tamam   Taverna €€
(☎28210 58639; Zambeliou 49) A taverna in an old converted Turkish bathhouse, with tables that spill out onto the street.

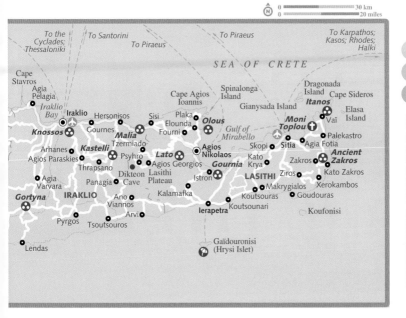

ⓘ Information

Tourist information office (☎ 28210 36155;
Kydonias 29; ⏰ 8am-2.30pm) Under the
Town Hall; is helpful and provides practical
information and maps.

ⓘ Getting There & Away

BOAT Daily ferries sail between Piraeus
(€30, nine hours) and the port of Souda,
9km southeast of Hania. Frequent buses (€1.30)
and taxis (€10) connect town and Souda.

BUS Frequent buses run along Crete's
northern coast to Iraklio (€11, 2¾ hours,
half-hourly), Rethymno (€6, one hour, half hourly)
and Kastelli-Kissamos (€4, one hour, 14 daily).

Samaria Gorge ΦΑΡΑΓΓΙ ΤΗΣ ΣΑΜΑΡΙΑΣ

Samaria Gorge (☎ 28250 67179; admission
€5; ⏰ 6am-3pm May–mid-Oct) is one of
Europe's most spectacular gorges and a
superb hike. Walkers should take rugged
footwear, food, drinks and sun protection
for this strenuous five- to six-hour trek.

You can do the walk as part of an
excursion tour, or do it independently
by taking the Omalos bus from the main
bus station in Hania (€5.90, one hour)
to the head of the gorge at Xyloskalo
(1230m) at 7.30am, 8.30am and 2pm.
It's a 16.7km walk out (all downhill) to
Agia Roumeli on the coast, from where
you take a boat to Hora Sfakion (€8, 1¼
hours, three daily) and then a bus back
to Hania (€6.50, 1½ hours, three daily).
You are not allowed to spend the night in
the gorge, so you need to complete the
walk in a day.

DODECANESE ΔΩΔΕΚΑΝΗΣΑ

Strung out along the coast of western
Turkey, the 12 main islands of the Dodecanese (*dodeca* means 12) have suffered a
turbulent past of invasions and occupa-
tions that has endowed them with a
fascinating diversity.

Conquered successively by the
Romans, the Arabs, the Knights of
St John, the Turks, the Italians, then

liberated from the Germans by British and Greek commandos in 1944, the Dodecanese became part of Greece in 1947. These days, tourists rule.

Rhodes ΡΟΔΟΣ

POP 98,000

Rhodes (Rodos in Greek) is the largest island in the Dodecanese. According to mythology, the sun god Helios chose Rhodes as his bride and bestowed light, warmth and vegetation upon her. Throw in an east coast of virtually uninterrupted sandy beaches and it's easy to understand why sun-starved northern Europeans flock here.

ⓘ Getting There & Away

AIR There are plenty of flights daily between Rhodes' **Diagoras airport** (RHO) and Athens, plus less regular flights to Karpathos, Kasos, Kastellorizo, Thessaloniki, Iraklio and Samos.

The airport is on the west coast, 16km southwest of Rhodes Town; 25 minutes and €2.20 by bus.

BOAT Rhodes is the main port of the Dodecanese and there is a complex array of departures. There are daily ferries from Rhodes to Piraeus (€53, 13 hours). In summer, catamaran services run up and down the Dodecanese daily from Rhodes to Symi, Kos, Kalymnos, Nisyros, Tilos, Patmos and Leros.

Rhodes Town

POP 56,000

A wander around Rhodes' World Heritage–listed Old Town is a must. It is reputedly the world's finest surviving example of medieval fortification, with 12m-thick walls. Throngs of visitors pack its busier streets and eating, sleeping and shopping options abound.

The cobbled **Odos Ippoton (Ave of the Knights)** is lined with magnificent medieval buildings, the most imposing of which is the **Palace of the Grand Masters** (☎22410 23359; admission €6; ⊙8.30am-3pm Tue-Sun), which was restored, but never used, as a holiday home for Mussolini.

The 15th-century Knight's Hospital now houses the **Archaeological Museum** (☎ 22410 27657; Plateia Mousiou; admission €3; ⏰ 8am-4pm Tue-Sun). The splendid building was restored by the Italians and has an impressive collection that includes the ethereal marble statue *Aphrodite of Rhodes*.

The pink-domed **Mosque of Süleyman**, at the top of Sokratous, was built in 1522 to commemorate the Ottoman victory against the knights, then rebuilt in 1808.

🛏 Sleeping

MARCO POLO MANSION
Boutique Hotel €€
(☎ 22410 25562; www.marcopolomansion.gr; Agiou Fanouriou 40, Old Town; d €90-150) In a 15th-century building in the Turkish quarter of the Old Town, this place is rich in Ottoman-era colours and features in glossy European magazines.

HOTEL ANDREAS
Pension €€
(☎ 22410 34156; www.hotelandreas.com; Omirou 28d, Old Town; s/d €55/70; ❄ 🛜) Tasteful Hotel Andreas has individually decorated rooms and terrific views from its terrace. Rates differ by room; check it all out online, and choose your room before you go. There's a minimum two-night stay, but most stay longer.

Eating & Drinking

TO MELTEMI
Taverna, Seafood €
(Kountourioti 8; mains €5-12) At the northern end of Mandraki Harbour is one place worth heading to. Gaze out on Turkey from this beachside taverna where the seafood is superb.

Inside the walls, Old Town has it all in terms of touts and over-priced tavernas trying to separate less savvy tourists from their euro. The back alleys tend to throw up better-quality eateries and prices.

ⓘ Information

Tourist information office (EOT; ☎ 22410 35226; cnr Makariou & Papagou; ⊙8am-2.45pm Mon-Fri) Has brochures, maps and *Rodos News*, a free English-language newspaper.

ⓘ Getting Around

BUS Rhodes Town has two bus stations a block apart next to the New Market. The west-side bus station serves the airport, Kamiros (€4.60, 55 minutes) and the west coast. The east-side bus station serves the east coast, Lindos (€4.70, 1½ hours) and the inland southern villages.

Around the Island

The **Acropolis of Lindos** (admission €6; ⊙8.30am-6pm Tue-Sun), 47km from Rhodes Town, is an ancient city spectacularly perched atop a 116m-high rocky outcrop. Below is the town of **Lindos**, a tangle of streets with elaborately decorated 17th-century houses.

The extensive ruins of **Kamiros** (admission €4; ⊙8am-5pm Tue-Sun), an ancient Doric city on the west coast, are well preserved, with the remains of houses, baths, a cemetery and a temple,

but the site should be visited as much for its lovely setting on a gentle hillside overlooking the sea.

Between Rhodes Town and Lindos, the **beaches** are packed. Venture further south to find good stretches of deserted sandy beach.

Kos ΚΩΣ

POP 17,900

Captivating Kos, only 5km from the Turkish peninsula of Bodrum, is popular with history buffs as the birthplace of Hippocrates (460–377 BC), the father of medicine. The island also attracts an entirely different crowd – sun-worshipping beach lovers from northern Europe who flock in on charter flights during summer. Tourism rules the roost, and whether you are there to explore the Castle of the Knights or to party till you drop, Kos should keep you happy for at least a few days.

◎ Sights & Activities

CASTLE OF THE KNIGHTS Castle
(☎ 22420 27927; admission €4; ⊙8am-2.30pm Tue-Sun) Built in the 14th century, this

Acropolis of Lindos, Rhodes

CHRISTER FREDRIKSSON/LONELY PLANET IMAGES ©

CHRIS CHRISTO/LONELY PLANET IMAGES ©

Don't Miss **Knossos ΚΝΩΣΣΟΣ**

Five kilometres south of Iraklio, **Knossos** (☎28102 31940; admission €6; ⏱8am-7pm Jun-Oct, to 3pm Nov-May) was the capital of Minoan Crete, and is now the island's major tourist attraction.

Knossos (k-nos-*os*) is the most famous of Crete's Minoan sites and is the inspiration for the myth of the Minotaur. According to legend, King Minos of Knossos was given a magnificent white bull to sacrifice to the god Poseidon, but decided to keep it. This enraged Poseidon, who punished the king by causing his wife Pasiphae to fall in love with the animal. The result of this odd union was the Minotaur – half-man and half-bull – who lived in a labyrinth beneath the king's palace, munching on youths and maidens.

In 1900 Arthur Evans uncovered the ruins of Knossos. Although archaeologists tend to disparage Evans' reconstruction, the buildings – incorporating an immense palace, courtyards, private apartments, baths, lively frescoes and more – give a fine idea of what a Minoan palace might have looked like.

Buses to Knossos (€1.30, three per hour; 20min) leave from Bus Station A.

castle protected the knights from the encroaching Ottomans, and was originally separated from town by a moat. That moat is now Finikon, a major street. Entrance to the castle is over the stone bridge behind the Hippocrates Tree.

ASKLIPIEION   Ruins
(☎22420 28763; adult/student €4/3; ⏱8am-7.30pm Tue-Sun) On a hill 4km southwest of Kos Town stand the extensive ruins of the renowned healing centre where Hippocrates practised medicine. Groups of doctors from all over the world come to visit.

ANCIENT AGORA   Ruins
The ancient agora, with the ruins of the **Shrine of Aphrodite** and **Temple of Hercules**, is just off Plateia Eleftherias. North of the agora is the **Hippocrates Plane Tree**, under which the man himself is said to have taught his pupils.

Archaeological Museum — Museum

(☏22420 28326; Plateia Eleftherias; admission €3; ⊙8am-2.30pm Tue-Sun) The focus of the collection here is sculpture from excavations around the island.

If the history is all too much, wander around and relax with the Scandinavians at the town **beach** past the northern end of the harbour.

Kos Town has recently developed a number of **bicycle paths** and renting a bike from one of the many places along the waterfront is a great option for getting around town and seeing the sights.

Sleeping

HOTEL AFENDOULIS — Hotel €

(☏22420 25321; www.afendoulishotel.com; Evripilou 1; s/d €35/50; ❄ @) Run by the charismatic English-speaking Alexis, this is a great place to relax and enjoy Kos. Port and bus station transfers are complimentary, and you can get your laundry done here.

PENSION ALEXIS — Pension €

(☏22420 28798; www.pensionalexis.com; Irodotou 9; s/d €25/35; ❄) This highly recommended place has long been a budget favourite with travellers. It has large rooms, some with shared facilities, and a relaxing veranda and garden.

Eating & Drinking

Restaurants line the central waterfront of the old harbour, but you might want to hit the backstreets for value.

Stadium Restaurant — Seafood €

(☏22420 27880; mains €9-16) On the long waterfront 500m southeast of the castle, Stadium serves succulent seafood at good prices, along with excellent views of Turkey.

ⓘ Information

Municipal tourist office (☏22420 24460; www.kosinfo.gr; Vasileos Georgiou 1; ⊙8am-2.30pm & 3-10pm Mon-Fri, 9am-2pm Sat) On the waterfront directly south of the port; provides maps and accommodation information.

Exas Travel (☏22420 28545; www.exas.gr) Near the Archaeological Museum in the heart of town to the southwest of the harbour; handles schedules, ticketing and excursions.

ⓘ Getting There & Around

AIR There are daily flights to Athens from Kos' **Ippokratis airport** (KGS), which is 28km southwest of Kos Town. International charters wing in throughout the summer and Easyjet operates scheduled flights from London. Get to/from the airport by bus (€4) or taxi (€25).

BOAT There are frequent ferries from Rhodes to Kos that continue to Piraeus (€46, 10 hours), as well as ferries heading the opposite way. Daily fast-boat connections head north to Patmos and Samos, and south to Symi and Rhodes.

TO TURKEY In summer boats depart daily for Bodrum in Turkey (€34 return, one hour).

BUS There is a good public bus system on Kos, with the bus station on Kleopatras, near the ruins at the back of town.

MINI-TRAIN Next to the tourist office is a blue mini-train for Asklipion (€5 return, hourly) and a green mini-train that does city tours (€4, 20 minutes).

Patmos ΠΑΤΜΟΣ

POP 3050

Patmos has a sense of 'spirit of place', and with its great beaches and relaxed atmosphere, is a superb place to unwind. Orthodox and Western Christians have long made pilgrimages to Patmos, for it was here that John the Divine ensconced himself in a cave and wrote the Book of Revelation.

◎ Sights & Activities

The **Cave of the Apocalypse** (admission free, treasury €6; ⊙8am-1.30pm daily & 4-6pm Tue, Thu & Sun), where St John wrote his divinely inspired Book of Revelation, is halfway between the port and *hora*. Take a bus from the port or hike up the **Byzantine path**, which starts from a signposted spot on the Skala–*hora* road.

The **Monastery of St John the Theologian** (admission free; ⊙8am-1.30pm

daily & 4-6pm Tue, Thu & Sun) looks more like a castle than a monastery and tops Patmos like a crown. It exhibits all kinds of monastic treasures.

Patmos' coastline provides secluded coves, mostly with pebble beaches. The best is **Psili Ammos**, in the south, reached by excursion boat from Skala port. **Lambi Beach**, on the north coast, is a pebble-beach lover's dream come true.

Sleeping

Blue Bay Hotel   Boutique Hotel €€
(☎ 22470 31165; www.bluebaypatmos.gr; s/d/tr €78/116/144; ❄ @) At the quieter southern end of Skala, this waterfront hotel has superb rooms, internet access, and breakfast included in its rates (which tumble outside the high season).

YVONNI STUDIOS   Rooms €
(☎ 22470 33066; www.12net.gr/yvonni; s/d €35/50) On the western side of Skala, these exceptionally clean and pleasant studios are fully self-contained and big on privacy. Call ahead for a booking or drop into Yvonni's gift shop in Skala and ask for Theo.

ℹ Information

TOURIST INFORMATION Tourist office
(☎ 22470 31666; ⏱ 8am-6pm Mon-Fri Jun-Sep) In the white building opposite the port in Skala, along with the post office and police station.

TRAVEL AGENCIES Apollon Travel (☎ 22470 31324; apollontravel@stratas.gr) On the waterfront; handles schedules and ticketing.

WEBSITES www.patmosweb.gr; www.patmos -island.com

ℹ Getting There & Away

BOAT Patmos is well connected, with ferries to Piraeus (€35, eight hours, two weekly) and south to Rhodes (€32, 7½ hours, two weekly). In summer daily catamarans head south to Kos and Rhodes, and north to Samos.

IONIAN ISLANDS
ΤΑ ΕΠΤΑΝΗΣΑ

The idyllic cypress- and fir-covered Ionian Islands stretch down the western coast of Greece from Corfu in the north to Kythira, off the southern tip of the Peloponnese.

View of beach, Kefallonia island (p773)

ADINA TOVY AMSEL/LONELY PLANET IMAGES ©

GEORGE TSAFOS/LONELY PLANET IMAGES ©

Mountainous, with dramatic cliff-backed beaches, soft light and turquoise water, they're more Italian in feel, offering a contrasting experience to other Greek islands.

Corfu KEPKYPA

POP 122,670

Many consider Corfu, or Kerkyra (*ker*-kih-rah) in Greek, to be Greece's most beautiful island – the unfortunate consequence of which is that it's often overrun with crowds.

ℹ️ Getting There & Away

AIR Ioannis Kapodistrias Airport (CFU; ☏26610 30180) is 3km from Corfu Town. Olympic Air (☏26610 22962) and Aegean Airlines (☏26610 27100) fly daily to Athens and a few times a week to Thessaloniki.

BOAT Ferries go to Igoumenitsa (€7, 1½ hours, hourly). In summer daily ferries and hydrofoils go to Paxi, and international ferries (see p776) stop in Patra (€38, six hours).

Corfu Town

POP 28,692

Built on a promontory and wedged between two fortresses, Corfu's Old Town is a tangle of narrow walking streets

through gorgeous Venetian buildings. Explore the winding alleys and surprising plazas in the early morning or late afternoon to avoid the hordes of day trippers seeking souvenirs.

👁️ Sights

Palaio Frourio   Fortress
(Old Fortress; adult/concession €4/2; ⏱8.30am-7pm May-Oct, 8.30am-3pm Nov-Mar) The Palaio Frourio stands on an eastern promontory; the **Neo Frourio** (New Fortress) lies to the northwest.

Archaeological Museum   Museum
(Vraïla 5; admission €4; ⏱8.30am-3pm Tue-Sun) Houses a collection of finds from Mycenaean to classical times.

Church of Agios Spiridon   Church
(Agios Spiridonos) This richly decorated church displays the remains of St Spiridon, paraded through town four times a year.

🛏️ Sleeping

Accommodation prices fluctuate wildly depending on season; book ahead.

Bella Venezia   Boutique Hotel €€
(☏26610 46500; www.bellaveneziahotel .com; N Zambeli 4; s/d incl breakfast from

€102/123; ❄️✳️📶) Impeccable and under-stated; contemporary rooms are decked out in cream linens and marbles.

Hotel Astron   Hotel €€
(📞26610 39505; hotel_astron@hol.gr; Donzelot 15, Old Port; s/d €65/70; ✳️📶) Recently renovated and with some sea views, light-filled rooms are managed by friendly staff.

Eating

To Dimarchio   Italian, Greek €€
(📞26610 39031; Plateia Dimarchio; mains €8-25) Relax in a luxuriant rose garden on a charming square. Attentive staff serve elegant, inventive dishes, prepared with the freshest ingredients.

Rouvás   Greek €
(📞26610 31182; S Desilla 13; mains €8-14; 🕐lunch) Resilient traditional cooking makes this a favourite lunch stop for locals.

ℹ️ Getting Around

Blue buses (€0.90 to €1.30) for villages near Corfu Town leave from Plateia San Rocco.

Around the Island

The **Corfu Trail** (www.corfutrail.org) traverses the island north to south.

To gain an aerial view of the gorgeous cypress-backed bays around **Paleokastritsa**, the west coast's main resort, go to the quiet village of **Lakones**. Further south, good beaches surround tiny **Agios Gordios**.

Ithaki IΘΑΚΗ
POP 3700

Odysseus' long-lost home in Homer's *Odyssey*, Ithaki (ancient Ithaca) remains a verdant, pristine island blessed with cypress-covered hills and beautiful turquoise coves.

Ferries run between Frikes, Fiskardo (Keffalonia), Nydri and Vasiliki (Lefkada).

Other ferries run to Sami (Keffalonia) and Patras. Check ever-changing routes and schedules at **Delas Tours** (📞26740 32104; www.ithaca.com.gr; Vathy).

Kefallonia ΚΕΦΑΛΛΟΝΙΑ
POP 39,500

This largest Ionian island is breathtakingly beautiful with rugged mountain ranges, rich vineyards, soaring coastal cliffs and golden beaches; it remains low-key out-side resort areas.

ℹ️ Getting There & Around

AIR Olympic Air (📞26710 41511) flights go to Athens from Keffalonia Airport (EFL; 📞26710 41511), 9km south of Argostoli.

BOAT Four Island Ferries operates seasonal routes between Fiskardo, Frikes (Ithaki), Nydri and Vasiliki (Lefkada). In Fiskardo, get tickets from Nautilus Travel (📞26740 41440) or the dock before departure. Trips average 90 minutes and cost €7 per person and €30 per car.

BUS Four daily buses connect Argostoli with Athens (€37.10, seven hours), via Patra (€21, four hours)

Paleokastritsa bay, Corfu island
PHOTOGRAPHER: HOLGER LEUE/LONELY PLANET IMAGES ©

Practicalities

- **Electricity** Two-pin European plugs; 230V @ 50Hz.

- **Smoking** Banned in enclosed public spaces.

- **Time** Two hours ahead of GMT.

- **Tipping** In restaurants a service charge is included, but rounding the bill for a small tip is expected.

- **TV & Video** Main broadcaster ERT, plus national networks including Alpha, Alter, ANT1, Mega, Skai and Star.

- **Weights & Measures** Metric.

CAR A car is best for exploring Kefallonia. Pama Travel (✆26740 41033; www.pamatravel.com; Fiskardo) rents cars and boats, books accommodation and has internet access.

Fiskardo

Pretty Fiskardo, with its pastel-coloured Venetian buildings set around a picturesque bay, was the only Kefallonian village not to be destroyed by the 1953 earthquake. Take lovely walks to sheltered coves for swimming.

Sleeping

Archontiko Historic Pension €€
(✆26740 41342; r from €80; ❄) People-watch from the balconies of these luxurious rooms in a restored stone mansion overlooking the harbour.

Eating

Tassia Seafood, Greek €€
(✆26740 41205; mains €10-25) This unassuming but famous Fiskardo institution run by Tassia Dendrinou, celebrated chef and writer, serves up excellent seafood and Greek dishes.

Vasso's Seafood €€
(✆26740 41276; mains €10-40) Whether it's fresh grilled fish or pasta with crayfish, Vasso's is *the* place to head for exceptional seafood.

Around the Island

Straddling a slender isthmus on the northwest coast, the petite pastel-coloured village of **Assos** watches over the ruins of a Venetian fortress perched upon a pine-covered peninsula.

Splendid **Myrtos Beach**, 13km south of Assos, is spellbinding from above, with postcard views from the precarious roadway.

SURVIVAL GUIDE
Directory A–Z

Accommodation

The prices quoted in this chapter for sleeping options are for 'high season' (usually July and August). During 'low season' (late October to late April) prices can be up to 50% cheaper, but a lot of places, especially on the islands, virtually close their shutters for winter. Websites will usually display these differences in price.

In this chapter we have used the following price ranges for sleeping options.

€€€	more than €150
€€	€60 to €150
€	less than €60

Business Hours

It is worth noting that the opening hours of businesses associated with tourists can be rather haphazard.

Banks 8am-2.30pm Mon-Thu; 8am-2pm Fri (in cities, also: 3.30-6.30pm Mon-Fri; 8am-1.30pm Sat)

Post offices 7.30am-2pm Mon-Fri (in cities 7.30am-8pm Mon-Fri; 7.30am-2pm Sat)

Restaurants 11am-3pm & 7pm-1am (varies greatly)

Street kiosks (*periptera*) early-late Mon-Sun

Supermarkets 8am-8pm Mon-Fri, 8am-3pm Sat

Food

In this chapter we have used the following price ranges for Eating options:

€€€	more than €40
€€	€15 to €40
€	less than €15

Gay & Lesbian Travellers

Homosexuality is generally frowned upon.

It is wise to be discreet and to avoid open displays of togetherness.

Athens has a busy gay scene that packs up and heads to the islands for summer.

Mykonos has long been famous for its bars, beaches and hedonism.

Money

ATMs Everywhere except the smallest villages.

Bargaining While souvenir shops will generally bargain, prices in other shops are normally clearly marked and non-negotiable; accommodation is nearly always negotiable outside peak season, especially for longer stays.

Cash This is king at street kiosks and small shops, especially in the countryside.

Changing currency Banks, post offices and currency exchange offices are all over the place and exchange all major currencies.

Credit cards Generally accepted, but may not be on smaller islands or in small villages.

Tipping The service charge is included on the bill in restaurants, but it is the custom to round up the bill; same for taxis.

Public Holidays

New Year's Day 1 January

Epiphany 6 January

First Sunday in Lent February

Greek Independence Day 25 March

Good Friday/Easter Sunday March/April

May Day (Protomagia) 1 May

Feast of the Assumption 15 August

Ohi Day 28 October

Christmas Day 25 December

St Stephen's Day 26 December

Courtyard of the monastery at Paleokastritsa (p773), Corfu island

CHRIS CHRISTO/LONELY PLANET IMAGES ©

Fishing boats moored in the harbour, Ithaki island (p773)

GEORGE TSAFOS/LONELY PLANET IMAGES ©

Telephone

Public phones are easy to use; pressing the 'i' button brings up the operating instructions in English.

Public phones are everywhere and all use phonecards.

PHONE CODES

Telephone codes are part of the 10-digit number within Greece.

The landline prefix is 2 and for mobiles it's 6.

PHONECARDS

Phonecards come in €3, €5 and €10 versions; local calls cost €0.30 for three minutes.

Discount-card schemes are available, offering much better value for money.

Visas

Visitors from most countries don't need a visa for Greece.

Countries whose nationals can stay in Greece for up to three months include Australia, Canada, all EU countries, Iceland, Israel, Japan, New Zealand and the USA.

Transport

Getting There & Away

Air

Most visitors arrive by air; mostly into Athens.

There are a growing number of scheduled services by budget airlines, eg Easyjet flies into Athens, Corfu, Hania, Iraklio, Kos, Mykonos, Rhodes, Santorini, Thessaloniki and Zakynthos.

Olympic Air (OA; www.olympicair.com) Privatised version of former national carrier, Olympic Airlines.

Aegean Airlines (A3; www.aegeanair.com)

Sea

Check out ferry routes, schedules and services online at www.greekferries.gr.

ITALY

Ancona In summer, there are three daily sailings to Patra (20 hours).

Bari Daily sailings to Patra (14½ hours) via Corfu (eight hours) and Keffalonia (14 hours); also daily to Igoumenitsa (11½ hours).

Venice In summer, up to 12 weekly sailings to Patra (30 hours) via Corfu (25 hours).

TURKEY

Boat services operate between Turkey's Aegean coast and the Greek Islands: Rhodes to Marmaris; Symi to Datça; Kos to Bodrum; Samos to Kuşadası; Chios to Çeşme; Lesvos to Ayvalik.

Getting Around

Greece has a comprehensive transport system and is easy to get around.

Air

Aegean Airlines (A3; www.aegeanair.com) The big competitor offers newer aircraft and similar prices on popular routes.

Astra Airlines (A2; www.astra-airlines.gr) Based in Thessaloniki; a newcomer flying limited routes.

Athens Airways (ZF; www.athensairways.com) New kid on the block.

Olympic Air (OA; www.olympicair.com) Recently privatised; has the most extensive network.

Sky Express (SHE; www.skyexpress.gr) Based in Iraklio, Crete; mainly flies routes that the big two don't.

Boat
FERRY

Ferries come in all shapes and sizes, from state-of-the-art 'superferries' on major routes, to ageing open ferries that operate local services.

Newer high-speed ferries are slashing travel times, but cost much more.

Tickets can be bought at the last minute at the dock, but in high season, some boats may be full – plan ahead.

CATAMARAN

High-speed catamarans have become an important part of the island travel scene.

Much less prone to cancellation in rough weather.

Fares are generally more expensive than ferries and about the same as hydrofoils.

HYDROFOIL

A faster alternative to ferries on some routes; take half the time, but cost twice as much.

Most routes will operate only during the high season.

Tickets for hydrofoils must be bought in advance and there is often seat allocation.

Bus

Long-distance buses are operated by **KTEL** (Koino Tamio Eispraxeon Leoforion; www.ktel.org).

Car & Motorcycle

EU-registered vehicles are allowed free entry into Greece for six months without road taxes; a green card (international third party insurance) is all that's required.

HIRE

High-season weekly rates start at about €280 for the smallest models, dropping to €200 in winter – add tax and extras.

Major companies will request a credit-card deposit.

Minimum driving age in Greece is 18, but most car-hire firms require a driver of 21 or over.

Mopeds and motorcycles are available for hire everywhere.

You need a valid motorcycle licence stating proficiency for the size of motorcycle you wish to rent – from 50cc upwards.

Mopeds and 50cc motorcycles range from €10 to €25 per day or from €25 per day for a 250cc motorcycle.

ROAD RULES

Drive on the right; overtake on the left (not all Greeks do this!).

Compulsory to wear seatbelts in the front seats, and in the back if they are fitted.

Drink-driving laws are strict; a blood alcohol content of 0.05% incurs a fine of around €150 and over 0.08% is a criminal offence.

Train
Greek Railways Organisation (OSE; www.ose.gr)

Greece has only two main lines:

Athens north to Thessaloniki and Alexandroupolis.

Athens to the Peloponnese.

Europe
In Focus

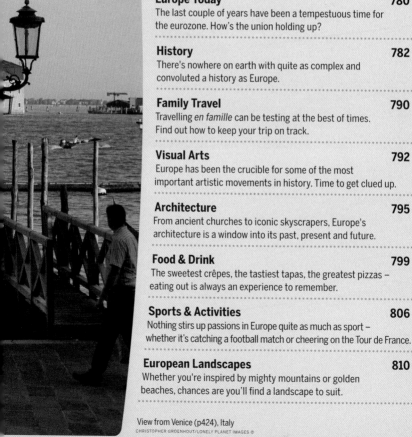

View from Venice (p424), Italy
CHRISTOPHER GROENHOUT/LONELY PLANET IMAGES ©

Europe
Today

> *Recent elections in many European countries have shown a collapse in support for socialist parties.*

Boom & Bust

Since the worldwide financial crash of late 2008, it's been a rocky ride for many of Europe's economies. Nearly all of the EU was officially in recession for most of 2009 and 2010, and only a handful of countries have since shown any sign of a concerted recovery.

While some of Europe's larger economies are beginning to show growth, it's been a different story for others. Since late 2009, the European Central Bank has been forced to hand out a series of hugely expensive bailouts in an attempt to stop some of the eurozone's most heavily indebted nations from sliding into bankruptcy. Greece was the first to be bailed out, with a €110 billion rescue package in May 2010, followed by €85 billion for

RICHARD I'ANSON/LONELY PLANET IMAGES ©

while the UK (along with many other nations) has introduced strict antiterrorism laws, which many people argue restrict the age-old right to peaceful protest.

The Rise of the Right

Recent elections in many European countries have shown a collapse in support for socialist parties. The majority of Western Europe is now governed by right-of-centre parties, and the far right looks to be on the rise.

While many commentators maintain that this is a predictable response to current economic problems and the general political climate, others have suggested that it could have a much deeper significance – perhaps even endangering Europe's long-held values of tolerance, harmony, freedom and social equality.

The End of Schengen?

French president Nikolas Sarkozy and Italian prime minister Silvio Berlusconi have suggested that in order to control illegal immigration there might be a need to place some restrictions on the Schengen Agreement, the landmark 1985 treaty that enables EU citizens to move freely across each other's borders.

This highly controversial proposal has caused considerable debate on all sides of the political spectrum. In response Cecilia Malmström, the EU's commissioner for home affairs, has agreed there might be a need to impose temporary border restrictions in 'exceptional circumstances'.

Exactly what these circumstances might be and what they mean for the future of Schengen is anyone's guess, but one thing's for certain – there are bound to be fireworks ahead.

Ireland in November and €78 billion for Portugal in May 2011.

With rumours swirling that Spain and Italy's economies could also be teetering on the brink, some economists have predicted that Europe's sovereign debt crisis could even threaten the long-term viability of the euro as a currency.

Freedoms & Fears

Freedom of speech, the right to privacy and human rights continue to be hot topics in Europe. Faced with a range of issues, from illegal immigration to international terrorism, many European governments have taken an increasingly hard-line stance. France recently made the highly controversial decision to ban Muslim women from wearing the veil in public,

History

Europe is a place where history seems to seep into every corner. It's literally everywhere you look: in the tumbledown remains of Greek temples and Roman bathhouses, in the fabulously ostentatious architecture of French chateaux and Austrian castles, in the winding streets and broad boulevards of its many stately cities. Understanding Europe's long and often troubled history is a crucial part of figuring out what makes this continent tick.

Prehistory

The first settlers arrived in Europe around two million years ago, but it wasn't until the end of the last major ice age between 12,000 BC and 8000 BC that humans really took hold. As the glaciers and ice sheets retreated, hunter-gatherer tribes extended their reach northwards in search of new land. Some of Europe's earliest human settlements were left behind by Neolithic tribes.

4500–2500 BC
Neolithic tribes build burial tombs, barrows, stone circles and alignments across Europe, including Stonehenge and Carnac.

Greeks & Romans

Europe's first great civilisations developed in Mycenae (about 90km southwest of Athens) and ancient Crete, but it was the Greeks and the Romans who left the most enduring mark. The civilisation of ancient Greece emerged around 2000 BC and made huge leaps forward in science, technology, architecture, philosophy and democratic principles. Many of the writers, thinkers and mathematicians of ancient Greece, from Pythagoras to Plato, still exert a profound influence on us to this day.

Hot on the heels of the Greeks came the Romans, who set about conquering most of Europe and devised the world's first recognisable democratic republic. At its height, Roman power extended all the way from Celtic Britain to ancient Persia (Iran), and the Romans' myriad achievements are almost too numerous to mention: they founded cities, raised aqueducts, constructed roads, laid sewers and built baths all over the continent, and produced a string of brilliant writers, orators, politicians, philosophers and military leaders who laid the foundations for modern Europe.

The Best...
Ancient Ruins

1 The Acropolis, Greece (p747)

2 The Colosseum, Italy (p397)

3 Stonehenge, England (p103)

4 Pompeii, Italy (p468)

The Dark Ages

By the 4th century AD, both the Greek and Roman empires had already seen their golden ages come and go. Greece had been swallowed by the kingdom of Macedonia, led by Alexander the Great, then by Rome itself in AD 146. Meanwhile, Rome's empire-building ambitions eventually proved too much, and a series of political troubles and military disasters resulted in the sacking of Rome (in 410) at the hands of the Goths. Although Roman emperors clung on to their eastern Byzantine empire for another thousand years, founding a new capital at Constantinople, Rome's period of dominance over Western Europe was well and truly over. A new era, the Dark Ages, had begun.

The next few centuries were marked by a series of conflicts in which the various kingdoms of the European mainland sought to gain political and strategic control. Eventually in the year 768, Charlemagne, King of the Franks, brought together much of Western Europe under what would later become known as the Holy Roman Empire.

2500–500 BC
Ancient Greeks break new ground in technology, science, art and architecture.

1st century BC–4 AD
The Romans conquer much of Europe. The Roman Empire flourishes under Augustus and his successors.

410
The sacking of Rome by the Goths brings an end to Roman dominance.

The Best...
Historic
Cities

Meanwhile, an alliance of Christian nations sent troops to reclaim the Holy Land from Islamic control in a series of campaigns collectively known as the Crusades. Later centuries saw ongoing conflict between European powers and the powerful Turkish Ottoman Empire as it slowly consolidated control of Asia Minor, Eastern Europe and parts of the Balkans.

Renaissance & Reformation

Europe's troubles rumbled on into the 14th and 15th centuries. In the wake of further conflicts and political upheavals, as well as the devastating outbreak of the Black Death (which is estimated to have wiped out somewhere between a third and half of Europe's population), control over the Holy Roman Empire passed into the hands of the Austrian Habsburgs, a political dynasty that was to become one of the continent's dominant powers. Meanwhile, the Italian city-states of Genoa, Venice, Pisa and Amalfi consolidated their control over the Mediterranean, establishing trading links with much of the rest of Europe and the Far East, and embarking on some of the first journeys in search of the New World.

In the mid-15th century, a new age of artistic and philosophical development broke out across the continent. The Renaissance encouraged writers, artists and thinkers all over Europe to challenge the accepted doctrines of theology, philosophy, architecture and art. The centre of this artistic tsunami was Florence, Italy, where such inspirational figures as Michelangelo and Leonardo da Vinci broke new ground in art and architecture. Meanwhile, another epoch-changing development was underway in Germany, thanks to the invention of the printing press – a key technological development devised by Johannes Gutenburg around 1440. The advent of 'movable type' made printed books available to the masses for the first time.

While the Renaissance largely challenged artistic ideas, the Reformation dealt with questions of religion. Challenging Catholic 'corruption' and the divine authority of the Pope, the German theologian Martin Luther established his own breakaway branch of the Church, to which he gave the name 'Protestantism', in 1517. Luther's stance was soon echoed by the English monarch Henry VIII, who cut ties with Rome in 1534 and went on to found his own (Protestant) Church of England, thus sowing the seeds for centuries of bloody conflict between Catholics and Protestants in Europe.

800
Charlemagne becomes the first Holy Roman Emperor.

1066
William the Conqueror defeats the English King Harold at the Battle of Hastings.

1340s
The Black Death reaches its peak in Europe, killing between 30% and 50% of Europe's population.

The New World

The schisms of the Church weren't the only source of tension. The discovery of the 'New World' in the mid-16th century led to a colonial arms race between the major European nations, in which each country battled to lay claim to the newly discovered lands – often enslaving or killing the local populace in the process.

More trouble was to follow during the Thirty Years' War (1618–48), which began as a conflict between Catholics and Protestants and eventually sucked in most of Europe's principal powers. The war was eventually ended by the Peace of Westphalia in 1648, and Europe entered a period of comparative stability.

Enlightenment

In the wake of the Enlightenment (see boxed text, p786), people in many areas of Europe became increasingly dissatisfied with the political status quo, which consolidated the majority of wealth, prestige and power in the hands of a few aristocrats and all-powerful monarchs. Trouble was brewing acoss Europe, and things came to a head in 1789 when armed mobs stormed the Bastille prison in Paris, kickstarting the French Revolution.

Renaissance frescoes, Piazza Navona (p403), Italy
OLIVIER CIRENDINI/LONELY PLANET IMAGES ©

15th century
The Italian Renaissance brings about a revolution in art, architecture and science.

1517
Martin Luther nails his demands to the church door in Wittenburg, sparking the start of the Reformation.

1789
France becomes a republic following the French Revolution. Thousands of aristocrats are executed by guillotine.

The Age of Reason

If there's one era that's defined Europe's philosophical landscape over the last few centuries, it's the Enlightenment (also known as the 'Age of Reason'). This was the period in the 18th century when science and rationality assumed supremacy over religious belief for the first time. Its emphasis on logic, education and liberal social values over the constraints of religious doctrine has influenced the work of countless poets, philosophers and politicians, and contributed to the outbreak of the French Revolution. Key figures of the movement include the antimonarchist, antireligious French writer Voltaire (1694–1778) and the German philosopher Immanuel Kant (1724–1804).

The Revolution began with high ideals, inspired by its iconic slogan of *liberté, egalité, fraternité* (liberty, equality, brotherhood, a phrase that still graces French banknotes and inspired the American Revolution). But before long things turned sour and heads began to roll. Hardline republicans seized control and demanded bloody retribution for centuries of oppression. Scores of aristocrats subsequently met their end under the guillotine's blade, including the French monarch Louis XVI, who was publicly executed in January 1793 in Paris' Place de la Concorde, followed soon after by his wife Marie Antoinette.

The Reign of Terror between September 1793 and July 1794 saw religious freedoms revoked, churches closed, cathedrals turned into 'Temples of Reason' and thousands beheaded. In the chaos, a dashing young Corsican general named Napoleon Bonaparte (1769–1821) seized his chance.

Napoleon assumed power in 1799 and in 1804 was crowned Emperor. He fought a series of stunning campaigns across Europe and conquered vast swathes of territory for the French empire but, following a disastrous campaign to conquer Russia in 1812, Napoleon's grip on power faltered and he was eventually defeated by a coalition of British and Prussian forces at the Battle of Waterloo in 1815. While his military ambitions ultimately ended in defeat, Napoleon's programme of civic and industrial reforms set the framework for political change across much of Europe.

Industry, Empire & WWI

Having vanquished Napoleon, Britain emerged as Europe's predominant power. With such innovations as the steam engine, the railway and the factory, Britain unleashed the Industrial Revolution and, like many of Europe's major powers (including France, Spain, Belgium and the Austro-Hungarian empire), set about developing its colonies across much of Africa, Australasia and the Middle and Far East.

18th & 19th centuries

The Industrial Revolution transforms European society.

1914

The assassination of Archduke Franz Ferdinand leads to the outbreak of WWI (1914–18).

Before long these competing empires clashed again, with predictable consequences. When the heir to the Austro-Hungarian throne, Archduke Franz Ferdinand, was assassinated in 1914, the blame fell on a Serbian nationalist by the name of Gavrilo Princip. Tensions broke out into open warfare just a month later, heralding the beginning of the bloodiest war ever fought on European soil. Allies lined up on opposing sides; Germany and Turkey sided with the Austro-Hungarians, while Britain, France, Russia and Italy (later joined by the USA) sided with the Serbians.

By the end of hostilities in 1918, huge tracts of northern France and Belgium had been razed and over 16 million people across Europe had been killed. In the Treaty of Versailles, the defeated powers of Austro-Hungary and Germany lost large areas of territory and found themselves crippled with a massive bill for reparations, sowing seeds of discontent that would be exploited a decade later by a young Austrian house painter by the name of Adolf Hitler.

The Best...
Royal Palaces

1 Windsor Castle, England (p94)

2 Château de Versailles, France (p216)

3 The Hofburg, Austria (p637)

4 Schloss Schönbrunn, Austria (p643)

IN FOCUS HISTORY

WWII

Hitler's rise to power was astonishingly swift. By 1936 he had risen to the role of Chancellor and, as the head of the Nazi Party, assumed total control of Germany's power structures. Having spent much of the 1930s building up a formidable war machine, assisting General Franco's nationalist forces during the Spanish Civil War, Hitler annexed former German territories in Austria and parts of Czechoslovakia, before extending his reach onwards into Poland in 1939.

The occupation of Poland proved the final straw. Britain, France and its Commonwealth allies declared war on Germany, which had formed its own alliance of convenience with the Axis powers of Italy and Japan. Hitler unleashed his blitzkrieg on an unsuspecting Europe, and within a few short months had conquered huge areas of territory across Eastern and central Europe, forcing the French into submission and driving the British forces to a humiliating retreat at Dunkirk. Europe was to remain under Nazi occupation for the next four years.

The Axis retained the upper hand until the Japanese attack on Pearl Harbor forced a reluctant USA into the war in 1941. Hitler's subsequent decision to invade Russia in 1941 proved to be a catastrophic error, resulting in devastating German losses that opened the door for the Allied invasion of Normandy in June 1944.

After several months of bitter fighting, Hitler's remaining forces were pushed back towards Berlin. Hitler committed suicide on 30 April 1945 and the Russians took

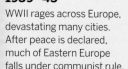

1939–45
WWII rages across Europe, devastating many cities. After peace is declared, much of Eastern Europe falls under communist rule.

1957
The European Economic Community (EEC) is formed by a collection of Western European countries.

1973
The EEC is enlarged to include the UK, Ireland and Denmark. Greece joins in 1981, followed by Spain and Portugal in 1986.

the city, crushing the last pockets of German resistance. By 8 May Germany and Italy had unconditionally surrendered to the Allied powers, bringing the long war in Europe to an end.

The Iron Curtain

Sadly, the cessation of hostilities wasn't the end of Europe's troubles. Differences of opinion between the Western powers and the communist Soviet Union soon led to a stand-off. The USSR closed off its assigned sectors – including East Berlin, East Germany and much of Eastern Europe – heralding the descent of the Iron Curtain and the beginning of the Cold War, a period of political tension and social division in Europe that endured for the next 40 years.

The era finally came to an end in 1989, when popular unrest in Germany resulted in the fall of the Berlin Wall. Germany was reunified in 1990; a year later the USSR was dissolved. Shortly afterwards Romania, Bulgaria, Poland, Hungary and Albania had implemented multiparty democracy. In Czechoslovakia, the so-called Velvet Revolution brought about the downfall of the communist government through mass demonstrations and other nonviolent means.

Galerie des Glaces (Hall of Mirrors) at Château de Versailles (p218), France
DENNIS JOHNSON/LONELY PLANET IMAGES ©

1989
The fall of the Berlin Wall heralds the downfall of oppressive regimes across much of Eastern Europe.

1993
The Maastricht Treaty leads to the formation of the EU.

2002
Twelve member states of the EU ditch their national currencies in favour of the euro.

Europe United

Elsewhere in Europe, the process of political and economic integration has continued apace since the end of WWII. The formation of the European Economic Community (EEC) in 1957 began as a loose trade alliance between six nations, but since its rebranding as the EU at the Treaty of Maastricht in 1993 its core membership has expanded to 27 countries. Sixteen nations have so far chosen to adopt the single currency, the euro, although divisions over the future direction and democratic accountability of Europe continue to rumble on in many of its constituent states.

One of the most divisive issues of recent years has been the implementation of the new European Constitution, which paved the way for the appointment of Europe's first ever fixed-term President, Herman Van Rompuy, who was appointed in 2009. EU advocates maintain that the Constitution was simply designed to make the EU run more efficiently, but Euro-sceptics see it as yet another sign of the inexorable move towards a European super-state.

Constitutional arguments are not the most pressing problems faced by the Eurozone, however. The continuing fallout from the worldwide economic crash of 2008 has resulted in a string of hugely expensive bailouts for Ireland, Greece and Portugal, with rumours that larger nations, including Italy and Spain, may be soon to follow. These economic crises have been damaging not just for the single currency, but also to the spirit of solidarity within the EU: many people have started to question why richer nations such as France and Germany should be held responsible for the economic mistakes of their more profligate European cousins.

Ironically, Europe probably needs its neighbours now more than ever, especially in a world that seems to be moving inexorably east towards the rising nations of China and India. Europe hasn't had its day just yet – but, like the rest of the world, it's facing an increasingly uncertain future.

2009

Belgian Prime Minister Herman Van Rompuy becomes the first permanent President of the EU.

2009–11

Europe is rocked by a series of financial crises, leading to costly bailouts for Ireland, Greece and Portugal.

GREG ELMS/LONELY PLANET IMAGES ©

Family Travel

Mother and child at the Guggenheim Museum (p341), Spain

DOMINIC BONUCCELLI/LONELY PLANET IMAG

Travelling with kids can be one long adventure or a nonstop nightmare. The key to fun and rewarding family travel is planning – planning your European trip together is not just an excellent way to avoid any unwelcome surprises on the road, it's also an excellent way to get everyone excited about the adventure ahead.

Travel

Children and young people qualify for cheap travel on nearly all types of public transport in Europe (usually around 50% of the adult fare). Look out for railcards and passes that qualify you for extra discounts – many cities offer passes that combine entry to sights and attractions with travel on public transport.

Travel distances can be long, so it's a good idea to break up the trip with things to see and do en route. Traffic is at its worst during holiday seasons, especially between June and August, and journey times are likely to be much longer during this period. Trains can be a great option for family travel – kids will have more space to move around, and can pack books, puzzles and computer games to keep them entertained along the way.

Sights & Attractions

Most attractions offer discounted entry for children (generally for 12 and unders, although this does vary). If you can, try to mix up educational activities with other things they're guaranteed to like – balance that visit to the Tate Modern or the Louvre with a trip to the London Aquarium or a day at Disneyland Paris, for example. The number one rule is to avoid packing too much in – you'll get tired, the kids will get irritable and tantrums are sure to follow. Plan carefully and you'll enjoy your time much more.

Hotels & Restaurants

It's always worth asking in advance whether hotels are happy to accept kids. Many are fully geared for family travel, with childrens' activities, child-minding services and the like, but others may impose a minimum age limit to deter guests with kids. Family-friendly hotels will usually be able to offer a large room with two or three beds to accommodate families, or at least neighbouring rooms with an adjoining door.

Dining out *en famille* is generally great fun, but again, it's always worth checking to see whether kids are welcome – generally the posher or more prestigious the establishment, the less kid-friendly they're likely to be. Many restaurants offer cheaper children's menus, usually based around simple staples such as steak, pasta, burgers and chicken. Most will also offer smaller portions of adult meals.

If your kids are fussy, buying your own ingredients at a local market can be a good way of getting them to experiment – they can choose their own food while simultaneously practising the local lingo.

Need to Know

- ○ **Changing facilities** Found at most supermarkets and major attractions.
- ○ **Cots and highchairs** Available in many restaurants and hotels, but ask ahead.
- ○ **Health** Generally good, but pack your own first-aid kit to avoid language difficulties.
- ○ **Kids' menus** Widely available.
- ○ **Nappies (diapers)** Sold everywhere, including pharmacies and supermarkets.
- ○ **Strollers** It's easiest to bring your own.
- ○ **Transport** Children usually qualify for discounts; young kids often travel free.

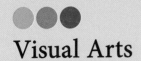

Visual Arts

Interior of Galleria degli Uffizi, Florence

ALBORNO ANDREA/PHOTOLIB

If there were a global league table measuring artistic importance, Europe would surely take top prize. Many of the major art movements of the last millennia can trace their origins back to European shores, and you'll find some of the world's top artistic institutions dotted across the continent.

Ancient Art

Europe's early civilisations left behind a wealth of artworks (particularly sculptures, monuments and pottery) that provide a fascinating window onto the ancient world. Art was a crucial part of everyday life for many ancient civilisations: decorative objects were a sign of status and prestige, while statues were used to venerate and honour the dead, and monuments and temples were lavishly decorated in an attempt to appease the gods.

The Acropolis Museum in Athens is one of the best places to explore the artistic legacy of the ancient world, but you'll find wonderful sculptures and artefacts from early civilisations dotted throughout Europe's top art museums. Perhaps the most famous is the Venus de Milo at the Louvre in Paris, thought to have been created sometime between 130 BC and 100 BC by the master sculptor Alexandros of Antioch.

Medieval Art

During the Middle Ages, the power of the church and its importance as an artistic patron meant that the majority of medieval art dealt with religious subjects. The Old Testament, the crucifixion, the apostles and the Last Judgment were particularly common topics. Some of the finest medieval artworks are actually woven into the fabric of Europe's churches and cathedrals in the form of carvings, sculptures and frescos painted onto panels or interior walls.

Flemish and German painting produced several important figures during the period, including Jan van Eyck (c.1390–1441) and Hans Memling (c.1430–94), known for their lifelike oils, and Hieronymus Bosch (1450–1516), known for his use of fantastic imagery and allegorical concepts.

The Renaissance

The Renaissance marked Europe's golden age of art. Artists such as Leonardo da Vinci (1452–1519), Michelangelo (1475–1564), Raphael (1483–1520), Titian (1487–1576) and Botticelli (1445–1510) introduced new techniques, colours and forms into the artistic lexicon, drawing inspiration from the sculptors and artists of the classical world.

Landscape and the human form, in particular, gained increasing importance during the Renaissance. Michelangelo's masterpiece, *David*, is often cited as the perfect representation of the human figure (despite the fact that the artist deliberately distorted its proportions in order to make it more pleasing to the eye). The sculpture is now on display at the Galleria dell'Accademia in Florence.

In the wake of the Renaissance came the great names of the Baroque period, epitomised by the Italian artist Caravaggio (1573–1610) and the Dutch artists Rembrandt (1606–99), Rubens (1577–1640) and Johannes Vermeer (1632–75). The Baroque artists employed light and shadow (*chiaroscuro*) to heighten the drama of a scene and give their work a photographic intensity.

Romanticism & Impressionism

During the 18th century, Romantic artists such as Caspar David Friedrich (1774–1840) and JMW Turner (1775–1851) explored the drama of the natural landscape – cloud-capped mountains, lonely hilltops, peaceful meadows and moody sunsets. Other artists, such as Théodore Géricault (1791–1824) and Eugène Délacroix (1798–1863), drew inspiration from French history and prominent people of the day. One of Spain's most important artists, Francisco Goya (1746–1828), covered everything from royal portraits to anguished war scenes, bullfight etchings and tapestry designs.

During the late 19th century, artists such as Claude Monet (1840–1926), Edgar Degas (1834–1917), Camille Pissarro (1830–1903), Edouard Manet (1832–83) and Pierre-Auguste Renoir (1841–1919) aimed to capture the general 'impression' of a scene rather than its strictly naturalistic representation (hence the name of their movement, 'Impressionism').

The Best... National Art Museums

1 National Gallery, London (p63)

2 Musée du Louvre, Paris (p179)

3 Uffizi Gallery, Florence (p442)

4 Prado, Madrid (p298)

5 Rijksmuseum, Amsterdam (p498)

The Best...
Modern Art
Galleries

1 Tate Modern, London
(p79)

2 Museu Picasso,
Barcelona (p322)

3 Guggenheim
Museum, Bilbao
(p341)

4 Centre Pompidou-
Metz (p236)

5 SMAK, Ghent
(p532)

Their bold experiments with light, colour and form segued into that of their successors, the Post-Impressionists such as Paul Cézanne (1839–1906), Vincent Van Gogh (1853–90) and Paul Gauguin (1848–1903).

From Fauvism to Conceptual Art

The upheavals of the 20th century brought great change and many new artistic movements. The Fauvists were fascinated by colour, typified by the work of Henri Matisse (1869–1954), while the Cubists, such as Georges Braque (1882–1963) and Pablo Picasso (1881–1973), broke their work down into abstract forms, drawing inspiration from a broad range of sources: from primitive art to the emerging science of psychoanalysis.

The Dadists and Surrealists took these ideas to their illogical extreme, exploring dreams and the subconscious: key figures include Réné Magritte (1898–1967) from Belgium, Max Ernst (1891–1976) from Germany, and Joan Miró (1893–1983) and Salvador Dalí (1904–89) from Spain.

The late 20th century has witnessed a myriad of artistic movements: abstract expressionism, neoplasticism, minimalism, formalism and pop art, to name a few. One of the most controversial movements of recent years has been conceptual art, which stresses the importance of the idea behind a work rather than its aesthetic value. Britain has a particularly vibrant conceptual art scene: key artists to look out for include Tracy Emin, the Chapman Brothers, Rachel Whiteread, Mark Wallinger and Damien Hirst (famous for his pickled sharks and diamond-encrusted skulls).

Architecture

Erechtheion temple, the Acropolis (p747), Athens

DENNIS JOHNSON / LONELY PLANET IMAGES ©

With an architectural heritage stretching back seven millennia, Europe is one long textbook for building buffs. From Greek temples to venerable mosques and modern skyscrapers, Europe's fascinating and complex architectural environment is bound to be one of the main highlights of your visit.

The Ancient World

Europe's oldest examples of architecture are the many hundreds of stone circles, henges, barrows, burial chambers and alignments built by Neolithic people between 4500 BC and 1500 BC. The most impressive examples of these ancient structures are at Brú Na Bóinne in Ireland, Carnac in Brittany and, of course, Stonehenge in the southwest of England. No one is quite sure what the purpose of these structures was, although theories abound. Some say they could be celestial calendars, burial monuments or tribal meeting places, although it's generally agreed these days that they served some sort of religious function.

Greek & Roman Architecture

Several ancient cultures have left their mark around the shores of the Mediterranean, including the Minoans (in Crete), the Etruscans

(in present-day Tuscany), the Mycenaeans (in the northeast Peloponnese) and, of course, the ancient Greeks and Romans. Athens is the best place to go to appreciate Greece's golden age: the dramatic monuments of the Acropolis perfectly illustrate the ancient Greeks' sophisticated understanding of geometry, shape and form, and set the blueprint for many of the architectural principles that have endured to the present day.

The Romans were even more ambitious than the Greeks with their architecture, and built a host of monumental structures designed to project the might and majesty of the Roman Empire. Roman architecture was driven by a combination of form and function – structures such as the Pont du Gard aqueduct in southern France show how the Romans valued architecture that looked beautiful but also served a practical purpose. It goes without saying that Rome has the greatest concentration of architectural treasures, including the famous Colosseum and the Roman Forum, but you'll find remains of Roman buildings scattered all over the continent.

Romanesque & Gothic Architecture

The solidity and elegance of ancient Roman architecture echoed through the 10th and 11th centuries in buildings constructed during the Romanesque period. Many of Europe's earliest churches are classic examples of Romanesque construction, using rounded arches, vaulted roofs, and massive columns and walls.

Even more influential was the development of Gothic architecture, which gave rise to many of Europe's most spectacular cathedrals. Tell-tale characteristics of Gothic architecture include the use of pointed arches, ribbed vaulting, great showpiece windows and flying buttresses. The famous cathedrals situated in Chartres, Cologne, Reims and Notre-Dame in Paris are ideal places to see Gothic architecture in action.

Interior of St Peter's Basilica, Rome

Renaissance & Baroque Architecture

The Renaissance led to a huge new range of architectural experiments. Pioneering Italian architects such as Brunelleschi, Michelangelo and Palladio shifted the emphasis away from Gothic austerity towards a more human approach. They combined elements of classical architecture with new building materials, and specially commissioned sculptures and decorative artworks. Florence and Venice are particularly rich in Renaissance buildings, but the movement's influence can be felt right across Europe – the showy chateaux in France's Loire Valley, for example, bear many hallmarks of the Renaissance movement.

Architectural showiness reached its zenith during the Baroque period, when architects pulled out all the stops to show off the wealth and prestige of their clients. Baroque buildings are all about creating drama and theatricality, and architects often employed swathes of craftsmen and used the most expensive materials available to create the desired effect. The lavish country estate of Castle Howard in northern England, Paris' Hôtel des Invalides and practically all of Salzburg's buildings showcase the ostentation and expense that underpinned Baroque architecture.

The Best...
Renaissance Buildings

1 Duomo, Florence (p439)

2 St Peter's Basilica, Rome (p399)

3 Palazzo Pitti, Florence (p443)

4 Sistine Chapel, Vatican City (p405)

5 Château de Chambord, Loire Valley (p239)

The Industrial Age

The 19th century was the great age of urban planning, when the chaotic streets and squalid slums of many of Europe's cities were swept away in favour of grand squares and ruler-straight boulevards. This was partly driven by an attempt to clean up the urban environment – most of Europe's cities were still plagued by disease, poor sanitation and squalid slums – but it also allowed architects to redesign the urban landscape to suit the industrial age, merging factories, public buildings, museums and residential suburbs into a seamless whole. One of the most obvious examples of urban remodelling was Baron Haussman's reinvention of Paris during the late 19th century, which resulted in the construction of the city's great boulevards and many of its landmark buildings.

Nineteenth-century architects also increasingly began to move away from the showiness and ornamentation of the Baroque and Rococo periods in favour of new materials such as brick, iron and glass. Neo-Gothic architecture was designed to emphasise permanence, solidity and power, reflecting the confidence of the industrial age. It was an era that also gave rise to many of Europe's great public buildings, including many landmark museums, galleries, libraries, city halls and train stations.

The 20th Century

By the turn of the 20th century, the worlds of art and architecture had both begun to experiment with new approaches to shape and form. The flowing shapes and archnatural forms of art nouveau had a profound influence on the work of Charles Rennie Mackintosh in Glasgow, the Belgian architect Victor Horta and the Modernista buildings of Antonio Gaudí.

The Best...
Modern
Buildings

1 Guggenheim
Museum, Bilbao
(p341)

2 Centre Pompidou-
Metz, Paris (p236)

3 The Kunsthaus,
Graz (p655)

4 The Reichstag
Dome, Berlin (p563)

5 The Eden Project,
Cornwall (p101)

Meanwhile, other architects stripped their buildings back to the bare essentials, emphasising strict function over form: Le Corbusier, Ludwig Mies van der Rohe and Walter Gropius (founder of the German Bauhaus movement) are among the most influential figures of the period.

Functional architecture continued to dominate much of mid-20th-century architecture, especially in the rush to reconstruct Europe's shattered cities in the wake of two world wars, although the 'concrete box' style of architecture has largely fallen out of fashion over recent decades. Europeans may have something of a love-hate relationship with modern architecture, but the best buildings eventually find their place – a good example of this is the inside-out Centre Pompidou in Paris, which initially drew howls of protest but is now considered one of the icons of 20th-century architecture. Regardless of whether you approve of the more recent additions to Europe's architectural landscape, one thing's for sure – you won't find them boring.

Food & Drink

Spaghetti alla Vongole, Italy

JEAN-BERNARD CARILLET / LONELY PLANET IMAGES ©

If there's one thing that unites Europe, it's a passion for food. The flavours you'll encounter will be wonderfully varied, from the spiciness of Mediterranean cuisine to the richness of French cheeses and the distinctiveness of German wurst. Some of the ingredients might not be to your taste, but you won't know till you try – so open your mind, swallow your preconceptions and tuck in. Bon appétit!

Britain

Britain might not have a distinctive cuisine, but it does have a thriving food culture. British chefs have gained a reputation as some of the most creative and imaginative in Europe, cherry-picking flavours, techniques and ingredients from across the continent. Britain's colonial legacy has also left it with a vibrant curry culture – a recent poll suggested that the nation's favourite food was chicken tikka masala.

Traditional Dishes

The Brits love a good roast, traditionally eaten on a Sunday and accompanied by crispy roast potatoes, thick gravy and cooked vegetables. The classic is roast beef with Yorkshire pudding (a crisp batter puff), but lamb, pork and chicken are equally popular. 'Bangers and mash' (sausages and mashed potato) and fish and chips (battered cod served with thick-cut potatoes) are also old favourites.

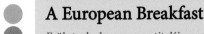

A European Breakfast

Frühstuck, desayuno, petit déjeuner – what you'll find on the breakfast table depends entirely on where you happen to be.

In Britain and Ireland, the traditional start to the day consists of a cooked breakfast ('fry-up') of eggs, bacon, sausages, mushroom, black pudding (blood sausage), fried bread, beans and tomatoes.

The Mediterranean approach is lighter. Spaniards usually start the day with coffee and a *tostada* (piece of toast) or *pastel/bollo* (pastry), while the French typically opt for coffee and a baguette with jam, a croissant or a *pain au chocolat*. Meanwhile, Italians prefer a cappuccino and *cornetto* (Italian croissant) at a cafe.

The biggest breakfasts are served in Germany, Austria and Switzerland, where you could survive for the entire day purely on what's served up on the breakfast table – from fresh breads, cakes and pastries to a smorgasbord of cold meats, cheeses, cereals and fruit. *Gut essen* indeed!

Specialities in Scotland include haggis served with 'tatties and neeps' (potato and turnip). Traditional Welsh dishes include *cawl* (broth, usually with lamb and leeks) and *bara lafwr* (savoury scones made with oatmeal and seaweed).

Cheese

Britain's favourite cheese is cheddar – a matured hard cheese with a pungent flavour – but there are many others to discover, including Wensleydale, Red Leicester and Stilton.

Drinks

Pubs serve a choice of generic lagers, but the traditional British brew is ale – served warm and flat in order to bring out the hoppy flavours. Ireland's trademark ale is stout – usually Guinness, although in Cork stout can mean a Murphy's or a Beamish, too.

France

French cuisine continues to set the pace for the rest of the world. Each region has its distinctive dishes: broadly, the hot south tends to favour dishes based around olive oil, garlic and tomatoes, while the cooler north favours root vegetables, rich gravies and creamy or buttery sauces. The French are famously unfussy about which bits of the animal they eat – kidney, liver and tongue are as much of a delicacy as a fillet steak or a prime rib.

Traditional dishes

Bouillabaisse is the signature southern dish, a hearty, saffron-scented fish stew that's best eaten in Marseille. *Soupe de poissons* (fish soup) is thinner and is usually served with spicy rouille, gruyère cheese and croutons.

The Alps are the place to try *fondue*, hunks of toasted bread dipped into thick cheese sauces. Brittany and Normandy are rich in seafood, especially mussels and oysters. Lyon's small local restaurants *(bouchons)* are renowned for their pig dishes, particularly *andouillette*, a sausage made from pig intestines.

Central France prides itself on its hearty cuisine, including *foie gras* (goose liver), *boeuf bourgignon* (beef cooked in red wine), *confit de canard* (duck cooked in preserved fat) and *truffes* (black truffles).

Cheese

France produces literally hundreds of different types of cheese. Some of the big names are camembert, brie, Livarot, Pont l'Évêque and Époisses (all soft cheeses); roquefort and Bleu d'Auvergne (blue cheeses); and Comté, cantal and gruyère (hard cheeses).

Drinks

France is Europe's biggest wine-producing nation. The principal regions are Alsace, Bordeaux, Burgundy, Languedoc, the Loire and the Rhône, all of which produce a mix of reds, whites and rosés. Then, of course, there's Champagne – home to the world's favourite bubbly, aged in centuries-old cellars beneath the hallowed fields around Reims and Épernay.

Italy

Italian cuisine is dominated by the twin staples of pizza and pasta, which are thought to have been eaten in Italy since Roman times. A full meal comprises an antipasto (starter), *primo* (pasta or rice dish), *secondo* (usually meat or fish), *contorno* (vegetable side dish or salad), *dolce* (dessert) and coffee. When eating out it's OK to mix and match any combination.

Traditional dishes

Italian pasta comes in a bewildering variety of shapes, from bow-shaped *farfalle* to twisty *fusilli*, ribbed *rigatoni* and long, flat *pappardelle*. Italian pasta is made with durum flour, which gives it a distinctive *al dente* bite; the type of pasta used is usually dictated by the type of dish being served (ribbed or shaped pastas hold sauce better, for example).

Italian pizza comes in two varieties: the Roman pizza with a thin crispy base, and the Neapolitan pizza, which has a higher, doughier base. The best are always prepared in a *forno a legna* (wood-fired oven). Flavours are generally kept simple – the best pizza restaurants often serve only a couple of toppings, such as *margherita* (tomato and mozzarella) and *marinara* (tomato, garlic and oregano).

Vegetarians & Vegans

Vegetarians will have a tough time in many areas of Europe – meat eating is still very much the norm, and eating fish is often seen as a vegetarian option. But you'll usually be able to find at least something meat free on most menus, though don't expect much choice. Vegans will have an even tougher time – cheese, cream and milk are an integral ingredient in most European cuisines.

Vegetable-based *antipasti* (starters), tapas, meze, pastas, side dishes and salads are all good ways of ensuring a meat-free meal. Shopping for yourself in local markets can also be a good way of trying the local food without having to compromise your principles.

Cheese

Like the French, the Italians pride themselves in their cheese-making abilities: again, there are hundreds of different types, but the biggest names are parmesan, ricotta and mozzarella.

Drinks

Most Italians drink beer with pizza and wine with other meals. Italy's wines run the gamut from big-bodied reds such as Piedmont's Barolo, to light white wines from Sardinia and sparkling prosecco from the Veneto.

The Netherlands & Belgium

Traditional Dishes

The Netherlands' colonial legacy has given the Dutch a taste for Indonesian and Surinamese-inspired meals like *rijsttafel* (rice table): an array of spicy dishes such as braised beef, pork satay and ribs, all served with white rice.

Other Dutch dishes to look out for are *erwertensoep*, a rich pea soup with onions, carrots, smoked sausage and bacon, *krokotten*, dough balls with various fillings that are crumbed and deep-fried, and, of course, there are *friet* (fries), which the Dutch like to claim they invented – here they're thin, crispy and eaten with mayonnaise rather than ketchup (tomato sauce).

The iconic dish to try in Belgium is *mosselen/moules* – a steaming cauldron of mussels served in their shells, usually accompanied on the side by a helping of *frites* (fries) and cold beer. Other dishes to sample include *balekkes/bouletten* (meatballs), *vlaamse stoverij/carbonade flamande* (a beer-based beef casserole) and *waterzooi* (a creamy chicken or fish stew), often accompanied by *stoemp* (a veg-and-potato mash).

Sweet Treats

From pralines to puddings, Europe provides endless opportunities to indulge in something sweet, sticky and sinful. Germans and Austrians are particularly known for their sweet tooth – treats include *Salzburger nockerl* (a fluffy soufflé) and *Schwarzwälder kirschtorte* (Black Forest cherry cake), plus many types of *apfeltasche* (apple pastry) and *strudel* (filled filo pastry). The Brits are another big cake-eating nation – a slice of cake or a dunked biscuit is an essential teatime ritual in the British Isles.

The Italians are famous for their *gelaterias* (ice-cream stalls; the best will be labelled *produzione propria*, indicating that it's handmade on the premises). Most Greek desserts are variations on pastry soaked in honey, such as *baklava* (thin layers of pastry filled with honey and nuts).

But it's the French who have really turned dessert into a fine art. Stroll past the window of any *boulangerie* (bakery) or patisserie and you'll be assaulted by temptations, from creamy *éclairs* (filled choux buns) and crunchy *macarons* (macaroons) to fluffy *madeleines* (shell-shaped sponge cakes) and wicked *gâteaux* (cakes).

Go on – you know you want to.

Cheese

The Dutch are keen on cheese: the best known varieties are edam and gouda, sometimes served as bar snacks with mustard.

Drinks

Beer is the tipple of choice. Small Dutch brewers like Gulpen, Haarlem's Jopen, Bavaria, Drie Ringen, Leeuw and Utrecht are all excellent. You'll find an even bigger choice in Belgium: look out for dark Trappist beers, golden beers such as Duuvel and the champagne-style lambic beers brewed around Brussels.

Spain

Spain's cuisine is typical of the flavours of Mediterranean cooking, making extensive use of herbs, tomatoes, onions, garlic, spices and lashings of olive oil.

Traditional dishes

The nation's signature dish is *paella*, consisting of rice, seafood and sometimes chicken or meat, simmered with saffron in a large pan. Valencia is considered *paella*'s spiritual home.

Spain also prides itself on its ham (especially *jamón serrano*, a cured ham similar to Italian parma ham) and spicy sausages (including *chorizo, lomo* and *salchichón*). These are often used in making the bite-size Spanish dishes known as *tapas* (or *pintxos* in the Basque region). Tapas is usually a snack, but it can also be a main meal – three or four dishes is generally enough for one person.

Drinks

Spain boasts the largest area (1.2 million ha) of wine cultivation in the world. La Rioja and Ribera del Duero are the principal wine-growing regions.

Cakes in a patisserie, France

Greece

Greece is known for its seafood – you'll find everything from swordfish to octopus on *taverna* menus. As with its Mediterranean neighbours, garlic, tomatoes and olives (either whole or as olive oil) feature heavily.

Traditional Dishes

The Greek form of tapas is *mezedhes*: common dishes include grilled octopus, kalamata olives, meatballs, fried sausages and fava beans, served with dips such as hummus (chickpeas), taramasalata (cod roe) and tzatziki (yoghurt, garlic and cucumber).

In Greece, large kebabs are known as *gyros*, while *souvlaki* is made from small cubes of meat cooked on a skewer; both are served in pitta bread with salad and sauces. Falafel (chickpea balls) are another much-loved Greek snack.

Cheese

Greece's main cheese is *feta*. Its strong, salty flavour is a key ingredient in many dishes and salads. *Halloumi* is a chewy cheese that is often cooked.

Drinks

The potent aniseed-flavoured spirit of *ouzo* has been the tipple of choice since time immemorial. It's traditionally mixed with water and ice (turning a cloudy white). Similar traditions exist in the south of France (where *pastis* is the tipple), Spain (*grappa*) and Turkey (*raki*).

Greek wines aren't as well known as other countries, but they can be very good.

Germany, Austria and Switzerland

The Germanic nations are all about big flavours and big portions. *Wurst* (sausage) is available in hundreds of forms, and is often served with *sauerkraut* (fermented cabbage).

Traditional Dishes

The most common types of *wurst* include *bratwurst* (spiced sausage), *weissewurst* (veal sausage), *blutwurst* (blood sausage) and many forms of schnitzel (breaded pork or veal cutlet, the key ingredient in Austria's signature dish, *Wiener schnitzel*).

Other popular mains include *Rippenspeer* (spare ribs), *Rotwurst* (black pudding), *Rostbrätl* (grilled meat) and *Putenbrust* (turkey breast). Potatoes are served as

The Art of the Sandwich

There's no such thing as a simple sandwich in Europe. Every nation has its own unique take.

In the UK, a sandwich is usually made with a square-sized loaf, cut in two; across the Channel in France and Belgium, they're more likely to make their sandwiches using a long baton-shaped baguette.

The Italians favour the *panini*, a pocket-shaped parcel of bread usually served piping hot, while the *pitta*, a flatbread served widely in Greece, is a close relation.

Bratkartoffeln (fried), *Kartoffelpüree* (mashed), Swiss-style *rösti* (grated then fried) or *Pommes Frites* (French fries).

The Swiss are known for their love of fondue and the similar dish of *raclette* (melted cheese with potatoes).

Cheese

Gouda, Emmental and gruyère are the best-known Swiss cheeses, while the Germans are known for their hard cheeses – especially *Allgäu Emmentaler* and *Bergkäse* (mountain cheese).

Drinks

Beer is the national beverage. *Pils* is the crisp pilsner Germany is famous for, often slightly bitter. *Alt* is darker and more full bodied. *Weizenbier* is made with wheat instead of barley malt and served in a tall, 500mL glass. *Helles bier* is light beer, while *Dunkles bier* is dark.

Germany is principally known for white wines – inexpensive, light and intensely fruity. The Rhine and Moselle Valleys are the largest wine-growing regions.

The Best...
Local Spirits

1 Whisky in Scotland (p132)

2 Pastis in the south of France (p259)

3 Ouzo in Greece (p742)

4 Grappa in Spain (p298)

5 Jenever in the Netherlands (p494)

The Czech Republic

Traditional Dishes

Like many nations in Eastern Europe, Czech cuisine is heavy and stodgy, principally revolving around meat, potatoes and root vegetables, dished up in stews, goulashes and casseroles. *Pečená kachna* (roast duck) is the quintessential Czech restaurant dish, while *klobása* (sausage) is an ideal post-pint snack. A regular meal accompaniment in the Czech Republic is *knedliky*, boiled dumplings made from wheat or potato flour.

Cheese

The Czechs aren't renowned for their cheese, though you'll probably try *nakládaný hermelín*, a soft cheese covered in a white rind, at least once.

Beer

The Czechs have a rich beer culture, with some of Europe's best *pivo* (beer), usually lager style. The Moravian region is the up-and-coming area for Czech wines.

Sports & Activities

Hiking in the Alps, Switzerland

BRUCE BI / LONELY PLANET IMAGES

With decades of sporting prowess under its belt and a landscape taking in everything from snow-flecked mountains to sapphire seas, Europe offers endless ways to get active. Hardcore hikers, cyclists, diving devotees and adrenaline junkies will all find plenty to keep them occupied. And if you really want to get under a nation's skin, you could do a lot worse than head for the nearest football ground...

Football

Football (*not* soccer, please) is Europe's number-one spectator sport, and tantamount to a religion in many corners of the continent. Europe's big nations battle it out every four years (with varying degrees of success) in the knockout European Championships; the most recent winner was Spain in 2008, with the next tournament scheduled to be jointly hosted by Poland and Ukraine in 2012.

Each country has it own top-flight domestic league (the Premier League in Britain, the Bundesliga in Germany, Serie A in Italy, La Liga in Spain, and so on) plus a series of lower divisions. The top teams from each league battle it out in the hotly contested Champions League in a bid to be crowned European champions, while lower-placed teams contest the UEFA Europa League. The football season varies from country to country, but it generally runs from sometime in August or September to anytime between May and July. Tickets for top sides such as Manchester United, Chelsea, Barcelona, Real Madrid, Bayern Munich, Juventus and Inter Milan are seriously expensive (if you can get hold of one, that is) – so if you're desperate to catch a match you'll probably have more luck going to see one of the lesser-ranked sides.

Cycling

Europe's hills and mountains don't seem to put people off getting into the saddle. Cycling is very popular in many areas of Europe, especially France, Italy and Austria: these countries have collectively produced some of the finest competitive cyclists the world has ever seen. Avid cyclists and fans stay glued to their screens or turn out to cheer along the roadside during the annual Tour de France, a gruelling long-distance road race that's been held nearly every year since 1903.

Roadbikes tend to be the most popular form of cycling in Europe, although mountain bikes are catching up fast – especially in mountainous areas such as the Alps, the Pyrenees and the Dolomites. For a more sedate pace (and a lot fewer hills), Belgium, the Netherlands and Luxembourg are all fantastic countries to explore in the saddle, with large areas of flat, rolling countryside and a welcoming, bike-friendly attitude.

The Best... Places to Explore by Bicycle

1 Amsterdam, the Netherlands (p494)

2 Kinderdijk, the Netherlands (p513)

3 The Loire Valley, France (p236)

4 Tuscany, Italy (p439)

5 Bohemia, the Czech Republic (p712)

IN FOCUS SPORTS & ACTIVITIES

Hiking

Keen hikers can spend a lifetime exploring Western Europe's many exciting trails. Probably the most spectacular are to be found in the Alps and the Italian Dolomites, which are criss-crossed with well-marked trails; food and accommodation are available along the way in season. The equally sensational Pyrenees are less developed, which can add to the experience as you'll often rely on remote mountain villages for rest and sustenance. Hiking areas that are less well known, but nothing short of stunning, are Corsica and Sardinia. The Picos de Europa range in Spain is also rewarding, while the Lake District, the Yorkshire Dales and the Scottish Highlands are among the UK's top hiking spots.

The best months for hiking are generally from June to September, although the weather can be unpredictable at any time of year. Be prepared: check the weather forecast before you head out and wear appropriate clothing, especially if you're planning on hiking through remote areas – if you get into trouble, help can be a long way away.

Most countries in Europe have national parks and other interesting areas that qualify as a hiker's paradise. Guided hikes are often available for those who aren't sure about their physical abilities or who simply don't know what to look for. Local tourist offices can provide all the info you need.

For really hardcore hikers, Europe now has several long-distance paths covering various countries, mostly making use of existing GR (*grande randonnée*) trails.

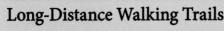

Long-Distance Walking Trails

○ **Camino de Santiago** (St James' Way; www.santiago-compostela.net) Spain's best-known long-distance trail traces the old pilgrimage route to Santiago de Compostela.

○ **Grand Italian Trail** Hiking trail that cuts 6166km across Italy.

○ **Haute Randonnée Pyrénéenne** High-altitude hiking through the Pyrenees.

○ **South West Coast Path** (www.swcp.org.uk) Most of Britain's stunning southwest coastline is accessible via this 630km trail.

○ **Via Alpina** (www.via-alpina.org) Network of five long-distance routes across the alpine regions of Slovenia, Austria, Germany, Liechtenstein, Switzerland, Italy, France and Monaco.

○ **West Highland Way** (www.west-highland-way.co.uk) Classic route through southern Scotland.

Skiing & Snowboarding

Winter sports are part of a way of life for residents of many European nations. The Austrians, Swiss, Germans and French are particularly snow-mad – between them they have produced many of the great names in skiing and snowboarding over the last century.

If you fancy taking to the pistes, you'll find hundreds of resorts located in the Alps and Pyrenees for downhill skiing and snowboarding. Cross-country skiing is also very popular in some areas, especially the Jura Mountains. Many resorts also offer other snowbound activities such as luging, bobsleighing and ice-climbing.

A skiing holiday can be expensive once you've added up the costs of ski lifts, accommodation and the inevitable après-ski sessions. Equipment hire, on the other hand, can be relatively cheap, and the hassle of bringing your own skis may not be worth it.

The ski season generally lasts from early December to late March, though at higher altitudes it may extend an extra month either side. Snow conditions can vary greatly from one year to the next and from region to region, but January and February tend to be the best (and busiest) months.

Ski resorts in the French and Swiss Alps offer great skiing and facilities, but are also by far the most expensive. Expect high prices in the German Alps, too, though Germany has some cheaper options available in the Black Forest and Harz Mountains. Austria is generally better value than France and Switzerland, especially in Carinthia. Prices in the Italian Alps are similar to those in Austria (although there are some upmarket exceptions), and can be relatively cheap given the right package.

Possibly the cheapest skiing in Western Europe is to be found in the Pyrenees in Spain and Andorra, and in the Sierra Nevada range in the south of Spain.

Water Sports

With the Mediterranean, the Atlantic, the Adriatic and the English Channel right on the doorstep, you won't be surprised to discover that messing about on the water is a popular European pastime.

Diving

It's not tropical, but that doesn't mean Europe isn't a great place to dive. Topaz waters and a spiky, volcanic geology make for spectacular diving all along the Mediterranean coast, while the clear waters and varied underwater life of the Adriatic have led to a flourishing dive industry there, especially in Croatia. Wreck-diving is a particular highlight – Europe's long maritime history, as well as its war-torn past, mean that the coastline is littered with underwater vessels. The many islands of the Mediterranean offer some of Europe's finest diving – Sicily's Aeolian Islands, Sardinia, Corsica and the Greek Islands all provide fantastic opportunities for underwater exploring.

If you're a novice diver, diving schools offering introductory dives and longer courses are available in many areas; make sure they're accredited by PADI or one of the equivalent organisations. If you're an experienced diver, remember your accreditation certificates and any other relevant paperwork if you're planning on renting equipment or undertaking more complex dives.

The Best...
Ski Resorts

1 Chamonix, France (p246)

2 Zermatt, Switzerland (p679)

3 St Moritz, Switzerland (p692)

4 Grindelwald, Switzerland (p685)

IN FOCUS SPORTS & ACTIVITIES

Boating, Canoeing & Kayaking

Europe's lakes, rivers and diverse coastlines offer a variety of boating options unmatched anywhere in the world. You can kayak in Switzerland, row on a peaceful Alpine lake, join a Danube River cruise from Amsterdam to Vienna, rent a sailing boat on the Côte d'Azur or putter along the extraordinary canal networks of Britain, Ireland or France – the possibilities are endless.

Surfing & Windsurfing

The best surfing in Europe is on the Atlantic coastline. Top spots include the Atlantic Coast in France (especially around Biarritz), the west coasts of Wales, Ireland, Scotland and southwest England, and Spain's Basque Country (San Sebastián, Zarautz and Mundaka).

Windsurfing is less dependent on geography, so you'll be able to catch a break anywhere there's some wind and open water. With its long beaches and ceaseless wind, Tarifa, near Cádiz in Spain, is considered to be Europe's windsurfing capital, but you'll find windsurfing spots all over the Med and the Adriatic.

Sailing

Sailing is a brilliant way to see Europe's coastline. Sailing between the Mediterranean's coast and islands is hugely popular, especially in Greece. Sailing courses are widely available, although renting your own boat can be an expensive option, so you'll need a few seagoing friends to make the expense worthwhile.

European Landscapes

View to Grindelwald Glacier, Switzerland

DAVID TOMLINSON / LONELY PLANET IMAGES

One of the great pleasures of travelling in Europe is the sheer diversity of the landscape. A single day's journey can carry you from the glittering beaches of the Mediterranean to the icy glaciers of the Alps, from snow-capped mountains and rolling hills to patchwork fields and azure seas. Europe is a place where it's simply impossible not to feel inspired by the scenery.

Mountains

In terms of sheer scale, there's one mountain range in Europe that's impossible to ignore, and that's the Alps. This jagged chain of peaks covers over 1200km between Nice and Vienna, straddling the borders of France, Italy, Germany, Austria and Switzerland en route. With a total area of almost 192,000 sq km, the Alps are not just Europe's largest mountain range, they're one of the largest mountain systems on earth. They're also home to Europe's highest peak, moody Mont Blanc (4810m), which looms above the Franco–Italian border and remains snowcapped most of the year.

While the Alps might look like an untouched wilderness, they're actually not as pristine as they appear. In contrast to many mountain ranges in North America, for example, heavy industry and urban development are permitted in many areas of the Alps (albeit under strict controls). Tourism is also seriously big business, with several hundred ski resorts now dotted across the Alpine peaks, collectively clocking up over 201 million skier days every year.

Thankfully, many areas have been protected from development by being designated national parks. Among the largest areas are the Parc National de la Vanoise and the Parc National des Écrins in France, the Swiss National Park in Switzerland and the Gran Paradiso National Park in Italy. Here you'll still be able to spot some of Europe's rarest wildlife, including ibexes, wolves, brown bears, lynxes, golden eagles, chamois and mouflons (a curly horned wild sheep).

To the east of the Alps lies one of Europe's other great mountain ranges, the Carpathians, which sprawl for 1500km across much of the Czech Republic and Eastern Europe. Slightly smaller in stature but no less spectacular are the Pyrenees, which stretch for just over 490km across the Franco–Spanish border; the 300km long Cantabria Mountains of northern Spain; and the various mountain ranges of Scotland, including the Grampians, Cairngorms and Highlands.

Coastlines & Beaches

Since Europe is surrounded on three sides by the sea, it's hardly surprising that the continent is home to some spectacular coastlines.

The Mediterranean draws the majority of visitors, thanks to its sparkling beaches and balmy summer temperatures. Spain, France, Greece and Italy all offer glorious stretches of coastline, but each area has a markedly different character: while package holidaymakers flock to the high-rise hotels sprawling along Spain's Costa Brava, for example, Italy's Amalfi Coast and the French Riviera are dotted with the kind of pretty coastal villages and picturesque harbours that hardly seem to have changed in the last hundred years.

Out to the west, Europe's Atlantic coast receives fewer visitors than the Med, mainly due to its chillier sea temperatures and less reliable weather. But while it might not always be the place for lounging around on the beach, the Atlantic swells are a boon for surfers: the west coasts of Spain, France, Ireland and southwest England offer some of the best surfing conditions anywhere in Europe.

But if it's coastline that floats your boat, it's hard to beat Britain. This sea-fringed island boasts the longest stretch of continuous coastline in Europe (over 17,000km in all), and unsurprisingly is home to some of its most impressive scenery: from the craggy cliffs of Cornwall to the wide open beaches of the Gower Peninsula and the stately rock stacks of western and northern Scotland.

Forests

Europe was once covered by a vast forest that stretched all the way from the Arctic Ocean to the Mediterranean Sea. In fact, it's thought that the forest probably covered around 80% of the continent. But since the Industrial Revolution somewhere between a half and two-thirds of the original tree cover has been lost. Large areas of forest

The Best...
Mountain
Experiences

1 Riding the cable car to the Aiguille du Midi (p246)

2 Taking a train to Europe's highest station, Jungfraujoch (p686)

3 Catching your first sight of the Matterhorn (p679)

4 Hiking the Picos di Europa (p316)

5 Gazing over Grindelwald's glaciers (p685)

The Best...
Beach
Destinations

1 Côte d'Azur, France
(p269)

2 Amalfi Coast, Italy
(p473)

3 Aegean Islands,
Greece (p763)

4 The French Atlantic
Coast (p252)

5 Southwest England
(p98)

have since been replanted, often with fast-growing non-native species such as pine, fir and conifer; around 5% of Europe's total forested area is now collectively protected by national agencies.

Outside eastern and Scandinavian Europe, the largest area of 'old growth' woodland is the Black Forest, covering around 12,000 sq km in the Baden-Württemberg region of southwest Germany. Other notable woodlands include the Landes Forest in southwest France, the forests of the Carpathian Mountains, and the New Forest in southern England.

Islands

Europe's seas are studded with countless islands. The highest concentration can be found in Greece, which is effectively a nation made up of numerous islands, including the Peloponnese, Cyclades and Dodecanese. Somewhat less frequented are the far-flung Ionian and Aegean Islands, each defined by its own unique character and decorated with a smattering of sandy beaches, secluded bays and hidden coves.

Many of the Mediterranean's islands are volcanic in origin. The Greek island of Santorini is all that remains of a vast volcano that exploded sometime between 1700 BC and 1500 BC. Others, such as Sicily and the nearby Aeolian Islands, remain highly active – Mt Etna and Mt Stromboli both still regularly blow their tops, with Etna thought to be overdue for a major eruption (the last serious explosion has been estimated to have occurred around 2000 years ago).

The largest islands in the Mediterranean are Sardinia (governed by Italy) and Corsica (governed by France). Both of these popular destinations are packed with French and Italian holidaymakers, and the beaches of both islands are busiest between July and September. Time your visit for the shoulder months, however, and you might well have the islands all to yourself.

Further afield, Britain has a string of islands that make ideal places for escaping the crowds. Forty-five kilometres off the tip of southwest Britain are the tiny Scilly Isles, only five of which are inhabited on a permanent basis. Off Scotland's west coast are the rocky Inner and Outer Hebrides, while further north are the Orkneys, home to some of Britain's most ancient settlements, and the isolated Shetland Islands, which mark the most northerly point in the British Isles.

Survival Guide

Horse and carriage in St Peter's Square (p401), The Vatican, Rome
RUTH EASTHAM & MAX PAOLI / LONELY PLANET IMAGES ©

Directory

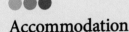

Accommodation

Where you stay in Europe may be one of the highlights of your trip. Quirky family-run inns, manic city hostels, languid and low-key beach resorts are just some of the places where you'll make both new memories and, more than likely, new friends.

Self-catering apartments and cottages are worth considering when travelling with a group, especially if you plan to stay somewhere for a while. During peak holiday periods, accommodation can be hard to find, and it's advisable to book ahead. Accommodation listings in this guide have been ordered by price, from budget to top end.

B&BS & GUEST HOUSES

In the UK and Ireland myriad B&Bs are real bargains in this field, where you get bed and breakfast in a private home. In some areas every second house will have a B&B sign out the front.

In other countries, similar private accommodation – though often without breakfast – may go under the name of pension, guest house, *Gasthaus, Zimmerfrei, chambre d'hôte* and so on. Although the majority of guest houses are simple affairs, there are more expensive ones where you'll find bathrooms and other luxuries.

With B&Bs especially, make certain that they are centrally located and not in some dull and distant suburb.

HOTELS

From fabulous five-star icons to workaday cheapies by train stations, the range of hotels in Western Europe is immense. You'll often find inexpensive hotels clustered around the bus and train station areas, which are always good places to start hunting; however, these areas can be charmless and scruffy. Look for moderately priced places closer to the interesting parts of town. Ask about breakfast; sometimes it's included, sometimes it's not.

Besides big booking sites such as **Hotels.com** (www.hotels.com), we've had good luck with the following discount booking sites:

Which Directory?

Readers should note there are two types of directory in this book: the Regional Directory and individual country directories. The bookwide Directory serves as a comprehensive resource for all the countries in this book. The country directories appear at the end of each country chapter.

DHR (www.dhr.com)

Direct Rooms (www.directrooms.com)

Hotel Club (www.hotelclub.net)

Hotel Info (www.hotel.info)

HRS (www.hrs.com)

LateRooms (www.laterooms.com)

RENTAL ACCOMMODATION

Rentals can be both advantageous and fun for families travelling together or for those staying in one place for a few nights. All rentals should be equipped with kitchens (or at least a kitchenette), which can save on the grocery bill and allow you to peruse the neighbourhood markets and shops, eating like the locals do. Some are a little more up-market with laundry facilities, parking and even daily maid services.

Book Your Stay Online

For more accommodation reviews by Lonely Planet authors, check out hotels.lonelyplanet.com/Europe. You'll find independent reviews, as well as recommendations on the best places to stay. Best of all, you can book online.

For leads, try the following websites:

HolidayHavens (www.holidayhavens.co.uk)

Holiday-Rentals (www.holiday-rentals.com)

Homelidays (www.homelidays.com)

Vacations-Abroad (www.vacations-abroad.com)

VacationRentalsByOwner (www.vrbo.com)

Business Hours

Standard business hours vary hugely in Western Europe, where dinner means midnight in Madrid and 7pm in the Netherlands. Some countries have embraced Sunday shopping and others haven't. See the country chapter directories for details.

Customs

Duty-free goods are not sold to those travelling from one EU country to another. For goods purchased at airports or on ferries *outside* the EU, the usual allowances apply for tobacco (200 cigarettes, 50 cigars or 250g of loose tobacco) – although some countries have

reduced this to curb smoking – and alcohol (1L of spirits or 2L of liquor with less than 22% alcohol by volume; 4L of wine). The total value of theses goods cannot exceed €300.

Gay & Lesbian Travellers

In cosmopolitan centres in Western Europe you'll find very liberal attitudes towards homosexuality. Belgium, the Netherlands and Spain have legalised full same-sex marriages. Many other countries allow civil partnerships that grant all or most of the rights of marriage.

London, Paris, Berlin, Madrid, Lisbon and Amsterdam have thriving gay communities and pride events. The Greek islands of Mykonos and Lesvos are popular gay beach destinations.

The following websites are useful:

Damron (www.damron.com) The USA's leading gay publisher offers guides to world cities.

Gay Journey (www.gayjourney.com) A mishmash of travel-related information, including lists of gay-friendly hotels in Europe.

Emergency Number

The EU-wide general emergency number is ☎112 (but ☎999 in the UK).

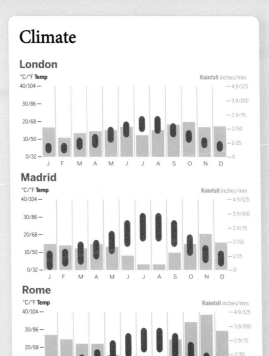

Climate

London

°C/°F **Temp**

Rainfall inches/mm

Madrid

°C/°F **Temp**

Rainfall inches/mm

Rome

°C/°F **Temp**

Rainfall inches/mm

International Lesbian and Gay Association (www.ilga.org) Campaigning group with some country-specific information on homosexual issues (not always up-to-date) and a conference calendar.

Spartacus International Gay Guide (www.spartacusworld.com) A male-only directory of gay entertainment venues in Europe.

Electricity

VOLTAGES & CYCLES

Most of Europe runs on 220-240V, 50Hz AC (as opposed to say, North America, where the electricity is 120V, 60 Hz AC). Chargers for phones, iPods and laptops *usually* can handle any type of electricity. If in doubt, read the small print. What you'll need are plug converters – see the following.

EU & CONTINENTAL EUROPE

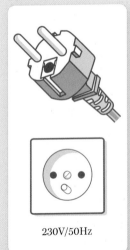

230V/50Hz

UK & IRELAND

230V/50Hz

PLUGS & SOCKETS

If your plugs are of a different design from the UK/Ireland and EU plugs, you'll need an adaptor. If you don't get one before travelling, shops in airports and train stations often have a selection of adaptors.

Health

It is unlikely that you will encounter unusual health problems in Western Europe, and if you do, standards of care are world class.

A few travelling tips:
- Bring medications in their original, clearly labelled containers.

- Bring a list of your prescriptions (photocopies of the containers are good) including generic names, so you can get replacements if your bags go on holiday – carry this info separately.

- If you have health problems that may need treatment, bring a signed and dated letter from your physician describing your medical conditions and medications.

- If carrying syringes or needles, have a physician's letter documenting their medical necessity.

- If you need vision correction, carry a spare pair of contact lenses or glasses, and/or bring your optical prescription with you.

INSURANCE

If you're an EU citizen, the European Health Insurance Card (EHIC) covers you for most medical care. EHIC will not cover you for nonemergencies or emergency repatriation. Citizens of other countries should find out if there is a reciprocal arrangement for free medical care between their country and the country visited. Find out in advance if your insurance plan will make payments directly to providers or reimburse you later for overseas health expenditures.

RECOMMENDED VACCINATIONS

No jabs are necessary for Western Europe. However, the World Health Organization (WHO) recommends that all travellers should be covered for diphtheria, tetanus, measles, mumps, rubella and polio, regardless of their destination.

Insurance

It's foolhardy to travel without insurance to cover theft, loss and medical problems. Start by seeing what your own insurance covers, be it medical, for home owners or renters. You may find that many aspects of travel in Western Europe are covered. If you need to purchase coverage, there's a wide variety of policies, so check the small print. Some policies specifically exclude 'dangerous activities', which can include scuba diving, motorcycling, winter sports, adventure sports or even hiking. Some pay doctors or hospitals directly, but most require you to pay upfront, save the documentation and then claim later. Check that the policy covers ambulances or an emergency flight home.

Internet Access

The number of internet cafes is plummeting. You'll may still find them in tourist areas and around big train stations.

- Hostels, hotels and other accommodation usually have wi-fi.

- Wi-fi (WLAN in Germany) access is best the further north in Western Europe you go (Greece and Portugal are laggards).

- Internet access places may add a surcharge of €1 to €5 per hour for using Skype.

Legal Matters

Most Western European police are friendly and helpful, especially if you have been a victim of a crime. You are required by law to prove your identity if asked by police, so always carry your passport, or an identity card if you're an EU citizen.

AGES OF CONSENT

You can generally purchase alcohol (beer and wine) between 16 and 18 years (usually 18 for spirits) but, if in doubt, ask. Although you can drive at 17 or 18 years, you might not be able to hire a car until you reach 25 years of age.

ILLEGAL DRUGS

Narcotics are sometimes openly available in Europe, but that doesn't mean they're legal. The Netherlands is most famed for its liberal attitudes, with 'coffee shops' openly selling cannabis. However, even there, it's a case of the police turning a blind eye.

Possession of cannabis is decriminalised but not legalised (apart from medicinal use). Don't take this relaxed attitude as an invitation to buy harder drugs; if you get caught, you'll be punished.

Equally, in Belgium, the possession of up to 5g of cannabis is legal but selling the drug isn't, so if you get caught at the point of sale you could be in trouble.

SMOKING

Cigarette smoking bans have been progressively introduced across Europe. Although outdoor seating has long been a tradition outside European cafes, it's had new impetus given that most Western European countries have banned smoking in public places, including restaurants and bars.

Money

For security and flexibility, diversify your source of funds. Carry an ATM card, credit card and cash.

ATMS

Every country covered in this book has international ATMs that allow you to withdraw cash directly from your home account, and this is the most common way European travellers access their money. You should always have a back-up option, however, as some readers have reported glitches with ATMs in various countries, even when their card worked elsewhere across Europe. In some remote villages, ATMs might also be scarce.

When you withdraw money from an ATM the amounts are converted and dispensed in local currency. However, there will be fees (see the boxed text, p818). If you're uncertain, ask your bank to explain.

Finally, remember to always cover the keypad when entering your PIN and make sure that there are no unusual devices attached to the machine; these can copy your card's details or cause it to stick in the machine. If your card disappears and the screen goes blank before you've even entered your PIN, don't enter it – especially if a 'helpful' bystander tells you to do so. If you find you are unable to retrieve your card from the machine, call your bank's emergency number as soon as possible.

CASH

Nothing beats cash for convenience...or risk. If you lose it, it's gone forever and very few travel insurers will come to your rescue. Those that do will limit the amount to somewhere around €300 or £200.

There is no reason to get local currency before arriving in Europe, especially as exchange rates for doing so in your home country are likely to be abysmal.

CREDIT CARDS

Credit cards are handy for major purchases such as air or rail tickets, and offer a lifeline in certain emergencies.

Visa and MasterCard/Eurocard are more widely accepted in Europe than Amex and Diners Club. There are, however, regional differences in the general acceptability of credit cards. In the UK, for example, you can usually flash your plastic in the most humble of budget restaurants; in Germany some restaurants don't take credit cards.

As with ATM cards, banks have loaded up credit cards with hidden charges for foreign purchases. Cash withdrawals on a credit card are almost always a much worse idea than using an ATM card due to the fees and high interest rates. Plus, purchases in currencies different from home are likely to draw various currency conversion surcharges that are simply there to add to the bank's profit. These can run up to 5% or more. Your best bet is to check these things before leaving and try to use a card that offers the best deal.

MONEY EXCHANGE

In general, US dollars and UK pounds are the easiest currencies to exchange in Western Europe. Get rid of Scottish and Welsh pounds before leaving the UK; nobody outside Britain will touch them.

Most airports, central train stations, big hotels and many border posts have banking facilities outside regular business hours, at times on a 24-hour basis. Post offices in Europe often perform banking tasks, tend to be open longer hours and outnumber banks in remote places.

The best exchange rates are usually at banks. *Bureaux de changes* usually – but not always – offer worse rates or charge higher commissions.

TAXES & REFUNDS

Sales tax applies to many goods and services in Western Europe (although the amount – 10% to 20% – is already built into the price of the item). Luckily, when non-EU residents spend more than a certain amount (around €75) they can usually reclaim that tax when leaving the country.

TIPPING

Adding another 5% to 10% to a bill for a meal for good service is common across Western Europe.

TRAVELLERS CHEQUES

Travellers cheques have been replaced by international ATMs and it's often difficult to find places that cash them.

Minimising ATM Charges

When you withdraw cash from an ATM overseas there are several ways you can get hit. Firstly, most banks add a hidden 2.75% loading to what's called the 'Visa/MasterCard wholesale' or 'interbank' exchange rate. In short, they're giving you a worse exchange rate than strictly necessary. Additionally, some banks charge their customers a cash withdrawal fee (usually 2% with a minimum €2 or more). If you're really unlucky, the bank at the foreign end might charge you as well. Triple whammy. If you use a credit card in ATMs you'll also pay interest – usually quite high interest – on the cash withdrawn.

Most experts agree that having the right bankcard is still cheaper than exchanging cash directly. It's also worth seeing if your bank has reciprocal agreements with banks where you are going that minimise ATM fees.

Safe Travel

On the whole, you should experience few problems travelling in Western Europe – even alone – as the region is well developed and relatively

The Euro

A common currency, the euro is the official currency used in 16 of the 27 EU states: Austria, Belgium, Cyprus, Finland, France, Germany, Greece, Ireland, Italy, Luxembourg, Malta, the Netherlands, Portugal, Slovakia, Slovenia and Spain. Denmark, Britain, Switzerland and Sweden have held out against adopting the euro for political reasons.

The euro has the same value in all EU member countries. The euro is divided into 100 cents. There are seven euro notes (five, 10, 20, 50, 100, 200 and 500 euros) and eight euro coins (one and two euros, then one, two, five, 10, 20 and 50 cents). One side is standard for all euro coins and the other side bears a national emblem of participating countries.

safe. But do exercise common sense. Whatever you do, don't leave friends and relatives back home worrying about how to get in touch with you in case of an emergency. Work out a list of places where they can contact you or, best of all, phone home now and then or email.

Also, leave a record (ie a photocopy) of your passport, credit and ATM cards and other important documents in a safe place. You can scan your documents and credit cards and post the file somewhere safe online, perhaps by emailing it to yourself. If things are stolen or lost, replacement is much easier when you have the vital details available.

DRUGS

Always treat drugs with a degree of caution. There are a lot of drugs available in Western Europe, sometimes quite openly (particularly in the Netherlands), but that doesn't mean they're legal. See p817 for details.

THEFT

Theft happens in Europe, and you have to be wary of theft by other travellers. The most important things to guard are your passport, papers, tickets and money – in that order.

You can lessen the risks further by being careful of snatch thieves. Cameras or shoulder bags are an open invitation for these people, who sometimes operate from motorcycles or scooters and expertly slash the strap before you have a chance to react. A small day pack is better, but watch your rear. Be very careful at cafes and bars; loop the strap of your bag around your leg while seated.

Pickpockets are most active in dense crowds, especially in busy train stations and on public transport during peak hours. A common ploy is for one person to distract you while another zips through your pockets. Beware of gangs of kids – who can look either dishevelled or well dressed – madly waving newspapers

and demanding attention. In the blink of an eye, a wallet or camera can go missing.

Telephone

Treat your hotel phone and its often hidden and outrageous rates the same way you'd treat a thief. Using wi-fi in the room for Skype is the most common way to connect.

MOBILE PHONES

Travellers can easily purchase prepaid mobile phones (from €30/£20) or SIM cards (from €10/£5). GSM cellular phones are compatible throughout all the countries in Western Europe.

If you bring your mobile phone from home:

o Check international roaming rates in advance; often they are extortionate.

o Check roaming fees for data usage for email and web connections; users of smart phones such as the iPhone can get socked with huge fees.

You can bring your mobile phone from home and buy a local SIM card to enjoy cheap local calling rates if it is (a) unlocked, and (b) compatible with European GSM networks.

Time

o **GMT/UTC** Britain, Ireland

o **Central European Time** (GMT/UTC +1) Andorra, Austria, Belgium, France, Germany, Greece, Italy, Liechtenstein, Luxembourg, Netherlands, Portugal, Spain, Switzerland

Climate Change & Travel

Every form of transport that relies on carbon-based fuel generates CO_2, the main cause of human-induced climate change. Modern travel is dependent on aeroplanes, which might use less fuel per kilometre per person than most cars but travel much greater distances. The altitude at which aircraft emit gases (including CO_2) and particles also contributes to their climate change impact. Many websites offer 'carbon calculators' that allow people to estimate the carbon emissions generated by their journey and, for those who wish to do so, to offset the impact of the greenhouse gases emitted with contributions to portfolios of climate-friendly initiatives throughout the world. Lonely Planet offsets the carbon footprint of all staff and author travel.

- **East European Time** (GMT/ UTC +2) Greece

- **Daylight Saving Time/ Summer Time** Last Sunday in March to the last Sunday in October.

Tourist Information

Tourist offices in Western Europe are common and almost universally helpful. They can find accommodation, issue maps, advise on sights and activities, and help with more obscure queries such as 'Where can I wash my clothes?'

Visas

With a valid passport you should be able to visit all countries in Western European for up to three months, provided you have some sort of onward or return ticket and/or 'sufficient means of support' (money).

In line with the Schengen Agreement, there are no passport controls at borders between Andorra, Austria, Belgium, Denmark, Finland, France, Germany, Greece, Iceland, Italy, Liechtenstein, Luxembourg, the Netherlands, Norway, Portugal, Spain, Sweden, Switzerland and many of the Eastern European EU members such as the Czech Republic.

Border procedures between EU and non-EU countries can still be thorough, though citizens of Australia, Canada, New Zealand and the USA don't need visas for tourist visits to any Schengen country or the UK.

Weights & Measures

The metric system is in use throughout most Western European countries. Be aware that in Britain, however, nonmetric equivalents are common (for example: distances continue to be given in miles and beer is sold in pints not litres).

Transport

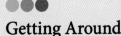

Getting There & Away

Major gateways to Western Europe include airports in London, Paris, Amsterdam, Frankfurt and Rome; however, with connections you can reach scores of airports across the continent.

For details on specific airports, see the Transport sections of the country chapters.

Getting Around

Travel within most of the EU, whether by air, rail or car, is made easier owing to the Schengen Agreement, which abolished border controls between most EU countries.

✈ AIR

Getting around Western Europe by air is very popular thanks to the proliferation of discount carriers and cheap fares. But with cheap fares come many caveats. First, some of the barebones carriers are just that. Discount leader Ryanair prides itself on nonreclining seats, nonexistent legroom and nonexistent window shades. At some of its far-flung airports customer service will also be nonexistent. Scores of other discount airlines are following this model.

A second caveat involves the airports. If you really want to go to Carcassonne in the south of France, then getting a €20 Ryanair ticket from London will be a dream come true. But if you want to go to Frankfurt in Germany and end up buying a ticket to 'Frankfurt-Hahn', you'll find yourself at a small airport 70km west of Frankfurt and two hours away by bus.

Although many people first think of budget carriers when they consider a cheap ticket in Western Europe, you should compare all carriers, including established ones like British Airways and Lufthansa, which serve major airports close to main destinations.

 BICYCLE

It is easy to hire bicycles in Western Europe and you can often negotiate good deals. Local tourist offices, hostels and hotels will have information on rental outlets. Occasionally you can drop off the bicycle at a different location so you don't have to double back on your route.

Urban bike-hire schemes where you check out a bike from one stand and return it to another after brief use have taken off in cities as huge as London and Paris.

Within Western Europe, bikes can sometimes be brought with you onto a train, subject to a small supplementary fee.

 BOAT

Most ferry companies adjust prices according to the level of demand (so-called fluid or dynamic pricing), so it may pay to offer alternative travel dates. Vehicle tickets usually include the driver and a full complement of passengers.

The main areas of ferry service for users of this book are between:

o Ireland and the UK

o Ireland and France

o The UK and the continent (especially France but also Belgium, the Netherlands and Spain)

o Italy and Greece

Compare fares and routes using **Ferry Savers** (www.ferrysavers.com).

 BUS

Buses sometimes have the edge in terms of costs, but are generally slower and much less comfortable than trains and not as quick or sometimes as cheap as airlines.

Europe's largest network of international buses is provided by a consortium of bus companies that operates under the name **Eurolines** (www.eurolines.com). There are many services and it is possible to travel very far for less than €100.

🚗 CAR & MOTORCYCLE

Travelling with your own vehicle allows increased flexibility and the option to get off the beaten track. Unfortunately, cars can be the proverbial ball and chain in city centres when you have to negotiate one-way streets or find somewhere

to park amid a confusing concrete jungle and a welter of expensive parking options.

DRIVING LICENCE

Proof of ownership of a private vehicle should always be carried (a Vehicle Registration Document for British-registered cars) when driving in Europe. An EU driving licence is acceptable.

Many non-European driving licences are valid in Europe. Some travel websites and auto clubs advise carrying an International Driving Permit (IDP), but this costly multilingual document sold by national auto clubs is not necessary in Europe – especially to rent a car.

FUEL

Fuel prices can vary enormously from country to country (though it's always more expensive than in North America or Australia) and may bear little relation to the general cost of living.

Unleaded petrol and diesel are available across Western Europe.

HIRE

The big international rental firms will give you reliable service and a good standard of vehicle. Usually you will have the option of returning the car to a different outlet at the end of the rental period. Rates vary widely but expect to pay somewhere between €25 and €70 per day.

No matter where you rent from, it is imperative to understand exactly what is included in your rental agreement (collision damage waiver, unlimited mileage etc). Make sure you are covered with an adequate insurance policy. And Americans should take note: less than 4% of European cars have automatic transmissions, so if you're afraid of a stick, you'll pay more than double for your car.

The minimum rental age is usually 21 or even 23, and you'll need a credit card.

Motorcycle and moped rental is easy to obtain in countries such as Italy, Spain, Greece and in the south of France.

INSURANCE

Third-party motor insurance is compulsory in Europe if you're driving your own car (rental cars usually come with insurance). Most UK motor-insurance policies automatically provide this for EU countries. Get your insurer to issue a Green Card (may cost extra): an internationally recognised proof of insurance, and check that it lists all the countries you intend to visit. Also ask your insurer for a European Accident Statement form. Never sign statements you can't read or understand – insist on a translation.

It's a good investment to take out a European motoring-assistance policy, such as the AA Five Star Service or the RAC European Motoring Assistance. Expect to pay about £50 for 14 days' cover, with a 10% discount for association members. Non-Europeans might find it cheaper to arrange international coverage with their national motoring organisation before leaving home. Ask your motoring organisation for details about free services offered by affiliated organisations around Western Europe.

○ Every vehicle travelling across an international border should display a sticker showing its country of registration.

ROAD CONDITIONS

Conditions and types of roads vary across Western Europe, but it is possible to make some generalisations. The fastest routes are four- or six-lane dual carriageways/highways, ie two or three lanes either side (motorway, autobahn, *autoroute, autostrada* etc). These roads are great for speed and comfort but driving can be dull, with little or no interesting scenery. Some of these roads incur expensive tolls (eg in Italy, France and Spain) or have a general tax for usage (Switzerland and Austria), but there will usually be an alternative route you can take. Motorways and other primary routes are almost always in good condition.

Road surfaces on minor routes are not perfect in some countries (eg Greece), although normally they will be more than adequate. These roads are narrower and progress is generally much slower. To compensate, you can expect much better scenery and plenty of interesting villages along the way.

ROAD RULES

With the exception of Britain and Ireland, driving is on the right-hand side of the road.

Take care with speed limits, as they vary from country to country. You may be surprised at the apparent disregard of traffic regulations in some places (particularly in Italy and Greece), but as a visitor it is always best to be cautious.

In many countries, driving infringements are subject to an on-the-spot fine. Always ask for a receipt.

European drink-driving laws are particularly strict. The blood-alcohol concentration (BAC) limit when driving is between 0.05% and 0.08%, but in certain areas it can be *zero* per cent. See the individual country chapters for more details on traffic laws.

PUBLIC TRANSPORT

Most Western European cities have excellent public transport systems, which comprise some combination of subways, trains, trams and buses. Service is usually comprehensive. Major airports generally have fast-train or subway links to the city centre. See the country chapters for more information.

TAXI

Taxis in Western Europe are metered and rates are generally high. There might also be supplements (depending on the country) for things such as luggage, the time of day, the location from which you boarded and for extra passengers. Good public transport networks make the use of taxis almost unnecessary, but if you need one in a hurry they can usually be found idling near train stations or outside big hotels. Spain, Greece and Portugal have lower fares, which makes taking a taxi more viable.

Don't underestimate the local knowledge that can be gleaned from taxi drivers. They can often tell you about the liveliest places in town and know all about events happening during your stay.

🚌 TRAIN

Trains are a popular way of getting around: they are comfortable, frequent and generally on time. The Channel Tunnel makes it possible to get from Britain to continental Europe using **Eurostar** (www.eurostar.com). See country chapters for more details.

For many people, travel in Europe would not be travel in Europe without trains. But the traditional image of compartments with little wine-bottle holders has been completely replaced by fast, modern trains that are more like much more comfortable versions of airplanes. Diners have mostly been replaced by snack bars or trolleys, although most people buy their food before boarding.

INFORMATION

Every national rail company has a website with schedule and fare information. Recommended sites:

Deutsche Bahn (DB; www.bahn.de) Excellent schedule and fare information in English for trains not just in Germany but across Europe.

The Man in Seat 61 (www.seat61.com) Invaluable train descriptions and details of journeys to the far reaches of the continent.

If you plan to travel extensively by train, you might enjoy the *Thomas Cook European Timetable,* which gives a cleverly condensed listing of train schedules and indicates where supplements apply or where reservations are necessary. The timetable is updated monthly and is available from

Discount Train Tickets Online

The railways offer many cheap ticket deals through their websites. It's always worth checking online for the same kinds of sales we now expect from budget airlines, including advance-purchase reductions, one-off promotions and special circular-route tickets.

Actually getting discount train tickets you've purchased online varies. Common methods include the following:

○ Reservation number issued with the reservation, which you use at a station ticket-vending machine (some UK lines).

○ Credit card you used to purchase the tickets used at a station ticket-vending machine (France, but non-French credit card holders must retrieve their tickets at a ticket window).

○ Ticket is emailed to buyer, who then prints it out (Germany).

○ Nonlocal credit cards aren't accepted online and you can't buy the discounted fares at the station (the Netherlands).

Thomas Cook (www.thomascookpublishing.com) outlets and bookshops in the UK (order online elsewhere in the world).

Note that European trains sometimes split en route in order to service two destinations, so even if you know you're on the right train, make sure you're in the correct carriage, too.

TICKETS

Normal international tickets are valid for two months, and you can make as many stops as you like en route. Used this way, a ticket from Paris to Vienna can serve as a mini-railpass, as long as you stay on the route shown on the ticket.

HIGHSPEED TRAINS

Western European trains (outside Greece and Portugal) are often fast, frequent and

usually comfortable. Highspeed networks (300km/h or more) continue to expand. For routes and journey times, see the table, p824.

Major highspeed trains that cross borders include the following:

Eurostar (www.eurostar.com) Links beautiful St Pancras station in London to Brussels and Paris in about two hours.

ICE (www.db.de) The fast trains of the German railways span the country and extend to Paris, Brussels, Amsterdam, Vienna and Switzerland.

TGV (www.sncf.com) The legendary fast trains of France reach into Belgium, Luxembourg, Germany, Switzerland and Italy (Milan).

Highspeed Trains

ROUTE	DURATION
Amsterdam–Paris	3hr
Barcelona–Madrid	3hr
Brussels–Cologne	2¼hr
London–Paris	2¼hr
Milan–Rome	4hr
Nuremberg–Munich	1hr
Paris–Frankfurt	3¾hr
Paris–Marseille	3hr
Zürich–Milan	3¾hr

Thalys (www.thalys.com) Links Paris with Brussels, Amsterdam and Cologne.

OTHER TRAINS

NIGHT TRAINS

The romantic image of the European night train is becoming a lot less common with the popularity of budget airlines; however, you can still find a good network of routes that run from the north to Italy. Besides the national railways, the following are three important night train operators:

Artesia (www.artesia.eu) Runs services between Paris and Rome and points in between.

Caledonian Sleeper (www.scotrail.co.uk) Links London overnight with Scotland (as far north as Inverness and Aberdeen).

City Nightline (www.citynightline.de) Operates night trains from Germany and the Netherlands south through Switzerland and Austria into Italy as well as France.

EXPRESS TRAINS

Slower but still reasonably fast trains that cross borders are often called EuroCity (EC) or InterCity (IC). Reaching speeds of up to 200km/h or more, they are comfortable and frequent. A good example is the Railjet service of Austria that reaches Munich and Zurich.

RESERVATIONS

On weekends and during holidays and the summer, it's a good idea to reserve seats on trains (which costs about €3 to €5). Some heavily discounted tickets bought online may include an assigned seat on a train, but most regular tickets are good for any train on the route. You can usually reserve ahead of time using a ticket machine in stations or at a ticket window.

On many highspeed trains, such as France's TGVs, reservations are mandatory.

RAIL PASSES

Think carefully about purchasing a rail pass. Spend a little time online on the national railways sites (see the individual country chapters) and determine what it would cost to do your trip by buying the tickets separately. More often than not, you'll find that you'll spend less than if you buy a Eurail pass.

Shop around, as pass prices can vary between different outlets. Once purchased, take care of your pass as it cannot be replaced or refunded if lost or stolen. Passes get reductions on Eurostar through the Channel Tunnel and on certain ferry routes (eg between France and Ireland). In the USA, **Rail Europe** (www.raileurope.com) sells a variety of rail passes (note that its individual train tickets tend to be more expensive than what you'll pay if buying from railways online or in stations).

Inter-Rail Pass Types

	ADULT 1ST CLASS	ADULT 2ND CLASS	UNDER 26 2ND CLASS
5 days of travel within 10 days	€374	€249	€159
10 days of travel within 22 days	€439	€359	€239
unlimited travel for 1 month	€899	€599	€399

EURAIL

There are so many different **Eurail** (www.eurail.com) passes to choose from that you need to have a good idea of your itinerary before purchasing one. These passes can be bought only by residents of non-European countries, and are supposed to be purchased before arriving in Europe. There are also two options: adults and people under 26 years.

Eurail passes are valid for unlimited travel on national railways and some private lines in Austria, Belgium, France, Germany, Greece, Ireland, Italy, the Netherlands, Spain and Switzerland (including Liechtenstein), plus several more neighbouring ones, and for some ferries between Italy and Greece. The UK is *not* covered by Eurail; it has its own Britrail pass (p171). Reductions are given on some other ferry routes and on river/lake steamer services in various countries and on the Eurostar to/from the UK.

Pass types include the following:

Eurail Global All the European countries (despite the much grander-sounding name) for a set number of consecutive days. For sample costs, see the table below.

Eurail Flexi

	10 DAYS IN 2 MONTHS	15 DAYS IN 2 MONTHS
Adult 1st class	US$832	US$1093
Under 26 2nd class	US$543	US$711

Eurail Flexi Offers travel for a set number of days within a period of time. For sample costs, see the table above.

Eurail Saver Two to five people *always* travelling together can save about 15% on the previously discussed pass types.

Eurail Selectpass Buyers choose which neighbouring countries it covers and for how long. Options are myriad and can offer significant savings over the previously discussed passes if, for example, you are going to only three or four countries. Use the Eurail website to calculate these.

EXTRA FEES

Eurail likes to promote the hop-on, hop-off aspect of its passes. But while German ICE trains may be used at will, French TGVs require a seat reservation and the catch is that these are not always available to pass holders on all trains. In addition, some of the highspeed services like Thalys trains require a fairly hefty surcharge from pass users: 1st class/2nd class €41/€26.

INTER-RAIL

The **Inter-Rail pass** (www.interrailnet.com) is available to European residents of more than six months standing (passport ID required). Terms and conditions vary slightly from country to country, but in the country of origin there is a discount of around 50% on the normal fares. The pass covers up to 30 countries.

Inter-Rail passes are generally cheaper than Eurail, but most fast trains require you to buy a seat reservation and pay a supplement of €3 to €40 depending on the route. For sample costs, see the table, p824. Inter-Rail passes are also available for individual countries. Compare these to passes offered by the national railways.

NATIONAL RAIL PASSES

If you're intending to travel extensively within one country, check what national rail passes are available as these can sometimes save you a lot of money; details can be found in the individual country chapters. In a large country such as Germany where you might be covering long distances, a pass can make sense, whereas in a small country such as the Netherlands it won't.

Eurail Global

	15 DAYS	1 MONTH
Adult 1st class	US$705	US$1135
Under 26 2nd class	US$458	US$739

A-Z

Language

Don't let the language barrier get in the way of your travel experience. This section offers basic phrases and pronunciation guides to help you negotiate your way around Europe. Note that in our pronunciation guides, the stressed syllables in words are indicated with italics.

To enhance your trip with a phrasebook (covering all of these languages in much greater detail), visit **lonelyplanet.com**. Lonely Planet iPhone phrasebooks are available through the Apple App store.

CZECH

Hello.	*Ahoj.*	*uh·*hoy
Goodbye.	*Na shledanou.*	*nuh·*skhle·duh·noh
Yes./No.	*Ano./Ne.*	*uh·*no/ne
Please.	*Prosím.*	*pro·*seem
Thank you.	*Děkuji.*	*dye·*ku·yi
Excuse me.	*Promiňte.*	*pro·*min'·te
Help!	*Pomoc!*	*po·*mots

Do you speak English?
Mluvíte anglicky? — *mlu·*vee·te *uhn·*glits·ki
I don't understand.
Nerozumím. — *ne·*ro·zu·meem
How much is this?
Kolik to stojí? — *ko·*lik to *sto·*yee
I'd like ..., please.
Chtěl/Chtěla bych ..., — khtyel/*khtye·*luh bikh ...
prosím. (m/f) — *pro·*seem
Where's (the toilet)?
Kde je (záchod)? — gde ye (*za·*khod)
I'm lost.
Zabloudil/ — *zuh·*bloh·dyil/
Zabloudila jsem. (m/f) — *zuh·*bloh·dyi·luh ysem

DUTCH

Hello.	*Dag.*	dakh
Goodbye.	*Dag.*	dakh
Yes.	*Ja.*	yaa
No.	*Nee.*	ney
Please.	*Alstublieft.*	al·stew·*bleeft*
Thank you.	*Dank u.*	dangk ew
Excuse me.	*Excuseer mij.*	eks·kew·*zeyr* mey
Help!	*Help!*	help

Do you speak English?
Spreekt u Engels? — spreykt ew *eng·*uhls
I don't understand.
Ik begrijp het niet. — ik buh·*khreyp* huht neet
How much is this?
Hoeveel kost het? — hoo·*veyl* kost huht
I'd like ..., please.
Ik wil graag ... — ik wil khraakh ...
Where's (the toilet)?
Waar zijn — waar zeyn
(de toiletten)? — (duh twa·*le·*tuhn)
I'm lost.
Ik ben verdwaald. — ik ben vuhr·*dwaalt*

FRENCH

Hello.	*Bonjour.*	bon·zhoor
Goodbye.	*Au revoir.*	o·rer·vwa
Yes.	*Oui.*	wee
No.	*Non.*	non
Please.	*S'il vous plaît.*	seel voo play
Thank you.	*Merci.*	mair·see
Excuse me.	*Excusez-moi.*	ek·skew·zay·mwa
Help!	*Au secours!*	o skoor

Do you speak English?
Parlez-vous anglais? — par·lay·voo ong·glay
I don't understand.
Je ne comprends pas. — zher ner kom·pron pa
How much is this?
C'est combien? — say kom·byun
I'd like ..., please.
Je voudrais ..., — zher voo·dray ...
s'il vous plaît. — seel voo play
Where's (the toilet)?
Où sont — oo son
(les toilettes)? — (lay twa·let)
I'm lost.
Je suis perdu(e). (m/f) — zhe swee·pair·dew

GERMAN

Hello.	*Guten Tag.*	*goo·*ten taak
Goodbye.	*Auf Wiedersehen.*	owf *vee·*der·zey·en
Yes.	*Ja.*	yaa
No.	*Nein.*	nain
Please.	*Bitte.*	*bi·*te
Thank you.	*Danke.*	*dang·*ke
Excuse me.	*Entschuldigung.*	ent·*shul·*di·gung
Help!	*Hilfe!*	*hil·*fe

Do you speak English?
Sprechen Sie Englisch?   shpre·khen zee *eng·*lish
I don't understand.
Ich verstehe nicht.   ikh fer·*shtey·*e nikht
How much is this?
Was kostet das?   vas *kos·*tet das
I'd like ..., please.
Ich hätte gern ..., bitte.   ikh *he·*te gern ... *bi·*te
Where's (the toilet)?
Wo ist   vaw ist
(die Toilette)?   (dee to·a·*le·*te)
I'm lost.
Ich habe mich verirrt.   ikh *haa·*be mikh fer·*irt*

ITALIAN

Hello.	*Buongiorno.*	bwon·*jor·*no
Goodbye.	*Arrivederci.*	a·ree·ve·*der·*chee
Yes.	*Sì.*	see
No.	*No.*	no
Please.	*Per favore.*	per fa·*vo·*re
Thank you.	*Grazie.*	*gra·*tsye
Excuse me.	*Mi scusi.*	mee *skoo·*zee
Help!	*Aiuto!*	a·*yoo·*to

Do you speak English?
Parla inglese?   *par·*la een·*gle·*ze
I don't understand.
Non capisco.   non ka·*pee·*sko
How much is this?
Quanto costa?   *kwan·*to *ko·*sta
I'd like ..., please.
Vorrei ..., per favore.   vo·*ray* ... per fa·*vo·*re
Where's (the toilet)?
Dove sono   *do·*ve *so·*no
(i gabinetti)?   (ee ga·bee·*ne·*ti)
I'm lost.
Mi sono perso/a. (m/f)   mee *so·*no *per·*so/a

GREEK

Hello.	Γεια σου.	yia su
Goodbye.	Αντίο.	a·*di·*o
Yes.	Ναι.	ne
No.	Όχι.	*o·*hi
Please.	Παρακαλώ.	pa·ra·ka·*lo*
Thank you.	Ευχαριστώ.	ef·kha·ri·*sto*
Excuse me.	Με συγχωρείτε.	me sing·kho·*ri·*te
Help!	Βοήθεια!	vo·*i·*thia

Do you speak English?
Μιλάς Αγγλικά;   mi·*las* ang·gli·*ka*
I don't understand.
Δεν καταλαβαίνω.   dhen ka·ta·la·*ve·*no
How much is this?
Πόσο κάνει;   *po·*so *ka·*ni
I'd like ..., please.
Θα ήθελα ...,   tha *i·*the·la ...
παρακαλώ.   pa·ra·ka·*lo*
Where's (the toilet)?
Που είναι (η τουαλέτα);   pu *i·*ne (i tu·a·*le·*ta)
I'm lost.
Έχω χαθεί.   *e·*kho kha·*thi*

SPANISH

Hello.	*Hola.*	*o·*la
Goodbye.	*Adiós.*	a·*dyos*
Yes.	*Sí.*	see
No.	*No.*	no
Please.	*Por favor.*	por fa·*vor*
Thank you.	*Gracias.*	*gra·*thyas
Excuse me.	*Disculpe.*	dees·*kool·*pe
Help!	*¡Socorro!*	so·*ko·*ro

Do you speak English?
¿Habla inglés?   a·bla een·*gles*
I don't understand.
No entiendo.   no en·*tyen·*do
How much is this?
¿Cuánto cuesta?   *kwan·*to *kwes·*ta
I'd like ..., please.
Quisiera ..., por favor.   kee·*sye·*ra ... por fa·*vor*
Where's (the toilet)?
¿Dónde están   *don·*de es·*tan*
(los servicios)?   (los ser·*vee·*thyos)
I'm lost.
Estoy perdido/a. (m/f)   es·*toy* per·*dee·*do/a

Behind the Scenes

Author Thanks

OLIVER BERRY

Special thanks for this book go to Mike Stack, Teio Meedendorp, Willemijn Kevenaar and Martina Švajcrová for agreeing to contribute their local expertise; to Jo Potts, Kirsten Rawlings and Tasmin Waby McNaughtan for keeping the book on track during authoring and editing; and to Lisa Dunford, who co-authored the first edition of *Discover Europe* with me. Biggest thanks of all go to the Lonely Planet authors who supplied the fantastic text on which this book is based.

Acknowledgments

Climate map data adapted from Peel MC, Finlayson BL & McMahon TA (2007) 'Updated World Map of the Köppen-Geiger Climate Classification', *Hydrology and Earth System Sciences*, 11, 163344.

Illustrations p70-1, p80-1, p120-1, p138-9, p142-3, p146-7, p192-3, p196-7, p218-19, p226-7, p260-1, p278-9, p300-1, p324-5, p328-9, p352-3, p360-1, p364-5, p392-3 and p424-5 by Javier Zarracina.

Cover photographs: Front: Château de Chambord, Loire Valley, France, Luca da Ros, SIME/4corners; Back: Canal at night, Amsterdam, the Netherlands, Jean-Pierre Lescourret, Lonely Planet Images.

Many of the images in this guide are available for licensing from Lonely Planet Images: www.lonelyplanetimages.com.

Our Readers

Many thanks to the travellers who used the last edition and wrote to use with helpful hints, useful advice and interesting anecdotes:

Fleur Boudo, Kaur Harvinder, Barbara Hollingworth, Tom Riley

This Book

This 2nd edition of *Discover Europe* was coordinat by Oliver Berry, and was researched and written by Brett Atkinson, Alexis Averbuck, Kerry Christiani, Mark Elliott, David Else, Duncan Garwood, Anthony Ham, Virginia Maxwell, Craig McLachlan, Caroline Sieg, Ryan Ver Berkmoes, Nicola Williams and Neil Wilson. This guidebook was commissioned in Lonely Planet's London office, and produced by the followir

Commissioning Editor Jo Potts
Coordinating Editors Justin Flynn, Bella Li
Coordinating Cartographer Andrew Smith
Coordinating Layout Designer Frank Deim
Managing Editors Bruce Evans, Tasmin Waby McNaughtan, Anna Metcalfe, Kirsten Rawlings
Managing Cartographers Alison Lyall, Herman So
Managing Layout Designer Chris Girdler
Assisting Editors Cathryn Game, Asha Ioculari, Catherine Naghten, Kristin Odijk, Sophie Splatt
Assisting Cartographers Mick Garrett, James Levers Xavier di Toro
Assisting Layout Designers Yvonne Bischofberger, Jane Hart, Carol Jackson, Jessica Rose, Wibowo Rusli, Jacqui Saunders, Wendy Wright
Cover Research Naomi Parker
Internal Image Research Aude Vauconsant
Language Content Branislava Vladisavljevic

Thanks to Shahara Ahmed, Judith Bamber, Melanie Dankel, Janine Eberle, Ryan Evans, Laura Jane, Yvonne Kirk, Nic Lehman, John Mazzocchi, Wayne Murphy, Trer Paton, Piers Pickard, Malisa Plesa, Averil Robertson, Lachlan Ross, Mik Ruff, Laura Stansfeld, Juan Winata

SEND US YOUR FEEDBACK

We love to hear from travellers – your comments kee us on our toes and help make our books better. Our well-travelled team reads every word on what you loved or loathed about this book. Although we cann reply individually to postal submissions, we always guarantee that your feedback goes straight to the a propriate authors, in time for the next edition. Each person who sends us information is thanked in the next edition, and the most useful submissions are rewarded with a free book.

Visit **lonelyplanet.com/contact** to submit you updates and suggestions or to ask for help. Our award-winning website also features inspirational travel stories, news and discussions.

Note: We may edit, reproduce and incorporate your comments in Lonely Planet products such as guidebooks, websites and digital products, so let know if you don't want your comments reproduce or your name acknowledged. For a copy of our privacy policy visit lonelyplanet.com/privacy.

Index

000 Map pages

G

H

000 Map pages

T

000 Map pages

How to Use This Book

These symbols will help you find the listings you want:

- ◉ Sights
- ✦ Activities
- ✉ Courses
- ✦ Tours
- ✿ Festivals & Events
- ▤ Sleeping
- ✖ Eating
- ◉ Drinking
- ✿ Entertainment
- 🔒 Shopping
- ⓘ Information/Transport

These symbols give you the vital information for each listing:

- ☎ Telephone Numbers
- ☉ Opening Hours
- ℗ Parking
- ⊖ Nonsmoking
- ❄ Air-Conditioning
- @ Internet Access
- 🛜 Wi-Fi Access
- 🏊 Swimming Pool
- 🌿 Vegetarian Selection
- 📖 English-Language Menu
- 👪 Family-Friendly
- 🐾 Pet-Friendly
- 🚌 Bus
- ⛴ Ferry
- Ⓜ Metro
- Ⓢ Subway
- ⊖ London Tube
- 🚃 Tram
- 🚆 Train

Reviews are organised by author preference.

Map Legend

Sights
- 🏖 Beach
- 🔺 Buddhist
- 🏰 Castle
- ✝ Christian
- 🕉 Hindu
- ☪ Islamic
- ✡ Jewish
- 🏛 Monument
- 🏛 Museum/Gallery
- 🏚 Ruin
- 🍷 Winery/Vineyard
- 🐾 Zoo
- ◎ Other Sight

Activities, Courses & Tours
- 🤿 Diving/Snorkelling
- 🛶 Canoeing/Kayaking
- ⛷ Skiing
- 🏄 Surfing
- 🏊 Swimming/Pool
- 🚶 Walking
- 🏄 Windsurfing
- ✦ Other Activity/Course/Tour

Sleeping
- ▤ Sleeping
- ⛺ Camping

Eating
- ✖ Eating

Drinking
- ◉ Drinking
- ◉ Cafe

Entertainment
- ✿ Entertainment

Shopping
- 🔒 Shopping

Information
- ✉ Post Office
- ⓘ Tourist Information

Transport
- ✈ Airport
- ⊗ Border Crossing
- 🚌 Bus
- 🚡 Cable Car/Funicular
- 🚲 Cycling
- ⛴ Ferry
- Ⓜ Metro
- 🚝 Monorail
- ℗ Parking
- Ⓢ S-Bahn
- 🚕 Taxi
- 🚉 Train/Railway
- 🚋 Tram
- ⊖ Tube Station
- Ⓤ U-Bahn
- • Other Transport

Routes
- Tollway
- Freeway
- Primary
- Secondary
- Tertiary
- Lane
- Unsealed Road
- Plaza/Mall
- Steps
- Tunnel
- Pedestrian Overpass
- Walking Tour
- Walking Tour Detour
- Path

Boundaries
- International
- State/Province
- Disputed
- Regional/Suburb
- Marine Park
- Cliff
- Wall

Population
- 😄 Capital (National)
- ◉ Capital (State/Province)
- ● City/Large Town
- ● Town/Village

Geographic
- 🏠 Hut/Shelter
- 🔆 Lighthouse
- 👀 Lookout
- ▲ Mountain/Volcano
- 🌴 Oasis
- ◉ Park
-)(Pass
- 🍴 Picnic Area
- 💧 Waterfall

Hydrography
- River/Creek
- Intermittent River
- Swamp/Mangrove
- Reef
- Canal
- Water
- Dry/Salt/Intermittent Lake
- Glacier

Areas
- Beach/Desert
- Cemetery (Christian)
- Cemetery (Other)
- Park/Forest
- Sportsground
- Sight (Building)
- Top Sight (Building)

NICOLA WILLIAMS

France Nicola Williams has lived in France and written about it for more than a decade. From her hillside home on the southern shore of Lake Geneva, it's a quick flit to the Alps (call her a ski fiend), Paris (art buff), Provence (food-and-wine lover). Paris this time meant stylish apartment living in St-Germain des Prés with husband extraordinaire Matthias and three trilingual kids with ants in their pants. Nicola blogs at tripalong.wordpress.com and tweets at @Tripalong.

Read more about Nicola at:
lonelyplanet.com/members/nicolawilliams

NEIL WILSON

Ireland Neil's first experiences of Ireland were a sailing trip to Kinsale in 1990 and a tour of Northern Ireland's Antrim coast in 1994. Since then he has returned regularly for holidays, hiking trips and guidebook research – this time round he finally climbed Carrauntoohil, Ireland's highest peak. Neil is a full-time travel writer based in Edinburgh, Scotland, and has written around 50 guidebooks, including the last four editions of Lonely Planet's *Ireland* guide.

Read more about Neil at:
lonelyplanet.com/members/neilwilson

MARK ELLIOT

Belgium In 1995, a chance encounter at a Turkmenistan camel market saw British-born author Mark Elliott tumble into the arms of his Belgian bride-to-be. He followed her home and is now well into a second decade living in the Benelux, still revelling in the crazy carnivals, fabulous festivals, classic castles and brilliant beer cafes that make this one of the world's most underestimated destinations.

Read more about Mark at:
lonelyplanet.com/members/markelliottauthor

DAVID ELSE

Britain David is a professional travel writer and author of more than 40 guidebooks, including numerous editions of Lonely Planet's guides to *Great Britain*, *England* and *Walking in Britain*. His knowledge comes from a lifetime of travel around the country – often on foot – a passion dating from university years, when heading for the hills was always more attractive than visiting the library. Originally from London, David has lived in Yorkshire, Wales and Derbyshire, and is currently based on the southern edge of the Cotswolds.

Read more about David at:
lonelyplanet.com/members/davidelse

DUNCAN GARWOOD

Italy Since moving to Italy in 1997, Duncan has travelled the length and breadth of the country numerous times, contributing to a raft of Lonely Planet *Italy* titles as well as newspapers and magazines. Each trip throws up special memories and this time it was a perfect beach moment in Sardinia – driving down a rough dirt track to find a deserted strip of sand lapped by limpid aquamarine waters. He currently lives in the Alban hills just outside of Rome.

Read more about Duncan at:
lonelyplanet.com/members/duncangarwood

ANTHONY HAM

Spain In 2002, Anthony arrived in Madrid on a one-way ticket. He has called the city home ever since and now lives with his madrileña wife and two daughters in a house overlooking their favourite plaza in the city. He has written more than 50 guidebooks for Lonely Planet, including *Spain* and *Madrid*. Researching this guide allowed him to rediscover his home city afresh (Malasaña is his new favourite barrio) and he particularly enjoyed losing himself in the villages of Aragón.

Read more about Anthony at:
lonelyplanet.com/members/anthony_ham

VIRGINIA MAXWELL

Italy Virginia has been travelling regularly in Italy for over 20 years, inspired by a love of Renaissance arts and architecture and an all-abiding passion for the country's food and wine. She is the coordinating author of Lonely Planet's *Tuscany & Umbria* and has covered Rome, Lazio and Tuscany for the *Italy* guidebook.

Read more about Virginia at:
lonelyplanet.com/members/virginiamaxwell

CRAIG MCLACHLAN

Greece Craig has researched the Greek Islands for four of the most recent Lonely Planet guidebooks to Europe. He is also a regular visitor to Greece as a tour leader, mainly guiding hiking groups through the mountains and gorges of Crete and around the Cyclades. A New Zealander, Craig spends the southern-hemisphere summer running an outdoor adventure company in Queenstown before heading north for the winter as a 'freelance anything'. He is also a karate instructor and Japanese interpreter. Check out www.craigmclachlan.com.

Read more about Craig at:
lonelyplanet.com/members/craigmclachlan

CAROLINE SIEG

Germany, Switzerland Half Swiss, half American, Caroline's relationship with Switzerland began when she and her family first moved to Lucerne when she was aged five. Several moves back and forth across the Atlantic ended when she settled to live in Zürich during high school and beyond, including a season working in a ski resort in the Valais. These days, Caroline heads to Switzerland as often as possible – to ski, indulge in cheese and chocolate, or to simply meander along the shores of Lake Zürich.

Read more about Caroline at:
lonelyplanet.com/members/carolinesieg

RYAN VER BERKMOES

Germany, The Netherlands Ryan Ver Berkmoes spent three years editing a magazine in Frankfurt, Germany, before embarking on a career with Lonely Planet. His first few jobs involved working on the Germany chapter of the fourth edition of *Western Europe*, as well as the first edition of *The Netherlands* – a country where they pronounce his name better than he can. He continues to write about both. These days he lives in Portland, Oregon. Follow him at ryanverberkmoes.com. He tweets at @ryanvb.

Read more about Ryan at:
lonelyplanet.com/members/ryanverberkmoes

Our Story

A beat-up old car, a few dollars in the pocket and a sense of adventure. In 1972 that's all Tony and Maureen Wheeler needed for the trip of a lifetime – across Europe and Asia overland to Australia. It took several months, and at the end – broke but inspired – they sat at their kitchen table writing and stapling together their first travel guide, *Across Asia on the Cheap*. Within a week they'd sold 1500 copies. Lonely Planet was born.

Today, Lonely Planet has offices in Melbourne, London and Oakland, with more than 600 staff and writers. We share Tony's belief that 'a great guidebook should do three things: inform, educate and amuse'.

Our Writers

OLIVER BERRY

Coordinating author, France Oliver has travelled the length and breadth of Europe while writing guides, books and features for Lonely Planet, including for the first edition of *Discover Europe*. He graduated in English from University College London and writes regularly on travel, film and music. When he is not on the road, Oliver lives in his home county of Cornwall in the southwest of England. You can see some of his latest work at www.oliverberry.com.

Read more about Oliver at:
lonelyplanet.com/members/oliverberry

BRETT ATKINSON

The Czech Republic Brett Atkinson has been travelling to Eastern Europe for more than 20 years: honeymooning in Bosnia, Croatia and Hungary, writing about the legacy of the communist era, and enjoying more than a few local beers. For his most recent extended research trip to the Czech Republic, he dived into Prague's emerging visual arts scene, trekked the spectacular valleys of the Bohemian Switzerland region, and continued to marvel at sunsets above Prague Castle. When he's not on the road for Lonely Planet, Brett's at home in Auckland, New Zealand, planning his next overseas sojourn with his wife Carol. He's contributed to more than 20 Lonely Planet titles and travelled to more than 60 countries. See www.brett-atkinson.net for details of his latest writing and travels.

ALEXIS AVERBUCK

Greece Alexis Averbuck lives in Hydra, Greece, and makes any excuse she can to travel the isolated back roads of her adopted land. She is committed to dispelling the stereotype that Greece is simply a string of sandy beaches. A travel writer for two decades, Alexis has lived in Antarctica for a year, crossed the Pacific by sailboat and written books on her journeys through Asia and the Americas. She's also a painter – see her work at www.alexisaverbuck.com.

Read more about Alexis at:
lonelyplanet.com/members/alexisaverbuck

KERRY CHRISTIANI

Austria Born in Essex, England, Kerry now lives in the Black Forest, Germany. On her second visit to Austria for Lonely Planet she discovered the truth about the Von Trapps in Salzburg, sweated out a rare heatwave in the Alps and climbed (almost) every mountain – and in doing so fell for the country and its great outdoors all over again. Kerry's wanderlust has taken her to six continents, inspiring numerous articles and some 20 guidebooks, including Lonely Planet's *Germany*, *Switzerland* and *France*.

Read more about Kerry at:
lonelyplanet.com/members/kerrychristiani

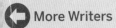 **More Writers** ....

Published by Lonely Planet Publications Pty Ltd
ABN 36 005 607 983
2nd edition – December 2011
ISBN 978 1 74220 131 3
© Lonely Planet 2011   Photographs © as indicated 2011
10 9 8 7 6 5 4 3 2 1
Printed in China